Financial Markets and Corporate Strategy

Financial Markets and Corporate Strategy

Third Edition

David Hillier, Mark Grinblatt and Sheridan Titman

Mc Graw Hill

Financial Markets and Corporate Strategy, Third Edition
David Hiller, Mark Grinblatt & Sheridan Titman
ISBN-13 9781526849496
ISBN-10 1-5268-4949-6

Published by McGrawHill Education
Unit 4, Foundation Park,
Roxborough Way,
Maidenhead
SL6 3UD
Website: www.mheducation.co.uk

British Library Cataloguing in Publication Data
A catalogue record for this book is available from the British Library

Library of Congress Cataloging in Publication Data
The Library of Congress data for this book has been applied for from the Library of Congress

Portfolio Manager: Felicity Baines
Content Developer: Maggie du Randt
Content Product Manager: Ali Davis
Marketing Manager: Ros Letellier

Cover design by Adam Renvoize
Printed and bound in the UK by CPI

Brief Table of Contents

Detailed Table of Contents

About the Authors

David Hillier is Associate Principal and Executive Dean of the University of Strathclyde Business School. A Professor of Finance, David was recognised as in the top 3 per cent of the most prolific finance researchers in the world over the past 50 years (Heck and Cooley, 2009) and appears regularly in the media as a business commentator. In addition, his YouTube channel of finance lectures (professordavidhillier) has attracted over half a million views worldwide.

David has acted as a World Bank consultant and provided consultancy advice to the NHS and several international stock exchanges. His executive clients include the Wise Group, Weir Group, Babcock, Wm Grant & Sons, Iberdrola and David Brown Gears. He has taught in many international environments, including China, Greece, Malaysia, the Netherlands, Oman, Bahrain, Switzerland, Tanzania and Romania. David sits on Scotland's skills agency, Skills Development Scotland, the CBI Scotland regional council and the MCR Pathways National Advisory Council. David has won many industry and academic awards, including the Institute of Directors Scotland Public Sector Director of the Year.

David publishes in the area of corporate finance. His PhD research is related to corporate insider trading, an area in which he is still very active. David's research has been funded by several international organisations, including the Italian and Spanish governments, the Thai Stock Exchange, Thai Securities and Exchange Commission, Thai Government Pension Fund, Australian Research Council, The Actuarial Profession, Rotman International Centre for Pension Management, and the Central Bank of Tanzania.

Mark Grinblatt is a Professor of Finance at the University of California, Los Angeles, Anderson School of Management. He has also acted as a consultant to numerous firms and as an associate editor for the *Journal of Financial and Quantitative Analysis* and the *Review of Financial Studies*.

Sheridan Titman is a Professor of Finance at the University of Texas. He is also a research associate of the National Bureau of Economic Research and has worked in a consulting capacity.

Preface

In the preface to the second European edition of *Financial Markets and Corporate Strategy,* I quoted from the first edition:

"I'm fully expecting things to change again over the next couple of years, as the world's economies adapt to the new reality of a harsher economic environment."

It has been ten years since I wrote those words, and I don't think anyone truly realised how much the financial markets and global economy would change in this time. We have seen the rise and fall of globalisation, the advent of cryptocurrencies and blockchain, Brexit, Covid-19, climate change, widespread disruption to international supply chains, rampant inflation, the rising economic might of China, and the Russian invasion of Ukraine.

All these tumultuous events have resulted in new dynamics in financial markets and corporate strategy. The power of banking institutions has waned, and other, newer forms of financing have become more popular. Private equity and securitisation is no longer the vibrant industry it once was, and hedge funds have become much more heavily regulated. State and foreign shareholders are now common in the ownership structure of many large firms, and new ways of management thinking come with new shareholders and investors.

Much of the book has been rewritten to reflect the many changes that have taken place in the financial markets over the past ten years. In particular, I've included much more on sustainability, which flavours a lot of the revised text. In addition, the chapters on financing, equity and debt markets have been overhauled to bring them up to date with the new economic paradigm in which corporations operate.

The old statement that 'nothing is as practical as a good theory' underlines a lot of the book's ethos, and whereas the corporate environment has changed significantly, the insights gained from theoretical models remain. I've endeavoured to develop the theory where possible from newly published research. I've also updated most chapters with new research published in the top journals since 2012. This was a significant undertaking, and, through necessity, I have had to omit some valuable papers. However, where possible, I refer to the most cited articles since 2012, and these are included in the reference list at the end of each chapter. I apologise in advance if some important work has been omitted, and I am more than happy to correspond with researchers on the future direction of the text.

We live in very interesting times. Unlike the Chinese proverb (or curse!), corporate managers should view the current global economic changes as an opportunity to grow their firm and create new value for investors. The pace of technological change is such that the corporate world is evolving at an incredible rate. It is thus hoped that the overview of financial markets provided in this book, together with its synthesis of current research and theory, will help managers not only adapt but thrive and prosper in this new economic reality.

David Hillier

Acknowledgements

I acknowledge the assistance of the following individuals who were invaluable in helping me finish the book.

Maggie du Randt of McGraw Hill has worked with me from the very start of this project and, over the past year, reviewed each chapter carefully and gave me detailed feedback and advice on each section. I'd also like to thank Ali Davis and Ros Letellier from the production and marketing team for their hard work in publishing this book.

The book has been reviewed in detail by many academic colleagues. In particular, I would like to recognise the efforts of the following people:

Charlotte Christiansen, Aarhus University
Lynn Hodgkinson, University of Wales Bangor
Daniel Hung, Durham University
Dr Piotr Korczak, University of Bristol
Stefan Arping, University of Amsterdam
Christian Riis Flor, University of Southern Denmark
Tommaso Gabrieli, City University of London
Hang Le, Sheffield University
Filip Zikes, Imperial College London
Cian Twomey, University of Galway
Ken Dyson, University of Ulster

As a social being, my work involves family and friends who have discussed my work and helped me in the past year of writing. Therefore, I take the opportunity to thank Paul and Louise Richards, Paul and Clare Lombardi, Pete and Katherine McCudden, Anne and Frank Walker, and Joe and Amanda Dunn and Monsignor Tom Monaghan.

Finally, many thanks to my family, who mean everything to me: my mum, Marion; Chris and Bonnie, Margaret, Cathie, Liam, John, Patrick, and Quentin; and Benjy, Danny, Con, Maria, Patrick, Saoirse, and Thomas, my grandson.

Most of all, to the love of my life: Mary-Jo.

David Hillier, 2022

Guided Tour

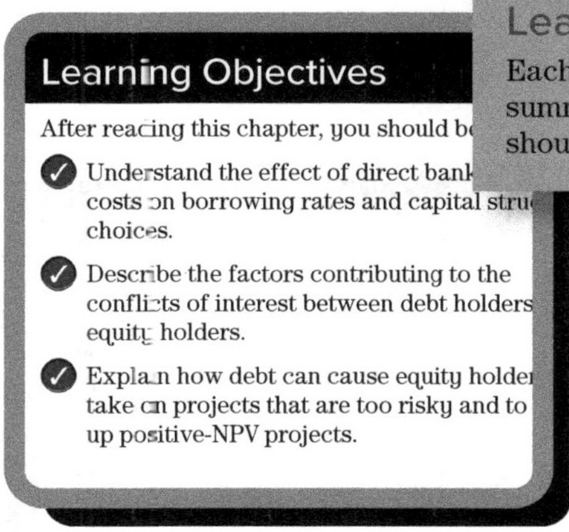

Learning Objectives

After reacing this chapter, you should b

- Understand the effect of direct bank costs on borrowing rates and capital stru choices.
- Describe the factors contributing to the conflicts of interest between debt holders equity holders.
- Explain how debt can cause equity holde take on projects that are too risky and to up positive-NPV projects.

Learning Objectives

Each chapter opens with a set of learning objectives, summarizing what knowledge, skills or understanding you should acquire from each chapter.

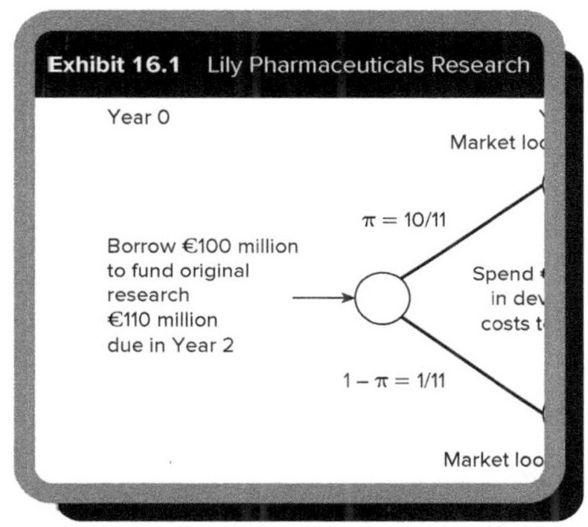

Exhibits

Each chapter provides a variety of figures and tables to demonstrate aspects of financial markets and corporate strategy presented in the text.

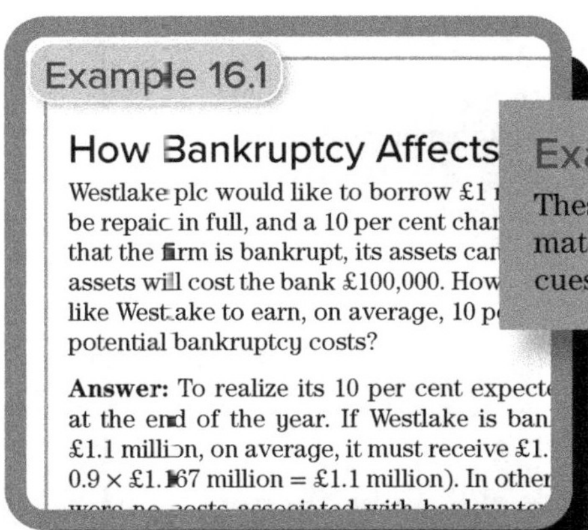

Example 16.1

How Bankruptcy Affects

Westlake plc would like to borrow £1 be repaid in full, and a 10 per cent cha that the firm is bankrupt, its assets ca assets will cost the bank £100,000. How like Westlake to earn, on average, 10 p potential bankruptcy costs?

Answer: To realize its 10 per cent expect at the end of the year. If Westlake is ban £1.1 million, on average, it must receive £1. 0.9 × £1.167 million = £1.1 million). In othe

Examples

These appear in the margins of the book adjacent to important material. They are designed to function as study guides, retrieval cues, and self-tests.

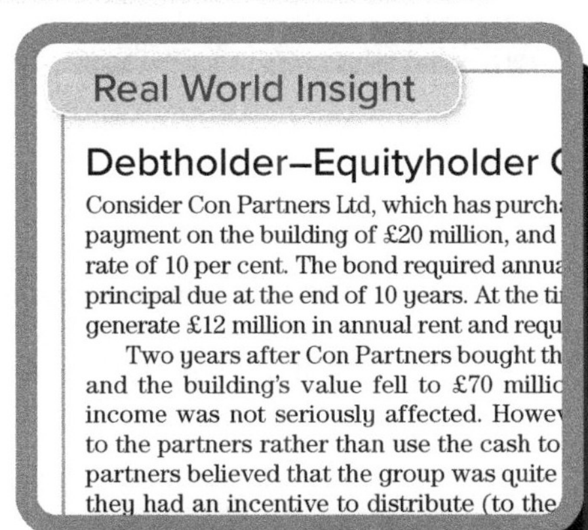

Real World Insight

Debtholder–Equityholder C

Consider Con Partners Ltd, which has purch payment on the building of £20 million, and rate of 10 per cent. The bond required annu principal due at the end of 10 years. At the ti generate £12 million in annual rent and requ

Two years after Con Partners bought th and the building's value fell to £70 milli income was not seriously affected. Howe to the partners rather than use the cash to partners believed that the group was quite they had an incentive to distribute (to the

Real World Insight

These exercises challenge you to think critically in evaluating popular truisms, scientific and pseudoscientific claims, and psychology's relevance to your own life.

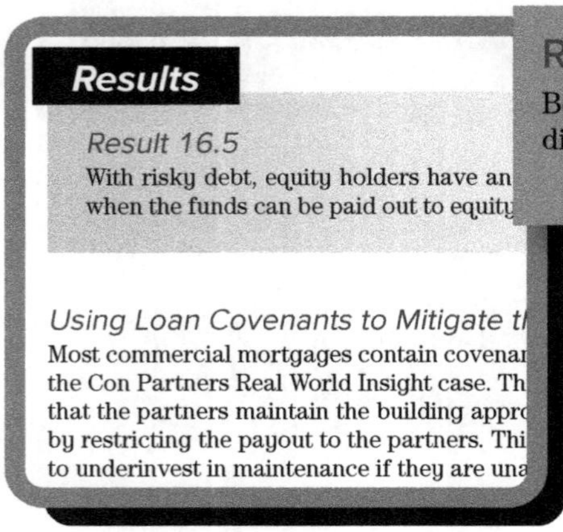

Results

With risky debt, equity holders have an
when the funds can be paid out to equity

Using Loan Covenants to Mitigate t

Most commercial mortgages contain covena
the Con Partners Real World Insight case. Th
that the partners maintain the building appr
by restricting the payout to the partners. Thi
to underinvest in maintenance if they are una

Results

Boxed for easy reference, the Results feature summarizes, in a digestible format, key points from the material just read.

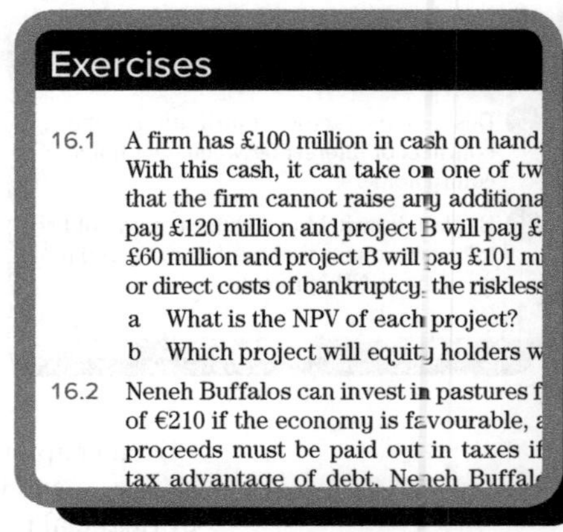

Exercises

16.1 A firm has £100 million in cash on hand,
With this cash, it can take on one of tw
that the firm cannot raise any additiona
pay £120 million and project B will pay £
£60 million and project B will pay £101 m
or direct costs of bankruptcy, the riskless
a What is the NPV of each project?
b Which project will equity holders w
16.2 Neneh Buffalos can invest in pastures f
of €210 if the economy is favourable,
proceeds must be paid out in taxes i
tax advantage of debt, Neneh Buffal

Exercises

These questions encourage you to review and apply the knowledge you have acquired from each chapter. They are a useful revision tool, and can also be used by your lecturer as assignments or practice exam questions.

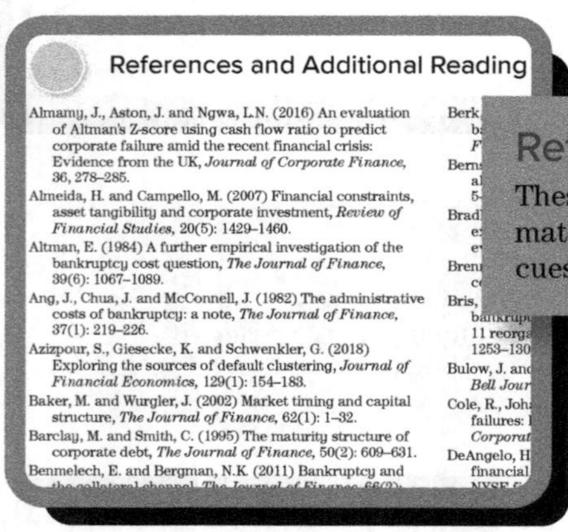

References and Additional Reading

Almamy, J., Aston, J. and Ngwa, L.N. (2016) An evaluation of Altman's Z-score using cash flow ratio to predict corporate failure amid the recent financial crisis: Evidence from the UK, *Journal of Corporate Finance*, 36, 278–285.
Almeida, H. and Campello, M. (2007) Financial constraints, asset tangibility and corporate investment, *Review of Financial Studies*, 20(5): 1429–1460.
Altman, E. (1984) A further empirical investigation of the bankruptcy cost question, *The Journal of Finance*, 39(6): 1067–1089.
Ang, J., Chua, J. and McConnell, J. (1982) The administrative costs of bankruptcy: a note, *The Journal of Finance*, 37(1): 219–226.
Azizpour, S., Giesecke, K. and Schwenkler, G. (2018) Exploring the sources of default clustering, *Journal of Financial Economics*, 129(1): 154–183.
Baker, M. and Wurgler, J. (2002) Market timing and capital structure, *The Journal of Finance*, 62(1): 1–32.
Barclay, M. and Smith, C. (1995) The maturity structure of corporate debt, *The Journal of Finance*, 50(2): 609–631.
Benmelech, E. and Bergman, N.K. (2011) Bankruptcy and

References and Additional Reading

These appear in the margins of the book adjacent to important material. They are designed to function as study guides, retrieval cues, and self-tests.

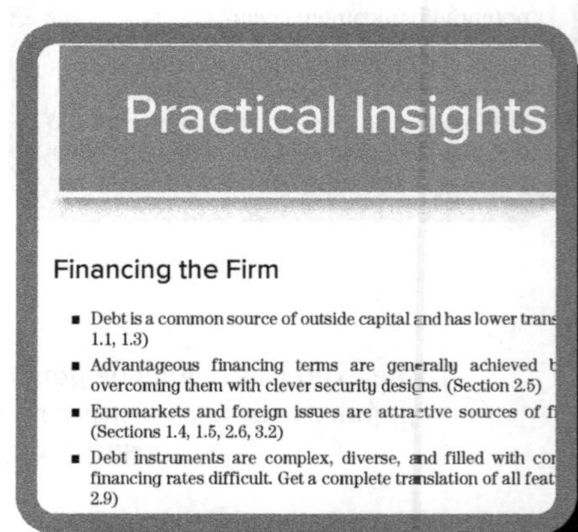

Practical Insights

Financing the Firm

- Debt is a common source of outside capital and has lower trans
1.1, 1.3)
- Advantageous financing terms are generally achieved b
overcoming them with clever security designs. (Section 2.5)
- Euromarkets and foreign issues are attractive sources of f
(Sections 1.4, 1.5, 2.6, 3.2)
- Debt instruments are complex, diverse, and filled with co
financing rates difficult. Get a complete translation of all feat
2.9)

Practical Insights

Practical Insights is a unique feature of this text (found at the end of each part) that contains guidelines to help you identify the important issues faced by financial managers.

Online Learning Centre

Accessed via Connect

McGraw Hill connect®

Students – Helping you to connect, learn and succeed

We understand that studying for your module is not just about reading this textbook. It's also about research, practice, revising key terms, preparing for assignments and passing exams. The Online Learning Centre provides you with a number of **FREE** resources to help you succeed on your module, including:

- Spreadsheet exercises
- PowerPoints
- Solution Manual
- Test Bank

Lecturer support – Helping you to help your students

The Online Learning Centre also offers lecturers adopting this book a range of resources designed to:

- **Enable faster course preparation** – time-saving support for your module
- **Provide high-calibre content to support your students** – resources written by your academic peers, who understand your need for rigorous and reliable content

The materials created specifically for lecturers adopting this textbook include:

- **Lecturer Outlines** to support your module preparation, with case notes, guide answers, teaching tips and more
- **PowerPoint presentations** to use in lectures
- **Image library** of artwork from the textbook

Visit www.mheducation.co.uk/textbooks/baldwin to access the student resources.
To request access to the instructor resources, contact your McGraw Hill representative.
https://www.mheducation.co.uk/customer-service/contact-a-rep

McGraw Hill

Mc Graw Hill **create**®

Let us help make our content your solution

At McGraw-Hill Education our aim is to help lecturers to find the most suitable content for their needs delivered to their students in the most appropriate way. Our **custom publishing solutions** offer the ideal combination of content delivered in the way which best suits lecturer and students.

Our custom publishing programme offers lecturers the opportunity to select just the chapters or sections of material they wish to deliver to their students from a database called CREATE™ at

http://create.mheducation.com/uk/

CREATE™ contains over two million pages of content from:

- textbooks
- professional books
- case books – Harvard Articles, Insead, Ivey, Darden, Thunderbird and BusinessWeek
- Taking Sides – debate materials

Across the following imprints:

- McGrawHill Education
- Open University Press
- Harvard Business Publishing
- US and European material

There is also the option to include additional material authored by lecturers in the custom product – this does not necessarily have to be in English.

We will take care of everything from start to finish in the process of developing and delivering a custom product to ensure that lecturers and students receive exactly the material needed in the most suitable way.

With a Custom Publishing Solution, students enjoy the best selection of material deemed to be the most suitable for learning everything they need for their courses – something of real value to support their learning. Teachers are able to use exactly the material they want, in the way they want, to support their teaching on the course.

Please contact **your local McGrawHill Education representative** with any questions or alternatively contact Marc Wright **e: marc.wright@mheducation.com**

PART

1

Financial Markets and Financial Instruments

Part contents

The title of this finance text is *Financial Markets and Corporate Strategy* because it reflects our belief that one must have a thorough understanding of financial markets to use financial theory to formulate corporate strategy. There are two aspects to this understanding. The first, to be studied in Part I, is that a corporate strategist needs to understand financial institutions. The second, studied in Part II, is that the strategist needs to know how to value securities in the financial markets.

Financial markets, from an institutional perspective, are covered in three chapters. Chapter 1 walks the reader through the decision-making process of raising funds, from whom, in what form, and with whose help. It also focuses on the legal and institutional environment in which securities are issued and compares the procedure for raising capital in developed and emerging markets.

Chapter 2 emphasizes the wide variety of debt instruments available to finance a firm's investments. However, the chapter is also designed to help the reader understand the terminology, pricing conventions and return computations found in debt markets. It also familiarize the reader with the secondary markets in which debt trades.

Chapter 3 covers equity securities, which are much less diverse than debt securities. The focus is on the secondary markets where equities are traded and the process by which firms 'go public', issuing publicly traded equity for the first time. Next, the chapter examines the pricing of equity securities during an initial public offering. Finally, it introduces some theories of market behaviour, which provide insights into how prices are determined in the secondary markets.

Chapter 1

Raising Capital: The Process and the Players

Learning Objectives

After reading this chapter, you should be able to:

- Describe how firms raise funds for new investment.
- Understand the process of issuing new securities.
- Comprehend the role played by financial institutions in raising capital.
- Discuss how capital is raised in countries in developed and emerging markets.
- Analyse trends in the capital markets.

Finance is the study of trade-offs between the present and the future. For an individual investor, an investment in the debt or equity markets means giving up something today to gain something in the future. There is a similar sense of giving up something today to gain something in the future for corporate investment in a factory, machinery or an advertising campaign.

The decisions of individual investors and corporations are intimately linked. To grow and prosper by wise investments in factories, machinery, advertising campaigns and so forth, most firms require access to capital markets. **Capital markets** are an arena in which firms and other institutions requiring funds to finance their operations come together with individuals and institutions that have money to invest. To invest wisely, both individuals and firms must thoroughly understand these capital markets.

Capital markets have grown in complexity and importance over the past ten years. As a result, the level of sophistication required by corporate financial managers has also grown. The amount of capital raised in external markets has increased dramatically, with an ever-increasing variety of available financial instruments. Moreover, the financial markets have become truly global, with thousands of securities trading around the clock worldwide.

To be a player in modern business requires a sophisticated understanding of the new, ever-changing institutional framework in which financing occurs. As a beginning, this chapter describes the workings of the capital markets and the general decisions firms face when they raise funds. Specifically, we focus on the classes of securities that firms issue, the role financial institutions play in raising capital, the regulatory environment in which money is raised, and the differences between countries' financial systems. The chapter concludes with a discussion of current trends in raising capital.

1.1 Financing the Firm

Households, firms, financial intermediaries, and the government all play a role in the financial system of developed economies. **Financial intermediaries** are institutions such as banks that collect the savings of individuals and corporations and funnel them to firms that use the money to finance their investments in plant, equipment, research and development, and so forth. We describe some of the most important financial intermediaries in Exhibit 1.1.

Exhibit 1.1 Description of Financial Intermediaries

Financial intermediary	Description
Bank (commercial and retail activity)	Takes deposits from individuals and corporations and lends these funds to borrowers
Bank (investment activity)	Raises money for corporations by marketing and selling securities
Insurance company	Invests money in securities, property and other assets to meet future insurance claims
Pension fund	Invests money in securities, property and other assets to pay pensions in the future
Charitable foundation	Invests the endowment of a non-profit organization such as a university
Mutual fund	Pools savings from individual investors to purchase securities
Hedge fund	Pools savings from individual wealthy and professional investors (who satisfy specific criteria relating to personal wealth and investor sophistication) to purchase securities using a variety of non-traditional investment strategies
Venture capital firm	Pools money from individual investors and other financial intermediaries to fund relatively small, new businesses, generally with private equity financing

In addition to financing firms indirectly through financial intermediaries, households finance firms directly by individually buying and holding equity (known as *shares* or *stocks*) and debt instruments (known as *bonds*). The government also plays a vital role in regulating the capital markets and taxing various financing alternatives.

Decisions Facing the Firm

Firms can raise investment capital from many sources with various financial instruments. The firm's *financial policy* describes the mix of financial instruments used to finance the firm.

Internal Capital

Firms raise capital internally (**internal capital**) by retaining their earnings and raise it externally by obtaining funds from the capital markets. Historically, this has been the primary source of financing for companies in developed markets. Exhibit 1.2 shows that, in the aggregate, the percentage of total investment funds that European firms generate internally – essentially retained earnings plus depreciation – is very high at just under 90 per cent (Ferrando and Lekpek 2018). Beck et al. (2008) argue that the variation in financing patterns worldwide is driven by the degree of financial and legal development within each country. Firms in emerging markets with newly developed financial structures are more likely to draw on internal financing than public debt or equity issues. In general, internal cash flows are typically insufficient to meet the total capital needs of most firms.

Exhibit 1.2 Financing Patterns in Europe

Financing Instrument	% of Firms
Internal finance	87%
Intra-group	6%
Bank loans	39%
Other bank finance	12%
Bonds	2%
Equity	1%
Leasing/hire purchase	22%
Factoring/invoicing	6%
Family/friends	2%
Grants	5%
Other	1%

The table shows the weighted percentage of firms using different sources of finance. Survey carried out by the European Investment Bank on 12,500 European firms across all 28 member states.

Source: Ferrando and Lekpek (2018).

External Capital

When a firm determines it needs external funds, it must access capital markets and decide on the funds to raise. Exhibit 1.3 illustrates the two primary sources of outside financing – debt and equity – and the common forms of debt and equity financing.[1]

Exhibit 1.3 Sources of External Capital

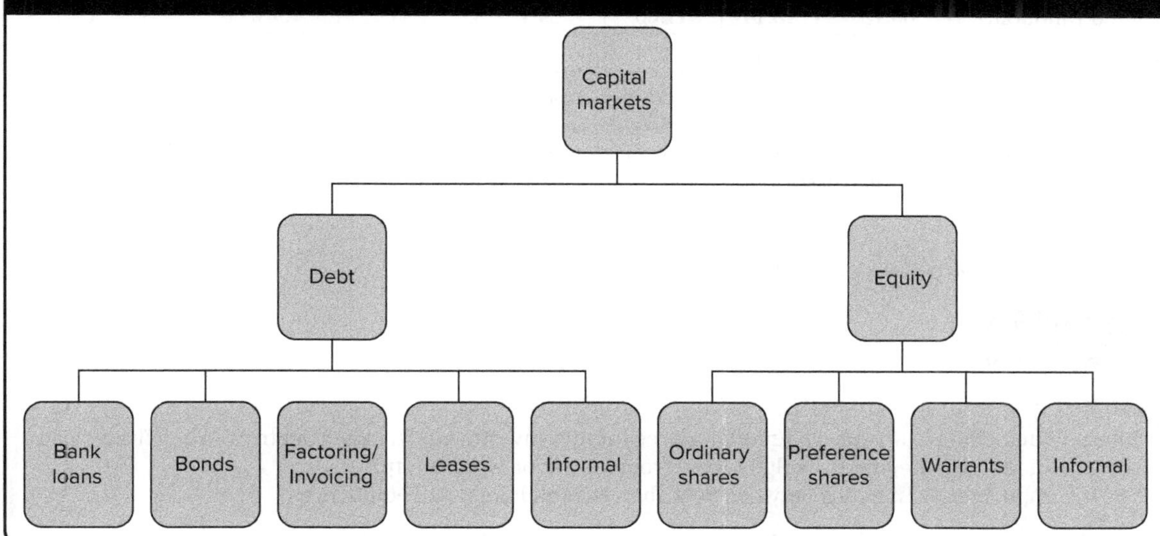

[1] The different sources of debt financing will be explored in detail in Chapter 2; the various sources of equity capital are examined in Chapter 3.

The main difference between **debt** and **equity** is that debt holders have a contract specifying that their claims must be paid in full before the firm can make payments to its equity holders. In other words, debt claims are **senior** or have priority over equity claims. A second important distinction between debt and equity is that payments to debt holders are generally viewed as a tax-deductible expense of the firm. In contrast, the dividends on an equity instrument are considered a payout of profits and are therefore not a tax-deductible expense.

Major corporations frequently raise outside capital by accessing the debt and equity markets. Debt can come from public debt markets or, more commonly, in the form of bank loans. Exhibit 1.4 extends Exhibit 1.2 and presents the average proportions of external funding from various sources for selected countries.

It is clear that, for most countries, bank loans are the most common form of external financing. However, there is still substantial variation across regions that affects corporate financial strategies. Informal finance, for example, is common in China, where moneylenders, family and cooperatives contribute capital for investment.[2] Supplier credit, where plant and equipment manufacturers provide financing for corporate investment, makes up between 5 and 10 per cent of funding for investments in many countries. Academics have largely ignored this important form of financing, yet it rivals equity and bank loans in countries such as France.

Exhibit 1.4 External Financing Patterns Around the World

Country	External finance	Bank	Equity	Leasing	Supplier credit	Development bank	Informal
Canada	48.55	23.45	8.39	2.39	3.39	5.93	5.00
China	29.93	10.17	2.41	1.63	2.41	4.63	5.93
Croatia	41.31	19.79	3.02	0.31	8.19	6.23	2.47
Czech Republic	32.50	13.90	0.66	3.90	3.75	6.84	3.46
France	30.91	6.76	5.76	4.30	7.36	1.42	1.67
Germany	54.29	16.84	23.13	0.74	0.94	8.52	4.13
Italy	77.71	49.67	6.88	1.67	5.83	1.17	4.17
Malaysia	40.62	13.81	4.76	3.48	13.81	4.05	0.71
Singapore	45.17	28.06	7.67	1.16	6.14	0.58	0.00
Spain	39.78	23.00	0.67	8.04	4.22	2.62	1.22
Sweden	43.42	19.70	8.33	1.22	6.16	3.43	1.12
Turkey	43.98	20.41	9.68	4.85	1.42	6.21	1.17
United Kingdom	36.12	13.14	11.56	2.91	7.47	0.58	0.47
United States	47.12	21.47	3.24	6.09	6.62	6.76	2.94

The figures given are firm averages for each country, and they are the proportion of investment financed by each source. External finance is the sum of bank, equity, leasing, supplier credit, development bank and informal finance. Bank finance includes financing from domestic as well as foreign banks. Development bank includes funding from both development and public sector banks. Informal includes funding from moneylenders and traditional or informal sources.

Source: Beck et al. (2008).

Result 1.1 summarises the discussion in this subsection.

Results

Result 1.1

Internal financing is the primary funding source for new investments in most countries. When firms raise external financing, they most likely borrow from a bank or issue equity.

The important distinctions between debt (bonds/bank loans) and equity are:

- Debt claims are senior to equity claims.
- Interest payments on debt claims are tax-deductible, but dividends on equity claims are not.

[2] See Ayyagari et al. (2010) for more on informal finance in China.

Real-World Insights

The UN Climate Change Conference, COP26, took place in Glasgow in October 2021. One of the objectives of COP26 was to mobilise $100 billion in Climate Finance every year. Achieving this objective would funnel significant new money into sustainability investments worldwide. In addition, the world's leaders called on financial institutions in every country to support this agenda by changing their investment criteria to incentivize projects and companies that had a strategic plan which included net zero targets.

According to the UK government, who organized the conference,

'We must work to unleash the trillions in private finance that are needed to power us towards net zero by the middle of the century. To do this, every financial decision needs to take climate into account. This includes all private investment decisions, but also all spending decisions that countries and international financial institutions are making as they roll out stimulus packages to rebuild economies from the pandemic.

'Companies need to be transparent about the risks and opportunities that climate change, and the shift to a net zero economy pose to their business. Central banks and regulators need to make sure that our financial systems can withstand the impacts of climate change and support the transition to net zero. It also means banks, insurers, investors and other financial firms committing to ensuring their investments and lending is aligned with net zero.'

The UK government's statement signals the challenge facing companies in the years ahead. Sustainability strategies are no longer an optional part of a company's toolkit. Now, every firm must consider how it will contribute to a world with net zero carbon emissions.

Who has the Biggest Capital Markets?

Ten years ago, to ask which country has the biggest stock market would have been a simple question. However, cross-border mergers and acquisitions of stock exchanges in the last few years make answering the question much more difficult. For example, the London Stock Exchange has been the subject of a takeover attempt by NASDAQ and the Deutsche Bourse. In addition, the London Stock Exchange acquired the Borsa Italia, Italy's primary exchange. Thus, stock markets are no longer national entities but instead consist of several exchanges.

Exhibit 1.5 presents a selection of stock exchanges with market capitalizations (US$ millions) as reported by the World Federation of Exchanges in 2021. The world's largest stock exchange is the New York Stock Exchange (NYSE), followed by NASDAQ, another exchange based in the US. The Asian markets follow some way behind, and then there are the European exchanges. A growing group of exchanges are in the Middle East and the Gulf. Of particular note is the Saudi Stock Exchange (also known as the Tadawul) which hosts one of the world's largest companies, Saudi Aramco.

All major stock exchanges are fully automated, but the whole process from order entry to trade settlement is carried out using computers. Gone are the days of crazy scenes where traders scream and shout at each other to get orders submitted. Technology has substantially reduced trading costs by removing many frictions in the trading process. Arguably, this increasing use of technology will have lowered the costs of raising finance for corporate firms (Hendershott et al. 2011)

1.2 Public and Private Sources of Capital

Firms raise money from public and private sources. Capital raised from public sources must be registered **securities,** which are publicly traded financial instruments. In every country, public securities must be registered with the domestic securities regulator. In Europe, individual countries have their own securities regulator. For example, in the UK, the regulator is the **Financial Conduct Authority (FCA);** in Germany, it is the **Federal Financial Services Agency (BaFin);** and, in the USA, the regulator is the **Securities and Exchange Commission (SEC).**

Public securities differ from private financial instruments because they can be traded on public **secondary markets** such as the London Stock Exchange or NYSE Euronext. Examples of publicly traded securities include ordinary shares (common stock), preference shares (preferred stock) and corporate bonds.

Exhibit 1.5 Comparison of Selected Equity Markets, 2021

Stock Exchange	Market Cap (US$ millions)	Stock Exchange	Market Cap (US$ millions)
NYSE	26,232,740	SIX Swiss Exchange	2,001,603
NASDAQ – US	19,060,372	Johannesburg Stock Exchange	1,051,529
Shanghai Stock Exchange	6,975,970	BME Spanish Exchanges	759,175
Japan Exchange Group	6,718,220	Moscow Exchange	694,739
Hong Kong Exchanges and Clearing	6,130,420	Singapore Exchange	652,615
Euronext	5,443,947	Bursa Malaysia	436,538
Shenzhen Stock Exchange	5,238,495	Abu Dhabi Securities Exchange	202,174
LSE Group	4,045,597	Qatar Stock Exchange	165,394
TMX Group	2,608,377	Vienna Stock Exchange	132,083
National Stock Exchange of India	2,552,464	Dubai Financial Market	92,658
Saudi Stock Exchange (Tadawul)	2,429,102	Athens Stock Exchange	50,987
Deutsche Boerse AG	2,284,109	Bahrain Bourse	24,608
NASDAQ Nordic and Baltics	2,110,440	Muscat Stock Exchange	16,481

Source: World Federation of Exchanges (2021).

Private capital comes in the form of bank loans or **private placements.** Private placements are financial claims exempted from the full registration requirements that apply to publicly listed securities. To qualify for private placement exemption, the issue must be restricted to a small group of sophisticated investors with minimum thresholds for income or wealth. Typically, sophisticated investors include insurance companies, pension funds and wealthy individuals. They also include venture capital firms, as noted in Exhibit 1.1.

Privately placed financial instruments cannot usually be sold on public markets unless they are subsequently registered with the domestic securities regulator, in which case they become publicly listed securities.

Public markets tend to be anonymous: that is, buyers and sellers can complete their transactions without knowing each other's identities. Because of the anonymous nature of trades on this market, uninformed investors risk trading with other investors who are vastly more informed because they have 'inside' information about a particular company and can profit from it. Insider dealing,[3] as this is known, is illegal, and uninformed investors are partially protected by laws preventing investors from buying or selling public securities based on **inside information.**

In contrast, privately placed debt and equity investors base their decisions on information that is not publicly known. Since traders in private markets are assumed to be sophisticated investors aware of each other's identities, inside information about privately placed securities is not as problematic. For example, suppose a potential buyer of a private debt instrument has reason to believe that the seller possesses material information they are not disclosing. In that case, the buyer can choose not to buy. If the seller misrepresents this information, the buyer can later sue. Because private markets are not anonymous, they are generally less liquid: that is, the transaction costs associated with buying and selling private debt and equity tend to be much higher than the costs of buying and selling public securities.

[3] It is important to make a distinction between insider dealing, which is illegal and based on private, specific and precise information, and insider trading, which is the regular trading activity of company insiders in their firm's securities.

Result 1.2 summarizes the advantages and disadvantages of private placements.

Results

Result 1.2

Corporations raise capital from both private and public sources. Some advantages associated with private sources are as follows.

- Terms of private bonds and equities can be customized for individual investors.
- There is no costly registration with the securities regulator.
- There is no need to reveal confidential information.
- They are easier to renegotiate.

Privately placed financial instruments can also have disadvantages. For example:

- Limited investor base.
- Less liquid.

The market for private securities issues has changed significantly since the global banking crisis of 2008. For many years, bank loans have been the most popular form of financing in many countries. However, the introduction of new banking regulations in 2010 and a need to reduce the overall size of loan portfolios led corporations to seek other funding sources.

Private placements have become popular throughout the world, but the market was severely affected by the global pandemic in 2020 and fell by 20 per cent. Nevertheless, there are signs that the demand for private placements is improving and will likely become more common in the coming years. Private placements are a convenient intermediate step between bank loans and full public listing, and they also allow firms to develop strong investor relations. Moreover, in recognition of the shift towards private placements, established stock exchanges have adjusted their product lines to capture private placement order flow. For example, NASDAQ (the second-largest stock exchange globally) has a portal to display and post interest in new private placements.

One area on which private capital has focused is environmental, society and governance (ESG) investments. With interest in sustainability and climate change exploding in recent years, investors are increasingly seeking out companies that meet their criteria for responsible investing. In the United States, $400 billion has been invested in ESG private capital between 2015 and 2020, with $100 billion invested in 2020 alone. ESG-related private debt and equity increased by 23 and 30 per cent per annum, respectively, over the period. Venture capital ESG investments also increased by 30 per cent per annum (McKinsey Global Private Markets Review, 2021)

1.3 The Environment for Raising Capital

Layers of regulation govern public debt and equity issues. These regulations certainly increase the costs of issuing public securities, but they also protect investors, which, in theory, should enhance their value. The significance of capital market regulations can be illustrated by contrasting the situation in Western Europe with that of some emerging markets, which are much less regulated. A significant risk in emerging markets is that shareholder rights will not be respected. This affects the market valuations of emerging-market stocks, which sometimes sell for substantially less than the value of their assets.

It is important to emphasize that the heterogeneity of domestic corporate environments can be substantial, and it is impossible to briefly explain all the differences across each country. Fortunately, researchers have identified several commonalities that effectively capture the main characteristics of different corporate environments. Specifically, these are the legal environment, financial development, and corporate ownership concentration.

It is also tempting to treat the European Union as a unified entity when discussing the environment for raising capital. However, variability in the regulatory regimes of EU member countries is just as significant as that between, say, China and the US. Therefore, one of the repeat messages in this textbook is that to understand corporate strategy, you must understand the financial markets, which means familiarizing yourself with differences in regulatory environments across countries.

The Legal Environment

The legal environment in which a corporation does business can impact its strategy and financing decisions. In a common law system, the law varies with the decisions of a country's courts, whereas under civil law, it is strictly interpreted with respect to an agreed-upon code or charter. France, Germany and Italy are examples of countries that follow civil law systems, whereas the UK, Ireland and the US follow common law.

The third form of legal system found in certain parts of the world is religious law, where religious principles form the basis of legal decisions. Islamic sharia law, followed by Iran, Saudi Arabia, and parts of Malaysia and Nigeria, is the most common form of religious law. Sharia law impacts financing activity because Islam does not allow interest payments in any economic transaction, and this means that interest-bearing financial loans are strictly forbidden.

Exhibit 1.6 presents a snapshot of countries that follow different legal systems. Many countries do not follow one system alone, and the exact legal environment can be a hybrid of two systems. For example, India's legal system is based on common law, but personal laws are driven by religious law depending on an individual's religion. Scotland has a different legal system from the rest of the UK, with most laws based on continental or Roman civil law. Commercial law in Scotland is an exception and is similar to the rest of the United Kingdom in this regard.

Exhibit 1.6 Legal Systems around the World

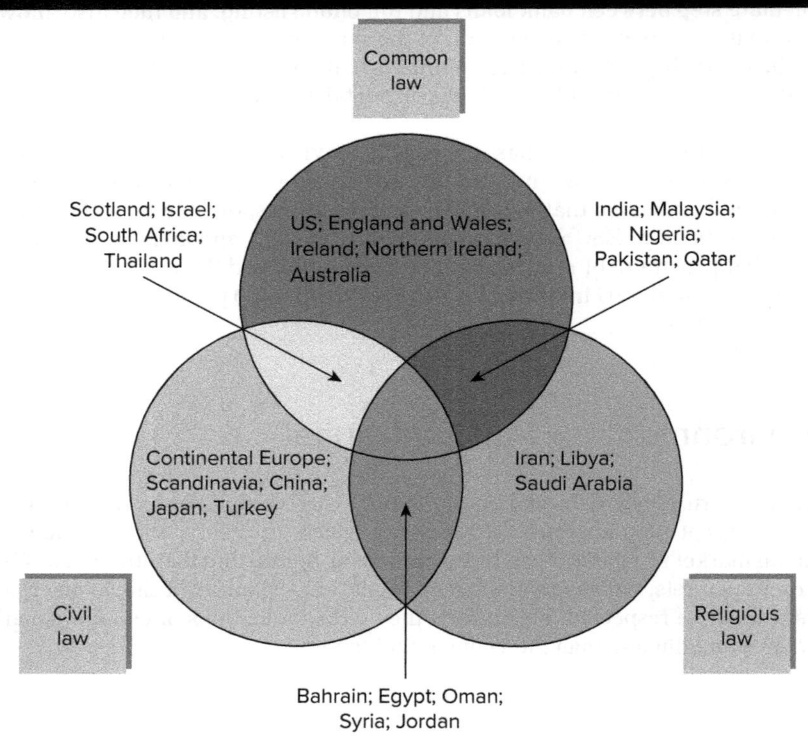

Because the corporate environment must respond quickly to different economic events, common law systems are better suited to adapt faster to these changes. This is because court cases can typically be resolved faster than changes in regulation through government statutes. Researchers[4] have examined differences in investor protection and law enforcement across various legal environments and have documented significant differences across countries. For example, common law countries tend to have stronger investor protection laws that are effectively and efficiently implemented, encouraging investment by external minority investors. Thus, financing strategies favouring outside investors (such as the public equity markets) tend to be more attractive in common law countries.

Law enforcement goes hand in hand with the form of the legal system, and the degree to which laws are implemented can significantly impact corporate financing activity. Even in Europe, law enforcement and corruption are exceptionally varied. Exhibit 1.7 presents the 2020 Corruption Perceptions Index as presented by Transparency International. The index is graded between 1 and 100, with a score of 1 indicating that a country is exceptionally corrupt. Scandinavian countries have very little corruption, but this tends to worsen as one goes further south through Europe. Consistent with their lack of economic development, emerging markets tend to have more corruption than developed countries.

Exhibit 1.7 Corruption around the World

Country	Score	Country	Score
Denmark	88	USA	67
Finland	85	Spain	62
Switzerland	85	Portugal	61
Singapore	85	Oman	54
Sweden	85	Italy	53
Norway	84	Saudi Arabia	53
Netherlands	82	Malaysia	51
Germany	80	Greece	50
United Kingdom	77	South Africa	44
Austria	76	Bahrain	42
Belgium	76	China	42
Japan	74	India	40
Ireland	72	Brazil	38
UAE	71	Russia	30
France	69	Somalia	12

Source: Transparency International UK.

The legal environment has a tangible impact on the cost of raising capital. Qi et al. (2010) looked into whether it was more expensive to issue debt in countries with weaker political institutions. They report that a one standard deviation improvement in political rights leads to a drop of 18.6 per cent in bond yields (a measure of bond risk and cost of raising debt capital). An influential factor is press freedom, potentially through its role as an independent monitor of firm performance.

The Financial System: Bank- and Market-Based Countries

In a bank-based financial system, banks play a significant role in facilitating money flows between investors with surplus cash and organizations that require funding. In market-based systems, financial markets take on the part of the financial intermediary and facilitate money flows between consumers and lenders. Corporations

[4] See La Porta et al. (1997, 1998) and Demirgüç-Kunt and Maksimovic (1998).

in countries with very well-developed financial markets find it easier to raise funds by issuing debt and equity to the public than through bank borrowing. Countries with bank-based systems have powerful banks that actively monitor corporations and are often involved in long-term strategic decisions.

Debate is still ongoing as to the relative merits and disadvantages of each type of system. Proponents of the bank-based view argue that these systems enhance market quality because banks expend considerable resources when they gather information on potential borrowers, and bank monitoring improves the decision-making of corporate managers. However, it has also been argued that corporations in market-based countries have a shorter-term focus than in bank-based countries because of the emphasis on share price and market performance. In addition, when banks are the primary source of funding to a company, managers may have longer investment horizons and be less willing to take risks.

On the other hand, market-based systems are arguably more efficient at financing companies because investors can profit easily from their research in liquid markets, which thus encourages trading. Moreover, in contrast to bank-based systems, countries with liquid financial markets increase the likelihood that poorly performing firms can be penalised through corporate takeovers. In addition, the variety of security instruments that are actively traded in market-based systems will improve a firm's risk management activities.

There are many ways in which a country's financial system can be classified as bank- or market-based. Exhibit 1.8 shows the level of domestic deposits in banks divided by stock market size for several countries. A country with a high ratio (above 1.5) could be regarded as a bank-based financial system, whereas market-based systems would have low values for this ratio. Note how the UK, South Africa and the US are market-based compared with most continental European countries.

Exhibit 1.8 Bank-versus Market-Based Financial Systems

Country	Deposit money banks' assets to GDP (%)	Stock market capitalisation to GDP (%)	Deposit money banks' assets/ Stock market capitali-sation	Country	Deposit money banks' assets to GDP (%)	Stock market capitali-sation to GDP (%)	Deposit money banks' assets/ Stock market capitali-sation
South Africa	77.91	245.42	**0.32**	Ireland	100.47	61.5	**1.63**
United States	60.2	143.31	**0.42**	Finland	101.88	57.22	**1.78**
Switzerland	177.55	219.31	**0.81**	UAE	102.65	54.09	**1.90**
Saudi Arabia	66.27	70	**0.95**	Germany	96.6	47.12	**2.05**
India	69.3	71.5	**0.97**	Spain	154.51	67.26	**2.30**
Belgium	81.08	80.37	**1.01**	Poland	68.15	29.3	**2.33**
United Kingdom	134.69	112.11	**1.20**	China	153.41	64.14	**2.39**
Oman	72.12	56.38	**1.28**	Russia	60.75	24.14	**2.52**
Netherlands	128.26	92.92	**1.38**	Norway	128.76	47.34	**2.72**
France	112.68	79.24	**1.42**	Denmark	184.59	61.18	**3.02**
Sweden	133.6	92.81	**1.44**	Austria	104.09	23.42	**4.44**
Bahrain	101.27	66.67	**1.52**	Italy	130.17	28.02	**4.65**
Australia	136.01	88.36	**1.54**	Greece	128.45	22.59	**5.69**

Source: World Bank and authors' own calculations.

Ownership Structure

Another factor that can affect business decision-making and corporate strategy is the ownership structure of companies. Ownership structure is the make-up and constitution of shareholdings in a firm. Most large companies are widely held in the UK and US, which means that no single investor has a significant ownership stake in a firm. In such environments, managers have greater power because no one investor has enough shares to become a majority owner. However, the rest of the world is characterized by closely held firms, where governments, families and banks are the principal shareholders. In these countries, the danger of the majority shareholder influencing corporate management to pursue objectives not aligned with minority shareholders can be high.

Exhibit 1.9 presents a breakdown of the ownership structure of all listed corporations for selected countries. Ownership structure has a massive impact on corporate objectives. Whereas all shareholders wish to maximize the value of their investment, how value is assessed differs according to the investor. For example, suppose a firm is widely held in a market-based economy, such as the UK, South Africa and the US. In that case, corporate objectives are likely to be focused on maximizing share price performance. Family firms have slightly different goals because managers must consider current shareholders and their descendants. This would suggest that managers of family firms have a longer-term perspective than other firms, which would influence the types of investment and funding they choose. Finally, firms with the government as significant shareholders would have to consider political objectives in addition to maximizing share value.

In many countries, financial institutions are the largest shareholders of companies, and this presents opportunities for financial managers because corporations can tap into existing financing resources when the need arises. However, there are challenges with having a financial institution as a major shareholder. Since the overriding objective of financial institutions is to maximize returns, they can pressure managers into providing short-term financial performance at the expense of long-term value gains. This behaviour is exacerbated when the institutional shareholder has its own short-term performance targets. Exhibit 1.10 presents the institutional ownership breakdown of selected countries. The power of financial institutions varies across countries, and in most domains, foreign financial institutions have a larger shareholding than domestic institutions. For example, in the UK, financial institutions owned 20.1 per cent of publicly listed firms in 2005, with 11.3 per cent of total market capitalization held by foreign financial institutions. However, this is not a uniform pattern with the US and Sweden notable counter-examples. Leuz et al. (2009) investigated the reasons for the global variation in foreign ownership and found that macro-level governance was a significant factor. Specifically, countries with poorer governance had lower levels of foreign ownership, particularly in those environments where information disclosure was inadequate.

Investment Banking

Just as governments are ubiquitous in issuing securities, so too are banks through their investment arms. Modern investment banking comprises two parts: the corporate business and the sales and trading business.

The Corporate Business

The corporate side of investment banking is a fee-for-service business: that is, the firm sells its expertise. The primary expertise of banks is underwriting securities, but they also sell other services. For example, they provide merger and acquisition advice in the form of prospecting for takeover targets, advising clients about the price to be offered for these targets, finding financing for a takeover, and planning takeover tactics or, on the other side, takeover defences. The major investment banking houses are also actively engaged in designing new financial instruments.

The Sales and Trading Business

Investment banks that underwrite securities sell them to the bank's institutional investors on the sales and trading end of their business. These investors include mutual funds, pension funds and insurance companies. Sales and trading also consist of public market making, trading for clients, and trading on the investment banking firm's own account.

Market making requires that the investment bank act as a **dealer** in securities, standing ready to buy and sell, respectively, at wholesale (**bid**) and retail (**ask**) prices. The bank makes money on the difference between the bid price and the ask price, or the **bid-ask spread.** Banks do this for corporate debt and equity securities and as dealers in government securities. In addition, investment banks trade securities using their own funds, known as **proprietary trading.** Proprietary trading is riskier for an investment bank than being a dealer and earning the bid-ask spread, but the rewards can be commensurately larger.

Exhibit 1.9 Corporate Ownership around the World

Country	State	Familes/ Indivi-duals	Private Firms	Closely Held	Widely Held Private Firms	Widely Held Public Firms	Widely Held Block-holder	Widely Held No Block-holder	Widely Held
Austria	8.3	19.8	39.6	**67.7**	7.3	7.3	17.7	0.0	**32.3**
Bahrain	19.5	12.2	9.8	**41.5**	4.9	7.3	41.5	4.9	**58.6**
Belgium	5.6	17.4	29.2	**52.2**	6.2	5.0	31.7	5.0	**47.9**
China	23.2	17.3	29.5	**70.0**	1.9	0.4	21.3	6.4	**30.0**
Denmark	0.6	7.1	17.3	**25.0**	5.8	5.1	55.8	8.3	**75.0**
Finland	7.1	8.8	15.0	**30.9**	0.9	4.4	53.1	10.6	**69.0**
France	2.9	29.2	24.9	**57.0**	5.8	5.2	29.8	2.2	**43.0**
Germany	3.6	26.2	25.3	**55.1**	6.4	7.2	28.5	2.8	**44.9**
Greece	3.1	51.5	12.7	**67.3**	1.3	7.9	22.3	1.3	**32.8**
India	5.6	21.0	13.6	**40.2**	0.9	6.1	40.0	12.8	**59.8**
Ireland	1.5	7.7	13.8	**23.0**	1.5	1.5	61.5	12.3	**76.8**
Italy	3.8	36.1	22.9	**62.8**	2.3	4.5	25.6	4.9	**37.3**
Malaysia	5.9	16.1	26.7	**48.7**	0.8	5.3	40.2	5.1	**51.4**
Netherlands	2.3	10.5	21.1	**33.9**	6.0	6.8	51.9	1.5	**66.2**
Norway	5.0	13.4	16.9	**35.3**	4.0	2.0	54.2	4.5	**64.7**
Oman	24.4	22.0	12.2	**58.6**	2.4	4.9	31.7	2.4	**41.4**
Russia	26.6	16.7	25.9	**69.2**	5.3	3.9	20.2	1.4	**30.8**
Saudi Arabia	12.6	11.8	14.3	**38.7**	5.0	5.0	49.6	1.7	**61.3**
Singapore	5.9	19.0	17.2	**42.1**	1.4	5.1	34.8	16.6	**57.9**
South Africa	0.5	6.8	12.1	**19.4**	4.9	14.1	52.4	9.2	**80.6**
Spain	3.8	22.0	12.1	**37.9**	5.5	7.7	47.3	1.6	**62.1**
Sweden	1.2	13.4	19.3	**33.9**	3.6	5.3	47.8	9.5	**66.2**
Switzerland	6.9	19.9	14.5	**41.3**	5.4	4.7	42.4	6.2	**58.7**
UAE	37.2	19.1	7.4	**63.7**	2.1	2.1	31.9	0.0	**36.1**
UK	0.9	10.1	5.7	**16.7**	1.2	2.7	66.3	13.1	**83.3**
US	0.2	16.2	6.2	**22.6**	3.4	2.4	57.0	14.6	**77.4**

Source: Adapted from Table 1, Aminadav, G. and Papaioannou, E. (2020). Corporate control around the world. *The Journal of Finance,* 75(3), 1191–1246. This table reports the share of controlled firms by type (family-controlled, government-controlled, controlled by a private firm with an unmatched ultimate owner, controlled by a widely held private firm, controlled by a widely held public firm), the share of widely held firms with at least one block (stake >5%), and the share of widely held corporations without any block. Identification of controlled corporations is based on the 20% absolute voting-rights cutoff.

Exhibit 1.10 Institutional Ownership by Country

	Market cap. ($ bn)	Total inst.	Foreign inst.	Foreign US inst.	Foreign non-US inst.	Domestic inst.	Indep. inst.	Mutual funds	Invest. adv.	Grey inst.	Bank trusts	Insur. comp.	Other inst.
US	19,541	65.7	6.0		6.0	59.6	44.0	18.1	25.9	19.0	7.5	2.6	9.0
UK	4,231	20.1	11.3	6.8	4.6	8.8	12.8	3.6	9.2	7.2	4.0	2.4	0.8
France	2,332	21.1	13.5	5.1	8.4	7.6	11.1	3.7	7.4	9.9	6.7	2.6	0.6
Germany	1,568	21.0	13.5	5.8	7.7	7.5	10.3	3.0	7.3	10.6	8.4	1.5	0.7
Sweden	445	33.8	12.9	5.1	7.8	21.0	17.2	8.9	8.3	16.4	6.2	2.9	7.3
Netherlands	796	32.4	30.8	14.0	16.8	1.6	20.6	5.3	15.3	11.5	7.9	2.4	1.1
Switzerland	1,137	22.9	19.5	10.1	9.4	3.3	14.0	5.2	8.8	8.7	6.4	1.2	1.1
Italy	1,013	13.6	11.1	2.9	8.3	2.5	7.1	2.7	4.5	6.4	5.0	1.1	0.3
Norway	226	21.1	13.5	5.8	7.7	7.6	11.7	3.7	8.0	9.2	5.1	1.2	2.9
Ireland	133	30.5	29.7	14.4	15.4	0.8	20.0	7.1	12.9	9.6	6.7	1.5	1.4
Belgium	441	9.8	7.8	2.3	5.5	2.0	4.6	1.5	3.1	5.2	3.7	1.2	0.2
Denmark	189	20.5	10.9	4.4	6.5	9.6	8.1	2.7	5.4	12.3	4.0	0.6	7.6
Spain	750	16.6	14.1	4.0	10.1	2.5	8.5	2.7	5.8	8.1	6.1	1.4	0.6
Singapore	240	10.8	9.2	4.6	4.6	1.7	8.2	3.4	4.9	2.5	1.7	0.5	0.3
Finland	235	33.8	28.7	13.1	15.6	5.1	18.8	6.4	12.3	14.7	8.1	2.2	4.4
South Africa	426	11.2	7.4	4.3	3.1	3.7	8.6	1.8	6.8	2.4	0.9	1.2	0.2
India	420	15.9	11.0	6.7	4.3	4.9	13.5	5.3	8.2	2.0	1.6	0.2	0.3
Austria	138	13.2	12.2	4.0	8.2	1.1	7.7	2.6	5.1	5.5	4.5	0.8	0.2
Greece	161	10.2	9.7	2.9	6.8	0.6	5.8	2.0	3.8	4.3	3.2	0.8	0.2

The table reports total institutional ownership, foreign institutional ownership by all institutions, US institutions and non-US institutions, domestic institutional ownership, ownership by independent institutions (mutual funds and independent investment advisers), and ownership by grey institutions (bank trusts, insurance companies, and other institutions) as a percentage of destination country stock market capitalization in December 2005.

Source: Ferreira and Matos (2008).

The Largest Investment Banks

Although there are many types of financial institutions that carry out investment banking, only the largest banks account for most of the activity in all lines of business. Exhibit 1.11 presents the top **underwriters**[5] in the EMEA (Europe, Middle East and Africa) area for 2020 and the amounts they underwrote.

Exhibit 1.11 Top Underwriters in the EMEA Region, 2020

Bookrunner	Rank 2020	Rank 2019	Proceeds US$mil	Market Share	Market Share Change	% of Deals
Morgan Stanley	1	3	18,524	8.9	1.2	77
Goldman Sachs & Co	2	2	18,397	8.8	0.9	99
JP Morgan	3	1	18,255	8.8	0.3	118
Citi	4	4	14,735	7.1	1.5	82
BofA Securities Inc	5	6	13,124	6.3	2.1	75
BNP Paribas SA	6	8	9,319	4.5	0.8	71
Barclays	7	9	9,104	4.4	1.6	62
Credit Suisse	8	5	8,786	4.2	−0.8	49
HSBC Holdings PLC	9	11	7,716	3.7	1.2	51
UBS	10	7	5,925	2.9	−1.0	40
Jefferies LLC	11	12	5,643	2.7	0.5	55
UniCredit	12	22	3,962	1.9	0.9	27
Numis	13	17	3,815	1.8	0.5	45
Credit Agricole CIB	14	14	3,414	1.6	−0.3	25
Societe Generale	15	10	3,401	1.6	−1.0	35
Deutsche Bank	16	13	3,387	1.6	−0.5	32
Carnegie Investment Bank AB	17	20	3,180	1.5	0.4	80
Berenberg	18	16	3,154	1.5	0.0	40
Davy	19	60	2,130	1.0	0.7	9
Santander Corp & Invest Bkg	20	19	2,054	1.0	−0.1	15
ABG Sundal Collier	21	41	1,998	1.0	0.4	59
Nordea	22	25	1,851	0.9	0.1	38
Danske Bank	23	48	1,814	0.9	0.5	32
VTB Capital	24	53	1,705	0.8	0.5	8
IMI – Intesa Sanpaolo	25	56	1,674	0.8	0.5	12
Industry Total			**208,125**	**100.0**		**1,229**

Source: EMEA Equity Capital Markets Review, Full Year 2020, Refinitiv

[5] The primary or lead underwriter in a security issue is known as the *bookrunner*.

The Underwriting Process

The essential outline of investment banking worldwide has been in place for almost a century and originated in the United States. The players have changed, of course, but the way they do business now is roughly the same as a century ago.

The underwriter of a security issue performs four main functions: (1) origination, (2) distribution, (3) risk bearing and (4) certification.

Origination

Origination involves advising the issuing firm about the type of security to issue, the timing of the issue and the pricing of the issue. Origination also means working with the firm to develop the **registration statement** and forming a syndicate of investment bankers to market the issue. The managing or lead underwriter performs all these tasks.

Distribution

The second function an underwriter performs is the **distribution,** or selling, of the issue. Distribution is generally carried out by a syndicate of banks formed by the lead underwriter. The banks in the syndicate are listed in the offer **prospectus,** along with how much of the issue each has agreed to sell.

Risk Bearing

The third function the underwriter performs is **risk bearing.** In most cases, the underwriter has agreed to buy a firm's new securities and resell them to its clients. **Fair practice rules** may prevent the underwriter from selling securities at a price higher than agreed, so the underwriter's upside is limited. Fair practice rules apply in several developed countries but are not universal. If the issue does poorly, the underwriter may be stuck with securities that may end up being sold at bargain prices. However, the actual risk underwriters take when marketing securities is generally limited since most issues are not priced until the day or even hours before they go on sale. Until that final pricing meeting, the underwriter is not committed to selling the issue.

Certification

An additional role of an underwriter is to certify the quality of an issue, which requires that the bank maintain a sound reputation in capital markets. An investment banker's reputation will quickly decline if the certification task is not performed correctly. Moreover, if an underwriter substantially misprices an issue, its future business is likely to be damaged, and it might even be sued. A study by Booth and Smith (1986) suggested that underwriters, aware of the costs associated with mispricing an issue, charge higher fees on issues that are harder to value.

The Underwriting Agreement

The **underwriting agreement** between a firm and its underwriter specifies what is being sold, the amount being sold and the selling price. The agreement also specifies the **underwriting spread,** which is the difference between the total proceeds of the offering and the net proceeds that go to the issuing firm, and the existence and extent of the **overallotment option.** This option, sometimes called the **'Green Shoe option'** after the firm that first used it, permits the investment banker to request that more shares be issued on the same terms as those already sold.

The underwriting agreement shows the fixed fees the firm must pay, including listing fees, taxes, regulator fees, transfer agent's fees, legal and accounting costs, and printing expenses. In addition to these fixed fees, firms may have to pay several other forms of compensation to the underwriters. For example, underwriters often receive warrants as part of their compensation.[6]

Classifying Offerings

If a firm is issuing equity to the public for the first time, it makes an **initial public offering (IPO).** If a firm is already publicly traded and is simply selling more equity, it is making a **seasoned offering (SEO).** Both IPOs and seasoned offerings can include both primary and secondary issues. In a **primary issue,** the firm raises

[6] See Barry et al. (1991). Also, Chapter 3 discusses warrants in more detail.

capital for itself by selling equity to the public; a **secondary issue** or an offer for sale is undertaken by existing large shareholders who want to sell a substantial number of shares they currently own.[7]

The Costs of Debt and Equity Issues

Exhibit 1.12 shows the direct costs of both seasoned equity offerings in the UK and US. Three things stand out. First, total issue costs decline as the gross proceeds of the offering increase for both US and UK companies. Thus, it appears that issuance costs are subject to substantial economies of scale. Second, issue costs in the USA are higher than in the UK for most levels of gross proceeds. Finally, and perhaps most important, the costs of issuing securities to the public are quite high. For example, total direct expenses are approximately 5 per cent in the UK, which rises to nearly 15 per cent for small issues.

Exhibit 1.12 Costs of New Issues

UK Rights Issues and Open Offers, Purged Sample		US SEOs	
Gross Proceeds (£m)	**Total Costs (%)**	**Gross Proceeds ($ m)**	**Total Costs (%)**
312.5+	2.17	500+	3.15
125.0–312.4	2.65	200–499.9	3.47
62.5–124.9	2.79	100–199.9	4.22
50.0–62.4	3.54	80–99.9	4.73
37.5–49.9	3.07	60–79.9	5.18
25.0–37.4	3.70	40–59.9	5.87
12.5–24.9	3.68	20–39.9	6.93
6.25–12.4	5.16	10–19.9	8.72
1.25–6.24	8.27	2–9.9	13.28
0.1–1.24	14.36		
Total	5.78		7.11
Median	4.28		

Source: Adapted from Armitage (2000), Table 1.

The total costs of selling securities fall into the following six main categories.

1. Gross spread: The gross spread consists of direct fees paid by the issuer to the underwriting syndicate – the difference between the price the issuer receives and the offer price.
2. Other direct expenses: These are direct costs incurred by the issuer that are not part of the compensation to underwriters. These costs include filing fees, legal fees, and taxes – all reported on the prospectus.
3. Indirect expenses: These costs are not reported on the prospectus and include management time spent working on the new issue.
4. Abnormal returns: In a seasoned issue of equity, the price of the existing shares drops on average by 3 per cent on the announcement of the issue. This drop is called the abnormal return.
5. Underpricing: For initial public offerings, losses arise from selling the equity below the true value.
6. Green Shoe option: The Green Shoe option gives the underwriters the right to buy additional shares at the offer price to cover overallotments.

[7]Sometimes the term 'secondary' means any non-IPO, even if the shares are primary. To avoid confusion, some investment bankers use the term 'add-on', meaning primary shares for an already public company.

Research on these issue costs provides several insights. First, with the possible exception of straight debt offerings, there are substantial economies of scale. The underwriter spreads are smaller on larger issues, and other direct costs fall sharply as a percentage of the amount raised – reflecting the fixed nature of such charges. Second, the costs associated with selling debt are substantially less than selling equity. Third, IPOs have higher expenses than SEOs, but the difference is not as significant as might originally be guessed. Fourth, straight bonds are cheaper to float than convertible bonds. Finally, higher-rated bonds are said to be investment grade, whereas lower-rated bonds are non-investment grade. Research has shown substantial economies of scale with debt offerings and that investment-grade issues have much lower direct costs, particularly for straight bonds.

Issuing securities to the public is a weighty decision, especially for smaller companies. Although there are many benefits, such as raising needed capital and spreading ownership, the costs cannot be ignored.

Result 1.3 summarises the main points of this subsection.

Results

Result 1.3

Issuing public debt and equity can be a lengthy and expensive process. Public debt issuance is relatively routine for large corporations, and the costs are relatively low. However, equity is much more costly to issue for large and small firms, and it is especially expensive for firms issuing equity for the first time.

Types of Underwriting Arrangement

Firm Commitment vs Best-Efforts Offering

A public offering can be executed on either a firm commitment or a best-efforts basis. In a **firm-commitment offering,** the underwriter agrees to buy the whole offering from the firm at a set price and offer it to the public at a slightly higher price. In this case, the underwriter bears the risk of not selling the issue, and the firm's proceeds are guaranteed. In a **best-efforts offering,** the underwriter and the firm fix a price, as well as the minimum and maximum number of shares to be sold. The underwriter then makes the 'best effort' to sell the issue. Investors express their interest by depositing payments into the underwriter's escrow account. If the underwriter has not sold the minimum number of shares after a specified period, usually 90 days, the offer is withdrawn, the money is refunded, and the issuing firm can try again later. Nearly all seasoned offerings are made with firm-commitment offerings. The more well-known firms that have IPOs tend to use firm-commitment offerings, but less-established firms tend to go public with best-efforts offerings.

Negotiated vs Competitive Offerings

The issuing firm can also choose between a negotiated and competitive offering. The firm negotiates the underwriting agreement with the underwriter in a **negotiated offering.** In a **competitive offering,** the firm specifies the underwriting agreement and puts it out to bid. In practice, firms rarely use competitive offerings except for a few utilities that are required to use them. This is somewhat puzzling since competitive offerings appear to have lower issue costs.[8]

Shelf Offerings

Another way to offer securities is through a **shelf offering.** Many countries allow firms to register more securities than they wish to issue. Only one registration statement needs to be lodged, allowing several issues of any amount (subject to the initial number of securities registered) to take place at any time without further notice to the regulator. Then, when the need for financing arises, the firm simply asks a bank for a bid to take the securities 'off the shelf' and sell them. If the issuing firm is not satisfied with this bid, it can shop among other banks for better offers.

[8] For a discussion of this matter, see Bhagat and Frost (1986).

Rights Offerings

Finally, there is the possibility of a **rights offering** for firms selling equity. Rights entitle existing shareholders to buy new shares in the firm at what is generally a discounted price. Rights offerings can be made without investment bankers or with them on a standby basis. A rights offering on a **standby basis** includes an agreement by the investment bank to take up any unexercised rights and exercise them, paying the subscription price to the firm in exchange for the new shares. In some cases, rights are actively traded after the firm distributes them.

1.4 Raising Capital in International Markets

Capital markets have truly become global. Firms raise funds from almost all parts of the world, not just in their own country. Similarly, investors provide capital for foreign as well as domestic firms. A firm can raise money internationally in two general ways: in what is known as the Euromarkets or in the domestic markets of various countries.

Euromarkets

The term 'Euromarkets' is a misnomer because the markets have no actual physical location. Instead, **Euromarkets** are simply a collection of large international banks that help firms issue bonds and make loans outside the firm's country. So firms domiciled in the United States could, for instance, issue dollar-denominated bonds, known as **Eurodollar bonds,** outside the United States, or yen-denominated bonds, known as **Euroyen bonds,** outside Japan. Similarly, a German multinational could borrow through the Euromarkets in either British pounds, Swiss francs or euros.

Direct Issuance

The second way to raise money internationally is to sell directly in the foreign markets, or what is called **direct issuance.** For example, a Thai corporation could issue a yen-denominated bond in the Japanese bond market. Or a Chinese firm might sell equity to US investors and become publicly listed on one of the US exchanges. Being a foreign issuer in a financial market means satisfying all the regulations that apply to domestic firms, as well as special regulations that might apply only to foreign issuers.

1.5 Islamic Financing

With the relative decline in Western bank credit compared with other environments, interest has grown concerning other financing sources, especially for those companies that operate and are owned by Muslims in the Middle East and Gulf region. As a result, financial institutions have developed securities and business practices reflecting Islamic values in response to the rapid expansion of firms from this region. This is known as *Islamic financing,* with the main characteristic being that interest of any kind is not allowed to be charged on financial securities.

The United Kingdom is at the forefront of Islamic financing in Western Europe, with 23 banks having Islamic financing divisions. Other European Islamic financing centres include Switzerland, France and Luxembourg. In the Middle East, Iran and Saudi Arabia hold the majority of the world's financial sharia-compliant assets (around $400 billion), with Bahrain acting as the financial centre for global trading. Malaysia is the leading country for Islamic financing in South East Asia. Islamic financing need not be confined only to Muslims, and in Malaysia, nearly a quarter of all users of Islamic products are non-Muslims.

Not having interest-bearing securities presents challenges to firms wishing to raise financing for investment projects. In response, Islamic banks have created innovative financing methods consistent with Islamic or sharia principles and have debt-like characteristics. The most common of these involve elements of profit-sharing, known as *Mudharabah,* joint ventures (*Musharaka*), leasing (*Ljara*) and compensation for facilitating the financing activity (*Murabahah*). Islamic securities that can be traded on exchanges are known as *Sukuk.*

1.6 Trends in Raising Capital

This chapter has so far provided a general overview of the process of how the modern firm raises capital across different regulatory environments. Much of what you have learned has remained the same for decades and, in some cases, for as long as a century. However, capital markets have changed dramatically over the past few years and will continue to change in the future. Financial technology has led to revolutions in how companies run their operations and trade. In addition, the world is experiencing the full effect of climate change, the global Covid pandemic has severely disrupted supply chains, and geopolitical issues are becoming significant barriers to trade and international trade capital flows. Although no one can predict the future, we should note several trends in the capital markets.

The New Economic Reality

The global pandemic in 2020 forced all countries to borrow and print money to mitigate the economic impact of lockdown restrictions, international travel seizing up and funding vaccination programmes for whole populations. After a sustained period of low interest rates and inflation, the world's economies need new growth to offset the record government spending between 2020 and 2022. Before the emergence of Covid, money was in cheap supply, and global supply chains were as efficient as possible.

Unfortunately, the corporate world is now a very different place. Standard theoretical paradigms, such as efficient capital markets, are no longer considered as appropriate as they once were. As a result, risk – its identification, measurement, and management – has become significantly more critical, and corporate models that once worked are no longer so powerful.

Global economies may recover within a few years, and the corporate world will settle into a new equilibrium over the coming years. New practices and views regarding how corporations do their business may also arise. Corporate strategy must also adapt to the new reality with the rapidly emerging importance of sustainability issues and climate change. Those companies that quickly adapt to the new environment will be successful. Those that do not will fail.

Financial Technology

In 2008, an anonymous programmer called Nakamoto proposed a new technology called blockchain to validate ownership of a virtual currency, bitcoin. A blockchain is an automated database created using cryptographic methods that makes it impossible to change data or information in a ledger of transactions retrospectively. As a result, it has a massive advantage over standard financial ledgers, which can be modified or hacked by enterprising criminals and fraudsters.

Blockchain has revolutionized financial transactions and, although the world has not yet fully moved to this new technology, it is almost certain it will become ubiquitous in business over the next ten to twenty years. The central application of blockchain is currently to track the ownership of financial assets using peer-to-peer technology, and this is only the start of the possibilities for its use. For example, most of the world's stock exchanges are actively investigating how blockchain can be used to trade equity, debt and derivative securities. Other blockchain applications include using it to track ownership of a wide range of assets, including property and land registrations, cars and fine art. It could also maintain public records such as driving licences, health service data, vaccination records and academic qualifications.

Since blockchain technology accurately records transactions in real-time on a distributed (that is, non-centralized) ledger, some commentators (for example, Yermack 2017) have argued that it could also be used to record all corporate transactions. The purpose of this would be to minimize fraud and misreporting of earnings. In addition, the technology would also reduce the likelihood of illegal insider trading by corporate executives because of the ability to track information flows.

Financial technology does not solely apply to blockchain technologies. Open banking has spread worldwide, with data on depositors' bank account transactions now available to appropriately certified non-bank companies. Open banking has created a whole new class of businesses looking to analyse spending patterns using artificial intelligence and big data to maximize the efficiency of short-term capital usage and identify the best insurance deals on the market for each user. In addition, open banking has allowed new entrants into the payment systems sector that banking institutions once monopolized. New payment mechanisms, such as Apple pay, have been developed using innovative technologies to allow contactless payments for goods and services.

New forms of lending and investing have been created, primarily through peer-to-peer platforms, crowdfunding and online fintech lenders, which fall outside traditional banking regulations. Buchak et al. (2018) examined fintech lending intermediaries and found they were more active in the refinancing market. They are also more expensive to borrow from, but the convenience of online transactions led to them capturing new market share. Crowdfunding has not substituted for other forms of financing but instead created a new platform for raising funds, particularly for new start-ups and small-scale entrepreneurs. It can also provide much-needed market demand information for new products. If a crowdfunding campaign is not successful, it is unlikely that the firm will find investors to commercialize a new product or service. Finally, crowdfunding allows companies to avoid set-up costs because it generates customer demand before the new product is produced (Bollaert et al. 2021).

The advent of new financial technologies has changed how companies, financial institutions, stock exchanges, investors and consumers engage. The future will likely bring just as profound a change in line with the expanding role of blockchains, artificial intelligence and big data in everyday business operations. Although we do not know what next year's new technology will be, we know that it will come and is likely to change how we do things that we currently take for granted.

International Finance

The emergence of China as a global economic power has led to a fundamental shift in the way Western companies undertake international trade. Only once before, when the United States became an industrial powerhouse in the 19th century, have European businesses been under so much threat from global competitors. Furthermore, the economic landscape will undoubtedly evolve further as the world recovers from the Covid pandemic. Increasing trade barriers between China and the west, the continuing impact of Brexit on European and UK firms, increased influence of China in emerging markets because of its Belt and Road initiative, a refocusing of business on local supply chains, and concerted moves to protect national industries and strategic resources will be the main drivers for this change.

It remains to be seen if financial technologies, such as blockchains, and cryptocurrencies, such as bitcoin and etherium, will lessen or remove the effects of a seemingly unstoppable move to a more polarized world. Cryptocurrencies allow investors and traders to bypass national government regulations and are truly decentralized trading platforms. Although China has stamped down on cryptocurrencies and made them effectively illegal, their trading has continued, and valuations have held up, as evidenced in Exhibit 1.13.

Exhibit 1.13 Bitcoin price history 2014–2022

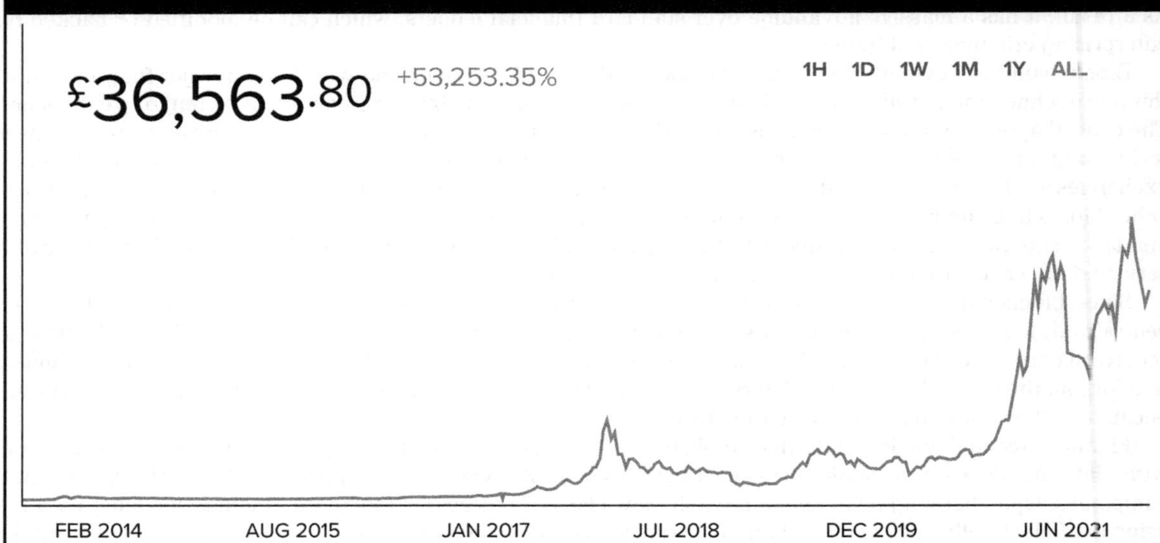

Source: Coinbase.

To understand how business practice will change over the coming decade, consider the world's trading blocs, especially the new free trade agreement, Regional Comprehensive Economic Partnership (RCEP), signed in 2020 by fifteen countries, including China, Australia, Japan, New Zealand and South Korea. Together, the countries that form RCEP account for 30 per cent of the world's global GDP and rivals NAFTA (North Atlantic Free Trade Agreement) and the EU in terms of economic power. Exhibit 1.14 presents the relative share of global imports and exports of each bloc. RCEP is characterized by net exporters, and so the new agreement, which eliminates tariffs on 90 per cent of goods traded, will increase the GDP of all the members.

Exhibit 1.14 Percentage of World Trade Held by Countries in EU, RCEP and NAFTA

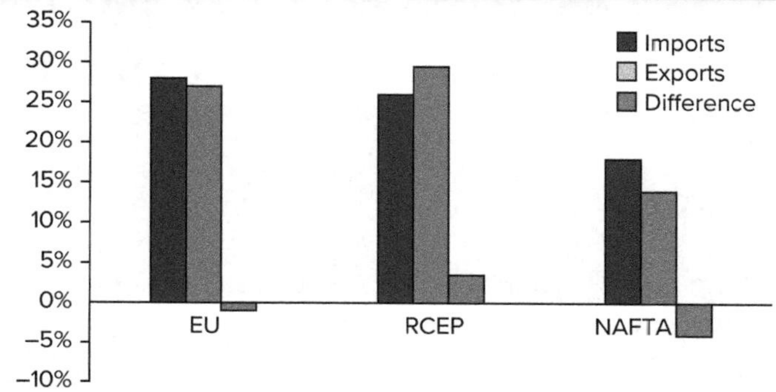

Source: International Trade Centre.

Closer to home, the effect of Brexit on the UK and European companies remain to be determined, and the arguments for and against the UK leaving the European Union are still politically charged with little opportunity for reasoned debate between camps. In addition, the beginning of the UK–EU trade agreement began at the beginning of 2020, and its impact was overwhelmingly dominated by the economic impact of the Covid pandemic. Unfortunately, it will take a few years more before ascertaining if Brexit has been a positive or negative experience for the UK and EU.

The preceding discussion tells us one thing. If British and European businesses are to achieve growth rates commensurate with previous decades, they will have to understand the changing geopolitical dynamics and how these will affect their business strategy. Regulatory, monetary and fiscal policies could dramatically change in the coming years because of the recovery required from the pandemic. To refund public finances, governments may need to increase corporate and income tax rates, reduce public spending and incentivize innovative new industries. With new approaches to international supply chains and increased political risk from international trade, the future is highly uncertain. This means that financial risk management will be even more necessary to manage exposures to currency volatility.

Sustainability and Climate Change

Interest in Environmental, Social and Governance (ESG) issues has exploded in recent years with the recognition that climate change will affect everyone if countries, businesses and individuals fail to make a concerted effort to avert potentially catastrophic shifts in global temperatures. When country leaders met in Glasgow at the end of 2021 for COP26, they urged business leaders to commit to sustainability principles. This appeal has galvanized a new generation of entrepreneurs and businesses in putting sustainability and climate change at the centre of their business strategies. In addition, financial institutions made significant commitments to ensure that sustainability was a critical factor in all lending or investing decisions.

To reflect the importance of sustainability in business strategy, the Governance and Accountability Institute reported that 92 per cent of all S&P 500 companies had published a sustainability report in 2020. Even among small to medium enterprises, 49 per cent of firms had published a sustainability report. As a result, sustainability and climate change are no longer topics for the margins but are now best practices for companies looking for new financing. Further, investors require companies to be clear about their approach to the environment and society.

Many firms now explicitly consider their business and strategic model within the UN Sustainable Development Goals framework and present these as part of their overall corporate governance framework to reflect this change. The goals span a range of socially optimal objectives and contribute to the environment and society in a small way. Exhibit 1.15 presents these in a graphical format.

Exhibit 1.15 UN Strategic Development Goals

Source: United Nations.

Charting the Future

The preceding discussion points to the following: change is coming to businesses and how they interact with the world. If corporations are unable or unwilling to change, it is probable that they will perform below expectations and may even cease to exist in the future. So how can corporations flourish in this new environment amid the emerging competitive pressures pressing in on them?

Despite the UK leaving the EU, both parties are still massive trading partners, and the EU is the most important market to the UK. However, UK–EU trade has become much more complex and costly for some industries, and affected firms have had to adapt their operations rapidly. The UK has now joined Switzerland and Norway as non-EU European countries, and this will have a long-lasting impact on the competitiveness of British and EU firms.

With so much change in the world, opportunities still exist and will continue to exist in the future. Technological advances, climate change, a renewed focus on sustainability, and even the rapidly evolving political environment will create new roads and avenues for companies to innovate. This innovation may be around new products, services, customer segments or even new industries. It is now up to individual companies to identify these opportunities and adapt their corporate strategy to take advantage of whatever comes their way in the next three to five years.

Results

Result 1.4

Current trends will fundamentally influence how corporations raise capital and do their business in the future. Key trends include technological advancement, sustainability and global political instability. In this new economic environment, corporate strategy must adapt if companies are to exploit the future challenges awaiting them.

1.7 Summary and Conclusions

Because of the changes taking place in the world, financial managers face choices that are very different now from those they faced several years ago. As a result, corporate finance professionals need an advanced knowledge of how financial markets operate, how financial instruments are priced, and how they can be used to add value to their company's business strategy.

This text is devoted to making its readers adept at dealing with the new world of finance and the challenges their companies will face in a post-pandemic world. The first step in developing the necessary skills is becoming familiar with what the new world looks like, who the players are and the choices to be made. In this vein, Chapter 1 has described the securities available for external financing, current trends in financing the firm, the institutional and regulatory environment in which securities are issued, the process of issuing securities and recent trends in raising capital. The following two chapters will provide a more detailed discussion of the international debt and equity markets.

Key Concepts

Result 1.1: Internal financing is the primary funding source for new investments in most countries. When firms raise external financing, they most likely borrow from a bank or issue equity.

The important distinctions between debt (bonds/bank loans) and equity are:

1. Debt claims are senior to equity claims.
2. Interest payments on debt claims are tax-deductible, but dividends on equity claims are not.

Result 1.2: Corporations raise capital from both private and public sources. Some advantages associated with private sources are as follows.

- Terms of private bonds and equities can be customized for individual investors.
- There is no costly registration with the securities regulator.
- There is no need to reveal confidential information.
- They are easier to renegotiate.

Privately placed financial instruments can also have disadvantages. For example:

- Limited investor base.
- Less liquid.

Result 1.3: Issuing public debt and equity can be a lengthy and expensive process. Public debt issuance is relatively routine for large corporations, and the costs are relatively low. However, equity is much more costly to issue for large as well as small firms, and it is especially expensive for firms issuing equity for the first time.

Result 1.4: Current trends will fundamentally influence how corporations raise capital and do their business in the future. Key trends include technological advancement, sustainability and global political instability. Therefore, corporate strategy in this new economic environment must adapt if companies are to exploit the future challenges awaiting them.

Key Terms

ask 13
best-efforts offering 19
bid 13
bid-ask spread 13
capital markets 3
competitive offering 19

dealer 13
debt 6
direct issuance 20
distribution 17
equity 6
Eurodollar bonds 20
Euromarkets 20
Euroyen bonds 20
Federal Financial Services Agency (BaFin) 7
financial intermediaries 4
fair practice rules 17
Financial Conduct Authority (FCA) 7
firm-commitment offering 19
Green Shoe option 17
initial public offering (IPO) 17
inside information 8
internal capital 4
market making 13
negotiated offering 19
origination 17
overallotment option 17
primary issue 17
private placements 8
proprietary trading 13
prospectus 17
registration statement 17
rights offering 20
risk bearing 17
seasoned offering (SEO) 17
secondary issue 18
secondary markets 7
securities 7
Securities and Exchange Commission (SEC) 7
senior 6
shelf offering 19
standby basis 20
underwriters 16
underwriting agreement 17
underwriting spread 17

Exercises

1.1 Companies can seek out many types of financing. Review the benefits and weaknesses of each and explain why a firm's legal and capital market environment may impact the funding decision.

1.2 Why is there a need for regulation? If a market was fully efficient, would there be a need for regulation?

1.3 What are the strengths and weaknesses of private and public sources of financing? Would these be different for small versus large firms? What about firms in developed markets versus emerging markets?

1.4 Are there any situations when corruption would be beneficial to financial markets? Provide examples to illustrate your answer.

1.5 Competitive underwritings appear cheaper than negotiated ones, but almost no firms use the former. Can you give some reasons for this?

1.6 Exhibit 1.8 presents some data illustrating the differences between bank and market-based countries. What are the weaknesses of this way of differentiating between the two systems? Can you think of better measures? What would these be?

1.7 Why do you think the UK, South Africa and the US have more widely held firms than other countries?

1.8 Choose a new trend that may affect the financial markets and business operations. Review how you believe companies and markets will be affected by this new trend. Use examples to evidence your arguments.

1.9 Insider dealing is illegal in most countries. What are the costs and benefits of prohibiting insider dealing?

1.10 Many companies simultaneously issue both equity and debt. Explain why they would do this.

1.11 Small firms tend to raise funds from private investors and venture capitalists. However, as these firms grow, they focus more on raising capital from the organized capital markets. Explain why this occurs.

1.12 In emerging markets, the functioning of primary markets is not well established. As a result, firms operating in this environment must use alternative methods of raising funds. Discuss the issues that companies face in raising funds in emerging markets.

1.13 Investment banks that are successful in raising capital for companies tend to advise on merger and takeover activities. Why do you think this happens? Discuss.

1.14 What are the principles underlying Islamic financing? Explain how an Islamic bank could replicate the products of Western banks. Provide some hypothetical examples to support your answer.

1.15 What is the difference between internal financing and external financing? Review the factors influencing a firm's choice between external and internal financing.

1.16 You plan to raise funds by following Islamic principles. You require funding today of 10 billion Bahraini dinars and would like to pay it back in equal amounts over ten years in monthly instalments. How would you do this?

References and Additional Reading

Abedifar, P., Molyneux, P. and Tarazi, A. (2013) Risk in Islamic banking, *Review of Finance*, 17(6): 2035–2096.

Aminadav, G. and Papaioannou, E. (2020) Corporate control around the world, *The Journal of Finance*, 75(3): 1191–1246.

Ayyagari, M., Demirgüç-Kunt, A. and Maksimovic, V. (2010) Formal versus informal finance: Evidence from China, *The Review of Financial Studies*, 23(8): 3048–3097.

Beck, T., Demirgüç-Kunt, A. and Maksimovic, V. (2008) Financing patterns around the world: Are small firms different?, *Journal of Financial Economics*, 89(3): 467–487.

Begenau, J. and Salomao, J. (2019) Firm financing over the business cycle, *The Review of Financial Studies*, 32(4): 1235–1274.

Bollaert, H., de Silanes, F.L. and Schwienbacher, A. (2021) Fintech and access to finance, *Journal of Corporate Finance*: 101941.

Booth, J.R. and Smith II, R.L. (1986) Capital raising, underwriting and the certification hypothesis, *Journal of Financial Economics*, 15(1–2): 261–281.

Buchak, G., Matvos, G., Piskorski, T. and Seru, A. (2018) Fintech, regulatory arbitrage, and the rise of shadow banks, *Journal of Financial Economics*, 130(3): 453–483.

Dittmann, I., Maug, E. and Schneider, C. (2010) Bankers on the boards of German firms: What they do, what they are worth, and why they are (still) there, *Review of Finance*, 14(1): 35–71.

Ferrando, A. and Lekpek, S. (2018) *Access to Finance and Innovative activity of EU firms: a Cluster Analysis* (No. 2018/02), EIB Working Papers.

Ferreira, M.A. and Matos, P. (2008) The colors of investors' money: The role of institutional investors around the world, *Journal of Financial Economics*, 88(3): 499–533.

Gillan, S.L., Koch, A. and Starks, L.T. (2021) Firms and social responsibility: A review of ESG and CSR research in corporate finance, *Journal of Corporate Finance*: 101889.

Hendershott, T., Jones, C.M. and Menkveld, A.J. (2011) Does algorithmic trading improve liquidity?, *The Journal of Finance*, 66(1): 1–33.

Kirilenko, A., Kyle, A.S., Samadi, M. and Tuzun, T. (2017) The flash crash: High-frequency trading in an electronic market, *The Journal of Finance*, 72(3): 967–998.

Leuz, C., Lins, K.V. and Warnock, F.E. (2009) Do foreigners invest less in poorly governed firms?, *The Review of Financial Studies*, 22(8): 3245–3285.

Qi, Y., Roth, L. and Wald, J.K. (2010) Political rights and the cost of debt, *Journal of Financial Economics*, 95(2): 202–226.

Spamann, H. (2010) The "antidirector rights index" revisited, *The Review of Financial Studies*, 23(2): 467–486.

Tian, X. (2011) The causes and consequences of venture capital stage financing, *Journal of Financial Economics*, 101(1): 132–159.

Yermack, D. (2017) Corporate governance and blockchains, *Review of Finance*, 21(1): 7–31.

Chapter 2

Debt Financing

Learning Objectives

After reading this chapter, you should be able to:

- Describe the primary sources of debt financing – bank loans, leases, commercial paper, asset-backed securities and debt instruments.
- Describe the various characteristics of the debt securities a firm can issue.
- Understand the principle of amortization for some types of debt securities.
- Describe the global environment in which firms issue debt securities.
- Discuss the operation of secondary markets for debt securities.
- Understand the concept of yield to maturity and how it relates to a coupon yield.
- Compute accrued interest for treasury securities and corporate securities.

A major provider of debt capital is the banking sector, and bank regulators continually update rules regarding the classification of debt instruments in financial institution balance sheets. For example, Basel III (fully implemented in January 2023) requires banks to maintain very low-risk debt in their reserves. Although this book is not about banks, most corporate bonds are sold to financial institutions, including banks, and therefore the regulation is important to all firms. One area where regulation has impacted corporate financing behaviour is in the way in which it deals with hybrid securities – financial instruments that have both debt and equity properties. Hybrids are popular financing choices for firms because there is a degree of flexibility in how these instruments are recognized in the balance sheet.

Hybrid securities combine characteristics of debt and equity in one financial instrument and, given their particular features, firms have flexibility in how these instruments are perceived. For example, a typical bond would have fixed interest coupon payments and a fixed face value (principal borrowed). However, a hybrid bond may allow interest payments to be skipped or the final principal payment to be postponed.

Chapter 1 noted that a significant source of external financing is debt.[1] Corporate managers, whose firms finance their operations by issuing debt, and investors who buy corporate debt need to thoroughly understand debt instruments and the institutional features of debt markets.

Debt instruments, also called **fixed-income investments**, are contracts containing a promise to pay a future stream of cash to investors who hold the contracts. The debt contract can be **negotiable**, a feature specified in the contract that permits its sale to another investor, or **non-negotiable**, which prohibits sale to another party. Generally, the promised cash flows of a debt instrument are periodic payments, but the parties involved can negotiate almost any sort of cash flow arrangement. Thus, a debt contract may specify the size and timing of interest payments and a schedule for repayment of **principal**, the amount owed on the loan. In addition to promises of future cash, a debt contract also establishes:

- The financial requirements and restrictions that the borrower must meet.
- The rights of the debtholder if the borrower **defaults** on any contracted payments or contractual terms in the debt contract.

The sheer variety of debt contracts generates a huge terminology and classification system for debt. A thorough education in this nomenclature and classification system is needed to apply many of the theoretical concepts developed in this text. For example, the simplest calculation of the returns of a financial instrument requires knowledge of the precise timing and magnitude of cash flows. Debt is full of conventions and shorthand language that reveal this cash flow information to knowledgeable participants in the debt market. To participate in the debt markets, one must be grounded in the culture of the debt markets.

This chapter should be used as a reference manual for the novice who wishes to participate in the debt markets. We begin this chapter by focusing on the four most common forms of debt contract that corporations employ to finance their operations: bank loans, leases, commercial paper, supplier credit and bonds (sometimes called notes). We then analyse the relationship between the price of a debt instrument and a commonly used measure of its promised return, the *yield to maturity*. This relationship between price and yield requires understanding of some concepts peculiar to debt: accrued interest, settlement conventions, yield quotation conventions and coupon payment conventions. Finally, we investigate the valuation of bonds in later chapters.

2.1 Bank Loans

Bank loans form a significant part of debt financing for companies. Although the amount of credit available from banks has declined from pre-financial crisis levels, it still dominates other forms of funding in many countries. Exhibit 2.1 presents a time series of bank loan data versus different financing types for the Eurozone area over the recent period. As can be seen, bank loans have declined significantly since 2008, and, in some years, more bank loans were paid back than new ones created.

Exhibit 1.4 from Chapter 1 presents how bank debt varies across countries. For example, in Italy, bank debt contributes approximately 50 per cent of financing to all new investments compared with only 13 per cent in the UK and 6.76 per cent in France.

Types of Bank Loan

Exhibit 2.2 shows the two general types of bank loan: lines of credit and loan commitments.

Lines of credit do not, in a practical sense, commit the bank to lend money because the bank is free to quote any interest rate it wishes at the time the borrowing firm requests funds. If the interest rate is too high, the firm will decline the available line of credit. The more formal contract, the loan commitment, specifies a preset interest rate. Sufi (2009) has shown that firms with high levels of cash flow can obtain lines of credit, but less liquid firms will rely on cash for their short-term capital requirements.

To understand the terms of a bank loan, you must have a thorough understanding of the floating interest rates generally used for these loans. Therefore, we turn to this topic next.

[1] It is a huge market. As of 2022, the total size of the global bond market (total debt outstanding) was estimated to be $119 trillion.

Exhibit 2.1 Financial Flows as a Percentage of GDP

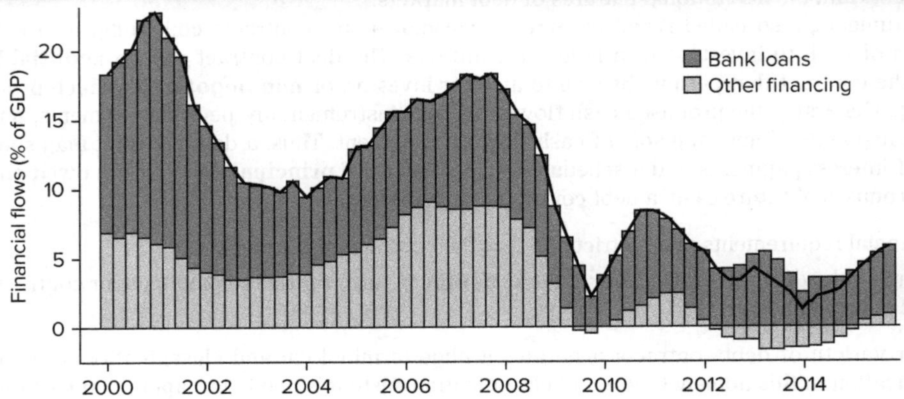

Source: Aldasoro, I. and Unger, R. (2017) *External financing and economic activity in the euro area – why are bank loans special?*, BIS Working Papers No. 622. Bank for International Settlements. © Bank for International Settlements. Available at: https://www.bis.org/publ/work622.htm. (Accessed 20 November 2019.)

Exhibit 2.2 Types of Bank Loan

Line of credit	An arrangement between a bank and a firm, typically for a short-term loan, whereby the bank authorizes the maximum loan amount, but not the interest rate, when setting up the line of credit.
Loan commitment	An arrangement that requires a bank to lend up to a maximum pre-specified loan amount at a pre-specified interest rate at the firm's request, as long as the firm meets the requirements established when the commitment was drawn up. There are two types of loan commitment: 1 A **revolver**, in which funds flow back and forth between the bank and the firm without any predetermined schedule; funds are drawn from the revolver whenever the firm wants them, up to the maximum amount specified; they may be subject to an annual clean-up in which the firm must retire all borrowings. 2 A **non-revolving loan commitment** in which the firm may not pay down the loan (known as a **takedown**) and then subsequently increase the amount of borrowing.

Floating Rates

Floating rates are interest rates that change over time. Both lines of credit and loan commitments are floating-rate loans, priced as a fixed spread over a prevailing **benchmark rate**, which is the floating interest rate specified in the contract. The spread usually depends on the default risk of the borrower. We shall discuss default risk in detail after describing some commonly used benchmark rates below.

Benchmark Rates

Exhibit 2.3 describes commonly used benchmark rates.

Exhibit 2.4 displays the benchmark rates prevailing in January 2022 in order of increasing loan maturity. Note that the rates were historically exceptionally low. The Eurozone is particularly noteworthy because, bar the thirty-year bond, all maturities have negative yields. A negative yield means that a lender would receive less money than invested at the end of the loan term. This is highly unusual and very unlikely to continue in the longer term.

Exhibit 2.3 Benchmark Rates for Floating-Rate Loans

<table>
<tr><td>Treasury rate</td><td>The yields on Treasury securities for various maturities range from 1 month to 30 years. These yields are computed from on-the-run Treasuries – that is, from the most recently auctioned Treasury issues that have the greatest liquidity.
■ Treasury bills are the zero-coupon Treasury issues, with maturities that range from one month to one year at issue. The bill rates for one-month, three-month and six-month maturities are the most popular Treasury-based benchmark rates.
■ Treasury notes are the coupon-paying issues with maturities from one year to 10 years at their initial issue date.
■ Treasury bonds are coupon-paying issues with maturities greater than ten years at their issue date. Their maximum maturity is 30 years.</td></tr>
<tr><td>Base rate (UK)/ marginal lending rate (Eurozone)</td><td>The base rate in the UK and marginal lending rate in the Eurozone are the rates that the Bank of England and European Central Bank pay on deposits lodged by other banks. These rates determine the minimum rate at which banks with deposits at the central bank can lend to each other overnight. For example, one bank may be short of reserves, requiring it to borrow excess reserves from another bank. The Federal Funds Rate is the US equivalent, and the SARB (South African Reserve Bank) Repo Rate is used in South Africa.</td></tr>
<tr><td>SONIA</td><td>The Sterling Overnight Index Average Rate (SONIA) is a benchmark rate set and governed by the Bank of England. SONIA is the average interest rate banks pay to borrow sterling overnight from other financial institutions and institutional investors.</td></tr>
<tr><td>€STR</td><td>The Euro Short Term Rate (€STR) is a benchmark rate governed by the European Central Bank. €STR is the average interest rate banks pay to borrow euros overnight from other financial institutions and institutional investors.</td></tr>
<tr><td>SOFR</td><td>The Secured Overnight Financing Rates (SOFR) is the average interest rate banks pay to borrow US dollars overnight from other financial institutions and other institutional investors.</td></tr>
<tr><td>Commercial paper rate</td><td>The yields on short-term, zero-coupon notes issued by major corporations.</td></tr>
</table>

Exhibit 2.4 Selected Benchmark Rates, January 2022

Maturity	UK	US	Eurozone
1 Month	0.18%	0.06%	**–0.64%**
3 Month	0.19%	0.10%	**–0.67%**
6 Month	0.16%	0.24%	**–0.63%**
2 Years	0.76%	0.78%	**–0.61%**
5 Years	0.90%	1.36%	**–0.43%**
10 Years	1.07%	1.64%	**–0.14%**
30 Years	1.21%	2.03%	**0.25%**

Source: *Financial Times*, 4 January 2022.

Creditworthiness and Spreads

Spreads to these benchmark rates are quoted in terms of basis points, where 100 basis points equal 1 per cent. For example, the spread of a borrower with almost no default risk might be SONIA plus 20 basis points, which means that if SONIA is at 0.55 per cent per year, the borrower pays 0.75 per cent per year. The creditworthiness of the borrower determines the spread over the benchmark rate. For example, a very creditworthy (AAA) firm may expect to pay 1.30 per cent on a long-term bond, compared with a less creditworthy (BAA) firm, which may need to pay 4.70 per cent, which is 340 basis points above the AAA rate.

Caps, Floors and Collars

Floating-rate lending agreements often have a **cap** (maximum interest rate) or a **floor** (minimum interest rate). For example, if a loan has a spread of 50 basis points to €STR, and €STR is at 0.1 per cent, but the cap is set at 0.45 per cent, then the interest rate charged on the loan will be the cap interest rate, 0.45 per cent, instead of the benchmark rate plus the spread, which would be 0.60 per cent. A **collared floating-rate loan** has a cap and a floor on the interest rate.

Loan Covenants

Lending agreements contain **loan covenants**, which are contractual restrictions imposed on the behaviour of the borrowing firm.[2] For instance, managers of the borrowing company may be required to meet minimum net worth constraints on a quarterly basis.[3] Borrowers may face restrictions on dividend payouts or the extent to which they can borrow from other sources. Alternatively, they may pledge certain assets as collateral, such as trade receivables (debtors) or inventory. If the firm defaults on the loan, the bank can claim the trade receivables or inventory in place of a forgone loan repayment.

2.2 Leases

A **lease** can be viewed as a debt instrument in which the owner of an asset, the **lessor**, gives the right to use the asset to another party, the **lessee**, in return for a set of contractually fixed payments. The contract between the lessor and the lessee defines:

- the length of time for which the lessee can or must use the asset
- the party responsible for maintenance of the asset
- whether the lessee has the right to buy the asset at the end of the leasing period and, if so, at what purchase price.

Driven by innovative providers and the demands of buyers, the volume of leasing has grown sharply since the mid-1970s, and in Europe the total amount of assets leased at the end of 2020 was €715 billion.[4] Since 2013, leasing volumes have increased each year across the region (including the UK). However, the global pandemic impacted all industry sectors, and this was reflected in an annual European growth rate of −14.2 per cent in 2020 (Lease Europe, 2020 Annual Report).

Leases are an allowable source of financing in Islamic countries, where interest payments from financial securities are forbidden. In line with the growth of Islamic financing products worldwide, the use of leases as a substitute for debt has provided significant impetus to its growing international importance.

The list of assets available for lease is almost endless. For example, it is possible to lease copiers from Xerox, computers from Apple and bulldozers from Caterpillar. In addition, many firms specialize in leasing. For example, GE Capital leases aeroplanes, automobiles, trucks, trailers, tank cars, medical devices, office equipment and even whole office buildings that they will erect for you in short order. Exhibit 2.5 illustrates the breakdown of new lease volumes in 2020 by asset class and industry sector, where most new leases are in the automobile sector. Consumer leasing (mostly made up of automobiles) consists of 30 per cent of total European leases in 2020.

---

[2] Covenants will be studied in greater depth later in this chapter when we focus on bonds.

[3] A net worth constraint requires book assets to exceed book liabilities by a threshold amount.

[4] Source: Lease Europe, 2020 Annual Report.

Exhibit 2.5 European Leasing Volumes by Asset Class and Industry Sector, 2020.]

Asset Class	Percentage of New Lease Volume (€358 billion)	Leasing Breakdown by Industrial Sector	Percentage of New Lease Volume (€358 billion)
Passenger cars	51%	Services	37%
Commercial vehicles	18%	Consumers	30%
Equipment	27%	Manufacturing, industry and construction	23%
Real estate	4%	Agriculture, forestry and fishing	5%
		Public sector	3%
		Other	1%

Exhibit 2.6 describes the two basic types of lease – operating leases and financial leases. Operating leases are more complicated to value than financial leases because of the uncertainty about the length of the lease.

Exhibit 2.6 Types of Lease

Operating lease	An agreement, usually short term, allowing the lessee to retain the right to cancel the lease and return the asset to the lessor. If the lessor bears the majority of risks and reward of the asset, the lease would be considered an operating lease.
Financial lease (or **capital lease**)	An agreement that generally extends over the asset's life and indicates that the lessee cannot return the asset except with substantial penalties. Financial leases include the **leveraged lease** (asset purchase financed by a third party), **direct lease** (asset purchase funded by the manufacturer of the asset) and **sale and leaseback** (asset purchased from the lessee by the lessor). If the lessee bears the majority of risks and reward of the asset, the lease would be considered a financial lease.

Accounting and Leases

Thirty years ago, a firm could arrange to use an asset through a lease and not disclose the asset or the lease contract on the balance sheet. Lessees had to report information on leasing activity only in the footnotes of their financial statements, which led leasing to be known as off-balance-sheet financing. Things have changed significantly in recent years, and leasing now has an accounting standard all to itself: IFRS 16 Leases.

Leases have different characteristics, affecting how they should be recorded in the firm's financial statements. The primary issue relates to the effective ownership of an asset, the risks and rewards of ownership, and to whom this should be attributed. Specifically, a lease is a finance lease if the lessee bears the majority of risks and reward of the asset, whereas it is viewed as an operating lease if the lessor carries the risk. The IFRS accounting treatment of leases (applicable to most European and South African companies, IFRS 16) underwent a substantial evolution in 2019, and there were several significant changes to the way leases impact the balance sheets of lessees (lessors were largely unimpacted by the changes).

2.3 Commercial Paper

The most commonly used short-term source of financing for corporations is commercial paper. As first defined in Chapter 1, commercial paper is a contract by which a borrower promises to pay a pre-specified amount to the lender of the commercial paper at some date in the future, usually one to six months. This pre-specified amount is generally paid off by issuing new commercial paper. On rare occasions, the borrower will not choose this rollover, perhaps because short-term interest rates are too high. In this case, the company pays off the commercial paper debt with a line of credit (announced in the commercial paper agreement) from a bank. This bank backing, along with the high quality of the issuer and the short-term nature of the instrument, makes commercial paper virtually risk free.[5]

The characteristics of commercial paper vary across countries. It usually has a life of less than a year, averaging 45 days, but may have a term of longer than one year. In 2020, the size of the commercial paper market was $1.1 trillion, and non-financial issuers represented about 20 per cent of the total market. Issuers tend to be high-quality, **prime-rated** financial institutions and international defaults are low.

Who Sells Commercial Paper?

Firms that lend money, such as bank holding companies, insurance companies and private consumer lenders, issue two-thirds of all commercial paper. The highest-quality non-financial corporations issue the remaining portion. While large financial firms issue their own commercial paper directly, much of it to money-market funds, non-financial firms issue their commercial paper through dealers.

Buyback Provisions

Most commercial paper can be sold to other investors, although this rarely occurs because the costs of such transactions are high. A consequence of this lack of secondary market activity is that virtually all issuers of commercial paper stand ready to buy back their commercial paper before maturity, often with little or no penalty. However, less than 1 per cent of commercial paper is redeemed prematurely.

2.4 Supplier Credit

A common way to finance major new asset purchases is through supplier trade credit. Common in import and export businesses, the supplier offers credit to the buyer so that payment can be deferred until later. Supplier credit varies from contract to contract, but there are various commonalities across the instruments. A buyer of new assets may lodge an initial payment representing a fixed percentage of the total contract cost with the remaining balance scheduled for payment through a promissory note, which promises payment by a scheduled date.

Supplier credit presents advantages to both buyers and sellers of assets. A buyer can receive a required asset upfront without significant capital expenditure in return for paying fixed instalments over the asset's life. For a seller, both the increased sales and the recurring revenue (assuming no default) provide ongoing liquidity for their operations.

Cuñat (2007) examines the properties of trade credit and argues that it has several benefits over and above bank loans for both the lender and borrower. For example, if a borrower is becoming unreliable with its payments, the supplier of trade credit can reduce the supply of any goods it provides, which will motivate the borrower to meet its obligations. Trade credit can also protect the borrower from any liquidity shocks it experiences during the firm's operations.

An Example of Supplier Credit

Importers and exporters frequently draw on supplier credit agreements because of the specific characteristics of the import–export business model. For example, if an importer buys goods from overseas with the express intention of selling them at a profit, it can purchase the item through supplier credit, with a payment date scheduled for after the buyer's own sell-on date. Given that the buyer does not need to pay the supplier until after receiving cash from its own customers, the buyer does not commit any of its own funds to the transaction.

2.5 Corporate Bonds

Bonds are tradable fixed-income securities. Exhibit 2.7 describes the most important features that bond issuers can set: covenants, option features, cash flow pattern (via coupon and principal schedule), maturity, price and rating. Much of the terminology used in referring to bonds derives from these features.

[5] In a few cases, lower-quality issuers offer collateral as a guarantee of payment.

Exhibit 2.7 Bond Features

Bond covenants (also called **bond indentures**)	The rules that specify the lender's rights and any restrictions on the borrower. Smith and Warner (1979) identified four kinds of bond covenant: asset covenants, dividend covenants, financing covenants and bonding covenants. Not all of these types are included in every bond.
Options	Bond features that allow both buyers and sellers to terminate the bond agreement, often requiring the party exercising the option to make certain payments or take on different risks. The most common embedded options are callability, convertibility and putability (see Exhibit 2.10).
Cash flow pattern	Specified by the annual interest payments, or **coupon**, as a percentage of the principal, schedule for payment of principal, known as **amortization**, and **face value**, a number that denominates the size of the bond.[a] ▪ Fixed-rate bonds typically pay half the stated coupon every six months. The **coupon rate**, which is the coupon stated as a percentage of the bond's face value, determines the coupon. Hence an 8 per cent coupon typically means two 4 per cent (for example, £4) payments per face value (for example, £100) per year. ▪ Floating-rate bonds are more complicated because of the many ways they can float. The interest rates on such bonds are typically some benchmark rate plus a fixed or a variable spread.[b]
Maturity	The maximum length of time the borrower has to pay off the bond principal in full. Corporate bond maturities are generally less than 30 years, but it is possible to sell bonds with longer maturities.
Price	The amount at which a bond sells, particularly in relation to the principal owed.
Bond rating	A sequence of letters and numbers that specifies the creditworthiness of a bond.

[a] *Face value is usually the principal at the bond's maturity date or the amount borrowed at the bond's issue date. For mortgages and other annuity bonds (defined later in this chapter), face values are the amount borrowed at the bond's issue date.*

[b] *More exotic floaters exist. For example, inverse floaters have coupons that rise as the benchmark rate falls. (See Chapter 23 for a discussion of inverse floaters.)*

Bond Covenants

As later chapters of this text point out, equity holders who control the firm can expropriate wealth from bondholders by making assets riskier, reducing assets through paying dividends and adding liabilities. Virtually all debt contracts contain covenants to restrict these kinds of activities. In the absence of such covenants, the incentives of equity holders to expropriate bondholder wealth would be reflected in the bond's coupon or price, resulting in higher borrowing rates.

Exhibit 2.8 classifies covenants by type.

Exhibit 2.8 Types of Bond Covenant

Asset covenant	Governs the firm's acquisition, use and disposition of assets.
Dividend covenant	An asset covenant that restricts the payment of dividends.
Financing covenant	Description of the amount of additional debt the firm can issue and the claims to assets that this additional debt might have in the event of default.
Bonding covenant	Description of the mechanism for enforcement of the covenants. It includes an independent audit of the company's financial statements, the appointment of a trustee to represent the bondholders and monitor the firm's compliance with bond covenants, periodic signatures by company officers that certify compliance with bond covenants, and **'lock-box mechanisms'**.[a]

[a] *A lock-box is a bank account whose beneficial owner is the debt holder. The cash in the account is a form of collateral for the bondholder. For example, when debt is collateralized by trade receivables, the cheques of the firm's 'trade receivables' clients are written to the bank and directed to the account held in the name of the debt holders.*

Asset Covenants

Among other things, asset covenants specify the bondholder's rights to the firm's assets in case of default. For example, some bonds are **senior bonds**, which give investors the right to liquidate or manage the assets to satisfy their claims before any of the holders of **junior bonds** (which have **subordinated claims** on a company's assets) receive payment. Other bonds are **secured bonds**, which means the firm has pledged specific assets to the bondholders in case of default. In addition, some asset covenants may prevent acquisitions of other companies.

Bonds are often named for their asset covenants. In addition to 'senior' and 'junior', the names used to refer to a bond depend on whether a bond is backed by collateral and, if so, what that collateral is. Exhibit 2.9 illustrates this point.

Exhibit 2.9 Bond Type Based on Asset Claims in Default

Secured bond	A bond for which the firm has pledged title to specific assets.
Mortgage bond	A type of secured bond giving lenders a first-mortgage lien on certain assets, such as land, a building or machinery. If the firm defaults, the lien allows the lender to foreclose and sell the assets.
Collateral trust bond	A type of secured bond involving assets placed in a trust. The trustee gives the assets to the bondholder in the event of default.
Equipment trust certificate	A type of secured bond with indentures that give lenders the right to specific pieces of equipment in the event of default.
Debenture	A type of unsecured bond. In the event of default, debenture holders are **unsecured creditors**, meaning they have a claim on all the firm's assets not already pledged.

Dividend Covenants

Dividend covenants are beneficial in preventing a manager from leaving bondholders penniless by simply liquidating the firm and paying out the liquidation proceeds as a dividend to shareholders. Bondholders view even partial payment of dividends as a liquidation of a portion of the firm's assets: thus, dividends *per se* are detrimental to bondholders. However, simply prohibiting dividends is not likely to be a good policy because it might cause the firm to waste cash by investing in worthless projects instead of using the money to pay dividends. Kalay (1982) described the typical form of a dividend covenant: a formula that defines an inventory of funds available for dividend payments. The inventory will depend on the size of earnings, new funds derived from equity sales and the dividends paid out so far.

Financing Covenants

Financing covenants prevent the firm from promiscuously issuing new debt, which would dilute the claims of existing bondholders to the firm's assets. Such covenants generally specify that any new debt has a subordinated claim to the assets. If a firm is permitted to issue new bonds having the same priority to the firm's assets as existing debt, the new loan amount is generally limited and often contingent on the financial health of the firm.

The debt contracts of companies with exceptional credit ratings generally do not contain subordination clauses. For these companies, 'straight' subordinated debt issues seldom exist. In contrast, convertible debt (discussed in the next section; see Exhibit 2.11) is generally subordinated to straight debt, even for high-quality issuers.

Financial Ratio Covenants

Both asset and financing covenants require the firm to maintain specific financial ratios. For instance, a covenant may specify a minimum value for **net working capital** – that is, current assets less current liabilities. Similarly, such covenants may prescribe a minimum **interest coverage ratio** – that is, the ratio of earnings to interest – or a minimum ratio of tangible assets to total debt. When the firm cannot meet the financial ratio conditions, it is technically in default, even when it has made the promised payments to bondholders.

Sinking Fund Covenants

One covenant related to financing is a **sinking fund provision**, which requires that a specific fraction of the issued bonds be retired before maturity. For example, a typical sinking fund on a 30-year bond might ensure that 25 per cent of the bonds are retired between years 10 and 20. The firm makes payments to the trustee, who then repurchases randomly chosen bonds. The trustee may do this in the open market or, more typically, retire the bonds by exercising the call provision in the bond. (See the subsection on bond options for details.)

Bonding Mechanism

Covenants generally specify a **bonding mechanism** or provision to ensure that the borrower upholds the bond indentures. For example, large bond issues require the appointment of a trustee to ensure that no violation of the bond indentures takes place.

Bond Options

A bond option gives the holder or the issuer a right to sell or buy the bond at a certain price within a specified period or under pre-identified situations. For example, a callable bond option gives an issuing company the right to call (that is, redeem) the bond at a price that is a specified percentage of face value. The price will typically vary according to the date the bond is called. Virtually all bonds with sinking fund provisions have this call feature so that the firm can implement the sinking fund if it is unable to find a sufficient number of bonds to repurchase on the open market.

Exhibit 2.10 describes the various types of options embedded in bonds.

Exhibit 2.10 Types of Bond Option

Callability	Allows the issuing firm to retire the bonds before maturity by paying a pre-specified price. Typically, the bond indenture contains a schedule of dates and the prices on those dates at which the firm can call the bonds. These call provisions: ■ Give firms protection from bondholders who refuse to renegotiate bond covenants that the firm believes, after the fact, are too restrictive. ■ Allow firms to retire high-coupon bonds when interest rates have fallen or when the firm's creditworthiness has improved. ■ Enable firms to implement sinking fund provisions. ■ Result in bonds that sell for lower prices than non-callable bonds. If covenants do not prevent the call from being financed by issuing new, lower interest rate debt, the bonds are called **refundable bonds**.
Convertibility	Gives the bondholder the option to convert the bond into another security, typically the ordinary equity of the firm issuing the convertible bond. The terms of the conversion option are specified in the bond covenants by indicating the conversion price or the number of shares that the bondholder can exchange for the bond.
Exchangeability	Gives the issuing firm the right to exchange the bond for a bond of a different type or ordinary equity in another company, which the issuer already owns. For example, the firm might be able to exchange a bond with floating-rate payments for one with fixed-rate payments.
Putability	Gives the bondholder the right, under certain circumstances, to sell the bond back to the firm. If the value of the outstanding bonds falls (perhaps owing to a proposal to leverage the firm much more highly or because of higher interest rates), bondholders could force the firm to buy back the outstanding bonds at an exorbitant price. Putable bonds sell for higher prices than non-putable bonds.

How Abundant are These Options?

Callable bonds are common and typically used for corporate and municipal bonds, and according to the Securities Industry and Financial Markets Association, 68.5 per cent of corporate bonds in 2016 were callable. Convertible bonds, which possess desirable properties for resolving certain bondholder–stockholder conflicts,[6] are frequently issued by small firms, although some large firms use them as well.

[6] See Chapter 16.

The Conversion Price of a Convertible Bond

The **conversion price** of a convertible bond is its face value divided by the number of shares into which each bond can be converted. It is the face value given up per share received upon conversion. The **conversion premium or discount** is the percentage difference between the conversion price and the stock price.

Example 2.1 illustrates the calculations.

Example 2.1

PGS ASA Convertible Bond Issue

In 2021, the Norwegian marine geophysical company, PGS ASA, raised NOK 116,162,097 (£9,712,192) with an unsecured convertible bond issue paying a coupon of 5 per cent per annum. Each bond had a conversion price of NOK 3, which means that the bond issue could be converted into (116,162,097 divided by 3 =) 38,720,699 new shares. However, the bond could only be converted during specific periods. When PGS issued its convertible bonds, its equity was valued at NOK 3.59, which means there was a conversion discount at issue of 16.4 per cent.

On 5 January 2022, the company announced it had received conversion notices from convertible bondholders representing NOK 67,101 to convert 67,101 bonds into 22,367 new shares. Note how this is calculated: convertible bond face value divided by conversion price equals the number of new shares.

Complex Debt Instruments

Many companies have more complex debt securities that combine the characteristics of callable, exchangeable and putable bonds. For example, Anixter International Inc., a global IT firm, has a convertible note that matures in 2033 and is callable (convertible) and putable. That is, if Anixter's share price rises above the conversion price, holders of the bond can convert the note into Anixter equity. Likewise, if interest rates rise and the value of the bond falls below the put price of the note, holders can sell the instrument to Anixter at the put price. This type of instrument also goes by the name of LYON (liquid yield option note).

Cash Flow Pattern

Bond types are often categorized by their cash flow pattern, as Exhibit 2.11 describes.

Exhibit 2.11 Bond Types Based on Coupon or Cash Flow Pattern

Straight-coupon bond (also called a **bullet bond**)[a]	A fixed-rate instrument in which the coupon is typically paid in two equal semi-annual instalments, with only the last instalment including the principal repayment.
Zero-coupon bond (also called a **pure discount bond**)	A bond that pays no periodic interest but has a single payment at maturity. These bonds are sold at a discount from their face value. The size of the discount depends on prevailing interest rates and the borrower's creditworthiness.
Deferred-coupon bond	A bond that permits the issuer to avoid interest payment obligations for a certain period (for example, five years). This allows cash-constrained firms some breathing space in the hope that their cash flows will grow. ▪ In one variation, the coupon deferral causes the bondholder to be paid in kind with additional bonds: hence the name **PIK (payment-in-kind) bonds**. ▪ In another variation, the coupon is at a fixed rate of zero: hence the name **Zerfix bond**.
Perpetuity bond (also called a **consol**)	A bond that lasts forever and pays only interest.[b]

Exhibit 2.11 *Continued*

Annuity bond	A bond that pays a mix of interest and principal for a finite amount of time. In contrast to a straight coupon bond, there is no balloon payment of principal at the bond's maturity date. This is similar to the cash flow streams paid in residential mortgages.

[a]In some circles, zero-coupon bonds, which do not pay interest periodically, are also considered bullets. We shall consider as bullets only those bonds that pay interest.

[b]Perpetuities although helpful in understanding bond pricing because of their mathematical properties, are extremely rare in practice. They are found chiefly in the United Kingdom, where they are generally referred to as consols.

Exhibit 2.12 contrasts the cash flow patterns for the five types of bonds described in Exhibit 2.11. First, note the pattern of cash flows for a straight-coupon bond. This pattern consists of a set of small, equal cash flows every period until the maturity date of the bond, at which time there is a much larger cash flow. The small, level, periodic cash flows are typically semi-annual coupons until the bond's maturity date. At maturity, the large **balloon payment**[7] of straight-coupon bonds reflects the payment of all the principal due in addition to the semi-annual coupon. The coupon is usually set so that the bond initially trades close to **par value** (for example, £100 selling price per £100 of face value).

Amortization of Annual Pay Annuity Bonds

The promised cash flows of some bonds resemble an annuity rather than a straight-coupon bond. For instance, residential mortgages and many commercial mortgages pay a level monthly payment, a portion of which is interest and another portion principal.

The right-hand side of Exhibit 2.13 illustrates the pattern of principal paydown for a 10-year annual pay mortgage over time (that is, its amortization) with interest charged at 10 per cent per annum. It shows that early in the life of this annuity bond, the largest portion of the payment is interest. However, with each subsequent payment, a greater part of the payment applies to the principal, and a smaller portion applies to interest. So, for example, £10,000 of the £100,000 first-year payment is interest, but this interest drops to £9,373 in the second year, even though the first- and second-year payments are identical.

The Amortization of an Annual Pay Fixed-Coupon Bond

The left-hand side of Exhibit 2.13 illustrates the amortization of a fixed-coupon bond. In contrast with the annuity on the right-hand side (the £10,000 first-year payment on the straight-coupon bond), there is no reduction in the principal balance due on the loan, and the borrower still owes £100,000 principal on the bond in year 2. In subsequent years only interest is covered by each £10,000 annual payment. Thus not until the final year of the bond is any principal paid. In this case, both the £10,000 in interest due and the entire £100,000 principal make up the final payment.

Amortization of Perpetuities and Zero-Coupon Bonds

The amortization of a perpetuity is identical to that of a straight-coupon bond except that, lacking a maturity date, there is never any payment of principal in one final balloon payment. In contrast, a zero-coupon bond has **negative amortization**. No payment is made, so the principal on which interest is owed grows over time.

Bond Prices: Par, Discount and Premium Bonds

Bonds are also categorized by their market price in relation to the amount of principal due, as Exhibit 2.14 illustrates. As time elapses, a straight-coupon bond traded at par when issued can become a discount or premium bond. This occurs either if riskless bonds of the same maturity experience price changes, which implies a change in interest rates, or if the credit risk of the bond changes.

[7] A balloon payment refers to a bond payment that is much larger than its other payments.

Exhibit 2.12 Cash Flows of Various Bond Types

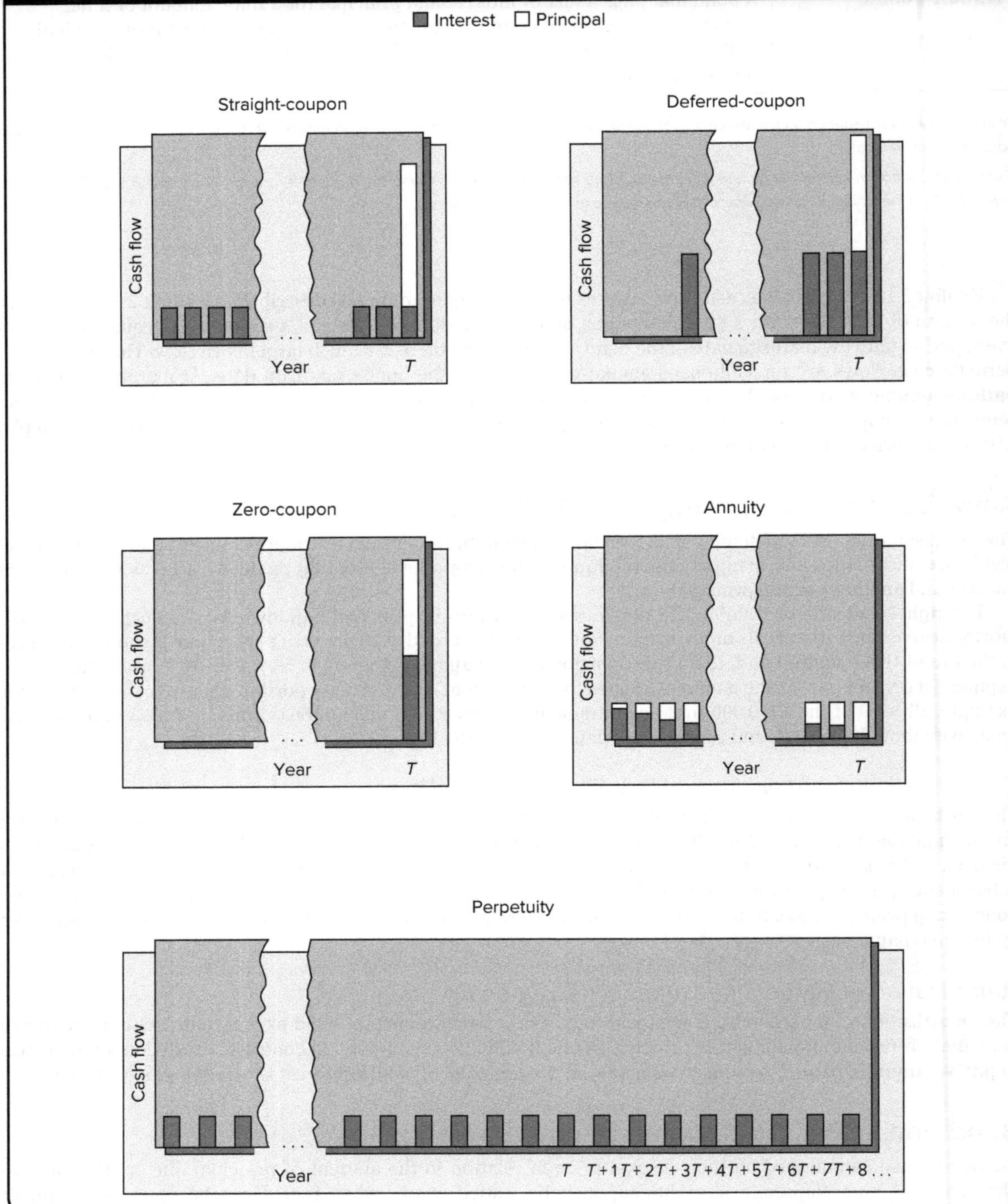

Exhibit 2.13 Amortization of Fixed-Coupon Bonds and Mortgages

Fixed-Coupon Bond			Mortgage				
Year	Interest	Principal	Year	Interest	Principal	Annual Payment	Remaining
1	10,000		1	10,000	6,275	16,275	93,725
2	10,000		2	9,373	6,902	16,275	86,823
3	10,000		3	8,682	7,592	16,275	79,231
4	10,000		4	7,923	8,351	16,275	70,880
5	10,000		5	7,088	9,187	16,275	61,693
6	10,000		6	6,169	10,105	16,275	51,588
7	10,000		7	5,159	11,116	16,275	40,472
8	10,000		8	4,047	12,227	16,275	28,245
9	10,000		9	2,825	13,450	16,275	14,795
10	10,000	100,000	10	1,480	14,795	16,275	0

Exhibit 2.14 Bond Type Based on Market Price

Premium bond	Bond with a quoted price that exceeds the face value of the bond
Par bond	Bond with a quoted price that equals the face value of the bond
Discount bond	Bond with a face value that exceeds the quoted price of the bond

Bonds issued at a discount are known as **original issue discount (OID)** bonds, which occurs when the coupon rate is set below the coupon rate of par bonds of the same maturity and credit risk. There may be no coupon, as in the case of zero-coupon bonds. Alternatively, the bond may pay a dual coupon; a **dual-coupon bond** has a low coupon initially and a higher coupon in later years. Dual coupons are typically found in high-yield bonds or bonds with high default risk (to be discussed later in this chapter).

Maturity

It is also possible to classify debt instruments based on their maturity. Generally, a **bill** or paper issue consists of a zero-coupon debt security with one year or less to maturity at the issue date. A **note** refers typically to a medium-term debt security with maturity at issue of 1–10 years. A **bond** generally refers to a debt security with more than ten years to maturity. However, these distinctions are not always so sharp. For example, the terms 'medium-term note', 'structured bond' and 'structured note' can refer to a particular type of debt security of almost any maturity. The term 'bond' also can be a generic term referring to any debt security, as we have used it here.

Duration

A helpful measure related to a bond's maturity is **duration**. We discuss this topic more fully in Section 23.2, but it is appropriate to introduce it here. Duration measures the bond's volatility over the remainder of its term and is used to hedge bond risk. Bonds with longer maturities tend to have longer durations, but it is not always the case. For example, bonds with most of their cash flows early will have a shorter duration than bonds with most cash flows towards the end of their lives.

Bond Ratings

A bond rating is a quality ranking of a specific debt issue. There are three major bond-rating agencies: Moody's, Standard & Poor's (S&P), and Fitch Ratings.

The Process of Obtaining a Rating

For a fee ranging from thousands of pounds to tens of thousands of pounds, each agency will rate the credit quality of a debt issue and follow that issue over its lifetime with annual or more frequent reviews. As a result, debt may be upgraded or downgraded, depending on the firm's financial condition.

A rating agency is hired to rate a bond before the firm offers it to the public. To produce a rating, the agency must first scrutinize the firm's financial statements and talk to senior management. After the agency notifies the firm of its initial rating, the firm's management generally provides additional information if it believes the rating is too low. Once the final rating is determined, the rating agency will continue to monitor the firm for any changes in its financial status.

The Ratings Designations and Their Meaning

Exhibit 2.15 shows the rating designations used by the three leading rating agencies and their meaning.

Exhibit 2.15 Summary of Rating Symbols and Definitions

Moody's	S&P	Fitch	Brief definition
Investment grade: high creditworthiness			
Aaa	AAA	AAA	Gilt edge, prime, maximum safety
Aa1	AA+	AA+	Very high grade, high quality
Aa2	AA	AA	
Aa3	AA–	AA–	
A1	A+	A+	Upper medium grade
A2	A	A	
A3	A–	A–	
Baa1	BBB+	BBB+	Lower medium grade
Baa2	BBB	BBB	
Baa3	BBB–	BBB–	
Distinctly speculative: low creditworthiness			
Ba1	BB+	BB+	Low grade, speculative
Ba2	BB	BB	
Ba3	BB–	BB–	
B1	B+	B+	Highly speculative
B2	B	B	
B3	B–	B–	

Exhibit 2.15 *Continued*

Moody's	S&P	Fitch	Brief definition
Investment grade: high creditworthiness			
Predominantly speculative: substantial risk or in default			
Caa	CCC+ CCC CCC–	CCC	Substantial risk, in poor standing
Ca	CC	CC	May be in default; extremely speculative
C	C	C	Even more speculative than those above
	CI		Income bonds; no interest being paid
	D	DDD DD D	Default

Source: Wilson, Richard and Frank Fabozzi. *The New Corporate Bond Market,* 1990 Probus Publishing Company.

The Relationship Between a Bond's Rating and Its Yield

Bond ratings can have an important influence on the promised rates of return of corporate bonds, known as *bond yields.* For instance, at the beginning of the global pandemic in March 2020, the spread between AAA-rated and BBB-rated bonds increased to nearly 500 basis points. Within two years, the spread had fallen to 120 basis points.

When Ederington et al. (1987) investigated the relationship between bond yields and ratings and accounting measures of creditworthiness, they found that both types of information influenced bond yields. Thus, according to their study, holding all else constant (for example, similar financial ratios, equal seniority, coupon, collateralization and options), a highly rated firm's bond would sell at a higher price than the bond of a firm with a lower rating.

Credit rating agencies have come in for significant levels of criticism in recent years. For example, many of the major US firms that collapsed in the early 2000s (e.g. Enron and Worldcom) had AAA ratings shortly before default. In 2007, AAA ratings were given to subprime mortgage assets that subsequently defaulted on their payments. The salient question is: do credit ratings reflect information that is already publicly available in the financial markets, or do they draw on private information? Brooks et al. (2004), using sovereign (country) credit ratings, showed that equity market valuations fell in countries that experienced credit rating downgrades, indicating that credit ratings impart new information to the market. This is also consistent with research that has examined corporate credit ratings (see, for example, Goh and Ederington 1993). Dittmar and Yuan (2008) report that the corporate and sovereign bond markets are very closely linked, with over 20 per cent of the information in emerging-market corporate bond yields explained by changes in their country's sovereign bond yields.

The High-Yield Debt Market

An **investment-grade rating** on a bond is a rating of Baa and above by Moody's, and BBB and above for the other two agencies. Because many large investors are prohibited from owning below-investment-grade bonds, also known as **high-yield bonds** or **junk bonds**, most firms strive to maintain an investment-grade rating. Despite these negative consequences, the growth of the high-yield bond market has been spectacular.

Issuance in the High-Yield Debt Market

High-yield bonds have been very popular in recent years as the financial markets have become better at hedging and managing risk. Before this innovation, bank loans were the only available sources of debt capital for small firms and leveraged buyouts. With the advent of the junk bond market, firms in need of debt financing found a public market willing to provide funding at a lower cost than the banks and often with more flexible covenants.

To its supporters, the evolution of the junk bond market illustrates how the financial markets respond to demand and create enormous value in doing so. Of course, there had always been high-yield debt. Before 1980, however, nearly all of it was made up of so-called **'fallen angels'** – that is, investment-grade debt that had been downgraded because the issuing firm had experienced financial distress. Nowadays, many smaller sub-investment-grade firms have high-yield debt. The market can accommodate these riskier investments because institutions can access credit derivatives to hedge the risk of all kinds of default.

The high-yield bond market has not yet become prevalent across the world. In many countries, only the most creditworthy organizations can issue debt or, at the very least, debt guaranteed by AAA banks.

Exhibit 2.16 presents the timeline of European bond issues together with a breakdown of high-yield issues by industry sector. Financial institutions are the most common issuers of high-yield bonds. In Europe, the value of high-yield bonds issued during 2020 was approximately €160 billion, up from €30 billion in 2009. Most non-financial high-yield bonds are issued to fund acquisitions. They are also used for general corporate purposes, to refinance expensive bank and acquisition debt, to acquire other firms' securities and, in some cases, to finance the purchase of new aircraft.

Exhibit 2.16 European Bond Issues

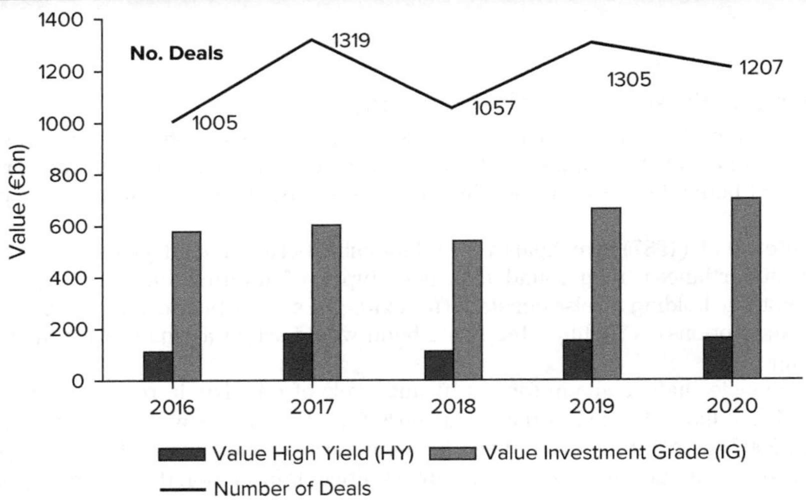

Source: PwC Debt Watch Europe Annual Review 2020.

The Default Experience and the Returns of High-Yield Debt

The junk bond market continues to be controversial. Early studies by Altman and Nammacher (1985), Altman (1987) and Weinstein (1986–1987) claimed that the probability of default on a typical junk bond was relatively low. In contrast, its return relative to a typical investment-grade bond was high, implying that junk bonds were a great buy. However, such studies underestimated default probabilities because they measured the default rate as the percentage of bonds defaulting in a year divided by the total amount of bonds outstanding.

Altman (1989) pointed out that the growth in the high-yield market meant that old issues with relatively high default rates were masked by the large volume of new issues with much lower default rates. In the first year after issue, bonds did have low default rates, in the range of 2–3 per cent, but once they had aged by 6–10 years, the proportion that ultimately defaulted rose to 20–30 per cent. As expected, this compares unfavourably with investment-grade debt, whose cumulative default rate is roughly 1–2 per cent after ten years.[8]

[8] Risk-free, short-term interest rates hit a peak of about 16 per cent in 1981.

Evidence on the value of investing in junk bonds is less clear-cut. Although the present consensus is that about 20–30 per cent of the junk bonds issued in any given year are likely to default eventually, the returns from holding junk bonds continue to be disputed. For example, Altman (1989) showed that default-adjusted spreads over Treasuries on high-yield bonds were large and positive, indicating that investors did well. However, because Altman adjusted only for default risk, his results must be viewed with scepticism.

Cornell and Green (1991) and Blume et al. (1991) reached different conclusions. Both studies found that, on average, the returns from holding junk bonds lie between the returns from holding high-grade bonds and those from holding ordinary equity. In addition, both studies concluded that the average returns experienced by investors in junk bonds compensated them fairly for the risk they bore.

In recent years, default rates on high-yield bonds have become quite volatile. For example, in 2020, the default rate reached 9 per cent compared with 2021, when US high-yield default rates were the lowest they had been since 2007, at less than 0.5 per cent.[9] This very low incidence of defaults is unlikely to continue in the foreseeable future, however, and high-yield bond defaults should grow to more than 3 per cent, primarily as a result of government support being withdrawn as economies emerge from the worldwide pandemic.

2.6 Asset-Backed Securities

Asset-backed securities are collateralized by cash flows from assets, such as mortgages and trade receivables. The process of packaging tiny investments into a larger portfolio and selling a security backed by the portfolio's cash flows is called **securitization** or **structured credit**. The mortgage-backed securities market is perhaps the pioneer in this vein, but other interesting examples abound, including credit cards, student loans, automobile loans and intellectual property rights. Asset-backed securities became one of the cheapest ways of turning a typically illiquid asset such as credit card revenue into ready cash and have been used in many countries.

The global credit crunch of 2007 and subsequent banking crisis was arguably caused by a proliferation of structured credit products, such as collateralized debt obligations (CDOs), in which the measurement of overall risk was extremely complicated. As a result, the market for asset-backed securities seized up entirely (see Exhibit 2.16), and only very recently has interest in these products re-emerged. However, it is unlikely that the market for asset-backed securities will ever reach the levels of the early 2000s, owing to more robust accounting standards and bank regulations.

Real-World Insights

In 1997 David Pullman, the celebrity entrepreneur, introduced the Bowie Bond. This asset-backed security, collateralized by royalties from the British singer David Bowie's entire music catalogue, was sold to Prudential Insurance Company of America for $55 million. The security was a 10-year bond, A-rated, and promised to pay the holder 7.9 per cent annually on the principal. As a result of this innovative instrument, other securities backed by intellectual property rights have been issued to the market, including Rod Bonds (Rod Stewart), Holland–Dozier–Holland Bonds (Motown), Bruce Springsteen and James Brown Bonds.

In 2022, Lyric Capital and Northleaf Capital Partners issued $308.8 million in asset-backed securities representing the royalties of The Who, Tim McGraw and other pop musicians. The 30-year bonds pay quarterly coupons on the royalties of the artists' back catalogues (52,729 songs published before 2013) with repayment of principal starting in December 2026. The maturity date of the bond is December 2051.

2.7 Green, Blue and ESG Bonds

Green, blue and ESG bonds are issued to fund projects or initiatives that improve the world's climate, sustainability or social objectives. Blue bonds focus entirely on sustainable marine investments and are a subset of green bonds. Any initiative that involved the UN Sustainable Development Goals would most likely be viewed as a corporate green or ESG bond. In line with the growing importance of climate change and awareness of the

[9] Amundi Research, 2021.

impact of industrial activity on the environment, green bonds have only been issued with regularity since 2014. Examples of green or ESG bonds may include financing renewable energy, clean transportation, sustainable water, environmentally safe buildings, conservation, and pollution control.

One of the largest issuers of green bonds is the World Bank, with over 170 issued bonds of just under \$15 billion. In 2020 alone, \$270 billion was raised through green bonds, and the total amount raised is well over \$1 trillion. In addition, green and ESG bonds attract tax incentives, and it is expected that these instruments will become significantly more common in the aftermath of COP26 in Glasgow, 2021, when financial institutions committed to prioritizing funding for sustainability linked investments.

Apart from the obvious reasons for improving the environment, companies may issue green bonds for other purposes (Flammer, 2021). First, they signal the firm's commitment to their investors and employees of its strategic commitment towards sustainability and ESG matters. Green and ESG bonds restrict a firm's activities, and the governance aspect of these instruments should assure investors. It is possible that green bonds are simply a tick box exercise and do not reflect the firm's genuine commitment to improving the environment. Issuing green bonds solely for branding or marketing is known as 'greenwashing'; and may be a driver in the new popularity of these types of bonds. The third purpose is to minimize the firm's cost of raising financing. If investors are content to forego financial returns in return for evidence that the borrower is committed to the environment, there will be a market niche for this particular financial security.

Flammer (2021) reports that the market responds positively to green bond issues and that the response is stronger when a firm announces its first green bond. Moreover, companies with green bonds have improved environmental performance after the issue date. Environment performance includes lower CO_2 emissions and higher ecological ratings. ESG funds are also more likely to increase shareholdings in firms with green bonds. Overall, Flammer's (2021) study found no evidence of greenwashing and reported only positive environmental benefits from these securities.

2.8 More Exotic Securities

One of the chief characteristics of financial markets is their ability to develop innovative financial instruments. This section explores a few examples of these innovations and the forces that drive them.

Macroeconomic Conditions and Financial Innovation

Occasionally, conditions that influence the macroeconomy lead to innovative debt securities. For example, due to the global Coronavirus pandemic, many governments have issued **Pandemic Bonds**. Pandemic bonds are like standard bonds in that investors receive coupons and principal at the bond's maturity. The difference comes in how much of the principal is paid. If there is no pandemic during the bond's life, investors receive 100 per cent of the principal. However, if there is a pandemic, investors will receive part or none of the initial principal. This is because the issuing government would use the principal to manage its response to an outbreak.

Another example is **Treasury Inflation Protected Securities (TIPS)**. These Treasury notes and bonds pay a lower coupon rate than ordinary Treasury securities, again saving the issuer (the government) a sizeable sum in the short run. To compensate investors for the lower coupon, the principal on which the coupon is paid grows each year – by the inflation rate as measured by the consumer price index.

Finally, a third example is the **Catastrophe Bond**. Catastrophe bonds are similar to pandemic bonds, except that the catastrophe event is specified. Typical catastrophic events include hurricanes, floods, weather events, volcano eruptions and earthquakes.

Financial Innovation in Emerging Capital Markets

Other frictions in the financial markets of some countries may drive financial innovation. Firms located in countries with emerging capital markets can be just as inventive as US firms. For example, a Russian automobile manufacturer issued 300,000 bonds convertible into the cars it made. If held to maturity, each bond was redeemable for one car. For people who wanted an automobile, buying the Avtovaz bond (as it was known) was an easy choice; at the time, the only other way to get a car in Russia was to pay a bribe to be put at the top of the waiting list.

Emerging markets have also begun to issue commodity-linked bonds paying an interest coupon linked to the price of the country's major export commodity or delivering the commodity itself. This is particularly useful when the cost of commodities increases, as has been the case in recent years. Typical commodity-linked bonds are tied to oil, gold, silver and other industrial metals.

The Junk Bond Market and Financial Innovation

The junk bond market has also been a driving force for innovative security design. Once the junk bond market took off, many innovations followed. For example, instead of straight bonds with high coupons, firms began to issue bonds with special features and embedded options. Thus they created Zerfix bonds (short for *zero* and *fixed* coupons), a deferred coupon bond that consisted of an initial zero coupon followed by a fixed coupon after 3–7 years. Zerfix bonds were intended to help the issuing firm conserve cash. Similarly, firms issued PIK bonds, which allowed them to pay either cash or additional bonds. Finally, as an implicit promise to retire or refinance debt, firms sold **increasing-rate notes (IRNs)**, which required the firm to increase the coupon quarterly at a predetermined rate in the range of 20–50 basis points.

A Perspective on the Pace of Financial Innovation

The pace of financial innovation has been remarkable, given that new security designs cannot be patented and are easily copied; once they are copied, their profitability to the inventor drops dramatically. To encourage such a rapid pace of innovation, successful security designs have to be phenomenally profitable to the inventor for that brief time before competitors introduce imitations.

Will the pace of financial innovation ever slow down? As long as governments continue to tax, regulate and restrain trade, firms will devise ways to minimize taxes, reduce the effectiveness of regulations and overcome trading frictions in the economy. Therefore we expect financial innovation to continue.

2.9 Raising Debt Capital in the Euromarkets

As suggested in Chapter 1, there are two general ways in which a firm can raise money internationally: in the Euromarkets or in the domestic markets of other countries. Firms using the Euromarkets can either sell bonds or take out loans. Firms can also sell debt directly to foreign investors or borrow from a foreign bank in various currencies.

Features of Eurobonds

A **Eurobond** typically has the following features:

- It is sold outside the country in whose currency it is denominated.
- It is a **bearer bond**, which means it is unregistered and payable to the person who carries it; losing a Eurobond is like losing a wallet filled with currency.[10]
- It is offered to investors in many countries, usually by an international syndicate of investment banks.
- It is generally sold only by large and well-known multinational firms.
- Its coupons are typically paid annually.

Because the Eurobond market is not located in any one country, it is self-regulated by the International Capital Market Association (ICMA), which has over 615 member firms in 65 countries. A typical issuer, such as a US multinational company, does not have to meet SEC requirements to sell a Eurobond security. This allows deals to be completed in just a few days and without the same level of bureaucracy as would be experienced with a domestic bond issue.

Eurocurrency Loans

Firms can also raise funds in the Euromarkets through a **Eurocurrency loan**. A Eurocurrency is a major currency on deposit in a bank outside the country of origin for the currency. Thus, when AT&T deposits dollars into the London branches of Barclays, its deposits become **Eurodollar deposits**. Similarly, when Toyota deposits yen in the London branches of Deutsche Bank or Mizuho Bank, the yen become Euroyen deposits. The banks loan the funds out short-term as SOFR, €STR, or SONIA loans to other major banks. Alternatively, banks may lend the funds as long-term Eurocurrency loans to a firm.

[10] While having a bearer bond means that you must physically clip a coupon onto the bond to obtain an interest payment, this is viewed by some governments as inconveniencing tax collectors more than bondholders.

Features of Eurocurrency Loans

The following features characterize long-term Eurocurrency loans:

- They are issued on a floating-rate basis, usually at a fixed spread above a benchmark, such as SONIA or €STR.
- The margin varies between about 50 and 300 basis points, depending on the credit risk of the borrowing firm or bank, with the benchmark SONIA or €STR rate generally reset every six months.
- They have a maturity of 3–10 years.
- They are issued by a syndicate of banks, which charge fixed fees of 0.25–1 per cent of the loan value. The syndicate allows great flexibility in the timing of takedowns of the loan commitment.

Why the Rates of Eurocurrency Loans are Relatively Low

For various reasons, lending rates in the Eurocurrency market are often lower than those in domestic markets. First, banks have no reserve requirements for Eurodeposits. Second, borrowers are large, well-known companies with good credit ratings, which diminishes the degree of investigation required by the lender firm. Finally, the lack of regulation means banks can price loans more aggressively in the Eurocurrency market than in the domestic market. For all these reasons, the market has grown substantially.

It is a simple matter to show how a lack of reserve requirements for Eurodeposits can impact the competitiveness of lending rates offered by domestic banks. For example, assume that a domestic bank must hold 11.5 per cent of all its assets in capital reserves, which earn no interest. Then, suppose a Eurobank, requiring no capital reserves on Eurocurrency loans, offers a Eurocurrency lending rate of 2 per cent. In that case, a domestic bank must earn 2.26 per cent (2/(1 – 0.115)) on a comparable loan to earn the same return. Thus, holding everything else constant, the capital reserve requirement of domestic banks will make them less competitive than Eurobanks offering the same product.

2.10 Primary and Secondary Markets for Debt

One of the biggest financial markets in the world is the bond market, but corporate bonds are not the big draw. Instead, government bonds are the focus of bond trading activity. In 2021, the Bank for International Settlements estimated that foreign companies' total international debt securities outstanding in the UK was $3.4 trillion. Data for selected countries are given in Exhibit 2.17.

Exhibit 2.17 Total Value of International Debt Securities Issued in Each Country

Country	Amount (US$bn)	Country	Amount (US$bn)
Austria	344	Italy	931
Bahrain	37	The Netherlands	2,296
Belgium	180	Norway	255
China	234	Oman	41.4
Denmark	141	South Africa	34.3
Finland	236	Spain	580
France	1,447	Sweden	453
Germany	1,351	Switzerland	126
Greece	80	United Arab Emirates	185
India	78	United Kingdom	3,361
Ireland	1,028	United States	2,445

Source: Bank for International Settlements Debt Securities Statistics, Table C3, Q3-2021.

The Primary and Secondary Market for Treasury Securities

The prices of Treasury securities are set initially in Treasury auctions, which are open to registered dealers, such as banks. The secondary market functions because dealers trade these securities through a telephone-linked network and telephone-linked brokers, who exist primarily to provide anonymity when these dealers trade with one another. Because the secondary markets do not occur on organized exchanges, the market is generally described as **over the counter (OTC)**. Treasury dealers make markets in Treasury securities by quoting bid-ask spreads. They finance many of their purchases with **repurchase agreements** (or repos, or simply RPs) – loans that use Treasury securities as collateral and thus need cash for only a small fraction of the purchase price, typically about 2 per cent.

Short sales,[11] which involve selling bonds that the seller does not own, use reverse RPs, the opposite side of a repurchase agreement. Dealers use these short sales in complicated trading strategies to offset interest rate risk from the purchases of other debt securities. The dealers borrow the Treasury securities, usually overnight, and provide loans to the security lender. The loan proceeds come out of the short sale.

The Primary and Secondary Market for Corporate Bonds

In contrast to the initial pricing of Treasury securities, the initial prices of corporate bonds, including notes, are typically set by the syndicate desk of the lead underwriter (bookrunner), which issues the bonds to its clients. The **syndicate desk** is where the sales and trading side of the bookrunner meets the bank's corporate side. The members of this desk price securities, talking simultaneously to the corporate issuer and the investment bank's salespeople, who obtain the prices at which they are likely to buy a particular issue from institutional clients. Then, until the moment of issue, the likely pricing of these bonds is quoted to the borrowing firm and investors as a spread to the Treasury security of closest maturity.

The secondary market for corporate debt tends to be an over-the-counter market consisting of many secondary market dealers in Treasuries. The dealers are also linked by phone and computerized quotation systems. Corporate bonds can be traded on exchanges, but the number of exchange-listed bonds has been dropping over time, and it is now a minor part of the market. However, as in all things related to financial markets, new developments evolve continuously, and the secondary bond market is no different.

Exhibit 2.18 provides secondary market pricing for UK Treasury securities on the over-the-counter market up to 40 years in maturity. Most corporate bonds are not actively traded. The illiquidity of these bonds stands in marked contrast to recently issued Treasury notes, Treasury bonds, and the equity of large corporations, which are all actively traded.

Exhibit 2.18 Secondary Market Pricing for Treasury Securities

Jan 05	Price £
	–
Tr 1.75pc '22	100.87
Tr 0.75pc '23	100.25
Tr 0.125pc '24	98.73
Tr 2pc '25	104.32
Tr 0.125pc '26	97.20
Tr 1.25pc '27	102.08
Tr 0.875pc '29	99.32
Tr 4.25pc '32	131.02
Tr 4.25pc '36	139.81
Tr 4.5pc '42	159.55
Tr 3.75pc '52	164.84
Tr 4pc '60	190.64

Source: FT.com. January 5, 2022.

[11] For more information on short sales, see Chapter 4.

2.11 Bond Prices, Yields to Maturity and Bond Market Conventions

Now that you are familiar with the varieties of bonds and the nature of the bond market, it is necessary to understand how bond prices are quoted. There are two languages for talking about bonds: the *language of prices* and the *language of yields*. It is essential to know how to speak both languages and translate one language easily into the other. Although people refer to various yields when discussing bonds, our focus is primarily on the **yield to maturity**. The discount rate (as defined later in Chapter 9, a rate of return applied with the arrow of time in reverse) makes the discounted value of the promised future bond payments equal to the bond's market price.

Exhibit 2.19 Bond Price–Yield Relationship

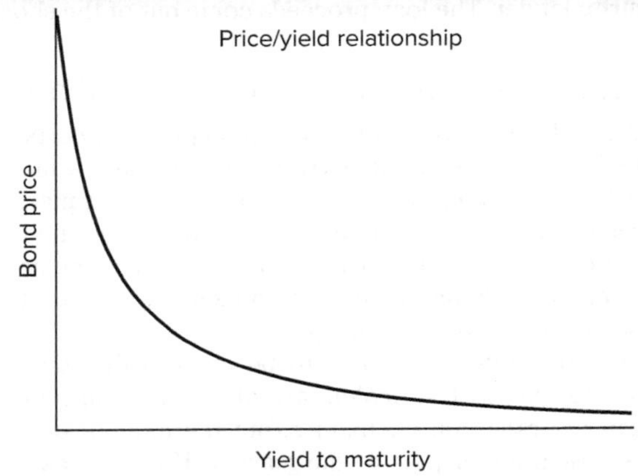

Exhibit 2.19 graphs the relationship between the yield to maturity and the bond's price. Increasing the yield to maturity decreases the present value (or current market price) of the bond's cash flows. Hence, there is an inverse relationship between bond price and yield. The price–yield curve also has a particular type of curvature. The curvature in Exhibit 2.19, known as **convex curvature**, occurs because the curve must always decline but at a decreasing rate as the yield increases. (See Chapter 23 for more detail.)

The results of this subsection can be summarized as follows.

Results

Result 2.1

For straight-coupon, deferred-coupon, zero-coupon, perpetuity and annuity bonds, the bond price is a downward-sloping convex function of the bond's yield to maturity.

Settlement Dates

Knowing the date to which the bond's future cash flows should be discounted is essential when computing a bond yield. The critical date is the date of legal exchange of cash for bonds, known as the **settlement date**. An investor who purchases a bond does not begin to accrue interest or receive coupons until the settlement date. In most countries, the settlement date for Treasury bonds is one trading day after a trade is executed; for government agency securities, settlement is two trading days after a transaction is completed; for corporate bonds, settlement is two trading days after an order is executed.

Alternatives to these settlement conventions are possible. However, requesting an unconventional settlement typically generates extra transaction costs for the buyer or seller making the request. These additional transaction costs are usually manifested in a disadvantageous price – higher for the buyer, lower for the seller – relative to the transaction price for a conventional settlement.

Accrued Interest

Yield computations require knowledge of which price to use. This would seem to be a simple matter except that, for bonds not in default, the price paid for a bond is not the same as its quoted price. The price actually paid for an interest-paying bond is understood by all bond market participants to be its quoted price plus accrued interest.

Accrued interest is the interest owed on the bond when purchased between coupon payment dates. For example, halfway between payment dates, accrued interest is half of the bond coupon. The sum of the bond's quoted price and the accrued interest is the amount of cash required to obtain the bond. This sum is the right price for computing the bond's yield to maturity.

The quoted price of a bond is called its **flat price**. The price actually paid for a bond is its **full price**. Thus, for a bond not in default, the full price is the flat price plus accrued interest. A price quote for a bond represents a quote per 100 currency units (£, $, €, etc.) of face value (for example, 99.903).

The accrued interest quotation convention prevents a quoted bond price falling by the coupon amount on the ex-coupon date. The ex-coupon date (**ex-date**) is when the bondholder becomes entitled to the coupon. If the bondholder sells the bond the day before the ex-date, the coupon goes to the new bondholder. If the bond is sold on or after the ex-date, the coupon goes to the old bondholder. In contrast, equities do not follow this convention when a dividend is paid. Therefore, share prices drop abruptly at the ex-date of a dividend, also called the *ex-dividend date.*

Accrued interest calculations are based on simple interest. Accrued interest is zero immediately on the ex-date. The coupon payment to the bondholder as of the ex-date reflects the payment in full of the bond interest owed. Just before the ex-date, accrued interest is the amount of the coupon to be paid. On days between ex-dates, we use the following formula:

$$\text{accrued interest} = \frac{\text{'days' elapsed}}{\text{'days' in current coupon period}} \times \text{coupon per coupon period}$$

'Days' appears in quotes because several day-count conventions for computing accrued interest exist in the bond market. These vary from bond to bond. Among these are actual/actual, actual/365, actual/360 and 30/360. The two most difficult accrued calculations are actual/actual and 30/360. Given the regional variations in day-count conventions, an investor must know how accrued interest is calculated before trading bonds. For Treasuries, a country's central bank will give information on conventions and, for a corporate bond, the exchange on which it is listed will provide the relevant information. For European (including the UK) Treasury securities and many corporate bonds, actual/ actual is used as a default. However, many corporate bonds in the UK also use 30/360.[12]

As noted earlier, many corporate securities, particularly those about to be issued, have prices quoted as a spread to Treasury securities of comparable maturity. The most popular interest rate derivative security, the **interest rate swap** (a contract to exchange fixed for floating interest rate payments),[13] has its price quoted as a spread to the yield of on-the-run Treasuries with the same maturity as the swap. Thus, it is essential to understand Treasuries' pricing and cash flow conventions because of their role as benchmark securities.

With the possible exception of the first coupon, Treasury notes and bonds pay coupons every six months. The maturity date of the bond determines the semi-annual cycle for coupon payments. For example, a bond with a 5 per cent coupon that matures on October 2028 pays interest every April and October. The amount of interest that accrues over an entire six-month period is half of the 5 per cent coupon, or £2.50 per £100 of face value. The number of days between October and April is not always the same because of the extra day every four years. This means that the accrued interest accumulating per day depends on the year and the relevant six-month period.

Although all settlement dates are business days, one or both coupon dates may fall on a non-business day – a weekend or holiday. This does not alter the accrued interest calculation but does affect the day a coupon is received because they do not get paid on non-business days. If the coupon is due to be received on a weekend or holiday, it will be received the next working day. Based on convention in the bond trading industry, both the yield to maturity and accrued interest calculations should assume that the coupon is received on its original date, even if it is a weekend or holiday.

[12] For more information on bonds that are traded on the London Stock Exchange, see the information document *Order Book for Retail Bonds; Accrued Interest – A Guide for Private Investors,* London Stock Exchange (2010).

[13] See Chapter 7 for a detailed description of interest rate swaps.

Example 2.2

How Settlement Dates Affect Accrued Interest Calculations

Compute the accrued interest on a (hypothetical) 10 per cent UK Treasury note maturing 15 March 2025, with a £100,000 face value, if purchased on Monday, 23 May 2023. What is the actual purchase price if the quoted price is 100.1875?

Answer: Since there is no legal holiday on 23 May (a weekday), the settlement date is 24 May, one trading day later. The prior coupon date is 15 March. The subsequent coupon date is 15 September. Thus the number of days since the last coupon is

16 days (March) + 30 days (April) + 23 days (May) = 69 days

The number of days between coupons is 184 days. Therefore, the accrued interest is £5 × (69/184) per £100 of face value, or approximately £1,875. Thus the actual purchase price is the sum of £100,187.50 and £1,875, or £102,062.5.

Accrued Interest for Corporate Securities that use 30/360

Many corporate bonds pay interest on a 30/360 basis. Thus to compute the number of days of accrued interest based on a 30-day month requires dividing by 360 and multiplying by the annualized coupon.

Here is the tricky part. To calculate the number of days elapsed since the last coupon was calculated based on a 30-day month, assume that each month has 30 days. Begin by counting the previous coupon date as day 1, and continue until reaching the 30th day of the month. (Do not forget to assume that February has 30 days.) The count continues for the following month until reaching the 30th day of the month. Then it continues for the next month, and so on, until reaching the settlement date. The settlement date is not counted for accrued interest because interest is assumed to be paid at the beginning of the coupon date – that is, midnight – and only full days are counted.

For example, there are 33 days of accrued interest if 31 January is the last coupon date and 3 March is the settlement date in the same year, whether or not it is a leap year. 31 January is day one even though the month exceeds 30 days; there are 30 days in February and two days in March before settlement. 29 February to 2 March in a leap year contains three days of accrued interest – two days in February and one in March. 28 February to 1 March also has three days of accrued interest, all in February, regardless of whether or not it is a leap year.

Example 2.3 provides a typical calculation.

Example 2.3

Computing Accrued Interest with 30/360 Day Counts

Compute the accrued interest on an 8 per cent corporate bond that settles on 30 June. The last coupon date was 25 February.

Answer: There are 125 days of accrued interest: 6 days in February; 30 in March, April and May; and 29 in June. 125/360 = 0.3472222. The product of 0.3472222 and €8 is €2.77778. Thus the bond has €2.77778 of accrued interest per €100 of face value.

2.11 Recent Research in Debt Financing

With the changing environment regarding debt, there has been a resurgence of interest in debt financing and the factors that drive pricing, contract design and availability. Agarwal and Hauswald (2010) report that the physical distance between the borrower and the lending bank is a factor in the debt financing decision. Banks must undertake an extended analysis of the credit applicant when making their lending decision, and a component of the information gathered is soft and proprietary. Given its nature, the quality of such information gets worse as the borrowing firm becomes less local. The borrower–lender distance effect has also been found in the municipal bond market by Butler (2008), and it could explain why banks exhibit a significant home-country bias in the loan portfolios (Carey and Nini 2007). Heightened competition between companies increases the cost of raising debt capital (Valta 2012). Competition within industries makes borrowing riskier because firms compete with other companies selling similar products or services, and this is priced by the market. Moreover, competition has an outsize effect on smaller firms with much larger competitors.

Some distance effects could be mitigated by having restrictive covenants that are regularly monitored and enforced. Covenants affect corporate decision-making and strategy, especially when the terms are in danger of being violated. For example, Chava and Roberts (2008) report that corporate investment declines sharply when a creditor threatens to accelerate the terms of a loan (possibly due to breaking the terms of the covenant). In addition, the cost of bank capital increases with the probability that a firm may be acquired because of the danger of covenants being violated in the event of a merger (Cremers et al. 2007; Chava et al. 2009). Demiroglu and James (2010) report that risk firms with fewer investment opportunities have more restrictive covenants. Interestingly, the covenants themselves lead to improvements in the measured variables. Highly restrictive covenants have other benefits in that violations do not impact corporate investment strategy as much as violations of loose covenants.

Covenants are just one type of transaction cost faced by borrowing firms, and a firm can incur various kinds of fees when arranging a loan or issuing a bond. Berg et al. (2016) report that 80 per cent of syndicated loans in the US have complex fee structures, which can be significant. Like bond covenants, fees are set to reflect the risks of the borrower and the likelihood of them defaulting in the future. Berg et al.'s (2016) research is particularly insightful because most traders measure the cost of debt without considering the fees incurred in setting up the loan or bond issue. A more appropriate cost of borrowing would incorporate these fees.

Several factors drive the choice of debt instrument to issue. Chen et al. (2010) argue that callable bonds shift risks from the firm to bondholders when a firm has more debt and poor or risky future investment opportunities. The length of bonds or loans is driven by expected future risks, with firms using a range of bond or loan terms to maturity to derisk the need to pay back the principal on a single date (Choi et al. 2018).

As discussed earlier, corporate bond prices are strongly related to their yield to maturity, with a bond's price negatively associated with its yield. Bao et al. (2011) show that an important factor in determining the yield to maturity of a bond is how liquid it is in the markets. The more liquid a bond, the lower its bond yield. Under certain conditions, illiquidity can have a stronger effect on bond yields than a firm's credit risk. Other factors driving bond prices and the cost of debt include ownership structure and, in particular, when the largest shareholder's voting power is significantly higher than its cash flow rights (Lin et al. 2011). In such situations, the cost of raising debt is substantially higher because the potential for large shareholders to influence management to their selfish ends will increase monitoring costs and credit risk.

Finally, new ways of raising debt using technological advances have appeared. The most common are peer-to-peer lending platforms, where lenders engage directly with borrowers over the internet. Tang (2019) finds that peer-to-peer lending substitutes bank loans for very small borrowers and complements banks for small loans. To date, peer-to-peer lending is only used for the smallest companies, but this may change as the market becomes more mature. Blockchain technology has great potential in making the peer-to-peer market more successful because it can reduce the risk of fraud and, ultimately, credit risk facing lenders.

2.12 Summary and Conclusions

This chapter has provided an introduction to the various sources of debt financing: bank loans, leases, supplier credit, commercial paper and debt securities. A large variety of debt financing is available. In addition, there are many ways to categorize debt instruments: by their covenants, options, cash flow patterns, pricing, maturity or rating.

One of the goals of this text is to bring the reader from having merely an abstract view of finance to being able to pick up a business newspaper or examine a computer screen and usefully employ the data displayed to value financial and real assets. Accomplishing this goal requires a substantial amount of knowledge about debt securities, some of which is found in this chapter.

In addition to learning how debt prices and yields are quoted, various skills are acquired in this chapter. Among them is knowing where to trade debt, where to issue debt, and what role debt plays in global capital markets. These skills are helpful to the corporate manager who needs to determine whether to finance investment with debt or equity securities.

To complete the institutional education of the financial manager, it is essential to explore in similar detail the main competitor to debt financing: equity financing. For this, we turn to Chapter 3.

Key Concepts

Result 2.1: For straight-coupon, deferred-coupon, zero-coupon, perpetuity and annuity bonds, the bond price is a downward-sloping convex function of the bond's yield to maturity.

Key Terms

accrued interest 51
amortization 35
annuity bond 39
asset covenant 35
asset-backed security 45
balloon payment 39
base rate 31
bearer bond 47
benchmark rate 30
bill 41
bond 41
bond covenant 35
bond indenture 35
bond rating 35
bonding covenant 35
bonding mechanism 37
bullet bond 38
callability 37
cap 32
capital lease 33
cash flow pattern 35
collared floating-rate loan 32
catastrophe bond 46
collateral trust bond 36
commercial paper rate 31
consol 39
conversion premium 38
conversion price 38
convertibility 37
convex curvature 50
coupon 35
coupon rate 35
debenture 36
default 29
deferred-coupon bond 38
direct lease 33
discount bond 38
dividend covenant 35
dual-coupon bond 41
duration 42
equipment trust certificate 36
Eurobond 47
Eurocurrency loan 47
Eurodollar deposit 47
exchangeability 37
ex-date 51
face value 35
fallen angels 44
Federal Funds Rate 31
financial lease 33
financing covenant 35
fixed-income investment 29
flat price 51
floating rate 30
floor 32
full price 51
high-yield bond 43
increasing-rate note (IRN) 47
interest coverage ratio 36
interest rate swap 51
investment-grade rating 43
junior bond 36
junk bond 43
lease 32
lessee 32
lessor 32
leveraged lease 33
line of credit 30
loan commitment 30
loan covenant 32
lock-box mechanism 35
marginal lending rate 31
maturity 35
mortgage bond 36
negative amortization 39
negotiable 29
net working capital 36
non-negotiable 29
non-revolving loan commitment 30
note 41
on-the-run Treasury 31
operating lease 33
option 35
original issue discount (OID) 41
over the counter (OTC) 49
pandemic bond 46
par bond 41
par value 39
perpetuity bond 39
PIK (payment-in-kind) bond 38

Exercises

2.1 Critics of rating agencies argue that because the firm pays rating agencies to rate the firm's debt, the rating agencies have the wrong incentives. What do you think of this argument? Can you think of ways to assess its validity?

2.2 Credit rating agencies experienced substantial criticism from the regulatory authorities for not predicting the global financial crisis in 2008. Why do you think this happened, and how did the agencies defend themselves?

2.3 Bank loans have become significantly less popular as a financing source since the financial crisis. However, they retain their importance in many countries and are the primary financing source for companies. Why do you think bank loans continue to be important in some countries but less popular in others? Explain.

2.4 The table below shows the cumulative default rates of rated bonds.

	AAA	AA	A	BBB	BB	BB	CCC/C
No. of issuers defaulting within:							
One year	0	0	0	3	15	88	145
Three years	0	1	6	29	148	646	272
Five years	0	3	13	71	303	1,116	314
Seven tears	2	6	28	105	411	1,389	331
Total	8	32	101	221	650	1,735	351
Percent of total defaults per time frame							
One year	0	0	0	1.2	6	35.1	57.8
Three years	0	0.1	0.5	2.6	13.4	58.5	24.9
Five years	0	0.2	0.7	3.9	16.6	61.3	17.3
Seven tears	0.1	0.3	1.2	4.6	18.1	61.1	14.6
Total	0.3	1	3.3	7.1	21	56	11.3

Source: S&P Global, '2020 Annual Global Corporate Default And Rating Transition Study'.

What conclusions can you draw from the table?

2.5 Today is 30 March. Consider a straight-coupon bond (or bank loan) with semi-annual interest payments at an 8 per cent annualized rate. Per €100 of face value, what is the semi-annual interest payment if the day count is based on the following methods?

a Actual/actual

b 30/360

c Actual/365 if the coupon payment date is 15 August.

d Actual/360 if the coupon payment date is 15 August.

2.6 Refer to the bond in exercise 2.5. What is the accrued interest for settlement of a trade on 1 August, with each of the four day-count methods? For parts *a* and *b*, assume that the coupon payment date is 15 August.

2.7 XYZ Corporation takes out a £1 million loan that semi-annually pays six-month SONIA + 50 bp on 5 March 2023. Assume that SONIA is at 1 per cent on 5 March 2023, 0.75 per cent on 5 September 2023, and 1.125 per cent on 5 March 2024. What are the first three interest payments on the loan? When are they paid?

2.8 A 5 per cent corporate bond maturing 14 November 2031 (originally a 25-year bond at issue) has a yield to maturity of 6 per cent (a 3 per cent discount rate per six-month period for each of its semi-annual payments) for the settlement date, 9 June 2022. What are the flat price, full price and accrued bond interest on 9 June 2022?

2.9 A bank loan to the Knowledge Company has a 50 basis point spread to €STR. If €STR is at 1 per cent, what is the interest rate on the bank loan?

2.10 If you were to issue a long-term bond to fund investment in China, would you include a call provision? What are the benefits of having a call provision? What are the costs? How do these answers change for a put provision? What are the other options that can be embedded into bond contracts?

2.11 Refer to exercise 2.10. Given that the investment is in China, how would you decide on an appropriate coupon rate to set on your bonds? Is the coupon rate the same as the required rate of return on the bond? Explain.

2.12 Empirically, share prices and bond prices have been shown to react only to a small degree to credit rating changes, if at all. Why do you think this is?

2.13 Governments, as well as companies, have credit ratings. What impact do you think a government's credit rating has on a company that operates in that country?

2.14 Refer to exercise 2.10. Assume that your bond issue has a credit rating from Moody's and S&P. However, Moody's has given a rating of Aaa and S&P has assigned a rating of BBB. What does this mean, and why do you think it could happen? Explain.

2.15 A controversy erupted regarding bond rating agencies when some agencies provided unsolicited bond ratings. Why do you think this is controversial?

References and Additional Reading

Agarwal, S. and Hauswald, R. (2010) Distance and private information in lending *The Review of Financial Studies*, 23(7): 2757–2788.

Altman, E. (1987) The anatomy of the high-yield bond market *Financial Analysts Journal*, 43(4): 12–25.

Altman, E. (1989) Measuring corporate bond mortality and performance *The Journal of Finance*, 44(4): 909–922.

Altman, E. and Nammacher, S. (1985) The default rate experience on high-yield corporate debt *Financial Analysts Journal*, 41(4): 25–41.

Bao, J., Pan, J. and Wang, J. (2011) The illiquidity of corporate bonds, *The Journal of Finance*, 66(3): 911–946.

Berg, T., Saunders, A. and Steffen, S. (2016) The total cost of corporate borrowing in the loan market: Do not ignore the fees, *The Journal of Finance*, 71(3): 1357–1392.

Blume, M.E., Keim, D.B., and Patel, S.A. (1991) Returns and volatility of low-grade bonds, 1977–1989 *The Journal of Finance*, 46(1): 49–74.

Brooks, R., Faff, R., Hillier, D. and Hillier, J. (2004) The national market impact of sovereign rating changes *Journal of Banking and Finance*, 28(1): 233–250.

Butler, A. (2008) Distance still matters: evidence from municipal bond underwriting *The Review of Financial Studies*, 21(2): 763–784.

Carey, M. and Nini, G. (2007) Is the corporate loan market globally integrated? A pricing puzzle *The Journal of Finance*, 62(6): 2969–3007.

Chava, S., and Roberts, M.R. (2008) How does financing impact investment? The role of debt covenants *The Journal of Finance*, 63(5): 2085–2121.

Chava, S. Livdan, D. and Purnanandam, A. (2009) Do shareholder rights affect the cost of bank loans? *The Review of Financial Studies*, 22(8): 2973–3004.

Chen, Z., Mao, C.X. and Wang, Y. (2010) Why firms issue callable bonds: Hedging investment uncertainty *Journal of Corporate Finance*, 16(4): 588–607.

Choi, J., Hackbarth, D. and Zechner, J. (2018) Corporate debt maturity profiles *Journal of Financial Economics*, 130(3): 484–502.

Cornell, B. and Green, K. (1991) The investment performance of low-grade bond funds *The Journal of Finance*, 46(1): 29–48.

Cremers, K.J. Martijn, Nair, V.B. and Wei, C. (2007) Governance mechanisms and bond prices *The Review of Financial Studies*, 20(5): 1359–1388.

Cuñat, V (2007) Trade credit: suppliers as debt collectors and insurance providers *The Review of Financial Studies*, 20(2): 491–527.

Demiroglu, C. and James, C.M. (2010) The information content of bank loan covenants *The Review of Financial Studies*, 23(10): 3700–3737.

Dittmar, R.F. and Yuan, K. (2008) Do sovereign bonds benefit corporate bonds in emerging markets? *The Review of Financial Studies*, 21(5): 1983–2014.

Ederington, L.H., Yawitz, J.B. and Roberts, B.E. (1987) The informational content of bond ratings *Journal of Financial Research*, 10(3): 211–226.

Flammer, C. (2021). Corporate green bonds. *Journal of Financial Economics*, 142(2), 499–516.

Goh, J.C. and Ederington, L.H. (1993) Is a bond rating downgrade bad news, good news, or no news for stockholders? *The Journal of Finance*, 48(5): 2001–2008.

Kalay, A. (1982) Stockholder–bondholder conflict and dividend constraints *Journal of Financial Economics*, 10(2): 211–233.

Lin, C., Ma, Y., Malatesta, P. and Xuan, Y. (2011) Ownership structure and the cost of corporate borrowing *Journal of Financial Economics*, 100(1): 1–23.

Smith, C. and Warner, J. (1979) On financial contracting: an analysis of bond covenants *Journal of Financial Economics*, 7(1979): 117–161.

Sufi, A. (2009) Bank lines of credit in corporate finance: an empirical analysis *The Review of Financial Studies*, 22(3): 1057–1088.

Tang, H. (2019) Peer-to-peer lenders versus banks: substitutes or complements?, *The Review of Financial Studies*, 32(5): 1900–1938.

Valta, P. (2012) Competition and the cost of debt *Journal of Financial Economics*, 105(3): 661–682.

Weinstein, M.I. (1986–1987) A curmudgeon's view of junk bonds *Journal of Portfolio Management*, 13(3): 76–80.

Chapter 3

Equity Financing

Learning Objectives

After reading this chapter, you should be able to:

- Describe the types of equity security a firm can issue.
- Provide an overview of the operation of secondary markets for equity.
- Describe the role of institutions in secondary equity markets and corporate governance.
- Describe the private equity market.
- Understand the process of going public.
- Discuss the concept of informational efficiency.

The global coronavirus pandemic illustrated the fragility of global supply chains in many sectors. Although disruption can be viewed negatively, it also presents opportunities to existing businesses and innovative entrepreneurs. With new business models and ways of working, expect to see creative ideas, products and services that speak to the new economic environment we are all working within. A subset of these new ideas will be successful and lead to equity issues to raise financing to scale up operations.

For example, although the world was under lockdown restrictions, 2021 had many high profile equity issues in the UK. The largest publicly listed issues were in new technology sectors, which were successful due to the pandemic. These were the food delivery service, Deliveroo; the technology branding company and the UK's largest IPO since 2015 (£1.88 billion), The Hut Group; the cybersecurity firm, Darktrace; the boot manufacturer, Dr Martens; the digital card company, Moonpig; and the biotech firm, Oxford Nanopore.

Before the pandemic, none of the above companies either existed or were at the scale required for a public equity issue. Likewise, the companies that will raise equity in five years are unlikely to exist now.

Chapter 2 discussed debt financing, an essential source of external capital for firms. We turn now to equity, another common source of external capital. Although debt and equity are alike in that both provide resources for investment in capital equipment, research and development, and training that allow firms to prosper, they differ in several important respects:

- Debt holder claims must be paid in full before the claims of equity holders can be paid.
- In most countries, equity holders elect the corporation's board of directors and thus ultimately control the firm.[1]
- Equity holders receive cash in the form of dividends, which are not tax-deductible to the corporation, whereas the interest payments of debt instruments are a tax-deductible expense.[2]

This chapter describes various equity instruments, how they are traded, and the individuals and institutions that own them. It examines the private equity industry, which has become very important to the financial markets in the last ten years. It also briefly discusses how equity is valued in practice in the capital markets. In addition, it examines the distinction between privately owned firms and publicly owned firms, which have a listing on a stock exchange. Finally, the chapter covers why a firm might want to have its equity publicly traded and the process by which a firm goes public.

3.1 Types of Equity Securities

Firms obtain equity capital either internally by earning money and retaining it or by issuing new equity securities. A firm can issue three different kinds of equity: ordinary shares, preference shares and warrants.

Ordinary Shares

Ordinary shares, or **common stocks**, are a share of ownership in a corporation, which usually entitles its holders to vote on its affairs. The ordinary shareholders are generally viewed as the firm's owners. They are entitled to the firm's profits after other contractual claims are satisfied and ultimately control how the firm operates.[3]

Many technology and founder-led firms have two classes of equity (**dual-class shares**), usually called class A and class B, which differ in votes per share. Dual-class shares are confined mainly to firms that are majority controlled by a person or group. There is quite a substantial variation by country in the frequency of dual-class share structures. In Exhibit 3.1, the percentages of Europe's largest 300 firms that do not have dual-class share structures (following a 'one share one vote' system) are presented. Approximately 35 per cent of all firms have a dual-class shares structure, but, as can be seen, there is not a consistent pattern across Europe. France (69 per cent), The Netherlands (86 per cent) and Sweden (75 per cent) have the highest proportions of dual-class firms, whereas in Belgium (0 per cent), Germany (3 per cent) and the UK (12 per cent) dual-class structures are uncommon.

As technology firms become more ubiquitous, we can expect more dual-class firms. This changing trend has already started with nearly 30 per cent of UK IPOs between 2017 and 2019 having more than one class of shares.

Although multiple voting rights are the main differentiating feature between most dual-class shares, other characteristics can separate share classes. *Voting rate ceilings* restrict voting power for an investor to a specified percentage of shares, irrespective of the actual shareholding. The exact ceiling percentage can vary but is usually between 5 and 20 per cent of total shares outstanding. *Ownership ceilings* forbid any shareholder from taking a holding of greater than a specified percentage of shares. *Priority shares* give the holders certain rights, such as appointing a representative to the board of directors or vetoing a proposal at an annual general meeting. *Golden shares* are found in former state-owned enterprises and technology firms, and they give the founder beneficial powers, such as veto capability against new shareholders. Finally, common in the Netherlands, depositary receipts are securities with an equity ownership stake without voting rights. The company's shares are held in a foundation, which then issues depository receipts to investors that mimic the cash flows of the underlying shares but have no voting rights. Frequently, the foundation's board of directors is linked to the underlying firm.

---

[1] In reality, however, managers may be influenced more by bankers and other debt holders with whom they must deal on a day-to-day basis than by shareholders, with whom they have much less contact. Issues relating to who controls corporations will be discussed in more detail in Chapter 18.

[2] In this way, many countries' tax codes favour debt over equity financing. The tax advantages of debt versus equity financing will be discussed in great detail in Chapters 13, 14 and 15.

[3] As Chapter 18 discusses, it is often difficult for shareholders to exercise their control.

Exhibit 3.1 Percentage of Companies with a 'One Share One Vote' Structure by Country

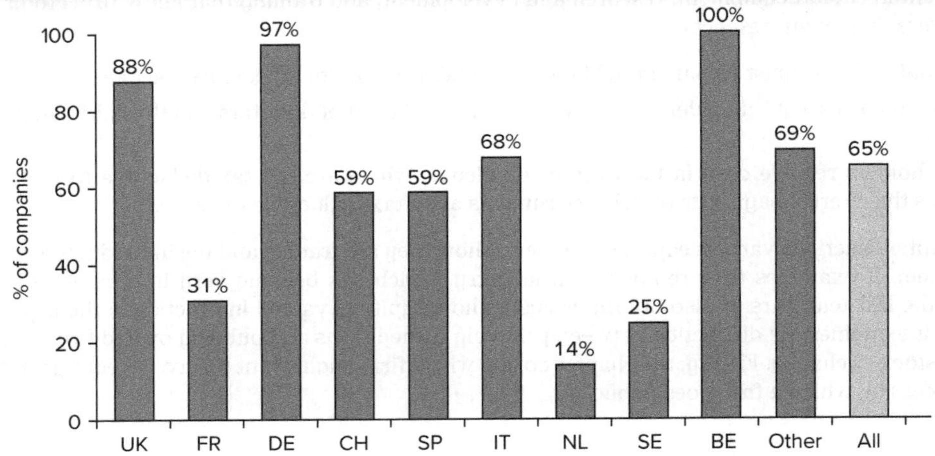

Source: 'Application of the One Share One Vote System in Europe', Deminor-Rating commissioned by the Association of British Insurers (2005).

Real-World Insights

We have already mentioned Deliveroo and The Hut Group in the context of recent IPOs. Both firms have dual-class share structures. Deliveroo has two classes of shares: Class A shares for all investors and Class B shares for the founder, Will Shu. Class B shares have 20 votes compared with Class A shares, which have one vote. Although the founder of Deliveroo has less than 3 per cent of total equity, he has more than 57 per cent of the voting rights, giving him overall control of the firm. The Hut Group has a hugely innovative share structure whereby the founder, Matt Moulding, has a single *golden share* that receives no dividends but gives enough votes to overrule any resolution seeking to change control of the firm.

A significant source of financing for many companies is preference shares, which generally sacrifice voting rights for higher priority rights in the case of company default. These are covered in more detail in the next section. Exhibit 3.2 presents a breakdown of dual-class share structures by country.

Exhibit 3.2 Percentage of Dual-Class Share Characteristics by Country (FTSE Eurofirst 300 Companies)

	Non-voting preference shares (%)	Multiple voting rights (%)	Voting right ceilings (%)	Ownership ceilings (%)	Priority shares (%)	Golden shares (%)	Depositary receipts (%)
UK	20	1	3	5	4	3	–
France	2	64	19	2	5	–	–
Germany	24	–	3	–	–	–	–
Switzerland	–	12	35	–	–	–	–
Spain	–	–	41	–	–	–	–
Italy	36	–	8	28	–	–	–
Netherlands	–	67	–	–	29	10	24
Sweden	–	75	6	–	–	–	–
Other	8	8	11	8	–	3	–

Source: 'Application of the One Share One Vote System in Europe', Deminor-Rating commissioned by the Association of British Insurers (2005).

Preference Shares

A **preference share**, or **preferred stock**, is a financial instrument that gives its holders a claim on a firm's earnings that must be paid before dividends on its ordinary shares can be paid. Preference shares hold a senior claim in reorganization or **liquidation**, which is the sale of the company's assets. However, the claims of preferred shareholders are always junior to the claims of the firm's debt holders. Preference shares are used much less than ordinary shares as a source of capital, although they are common in the UK.

Preference shares are like debt in that dividends are fixed at the time of sale. In some cases, preference shares have a maturity date, much like a bond. In other cases, preference shares are more like ordinary shares because they do not have a maturity date. Preference shares are almost always **cumulative**: if the corporation stops paying dividends, the unpaid dividends accumulate and must be paid in full before any dividends can be paid to ordinary shareholders. At the same time, a firm generally cannot be forced into bankruptcy for not paying its preferred dividends.[4] The voting rights of preference shares differ from instrument to instrument. Preferred shareholders do not always have voting rights, but they often obtain voting rights when the preferred dividends are suspended.

Reasons for Issuing Preference Shares

There are several reasons why firms would choose to issue preference shares instead of straight debt or equity. A factor that has become significantly more important is financial institution capital adequacy. Banks and other financial institutions must, by law, maintain minimum levels of cash or cash-like securities, known as Tier 1 Capital. Preference shares are categorized as Tier 1 Capital and, consequently, many banks have this type of security to maintain their capital ratios. Another reason for issuing preference shares is to manage the firm's leverage. A high leverage (debt to equity) ratio implies enhanced financial risk. Since preference shares have debt-like characteristics but are defined as equity in the financial accounts, using this instrument instead of debt can reduce a firm's financial leverage. Linked to the leverage issue, companies are also concerned about their credit rating. Since preference shares are classified as equity, their benefits over straight debt can also be received through firms receiving a better credit rating.

Convertible Preference Shares

Convertible preference shares are similar to the convertible debt instruments described in Chapter 2. These instruments have the properties of preference shares before being converted but can be converted into the issuer's ordinary shares at the preferred shareholder's discretion. In addition to the standard features of preference shares, convertible preference shares specify the number of ordinary shares into which each preference share can be converted.

Adjustable-Rate Preference Shares

This kind of preference share goes by various acronyms, including ARPS (**adjustable-rate preference shares**), DARTS (Dutch auction-rate stock), APS (auction preference shares) and RP (remarketed preferred). In each form of ARPS, the dividend is adjusted quarterly (sometimes monthly) by an amount determined by the change in some short-term benchmark interest rate.

Income Preferred Securities

One of the most significant advantages of preference shares is that they allow corporations to issue a debt-like security without lowering the ratings on their existing debt. However, in contrast to a debt security with its tax-deductible interest, preference shares have the disadvantage that their dividends are not tax-deductible. In response to the desire for a security that provides the best of debt and preferred equity, investment bankers have developed a security they call either IPS (income preferred securities) or trust preferred securities. An IPS is a preference share issued by a subsidiary or trust (specially formed for this purpose) of the company located in a tax haven, such as the Bahamas.

Warrants

There are several other equity-related securities that firms issue to finance their operations. For example, firms sometimes issue **warrants**, which are long-term call options on the issuing firm's equity. **Call options**[5] give their holders the right to buy shares of the firm at a pre-specified price for a given period. These options are

---

[4] For the newer kinds of preference share, discussed below, preference shareholders can sometimes force the firm into bankruptcy.
[5] Call options will be discussed in more detail in Chapters 7 and 8.

often included as part of a **unit offering**, which includes two or more securities offered as a package. For example, firms might try to sell one ordinary share and one warrant as a unit. Schultz (1990) suggested that this kind of unit offering serves as a form of staged financing in which investors have an option either to invest more in the firm if it is successful or to shut it down by refusing to invest at the option's pre-specified price. Warrants are often bundled with a firm's bond and preference share offerings.

The Volume of Global Equity Financing

Exhibit 3.3 shows the distribution of equity financing across the world in 2020. The locus of investment is in the Asia-Pacific region, particularly China. An interesting pattern in financing is the sectors that were attracting the most interest in 2020. The High Technology sector was the most popular market in the Americas and EMEA regions compared to Industrials in Asia-Pacific and Japan. In addition, financial sector IPOs were the second most popular area in Asia-Pacific.

Exhibit 3.3 Global Equity Financing Proceeds in 2020

Region	Proceeds ($mill)	Number of Deals	Average Deal Size ($millions)	Most Active Sector	Second Most Active Sector
Americas	390,130	1,131	345	Technology	Healthcare
Asia Pacific	407,099	3,106	131	Industrials	Financials
EMEA	208,125	1,229	169	Technology	Industrials
Japan	39,282	190	207	Industrials	Financials

Source: Refinitiv, Global Equity Capital Markets Review 2020.

3.2 The Globalization of Equity Markets

Corporations sometimes raise capital from foreign investors by listing ordinary equity on foreign exchanges. For instance, Vodafone plc has equity listed on the London Stock Exchange and exchanges in Germany and the US. The process of listing securities in foreign countries means complying with all local regulations, possibly including some that apply specifically to foreign issuers. Investors may also buy foreign equities directly on foreign exchanges or through financial institutions such as banks.

Many firms now raise capital outside their domestic country in financial market centres, such as London, Shanghai or New York. In recent years there has been a substantial shift in the location of IPOs, with much of the order flow migrating from the US to other areas, most notably Asia (China and Hong Kong).

In almost all countries, shareholder rights and equity market development lag behind the world's major financial centres of the US, Europe (mainly Germany, The Netherlands, Switzerland, France and Sweden), and the UK. It is natural, then, for many foreign firms to list their equities in these markets. Unfortunately, companies must meet stringent requirements to be listed on stock exchanges like London or New York. For example, US financial disclosure requirements are the strictest globally, and many foreign firms face high costs relative to other countries in producing US-style financial statements. **Depository receipts (DRs)** provide a way to get around foreign listing problems. With a depository receipt, a foreign firm deposits its shares with a bank in New York, London, Zurich or Tokyo (the major depository receipt centres). The bank then issues a depository receipt, a security that has a legal claim on the cash flows from the deposited shares. In other words, the bank holding the shares receives the equity's dividends, which it pays to the holder of the depository receipt after deducting a small fee.

There are two types of depository receipts. The most common type is known as an **American depository receipt (ADR)**, which is a depository receipt issued in the US market. The other is the **global depository receipt (GDR)**, corresponding to a depository receipt issued outside the US. Trading in DRs has grown massively in recent years. In 2020, over $1.3 trillion of DRs were traded, compared with just under $660 billion in 2002.[6]

[6] Source: BNYMellon website, www.bnymellon.com.

3.3 Secondary Markets for Equity

As discussed in Chapter 1, the advantage of publicly traded securities is that they can be sold later in public secondary markets. This section discusses the types of secondary equity markets and how each type operates.

Types of Secondary Market for Equity

Secondary equity markets can be organized either as an exchange or an over-the-counter market. An **exchange** is a physical location where buyers and sellers buy and sell securities. NYSE Euronext and the London and Tokyo stock exchanges are good examples of organized secondary markets for equities. An **over-the-counter (OTC) market**, in contrast, allows buyers and sellers to transact without meeting at one physical place. For example, OTC transactions often occur over computer networks, such as the debt-based Euromarkets described previously. The National Association of Security Dealers Automated Quotation System (NASDAQ) market in the United States is a noteworthy example of a computer-linked OTC equity market.

Two alternatives to the traditional exchange-based and OTC-based markets, known as the third and fourth markets, include elements of both OTC and exchange markets. The **third market** comprises exchange-listed equities that a broker can buy and sell over the counter. The **fourth market** consists of large investors who trade exchange-listed equities among themselves, bypassing the exchange. Generally, the trades take place through an electronic communication network or **ECN**. Although it is difficult to obtain data on transaction costs in alternative markets, an estimate of the cost of trading on the exchange floor is £0.025 to £0.05 per share. In contrast, the costs of trading in the off-exchange markets can be as low as £0.005 per share.

In all markets, trading is done by brokers, dealers, or both. A **broker** facilitates a trade between a buyer and a seller by bringing the two parties together. Brokers profit by charging a brokerage commission for this service. Alternatively, *dealers* buy and sell securities directly: they maintain an inventory in the security and stand willing to take the opposite side of a buy or sell. Dealers make their money on the bid-ask spread, buying at the bid price and selling at the ask.

Exchanges

There are numerous exchanges worldwide that trade everything from equities and bonds to options and futures contracts. All exchanges have listing requirements. For example, the main market of the London Stock Exchange requires firms to have a minimum market capitalization of £700,000 and three years of fully audited financial statements. In contrast, the market for smaller companies in London, known as the Alternative Investment Market (AIM), has no market capitalization requirements.

Most exchanges have electronic trading systems. Traders submit orders to an **electronic limit order book**, and these are crossed with other orders that have previously been submitted to the system and executed. Sometimes a large order may be crossed with several other orders, and a weighted average transaction price is reported. Two general types of orders can be submitted to an order book. A **market order** is an order to buy or sell at the prevailing market price. For small-sized orders, this usually means purchasing at the best quoted ask price and selling at the best quoted bid price. A **limit order** is an offer to buy or sell at a pre-specified share price.

A notable exception to the electronic limit order book system is on NASDAQ. Its trading system is known as a **competitive dealer market**. Here, dealers record quotes and trades manually, and they are linked by a computer system that allows them to see all the quotes on a particular equity. The typical firm listed on NASDAQ has approximately ten dealers active in trading. However, some equities can have as few as one registered dealer only. Each dealer provides a bid-ask quote and a '**depth**' – that is, how many shares it is willing to buy at the bid price and sell at the ask price. Of course, there is no requirement that the quote is competitive.

Electronic Communication Networks (ECNs)

ECNs have become increasingly popular places to trade equities, particularly after the exchanges and dealer markets are closed for the day and before they open. Many are open to individuals as well as to institutions. The most popular ECNs are Instinet, Archipelago, Brut, Bloomberg's Tradebook, SelectNet and Island.

3.4 Equity Market Informational Efficiency and Capital Allocation

Part II of this book examines, in detail, various methods that can be used to value equities. These methods assume that security prices satisfy what financial economists call the **efficient markets hypothesis.** Fama (1970) summarizes the idea of an efficient market as a market in which prices fully reflect available information. In other words, financial market prices are close to their intrinsic values and hence do not offer investors high expected returns without exposing them to high risks.

Economists are concerned about the efficiency of share prices because they affect how capital is allocated throughout the economy. To understand this, consider the large number of IPOs during the global pandemic between 2020 and 2022. Pre-covid, firms would have gone through the full IPO process of roadshows, prospectuses, conferences and stock exchange listing, assuming that the prices achieved in the financial markets would be reflective of underlying asset values. However, the uncertainty created by the pandemic made this an unattractive option for many companies because the issue price would be as much dependent on the sentiment of the volatile market participants as it is the business fundamentals of the company seeking financing.

The capital markets continually innovate and a vehicle for raising funds, **special purpose acquisition companies** (SPACs), became extremely popular during the pandemic period. A SPAC is a company created specifically to acquire another private company. The SPAC undergoes its own IPO and lists on the stock market. It has no other operations and may have an acquisition target in mind when it is listed, but this would generally not be known at the time of stock exchange listing. SPACs go through the same IPO process as any other firm and appoint underwriters to market their issue. The capital raised in a SPAC IPO is kept in an interest-bearing account and can only be used for an acquisition. If the acquisition doesn't occur within a specified period, typically two years, the money is returned to the shareholders. Shareholders must also sign off at an EGM any acquisition proposed by the SPAC's management.

The market's enthusiastic acceptance of SPAC IPOs had a major effect on equity financing and capital allocation. Many firms choose to be acquired by a SPAC, which allows them to be indirectly listed on the stock exchange without going through the IPO process. Moreover, a SPAC acquisition could be completed within two to three months at a negotiated price compared with a potential twelve-month process with an uncertain issue price for a traditional IPO. Although most SPACs are in the US, with around 200 IPOs in 2021 compared with only two in 2010, the European market has also experienced a significant increase, with 35 SPAC IPOs in 2021 compared with four in 2020. Sadly SPAC performance hasn't been great compared with traditional IPOs over the same period. According to an article by Bloomberg in 2021[7], the average gain for traditional US IPOs between 2018 and 2021 was 61 per cent, compared with only 11 per cent for SPACs.

The critical point to remember from the SPAC example is that the stock market provides valuable signals that indirectly lead to the allocation of capital to various sectors of the economy. The explosion of SPAC IPOs during the pandemic signalled a potentially more efficient way of raising financing during highly volatile periods. The success of one or two SPAC IPOs would have undoubtedly led to followers seeking similar funding. However, it's possible that the market provided too much capital to SPACs, and this would have meant other financing opportunities would have been unsuccessful due to lesser demand. Over the coming years, and once the pandemic has lessened in impact, we shall discover whether the SPAC IPOs were a temporary fad that misallocated capital in the economy or have become an alternative mode of raising financing in the capital markets.

Results

Result 3.1

The stock market plays a vital role in allocating capital. Sectors of the economy that experience favourable share price returns or media interest can more easily raise new funding for investment. Given this, the stock market is likely to allocate capital more efficiently if market prices accurately reflect the investment opportunities within an industry.

[7] 'Wall Street is Churning Out SPACs at Investors' Peril', *Bloomberg,* 16 November 2021.

3.5 Private Equity

Since 2010, the size of the global **private equity** market has grown significantly, and in 2020, global private equity fundraising stood at $503 billion, up from $155 billion in 2010, with $7.3 trillion private equity assets under management. Private equity is any type of share ownership that is not listed on a public exchange and cannot, therefore, be traded in the public equity markets. It is in direct competition to SPACs in financing private firms. The amount of 'dry powder' in private equity funds can give insights into future trends in private equity investment. Dry powder is unspent capital committed to investment in the future. Exhibit 3.4 shows the growth in dry powder by fund type. Much of the change in private equity has been in lending, but there is significant capital awaiting investment in equity.

Exhibit 3.4 Growth in Private Equity Dry Powder 2020 vs 2010 by Fund Type

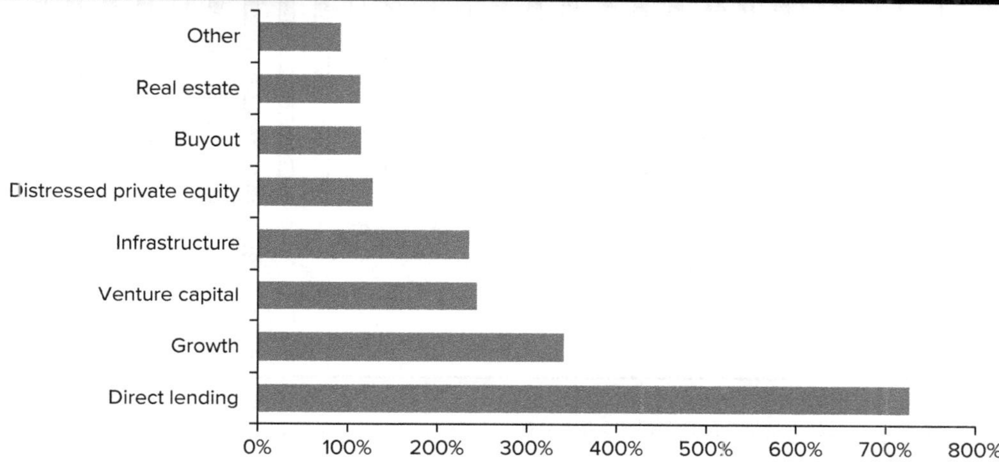

Source: Global Private Equity Report 2020, Bain & Company.

Across Europe, there are wide variations in the attractiveness of countries with respect to private equity. For example, Groh et al. (2010) created an attractiveness index based on 42 different parameters and showed that the UK and Ireland were the most attractive locations in Europe (see Exhibit 3.5). However, although the UK and Ireland are similar to most other countries in Europe, they differ in terms of the size and liquidity of their financial markets, together with the strength of corporate governance rules and investor protection.

There are three types of private equity. **Venture capital** focuses on the very early stages of a firm's development and provides funding to start-ups and new firms with excellent growth potential. **Mezzanine financing** provides funds for firms with growth potential and need additional financing for listing in the capital markets. Finally, private equity funds can buy out companies with future growth opportunities, restructure their assets or operations, or act as **strategic investors** in emerging-market companies.

Because private equity is not allowed to be traded on public stock markets, the investment is long term and illiquid. This is a significant disadvantage of this type of investment and, as a result, it requires higher returns than other, more liquid asset classes. Private equity investors can earn a return on their investment in three main ways. First, the invested firm may be taken to the markets through an IPO, and the private equity can be re-registered and sold to the public. Second, the invested firm may be acquired or merged with another company, and the private equity fund will sell its stake to the acquirer. Third, the private equity fund may sell its shares privately to another private equity investor.

3.6 The Decision to Issue Shares Publicly

Many economists believe that the relatively liquid equity markets and the active new issues market provide a competitive advantage to young firms in developed markets. However, in less developed countries and emerging markets, where access to good capital markets is difficult, entrepreneurs and venture capitalists find

Exhibit 3.5 Private Equity Attractiveness Index

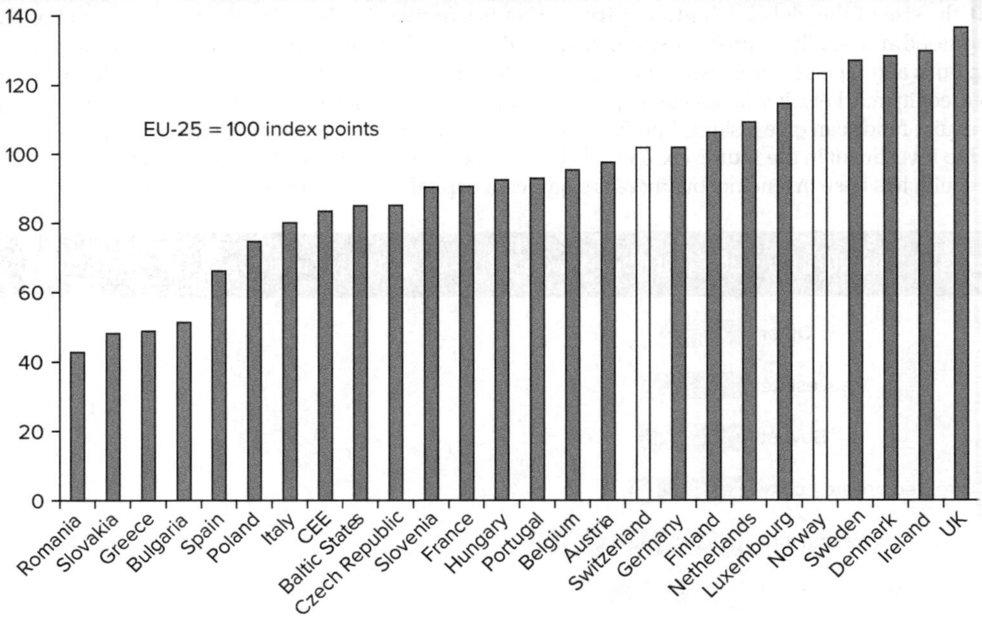

Source: Groh et al. (2010).

it almost impossible to cash out or diversify their holdings. This, in turn, makes it more expensive to start a firm and reduces the rate at which firms are created.

Although the most common motives for public offerings are to minimize the cost of financing, access new financing sources and improve financial flexibility, there are several other practical reasons for listing on a stock exchange. Bancel and Mittoo (2009) surveyed European CFOs and reported that enhanced visibility and credibility, as well as strategic and reputational concerns, are also significant factors. Celikyurt et al. (2010) report that many firms become publicly listed to raise cash for future acquisitions. In recent years, an increasing number of firms have issued shares (IPO and SEO) simply to increase cash liquidity, primarily as a precautionary motive (McLean 2011). Hsu et al. (2010) find that a successful IPO reduces the advantages of a firm's competitors because the newly public firm has loosened financial constraints, quality certification from the IPO's bookrunner, and extant knowledge of the capital markets. Ultimately, the decision to go public is complex and unrelated solely to financing. To understand why firms go public, one must also consider their strategic goals and objectives.

The IPO market for equity is both large and active. Exhibit 3.6 shows the annual number of firms going public and the total annual proceeds raised by those firms in the United Kingdom. As can be seen, the IPO market is cyclical, with the early 1980s and 1990s being particularly quiet. This compares with the boom years of the mid-1980s, mid-1990s, 2000 and 2004–2007. Since the financial crisis of 2008, the number of IPOs has been considerably lower than in earlier years. Some of the reasons for this cyclical behaviour are discussed below.

Demand- and Supply-Side Explanations for IPO Cycles

There are both demand-side and supply-side explanations for the cyclical nature of the IPO market. On the demand side, there are periods when an especially large number of new firms, which are unlikely to obtain private funding at attractive terms, have investment projects that need to be funded. The Internet start-ups of the early 2000s are good examples. On the supply side, there might be periods when investors and institutions that traditionally invest in IPOs have a lot of money to invest. This could happen, for example, if a large inflow of cash went into mutual funds that invest in small stocks.[8]

[8] See Choe et al. (1993) for a discussion and evidence on demand-side effects. Loughran and Ritter (1995) discuss and provide evidence of supply-side explanations of the hot issue market.

Exhibit 3.6 Number of Offerings and Average Initial Return of UK IPOs in 1980–2020

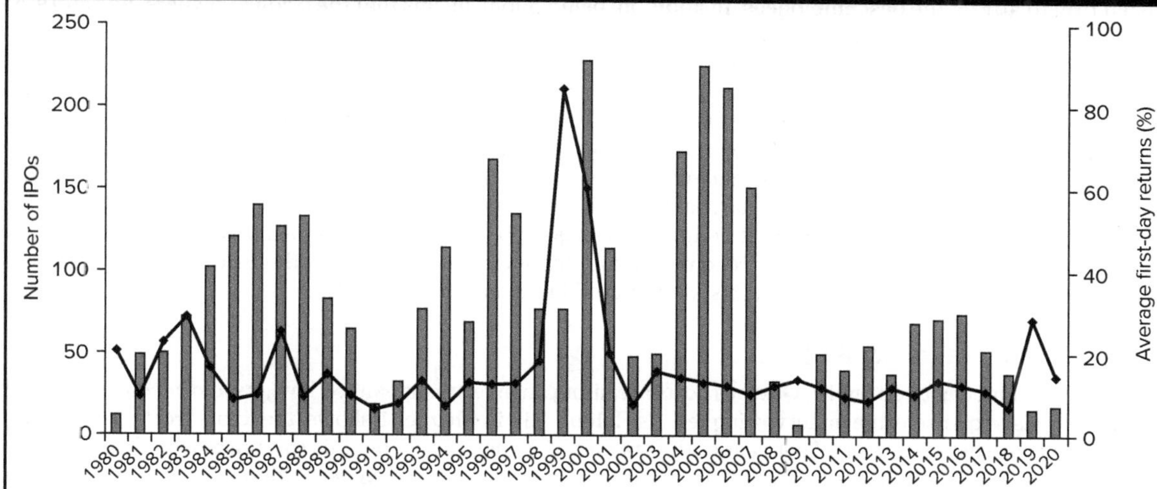

Source: Professor Jay Ritter's University of Florida web page, http://bear.cba.ufl.edu/ritter.

A firm considering going public would be interested in knowing whether **hot issue periods** – periods during which large numbers of firms are going public – are driven by greater demand from firms requiring financing or by a larger supply of public funds looking for new investment opportunities. If the hot issue periods are demand driven, entrepreneurs may wish to avoid going public during that time because the competition for funds would suggest that the firm might get a better price by waiting. However, the supply-side explanation indicates the opposite: IPOs are cyclic because entrepreneurs time their initial public offerings to correspond with the greater supply of available funding and thereby get better deals in the hot issue periods. Loughran and Ritter's (1995) empirical study suggested that the post-issue share price returns of firms that go public in hot issue periods are low, supporting the supply-side explanation. This means that entrepreneurs may benefit by timing their IPOs so that they come out in hot issue periods. From an investor's perspective, however, this would not be a good time to buy IPOs. Ivanov and Lewis (2008) and Kim and Weisbach (2008) provide evidence that both explanations may be valid because improvements in business conditions and investor sentiment lead to more IPOs.

Results

Result 3.2

IPOs are cyclic and frequently observed in some years while not in others. The available evidence suggests that hot issue periods are characterized by an ample supply of available capital. Given this interpretation, firms are better off going public during a hot issue period.

The Benefits of Going Public

For executives of many small firms, listing on a stock exchange can be viewed as a measure of success. However, many firms choose never to raise money from the public equity markets and have been very successful. Firms may go public for various reasons. First, they may obtain capital at more attractive terms from the public markets. For example, companies in 'hot potato' industries that are constantly in the news find public markets to be a cheaper source of financing because of investor enthusiasm for their products. However, some firms that go public issue very few shares in their IPO and do not need the raised capital. For example, Bodnaruk et al. (2008) found that, for Swedish firms, the controlling shareholder had most to gain from going public, especially when they had lower wealth. In some cases, the major shareholder may make the listing decision rather than the senior executives.

Given that publicly traded shares can be traded without much difficulty, the equity of a listed firm may be considered a more attractive form of compensation than the equity of a private firm, making it easier for the listed firm to attract the best employees. In addition, being public means that the original owners, investors, and old and new managers can cash out of the firm and diversify their portfolios.

An additional advantage of being public is that share prices in the public markets provide a valuable source of information for managers. Every day, investors buy and sell shares, thereby rendering their judgements about the firm's prospects. Although the market isn't infallible, it can be a useful reality check. For example, a manager would probably think twice about expanding the firm's core business after its share price fell. This is because a falling share price indicates that investors and analysts have unfavourable information about a firm's prospects, which would tend to imply that an expansion would not be warranted.

Finally, some managers believe that going public is good publicity. For example, listing the firm's equity on a national exchange may bring name recognition and increase its credibility with customers, employees and suppliers. In some businesses, though, this kind of credibility matters very little.

The Costs of Going Public

It costs a lot of money to go public. Obvious costs are hiring an investment banker, lawyers and accountants, but by far, the biggest expense is the underwriting fee. As Exhibit 1.12 in Chapter 1 shows, the total direct costs of taking a firm public are between 6 and 7 per cent of the amount of money raised, but this can range from 2 to 13 per cent depending on the size of the issue. Exhibit 3.7 provides a breakdown of US underwriting fees in 2020 by deal size. According to the OECD[9], underwriting fees in European IPOs are less than half of their US counterparts.

Exhibit 3.7 Average Underwriter Fee in US IPOs, 2020, by Deal Size

DEAL SIZE ($)	UNDERWRITER FEE AS % OF GROSS PROCEEDS
25M TO 99M	7%
100M TO 249M	6.80%
250M TO 499M	6.10%
500M TO 1BN	5.40%
GREATER THAN 1BN	3.50%

Source: Statista (2020).

While direct costs may be significant, there is an additional and equally important cost of going public. The price at which the investment banker sells the issue to the original investors is generally 10 to 15 per cent below the price at which the equity trades in the secondary market shortly after that. However, the underpricing can be much larger in many countries. In addition, underpricing is greater for firms that are more difficult to value, such as smaller companies or those with less track record of operations (Lowry et al. 2010). Similarly, firms with higher levels of uncertain text in regulatory filings also have more underpricing (Loughran and McDonald 2013). Regardless of the reason for the observed underpricing of new issues, firms should add the typical percentage of underpricing to their cost of going public. Considering all these, the total cost of going public could exceed 25 per cent of the amount raised in the IPO, or even more in some countries. However, firms often raise very little in the IPO, so the cost as a fraction of the firm's total value is generally considerably smaller.

Once a firm is public, it faces other costs that private firms do not bear. For example, public firms must provide periodic financial statements to their stock exchange. They also must hold regular shareholder meetings and communicate with institutional shareholders and financial analysts. Because a public firm's communication with its shareholders must be transparent and informative, any data provided to shareholders will also be available to competitors, which may put the firm at a competitive disadvantage.

Because a public corporation is more visible than a private company, it may be pressured to do things in ways that it would not do otherwise. For example, Jensen and Murphy (1990) argue that the mandated disclosure of senior remuneration constrains firms from paying their executives too much. In addition, shareholders may pressure managers to make socially responsible investment choices that they might not otherwise consider.

[9] OECD *Business Finance Outlook*, 2017.

Result 3.3 summarizes the discussion in the last two subsections.

Results

Result 3.3

The advantages and disadvantages of going public are as follows.

Advantages:

- Better access to capital markets
- Shareholders gain liquidity
- Original owners can diversify
- External capital markets provide monitoring and information
- Enhances the firm's credibility with customers, employees and suppliers.

Disadvantages:

- It is expensive
- The costs of dealing with shareholders
- Information is revealed to competitors
- Public pressure.

In general, a firm should go public when the benefits exceed the costs.

The Process of Going Public

Taking a company public is a lengthy process that usually requires several months.

The Registration Statement

Once the firm chooses an underwriter, it begins assembling the data required for the registration statement. This includes the audited financial statements and a complete description of the firm's business: products, prospects and possible risks (for example, reliance on specific customers or contracts and dependence on key personnel). The underwriters are legally responsible for ensuring that the registration statement discloses all material information about the firm. **Material information** is information that, if omitted, would significantly alter the firm's value.

Marketing the Issue

The underwriter is also responsible for forming the underwriting syndicate, marketing the equity, and allocating shares among syndicate members. Marketing the equity may involve 'roadshows' in which the firm's management and the underwriter explain and try to sell the IPO to institutional investors. These presentations enable investors to get a feel for management and, equally important, allow the underwriter to estimate the demand for an issue. Although 'expressions of interest' from potential buyers are non-binding, they influence the offer price, the number of shares and allocations to particular investors. A *pathfinder* prospectus is usually issued containing relevant information about the firm to aid possible investors in their decision-making. An offer price, potential yields and expected financial ratios will not typically be provided at this stage.

Pricing the Issue

Once the regulator approves the registration statement, the process of going public can move into its final stage of pricing the issue, determining the number of shares to be sold and distributing the shares to investors. In many cases, the IPO is oversubscribed. An **oversubscribed offering** means that investors want to buy more shares than the underwriter plans to sell. For example, when Coal India went public, the underwriters had €2.46 billion to raise. However, the issue was substantially oversubscribed, attracting over €20 billion of declared interest from foreign investors alone.

Book Building vs Fixed-Price Method

How investment bankers price and market a new issue, as described above, is called the **book-building process**. The principal thing to note about the book-building process is that it allows the investment banker to gauge the demand for the issue and, as a result, price the issue more accurately. Consequently, this book-building process has become increasingly popular for IPOs marketed internationally.

Until recently, most IPOs were sold with the **fixed-price method**. For example, fixed-price offerings in the United Kingdom advertise the number of shares and the offer price by prospectus 14 days before applications are accepted from interested investors. The main distinction between the fixed-price and book-building methods is that, with the former method, the investment bank is less able to gauge investor demand. In addition, investors in fixed-price offerings are generally allocated shares in oversubscribed offerings using some fixed formula. For example, if a company offers 1 million shares to investors, and investors, in the aggregate, request 2 million shares, each investor may receive only half of what they requested. In other words, shares may be allocated on a *pro-rata* basis. There are, however, frequent deviations from these *pro-rata* allocations. For example, in some cases, underwriters can discriminate in favour of small investors, giving them a larger proportion of the shares they request. In contrast to the book-building method, where the underwriter has considerable discretion in fixed-price offerings, investment banks generally have little leeway in allocating the shares of new issues.

Ljungqvist et al. (2003) considered the use of book building by examining 2,051 IPOs in over 60 countries around the world. They showed that it was used in most of their sample, particularly for Europe and South America, where governments typically do not limit the choices of issuers. However, in Asia, where regulations tend to be more restrictive, the shift to book building has not been as rapid, and only in Japan and China is it regularly used. In many countries, the underwriter uses a hybrid method – a book-building method for allocating the shares to institutions and a fixed-price method for allocating shares to individual investors. There has also been a small number of IPOs sold through auctions on the Internet; the most notable example is Google (now Alphabet inc.).

Book-building has several advantages (not necessarily financial) over fixed-price issues. Degeorge et al. (2007) considered public offerings in France. They found that the main benefits from the book-building process came from the proactive advertising of the issue before the issue date, which increased interest. Interestingly, there was little difference in value benefit between the two methods. However, Busaba and Chang (2010) found that if there is the possibility of informed trading after the issue date, more underpricing would be required for book-building and fixed-price IPOs. If an underwriter is able to sell to only a small subset of large investors, book-building will produce higher proceeds. However, if this is not the case, a fixed price IPO to retail investors will raise more capital.

3.7 Equity Returns Associated with IPOs of Ordinary Equity

The Underpricing of IPOs

The cost associated with the underpricing of new issues is a significant cost associated with going public. Researchers generally measure underpricing as the average initial returns measured over the first trading day (the percentage increase from the offering price to the first closing price). Almost universally, researchers have found IPO underpricing of varying degrees. Exhibit 3.8 presents average initial IPO returns for selected countries. In some countries (for example, Saudi Arabia, China, UAE), underpricing is enormous and, in general, this is replicated across less developed economies. The difference in underpricing between the United Kingdom (15.7 per cent), where fixed-price offers dominate, and the United States (17.2 per cent), where book building dominates, is not particularly large.

Exhibit 3.8 Equal Weighted Average Initial IPO Returns for Selected Countries

Country	Average Initial Return (%)	Country	Average Initial Return (%)	Country	Average Initial Return (%)
Austria	6.2	**India**	84.0	**Singapore**	25.8
Belgium	11.0	**Ireland**	21.6	**South Africa**	17.2
China	170.2	**Israel**	13.8	**Spain**	9.2
Denmark	7.4	**Italy**	13.1	**Sweden**	25.9

Exhibit 3.8 Continued

Country	Average Initial Return (%)	Country	Average Initial Return (%)	Country	Average Initial Return (%)
Finland	14.2	**Malaysia**	50.3	**Switzerland**	25.2
France	9.7	**Netherlands**	13.3	**UAE**	270.1
Germany	21.8	**Norway**	6.7	**UK**	15.7
Greece	50.8	**Saudi Arabia**	239.8	**US**	17.2

Source: Professor Jay R. Ritter's website, University of Florida, https://site.warrington.ufl.edu/ritter/files/International.pdf

What Are the Long-term Returns of IPOs?

A series of papers – Ritter (1991), Loughran et al. (1994), Aggarwal and Rivoli (1990), Gompers and Lerner (2003) and Gao et al. (2006) – have shown that the long-term return to investing in IPOs is surprisingly low. Exhibit 3.10 presents three-year post-IPO buy and hold returns for US firms (1980–2019) by firm size. Three measures of long-term returns are recorded. First, there are positive long-term raw returns for all sizes apart from the smallest IPOs. However, once these returns are adjusted to reflect how well the market or similar style firms performed, the underperformance of IPOs is clear. Given these returns, the terminal value of an IPO portfolio after three years would be only 85 per cent of the value of a portfolio that invested in all stocks and 95 per cent of the value of a portfolio of firms with a similar style. The evidence reviewed in Loughran et al. (1994) shows that investors in Brazil, Finland, Germany and the United Kingdom would have been just as disappointed with their investments in IPOs as investors in the United States. Chemmanur et al. (2010) report that institutional trading around IPOs can predict long-term returns, especially in firms where institutions have been involved in the IPO.

Exhibit 3.10 Long-run Returns on IPOs Categorized by the Pre-issue Sales of the Firm, 1980–2019

			Average 3-year Buy-and-hold Return		
Sales (in 2019$)	Number of IPOs	Average First-day Return	IPOs	Market-adjusted	Style-adjusted
0–9.999 mm	1,681	21.4%	−6.3%	−42.5%	−27.0%
10–19.999 mm	699	28.1%	3.8%	−34.8%	−13.7%
20–49.999 mm	1,485	22.9%	24.2%	−18.9%	−2.1%
50–99 999 mm	1,399	18.0%	27.7%	−15.1%	−5.9%
100–499.999 mm	2,208	13.2%	45.6%	3.1%	9.0%
500 mm and up	1,138	9.4%	37.5%	1.7%	1.4%
0–99.999 mm	5,264	21.8%	12.7%	−27.5%	−12.6%
100 mm and up	3,346	11.9%	42.8%	2.7%	6.4%
1980–2019	8,610	17.9%	24.4%	−15.8%	−5.2%

Source: Professor Jay R. Ritter's website, University of Florida, https://site.warrington.ufl.edu/ritter/files/IPO-statistics-longrun.pdf

Autore et al. (2009) report that the intended use of funds can influence post-offer performance. Firms with specific investment plans perform better than similar equity issues that use the money raised for general business purposes. Having a particular project in mind signals profitable investment opportunities, whereas general-purpose equity issues may simply be evidence of market timing. Consistent with Autore et al. (2009), Billett et al. (2011) argue that most prior empirical studies have ignored events after an IPO and, as a result, have not considered firm decisions post-IPO. They collected information on all post-IPO financing activities and found that the IPO decision itself was not associated with poor long-term market performance, but those firms who regularly went to the markets for financing did experience negative long-term returns.

Going public may also affect a firm's innovation strategy, which could indirectly affect long-term returns. Bernstein (2015), using patent data, found that internal innovation falls after an IPO because of fewer innovative inventors. There is also a drop in inventor productivity after an IPO. To compensate, publicly listed firms buy in new talent and acquire external innovation.

3.8 What Explains Underpricing?

The tendency of IPOs to be underpriced is of interest for several reasons. For example, the underpricing of IPOs increases the cost of going public and may thus deter some firms from going public. However, to investors, underpriced IPOs appear to provide the 'free lunch', or the sure thing, of which they dream. Before many firms go public, it is widely reported in the media that their shares will be substantially oversubscribed at the initial offering price. As a result, underpriced equities commonly trade well above the issue price in the secondary market. Indeed, investors who buy at the offering price and then sell their shares immediately in the secondary market can make substantial profits.

How Do I Get These Underpriced Shares?

As with most free lunches, there are hidden costs to the allocation of underpriced new issues. It is impossible to simply open a brokerage account and expect to buy many new issues at the offering price. Investors should consider why underwriters underprice new issues before they attempt to realize the apparent profit opportunity in this market.

The Incentives of Underwriters

Underwriters weigh the costs and benefits of raising or lowering an offering price. Pricing an issue too low adds to the cost of going public. Therefore, underwriters try to price their issues as high as possible to attract clients. This tendency, however, is offset by the possibility that the issue may not sell if it is priced too high, leaving the underwriter saddled with unsold shares. Because the cost of having unsold shares is borne directly (firm commitment) or indirectly, as a loss of reputation (best efforts), by the underwriter, it may have a substantial influence on the pricing choice and may lead the underwriter to underprice the issue.

There is a potential conflict of interest between underwriters and issuing firms because of their differing incentives and the underwriter's better information about market conditions. Given superior information, the underwriter has a substantial say on the price of an issue. This will not be a problem if the underwriter has the same incentives as the issuing firm, but that is unlikely. The underwriter's incentive is to set the offering price low enough to ensure that all the shares will sell without much effort and without subjecting the underwriter to excessive risk. Underpricing the issue makes the underwriter's job more manageable and less risky.

An underwriter may underprice an issue because of costs arising from potential investor lawsuits if share price performance in the months immediately after the issue date is poor. Tinic (1988) examined this possibility, arguing that concerns about being sued increased following the Securities Act of 1933. Comparing a pre-1933 sample of issues with a post-1933 sample, Tinic found that the initial return, or the degree of underpricing, was much higher after the 1933 Act, which supports this theory. However, Drake and Vetsuypens (1993) examined 93 firms that were sued after their IPOs. Underpricing did not appear to be a factor in driving the lawsuits. International studies of underpricing have also provided contradictory evidence on the role of litigation in IPO underpricing. Outside the US, the risk that underwriters will be sued is minimal, and yet underpricing still occurs.

Investors use all available information when they assess the attractiveness of an IPO, and one way in which a firm can reduce uncertainty is to have a credit rating. An and Chan (2008) found that having a credit rating (and not necessarily the credit rating itself) can reduce the underpricing common in IPOs.

The Case Where the Managers of the Issuing Firm Have Better Information than Investors

Often firms go public as a precursor to a larger seasoned issue shortly after. This allows managers to test the waters with a small issue and raise additional equity capital if that issue is successful. Investment bankers have frequently suggested that it is an excellent idea to underprice the initial offering in these circumstances to make investors feel better about the secondary issue. The belief is that investors will be more likely to subscribe to a firm's seasoned offering after making money in the IPO.

Several academic papers have noted that entrepreneurs who expect their firms to do well and have opportunities for further investment will have the greatest incentive to underprice their shares.[10] These papers argue that investors understand that only the best-quality firms have the motivation to underprice their issues. Therefore, these investors take a more favourable view of the subsequent issues of firms that underpriced their IPOs. Thus, the incentive to underprice an issue is determined by a firm's intention to seek further outside financing. Although this argument seems plausible, empirical research on the pricing of new issues provides little support for this hypothesis.[11]

The Case Where Some Investors Have Better Information than Other Investors

If IPOs tend to be underpriced, does it make sense to place orders for all available IPOs? To understand the risk of this strategy, recall the famous line by Groucho Marx, who said, 'I would never join a club that would have me for a member'. To have an IPO allocated to you is a bit like being invited to join an exclusive club. Since the hot issues are underpriced, there is usually excess demand, making it unlikely you will be allotted your full order amount. So while it might be nice to be asked to join a club, you have to query whether the club is really so exclusive if you have been asked to join. Likewise, it is important to ask why you have been successful in getting your full allocation of shares if an IPO is really so hot.

To understand this argument, suppose that there are two kinds of investors: the informed and the uninformed. Informed investors know the true value of the shares, perhaps through costly research. Hence, they will put in an order for the IPO only when the shares are underpriced. Uninformed investors do not know what shares are worth and submit orders for a cross-section of IPOs. Unfortunately, they get allocated 100 per cent of the overpriced 'dogs' and only a fraction of the underpriced 'stars'.

If new issues are not underpriced, uninformed investors will, on average, systematically lose money. The allocation of the dogs to investors is an example of what economists refer to as the **winner's curse,** a term derived from an analysis of auctions, in which the bidder who wins the auction ultimately realizes that they were willing to pay more for the object than everyone else in the room – and thus overpaid. Similarly, an investor allocated shares in an IPO could be subject to the winner's curse if they are allocated shares because more informed investors have chosen not to purchase them. Because of this winner's curse, individuals aware of their lack of knowledge avoid auctions, and uninformed investors generally avoid buying IPOs.

Underwriters, wanting to broaden the appeal of issues, may underprice share issues to induce uninformed investors to buy. One implication of this line of reasoning is that riskier IPOs that are more subject to the winner's curse must be underpriced more, on average, than less risky IPOs.

Several banks in the US have been successfully sued by investors who alleged a discriminatory allocation of shares in hot IPOs. Some underwriters allegedly allocated more shares in hot IPOs to their most favoured and financially lucrative clients to attract future business. This meant that less-informed investors were unlikely to partake in these successful offerings. Aggarwal et al. (2002) provide evidence consistent with this allegation by showing that large institutions earned more on their IPO allocations than smaller retail investors. The main reason for this superior performance was that they were allocated more equity in the IPOs with greater price appreciation. Dorn (2009) shows that individual or retail investors consistently overpay in German IPOs compared with the aftermarket price.

Koh and Walter's (1989) study of IPOs in Singapore and Keloharju's (1993) study of IPOs in Finland provide more direct tests of the winner's curse. These countries use the fixed-price method to distribute and allocate shares, and the degree of rationing is public knowledge. The results of both studies show that: (1) buyers receive more shares of the overpriced issues and fewer shares of the underpriced issues; and (2) since investors receive a greater allocation of the bad issues, on average, they realize zero profits from buying IPO shares, even though the shares are underpriced.

Lowry et al. (2010) report that issue date returns are more volatile in firms that are difficult to value because of information asymmetry. One way to reduce this asymmetric information problem is to list the firm's existing (private) shares on an exchange and subsequently issue new shares. By following this sequential process,

[10] This explanation for underpricing new issues is developed in papers by Allen and Faulhaber (1989), Grinblatt and Hwang (1989), Welch (1989), Chemmanur (1993) and Francis et al. (2010).

[11] Garfinkel (1993), Jegadeesh et al. (1993) and Michaely and Shaw (1994) look at the relationship between the amount by which an issue is underpriced and whether the issuer subsequently follows with a secondary offering. All conclude that there is no such relationship.

valuation uncertainty can be reduced, as interest in existing shares can be ascertained before the offer date. In many countries, a company is typically listed, with shares being issued simultaneously. However, in the United Kingdom, it is possible to have a sequential offering. Derrien and Kecskés (2007) report that uncertainty is reduced, underpricing occurs less often and financing costs are lower for sequential offerings.

The Case Where Investors Have Information that the Underwriter Does Not

The winner's curse provides a reasonable explanation for underpricing in countries that use the fixed-price method. The model also provides a necessary lesson for uninformed investors who know about the underpricing of new issues and see this as a profit opportunity. However, the Winner's Curse may not fully explain why issues tend to be underpriced in the book-building approach to new issues.

Recall that with the book-building procedure, underwriters rely on information learned from potential investors when they price the IPO. If investors express enthusiasm for the issue, the underwriter raises the price. If investors are less enthusiastic, the underwriter lowers the price.

Because their information affects the price, investors have an incentive to distort their true opinions of an IPO. In particular, investors might appear pessimistic about the issuing firm's prospects in the hope of getting allocated shares of the issue at a more favourable price. Obtaining truthful information may be especially difficult when there are influential investors whose decisions are likely to influence the decisions of others.[12] Influential investors play an important role in the success or failure of an offer because smaller investors may ignore their own information and decide whether to subscribe to an issue based on the stated opinions of market leaders. For example, if a very large investment house, such as Fidelity, expresses no interest in an issue, small investors may choose to ignore their own information and decide not to participate in the offering, causing the IPO to fail.

Benveniste and Spindt (1989) and Benveniste and Wilhelm (1990) suggested that the way in which investment banks price and allocate the shares of new issues when they use a book-building process may make it easier for them to elicit credible information from their large investors. Binay et al. (2007) show that the investor–underwriter relationship is significant in allocating IPOs because of trust built from past dealings and that regular investors participate more often in underpriced issues. Jenkinson and Jones (2009b) go so far as to suggest that the investor–underwriter relationship is the most important driver in IPO allocation and that information production or revelation is of secondary importance.

Individual investors hoping to gain from investing in underpriced new issues should be aware that not all IPOs are underpriced and that they may not be in a position to obtain those IPOs that are. To make matters even more difficult, Kaustia and Knüpfer (2008) have suggested that the demand for IPOs may not even be rational. They found a strong link between past IPO returns and future subscriptions for new issues in Finland, irrespective of the quality of the individual IPO. Investor sentiment, as this is known, is increasingly being viewed as an important driver in many areas of finance, not just equity IPOs.

Bringing the Evidence Together

The preceding discussion clearly shows no single factor driving the underpricing of new equity issues. Bolton et al. (2018) reviewed the IPO literature to date across different countries and analysed the collective findings of this research. It is fair to say that the results are not conclusive or indicative of a clear explanation for underpricing. The main factors explaining underpricing that they considered were: positive media attention before the IPO date; local bias; recent market return; recent IPO activity; top-tier underwriters; VC-backed IPOs; an integer offer price; the IPO has a strong order flow; the underwriter has made a firm commitment to sell the issue; or the IPO is high-tech.

Exhibit 3.9 presents an overview of the international evidence on the determinants of IPO underpricing across countries. A '+' entry means a positive relationship between the characteristic and IPO underpricing; A '–' entry means a negative relationship and '0' means that no association exists. So, for example, in all countries, recent market performance is strongly associated with greater levels of underpricing. European IPOs tend to have similar drivers, but what explains the difference in findings between China and other countries? More research is required to ascertain the different results, which may be due to regulatory differences skewing the Chinese results.

---

[12] Benveniste and Wilhelm (1997) report that Fidelity, one such market leader, buys about 10 per cent of all newly issued shares.

Exhibit 3.9 Determinants of Underpricing by Country

Country	Offer Size	Recent Market Return	Recent IPO Activity	Stock Market Turnover	Top Tier Under-writer	VC Backed IPO	Firm Commit-ment	High-Tech Firm
United States	–	+	+	–	+	+	–	+
China	–	+	–	–	–	–	–	–
United Kingdom	–	+	+	+	–	–	–	+
France	0	+	+		0	–	0	+
Singapore	–	+	0	+	0	–	0	0
Germany	0	+	+	0	0	–	–	+
Malaysia	–	+	+	0	0	0	0	+
India	–	+	0	0	–	0	–	0

Source: Adapted from Table 4.2 of Boulton, T., Smart, S. and Zutter, C. (2018) *Determinants of variation in IPO underpricing. The Oxford Handbook of IPOs,* 81. Oxford University Press.

3.9 Seasoned Equity Offerings

When a company goes to the equity markets for a second, third or subsequent time, it is referred to as a **Seasoned Equity Offering**. Seasoned Equity Offerings (SEOs) follow the same process as IPOs with one difference: the share price is known beforehand. The incentives to set an issue price below the market value remain, but the quality of information on the actual value of the shares is much more robust, reducing the risk faced by the underwriter and issuing firm.

To proceed with an SEO, the firm must usually offer the new equity to existing shareholders before having a broader public issue. The reason is that existing shareholders must be allowed to maintain their proportionate holdings in the firm, and we call this a pre-emptive right. Not all firms have pre-emptive rights, but in Europe and most of the world, they are common and stated in the articles of incorporation. If a firm offers pre-emptive rights to its shareholders, it must first offer any new equity issue to existing shareholders. This assures each owner their proportionate share. If the articles of incorporation do not include a pre-emptive right, the firm has a choice of offering the issue of equity directly to existing shareholders or to the public. Holderness (2018) found that rights offerings will predominate wherever shareholder approval is required, but public issues will be more common if managers can bypass shareholders.

An equity issue to existing shareholders is called a rights issue or rights offering. Here each shareholder is issued an option to buy a specified number of new shares from the firm at a specified price within a specified time, after which the rights expire. The rights issue terms are evidenced by certificates known as share warrants or rights. Such rights are often traded on securities exchanges or over the counter. Rights issues have some interesting advantages relative to cash offers. For example, they appear cheaper for the issuing firm than cash offers. In fact, a firm can undertake a rights issue without using an underwriter, whereas, as a practical matter, an underwriter is almost a necessity in a cash offer.

Rights issues are typically arranged using **standby underwriting**. In standby underwriting, the issuer makes a rights issue, and the underwriter makes a firm commitment to 'take up' (that is, purchase) the unsubscribed portion of the issue. As a result, the underwriter usually gets a **standby fee** and additional amounts based on the securities taken up.

Standby underwriting protects the firm against undersubscription, which can occur if investors throw away rights or if bad news causes the market price of the equity to fall below the subscription price.

In practice, only a small percentage (fewer than 10 per cent) of shareholders fail to exercise valuable rights. This failure can probably be attributed to ignorance or holidays. Furthermore, shareholders are usually given an **oversubscription privilege**, enabling them to purchase unsubscribed shares at the subscription price. The oversubscription privilege makes it unlikely that the corporate issuer would turn to its underwriter for help

Motivations for Seasoned Equity Offerings

Asquith and Mullins (1986), Masulis and Korwar (1986) and Baker and Wurgler (2002) find that firms undertaking equity issues typically have high market values before the issue. However, Carlton et al. (2006) put forward the argument that small firms having high growth opportunities but lacking cash may also go to the market, in contrast to mature firms with poor growth opportunities that fall back on internal funds to finance new investment. If the Carlton et al. (2006) hypothesis holds, high growth firms will dominate the SEO market.

It is not clear from the extant research evidence what motivates firms to go to the equity markets for a second time. DeAngelo et al. (2010) test both of these theories (market timing vs lifecycle) and find that neither provides a compelling explanation for seasoned equity offerings. DeAngelo et al. (2010) find that without the proceeds from the SEO, 62.6 per cent of issues would run out of cash, and 81.1 per cent had below normal cash balances within a year of the SEO. They argue that the driving reason for SEOs is a short-term cash need, with market timing and firm lifecycle being only of minor importance.

3.10 The Going-Private Decision

In the early to mid-2000s, the number of firms that went from being public to private grew massively. Although this has traditionally been viewed as being driven by the growth in private equity funding, there had to have been strategic reasons for managers to go down this route. Marosi and Massoud (2007) and Bharath and Dittmar (2010) considered this issue for US going-private decisions. They found that whereas the decision to initially list was because of the reasons outlined earlier, the choice between being public (as opposed to becoming listed) and going private was more to do with maintaining control of the firm and accessing new capital sources. Firms that went private had higher information costs (proxied by low analyst following and institutional ownership) and lower stock market liquidity than comparable firms. In addition, increased regulatory costs caused by the introduction of the Sarbanes–Oxley Act (2002) were a significant factor in firms seeking to delist.

Renneboog et al. (2007) considered UK going-private decisions and investigated several motivations for such a decision. Upon announcement of a public to private transaction, shareholders received an average premium of 40 per cent on their existing shares in addition to a 30 per cent share price reaction. The authors suggest that the wealth gains were caused by undervaluation, reduced tax payments and realignment of incentives.

3.10 Summary and Conclusions

This chapter has reviewed some of the institutional features of the global equity markets. It described the various equity instruments, the types of investors who hold these equity investments and the markets on which they are traded. It pointed out that there are fewer types of equity security than debt securities. Although the equity markets are less dominated by institutions than the debt markets are, it is still the case that, in many countries, more than half of all equities are held by institutions.

The chapter also discussed the process by which firms go public. When firms go public, they transform their private equity, which cannot be traded, into public equity traded in the stock markets. Our discussion of firms' incentives to go public raised several questions that will be addressed in more detail in later chapters. For example, since firms generally raise substantial amounts of new equity when they go public, the decision to go public must be considered along with the firm's capital structure choice, which is examined in Part IV of this text. Going public also affects shareholders' influence on a corporation's management, which is explored in Part V of this text. Finally, the decision to go public is strongly influenced by the difference between the firm's fundamental value, as perceived by senior management, and the price obtained for the shares in the public markets. However, this type of comparison requires additional knowledge of what determines both fundamental values and market prices. The determination of these values is considered in Parts II and III of this text.

Key Concepts

Result 3.1: The stock market plays a vital role in allocating capital. Sectors of the economy that experience favourable stock returns can more easily raise new capital for investment. Given this, the stock market is likely to allocate capital more efficiently if market prices accurately reflect the investment opportunities within an industry.

Result 3.2: IPOs are observed frequently in some years and not in others. The available evidence suggests that the hot issue periods are characterized by an ample supply of available capital. Given this interpretation, firms are better off going public during a hot issue period.

Result 3.3: The advantages and disadvantages of going public are as follows.

Advantages:

- Better access to capital markets
- Shareholders gain liquidity
- Original owners can diversify
- Monitoring and information are provided by external capital markets
- Enhances the firm's credibility with customers, employees and suppliers.

Disadvantages:

- It is expensive
- The costs of dealing with shareholders
- Information is revealed to competitors
- Public pressure.

In general, a firm should go public when the benefits exceed the costs.

Key Terms

Exercises

3.1 AB Electrolux is a Swedish electrical appliance maker. Alecta, an occupational pensions specialist, is one of the company's major shareholders. AB Electrolux has two classes of shares: class A and class B. There are 9.5 million class A shares outstanding, each entitled to 10 votes. There are 272 million class B shares outstanding with one vote per share. Alecta owns 500,000 million shares of class A equity and 16.2 million shares of class B equity. What percentage of the total votes does Alecta control?

3.2 Accurately pricing a new issue can be costly. Explain why underwriters desire a reputation for pricing new issues as accurately as possible. Describe the actions they take to ensure accuracy.

3.3 Suppose a firm wants to make a £75 million IPO of equity. Estimate the transaction costs associated with the issue.

3.4 Suppose your firm wants to issue a security that pays a guaranteed fixed payment plus an additional benefit when the firm's share price increases. Describe how such a security can be designed, and name existing securities with this characteristic.

3.5 When underwriters bring a new firm to market, do you think they have conflicting incentives? What might these be, and what are their causes?

3.6 Before the Internet bubble burst in 2000 and 2001, internet IPOs were substantially more underpriced than the IPOs issued in earlier periods. Discuss why you think this may have happened.

3.7 You are interested in buying 100 shares of Correndo SpA. The current bid price is €18, and the ask price is €19. Suppose you submit a market order. At what price is your order likely to be filled? What are the advantages and disadvantages of submitting a limit order to purchase the shares at €17.9 versus putting in a market order?

3.8 You own 100 per cent of your company's equity and wish to sell all your shares in an IPO. How do you think the market would react to this?

3.9 Chilites has just gone public. Under a firm commitment agreement, Chilites received €6.75 for each of the 10 million shares sold. The initial offering price was €7 per share, and the equity rose to €9 per share in the first few minutes of trading. Chilites paid €4 million in direct legal and other costs and €2 million in indirect costs. What was the flotation cost as a percentage of funds raised?

3.10 Carlyle plc and Mullan plc have both announced IPOs at £40 per share. One of these is undervalued by £11, and the other is overvalued by £6, but you have no way of knowing which is which. You plan on buying 1,000 shares of each issue. If an issue is underpriced, it will be rationed, and only half of your order will be filled. What would your profit be if you could get 1,000 shares in Carlyle and 1,000 shares in Mullan? What profit do you expect? What principle have you illustrated?

References and Additional Reading

Aggarwal, R. and Rivoli, P. (1990) Fads in the initial public offering market *Financial Management*, 19(4): 45–57.

Aggarwal, R., Prabhala, N. and Puri, M. (2002) Institutional allocation in initial public offerings: empirical evidence *The Journal of Finance*, 57(3): 1421–1442.

Allen, F. and Faulhaber, G. (1989) Signaling by underpricing in the IPO market *Journal of Financial Economics*, 23(2): 303–323.

An, H. and Chan, K.C. (2008) Credit ratings and IPO pricing *Journal of Corporate Finance*, 14(5): 584–595.

Autore, D.M., Bray, D.E. and Peterson, D.R. (2009) Intended use of proceeds and the long-run performance of seasoned equity issuers *Journal of Corporate Finance*, 15(3): 358–367.

Bancel, F. and Mittoo, U.R. (2009) Why do European firms go public? *European Financial Management*, 15(4): 844–884.

Benveniste, L. and Spindt, P. (1989) How investment bankers determine the offer price and allocation of new issues *Journal of Financial Economics*, 24(2): 343–361.

Benveniste, L. and Wilhelm, W. (1990) A comparative analysis of IPO proceeds under alternative regulatory environments *Journal of Financial Economics*, 28(1–2): 173–207.

Benveniste, L. and Wilhelm, W. (1997) Initial public offerings: going by the book *Journal of Applied Corporate Finance*, 10: 98–108.

Bernstein, S. (2015). Does going public affect innovation?. *The Journal of Finance*, 70(4): 1365–1403.

Bharath, S.T. and Dittmar, A.K. (2010) Why do firms use private equity to opt out of public markets? *The Review of Financial Studies,* 23(5): 1771–1818.

Billett, M.T., Flannery, M.J. and Garfinkel, J.A. (2011) Frequent issuers' influence on long-run post-issuance returns *Journal of Financial Economics,* 99(2): 349–364.

Binay, M.M., Gatchev, V.A. and Pirinsky, C.A. (2007) The role of underwriter–investor relationships in the IPO process *Journal of Financial and Quantitative Analysis,* 42(3): 785–809.

Bodnaruk, A., Kandel, E., Massa, M. and Simonov, A. (2008) Shareholder diversification and the decision to go public *The Review of Financial Studies,* 21(6): 2780–2824.

Busaba, W.Y. and Chang, C. (2010) Bookbuilding vs. fixed price revisited: the effect of aftermarket trading *Journal of Corporate Finance,* 16(3): 370–381.

Celikyurt, U., Sevilir, M. and Shivdasani, A. (2010) Going public to acquire? The acquisition motive in IPOs *Journal of Financial Economics,* 96(3): 345–363.

Chemmanur, T. J., Hu, G., and Huang, J. (2010). The role of institutional investors in initial public offerings. *The Review of Financial Studies,* 23(12): 4496–4540.

Choe, H., Masulis, R. and Nanda, V. (1993) Common stock offerings across the business cycle: theory and evidence *Journal of Empirical Finance,* 1(1): 3–31.

DeAngelo, H., DeAngelo, L. and Stulz, R.M. (2010). Seasoned equity offerings, market timing, and the corporate lifecycle, *Journal of Financial Economics,* 95(3): 275–295.

Degeorge, F., Derrien, F. and Womack, K.L. (2007) Analyst hype in IPOs: explaining the popularity of bookbuilding *The Review of Financial Studies,* 20(4): 1021–1058.

Derrien, F. and Kecskés, A. (2007) The initial public offerings of listed firms *The Journal of Finance,* 62(1): 447–479.

Dorn, D. (2009) Does sentiment drive the retail demand for IPOs? *Journal of Financial and Quantitative Analysis,* 44(1): 85–108.

Drake, P. and Vetsuypens, M. (1993) IPO underpricing and insurance against legal liability *Financial Management,* 22(1): 64–73.

Fama, E. (1970) Efficient capital markets: a review of theory and empirical work *The Journal of Finance,* 25(2): 383–417.

Francis, B.B., Hasan, I., Lothian, J.R. and Sun, X. (2010) The signaling hypothesis revisited: evidence from foreign IPOs *Journal of Financial and Quantitative Analysis,* 45(1): 81–106.

Gao, Y., Mao, C.X. and Zhong, R. (2006) Divergency of opinion and long-term performance of initial public offerings *Journal of Financial Research,* 29(1): 113–129.

Garfinkel, J. (1993) IPO underpricing, insider selling, and subsequent equity offerings: is underpricing a signal of quality? *Financial Management,* 22(1): 74–83.

Gompers, P. and Lerner, J. (2003) The really long-run performance of initial public offerings: the pre-Nasdaq evidence *The Journal of Finance,* 58(4): 1355–1392.

Grinblatt, M. and Hwang, C.-Y. (1989) Signaling and the pricing of new issues *The Journal of Finance,* 44(2): 393–420.

Groh, A.P., Von Liechtenstein, H. and Lieser, K. (2010) The European venture capital and private equity country attractiveness indices *Journal of Corporate Finance,* 16(2): 205–224.

Holderness, C.G. (2018). Equity issuances and agency costs: The telling story of shareholder approval around the world, *Journal of Financial Economics,* 129(3): 415–439.

Hsu, H.-C., Reed, A.V. and Rocholl, J. (2010) The new game in town: competitive effects of IPOs *The Journal of Finance,* 65(2): 495–528.

Ivanov, V. and Lewis, C.M. (2008) The determinants of market-wide issue cycles for initial public offerings *Journal of Corporate Finance,* 14(5): 567–583.

Jegadeesh, N., Weinstein, M. and Welch, I. (1993) An empirical investigation of IPO returns and subsequent equity offerings *Journal of Financial Economics,* 34(2): 153–175.

Jenkinson, T. and Jones, H. (2009b) IPO pricing and allocation: a survey of the views of institutional investors *Review of Financial Studies,* 22(4): 1477–1504.

Jensen, M. and Murphy, K. (1990) CEO incentives: it's not how much you pay but how *Journal of Applied Corporate Finance,* 3(1990): 36–49.

Kaustia, M. and Knüpfer, S. (2008) Do investors overweight personal experience? Evidence from IPO subscriptions *The Journal of Finance,* 63(6): 2679–2702.

Keloharju, M. (1993) The winner's curse, legal liability, and the long-run price performance of initial public offering in Finland *Journal of Financial Economics,* 34: 251–277.

Kim, W. and Weisbach, M.S. (2008) Motivations for public equity offers: an international perspective *Journal of Financial Economics,* 87(2): 281–307.

Koh, F. and Walter, T.(1989) A direct test of Rock's model of the pricing of unseasoned issues *Journal of Financial Economics,* 23(2): 251–272.

Ljungqvist, A., Jenkinson, T. and Wilhelm, W. (2003) Global integration in primary equity markets: the role of US banks and US investors *The Review of Financial Studies,* 16(1): 63–99.

Loughran, T., and McDonald, B. (2013) IPO first-day returns, offer price revisions, volatility, and form S-1 language, *Journal of Financial Economics,* 109(2): 307–326.

Loughran, T. and Ritter, J. (1995) The new issues puzzle *The Journal of Finance,* 50(1): 23–52.

Loughran, T., Ritter, J. and Rydqvist, K. (1994) Initial public offerings: international insights *Pacific-Basin Finance Journal,* 2(2–3): 165–199.

Lowry, M., Officer, M.S. and Schwert, G.W. (2010) The variability of IPO initial returns, *The Journal of Finance,* 65(2): 425–465.

Marosi, A. and Massoud, N. (2007) Why do firms go dark? *Journal of Financial and Quantitative Analysis,* 42(2): 421–442.

McLean, R.D. (2011) Share issuance and cash savings *Journal of Financial Economics,* 99(3): 693–715.

Michaely, R. and Shaw, W. (1994) The pricing of initial public offerings: tests of adverse selection and signaling theories *The Review of Financial Studies,* 7(2): 279–319.

Renneboog, L., Simons, T. and Wright, M. (2007) Why do public firms go private in the UK? The impact of private equity investors, incentive realignment and undervaluation *Journal of Corporate Finance,* 13(4): 591–628.

Ritter, J. (1991) The long-run performance of initial public offerings *The Journal of Finance,* 46: 3–27.

Schultz, P. (1990) Unit initial public offerings: a form of staged financing *The Journal of Financial Economics,* 34(2): 199–229.

Tinic, S. (1988) Anatomy of initial public offerings of common stock *The Journal of Finance,* 43(4): 789–822.

Welch, I. (1989) Seasoned offerings, imitation costs and the underwriting of IPOs *The Journal of Finance,* 44(2): 421–449.

Practical Insights for Part I

Financing the Firm

- Debt is a common source of outside capital and has lower transaction costs than equity financing. (Sections 1.1, 1.3)
- Advantageous financing terms are generally achieved by understanding investors' frictions and overcoming them with clever security designs. (Section 2.5)
- Euromarkets and foreign issues are attractive sources of financing. It pays to be familiar with them. (Sections 1.4, 1.5, 2.6, 3.2)
- Debt instruments are complex, diverse, and filled with conventions that make comparisons between financing rates difficult. Get a complete translation of all features and rate conventions. (Sections 2.1–2.5, 2.9)
- Equity capital obtained during hot issue periods may be cheaper for the issuer than equity capital obtained at other times. (Section 3.6)
- Include underpricing, which can be more than 50 per cent in some countries, when figuring out the total cost of IPO equity financing. (Section 3.6)
- Public capital is generally cheaper but comes with a host of hidden costs that make it unattractive to some firms. In particular, one should factor in the costs of regulations imposed by government agencies and exchanges on capital costs obtained from public sources. Because of these costs, most small firms obtain outside capital from private sources. (Sections 1.2, 1.3, 3.6)

Knowing Whether and How to Hedge Risk

- Before hedging, it is essential to be familiar with the securities and derivatives used for hedging and the arenas in which these financial instruments trade. (Sections 2.5, 2.8, 3.3)
- Issuing securities or entering into contractual agreements often requires the aid of a trusted investment banker and thus knowledge of how such bankers operate. (Section 1.3)

Allocating Capital for Real Investment

- Stock prices can provide valuable information about the profitability of projects in a firm or an industry. (Section 3.4)

Allocating Funds for Financial Investments

- Most debt instruments are not traded very actively. Such illiquidity needs to be accounted for when making investment decisions. (Section 2.8)
- When there are restrictions on investment for tax, regulatory or contractual reasons, the wide variety of financial instruments available can allow one to skirt these restrictions. (Sections 2.5, 2.6, 2.7, 3.1)
- Historically, IPOs have been good short-term investments, especially for investors who can obtain hot issues. (Sections 3.7, 3.8)
- Historically, the typical IPO has been a bad long-term investment. (Section 3.7)

- When investing in debt instruments, one must have total mastery of all debt quotation conventions. (Section 2.9)
- Preferred stock investment is often motivated by tax considerations. (Section 3.1)
- Although generally not traded, commercial paper will typically be redeemed early by the issuing corporation if the investor requests it. It is almost as safe as Treasury bills yet offers more attractive rates, especially to tax-advantaged institutions, such as pension funds. (Section 2.4)

PART 2

Valuing Financial Assets

Part contents

The modelling of how prices are determined in markets for financial assets (for example, equities, bonds and derivatives) differs from how prices are modelled for consumer goods in economics. For instance, in economics, the prices of goods, such as cookers and butter, are determined by specifying how consumer preferences for cookers and butter interact with the technology of producing them. By contrast, Finance is focused on valuing assets *in relation to the values of other assets.*

This difference in focus often allows the field of Finance to dispense with the language of preferences (for example, utility functions, indifference curves) and the language of production technology (for example, marginal cost), which is so often used in economics. Instead, financial valuation has its own language. It uses terms like *arbitrage, diversification, portfolios, tracking* and *hedging.*

The following five chapters illustrate this point nicely. Chapter 4 introduces portfolios, which are simply combinations of financial assets and the tools needed to manage them. Understanding the concepts presented in this chapter provides the framework that we shall use to value a financial asset in relation to other financial assets. In particular, most of the valuation of financial assets in Chapters 5–8 is based on comparing the financial asset to be valued with a portfolio whose value or rate of expected appreciation is known. The latter portfolio, known as the *tracking portfolio,* is designed to have risk attributes identical to the stock, bond, option or other financial assets that one is trying to value.

The ability to form portfolios also leads to another significant insight: diversification. Diversification means that investors might eliminate some types of risk by holding many different financial assets. The implications of diversification are profound. In particular, it implies that the tracking portfolio with which one compares a financial asset need not match the asset being valued in *all* risk dimensions – only in those risk dimensions that cannot be diversified away.

We use the theme of the tracking portfolio throughout much of this text. It is first developed in Chapter 5, where the portfolio tools from Chapter 4 are applied to determine how to invest optimally. The first major valuation model, the *Capital Asset Pricing Model,* is developed. This model suggests that the expected returns of all investments are determined by their market risk. In this model, each financial asset is tracked by a combination of a risk-free security and a special investment known as the *market portfolio.* The precise weighting of the combination varies from asset to asset and is determined by the asset's market risk. The expected return of this tracking portfolio has to be the same as the expected return of the tracked asset. The tracked asset's market risk determines the composition of the tracking portfolio. Thus it indirectly determines the expected return of the tracked asset. In this sense, the Capital Asset Pricing Model values each asset in relation to its tracking portfolio.

The theme of the tracking portfolio is carried further in Chapter 6, where we develop a statistical tool known as a *factor model* and show how combining factor models with the clever formation of portfolios leads to a valuation insight known as the *arbitrage pricing theory.* According to this theory, the expected returns of assets are determined by their factor risk. With the arbitrage pricing theory, each financial asset is tracked by a risk-free security and special investments known as *factor portfolios.* The expected return of this factor-based tracking portfolio determines the expected return of the tracked asset.

An *arbitrage opportunity* will arise if the expected return relationship between the tracked asset and its tracking portfolio does not hold. This concept leads to powerful insights into valuation. An arbitrage opportunity, which essentially is a money tree, is a set of trades that make money without risk. Specifically, an arbitrage opportunity requires no up-front cash and results in riskless profits in the future.[1]

The arbitrage opportunity that arises when the valuation relationship between an asset and its tracking portfolio is violated involves buying the misvalued investment and hedging its risk by taking an opposite position in its tracking portfolio, or vice versa. This arbitrage opportunity exists not only because of the ability to form tracking portfolios that match the factor risk of the investment being valued but also because of the ability to form diversified portfolios, first discussed in Chapter 4.

Diversification plays no role in derivatives valuation, discussed in Chapters 7 and 8. This is because the tracking portfolio, in this case, a combination of the underlying financial asset to which the derivative is related and a risk-free asset, tracks the derivative perfectly. Once again, arbitrage opportunities are available unless the derivative security has the same price as its tracking portfolio.

The perfect tracking of derivatives comes at the cost of additional complexity. A dynamic strategy in which the weighting of this combination is constantly changing is typically required to form the tracking portfolio of a derivative. This can make the valuation formulae for derivatives appear complex in relation to the valuation formulae developed in Chapters 5 and 6.

[1] Chapters 7–8 provide a variation of this definition: riskless cash today and no future cash paid out.

All the key insights developed in Part II are essential for investment in financial assets and the regular valuation of tangible assets (for instance, machines and factories) in corporations. The analysis of real asset valuation is developed in Part III of the text. The techniques developed in Part II are also helpful in understanding some aspects of financial structure developed in Part IV of the text, and the theory of risk management, developed in Part VI of the text. In particular, we use the mathematics of portfolios repeatedly and make liberal use of tree diagrams, which are seen in great detail in Chapters 7 and 8 in much of our later analysis. Finally, portfolio tools and financial asset valuation help us to understand some issues in corporate control, asymmetric information and acquisition valuation, developed in Part V of the text. Therefore Part II is central to what follows. Even students with a background in investment theory should review these chapters before proceeding to the remainder of the text, which is devoted almost entirely to corporate applications.

Chapter 4

Portfolio Tools

Learning Objectives

After reading this chapter, you should be able to:

- Compute both the covariance and the correlation between two returns, given historical data.
- Identify a mean-standard deviation diagram and be familiar with its basic elements.
- Use means and covariances for individual asset returns to calculate the mean and variance of the return of a portfolio of n assets.
- Use covariances between equity returns to compute the covariance between the return on an equity and the return on a portfolio.
- Understand the implications of the statement that 'the covariance is a marginal variance' for small changes in the composition of a portfolio.
- Compute the minimum variance portfolio of a set of risky assets, and interpret the equations that need to be solved in this computation.

The financial markets have gone through massive changes since the second edition of *Financial Markets and Corporate Strategy: European Edition* was published in 2012. At the time, Europe was experiencing its sovereign debt crisis, when some European governments struggled to repay debts they took out in the global financial crisis of 2008. The next change occurred around the UK Brexit vote in 2016. Planning for the referendum took a year, and the 12 months before the vote saw sustained falls in stock market valuations. Once the vote confirmed that the UK was leaving the European Union, the value of sterling fell in comparison to the euro and this increased stock market valuations in the UK. Finally, 2020 saw the emergence of the Coronavirus pandemic and stock market valuations collapsed by at least 20 per cent across the world in March 2020. Stock markets have steadily climbed since that nadir, and by 2022, valuations had returned to pre-pandemic levels. How does one make sense of stock market movements, the share price returns of companies and the day-to-day volatility of equities? This chapter helps us begin to find out.

The modern theory of how to invest, initially developed by Nobel Laureate in Economics Harry Markowitz, plays a role in almost every area of financial practice and can be a valuable tool for important managerial decisions. This theory was developed to help investors form a **portfolio** – a combination of investments – that achieves the highest possible expected return[2] for a given level of risk. The theory assumes that investors are **mean-variance optimizers:** that is, seekers of portfolios with the lowest possible return *variance* for any given level of mean (or expected) return. This suggests that the **variance** of an investment return, a measure of how dispersed its return outcomes are, is the appropriate measure of risk.[3]

The term coined by Markowitz for this theory, **mean-variance analysis,** describes mathematically how the risk of individual securities contributes to the risk and return of portfolios. This is of great benefit to portfolio managers making **asset allocation** decisions, which determine how much of their portfolio should be earmarked for each of the many broad investment classes (for example, equity, debt, property and emerging-market securities).

Mean-variance analysis is also valuable for corporate managers. Financing represents the opposite side of investing. Just as portfolio tools help investors to understand the risk they bear, they also help a corporate manager to understand how financial structure affects the corporation's risk. Moreover, most large corporations contain many different investment projects: thus, a corporation can be considered a portfolio of real assets. Although the objectives of a corporate manager differ from those of a portfolio manager, the corporate manager is interested in how the risk of individual investments affects the overall risk of the entire corporation. Mean-variance analysis provides the necessary tools to evaluate the contribution of an investment project to the expected return and variance of a corporation's earnings. In addition, corporate managers use mean-variance analysis to manage the firm's overall risk.[4] Finally, mean-variance analysis is the foundation of the most commonly used tool for project and securities valuation, the Capital Asset Pricing Model (CAPM), a theory that relates risk to return (see Chapter 5).

Diversification, the holding of many securities to lessen risk, is the most important concept introduced in this chapter. It means that portfolio managers or individual investors balance their investments among several securities to reduce risk. As a portfolio manager or individual investor adds more equities to their portfolio, the additional equities *diversify* the portfolio if they do not covary (that is, move together) too much with other equities in the portfolio. Because equities from similar geographic regions and industries tend to move together, a portfolio is diversified if it contains companies from various regions and industries. Similarly, firms often prefer to diversify, selecting investment projects in different sectors to lower the firm's overall risk. Diversification is one factor that corporate managers consider when deciding how much of a corporation's capital to allocate to operations in Europe, Asia and the United States or, for example, when determining how much to invest in various product lines. Diversification is also relevant to a firm's pension fund and its financial risk management.

Many pension funds place a portion of their assets with hedge funds, acting indirectly as a 'fund of funds'. The managers of funds of funds fully understand the principle of diversification. They know that placing capital with many hedge fund managers reduces risk and that a precise quantitative weighting of the fund managers in their portfolio can reduce risk even further. This chapter provides tools that are part of an essential toolkit for running a fund of funds, whether explicitly or implicitly (as a pension fund trustee who allocates capital to hedge fund managers).

While the principle of diversification is well known, even by students new to Finance, implementing mean-variance analysis – for example, coming up with the weights of portfolios with desirable properties, such as a portfolio with the lowest variance – requires some work. This chapter will examine some of the preliminaries needed to understand how to implement mean-variance analysis. It shows how to compute summary statistics for security returns – specifically, *means, variances, standard deviations, covariances* and *correlations* – all of

---

[2] A **return** is profit divided by amount invested. Formally, the return, R, is given by the formula

$$R = \frac{P_1 + D_1 - P_0}{P_0}$$

where

P_1 = end-of-period value of the investment
P_0 = beginning-of-period value of the investment
D_1 = cash distributed over the period.

The three variables for determining a return are thus: beginning-of-period value; end-of-period value; and cash distributed. Beginning-of-period value is the amount paid for the investment. Similarly, end-of-period value is the price that one would receive for the investment at the end of the period. One need not sell the investment to determine its end-of-period value. Finally, the cash distributions are determined by the type of investment: cash dividends for equity, or coupon payments for bonds.

[3] Other measures of risk exist, but variance is still the predominant measure used by portfolio managers and corporate managers.

[4] See Chapter 22.

which are discussed later in the chapter. These are the raw inputs for mean-variance analysis. It is impossible to implement the insights of Markowitz without first knowing how to compute these raw inputs.

This chapter also shows how the means, variances and covariances of securities in a portfolio determine the means and variances of portfolios. Perhaps the critical insight a portfolio manager could learn from this analysis is that the desirability of a particular investment is determined less by the variance of its return and more by how it covaries with other assets in the portfolio.

4.1 Portfolio Weights

To build the skills to implement mean-variance analysis, we must develop mathematical ways of representing portfolios.

The **portfolio weight** for stock *j*, denoted x_j, is the fraction of a portfolio's wealth held in stock *j*: that is,

$$x_j = \frac{\text{money held in stock } j}{\text{monetary value of the portfolio}}$$

By definition, portfolio weights must sum to 1.

The Two-Stock Portfolio

Example 4.1 illustrates how to compute portfolio weights for a two-stock portfolio.

Example 4.1

Computing Portfolio Weights for a Two-Stock Portfolio

A portfolio consists of £1 million in Vodafone equity and £3 million in Unilever equity. What are the portfolio weights of the two equities?

Answer: The portfolio has a total value of £4 million. The weight on Vodafone is £1,000,000/£4,000,000 = 0.25 or 25 per cent, and the weight on Unilever is £3,000,000/£4,000,000 = 0.75 or 75 per cent.

Short Sales and Portfolio Weights

In Example 4.1, both portfolio weights are positive. However, in many markets, investors can **sell short** certain securities, which means that they can sell investments that they do not currently own. To sell short shares or bonds, the investor must borrow the securities from someone who owns them. This is known as taking a **short position** in a security. To close out the short position, the investor buys the investment back and returns it to the original owner.

To sell short certain other investments, one takes a position in a contract where money is received upfront and paid back at a later date. For example, borrowing from a bank can be considered selling short or, equivalently, taking a negative position in an investment held by the bank – namely, your loan. For the same reason, a corporation that issues a security (for example, a bond) can be thought of as having a short position in the security.

Regardless of the mechanics of selling short, it is only relevant for our purposes to know that *selling short an investment is equivalent to placing a negative portfolio weight on it.* In contrast, a **long position,** achieved by buying an investment, has a positive portfolio weight. To compute portfolio weights when some investments are sold short, sum the amount invested in each asset, treating shorted (or borrowed) investments as negative numbers. Then divide each investment by the sum. For example, a position with €500,000 in a security and €100,000 borrowed from a bank has a total investment of €400,000 (= €500,000 – €100,000). Dividing €500,000 and –€100,000 by the total investment of €400,000 yields the portfolio weights of 1.25 and –0.25 on the security and the bank investment, respectively. Note that the weights in a portfolio must sum to 1.

Feasible Portfolios

To decide which portfolio is best, it is important to mathematically characterize the universe of **feasible portfolios,** which is the set of portfolios in which one can invest. For example, if you can invest in only two securities and cannot sell short either, the feasible portfolios are characterized by all pairs of non-negative weights that sum to 1. On the other hand, if short sales are allowed, any pair of weights that adds to 1 characterizes a feasible portfolio.

Example 4.2 illustrates the concept of feasible portfolio weights.

Example 4.2

Feasible Portfolio Weights

Suppose the world's financial markets contain only two equities, Vodafone and Unilever. Describe the feasible portfolios.

Answer: In this two-equity world, the feasible portfolios consist of any two numbers, x_{Voda} and x_{Uni}, for which $x_{BA} = 1 - x_{\text{Voda}}$. Examples of feasible portfolios include:

1 $x_{\text{Voda}} = 0.5$ $\quad x_{Uni} = 0.5$

2 $x_{\text{Voda}} = 1$ $\quad x_{Uni} = 0$

3 $x_{\text{Voda}} = 2.5$ $\quad x_{Uni} = -1.5$

4 $x_{\text{Voda}} = \sqrt{2}$ $\quad x_{Uni} = 1 - \sqrt{2}$

5 $x_{\text{Voda}} = -\frac{1}{3}$ $\quad x_{Uni} = \frac{4}{3}$

An infinite number of such feasible portfolios exist because an infinite number of pairs of portfolio weights solve $x_{Uni} + x_{\text{Voda}} = 1$.

The Many-Security Portfolio

The universe of securities available to most investors is large. Thus it is more realistic to consider portfolios of more than two securities, as in Example 4.3.

Example 4.3

Computing Portfolio Weights for a Portfolio of Many Securities

Describe the weights of a €40,000 portfolio invested in four securities. The amounts invested in each security are as follows:

Security	1	2	3	4
Amount	€20,000	–€5,000	€0	€25,000

Answer: Dividing each of these investment amounts by the total investment amount, €40,000, gives the weights:

$$x_1 = 0.5 \quad x_2 = -0.125 \quad x_3 = 0 \quad x_4 = 0.625$$

For an arbitrary number of assets, we represent securities with algebraic notation (see Exhibit 4.1). To simplify the language of this discussion, we refer to the risky assets selected by an investor as securities, which can represent equities, bonds and options, or tangible assets like machines, factories and real estate. It is also possible to generalize the 'risky assets' to include hedge funds or mutual funds, in which case the analysis applies to portfolios of portfolios!

The following few sections elaborate on each of the items in Exhibit 4.1.

Exhibit 4.1 Notation

Term	Notation
Portfolio return	$\tilde{R}_p$
Expected portfolio return (mean portfolio return)	$\bar{R}_p$ or $E(\tilde{R}_p)$
Portfolio return variance	σ_p^2 or $\sigma^2(\tilde{R}_p)$
Portfolio weight on security i	x_i
Security i's return	$\tilde{r}_i$
Security i's expected return	$\bar{r}_i$ or $E(\tilde{r}_i)$
Security i's return variance	σ_i^2 or $\text{var}(\tilde{r}_i)$
Covariance of security i and security j's returns	σ_{ij} or $\text{cov}(\tilde{r}_i, \tilde{r}_j)$
Correlation between security i and security j's returns	ρ_{ij} or $\rho(\tilde{r}_i, \tilde{r}_j)$

4.2 Portfolio Returns

There are two equivalent methods to compute portfolio returns. The **ratio method** divides the portfolio's value at the end of the period (plus distributed cash, such as dividends) by the portfolio value at the beginning of the period and then subtracts 1 from the ratio. The **portfolio-weighted average method** weights the returns of the investments in the portfolio by their respective portfolio weights and then sums the weighted returns.

Example 4.4 illustrates both methods.

Example 4.4

Computing Portfolio Returns for a Two-Security Portfolio

A £4,000,000 portfolio consists of £1,000,000 of Vodafone equity and £3,000,000 of Unilever equity. If Vodafone shares have a return of 10 per cent and Unilever shares have a return of 5 per cent, determine the portfolio return using (1) the ratio method and (2) the portfolio-weighted average method.

Answer: (1) For £1,000,000 of Vodafone shares to have a 10 per cent return, the end-of-period value plus dividends for the equity must amount to £1,100,000. Similarly, the end-of-period value of the Unilever shares plus dividends must amount to £3,150,000 to yield a 5 per cent return. Hence, the portfolio's end-of-period value is £4,250,000, the sum of £1,100,000 and £3,150,000, implying that the return on the portfolio is

$$\frac{£4{,}250{,}000}{£4{,}000{,}000} - 1 = 0.0625 \quad \text{or} \quad 6.25\%$$

(2) The portfolio weight is 0.25 for Vodafone and 0.75 for Unilever. Thus the portfolio-weighted average return is 0.25(0.1) + 0.75(0.05) = 0.0625 = 6.25%.

For N securities, indexed from 1 to N, the portfolio return formula becomes

$$\tilde{R}_p = x_1\tilde{r}_1 + x_2\tilde{r}_2 + \ldots + x_N\tilde{r}_N = \sum_{i=1}^{N} x_i\tilde{r}_i \qquad (4.1)$$

4.3 Expected Portfolio Returns

So far, we have looked at actual investment returns. However, no-one has the luck to invest with perfect foresight. Consequently, finance theory and mean-variance analysis focus on the anticipated future returns of investments. A variety of future return outcomes are likely to exist for a given risky investment, each occurring with a specific probability. To compute the **expected return** (also called the **mean return**), weight each of the return outcomes by the probability of the outcome and sum the probability-weighted returns over all outcomes.

The examples below sometimes assume that we know these outcomes and their probabilities. However, in practice, one often estimates the expected return by computing the historical average return. A typical period for such a computation can be anywhere from 5 to 50 years in the past.

Example 4.5 shows how to estimate expected returns from historical data.

Example 4.5

Estimating an Expected Return for a Portfolio of Large Company Equities

A stock index portfolio had returns of 5.69 per cent in 2006, 2.21 per cent in 2007, −19.43 per cent in 2008 and 32.55 per cent in 2009. If the returns between 2006 and 2009 are unbiased estimates of future returns, what is your assessment of the expected return on the stock index portfolio?

Answer: The average of the four returns is 5.255 per cent per year.

Average returns calculated from past data are only estimates of the true unobserved return that governs the probability distribution of future return outcomes. If other periods were used or, alternatively, longer or shorter periods, the estimated expected return would be different. Therefore, care must be taken when using historical returns to proxy for future expected returns because there is no *a priori* reason why the past should be the best predictor of the future.

Portfolios of Two Securities

Expected returns have some useful properties.

1 The expected value of a constant times a return is the constant times the expected return: that is,

$$E(x\tilde{r}) = xE(\tilde{r}) \tag{4.2}$$

2 The expected value of the sum or difference of two returns is the sum or difference between the expected returns themselves: that is,

$$E(\tilde{r}_1 + \tilde{r}_2) = E(\tilde{r}_1) + E(\tilde{r}_2) \text{ and } E(\tilde{r}_1 - \tilde{r}_2) = E(\tilde{r}_1) - E(\tilde{r}_2) \tag{4.3}$$

Combining these two equations implies the following.

3 The expected return of a portfolio is the portfolio-weighted average of the expected returns: that is, for a portfolio of two securities,

$$E(\tilde{R}_p) = E(x_1\tilde{r}_1 + x_2\tilde{r}_2) = x_1E(\tilde{r}_1) + x_2E(\tilde{r}_2) \tag{4.4a}$$

As Example 4.6 shows, using algebraic symbols for weights leads to formulae that often contain valuable insights.

Example 4.6

Expected Portfolio Returns with Arbitrary Weights

The Palisades Quant Fund has a portfolio weight of x in the Eurostoxx 50 index, which has an expected return of 11 per cent. The fund's investment in Treasury bills, with a portfolio weight of $1 - x$, earns 5 per cent. What is the expected return of the portfolio?

Answer: Using equation (4.4a), the expected return is

$$E(\widetilde{R}_p) = 0.11x + 0.05(1 - x) = 0.05 + 0.06x$$

Selling short an investment with a low expected return (that is, borrowing at a low rate) and using the proceeds to increase a position in an investment with a high expected return results in a larger expected return than can be achieved by investing only in the investment with the high expected return. This is known as **leveraging an investment.**

Example 4.6, for instance, illustrates that the larger x is, the larger the portfolio's expected return. If x is greater than 1, implying that $1 - x$ is negative (and that there is risk-free borrowing), the expected return will exceed 11 per cent. In theory, an investor can achieve arbitrarily high expected returns by taking a large positive position in the asset with the higher expected return and taking a large negative position in the asset with the lower expected return (that is, by making x arbitrarily large). For example, suppose the investor in Example 4.6 uses £200,000 of their own money for investment. In that case, they could achieve an expected return of 161 per cent by borrowing an additional £5 million at 5 per cent and investing the proceeds in the equity portfolio. (In the real world, a bank would be unwilling to make such a loan because the investor would be likely to default if the equity portfolio declined in value too much.) In this case, x is 26.

Portfolios of Many Securities

The formula for the mean return of a portfolio consisting of many securities directly extends the two-asset formula shown in equation (4.4a). As with two securities, it is necessary to know only the expected returns of individual securities and the portfolio weights. Taking the expectation of both sides of the portfolio return formula (equation (4.1)) and applying the properties of expected returns given in equations (4.2) and (4.3) gives the following result.

Results

Result 4.1

The expected portfolio return is the portfolio-weighted average of the expected returns of the individual stocks in the portfolio:

$$\overline{R}_p = \sum_{i=1}^{N} x_i \overline{r}_i \qquad (4.4b)$$

4.4 Variances and Standard Deviations

Example 4.6 illustrates that it is possible to generate arbitrarily large expected returns by buying the investment with the largest expected return and selling short the investment with the lowest expected return.[5] The force that prevents investors from doing this is risk. When leveraging a portfolio to achieve higher expected returns, the investor also increases the portfolio's risk.

[5] If investors are **risk neutral,** which means that they do not care about risk, they would select portfolios solely on the basis of expected return. However, most investors are concerned with risk as well as expected returns.

Return Variances

The concern investors have for losses is known as **risk aversion.** A fundamental research area of finance theory is how to define and quantify risk. Mean-variance analysis defines the risk of a portfolio as the variance of its return.

To compute return variances, the examples below assume that there are a finite number of possible future return outcomes, that we know what these outcomes are, and that we know the probability of each outcome. Given these possible return outcomes:

1. Compute the demeaned returns. (To find the **demeaned returns** simply subtract the mean return from each of the potential return outcomes).
2. Square the demeaned returns.
3. Take the probability-weighted average of these squared numbers.

The **variance** of a return is the expected value of the squared demeaned return outcomes: that is

$$\text{var}(\tilde{r}) = E[(\tilde{r} - \bar{r})^2]$$

where $\tilde{r}$, the return of the investment, is a random variable, and $\bar{r}$, the expected return of the investment, is a statistic that helps to summarize the distribution of the random variable.

A valuable property of variances is that the variance of a constant times a return is the square of that constant times the variance of the return: that is,

$$\text{var}(x\tilde{r}) = x^2 \text{ var}(\tilde{r}) \tag{4.5}$$

Estimating Variances: Statistical Issues

The variances in Example 4.7 are based on return distributions computed with a *forward-looking approach.* With this approach, the analyst estimates the variances and covariances by specifying the returns in different scenarios or states of the economy that could occur in the future. We have simplified this process by giving you the outcomes and probabilities. In practice, this involves much guessing and is quite challenging to implement. More commonly, the variance is computed by averaging squared historical demeaned returns, as outlined in Example 4.8.

Example 4.7

Computing Variances

Compute the variance of the return of a €400,000 investment in the hypothetical company SINTEL. Assume that over the next period, SINTEL earns 20 per cent $\frac{8}{10}$ of the time, loses 10 per cent $\frac{1}{10}$ of the time and loses 40 per cent $\frac{1}{10}$ of the time.

Answer: The mean return is

$$0.8(20\%) + 0.1(-10\%) + 0.1(-40\%) = 11\%$$

Subtract the mean return from each of the return outcomes to obtain the demeaned returns.

$$20\% - 11\% = 9\% = 0.09$$
$$-10\% - 11\% = -21\% = -0.21$$
$$-40\% - 11\% = -51\% = -0.51$$

The variance is the probability-weighted average of the square of these three numbers:

$$\text{var} = 0.8\,(0.09)^2 + 0.1\,(-0.21)^2 + 0.1\,(-0.51)^2 = 0.0369$$

Example 4.8

Estimating Variances with Historical Data

Recall from Example 4.5 that the annual returns of a stock index portfolio were 5.69 per cent, 2.21 per cent, −19.43 per cent and 32.55 per cent, respectively, and that the average of these four numbers was 5.255 per cent.

Answer: Subtracting the average return of 5.255 per cent from each of these four returns results in demeaned returns of 0.435, −3.045, −24.685 and 27.295 per cent, respectively. Thus the average squared demeaned return is

$$\frac{(0.435)^2 + (-3.045)^2 + (-24.685)^2 + (27.295)^2}{4} = 340.957$$

It is important to stress that the number computed in Example 4.8 is only an estimate of the true variance. For instance, if we used only years −2 to 0 data (2.21, −19.43 and 32.55 per cent), our variance estimate would be 454.546. Several fine points are worth mentioning when estimating variances with historical data on returns. First, in contrast with means, one often obtains a more precise variance estimate with more frequent data. Hence, when computing variance estimates, weekly returns would be preferred to monthly returns, monthly returns to annual returns, and so on.[6] Daily data often present problems because of how trading affects observed prices.[7] If the data are sufficiently frequent, a year of weekly data can provide a reasonably accurate estimate of the true variance. By contrast, the mean return of an equity is generally estimated imprecisely, even with years of data.

Some statisticians recommend computing estimated variances by dividing the summed squared demeaned returns by one less than the number of observations rather than by the number of observations.[8] In Example 4.8, this would result in a variance estimate equal to 4/3 times the existing estimate, or 0.0667.

In some instances–for example, when valuing property in emerging economies–historical data may not be available for a variance estimation. In this case, the forward-looking approach is the only alternative for variance computation. Chapter 11 discusses in a bit more detail how to do this.

Standard Deviation

Squaring returns (or demeaned returns) to compute the variance often leads to confusion when returns are expressed as percentages. It would be convenient to have a measure of average dispersion from the mean that is expressed in the same units as the variable itself. One such measure is the standard deviation. The **standard deviation** (denoted σ or $\sigma(\tilde{r})$), is the square root of the variance. One typically reports the standard deviation of a return in per cent per year whenever returns are reported in units of per cent per year. This makes it easier to think about how dispersed a distribution of returns really is. For example, a security with an expected annual return of 12 per cent and an annualized standard deviation of 10 per cent has a typical deviation from the mean of about 10 per cent. Thus, observing annual returns as low as 2 per cent or as high as 22 per cent would not be unusual.

The standard deviation possesses the following useful property. The standard deviation of a constant times a return is the constant times the standard deviation of the return: that is,

$$\sigma(x\tilde{r}) = x\sigma(\tilde{r}) \tag{4.6}$$

This result follows from equation (4.5) and the mathematical property that the square root of the product of two numbers is the product of the square root of each of the numbers.

[6] To obtain an annualized variance estimate from weekly data, multiply the weekly variance estimate by 52; to obtain it from monthly data, multiply the monthly estimate by 12; and so on.

[7] This stems from dealers buying at the bid and selling at the ask, as described in Chapter 3, which tends to exacerbate variance estimates.

[8] This altered variance estimate is unbiased – that is, tending to be neither higher nor lower than the true variance. The variance computations here do not make this adjustment.

4.5 Covariances and Correlations

To compute the variance of a portfolio return, it is essential to understand covariances and correlations, which measure the degree to which a pair of returns move together. A positive covariance or correlation means that the two returns tend to move in the same direction: that is, when one return is above its mean, the other tends to be above its mean. Conversely, a negative covariance or correlation means that the returns tend to move in opposite directions.

Covariance

The **covariance** is a measure of relatedness that depends on the unit of measurement. For example, the height of parents covaries positively with their children's height. However, the size of the covariance will differ depending on the units used (for example, inches, feet, metres or centimetres). The covariance measured in inches will be 144 times (12 × 12) the covariance measured in feet. For this reason, it is often convenient to employ a measure of relatedness that does not depend on the unit of measurement. Correlation, which is discussed shortly, is such a measure.

The covariance between two returns (often denoted by σ_{12} for securities 1 and 2) is the expected product of their demeaned outcomes: that is,

$$\sigma_{12} = E[(\tilde{r}_1 - \bar{r}_1)(\tilde{r}_2 - \bar{r}_2)]$$

Covariances and Joint Distributions

To compute a covariance between two returns, it is necessary to pair each outcome for one return with a corresponding outcome for the other return. The set of probabilities attached to each pair is known as the **joint distribution** of the two returns. Example 4.9 calculates variances using the forward-looking approach, but it shows that it is impossible to calculate a covariance from the information typically used to compute return variances and means.

Example 4.9

Distributions Where Covariance Information is Unavailable

Is it possible to compute the means, variances and covariances of the two equity returns described below? If so, calculate them.

Equity A		Equity B	
Probability	**Return outcome**	**Probability**	**Return outcome**
$\frac{1}{3}$	0.1	$\frac{3}{4}$	0
$\frac{1}{2}$	0.2	$\frac{1}{4}$	0.5
$\frac{1}{6}$	0.3		

Answer: The covariance between the returns of equities A and B cannot be computed because there is no information about how the various outcomes pair up: that is, the joint distribution of the returns is not reported. The mean returns are $E(\tilde{r}_A) = \frac{11}{60} = 0.183333$ and $E(\tilde{r}_B) = \frac{1}{8} = 0.125$, implying that the variances are

$$\text{Var}(\tilde{r}_A) = 0.00472 = \frac{1}{3}\left(0.1 - \frac{11}{60}\right)^2 + \frac{1}{2}\left(0.2 - \frac{11}{60}\right)^2 + \frac{1}{3}\left(0.3 - \frac{11}{60}\right)^2 = \frac{17}{3{,}600}$$

$$\text{Var}(\tilde{r}_B) = 0.04688 = \frac{3}{4}\left(0 - \frac{1}{8}\right)^2 + \frac{1}{4}\left(0.5 - \frac{1}{8}\right)^2 = \frac{3}{64}$$

To compute a covariance with the forward-looking approach, determine the probability-weighted average of the product of the two demeaned returns associated with each of the paired outcomes using the joint distribution, as Example 4.10 illustrates.

Example 4.10

Computing the Covariance from a Joint Distribution

Given the following joint distribution, determine the covariance between the returns of equities A and B.

Event	Probability	Return A	Return B
1	$\frac{1}{6}$	0.1	0
2	$\frac{1}{6}$	0.1	0.5
3	$\frac{1}{2}$	0.2	0
4	0	0.2	0.5
5	$\frac{1}{12}$	0.3	0
6	$\frac{1}{12}$	0.3	0.5

Answer: The covariance calculation sums the probability-weighted product of the demeaned outcomes. The mean return for equity A is $\frac{11}{60}$, and the mean return for equity B is $\frac{1}{8}$, which implies that

$$\begin{aligned}\text{cov} &= \frac{1}{6}\left(0.1-\frac{11}{60}\right)\left(0-\frac{1}{8}\right)+\frac{1}{6}\left(0.1-\frac{11}{60}\right)\left(0.5-\frac{1}{8}\right)+\frac{1}{2}\left(0.2-\frac{11}{60}\right)\left(0-\frac{1}{8}\right)+0\\&\quad+\frac{1}{2}\left(0.3-\frac{11}{60}\right)\left(0-\frac{1}{8}\right)+\frac{1}{12}\left(0.3-\frac{11}{60}\right)\left(0.5-\frac{1}{8}\right)\\&= -0.00208333 \text{ (approximately)}\end{aligned}$$

Estimating Covariances with Historical Data

As with means and variances, the forward-looking approach is challenging to implement in practice. Typically, covariances are estimated by looking at the average demeaned product of historical returns, as Example 4.11 illustrates.

Example 4.11

Computing the Covariance from Historical Returns

Determine the covariance between the returns of our stock index portfolio and a portfolio of corporate bonds, given the following annual returns.

−3	5.69	−1.41	0.435	−1.965	−0.854775
−2	2.21	2.95	−3.045	2.395	−7.292775
−1	−19.43	0.64	−24.685	0.085	−2.098225
0	32.55	0.04	27.295	−0.515	−14.056925

Answer: Recall from Example 4.8 that the average stock portfolio return is 5.255 per cent. The average corporate bond return is 0.555 per cent. Hence, the covariance estimate is the mean average of the numbers in the final column, which is –6.076.

Variance is a Special Case of the Covariance

It is useful to remember that the variance of a return is merely a special case of a covariance. The variance measures the covariance of a return with itself: that is,

$$\text{cov}(\tilde{r}, \tilde{r}) = \text{var}(\tilde{r})$$

This identity follows directly from comparing the formulae for the variance and the covariance.

Translating Covariances into Correlations

The **correlation** between two returns, denoted *r*, is the covariance between the two returns divided by the product of their standard deviations: that is,

$$\rho(\tilde{r}_1, \tilde{r}_2) = \frac{\text{cov}(\tilde{r}_1, \tilde{r}_2)}{\sigma_1 \sigma_2} \tag{4.7}$$

Applying equation (4.7) to Example 4.11 yields a correlation between the stock portfolio returns and the corporate bond portfolio of –0.2095.

The correlation can be thought of as a covariance where all random variables have been rescaled to have a variance of 1: that is,

$$\rho(\tilde{r}_1, \tilde{r}_2) = \text{cov}\left(\frac{\tilde{r}_1}{\sigma_1}, \frac{\tilde{r}_2}{\sigma_2}\right)$$

Because of this rescaling, all correlations are between –1 and +1. A coefficient of +1 is defined as a perfect positive correlation: the returns *always* move together. A coefficient of –1 is defined as a perfect negative correlation: the returns *always* move in opposite directions. Perfectly positively or perfectly negatively correlated random variables have paired outcomes that plot as a straight line in an *X*–*Y* graph.

Translating Correlations into Covariances

A formula for translating correlations into covariances can be obtained by rearranging equation (4.7) as follows:

$$\text{cov}(\tilde{r}_1, \tilde{r}_2) = \rho(\tilde{r}_1, \tilde{r}_2)\sigma_1\sigma_2$$

More generally, given securities *i* and *j*,

$$\sigma_{ij} = \rho_{ij}\sigma_i\sigma_j \tag{4.8}$$

The following section uses this equation to compute portfolio variances from correlations.

4.6 Variances of Portfolios and Covariances between Portfolios

Return covariances are critical inputs for computing the variance of security portfolio returns.

Variances for Two-Security Portfolios

Consider an investor who holds an airline's equity and is considering adding a second equity to their portfolio. Naturally, you would expect the new portfolio to have more variability if the second equity were another airline as opposed to, say, a pharmaceutical company. After all, the prices of two airline equities are more likely to move together than the prices of an airline and a pharmaceutical firm. In other words, if the returns of two securities covary positively, a portfolio that has positive weights on both securities will have a higher return variance than if they covary negatively.

Computing Portfolio Variances with Given Inputs

To verify this relationship between portfolio variance and the covariance between a pair of securities, expand the formula for the variance of a portfolio:

$$\text{var}(x_1\tilde{r}_1 + x_2\tilde{r}_2) = E\{[x_1\tilde{r}_1 + x_2\tilde{r}_2 - E(x_1\tilde{r}_2 + x_2\tilde{r}_2)]^2\}$$

It is possible to rewrite this equation as

$$\begin{aligned}\text{var}(x_1\tilde{r}_1 + x_2\tilde{r}_2) &= E\{[x_1\tilde{r}_1 + x_2\tilde{r}_2 - (x_1\bar{r}_1 + x_2\bar{r}_2)]^2\}\\ &= E\{[x_1(\tilde{r}_1 - \bar{r}_1) + x_2(\tilde{r}_2 - \bar{r}_2)]^2\}\end{aligned}$$

Squaring the bracketed term and expanding yields

$$\begin{aligned}\text{var}(x_1\tilde{r}_1 + x_2\tilde{r}_2) &= E[x_1^2(\tilde{r}_1 + \bar{r}_1)^2 + x_2^2(\tilde{r}_2 + \bar{r}_2)^2 + 2x_1x_2(\tilde{r}_1 - \bar{r}_1)(\tilde{r}_2 + \bar{r}_2)]\\ &= x_1^2E[(\tilde{r}_1 - \bar{r}_1)^2] + x_2^2E[(\tilde{r}_2 - \bar{r}_2)^2] + 2x_1x_2E[(\tilde{r}_1 - \bar{r}_1)(\tilde{r}_2 - \bar{r}_2)]\\ &= x_1^2\,\text{var}(\tilde{r}_1) + x_2^2\,\text{var}(\tilde{r}_2) + 2x_1x_2\,\text{cov}(\tilde{r}_1, \tilde{r}_2)\\ &= x_1^2\sigma_1^2 + x_2^2\sigma_2^2 + 2x_1x_2\sigma_{12}\end{aligned} \tag{4.9a}$$

Equation (4.9a) indicates that the variance of a portfolio of two investments is the sum of the products of the squared portfolio weights and the variances of the investment returns, plus a third term, which is twice the product of the two portfolio weights and the covariance between the investment returns. Thus, consistent with the intuition provided above, when the portfolio has a positive weight on both securities, the larger the covariance, the larger is the portfolio variance.

Example 4.12 illustrates how to apply equation (4.9a).

Example 4.12

Computing the Standard Deviation of Portfolios of Two Assets

Asset A has a standard deviation (s_A) of 30 per cent per year. Asset B has a standard deviation (s_B) of 10 per cent per year. The annualized covariance between the returns of the two assets (s_{AB}) is 0.0002. Compute the standard deviation of portfolios with the following sets of portfolio weights:

1 $x_A = 0.75$ $x_B = 0.25$
2 $x_A = 0.25$ $x_B = 0.75$
3 $x_A = 1.5$ $x_B = -0.5$
4 $x_A = x$ $x_B = 1 - x$

Answer: The assets' variances are the squares of their standard deviations. The variance of asset A's return is therefore 0.09, and asset B's is 0.01. Applying equation (4.9a) gives the variances for the four cases:

1 $0.75^2(0.09) + 0.25^2(0.01) + 2(0.75)(0.25)(0.0002) + 0.051325$
2 $0.25^2(0.09) + 0.75^2(0.01) + 2(0.75)(0.25)(0.0002) + 0.011325$
3 $1.5^2(0.09) + (-0.5)^2(0.01) + 2(1.5)(-0.5)(0.0002)\ -0.2047$
4 $0.09x^2 - 0.01(1 - x)^2 - 2(0.0002)x(1 - x)$

Because these are variances, the standard deviations are the square roots of these results. They are approximately:

1 22.65%
2 10.64%
3 45.24%
4 $\sqrt{0.09x^2 + 0.01(1 - x)^2 + 2(0.0002)x(1 - x)}$

Using Historical Data to Derive the Inputs: The Backward-Looking Approach

Example 4.12 calculates the standard deviations of portfolios of two assets, where the variances (or standard deviations) and covariances of the assets are given to us. As noted earlier, these variances and covariances must be estimated. A common approach is to look backwards, using variances and covariances computed from historical returns to estimate future variances and covariances. Example 4.13 shows how to use this approach to predict the variance following a major merger.

Example 4.13

Predicting the Return Variance of AT&T-BellSouth Following the Merger of AT&T and BellSouth

At the beginning of 2022, Microsoft Inc. acquired the video game company Activision Inc. for $68.7 billion cash, which led to a combined market capitalization of $2.3 trillion. Exhibit 4.2 presents the 12-monthly returns of Microsoft and Activision in the year before the announcement. Note that the returns are given for the period January to December 2020. This is so that any speculation regarding the merger, which took place during 2021, has no impact on our calculations. Predict the variance of the merged entity using these data. Assume that Activision is $\frac{1}{3}$ of the merged entity for your answer.

Exhibit 4.2 Monthly Returns for Microsoft and Activision from January 2020 to December 2020

DATE	MICROSOFT	ACTIVISION
JAN 2020	7.95%	−1.58%
FEB 2020	−4.83%	−0.60%
MAR 2020	−2.39%	2.32%
APR 2020	13.63%	7.15%
MAY 2020	2.25%	13.69%
JUN 2020	11.37%	5.45%
JUL 2020	0.74%	8.87%
AUG 2020	10.01%	1.08%
SEP 2020	−6.51%	−3.08%
OCT 2020	−3.74%	−6.45%
NOV 2020	5.73%	4.95%
DEC 2020	4.17%	16.82%

Source: Yahoo! Finance.

Answer: The variances of Microsoft and Activision's monthly returns are 0.00452 and 0.00471, respectively, and the covariance between them is 0.00150. Thus, the monthly return variance of the combined entity is

$$\left(\frac{2}{3}\right)^2(0.00452)+\left(\frac{1}{3}\right)^2(0.00471)+2\left(\frac{2}{3}\right)\left(\frac{1}{3}\right)(0.00150)=0.00320$$

The covariance between Microsoft and Activision means that the benefit of the merger arising from diversification alone is relatively low. The main reason behind the merger was that Microsoft felt that the combined entity would capture economies of scale from the video games market on the Xbox and other consoles.

Correlations, Diversification and Portfolio Variances

Substituting equation (4.8) – the formula for computing covariances from correlations and standard deviations – into equation (4.9a), the portfolio variance formula, generates a formula for the variance of a portfolio given the correlation instead of the covariance:

$$\mathrm{var}(x_1\tilde{r}_1 + x_2\tilde{r}_2) = x_1^2\sigma_1^2 + x_2^2\sigma_2^2 + 2x_1x_2\rho_{12}\sigma_1\sigma_2 \tag{4.9b}$$

Equation (4.9b) illustrates the principle of diversification. For example, if both asset variances are 0.04, a portfolio that is half invested in each asset has a variance of

$$0.02 + 0.02\rho = 0.25(0.04) + 0.25(0.04) + 2(0.5)(0.5)\rho_{12}(0.2)(0.2)$$

This variance is lower than the variance of either asset as long as *r* is less than 1. Since *r* is generally less than 1, more assets almost always imply lower variance.

Equation (4.9b) also yields the following result.

Results

Result 4.2

Given positive portfolio weights on two assets, the lower the correlation, the lower the variance of the portfolio.

Portfolio Variances When One of the Two Investments in the Portfolio is Riskless

A special case of equation (4.9b) occurs when one of the investments in the portfolio is riskless. For example, if investment 1 is riskless, then σ_1 and σ_{12} are both zero. In this case, the portfolio variance is

$$x_2^2\sigma_2^2$$

The standard deviation is either

$$x_2\sigma_2 \text{ if } x_2 \text{ is positive}$$

or

$$-x_2\sigma_2 \text{ if } x_2 \text{ is negative}$$

Hence, when σ_1 is zero, the formula for the standard deviation of a portfolio of two investments is the absolute value of the portfolio-weighted average of the two standard deviations, 0 and σ_2. Note also that since $x_2 = (1 - x_1)$, a positive weight on a risk-free asset and risky asset return, which necessarily implies that both weights are less than 1, reduces variance relative to a 100 per cent investment in the risky asset. Moreover, a negative weight on a risk-free asset (implying that $x_2 > 1$) results in a larger variance than a 100 per cent investment in the risky asset. Hence, leverage increases risk (see part *b* of exercise 4.18).

Portfolio Variances When the Two Investments in the Portfolio Have Perfectly Correlated Returns

Equation (4.9b) also implies that when two securities are perfectly positively or negatively correlated, it is possible to create a riskless portfolio from them: that is, one with a variance and standard deviation of zero, as Example 4.14 illustrates.[9]

For the portfolio in Example 4.14, the standard deviation, the square root of the variance, is the absolute value of $0.5x + 0.4(1 - x)$. This is the portfolio-weighted average of the standard deviations. In summary, we have the following result.

[9] Perfect correlations often arise with derivative securities. A **derivative** is a security whose value depends on the value of another security. For example, the value of a call option written on an asset – the right to buy the asset for a given amount – described in Chapter 3, or a put option – the right to sell the asset for a given amount – described in Chapter 2, depends entirely on the value of the underlying asset. Derivative securities are discussed further in Chapters 7 and 8.

Results

Result 4.3

The standard deviation of either (1) a portfolio of two investments where one of the investments is riskless, or (2) a portfolio of two investments that are perfectly positively correlated is the absolute value of the portfolio-weighted average of the standard deviations of the two investments.

Example 4.14

Forming a Riskless Portfolio from Two Perfectly Correlated Securities

The Acquiring Corporation has just announced plans to purchase the Target Corporation, which started trading for £50 per share just after the announcement. In one month, shareholders of the Target Corporation will exchange each share of Target Corporation equity that they own for two shares of Acquiring Corporation equity, which currently sells for £20 per share, plus £10 in cash. As a consequence of this announcement, shares of the Target Corporation began to move in lockstep with shares of the Acquiring Corporation. Although returns on the two equities became perfectly positively correlated once the announcement occurred, the cash portion of the exchange offer made the shares of the Target Corporation less volatile than the shares of the Acquiring Corporation. Specifically, immediately after the announcement, the standard deviation of the returns of the Acquiring Corporation's shares is 50 per cent per annum. In contrast, those of the Target Corporation have a standard deviation of 40 per cent per annum. What portfolio weights on the Target and Acquiring Corporations would generate a riskless investment during the month before the actual merger?

Answer: Using equation (4.9b), the portfolio weights x and $1 - x$ on the Acquiring and Target Corporation's shares, respectively, make the variance of the portfolio's return

$$0.5^2x^2 + 0.4^2(1-x)^2 + 2x(1-x)(0.5)(0.4) - [0.5x + 0.4(1-x)]^2$$

which equals zero when $x = -4$. Thus the weight on Acquiring is –4, and the weight on Target is 5.

For special cases (1) and (2), Result 4.3 suggests that when the weight on the riskier of the two assets is positive, the equations for the standard deviation and of the mean of the portfolio are the portfolio-weighted averages of the individual asset return standard deviations and the individual asset return means, respectively,

Portfolios of Many Assets

To compute the variance of a portfolio of many assets, one needs to know:

- the variances of the returns of each asset in the portfolio
- the covariances between the returns of each pair of assets in the portfolio
- the portfolio weights.

A Portfolio Variance Formula Based on Covariances

Given the information described above, one can compute the variance of the return of a portfolio of an arbitrary number of assets using Result 4.4.

Results

Result 4.4

The formula for the variance of a portfolio return is given by

$$\sigma_p^2 = \sum_{i=1}^{N}\sum_{j=1}^{N} x_i x_j \sigma_{ij} \qquad (4.9c)$$

where σ_{ij} is the covariance between the returns of assets i and j.

Example 4.15 illustrates how to apply equation (4.9c).

In equation (4.9c), note that σ_{ij} is the variance of the ith asset return when $j = i$, and that N^2 terms are summed. Therefore, the expression for the variance of a portfolio contains N variance terms (one for each asset) but $N^2 - N$ covariance terms. For a portfolio of 100 assets, the expression would thus have 100 variance terms and 9,900 covariance terms. Clearly, the covariance terms are more important determinants of the portfolio variance for large portfolios than the individual variances.

Example 4.15

Computing the Variance of a Portfolio of Three Assets

Consider three assets denoted 1, 2 and 3. The covariance between the daily returns of assets 1 and 2 is 0.000595. Between assets 2 and 3, the covariance is 0.000223, and between 1 and 3, it is 0.000239. The variances of the three equities are respectively 0.003068, 0.00076 and 0.000366, and the weights on the three assets are: $x_1 = \frac{1}{3}$, $x_2 = \frac{1}{6}$, and $x_3 = \frac{1}{2}$. Calculate the variance of the portfolio. Notice how the portfolio variance is less than the variance of all of the individual assets. This is the benefit of diversification.

Answer: From equation (4.9c), the variance of the portfolio is

$$\begin{aligned}
&x_1x_1\sigma_{11} + x_2x_2\sigma_{22} + x_3x_3\sigma_{33} + 2x_1x_2\sigma_{12} + 2x_1x_3\sigma_{13} + 2x_2x_3\sigma_{23}\\
&= \left(\frac{1}{3}\right)\left(\frac{1}{3}\right)0.0031 + \left(\frac{1}{6}\right)\left(\frac{1}{6}\right)0.00076 + \left(\frac{1}{2}\right)\left(\frac{1}{2}\right)0.00037 + 2\left(\frac{1}{3}\right)\left(\frac{1}{6}\right)0.0006 + 2\left(\frac{1}{3}\right)\left(\frac{1}{2}\right)0.0002\\
&\quad + 2\left(\frac{1}{6}\right)\left(\frac{1}{2}\right)0.00022\\
&= 0.000636
\end{aligned}$$

Note that several terms in the expression for a portfolio's variance repeat; for example, see equation (4.9c) and the answer to Example 4.15. Therefore, you sometimes will see equation (4.9c) written as

$$\sigma_p^2 = \sum_{j=1}^{N} x_j^2\sigma_j^2 + 2\sum_{i<j} x_i x_j \sigma_{ij}$$

For two assets, this reads as

$$\sigma_p^2 = x_1^2\sigma_1^2 + x_2^2\sigma_2^2 + 2x_1x_2\sigma_{12}$$

A Portfolio Variance Formula Based on Correlations

Covariances can also be computed from the corresponding correlations and either the variances or standard deviations of the asset returns. For example, substituting equation (4.8), $\sigma_{ij} = \rho_{ij}\sigma_i\sigma_j$, into equation (4.9c) yields an equation for the variance of a portfolio of many assets in terms of correlations and standard deviations:

$$\sigma_p^2 = \sum_{i=1}^{N}\sum_{j=1}^{N} x_i x_j \rho_{ij}\sigma_i\sigma_j$$

Covariances between Portfolio Returns and Asset Returns

Some of the portfolios that we shall be interested in (for example, the minimum variance portfolio) can be found by solving for the weights that generate portfolios that have pre-specified covariances with individual assets. Here, the following result is often used.

Results

Result 4.5

For any asset, indexed by k, the covariance of a portfolio's return with asset k's return is the portfolio-weighted average of the covariances of the returns of the investments in the portfolio with asset k's return: that is,

$$\sigma_{pk} = \sum_{i=1}^{N} x_i \sigma_{ik}$$

4.7 The Mean-Standard Deviation Diagram

It is time to put all this information together. This section focuses on a graph that will help you to understand how investors should view the trade-offs between means and variances when selecting portfolio weights for their investment decisions. This graph, known as the **mean-standard deviation diagram,** plots the means (Y-axis) and the standard deviations (X-axis) of all feasible portfolios to develop an understanding of the feasible means and standard deviations that portfolios generate. The mastery of what you have just learned – how the construction of portfolios generates alternative mean and standard deviation possibilities – is critical to understanding this graph and its implications for investment and corporate financial management.

Combining a Risk-Free Asset with a Risky Asset in the Mean-Standard Deviation Diagram

When Both Portfolio Weights Are Positive

Results 4.1 and 4.3 imply that both the mean and the standard deviation of a portfolio of a riskless investment and a risky investment are the portfolio-weighted averages of the means and the standard deviations of the riskless and risky investment, respectively, when the portfolio weight on the risky investment is positive. This implies that the positively weighted portfolios of the riskless and risky investment lie on a line segment connecting the two investments in the mean-standard deviation diagram. This is a special case of the following more general mathematical property.

Results

Result 4.6

Whenever the portfolio mean and standard deviation are portfolio-weighted averages of the means and the standard deviations of two investments, the portfolio mean-standard deviation outcomes are graphed as a straight line connecting the two investments in the mean-standard deviation diagram.

As suggested above, the portfolios that combine a position in a risk-free asset (investment 1 with return r_f) with a long position in a risky investment (investment 2 with return $\tilde{r}_2$) have the property needed for Result 4.6 to apply and thus plot as the topmost straight line (line AB) in Exhibit 4.3.

To demonstrate this, combine the equation for the mean and standard deviation of such a portfolio

$$\begin{aligned} \overline{R}_p &= x_1 r_f + x_2 \overline{r}_2 \\ \sigma_p &= x_2 \sigma_2 \end{aligned} \qquad (4.10)$$

to express the mean of the return of a portfolio of a riskless and a risky investment as a function of its standard deviation. When the position is long in investment 2, the risky investment, we can rearrange the standard deviation equation to read

$$x_2 = \frac{\sigma_p}{\sigma_2}$$

which implies that

$$x_1 = 1 - \frac{\sigma_p}{\sigma_2}$$

Substituting these expressions for x_1 and x_2 into the expected return equation, equation (4.10), yields

$$\bar{R}_p = r_f + \frac{\bar{r}_2 - r_f}{\sigma_2}\sigma_p$$

This equation is a straight line going from point A, representing the risk-free investment (at $\sigma_p = 0$), through the point representing the risky investment (at $\sigma_p = \sigma_2$). The line thus has an intercept of r_f and a slope of $(\bar{r}_2 - r_f)/\sigma_2$.

Exhibit 4.3 Mean-Standard Deviation Diagram: Portfolios of a Risky Asset and a Riskless Asset

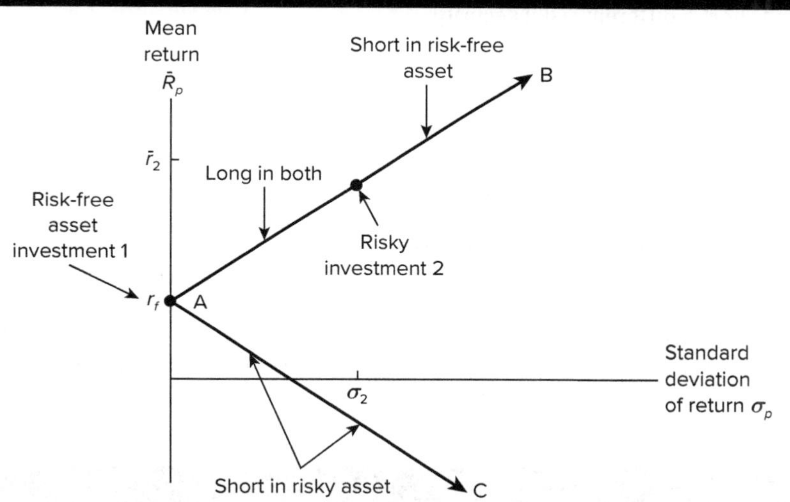

When the Risky Investment Has a Negative Portfolio Weight

When the new portfolio is short in the risky investment, the formula for the standard deviation is

$$\sigma_p = -x_2\sigma_2$$

which implies that

$$x_2 = -\frac{\sigma_p}{\sigma_2}$$

To make the weights sum to 1,

$$x_1 = 1 + \frac{\sigma_p}{\sigma_2}$$

When these two portfolio weight expressions are substituted into the formula for the expected return, equation (4.10), they yield

$$\bar{R}_p = r_f - \frac{\bar{r}_2 - r_f}{\sigma_2}\sigma_p$$

This also is the equation of a straight line. This line is graphed as the bottom line (AC) in Exhibit 4.3 Since the risky investment has a negative weight, and the graph has a mean return for the risky investment that is larger than the return of the risk-free asset, the slope of this line is negative. The more one shorts the (risky) high expected return asset, the lower is the portfolio's expected return, and the higher is the portfolio's standard deviation.

When the Risk-Free Investment Has a Negative Portfolio Weight

Consistent with our earlier discussions, Exhibit 4.3 shows that when the risk-free security is sold short, the portfolio will be riskier than a position that is 100 per cent invested in $\tilde{r}_2$. This leads to the following result.

Results

Result 4.7

When investors employ risk-free borrowing (that is, leverage) to increase their holdings in a risky investment, the risk of the portfolio increases.

Depending on the portfolio weights, risk also may increase when the holdings of a risky investment are increased by selling short a different risky security.

Portfolios of Two Perfectly Positively Correlated or Perfectly Negatively Correlated Assets

Perfect Positive Correlation

Exhibit 4.4 shows the plotted means and standard deviations from portfolios of two perfectly positively correlated assets. Points A and B on the line, designated, respectively, as '100 per cent in asset 1' and '100 per cent in asset 2', correspond to the mean and standard deviation pairings achieved when 100 per cent of an investor's wealth is held in one of the two investments. Bold segment AB graphs the means and standard deviations achieved from portfolios with positive weights on the two perfectly correlated assets. Moving up the line from point A towards point B places more weight on the investment with the higher expected return (asset 2). Above point B, the portfolio is selling short asset 1 and going 'extra long' (weight exceeds 1) in asset 2. Below point A, the portfolio is selling short asset 2.

Exhibit 4.4 Mean-Standard Deviation Diagram: Portfolios of Two Perfectly Positively Correlated Assets

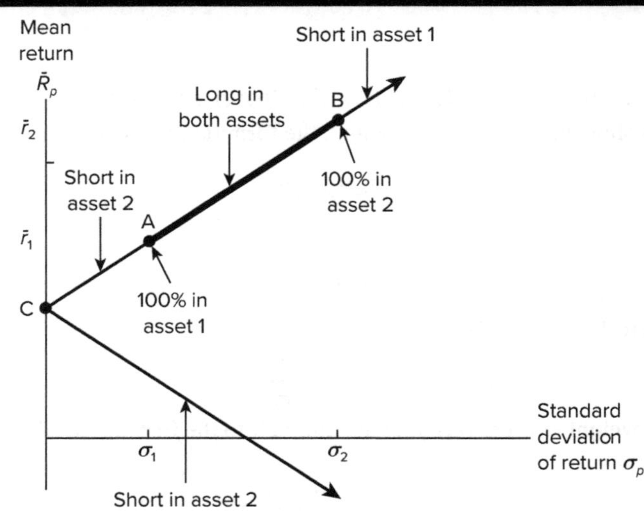

Exhibit 4.4 demonstrates that it is possible to eliminate risk – that is, to achieve zero variance – with a portfolio of two perfectly positively correlated assets.[10] To do this, it is necessary to be long in one investment and short in the other in proportions that place the portfolio at point C.

The graph of portfolios of two perfectly positively correlated, but risky, investments has the same shape (a pair of straight lines) as the graph for a portfolio of a riskless and a risky investment. This should not be surprising because a portfolio of the two perfectly correlated investments is itself a riskless asset. The feasible means and standard deviations generated from portfolios of, say, the riskless combination of assets 1 and 2, on the one hand, and asset 2, on the other, should be identical to those generated by portfolios of assets 1 and 2 themselves. Also, when the portfolio weights on both investments are positive, the mean and the standard deviation of a portfolio of two perfectly correlated investments are portfolio-weighted averages of the means and standard deviations of the individual assets. Consistent with Result 4.6, such portfolios are on a line connecting the two investments whenever the weighted average of the standard deviations is positive.

Perfect Negative Correlation

For similar reasons, a pair of perfectly negatively correlated risky assets graphs as a pair of straight lines. However, in contrast to a pair of perfectly positively correlated investments, the investor eliminates variance by being long in both investments when two investments are perfectly negatively correlated.

Example 4.16

Forming a Riskless Portfolio from Two Perfectly Negatively Correlated Securities

Over extremely short time intervals, the return of IBM is perfectly negatively correlated with the return of a put option on the company. The standard deviation of the return on IBM equity is 18 per cent per year, and the standard deviation of the return on the option is 54 per cent per year. What portfolio weights on IBM and its put option create a riskless investment over short time intervals?

Answer: The variance of the portfolio, using equation (4.9b), is

$$0.18^2x^2 + 0.54^2(1-x)^2 - 2x(1-x)(0.18)(0.54) = [0.18x - 0.54(1-x)]^2$$

This expression is 0 when $x = 0.75$. Thus, the weight on IBM equity is $\frac{3}{4}$, and the weight on the put option is $\frac{1}{4}$.

The Feasible Means and Standard Deviations from Portfolios of Other Pairs of Assets

We noted in the last subsection that, with perfect positive correlation, the standard deviation of a portfolio with positive weights on both assets equals the portfolio-weighted average of the two standard deviations. Consider the case where risky investments have less than perfect correlation ($\rho < 1$). Result 4.2 states that the lower the correlation, the lower the portfolio variance. Therefore, the standard deviation of a portfolio with positive weights on both assets is less than the portfolio-weighted average of the two standard deviations, which gives the curvature to the left shown in Exhibit 4.5. The degree to which this curvature occurs depends on the correlation between the returns. Consistent with Result 4.2, the smaller the correlation, ρ, the more distended the curvature. The ultimate curvature is the pair of lines generated with a perfect negative correlation, $\rho = -1$, the smallest correlation possible.[11]

---

[10] This also was shown in Example 4.14.

[11] Although not pictured in Exhibit 4.5, smaller correlations increase the standard deviation when short sales of one of the investments occurs.

Exhibit 4.5 Mean Standard Deviation Diagram: Portfolios of Two Risky Securities with Arbitrary Correlation, r

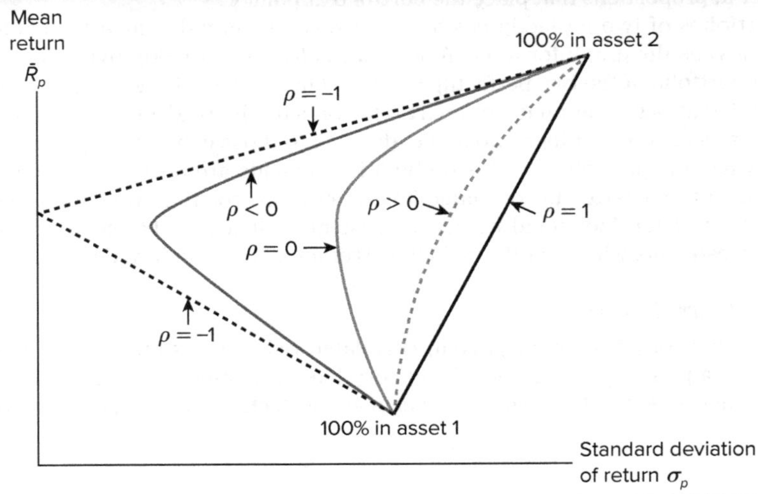

The combination of the two assets that has minimum variance is a portfolio with positive weights on both, only if the correlation between their returns is not too large. For sufficiently large correlations, the **minimum variance portfolio,** the portfolio of risky investments with the lowest variance, requires a long position in one investment and a short position in the other.[12]

4.8 Interpreting the Covariance as a Marginal Variance

It is helpful to interpret the covariance between the asset return and portfolio return as the asset's **marginal variance,** which is the change in the variance of a portfolio for a slight increase in the portfolio weight of the asset.

Results

Result 4.8

An asset's return covariance with a portfolio return is proportional to the variance added to the portfolio return when the asset's portfolio weight is increased by a small amount, keeping the weighting of other assets fixed by financing the additional holdings of the asset with another investment that has zero covariance with the portfolio.

A Proof Using Derivatives from Calculus

To show that the covariance is a marginal variance, add m, per unit of cash invested in the portfolio of asset k to the portfolio, and finance this purchase by borrowing m of a risk-free security with return r_f, which, being risk-free, has zero variance and a zero covariance with the portfolio. If, before the addition of asset k, the portfolio had return $\tilde{R}_p$, the new portfolio return, $\tilde{R}$, is

$$\tilde{R} = \tilde{R}_p + m(\tilde{r}_k - r_f)$$

[12] While short positions are not displayed in Exhibit 4.5, they can easily be added to an analogous diagram. See exercise 4.20.

where r_f is the risk-free return. Because the risk-free return is constant and does not affect the variance, we know from the portfolio variance formula, equation (4.9a), that the variance of this portfolio, σ^2, is

$$\sigma^2 = \text{var}\left[\tilde{R}_p + m(\tilde{r}_k - r_f)\right] = \sigma_p^2 + m^2\sigma_k^2 + 2m\sigma_{pk} \tag{4.11}$$

where

$$\sigma_p^2 = \text{var}(\tilde{R}_p),\ \sigma_k^2 = \text{var}(\tilde{r}_k),\ \text{and}\ \sigma_{pk} = \text{cov}(\tilde{R}_p, \tilde{r}_k)$$

The derivative of the variance in equation (4.11) with respect to m is

$$\frac{d\sigma^2}{dm} = 2(m\sigma_k^2 + \sigma_{pk})$$

Evaluate this derivative at $m = 0$ to determine how the portfolio variance is affected by a marginal addition of asset k. At $m = 0$, the derivative has the value

$$\frac{d\sigma^2}{dm} = 2\sigma_{pk} \tag{4.12}$$

Equation (4.12) implies that adding asset k to the portfolio increases the portfolio variance if the return on the asset covaries positively with the portfolio return. Conversely, the addition of asset k decreases the portfolio variance if its return covaries negatively with the portfolio return. This result applies only for small m (that is, for a sufficiently small amount of asset k added to the portfolio). Moreover, it assumes that this amount is appropriately financed with an opposite, and similarly small, short position in the risk-free asset so that the new portfolio weights still sum to 1 after the asset is added to the portfolio.

Numerical Interpretations of the Marginal Variance Result

Increasing an Asset Position Financed by Reducing or Selling Short the Position in the Risk-Free Asset

The marginal variance result of the last subsection generates predictions about the impact of marginal changes in the weights of a portfolio. For example, consider a £100,000 portfolio that has £60,000 invested in HSBC, £30,000 invested in Vodafone and £10,000 invested in risk-free government Treasury bills. If HSBC's return positively covaries with the return on this £100,000 portfolio and Vodafone's return negatively covaries with it, then the marginal variance result implies the following.

1 A portfolio with £60,001 invested in HSBC, £30,000 in Vodafone and £9,999 invested in Treasury bills will have a higher return variance than the original portfolio – £60,000 in HSBC, £30,000 in Vodafone and £10,000 in T-bills – because, at the margin, it has an additional £1 invested in the positively covarying equity, financed by reducing investment in the risk-free asset by £1.

2 A portfolio with £60,000 invested in HSBC, £30,001 in Vodafone and £9,999 invested in Treasury bills will have a lower return variance than the original portfolio, because, at the margin, it has an additional £1 invested in the negatively covarying equity, financed by reducing investment in the risk-free asset by £1.

3. A portfolio with £59,999 invested in HSBC, £30,000 in Vodafone and £10,001 invested in Treasury bills will have a lower return variance than the original portfolio, because, at the margin, it has £1 less invested in the positively covarying equity and an additional £1 invested in the risk-free asset.[13]

Increasing an Asset Position Financed by Reducing or Shorting a Position in a Risky Asset

To generalize the interpretation of the covariance as a marginal variance, substitute the returns of some asset for the risk-free asset in equation (4.11). In this case, the marginal variance is proportional to the difference in the covariances of the returns of the two assets with the portfolio. Adding a bit of the difference between two asset returns is equivalent to increasing the portfolio's position slightly in the first asset and decreasing its position slightly by an offsetting amount in the second asset.

[13] We have confidence in these results because the change in the portfolio is small. Specifically, $m = 0.00001$ in cases 1 and 2 and $m = -0.00001$ in case 3.

In the HSBC, Vodafone and Treasury bill example, suppose that HSBC's return has a covariance of 0.03 with the return of the £100,000 portfolio, while Vodafone's return has a covariance of –0.01. In this case, the following applies.

1. A portfolio with £60,001 invested in HSBC, £29,999 in Vodafone and £10,000 in Treasury bills will have a higher return variance than the original portfolio, because, at the margin, it has an additional £1 invested in positively covarying equity, financed by reducing investment in an equity with a lower covariance by £1.
2. A portfolio with £59,999 invested in HSBC, £30,001 in Vodafone and £10,000 in Treasury bills will have a lower return variance than the original portfolio, because, at the margin, it has an additional £1 invested in the negatively covarying equity, financed by reducing investment in an equity with a higher covariance by £1.

Example 4.17

How to Use Covariances Alone to Reduce Portfolio Variance

Vodafone and Unilever shares have respective covariances of 0.001 and 0.002 with a portfolio. Vodafone and Unilever are already in the portfolio. Now, change the portfolio's composition slightly by holding a few more Vodafone shares and reducing Unilever's holding by an equivalent sterling amount. Does this increase or decrease the variance of the overall portfolio?

Answer: This problem takes an existing portfolio and adds some Vodafone equity to it, financed by selling short an equal amount of Unilever (which is equivalent to reducing an existing Unilever position). The new return is

$$\tilde{R}_p + m(\tilde{r}_{\text{Voda}} - \tilde{r}_{Uni})$$

The covariance of $\tilde{r}_{\text{Voda}} - \tilde{r}_{Uni}$ with the portfolio is 0.001 – 0.002, which is negative. If m is small enough, the new portfolio will have a smaller variance than the old portfolio. More formally, taking the derivative of the variance of this expression with respect to m and evaluating the derivative at $m = 0$ yields

$$2\left[\text{COV}\left(\tilde{r}_{\text{Voda}}, \tilde{R}_p\right) - \text{cov}\left(\tilde{r}_{Uni}, \tilde{R}_p\right)\right]$$

which is negative.

Result 4.9 summarizes the conclusions of this section.

Results

Result 4.9

If the difference between the covariances of the returns of assets A and B with the portfolio's return is positive, increasing the portfolio's holding in asset A slightly and reducing the position in asset B by the same amount increases the portfolio return variance. Conversely, if the difference is negative, this change will decrease the portfolio return variance.

Why Asset Variances Have no Effect on the Marginal Variance

It is somewhat surprising that the variances of individual assets play no role in the computation of what has been termed the *marginal variance.* However, bear in mind that computations involving infinitesimal changes in a portfolio require the use of calculus. In the HSBC and Vodafone examples, the portfolio changes, although extremely small, are not infinitesimal, and the variance of HSBC and Vodafone affects the variance of the new portfolio return. However, the portfolio changes are so small that any effect from the variances of HSBC and Vodafone are minuscule enough to be swamped by the covariance effect.

The lesson about covariance as a marginal variance is essential, because it allows us to understand the necessary conditions for identifying the precise portfolio weights of portfolios that investors and corporate financial managers find useful. The first of these portfolios is introduced in the next section.

4.9 Finding the Minimum Variance Portfolio

This section illustrates how to compute the weights of the minimum variance portfolio, an interesting portfolio for various reasons. Highly risk-averse investors will select this portfolio if no risk-free investment is available. In addition, this portfolio is helpful for understanding many risk management problems.[14] This section discusses insights about covariance as a marginal variance presented in the last section to develop a set of equations that, when solved, identify the weights of this portfolio.

Properties of a Minimum Variance Portfolio

The previous section discussed how to adjust the portfolio weights of assets in a portfolio to lower the portfolio's variance by following these steps.

1. Take two asset returns that have different covariances with the portfolio's return.
2. Take on a small additional positive investment (that is, a slightly larger portfolio weight) in the low-covariance asset and an additional negative offsetting position (that is, a slightly lower portfolio weight) in the high-covariance asset.

With this process, the portfolio's variance can be lowered until all assets in the portfolio have identical covariances with the portfolio's return. When all assets have the same covariance with the portfolio's return, more tinkering with the portfolio weights at the margin will not reduce variance, implying that a minimum variance portfolio has been obtained.

Results

Result 4.10

The portfolio of a group of assets that minimizes return variance is the portfolio with a return that has an equal covariance with every asset return.

Identifying the Minimum Variance Portfolio of Two Assets

The two-asset problem in Example 4.18 illustrates the procedure for finding this type of portfolio. This implies that a short position in the DFA small cap fund reduces variance relative to a portfolio with a 100 per cent position in the S&P. Indeed, until we reach the 132 per cent investment position in the S&P index, additional shorting of the DFA fund to finance the more than 100 per cent position in the S&P index reduces variance.

Example 4.18

Forming a Minimum Variance Portfolio for Asset Allocation

Historically, the return of the S&P 500 Index (S&P) has had a correlation of 0.8 with the return of the Dimensional Fund Advisors small-cap fund, which is a portfolio of small equities that trade primarily on NASDAQ. S&P has a standard deviation of 20 per cent per year: that is, $\sigma_{S\&P} = 0.2$. The DFA small-cap fund return has a standard deviation of 39 per cent per year: that is, $\sigma_{DFA} = 0.39$. What portfolio allocation between these two investments minimizes variance?

[14] See Chapter 21 for a discussion of risk management.

Answer: Treat the two indices as if they were two individual assets. If x is the weight on the S&P, the covariance of the portfolio with the S&P index (using Result 4.5) is

$$\begin{aligned}\mathrm{cov}\left[x\tilde{r}_{\mathrm{S\&P}} + (1-x)\tilde{r}_{\mathrm{DFA}}, \tilde{r}_{\mathrm{S\&P}}\right] &= x\,\mathrm{cov}(\tilde{r}_{\mathrm{S\&P}}, \tilde{r}_{\mathrm{S\&P}}) + (1-x)\,\mathrm{cov}(\tilde{r}_{\mathrm{DFA}}, \tilde{r}_{\mathrm{S\&P}}) \\ &= 0.2^2x + (0.2)(0.39)(0.8)(1-x) \\ &= -0.22x + 0.062\end{aligned}$$

The covariance of the portfolio with the return of the DFA fund is

$$\begin{aligned}\mathrm{cov}\left[x\tilde{r}_{\mathrm{S\&P}} + (1-x)\tilde{r}_{\mathrm{DFA}}, \tilde{r}_{\mathrm{DFA}}\right] &= x\,\mathrm{cov}(\tilde{r}_{\mathrm{S\&P}}, \tilde{r}_{\mathrm{DFA}}) + (1-x)\mathrm{cov}(\tilde{r}_{\mathrm{DFA}}, \tilde{r}_{\mathrm{DFA}}) \\ &= x(0.2)(0.39)(0.8) + (1-x)(0.39)^2 \\ &= -0.090x + 0.152\end{aligned}$$

Setting the two covariances equal to each other and solving for x gives

$$\begin{aligned}-0.022x + 0.062 &= -0.090x + 0.152, \quad \text{or} \\ x &= 1.32 \text{ (approximately)}\end{aligned}$$

Thus placing weights of approximately 132 per cent on the S&P index and –32 per cent on the DFA fund minimizes the variance of the portfolio of these two investments.

Example 4.18 implies that a short position in the DFA small-cap fund reduces variance relative to a portfolio with a 100 per cent position in the S&P. Indeed, until we reach the 132 per cent investment position in the S&P index, additional shorting of the DFA fund to finance the more than 100 per cent position in the S&P index reduces variance.

For example, consider what happens to the variance of a portfolio that is 100 per cent invested in the S&P 500 when its weights are changed slightly. Increase the position to 101 per cent invested in the S&P, the increase financed by selling short 1 per cent in the DFA small-cap fund. The covariance of the DFA small-cap fund with the initial position of 100 per cent invested in S&P is 0.06 = (0.8)(0.39)(0.2), and the covariance of the S&P with itself is a lower number, 0.04 = (0.2)(0.2). Moreover, variances do not matter for such minor changes, only covariances. Hence increasing the S&P position from 100 per cent and reducing the DFA position from 0 per cent reduces variance.

Identifying the Minimum Variance Portfolio of Many Assets

With N assets, we recommend a two-step process, based on Result 4.10, to find the portfolio that has the same covariance with every asset. First, solve N equations with N unknowns. Then rescale the portfolio weights. Example 4.19, using a portfolio of three assets, illustrates the technique.

Solving for the minimum variance portfolio of many assets usually requires a computer.[15]

Example 4.19

Finding the Minimum Variance Portfolio

Suntharee Beers, a Thai firm, wants to branch out internationally. Recognizing that the markets in Japan and Europe are difficult to break into, it is contemplating capital investments to open franchises in India (investment 1), Russia (investment 2) and China (investment 3). Given that Suntharee has a fixed amount of capital to invest in foreign franchising and recognizing that such investment is risky, Suntharee wants to find

[15] Many software packages, including spreadsheets, can be used to obtain a numerical solution to this type of problem. The solution usually requires setting up a matrix (or array) of covariances, where the row i and column j of the matrix is the covariance between the returns of assets i and j, denoted σ_{ij}. Instruct the software to first *invert the matrix,* which is an important step that the computer uses to solve systems of linear equations, and then to sum the columns of the inverted covariance matrix, which is the same as summing the elements in each row. The sum of the columns is then rescaled so that the entries sum to 1. The matrix inversion method is partly analogous to the substitution method in Example 4.19. In Microsoft Excel, matrix inversion uses the function MINVERSE.

the minimum variance investment proportions for these three countries. Solve Suntharee's portfolio problem. Assume that the returns of the franchise investments in the three countries have the following covariances.

	Covariance with		
	India	Russia	China
India	0.002	0.001	0
Russia	0.001	0.002	0.001
China	0	0.001	0.002

Answer: Treat franchise investment in each country as a portfolio investment problem.

Step 1: Solve for the 'weights' that make the covariance of each of the three country returns a constant. These 'weights' are not true weights because they do not necessarily sum to 1. (Some constants will result in weights that add to 1. However, it is easier to pick first any constant and later rescale the weights.) Let us use '1' as that constant. The first step is to simultaneously solve three equations:

$$0.002x_1 + 0.001x_2 + 0x_3 = 1$$
$$0.001x_1 + 0.002x_2 + 0.001x_3 = 1$$
$$0x_1 + 0.001x_2 + 0.002x_3 = 1$$

The left-hand side of the first equation is the covariance of the return of a portfolio with weights x_1, x_2, x_3 with the return of asset 1 (using Result 4.5). The first equation shows that this covariance must equal 1. The other two equations make identical statements about covariances with assets 2 and 3.

Now, solve these equations with the substitution method. Rewrite the first and third equations as

$$x_1 = 500 - \frac{x_2}{2}$$

$$x_3 = 500 - \frac{x_2}{2}$$

Substituting these values of x_1 and x_2 into the second equation yields

$$0.001x_2 = 0$$

or

$$x_2 = 0$$

Substitution of this value into the remaining two equations implies that

$$x_1 = 500$$
$$x_3 = 500$$

Step 2: Rescale the portfolio weights so that they add to 1. After rescaling, the computed solution is

$$x_1 = 0.5 \quad x_2 = 0 \quad x_3 = 0.5$$

4.10 Summary and Conclusions

This chapter presented basic concepts in probability and statistics that are fundamental to most of investment theory and much of corporate Finance. In particular, to prepare you for using the mean-variance model, this chapter examined means, variances, standard deviations, covariances and correlations. It also computed the means, variances and covariances of portfolios given the means, variances and covariances of the individual securities.

This chapter also interpreted the covariance as a marginal variance, using this insight to derive a formula for the minimum variance portfolio. The return of such a portfolio has the same covariance with the return of every security in the portfolio.

Chapter 5 takes the analysis one step further by analysing the mean-standard deviation diagram in greater depth, identifying other interesting portfolios, developing a theory of the optimal investment mix of assets, and deriving a theory of the relationship between risk and mean return. All this is predicated on the basic mathematics and intuition developed in this chapter.

Key Concepts

Result 4.1: The expected portfolio return is the portfolio-weighted average of the expected returns of the individual assets in the portfolio:

$$\bar{R}_p = \sum_{i=1}^{N} x_i \bar{r}_i$$

Result 4.2: Given positive portfolio weights on two assets, the lower the correlation, the lower the variance of the portfolio.

Result 4.3: The standard deviation of either (1) a portfolio of two investments where one of the investments is riskless, or (2) a portfolio of two investments that are perfectly positively correlated is the absolute value of the portfolio-weighted average of the standard deviations of the two investments.

Result 4.4: The formula for the variance of a portfolio return is given by

$$\sigma_p^2 = \sum_{i=1}^{N} \sum_{j=1}^{N} x_i x_j \sigma_{ij}$$

where σ_{ij} is the covariance between the returns of assets i and j.

Result 4.5: For any asset, indexed by k, the covariance of the return of a portfolio with the return of asset k is the portfolio-weighted average of the covariances of the returns of the investments in the portfolio with asset k's return: that is,

$$\sigma_{pk} = \sum_{i=1}^{N} x_i \sigma_{ik}$$

Result 4.6: Whenever the portfolio mean and standard deviations are portfolio-weighted averages of the means and standard deviations of two investments, the portfolio mean-standard deviation outcomes are graphed as a straight line connecting the two investments in the mean-standard deviation diagram.

Result 4.7: When investors employ risk-free borrowing (that is, leverage) to increase their holdings in a risky investment, the risk of the portfolio increases.

Result 4.8: The covariance of an asset return with the return of a portfolio is proportional to the variance added to the portfolio return when the asset's portfolio weight is increased by a small amount, keeping the weighting of other assets fixed by financing the additional holdings of the asset with another investment that has zero covariance with the portfolio.

Result 4.9: If the difference between the covariances of the returns of assets A and B with the return of a portfolio is positive, slightly increasing the portfolio's holding in asset A and reducing its position in asset B by the same amount increases the portfolio return variance. If the difference is negative, the change will decrease the portfolio return variance.

Result 4.10: The portfolio of a group of assets that minimizes return variance is the portfolio with a return that has an equal covariance with every asset return.

Key Terms

Exercises

4.1 Prove that $E[(\tilde{r}-\bar{r})^2] = E(\tilde{r}^2) - \bar{r}^2$ using the following steps:

a Show that $E[(\tilde{r}-\bar{r})^2] = E(\tilde{r}^2 - 2\tilde{r}\bar{r} + \bar{r})^2$.

b Show that the expression in part *a* is equal to $E(\tilde{r}^2) - 2E(\tilde{r}\bar{r}) + \bar{r}^2$.

c Show that the expression in part *b* is equal to $E(\tilde{r}^2) - 2\bar{r}^2 + \bar{r}^2$. Then add.

4.2 Derive a formula for the weights of the minimum variance portfolio of two assets using the following steps.

a Compute the variance of a portfolio with weights x and $1-x$ on assets 1 and 2, respectively. Show that you get

$$\text{var}(\widetilde{R}_p) = x^2\sigma_1^2 + (1-x)^2\ \sigma_2^2 + 2x(1-x)\rho\sigma_1\sigma_2$$

b Take the derivative with respect to x of the expression in part *a*. Show that the value of x that makes the derivative 0 is

$$x = \frac{\sigma_2^2 - \rho\sigma_1\sigma_2}{\sigma_1^2 + \sigma_2^2 - 2\rho\sigma_1\sigma_2}$$

c Compute the covariance of the return of this minimum variance portfolio with assets 1 and 2.

4.3 Compute the expected return and the variance of the return of the equity of Gamma Corporation. Gamma equity has a return of:

- 24 per cent with probability $\frac{1}{4}$
- 8 per cent with probability $\frac{1}{8}$
- 4 per cent with probability $\frac{1}{2}$
- −16 per cent with probability $\frac{1}{8}$.

4.4 If the ratio of the return variances of equity A to equity B is denoted by q, find the portfolio weights for the two equities that generate a riskless portfolio if the returns of the two equities are (a) perfectly negatively correlated or (b) perfectly positively correlated.

4.5 Iain invests €10,000 in Michelin shares with a €3 annual dividend selling at €85 per share, and €15,000 in Société Générale shares with €6 annual dividend at €120 per share. The following year, Michelin shares are trading at €104 per share while Société Générale shares trade at €113. Calculate Iain's portfolio weights and returns.

4.6 Helix, a Chinese national, decides to buy a 6 per cent, 10-year straight-coupon bond for RMB10,000, which pays annual coupons of RMB600 at the end of each year. At the end of the first year, the bond is trading at RMB11,500. At the end of the second year, the bond trades at RMB10,000.

a What is Helix's return over the first year?

b What is Helix's return over the second year?

c What is the average return per year for the two-year period? Use the arithmetic average.

4.7 Helix's portfolio consists of RMB1,000,000 in face value of the bonds described in exercise and an RMB800,000 bank CD that earns 3.5 per cent per year for the first year and 3.0 per cent the second year. Calculate *a*, *b* and *c* as in exercise 4.6.

4.8 Show that the return of the minimum variance portfolio in Example 4.17, that is, 75 per cent Vodafone and 25 per cent British Airways put option, has the same covariance with Vodafone's equity return as it does with the put option. Show that no other portfolio of the two equities has this property.

Exercises 4.9–4.17 make use of the following data.

ABCO is a conglomerate that has €4 billion in ordinary equity. Its capital is invested in four subsidiaries: entertainment (ENT), consumer products (CON), pharmaceuticals (PHA) and insurance (INS). The four subsidiaries are expected to perform differently, depending on the economic environment.

	Investment (€ millions)	Poor economy (%)	Average economy (%)	Good economy (%)
ENT	1,200	+20	–5	–8
CON	800	+15	+10	–20
PHA	1,400	–10	–5	+27
INS	600	–10	+10	+10

4.9 Assuming (1) that the three economic outcomes have an equal likelihood of occurring, and (2) that the good economy is twice as likely to take place as the other two:

a Calculate individual expected returns for each subsidiary.

b Calculate implicit portfolio weights for each subsidiary, and an expected return and variance for the equity in the ABCO conglomerate.

4.10 Assume, in exercise 4.9 that ABCO also has a pension fund, which has a net asset value of €5 billion, implying that ABCO's equity is really worth €9 billion instead of €4 billion. The €5 billion in pension funds is invested in short-term government risk-free securities yielding 5 per cent per year. Recalculate parts *a* and *b* of exercise 4.9 to reflect this.

4.11 Assume, in exercise 4.9 that ABCO decides to borrow €8 billion at 5 per cent interest to triple its current investment in each of its four lines of business. Assume that this new investment has the same per monetary return outcomes as the old investment.

a Answer parts *a* and *b* of exercise 4.9 given the new investment.

b How does this result compare with the results from exercise 4.9? Why?

c To whom does this return belong? Why?

4.12 ABCO's head of risk management now warns of focusing on expected returns to the exclusion of risk measures such as variance. ABCO decides to measure return variance.

a For each ABCO subsidiary, compute the return variance with the standard formula

$$\text{var}(\tilde{r}) = E[(\tilde{r} - \bar{r})^2]$$

(i) if the three economic scenarios are equally likely

(ii) if the good economic scenario is twice as likely as the other two.

b Show that the alternative variance formula, $E(\tilde{r}^2) - [E(\tilde{r})^2]$, from exercise 4.1, yields the same results.

4.13 Assuming that the three economic scenarios are equally likely, compute the covariances and the correlation matrix for the four ABCO subsidiaries. Show that an alternative covariance formula, $\text{cov}(\tilde{r}_1, \tilde{r}_2) = E(\tilde{r}_1, \tilde{r}_2)^2 - E(\tilde{r}_1)E(\tilde{r}_2)$, generates the same covariances.

4.14 ABCO is considering selling off two of its four subsidiaries and reinvesting the proceeds in the remaining two subsidiaries, keeping the same relative investment proportions in the surviving two. Assuming that the three economic scenarios are equally likely, compute the return variance of the €4 billion in ABCO equity for each of the six possible pairs of subsidiaries remaining.

4.15 For each of the six cases in exercise 4.14, ABCO wants to consider what would happen to the return variance of ABCO's €4 billion in equity if it revised the relative investment proportions in the two remaining subsidiaries. In particular, for each of the six possible sell-off scenarios, what proportion of the €4 billion should be invested in the two remaining subsidiaries if ABCO were to minimize its variance? Assume that short sales are not permitted.

4.16 Draw six mean-standard deviation diagrams, one for each of the six remaining pairs of subsidiaries in exercise 4.15. Mark the individual subsidiaries, the minimum variance combination assuming no short sales, and ABCO's return variance for a 50/50 per cent combination.

4.17 How does your answer to exercise 4.16 change if short sales are permitted?

4.18 The three-asset portfolio in Example 4.15 is combined with a risk-free investment.

a What are the variance and standard deviation of the return of the new portfolio if the percentage of wealth in the risk-free asset is 25 per cent? What are the portfolio weights of the four assets in the new portfolio?

b Repeat the problem with –50 per cent as the weight on the risk-free asset.

4.19 From Example 4.15, the covariances between the returns of AIB, CRH and Ryanair are given in the table below.

	AIB	CRH	Ryanair
AIB	0.000325	0.000190	0.000185
CRH	0.000190	0.000316	0.000174
Ryanair	0.000185	0.000174	0.000498

Compute the minimum variance portfolio of these three equities.

4.20 Graph a generalization of Exhibit 4.5 that includes portfolios with short positions in one of the two investments.

4.21 In Example 4.5, we examined the returns on the FTSE 100 between 2006 and 2009. In 2007 and 2008, the market went through a very difficult period as a result of the poor economic conditions at the time. Did other markets experience the same problem? Collect annual data for the CAC40 (France), DAX (Germany), AEX (The Netherlands) and OMX (Sweden) and calculate the expected return and variance of these indices, using data for the same period.

4.22 A portfolio consists of the following three assets, whose performance depends on the economic environment.

	Investment (£)	Good (%)	Bad (%)
Asset 1	500	+13	–20
Asset 2	1,250	+6	+3
Asset 3	250	–7	+2

Assuming that the good economic environment is twice as likely as the bad one, compute the expected return and variance of the portfolio.

What if £1,000 of asset 4, which has a mean return of 4 per cent, a variance of 0.02 and is uncorrelated with the preceding portfolio, is added to the portfolio? How will this change the expected return and variance of the total investment?

4.23 You wish to diversify your investment portfolio, and have decided to invest in international equities. The table below provides monthly index levels during 2009 and 2010 for four countries: Hang Seng Index (Hong Kong), OMX Copenhagen 20 (Denmark), DAX (Germany) and the FTSE 100 (UK).

Hang Seng	OMX Copenhagen	DAX	FTSE 100
21,752.87	324.16	5,414.96	5,044.5
21,821.50	327.20	5,625.95	5,190.7
21,872.50	336.69	5,957.43	5,412.9
20,121.99	354.85	5,608.79	5,188.5
20,608.70	354.77	5,598.46	5,354.5
21,239.35	383.04	6,153.55	5,679.6

Date	Hang Seng	OMX	Copenhagen	DAX	FTSE 100
Apr 2010	21,108.59	411.50	6,135.70	5,553.3	
May 2010	19,765.19	388.69	5,964.33	5,188.4	
June 2010	20,128.99	393.02	5,965.52	4,916.9	
July 2010	21,029.81	410.83	6,147.97	5,258	
Aug 2010	20,536.49	396.38	5,925.22	5,225.2	
Sep 2010	22,358.17	416.96	6,229.02	5,548.6	
Oct 2010	23,096.32	424.20	6,601.37	5,675.2	
Nov 2010	24,700.30	432.89	6,723.41	5,815.2	

Source: Yahoo! Financey.

a. Calculate the monthly returns to each index.
b. Calculate the expected return and variance of each of the indices.
c. Calculate the covariance between each of the indices.
d. Calculate the expected return and variance of a portfolio with equal weights in each region.
e. Calculate the weights of each investment in the minimum variance portfolio.
f. Calculate the expected return and variance of the minimum variance portfolio.

References and Additional Reading

Constantinides, G. and Malliaris, A.G. (1995) Portfolio theory in Robert Jarrow, V. Maksimovic and W. Ziemba (eds) *Handbooks in Operations Research and Management Science: Volume 9, Finance*, Amsterdam: Elsevier Science, 1–30.

Markowitz, H. (1952) Portfolio selection *Journal of Finance*, 7(1): 77–91.

Merton, R. (1972) An analytic derivation of the efficient portfolio frontier *Journal of Financial and Quantitative Analysis*, 7(4): 1851–1872.

Sharpe, W. (1970) *Portfolio Theory and Capital Markets*, New York: Mc Graw-Hill.

Tobin, J. (1958) Liquidity preference as behavior towards risk *Review of Economic Studies*, 25(2): 65–86.

Chapter 5

Mean-Variance Analysis and the Capital Asset Pricing Model

Learning Objectives

After reading this chapter, you should be able to:

- Understand the importance of the mean-standard deviation diagram, and know how to locate within it the efficient frontier of risky assets, the capital market line, the minimum variance portfolio and the tangency portfolio.
- Compute and use both the tangency portfolio and the efficient frontier of risky assets.
- Understand the linkage between mean-variance efficiency and risk-expected return equations.
- Describe how to calculate the beta of a portfolio, given the betas and weights of individual assets in the portfolio.
- Comprehend what the market portfolio is, what assumptions are needed for the market portfolio to be the tangency portfolio – that is, for the Capital Asset Pricing Model (CAPM) to hold – and the empirical evidence for the CAPM.

Many investors now look to international funds or international asset classes to diversify their portfolio risk. However, choosing the country components of a global portfolio can be problematic. For example, in recent years, many country asset markets have moved in broadly similar directions at the same time. This trend towards higher correlations across country asset markets has led investors to investigate new alternative asset classes, such as cryptocurrency, property and commodities. There has also been a significant increase in demand for investments in China and India.

An examination of the correlation matrix of monthly returns of the FTSE 100 (UK), AEX (Netherlands), OMX (Sweden), FTSE/JSE Top 40 (South Africa), S&P 500 (US) and Shanghai Composite (China) for the period January 2010 to December 2021 shows just how strong the market relationships were. The correlation between European and US indices is exceptionally high and above 0.75 in all cases. In contrast, China has a much lower correlation with the US and Europe, and South Africa has correlations lower than European countries but significantly higher than China. This suggests that diversification benefits European investors by investing in Asia and potentially South Africa.

	FTSE 100	AEX	OMX	JSE	S&P500	Shanghai
FTSE 100	1					
AEX	0.82	1				
OMX	0.76	0.84	1			
JSE	0.65	0.63	0.67	1		
S&P500	0.80	0.80	0.82	0.69	1	
Shanghai	0.32	0.32	0.34	0.38	0.40	1

The annualized means and standard deviations for the equity index returns associated with the six regions were estimated as follows.

	FTSE 100	AEX	OMX	JSE	S&P500	Shanghai
Mean (%)	7.05%	11.53%	14.69%	12.05%	15.04%	2.84%
Standard Deviation (%)	13.54%	14.83%	15.12%	13.87%	15.55%	20.72%

Compared with other countries, the Shanghai Composite Index performed very poorly between 2010 and 2021. However, at the same time, its standard deviation was the highest of all six countries.

When most investors think about quantifying the risk of their portfolios, they think about the variance or standard deviation of their portfolio's return. While variance is not the only way to quantify risk, it is the most widely used measure. This chapter analyses the portfolio selection problem of an investor who uses variance as the sole measure of a portfolio's risk. In other words, the investor wishes to select a portfolio that has the maximum expected return, given the variance of its future returns. To do this, they must understand the trade-off between mean and variance.

Chapter 4 introduced the analysis of this trade-off, known as *mean-variance analysis*. To analyse problems like those in the opening vignette, however, one needs to develop mean-variance analysis in more depth. For example, based on the data in the vignette, one can show that a portfolio invested 43.92 per cent in the FTSE 100 index and 56.08 per cent in the S&P 500 index could earn the same mean return as a portfolio invested 100 per cent in the AEX. At the same time, this UK/US equity portfolio would have a standard deviation of 13.94 per cent per year compared with the AEX standard deviation of 14.83 per cent per year. Mastery of certain portions of this chapter is a requirement for understanding how to develop superior portfolio weights in situations like this.

As one of the cornerstones of financial theory, mean-variance analysis is significant enough to have been mentioned in two Nobel Prizes in economics: James Tobin in 1981 and Harry Markowitz in 1990. While an important tool in its own right, mean-variance analysis also indirectly generated a third Nobel Prize for William Sharpe in 1990 for developing the Capital Asset Pricing Model (CAPM), a model of the relation of risk to expected return.[1] This chapter will examine this model, which follows directly from mean-variance analysis.

The chapter is organized into three major parts. After a brief introduction to applications of mean-variance analysis and the CAPM in use today, the first part focuses on the trade-off between mean and variance and uses the tools developed in this chapter to design optimal portfolios. The second part looks at the risk–expected return relation derived from mean-variance analysis, focusing on the CAPM as a special case. The last part examines how to implement the CAPM and analyses the empirical evidence about the CAPM.

[1] Sharpe (1964) shares credit for the CAPM with Lintner (1965).

5.1 Applications of Mean-Variance Analysis and the CAPM in Use Today

Mean-variance analysis and the Capital Asset Pricing Model (CAPM) have practical applications for professional investors and individuals working in corporate finance.

Investment Applications of Mean-Variance Analysis and the CAPM

As tools for illustrating how to achieve higher average returns with lower risk, mean-variance analysis and the CAPM are routinely applied by brokers, pension fund managers and consultants when formulating investment strategies and giving financial advice. For example, mean-variance analysis is widely used in deciding the allocation of assets such as bonds, equities, cash and property across industries, countries and asset classes.

Corporate Applications of Mean-Variance Analysis and the CAPM

A firm grasp of mean-variance analysis and the CAPM is becoming increasingly relevant for the corporate manager. In a world where managers of firms with declining share prices are likely to lose their jobs in a takeover or restructuring, the need to understand the determinants of share value and what actions to take to increase this value in response to the pressures of shareholders and directors has never been greater.

For example, corporations can use mean-variance analysis to hedge their risks optimally and diversify their real investment projects portfolios. However, one of the lessons of the CAPM is that, while diversifying investments can reduce the variance of a firm's share price, it does not reduce the firm's **cost of capital**, which is a weighted average of the expected rates of return required by the financial markets for a firm's debt and equity. As a result, a corporate diversification strategy can create value for a corporation only if the diversification increases the expected returns of the real asset investments of the corporation.[2]

Corporations also use the CAPM and mean-variance analysis to evaluate their capital expenditure decisions. Financial managers use the insights of mean-variance analysis and the CAPM to derive meaningful conclusions about valuing real assets and understand how debt financing affects the risk and the required return of equity.[3]

5.2 The Essentials of Mean-Variance Analysis

To illustrate how to use the mean-standard deviation diagram for investment decisions, it is necessary first to understand where all possible investments lie in the diagram. Therefore, the first subsection discusses what the diagram implies about the feasible mean-standard deviation outcomes that can be achieved with portfolios. The second subsection analyses the assumptions of mean-variance analysis and discusses which feasible mean-standard deviation outcomes are desirable.

The Feasible Set

The **feasible set** of the mean-standard deviation diagram – the shaded area in Exhibit 5.1 and its boundary – is the set of mean and standard deviation outcomes achieved from all feasible portfolios, plotted with mean return on the vertical axis and standard deviation on the horizontal axis.[4]

To simplify exposition, Exhibit 5.1 assumes that the feasible set is formed from portfolios of only four assets, the four points inside the hyperbolic-shaped boundary of the shaded area. This hyperbolic shape occurs whenever a risk-free security or portfolio is not available. This and the following few sections analyse the problem of optimal investment when a risk-free investment both is and is not available.

---

[2] Chapters 21 and 22 provide further discussion of this application.

[3] Chapters 11 and 13 provide further discussion of this application.

[4] At one time, mean-variance analysis was conducted by studying a diagram where the axes were the mean and variance of the portfolio return. However, certain important portfolio combinations lie on a straight line in the mean-standard deviation diagram but on a curved line in the mean-variance diagram. Although the focus today is on the simpler mean-standard deviation analysis, the name 'mean-variance analysis' has stuck with us.

Exhibit 5.1 The Feasible Set

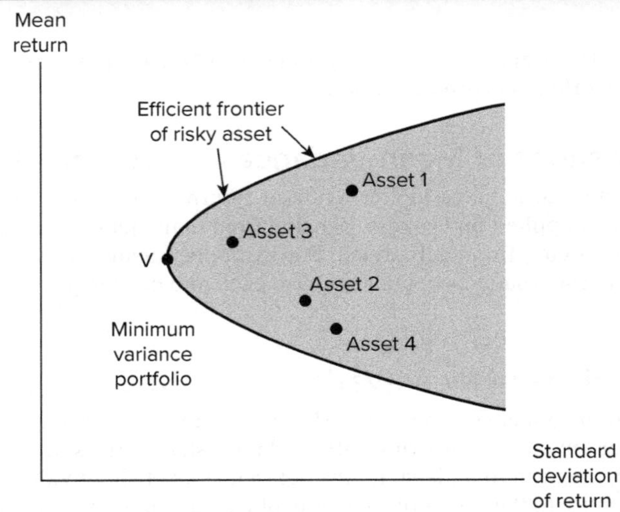

Chapter 4 noted that the mean and variance of the return of a portfolio are wholly determined by three characteristics of each asset in the portfolio:

1 The mean return of each asset, also known as the expected return
2 The variance of the return of each asset
3 The covariances between the return of each asset and the returns of other assets in the portfolio.

Hence knowing means, variances and covariances for a group of investments is all that is needed to obtain a figure like that found in Exhibit 5.1.

As seen in Exhibit 5.1, investors achieve higher means and lower variances by 'moving to the north-west', or up and to the left, while staying within the feasible set. One of the goals of this chapter is to learn how to identify the weights of the portfolios on the upper-left or 'north-west' boundary of this shaded area. These portfolios are known as **mean-variance efficient portfolios**.

The Assumptions of Mean-Variance Analysis

The identification of the weights of the portfolios on the north-west boundary is useful only if investors prefer to be on the north-west boundary and if there are no frictions or impediments to forming such portfolios. Thus, it should not be surprising that the two assumptions of mean-variance analysis are as follows.

1 In making investment decisions today, investors care only about the means and variances of the returns of their portfolios over a particular period (for example, the next week, month or year). So, naturally, their preference is for higher means and lower variances.
2 Financial markets are *frictionless* (to be defined shortly).

These assumptions allow us to use the mean-standard deviation diagram to determine which portfolios are better than others. As a tool in the study of optimal investment, the diagram can help rule out **dominated portfolios**, plotted as points in the diagram that lie below and to the right (that is, to the south-east) of some other feasible portfolio. These portfolios are dominated because other feasible portfolios have higher mean returns and lower return variances, and thus are better.

The Assumption that Investors Care only about the Means and Variances of Returns

The first assumption of mean-variance analysis – that investors care only about the mean and variance[5] of their portfolio return and prefer higher means and lower variances – is based on the notion that investors

[5] The standard deviation, the square root of the variance, can be substituted for 'variance' in this discussion, and *vice versa*.

prefer portfolios that generate the greatest amount of wealth with the lowest risk. Mean-variance analysis assumes that the return risk, or uncertainty, that concerns investors can be summarized entirely by the return variance. Investors prefer a higher mean return because it implies that, on average, they will be wealthier. A lower variance is preferred because there will be less dispersion in the possible wealth outcomes. Investors are generally thought to be *risk-averse* – that is, they dislike dispersion in their possible wealth outcomes.

Statisticians have shown that the variance fully summarizes the dispersion of any normally distributed return. The motivation behind using variance as the proper measure of dispersion for analysing investment risk is the close relationship between the observed distribution of many portfolio returns and the normal distribution.

The Assumption that Financial Markets Are Frictionless

The second assumption of mean-variance analysis – frictionless markets – is actually a collection of assumptions designed to simplify the computation of the feasible set. In **frictionless markets**, all investments are tradable at any price and in any quantity, both positive or negative (that is, there are no short sales restrictions). In addition, there are no transaction costs, regulations or tax consequences of asset purchases or sales.

How Restrictive Are the Assumptions of Mean-Variance Analysis?

Because both of these assumptions are strong, the simplicity gained from making them comes at some cost. For example, Fama (1976) noted that the returns of individual equities are not distributed normally (although the returns of portfolios tend to be more normally distributed). Moreover, investors can generate distinctly non-normal returns – for example, by buying index options or by using option-based portfolio insurance strategies.[6] Given two portfolio strategies with the same mean and variance, an investor who cares primarily about large losses might prefer the investment with the smaller maximum loss. Unfortunately, the variance does not capture precisely the risk that these investors wish to avoid.

An additional objection to mean-variance analysis, which applies even if returns are distributed normally, is that investors do not view their portfolio's return in isolation, as the theory suggests. Most investors are concerned about how the pattern of their portfolio returns relates to the overall economy as well as to other factors affecting their well-being. Some investors, for example, might prefer a portfolio that tends to have a high return in the middle of a recession, when the added wealth may be needed, to an otherwise equivalent portfolio that tends to do well at the peak of a business cycle. The former investment would act as insurance against being laid off from work. Similarly, many investors are willing to offset some level of expected return performance to constrain their investments to meet environmental, social or governance criteria.

Because it is a collection of assumptions, the assumption of frictionless markets may or may not be critical, depending on which assumption one focuses on. Relaxing portions of this collection of assumptions often leads to the same results, but at the cost of much greater complexity. In other cases, relaxing some of these assumptions leads to different results. In most instances, however, the basic intuitive lessons from this chapter's relatively simple treatment remain the same: portfolios dominate individual assets; covariances are more important than variances for risk-return equations; and optimal portfolios, in a mean-variance sense, can generally be found if one knows the inputs.

5.3 The Efficient Frontier and Two-Fund Separation

The top half of the boundary in Exhibit 5.1 is sometimes referred to as the efficient frontier of risky assets. The **efficient frontier** represents the means and standard deviations of the mean-variance efficient portfolios. The efficient frontier is the most efficient trade-off between mean and variance. By contrast, an inefficient portfolio, such as a 100 per cent investment in, for example, research and development companies, wastes risk by not maximizing the mean return for the risk it contains. A more efficient portfolio-weighting scheme can earn a higher mean return and have the same variance (or, alternatively, the same mean and a lower variance).

The Quest for the Holy Grail: Optimal Portfolios

Based on the assumptions of the last section, the efficient frontier is the 'holy grail' – that is, the efficient frontier is where an investor wants to be. Of course, the efficient frontier contains many portfolios and which of these portfolios investors select depends on their personal trade-off between mean and variance. For example, the leftmost point

[6] Options and portfolio insurance strategies are discussed in Chapter 8.

of Exhibit 5.1's frontier is point V, which characterizes the mean and standard deviation of the minimum variance portfolio. This portfolio will attract only those investors who dislike variance so much that they are willing to forgo substantial mean returns to minimize variance. Other investors, eager to experience higher variance in exchange for higher mean returns, will select portfolios on the efficient frontier above point V in Exhibit 5.1.

Chapter 4 noted that point V, the minimum variance portfolio, is a unique portfolio weighting that can be identified by solving a set of equations. In most instances, each mean-standard deviation point on the boundary is achieved with a *unique* portfolio of assets. However, many asset combinations can achieve a given mean-standard deviation outcome on the interior of the feasible set.

Because investors who treat variance as the sole measure of risk want to select mean-variance efficient portfolios, it is useful to learn how to construct them. Identifying these special portfolios is greatly simplified by learning about an important property known as two-fund separation.

Two-Fund Separation

Two-fund separation means that it is possible to divide the returns of all mean-variance efficient portfolios into weighted averages of the returns of two portfolios. The weights may change as one moves along the efficient frontier, but the two separating portfolios remain the same.

This insight follows from the following slightly more general result.

Results

Result 5.1

All portfolios on the mean-variance efficient frontier can be formed as a weighted average of any two portfolios (or funds) on the efficient frontier.

Result 5.1 can be generalized even further. Two funds generate not only the north-west boundary of efficient portfolios but all the portfolios on the boundary of the feasible set: north-west plus south-west (or lower left boundary). This implies that once any two funds on the boundary are identified, it is possible to create *all* other mean-variance efficient portfolios from these two funds!

Exhibit 5.2 highlights four boundary portfolios, denoted A, B, C and D, and the minimum variance portfolio, V. All the portfolios on the western (or left-hand) boundary of the feasible set are weighted averages of portfolios A and B, as well as averages of C and D, B and D, or B and V, and so on. Moreover, *any* weighted average of two boundary portfolios is itself on the boundary.

Exhibit 5.2 Two-Fund Separation and the Boundary of the Feasible Set

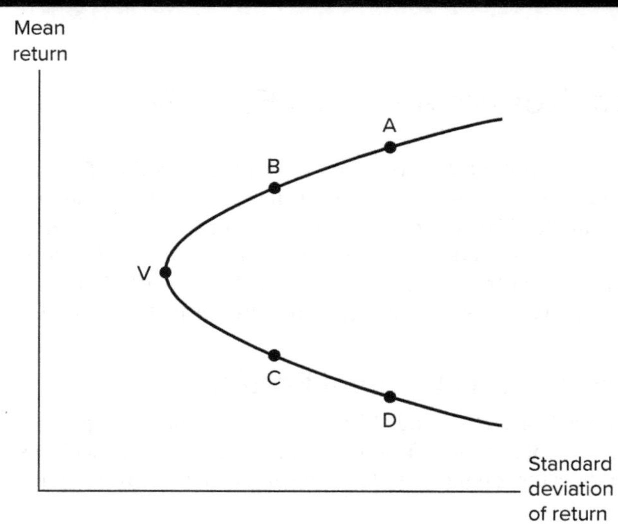

Example 5.1 illustrates two-fund separation.

Example 5.1

Two-Fund Separation and Portfolio Weights on the Boundary

Consider a mean-standard deviation diagram constructed from five assets. One of its boundary portfolios has the weights

$$x_1 = 0.2,\ x_2 = 0.3,\ x_3 = 0.1,\ x_4 = 0.1 \text{ and } x_5 = 0.3$$

The other portfolio has equal weights of 0.2 on each of the five assets. Determine the weights of the five assets for all other boundary portfolios.

Answer: The remaining boundary portfolios are described by the weighted averages of the two portfolios (or funds). Portfolio weights (0.2, 0.3, 0.1, 0.1, 0.3) describe the first fund. Weights (0.2, 0.2, 0.2, 0.2, 0.2) describe the second fund. Thus, letting w denote the weight on the first fund, it is possible to define all boundary portfolios by portfolio weights x_1, x_2, x_3, x_4 and x_5 that satisfy the equations

$$\begin{aligned} x_1 &= 0.2w + 0.2(1 - w) \\ x_2 &= 0.3w + 0.2(1 - w) \\ x_3 &= 0.1w + 0.2(1 - w) \\ x_4 &= 0.1w + 0.2(1 - w) \\ x_5 &= 0.3w + 0.2(1 - w) \end{aligned}$$

For example, if the new boundary portfolio is equally weighted between the two funds ($w = 0.5$), its portfolio weights on assets 1–5 are, respectively, 0.2, 0.25, 0.15, 0.15 and 0.25. For ($w = -1.5$), the boundary portfolio weights on assets 1–5 are, respectively, 0.2, 0.05, 0.35, 0.35 and 0.05.

Example 5.2 finds a specific portfolio on the boundary generated in the last example.

Example 5.2

Identifying a Specific Boundary Portfolio

If the portfolio weight on asset 3 in Example 5.1 is –0.1, what is the portfolio weight on assets 1, 2, 4 and 5?

Answer: Solve for the w that makes $0.1w + 0.2(1 - w) = -0.1$. The answer is $w = 3$. Substituting this value into the other four portfolio weight equations in Example 5.1 yields a boundary portfolio with respective weights of 0.2, 0.5, –0.1, –0.1 and 0.5.

One insight gained from Examples 5.1 and 5.2 is that whenever an asset has the same weight in two portfolios on the boundary, as asset 1 does in the last two examples, it must have the same weight in all portfolios on the boundary. More typically, as with other assets in these examples, observe that:

- some assets have a portfolio weight that continually increases as w increases
- other assets have a portfolio weight that continually decreases as w increases.

Although these insights help characterize the boundary, they do not precisely identify the portfolios on the boundary. This chapter will address this topic after describing how a risk-free asset affects the analysis.

5.4 The Tangency Portfolio and Optimal Investment

So far, this chapter has studied how to invest optimally by looking at the portfolios formed only from risky assets. Generally, whenever an additional asset is added to the set of investments held in a portfolio, the feasible set of the mean-standard deviation diagram expands. The risk-free asset is no exception, but it is notable for the manner in which it changes the shape of the feasible set and the efficient frontier.

Chapter 4 indicated that portfolios of a risk-free investment and a risky investment lie on a straight line in the mean-standard deviation diagram. Because of this, the addition of a risk-free asset to the analysis of risky assets not only greatly expands the feasible set but also changes the shape of the efficient frontier from a hyperbola to a straight line. This dramatically reduces our search for the optimal portfolio.

Indeed, as this chapter will show, when there is a risk-free investment, only one 'key' portfolio needs to be found because of the principle of two-fund separation (that is, the efficient frontier can be generated by only two portfolios). This was illustrated in the last section where, because the analysis precluded the existence of a risk-free investment, the two portfolios that generated the efficient frontier were necessarily risky portfolios: that is, they had positive variance. However, a risk-free investment, if one exists, will be the minimum variance investment and thus must be on the efficient frontier. This greatly simplifies the problem of the optimal investment mix because we now need to be concerned with only one efficient risky portfolio. Because of two-fund separation, this efficient risky portfolio and the risk-free asset generate the entire boundary of the feasible set.

The following analysis illustrates how to derive the weights of this efficient risky portfolio. It is appropriate to call this the **tangency portfolio** for reasons that will become clear shortly. This portfolio represents the unique optimal portfolio that contains no investment in the risk-free asset.

Optimal Investment when a Risk-Free Asset Exists

The shaded region and its black boundary in Exhibit 5.3 represent the feasible portfolios composed only of risky assets. Consider three risky asset portfolios, represented by points A, B and T, and combine each of them separately with a risk-free investment. As we saw in the last chapter, such combinations generate a straight line. Point T identifies the tangency portfolio. The line connecting the risk-free return with point T is designated as the **capital market line**, or **CML**. As we discuss below, the capital market line represents the portfolios that optimally combine all investments.

Exhibit 5.3 Combining Risky Portfolios with a Risk-Free Portfolio

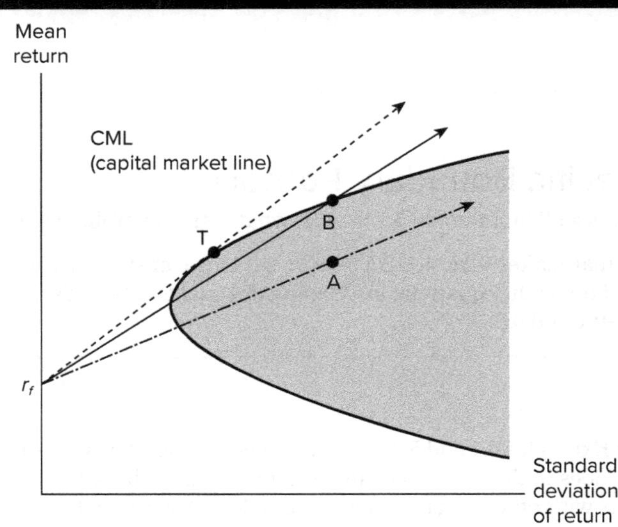

The Tangency Portfolio and the Capital Market Line

It should be clear that portfolio T is the best of the three asset portfolios since line CML, which connects T with the risk-free investment (at point r_f), lies above the other two lines. More generally, the line going through portfolio T is tangent to the efficient frontier of *risky* investments; as a result, no feasible portfolio lies northwest of this line. Investors want to invest in portfolios that have the best trade-off between mean and variance, and such portfolios all lie on this line. Result 5.2 summarizes this vital point.

Results

Result 5.2

Under the assumptions of mean-variance analysis and assuming the existence of a risk-free asset, all investors will select portfolios on the capital market line.

Result 5.2 states that the capital market line is the key to optimal investment for every investor interested in maximizing expected return for a given amount of variance risk. Extremely risk-averse investors will select a portfolio close to the risk-free asset, achieving a low expected return and a low variance for their future wealth. Investors who are only slightly risk-averse will select a portfolio high up on the CML, possibly above T if they choose to sell short the risk-free asset. They would achieve a higher expected return than more risk-averse investors, but the larger variance also makes the *possibility* of realizing large losses quite high.

The Equation of the Capital Market Line

Line CML is represented by the equation

$$\bar{R}_p = r_f + \frac{\bar{R}_T - r_f}{\sigma_T}\sigma_p \tag{5.1}$$

where $\bar{R}_T$ and σ_T are, respectively, the mean and standard deviation of the tangency portfolio's return, and r_f is the return of the risk-free asset. As the steepest-sloped line available from combining a risk-free investment with any risky investment, the CML plots the set of mean-variance efficient portfolios that can be achieved by combining the risky assets with a risk-free investment. All the portfolios above r_f on line CML – as weighted averages of the weights of portfolio T and the risk-free asset – have the same relative proportions invested in any two risky assets as portfolio T. For example, if the ratio of portfolio T's weight on asset A to its weight on asset B is 1:6, all portfolios on line CML have relative weights on these two assets in the ratio 1:6. However, the actual portfolio weights on assets A and B will scale down proportionately as one moves down line CML towards the risk-free asset.

Empirical Estimates of the Slope of the Capital Market Line

The slope of the capital market line, $(\bar{R}_T - r_f)/\sigma_T$, is a ratio that measures the trade-off between risk and return. Larger ratios imply that the financial markets offer greater expected return improvements for given increases in risk.

The historical returns of some popular investment portfolios help to characterize the numerator and denominator of the ratio. The numerator of the ratio, $(\bar{R}_T - r_f)$, is often referred to as a *risk premium*.[7] The USA has the most extended data series for returns, and it is useful to examine the slope of the capital market line for the country. Other countries have data for much shorter periods, and, as a result, calculations of risk premiums and slopes will be influenced by time period differences.

Using an average T-bill return of 3.33 per cent as the risk-free rate, Exhibit 5.4 notes that the risk premium of large US equities has been about 8.51 per cent per year while the standard deviation has been approximately 19.46 per cent per year, generating a ratio of 0.44. For a portfolio of small-capitalization equities – that is, small companies – the ratio is 0.41. Some portfolios of these investments have even steeper slopes. Hence, the capital market line based on the optimal combination of all investments should have a ratio greater than 0.44. In other words, for investments on the capital market line, an increase in standard deviation from 10 per cent to 20 per cent per year will generate more than a 4.4 per cent per year increase in expected return.

---

[7] The **risk premium** of a security or portfolio is its expected return less the risk-free return.

Exhibit 5.4 Means, Standard Deviations, Risk Premiums and Mean-Standard Deviation Slopes for US Securities 1926–2021

Portfolio	Mean return [a] (%)	Risk premium [a] (%)	Standard deviation [a] (%)	Slope
Large-cap assets	11.84	8.51	19.46	0.44
Small-cap assets	16.52	13.19	32.11	0.41
Long-term government bonds	5.13	1.8	7.68	0.23

Source: [a] © Computed using data from Stocks, Bonds, Bills & Inflation 2000 Yearbook™, Ibbotson Associates, Chicago, IL. Data for 2000–2021 come from Refinitiv. Risk premiums are based on the average T-bill return of 3.33 per cent. Means are averages of annual returns. Standard deviations are sample standard deviations of annual returns.

When using statistics like these, one must be extremely careful since the sample period is extremely important for calculations. Short-period fluctuations can severely distort the risk-return relationships for security classes. Taking the UK as an example, the FTSE 100 was 7,286 at the beginning of 2020, falling to 5,672 by March, increasing again to 6,169 by June of the same year and falling 10 per cent by October to under 5,577 before growing again to 6,407 by the end of the year. The overall mean return on the FTSE 100 was negative over this period, so the slope of the CML for UK equities using month returns was also negative! As a rule, one should use the longest possible period when undertaking an analysis of this kind.

Identification of the Tangency Portfolio

Because the tangency portfolio is generally a unique combination of individual assets and is the key to identifying the other portfolios on the capital market line, determining the weights of the tangency portfolio is an important and valuable exercise.

The Algebraic Formula for Finding the Tangency Portfolio

For all investments – efficient ones, such as the portfolios on the capital market line and the dominated investments – the following result applies.

Results

Result 5.3

The ratio of the risk premium of every asset and portfolio to its covariance with the tangency portfolio is constant: that is, denoting the return of the tangency portfolio as $\tilde{R}_T$,

$$\frac{\bar{r}_i - r_f}{\text{cov}(\tilde{r}_i, \tilde{R}_T)}$$

is identical for all assets.

Result 5.3 suggests an algebraic procedure for finding the tangency portfolio similar to the technique used to find the minimum variance portfolio. Recall that, to find the minimum variance portfolio, it is necessary to find the portfolio that has equal covariances with every asset. To identify the tangency portfolio, find the portfolio that has a covariance with each asset that is a constant proportion of the asset's risk premium. This proportion, while unknown in advance, is the same across assets and is whichever proportion makes the portfolio weights sum to 1. This suggests that, to derive the portfolio weights of the tangency portfolio:

1 Find 'weights' (they do not need to sum to 1) that make the covariance between the return of each asset and the return of the portfolio constructed from these weights equal to the asset's risk premium.

2 Then rescale the weights to sum to 1 to obtain the tangency portfolio.

A Numerical Example Illustrating How to Apply the Algebraic Formula

Example 5.3 illustrates how to use Result 5.3 to compute the weights of the tangency portfolio.

Example 5.3

Identifying the Tangency Portfolio

Suntharee Beers (from Example 4.19) wants to find the tangency portfolio of capital investments from franchising in three less-developed countries. Recall that covariances between franchising operations in India (investment 1), Russia (investment 2) and China (investment 3) were as shown in the following table.

	Covariance with		
	India	**Russia**	**China**
India	0.002	0.001	0
Russia	0.001	0.002	0.001
China	0	0.001	0.002

Find the tangency portfolio for the three investments when they have expected returns of 15 per cent, 17 per cent and 17 per cent, respectively, and the risk-free return is 6 per cent per year.

Answer:

Step 1: Solve for the portfolio 'weights' that make the portfolio's covariance with each asset equal to their risk premiums. These weights are not true weights, because they do not necessarily sum to 1. The first step is the simultaneous solution of the three equations:

$$0.002x_1 + 0.001x_2 + 0x_3 = 0.15 - 0.06$$
$$0.001x_1 + 0.002x_2 + 0.001x_3 = 0.17 - 0.06$$
$$0x_1 + 0.001x_2 + 0.002x_3 = 0.17 - 0.06$$

The left-hand side of the first equation is the covariance of a portfolio with weights x_1, x_2 and x_3 with asset 1. Thus the first equation states that this covariance must equal 0.09. The other two equations make analogous statements about covariances with assets 2 and 3.

Using the substitution method, the first and third equations can be rewritten to read

$$x_1 = 45 - \frac{x_2}{2}$$

$$x_3 = 55 - \frac{x_2}{2}$$

Upon substitution into the second equation, they yield

$$0.001x_2 = 0.01, \text{ or } x_2 = 10$$

Substituting this value for x_2 into the remaining two equations implies that

$$x_1 = 40 \text{ and } x_3 = 50$$

Step 2: Rescale the portfolio weights so that they add to 1. After rescaling, the solution for the weights of the tangency portfolio is

$$x_1 = 0.4, x_2 = 0.1 \text{ and } x_3 = 0.5$$

The Intuition for the Algebraic Formula

Why is the ratio of the risk premium to the covariance so relevant? Consider the case where the ratio of an asset's risk premium to its covariance with the candidate tangency portfolio differs from asset to asset. In this case, it is possible to slightly alter the portfolio's weights to increase its mean return while lowering its variance.

This can be done by slightly increasing the weight on an asset with a high ratio of risk premium to marginal variance while slightly decreasing the weight on an asset with a low ratio and altering the weight on the risk-free asset so that the weights add up to 1. This action implies that the candidate tangency portfolio was not on the capital market line in the first place.

A Numerical Illustration of How to Generate a Mean-Variance Improvement

Example 5.4 demonstrates how to achieve this mean-variance improvement by taking a portfolio for which the ratio condition in Result 5.3 is violated and constructing a new portfolio that is mean-variance superior to it.

Example 5.4

Developing a Superior Portfolio when Risk Premiums are not Proportional to Covariances

The return of ACME plc shares has a covariance with your investment portfolio of 0.001 per year and a mean return of 20 per cent per year, while ACYOU plc shares have a return covariance of 0.002 with the same portfolio and a mean return of 40 per cent per year. The risk-free rate is 10 per cent per year. Prove that you have not chosen the tangency portfolio.

Answer: To prove this, construct a **self-financing** (that is, zero-cost) investment of ACME, ACYOU and the risk-free asset with a negative marginal variance and a positive marginal mean. Adding this self-financing investment to your portfolio generates a new portfolio with a higher expected return and lower variance. Letting the variable m represent a small number per euro invested in your portfolio, this self-financing investment is long €0.99m in ACYOU plc, short €1.99m in ACME plc and long €1m in the risk-free asset. When added to your portfolio, this self-financing investment increases the expected return by

$$0.99m(40\%) - 1.99m(20\%) + m(10\%) = 9.8m\% \text{ per year}$$

However, if m is sufficiently small, the addition of this portfolio to the existing portfolio reduces return variance because the covariance of the self-financing portfolio of the three assets with your portfolio is

$$0.99m(0.002) - 1.99m(0.001) = -0.00001m$$

A negative covariance means a negative marginal variance when the added portfolio is sufficiently small.

The risk premium-to-covariance ratio from Result 5.3 should be the same whether the ratio is measured for individual assets, projects that involve investment in real assets, or portfolios. For example, using the tangency portfolio in place of asset i, the ratio of the tangency portfolio's risk premium to its covariance with itself (that is its variance) should equal the ratio in Result 5.3, or[8]

$$\frac{\bar{r}_i - r_f}{\text{cov}(\tilde{r}_i, \tilde{R}_T)} = \frac{\bar{R}_T - r_f}{\text{var}(\tilde{R}_T)} \tag{5.2}$$

5.5 Finding the Efficient Frontier of Risky Assets

One can reasonably argue that no risk-free asset exists. While many default-free securities such as Treasury bills are available to investors, even a one-month T-bill fluctuates in value unpredictably from day to day. Thus, when the investment horizon is shorter than a month, this asset is definitely not 'risk-free'. In addition, investors would not consider a foreign government Treasury bill a risk-free investment. A South African investor, for example, views the certain pound sterling pay-off at the maturity of a UK T-bill as risky because it must be translated into rand at an uncertain exchange rate. Even to an investor with a one-month horizon,

[8] Section 5.7 develops more intuition for equation (5.2) and (the equivalent) Result 5.3.

the purchasing power of an asset, not just its nominal value, is critical. Thus, the inflation-adjusted returns of Treasury bills are risky, even when calculated to maturity. Also, in many settings, there may be no risk-free asset. For example, a variety of investment and corporate finance problems preclude investment in a risk-free asset. For these reasons, it is useful to learn how to compute all the portfolios on the (hyperbolic-shaped) boundary of the feasible set of risky investments, detailed in Exhibit 5.1. This section uses the insights from Section 5.4 to find this boundary.

Because of two-fund separation, identifying any two portfolios on the boundary is enough to construct the entire set of risky portfolios that minimize variance for a given mean return. Use the minimum variance portfolio of the risky assets as one of the two portfolios since computing its weights is so easy. For the other portfolio, note that (with one exception)[9] it is possible to draw a tangent line from every point on the vertical axis of the mean-standard deviation diagram to the hyperbolic boundary. We shall refer to the point of tangency as the *hypothetical tangency portfolio*. Hence:

1 Select any return that is less than the expected return of the minimum variance portfolio.
2 Compute the hypothetical tangency portfolio by pretending that the return in step 1 is the risk-free return, even if a risk-free asset does not exist.
3 Take weighted averages of the minimum variance portfolio and the hypothetical tangency portfolio found in step 2 to generate the entire set of mean-variance efficient portfolios; the weight on the minimum variance portfolio must be less than 1 to be on the top half of the hyperbolic boundary.

Example 5.5 illustrates this three-step technique.

Since the financial markets contain numerous risky investments available to form a portfolio, finding the efficient frontier of risky assets in realistic settings is best left to a computer. Examples in this chapter, such as Example 5.5, which are simplified so that these calculations can be performed by hand, illustrate basic principles that you can apply to solve more realistic problems.[10]

Example 5.5

Finding the Efficient Frontier When No Risk-Free Asset Exists

Find the portfolios on the efficient frontier constructed from investment in the three franchising projects in Example 5.3 (and Example 4.19).

Answer: Solve for the portfolio 'weights' that make the portfolio's covariance with each asset equal to the asset's risk premium. (In this example, 'risk premium' refers to the expected return less some hypothetical return that you select.) Then rescale the weights so that they sum to 1. If the hypothetical return is 6 per cent, the weights (unscaled) are given by the simultaneous solution of the three equations

$$0.002x_1 + 0.001x_2 + 0x_3 = 0.15 - 0.06$$
$$0.001x_1 + 0.002x_2 + 001x_3 = 0.17 - 0.06$$
$$0x_1 + 0.001x_2 + 0.002x_3 = 0.17 - 0.06$$

The solution to these equations, when rescaled, generate portfolio weights of

$$x_1 = 0.4,\ x_2 = 0.1 \text{ and } x_3 = 0.5$$

(Not surprisingly, with a hypothetical risk-free return in this example that is identical to the risk-free return in Example 5.3, the weights in the two examples, 0.4, 0.1 and 0.5, match. Alternatively, instead of subtracting

[9] The exception is at the expected return of the minimum variance portfolio, point V in Exhibit 5.2.

[10] Many software packages, including spreadsheets, can be used to obtain a numerical solution to this type of problem. The solution usually requires inverting the covariance matrix, an important step that the computer uses to solve systems of linear equations. Then sum 'weighted' columns of the inverted covariance matrix, which is the same as taking weighted sums of the elements in each row of the matrix, where the 'weight' on column *i* is the risk premium of investment *i*. Next, rescale the 'weighted' sum of the columns, itself a column, so that its entries sum to 1. Entry *j* of the rescaled column is the weight on investment *j* in the tangency portfolio. In Microsoft Excel, the function MINVERSE inverts a matrix, and the function MMULT multiplies the inverted matrix and the column of risk premiums, which is the same as summing weighted columns.

0.06 from the expected returns on the right-hand side of the first three equations, you could have subtracted other numbers – for example, 0.04 or zero. If 0.04 had been used instead of 0.06, the right-hand side of the first three equations would be 0.11, 0.13 and 0.13, respectively, instead of 0.09, 0.11 and 0.11. If zero had been used, the right-hand side would be 0.15, 0.17 and 0.17, respectively.)

For the other portfolio, use the minimum variance portfolio (which was computed in Example 4.19 to be)

$$x_1 = 0.5,\ x_2 = 0 \text{ and } x_3 = 0.5$$

Thus the portfolios on the boundary of the feasible set are described by

$$\begin{aligned} x_1 &= 0.4w + 0.5(1 - w) \\ x_2 &= 0.1w \\ x_3 &= 0.5w + 0.5(1 - w) = 0.5 \end{aligned}$$

Those with $w > 0$ are on the top half of the boundary and are mean-variance efficient.

5.6 How Useful is Mean-Variance Analysis for Finding Efficient Portfolios?

One difficulty in employing mean-variance analysis to find mean-variance efficient portfolios is that true means and covariances are generally unobservable. The real world requires that they be estimated. Since there is an incredibly large number of assets and other investments to choose from, the full implementation of mean-variance analysis as a tool for portfolio management seems limited. First, the calculation of the necessary inputs appears to be an almost heroic undertaking, given that there can be thousands of equities traded on individual stock exchanges. Second, the estimated means and covariances will differ from the true means and covariances for virtually all of these securities because of sample period variations.

The difficulties in applying mean-variance analysis to determine the efficient portfolios of *individual* assets can be overcome with additional assumptions. When added to those of mean-variance analysis, these assumptions enable the analyst to deduce the efficient portfolios rather than compute them from historical covariances and historical means. (We shall explore one theory based on additional assumptions, the CAPM, in this chapter.)[11]

Moreover, these considerations are far less important for the applicability of mean-variance analysis to smaller types of problem, such as asset allocation across asset classes (that is, what fraction of the investor's wealth should be in bonds, assets, cash, and so on), countries (that is, what fraction of wealth should be in Africa, Asia, Europe, the United States, etc.) or industries. These simpler problems are more manageable from a computational standpoint and generally have estimated covariances and means closer to their true values because the fundamental 'assets' in this case are broad-based portfolios rather than individual assets.[12] These considerations also do not limit the use of mean-variance analysis for hedging in corporate finance.[13]

5.7 The Relation between Risk and Expected Return

A secondary benefit of identifying a mean-variance efficient portfolio is that it generates an equation that relates the risk of an asset to its expected return. Knowing the relationship between risk and expected return has a variety of applications; among these are the evaluation of the performance of professional fund managers, the

[11] A second approach, known as factor modelling, discussed in Chapter 6, is a statistical method for reducing the problem of estimating covariances to one of manageable size in order to derive insights about optimal portfolios. If the statistical assumptions correspond to reality, the covariance estimates obtained may be precise. Moreover, with this second approach, the mean returns necessary to find the optimal portfolios reduce to a problem of estimating the means of a few broad-based portfolios of large numbers of assets. As suggested in our discussion of asset allocation, mean-variance analysis is more feasible in this case.

[12] Estimates of portfolio means and standard deviations are more accurate than those for individual assets, because random estimation errors across assets tend to cancel one another in a portfolio.

[13] The practice of hedging is discussed in Chapter 22.

determination of required rates of return to set fair rates for regulated utilities and the valuation of corporate investment projects.

As an example of the last application, suppose that the UK online grocery retailer, Ocado plc, wants to expand its operations into Europe. It has estimated the expected future cash flows from such an investment. To determine whether this expansion improves the firm's value, the expected future cash flows from the expansion need to be translated into a value in today's British pounds. Ocado can compute this by discounting the expected future cash flows at the rate of return required by the financial markets on investments of similar risk.[14]

A popular assumption in estimating this required rate of return is that the expansion project has the same required return as Ocado's equity. However, it would be foolish for Ocado to estimate this required rate of return by taking the average of its historical share price returns. For example, Ocado's equity appreciated more than ten-fold in the ten years following its initial public offering in 2017. It would be highly unusual for this incredible track record to be repeated. In other words, because of its remarkable performance in its first ten years as a publicly-traded company, Ocado's average historical share price return substantially exceeds the expected rate of return required by investors looking ahead.

Because asset returns have such high variances, Ocado's problem is familiar to many corporations. If historical data provide unreliable estimates of the true expected rates of return of the equity of individual corporations, how do these companies obtain such estimates? Fortunately, the difficulty in estimating expected returns is not shared by measures of return risk. Reasonably accurate estimates of return risk can be obtained if one knows the tangency portfolio. In this case, a theory that relates the variables that one can estimate well (the risk measures) to the variables that are problematic to estimate (the expected returns of individual companies) could be helpful to companies like Ocado. Later parts of this chapter estimate Ocado's risk and expected return using such a theory.

Relevant Risk and the Tangency Portfolio

When a risk-free asset exists, the relationship between the relevant risk of an investment and its expected return can be derived directly from equation (5.2). Specifically, equation (5.3) is obtained by moving the covariance of the investment with the tangency portfolio to the right-hand side of equation (5.2):

$$\bar{r} - r_f = \frac{\text{cov}(\tilde{r}, \tilde{R}_T)}{\text{var}(\tilde{R}_T)} (\bar{R}_T - r_f) \tag{5.3}$$

(For simplicity of notation, we have dropped the i subscript.)

Equation (5.3) describes the relationship between the expected return of an investment and a measure of its risk. In this case, the relevant measure of risk is the covariance between the returns of the tangency portfolio and the investment.[15]

Example 5.6 illustrates how to apply equation (5.3).

Example 5.6

Implementing the Risk-Return Equation

Assume that the French risk-free return is 6 per cent. The return of Alcatel-Lucent shares has a covariance with the return of the tangency portfolio that is 50 per cent larger than the corresponding covariance for France Telecom equity. The expected return of France Telecom is 12 per cent per year. What is the expected return of Alcatel-Lucent shares?

Answer: The risk premium of France Telecom equity is 6 per cent per year (the expected return minus the risk-free return: 12 per cent less 6 per cent). Alcatel-Lucent's risk premium must be 50 per cent larger, or 9 per cent per year. Adding the risk-free return to this number yields 15 per cent, the expected return of Alcatel-Lucent.

---

[14] Discounting means dividing by a power of the following sum: one plus a rate of return. It is formally defined in Chapter 9.

[15] Section 5.8 discusses how this equation is altered by the absence of a risk-free asset in the economy.

Betas

The first factor in the product on the right-hand of equation (5.3) is commonly referred to as **beta** and typically denoted by the Greek letter *b*: that is,

$$\beta = \frac{\text{cov}(\tilde{r}, \tilde{R}_T)}{\text{var}(\tilde{R}_T)}$$

This notation is used because the right-hand of equation (5.3) also happens to be the formula for the slope coefficient in a regression, which commonly uses *b* to denote the slope. With this notation, equation (5.3) becomes

$$\bar{r} - r_f = \beta(\bar{R}_T - r_f) \tag{5.4}$$

The Securities Market Line versus the Mean-Standard Deviation Diagram

Panel A of Exhibit 5.5 plots the familiar mean-standard deviation diagram. For the same financial market, panel B to the right of panel A plots what is commonly known as the securities market line. The **securities market line** is a line relating two important attributes for all the investments in the financial market. In equation (5.4), it is the graphical representation of mean return versus beta. The four securities singled out in both panels are the same in both diagrams. The tangency portfolio is also the same in both panels.

Exhibit 5.5 The Relation between the Mean-Standard Deviation Diagram and a Mean Beta Diagram

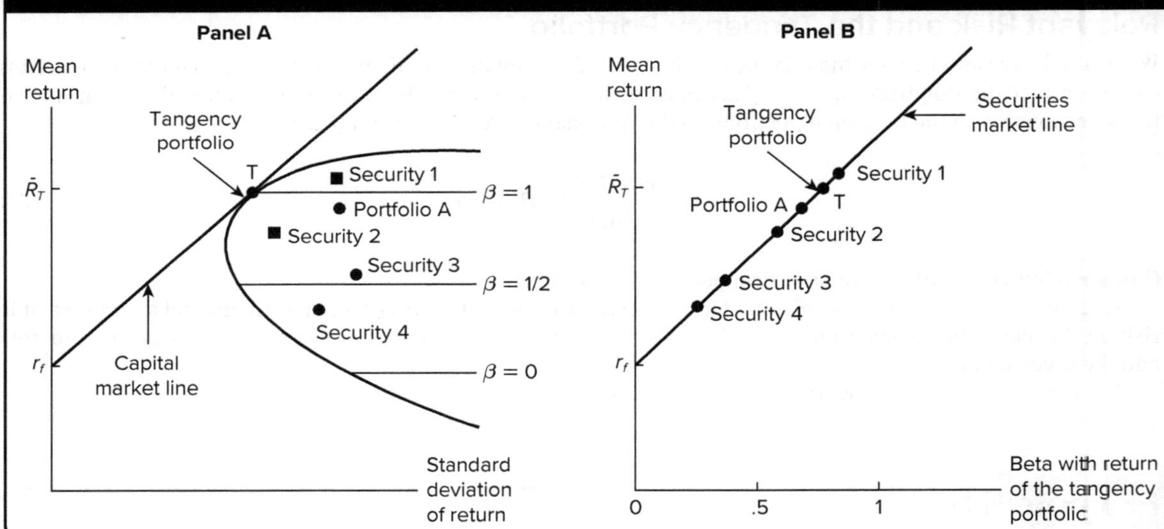

Note that, in panel B, the tangency portfolio has a beta of 1, because the numerator and denominator of the ratio used to compute its beta are identical. The risk-free asset necessarily has a beta of zero; being constant, its return cannot covary with anything. Each portfolio on the capital market line (see panel A), a weighted average of the tangency portfolio and the risk-free asset, has a location on the securities market line found by taking the same weighted average of the points corresponding to the tangency portfolio and the risk-free asset.[16] What is special about the securities market line is that all investments in panel A lie on the line: both the efficient portfolios on the capital market line and the dominated investments to the right of the capital market line.

Exhibit 5.5 purposely places the two graphs side by side to illustrate the critical distinction between the securities market line and the mean-standard deviation diagram. The difference between panels A and B is reflected on the horizontal axis. Panel A shows the standard deviation on this axis, whereas panel B shows the

[16] For this weighting of two portfolios, think of the risk-free asset as a portfolio with a weight of 1 on the risk-free asset and 0 on all the other assets.

beta with the return of the tangency portfolio, which is proportional to the marginal variance. Thus, although investments with the same mean return can have different standard deviations, as seen in panel A, they must have the same beta, as seen in panel B. For example, in panel A, all of the points on the grey line to the right of point T, labelled '$\beta = 1$', are portfolios with the same beta as the tangency portfolio. In panel B, all these portfolios – even though they are distinct in terms of their portfolio weights and standard deviations – plot at precisely the same point as the tangency portfolio. For the same reason, all points on the grey horizontal line to the right of the risk-free asset in the mean-standard deviation diagram, designated '$\beta = 0$', are portfolios with a beta of 0 even though they have positive and differing standard deviations. In the mean-beta diagram, which graphs the securities market line in panel B, these portfolios plot at the same point as r_f.[17]

Portfolio Betas

An important property of beta is found in Result 5.4.[18]

Results

Result 5.4

The beta of a portfolio is a portfolio-weighted average of the betas of its individual securities: that is,

$$\beta_p = \sum_{i=1}^{N} x_i \beta_i$$

where

$$\beta_i = \frac{\text{cov}(\tilde{r}_i, \tilde{R}_T)}{\text{var}(\tilde{R}_T)}$$

Thus, a portfolio that is 75 per cent invested in an asset with a beta of 1.2 and 25 per cent invested in an asset with a beta of 0.8 has a beta of 1.1, since

$$1.1 = 0.75(1.2) + 0.25(0.8)$$

Contrasting Betas and Covariances

Note that betas and covariances are essentially the same measures of marginal variance. Beta is simply the covariance divided by the same constant for every asset. For historical reasons and ease of estimation with regression, beta has become the more popular scaling of marginal variance. In principle, however, both are equally good as measures of marginal risk.

Marginal Variance versus Total Variance

Previously, this text defined a portfolio's risk as the variance of its return. However, to determine the expected rate of return on an investment, the relevant risk is beta (or covariance) computed with respect to the tangency portfolio.

Beta versus Variance as a Measure of Risk

Why is beta and not variance the relevant measure of risk? An analogy from economics may shed some light on this question. A central tenet of economics is that the market price of a good is equal to the marginal cost of producing one more unit of the good. Thus the total cost of production or the average cost of production does not matter for pricing; only the *marginal* cost matters. In finance, the marginal variance (that is, the covariance of an investment with the return of an investor's optimal portfolio) determines the incremental risk

[17] Because mean return and beta plot on a straight line (see panel B), all investments with the same mean return have the same beta, and all investments with the same beta have the same mean return.

[18] Because β is merely the covariance of security i with the tangency portfolio divided by a constant, Result 5.4 is a direct extension of Result 4.5 in Chapter 4: the covariance of the return of a portfolio with the return of an asset is the portfolio-weighted average of the covariances of the investments in the portfolio with the asset return.

from adding a small amount of the investment to the portfolio. Therefore it is not surprising that required rates of return on risky investments are determined by their marginal variances.

Tracking Portfolios in Portfolio Management and as a Theme for Valuation

Investment professionals often use **tracking portfolios** – portfolios designed to match specific attributes of target portfolios – for the purpose of managing an index fund at a low transaction cost. This text generalizes the concept of a tracking portfolio to develop valuation models. Understanding tracking portfolios is critical for understanding the role of portfolios and portfolio theory in corporate finance and strategy.

Uses of Tracking Portfolios in Investment Management

Investment professionals often need to **track**, that is, replicate the return characteristics of large portfolios using a relatively small number of assets. For example, many portfolio managers are asked to create portfolios that 'track' a market index in the hope of beating it. In what follows, it will sometimes be important to distinguish between perfect and imperfect tracking.

Portfolio A tracks portfolio B perfectly if the difference in the returns of the portfolios is a constant

Exhibit 5.6 illustrates the values of the Eurostoxx 50 index and a simulated tracking portfolio over two years, 2020–2022. Notice how, during some periods, there is quite a difference, known as tracking error, between the actual value of the Eurostoxx 50 and the tracking portfolio.

Exhibit 5.6 Value of the Eurostoxx 50 and its Tracking Portfolio between 2020 and 2022

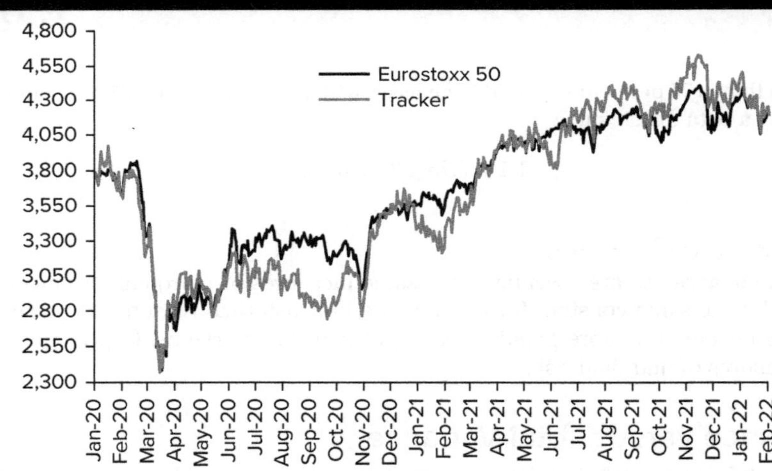

In a typical tracking strategy, the investment professional selects about 50 assets that they believe are underpriced, and then weights each of the underpriced assets in a portfolio in a way that minimizes the variance of the difference between the return of the managed portfolio and the return of the index (in our example, the Eurostoxx 50). Although such a portfolio may not track the index perfectly, it can come close to doing so. Moreover, as we shall see, tracking strategies can lead to important insights into the risk–expected return equation.

Uses of Tracking Portfolios as a Theme in this Text

One of the key themes in this text is that it is possible to think about tracking almost any investment. One can track an individual equity security, a real asset such as a factory or an index of assets. In contrast to the almost perfect tracking of broad-based investment portfolios or derivatives (which have complicated tracking strategies), tracking an individual security or real asset generally involves substantial tracking error.[19] In these

[19] The tracking of broad-based portfolios is discussed in Chapter 6; that of derivatives in Chapters 7 and 8.

cases, the best tracking portfolio is one that comes as close as possible to matching the returns of the tracked investment. This kind of tracking portfolio minimizes the variance of the tracking error.

In this chapter, where asset k is tracked with a portfolio of the risk-free asset (weight $1 - b$) and the tangency portfolio (weight b), the best tracking portfolio is the one whose tracking weight, b, is the same as the asset's beta: that is,

$$b = b_k$$

A tracking portfolio generated with this 'best' tracking weight has the same marginal variance as asset k.[20] The central insight derived from this best tracking portfolio is summarized in Result 5.5.

Results

Result 5.5

If an asset and its tracking portfolio have the same *marginal variance* with respect to the tangency portfolio, then the asset and its tracking portfolio must have the same *expected return.*

This result was partly illustrated in Exhibit 5.5, where we learned that all investments with the same beta have the same expected return. However, this beta must be computed with respect to a mean-variance efficient portfolio like the tangency portfolio. Portfolios that lie inside the efficient frontier of risky assets, like Portfolio A or Security 2 in Exhibit 5.5, will not do.

5.8 The Capital Asset Pricing Model

Implementing the risk–expected return relationship requires observation of the tangency portfolio. However, it is impossible to derive the tangency portfolio simply from observed historical returns on large numbers of assets. First, such an exercise would be extraordinarily complex and inaccurate, requiring thousands of covariance estimates. Moreover, using historical average returns to determine means, and historical return data to estimate the covariances and variances, would only create a candidate tangency portfolio that would be useless for generating forward-looking mean returns. The required rates of return derived from a risk-return relationship based on betas with respect to such a tangency portfolio would simply be the average of the historical rates of return used to find the tangency portfolio. In the case of Ocado from Section 5.7, this procedure would generate Ocado's large historical average return as its expected return which, as suggested earlier, is a bad estimate. Clearly, other approaches for identifying the true tangency portfolio are needed.

To put some economic substance into the risk-expected return relationship described by equation (5.4), it is necessary to develop a theory that identifies the tangency portfolio from sound theoretical assumptions. This section develops one such theory, generally referred to as the **Capital Asset Pricing Model (CAPM)**, which, as noted earlier, is a model of the relationship of risk to expected returns.

The central insight of the CAPM is that the variance of an asset by itself is *not* an important determinant of the asset's expected return. Instead, what is important is the market beta of the asset, which measures the covariance of the asset's return with the return on a market index, scaled by the variance of that index.

Assumptions of the CAPM

As noted earlier, the two assumptions of mean-variance analysis are that:

1. Investors care only about the mean and variance of their portfolio's returns.
2. Markets are frictionless.

To develop the CAPM, one additional assumption is needed:

3. Investors have **homogeneous beliefs**, which means that all investors reach the same conclusions about the means and standard deviations of all feasible portfolios.

[20] This conclusion, which implies that tracking portfolios with these weights are optimal hedges, is proved in Chapter 22.

The assumption of homogeneous beliefs implies that investors will not try to outsmart one another and 'beat the market' by actively managing their portfolios. On the other hand, the assumption does not imply that investors can merely throw darts to pick their portfolios. A scientific examination of means, variances and covariances may still be of use, but every person will arrive at the same conclusions about the mean and standard deviation of each feasible portfolio's return after their own scientific examination.

The Conclusion of the CAPM

From these three assumptions, theorists developed the CAPM, which concludes that the tangency portfolio must be the market portfolio. The following section details this portfolio and how practitioners implement it in the CAPM.

The Market Portfolio

The **market portfolio** is a portfolio where the weight on each asset is the market value (also called the **market capitalization**) of that asset divided by the market value of all risky assets.

In Example 5.7, the return of the market portfolio, $0.371\tilde{r}_{DT} + 0.168\tilde{r}_{BMW} + 0.461\tilde{r}_{MB}$, is the relevant return with which one computes the betas of the three assets if the CAPM is true. The betas determine the expected returns of the three assets. Of course, the world contains many investment assets, not just three assets from Germany, implying that the actual market portfolio has a weight on every asset in the world.

Example 5.7

Computing the Weights of the Market Portfolio

Consider a hypothetical economy with only three investments: the assets of Deutsche Telekom (DT), BMW, and Mercedes-Benz Group (MB). The approximate prices per share of these three assets are €13.72, €44.99 and €70.60, respectively. The approximate number of shares outstanding for the three firms are 4.367 billion (DT), 0.603 billion (BMW) and 1.057 billion (MB). What are the portfolio weights of the market portfolio?

Answer: The market capitalization of the assets is:

DT = €13.72 × 4.367 billion = €59.92 billion
BMW = €44.99 × 0.603 billion = €27.13 billion
MB = €70.60 × 1.057 billion = €74.66 billion
Total market capitalization = €161.71 billion

The market portfolio's weights (with decimal approximations) on the three assets are therefore

DT = €59.92 billion/€161.71 billion = 0.371
BMW = €27.13 billion/€161.71 billion = 0.168
MB = €74.66 billion/€161.71 billion = 0.461

With all the world's assets to consider, the task of calculating the market portfolio is obviously impractical. As claims to the real assets of corporations, all assets and corporate bonds listed on all world exchanges and those traded over the counter would have to be included, along with all real estate.

Since many of these investments are not traded frequently enough to obtain prices for them, one must use a proxy for the market portfolio. An often-used proxy is a **value-weighted portfolio**, meaning that the portfolio weight on each of its assets is proportional to the market value of that asset. Nearly every stock exchange in the world will have a value-weighted index. Examples are the S&P 500 in the USA, the FTSE All-Share Index in the UK, the Euronext 50 in the Eurozone and the FTSE/JSE Index in South Africa. Still, these proxies ignore vast markets (for example, residential and commercial property, the Tokyo Stock Exchange and the Tokyo real estate market), making them poor substitutes for the true world market portfolio.

Why the Market Portfolio is the Tangency Portfolio

Example 5.7 considered a hypothetical world that contained only three risky investments: the assets of Deutsche Telekom, BMW and Mercedes-Benz Group AG. Suppose that there is also a risk-free asset available for investment and that only two investors exist in this world: Jack and Jill.

What portfolio will Jack select? Mean-variance analysis implies that Jack will hold the tangency portfolio and either a long or a short position in the risk-free investment. The proportion of his portfolio in the risk-free investment will depend on Jack's aversion to risk. Jill will also invest in some combination of the tangency portfolio and the risk-free investment.

In Example 5.7, the market values of Deutsche Telekom, BMW and Mercedes-Benz Group AG are €59.92 billion, €27.13 billion and €74.66 billion, respectively. Since Jack and Jill are the only two investors in the world, their joint holdings of Deutsche Telekom, BMW and Mercedes-Benz Group AG must also total €59.92 billion, €27.13 billion and €74.66 billion. Therefore, it should be apparent that the tangency portfolio must contain some shares of BMW. Otherwise, neither Jack nor Jill will hold BMW shares, implying that the supply of BMW equity (€27.13 billion) would not equal its demand (€0).

If supply equals demand, and Jack and Jill both hold the tangency portfolio, then Jack must hold the same fraction of all the outstanding shares of the three assets. That is, *if* Jack holds one half of the 4.367 billion shares of Deutsche Telekom, he must also hold one half of the 0.603 billion shares of BMW and one half of the 1.057 billion shares of Mercedes-Benz Group. In this case, Jill would own the other half of all three equities. The respective proportions of their total asset investment spent on each of the three equities will thus be the market portfolio's proportions: that is, approximately 0.371, 0.168 and 0.461 (see Example 5.7).

To understand why this must be true, consider what would happen if Jack held one half of the shares of BMW but only one-third of Mercedes-Benz Group's shares. In this case, the ratio of Jack's portfolio weight on BMW to his weight on Mercedes-Benz Group would *exceed* the 0.168/0.461 ratio of their weights in the market portfolio. This implies that Jill would have to hold one half of the shares of BMW and two-thirds of the shares of Mercedes-Benz Group for supply to equal demand. But then the ratio of Jill's weight on BMW to her weight on Mercedes-Benz Group, being *less than* the 0.168/0.461 ratio of the market portfolio, would differ from Jack's, implying that Jack and Jill could not both be on the capital market line.

In short, because both Jack and Jill hold the tangency portfolio, they hold the risky investments in the exact same proportions. Because their holdings of risky assets add up to the economy's supply of risky assets, the market portfolio must also consist of risky investments allocated with these same proportions. It follows that the market portfolio is the tangency portfolio. The same conclusion, summarized in Result 5.6, is reached whether there are two investors in the world or billions.

Results

Result 5.6

Under the assumptions of the CAPM, and if a risk-free asset exists, the market portfolio is the tangency portfolio and, by equation (5.4), the expected returns of financial assets are determined by

$$\bar{r} - r_f = \beta(\bar{R}_M - r_f) \tag{5.5}$$

where $\bar{R}_M$ is the mean return of the market portfolio, and β is the beta computed against the return of the market portfolio.

Equation (5.5) is a special case of equation (5.4) with the market portfolio used as the tangency portfolio. By identifying the tangency portfolio, the CAPM provides a risk-return relationship that is not only implementable but is implemented in practice.

Result 5.6 is not significantly affected by the absence of a risk-free asset or by different borrowing and lending rates. In these cases, the market portfolio is still mean-variance efficient with respect to the feasible set of portfolios constructed solely from risky assets. Equation (5.5) remains the same, except that r_f is replaced by the expected return of a risky portfolio with a beta of zero.

Implications for Optimal Investment

In addition to the implementable relationship between risk and expected return, described by equation (5.5), the CAPM also implies a rule for optimal investment.

Results

Result 5.7

Under the assumptions of the CAPM, if a risk-free asset exists, every investor should optimally hold a combination of the market portfolio and a risk-free asset.

According to the CAPM, the significant difference between the portfolios of Jack and Jill derives entirely from their differing weights on the risk-free asset. This is demonstrated in Example 5.8.

Example 5.8

Portfolio Weights that Include the Risk-Free Asset

Consider one-month Treasury bills as the risk-free asset. Ten million T-bills are issued for €9,900 each. Jack holds 7 million T-bills, and Jill holds 3 million. If Jack has €200 billion in wealth, what are the portfolio weights of Jack and Jill, given the data in the previous example, which indicated that the aggregate wealth invested in risky assets is €161.71 billion?

Answer: The total wealth in the world is the value of the risky assets, €161.71 billion, plus the value of the T-bills, €99 billion, which sum to a total of €260.71 billion. Thus, if Jack has €200 billion, Jill has €60.71 billion. Jack spends €69.3 billion on T-bills, which makes his portfolio weight on T-bills €69.3 billion/€200 billion = 0.347. Jill spends €29.7 billion on T-bills, making her T-bill portfolio weight approximately 0.489. Thus, Jack owns €130.7 billion/€161.71 billion of the shares of the three risky equities, and Jill owns €31.01 billion/€161.71 billion. After some calculation, Jack's four portfolio weights (respectively, the risk-free asset, Deutsche Telekom, BMW and Mercedes-Benz Group AG) are approximately 0.347, 0.242, 0.109 and 0.302, and the weights for Jill are 0.489, 0.189, 0.086 and 0.236.

Note that, from Example 5.8, the last three weights in Jack's and Jill's portfolios – that is, weights of 0.242, 0.109 and 0.302 (Jack), and 0.189, 0.086 and 0.236 (Jill), on Deutsche Telekom, BMW and Mercedes-Benz Group AG, respectively – are the market portfolio's weights if they are rescaled to sum to 1. This result follows from both Jack's and Jill's portfolios being combinations of the tangency (market) portfolio and the risk-free asset.

To understand the importance of Result 5.7, think again about the inputs needed to find the tangency portfolio. With thousands of securities to choose from, an investor would need to calculate thousands of mean returns and millions of covariances. Such a daunting task would undoubtedly require a professional portfolio manager. However, the CAPM suggests that none of this is necessary; investors can do just as well by investing in the market portfolio.

The last 30 years have witnessed tremendous growth in passively managed index portfolios as vehicles for investment in the pension fund, mutual fund and life insurance industries. These portfolios attempt to mimic the return behaviour of value-weighted portfolios like the FTSE 100 or Eurostoxx 50. One of the primary reasons behind this trend was the popularization of the CAPM, a theory that suggested that the mean-standard deviation trade-off from investing in the market portfolio cannot be improved upon.

5.9 Estimating Betas, Risk-Free Returns, Risk Premiums and the Market Portfolio

To implement the risk-expected return relationship of the CAPM, it is necessary to estimate its parameters. These include the risk-free return, beta and market risk premium. We also have to know the composition of the market portfolio to compute the last two parameters.

Risk-Free or Zero-Beta Returns

Most academic studies of the CAPM have used short-term Treasury bill returns as proxies for the risk-free return. However, as Black et al. (1972), among others, have noted, this rate seems to be lower than the typical average return of a zero-beta risky asset. An alternative is to use the zero-beta expected return estimate from fitting the intercept in the risk-expected return equation to all assets.

Beta Estimation and Beta Shrinkage

Beta, as mentioned previously, is the notation for the covariance divided by the variance of the market return, because this ratio is the appropriate slope coefficient in a regression. In practice, one never obtains the true beta, but it is possible to obtain an estimate. Estimation with historical data is easy after recognizing that the ratio of covariance to variance is a slope coefficient, which can be obtained from a linear regression. The left-hand variable in the regression is the asset's return on which beta is being estimated; the right-hand side is a proxy for the market return (for example, the return on the FTSE 100 or Eurostoxx 50). Many spreadsheets and calculators have built-in regression routines that will use these data to estimate beta as the regression slope coefficient.

Example 5.9 provides real-world data and illustrates both a beta calculation and the estimation of expected return using beta.

A variety of statistical methods can improve the beta estimate. These methods usually involve taking some weighted average of 1 and the beta estimated with a software package. Parts *b* and *c* of Example 5.9 show how important it is to use the correct time period in your calculations.

Example 5.9

Estimating Beta and the Expected Return for Adyen NV

Historical monthly returns (in %) for Adyen NV and the Eurostoxx 50 Index are given below.

Date	Adyen NV	Eurostoxx 50	Date	Adyen NV	Eurostoxx 50
Feb–2019	1.90%	4.39%	Sep–2020	11.29%	–2.41%
Mar–2019	5.76%	1.62%	Oct–2020	–7.95%	–7.37%
Apr–2019	3.95%	4.86%	Nov–2020	10.67%	18.06%
May–2019	–0.66%	–6.66%	Dec–2020	18.91%	1.72%
Jun–2019	–5.85%	5.89%	Jan–2021	–9.74%	–2.00%
Jul–2019	1.24%	–0.20%	Feb–2021	11.43%	4.45%

Improving the Beta Estimated from Regression

Example 5.9 estimated the beta of Adyen NV with a simple regression of monthly Adyen returns on the corresponding returns of a proxy for the market portfolio (Eurostoxx NV). The better beta estimates, alluded to above, account for estimation error. One source of estimation error arises simply because Adyen NV's equity returns are volatile: therefore, estimates based on those returns are imprecise.[21] A second source of estimation error arises because price changes for some equities (usually the smaller capitalization equities) seem to lag the changes of other equities, either because of non-trading or because of stale limit orders – that is, limit orders that were executed as a result of the investor failing to update the order as new information about the asset became available.

[21] Just as a coin tossed 10 times can easily have a 'heads' outcome 60 per cent of the time (or six times), even if the true probability of a 'heads' outcome is 50 per cent, the average historical returns of equities are rarely equal to their true mean returns.

Date	Adyen NV	Eurostoxx 50	Date	Adyen NV	Eurostoxx 50
Aug–2019	−4.10%	−1.16%	Mar–2021	−0.65%	7.78%
Sep–2019	−8.26%	4.16%	Apr–2021	7.25%	1.42%
Oct–2019	4.14%	0.98%	May–2021	−7.40%	1.63%
Nov–2019	10.61%	2.75%	Jun–2021	9.00%	0.61%
Dec–2019	5.00%	1.12%	Jul–2021	11.11%	0.62%
Jan–2020	13.68%	−2.78%	Aug–2021	19.44%	2.62%
Feb–2020	−4.07%	−8.55%	Sep–2021	−11.68%	−3.53%
Mar–2020	−3.34%	−16.30%	Oct–2021	8.10%	5.00%
Apr–2020	16.95%	5.06%	Nov–2021	−6.24%	−4.41%
May–2020	31.27%	4.18%	Dec–2021	−5.56%	5.79%
Jun–2020	9.51%	6.03%	Jan–2022	−22.60%	−2.88%
Jul–2020	9.38%	−1.85%	Feb–2022	−8.27%	−2.27%
Aug–2020	−0.28%	3.09%			

a What is the annualized expected return required by investors in Adyen NV equity as estimated by averaging the monthly returns and multiplying by 12?

b What is the annualized expected return required by investors in Adyen NV equity as estimated from the CAPM, using the Eurostoxx 50 as the market portfolio and 0.55 per cent for the risk-free (or zero-beta) return?

c What is the annualized expected return required by investors in Adyen NV shares as estimated from the CAPM, using data solely from 2021? Assume the risk-free (or zero-beta) return is 0.55 per cent.

Answer:

a Averaging the monthly returns of Adyen NV and multiplying by 12 generates an annualized expected return of 36.95 per cent.

b The beta estimated by regressing the returns of Adyen NV on the returns of the Eurostoxx is 0.67. The annualized average return of the Eurostoxx 50 over the period is 10.20 per cent. Hence, using equation (5.5), the expected return of Adyen NV is

$$0.55\% + 0.67(10.20\% - 0.55\%) = 6.99\%$$

c The beta estimated for 2021 returns is 0.69. The annualized average return of Eurostoxx 50 using data for 2021 only is 25.06 per cent (multiply the average monthly return in 2021 by 12). Using equation (5.5), the expected return for Adyen NV is

$$0.55\% + 0.69(19.98\% - 0.55\%) = 21.04\%$$

This is much closer to the actual Adyen NV return of 25.06 per cent.

To understand the importance of estimation error, consider a case where last year's returns are used to estimate the betas of four very similar firms, denoted as firms A, B, C and D. The estimated betas are $\beta_A = 1.4$, $\beta_B = 0.8$, $\beta_C = 0.6$ and $\beta_D = 1.2$. However, because these are estimated betas, they contain estimation error. As a result, the true betas are probably not as divergent as the estimated betas. Given these estimates, it is likely that asset A has the highest beta and asset C the lowest. Our best guess, however, is that the beta of asset A is overestimated, and the beta of asset C is underestimated.[22]

The Bloomberg Adjustment

Bloomberg, an investment data service, adjusts estimated betas with the following formula:

$$\text{adjusted beta} = 0.67 \times \text{unadjusted beta} + 0.33$$

which would increase Adyen's beta from 0.67 to 0.78.

In general, the **Bloomberg adjustment** formula lowers betas exceeding 1 and increases betas under 1.

Adjusting for the Lagging Reaction of the Prices of Small Company Shares to Market Portfolio Returns

It also may be necessary to make additional adjustments to small firms' betas because the returns of the shares of small companies tend to react to market returns with a lag. This delayed reaction creates a downward bias in the beta estimates of these smaller capitalization equities since only part of the effect of market movements on the returns of these assets is captured by their contemporaneous covariances. The bias can be significant when one estimates the betas from daily returns. For this reason, analysts should avoid daily returns and instead estimate betas with weekly or monthly returns, where the effect of delayed reaction tends to be less severe. However, a paper by Handa et al. (1989) suggests that the monthly betas of small capitalization equities may also be underestimated compared with yearly betas.[23]

The following simple procedure for adjusting the betas of smaller cap assets can compensate for the lagged adjustment. First, add the lagged market return as an additional right-hand-side variable in the beta estimation regression. Then sum the two slope coefficients in the regression – the slope coefficient on the market return that is contemporaneous with the asset return and the slope coefficient on the lagged market return – to obtain the adjusted beta. One could further refine this adjusted beta with the Bloomberg technique.

A Result to Summarize the Beta Adjustments

Result 5.8 summarizes this subsection.

Results

Result 5.8

Betas estimated from standard regression packages may not provide the best estimates of an asset's true beta. Better beta estimates can be obtained by taking into account the lead-lag effect in asset returns and the fact that relatively high beta estimates tend to be overestimates and relatively low beta estimates tend to be underestimates.

Estimating the Market Risk Premium

One can estimate the expected market return by averaging the past returns of the market portfolio. It is natural to assume that the longer the time series, the better the statistical estimate of the expected market return would be. However, some empirical evidence suggests that the mean returns of market portfolios such as the FTSE 100 change over time, providing an argument for using a shorter historical time series, although the one year used in Example 5.9 may be too short. In addition, changes in the market portfolio's expected return appear to be predictable from variables such as the level of interest rates, the aggregate dividend yield and the

[22] To understand why this is true, think about your friends who scored 770 on their GMATs or SATs. While it is true that most people who score 770 are smart, scoring that high might also require some luck: thus, those with the best scores may not be quite as smart as their 770 score would indicate. Similarly, the asset with the highest estimated beta in a given group may not really be as risky as its beta would indicate. The asset with the highest estimated beta in a group is likely to have a high estimation error in addition to having a high actual beta.

[23] In the absence of these considerations, the smaller the return horizon, the more precise is the beta estimate. Our preferred compromise horizon for large firms is weekly data. An alternative is to employ daily data but make a statistical correction to the beta estimation procedure. See Scholes and Williams (1977) and Dimson (1979) for details on these statistical corrections.

realized market return over the previous three to five years. Assuming that a model predicting the market's expected return is accurate and holds over long periods, one should estimate the model's parameters with as much historical data as possible. Current levels of the predictor variables should then be used to forecast the market's expected return.

To compute the market portfolio's risk premium, subtract a risk-free return from the expected return estimate. It is also possible to estimate the risk premium directly by averaging the market portfolio's historical **excess returns**, which are its returns in excess of the risk-free return. However, this is sensible only if the risk premium is stable over time. Empirical evidence suggests that the mean of the market return itself is more stable than the mean of the excess return. Hence, we do not recommend averaging historical excess returns to estimate the risk premium.

Identifying the Market Portfolio

Of course, the entire analysis here presumes that the analyst can identify the weights of the market portfolio. Previously, our discussion focused on several common proxies for the market portfolio, which were selected because, like the market portfolio, they were value-weighted portfolios. However, they contain only a small set of the world's assets. Therefore always keep in mind that these are merely proxies and that the usefulness of the CAPM depends on whether or not these proxies work. The following section discusses the evidence about how well these proxies do as candidates for the tangency portfolio.

5.10 Empirical Tests of the CAPM

In Part III of this text, the CAPM is used as a tool for obtaining the required rates of return needed to evaluate corporate investment projects. The relevance of CAPM applications is determined by the ability of the theory to predict these required rates of return. Given the importance of this topic, financial economists have conducted hundreds of studies that examine the extent to which the expected returns predicted by the CAPM fit the data. This section describes the results of these studies.

In empirical tests of the CAPM, the returns of low-beta assets are much too high relative to its predictions, and the returns of high-beta assets are much too low. More importantly, several asset characteristics explain historical average returns much better than the CAPM beta. These characteristics include, among others, the firm's market capitalization – that is, the market value of the firm's outstanding shares, the ratio of the firm's market value to book value, or **market-to-book ratio**, and **momentum**, defined as the asset's return over the previous six months.[24] Interestingly, investment funds exist to exploit all three characteristics. The current interpretation of these empirical findings, discussed in greater depth below, is that the CAPM does not properly describe the relationship between risk and expected return.

Can the CAPM Really Be Tested?

Applications and tests of the CAPM require the use of market proxies such as the FTSE 100 because, as noted earlier, the exact composition of the market portfolio is unobservable. In an influential article, Roll (1977) pointed out that the unobservability of the market portfolio made the CAPM inherently untestable. So previous tests that used proxies for the market provided almost no evidence that could lead one to accept or reject the CAPM. Roll's logic was as follows.

1. A portfolio always exists with the property that the expected returns of all securities are related linearly to their betas, calculated with respect to that portfolio. (Equation (5.4) shows this is a mean-variance efficient or tangency portfolio.)
2. Even if the theory is wrong, the portfolio used as a market proxy may turn out to be mean-variance efficient, in which case the tests will incorrectly support the theory.
3. Alternatively, the proxy may not be mean-variance efficient, even though the theory is correct, in which case the theory is incorrectly rejected.

[24] Momentum investment strategies that rank assets based on their returns in the past 3 months, 9 months or 12 months seem to work equally well. The choice of 6 months for our discussion is arbitrary.

Applications of the CAPM in corporate finance and portfolio management share this problem of observability with the CAPM tests. Is it possible to apply a model like the CAPM if it cannot be tested because its most crucial components cannot be observed?

Although academics have debated whether the CAPM is testable, without arriving at a consensus, the model is applied by practitioners, using various portfolios as proxies for the market. In these industry applications, appropriate expected returns are obtained from any market proxy that is mean-variance efficient, whether the CAPM actually holds or, equivalently, whether the 'true' market portfolio is mean-variance efficient. Therefore the appropriateness of the various applications of the CAPM rests not on whether the CAPM holds but on whether the market proxy (such as the FTSE 100) used to apply the CAPM is mean-variance efficient. Accordingly, purported tests of the CAPM that use these proxies for the market are, in fact, tests of the mean-variance efficiency of the proxies, and are of interest for precisely this reason.

We summarize this discussion as follows.

Results

Result 5.9

Testing the CAPM may be problematic because the market portfolio is not directly observable. Applications of the theories use various proxies for the market. Although the results of empirical tests of the CAPM that use these proxies cannot be considered conclusive, they provide valuable insights about the appropriateness of the theory as implemented with the specific proxies used in the test.

Example 5.10 illustrates why it is important to test the CAPM using proxy portfolios applied in practice.

Example 5.10

Using a Proxy to Estimate the Cost of Capital

Bongout SA would like to obtain an estimate of the expected rate of return on its equity. Analysts estimate that the equity's beta with respect to the CAC 40 Index of largest French companies is about 1, and the expected rate of return on the CAC 40 is estimated to be 13.5 per cent. Is the expected return on Bongout's equity 13.5 per cent?

Answer: If the CAC 40 is a mean-variance efficient portfolio, 13.5 per cent is a reasonable estimate of Bongout's expected return, regardless of whether the CAPM is correct. If the CAC 40 is not mean-variance efficient, the estimate will not be valid.

Most tests of the CAPM have used some value-weighted portfolio of all equities in a market as a proxy for the true market portfolio. If empirical tests strongly reject the mean-variance efficiency of value-weighted portfolios, then you must be sceptical of applications that use similar portfolios to calculate expected returns. However, if these same tests provide strong support for the model, you can be comfortable with applications that use value-weighted portfolios, such as the FTSE 100. Fortunately, Levy and Roll (2010) have investigated the mean-variance efficiency of market proxy portfolios with a novel methodology. For every market proxy, they find that minor variations in sample parameters (and within estimation error bounds) can ensure that the proxy is mean-variance efficient, providing strong evidence that the CAPM is valid.

Our view is that if the portfolio used as a market proxy is mean-variance efficient, even if the theory is wrong – Roll's situation (2) – we can use the proxy even if there is no initially apparent theoretical justification for its use. The danger is that a hunt for a mean-variance efficient proxy based mainly on empirical fit and not on a sound theoretical footing is unlikely to have the same fit in the future. However, some balance between theory and empirical fit may be the best we can do.[25]

[25] This will be discussed further in Chapter 6, where enquiries into efficiency are a bit less dismal than those presented here.

Is the Value-Weighted Market Index Mean-Variance Efficient?

To understand the nature of the various tests of the CAPM, it is helpful to first contrast the model with the empirical tests that use historical data. The CAPM provides predictions about how the expected rates of return of securities relate to their betas. Unfortunately, the analyst does not observe the expected returns or the betas. The tests assume that, in large samples, the average historical return of each asset approximates its expected return, and that the estimated betas approximate the true betas. Of course, the CAPM will not hold exactly with these estimated betas and estimated expected returns. Research on the CAPM performs statistical tests to determine whether the observed deviations from the model occurred because of estimation error (for example, the averages of the realized returns may have been very different from the expected returns) or because the model was wrong.

Cross-Sectional Tests of the CAPM

In the early 1970s, extensive tests were conducted to determine whether the CAPM was consistent with the observed distribution of the returns of stock-exchange-listed equities. One of the earliest procedures to test the CAPM involved a two-step approach. First, betas were estimated with a set of time-series regressions, one for each security. (In a **time-series regression**, each data observation corresponds to a date in time: for example, the returns on HSBC and the FTSE 100 in January 2022 might be the respective left-hand-side and right-hand-side values for a single observation.) Each of these regressions, one for each security j, can be represented by the equation

$$r_{jt} = \alpha_j + \beta_j R_{Mt} + \varepsilon_{jt} \tag{5.6}$$

where

α_j = the regression's intercept
β_j = the coefficient of the regression's slope
r_{jt} = the month t return of asset j
R_{Mt} = the month t return of the value-weighted portfolio of London Stock Exchange equities
ε_{jt} = the month t regression residual for asset j

Exhibit 5.7 graphs the data and line of best fit for a beta regression involving the returns of Adyen NV shares, using the monthly data from Example 5.9. The slope of the line of best fit is the beta, which is 0.67 for Adyen.

The second step obtains estimates of the intercept and slope coefficient of a single **cross-sectional regression**, in which each data observation corresponds to an asset. (For example, Adyen NV's average return and beta might be the respective left- and right-hand-side values for a single observation.)[26] This equation can be represented algebraically as

$$\bar{r}_j = \gamma_0 + \gamma_1 \hat{\beta}_j + \gamma_2 \text{CHAR}_j + \delta_j \tag{5.7}$$

where

$\bar{r}_j$ = average monthly historical return of asset j, each j representing a stock-exchange-listed asset
β_j = estimated slope coefficient from the time-series regression described in equation (5.6)
CHAR_j = a characteristic of asset j unrelated to the CAPM, such as firm size
γ_s = intercept and slope coefficients of the regression
δ_j = asset j regression residual.

The second step regression, equation (5.7), should have the following features if the CAPM is true.

- The intercept, γ_0, should be the risk-free return.
- The slope, γ_1, should be the market portfolio's risk premium.
- γ_2 should be zero since variables other than beta (for example, return variance or firm size), represented as CHAR_j, should not explain the mean returns once beta is accounted for.

[26] Fama and MacBeth (1973) used an innovative procedure to overcome a bias in statistical inference arising from correlated residuals in the cross-sectional regression. This involves running one cross-sectional regression for each observation in time, and averaging the slope coefficients. Also, these researchers ran their tests on beta-grouped portfolios rather than on individual assets.

Exhibit 5.7 Adyen NV: Monthly Returns (February 2019–February 2022)

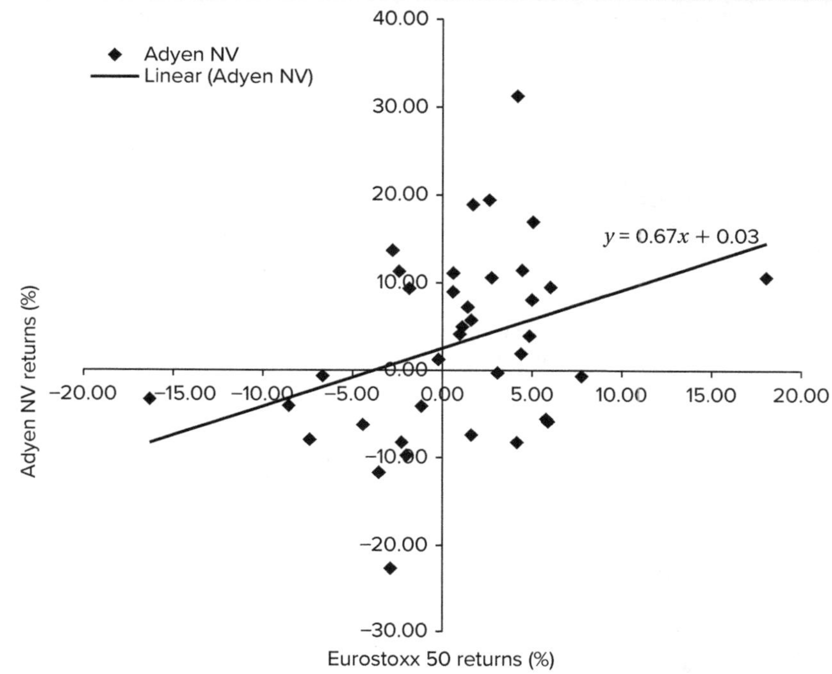

Exhibit 5.8, which illustrates hypothetical data and fit for the cross-sectional regression, indicates data consistent with the CAPM. In particular, the intercept is the risk-free return, and the slope is the risk premium of the market portfolio. In contrast, the four panels in Exhibit 5.9 portray data that are inconsistent with the theory: in panel A, the intercept is wrong; in panel B, the slope is wrong; in panel C, securities appear to lie on a curve rather than on a line; in panel D, the deviations of the mean returns from the securities market line are plotted against firm size. The evidence of a relationship between returns (after accounting for beta) and firm size would imply a rejection of the CAPM.

Exhibit 5.8 Second Step Regression Data Consistent with the CAPM

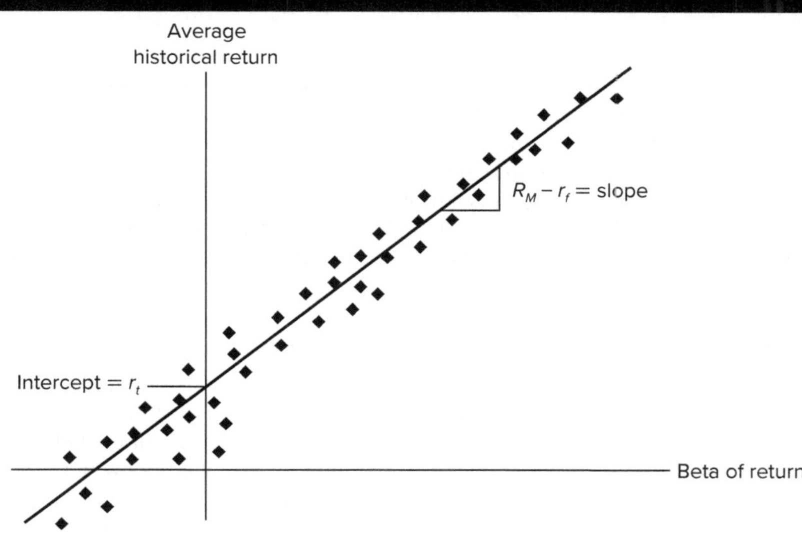

Exhibit 5.9 Second Step Regression Data Inconsistent with the CAPM

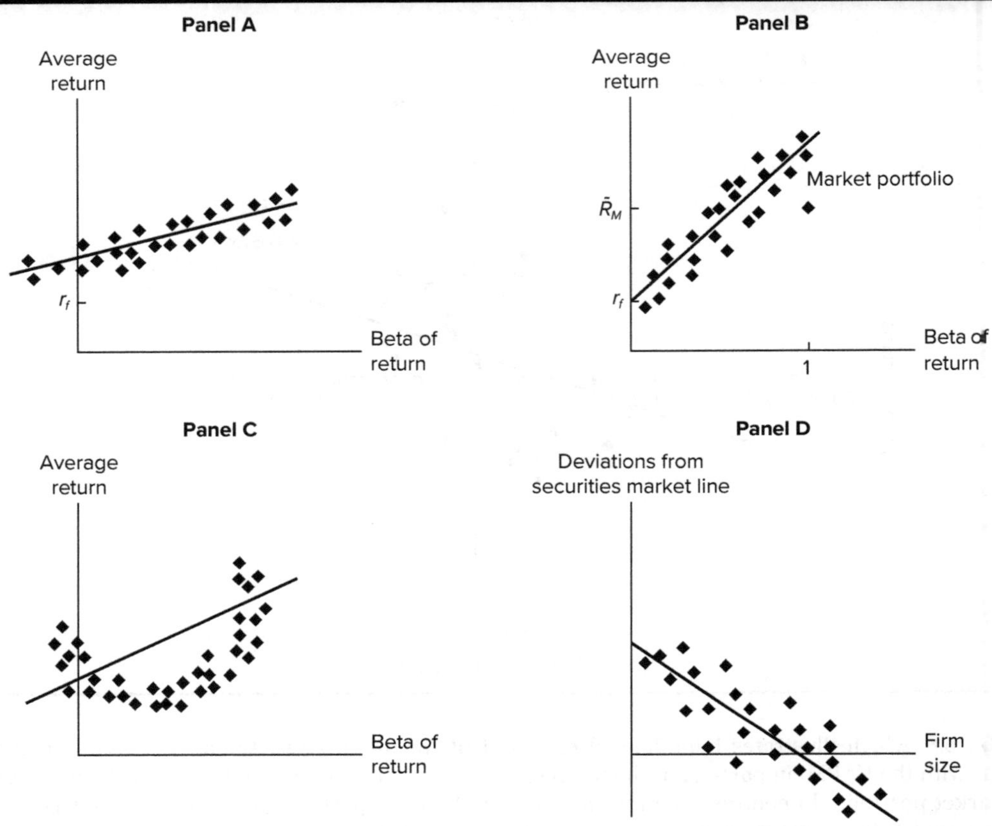

Time-Series Tests of the CAPM

The second set of CAPM tests, introduced by Black et al. (1972), examine the restrictions on the intercepts of time-series market model regressions. Consider the regression

$$r_{jt} - r_f = \alpha_j + \beta_j(R_{Mt} - r_f) + Z_{jt} \tag{5.8}$$

It is substantially identical to the regression in equation (5.6),[27] except that excess returns are used instead of returns. The CAPM implies that the intercept, αj, in equation (5.8) is zero for every asset or portfolio. Researchers have tested the CAPM with this approach, using the returns of portfolios formed from characteristics such as the security's prior beta, firm size and the ratio of the market value of an asset to its book value to estimate the coefficients in equation (5.8). For example, one could test the CAPM by regressing the excess returns of a portfolio consisting of the 100 equities in a market with the smallest capitalization on the excess returns of a market proxy. The CAPM predicts that the intercepts from such regressions should be zero. However, if the CAPM underestimates the returns of small-capitalization assets, the intercepts in regressions that involve small company assets will be positive.

Results of Cross-Sectional and Time-Series Research

Both time-series and cross-sectional tests find evidence generally unsupportive of the CAPM. Commensurate with the model's importance to modern finance theory, the number of studies that test the CAPM is vast, and full coverage is beyond the scope of this text. However, in this section, we will consider the most important recent studies that look specifically at beta, and in the next chapter, we will review important recent research on other risk factors.

[27] Betas estimated from the two regressions are almost always nearly identical.

The first empirical tests of the CAPM occurred in the 1970s and supported the model. Using data from US stock markets, researchers (e.g. Black 1972; Fama and French 1973) showed that the average return on a portfolio of stocks was positively related to the beta of the portfolio – a finding consistent with the CAPM. Some evidence, however, was less consistent with the CAPM. For example, Black (1972) found that the Security Market Line was too flat, and the zero-beta portfolio had a higher average return than the risk-free asset.

Although a large body of empirical work developed in the following decades, often with varying results, the CAPM was not seriously called into question until the 1990s. Two papers by Fama and French (1992, 1993) found that, for US firms, the relationship between average return and beta was virtually non-existent and that the average return on a security is negatively related to both the firm's price-earnings (PE) ratio and the firm's market-to-book (MB) ratio. Other research has shown that securities with strong past price momentum tend to have higher returns in the near future (Carhart 1997).

Fama and French (2015, 2016, 2017) extended their earlier analysis by adding two additional factors to the cross-sectional beta regression. The first variable (RMW) relates to profitability and is captured by the average return on the strongest operating profitability portfolios minus the average return on the weakest operating profitability portfolios. Profitability is measured as *'revenue minus the cost of goods sold, minus selling, general, and administrative expenses, minus interest expense, all divided by book equity'*. The second variable is CMA, which captures the average return on the most conservative investment portfolios minus the average return on the most aggressive investment portfolios. Investment is measured as *'the change in total assets from the fiscal year ending in year $t-2$ to the fiscal year ending in $t-1$, divided by $t-2$ total assets'*.

Fama and French (2016) provide additional damning evidence on the power of beta. Specifically, average returns are positively related to RMW and negatively associated with CMA, virtually removing the explanatory power of beta in average US returns. Fama and French (2017) subsequently tested their model on European stock returns and found that the profitability factor (RMW) has explanatory power for average returns, but the investment factor (CMA) adds little information. If confirmed by other research, these studies would be quite damaging to the CAPM. After all, the CAPM states that the expected returns on equities should be related only to beta and not to other factors such as PE, MB, momentum or RMW.

Other factors have also been found to be important. Medhat and Schmeling (2022) report on a short-term momentum effect that is just as important as Carhart's (1997) price momentum factor. Sorting companies by the previous month's return and turnover, Medhat and Schmeling (2022) report significant reversal for low-turnover stocks and momentum for high turnover stocks.

We have already shown that, in the absence of frictions, a rational risk-averse investor will construct a portfolio that combines both the risk-free asset and optimal market portfolio, and this maximises the portfolio's reward to risk ratio. The risk-free asset or market portfolio weights may be positive or negative but must add up to 1. Therefore, if the weight of one asset is negative, the other asset in the portfolio must have a weight greater than 1. This is equivalent to borrowing in one asset (negative weighting) and investing the borrowed funds in the other asset (weighting greater than 1). Such a portfolio is known as leveraged. Moreover, a portfolio with a negative weighting on the risk-free asset will have a higher expected return than the market portfolio.

Frazzini and Pederson (2014) show that if investors are constrained in their ability to borrow but wish to achieve a return higher than the market (portfolio beta > 1), they must construct a sub-optimal portfolio that is overweighted in high-beta assets. This unlevered high-beta portfolio will necessarily be dominated by a levered portfolio with the same beta. Moreover, because high-beta assets are in excess demand, their prices will be too high, leading to low risk-adjusted returns and a flatter security market line than would be expected. Hong and Sraer (2016) found that if the overpricing was high enough, expected returns might actually decrease with beta.

If there are enough investors with borrowing constraints, unconstrained arbitrageurs can exploit the overpriced high-beta stocks and 'bet against beta'. The *betting against beta* portfolio would be short (negative portfolio weight) in high beta assets and be long (weighting greater than 1) in low-beta assets. Frazzini and Pederson (2014) found that such a portfolio generated significantly positive risk-adjusted returns in twenty countries, including the UK, US, and all European states, except Austria. Exhibit 5.10 presents the Sharpe (risk-reward) ratios for selected countries for this strategy.

Many researchers have criticized the research carried out by studies like Fama and French (2015, 2016, 2017) and Frazzini and Pederson (2014). First, although Fama and French and Frazzini and Pederson (2014) cannot reject the hypothesis that average returns are unrelated to beta, they also cannot reject the hypothesis that average returns are related to beta exactly as specified by the CAPM. In other words, although 50 plus years of data seem like a lot, there may simply not be enough observations to test the CAPM properly. Second, PE, MB, momentum, RMW, BAB are only five of an infinite number of possible factors. Thus the relationship between average return and these variables may be spurious, being nothing more than the result of data mining or methodological issues.[28] Third, stock returns are positively related to beta over a very long period (more than seventy years). There appears to be no compelling reason for emphasizing a shorter period than this

Exhibit 5.10 Sharpe Ratios of Betting against Beta (BAB) Portfolios across Selected Countries

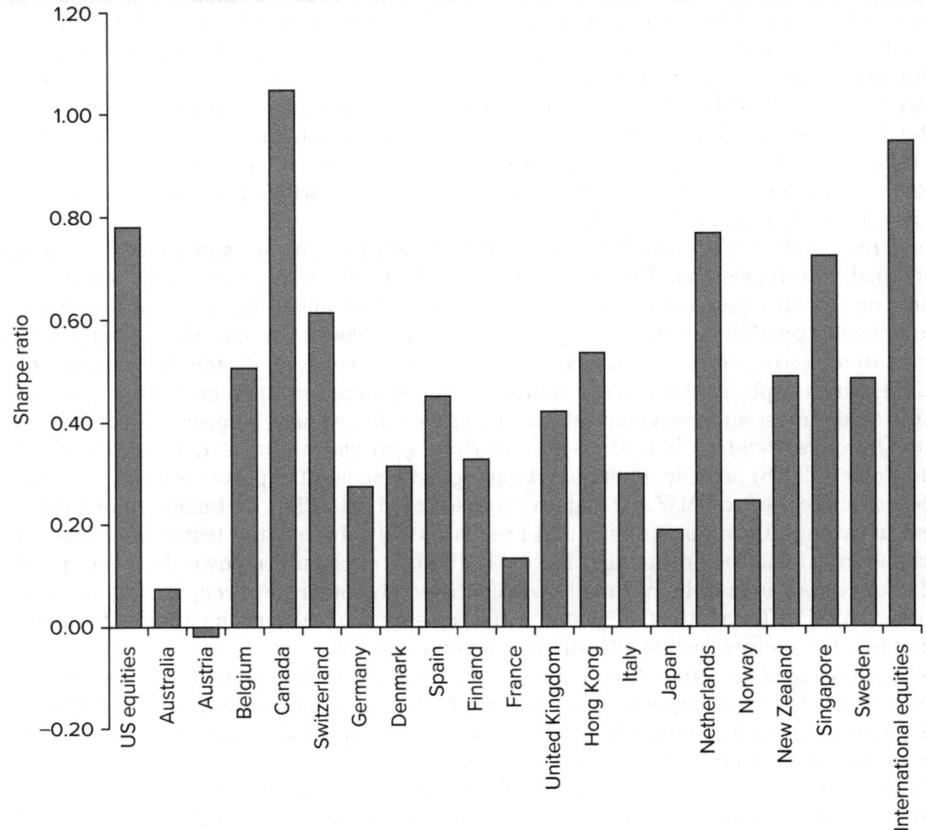

Source: Adapted from Figure 2, Frazzini, A., & Pedersen, L. H. (2014). Betting against beta. Journal of Financial Economics, 111(1), 1-25. Betting against beta (BAB) Sharpe ratios by country. Exhibit 5.10 shows annualized Sharpe ratios of BAB factors across selected countries. To construct the BAB factor, all securities are assigned to one of two portfolios: low beta and high beta. Securities are weighted by the ranked betas, and the portfolios are rebalanced every calendar month. Both portfolios are rescaled to have a beta of one at portfolio formation. The BAB factor is a self-financing portfolio that is long the low-beta portfolio and shorts the high-beta portfolio. Sharpe ratios are annualized.

one. Fourth, average returns are positively related to beta over shorter periods when annual data, rather than monthly data, are used to estimate beta. There appears to be no compelling reason for preferring either monthly data over annual data, or vice versa. Thus, we believe that although findings from cross-sectional tests are quite intriguing, we cannot view them as the final word.

Result 5.10 summarizes the results of this subsection.

Results

Result 5.10

Research using historical data indicates that cross-sectional differences in asset returns are related to several characteristics, including market capitalization, market-to-book ratios, momentum and a betting against beta factor. Controlling for these factors, these studies find little or no relationship between the CAPM beta and returns over the historical periods studied.

[28] Despite the research attracting thousands of citations, Novy-Marx and Velikov (2021) criticise Frazzini and Pederson (2014) on a number of levels and argue that the Frazzini and Pederson (2014) methodology cannot 'be achieved in practice', making the study hypothetical in nature.

Interpreting the CAPM's Empirical Shortcomings

There are two explanations for the poor ability of the CAPM to explain average asset returns. The first has to do with the possibility that the various proxies for the market portfolio do not fully capture all the relevant risk factors in the economy. According to this explanation, firm characteristics, such as size and market-to-book ratios, are highly correlated with the sensitivities of assets to risk factors not captured by proxies for the market portfolio. For example, if investors believe that large firms benefit more than small firms from economic factors that lead to increased layoffs or wage reductions, they may prefer investing in the assets of the large firms, even if the expected returns of large firms are lower.

A second explanation of the CAPM's poor performance is that it is simply a false theory because investors have behavioural biases against classes of assets that have nothing to do with the mean and marginal risk of the returns on assets. The smaller capitalization assets and assets with lower market-to-book ratios may require a higher expected rate of return if investors shy away from them for behavioural reasons. For example, firms with low market-to-book ratios are generally considered to have poor prospects. Indeed, that is why their market values are so low relative to their book values. By contrast, firms with high market-to-book ratios are considered to be those with the brightest futures.

One behavioural explanation for the higher returns of the distressed, or near bankrupt, firms is that some portfolio managers find it more costly to lose money on distressed firms. There is a saying that 'portfolio managers can't get fired buying Apple shares'. The basic argument is that if portfolio managers buy Apple shares and then lose money, it isn't their fault because the conventional wisdom is that the firm is an excellent investment. Contrast this with an investment that has fallen precipitously in value and is under threat of bankruptcy. Examples abound of firms like this. Money managers would find it very difficult to justify investing in firms like these because they would probably be fired if the firm did go bankrupt. What this means is that a money manager might find it riskier, from a personal perspective, to buy a distressed company's shares, even if the actual return distribution of the shares is similar to that of a financially healthy firm. If this were true, the distressed firm would require a higher expected rate of return.

Are These CAPM Anomalies Disappearing?

There is evidence to suggest that at least some of the anomalies described in this section are disappearing. For example, Zaremba et al. (2020) investigate 53 anomalies across 64 countries from 1973 to 2018. Over the longer term, they found that anomalies presented in the literature can lead to profitable trading strategies. However, Zaremba et al. (2020) present convincing evidence that these strategies are no longer profitable, especially in developed markets. The authors consider several different explanations for this pattern, such as the market learning from and adapting to academic findings and changing profitability, but eventually, they put the disappearing anomalies down to increased capital market efficiency, which, in turn, leads to lower return predictability across the world.

Variations of the CAPM

The CAPM relates an individual security's expected return to the expected return on the market portfolio through its systematic risk, beta. Beta measures the sensitivity of an investor's wealth to movements in the underlying market portfolio. Many academics have argued that wealth, on its own, is not important in pricing securities. Instead, it is the effect of an investment on an investor's consumption, or spending power, that is relevant. So, the more an investment makes consumption riskier, the higher should be its expected returns.

This view has led to a variation of the CAPM, known as the Consumption Capital Asset Pricing Model, or CCAPM. In the CAPM, systematic risk, or beta, measures the covariance of security returns with market returns. However, the CCAPM beta is slightly more complicated. We express the CCAPM as follows:

$$\underbrace{\bar{R}}_{\substack{\text{expected}\\ \text{return}\\ \text{on a security}}} = \underbrace{R_f}_{\substack{\text{risk-free}\\ \text{rate}}} + \underbrace{\beta_c}_{\substack{\text{consumption}\\ \text{beta of the}\\ \text{security}}} \times \underbrace{(\bar{R}_{mt} - R_f)}_{\substack{\text{difference between}\\ \text{expected return on market}\\ \text{and risk-free rate}}} \qquad (5.9)$$

where the consumption beta, β_c, is equal to:

$$\beta_C = \frac{\text{cov}(\overline{R}, \text{consumption growth})}{\text{cov}(\overline{R}_M, \text{consumption growth})} \quad (5.10)$$

In the CCAPM, if a security has a higher expected return when consumption growth is higher, its consumption beta will be high. Similarly, a low covariance between security returns and consumption growth will lower CCAPM beta.

Another variation in the CAPM recognizes that not all of an individual's wealth comes from financial assets. In recent years, many people increased their wealth through investment in non-financial **human capital** assets such as housing and property. This has been particularly true in Europe (mainly the UK, Ireland and Eastern Europe), where property values have been rapidly growing each year. The same high property growth rates have been observed in China, Hong Kong and India. The human capital CAPM, or HCAPM, incorporates both sources of wealth creation. According to the HCAPM, the return on the expected market portfolio is a linear combination (weighted by the relative investment of assets) of the expected return on the underlying financial portfolio and the underlying non-financial portfolio. If δ represents the fraction of total wealth invested in non-financial assets (or human capital), and $\overline{R}_{NF}$ and $\overline{R}_F$ represent the expected returns on non-financial and financial assets respectively, the expected return on the market is given by:

$$\overline{R}_M = \delta\overline{R}_{NF} + (1 - \delta)\overline{R}_F \quad (5.11)$$

The expected return on financial assets is simply the market portfolio of the CAPM. In contrast, the expected return on non-financial assets is typically growth in average earnings or labour income. The HCAPM has the same form as the standard CAPM. However, if the expected return on the market portfolio is disaggregated into its two components, the expected return on a security can be expressed as a linear function of its financial and non-financial betas. In this form, the expected return on a security is shown as follows:

$$\overline{R} = \beta_0 + \beta_F\overline{R}_F + \beta_{NF}\overline{R}_{NF} \quad (5.12)$$

In recent years, a variant of the CCAPM, known as the extrapolative capital asset pricing model, or X-CAPM, has emerged as an interesting model to explain aggregate stock returns. The model's basic premise is that a subgroup of all investors form expectations of future stock returns based on past return information. When both groups of investors are combined in a CCAPM-type specification, the model captures many of the observed behaviours of stock returns.

To understand how the X-CAPM model works in practice, consider the dividend pricing model:

$$P_0 = \frac{Div_1}{r} \Rightarrow \frac{Div_1}{r} - P_0 = 0 \quad (5.13)$$

If $\frac{Div_1}{r} > P_0$, we would expect prices to increase and stock returns to be positive. The converse is true for $\frac{Div_1}{r} < P_0$ and prices will fall, leading to negative returns. If there is a proportion of investors who extrapolate historical information to form expectations of future returns, then the difference $\frac{Div_1}{r} - P_0$ will be autocorrelated over time. Barberis et al. (2015) found that this difference measure was a good predictor of future share price returns, and Barberis et al. (2018) found that the extrapolation concept can also explain pricing bubbles in stock markets.

Although both the CCAPM and HCAPM are theoretically sound, the models do not tend to be used in practice because of difficulties in using the models with actual data. For example, the CCAPM requires reliable data on total consumption growth, and the HCAPM utilizes data on non-financial wealth, both of which are rarely available on a continuing basis. For this reason, the standard CAPM is the most commonly used theoretical model in corporate finance.

Real-World Insights

The CAPM assumes that an investor has the entire universe of assets to choose from, and this leads to the optimal market portfolio. However, when an investor voluntarily chooses to restrict their investment choices to a subset of assets, the resultant market proxy will be less efficient than the market portfolio, resulting in a lower Sharpe (reward to risk) ratio. What does this mean for those who wish to prioritise environmental, societal or governance concerns? Are socially aware investors destined to bear lower returns or greater portfolio risk than their non-ESG promoting counterparts? This thorny issue has spawned several papers (e.g. Baker et al. 2018; Idzorek et al. 2021; Pederson et al. 2021; Zerbib 2020) attempting to justify why restricted portfolios, like ESG funds, may lead to optimal portfolio formation even though the full range of investment assets is unavailable.

An interesting new model is the Popularity Asset Pricing Model (PAPM) proposed by Idzorek et al. (2021). The PAPM builds on Fama and French (2007), who proposed two additional risk factors to the standard CAPM: 'Disagreement' and 'Tastes'. 'Disagreement' and 'Tastes' correspond to heterogeneous expectations and permanent investor preferences for specific stocks, respectively, and reflect today's world where investors have created strong movements for sustainable investment. Given the increasing popularity of sustainability issues and climate change, investor preferences for firms with strong ESG credentials will lead to higher demand for this market segment resulting in permanently higher prices and lower expected returns for these ESG equities. The opposite is true for sin stocks, such as firms involved in gambling, weapons and extractive industries, where investor disdain will lead to lower prices and higher expected returns. In such an environment, there will be no single optimal portfolio, and each investor will have their own personalised optimal portfolio based on individual tastes. Idzorek et al. (2021) argue that the CAPM is a special case of the PAPM where disagreement is zero (homogeneous expectations), and everyone has the same taste for securities. When this happens, the PAPM collapses to the CAPM.

5.11 Summary and Conclusions

This chapter analysed various features of the mean-standard deviation diagram, developed a condition for deriving optimal portfolios and showed that this condition has implications for valuing financial assets. The chapter also showed that the beta used in this valuation relationship, the relationship between risk and expected return, is an empty concept unless it is possible to identify the tangency portfolio. The Capital Asset Pricing Model is a theory that identifies the tangency portfolio as the market portfolio, making it a powerful tool for valuing financial assets. As later chapters illustrate, it is also useful for valuing real assets.

Valuation plays a significant role in corporate finance. Part III will discuss that when firms evaluate capital investment projects, they need to estimate the project's required rate of return. Moreover, valuation often plays a crucial role in determining how corporations finance their new investments. Many firms are reluctant to issue equity when they believe that their equity is undervalued. To value their equity, they need an estimate of its expected rate of return; the Capital Asset Pricing Model is currently one of the most popular methods used to determine this.

The empirical tests of the CAPM contradict its predictions. Indeed, the most recent evidence fails to find a positive relationship between the CAPM beta and average rates of return on equities, finding instead that equity characteristics, such as firm size and market-to-book ratios, provide very good predictions of an equity's return. Does this mean that the CAPM is a useless theory?

One response to the empirical rejection of the CAPM is that there are additional aspects of risk not captured by the market proxies used in the CAPM tests. If this is the case, the CAPM should be used but augmented with additional factors that capture those aspects of risk. Chapter 6, which discusses multifactor models, considers this possibility. Another possibility is that the model is fundamentally unsound and that investors do not act nearly as rationally as the theory suggests. If this is the case, however, investors should find beta estimates even more valuable because they can be used to construct portfolios that have relatively low risk without giving up anything in the way of expected return. Finally, the empirical tests carried out on the CAPM are possibly biased, resulting in an incorrect rejection of the null hypothesis of a zero CAPM intercept when it is true.

This chapter provides a unique treatment of the CAPM in its concentration on the more general proposition that the CAPM 'works' as a useful financial tool if its market proxy is a mean-variance efficient portfolio and does not work if the proxy is a dominated portfolio. To date, the empirical evidence has suggested that the proxies used for the CAPM appear to be dominated. However, this does not preclude the possibility that some modification of the proxy may ultimately prove to be useful. As you will see in Chapter 6, research along these lines currently appears to be making great strides.

We should also stress that testing the CAPM requires examining data in the fairly distant past, to a period before stock market professionals, portfolio managers and corporations used the CAPM. However, corporations interested in valuing either investment projects or their own assets have no interest in the historical relevance of the CAPM; they are interested only in whether the model provides reasonable estimates of current required rates of return. As economists, we like to think that investors act as if they are trained in the nuances of modern portfolio theory, even though beta was a relatively unknown Greek letter to investors of the 1960s. However, as educators, we like to believe that we do make a difference and that our teaching and research have made a difference. Given those beliefs, we at least want to entertain the possibility that current required rates of return reflect the type of risk suggested by the CAPM, even if rates of return did not reflect this type of risk in the past. Some evidence of this is that the size effect has dramatically diminished, if it has not disappeared entirely, since the early 1980s, when practitioners began to focus on the academic research in this subject. The same is true of the market-to-book effect.

Key Concepts

Result 5.1: All portfolios on the mean-variance efficient frontier can be formed as a weighted average of any two portfolios (or funds) on the efficient frontier.

Result 5.2: Under the assumptions of mean-variance analysis and assuming the existence of a risk-free asset, all investors will select portfolios on the capital market line.

Result 5.3: The ratio of the risk premium of every asset and portfolio to its covariance with the tangency portfolio is constant: that is, denoting the return of the tangency portfolio as $\tilde{R}_T$,

$$\frac{\bar{r}_i - r_f}{\text{cov}(\tilde{r}_i, \tilde{R}_T)}$$

is identical for all assets.

Result 5.4: The beta of a portfolio is a portfolio-weighted average of the betas of its individual securities: that is,

$$\beta_p = \sum_{i=1}^{N} x_i \beta_i$$

where

$$\beta_i = \frac{\text{cov}(\tilde{r}_i, \tilde{R}_T)}{\text{var}(\tilde{R}_T)}$$

Result 5.5: If an asset and its tracking portfolio have the same *marginal variance* with respect to the tangency portfolio, then the asset and its tracking portfolio must have the same *expected return.*

Result 5.6: Under the assumptions of the CAPM, and if a risk-free asset exists, the market portfolio is the tangency portfolio and, by equation (5.4), the expected returns of financial assets are determined by

$$\bar{r} - r_f = \beta(\bar{R}_M - r_f) \tag{5.5}$$

where $\bar{R}_M$ is the mean return of the market portfolio, and β is the beta computed against the return of the market portfolio.

Result 5.7: Under the assumptions of the CAPM, if a risk-free asset exists, every investor should optimally hold a combination of the market portfolio and a risk-free asset.

Result 5.8: Betas estimated from standard regression packages may not provide the best estimates of an asset's true beta. Better beta estimates can be obtained by taking into account the lead-lag effect in equity returns and the fact that relatively high beta estimates tend to be overestimates and relatively low beta estimates tend to be underestimates.

Result 5.9: Testing the CAPM may be problematic because the market portfolio is not directly observable. Applications of the theories use various proxies for the market. Although the results of empirical tests of the CAPM that use these proxies cannot be considered conclusive, they provide valuable insights about the appropriateness of the theory as implemented with the specific proxies used in the test.

Result 5.10: Research using historical data indicates that cross-sectional differences in asset returns are related to several characteristics, including market capitalization, market-to-book ratios, momentum and a betting against beta factor. Controlling for these factors, these studies find little or no relationship between the CAPM beta and returns over the historical periods studied.

Key Terms

Exercises

5.1 Here are some general questions and instructions to test your understanding of the mean standard deviation diagram.

a Draw a mean-standard deviation diagram to illustrate combinations of a risky asset and the risk-free asset.

b Extend this concept to a diagram of the risk-free asset and all possible risky portfolios.

c Why does one line, the capital market line, dominate all other possible portfolio combinations?

d Label the capital market line and tangency portfolio.

e What condition must hold at the tangency portfolio?

Exercises 5.2–5.9 use the following information about the hypothetical mean returns and covariances for three German companies: Deutsche Lufthansa, Volkswagen and BMW.

Company	Correlation with					
	Deutsche Lufthansa	Volkswagen	BMW	Expected return (%)	Historical return (%)	Standard deviation (%)
Deutsche Lufthansa	1	−0.23	0.58	17	12.8	37.0
Volkswagen	−0.23	1	−0.18	12	15.9	76.3
BMW	0.58	−0.18	1	40	23.1	35.8

5.2 Compute the tangency portfolio weights, assuming that a risk-free asset yields 5 per cent.

5.3 How does your answer to exercise 5.2 change if the risk-free rate is 3 per cent? 7 per cent?

5.4 Draw a mean-standard deviation diagram and plot Deutsche Lufthansa, Volkswagen and BMW on this diagram, as well as the three tangency portfolios found in exercises 5.2 and 5.3.

5.5 Show that an equally weighted portfolio of Deutsche Lufthansa, Volkswagen and BMW can be improved upon with marginal variance-marginal mean analysis.

5.6 Repeat exercises 5.2 and 5.3, but use a spreadsheet to solve for the tangency portfolio weights of Deutsche Lufthansa, Volkswagen and BMW in the three cases. The solution of the system of equations requires you to invert the matrix of covariances above and then to post-multiply the inverted covariance matrix by the column of risk premiums. The solution should be a column of cells, which needs to be rescaled so that the weights sum to 1.

5.7 a Compute the betas of Deutsche Lufthansa, Volkswagen and BMW with respect to the tangency portfolio found in exercise 5.2.

b Then compute the beta of an equally weighted portfolio of the three assets.

5.8 Using the fact that the hyperbolic boundary of the feasible set of the three assets is generated by any two portfolios:

a Find the boundary portfolio that is uncorrelated with the tangency portfolio in exercise 5.2.

b What is the covariance with the tangency portfolio of all inefficient portfolios with the same mean return as the portfolio found in part *a*?

5.9 What is the covariance of the return of the tangency portfolio from exercise 5.2 with the return of all portfolios that have the same expected return as Deutsche Lufthansa?

5.10 Using a spreadsheet, compute the minimum variance and tangency portfolios for the universe of three Norwegian equities (TGS Nopec Geophysical Co SA, Clavis Pharma ASA and Sevan Marine ASA), described below. Assume the risk-free return is 5.63 per cent. See exercise 5.6 for detailed instructions.

Asset	Correlation with					
	TGS Nopec	Clavis Pharma	Sevan Marine	Expected return (%)	Historical return (%)	Standard deviation (%)
TGS Nopec	1	0.11	0.14	16	26.30	48.16
Clavis Pharma	0.11	1	0.32	10	40.39	88.47
Sevan Marine	0.14	0.32	1	30	–49.08	71.60

5.11 Kato plc has the following simplified balance sheet (based on market values).

Assets	Liabilities and equity
	Debt
£10 billion	£6 billion
	Ordinary shares
	£4 billion

a The debt of Kato earns the risk-free return of 6 per cent per year. Kato's equity has a mean return of 12 per cent per year, a standard deviation of 30 per cent per year and a beta of 0.9. Compute the mean return, beta and standard deviation of the assets of Kato. *Hint:* view the assets as a portfolio of debt and equity.

b If the CAPM holds, what is the mean return of the market portfolio?

c How does your answer to part *a* change if the debt is risky, has returns with a mean of 7 per cent, a standard deviation of 10 per cent, a beta of 0.2 and a correlation of 0.3 with the return of Kato's equity?

5.12 The following are adjusted closing prices for Lloyd's Banking Group plc and the corresponding closing index values of the FTSE 100.

Month	Lloyd's Banking Group	FTSE 100
Mar–19	62.14	7,279.19
Apr–19	62.57	7,418.22
May–19	57.26	7,161.71
Jun–19	56.59	7,425.63
Jul–19	53.33	7,586.78
Aug–19	49.83	7,207.18
Sep–19	54.12	7,408.21
Oct–19	56.8	7,248.38
Nov–19	61.15	7,346.53
Dec–19	62.5	7,542.44
Jan–20	56.79	7,286.01
Feb–20	50.2	6,580.61
Mar–20	32	5,671.96
Apr–20	32.24	5,901.21
May–20	29.87	6,076.60
Jun–20	31.18	6,169.74
Jul–20	26.29	5,897.76
Aug–20	28.35	5,963.57
Sep–20	26.36	5,866.10
Oct–20	28.02	5,577.27
Nov–20	35.62	6,266.19
Dec–20	36.44	6,460.52
Jan–21	33	6,407.46
Feb–21	39	6,483.43
Mar–21	42.53	6,713.63
Apr–21	45.44	6,969.81
May–21	49.89	7,022.61
Jun–21	46.69	7,037.47
Jul–21	45.63	7,032.30
Aug–21	43.78	7,119.70

Month	Lloyd's Banking Group	FTSE 100
Sep–21	46.57	7,086.42
Oct–21	50.22	7,237.57
Nov–21	46.8	7,059.45
Dec–21	47.8	7,384.54
Jan–22	51.05	7,464.37
Feb–22	51.72	7,576.22

Using a spreadsheet, compute Lloyd's Banking Group's beta. Then apply the Bloomberg adjustment to derive the adjusted beta.

5.13 What value must ACYOU Corporation's expected return be in Example 5.4 to prevent us from forming a combination of Henry's portfolio, ACME, ACYOU and the risk-free asset that is mean-variance superior to Henry's portfolio?

5.14 Assume that the tangency portfolio for equities allocates 80 per cent to the DAX index and 20 per cent to the AEX index. This tangency portfolio has an expected return of 13 per cent per year and a standard deviation of 8.8 per cent per year. The beta for the DAX index, computed with respect to this tangency portfolio, is 0.54. Compute the expected return of the DAX index, assuming that this 80/20 per cent mix really is the tangency portfolio when the risk-free rate is 5 per cent.

5.15 Exercise 5.14 assumed that the tangency portfolio allocated 80 per cent to the DAX index and 20 per cent to the AEX index. The beta for the DAX index with this tangency portfolio is 0.54. Compute the beta of a portfolio that is 50 per cent invested in the tangency portfolio and 50 per cent invested in the DAX index.

5.16 Using data only from 2019–2022, redo Example 5.9. Which differs more from the answer given in Example 5.9: the expected return estimated by averaging the monthly returns or the expected return obtained by calculating beta and employing the risk-expected return equation? Why?

5.17 Estimate the Bloomberg-adjusted betas for the following companies.

Company	Unadjusted beta
BP	1.10
BT Group	1.26
Compass Group	0.68
HSBC Holdings	1.13
Lloyds Banking Group	2.11
Royal Bank of Scotland Group	2.33
Tate & Lyle	0.81

5.18 Compute the tangency and minimum variance portfolios, assuming only two equities: African Rainbow and Impala Platinum. The expected returns of African Rainbow and Impala Platinum are 0.15 and 0.14, respectively. The variances of their returns are 0.04 and 0.08, respectively. The covariance between the two is 0.02. Assume that the risk-free rate is 6 per cent.

5.19 There exists a portfolio P with an expected return of 11 per cent. Asset I has a covariance with P of 0.004, and Asset II has a covariance with P of 0.005. If the expected returns on Assets I and II are 9 per cent and 12 per cent, respectively, and the risk-free rate is 5 per cent, then is it possible for portfolio P to be the tangency portfolio?

5.20 The expected return of the JSE Index, which you can assume is the tangency portfolio, is 16 per cent and has a standard deviation of 25 per cent per year. The expected return of SABMiller is unknown, but it has a standard deviation of 20 per cent per year and a covariance with the JSE Index of 0.10. If the risk-free rate is 6 per cent per year:

a Compute SABMiller's beta.

b What is SABMiller's expected return given the beta computed in part *a?*

c If ABSA Bank has half the expected return of SABMiller, then what is ABSA Bank's beta?

d What is the beta of the following portfolio?

0.25 in SABMiller
0.10 in ABSA Bank
0.75 in the JSE Index portfolio
0.20 in Mondi (where $\beta_{Mondi} = 0.80$)
0.10 in the risk-free asset

e What is the expected return of the portfolio in part *d?*

References and Additional Reading

Baker, M., Bergstresser, D., Serafeim, G. and Wurgler, J. (2018) *Financing the response to climate change: The pricing and ownership of US green bonds* (No. w25194). National Bureau of Economic Research.

Barberis, N., Greenwood, R., Jin, L. and Shleifer, A. (2015) 'X-CAPM: An Extrapolative Capital Asset Pricing Model', *Journal of Financial Economics,* 115(1): 1–24.

Barberis, N., Greenwood, R., Jin, L. and Shleifer, A. (2018) 'Extrapolation and Bubbles', *Journal of Financial Economics,* 129(2): 203–227.

Basak, S. and Chabakauri, G. (2010) Dynamic mean-variance asset allocation. *The Review of Financial Studies,* 23(8): 2970–3016.

Bessembinder, H. (2018) Do stocks outperform treasury bills?, *Journal of financial economics,* 129(3): 440–457.

Black, F. (1972) 'Capital market equilibrium with restricted borrowing', *Journal of Business,* 45(3): 444–455.

Black, F., Jensen. M.C. and Scholes, M.S. (1972) The capital asset pricing model: some empirical tests in M. Jensen (ed.) *Studies in the Theory of Capital Markets.* New York: Praeger, 79–121.

Carhart, M.M. (1997) On persistence in mutual fund performance. *The Journal of Finance,* 52(1): 57–82.

Fama, E. (1976) *Foundations of Finance.* New York: Basic Books.

Fama, E.F. and MacBeth, J.D. (1973) Risk, return, and equilibrium: empirical tests *The Journal of Political Economy,* 81(3): 607–636.

Fama, E.F. and French, K.R. (1992) The cross-section of expected stock returns *The Journal of Finance,* 47(2): 427– 465.

Fama, E.F. and French, K.R. (1996) The CAPM is wanted, dead or alive *The Journal of Finance,* 51(5): 1947–1958.

Fama, E.F. and French, K.R. (2007) Disagreement, tastes, and asset prices. *Journal of financial economics,* 83(3): 667–689.

Fama, E.F. and French, K.R. (2015) A Five-factor Asset Pricing Model *Journal of Financial Economics,* 116(1): 1–22.

Fama, E.F. and French, K.R. (2016) Dissecting Anomalies with a Five-factor Model *The Review of Financial Studies,* 29(1): 69–103.

Fama, E.F. and French, K.R. (2017) International Tests of a Five-factor Asset Pricing Model *Journal of Financial Economics,* 123(3): 441–463.

Frazzini, A. and Pedersen, L.H. (2014) Betting against beta. *Journal of Financial Economics,* 111(1): 1–25.

Handa, P., Kothari, S.P. and Wasley, C. (1989) The relation between the return interval and betas: implications for the size effect *Journal of Financial Economics,* 23(1): 79–100.

Hong, H. and Sraer, D.A. (2016) Speculative betas, *The Journal of Finance,* 71(5): 2095–2144.

Levy, M. and Roll, R. (2010) The market portfolio may be mean/variance efficient after all: the market portfolio. *The Review of Financial Studies,* 23(6): 2464–2491.

Idzorek, T.M. Kaplan, P.D. and Ibbotson, R. G. (2021) The popularity asset pricing model. Available at SSRN 3451554.

Medhat, M. and Schmeling, M. (2022) Short-term momentum. *The Review of Financial Studies,* 35(3): 1480–1526.

Novy-Marx, R., & Velikov, M. (2022). Betting against betting against beta. *Journal of Financial Economics,* 143(1), 80–106.

Roll, R.W. (1977) A critique of the asset pricing theory's tests; Part I: On past and potential testability of the theory *Journal of Financial Economics,* 4(2): 129–176.

Pástor, L., Stambaugh, R. F., & Taylor, L. A. (2021). Sustainable investing in equilibrium. *Journal of Financial Economics,* 142(2), 550–571.

Pedersen, L.H., Fitzgibbons, S. and Pomorski, L. (2021) Responsible investing: The ESG-efficient frontier, *Journal of Financial Economics,* 142(2): 572–597.

Savov, A. (2011) Asset pricing with garbage, *The Journal of Finance,* 66(1): 177–201.

Zaremba, A., Umutlu, M., & Maydybura, A. (2020). Where have the profits gone? Market efficiency and the disappearing equity anomalies in country and industry returns. *Journal of Banking & Finance,* 121, 105966.

Zerbib, O.D. (2020, October) A sustainable capital asset pricing model (S-CAPM): Evidence from green investing and sin stock exclusion, in *Proceedings of Paris December 2020 Finance Meeting EUROFIDAI-ESSEC.*

Chapter 6

Factor Models

Learning Objectives

After reading this chapter, you should be able to:

- Decompose the variance of a security into market-related and non-market-related components, as well as common factor and firm-specific components, and comprehend why this variance decomposition is important for valuing financial assets.
- Identify the expected return, factor betas, factors and firm-specific components of a security from its factor equation.
- Explain how the principle of diversification relates to firm-specific risk.
- Compute the factor betas for a portfolio, given the factor betas of its component securities.
- Design a portfolio with a specific configuration of factor betas in order to create pure factor portfolios, as well as portfolios that perfectly hedge an investment's endowment of factor risk.
- Know what the arbitrage pricing theory (APT) equation means and what the empirical evidence says about the APT. You should also be able to use your understanding of the APT equation to form arbitrage portfolios when the equation is violated.

Between 1 January 2021 to 31 December 2021, the FTSE All Shares Index grew by 18.32 per cent, outpacing house prices, which appreciated by 10.17 per cent. In contrast, gold fell by 2.57 per cent over the same period, and gilts (high-quality corporate bonds) performed even worse, falling by 7.16 per cent. If one were to make the same comparison for previous years, we would see very different patterns. Take 2020, for example. Gold was the best performer, and equities were the worst-performing asset class!

Year	Inflation	Cash	Gilts	Equities	Houses	Gold
2002	2.94%	3.86%	10.52%	–22.68%	28.36%	11.57%
2003	2.80%	3.56%	1.23%	20.86%	8.29%	10.02%
2004	3.49%	4.44%	6.29%	12.84%	10.70%	–3.08%
2005	2.20%	4.55%	8.26%	22.04%	6.29%	31.06%
2006	4.44%	4.65%	–1.13%	16.75%	10.37%	8.95%
2007	4.04%	5.53%	6.18%	5.32%	7.00%	28.88%
2008	0.95%	4.28%	18.22%	–29.93%	–14.93%	42.75%
2009	2.39%	0.49%	–5.05%	30.12%	4.43%	14.77%
2010	4.77%	0.50%	9.17%	14.51%	0.37%	32.82%
2011	4.82%	0.48%	16.15%	–3.46%	–0.98%	12.28%
2012	3.09%	0.31%	3.25%	12.30%	1.07%	0.88%
2013	2.68%	0.30%	–8.35%	20.81%	5.41%	–29.37%
2014	1.61%	0.38%	14.64%	1.18%	7.70%	5.89%
2015	1.21%	0.46%	–0.09%	0.98%	6.91%	–6.95%
2016	2.49%	0.35%	8.70%	16.75%	5.16%	31.58%
2017	4.12%	0.24%	1.73%	13.10%	4.56%	1.94%
2018	2.70%	0.58%	0.43%	–9.48%	1.95%	4.64%
2019	2.20%	0.74%	5.51%	19.17%	0.90%	15.15%
2020	1.21%	0.15%	7.05%	–9.82%	7.08%	19.42%
2021	7.54%	0.06%	–7.16%	18.32%	10.17%	–2.57%

Source: BullionVault. Inflation: UK long-run Retail Price Index; Cash: 3-month UK Treasury Bill Rate; Gilts: 10-year UK Gilts (yield + capital value); Shares: FTSE All-Shares Index; Houses: HM Land Registry; Gold: London Gold Fix (£s).

The correlation matrix for Inflation, Cash, Gilts, Shares, Houses, and Gold returns is striking in how different asset classes move in line with each other. For example, note how inflation and gilts have a positive correlation with equities while gold is negatively correlated.

	Inflation	Cash	Gilts	Equities	Houses	Gold
Inflation	1					
Cash	–0.04	1				
Gilts	–0.30	0.25	1			
Equities	0.32	–0.16	–0.60	1		
Houses	0.20	0.19	–0.25	0.08	1	
Gold	–0.17	0.36	0.65	–0.25	–0.34	1

Do asset classes such as gold and property have an incremental explanatory effect on equity returns over and above the standard market index? This chapter provides some insights.

This chapter introduces **factor models,** which are equations that break down the returns of securities into two components. A factor model specifies that the return of each risky investment is determined by:

- a relatively small number of **common factors**, which are proxies for those events in the economy that affect a large number of different investments
- a risk component that is unique to the investment.

Take, for example, the multinational energy firm, BP. Changes in BP's share price can be partly attributed to a set of **macroeconomic variables**, such as changes in interest rates, inflation, productivity, and global conflict, which are common factors because they affect the prices of most securities. In addition, changes in BP's share price are affected by the success of new product innovations, cost-cutting efforts, a major oil leak in the Caribbean, the discovery of an illegal corporate act, a management change and so forth. These components of BP's return are considered **firm-specific components** because they affect only that firm and not the returns of other investments.

In many applications, it is possible to ignore the firm-specific components of returns in portfolios with many securities. The return variances of these portfolios are determined almost entirely by the common factors and are virtually unaffected by the firm-specific components. Since these are the kinds of portfolio that most investors should and will hold, the risk of a security generated by these firm-specific components – **firm-specific risk** – does not affect the overall desirability of these types of portfolios.

Although common factors affect the returns of numerous investments, the sensitivities of an investment's returns to the factors differ from investment to investment. For example, the share price of an electric utility may be much more sensitive to changes in interest rates than that of a soft drinks firm. These **factor betas,**[1] or **factor sensitivities** as they are sometimes called, are similar to the market betas discussed in the last chapter, which also differ from security to security.

Factor models are valuable tools for risk analysis, hedging and portfolio management. The chapter's opening vignette illustrates why it is important to understand the multiple sources of risk that can affect an investment's return.[2]

If securities were sensitive to only one common factor, the returns of most funds would be highly correlated with one another. However, securities are subject to multiple sources of **factor risk**, which is return variability generated by common factors. Some factors tend to affect large and small firms differently. Some affect growth-orientated companies differently from securities in slower-growth industries. This means that we may witness some funds doing well while others do poorly over any day, week, month or year. A fund, as well as a firm, should be very conscious of the factor risk to which it is exposed.

Factor models not only describe how unexpected changes in various macroeconomic variables affect an investment's return; they can also be used to provide estimates of the expected rate of return of an investment. Section 6.10 uses factor models to derive the **arbitrage pricing theory (APT)**, developed by Ross (1976), which relates the factor risk of an investment to its expected rate of return. It is termed the *arbitrage pricing theory* because it is based on the no-arbitrage principle.[3]

As a theory, the APT is applied in much the same way as the Capital Asset Pricing Model (CAPM). However, it requires less restrictive assumptions about investor behaviour than the CAPM, is more amenable to empirical tests, and in many cases can be applied more easily than the CAPM. Moreover, the APT is an alternative to the CAPM because of the CAPM's empirical shortcomings, described in Chapter 5. Specifically, the equities of small-capitalization firms and companies with low market-to-book ratios generally have much higher returns than the CAPM predicts. The hope is that, with APT factors, additional aspects of risk beyond market risk can be taken into account, and the high average returns of both the smaller cap equities and the low market-to-book equities can be explained.

Although investors often view the CAPM and the APT as competing theories, both can benefit investors and corporate finance practitioners. For example, the empirical evidence described at the end of Chapter 5 suggests that applications of the CAPM using traditional market proxies, such as the FTSE 100, fail to explain the cross-sectional pattern of past equity returns. An analysis of factor models provides insights into why the CAPM failed. Unfortunately, the greater flexibility of the APT, which allows it to explain *past* average returns much better than the CAPM, comes at a cost. Because the APT is less restrictive than the CAPM, it also provides less guidance about how expected *future* rates of return should be estimated.

---

[1] Statisticians also refer to these as factor loadings.

[2] Chapter 22 discusses risk analysis and hedging with factor models in greater depth.

[3] An **arbitrage opportunity** is a set of trades that make money without risk.

6.1 The Market Model: The First Factor Model

The simplest possible factor model is a **one-factor model**, which is a factor model with only one common factor. It is often convenient to consider this one factor as the market factor and refer to it as the **market model**. Intuition for the CAPM is often based on the properties of the market model. However, as this section shows, the CAPM is not necessarily linked to the market model: thus, this intuition for the CAPM is often wrong.

The Market Model Regression

To understand the market model, consider the regression used to estimate market betas in Chapter 5. There we estimated beta as the slope coefficient in a regression of the Adyen NV equity return on the Eurostoxx 50 return, and pictured the regression as the line of best fit for the points in Exhibit 5.7. The algebraic expression for the regression is simply equation (5.6), explicitly applied to Adyen NV:

$$\tilde{r}_{\text{Adyen}} = \alpha_{\text{Adyen}} + \beta_{\text{Adyen}} \widetilde{R}_{\text{Eurostoxx 50}} = \tilde{\varepsilon}_{\text{Adyen}} \tag{6.1}$$

With monthly estimates from 2019 through 2020, the estimates are;

α_{Adyen} = regression intercept = 0.03

β_{Adyen} = regression slope coefficient (Adyen's market beta) = 0.67

$\tilde{\varepsilon}_{\text{Adyen}}$ = regression residual, which is constructed to have a mean of zero

By the properties of regression, $\tilde{\varepsilon}_{\text{Adyen}}$ and $\widetilde{R}_{\text{Eurostoxx 50}}$ are uncorrelated.

Ignoring the constant, α_{Adyen}, equation (6.1) decomposes the uncertain return of Adyen into two components:

1 A component that can be explained by movements in the market factor – this component is the product of the beta and the Eurostoxx 50 return.

2 A component that is not the result of market movements, the regression residual, $\tilde{\varepsilon}_{\text{Adyen}}$.

The Market Model Variance Decomposition

Because $\tilde{\varepsilon}_{\text{Adyen}}$ and $\widetilde{R}_{\text{Eurostoxx 50}}$ are uncorrelated, and because α_{Adyen} is a constant that does not affect variances, the variance of the return on Adyen equity can be broken down into a corresponding set of two terms:

$$\sigma^2_{\text{Adyen}} = var(\beta_{\text{Adyen}} \widetilde{R}_{\text{Eurostoxx 50}}) + var(\tilde{\varepsilon}_{\text{Adyen}}) = \beta^2_{\text{Adyen}} var(\widetilde{R}_{\text{Eurostoxx 50}}) + var(\tilde{\varepsilon}_{\text{Adyen}}) \tag{6.2}$$

A Glossary of Risk Terms

The first term on the right-hand side of equation (6.2), $\beta^2_{\text{Adyen}} var(\widetilde{R}_{\text{Eurostoxx 50}})$, is referred to variously as Adyen's 'systematic', 'market' or 'non-diversifiable' risk. The remaining term, $var(\tilde{\varepsilon}_{Adyen})$, is referred to as its 'unsystematic', 'non-market' or 'diversifiable' risk.[4] We prefer to use *systematic* and *unsystematic* risk since *diversifiable* and *non-diversifiable* risk is misleading in most instances. The following definitions are more precise.

1 The security's **systematic (market) risk** is the portion of the security's return variance explained by market movements. Conversely, the **unsystematic (non-market) risk** is the portion of return variance that market movements cannot explain.

2 **Diversifiable risk** is virtually eliminated by holding portfolios with small weights on every security (lest investors put most of their eggs in one basket). Since the weights have to sum to 1, such portfolios, known as **well-diversified portfolios**, contain large numbers of securities. **Non-diversifiable risk** cannot generally be eliminated, even approximately, in portfolios with small weights on large numbers of securities.

---

[4] Other terms that are synonymous with 'diversifiable risk' are 'unique risk' and 'firm-specific risk'. We shall elaborate on the latter term and diversification shortly.

Regression R-Squared and Variance Decomposition

A commonly used statistic from the regression in equation (6.1), known as the **R-squared**,[5] measures the fraction of the return variance due to systematic risk. First, generalize the regression in equation (6.1) to an arbitrary asset (asset i) and an arbitrary market index with return, $\widetilde{R}_M$. This yields

$$\tilde{r}_i = \alpha_i + \beta_i \widetilde{R}_M + \tilde{\varepsilon} \tag{6.3}$$

Exhibits 6.1 and 6.2 graph data points for two such regressions: one for a company with mostly systematic risk (high R-squared in Exhibit 6.1), the other for a company with mostly unsystematic risk (low R-squared in Exhibit 6.2). The horizontal axis in both exhibits describes the value of the regression's independent variable, which is the market return. The vertical axis represents the regression's dependent variable, which is the company's share price return.

Exhibit 6.1 High R-Squared Regression

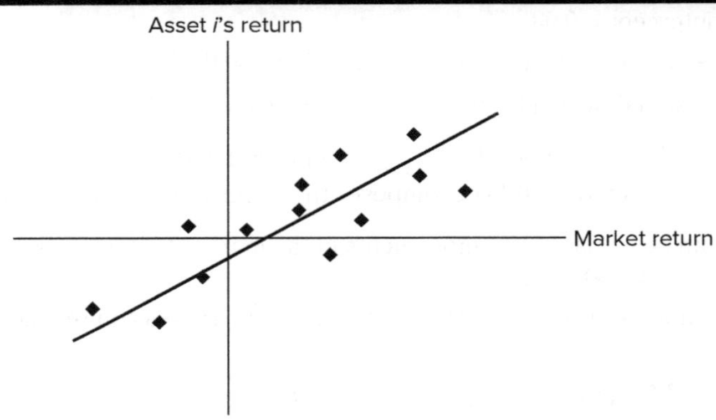

Exhibit 6.2 Low R-Squared Regression

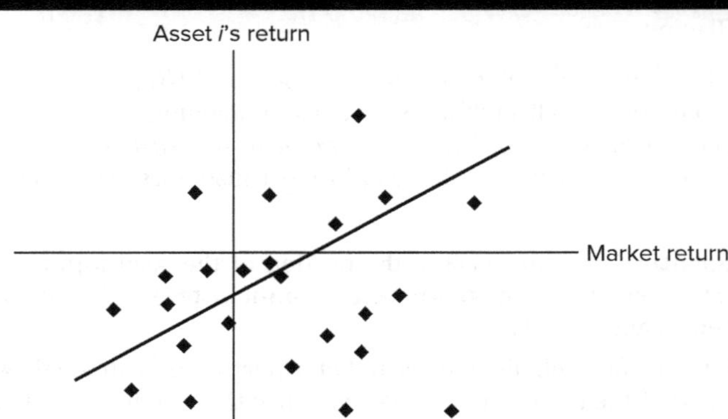

[5] In the case of Adyen, one measures R-squared as the ratio of the first term on the right-hand side of equation (6.2) to the sum of the two terms on the right-hand side. This ratio is a number between 0 and 1. In addition to the interpretation given here, one often refers to R-squared as a measure of how close the regression fits historical data. R-squared is also the square of the correlation coefficient between $\tilde{r}$ and $\widetilde{R}_M$.

Diversifiable Risk and Fallacious CAPM Intuition

The intuition commonly provided for the CAPM risk–expected return relationship is that systematic risk is non-diversifiable. Thus investors must be compensated with higher expected rates of return for bearing such risk.[6] In contrast, one often hears unsystematic risk referred to as being 'diversifiable', implying that additional expected returns are not required for bearing unsystematic risk. Although this intuition is appealing, it is somewhat misleading because, as shown below, some of the risk generated by the market model residual is not necessarily diversifiable.

For example, risk from the residual in Adyen's market model regression is not diversifiable because it is likely to pick up common factors to which Adyen is especially sensitive. An unanticipated increase in interest rates is likely to have a negative effect on most equities. In addition, interest rate risk is non-diversifiable because it is not eliminated by holding well-diversified portfolios. Instead, interest rate risk is a common factor.

Take Volkswagen as an example. Its share price is clearly affected by interest rate risk. New car sales plummet when buyers find the rates on car loans prohibitively expensive. Indeed, interest rate increases are much more likely to affect the return on Volkswagen's equity than the return on the market portfolio. So, where does the interest rate effect show up in equation (6.3)? Some of the impact of the increase in interest rates will be reflected in the systematic component of Volkswagen's return – Volkswagen's beta times the market return – but this is not enough to explain the further decline in Volkswagen's share price relative to the market. The rest of the interest rate effect shows up in Volkswagen's regression residual.

Since the change in interest rates, clearly a non-diversifiable risk factor, affects the market model regression residual, all the risk associated with the residual, $\tilde{\varepsilon}_i$, cannot be viewed as diversifiable. Although one can construct portfolios with specific weights that eliminate interest rate risk (with methods developed in this chapter),[7] *most* portfolios with small portfolio weights on large numbers of securities do not eliminate this source of risk.

Residual Correlation and Factor Models

If the market model is to be useful for categorizing diversifiable and non-diversifiable risk, the market portfolio's return must be the only source of correlation between different securities. As discussed above, this generally will not be true. However, if it is true, it must be the case that the return of security i can formally be written as

$$\tilde{r}_i = \alpha_i + \beta_i \tilde{R}_M + \tilde{\varepsilon}_i$$

where

$\tilde{R}_M$ is the return on the market portfolio

$\tilde{\varepsilon}_i$ and $\tilde{R}_M$ are uncorrelated

the $\tilde{\varepsilon}_i$ of different securities have means of zero and

the $\tilde{\varepsilon}_i$ of different securities are uncorrelated with each other.[8]

The fact that the $\tilde{\varepsilon}_i$ of the different securities are all uncorrelated with each other is the critical distinction between the one-factor market model expressed above and the more general 'return generating process' – equation (6.3) without the uncorrelated $\tilde{\varepsilon}$ assumption – used in discussions of the CAPM.

This 'one-factor model' has only one common factor, the market, generating returns. Each security's residual return, $\tilde{\varepsilon}_i$, is determined independently of the common factors. Because these $\tilde{\varepsilon}_i$ are uncorrelated, each $\tilde{\varepsilon}_i$ represents a change in firm value that is genuinely firm-specific. As the next section shows, firm-specific components of this type have virtually no effect on the variability of the returns of a well-balanced portfolio of many securities. Hence, in the one-factor model, return variability due to firm-specific components – that is, firm-specific risk – is diversifiable.

---

[6] Note that the market model regression, which uses realized returns, differs from the CAPM, which uses mean returns. If the CAPM holds, $\alpha_i = (1 - \beta_i) r_f$ in equation (6.3). Exercise 6.9 asks you to prove this.

[7] Factor risk, in general, can be eliminated with judicious portfolio weight choices, as will be noted shortly.

[8] With a finite number of assets, some negligible but non-zero correlation must exist between residuals in the market model, because the market portfolio-weighted average of the residuals is identically zero. We do not address this issue, because the effect is trivially small.

Even though the interest rate discussion above suggests that a one-factor market model is unlikely to hold in reality, studying this model helps to clarify the meaning of diversifiable and non-diversifiable risk. After a brief discussion of the mathematics and practical implementation of diversification, this chapter turns to more realistic multifactor models built upon the intuition of diversifiable versus non-diversifiable risk.

6.2 The Principle of Diversification

Everyone familiar with the cliché 'Don't put all your eggs in one basket' knows that the fraction of heads observed for a coin tossed 1,000 times is more likely to be closer to one-half than a coin tossed ten times. Yet coin tossing is not a perfect analogy for investment diversification. Factor models help us break up the returns of securities into two components: a component for which coin tossing as an analogy fails miserably (common factors) and a component for which it works perfectly (the firm-specific components).

Insurance Analogies to Factor Risk and Firm-Specific Risk

To further our intuition about these two risk components, consider two different insurance contracts: fire and health insurance. Fires are reasonably independent events across homes (or, at the very least, fires are independent events across neighbourhoods). Thus the fire-related claims on each company are reasonably predictable each year. Due to the near-perfect diversifiability of these claims, fire insurance companies tend to charge the expected claim for this diversifiable type of risk (adding a charge for overhead and profit). By contrast, health insurance has a mixture of diversifiable and non-diversifiable risk components. For example, diseases that require costly use of the medical care system do not tend to afflict large portions of the population simultaneously. As the Covid pandemic proves, however, health insurance companies cannot completely eliminate some kinds of risk by having a large number of policyholders. Should the coronavirus mutate into a more easily transmittable deadly disease, many health insurers would be forced into bankruptcy. As a result, insurers should charge more than the expected loss (that is, a risk premium) for the financial risk they bear from pandemics.

Factor risk is not diversifiable because the factors are common to many securities. This means that the returns due to each factor's realized values are perfectly correlated across securities. For example, in a one-factor market model, a portfolio with equal weights on 1,000 securities, each with the same market model beta, has the same market beta (and thus the same systematic risk) as each of the portfolio's individual securities.[9] This holds true in more general factor models, as the next section shows. Thus even the most extreme diversification strategy, such as placing an equal number of eggs in all the baskets, does not reduce that portion of the return variance due to factor risk.

Quantifying the Diversification of Firm-Specific Risk

By contrast, it is relatively straightforward to demonstrate that the $\tilde{\varepsilon}$ risk of securities is diversified away in large portfolios because the $\tilde{\varepsilon}$ are uncorrelated across securities. Let us begin with two securities, denoted 1 and 2, each with uncorrelated $\tilde{\varepsilon}$ that have identical variances of, say, 0.1. By the now-familiar portfolio variance formula from Chapter 4, an equally weighted portfolio of the two securities – that is, $x_1 = x_2 = 0.5$ – has the firm-specific variance

$$\text{var}(\tilde{\varepsilon}_p) = x_1^2\text{var}(\tilde{\varepsilon}_1) + x_2^2\text{var}(\tilde{\varepsilon}_2) = 2(0.25)(0.1) = 0.05$$

Thus a portfolio of two securities halves the firm-specific variance of each of the two securities.

An equally weighted portfolio of 10 securities, each with equal firm-specific variance, has the firm-specific variance

$$\begin{aligned}\text{var}(\tilde{\varepsilon}_p) &= x_1^2\text{var}(\tilde{\varepsilon}_1) + x_2^2\text{var}(\tilde{\varepsilon}_2) + \cdots + x_{10}^2\text{var}(\tilde{\varepsilon}_{10}) \\ &= 0.01(0.1) + 0.01(0.1) + \cdots + 0.01(0.1) \\ &= 10(0.01)(0.1) = 0.01\end{aligned}$$

This is one-tenth of the firm-specific variance of any of the individual securities.

[9] See Chapter 5, Result 5.4.

Continuing this process for N securities shows that the firm-specific variance of the portfolio is $1/N$ times the firm-specific variance of any individual security and that the standard deviation is inversely proportional to the square root of N. Exhibit 6.3 summarizes these results by plotting the standard deviation of the firm-specific standard deviation of a portfolio against the number of securities in the portfolio. It becomes evident that firm-specific risk is rapidly diversified away as the number of securities in the portfolio increases.[10]

Exhibit 6.3 Firm-Specific Standard Deviation of a Portfolio

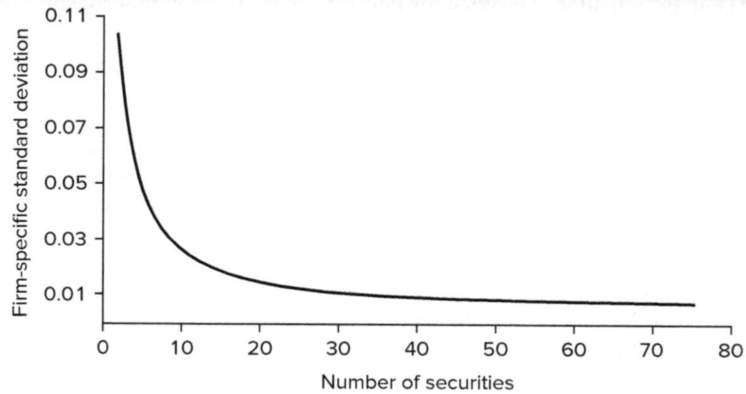

A good rule of thumb is that a portfolio with these weights will have a firm-specific variance inversely proportional to the number of securities. This implies the following result about standard deviations.

Results

Result 6.1

If security returns follow a factor model (with uncorrelated residuals), portfolios with approximately equal weight on all securities have residuals with standard deviations that are approximately inversely proportional to the square root of the number of securities.

6.3 Multifactor Models

The one-factor market model provides a simple description of security returns, but, unfortunately, it is unrealistic. For example, when securities are sensitive to interest rate risk as well as to market risk and firm-specific risks, the interest rate risk generates correlation between the market model residuals, implying that more than one common factor generates security returns.

The Multifactor Model Equation

The algebraic representation of a **multifactor model** – that is, a factor model with more than one common factor – is given by the equation

$$\tilde{r}_1 = \alpha_i + \beta_{i1}\tilde{F}_1 + \beta_{i2}\tilde{F}_2 + \cdots + \beta_{iK}\tilde{F}_K + \tilde{\varepsilon}_i \quad (6.4)$$

[10] When firm-specific variances are unequal, the portfolio of the N securities that minimizes var($\tilde{\varepsilon}_p$) has weights that are inversely proportional to the variances of the $\tilde{\varepsilon}_i$. These weights result in a firm-specific variance for the portfolio that is equal to the product of the inverse of the number of securities in the portfolio and the inverse of the average precision of a security in the portfolio, where the precision of security i is 1/var($\tilde{\varepsilon}_i$). As the number of securities in the portfolio increases, the firm-specific variance rapidly gets smaller with large numbers of securities in this portfolio. Although the inverse of the average precision is not the same as the average variance unless all the variances are equal, the two will probably be reasonably close.

The assumption behind equation (6.4) is that securities' returns are generated by a relatively small number of common factors, each factor symbolized by a subscript *F*, for which different securities have different sensitivities, or β, along with *uncorrelated* firm-specific components, the $\tilde{\varepsilon}$, which contribute negligible variance in well-diversified portfolios.

Interpreting Common Factors

The *F* in equation (6.4) can be considered proxies for *new* information about macroeconomic variables, such as industrial production, inflation, interest rates, oil prices and share price volatility. Because the *F* represent new information, they are generally scaled to have means of zero, which also has the convenient benefit of allowing the α to be interpreted as the mean (or expected) returns of securities.

Investors and other market participants obtain information about these macroeconomic factors from various sources, including economic announcements, such as employment, inflation and interest rate announcements. Other important regularly scheduled announcements are the merchandise trade deficit, the producer price index, money supply growth and the weekly jobless claims report. In addition, irregular news events such as the testimony or press releases of important policymaking officials, or actions taken by central banks can also provide information about important macroeconomic forces.

Sometimes, a seemingly non-financial event, such as the Russian invasion of Ukraine, will affect these fundamental forces. When Russia sent tanks into eastern Ukraine in 2022, gas and oil prices shot up while bond and share prices fell dramatically.

Several factor model 'interpretations' explain why share prices fell at the time of Ukraine's invasion. One interpretation is that higher expected import prices for gas and oil may have lowered corporate earnings because energy prices are an important cost of production. Alternatively, these political events may have changed investor expectations about the inflation factor or altered the risk of most securities because of an increase in uncertainty about future inflation, interest rates and the **gross domestic product (GDP)**, which is a measure of the value of an economy's production of goods and services.

In sum, a common factor is an economic variable (or portfolio return that acts as a proxy for an economic variable) that significantly affects the returns of broad market indices rather than individual securities alone. Common factors affect returns by changing discount rates, earnings prospects, or both.

6.4 Estimating the Factors

There are three ways to estimate the common factors in a factor model:

1. Use a statistical procedure, such as *factor analysis,* to determine **factor portfolios**, which are portfolios of securities designed to mimic the factors.
2. Use macroeconomic variables such as interest rate changes and changes in economic activity as proxies for the factors.
3. Use firm characteristics, such as firm size, to form portfolios that act as proxies for the factors.

Exhibit 6.4 illustrates the advantages and disadvantages of the various methods. We now elaborate on each of these factor-estimation techniques individually.

Using Factor Analysis to Generate Factor Portfolios

Factor analysis is a statistical estimation technique based on the idea that the covariances between security returns provide information that can be used to determine the common factors that generate the returns. Factor structures determine the covariance between security returns (see Section 6.6). Factor analysis starts with the covariance and discovers which factor structure best explains it.

With only two securities, it is possible to construct a single factor and a pair of factor betas that perfectly explain their covariance. However, when there are many securities, the best factor analysis estimates can only approximately explain the covariances, measured from historical returns, between all pairs of securities. Therefore, the factors and factor betas generated by factor analysis are those that provide the best possible explanation of the covariances estimated from historical security returns.

Exhibit 6.4 Summary of the Three Different Ways to Construct Factors

Estimation method	Advantages	Disadvantages
Factor analysis A purely statistical procedure for estimating factors, and the sensitivity of returns to them	Provides the best estimates of the factors, given its assumptions	The assumption that covariances are constant is crucial and is probably violated in reality; does not 'name' the factors
Macroeconomic variables Uses macroeconomic time-series that capture changes in productivity, interest rates and inflation to act as proxies for the factors generating security returns	Provides the most intuitive interpretation of the factors	Implies that the appropriate factors are the unanticipated changes in the macro variables. Unanticipated changes in variables such as aggregate productivity and inflation may be challenging to measure in practice
Firm characteristics Uses firm characteristics such as firm size or market-to-book ratio, which are known to be related to equity returns, to form factor portfolios	More intuitive than the factor analysis portfolios; formation does not require constant covariances	Portfolios selected on the basis of past return anomalies, which are factors only because they explain historical 'accidents', may not be good at explaining expected returns in the future

The advantage of forming factors based on factor analysis is that the factors selected best explain the covariances between all securities. In theory, if covariances do not change over time, the factors derived from factor analysis are precisely the factors desired. However, the downside to factor analysis is that it gives little insight into the economic variables to which factors are linked. For example, corporate managers would like to be able to relate the riskiness of their firm to factors such as interest rate changes and exchange rate changes, but it is difficult to 'name' the factors with the purely statistical factor analysis approach. The second problem is that the technique assumes that the return covariances do not change over time. As a result, the technique is severely disadvantaged in its ability to explain, for example, why the return variability of an equity increases following a significant decline in its share price.

Using Macroeconomic Variables to Generate Factors

A second approach for estimating the factors and factor betas is to use macroeconomic variables as proxies for the common factors. This approach takes a large set of macroeconomic variables such as changes in unemployment, inflation, interest rates, oil prices and so forth. It then limits the number of factors to, say, five, and then examines which five of a more extensive set of macroeconomic variables best explain the observed pattern of security returns.

An initial attempt to identify which common factors have the greatest influence on US share prices was undertaken in empirical research by Chan et al. (1985) and Chen et al. (1986). These authors found that the following five factors best explain the correlations between stock returns.

1. Changes in the monthly growth rate of the GDP, which alters investor expectations about future industrial production and corporate earnings.
2. Changes in the default risk premium, measured by the spread between the yields of AAA and Baa bonds of similar maturity. As this spread widens, investors become more concerned about default.
3. Changes in the spread between the yields of long-term and short-term government bonds: that is, the average slope of the term structure of interest rates as measured by the yields on US Treasury notes and bonds. This would affect the discount rates for obtaining present values of future cash flows.
4. Unexpected changes in the price level, as measured by the difference between actual and expected inflation. Unexpectedly high or low inflation alters the values of most contracts. These include contracts with suppliers and distributors, and financial contracts such as a firm's debt instruments.
5. Changes in expected inflation, as measured by changes in the short-term T-bill yield. Changes in expected inflation affect government policy, consumer confidence and interest rate levels.

One of the main advantages of using the macroeconomic variables approach is that it names the factors. As a result, corporate managers who want economic intuition about the sources of risk most likely to affect their cost of capital tend to prefer this approach.[11]

On the other hand, it may be difficult to measure the *unexpected* changes in the macroeconomic variables, which are needed to act as proxies for the factors. As a result, some variables with semi-predictable movements, such as oil prices, may not show up as factors with this procedure when they really are factors.[12] Another disadvantage is that some potentially important factors may be extremely difficult to quantify. For example, political changes, such as the invasion of a country by a hostile neighbour, can have a potentially enormous effect on security returns. However, constructing an index that reflects changes in the world's political environment is difficult.[13]

Using Characteristic-Sorted Portfolios to Estimate the Factors

Factors can also be estimated by using portfolios whose formation is based on firm characteristics. In theory, e selection of these characteristics should be based on the common factors that make securities move up and down together. Thus, if growth and value tend to have similar returns, then the return of a value portfolio or a growth portfolio, or some combination of the two, should be a factor. However, in practice, the growth versus value characteristic is selected not because of the degree to which it makes groups of equities move up or down together but because it is associated with high and low average equity returns. The rationale behind using the characteristic-based proxies for the factors tied to average returns is due to the APT's link between risk premiums and factor sensitivities, as described later in this chapter. If the risk premium (expected return less the risk-free rate) associated with a characteristic, such as size, represents compensation for a specific kind of factor risk, then portfolios consisting of equities grouped on that characteristic are likely to be highly sensitive to that kind of factor risk.

Given that covariances may change over time, portfolios formed in this way may provide better proxies for these common factors than portfolios created with factor analysis. They also have the advantage of using the returns of financial securities, which, being largely unpredictable, give this method an edge over the macroeconomic variables approach in measuring the unexpected changes that the factors are supposed to capture. On the other hand, if there is no link between the return premiums of equities and factor sensitivities, then this method is not picking up true factors that explain covariances but simply those portfolios consisting of equities that the financial markets appear to be mispricing.

6.5 Factor Betas

The magnitudes of a security's factor betas describe how sensitive the security's return is to changes in the common factors.

What Determines Factor Betas?

Consider how the share prices of Volkswagen, an automobile manufacturer, and Netflix, an online entertainment firm, react differently to factors. Auto sales are highly linked to overall economic activity. Therefore the returns on holding Volkswagen shares should be very sensitive to changes in industrial production. In contrast, online streaming is not as related to the business cycle as car purchases, so Netflix should prove less sensitive to this factor. Hence Volkswagen should have a larger factor beta on the industrial production factor than Netflix. If consumers watch more online television during recessions than at other times, substituting cheap online streaming entertainment for expensive vacations during tough times, Netflix might even have a negative factor beta on the industrial production factor.

[11] See Chapter 11.

[12] A remedy that was not available at the time of these studies is to use futures prices that can serve as a proxy for common factors such as unexpected changes in oil prices.

[13] See Erb et al. (1995) for a discussion of political risk and stock returns.

Factor Models for Portfolios

Like their single-factor counterparts, multifactor portfolio betas are the portfolio-weighted averages of the betas of the securities in the portfolio. For example, if equity A's beta on the inflation factor is 2 and equity B's is 3, a portfolio with weights of 0.5 on equity A and 0.5 on equity B has a factor beta of 2.5 on this factor.

Results

Result 6.2

The factor beta of a portfolio is the portfolio-weighted average of the individual securities' betas on that factor.

Given the *K*-factor model (or factor model with *K* distinct factors) of equation (6.4) for each security i, a portfolio of N securities with weights x_i on security i and return $\tilde{R}_p = x_1\tilde{r}_1 + x_2\tilde{r}_2 + \cdots + x_N\tilde{r}_N$, has a factor equation of

$$\tilde{R}_p = \alpha_p + \beta_{p1}\tilde{F}_1 + \beta_{p2}\tilde{F}_2 + \cdots + \beta_{pK}\tilde{F}_K + \tilde{\varepsilon}_p$$

where

$$\begin{aligned}
\alpha_p &= x_1\alpha_1 + x_2\alpha_2 + \cdots + x_N\alpha_N \\
\beta_{p1} &= x_1\beta_{11} + x_1\beta_{21} + \cdots + x_N\beta_{N1} \\
\beta_{p2} &= x_1\beta_{12} + x_1\beta_{22} + \cdots + x_N\beta_{N2} \\
&\cdots \\
\beta_{pK} &= x_1\beta_{1K} + x_2\beta_{2K} + \cdots + x_N\beta_{Nk} \\
\tilde{\varepsilon}_p &= x_1\tilde{\varepsilon}_1 + x_1\tilde{\varepsilon}_2 + \cdots + x_N\tilde{\varepsilon}_N
\end{aligned}$$

Example 6.1 shows that the factor beta is a portfolio-weighted average of the factor betas of the securities in the portfolio, but it also shows that the alphas (α) and the epsilons ($\tilde{\varepsilon}$) of the portfolios are portfolio-weighted averages of the alphas and epsilons of the securities.

Example 6.1

Computing Factor Betas for Portfolios

Consider the following two-factor model for the returns of three securities that are listed on Euronext: Carrefour (security A), Michelin (security B) and Cap Gemini (security C). Data are hypothetical.

$$\begin{aligned}
\tilde{r}_A &= 0.03 + \tilde{F}_1 - 4\tilde{F}_2 + \tilde{\varepsilon}_A \\
\tilde{r}_B &= 0.05 + 3\tilde{F}_1 - 2\tilde{F}_2 + \tilde{\varepsilon}_B \\
\tilde{r}_C &= 0.10 + 1.5\tilde{F}_1 - 0\tilde{F}_2 + \tilde{\varepsilon}_C
\end{aligned}$$

Using Result 6.2, write out the factor equation for a portfolio that (a) equally weights all three securities and (b) has weights $X_A = -5$, $X_B = 1.5$ and $X_C = 0$.

Answer:

(a)

$$\alpha_p = \frac{1}{3}(0.03) + \frac{1}{3}(0.05) + \frac{1}{3}(0.10) = 0.06$$

$$\beta_{p1} = \frac{1}{3}(1) + \frac{1}{3}(3) + \frac{1}{3}(1.5) = 1.833$$

$$\beta_{p2} = \frac{1}{3}(-4) + \frac{1}{3}(2) + \frac{1}{3}(0) = -0.667$$

Thus

$$\tilde{R}_p = 0.06 + 1.833\tilde{F}_1 - 0.667\tilde{F}_2 + \tilde{\varepsilon}_p$$

where

$$\tilde{\varepsilon}_p \text{ is an average of the three } \varepsilon$$

(b)

$$\alpha_p = -0.5(0.03) + 1.5(0.05) + 0(0.10) = 0.06$$
$$\beta_{p1} = -0.5(1) + 1.5(3) + 0(1.5) = 4$$
$$\beta_{p2} = -0.5(-4) + 1.5(2) + 0(0) = 5$$

Thus

$$\tilde{R}_p = 0.06 + 4\tilde{F}_1 + 5\tilde{F}_2 + \tilde{\varepsilon}_p$$

where

$$\tilde{\varepsilon}_p = -0.5\tilde{\varepsilon}_A + 1.5\tilde{\varepsilon}_B$$

6.6 Using Factor Models to Compute Covariances and Variances

This section demonstrates that the correlation or covariance between the returns of any pair of securities is determined by the factor betas of the securities. It then discusses how to use factor betas to compute more accurate covariance estimates. When using mean-variance analysis to identify the tangency and minimum variance investment portfolios, the more accurate the covariance estimate, the better the estimate of the weights of these critical portfolios.

Computing Covariances in a One-Factor Model

Since the ε in the factor equations described in the last section are assumed to be uncorrelated with each other and the factors, the only source of correlation between securities has to come from the factors. The following example illustrates the calculation of covariance in a one-factor model.

Example 6.2

Computing Covariances from Factor Betas

The following equations describe the hypothetical annual returns for two equities, Amazon and Boeing, where $\tilde{F}$ is the change in the GDP growth rate, and A and B represent Amazon and Boeing, respectively.

$$\tilde{r}_A = 0.10 + 2\tilde{F} + \tilde{\varepsilon}_A$$
$$\tilde{r}_B = 1.5 + 3\tilde{F} + \tilde{\varepsilon}_B$$

The $\tilde{\varepsilon}$ are assumed to be uncorrelated with each other as well as with the GDP factor, and the factor variance is assumed to be 0.0001. Compute the covariance between the two equity returns.

Answer:

$$\sigma_{AB} = \text{cov}\left(0.10 + 2\tilde{F} + \tilde{\varepsilon}_A,\ 1.5 + 3\tilde{F} + \tilde{\varepsilon}_B\right)$$
$$= \text{cov}\left(2\tilde{F} + \tilde{\varepsilon}_A,\ 3\tilde{F} + \tilde{\varepsilon}_B\right)$$

since constants do not affect covariances. Expanding this covariance, using the principles developed in Chapter 4, yields

$$\sigma_{AB} = \text{cov}\left(2\tilde{F},\ 3\tilde{F}\right) + \text{cov}\left(2\tilde{F},\ \tilde{\varepsilon}_B\right) + \text{cov}\left(\tilde{\varepsilon}_A,\ 3\tilde{F}\right) + \text{cov}\left(\tilde{\varepsilon}_A,\ \tilde{\varepsilon}_B\right)$$
$$= \text{cov}\left(2\tilde{F},\ 3\tilde{F}\right) + 0 + 0 + 0$$

Thus the covariance between the returns is the covariance between $2\tilde{F}$ and $3\tilde{F}$, which is 6 $\text{var}\left(\tilde{F}\right)$, or 0.0006.

The pair of equations for $\tilde{r}_A$ and $\tilde{r}_B$ in Example 6.2 represents a one-factor model for equities A and B. Notice the subscripts in this pair of equations. The $\tilde{\varepsilon}$ have the same subscripts as the returns, implying that they represent risks specific to either equity A or B. The value that each $\tilde{\varepsilon}$ takes on provides no information about the value the other $\tilde{\varepsilon}$ acquires. For example, $\tilde{\varepsilon}_A$, taking on the value 0.2, provides no information about the value of $\tilde{\varepsilon}_B$. The GDP factor, represented by $\tilde{F}$, has no A or B subscript, implying that this macroeconomic factor is a common factor affecting both equities. Since the firm-specific components of these returns are determined independently, they do not affect the covariance of the returns of these equities. The common factor provides the sole source of covariation. As a result, the covariance between the equity returns is determined by the variance of the factor and the sensitivity of each equity's return to the factor. The more sensitive the equities are to the common factor, the greater is the covariance between their returns.

Computing Covariances from Factor Betas in a Multifactor Model

Example 6.3 illustrates how return covariances are calculated within a two-factor model.

In Example 6.3, the covariances between the returns of any two securities are determined by the sensitivities of their returns to factor realizations and the variances of the factors. If some of the factors have high variances or, equivalently, if a number of security returns are particularly sensitive to the factors, then those factors will account for a large portion of the covariance between the returns. More generally, covariances can be calculated as shown in Result 6.3.

Example 6.3

Computing Covariances from Factor Betas in a Two-Factor Model

Consider the hypothetical returns of the three securities A, B and C, given in Example 6.1. Compute the covariances between the returns of each pair of securities, assuming that the two factors are uncorrelated with each other and that both factors have variances of 0.0001.

Answer: Since the two factors, denoted $\tilde{F}_1$ and $\tilde{F}_2$, are uncorrelated with each other, and since the $\tilde{\varepsilon}$ are uncorrelated with each of the two factors and with each other:

$$\text{cov}\left(\tilde{r}_A,\ \tilde{r}_B\right) = 3\ \text{var}\left(\tilde{F}_1\right) - 8\ \text{var}\left(\tilde{F}_2\right) = -0.005$$
$$\text{cov}\left(\tilde{r}_A,\ \tilde{r}_C\right) = 1.5\ \text{var}\left(\tilde{F}_1\right) = 0.00015$$
$$\text{cov}\left(\tilde{r}_B,\ \tilde{r}_C\right) = 4.5\ \text{var}\left(\tilde{F}_1\right) = -0.00045$$

Results

Result 6.3

Assume that there are K factors uncorrelated with each other and that the factor models respectively describe the returns of securities i and j

$$\tilde{r}_i = \alpha_i + \beta_{i1}\tilde{F}_1 + \beta_{i2}\tilde{F}_2 + \cdots \beta_{iK}\tilde{F}_K + \tilde{\varepsilon}_i$$

$$\tilde{r}_j = \alpha_i + \beta_{j1}\tilde{F}_1 + \beta_{j2}\tilde{F}_2 + \cdots \beta_{jK}\tilde{F}_K + \tilde{\varepsilon}_j$$

Then the covariance between $\tilde{r}_i$ and $\tilde{r}_j$ is

$$\sigma_{ij} = \beta_{i1}\beta_{j1}\text{var}(\tilde{F}_1) + \beta_{i2}\beta_{j2}\text{var}(\tilde{F}_2) + \cdots + \beta_{iK}\beta_{jK}\text{var}(\tilde{F}_K) \quad (6.5)$$

Result 6.3 states that covariances between security returns are determined entirely by the variances of the factors and the factor betas. The firm-specific components, $\tilde{\varepsilon}_i$ and $\tilde{\varepsilon}_j$, play no role in this calculation. If the factors are correlated, the $\tilde{\varepsilon}$ are still irrelevant for covariance calculations. In this case, however, additional terms must be appended to equation (6.5) to account for the covariances between common factors. Specifically, the formula becomes

$$\sigma_{ij} = \sum_{m=1}^{K}\sum_{n=1}^{K}\beta_{im}\beta_{jn}\text{cov}(\tilde{F}_m, \tilde{F}_n)$$

Factor Models and Correlations between Security Returns

In a multifactor model, the returns of securities that have similar configurations of factor betas are likely to be highly correlated with each other. In contrast, those that have differing factor beta patterns are likely to be less correlated with each other.

In an examination of three British equities that are members of the London Stock Exchange – BP, Fresnillo and GlaxoSmithKline – one is likely to find that the returns of BP (oil industry) and Fresnillo (precious metals) have the highest correlation. In contrast, GlaxoSmithKline (pharmaceuticals) has less correlation with the other two. Indeed, monthly returns bear this out. For example, the correlation between BP and Fresnillo is 0.44, whereas GlaxoSmithKline's correlations with these two firms are 0.21 and 0.08, respectively.

The higher correlation between BP and Fresnillo occurs not because they both extract commodities but because both companies are highly sensitive to the interest rate and industrial production factors. On the other hand, GlaxoSmithKline is less likely to be sensitive to the industrial production factor and possibly not at all to the interest rate factor.

Applications of Factor Models to Mean-Variance Analysis

Result 6.3 is used by portfolio managers who estimate covariances to determine optimal portfolio weights. Computing the tangency portfolio or the minimum variance portfolio in mean-variance analysis requires the estimation of covariances for each possible pairing of securities. There are over 1,000 equities listed on the London Stock Exchange, for example. To estimate the optimal portfolio weights in the tangency or minimum variance portfolio, you would need to calculate more than 1 million covariances between different securities, in addition to over 1,000 variances. Calculating more than 1 million numbers is a Herculean task. If a five-factor model is accurate enough to describe the covariance process, only five-factor betas per security, or about 5,000 calculations, would be needed in addition to variance calculations for each of 1,000 securities (and five factors). While 5,000 calculations is a daunting task, it is far less daunting than 1 million calculations.

One of the original reasons for developing the one-factor market model was to reduce the computational effort needed to determine covariances. Researchers, however, discovered that the market model added more than computational simplicity. The correlations, and consequently the covariances, estimated from the one-factor market model were, on average, better predictors of future correlations than the correlations calculated directly from past data (see Elton et al. 1978). The correlations and covariances based on multiple factor models might do even better.[14]

Using Factor Models to Compute Variances

Like the market model, factor models provide a method for breaking down the variance of a security return into the sum of a diversifiable and a non-diversifiable component. For a one-factor model, where

$$\tilde{r}_i = \alpha + \beta_i \tilde{F} + \tilde{\varepsilon}_i$$

return variance can be decomposed as follows:

$$\text{var}(\tilde{r}_i) = \beta_i^2 \text{var}(\tilde{F}) + \text{var}(\tilde{\varepsilon}_i)$$

The first term in the variance equation algebraically defines factor risk; the second term is firm-specific risk. The fraction of risk that is factor-related is the R-squared statistic from a regression of the returns of security i on the factor. Result 6.4 summarizes this more generally in a multifactor setting.

Results

Result 6.4

When K factors are uncorrelated with each other, and security I is described by the factor model

$$\tilde{r}_i = \alpha_i + \beta_{i1}\tilde{F}_1 + \beta_{i2}\tilde{F}_2 + \cdots + \beta_{iK}\tilde{F}_K + \tilde{\varepsilon}_i$$

the variance of B_i can be decomposed into the sum of $K + 1$ terms:

$$\text{var}(\tilde{r}_i) = \beta_{i1}^2 \text{var}(\tilde{F}_1) + \beta_{i2}^2 \text{var}(\tilde{F}_2) + \cdots + \beta_{iK}^2 \text{var}(\tilde{F}_K) + \text{var}(\tilde{\varepsilon}_i)$$

In this variance decomposition, the sum of the first K terms is the factor risk of the security, and the last term is the firm-specific risk. Example 6.4 applies the decomposition given in Result 6.4.

Example 6.4

Decomposing Variance Risk

Assume that the two factors in Example 6.1 each have a variance of 0.0001 and that the $\tilde{\varepsilon}$ of the three securities have variances of 0.0003, 0.0004 and 0.0005, respectively. First, compute the factor risk and the firm-specific risk of each of the three securities in Example 6.1. Then calculate the return variance. The factor equations for the three securities in the example are repeated here:

$$\tilde{r}_A = 0.03 + \tilde{F}_1 - 4\tilde{F}_2 + \tilde{\varepsilon}_A$$
$$\tilde{r}_B = 0.05 + 3\tilde{F}_1 - 2\tilde{F}_2 + \tilde{\varepsilon}_B$$
$$\tilde{r}_C = 0.10 + 1.5\tilde{F}_1 - 0\tilde{F}_2 + \tilde{\varepsilon}_C$$

[14] Recall that mean-variance analysis ideally requires the true covariances that generate securities' returns. However, just as a fair coin does not turn out to be heads 50 per cent of the time in a series of tosses, historical covariances based on a few years of data also will deviate from the true covariances. In the experience of modern science, simple models that capture the underlying structure of a phenomenon are more accurate at prediction than mere extrapolations of data. Here, for factor models to so dominate the inferences drawn from chance correlations based on past data, they must be capturing some of the underlying structure of the true covariances.

Answer: The variance equation in Result 6.4 implies the following.

Security	(1) Factor risk	(2) Firm-specific risk	(3) = (1) + (2) return variance
A	1(0.0001) + 16(0.0001) = 0.0017	0.0003	0.002
B	9(0.0001) + 4(0.0001) = 0.0013	0.0004	0.0017
C	2.25(0.0001) + 0 = 0.000225	0.0005	0.000725

6.7 Factor Models and Tracking Portfolios

Having learned about several applications of factor models, such as estimating covariances and decomposing variances, we now turn to what is perhaps the most important application of these models: designing a portfolio that targets a specific factor beta configuration to track the risk of an asset, a liability or a portfolio.[15] The tracking application is not only useful for hedging and for allocating capital, but it is the foundation of the no-arbitrage risk-return relationship derived in Section 6.10.

Tracking Portfolios and Corporate Hedging

Assume that BMW, which has extensive sales in the United States, knows that, for every 10 per cent depreciation in the US dollar, its equity declines by 1 per cent, and, for every 10 per cent appreciation in the US dollar, BMW's equity increases by 1 per cent. Similarly, a weakening of the US economy, which would reduce purchases of BMW prestige cars in the United States, might result in BMW's share price dropping by 5 per cent for every 10 per cent decline in the growth of US GDP. Hence BMW has two sources of risk in the USA: currency risk and a slowing of the US economy.

BMW can hedge these sources of risk by selling short a portfolio that tracks the sensitivity of BMW's equity to these two sources of risk. A short position in such a tracking portfolio, which might be composed of German and US equities, as well as currency instruments, would (1) appreciate in value by 1 per cent for every 10 per cent depreciation of the US dollar and (2) increase in value by 5 per cent when the USA experiences a 10 per cent decline in the growth of its GDP. A factor model allows BMW to measure the sensitivity of all securities to these two sources of risk and identify the portfolio weights needed to form this type of tracking portfolio.

Generally, in a context where factor models are used, tracking portfolios are well diversified – that is, they have little or no firm-specific risk.

Capital Allocation Decisions of Corporations and Tracking Portfolios

The tracking portfolio strategy also has value for advising corporations on allocating investment capital. A central theme of this text is that corporations create value whenever they allocate capital for real investment projects to earn returns that exceed those of the project's tracking portfolio. Moreover, the corporation does not have to sell short the tracking portfolio to create wealth. That can be achieved by the company's equity investors if they find that such arbitrage is consistent with their plans for selecting optimal portfolios. What is important is that the tracking portfolio is used as an appropriate benchmark for determining whether the real investment is undervalued.

Designing Tracking Portfolios

A tracking portfolio is constructed by first measuring the factor betas of the investment one wishes to track. Having identified the target configuration of factor betas, how do we build a portfolio of financial securities with the target configuration?

[15] Chapter 5 introduced tracking portfolios.

Knowing how to compute the factor betas of portfolios from the factor betas of the individual investments enables an analyst to design portfolios with any targeted factor beta configuration from a limited number of securities. The only mathematical tool required is the ability to solve systems of linear equations.

A Step-by-Step Recipe

To design a tracking portfolio, one must follow a sequence of steps:

1. Determine the number of relevant factors.[16]
2. Identify the factors with one of the three methods discussed in Section 6.4, and compute factor betas.
3. Next, set up one equation for each factor beta. On the left-hand side of the equation is the tracking portfolio's factor beta as a function of the portfolio weights. On the right-hand side of the equation is the target factor beta.
4. Then solve the equations for the tracking portfolio's weights, making sure that the weights sum to 1.

For example, to target the beta with respect to the first factor in a K-factor model, the equation would be

$$x_1\beta_{11} + x_2\beta_{21} + \cdots + x_N\beta_{N1} = \text{target beta on factor 1}$$

The betas on the left-hand side and target beta on the right-hand side would appear as numbers, and the x (the portfolio weights) would remain as unknown variables that have to be solved for. The equation targeting the beta with respect to the second factor would be

$$x_1\beta_{12} + x_2\beta_{22} + \cdots + x_N\beta_{N2} = \text{target beta on factor 2}$$

Proceed in this manner until each factor has one target beta equation. Then add a final equation that forces the portfolio weights to sum to 1:

$$x_1 + x_2 + \cdots + x_N = 1$$

Solving all these equations for the portfolio weights, $x_1, x_2, \ldots, x_N$, designs a tracking portfolio with the proper factor betas. Example 6.5 illustrates how to do this.

Example 6.5

Designing a Portfolio with Specific Factor Betas

Consider the three securities in Examples 6.1, 6.3 and 6.4. You are informed that the aggregate market index has a factor beta of 2 on the first factor and a factor beta of 1 on the second factor. Design a portfolio consisting of A, B, and C with a factor beta of 2 on the first factor and 1 on the second factor, which thus tracks the aggregate market index.

Answer: To design a portfolio with these characteristics, it is necessary to find portfolio weights, x_A, x_B, x_C, that make the portfolio-weighted averages of the betas equal to the target betas. To make the weights sum to 1, x_A, x_B and x_C must satisfy

$$x_A + x_B + x_C = 1$$

To have a factor beta of 2 on the first factor implies that

$$1x_A + 3x_B + 1.5x_C = 2$$

To have a factor beta of 1 on the second factor implies that

$$-4x_A + 2x_B + 0x_C = 1$$

[16] The number of factors, which can often be found in the finance research literature, is based on statistical tests.

Substituting the value of x_C from the first equation into the other two equations implies that

$$1x_A + 3x_B + 1.5(1 - x_A - x_B) = 2 \text{ (i)}$$

$$-4x_A + 2x_B = 1 \text{ (ii)}$$

Equation (i), above, is now solved for x_B. This value, when substituted into equation (ii), eliminates x_B from equation (ii), so that it now reads

$$-4x_A + \frac{2}{3}\left(x_A + 1\right) = 1$$

This equation has $x_A = -0.1$ as its solution. Since equation (i) reduces to

$$x_B = \frac{x_A + 1}{3}$$

$$x_B = 0.3$$

this implies that

$$x_C = 0.8$$

The Number of Securities Needed to Design Portfolios with Specific Target Beta Configurations

Example 6.5 could have used any configuration of target betas on the two factors and derived a solution. Hence it is possible to design a portfolio with almost any factor beta configuration from a limited number of securities. In a two-factor model, only three securities were needed to create investments with any factor beta pattern. In a five-factor model, six securities would be necessary to tailor the factor risk. In a K-factor model, $K + 1$ securities would be needed.

An Interesting Target Beta Configuration

An important application of the design of portfolios with specific factor configurations is the design of *pure factor portfolios*. As discussed in the next section, these portfolios can be thought of as portfolios that track the factors. As a result, they make it easier to see that factor models imply a useful risk–expected return relationship.

6.8 Pure Factor Portfolios

This section uses the technique developed in the last section to construct pure factor portfolios. **Pure factor portfolios** are portfolios with a sensitivity of 1 to one of the factors and 0 to the remaining factors. Such portfolios, which have no firm-specific risk, provide an intuitive framework for thinking about the implications of factor models. As a result, some portfolio managers use them to determine their optimal portfolios.

Constructing Pure Factor Portfolios from More Primitive Securities

In a K-factor model, it is possible to construct K pure factor portfolios, one for each factor, from any $K + 1$ investments that lack firm-specific risk.[17] Example 6.6 illustrates the construction.

[17] Since many investments have firm-specific risk, pure factor portfolios, in practice, may need to be generated from $K + 1$ well-diversified portfolios.

The Risk Premiums of Pure Factor Portfolios

The respective risk premiums of the K-factor portfolios in a K-factor model are typically denoted as $\lambda_1, \lambda_2, \ldots, \lambda_K$. In other words, the expected return of factor portfolio 1 is $r_f + \lambda_1$, etc. Example 6.7 computes the expected returns and risk premiums of the factor portfolios constructed in Example 6.6.

What Determines the Risk Premiums of Pure Factor Portfolios?

Pure factor portfolios, being risky, generally have expected returns that differ from the risk-free return. Some factors may carry a positive risk premium; others, such as factor portfolio 2 in Example 6.7, may have a zero or negative risk premium. Whether a factor portfolio has a positive or a negative risk premium depends on the aggregate supply of the factor in the financial markets and investors' tastes. If the assumptions of the CAPM are valid, then the risk premiums of the factor portfolios are proportional to their covariances with the return of the market portfolio.[18]

Why the Interest in Pure Factor Portfolios?

From a computational standpoint, it is easier to track an investment with a portfolio of the factor portfolios than with a portfolio of more basic investments, such as individual assets. For example, an investment with a beta of 0.25 on factor 1 and 0.5 on factor 2 is tracked by a portfolio with weights of 0.25 on factor portfolio 1 and 0.5 on factor portfolio 2. A 0.25 weight on the risk-free asset is also needed to make the weights sum to 1.

Example 6.6

Finding Weights that Design Pure Factor Portfolios

What are the weights of the two pure factor portfolios constructed from three UK pharmaceutical firms: AstraZeneca (a), GlaxoSmithKline (g) and ICI (i), assuming the following hypothetical factor equations with factor means of zero?

$$\tilde{r}_A = 0.08 + 2\tilde{F}_1 + 3\tilde{F}_2$$
$$\tilde{r}_G = 0.10 + 3\tilde{F}_1 + 2\tilde{F}_2$$
$$\tilde{r}_I = 0.10 + 3\tilde{F}_1 + 5\tilde{F}_2$$

Answer: To construct the factor portfolio that is only sensitive to factor 1, find portfolio weights x_1, x_2 and x_3 that result in a portfolio with a target factor beta of 1 on the first factor:

$$2x_A + 3x_G + 3x_I = 1$$

To generate a factor beta of 0 on the second factor, the portfolio weights need to satisfy

$$3x_A + 2x_G + 5x_I = 0$$

Since $x_A + x_G + x_I = 1$, the substitution for x_I in the two previous equations implies that

$$2x_A + 3x_G + 3(1 - x_A - x_G) = 1$$
$$3x_A + 2x_G + 5(1 - x_A - x_G) = 0$$

[18] If the factors are uncorrelated with each other, the covariance of a factor with the return of the market portfolio is determined by the market portfolio's factor beta on that factor. In this case, the factor will have a positive risk premium if the market portfolio has a positive factor beta on a factor, and vice versa. The economic intuition for this is straightforward: under the assumptions of the CAPM, investors must be induced to hold the market portfolio so that supply is equal to demand; this is the same as inducing them to hold the factors in exactly the same proportions as they are contained in the market portfolio. Hence, if the market portfolio has a negative beta on a factor, implying that the factor is in negative supply, investors must be induced to short the factor so that the supply of the factor is equal to its demand. To induce an investor to short a factor, the action must carry a reward. If the factor itself has a negative risk premium, short positions in it earn a positive reward. The opposite holds true for factors on which the market portfolio has a positive factor beta.

or

$$-x_A = -2$$
$$-2x_A - 3x_G = -5$$

Thus

$$x_A = 2, x_G = \frac{1}{3}, \text{ and } x_I = -\frac{4}{3}$$

To find factor portfolio 2, set $x_I = 1 - x_A - x_G$ and solve the following:

$$2x_A + 3x_G + 3(1 - x_A - x_G) = 0$$
$$3x_A + 2x_G + 5(1 - x_A - x_G) = 1$$

The solution is

$$x_A = 3,\ x_G = -\frac{2}{3} \text{ and } x_I = -\frac{4}{3}$$

Example 6.7

The Factor Equations of Pure Factor Portfolios

Write out the factor equations for the two factor portfolios in Example 6.6, and determine their risk premiums if the risk-free rate is 4 per cent.

Answer: The expected returns for factor portfolios 1 and 2 are their respective portfolio-weighted averages of the expected returns of the individual securities, which implies that

$$\alpha_{p1} = 2(0.08) + \frac{1}{3}(0.10) - \frac{4}{3}(0.10) = 0.06$$
$$\alpha_{p2} = 3(0.08) - \frac{2}{3}(0.10) - \frac{4}{3}(0.10) = 0.04$$

Thus the factor equation for factor portfolio 1 is

$$\tilde{R}_{p1} = 0.06 + \tilde{F}_1 + 0\tilde{F}_2$$

For factor portfolio 2, the factor equation is

$$\tilde{R}_{p2} = 0.04 + 0\tilde{F}_1 + \tilde{F}_2$$

The risk premiums are, respectively,

(factor portfolio 1) $\lambda_1 = 0.06 - 0.04 = 0.02$

(factor portfolio 2) $\lambda_2 = 0.04 - 0.04 = 0$

The construction of this tracking portfolio is easy because each of the building blocks has only one function: only the weight on factor portfolio 1 affects the tracking portfolio's factor 1 beta; only the weight on factor portfolio 2 affects the tracking portfolio's factor 2 beta; the risk-free asset is used only to make the portfolio weights sum to 1, after the other two weights are determined. Thus it is straightforward to construct tracking portfolios after first taking the intermediate step of forming factor portfolios. The following section uses this insight.

6.9 Tracking and Arbitrage

The previous sections illustrate how to construct portfolios with any pattern of factor betas from a limited number of securities. With more securities, the additional degrees of freedom in the selection of portfolio weights make the task of targeting a specific factor beta configuration even easier. Because a sufficiently large number of securities in the portfolio makes it likely that these portfolios will have negligible firm-specific risk, it is usually possible to construct portfolios that perfectly track investments that have no firm-specific risk. This is done by forming portfolios of the pure factor portfolios that have the same factor betas as the investment one wishes to track. The factor equations of the tracking portfolio and the tracked investment will be identical except for the α. By assumption, there are no Z terms in these factor equations. Hence the return of the tracking portfolio and the tracked investment can, at most, differ by a constant: the difference in their α, which is the difference in their expected returns.

If the factor betas of the tracking portfolio and the tracked investment are the same, but their expected returns differ, there will be an arbitrage opportunity. For example, if the tracking portfolio has a higher expected return, investors can buy that portfolio and sell short the tracked investment and receive risk-free cash in the future without spending any money today.

Using Pure Factor Portfolios to Track the Returns of a Security

Example 6.8 illustrates how to use factor portfolios and the risk-free asset to track the returns of another security.

Example 6.8

Tracking and Arbitrage with Pure Factor Portfolios

Given a two-factor model, find the combination of a risk-free security with a 4 per cent return and the two pure factor portfolios from Example 6.6 that tracks security j, which is assumed to have a factor equation of

$$\tilde{r} = 0.086 + 2\tilde{F}_1 - 0.6\tilde{F}_2$$

Then find the expected return of the tracking portfolio and determine whether arbitrage exists. Recall that the factor equations for the two pure factor portfolios (see Example 6.7) were respectively given by

$$\tilde{R}_{p1} = 0.06 + \tilde{F}_1 + 0\tilde{F}_2$$
$$\tilde{R}_{p2} = 0.04 + 0\tilde{F}_1 + \tilde{F}_2$$

Answer: To track security j's two factor betas, place a weight of 2 on factor portfolio 1 and a weight of –0.6 on factor portfolio 2. Since the weights now sum to 1.4, a weight of –0.4 must be placed on the risk-free asset. The expected return of this portfolio is the portfolio-weighted average of the expected returns of the risk-free asset, factor portfolio 1 and factor portfolio 2, which is

$$-0.4(0.04) + 2(0.06) - 0.6(0.04) = 0.08$$

An arbitrage opportunity exists because this expected return of 8 per cent differs from the 8.6 per cent return of the tracked security, as indicated by the 0.086 intercept (and the standard convention, discussed earlier, that the means of the factors are zero).

The Expected Return of the Tracking Portfolio

In Example 6.8, the tracking portfolio for security j is a weighted average of the two factor portfolios and the risk-free asset. Factor portfolio 1 is used solely to generate the target factor 1 beta. Factor portfolio 2 is used solely to generate the target sensitivity to factor 2. The risk-free asset is used only to make the weights of the tracking portfolio sum to 1. Note that the expected return of this tracking portfolio is

$$\text{Expected return} = (1 - \beta_{i1} - \beta_{i2}) + \beta_{i1}(r_f + \lambda_1) + \beta_{i2}(r_f + \lambda_2)$$

where β_{ij} is the factor beta of the tracked investment on factor j (and thus also the weight on pure factor portfolio j), and λ_j is the risk premium of factor portfolio j (making $r_f + \lambda_j$ its expected return). The expression above for the expected return is also written in an equivalent form:

$$\text{Expected return} = r_f + \beta_{i1}\lambda_1 + \beta_{i2}\lambda_2$$

Result 6.5 generalizes Example 6.8 as follows.

Results

Result 6.5

An investment with no firm-specific risk and a factor beta of β_{ij} on the jth factor in a K-factor model is tracked by a portfolio with weights of β_{i1} on factor portfolio 1, β_{i2} on factor portfolio 2, . . . , β_{iK} on factor portfolio K, and $1 - \sum_{j=1}^{K}\beta_{ij}$ on the risk-free asset. The expected return on this tracking portfolio is therefore

$$r_f + \beta_{i1}\lambda_1 + \beta_{i2}\lambda_2 + \cdots + \beta_{ik}\lambda_k$$

where $\lambda_1, \lambda_2, \ldots, \lambda_K$ denote the risk premiums of the factor portfolios, and r_f is the risk-free return.

Decomposing Pure Factor Portfolios into Weights on More Primitive Securities

Factor portfolios are themselves combinations of individual securities, like equities and bonds. In Example 6.8, the portfolio with weights of –0.4 on the risk-free security, 2 on factor portfolio 1 and –0.6 on factor portfolio 2 can be further broken down. Recall from Example 6.6 that factor portfolio 1 has respective weights of $(2, \frac{1}{3}, -\frac{4}{3})$ on the three individual securities, and factor portfolio 2 has corresponding weights of $(3, -\frac{2}{3}, -\frac{4}{3})$. Hence a weight of 2 on factor portfolio 1 is really a weight of 4 on security A, $\frac{2}{3}$ on security B and $-\frac{8}{3}$ on security C. Likewise, a weight of –0.6 on factor portfolio 2 is really a weight of –1.8 on security A, 0.4 on security B and 0.8 on security C. Summing the weights for each security found in Example 6.6 implies that, at a more fundamental level, our tracking portfolio in Example 6.8 consisted of weights of 2.2, $\frac{16}{15}$ and $-\frac{28}{15}$ on securities A, B and C, respectively, plus a weight of –0.4 on the risk-free asset.[19] Thus, it makes no difference in the last example whether one views the tracking portfolio as being generated by stocks A, B and C or by pure factor portfolios.

6.10 No Arbitrage and Pricing: The Arbitrage Pricing Theory

Because firm-specific risk is relatively unimportant to investors who hold well-diversified portfolios, it is reasonable to pretend that firm-specific risk does not exist and analyse the risk of securities by focusing only on their factor betas. If most investors do not have to bear firm-specific risk because they hold well-diversified portfolios, our analysis of the relationship between risk and return will be unaffected by this omission.

If two investments track each other perfectly and have different expected returns, then, in the absence of transaction costs and related market frictions, an investor can achieve riskless profits by purchasing the investment with the higher expected return and selling short the investment with the lower expected return. It is possible to demonstrate that such arbitrage opportunities will exist only if securities' returns do not satisfy an equation that relates the expected returns of securities to their factor betas. As noted previously, this risk–expected return relationship is known as the arbitrage pricing theory (APT).

[19] Moreover, even a risk-free security could have been formed from securities A, B and C in Example 6.6, so it is possible to break this down to an even more basic level.

The Assumptions of the Arbitrage Pricing Theory

The APT requires only four assumptions:

1 Returns can be described by a factor model.
2 There are no arbitrage opportunities.
3 There are many securities, so it is possible to form portfolios that diversify the firm-specific risk of individual securities. This assumption allows us to pretend that firm-specific risk does not exist.
4 The financial markets are frictionless.

This section derives the APT. To keep the analysis relatively simple, consider investments with no firm-specific risk.

Arbitrage Pricing Theory with No Firm-Specific Risk

Consider investment I with returns generated by the K-factor model represented by

$$\tilde{r}_i = \alpha_i + \beta_{i1}\tilde{F}_1 + \beta_{i2}\tilde{F}_2 + \cdots + \beta_{iK}\tilde{F}_K \tag{6.6}$$

Equation (6.6) has no $\tilde{\varepsilon}_i$ term: thus, there is no firm-specific risk. As Result 6.5 noted, one way to track the return of this investment is to form a portfolio with weights of $1 - \sum_{j=1}^{K}\beta_{ij}$ on the risk-free security, β_{i1} on factor portfolio 1, β_{i2} on factor portfolio 2, . . . , and finally β_{iK} on factor portfolio K. Recall that these factor portfolios can be generated either from a relatively small number of securities with no firm-specific risk or from a very large number of securities where the firm-specific risk is diversified away.

The expected return of the portfolio that tracks investment I is

$$r_f + \beta_{i1}\lambda_1 + \beta_{i2}\lambda_2 + \beta_{iK}\lambda_k$$

where $\lambda, \ldots, \lambda_k$ are the risk premiums of the factor portfolios.

It should be immediately apparent that an arbitrage opportunity exists – unless the original investment and its tracking portfolio have the same expected return – because a long position in investment i and an offsetting short position in the tracking portfolio has no risk and no cost. For example, if the equity of Adidas is investment i, buying €1 million of Adidas and selling short €1 million of the tracking portfolio would require no upfront cash. Moreover, since the factor betas of the long and short positions match exactly, any movements in the value of Adidas equity due to factor realizations would be completely offset by exactly opposite movements in the value of the short position in the tracking portfolio. Hence, if the expected return of Adidas equity exceeds the expected return of the Adidas tracking portfolio, an investor obtains a riskless positive cash inflow at the end of the period. For example, if the Adidas expected return exceeds the tracking portfolio's by 2 per cent, the investor would receive

$$€1{,}000{,}000 \times 0.02 = €20{,}000$$

Since this cash does not require any upfront money and is obtained without risk, buying Adidas and shorting its tracking portfolio represents an arbitrage opportunity. Similarly, if the expected return of Adidas equity were smaller than the expected return of the tracking portfolio, a short position in Adidas equity and an offsetting long position in its tracking portfolio would provide an arbitrage opportunity. To prevent arbitrage, the expected return of Adidas and its tracking portfolio must be equal.

Result 6.6 states this formally.

Results

Result 6.6

An arbitrage opportunity exists for all investments with no firm-specific risk unless

$$\bar{r}_i = r_f + \beta_{i1}\lambda_2 + \beta_{i2}\lambda_2 + \cdots + \beta_{iK}\lambda_K \tag{6.7}$$

where $\lambda_1, \ldots \lambda_k$ applies to all investments with no firm-specific risk.

The equation of the arbitrage pricing theory, equation (6.7), is a relationship between risk and expected return that must hold in the absence of arbitrage opportunities. On the left-hand side of the equation is the expected return of an investment. On the right-hand side is the expected return of a tracking portfolio with the same factor betas as the investment. Equation (6.7) thus depicts a relationship where there is no arbitrage: the equals sign merely states that the expected return of the investment should be the same as that of its tracking portfolio.

Graphing the APT Risk-Return Equation

In the one-factor case, the graph of equation (6.7) observed in Exhibit 6.5 is very similar to the graph of the security market line (depicted in panel B of Exhibit 5.5). On one axis is the beta or factor beta of a security; on another axis is its mean return. In this case, the risk–return relationship graphs as a straight line. According to the results in this section, if there is no arbitrage, all investments must lie on this line.

Exhibit 6.5 The APT Relation between the Mean Return of a Security and its Factor Betas

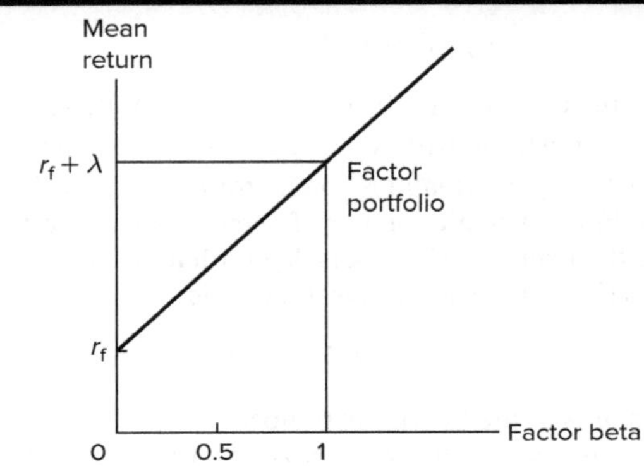

In the two-factor case, equation (6.7) graphs as a plane in three dimensions (see Exhibit 6.6). The location and slope of the plane are determined by the risk-free return, which is the height of the plane above the origin and the two risk premiums, or λ, of the pure factor portfolios. All investments must lie on this plane if there is no arbitrage.

Exhibit 6.6 Relationship between the Mean Return of a Security and its Factor Betas in a Multifactor Model

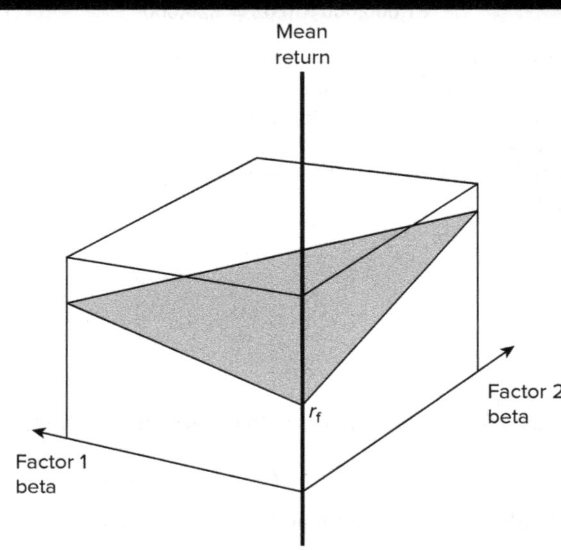

Verifying the Existence of Arbitrage

To learn whether the arbitrage pricing theory holds, do not look at graphs (which is impossible if there are more than two factors) or form tracking portfolios. Instead, determine whether a single set of λ can generate the expected returns of all the securities. For example, one can use the returns and factor sensitivities of $K > 1$ securities to solve equation (6.7) for the K λ. If these λ also generate the expected returns of all the other securities, the APT holds; if they do not, the APT is violated, and there is an arbitrage opportunity (assuming that the factor model assumption holds). Example 6.9 illustrates the procedure for testing whether a single set of λ have this property.

Example 6.9

Determining Whether Arbitrage Exists

Let the following two-factor model describe the returns to four securities: three risky securities indexed 1, 2 and 3, and a risk-free security:

$$\tilde{r}_f = 0.05$$
$$\tilde{r}_1 = 0.06 + 0\tilde{F}_1 + 0.02\tilde{F}_2$$
$$\tilde{r}_2 = 0.08 + 0.02\tilde{F}_1 + 0.01\tilde{F}_2$$
$$\tilde{r}_3 = 0.15 + 0.04\tilde{F}_1 + 0.04\tilde{F}_2$$

Is there an arbitrage opportunity?

Answer: The APT risk–expected return equation is

$$\bar{r}_i = r_f + \beta_{i1}\lambda_1 + \beta_{i2}\lambda_2$$

For securities 1 and 2, this reads

$$0.06 = 0.05 + 0\lambda_1 + 0.02\lambda_2$$

and

$$0.08 = 0.05 + 0.02\lambda_1 + 0.01\lambda_2$$

The first of these two equations implies that $\lambda_2 = 0.5$. Substituting this value for λ_2 into the second equation gives $\lambda_1 = 1.25$. Using these values for the APT equation of security 3, check to see whether

$$0.15 = [0.05 + 0.04(1.25) + 0.04(0.5)] = 0.12$$

Since the right-hand side term in brackets equals 0.12, which is less than the value on the left-hand side, 0.15, there is arbitrage. A long position in security 3 (the high expected return security) and an equal short position in its tracking portfolio, formed from securities 1, 2 and the risk-free security, generates arbitrage.

In Example 6.9, if the expected return of security 3 had been equal to 0.12, there would be no arbitrage. However, because its expected return of 0.15 exceeded the 0.12 expected return of its tracking portfolio, the no-arbitrage risk-return relationship of equation (6.7) is violated. Although this provides a prescription for generating arbitrage, it does not determine whether security 3 is underpriced or if its tracking portfolio is overpriced. Based on this example, one only knows that security 3 is underpriced *relative* to its tracking portfolio.

An alternative method for identifying the existence of arbitrage is to test directly whether a unique set of λ generate the expected returns of the securities. In this case, solve for the set of λ using one group of securities (the number of securities in the set is 1 plus the number of factors). Then solve again, using a different group of securities. If the different sets of λ are the same, there is no arbitrage; if they differ, there is arbitrage. Example 6.10 illustrates this technique.

Example 6.10

Determining whether Factor Risk Premiums are Unique

Use the data provided in Example 6.9 to determine whether there is an arbitrage opportunity by comparing the pair of λ found in Example 6.9 with the pair of λ found by using securities 2, 3 and the risk-free asset.

Answer: The APT risk–expected return equation says

$$\tilde{r}_i = r_f + \beta_{i1}\lambda_1 + \beta_{i2}\lambda_2$$

Example 6.9 found that using the risk-free asset and securities 1 and 2 to solve for λ_1 and λ_2 yields

$$\lambda_1 = 1.25 \text{ and } \lambda_2 = 0.5$$

Using securities 2 and 3 and the risk-free asset to solve for the λ requires solving the following pair of equations:

$$0.08 = 0.05 + 0.02\lambda_1 + 0.01\lambda_2$$

$$0.15 = 0.05 + 0.04\lambda_1 + 0.04\lambda_2$$

The first equation of the pair immediately above says $\lambda_2 = 3 - 2\,\lambda_1$. Substituting this into the second equation and solving for λ_1 yields $\lambda_1 = 0.5$, which, when substituted back into the first equation, yields $\lambda_2 = 2$. Since this pair of λ differs from the first pair, the APT equation does not hold, and there is arbitrage.

If security 3 in the last example had an expected return of 0.12, the second pair of λ would have been identical to the first pair. This would be indicative of no arbitrage.

Exhibits 6.7 and 6.8 illustrate this technique in a slightly more general fashion. They graph the factor risk premiums consistent with the APT risk–expected return equation (6.7) for each of the three risky securities in the last example. The horizontal axis corresponds to λ_1 and the vertical axis corresponds to λ_2. As you can see, solving systems of equations is identical to finding out where lines cross. The intersection of lines for securities 1 and 2 represents the first pair of factor risk premiums, and the intersection of lines for securities 2 and 3 the second pair. In Exhibit 6.7, the intersection point for the lines that correspond to securities 1 and 2, at point A, is not on the line for security 3. To preclude arbitrage, which would be the case if the expected return of security 3 was 0.12, all three of these lines would have to intersect at the same point: point A in Exhibit 6.8. Any other securities that exist would also require corresponding lines that go through this point.

Exhibit 6.7 Risk Premiums (/1 and /2) That Are Inconsistent with No Arbitrage for Three Securities

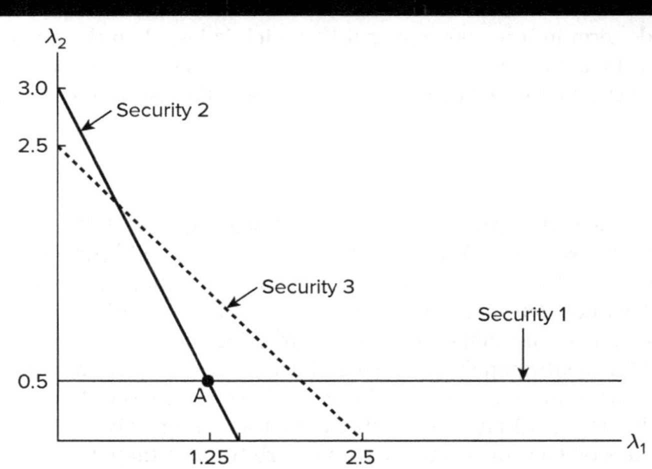

Exhibit 6.8 Risk Premiums (/1 and /2) That Are Consistent with No Arbitrage for Three Securities

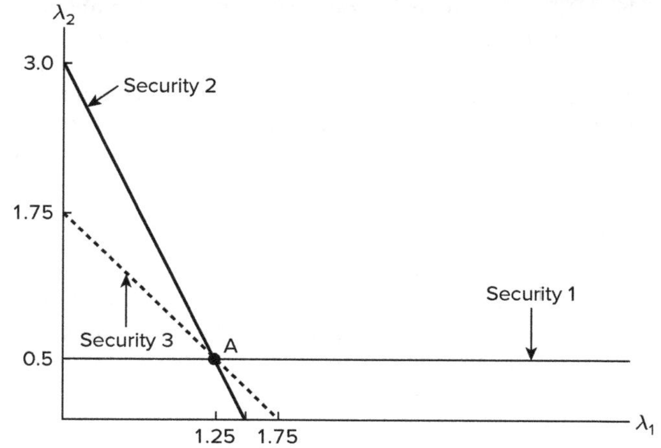

The Risk–Expected Return Relationship for Securities with Firm-Specific Risk

Up to this point, this chapter has examined the risk–expected return relationship of portfolios and securities that have no firm-specific risk. However, with a sufficiently large number of securities, the APT risk–expected return equation (6.7) must also hold, at least approximately, for individual securities that contain firm-specific risk.

Violations of the APT Equation for a Small Set of Securities Do Not Imply Arbitrage

As the previous section showed, an arbitrage opportunity exists whenever portfolios without firm-specific risk violate the APT risk–expected return equation. However, a relatively small number of securities with firm-specific risk can violate the APT equation (equation (6.7)) without providing an arbitrage opportunity. To understand this, consider the investment opportunity that would be offered if Credit Agricole, a French bank, were underpriced and provided investors with an expected return 5 per cent above the expected return expressed by the APT equation. Although this provides an excellent investment opportunity, it does not offer a risk-free arbitrage opportunity. Investors who want to take advantage of this underpricing must hold a significant percentage of Credit Agricole equity in their portfolios, which will expose them to Credit Agricole's firm-specific risk.

Violations of the APT Equation by Large Numbers of Securities Imply Arbitrage

Now consider what would happen if 300 equities had expected returns that exceeded the expected returns given by the APT equation. If this were so, it would be possible to form a portfolio of those equities that virtually eliminates firm-specific risk. However, since this diversified portfolio also must be mispriced by the APT equation, an arbitrage opportunity will exist. An investor can achieve these arbitrage gains by:

1 forming a portfolio of these 300 equities that diversifies away almost all of the firm-specific risk
2 eliminating the factor risk of the portfolio in item 1 by taking offsetting positions in the factor portfolios.

This argument suggests that the number of securities mispriced by the APT must not exceed the minimum needed to form a portfolio that virtually eliminates firm-specific risk. The number that can be mispriced depends on what one means by 'virtually eliminate'. Completely eliminating firm-specific risk requires an infinite number of securities. In a realistic setting with a large but finite number of securities, the no-arbitrage assumption does not need all stocks to satisfy the APT risk–expected return equation. However, with large numbers of assets, it does imply that the pricing model, equation (6.7), should hold reasonably closely for most assets.

Combining the APT with CAPM Intuition for Insights about How Much Deviation is Permitted

Given firm-specific risk, the APT's factor models, combined with intuition about market equilibrium from the CAPM, generate a model in which the APT equation holds almost perfectly for all securities. The CAPM tells us that those components of a security's risk that are independent of the market should not affect its expected returns. Since the market portfolio contains many securities, its return contains little firm-specific risk. Hence the firm-specific component of a security's risk has virtually no effect on its covariance with the market, and thus should not affect expected rates of return.[20] This argument suggests that equation (6.7) should hold almost exactly even for those investments with a great deal of firm-specific risk.

Implications of the APT for Optimal Portfolios

If the APT risk–expected return equation holds exactly, rather than approximately, there is no risk premium attached to firm-specific variance. This suggests that the tangency portfolio contains no firm-specific risk and thus must be some combination of the factor portfolios. Since the optimal portfolio for investors is a combination of the tangency portfolio and the risk-free asset, optimal investment portfolios are composed of weightings of the K factor portfolios and the risk-free investment. Such optimal portfolios contain the optimal mix of factor risk but have no firm-specific risk.

6.11 Estimating Factor Risk Premiums and Factor Betas

Factor risk premiums are needed to implement the APT. Typically, these have been estimated from the average historical risk premiums of factor portfolios – that is, their historical average returns in excess of the risk-free return. Since historical averages are not true means, considerable statistical error is associated with the factor risk premiums.[21]

To estimate factor betas when factors are pre-specified, either as macroeconomic factors or as portfolios tied to firm characteristics, one must use a regression of the historical returns of the security against the historical factor realizations. The slope coefficients in this regression are the factor betas. With a factor analysis implementation of a factor model, both the factor portfolios and the factor betas are generated directly as outputs of the factor analysis procedure. However, in this case, the resulting factor betas are still identical to multiple regression slope coefficients from a regression of historical returns against historical factor realizations.

6.12 Empirical Tests of Factor Models

As Chapter 5 noted, some researchers have suggested that market prices do not reflect fundamental long-term values because characteristics such as size, market-to-book and momentum explain average stock returns better than the CAPM beta. As a result, investors can realize superior performance by buying the stocks of small-capitalization companies with low market-to-book ratios, which have performed well over the past 3 to 12 months. If this were true, it would have important implications for the way corporations make financing decisions and how investors select their portfolios. In an irrational market, for example, corporations may lower their costs of capital by timing their share issues to correspond to periods when the shares are overpriced.

---

[20] This intuition is provided in models by Dybvig (1983), Grinblatt and Titman (1983), Connor (1984) and Wei (1988).

[21] We believe that just as beta estimates can be improved with a statistical adjustment, so can factor risk premiums. The insights of the last section, which combine the CAPM with the APT, imply that the risk premiums of the factor portfolios should be their CAPM betas times the risk premium of the market portfolio. To the extent that investors have some confidence in the CAPM risk–expected return relationship, they should make some comparison between the risk premiums for the factors that would exist if the CAPM were true and the risk premiums estimated by averaging historical data. For those factors with historical risk premiums that deviate substantially from their CAPM-predicted risk premiums, it is possible to improve the estimated risk premium by taking a weighted average of the historical risk premium and the CAPM-predicted risk premium. The weighting would depend on the relative confidence one has in the historical estimate over the CAPM estimate. To the extent that the factor has been extremely volatile, one has less confidence in the historical estimate of the factor risk premium. To the extent that the CAPM predictions for all risk premiums seem to bear little relation to the historical averages, one has less confidence in the CAPM estimates of the factor risk premiums.

However, not all researchers share this view of financial markets. Others have argued that the return premiums associated with these characteristics arise because equities with these characteristics are exposed to systematic risk factors. Since this risk is not reflected in the CAPM betas of the equities, a multifactor model like the APT is needed to explain the returns.

Some researchers have argued that low market-to-book equities are more sensitive to swings in the business cycle and changes in credit conditions because the companies are more likely to have their financing cut off during an economic downturn, and that the added sensitivity to these economic factors is not reflected in their covariation with an aggregate market index such as the FTSE 100. In other words, returns are generated by multiple factors, as described by factor models, and small capitalization and low market-to-book stocks may have high betas on factors under-represented by the FTSE 100.

Unfortunately, because the virtually limitless range of factors that can be used, the theoretical and empirical literature is not as well developed as the literature on the CAPM, and the results are less conclusive. Consequently, the debate about whether these effects are driven by psychological behaviour or by the sensitivity of equities to risk factors that researchers have ignored is not yet resolved. With this caveat in mind, the remainder of this section explores what is known about factor models and the APT.

Empirical Implications of Factor Models and the APT

There are three implications.

1. The expected return of any portfolio with factor betas that are all equal to zero is the risk-free rate.
2. The expected returns of securities increase linearly with increases in a given factor beta.
3. No other characteristics of securities other than factor betas determine expected returns.

Evidence from Factor Analysis Studies

Roll and Ross (1980) published one of the first tests using factor analysis. Because of the computational limitations of standard statistical factor analysis programs, they were forced to estimate factors on small numbers of equities. In a test of 42 groups of 30 securities each, they found that in 88.1 per cent of the groups, there was at least one factor with a non-zero risk premium; in 57.1 per cent of the groups, at least two with non-zero risk premiums; and in about one-third of the groups, at least three factors with non-zero risk premiums. Roll and Ross concluded that at least three factors are important for the APT's risk–expected return relation, but probably no more than four are important.

Other papers used procedures that allow researchers to generate factor portfolios from much larger data sets. These include works by Chen (1983), Connor and Korajczyk (1988) and Lehmann and Modest (1988), who were all particularly interested in whether the factors explain the size effect.[22] Chen (1983) claimed that his factors explain the size effect: after controlling for differences in factor sensitivities between large and small firms, the return premium for size becomes negligible. However, Lehmann and Modest (1988) argued that there is still a size effect, even after controlling for these differences.

In a shift away from the original unconditional factor model analyses that focus only on returns, Ludvigson and Ng (2007) used conditioning information and dynamic factor analysis to estimate the factors that jointly predict future excess returns and volatility. They found three new factors, unrelated to the traditional ones tested in prior literature, related to volatility, the risk premium and 'real' factors.

Evidence from Studies with Macroeconomic Factors

Chen et al. (1986), who analysed several macroeconomic factors, found that the factors representing the growth rate in GDP, the yield spread between long-and short-term government bonds and changes in default spreads had significant effects on risk premiums. The two inflation factors had a weaker but still significant effect. They also performed tests using consumption and oil prices as factors and found that neither affected the expected returns of equities. In addition, when added to the regression, the return of the market index could not explain expected returns.

Chan et al. (1985) examined the size effect in the context of the Chen et al. model. They created 20 size-ranked portfolios and estimated the factor sensitivities of each portfolio to the five Chen et al. factors as well

[22] The market-to-book ratio and the momentum effect had not attracted much academic attention at the time these papers were written.

as the equal-weighted NYSE portfolio. They found that the difference in residuals between the portfolio of the smallest firms and that of the largest is positive but not statistically significant. They also conducted a test using the logarithm of firm size as an independent variable and found its coefficient to be insignificantly different from zero in the multifactor model. The authors concluded that the multi-factor model explains the size anomaly.[23]

Jagannathan and Wang (1996) used some of the Chen et al. macro factors to predict time-series changes in the risk premiums associated with the factors and added an additional macro factor, aggregate labour income, to explain the average stock returns. Several interesting observations come from the Chan et al. (1985), and Jagannathan and Wang (1996) papers, which provide some insights into the small firm effect:

- Small company equity returns appear to be highly correlated with changes in the spread between Baa and default-free bonds.
- The spread seems to be a reasonably good predictor of future market returns.
- Small companies have higher market betas when the spread is higher.
- Small company equity returns seem to covary more with per capita labour income than the returns of large company equities.

The first and last points imply that it is possible, at least in part, to explain the small-firm effect using a standard APT-type model that identifies the default spread and labour income as systematic factors associated with positive risk premiums. The middle two observations suggest that small firms, in essence, successfully 'time the market'. In other words, small firms have higher betas when the market risk premium is highest. The explanation of the small firm effect that comes from these studies is that small-cap equities have higher returns than large-cap equities because they are riskier in two aspects: (1) their returns are more sensitive to the short-term business cycle, and credit movements that seem to be captured by the spread between high- and low-grade bonds and changes in aggregate labour income; (2) small-cap equities are especially sensitive to movements in the overall market when the market is the most risky. This means that the CAPM beta of the shares of a typical small company underestimates the equity's true risk.

Evidence from Studies that Use Firm Characteristics

As covered in Chapter 5, Fama and French (2015, 2016, 2017) suggested a five-factor model composed of the following five zero-cost (that is, self-financing) portfolios:

1. A long position in the value-weighted index portfolio and a short position in T-bills – the difference between the realized return of the value-weighted market index and the return of Treasury bills.
2. A long position in a portfolio of low market-to-book equities and a short position in high market-to-book equities.
3. A long position in a portfolio of small capitalization equities and a short position in a portfolio of large capitalization equities.
4. A long position in a portfolio of high operating profitability portfolios and a short position in a portfolio of low operating profitability equities.
5. A long position in a portfolio of the most conservative investments and a short position in a portfolio of the most aggressive investments. Investment is measured as *'the change in total assets from the fiscal year ending in year t–2 to the fiscal year ending in t–1, divided by t–2 total assets'*.

Fama and French (2016) asserted that the five factors explain most of the risk premiums of equities, including those that cannot be accounted for by the CAPM. Although Fama and French (2015, 2016, and 2017) have received thousands of citations, there are many other studies that have found equally compelling factors. A list of recent research studies is presented in Exhibit 6.9.

[23] Fama and French (1993) dispute this conclusion. They argue that the Chen et al. macroeconomic factors cannot explain the firm size effect.

Exhibit 6.9 Recent Empirical Research on Factor Models and the APT

Research Study	Factor	Main Findings
Boyer (2011)	Index Labels	Economically meaningless index labels change stock return behaviour.
Hou et al. (2011)	Momentum; Cash Flow to Price	Momentum and Cash Flow to Price capture significant time-series variation. Study was on 27,000 equities from 49 countries.
Novy-Marx (2012)	Momentum	The momentum factor is driven by firms' performance twelve to seven months prior to portfolio formation.
Fama and French (2012)	Size, Value, Momentum	The size, value and momentum factors are valid in all regions, except Japan.
Asness et al. (2013)	Value, Momentum	Value and momentum are important factors.
Garcia (2013)	Sentiment	Stock market sentiment is an important factor during recessions.
Eisfeldt and Papanikolaou (2013)	Organization Capital	Firms with more organization capital have average returns that are 4.6% higher than firms with low organization capital.
Kelly and Pruitt (2013)	Size, Value, Momentum	Returns and cash flow growth are highly predictable.
Hirshleifer et al. (2013)	Innovative Efficiency	Innovative efficiency is an important factor.
Novy-Marx (2013)	Gross Profitability	Gross profitability is an important factor.
Bebchuk et al. (2013)	Corporate Governance	This factor is no longer relevant since 2000.
Fama and French (2015)	Size, Value, Gross Profitability, Investment	The five-factor model performs better than the three-factor model (Size, Value).
Barroso and Santa-Clara (2015)	Risk-managed momentum	Risk-managed momentum doubles the Sharpe ratio of the momentum factor.
Amihud et al. (2015)	Illiquidity	Illiquidity is an important factor in 45 countries.
Harvey et al. (2016)	N/A	A methodological paper that addresses the problem of data-mining in factor studies.
Fama and French (2016)	Size, Value, Gross Profitability, Investment	A paper that looks into what is driving the Gross Profitability and Investment factor performance.
Fama and French (2017)	Size, Value, Gross Profitability, Investment	International study looking to extend Fama and French (2016).
He et al. (2017)	Intermediary Capital Risk	Shocks to the equity capital ratio of financial intermediaries are important in explaining the cross-section of returns.

Exhibit 6.9 *Continued*

Research Study	Factor	Main Findings
Stambaugh and Yuan (2017)	Mispricing factors	Two mispricing factors are important in explaining the cross-section of returns.
Barillas and Shanken (2018)	Various	This is a methodology paper that introduces a new test of asset pricing models. Momentum, value and profitability factors are important.
Fama and French (2018)	Size, Value, Gross Profitability, Investment, Momentum	The paper considers variations and the six-factor model, which is the Fama-French five-factor model pluse momentum.
Linnainmaa and Roberts (2018)	Various	Out of sample testing of factor models lead to less anomalies, and therefore identified factors are most likely a result of data-snooping.
Kelly et al. (2019)	Methodological	Introduces a new factor analysis methodology to identify factors. The method is called Instrumental Principal Component Analysis.
Feng et al. (2020)	Methodological	Proposes a new model selection method to identifying important new factors.
Schneider et al. (2020)	Betting against Beta, Betting against Volatility	Coskewness risk drives the performance of Betting against Beta and Betting against Volatility factors. Skewness is a big driver of returns.
Jacobs and Müller (2020)	International study	The US is the only country where an identified factor leads to a decline in the anomaly. In other countries the factors remain significant once identified.
Kozak et al. (2020)	Stochastic Discount Factors	A stochastic discount factor created from a small number of principal components outperforms characteristics-sparse SDFs formed using the four or five factor models of Fama-French or Carhart.
Harvey and Liu (2021)	Methodological	A new methodological approach to identifying appropriate factors.
Clarke (2022)	Level, Slope, Curve	A new methodological approach that results in novel factors.

6.13 Summary and Conclusions

A factor model is a decomposition of the returns of securities into two categories: (1) a set of components correlated across securities; and (2) a component that generates firm-specific risk and is uncorrelated across securities. The components that determine correlations across securities – common factors – are variables that represent some fundamental macroeconomic conditions. The components that are uncorrelated across securities represent firm-specific information.

The firm-specific risk, but not the factor risk, is diversified away in most large well-balanced portfolios. However, through a judicious choice of portfolio weights, it is possible to tailor portfolios with any factor beta configuration desired.

The arbitrage pricing theory is based on two ideas: first, factor models can describe the returns of securities; second, arbitrage opportunities do not exist. Using these two assumptions, it is possible to derive a multifactor version of the CAPM risk–expected return equation that expresses the expected returns of each security as a function of its factor betas. However, to test and implement the model, one must first identify the actual factors.

There are substantial differences between a multifactor APT and the CAPM that favour the use of the APT in place of the CAPM. In contrast to the CAPM, the multifactor APT allows for the possibility that investors hold very different risky portfolios. In addition, the assumptions behind the CAPM seem relatively artificial when compared with those of the APT.

In choosing the multifactor APT over the CAPM, one must recognize that the research into what the factors are is still in its infancy. The three methods of implementing the multifactor APT are more successful than the CAPM in explaining historical returns. However, it appears that firm characteristics such as size, market-to-book and momentum explain average historical returns more successfully. Until we can better determine what the factors are and which factors explain expected returns, the implications of APT will be fraught with ambiguity and are likely to be controversial.

Even if the CAPM and the APT do not hold in reality, the theories may still be useful to portfolio managers. Recall that, according to the CAPM, the market compensates investors who bear systematic risk by providing higher rates of return. If this hypothesis is false, portfolio managers can match the market portfolio in terms of expected returns with a far less risky portfolio by concentrating on equities with low betas. The evidence in this chapter suggests that, in addition to buying low-beta equities, investors should tilt their portfolios towards smaller cap firms with low market-to-book ratios and high momentum. However, we stress that these suggestions are based on past evidence, which may not be indicative of future events. As you know, economists do reasonably well explaining the past but are generally a bit shaky in predicting the future.

Despite any shortcomings that these theories exhibit when measured against historical data, the CAPM and APT have become increasingly important tools for evaluating capital investment projects.[25] They provide an increasingly effective framework for corporate financial analysts who can use them appropriately while understanding their limitations.

Key Concepts

Result 6.1: If securities' returns follow a factor model (with uncorrelated residuals), portfolios with approximately equal weight on all securities have residuals with standard deviations that are approximately inversely proportional to the square root of the number of securities.

Result 6.2: The factor beta of a portfolio on a given factor is the portfolio-weighted average of the individual securities' betas on that factor.

Result 6.3: Assume that there are K factors uncorrelated with each other and that the returns of securities i and j are respectively described by the factor models:

$$\tilde{r}_i = \alpha_i + \beta_{i1}\tilde{F}_1 + \beta_{i2}\tilde{F}_2 + \cdots + \beta_{iK}\tilde{F}_K + \tilde{\varepsilon}_i$$
$$\tilde{r}_j = \alpha_j + \beta_{j1}\tilde{F}_1 + \beta_{j2}\tilde{F}_2 + \cdots + \beta_{jK}\tilde{F}_K + \tilde{\varepsilon}_j$$

Then the covariance between $\tilde{r}_i$ and $\tilde{r}_j$ is

$$\sigma_{ij} = \beta_{i1}\beta_{j1}\text{var}(\tilde{F}_1) + \beta_{i2}\beta_{j2}\text{var}(\tilde{F}_2) + \cdots + \beta_{iK}\beta_{jK}\text{var}(\tilde{F}_K)$$

Result 6.4: When K factors are uncorrelated with each other and security i is described by the factor model

$$\tilde{r}_i = \alpha_i + \beta_{i1}\tilde{F}_1 + \beta_{i2}\tilde{F}_2 + \cdots + \beta_{iK}\tilde{F}_K + \tilde{\varepsilon}_i$$

the variance $\tilde{r}_i$ can be decomposed into the sum of $K + 1$ terms:

$$\text{var}(\tilde{r}_i) = \beta_{i1}^2 \text{var}(\tilde{F}_1) + \beta_{i2}^2 \text{var}(\tilde{F}_2) + \cdots + \beta_{iK}^2 \text{var}(\tilde{F}_K) + \text{var}(\tilde{\varepsilon}_1)$$

Result 6.5: An investment with no firm-specific risk and a factor beta of β_{ij} on the jth factor in a K-factor model is tracked by a portfolio with weights of β_{i1} on factor portfolio 1, β_{i2} on factor portfolio 2, . . . β_{iK}, on factor portfolio K, and $1 - \sum_{j=1}^{K}\beta_{ij}$ on the risk-free asset. The expected return of this tracking portfolio is therefore

$$r_f + \beta_{i1}\lambda_1 + \beta_{i2}\lambda_2 + \cdots + \beta_{ik}\lambda_k$$

where $\lambda_1, \lambda_2, \ldots, \lambda_k$ denote the risk premiums of the factor portfolios, and r_f is the risk-free return.

Result 6.6: An arbitrage opportunity exists for all investments with no firm-specific risk unless:

$$\tilde{r}_i = r_f + \beta_{i1}\lambda_1 + \beta_{i2}\lambda_2 + \cdots + \beta_{iK}\lambda_K$$

where $\lambda_1, \ldots, \lambda_k$ applies to all investments with no firm-specific risk.

Key Terms

arbitrage opportunity 162
arbitrage pricing theory (APT) 162
common factor 162
diversifiable risk 163
factor analysis 168
factor beta 162
factor model 162
factor portfolio 168
factor risk 162
factor sensitivity 162
firm-specific component 162
firm-specific risk 162
gross domestic product (GDP) 168
macroeconomic variable 162
market model 163
multifactor model 167
non-diversifiable risk 165
one-factor model 163
pure factor portfolio 178
R-squared 164
systematic (market) risk 163
unsystematic (non-market) risk 163
well-diversified portfolio 163

Exercises

6.1 Prove that the portfolio-weighted average of a security's sensitivity to a particular factor is the same as the covariance between the return of the portfolio and the factor divided by the variance of the factor if the factors are uncorrelated with each other. Do this with the following steps:

1 Write out the factor equation for the portfolio by multiplying the factor equations of the individual securities by the portfolio weights and adding.
2 Group terms that multiply the same factor.
3 Replace the factor betas of the individual security returns with the covariance of the security return with the factor divided by the variance of the factor.
4 Show that the portfolio-weighted average of the covariances that multiply each factor is the portfolio return's covariance with the factor.

The rest is straightforward.

6.2 What is the minimum number of factors needed to explain the expected returns of a group of ten securities if the securities' returns have no firm-specific risk? Why?

6.3 Consider the following two-factor model for the returns of three securities. Assume that the factors and epsilons have means of zero. Also, assume that the factors have variances of 0.01 and are uncorrelated with each other.

$$\tilde{r}_A = 0.13 + 6\tilde{F}_1 + 4\tilde{F}_2 + \tilde{\varepsilon}_A$$
$$\tilde{r}_B = 0.15 + 2\tilde{F}_1 + 2\tilde{F}_2 + \tilde{\varepsilon}_B$$
$$\tilde{r}_C = 0.07 + 5\tilde{F}_1 + 1\tilde{F}_2 + \tilde{\varepsilon}_C$$

If $\text{var}(\tilde{\varepsilon}_A) = 0.01\text{var}(\tilde{\varepsilon}_B) = 0.4\text{var}(\tilde{\varepsilon}_C) = 0.02$, what are the variances of the returns of the three securities, as well as the covariances and correlations between them?

6.4 What are the expected returns of the three securities in exercise 6.3?

6.5 Write out the factor betas, factor equations and expected returns of the following portfolios.

1 A portfolio of the three equities in exercise 6.3 with £20,000 invested in A, £20,000 invested in B and £10,000 invested in C.

2 A portfolio consisting of the portfolio formed in part 1 of this exercise and £3,000 short position in C of exercise 6.3.

6.6 How much should be invested in each of the equities in exercise 6.3 to design two portfolios? The first portfolio has the following attributes:

factor 1 beta = 1

factor 2 beta = 0

The second portfolio has the attributes:

factor 1 beta = 0

factor 2 beta = 1

Compute the expected returns of these two portfolios. Then compute the risk premiums of these two portfolios assuming that the risk-free rate is the 'zero-beta rate' implied by the factor equations for the three equities in exercise 6.3. This is the expected return of a portfolio with factor betas of zero.

6.7 Two equities, Uni and Due, have returns that follow the one-factor model:

$$\tilde{r}_{\text{Uni}} = 0.11 + 2\tilde{F} + \tilde{\varepsilon}_{\text{Uni}}$$
$$\tilde{r}_{\text{Due}} = 0.17 + 5\tilde{F} + \tilde{\varepsilon}_{\text{Due}}$$

How much should be invested in each of the two equities to design a portfolio that has a factor beta of 3? What is the expected return of this portfolio, assuming that the factors and epsilons have means of zero?

6.8 Describe how you might design a portfolio of the 40 largest equities that mimic the FTSE 100. Why might you prefer to do this instead of investing in all 100 of the FTSE 100 companies?

6.9 Prove that $\alpha_i = (1 - \beta_i)r_f$ in equation (6.3), assuming the CAPM holds. To do this, take expected values of both sides of this equation and match up the values with those of the equation for the CAPM's securities market line.

6.10 Compute the firm-specific variance and firm-specific standard deviation of a portfolio that minimizes the firm-specific variance of a portfolio of 20 securities. The first 10 securities have firm-specific variances of 0.10. The second 10 securities have firm-specific variances of 0.05.

6.11 Find the weights of the two pure factor portfolios constructed from the following three securities:

$$r_1 = 0.06 + 2\tilde{F}_1 + 2\tilde{F}_2$$
$$r_2 = 0.05 + 3\tilde{F}_1 + 1\tilde{F}_2$$
$$r_3 = 0.04 + 3\tilde{F}_1 + 0\tilde{F}_2$$

Then write out the factor equations for the two pure factor portfolios, and determine their risk premiums. Assume a risk-free rate that is implied by the factor equations and no arbitrage.

6.12 Assume that the factor model in exercise 6.11 applies again. If there exists an additional asset with the factor equation

$$r_4 = 0.08 + 1\widetilde{F}_1 + 0\widetilde{F}_2$$

does an arbitrage opportunity exist? If so, describe how you would take advantage of it.

6.13 Use the information provided in Example 6.10 to determine the coordinates of the intersection of the solid and dotted lines in Exhibit 6.7.

References and Additional Reading

Abeysekera, S.P. and Mahajan, A. (1987) A test of the APT in pricing UK stocks *Journal of Business Finance & Accounting*, 14(3): 377–391.

Acharya, V.V., Pedersen, L.H., Philippon, T. and Richardson, M. (2017) Measuring systemic risk. *The Review of Financial Studies*, 30(1): 2–47.

Admati, A.R. and Pfleiderer, P. (1985) Interpreting the factor risk premia in the arbitrage pricing theory *Journal of Economic Theory*, 35(1): 191–195.

Amihud, Y., Hameed, A., Kang, W. and Zhang, H. (2015) The illiquidity premium: International evidence *Journal of Financial Economics*, 117(2): 350–368.

Asness, C.S., Moskowitz, T.J. and Pedersen, L.H. (2013) Value and momentum everywhere *The Journal of Finance*, 68(3): 929–985.

Bai, J., Bali, T.G. and Wen, Q. (2019) Common risk factors in the cross-section of corporate bond returns. *Journal of Financial Economics*, 131(3): 619–642.

Barillas, F. and Shanken, J. (2018) Comparing asset pricing models. *The Journal of Finance*, 73(2): 715–754.

Barroso, P. and Santa-Clara, P. (2015) Momentum has its moments. *Journal of Financial Economics*, 116(1): 111–120.

Bebchuk, L.A., Cohen, A. and Wang, C.C. (2013) Learning and the disappearing association between governance and returns. *Journal of Financial Economics*, 108(2): 323–348.

Berry, M.A., Burmeister, E. and McElroy, M.B. (1988) Sorting out risks using known APT factors *Financial Analysts Journal*, 44(2): 29–42.

Bower, D., Bower, R.S. and Logue, D.E. (1984) Arbitrage pricing theory and utility stock returns *The Journal of Finance*, 39(4): 1041–1054.

Boyer, B.H. (2011) Style-related comovement: Fundamentals or labels?, *The Journal of Finance*, 66(1): 307–332.

Brown, S.J. (1989) The number of factors in security returns *The Journal of Finance*, 44(5): 1247–1262.

Brown, S.J. and Weinstein, M.I. (1983) A new approach to testing asset pricing models: the bilinear paradigm *The Journal of Finance*, 38(3): 711–743.

Chan, K.C., Chen, N. and Hsieh, D. (1985) An exploratory investigation of the firm size effect *Journal of Financial Economics*, 14(3): 451–471.

Chan, L.K., Hamao, Y. and Lakonishok, J. (1991) Fundamentals and stock returns in Japan *The Journal of Finance*, 46(5): 1739–1789.

Chen, N. (1983) Some empirical tests of the theory of arbitrage pricing *The Journal of Finance*, 38(5): 1393–1414.

Chen, N., Roll, R. and Ross, S.A. (1986) Economic forces and the stock market *Journal of Business*, 59(3): 383–403.

Cho, D.C. (1984) On testing the arbitrage pricing theory: inter-battery factor analysis *The Journal of Finance*, 39(5): 1485–1502.

Cho, D.C., Elton, E.J. and Gruber, M.J. (1984) On the robustness of the Roll and Ross arbitrage pricing theory *Journal of Financial Quantitative Analysis*, 19(1): 1–10.

Cho, D.C., Eun, C.S. and Senbet, L.W. (1986) International arbitrage pricing theory: an empirical investigation *The Journal of Finance*, 41(2): 313–329.

Chui, A.C., Titman, S. and Wei, K.J. (2010) Individualism and momentum around the world, *The Journal of Finance*, 65(1): 361–392.

Clarke, C. (2021) The level, slope, and curve factor model for stocks, *Journal of Financial Economics*.

Cochrane, J.H. (2022). Portfolios for long-term investors. *Review of Finance*, 26(1): 1–42.

Connor, G. (1984) A unified beta pricing theory *Journal of Economic Theory*, 34(1): 13–31.

Connor, G. and Korajczyk, R. (1988) Risk and return in an equilibrium APT: application of a new test methodology *Journal of Financial Economics*, 21(2): 255–289.

Cragg, J.G. and Malkiel, B.G. (1982) *Expectations and the Structure of Share Prices*. Chicago: University of Chicago Press.

Daniel, K. and Titman, S. (1997) Evidence on the characteristics of cross-sectional variation in stock returns *The Journal of Finance*, 52(1): 1–33.

Dong, X., Li, Y., Rapach, D. and Zhou, G. (2021). Anomalies and the expected market return. *Baruch College Zicklin School of Business Research Paper*, (2020–02): 02.

Duffie, D. (2010). Presidential address: Asset price dynamics with slow-moving capital, *The Journal of Finance*, 65(4): 1237–1267.

Dybvig, P.H. (1983) An explicit bound on deviations from APT pricing in a finite economy *Journal of Financial Economics*, 12(4): 483–496.

Dybvig, P.H. and Ross, S.A. (1985) Yes, the APT is testable *Journal of Finance*, 40(4): 1173–1188.

Eisfeldt, A.L. and Papanikolaou, D. (2013) Organization capital and the cross-section of expected returns, *The Journal of Finance,* 68(4): 1365–1406.

Elton, E.J., Gruber, M.J. and Urich, T.J. (1978) Are betas best? *The Journal of Finance,* 33(5): 1375–1384.

Erb, C., Harvey, C. and Viskanta, T. (1995) Country credit risk and global portfolio selection *Journal of Portfolio Management,* 21(2): 74–83.

Fama, E. and French, K. (1993) Common risk factors in the returns on stocks and bonds *Journal of Financial Economics,* 33(1): 3–56.

Fama, E.F., and French, K.R. (2012) Size, value, and momentum in international stock returns, *Journal of Financial Economics,* 105(3): 457–472.

Fama, E.F. and French, K.R. (2015) A five-factor asset pricing model, *Journal of Financial Economics,* 116(1): 1–22.

Garcia, D. (2013) Sentiment during recessions, *The Journal of Finance,* 68(3): 1267–1300.

Fama, E.F. and French, K.R. (2016) Dissecting anomalies with a five-factor model, *The Review of Financial Studies,* 29(1): 69–103.

Fama, E.F. and French, K.R. (2017) International tests of a five-factor asset pricing model, *Journal of Financial Economics,* 123(3): 441–463.

Fama, E.F. and French, K.R. (2018) Choosing factors. *Journal of Financial Economics,* 128(2): 234–252.

Feng, G., Giglio, S. and Xiu, D. (2020) Taming the factor zoo: A test of new factors, *The Journal of Finance,* 75(3): 1327–1370.

Gehr, Adam Jr (1978) Some tests of the arbitrage pricing theory *Journal of the Midwest Finance Association,* 7(4): 91–105.

Grinblatt, M. and Titman, S. (1983) Factor pricing in a finite economy *Journal of Financial Economics,* 12(4): 497–507.

Gultekin N.B. and Rogalski, R.J. (1985) Government bond returns, measurement of interest rate risk, and the arbitrage pricing theory *The Journal of Finance,* 40(1): 43–61.

Hamao, Y. (1988) An empirical examination of the arbitrage pricing theory: using Japanese data *Japan and the World Economy,* 1(1): 45–61; reprinted in E. J. Elton and M.J. Gruber (eds) (1990) *Japanese Capital Markets* (1990). New York: Harper & Row.

Harvey, C. R., & Liu, Y. (2021). Lucky factors. *Journal of Financial Economics,* 141(2), 413–435.

Harvey, C.R., Liu, Y. and Zhu, H. (2016). . . . and the cross-section of expected returns, *The Review of Financial Studies,* 29(1): 5–68.

He, Z., Kelly, B. and Manela, A. (2017) Intermediary asset pricing: New evidence from many asset classes, *Journal of Financial Economics,* 126(1): 1–35.

Hirshleifer, D., Hsu, P.H. and Li, D. (2013) Innovative efficiency and stock returns, *Journal of Financial Economics,* 107(3): 632–654.

Hou, K., Karolyi, G.A. and Kho, B.C. (2011) What factors drive global stock returns?, *The Review of Financial Studies,* 24(8): 2527–2574.

Huberman, G. (1982) A simple approach to arbitrage pricing theory *Journal of Economic Theory,* 28(1): 183–191.

Huberman, G., Kandel, S. and Stambaugh, R. (1987) Mimicking portfolios and exact arbitrage pricing *Journal of Finance,* 42(4): 873–888.

Hughes, P.J. (1984) A test of the arbitrage pricing theory using Canadian security returns *Canadian Journal of Administrative Science,* 1(2): 195–214.

Ingersoll, J.E. (1984) Some results in the theory of arbitrage pricing *Journal of Finance,* 39(4): 1021–1039.

Jacobs, H. and Müller, S. (2020) Anomalies across the globe: Once public, no longer existent?, *Journal of Financial Economics,* 135(1): 213–230.

Jagannathan, R. and Wang, Z. (1996) The conditional CAPM and the cross-section of expected returns *Journal of Finance,* 51(1): 3–53.

Jobson, J.D. (1982) A multivariate linear regression test of the arbitrage pricing theory *Journal of Finance,* 37(4): 1037–1042.

Jones, R.C. (1990) Designing factor models for different types of stock *Financial Analysts Journal,* 46(2): 25–30.

Kelly, B. and Pruitt, S. (2013). Market expectations in the cross-section of present values, *The Journal of Finance,* 68(5): 1721–1756.

Kelly, B.T., Pruitt, S. and Su, Y. (2019) Characteristics are covariances: A unified model of risk and return, *Journal of Financial Economics,* 134(3): 501–524.

Koijen, R.S., Moskowitz, T.J., Pedersen, L.H. and Vrugt, E.B. (2018) Carry, *Journal of Financial Economics,* 127(2): 197–225.

Kozak, S., Nagel, S. and Santosh, S. (2018) Interpreting factor models. *The Journal of Finance,* 73(3): 1183–1223.

Kozak, S., Nagel, S. and Santosh, S. (2020) Shrinking the cross-section, *Journal of Financial Economics,* 135(2): 271–292.

Kuwahara, H. and Marsh, T.A. (1992) The pricing of Japanese equity warrants *Management Science,* 38(11): 1610–1641.

Lee, K.H. (2011) The world price of liquidity risk. *Journal of Financial Economics,* 99(1): 136–161.

Lehmann, B.N. and Modest, D.M. (1988) The empirical foundations of the arbitrage pricing theory *Journal of Financial Economics,* 21(2): 213–254.

Levine, R. (1989) An international arbitrage pricing model with PPP deviations *Economic Inquiry,* 27(4): 587–599.

Linnainmaa, J.T. and Roberts, M.R. (2018) The history of the cross-section of stock returns. *The Review of Financial Studies,* 31(7): 2606–2649.

Litterman, R. and Scheinkman, J. (1991) Common factors affecting bond returns *Journal of Fixed Income,* 1(1): 54–61.

Ludvigson, S.C. and Ng, S. (2007) The empirical risk–return relation: a factor analysis approach *Journal of Financial Economics,* 83(1): 171–222.

McCulloch, R. and Rossi, P.E. (1991) A Bayesian approach to testing the arbitrage pricing theory *Journal of Econometrics,* 49(1–2): 141–168.

McElroy, M.B. and Brumeister, E. (1988) Arbitrage pricing theory as a restricted nonlinear multivariate regression model *Journal of Business & Economic Statistics,* 6(1): 29–42.

Mitton, T. (2022) Methodological variation in empirical corporate finance, *The Review of Financial Studies,* 35(2): 527–575.

Novy-Marx, R. (2012) Is momentum really momentum?. *Journal of Financial Economics,* 103(3): 429–453.

Novy-Marx, R. (2013) The other side of value: The gross profitability premium, *Journal of Financial Economics,* 108(1): 1–28.

Reinganum, M. (1981) The arbitrage pricing theory: some simple tests *Journal of Finance*, 36(2): 313–321.

Roll, R., and Ross, S.A. (1980) An empirical investigation of the arbitrage pricing theory *Journal of Finance*, 35(5): 1073–1103.

Rosenberg, B. (1974) Extra-market components of covariance in security returns *Journal of Financial and Quantitative Analysis*, 9(2): 263–274.

Ross, S.A. (1976) The arbitrage theory of capital asset pricing *Journal of Economic Theory*, 13(3): 341–360.

Schneider, P., Wagner, C. and Zechner, J. (2020) Low-Risk Anomalies?. *The Journal of finance*, 75(5): 2673–2718.

Shanken, J. (1982) The arbitrage pricing theory: is it testable? *Journal of Finance*, 37(5): 1129–1140.

Shanken, J. and Weinstein, M.I. (1990) Macroeconomic variables and asset pricing: estimation and tests Working paper, University of Rochester, July.

Sharpe, W.F. (1984) Factor models, CAPMs, and the APT *Journal of Portfolio Management*, 11(1): 21–25.

Stambaugh, R.F., and Yuan, Y. (2017). Mispricing factors. *The Review of Financial Studies*, 30(4): 1270–1315.

Warga, A. (1989) Experimental design in tests of linear factor models *Journal of Business and Economic Statistics*, 7(2): 191–198.

Wei, K.C.J. (1988) An asset pricing theory unifying the CAPM and APT *Journal of Finance*, 43(4): 881–892.

Wei, K.C.J., Lee, C.F. and Chen, A.H. (1991) Multivariate regression tests of the arbitrage pricing theory the instrumental variable approach *Review of Quantitative Finance and Accounting*, 1: 191–208.

Winkelmann, M. (1984) Testing APT for the German stock market In *Proceedings of the 11th Annual Meeting of the European Finance Association*, Manchester, England, Sept. 1984.

Chapter 7

Pricing Derivatives

Learning Objectives

After reading this chapter, you should be able to:

- Explain what a derivative is, and how basic derivatives, such as futures, forwards, options and swaps, work.
- Use the binomial model to construct a derivative's tracking portfolio, and understand its importance in valuing the derivative.
- Understand how to form arbitrage portfolios if a derivative's market price differs from its model price.
- Use risk-neutral valuation methods to solve for the no-arbitrage prices of any derivative in a binomial framework, and understand why risk-neutral solutions to the valuation problems of derivatives are identical to solutions based on tracking portfolios.

Derivative instruments can be exceedingly complicated, and even executives in large firms find them challenging to understand. Take Palladium Hotel Group as an example. The company is one of Spain's largest hotel groups, yet it was almost destroyed by following complex derivative strategies to minimize its risk. When derivatives are used to manage risk, the derivatives portfolio is known as a hedge book because the company wishes to hedge its risk. A firm may create a hedge book with its own team, or it can outsource this if it feels it doesn't have the skillset to manage a derivative portfolio on a day to day basis. Thinking it was taking the less risky option, Palladium hired Deutsche Bank to manage its derivative portfolio. In 2021, Palladium sued Deutsche Bank, alleging that it was sold derivatives it did not understand. To give some context, Palladium's annual sales are around €700 million a year with an EBITDA of just above €150 million. Palladium was not a small company, but at one point in the firm's dealings, it had an outstanding notional amount of derivatives amounting to €5.6 billion! Furthermore, Palladium alleged that the fees and losses associated with the contract were so large it had to take out substantial loans to cover them. Deutsche Bank had a different view of things, and they argued that Palladium was a 'sophisticated investor with extensive experience of using derivatives'. Either way, the Palladium experience illustrates how dangerous these instruments can be.

In the last few decades, the world's financial markets have experienced an unprecedented boom that revolved around the development of new financial products known as derivatives. A **derivative** is a financial instrument whose value today or at some future date is derived entirely from the value of another asset (or a group of other assets), known as the **underlying asset** (or assets). Examples of derivatives include interest rate futures contracts, options on futures, mortgage-backed securities, interest rate caps and floors, swap options, commodity-linked bonds, zero-coupon Treasury strips, and all sorts of options, contractual arrangements and bets related to the values of other more primitive securities.

Derivatives have now entered into the public discourse and political debate, as anyone who has read a newspaper in recent years is aware. Derivatives are inherently complex and most executives do not fully understand the pricing and pay-off dynamics of these financial instruments. The opening vignette discussed the litigation raised by Palladium Hotel Group against Deutsche Bank in 2021. However, other scandals, just as serious, have occurred, including that of Société Générale in 2008, Long-Term Capital Management in 1998, Metallgesellschaft AG in 1993, and Gibson Greetings, Orange County, Procter & Gamble and Barings Bank in 1994. Warren Buffet, a US financial mogul, even went so far as to call derivatives 'financial weapons of mass destruction'.

Despite these scandals, derivatives remain incredibly popular among investors and corporations, because they represent low-transaction-cost vehicles for managing risk, and for betting on the price movements of various securities. Corporations such as BMW, with substantial revenues from the USA, enter into currency swaps and currency forward rate agreements to eliminate currency risk. Pension fund managers, with large exposure to share price movements, buy put options on stock indices to place a floor on their possible losses. Mutual funds that have accumulated large profits may short stock index futures contracts in order to effectively realize capital gains in an appreciating stock market without selling equity, thereby avoiding unnecessary taxes. The list of profitable uses of derivatives is extensive.

The most important use of derivatives is a risk-reduction technique known as *hedging*,[1] which requires a sound understanding of how to value derivatives. Derivatives hedging is based on the notion that the change in the value of a derivative position can offset changes in the value of the underlying asset. However, it is impossible to understand how a derivative's value changes without first understanding what the proper value is.

Some derivatives are straightforward to value, and others are complicated. Every year, significant amounts of cash are made and lost by speculators willing to test their skills and their models by placing bets on what they believe are misvalued derivatives.

The major breakthrough in the valuation of derivatives started with a simple call option. At about the same time that options began trading on an organized exchange (in 1973 at the Chicago Board Options Exchange), two finance professors at the Massachusetts Institute of Technology, Fischer Black and Myron Scholes, came out with a formula, commonly known as the Black–Scholes formula, which related the price of a call option to the price of the equity to which the option applies. This formula was the start of a revolution for both academics and practitioners in their approach to finance. It generated a Nobel Prize in Economics for Myron Scholes and Robert Merton (who provided many key insights in option pricing theory). (Fischer Black passed away before the prize was awarded.)

The Black–Scholes model that led to the development of the formula is now part of a family of valuation models, most of which are more sophisticated than the Black–Scholes model. This family, known as *derivative valuation models,* is based on the now familiar principle of no arbitrage or law of one price. No-arbitrage valuation principles can determine the fair market price of almost any derivative. Knowledge of these principles is common in the financial services industry. Therefore it is often possible to tailor a security that is ideally suited to a corporation's needs, and to identify a set of investors who will buy that security. Investment banks and other financial intermediaries that design the security concern themselves largely with what design will be attractive to corporations and investors. These intermediaries do not worry about the risks of taking bets opposite to those of their customers when they 'make markets' in these derivatives, because they can determine, to a high degree of precision, what the derivative is worth, and they know how to hedge their risks.[2]

The analysis of derivatives in this chapter begins by exploring some of the derivatives encountered by the corporate financial manager and the sophisticated investor, followed by an examination of valuation principles that apply to all derivatives.[3]

---

[1] Hedging is covered in depth in Part VI.

[2] An investment bank will often serve as an over-the-counter market maker in the derivative it creates, standing ready to buy the derivative at a bid price and sell it at an ask price.

[3] The valuation of options, one of the most popular derivatives, is covered in depth in Chapter 8, which also touches briefly on forward prices for some complex assets such as bonds, commodities and foreign exchange.

7.1 Examples of Derivatives

This section introduces several derivatives: forwards and futures, swaps, options, corporate bonds, mortgage-backed securities and structured notes. The section also introduces derivatives that are implicit in real assets.

Forwards and Futures

A **forward contract** represents the obligation to buy (sell) a security or commodity at a pre-specified price, known as the **forward price**, at some future date. Forward contracts are inherent in many business contracts, and have been in existence for hundreds of years. Exhibit 7.1 illustrates the exchange that takes place at the **maturity date**, or **settlement date**, of the forward contract. At maturity, the person or firm with the long position pays the forward price to the person with the short position, who in turn delivers the asset underlying the forward contract. **Futures contracts** are a special type of forward contract that trade on organized exchanges known as **futures markets**.

Exhibit 7.1 The Exchange of an Asset for Cash in a Forward Contract at Maturity

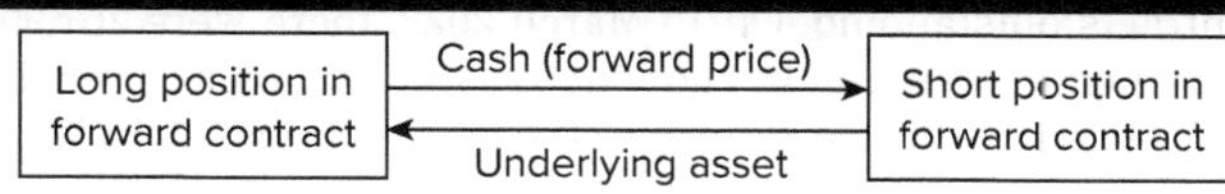

Exhibit 7.2 introduces forward rates for the euro against the pound for a variety of maturity dates. For example, the pound had a foreign exchange rate on Wednesday 16 March of 0.84305 British pounds to the euro. However, the 12-month forward rate was 0.85715 pounds to the euro. This means that one could have agreed that day to have exchanged a single euro for £0.85715 twelve months hence.

Exhibit 7.2 Pound/Euro forward rates as at 16 March 2022

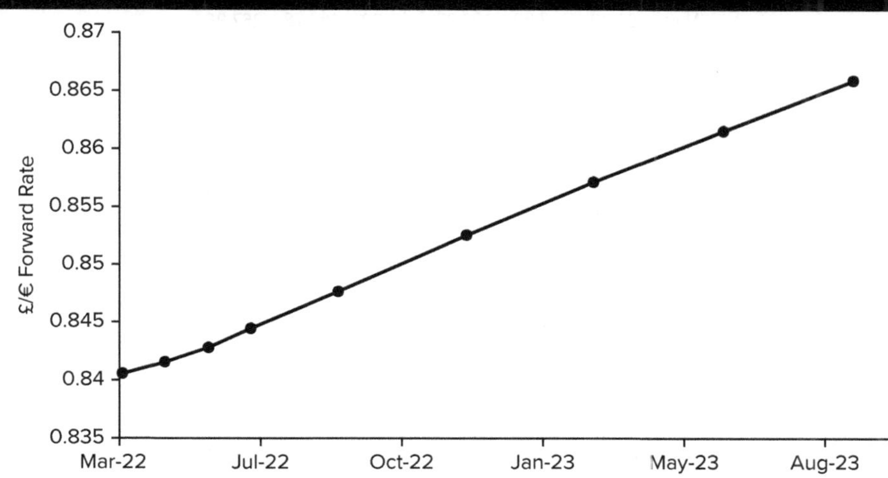

Source: FXEmpire.Com

Markets for Forwards and Futures

The first organized futures trading market, the Chicago Board of Trade, dates back to the US Civil War. Although the Board's early trading records were lost in the Great Chicago Fire of 1871, we know that the earliest futures contracts were probably limited to agricultural commodities that were grown in the US Midwest.

Today, futures and forward markets are also well known for the trading of contracts on financial securities, such as Treasury bonds, stock indices, short-term interest rate instruments, and currencies. There are futures markets in almost every type of financial commodity, including:

- currency futures
- interest rate futures
- bond futures
- equity futures
- soft commodity futures.

Across the world there are 98 futures markets: the most important of these are CME Group, Euronext, Eurex and The Intercontinental Exchange. They trade all types of futures contract, including financial, agricultural and energy futures and, combined, make up some of the largest markets in the world. The most important financial forward market is the interbank forward market for currencies, particularly dollars for yen and dollars for euros.

Exhibit 7.3 shows data for some oil and gas contracts traded on the New York Mercantile Exchange (NYMEX). Taking the Crude Oil NYMEX futures contract as an example, the table presents price and volume data for futures contracts to buy 1,000 barrels of crude oil. The column on the far right is the **open interest**, which is the number of contracts outstanding. On 15 March 2022, there were 267,960 May 2022 contracts and 183,210 June 2022 contracts. Open interest can be thought of as the number of bets between investors about oil and gas prices. The column labelled 'Sett price' describes the closing price for 15 March 2022. This price is used, along with the previous day's settlement price, to determine how much cash is exchanged between parties to the contract that day. The contracts maturing in May 2022 and June 2022 specify settlement prices of $94.79 and $92.83 per barrel, respectively.

Exhibit 7.3 Futures Prices for Oil and Gas, 15 March 2022

CRUDE OIL
NYMEX (1,000 barrels; $/barrel)

	Sett price	Day's chge	High	Low	Vol 000s	O int 000s
Apr	96.44	−7.91	102.58	93.53	367.41	141.24
May	94.79	−7.58	100.92	92.20	182.28	267.96
Jun	92.83	−6.73	98.39	90.37	139.51	183.21
Jul	90.87	−6.13	95.94	88.53	53.15	94.31
Total					**995.54**	**1860.42**

HEATING OIL
NYMEX (42,000 US galls; c/US galls)

Apr	3.0297	−0.2908	3.2600	2.9330	28.39	42.74
May	2.9458	−0.2463	3.1307	2.8635	28.14	56.25
Jun	2.8902	−0.2084	3.0153	2.8128	18.70	35.88
Jul	2.8499	−0.1820	2.9325	2.7791	10.63	16.43
Total					**113.55**	**238.99**

NATURAL GAS
NYMEX (10,000 mmBtu; $/mmBty)

Apr	4.568	−0.059	4.682	4.459	80.26	79.44
May	4.617	−0.053	4.722	4.509	48.87	205.04
Jun	4.670	−0.050	4.764	4.562	15.26	70.08
Jul	4.727	−0.049	4.824	4.620	11.92	88.04
Total					**226.34**	**1088.62**

Source: FT.Com

Distinguishing Forwards from Futures

The essential distinction between a forward and a futures contract lies in the timing of cash flows. With a forward contract, cash is paid for the underlying asset only at the maturity date, T, of the contract. It is useful to think of this cash amount, the forward price, F_0, which is set prior to maturity, at date 0, as the sum of

- What one would pay for immediate delivery of the underlying asset at the maturity date, T, without the forward contract: this is known as the **spot price** at maturity – essentially, the prevailing market price of the underlying asset; call this S_T.
- The profit (or loss) incurred as a result of having to pay the forward price in lieu of this spot price: this is $F_0 - S_T$.

With a futures contract, the price paid at maturity is the spot price, which is identical to the final day's futures price, F_T. The profit (or loss) is received (or paid) on a daily basis instead of in one large amount at the maturity date. The amount the buyer receives from (or pays to) the seller of the futures contract is the one-day appreciation (or depreciation) of the futures price. For example, if the futures price of oil rises from $90 a barrel to $92 a barrel from Monday to Tuesday, the buyer of a futures contract on 1,000 barrels receives $2,000 from the seller on Tuesday. This procedure, known as **marking to market**, reduces the risk of default, because the amounts that each side has to pay on a daily basis are relatively small. Moreover, it facilitates early detection in the event that one party to the contract lacks sufficient cash to pay for his or her losses.

The marking to market takes place automatically, by transferring funds between the margin accounts of the two investors agreeing to the contract. These **margin accounts** are simply deposits placed with brokers as security against default.

Example 7.1 illustrates how marking to market works.

Example 7.1

Marking to Market with NYMEX Crude Oil Futures

Elly has a long position in the NYMEX November futures contract to buy 1,000 barrels of crude oil. Bernard has a short position in the same contract. If the futures price for the November crude oil contract is $91.44 on 4 October, but it falls to $91.22 on 5 October, falls further to $91.02 on 6 October, and rises to $91.65 on 7 October, describe the cash payments and margin accounts of Elly's long and Bernard's short position. Assume that each of the margin accounts of Elly and Bernard initially contains $1,000.

Answer: The marking-to-market feature implies that the margin accounts of the long and short positions are as described in Exhibit 7.4.

Exhibit 7.4

Date	Elly's long margin ($)	Change from day before ($)	Bernard's short margin ($)	Change from day before ($)
4 October	1,000	–	1,000	–
5 October	780	–220	1,220	220
6 October	580	–200	1,420	200
7 October	1,010	430	990	–430

With a few exceptions, notably long-term interest rate contracts, the distinction in the timing of cash flows from profits or losses has a negligible effect on the fair market price agreed to in forward and futures contracts (see Grinblatt and Jegadeesh 1996). Hence this text treats forward and futures prices as if they are identical.

If day 0 forwards and futures prices for contracts maturing on day T are identical, it is easy to see that the total profit (excluding interest on cash balances) is identical with both the forward and the futures contract. With the *forward* contract, the profit is

$$S_T - F_0, \text{ all earned in cash on date } T$$

With the *futures* contract, at the same futures price of F_0 set at date 0, the profit is the same:

$$S_T - F_0$$

But this total profit is earned piecemeal, with

$F_1 = F_0$ the difference between the day 1 and day 0 futures prices earned (lost) on date 1
$F_2 = F_1$ earned (lost) on date 2
$F_3 = F_2$ earned (lost) on date 3

and so forth until the final days before maturity, when

$F_{T-1} - F_{T-2}$ is earned on date $T - 1$ and
$S_T - F_T$ is earned on date T.

The day-to-day futures profits still sum to the same amount, $S_T - F_0$, but the timing of the cash differs from the forward contract.

Swaps

A **swap** is an agreement between two investors, or **counterparties** as they are sometimes called, to periodically exchange the cash flows of one security for the cash flows of another. The last date of exchange determines the **swap maturity**. For example, a fixed-for-floating **interest rate swap** (see Exhibit 7.5) exchanges the cash flows of a fixed-rate bond for the cash flows of a floating-rate bond. The **notional amount** of the swap represents the size of the principal on which interest is calculated.

Exhibit 7.5 The Cash Flows of a Five-Year Semi-Annual Fixed-for-Floating Interest Rate Swap: $100

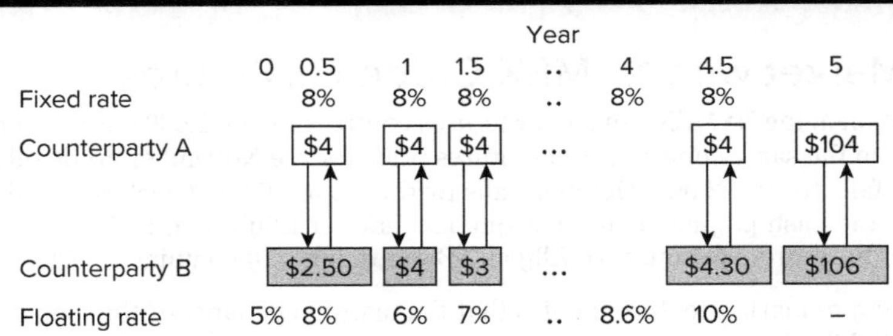

Netting in an Interest Rate Swap

The cash flows in an interest rate swap are netted so that periodically (typically every six months) only one of two swap counterparties pays cash and the other receives cash. In a typical swap, the floating rate is SONIA (UK), €STR (EU) or SOFR (US) plus some pre-specified percentage.[4] Example 7.2 illustrates how netting affects swap payments.

Example 7.2

Netting Payments in an Interest Rate Swap

If the fixed interest rate in a swap with semi-annual payments is 8 per cent per year (4 per cent for six months) and the floating interest rate is 8.6 per cent per year, how much does the party who pays the floating rate and receives the fixed rate receive or pay? What would happen to that party if, six months later, the floating interest rate had increased to 10 per cent per annum?

Answer: At year 4.5, counterparty A swaps its fixed payments of \$4 (= (8%/2) × \$100) with counterparty B's floating payments (= floating rate%/2 × \$100), as seen in Exhibit 7.5. Counterparty B would thus *pay* \$0.30 (= (8.6% – 8%)/2 × \$100) per \$100 of notional amount to counterparty A. If interest rates at year 4.5 increase to 10 per cent, counterparty B *pays* \$100 (= (10% – 8%)/2 × \$100) per \$100 of notional amount to counterparty A at year 5.

[4] Swaps are often used in conjunction with interest rate caps and floors, which are also popular derivatives. Caps pay when prevailing interest rates exceed a pre-specified rate, and floors pay if the pre-specified rate exceeds the prevailing rate. See Chapter 2 for further discussion.

Growth of the Interest Rate Swap Market

Interest rate swaps are one of the great derivatives success stories. At the end of 1987, the aggregate notional amount of interest rate swaps outstanding was less than $800 billion. By 2022, the estimated notional amount of interest rate swaps exceeded $380 trillion, more than half the entire interest rate derivatives market ($610 trillion) – many times the value of all US equities ($37.7 trillion)!

Currency Swaps

A *currency swap* (see Chapter 2) exchanges cash flow streams in two different currencies. Typically, it involves the periodic exchange of the cash flows of a par bond denominated in one currency for those of a par bond denominated in another currency. In contrast with a fixed-for-floating interest rate swap, which nets out the identical principal of the two bonds at maturity and thus exchanges only interest payments, the typical currency swap exchanges principal, which is denominated in two different currencies, at the maturity date of the swap.

The typical forward contracts, futures contracts and swap contracts are self-financing, or **zero-cost instruments**[5] – that is, the terms of these contracts are set so that one party does not have to pay the other to enter into the contract. In many instances, margin or collateral is put up by both parties, which protects against default in the event of extreme market movements, but this is not the same as paying someone to enter into the contract, because the terms of the contract are more favourable to one side than the other. There are exceptions to this zero-cost feature, however. Financial contracts can be modified in almost every way imaginable.

Options

Options exist on countless underlying securities. For example, there are swap options, bond options, equity options and options that are implicit in many securities, such as callable bonds, convertible preference shares, and caps and floors, which are options on interest rates.[6]

Options give their buyers the right, *but not the obligation,* to buy (call option) or sell (put option) an underlying security at a pre-specified price, known as the **strike price**. The value of the underlying security determines whether the right to buy or sell will be exercised, and how much the option is worth when exercised.

Most options have a limited life and expire at some future **expiration date**, denoted as *T*. Some options, which are called American options (see Chapter 8), permit exercise at any date up to *T*; others, which are called European options (see Chapter 8), permit exercise only on date *T*.

Example 7.3

Payments in a Currency Swap

Describe the exchange of payments in a fixed-for-fixed dollar–yen currency swap with annual payments and a $100 notional amount, as shown in Exhibit 7.6. The dollar bond has an interest rate of 7 per cent, the yen bond has an interest rate of 5 per cent and the current exchange rate is ¥80/$.

Answer: Here, the interest rates of both bonds are fixed, but each is denominated in a different currency. Thus counterparty A will exchange its $7 [= (7%)$100] fixed payments with counterparty B's fixed payments of ¥400 [= (5%)$100 (¥80/$)], as illustrated in Exhibit 7.6.

Exhibit 7.6 The Cash Flows of a Five-Year Annual Yen-Dollar Fixed-Rate Currency Swap: $100 Notional

	Year 1	2	3	4	5
Dollar rate ($100)	7%	7%	7%	7%	7%
Counterparty A	$7	$7	$7	$7	$107
	↓↑	↓↑	↓↑	↓↑	↓↑
Counterparty B	¥400	¥400	¥400	¥400	¥8,400
Yen rate (¥8,000)	5%	5%	5%	5%	5%

[5] See Chapter 5 for the first use of the term *self-financing*.

[6] See Chapter 2.

Values of Calls and Puts at Expiration

Exhibit 7.7 outlines the values of a call and put at their expiration date, T, as a function of S_T, the value of the underlying asset (for example, here, a share of equity) at that date. Exhibit 7.7 shows that if an option is exercised at T, its value is the difference between the share price and the strike or exercise price (call), or between the strike price and the share price (put). For example, if the equity is selling at £105 at the expiration date, a call option with a strike price of £100 is worth £5, because holding it is like having a coupon that allows the holder to buy equity at £5 off the going rate. If the equity is selling for £117, the call option is like a coupon for a £17 mark-off. If the equity is selling for £94, the option is worthless, since it is better to buy the equity at the market price than to exercise the option and pay the price specified by the option. Exercise of a put allows the option holder to sell the equity at an unfairly high price. For example, the right to sell a share of equity worth £48 at a price of £50 is worth £2.

Exhibit 7.7 The Value of a Call Option and a Put Option at Expiration

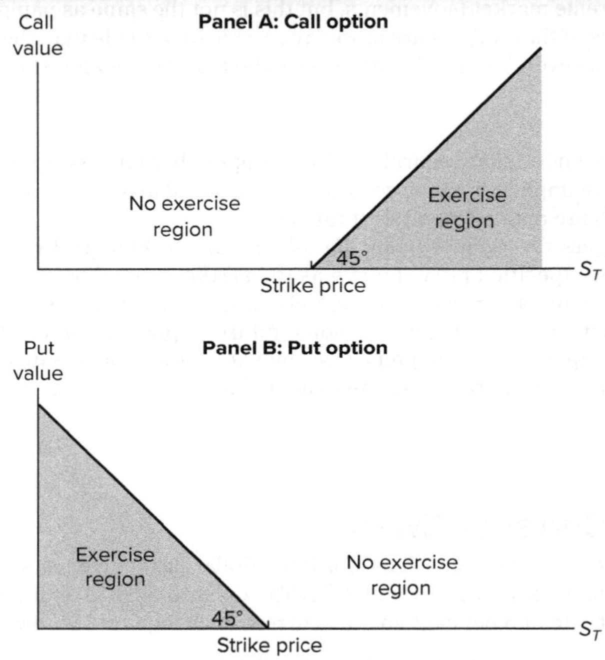

Panel A in Exhibit 7.7 (a call) illustrates this point more generally. The horizontal axis represents S_T, the price of the equity at expiration date T, and the vertical axis represents the value of the call at date T. If the share price is below the strike price of the call, the call option will not be exercised. Thus the call has zero value. If the share price is greater than the strike price, the value of the call rises by one pound for each pound increase in the share price. The value of the call at date T equals the maximum of either (1) zero or (2) S_T less the strike price.

Panel B of Exhibit 7.7 (a put) shows that the opposite relation holds between the value of the put and the value of the equity. Recall that the holder of a put possesses the right to *sell* the equity at the strike price. Thus the value of the put at date T equals the maximum of either (1) zero or (2) the strike price less S_T.

In contrast to forwards, futures and swaps, options benefit only one side of the contract – the side that receives the option. Hence the investor who receives an option pays for it up front, regardless of the terms of the option.

Exchange-Traded Options

Options are an important segment of the international securities markets and, according to the Bank for International Settlements, and amounted to 33.31 billion contracts in 2021, up from 9.42 billion in 2013.

Exchange-traded options constitute the bulk of traded options, although options on futures contracts, swaps and bonds are also extremely popular.

Exhibit 7.8 presents the range of March call and put options that existed for Vodafone plc on 17 March 2022. At 1.13 pm, the share price of Vodafone was £124.34, and options with exercise or strike prices ranged from £1 to £160. Since call options with lower exercise prices lead to greater profits, these options will be more valuable. Similarly, put options with higher exercise prices will have greater value, because they lead to higher profits.

Exhibit 7.8 March American Call Option Prices for Vodafone plc on Eurex, 17 March 2022

Call Settlement	Strike	Put Settlement
0.25	160	35.75
0.25	155	30.75
0.25	150	25.75
0.25	145	20.75
0.25	140	15.75
0.25	135	10.75
0.5	130	6
1.5	125	2
4.75	120	0.5
9.5	115	0.25
14.25	110	0.25
19.25	105	0.25
24.25	100	0.25
26.25	98	0.25
123.25	1	0.25

Source: Eurex.

It is also important to understand other option terminology. The underlying asset of a call (or put) option that is **in the money** has a current price that is greater (less) than the strike price. The underlying asset of a call (or put) option that is **out of the money** has a current price that is less (greater) than the strike price. An option **at the money** is one for which the strike price and underlying asset's price are the same.[7] As you can see from Exhibit 7.8, the Vodafone call options are out of the money for exercise prices above £124.34, and in the money for exercise prices less than £124.34.

Investors seem to be most interested in options that are slightly out of the money. Hence most exchange-traded options are initially designed to be slightly out of the money. As the underlying asset's price changes, however, they can evolve into at-the-money or in-the-money options.

Corporations are not involved in exchange-based trading of options on their equity. These options, like most derivatives, are merely complicated bets between two counterparties. Hence the number of long positions in an option is exactly the same as the number of short positions. This feature also applies to options traded in loosely organized 'over-the-counter markets' between institutions such as banks, pension funds and corporations.

[7] As implied by the terms, an *in-the-money* option means that exercising the option is profitable (excluding the cost of the option). Similarly, *at the money* and *out of the money* imply that exercising the option produces zero cash flow and negative cash flow, respectively, and thus exercise should not be undertaken.

Dealing with a single counterparty can be burdensome when liquidating or exercising an option position. If the call or put seller does not perform according to the option contract (that is, does not deliver the cash or underlying asset required in exercising the option), there is a high probability that a costly lawsuit will ensue. The institutional over-the-counter options markets mitigate this possibility by investigating the creditworthiness of each counterparty before entering into the contract. As a result, different option prices exist for different option sellers, depending on their degree of creditworthiness.

The organized exchanges solve the problem of counterparty default risk differently. Instead of performing the investigation function, each exchange uses a **clearing house**, which is a corporation set up by the exchange and its member brokers to act as a counterparty to all option contracts. All options are legal contracts between the investor and the clearing house. When an investor exercises an option, the clearing house's computer randomly selects one of the outstanding short positions in the option, and requires the holder of this short position either to buy or to sell the underlying security at the exercise price under the terms of the investor's contract with the clearing house. The clearing house mitigates the need for lawsuits by requiring those who short options to put up margin and have their creditworthiness verified by their brokers. In the rare instance of a lawsuit, the clearing house is responsible for suing the counterparty.

The eagerness of investors to place bets with option-like pay-offs determines the number of outstanding exchange-listed options. This number increases by one when an investor places an order to sell an option that he or she does not have and the order is executed. In option markets, the procedure for shorting an option is commonly referred to as **writing an option**. When an order to write an option is executed, the clearing house acts as the legal intermediary between the two parties, announcing that there is an increase in the number of contracts outstanding. Hence the mechanism for shorting most options differs from that for shorting equities and bonds, which requires some form of borrowing of securities to execute a short sale because the number of outstanding shares is fixed by the original issuer. Conversely, when an investor cancels a long position in an option by selling it, and someone else – not necessarily the investor from whom the option was purchased – with a short position simultaneously agrees that this is a fair price at which to close out his or her short position, the clearing house closes out its contracts with both parties. This leaves one option contract fewer outstanding.

Warrants

Warrants are options, usually calls, that companies issue on their own equity (see Chapter 3). In contrast to exchange-traded options, which are mere bets between investors on the value of a company's underlying equity – in which the corporation never gets involved – warrants are contracts between a corporation and an investor.

Warrants have become very popular in the last 20 years through their other title of *executive and employee stock options*. Warrants are also sources of capital for newer growth firms, and are common in some countries, such as Japan, where they are often linked to a bond issue.

Most of the warrants used to finance companies are traded on stock exchanges. These warrants can be sold short by borrowing them from a warrant holder in the same way that the equity is sold short (see Chapter 4).[8] Thus the number of warrants is fixed for a given issue. Warrants issued as employee compensation are generally not traded.

The major distinction between a warrant and other types of call option is that the company issues additional equity when an investor exercises a warrant. Upon exercise, the equity is sold to the warrant holder at the strike price. Since exercise occurs only when the strike price is less than the current share price, the exercise of the warrant involves the issuance of new shares of equity at bargain prices. The new shares dilute the value of existing shares. Because of this dilution, option pricing models used to value warrants differ from option pricing models used to value exchange-traded options. For example, consider Air France-KLM, an international air carrier, which is trading at €3.87 a share. Warrants with a strike price of €9 that expire in one year might be worth €6; they are worth slightly more than €6 if one values them with models that do not account for the dilution. Generally, the percentage of a corporation's equity represented by warrants is so small that one can ignore the effect of dilution, and value them like any other option. Hence, for the example of Air France-KLM, the difference between €6 (the value with dilution) and €6.01 (the value assuming no dilution) might be a realistic portrayal of the warrant dilution effect.[9]

---

[8] This is in notable contrast to exchange-traded options, where a short position is created along with every long position, because both positions merely represent the sides of a 'bet' between parties.

[9] It is important to note that exchange-traded options and otherwise identical warrants necessarily have the same value. Hence, if both warrants and identical exchange-traded options exist at the same time, the dilution effect of the warrants must be taken into account in valuing both the warrant and the exchange-traded options. However, this is rarely done in practice.

Embedded Options

In addition to warrants, a number of corporate securities have option-like components. For example, when a corporation issues a convertible bond, it gives the bondholder the option to exchange the bond for a pre-specified number of shares of equity in the corporation. Similarly, many long-term corporate bonds are callable or refundable bonds, which means that the corporation has the option to buy back the bonds at a pre-specified price after a certain date.

Options are also implicit in simple equity and simple debt, even when they lack a call or conversion feature. One can look at the ordinary equity of a firm with debt on its balance sheet as a call option that allows the equity holders the right, but not the obligation, to purchase the firm's assets from the debt holders by repaying the debt. Such common equity can be valued *in relation to the assets* as a derivative.[10] Similarly, one can look at simple corporate debt as risk-free debt and a short position in a put option that effectively (through the default option) allows the put option holder to sell the firm's assets to the debt holders for a price equal to the outstanding debt obligation: thus corporate debt can be valued in relation to the assets (or the equity) with the techniques developed in this chapter.

Real Assets

Investors can view many real assets as derivatives. For example, a copper mine can be valued in relation to the price of copper.[11] Sometimes other derivatives, such as options, are implicit in these real assets. For example, the option to shut down a copper mine often needs to be accounted for when valuing a mine. These implicit options also can be valued with the techniques developed here.

Structured Notes

A large percentage of the new issues of traded debt securities issued by corporations are in the form of *structured notes* (see Chapter 2), which are bonds of any maturity sold in small amounts by means of a previously shelf-registered offering (see Chapter 1). They are customized for investors, in that they often pass on the cash flows of derivative transactions entered into by the issuer.

Examples of structured notes include inverse floaters, which have coupons that decline as interest rates increase bonds with floating-rate coupons part of the time and fixed-rate coupons at other times; and bonds with coupons that depend on the return of a benchmark market index, an exchange rate, a constant times a squared benchmark interest rate, such as SONIA, or a commodity price. Basically, anything goes.

Why are structured notes so popular? From an economic perspective, structured notes are derivatives. From a legal and public relations standpoint, however, they are bonds, 'blessed' by the regulatory authorities, investment banks and ratings agencies. Some investors, such as state pension funds, may be prohibited from investing in derivatives directly. One hypothesis about the popularity of structured notes is that they permit an investor to enter into a derivatives transaction while appearing to the public like an investor in the conservative bonds of an AAA-rated corporation.

7.2 The Basics of Derivatives Pricing

Derivatives valuation has two basic components. The first is the concept of perfect tracking. The second is the principle of no arbitrage. A fair market price for a derivative, obtained from a derivatives valuation model, is simply a no-arbitrage restriction between the tracking portfolio and the derivative.

Perfect Tracking Portfolios

All derivative valuation models make use of a fundamental idea: *it is always possible to develop a portfolio consisting of the underlying asset and a risk-free asset that perfectly tracks the future cash flows of the derivative.* As a result, in the absence of arbitrage, the derivative must have the same value as the tracking portfolio.[12] A perfect *tracking portfolio* is a combination of securities that perfectly replicates the future cash flows of another investment.

---

[11] See Chapter 12.

[12] In this text, the models developed to value derivatives assume that perfect tracking is possible. In practice, however, transaction costs and other market frictions imply that investors can, at best, attain only almost perfect tracking of a derivative.

The perfect tracking, used to value derivatives, stands in marked contrast to the use of tracking portfolios (discussed in Chapters 5 and 6) to develop general models of financial asset valuation. There our concern was with identifying a tracking portfolio with the same systematic risk as the investment being valued. Such tracking portfolios typically generate substantial tracking error (see Exhibit 5.6). We did not analyse tracking error in Chapters 5 and 6 because the assumptions of those models implied that the tracking error had zero present value and thus could be ignored. This places a high degree of faith in the validity of the assumptions of those models. The success of derivative valuation models rests largely on the fact that derivatives can be almost perfectly tracked, which means that we do not need to make strong assumptions about how tracking error affects value.

No Arbitrage and Valuation

In the absence of tracking error, arbitrage exists if it costs more to buy the tracking portfolio than the derivative, or vice versa. Whenever the derivative is cheaper than the tracking portfolio, arbitrage is achieved by buying the derivative and selling (or shorting) the tracking portfolio. On initiating the arbitrage position, the investor receives cash, because the cash spent on the derivative is less than the cash received from shorting the tracking portfolio. Since the future cash flows of the tracking portfolio and the derivative are identical, buying one and shorting the other means that the future cash flow obligations from the short sales position can be met with the future cash received from the position in the derivative.[13]

Applying the Basic Principles of Derivatives Valuation to Value Forwards

This subsection considers several applications of the basic principles described above, all of which are related to forward contracts.

Valuing a Forward Contract

Models used to value derivatives assume that arbitrage is impossible. Example 7.4 illustrates how to obtain the fair market value of a forward contract using this idea, and how to arbitrage a mispriced forward contract.

Example 7.4

Valuing a Forward Contract on a Share of Equity

Consider the obligation to buy a share of Raiffeisen Bank International one year from now for €130. Today, the equity sells for €116 per share. Assume that Raiffeisen Bank International will pay no dividends over the coming year. One-year zero-coupon bonds that pay €130 one year from now currently sell for €122. At what price are you willing to buy or sell this obligation?

Answer: Compare the cash flows today and one year from now for two investment strategies. Under strategy 1, the forward contract, the investor acquires today the obligation to buy a share of Raiffeisen Bank International one year from now at a price of €130. Upon paying €130 for the equity at that time, the investor immediately sells it for cash. Strategy 2, the tracking portfolio, involves buying a share of Raiffeisen Bank International today and selling short €130 in face value of one-year zero-coupon bonds to partly finance the purchase. The equity is sold one year from now to finance (partly or fully) the obligation to pay the €130 owed on the zero-coupon bonds. Denoting the share price one year from now by the random number G_1, the cash inflows and costs from these two strategies are as shown in the table.

	Cash flow today (3)	Cash flow one year from today (3)
Strategy 1 (forward)	6	$\tilde{S}_1-130$
Strategy 2 (tracking portfolio)	122–116	$\tilde{S}_1-130$

[13] Usually, it is impossible to track a *mispriced* derivative perfectly, although a forward contract is an exception. However, any mispriced derivative that does not converge immediately to its no-arbitrage value can be taken advantage of further to earn additional arbitrage profits, using the tracking portfolio strategy outlined in this chapter.

Since strategies 1 and 2 have identical cash flows in the future, they should have the same cost today to prevent arbitrage. Strategy 2 costs €6 today. Strategy 1, the obligation to buy the equity for €130 one year from now, should also cost €6. If it costs less than €6, then going long in strategy 1 and short in strategy 2 (which, when combined, means acquiring the obligation, selling short a share of Raiffeisen Bank International and buying €130 face amount of the zero-coupon bonds) has a positive cash inflow today, and no cash flow consequences in the future. This is arbitrage. If the obligation costs more than €6, then going short in strategy 1 and going long in strategy 2 (short the obligation, buy a share of equity, and short €130 face amount of the zero-coupon bonds) has a positive cash inflow today and no future cash flows. Thus the investor would be willing to pay €6 as the fair value of the attractive obligation to buy Raiffeisen International for €130 one year from now.

Result 7.1 generalizes Example 7.4.

Results

Result 7.1

The no-arbitrage value of a forward contract on a share of equity (the obligation to buy a share of equity at a price of K, T years in the future), assuming the equity pays no dividends prior to T, is

$$S_0 - \frac{K}{(1 + r_f)^T}$$

where

S_0 = current share price

and

$K/(1 + r_f)^T$ = the current market price of a default-free zero-coupon bond paying K, T years in the future.

Obtaining Forward Prices for Zero-Cost Forward Contracts

The value of the forward contract is zero for a contracted price, K, that satisfies

$$S_0 - \frac{K}{(1 + r_f)^T} = 0$$

namely,

$$K = S_0(1 + r_f)^T$$

Whenever the contracted price K is set so that the value of forward is zero, the contracted price is known as the *forward price.* At date 0, this special contracted price is denoted as F_0.[14] Assuming that no money changes hands today as part of the deal, the forward price, $F_0 = S_0(1 + r_f)^T$, represents the price at which two parties would agree today represents fair compensation for the non-dividend-paying equity T years in the future. It is fair in the sense that no arbitrage takes place with this agreed-on forward price. We summarize this important finding in Result 7.2.

Results

Result 7.2

The forward price for settlement in T years of the purchase of a non-dividend-paying equity with a current share price of S_0 is

$$F_0 = S_0(1 + r_f)^T$$

[14] As mentioned earlier, 'off-market' forward prices, resulting in non-zero-cost contracts, exist. Usually, however, forward price refers to the cash required in the future to buy the forward contract's underlying investment under the terms specified in a *zero-cost* contract.

Currency Forward Rates

Currency forward rates are a variation on Result 7.2. Specifically, this is shown by the following result.

Results

Result 7.3

In the absence of arbitrage, the forward currency rate F_0 (for example, euros/dollar) is related to the current exchange rate (or **spot rate**), S_0, by the equation

$$\frac{F_0}{S_0} = \frac{1 + r_{\text{foreign}}}{1 + r_{\text{domestic}}}$$

where

r = the return (unannualized) on a domestic or foreign risk-free security over the life of the forward agreement, as measured in the respective country's currency.

To understand this result, compare the riskless future pay-offs of two strategies (A and B) that invest one US dollar today. Suppose that one US dollar currently buys 0.71 euros; that is, $S_0 = 0.71$. If the interest rate on euros is 4 per cent (that is, $r_{\text{foreign}} = 0.04$), the three-part strategy A involves contracting today to:

1. convert US$1 to €0.71
2. invest the euros at 4 per cent and receive €0.7384 (4 per cent more than 0.71) one year from now
3. convert the €0.7384 back to $0.7384/F_0$ dollars one year from now (at the euros per US dollar forward rate F_0 agreed to today).

Let's now compare strategy A with strategy B, which consists of taking the same dollar and investing it in the United States, earning 3 per cent (that is, $r_{\text{domestic}} = 0.03$), which produces US$1.03 one year from now.

To prevent arbitrage, strategy A has to generate the same pay-off next year as the US$1.03 generated by strategy B. This can happen only if

$$\frac{(0.71)(1.04)}{F_0} = 1.03$$

Or, equivalently,

$$\frac{F_0}{0.71} = \frac{1 + 0.04}{1 + 0.03}$$

which is the equation obtained if applying Result 7.3 directly.

By subtracting 1 from each side of the equation in Result 7.3 and simplifying, we obtain

$$\frac{F_0}{S_0} - 1 = \frac{r_{\text{foreign}} - r_{\text{domestic}}}{1 + r_{\text{domestic}}}$$

Note that the right-hand-side quotient of this equation is approximately the same as its numerator, $r_{\text{foreign}} - r_{\text{domestic}}$. Thus Result 7.3 implies that the **forward rate discount** relative to the spot rate is[15]

$$\frac{F_0 - S_0}{S_0}\left(= \frac{F_0}{S_0} - 1\right)$$

[15] It is a discount instead of a premium because exchange rates are measured as units of foreign currency that can be purchased per unit of domestic currency. Depending on the currency, it is sometimes customary to express the exchange rate as the number of units of domestic currency that can be purchased per unit of foreign currency. In this case, r_{foreign} and r_{domestic} are reversed in Result 7.3 and in the approximation of Result 7.3 expressed in this sentence. Moreover, we would refer to $F_0/S_0 - 1$ as the forward rate premium.

which represents the percentage discount at which one buys foreign currency in the forward market relative to the spot market, is approximately the same as the interest rate differential, $r_{\text{foreign}} - r_{\text{domestic}}$. For example, if the one-year interest rate in Switzerland is 10 per cent and the one-year interest rate in the United States is 8 per cent, then a US company can purchase Swiss francs forward for approximately 2 per cent less than the spot rate, which is reflected by F_0 being about 2 per cent larger than S_0.

Result 7.3 is sometimes known as the **covered interest rate parity relation**. This relationship describes how forward currency rates are determined by spot currency rates and interest rates in the two countries. Example 7.5 illustrates how to implement the covered interest rate parity relation.

Example 7.5

The Relationship Between Forward Currency Rates and Interest Rates

Assume that six-month SOFR on Canadian funds is 4 per cent and the US$ Eurodollar rate (six-month €STR on US funds) is 10 per cent, and that both rates are default free. What is the six-month forward Can$/US$ exchange rate if the current spot rate is Can$1.25/US$? Assume that six months from now is 182 days.

Answer: As noted in Chapter 2, SOFR is a zero-coupon rate based on an actual/360-day count. Hence:

	Canada	United States
Six-month interest rate (unannualized)	$2.02\% = \frac{182}{360} \times 4\%$	$5.06\% = \frac{182}{360} \times 10\%$

By Result 7.3, the forward rate is $\frac{\text{Can\$}1.21}{\text{US\$}}\left(= \frac{1.0202}{1.0506} \times 1.25\right)$.

7.3 Binomial Pricing Models

In derivative valuation models, the *current* price of the underlying asset determines the price of the derivative *today*. This is a rather surprising result, because, in most cases, the link between the price of the derivative and the price of the corresponding underlying asset is usually obvious only at some future date. For example, the forward contract described in Example 7.4 has a price equal to the difference between the share price and the agreed-upon settlement price, but only at the settlement date one year from now. A call option has a known value at the expiration date of the call when the share price is known.

Tracking and Valuation: Static Versus Dynamic Strategies

The pricing relation of a derivative with an underlying asset in the future translates into a no-arbitrage pricing relation in the present because of the ability to use the underlying asset to perfectly track the derivative's future cash flows. Example 7.4 illustrates an investment strategy in the underlying asset (a share of Raiffeisen equity) and a risk-free asset (a zero-coupon bond) that tracks the pay-off of the derivative at a future date when the relationship between their prices is known. In the absence of arbitrage, the tracking strategy must cost the same amount today as the derivative.

The tracking portfolio for a forward contract is particularly simple. As Example 7.4 illustrates, forward contracts are tracked by static investment strategies: that is, buying and holding a position in the underlying asset and a risk-free bond of a particular maturity. The buy and hold strategy tracks the derivative, the forward contract, because the future pay-off of the forward contract is a linear function of the underlying asset's future pay-off. However, most derivatives have future pay-offs that are not linear functions of the pay-off of the underlying asset. Tracking such non-linear derivatives requires a dynamic strategy: the holdings in the underlying asset and the risk-free bond need to change frequently in order to perfectly track the derivative's future pay-offs. With a call option on an equity, for example, tracking requires a position in the equity and a risk-free bond, where the number of shares of equity in the tracking portfolio goes up as the share price goes up and decreases as the share price goes down.

The ability to perfectly track a derivative's pay-offs with a dynamic strategy requires that the following conditions be met:

- The price of the underlying security must change smoothly: that is, it does not make large jumps.
- It must be possible to trade both the derivative and the underlying security continuously.
- Markets must be frictionless (see Chapter 5).[16]

If these conditions are violated, the results obtained will generally be approximations. One notable exception to this relates to the first two assumptions. If the price of the underlying security follows a very specific process, known as the binomial process, the investor can still perfectly track the derivative's future cash flows.

With the **binomial process**, the underlying security's price moves up or down over time, but can take on only *two* values at the next point at which trading is allowed – hence the name 'binomial'. This is certainly not an accurate picture of a security's price process, but it is a better approximation than you might at first think, and it is very convenient for illustrating how the theory of derivative pricing works. Academics and practitioners have discovered that the dynamic tracking strategies developed from binomial models are usually pretty good at tracking the future pay-offs of the derivative. Moreover, the binomial fair market values of most derivatives approximate the fair market values given by more complex models, often to a high degree of accuracy, when the binomial periods are small and numerous.

Binomial Model Tracking of a Structured Bond

Exhibit 7.9 illustrates what are known as binomial trees. The tree at the top represents the possible price paths for the CAC-40, the index of the 40 largest French equities, and is the underlying security in our example. The leftmost point of this tree, 4,460, represents the value of the CAC-40 today. The lines connecting 4,460 with the next period represent the two possible paths that the CAC-40 can take. The two values at the end of those lines, 4,906 and 4,014, represent the two possible values that the CAC-40 can assume one period from today. In the binomial process, one refers to the two outcomes over the next period as the **up state** and the **down state**. Hence 4,906 and 4,014 represent the pay-offs of the CAC-40 in the up state and down state, respectively.[17]

Exhibit 7.9 One-Period Binomial Trees

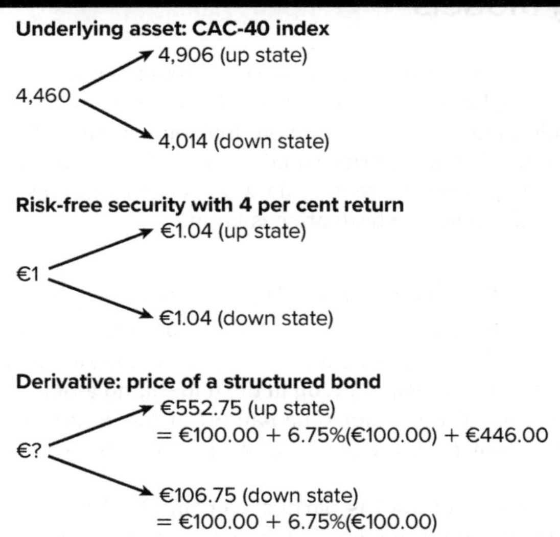

[16] Most of the models analysed here assume that the risk-free rate is constant. If the short-term risk-free return can change over time, perfect tracking can be achieved with more complicated tracking strategies. In many instances, formulae for valuing derivatives (for example, options) based on these more complex tracking strategies can be derived, but they will differ from those presented here. These extensions of our results are beyond the scope of this text.

[17] For reasons that will become clearer in Chapter 8, we assume that the future pay-offs of the CAC-40 include dividend payments.

The middle tree models the price paths for a risk-free security paying 4 per cent per period. This security is risk free because each €1.00 invested in the security pays the same amount, €1.04, at the nodes corresponding to both the up and the down states. The bottom tree models the price paths for the derivative, which in this case is a structured bond. The upper node corresponds to the pay-off of the structured bond when the up state occurs (which leads to a CAC-40 increase of 446 points to 4,906); the lower node represents the down state, which corresponds to a CAC-40 value of 4,014. The structured bond pays €552.75, €100.00 in principal plus 6.75 per cent interest at the maturity of the bond one period from now. In addition, if the CAC-40 goes up in value, there is an additional payment of €1 for every 1 point increase in the CAC-40. Since this occurs only in the up state, the pay-off of the structured bond at the up state node is €552.75, whereas the pay-off at the down-state node is €106.75.

The structured bond pictured in Exhibit 7.9 is a simplified characterization of a number of these bonds. Investors, such as pension fund managers, who are prohibited from participating directly in the equity markets have attempted to circumvent this restriction by investing in corporate debt instruments such as structured bonds that have pay-offs tied to the appreciation of an equity index. Of course, a corporation that issues such a bond needs compensation for the future payments it makes to the bond's investors. Such payments reflect interest and principal, as well as a pay-off that enables the investor to enjoy upside participation in the stock market. Generally, the corporation cannot observe a fair market price for derivatives, such as structured bonds, because they are not actively traded. The question mark at the leftmost node of the bottom tree in Exhibit 7.9 reflects that a fair value is yet to be determined. The next section computes this fair value using the principle of no arbitrage. It involves identifying a portfolio of financial instruments that are actively traded, unlike the structured bond. This portfolio has the property that its future cash flows are identical to those of the structured bond.

Using Tracking Portfolios to Value Derivatives

Since each node has only two future values attached to it, binomial processes allow perfect tracking of the value of the derivative with a tracking portfolio consisting of the underlying security and a risk-free bond. After identifying the tracking portfolio's current value from the known prices of its component securities, the derivative can be valued. This is the easy part, because, according to the principle of no arbitrage, the value of the derivative is the same as that of its tracking portfolio.

Identifying the Tracking Portfolio

Finding the perfect tracking portfolio is the major task in valuing a derivative. With binomial processes, the tracking portfolio is identified by solving two equations in two unknowns, where each equation corresponds to one of the two future nodes to which one can move.

The equation corresponding to the *up node* is

$$\Delta S_u + B(1 + r_f) = V_u \tag{7.1}$$

where

Δ = number of units (shares) of the underlying asset
B = amount of money in the risk-free security
r_f = risk-free rate
S_u = value of the underlying asset at the up node
V_u = value of the derivative at the up node.

The left-hand side of equation (7.1), $\Delta S_u + B(1 + r_f)$, is the value of the tracking portfolio at the up node. The right-hand side of the equation, V_u, is the value of the derivative at the up node. Equation (7.1) thus says that, at the up node, the tracking portfolio, with Δ units of the underlying asset and B units of the risk-free security, should have the same up-node value as the derivative: that is, it perfectly tracks the derivative at the up node.

Typically, everything is a known number in an expression like equation (7.1), except for Δ and B. In Exhibit 7.9, for example, where the underlying asset is the CAC-40 and the derivative is the structured bond, the known corresponding values are

$$r_f = 0.04$$

$$S_u = 4,906$$

and

$$V_u = €552.75$$

Thus, to identify the tracking portfolio for the derivative in Exhibit 7.9, the first equation that needs to be solved is

$$4{,}906\Delta + B(1.04) = €552.75 \quad (7.1a)$$

Equation (7.1) represents one linear equation with two unknowns, Δ and *B*. Pair this equation with the corresponding equation for the down node:

$$\Delta S_d + B(1 + r_f) = V_d \quad (7.2)$$

For the numbers in Exhibit 7.9, this is

$$4{,}014\Delta + B(1.04) = €106.75 \quad (7.2a)$$

Solving equations (7.1) and (7.2) simultaneously yields a unique solution for Δ and *B*, which is typical when solving two linear equations for two unknown variables.

Example 7.6 illustrates this technique for the numbers given in Exhibit 7.9, and provides some tips on methods for a quick solution.[18]

Finding the Current Value of the Tracking Portfolio

The fair market value of the derivative equals the amount it costs to buy the tracking portfolio. Buying Δ shares of the underlying security today at a cost of *S* per share, and *B* of the risk-free asset, cost $\Delta S + B$ in total. Hence the derivative has a no-arbitrage price of

$$V = \Delta S + B \quad (7.3)$$

This calculation is demonstrated in Example 7.7.

Result 7.4 summarizes the results of this section.

Results

Result 7.4

To determine the no-arbitrage value of a derivative, find a (possibly dynamic) portfolio of the underlying asset and a risk-free security that perfectly tracks the future pay-offs of the derivative. The value of the derivative equals the value of the tracking portfolio.

Example 7.6

Finding the Tracking Portfolio

A unit of the CAC-40 sells for €4,460 today. One period from now, it can take on one of two values each associated with a good or a bad state. If the good state occurs, it is worth €4,906. If the bad state occurs, it is worth €4,014. If the risk-free interest rate is 4 per cent per period, find the tracking portfolio for a structured bond that has a value of €552.75 next period if the CAC-40 unit sells for €4,906, and $106.75 if the CAC-40 sells for €4,014.

Answer: A quick way to find the tracking portfolio of the CAC-40 and the risk-free asset is to look at the differences between the up and down node values of both the derivative and the underlying asset. (This is equivalent to subtracting equation (7.2a) from (7.1a) and solving for Δ.) For the derivative, the structured bond, the difference is €446 = €552.75 – €106.75, but for the CAC-40 it is €892 = €4,906 – €4,014.

Since the tracking portfolio has to have the same €446 difference in outcomes as the derivative, and since the amount of the risk-free security held will not affect this difference, the tracking portfolio has to

[18] Example 7.6 tracks the structured bond over the period with a static portfolio in the CAC-40 and a riskless security. With multiple periods, readjust these weights as each new period begins to maintain perfect tracking of the option's value. This readjustment is discussed in more detail shortly.

hold 0.5 (€446/€892) units of the CAC-40. If it held more than 0.5 units, for example, the difference in the tracking portfolio's future values would exceed €446. Given that Δ is 0.5 units of the CAC-40, and that B euros of the risk-free asset are held in addition to 0.5 units, the investor perfectly tracks the derivative's future value only if he or she selects the correct value of B. To determine this value of B, study the two columns on the right-hand side of the table, which outlines the values of the tracking portfolio and the derivative in the up and down states next period.

	Today's value	Next period value	
		Up state	Down state
Tracking portfolio	0.5(€4,460) + B	0.5(€4,906) + 1.04B	0.5(€4,014) + 1.04B
Derivative	?	€552.75	€106.75

Comparing the two up-state values in the middle column implies that the amount of the risk-free security needed to perfectly track the derivative next period solves the equation

$$€2{,}453 + 1.04B = €552.75$$

Thus $B = -€1{,}900.25/1.04$ or $-€1{,}827.16$. (The minus sign implies that €1,827.16 is borrowed at the risk-free rate.) Having already chosen Δ to be 0.5, this value of B also makes the down-state values of the tracking portfolio and the derivative the same.

Example 7.7

Valuing a Derivative Once the Tracking Portfolio is Known

What is the no-arbitrage value of the derivative in Example 7.6? See Exhibit 7.9 for the numbers to use in this example.

Answer: The tracking portfolio, which requires buying 0.5 units of the CAC-40 (for €4,460 per unit) and borrowing €1,827.16 at the risk-free rate, costs

$$€402.8365 = 0.5(€4{,}460) - €1{,}827.16$$

To prevent arbitrage, the derivative should also cost the same amount.

Risk-Neutral Valuation of Derivatives: The Industry Approach

One of the most interesting things about Examples 7.6 and 7.7 is that there was no mention of the probabilities of the up and down states occurring. The probability of the up move determines the mean return of the underlying security, yet the value of the derivative *in relation to the value of the underlying asset* does not depend on this probability.

In addition, it was not necessary to know how risk averse the investor was.[19] If the typical investor is risk neutral, slightly risk averse, highly risk averse or even risk loving, one obtains the same value for the derivative *in relation to the value of the underlying asset*, regardless of investor attitudes towards risk. Why is this? Well, whenever arbitrage considerations dictate pricing, risk preferences should not affect the relation between the value of the derivative and the value of the underlying asset. Whether risk neutral, slightly risk averse or highly risk averse, you would still love to obtain something for nothing with 100 per cent certainty. The valuation approach this chapter develops is simply a way to determine the unique pricing relation that rules this out.

Result 7.5 summarizes this important finding.

[19] Given two investments with the same expected return but different risk, a risk-averse individual prefers the investment with less risk. To make a risk-averse individual indifferent between the two investments, the riskier investment would have to carry a higher expected return.

Results

Result 7.5

The value of a derivative, relative to the value of its underlying asset, does not depend on the mean return of the underlying asset or investor risk preferences.

Why Mean Returns and Risk Aversion Do Not Affect the Valuation of Derivatives

The reason why information about probabilities or risk aversion does not enter into the valuation equation is that such information is already captured by the price of the underlying asset on which we base our valuation of the derivative. For example, assume the underlying asset is an equity. Holding risk aversion constant, the more likely the future share price is up and the less likely the share price is down, the greater the current share price will be. Similarly, holding the distribution of future share price outcomes constant, if the typical investor is more risk averse, the current share price will be lower. However, the wording of Result 7.5 is about the value of the derivative *given the current share price.* Thus Result 7.5 is a statement that, *once the share price is known,* risk aversion and mean return information are superfluous, not that they are irrelevant.

An Overview of How the Risk-Neutral Valuation Method is Implemented

Result 7.5 states that the no-arbitrage price of the derivative in relation to the underlying security is the same, regardless of risk preferences. This serves as the basis for a trick known as the risk-neutral valuation method, which is especially useful in valuing the more complicated derivatives encountered in practice.

The **risk-neutral valuation method** is a three-step procedure for valuing derivatives:

1. Identify *risk-neutral probabilities* that are consistent with investors being risk neutral, given the current value of the underlying asset and its possible future values. **Risk-neutral probabilities** are a set of weights applied to the future values of the underlying asset along each path. The *expected* future asset value generated by these probabilities, when discounted at the risk-free rate, equals the current value of the underlying asset.
2. Multiply each risk-neutral probability by the corresponding future value for the derivative, and sum the products together.
3. **Discount** the sum of the products in step 2 (the probability-weighted average of the derivative's possible future values) at the risk-free rate. This simply means that we divide the result in step 2 by the sum of 1 plus the risk-free rate.

The major benefit of the risk-neutral valuation method is that it requires fewer steps to value derivatives than the tracking portfolio method. However, it is not really a different method, but a shortcut for going through the tracking portfolio method's valuation steps, developed in the last section. As such, it is easier to program into a computer, and has become a fairly standard tool in financial markets. Moreover, it has its own useful insights that aid in the understanding of derivatives.

The risk-neutral valuation method obtains derivative prices in the risk preference scenario that is easiest to analyse – that of risk-neutral preferences. Although this scenario may not be the most realistic, pretending that everyone is risk neutral is a perfectly valid way to derive the correct no-arbitrage value that applies in all risk preference scenarios.

The next three subsections walk through the three-step procedure in detail.

Step 1: Obtaining Risk-Neutral Probabilities

Example 7.6 has a unique probability p of the good state occurring, which implies that the underlying asset, the CAC-40, is expected to appreciate at the risk-free rate. Example 7.8 solves for that probability.

Example 7.8

Attaching Probabilities to Up and Down Nodes

For Example 7.6, solve for the probability of the up state occurring that is consistent with expected appreciation of the underlying asset at the 4 per cent risk-free rate. (See Exhibit 7.9 for the numbers to use in this example.)

Answer: With a 4 per cent risk-free rate per period in Example 7.6, the expected value of the CAC-40 in the next period if investors are risk neutral is 104 per cent of the current value, €4,460. Hence the risk-neutral probability p that makes the expected future value of the underlying asset 104 per cent of today's value solves

$$€4{,}460(1.04) = €4.906\pi + €4{,}014(1 - \pi)$$

Thus $\pi = 0.7$.

Note from Example 7.8 that 0.7 is the risk-neutral probability, not the actual probability, of the good state occurring, which remains unspecified. The risk-neutral probability is simply a number consistent with €4,460 as the current value of the underlying asset and with the assumption that investors are risk neutral, an assumption that may not be true.

The ability to form risk-free investments by having a long position in the tracking portfolio and a short position in the derivative, or vice versa, is what makes it possible to ignore the true probabilities of the up and down states occurring. This is a subtle point. In essence, we are pretending to be in a world that we are not in – a world where all assets are expected to appreciate at the risk-free rate. To do this, throw away the true probabilities of up and down moves and replace them with up and down probabilities that make future values along the binomial tree consistent with risk-neutral preferences.

Step 2: Probability-Weight the Derivative's Future Values and Sum the Weighted Value

Having computed the risk-neutral probabilities for the underlying asset, apply these same probabilities to the future outcomes of the value of the derivative to obtain its risk-neutral expected future value. This is its expected *future* value, assuming that everyone is risk neutral, which is not the same as the derivative's true expected value.

Step 3: Discount at the Risk-Free Rate

Discounting the risk-neutral expected value at the risk-free rate gives the no-arbitrage present value of the derivative. By discounting, we mean that we divide a number by the sum of 1 plus an interest rate (or 1 plus a rate of return). In this particular case, the number we discount is the derivative's expected future value, assuming everyone is risk neutral. The discount rate used here is the risk-free rate, meaning that we simply divide by the sum of 1 and the risk-free rate. It generally shrinks the number that we are dividing by, reflecting the fact that money today has earning power.

We shall have much more to say about why we discount and how we discount in the next part of the text, particularly in Chapter 9. We have already been discounting in this part of the text without specifically referring to it. For example, the no-arbitrage value of the forward contract (see Result 7.1) requires that we discount the price we pay, K, at the risk-free rate – in this case, over multiple periods. Without elaborating on this in too much detail, suffice it to say that discounting is a procedure for taking a future value and turning it into a present value, the latter being a number that represents a fair current value for a payment or receipt of cash in the future. Hence the discounted value of K in Result 7.1 turns a future payment of K into its present value, which we shall denote by PV(K). Similarly, the discounting of the risk-neutral expected future value of a derivative is a way of turning that expected future value into a present value.

Example 7.9 demonstrates how to value derivatives using the risk-neutral valuation method.

Example 7.9

Using Risk-Neutral Probabilities to Value Derivatives

Apply the risk-neutral probabilities of 0.7 and 0.3 from Example 7.8 to the cash flows of the derivative of Example 7.6 and discount the resulting risk-neutral expected value at the risk-free rate. (See Exhibit 7.9 for the numbers to use in the example.)

Answer: 0.7(€552.75) + 3(€106.75) yields a risk-neutral expected future value of €418.95, which has a discounted value of €418.95/1.04 = €402.8365.

Relating Risk-Neutral Valuation to the Tracking Portfolio Method

It is indeed remarkable, but not coincidental, as our earlier arguments suggested, that Examples 7.9 and 7.7 arrive at the same answer. Indeed, this will always be the case, as the following result states.

It is worth repeating that one cannot take the true expected future value of a derivative, discount it at the risk-free rate, and hope to obtain its true present value. The true expected future value is based on the true probabilities, not the risk-neutral probabilities.

Results

Result 7.6

Valuation of a derivative based on no arbitrage between the tracking portfolio and the derivative is identical to risk-neutral valuation of that derivative.

A General Formula for Risk-Neutral Probabilities

One determines risk-neutral probabilities from the returns of the underlying asset at each of the binomial outcomes, and not by the likelihood of each binomial outcome. The risk-neutral probabilities, π, are those probabilities that make the 'expected' return of an asset equal the risk-free rate. That is, π must solve

$$\pi u + (1 - \pi)d = 1 + r_f$$

where

r_f = risk-free rate
$u = 1 +$ per-period rate of return of the underlying asset at the up node
$d = 1 +$ per-period rate of return of the underlying asset at the down node.

When rearranged, this becomes

$$\pi = \frac{1 + r_f - d}{u - d} \tag{7.4}$$

Risk-Neutral Probabilities and Zero-Cost Forward and Futures Prices

One infers risk-neutral probabilities from the terms and market values of traded financial instruments. Because futures contracts are one class of popularly traded financial instruments with known terms (the futures price) and known market values, it is often useful to infer risk-neutral probabilities from them.

For example, corporations often enter into derivative contracts that involve options on real assets. Indeed, in the next section we shall consider a hypothetical case involving the option to buy jet aeroplanes. To value this option correctly, using data about the underlying asset, the jet aeroplanes, is a heroic task. For reasons beyond the scope of this text, the future values postulated for an asset such as a jet aeroplanes must be adjusted in a complex way to reflect maintenance costs on the plane, revenue from carrying passengers or renting the plane out, obsolescence, and so forth. In addition, the no-arbitrage-based valuation relationship derived is hard to envisage if one is required to 'sell short a jet aeroplanes' to take advantage of an arbitrage.

In these instances, corporations often use forward and futures prices as inputs for their derivative valuation models.[20] Such forwards and futures, while derivatives themselves, can be used to value derivatives for which market prices are harder to come by, such as jet aeroplanes options, without any of the complications alluded to above.

To use the prices of zero-cost forwards or futures to obtain risk-neutral probabilities, it is necessary to modify slightly the risk-neutral valuation formulae developed above. We begin with futures, and later argue that forwards should satisfy the same formula.

[20] Another related method of valuing derivatives is the *state price valuation method,* which was derived from research in mathematical economics in the 1950s by Gerard Debreu, a 1986 Nobel Prize winner, and Kenneth Arrow, a 1974 Nobel Prize winner. Since a state price is the risk-neutral probability times the risk-free rate, the state price valuation technique yields the same answers for derivatives as the two other methods discussed earlier.

Recall that futures prices are set so that the contract has zero fair market value. The amount earned on a futures contract over a period is the change in the futures price. This profit is marked to market in that the cash from this profit is deposited in – or, in the case of a loss, taken from – one's margin account at a futures brokerage firm. Thus a current futures price of F, which can appreciate in the next period to F_u in the up state or depreciate to F_d in the down state, corresponds to margin cash inflow $F_u - F$ if the up state occurs, and a negative number, $F_d - F$ (a cash outflow of $F - F_d$) if the down state occurs. (We omit time subscripts here to simplify notation.) In a risk-neutral setting with p as the risk-neutral probability of the up state, the expected cash received at the end of the period is

$$\pi(F_u - F) + (1 - \pi)(F_d - F)$$

The investor in futures spends no money to receive this expected amount of cash. Thus, in a risk-neutral world, the zero cost of entering into the contract should equal the discounted[21] expected cash received at the end of the period: that is,

$$0 = \frac{\pi(F_u - F) + (1 - \pi)(F_d - F)}{1 + r_f}$$

Rearranging this equation implies the following result.

Results

Result 7.7

The no-arbitrage futures price is the same as a weighted average of the expected futures prices at the end of the period, where the weights are the risk-neutral probabilities: that is,

$$F = \pi F_u + (1 - \pi)F_d \qquad (7.5)$$

If the end of the period is the maturity date of the futures contract, then $F_u = S_u$ and $F_d = S_d$, where S_u and S_d respectively, are the spot prices underlying the futures contract. Substituting S_u and S_d into the last equation implies that, for this special case,

$$F = \pi S_u + (1 - \pi)S_d$$

We can generalize this as follows:

Results

Result 7.8

The no-arbitrage futures price is the risk-neutral expected future spot price at the maturity of the futures contract.

Result 7.8 is a general result that holds in both a multi-period and a single-period setting. For example, a futures contract in January 2023 that is two years from maturity has a January 2023 futures price equal to the risk-neutral expected spot price in January 2025.

Example 7.10 illustrates how futures prices relate to risk-neutral probabilities.

[21] The discount rate does not matter here. With a zero-cost contract, expected future profit has to be zero.

Example 7.10

Using Risk-Neutral Probabilities to Obtain Futures Prices

Apply the risk-neutral probabilities of 0.7 and 0.3 from Example 7.8 to derive the futures price of the CAC-40. Exhibit 7.10, which modifies a part of Exhibit 7.9, should aid in this calculation.

Exhibit 7.10 Futures Prices

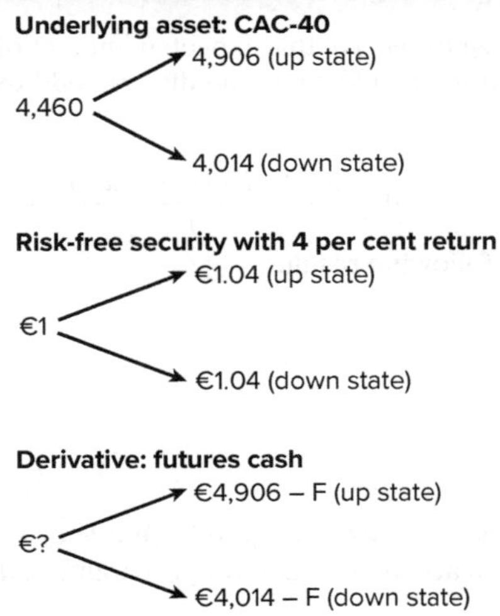

Answer: Using Result 7.8, the CAC-40 futures price is €4,638.40 = 0.7(€4,906) + 3(€4,014). Note that, consistent with Result 7.2, this is the same as €4,460(1.04), which is the future value of the spot price from investing it at the 4 per cent risk-free rate of interest.

It is also possible to rearrange equation (7.5) to identify the risk-neutral probabilities, π and $1 - \pi$, from futures prices. This yields

$$\pi = \frac{F - F_d}{F_u - F_d} \tag{7.6}$$

Example 7.11 provides a numerical illustration of this.

Earlier in this chapter, we mentioned that futures and forward prices are essentially the same, with the notable exception of long-term interest rate contracts. Hence the evolution of forward prices for zero-cost contracts could just as easily be used to compute risk-neutral probabilities. This would be important to consider in Example 7.11, because forward prices for aeroplanes exist, but futures prices do not.

Example 7.11

Using Futures Prices to Determine Risk-Neutral Probabilities

If futures prices for Boeing 777 aeroplanes can appreciate by 10 per cent (up state) or depreciate by 10 per cent (down state), compute the risk-neutral probabilities for the up and down states.

Answer: In the up state, $F_u = 1.1F$; in the down state, $F_d = 0.9F$. Thus, applying equation (7.6), the risk-neutral probability for the up state, $\pi = 0.5 = F - 0.9F/1.1F - 0.9F$, making $1 - \pi = 0.5$ as well.

In applying equations (7.5) and (7.6) to forwards rather than futures, it is important to distinguish the evolution of forward prices on new zero-cost contracts from the evolution of the value of a forward contract. For example, in January 2023 International Airlines Group (AIG) may enter into a forward contract with Boeing to buy Boeing 777s one year hence (that is, in January 2024), at a pre-specified price. Most likely, this pre-specified price is set so that the contract has zero up-front cost to IAG. However, as prices of 777s increase or decrease over the next month (February 2023), the value of the forward contract becomes positive or negative, because the old contract has the *same forward price*. Equations (7.5) and (7.6) would not apply to the value of this contract. Instead, these equations compare the forward price for 777s at the beginning of the month with subsequent forward prices for new contracts to buy 777s *at the maturity of the original contract* – that is, new contracts in subsequent months that mature in January 2024. Such new contracts would be zero-cost contracts.

It is also possible to use the binomial evolution of the *value*, not the *forward price* of the old British Airways forward contract, to determine the risk-neutral probabilities. However, because this contract sometimes has positive and sometimes negative value, one needs to use equation (7.4) for this computation.

It is generally impossible to observe a binomial path for the value of a single forward contract when that contract is not actively traded among investors (and it usually isn't). In contrast, parameters that describe the path of forward prices for new zero-cost contracts are usually easier to observe and estimate.

7.4 Multi-Period Binomial Valuation

Risk-neutral valuation methods can be applied whenever perfect tracking is possible. When continuous and simultaneous trading in the derivative, the underlying security and a risk-free bond takes place, and when the value of the tracking portfolio changes smoothly (i.e. it makes no big jumps) over time, perfect tracking is usually feasible. To the extent that one can trade almost continuously and almost simultaneously in the real world, and to the extent that prices do not move too abruptly, a derivative value obtained from a model based on perfect tracking may be regarded as a very good approximation of the derivative's fair market value.

When large jumps in the value of the tracking portfolio or the derivative can occur, perfect tracking is generally not possible. The binomial process that we have been discussing is an exception where jumps occur and perfect tracking is still possible.

How Restrictive Is the Binomial Process in a Multi-Period Setting?

Initially, at least, it appears as though the assumption of a binomial process is quite restrictive – more restrictive in fact than the continuous trading and price movement assumptions that permit tracking. Why, then, are we so focused on binomial processes for prices, rather than focusing on the processes where prices move continuously? We prefer to discuss tracking with binomial processes instead of with continuous processes because the latter, requiring advanced mathematics, is more complex to present. Moreover, binomial processes are not as restrictive as they might at first seem.

Although binomial processes permit only two outcomes for the next period, one can define a period to be as short as one likes, and one can value assets over multiple periods. Paths for the tracking portfolio when periods are short appear much like the paths seen with the continuous processes. Hence it is useful to understand how multi-period binomial valuation works. Another advantage of multi-period binomial models is that the empirical accuracy of the binomial pricing model increases as time is divided into finer binomial periods, which implies that there are more binomial steps.

Numerical Example of Multi-Period Binomial Valuation

Example 7.12 determines the current fair market price of a derivative whose value is known two binomial periods later. However, it will be necessary to program a computer or use a spreadsheet to value derivatives over large numbers of short binomial periods.

Example 7.12

Valuing a Derivative in a Multi-Period Setting

As the financial analyst for IAG, you have been asked to analyse Boeing's offer to sell options to buy 200 new 777 aeroplanes six months from now for $83 million per plane. You divide up the six months into two three-month periods and conclude – after analysing historical forward prices for new 777s – that a reasonable assumption is that new forward prices, currently at $100 million per plane, can jump up by 10 per cent or down by 10 per cent in each three-month period. By this, we mean that new three-month forward prices tend to be either 10 per cent above or 10 per cent below the new six-month forward prices observed three months earlier. Similarly, spot prices for 777s tend to be 10 per cent above or 10 per cent below the new three-month forward prices observed three months earlier. Thus the Boeing 777 jet option is worth $38 million per plane if the forward price jumps up twice in a row, and $16 million if it jumps up only once in the two periods. If the forward price declines by 10 per cent in the first three-month period and declines by 10 per cent again in the second three-month period, the option that Boeing has offered IAG will not be exercised, because the pre-specified 777 purchase price of the option will then be higher than the price IAG would pay to purchase 777s directly. What is the fair price that IAG should be willing to pay for an option to buy one aeroplane, assuming that the risk-free rate is 0 per cent?

Answer: Exhibit 7.11 graphs, above each node, the path of the new forward prices that (as described above) are relevant for computing risk-neutral probabilities. Below each node are the option values that one either knows or has to solve for. The leftmost point represents today. Movements to the right along lines connecting the nodes represent possible paths that new zero-cost forward prices can take. If there are two up moves, the forward (and spot) price is $121 million per plane. Two down moves mean it is $81 million per plane. One up and one down move, which occur along two possible paths, results in a $99 million price per plane.

Solve this problem by working backwards through the tree diagram, using the risk-neutral valuation technique. Exhibit 7.11 labels the nodes in the tree diagram at the next period as U and D (for up and down), and as UU, UD and DD for the period after that. Begin with a look at the U, UU, UD trio from Exhibit 7.11.

Exhibit 7.11 Forward Price Paths (in $ millions) and Derivative Values (in $ millions) in a Two-Period Binomial Tree

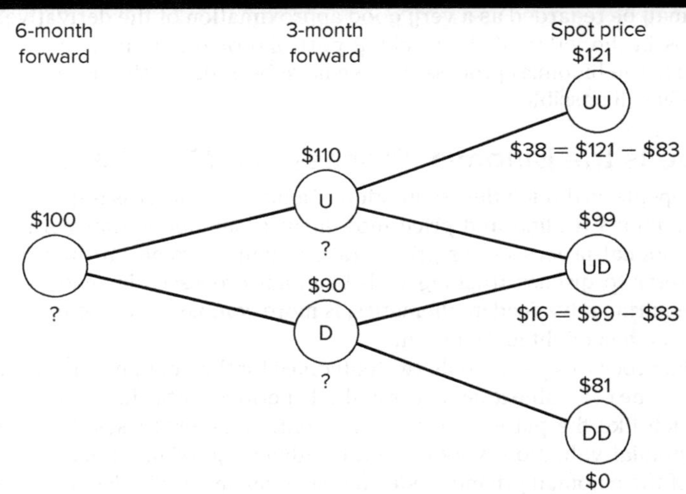

At node U the forward price is $110 million per plane. Using the risk-neutral valuation method, solve for the p that makes $121\pi + 9(1 - \pi) = 110$. Thus $\pi = 0.5$. The value of the option at U is

$$0.5(\$38 \text{ million}) + 0.5(\$16 \text{ million}) = \$27 \text{ million}$$

At node D the forward price is $90 million per plane. Solving $99\pi + 81(1 - \pi) = 90$ identifies the risk-neutral probability $\pi = 0.5$. This makes the option worth

$$0.5(\$16 \text{ million}) + 0.5(\$0) = \$8 \text{ million}$$

The derivative is worth either $27 million (node U) or $8 million (node D) at the next trading date. To value it at today's date, multiply these two outcomes by the risk-neutral probabilities. These are again $\pi = 0.5$ and $1 - \pi = 0.5$. Thus the value of the derivative is

$$\$17.5 \text{ million} = 0.5(\$27 \text{ million}) + 0.5(\$8 \text{ million})$$

In Example 7.12, the derivative is an option to buy aeroplanes. The 'underlying asset', basically a financial instrument that helps determine risk-neutral probabilities, is a set of forward contracts on aeroplanes. The binomial tree for the underlying forward price (above the nodes) and derivative values (below the nodes) is given in Exhibit 7.11.

Algebraic Representation of Two-Period Binomial Valuation

Let us try to represent Example 7.12 algebraically. Let V_{uu}, V_{ud} and V_{dd} denote the three values of the derivative at the final date. To obtain its node U value, V_u, Example 7.12 took p (which equals 0.5) and computed

$$V_u = \frac{\pi V_{uu} + (1-\pi)V_{ud}}{1+r_f}$$

(Since r_f was zero in the example, there was no reason to consider it, but it needs to be accounted for in a general formula.) To obtain its node D value, V_d, the example computed

$$V_d = \frac{\pi V_{uu} + (1-\pi)V_{ud}}{1+r_f}$$

To solve for today's value, V, Example 7.12 computed

$$\begin{aligned} V &= \frac{\pi V_u + (1-\pi)V_d}{1+r_f} \\ &= \pi\frac{\pi V_{uu} + (1-\pi)V_{ud}}{(1+r_f)^2} + \left(1-\pi\right)\frac{\pi V_{ud} + (1-\pi)V_{dd}}{(1+r_f)^2} \\ &= \frac{\pi^2 V_{uu} + 2\pi(1-\pi)V_{ud} + (1-\pi)^2 V_{dd}}{(1+r_f)^2} \end{aligned} \tag{7.7}$$

This is still the discounted expected future value of the derivative, with an expected value that is computed with risk-neutral probabilities rather than true probabilities. The risk-neutral probability for the value V_{uu} is the probability of two consecutive up moves, or π^2. The probability of achieving the value V_{ud} is $\pi p(1-\pi)$, since two paths (down–up or up–down) get you there, each with probability of $\pi(1-\pi)$. The probability of two down moves is $(1-\pi)^2$. Thus the risk-neutral expected value of the derivative two periods from now is the numerator in equation (7.7). Discounting this value by the risk-free rate over two periods yields the present value of the derivative, V. Of course, the same generic result applies when extending the analysis to three periods or more. To value the security today, take the discounted expected future value at the risk-free rate.

Note that, in principle, π can vary along the nodes of tree diagrams. However, in Example 7.12 π was the same at every node because u, d and r_f, which completely determine π, are the same at each node, making π the same at each node. If this is not the case, it is necessary to compute each node's appropriate π from the u, d and r_f that apply at that node.

7.5 Valuation Techniques in the Financial Services Industry

Investment banks, commercial banks and some institutional investors have made sizeable investments in the technology of pricing derivatives. Cheap computing power and expensive brain power are the main elements of this technology.

Numerical Methods

The techniques for valuing virtually all the new financial instruments developed by Wall Street firms consist primarily of **numerical methods**: that is, no algebraic formula is used to compute the value of the derivative as a function of the value of the underlying security. Instead, a computer is fed a number corresponding to the price of the underlying security, along with some important parameter values. The computer then executes a program that derives the numerical value of the derivative and, sometimes, additional information such as the number of shares of the underlying security in the tracking portfolio.

Binomial-Like Numerical Methods

These numerical methods fall into several classes. One class is the binomial approach used throughout this chapter. Some investment banks employ the binomial approach to value callable corporate bonds (see exercise 7.4) for their clients. This binomial approach is also commonly used in spreadsheets by graduates working in corporate finance, sales and trading, who need to find 'quick and dirty' valuation results for many derivatives.

One potential hitch in the binomial method is that it is necessary to specify the values of the underlying security along all nodes in the tree diagram. This requires estimation of u and d, the amounts by which the security can move up and down from each node. There are several ways to simplify the process. First, the binomial method can be used to approximate many kinds of continuous distribution if the time periods are cut into extremely small intervals. One popular continuous distribution is the lognormal distribution. The natural logarithm of the return of a security is normally distributed when the price movements of the security are determined by the lognormal distribution. Once the annualized standard deviation, σ, of this normal distribution is known, u and d are estimated as follows:

$$u = e^{\sigma\sqrt{T/N}}$$

$$d = \frac{1}{u}$$

where

T = number of years to expiration
N = number of binomial periods
e = the exponential constant (about 2.7183).

Thus

$$\sqrt{\frac{T}{N}} = \text{square root of the number of years per binomial period}$$

Depending on the problem, the available computing power and the time pressures involved, the valuation expert can model the binomial steps, T/N, as anywhere from one day to six months.[22]

Numerical analysis of derivatives with binomial approaches is often modified slightly to account for inefficient computing with the binomial approach. For one, the value of the derivative is affected more by what happens to the underlying asset in the near term and in the middle of the binomial tree, because that is where the risk-neutral probabilities are greatest, and risk-free discounting has the least impact on the current value of the derivative. Hence derivative valuation experts typically modify the binomial method to compute near-term future values and future values in the middle of the binomial tree more intensively and thus more precisely. Often, the tree is modified to a rectangular grid shape.[23]

Simulation

An additional method that firms use to value derivatives is **simulation**, a method that uses random numbers obtained from a computer to generate outcomes, and then averages the outcomes of some variable to obtain values. Simulations are generally used when the derivative value at each node along the tree diagram depends only on the simulation path taken, rather than on a comparison with action-contingent values of the derivative along other paths followed by the underlying asset. Derivatives that can be valued with simulation include forwards and European options, but they exclude, for example, mortgages and American put options.

A simulation starts with the initial price of the underlying security. Then a random number generated by a computer determines the value for the underlying security at the next period. This process continues to the end of the life of the derivative. At that point, a single path for the underlying security over a number of periods has been constructed, and an associated path for the derivative (whose value *derives* from the underlying security) has been computed. Usually, one generates derivative values along the single path by discounting back, one period at a time, the terminal value of the derivative. The discounting is made at the short-term risk-free rate, which may itself have its own simulated path!

---

[22]Chapter 8 describes how to estimate s from historical data.

[23] Other approaches are also available for valuing derivatives. One method, developed by Schwartz (1977), models the process for the underlying security as a continuous process, and uses stochastic calculus and no-arbitrage conditions to derive a differential equation for the derivative. It is possible to solve the differential equation with numerical methods that have been devised in mathematics, including the implicit finite difference method. Explicit methods for solving the differential equation are tied directly to the risk-neutral valuation method.

A second path for the underlying security is then generated, the derivative value is calculated for that path, and an initial derivative value for the second path is computed. This process continues until anywhere from 100 to 100,000 simulated paths have been analysed. The initial value of the derivative over each path is then averaged to obtain the fair market value of the derivative.

The Risk-Free Rate Used by Industry Practitioners

All derivative valuation procedures make use of a short-term risk-free return. The most commonly used input is SONIA, €STR or SOFR. Most academic research focuses on the short-term Treasury bill rate as the 'risk-free rate', but this research fails to recognize that only governments can borrow at this rate, while arbitrage opportunities between a tracking portfolio and a mispriced derivative may require uncollateralized risk-free borrowing by a high-quality borrower. The rate at which such borrowing takes place is much closer to a floating benchmark like SONIA (UK) or €STR (EU) than to the T-bill rate.[24]

7.6 Market Frictions and Lessons from the Fate of Amaranth Advisors

Real World Insights

Amaranth Investors

In 2006, Amaranth Advisors LLC, a hedge fund, collapsed after losing $6.5 billion in only one week from trading in natural gas derivative contracts. Using a derivative trading strategy called 'spread trading', it made massive profits in 2005 from speculating that prices would move significantly within the month. In August 2005, Hurricane Katrina hit the USA, causing more than $100 billion worth of damage, damaging 30 oil platforms and nine oil refineries, and reducing oil-producing capacity in the region to less than one-quarter of normal production levels. The company speculated on similar events happening in March and April in 2007 and 2008. Specifically, it went 'long' in March contracts and 'short' in April contracts, meaning that it would gain when March contracts increased in value and April contracts decreased in value – earning money on the spread. Instead, the opposite happened. The difference in value of March and April contracts at the end of August 2006 was $2.49, and by the end of September the spread had collapsed to only $0.58, resulting in the massive loss to Amaranth Advisors, whose value fell 65 per cent from $9 billion. By the end of September 2006, the firm was in liquidation.

The valuation models discussed in this chapter assume that a portfolio can be formed that perfectly tracks the cash outflows and inflows of the derivative security being evaluated. However, this is not the same as perfectly tracking the value of a derivative security at all points in time in the future. Usually, it is impossible to perfectly track the *value* of a *mispriced* derivative security at all future dates before the derivative security terminates. At least in theory, and perhaps in most cases, this is not a terribly relevant consideration. A mispriced derivative that does not immediately converge to its no-arbitrage value provides an opportunity to earn additional arbitrage profits, using the tracking portfolio strategy outlined in this chapter.

An exception occurs when the arbitrageur has limited financial resources, and when price changes can have cash flow implications.[25] This is, indeed, the lesson of Amaranth Advisors (see the Real World Insights in this section). To illustrate what happened to Amaranth, let's take a simple example that does not involve derivatives. Suppose that there are two zero-coupon bonds, Bond A and Bond B, each paying €1 million one year from now. Thus these bonds generate a single future cash inflow of €1 million to anyone who buys them. If Bond A currently sells for €900,000 and Bond B sells for €910,000, Bond A is underpriced relative to Bond

[24] A further discussion of this subject is found in Grinblatt (1995). This chapter's results on currency forward rates require longer-term risk-free rates. Implied zero-coupon interest rates in the floating benchmark market (known as *Eurocurrency rates*) appear to be the correct interest rates to use for this relationship. For horizons in excess of one year, the fixed rate on one side of an interest rate swap that is exchanged for a floating benchmark like SONIA or €STR provides the correct risk-free rate for the equation in Result 7.3.

B. It is thus possible to earn €10,000 in arbitrage profits simply by acquiring Bond A and short-selling Bond B. This is an oversimplification of the kind of strategy that Amaranth Advisors might have engaged in. In a market without frictions, next week's value would not be very relevant to the effectiveness of the arbitrage. For example, if Bond B's value appreciated to €920,000, while Bond A's value declined to €890,000, there would be a €20,000 paper loss in the portfolio position. However, as long as the positions were held for the long term, there would be no cash flow ramifications. Indeed, next week, one could replicate the same arbitrage position, capturing an additional €30,000 in arbitrage profits, the spread between the €920,000 price of shorted Bond B and acquired Bond A.

Suppose, however, that the broker who holds custody of these positions on behalf of Amaranth Advisors requires them to mark the positions to market, much as an oil futures contract is marked to market (see the previous section). In this case, as the spread between the prices of Bonds B and A widens from €10,000 to €30,000 over the course of the next week, the investor has to post an additional €20,000. This is a cash outflow that prevents perfect tracking between the future cash flows of Bonds A and B.

These cash flow implications, which can be a nuisance when an additional €20,000 is needed, can become a major problem if additional millions of euros are needed. This was part of the predicament faced by Amaranth Advisors. Its positions were leveraged to magnitudes that required major institutional financing. If it could not come up with the necessary capital, it would be forced to liquidate the positions, turning the paper loss into an actual cash outflow, negating what appeared, just a week earlier, to be a sure arbitrage.

Because of the inability to overcome financing constraints (which, indeed, may have allowed what seemed like arbitrage opportunities to exist in the first place), the paper losses of Amaranth Advisors became real losses, turning what seemed like arbitrage opportunities into massive cash losses for the fund.

7.7 Equities as Call Options on the Firm

A novel way of considering equity is as a call option on the firm. To understand this, consider a hypothetical firm that has issued debt to help finance a new venture. The debt of £1 million must be paid back in one year and there are four equal potential scenarios:

	Outright Failure	Moderately Unsuccessful	Moderately Successful	Very Successful
Cash flow before interest and principal	£500,000	£900,000	£1,100,000	£2,000,000
Interest and principal	–£500,000	–£900,000	–£1,000,000	–£1,000,000
Cash flow to shareholders	0	0	£100,000	£1,000,000

Shareholders receive nothing if the firm's cash flows are less than £1 million because all of the cash flows go to the bondholders. However, the shareholders earn a pound for every pound that the firm receives above £1 million. Notice that this is exactly the same as the payoff from a call option with a strike price of £1,000,000. But what is the underlying asset upon which the equity is a call option? The underlying asset is the firm itself. That is, we can view the *bondholders* as owning the firm. The shareholders have a call option on the firm with an exercise price of £1 million.

If the firm's cash flow is above £1 million, the shareholders would choose to exercise this option. In other words, they would buy the firm from the bondholders for £1 million. Their net cash flow is the difference between the firm's cash flow and their £1 million payment. This would be £1 million (= £2m – £1m) if the business is very successful and £100,000 (= £1.1m – £1m) if it is moderately successful.

Should the value of the firm's cash flows be less than £1 million, the shareholders would not choose to exercise their option. Instead, they would walk away from the firm, as any call option holder would do. The bondholders would then receive the firm's entire cash flow.

[25] This issue is discussed in more detail in Shleifer and Vishny (1997).

7.8 Summary and Conclusions

This chapter examined one of the most fundamental contributions to financial theory: the pricing of derivatives. The price movements of a derivative are perfectly correlated over short time intervals with the price movements of the underlying asset on which it is based. Hence a portfolio of the underlying asset and a riskless security can be formed that perfectly tracks the future cash flows of the derivative. To prevent arbitrage, the tracking portfolio and the derivative must have the same cost.

The no-arbitrage cost of the derivative can be computed in several ways. One method is direct. It forms the tracking portfolio at some terminal date and works backwards to determine a portfolio that maintains perfect tracking. The initial cost of the tracking portfolio is the no-arbitrage cost of the derivative. An alternative, but equivalent, approach is the risk-neutral valuation method, which assigns risk-neutral probabilities to the cash flow outcomes of the underlying asset that are consistent with that asset earning, on average, a risk-free return. Applying a risk-free discount rate to the expected future cash flows of the derivative gives its no-arbitrage present value. Both methods lend their unique insights to the problem of valuing derivatives, although the tracking portfolio approach seems to be slightly more intuitive. Computationally, the risk-neutral approach is easier to program.

To keep this presentation relatively simple, we have relied on binomial models, which provide reasonable approximations for the values of most derivatives. The binomial assumptions are usually less restrictive than they might at first seem, because the time period for the binomial jump can be as short as one desires. As the time period gets shorter, the number of periods gets larger. A binomial jump to one of two values every minute can result in 2^{60} (more than a billion) possible outcomes at the end of an hour. Defining the time period to be as short as one pleases means that the binomial process can approximate to any degree almost any probability distribution for the return on an investment over almost any horizon.

This chapter focused mainly on the general principles of no-arbitrage valuation, although it applied these principles to value simple derivatives. Many other applications exist. For example, the exercises that follow this chapter value risky bonds, callable bonds and convertible bonds. The following chapter focuses in depth on one of the most important applications of these principles, option pricing.

Key Concepts

Result 7.1: The no-arbitrage value of a forward contract on a share of equity (the obligation to buy a share of equity at a price of K, T years in the future), assuming the equity pays no dividends prior to T, is

$$S_0 - \frac{K}{(1+r_f)^T}$$

where

S_0 = current share price

and

$K/(1 + r_f)^T$ = the current market price of a default-free zero-coupon bond paying K, T years in the future.

Result 7.2: The forward price for settlement in T years of the purchase of a non-dividend-paying equity with a current price of S_0 is

$$F_0 = S_0(1 + r_f)^T$$

Result 7.3: In the absence of arbitrage, the forward currency rate F_0 (for example, euros/dollar) is related to the current exchange rate (or spot rate), S_0, by the equation

$$\frac{F_0}{S_0} = \frac{1 - r_{\text{foreign}}}{1 + r_{\text{domestic}}}$$

where

r = the return (unannualized) on a domestic or foreign risk-free security over the life of the forward agreement, as measured in the respective country's currency.

Result 7.4: To determine the no-arbitrage value of a derivative, find a (possibly dynamic) portfolio of the underlying asset and a risk-free security that perfectly tracks the future pay-offs of the derivative. The value of the derivative equals the value of the tracking portfolio.

Result 7.5: The value of a derivative, relative to the value of its underlying asset, does not depend on the mean return of the underlying asset or investor risk preferences.

Result 7.6: Valuation of a derivative based on no arbitrage between the tracking portfolio and the derivative is identical to risk-neutral valuation of that derivative.

Result 7.7: The no-arbitrage futures price is the same as a weighted average of the expected futures prices at the end of the period, where the weights are the risk-neutral probabilities: that is,

$$F = \pi F_u + (1 - \pi)F_d$$

Result 7.8: The no-arbitrage futures price is the risk-neutral expected future spot price at the maturity of the futures contract.

Key Terms

Exercises

7.1 Using risk-neutral valuation, derive a formula for a derivative that pays cash flows over the next two periods. Assume the risk-free rate is 4 per cent per period.

The underlying asset, which pays no cash flows unless it is sold, has a market value that is modelled in the following tree diagram:

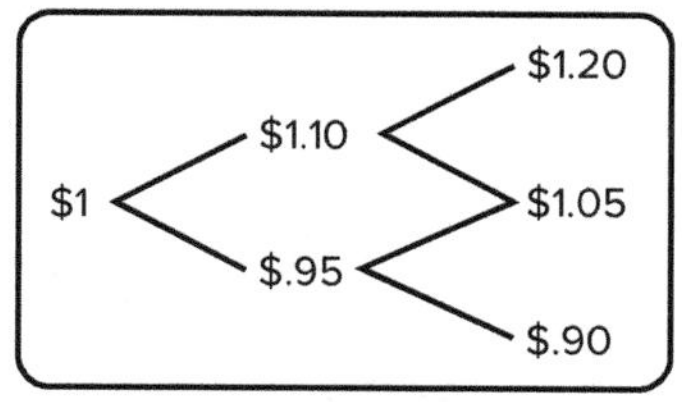

The cash flows of the derivative that correspond to the above tree diagram are:

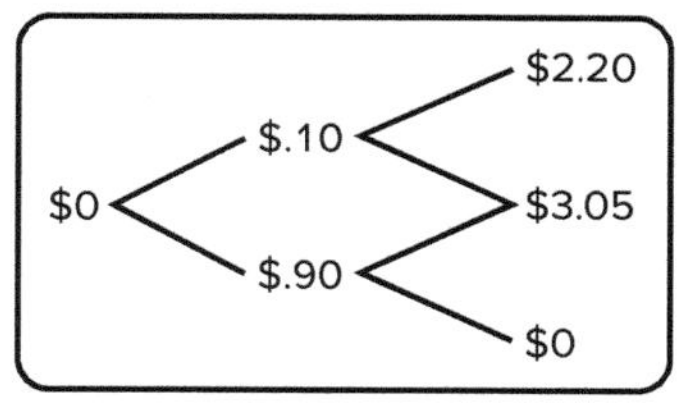

Find the present value of the derivative.

7.2 A convertible bond can be converted into a specified number of shares at the option of the bondholder. Assume that a convertible bond can be converted to 1.5 shares. A single share of this equity has a price that follows the binomial process:

Date 0 Date 1

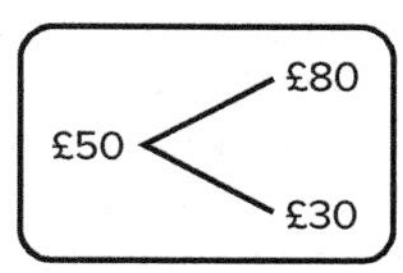

The equity does not pay a dividend between dates 0 and 1.

If the bondholder never converts the bond to equity, the bond has a date 1 pay-off of £100 + x, where x is the coupon of the bond. The conversion to equity may take place either at date 0 or at date 1 (in the latter case, upon revelation of the date 1 share price).

The convertible bond is issued at date 0 for £100. What should x, the equilibrium coupon of the convertible bond per £100 at face value, be if the risk-free return is 15 per cent per period and there are no taxes, transaction costs or arbitrage opportunities? Does the corporation save on interest payments if it issues a convertible bond in lieu of a straight bond? If so, why?

7.3 Value a risky corporate bond, assuming that the risk-free interest rate is 4 per cent per period, where a period is defined as six months. The corporate bond has a face value of €100 payable two periods from now, and pays a 5 per cent coupon per period: that is, interest payments of €5 at the end of both the first period and the second period.

The corporate bond is a derivative of the assets of the issuing firm. Assume that the assets generate sufficient cash to pay off the promised coupon one period from now. In particular, the corporation has set aside a reserve fund of €5/1.04 per bond to pay off the promised coupon one period from now. Two periods from now, there are three possible states. In one of those states, the assets of the firm are not worth much and the firm defaults, unable to generate a sufficient amount of cash. Only €50 of the €105 promised payment is made on the bond in this state.

The exhibit below describes the value of the firm's assets per bond (less the amount in the reserve fund maintained for the intermediate coupon) and the cash pay-offs of the bond. The non-reserved assets of the firm are currently worth €100 per bond. At the U and D nodes the reserve fund has been depleted, and the remaining assets of the firm per bond are worth €120 and €90, respectively, while they are worth €300, €110 and €50, respectively, in the UU, UD and DD states two periods from now.

Paths for (a) the Value of the Firm's Assets Per Bond (Above the Node); and (b) Cash Pay-offs of a Risky Bond (Below the Node); in a Two-Period Binomial Tree Diagram

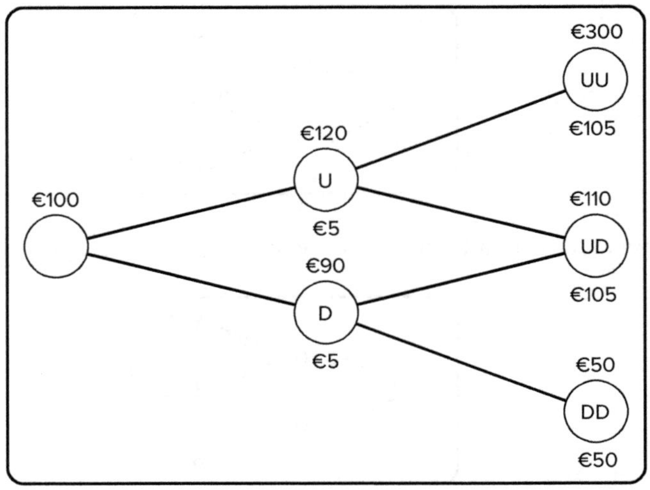

7.4 In many instances, whether a cash flow occurs early or not is a decision of the issuer or holder of the derivative. One example of this is a callable bond, which is a bond that the issuing firm can buy back at a pre-specified call price. Valuing a callable bond is complicated, because the early call date is not known in advance – it depends on the future path followed by the underlying security. In these cases, it is necessary to compare the value of the security – assuming it is held a while longer – with the value obtained from cash by calling the bond or prematurely exercising the call option. To solve these problems, you must work backwards in the binomial tree to make the appropriate comparisons and find the nodes in the tree where intermediate cash flows occur.

Suppose that, in the absence of a call, a callable corporate bond with a call price of €100 plus accrued interest has cash flows identical to those of the bond in exercise 7.3. (In this case, accrued interest is the €5 coupon if it is called cum-coupon at the intermediate date, and 0 if it is called ex-coupon.) What is the optimal call policy of the issuing firm, assuming that the firm is trying to maximize shareholder wealth? What is the value of the callable bond? *Hint:* keep in mind that maximizing shareholder wealth is the same as minimizing the value of the bond.

7.5 Consider an equity that can appreciate by 50 per cent or depreciate by 50 per cent per period. Three periods from now, an equity with an initial value of £32 per share can be worth (1) £108 – three up moves; (2) £36 – two up moves, one down move; (3) £12 – one up move, two down moves; or (4) £4 – three down moves. Three periods from now, a derivative is worth £78 in case (1), £4 in case (2) and £0 otherwise. If the risk-free rate is 10 per cent throughout these three periods, describe a portfolio of the equity and a risk-free bond that tracks the pay-off of the derivative and requires no future cash outlays. Then fill in the question marks in the accompanying exhibit, which illustrates the price paths of the equity and the derivative. *Hint:* you need to work backwards. Use the risk-neutral valuation method to check your work.

Three-Period Binomial Tree Diagram: (a) Underlying Security's Price (Above Node); (b) Derivative's Price (Below Node).

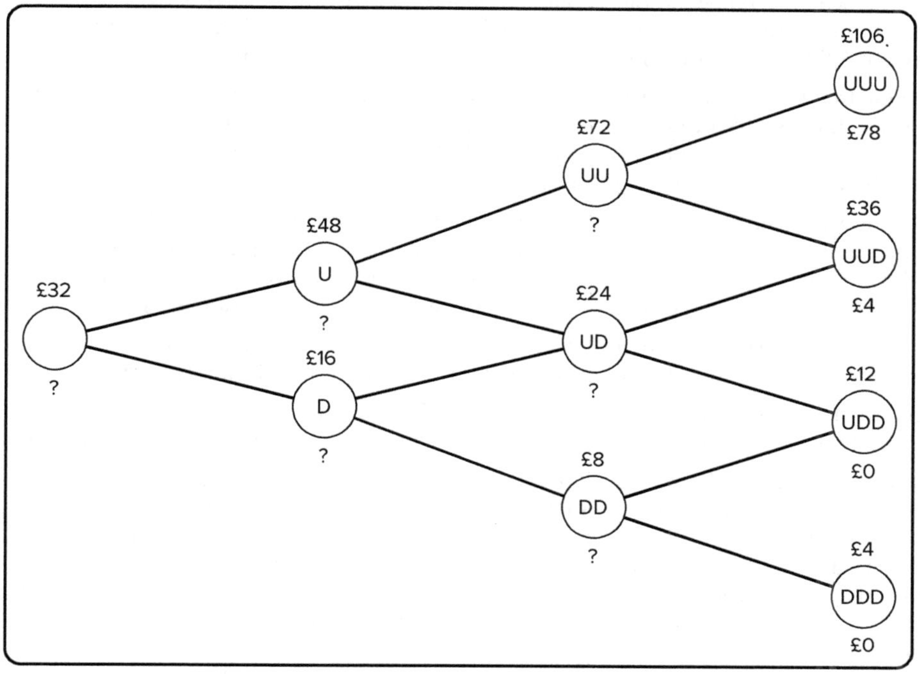

7.6 Consider a forward contract on Tesco plc requiring purchase of one share of Tesco equity for £4.90 in six months. The Tesco share price is currently £4.70. Assume that it pays no dividends over the coming six months. Six-month zero-coupon bonds are selling for £98 per £100 of face value.

a If the forward is selling for £0.25, is there an arbitrage opportunity? If so, describe exactly how you could take advantage of it.

b Assume that, three months from now, (i) the share price has risen to £4.80 and (ii) three-month zero-coupon bonds are selling for £99. How much has the fair market value of your forward contract changed over the three months that have elapsed?

7.7 Assume that forward contracts to purchase one share of Kingfisher plc and Reuters plc for £2.00 and £7.00, respectively, in one year are currently selling for £0.25 and £0.45. Assume that neither company pays a dividend over the coming year, and that one-year zero-coupon bonds are selling for £96 per £100 of face value. The current share prices of Kingfisher and Reuters are £1.87 and £6.60, respectively.

a Are there any arbitrage opportunities? If so, describe how to take advantage of them.

b What is the fair market price of a forward contract on a portfolio composed of one-half of Kingfisher and one-half of Reuters, requiring that £4.50 be paid for the portfolio in one year?

c Is this the same as buying one-half of a forward contract on each of Kingfisher and Reuters? Why or why not? (Show pay-off tables.)

d Is it generally true that a forward on a portfolio is the same as a portfolio of forwards? Explain.

7.8 Assume that the one-year Eurodollar (12-month LIBOR for US$) rate is 5.27 per cent and the Eurosterling rate (12-month LIBOR for the UK £) is 4.28 per cent. What is the theoretical 12-month forward $/£ exchange rate if the current spot exchange rate is $2.04/£?

7.9 Assume that share prices for EMC plc can appreciate by 15 per cent or depreciate by 10 per cent, and that the risk-free rate is 5 per cent over the next period. How much should you pay for a forward contract that will allow you to buy EMC for £23 if the value of EMC today is £22.75 and the actual probability of the up state occurring is 75 per cent?

7.10 A share price follows a binomial process for two periods. In each period, it either increases by 20 per cent or decreases by 20 per cent. Assuming that the equity pays no dividends, value a derivative that, at the end of the second period, pays £10 for every up move of the share price that occurred over the previous two periods. Assume that the risk-free rate is 6 per cent per period.

7.11 An equity has a 30 per cent per year standard deviation of its log returns. If you are modelling the share price to value a derivative maturing in six months with eight binomial periods, what should u and d be?

7.12 Find the risk neutral probabilities and zero-cost date 0 forward prices (for settlement at date 1) for the equity in exercise 7.2. As in that exercise, assume a risk-free rate of 15 per cent per period.

7.13 A European 'Tootsie Square' is a financial contract that, at maturity, pays off the square of the price of the underlying asset on which it is written. For instance, if the price of the underlying asset is £3 at maturity, the Tootsie Square contract pays off £9. Consider a *two-period* Tootsie Square written on Vodafone plc, which is currently trading at £1.795 per share. In each period, the price either rises 10 per cent or falls by 5 per cent (i.e. after one period, the share price of Vodafone can either rise to £1.9745 or fall to £1.7053). The probability of a rise is 0.5. The risk-free interest rate is 4 per cent *per period.*

a Determine the price at which you expect the Tootsie Square on Vodafone to trade.

b Suppose that you wanted to form a portfolio to track the pay-off on the Tootsie Square over the first period. How many shares of Vodafone should you hold in this portfolio?

References and Additional Reading

Arrow, K.J. (1964) The role of securities in the optimal allocation of risk-bearing *Review of Economic Studies,* 31(2): 91–96.

Balducci, V., Doraiswani, K., Johnson, C. and Showers, J. (1990) *Currency Swaps: Corporate Applications and Pricing Methodology,* pamphlet, Salomon Brothers, Inc., Bond Portfolio Analysis Group, New York.

Black, F. and Scholes, M. (1973) The pricing of options and corporate liabilities *Journal of Political Economy,* 81(3): 637–659.

Breeden, D.T. and Litzenberger, R.H. (1978) Prices of state-contingent claims implicit in option prices *Journal of Business,* 51(4): 621–651.

Cox, J.C. and Ross, S.A. (1976) The valuation of options for alternative stochastic processes *Journal of Financial Economics,* 3(1–2): 145–166.

Cox, J.C. and Rubinstein, M. (1985) *Options Markets.* Englewood Cliffs, NJ: Prentice Hall

Cox, J.C. Ross, S.A. and Rubinstein, M. (1979) Option pricing: a simplified approach *Journal of Financial Economics,* 7(3): 229–263.

Grinblatt, M. (1995) An analytic solution for interest rate swap spreads Working Paper, University of California, Los Angeles.

Grinblatt, M. and Jegadeesh, N. (1996) The relative pricing of Eurodollar futures and forwards *Journal of Finance,* 51(4): 1499–1522.

Grinblatt, M. and Longstaff, F. (2000) Financial innovation and the role of derivative securities: an empirical analysis of the Treasury STRIPS program *The Journal of Finance,* 55(3): 1415–1436.

Harrison, M.J. and Kreps, D.M. (1979) Martingales and arbitrage in multiperiod securities markets *Journal of Economic Theory,* 20(3): 381–408.

Hull, J.C. (1997) *Options, Futures, and Other Derivatives,* 3rd edn. Upper Saddle River, NJ: Prentice Hall.

Ingersoll, J. (1987) *Theory of Financial Decision Making.* Totowa, NJ: Rowman & Littlefield.

Jarrow, R. and Turnbull, S. (1996) *Derivative Securities.* Cincinnati, OH: South-Western Publishing.

Lewis, M. (1989) *Liar's Poker: Rising through the Wreckage on Wall Street.* New York: W.W. Norton.

Merton, R.C. (1973) Theory of rational option pricing *Bell Journal of Economics and Management Science,* 4(1): 141–183.

Rendelman, R.J. Jr, and Bartter, B.J. (1979) Two-state option pricing *The Journal of Finance,* 34(5): 1093–1110.

Ross, S.A. (1978) A simple approach to the valuation of risky streams *Journal of Business,* 51(3): 453–475.

Rubinstein, M. (1994) Presidential address: implied binomial trees *The Journal of Finance,* 49(3): 771–818.

Schwartz, E. (1977) The valuation of warrants: implementing a new approach *Journal of Financial Economics,* 4(1): 79–93.

Shleifer, A. and Vishny, R. (1997) The limits of arbitrage *The Journal of Finance,* 52(1): 35–55.

Chapter 8

Options

Learning Objectives

After reading this chapter, you should be able to:

- Explain the basic put–call parity formula, how it relates to the value of a forward contract, and the types of option to which put–call parity applies.
- Relate put–call parity to a boundary condition for the minimum call price, and know the implications of this boundary condition for pricing American call options and determining when they should be exercised.
- Gather the information needed to price a European option with (a) the binomial model and (b) the Black–Scholes model, and then implement these models to price an option.
- Understand the Black–Scholes formula in the following form

  $$S_0N(d_1) - \text{PV}(K)N(d_1 - \sigma\sqrt{\text{T}})$$

  And interpret $N(d_1)$.
- Provide examples that illustrate why an American call on a dividend-paying stock or an American put (irrespective of dividend policy) might be exercised prematurely.
- Understand the effect of volatility on option prices and premature exercise.

As financial technology becomes a staple of retail financial planning, new financial instruments utilizing mobile financial apps have become common, in line with a rapidly emerging interest in financial trading by tech-savvy investors. In 2021, Gamestop's share price exploded by 1,500% on the back of trading by Reddit users looking to exploit overactive short-selling activity by hedge funds. This would never have happened even two years before because the retail market has never been this informed or skilled at trading. A new instrument targeted to these types of investors is the micro e-mini option. The micro e-mini option is a derivative instrument with only a 2× contract multiplier on the underlying asset. This is in contrast to standard options with 100× or more contract multipliers. Having such a low multiplier means that transaction sizes in these options can be small, which thus opens up the market to retail traders who wish to trade twenty-four hours per day. Within two years of the instrument launching in 2019, trading volumes exploded to over 40,000 transactions in any one day. With the new popularity of micro options, retail investors will need to become familiar with the intricacies of option valuation and the various models used to price these instruments.

One of the most important applications of the theory of derivatives valuation is the pricing of options. Options, introduced earlier in the text, are ubiquitous in financial markets and, as seen in this chapter and in much of the remainder of this text, are often found implicitly in numerous corporate financial decisions and corporate securities.

Options have long been important to portfolio managers. In recent years they have become increasingly important to corporate treasurers. There are several reasons for this. For one, a corporate treasurer needs to be educated about options for proper oversight of the pension funds of the corporation. In addition, the treasurer needs to understand that options can be useful in corporate hedging,[1] and are implicit in many securities that the corporation issues, such as convertible bonds, mortgages and callable bonds.[2] Options are also an important form of executive compensation and, in some cases, a form of financing for the firm.

This chapter applies the no-arbitrage tracking portfolio approach to derive the 'fair market' values of options, using both the binomial approach and a continuous-time approach known as the Black–Scholes model. It then discusses several practical considerations and limitations of the binomial and Black–Scholes option valuation models. Among these is the problem of estimating volatility. The chapter generalizes the Black–Scholes model to a variety of underlying securities, including bonds and commodities. It concludes with a discussion of the empirical evidence for the Black–Scholes model.

8.1 A Description of Options and Options Markets

There are two basic types of option: call options and put options. The next subsection elaborates on an additional important classification of options.

European and American Options

- A **European** call (put) **option** is the right to buy (sell) a unit of the underlying asset at the strike price, *at a specific point in time,* the expiration or exercise date.
- An **American** call (put) **option** is the right to buy (sell) a unit of the underlying asset *at any time on or before* the expiration date of the option.

Most of the options that trade on organized exchanges are American options. For example, Eurex, a European derivatives exchange, trades American options, primarily on equities and equity indices such as the FTSE 100, CAC40 and Bel-20. European options are available, but they are not as popular as their American counterparts, because they can be exercised only on one date, the expiration date.

European options are easier to value than American options, because the analyst need be concerned only about their value at one future date. However, in some circumstances, which will be discussed shortly, European and American options have the same value. Because of their relative simplicity, and because the understanding of European option valuation is often the springboard to understanding the process of valuing the more popular American options, this chapter devotes more space to the valuation of European options than to American options.

The Four Features of Options

Four features characterize a simple option, the offer of the right to buy (call) or the right to sell (put). These are:

1. an underlying risky asset that determines the option's value at some future date[3]
2. a strike price

---

[1] Hedging is discussed in Chapter 22.

[2] Callable bonds give the corporation the right to redeem the outstanding bonds before maturity by paying a premium to bondholders. Therefore it is an option that the firm can choose to exercise by 'calling' the bonds. Typically, this will occur when interest rates are low. See Chapter 2.

[3] Typically, the underlying asset is ordinary equity, a portfolio of equities, foreign currencies or futures contracts, but there are many other assets or portfolios of assets on which options can be written. We use the term 'asset' loosely here to mean anything that has an uncertain value over time, be it an asset, a liability, a contract or a commodity. There is a vast over-the-counter market between financial institutions in which options of almost any variety on virtually any underlying asset or portfolio of assets are traded.

3 an **exercise commencement date,** before which the option cannot be exercised

4 an expiration date beyond which the option can no longer be exercised.

Because European options can be exercised only on their expiration dates, their commencement and expiration dates are the same. American options, which can be exercised at any time on or before their expiration dates, have commencement dates that coincide with their dates of initial issuance.[4]

8.2 Option Expiration

Exhibit 8.1, first seen in Chapter 7, graphs the value of a call and put option at the expiration date against the value of the underlying asset at expiration. In this chapter, we attach some algebra to the graphs of call and put values. For expositional simplicity, we shall often refer to the underlying asset as a share of ordinary equity, but our results also apply to options on virtually any financial instrument.

Exhibit 8.1 The Value of a Call Option and a Put Option at Expiration

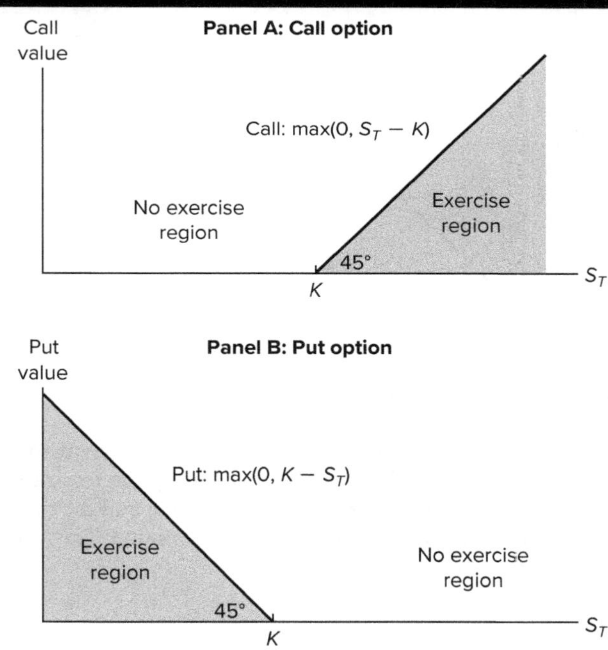

The uncertain future share price at the expiration date, T, is denoted by S_T. The strike or exercise price is denoted by K. The expiration value for the call option is the larger of zero and the difference between the share price at the expiration date and the strike price, denoted by $\max(0, S_T - K)$. For the put option, the expiration value is $\max(0, K - S_T)$.

Note that the two graphs in Exhibit 8.1 never lie below the horizontal axis. They either coincide with the axis or lie above it on the 45° line. In algebraic terms, the expressions for the future call value, $\max(0, S_T - K)$, and the future put value, $\max(0, K - S_T)$, are never negative. Recall from Chapter 7 that options can never have a negative value, because options expire unexercised if option exercise hurts the option holder. The absence of a negative future value for the option and the possibility of a positive future value make paying for an option worthwhile.

[4] Deferred American options, not discussed here, have issue dates that precede their commencement dates.

Future cash flows are never positive when writing an option. Exhibit 8.2 illustrates the value at expiration of the short position generated by writing an option. When the call's strike price, K, exceeds the future share price S_T (or S_T exceeds K for the put), the option expires unexercised. On the other hand, if S_T exceeds K, the call writer has to sell a share of equity for less than its fair value. Similarly, if K exceeds S_T, the put writer has to buy a share of equity for more than it is worth. In all cases, there is no positive future cash flow to the option writer. To compensate the option writer for these future adverse consequences, the option buyer pays money to the writer to acquire the option.

Exhibit 8.2 The Value of Short Positions in Call and Put Options at Expiration

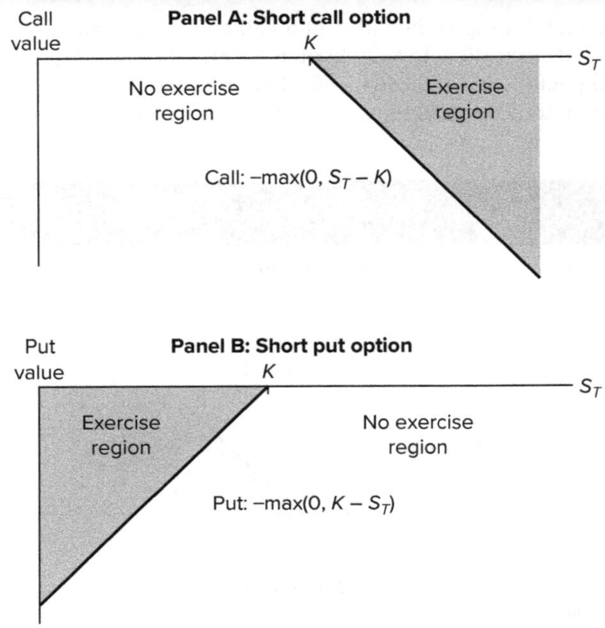

Finally, observe that the non-random number S_0, which denotes the current share price, does not appear in Exhibits 8.1 and 8.2 because the focus is only on what happens at option expiration. One of the goals of this chapter is to translate the future relationship between the equity value and the option value into a relationship between the current value of the equity and the current value of the option. The next section illustrates the type of reasoning used to derive such a relation.

8.3 Put–Call Parity

With some rudimentary understanding of the institutional features of options behind us, we now move on to analyse their valuation. One of the most important insights in option pricing, developed by Stoll (1969), is known as the **put–call parity formula**. This equation relates the prices of European calls to the prices of European puts. However, as this section illustrates, this formula also is important because it has a number of implications that go beyond relating call prices to put prices.

Put–Call Parity and Forward Contracts: Deriving the Formula

Exhibit 8.3 illustrates the value of a long position in a European call option at expiration and a short position in an otherwise identical put option. This combined pay-off is identical to the pay-off of a forward contract, which is the obligation (not the option) to buy the underlying asset for K at the expiration date.[5]

[5] In contrast to options, forward contracts – as obligations to purchase at pre-specified prices – can have positive or negative values. Typically, the strike price of a forward contract is set initially, so that the contract has zero value. In this case, the pre-specified price is known as the forward price. See Chapter 7 for more detail.

Exhibit 8.3 The Value at Expiration of a Long Position in a Call Option and a Short Position in a Put Option with the Same Features

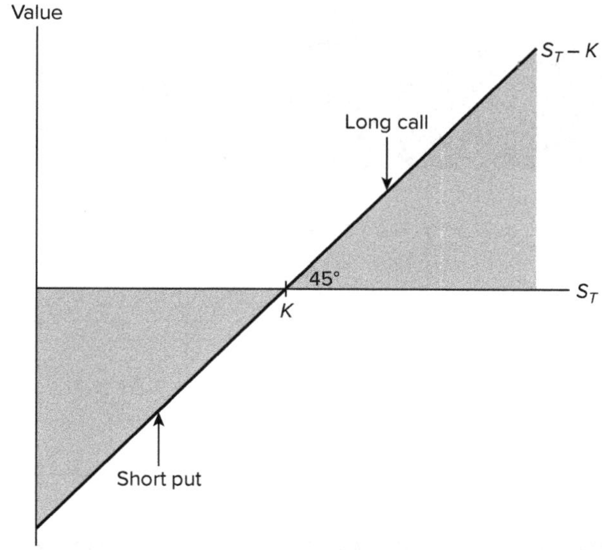

Result 7.1 in Chapter 7 indicated that the value of a forward contract with a strike price of K on a non-dividend-paying stock is $S_0 - K/(1 + r_f)^T$, the difference between the current share price and the present value of the strike price (which we also denote as PV(K)), obtained by discounting K at the risk-free rate. The forward contract has this value because it is possible to track this pay-off perfectly by purchasing one share of equity and borrowing the present value of K.[6] Since the tracking portfolio for the forward contract, with future (random) value $\tilde{S}_T - K$, also tracks the future value of a long position in a European call and a short position in a European put (see Exhibit 8.3), to prevent arbitrage, the tracking portfolio and the tracked investment must have the same value today.

Results

Result 8.1

(*The put–call parity formula.*) If no dividends are paid to holders of the underlying equity prior to expiration, then, assuming no arbitrage,

$$c_0 - p_0 = S_0 - \text{PV}(K) \qquad (8.1)$$

That is, a long position in a call and a short position in a put sells for the current share price less the strike price discounted at the risk-free rate.

Using Tracking Portfolios to Prove the Formula

Exhibit 8.4a, which uses algebra, and 8.4b, which uses numbers, illustrate this point further. The columns in the exhibits compare the value of a forward contract implicit in buying a call and writing a put (investment 1) with the value from buying the equity and borrowing the present value of K (investment 2, the tracking portfolio), where K, the strike price of both the call and put options, is assumed to be 50 in Exhibit 8.4b. Column (1) makes this comparison at the current date. In this column, C_0 denotes the current value of a European call and p_0 the current value of a European put, each with the same time to expiration. Columns (2) and (3) in Exhibit 8.4a make the comparison between investments 1 and 2 at expiration, comparing the future values of investments 1 and 2 in the exercise and no exercise regions of the two European options. To represent the uncertainty of the

[6] Example 7.4 in Chapter 7 proves this.

future share price, Exhibit 8.4b assumes three possible future share prices at expiration: $S_T = 45$, $S_T = 52$ and $S_T = 59$, which correspond to columns (2), (3) and (4), respectively. In Exhibit 8.4b, columns (3) and (4) have call option exercise, while column (2) has put option exercise.

Exhibit 8.4a Comparing Two Investments (Algebra)

Investment	Cost of acquiring the investment today (1)	Cash flows at the expiration date if S at that time is:	
		$\tilde{S}_T < K$ (2)	$\tilde{S}_T > K$ (3)
Investment 1: Buy call and write put = long position in a call and short position in a put	$C_0 - P_0$ $= C_0$ $-P_0$	$\tilde{S}_T - K$ $= 0$ $-(K - \tilde{S}_T)$	$\tilde{S}_T - K$ $= \tilde{S}_T - K$ -0
Investment 2: Tracking portfolio = buy equity and borrow present value of K	$S_0 - \mathrm{PV}(K)$ $= S_0$ $-\mathrm{PV}(K)$	$\tilde{S}_T - K$ $= \tilde{S}_T$ $-K$	$\tilde{S}_T - K$ $= \tilde{S}_T$ $-K$

Exhibit 8.4b Comparing Two Investments (Numbers) with $K = [50$

Investment	Cost of acquiring the investment today (1)	Cash flows at the expiration date if S at that time is:		
		€45 (2)	€52 (3)	€59 (4)
Investment 1: Buy call and write put = long position in a call and short position in a put	$C_0 - P_0$ $= C_0$ $-P_0$	−€5 = 0 −(€50 − €45)	€2 = (€52 − €50) −0	€9 = (€59 − €50) −0
Investment 2: Tracking portolio = buy equity and borrow present value of K	$S_0 - \mathrm{PV}(€50)$ $= S_0$ $-\mathrm{PV}(€50)$	−€5 = €45 −€50	€2 = €52 −€50	€9 = €59 −€50

Since the cash flows at expiration from investments 1 and 2 are both $\tilde{S}_T - K$, irrespective of the future value realized by $\tilde{S}_T$, the date 0 values of investments 1 and 2 observed in column (1) have to be the same if there is no arbitrage. The algebraic statement of this is equation (8.1).

An Example Illustrating How to Apply the Formula

Example 8.1 illustrates an application of Result 8.1.

Example 8.1

Comparing Prices of At-the-Money Calls and Puts

An at-the-money option has a strike price equal to the current share price. Assuming no dividends, what sells for more: an at-the-money European put or an at-the-money European call?

Answer: From put–call parity, $c_0 - p_0 = S_0 - \mathrm{PV}(K)$. If $S_0 = K$, $c_0 - p_0 = K - \mathrm{PV}(K) > 0$. Thus the call sells for more.

Arbitrage When the Formula is Violated

Example 8.2 demonstrates how to achieve arbitrage when equation (8.1) is violated.

Put–Call Parity and a Minimum Value for a Call

The put–call parity formula provides a lower bound for the current value of a call, given the current share price. Because it is necessary to subtract a non-negative current put price, p_0, from the current call price, c_0, in order to make $c_0 - p_0 = S_0 - \text{PV}(K)$, it follows that

$$C_0 \geq S_0 - \text{PV}(K) \tag{8.1a}$$

Thus the minimum value of a call is the current price of the underlying equity, S_0, less the present value of the strike price, PV(K).

Example 8.2

Generating Arbitrage Profits When there is a Violation of Put–Call Parity

Assume that a one-year European call on a €45 share of equity with a strike price of €44 sells for c_0 – €2 and a European put on the same equity (S_0 = €45), with the same strike price (€44) and time to expiration (one year), sells for P_0 = €1. If the one-year, risk-free interest rate is 10 per cent, the put–call parity formula is violated and there is an arbitrage opportunity. Describe it.

Answer: PV(K) = €44/1.1 = €40. Thus $C_0 - P_0$ = €1 is less than S_0 – PV(K) = €5. Therefore buying a call and writing a put is a cheaper way of producing the cash flows from a forward contract than buying equity and borrowing the present value of K. Pure arbitrage arises from buying the cheap investment and writing the expensive one: that is,

1 Buy the call for €2.
2 Write the put for €1.
3 Sell short the equity and receive €45.
4 Invest €40 in the 10 per cent risk-free asset.

This strategy results in an initial cash inflow of €4.

- If the share price exceeds the strike price at expiration, exercise the call, using the proceeds from the risk-free investment to pay for the €44 strike price. Close out the short position in the equity with the share received at exercise. The worthless put expires unexercised. Hence there are no cash flows and no positions left at expiration, but the original €4 is yours to keep.
- If the share price at expiration is less than the €44 strike price, the put will be exercised and you, as the put writer, will be forced to receive a share of equity and pay €44 for it. The share you acquire can be used to close out your short position in the equity, and the €44 strike price comes out of your risk-free investment. The worthless call expires unexercised. Again, there are no cash flows or positions left at expiration. The original €4 is yours to keep.

Put–Call Parity and the Pricing and Premature Exercise of American Calls

This subsection uses equation (8.1) to demonstrate that the values of American and European call options on non-dividend-paying equities are the same. This is a remarkable result and, at first glance, a bit surprising. American options have all the rights of European options, plus more: thus values of American options should equal or exceed the values of their otherwise identical European counterparts. In general, American options may be worth more than their European counterparts, as this chapter later demonstrates with puts. What is surprising is that they are *not always* worth more.

Premature Exercise of American Call Options on Equities with No Dividends before Expiration

American options are worth more than European options only if the right of premature exercise has value. Before expiration, however, the present value of the strike price of any option, European or American, is less than the strike price itself: that is, PV(K) < K. Inequality (8.1a) – which, as an extension of the put–call parity formula, assumes no dividends before expiration – is therefore the strict inequality

$$c_0 > S_0 - K \tag{8.1b}$$

before expiration, which must hold for both European and American call options. Inequality (8.1b) implies Result 8.2.

Results

Result 8.2

It never pays to exercise an American call option prematurely on an equity that pays no dividends before expiration.

One should never prematurely exercise an American call option on an equity that pays no dividends before expiration because exercising generates cash of $S_0 - K$, while selling the option gives the seller cash of c_0, which is larger by inequality (8.1b). This suggests that waiting until the expiration date always has some value, at which point exercise of an in-the-money call option should take place.

What if the market price of the call happens to be the same as the call option's exercise value? Example 8.3 shows that there is arbitrage if an American call option on a non-dividend-paying equity does not sell for (strictly) more than its premature exercise value before expiration.

Example 8.3

Arbitrage When a Call Sells for its Exercise Value

Consider an American call option with a £4.00 strike price on Rentokil, a UK pest control firm. Assume that the equity sells for £4.50 a share, and pays no dividends to expiration. The option sells for £0.50 one year before expiration. Describe an arbitrage opportunity, assuming the interest rate is 10 per cent per year.

Answer: Sell short a share of Rentokil and use the £4.50 you receive to buy the option for £0.50 and place the remaining £4.00 in a savings account. The initial cash flow from this strategy is zero. If the equity is selling for more than £4.00 at expiration, exercise the option and use your savings account balance to pay the strike price. Although the equity acquisition is used to close out your short position, the £0.40 interest (£4.00 × 0.1) on the savings account is yours to keep. If the share price is less than £4.00 at expiration, buy the equity with funds from the savings account to cancel the short position. The £0.40 interest in the savings account and the difference between the £4.00 (initial principal in the savings account) and the share price is yours to keep.

Holding onto an American call option instead of exercising it prematurely is like buying the option at its current exercise value in exchange for its future exercise value: that is, not exercising the option means giving up the exercise value today in order to maintain the value you will get from exercise at a later date. Hence the cost of not exercising prematurely (that is, waiting) is the lost exercise value of the option.

Example 8.3 shows that the option to exercise at a later date is more valuable than the immediate exercise of an option. An investor can buy the option for £0.50, sell the equity short and gain an arbitrage opportunity by exercising the option in the future if it pays to do so. Thus the option has to be worth more than the £0.50 it costs. It follows that holding on to an option already owned has to be worth more than the £0.50 received from early exercise (see exercise 8.1 at the end of the chapter).

When Premature Exercise of American Call Options Can Occur

Result 8.2 does not necessarily apply to an underlying security that pays cash prior to expiration. This can clearly be seen in the case of an equity that is about to pay a liquidating dividend. An investor needs to exercise an in-the-money American call option on the equity before the **ex-dividend date** of a liquidating dividend, which is the last date one can exercise the option and still receive the dividend.[7] The option is worthless thereafter, since it represents the right to buy a share of a company that has no assets. All dividends dissipate some of a company's assets. Hence, for similar reasons, even a small dividend with an ex-dividend date shortly before the expiration date of the option could trigger an early exercise of the option.

Early exercise is also possible when the option cannot be valued by the principle of no arbitrage, as would be the case if the investor was prohibited from selling short the tracking portfolio. This issue arises in many executive share options. Executive share options awarded to the company's CEO may make the CEO's portfolio more heavily weighted towards the company than prudent mean-variance analysis would dictate it should be. One way to eliminate this diversifiable risk is to sell short the company's equity (a part of the tracking portfolio), but the CEO and most other top corporate executives who receive such options are prohibited from doing this. Another way is to sell the options, but this too is prohibited. The only way for an executive to diversify is to exercise the option, take the equity, and then sell the shares. Such sub-optimal exercise timing, however, does not capture the full value of the executive share option. Nevertheless, the CEO may be willing to lose a little value to gain some diversification.

Except for these two cases – one in which the underlying asset pays cash before expiration and the other, executive share options, for which arbitraging away violations of inequality (8.1b) is not possible because of market frictions – one should not prematurely exercise a call option.

When dividends or other forms of cash on the underlying asset are paid, the appropriate timing for early exercise is described in the following generalization of Result 8.2.

Results

Result 8.3

An investor does not capture the full value of an American call option by exercising between ex-dividend or (in the case of a bond option) ex-coupon dates.

Only at the ex-dividend date, just before the drop in the price of the security caused by the cash distribution, is such early exercise worthwhile.

To understand Result 8.3, consider the following example. Suppose it is your birthday, and Aunt Michelle sends you one share of Allianz equity, an insurance firm listed on the Frankfurt Stock Exchange. Uncle Kevin, however, gives you a gift certificate entitling you to one share of Allianz equity on your next birthday, one year hence. Provided that Allianz pays no dividends within the next year, the values of the two gifts are the same. The value of the deferred gift is the cost of Allianz equity on the date of your birthday. Putting it differently, in the absence of a dividend, the only right obtained by receiving a security early is that you will have it at that later date. You might retort that if you wake up tomorrow and think Allianz's share price is going down, you will sell Aunt Michelle's Allianz share, but you are forced to receive Uncle Kevin's share. However, this is not really so, because at any time you think Allianz's share price is headed down, you can sell short Allianz and use Uncle Kevin's gift to close out your short position. In this case, the magnitude and timing of the cash flows from Aunt Michelle's gift of Allianz, which you sell tomorrow, are identical to those from the combination of Uncle Kevin's gift certificate and the Allianz short position that you execute tomorrow. Hence you *do not* create value by receiving shares on non-dividend-paying equities early, but you *do* create value by deferring the payment of the strike price – increasing wealth by the amount of interest collected in the period before exercise.

Thus with an option, or even with a forward contract on a non-dividend-paying security, paying for the security at the latest date possible makes sense. With an option, however, you have a further incentive to wait:

[7] Ex-dividend dates, which are ex-dates for dividends (see Chapter 2 for a general definition of ex-dates), are determined by the record dates for dividend payments and the settlement procedures of the securities market. The record date is the date when the legal owner of the equity is put on record for purposes of receiving a corporation's dividend payment. On NYSE Euronext, an investor is not the legal owner of an equity until three business days after the order has been executed. This makes the ex-date three business days before the record date.

if the security later goes down in value, you can choose not to acquire the security by not exercising the option, and if it goes up, you can exercise the option and acquire the security.

Premature Exercise of American Put Options

The value from waiting to see how the security turns out also applies to a put option. With a put, however, the option holder receives rather than pays out cash upon exercise, and the earlier the receipt of cash, the better. With a put, an investor trades off the interest earned from receiving cash early against the value gained from waiting to see how things will turn out. A put on an equity that sells for pennies with a strike price of £4.00 probably should be exercised. At best, waiting can provide only a few more pennies (the equity cannot sell for less than zero), which should easily be covered by the interest on the £4.00 received.

Relating the Price of an American Call Option to an Otherwise Identical European Call Option

If it is never prudent to exercise an American call option prior to expiration, then the right of premature exercise has no value. Thus in cases where this is true (for example, no dividends), the no-arbitrage prices of American and European call options are the same.

Results

Result 8.4

If the underlying equity pays no dividends before expiration, then the no-arbitrage values of American and European call options with the same features are the same.

Put–Call Parity for European Options on Dividend-Paying Equities

If there are riskless dividends, it is possible to modify the put–call parity relationship. In this case, the forward contract with price $c_0 - p_0$ is worth less than the equity minus the present value of the strike price, $S_0 - \text{PV}(K)$. Buying a share of equity and borrowing PV(K) now also generates dividends that are not received by the holder of the forward contract (or, equivalently, the long call plus short put position). Hence, although the tracking portfolio and the forward contract have the same value at expiration, their intermediate cash flows do not match. Only the tracking portfolio receives a dividend prior to expiration. Hence the value of the tracking portfolio (investment 2 in Exhibit 8.4) exceeds the value of the forward contract (investment 1) by the present value of the dividends, denoted PV(div) (with PV(div) obtained by discounting each dividend at the risk-free rate and summing the discounted values).

Results

Result 8.5

(*Put–call parity formula generalized.*) $c_0 - p_0 - S_0 - \text{PV}(K) - \text{PV}(\text{div})$. The difference between the no-arbitrage values of a European call and a European put with the same features is the current share price less the sum of the present value of the strike price and the present value of all dividends to expiration.

Example 8.4 applies this formula to illustrate how to compute European put values in relation to the known value of a European call on a dividend-paying equity.

Put–Call Parity and Corporate Securities as Options

Important option-based interpretations of corporate securities can be derived from put–call parity. Equity can be thought of as a call option on the assets of the firm.[8] This arises because of the limited liability of corporate equity holders. Consider a simple two-date model (dates 0 and 1) in which a firm has debt with a

[8] See Chapters 7 and 16 for more information on this subject.

face value of K to be paid at date 1, assets with a random pay-off at date 1, and no dividend payment at or before date 1. In this case, equity holders have a decision to make at date 1. If they pay the face value of the debt (the strike price), they receive the date 1 cash flows of the assets. On the other hand, if the assets at date 1 are worth less than the face value of the debt, the firm is bankrupt, and the equity holders walk away from the firm with no personal liability. Viewed from date 0, this is simply a call option to buy the firm's assets from the firm's debt holders.[9]

Example 8.4

Inferring Put Values from Call Values on a Dividend-Paying Stock

Assume that the shares of Accor, a French hotel group, currently sell for €100. A European call on Accor has a strike price of €121, expires two years from now, and currently sells for €20. What is the value of the comparable European put? Assume the risk-free rate is 10 per cent per year and that Accor is certain to pay a dividend of €2.75 one year from now.

Answer: From put–call parity

$$€20 - p_0 = €100 - \frac{€121}{1.1^2} - \frac{€2.75}{1.1}$$

or

$$p_0 = -(€100 - €100 - €2.50 - €20) = €22.50$$

Since the value of debt plus the value of equity adds up to the total value of assets at date 0, one also can view corporate bonds as a long position in the firm's assets and a short position in a call option on the firm's assets. With S_0 now denoting the current value of the firm's assets, c_0 denoting the current value of its equity, K denoting the face value of the firm's debt, and D_0 as the market (current) value of its debt, the statement that bonds are assets less a call option is represented algebraically as

$$D_0 = S_0 - c_0$$

However, when using the no-dividend put–call parity formula, $c_0 - p_0 = S_0 - \text{PV}(K)$, to substitute for c_0 in this expression, risky corporate debt is

$$D_0 = \text{PV}(K) - p_0$$

One can draw the following conclusion, which holds even if dividends are paid prior to the debt maturity date.

Results

Result 8.6

It is possible to view equity as a call option on the assets of the firm and to view risky corporate debt as riskless debt worth PV(K) plus a short position in a put option on the assets of the firm ($-p_0$) with a strike price of K.

Because corporate securities are options on the firm's assets, any characteristic of the assets of the firm that affects option values will alter the values of debt and equity. One important characteristic of the underlying asset that affects option values, presented later in this chapter, is the variance of the asset return. Result 8.6 also implies that the more debt a firm has, the less in the money is the implicit option in equity. Thus knowing how option risk is affected by the degree to which the option is in or out of the money may shed light on how

[9] This analysis is easily modified to accommodate riskless dividends. In this case, equity holders have a claim to a riskless dividend plus a call option on the difference between the firm's assets and the present value of the dividend. The dividend-inclusive put–call parity formula can then be used to interpret corporate debt.

the mix of debt and equity affects the risk of the firm's debt and equity securities. Finally, because equity is an option on the assets of the firm, a call option on the equity of a firm is really an option on an option, or a **compound option.**[10] The binomial derivatives valuation methodology developed in Chapter 7 can be used to value compound options.

Put–Call Parity and Portfolio Insurance

Portfolio insurance is an option-based investment that, when added to the existing investments of a pension fund or mutual fund, protects the fund's value at a target horizon date against drastic losses. These options have the desirable feature of unlimited upside potential with limited downside risk. Exhibit 8.5 demonstrates that if portfolios are composed of:

- a call option, expiring on the future horizon date, with a strike price of K, and
- riskless zero-coupon bonds worth F, the floor amount, at the option expiration date,

the portfolio's value at the date the options expire would never fall below the value of the riskless bonds, the floor amount, at that date. If the underlying asset of the call option performed poorly, the option would expire unexercised; however, because the call option value in this case is zero, the portfolio value would be the value of the riskless bonds. If the underlying asset performed well, the positive value of the call option would enhance the value of the portfolio beyond its floor value. In essence, this portfolio is insured.

Exhibit 8.5 Horizon Date Values of the Two Components of an Insured Portfolio

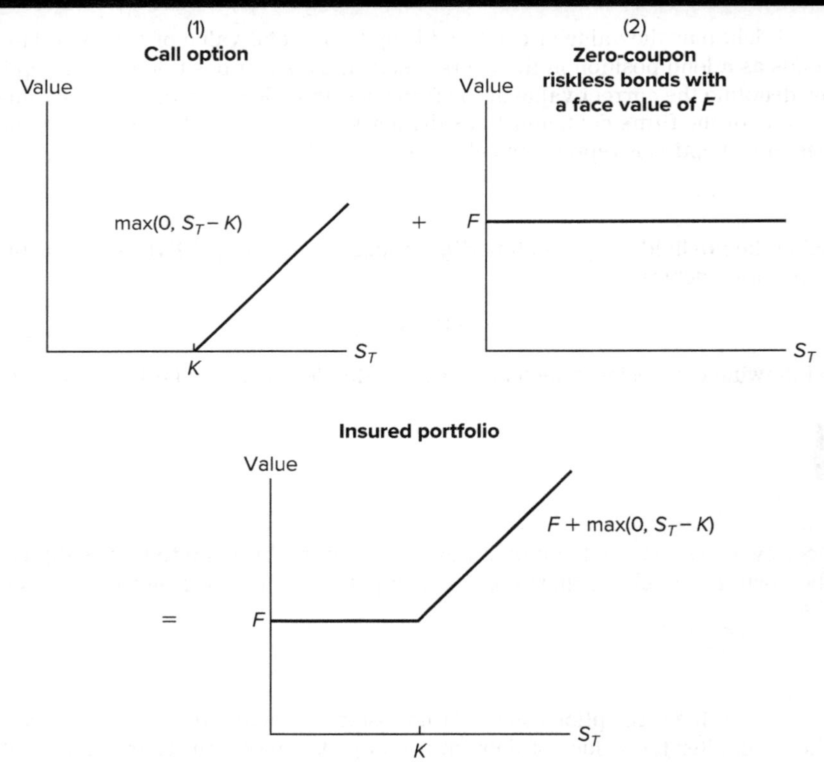

[10] The valuation of compound options was first developed in Geske (1979).

[11] Proper risk management is important in the management of portfolios and corporations. A casual reading of the business press would have you believe that all derivative securities are extremely risky. Here, however, the acquisition of protective puts can reduce risk by placing a floor on one's losses.

The present value of the two components of an insured portfolio is

$$c_0 + \text{PV}(F)$$

where PV(F) is the floor amount, discounted at the risk-free rate.

The problem is that the portfolios of pension funds and mutual funds are not composed of riskless zero-coupon bonds and call options. The challenge is how to turn them into something with similar payoffs. Portfolio insurance is the acquisition of a put on an equity index. The put's strike price determines an absolute floor on losses due to movements in the equity index. The put can be either purchased directly or produced synthetically by creating the put's tracking portfolio (see Chapter 7). Because of the lack of liquidity in put options on equity indices at desired strike prices and maturities, the tracking portfolio is typically constructed from a dynamic strategy in stock index futures. For a fee, financial institutions could tailor a strategy to meet a fund's insurance objectives.[11]

To understand how portfolio insurance works, note that the extended put–call parity formula in Result 8.5, $c_0 - p_0 = S_0 - \text{PV}(K) - \text{PV}(\text{div})$, implies that the *present value* of the desired insured portfolio is

$$c_0 + \text{PV}(F) = S_0 + p_0 - [\text{PV}(\text{div}) + \text{PV}(K) - \text{PV}(F)]$$

where

S_0 = the current value of the uninsured equity portfolio
p_0 = the cost of a put with a strike price of K
PV(div) = the present value of the uninsured equity portfolio's dividends.

The left-hand side of the equation is the present value of a desired insured portfolio with a floor of F. The right-hand side implies that if an investor starts with an uninsured equity portfolio at a value of S_0, he or she must acquire a put.

If there is to be costless portfolio insurance (that is, no liquidation of the existing portfolio to buy the portfolio insurance), the left-hand side of the equation must equal S_0. With such costless insurance, the expression in brackets above must equal the cost of the put. This implies that the floor amount, F, and the strike price of the put, K, which also affects p_0, must be chosen judiciously.

Real World Insights

Sustainability

Since COP26 at the end of 2021, there has been a considerable growth in derivatives linked to sustainability key performance indicators (KPIs). A sustainability linked derivative (SLD) has a payoff directly tied to an ESG target. An example of an SLD was issued by the global financial institution, ING, and was based on an interest rate swap. The standard contract was to swap a $1 billion five-year floating rate for a fixed rate. However, the innovation is that there is a positive or negative spread tied to the borrower meeting sustainability KPIs. If the borrowing company meets sustainability KPIs written into the SLD when it is issued, it will pay less in interest payments, thereby incentivizing behaviors towards improving climate change.

8.4 Binomial Valuation of European Options

Chapter 7 illustrated how to value any derivative security with the risk-neutral valuation method. Valuing European options with this method is simply a matter of applying the risk-neutral probabilities to the expiration date values of the option and discounting the risk-neutral weighted average at the risk-free rate. This section applies the risk-neutral valuation method to algebraic symbols that represent the binomial expiration date values of a European call option in order to derive an analytic formula for valuing European call options. (Put–call parity can be used to obtain the European put formula.) To simplify the algebra, assume that the one-period risk-free rate is constant, and that the ratio of price in the next period to price in this period is always u or d.

This section first analyses the problem of valuing a European call one period before expiration. It then generalizes the problem to one of valuing a call T periods before expiration. According to Result 8.4, if there are no dividends, the formula obtained also applies to the value of an American call.

Exhibit 8.6 illustrates the investor's view of the tree diagram one period before the option expiration date. Both the values of the equity (above the nodes) and the call option (below the nodes) are represented.[12] We noted in Chapter 7 that it is possible to value the cash flows of any derivative security after computing the risk-neutral probabilities for the equity. The hypothetical probabilities that would exist in a risk-neutral world must make the expected return on the equity equal the risk-free rate. The risk-neutral probabilities for the up and down moves that do this, π and $1 - \pi$, respectively, satisfy:

$$\pi = \frac{1 + r_f - d}{u - d}$$

Exhibit 8.6 Tree Diagram for the Value of the Equity (Above Node) and the Call Option (Below Node) Near the Expiration Date

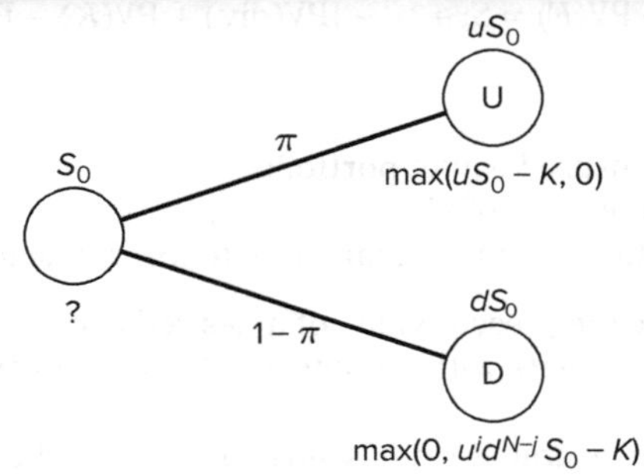

and:

$$1 - \pi = \frac{u - 1 - r_f}{u - d}$$

where:

u = ratio of next period's share price to this period's price if the up state occurs
d = ratio of next period's share price to this period's price if the down state occurs
r_f = risk-free rate.

Discounting the risk-neutral expected value of the expiration value of the call at the risk-free rate yields the proper no-arbitrage call value, c_0, as a function of the share price, S_0, in this simple case, namely,

$$c_0 = \frac{\pi \max(uS_0 - K,\ 0) + (1 - \pi)\max(ds_0 - k,\ 0)}{1 + r_f}$$

With N periods to expiration, the risk-neutral expected value of the expiration value of the call, discounted at the risk-free rate, again generates the current no-arbitrage value of the call. Now, however, there are $N + 1$ possible final call values, each determined by the number of up moves, 0, 1, . . . , N. There is only one path for N up moves, and the risk-neutral probability of arriving there is π^N. The value of the option with a strike price of K at this point is $\max(0, u^N S_0 - K)$. For $N - 1$ up moves, the value of the option is $\max(0, u^{N-1}S_0 - K)$, which multiplies the risk-neutral probability of $\pi^{N-1}(1 - \pi)$. However, there are N such paths, one for each of the N dates at which the single down move can occur. For $N - 2$ up moves, each path to $\max(0, u^{N-2}d^2S_0 - K)$ has a risk-neutral probability of $\pi^{N-2}(1 - \pi)^2$. There are $N(N - 1)/2$ such paths.

[12] The expiration date prices of the equity and call are at the two circular nodes on the right-hand side of the tree diagram, U and D, in Exhibit 8.6. The prices one period before are at the single node on the left-hand side.

In general, for j up moves, $j = 0, \ldots, N$, each path has a risk-neutral probability of $\pi^j(1-\pi)^{N-j}$, and there are $N!/[j!(N-j)!]$ such paths to the associated value of $\max(0, u^j d^{N-j} S_0 - K)$.[13] Therefore the 'expected' future value of a European call option, where the expectation uses the risk-neutral probabilities to weight the outcome, is

$$\sum_{j=0}^{N} \frac{N!}{j!(N-j)!} \pi^j (1-\pi)^{N-j} \max(0, u^j d^{N-j} S_0 - K)$$

This expression, discounted at the risk-free rate of r_f per binomial period, gives the value of the call option.

Example 8.5 applies this formula numerically.

Results

Result 8.7

(*The binomial formula.*) The value of a European call option with a strike price of K and N periods to expiration on an expiration with no dividends to expiration and a current value of S_0 is

$$c_0 = \frac{1}{(1+r_f)^N} \sum_{j=0}^{N} \frac{N!}{j!(N-j)!} \pi^j (1-\pi)^{N-j} \max(0, u^j d^{N-j} S_0 - K) \quad (8.2)$$

where

r_f = risk-free return per period
π = risk-neutral probability of an up move
u = ratio of the share price to the prior share price, given that the up state has occurred over a binomial step
d = ratio of the share price to the prior share price, given that the down state has occurred over a binomial step

8.5 Binomial Valuation of American Options

Example 8.5

Valuing a European Call Option with the Binomial Formula

Use equation (8.2) to find the value of a three-month at-the-money call option on Smith Group plc trading at £32 a share. To keep the computations simple, assume that $r_f = 0$, $u = 2$, $d = 0.5$, and the number of periods (computed as months), $N = 3$.

Answer: Exhibit 8.7 illustrates the tree diagram for Smith Group's equity and call option. The shares can have a final value (seen on the right-hand side of the diagram) of £256 (three up moves to node UUU), £64 (two up moves to node UUD), £16 (one up move to node UDD) or £4 (0 up moves to node DDD). The corresponding values for the option are £224 = $u^3 S_0 > K$, £32 = $u^2 d S_0 > K$, £0 and £0. Since $\pi = 1/3 = (1 + r_f - d)/(u - d)$ and $(1 - \pi) = 2/3$ for these values of u, d and r_f, the expected future value of the option using risk-neutral probabilities is

$$\left(\frac{1}{3}\right)^3 (£256 - £32) + 3\left(\frac{1}{3}\right)^2\left(\frac{2}{3}\right)(£64 - £32) + 3\left(\frac{1}{3}\right)\left(\frac{2}{3}\right)^2(£0) + \left(\frac{2}{3}\right)^3(£0) = £15.41$$

[13] The expression $n!$ means $n(n-1)(n-2) \cdots \times 3 \times 2 \times 1$, with the special case of 0! being equal to 1.

Exhibit 8.7 Binomial Tree Diagram for the Value of Smith Group Equity (Above Node) and the Smith Group Call Option (Below Node)

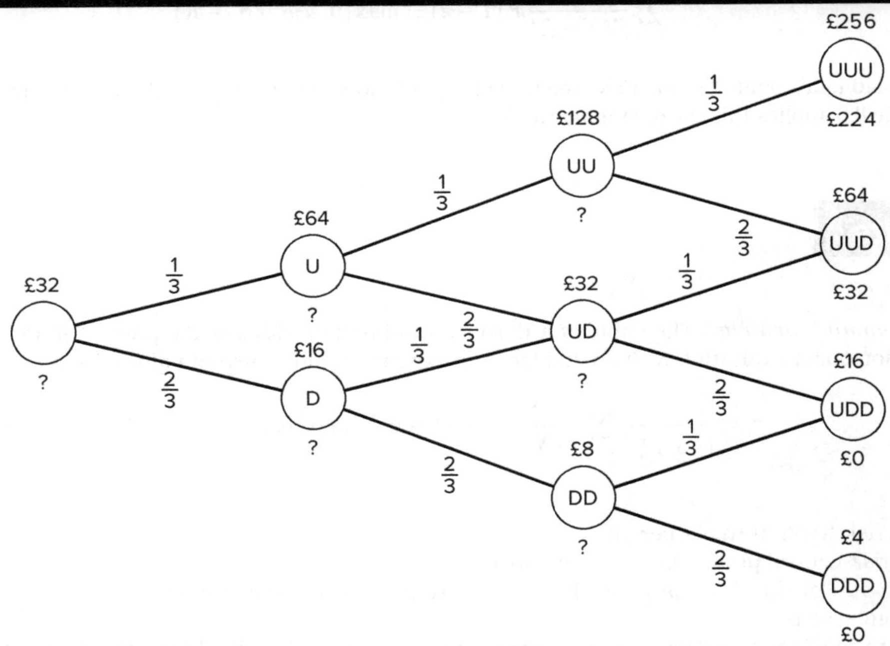

Since the discount rate is 0, £15.41 is also the value of the call option.

The previous section derived a formula for valuing European calls.[14] This section illustrates how to use the binomial model to value options that may be prematurely exercised. These include American puts and American calls on dividend-paying equities.

American Puts

The procedure for modelling American option values with the binomial approach is similar to that for European options. As with European options, work backwards from the right-hand side of the tree diagram. At each node in the tree diagram, look at the two future values of the option, and use risk-neutral discounting to determine the value of the option at that node. In contrast to European options, however, this value is only the value of the option at that node, provided that the investor holds on to it for one more period. If the investor exercises the option at the node, and the underlying asset is worth S at the node, then the value captured is $S - K$ for a call and $K - S$ for a put, rather than the discounted risk-neutral expectation of the values at the two future nodes, as was the case for the European option.

This suggests a way to value the option, assuming that it will be optimally exercised. Working back-wards, at each node, compare (1) the value from early exercise of the option with (2) the value of waiting one more period and achieving one of two values. The value to be placed at that decision node is the larger of the exercise value and the value of waiting. Example 8.6 illustrates this procedure for an American put.

Note that, even with the possibility of early exercise, it is still possible to track the put option in Example 8.6 with a combination of BBVA equity and a risk-free asset. However, the tracking portfolio here is different from that for a European put option with comparable features. In tracking the American put, the major difference is due to what happens at node D in Exhibit 8.8, when early exercise is optimal. To track the option value, do

[14] As suggested earlier, American calls on equities that pay no dividends until expiration can be valued as European calls with the method described in the last section.

not solve for a portfolio of the equity and the risk-free security that has a value of €3.00 if an up move occurs and €12.00 if a down move occurs, but solve for the portfolio that has a value of €3.00 if an up move occurs and €17.50 if a down move occurs. This still amounts to solving two equations with two unknowns. With the European option, the variation between the up and down state is –€9.00. With the American option in Example 8.6, the variation is –€14.50. Since the variation in the share price between nodes U and D is €30 (= €40 – €10), –0.3 (= –€9/€30) of a share perfectly tracks a European option, and –0.483333 (= –€14.50/€30) of a share perfectly tracks an American option. The associated risk-free investments solve

$$-0.3(€40) + 1.25x = €3 \text{ or } x = €12 \text{ for the European put}$$

$$-0.483333(€40) + 1.25x = €3 \text{ or } x = €17.867 \text{ for the American put}$$

Exhibit 8.8 Binomial Tree Diagram for the Price of BBVA Equity (Above Node) and an American Put Option (Below Node) with K = €27.50 and T = 2

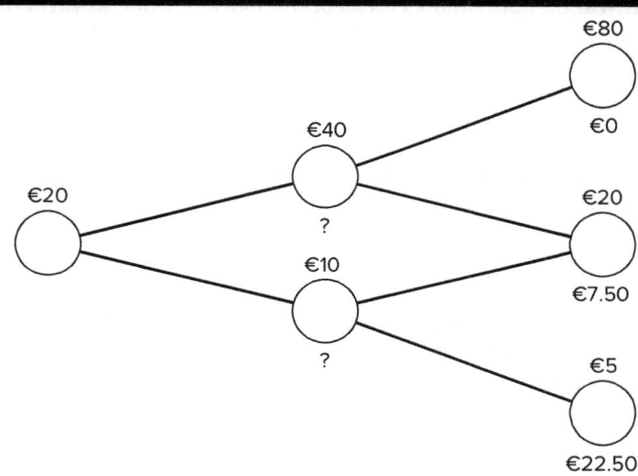

Example 8.6

Valuing an American Put

Assume that, in each period, the non-dividend-paying equity of BBVA, a major Spanish bank, can either double or halve in value: that is, $u = 2$, $d = 0.5$. If the initial share price is €20 per share and the risk-free rate is 25 per cent per period (this is incredibly high, but we need it to make our example work!), what is the value of an American put expiring two periods from now with a strike price of €27.50?

Answer: Exhibit 8.8 outlines the path of BBVA's equity and the option. At each node in the diagram, the risk-neutral probabilities solve

$$\frac{2\pi + 0.5(1 - \pi)}{1.25} = 1$$

Thus $\pi = 0.5$ throughout the problem.

In the final period, at the far right-hand side of the diagram, the equity is worth €80, €20 or €5. From node U, where the share price is €40, the price can move to €80 (node UU) with an associated put value of €0, or it can move to €20 (node UD), which gives a put value of €7.50. There is no value from early exercise at node U, because the €40 share price exceeds the €27.50 strike price. This means that the put option at node U is worth the discounted expected value of the €0 and €7.50 outcomes, or

$$\frac{0\pi + €7.50(1-\pi)}{1.25} = €3.00$$

From node D, where the share price is €10 a share, early exercise leads to a put value of €17.50. Compare this with the value from not exercising and waiting one more period, which leads to share prices of €20 (node UD) and €5 (node DD), and respective put values of €7.50 and €22.50. The value of these two outcomes is

$$\frac{€7.50\pi + €22.50(1-\pi)}{1.25} = €12.00$$

This is less than the value from early exercise. Therefore the optimal exercise policy is to exercise when the share price hits €10 at node D.

From the leftmost node, there are two possible subsequent values for the equity. If the share price rises to €40 a share (node U), the put, worth €3, should not be exercised early. If the share price declines to €10 a share (node D), the put is worth €17.50, achieved by early exercise. If the market sets a price for the American put, believing it will be optimally exercised, the market value at this point would be €17.50. To value the put at the leftmost node, weight the €3.00 and €17.50 outcomes by the risk-neutral probabilities and discount at the risk-free rate. This value is

$$\frac{€3.00\pi + €17.50(1-\pi)}{1.25} = €8.20$$

Early exercise leads to a €7.50 put at this node, which is inferior. Thus the value of the put is €8.20, and it pays to wait another period before possibly exercising.

This also implies that the European put is worth −0.3(€20) + €12 = €6, which is €2.20 less than the American put. One can also compute this €2.20 difference by multiplying $1 - \pi$ (which is 0.5) by the €5.50 difference between the non-exercise value and the actual value of the American put at node D, and discounting back one period at a 25 per cent rate.

Valuing American Options on Dividend-Paying Equities

An equity that pays dividends has two values at the node representing the ex-dividend date: (1) the **cum-dividend value** of the equity, which is the value of the equity prior to the ex-dividend date; and (2) the **ex-dividend value,** the share price after the ex-dividend date, which is lower by the amount of the dividend, assuming no taxes. At the ex-dividend date, arbitrage forces dictate that the share price should drop by the amount of the present value of the declared dividend (which is negligibly less than the amount of the dividend, since a cheque is generally mailed a few weeks after the ex-dividend date. Our analysis ignores this small amount of discounting).[15]

It never pays to exercise an American put just before the ex-dividend date. For example, if the dividend is £5 per share, a put that is about to be exercised is worth £5 more just after the ex-dividend date than it was prior to it. By contrast, it makes sense to exercise an American call just before the ex-dividend date, if one chooses to exercise prematurely at all. If the call is in the money both before and after the ex-date of a £5 dividend, the exercise value of the call is £5 higher before the ex-dividend date than after it.

The assumption that dividends are riskless creates a problem if an investor is not careful. For example, it may be impossible to have a risk-free dividend if the ex-date is many periods in the future and large numbers of down moves occur. In taking this 'bad path' along the binomial tree, an investor might find that a riskless dividend results in a *negative* ex-dividend value for the equity – which is impossible. There are two ways to

[15] If investors know that the share price will drop by less than the dividend amount, buying the equity just before it goes ex-dividend and selling just after it goes ex-dividend means a loss equal to the drop in the share price, which is more than offset by the dividend received. If the share price drops by more than the dividend, selling short the equity just before it goes ex-dividend and buying it back just after is also an arbitrage opportunity. With taxes, share prices may fall by less than the amount of the dividend. For more detail, see Chapter 15.

model the dividend process that avoid such problems. One approach, which works but is difficult to implement, assumes that the size of the dividend depends on the path that the share price takes. After all, if an equity declines substantially in value, the company may reduce or suspend the dividend. This requires the ability to model the dividend accurately along all paths a share price might take. Such a dividend would be a risky cash flow, because the path the share price will follow is unknown in advance.

Example 8.7

Valuing an American Call Option on a Dividend-Paying Equity

Assume that BBVA pays a dividend, and that the values above each node in Exhibit 8.8 represent the price process for BBVA equity stripped of its rights to a risk-free dividend of €6.25 paid at nodes U and D (which is assumed to be the only dividend prior to expiration). (1) Describe the tree diagram for the actual share price, assuming a risk-free rate of 25 per cent, and (2) value an American call option expiring in the final period with a strike price of €20.

Answer: (1) At the expiration date, on the far right of Exhibit 8.8, the actual share price and the ex-dividend share price are the same: the dividend has already been paid! At the intermediate period, each of the two nodes has two values for the equity. Ex-dividend, the share prices are €40 and €10 at nodes U and D, respectively, and the corresponding cum-dividend values are €46.25 and €16.25, derived by adding the €6.25 dividend to the two ex-dividend share prices. Since the present value of the €6.25 dividend is €5.00 one period earlier, the actual share price at the initial date is

$$€20 + \frac{€6.25}{€1.25} = €25$$

(2) The value of the option at the intermediate period requires a comparison of its exercise value with its value from waiting until expiration. Exercising just before the ex-dividend date generates €46.25 – €20.00 = €26.25 at the U node. The value from not exercising is the node U value of the two subsequent option expiration values, €60 (= €80 – €20) at node UU and €0 at node UD. Example 8.6 found that the two risk-neutral probabilities are each 0.5. Hence this value is

$$\frac{€60\pi + €0(1-\pi)}{1.25} = €24$$

Since €24.00 is less than the value of €26.25 obtained by exercising at node U, early exercise just prior to the ex-dividend instant is optimal. At the D node, the option is worth 0 since it is out of the money (cum-dividend) at node D and is not in the money for either of the two stock values at the nodes UD and DD at expiration. The initial value of the option is therefore

$$\frac{€26.25\pi + €0(1-\pi)}{1.25} = €10.50$$

A second approach is to ignore the dividend and model the path taken by the value of the equity stripped of its dividend rights between the initial date of valuation and the expiration date of the option. For the binomial process, start out with a price $S_0^* = S_0$ – PV (dividends to expiration). Then select a constant u and d to trace out the binomial tree at all dates t for S_t^*. To obtain the tree diagram for the actual value of the equity, S_t, add back the present value of the risk less dividend(s). With this method (see Example 8.7), an investor never has to worry about the value of the underlying equity being less than the dividend.

As in the case of put valuation (see Example 8.6), the American call option in Example 8.7 is worth more than a comparable European call option. If the option in this example had been a European option, it would have been worth €9.60 = [(0.5) €24 + (0.5) €0]/1.25. This is smaller than the American option value, because the right of premature exercise is used at node U and therefore has value.

Any suboptimal exercise policy lowers the value of the premature exercise option and transfers wealth from the buyer of the American option to the seller. This issue often arises in corporations, which are well known to exercise the American option implicit in callable bonds that they issue at a much later date than is optimal. Such suboptimal exercise transfers wealth from the corporation's equity holders to the holders of the callable bonds.

8.6 Black–Scholes Valuation

Up to this point, we have valued derivatives using **discrete models** of share prices, which consider only a finite number of future outcomes for the share price, and only a finite number of points in time. We now turn our attention to **continuous-time models.** These models allow for an infinite number of share price outcomes, and they can describe the distribution of equity and option prices at any point in time.

Black–Scholes Formula

Chapter 7 noted that if time is divided into large numbers of short periods, a binomial process for share prices can approximate the continuous-time lognormal process for these prices. Here, particular values are selected for u and d that are related to the standard deviation of the stock return, which also is known as the equity's **volatility.** The limiting case where the time periods are infinitesimally small is one where the binomial formula developed in the last section converges to an equation known as the **Black–Scholes formula.**

The Black–Scholes formula provides no-arbitrage prices for European call options and American call options on underlying securities with no cash dividends until expiration (because such options should have the same values as European call options with the same features). The Black–Scholes formula is also easily extended to price European puts (see exercise 8.2). Finally, the formula reasonably approximates the values of more complex options. For example, to price a call option on an equity that pays dividends, one can calculate the Black–Scholes values of options expiring at each of the ex-dividend dates and those expiring at the true expiration date. The largest of these option values is a quick and often accurate approximation of the value obtained from more sophisticated option pricing models. This largest value is known as the **pseudo-American value** of the call option.

Results

Result 8.8

(*The Black–Scholes formula.*) If an equity that pays no dividends before the expiration of an option has a return that is lognormally distributed, can be continuously traded in frictionless markets and has a constant variance, then, for a constant risk-free rate,[16] the value of a European call option on that equity with a strike price of K and T years to expiration is given by

$$c_0 = S_0 N(d_1) - \text{PV}(K)N(d_1 - \sigma\sqrt{T}) \tag{8.3}$$

where

$$d_1 = \frac{\ln[S_0/\text{PV}(K)]}{\sigma\sqrt{T}} + \frac{\sigma\sqrt{T}}{2}$$

The Greek letter σ is the annualized standard deviation of the natural logarithm of the stock return, ln( ) represents the natural logarithm, and $N(z)$ is the probability that a normally distributed variable with a mean of zero and variance of 1 is less than z.

Example 8.8 illustrates how to use a normal distribution table to compute Black–Scholes values.

The difference between the strike price and the underlying price is £0.04. Therefore the estimate of £0.21 for the value of the call option reflects the time value of the BP option and the probability that the price in the future will be above £6.20.

[16] The formula also holds if the variance and risk-free rate can change in a predictable way. In the former case, use the average volatility (the square root of the variance) over the life of the option. In the latter case, use the yield associated with the zero-coupon bond maturing at the expiration date of the option. If the risk-free rate or the volatility changes in an unpredictable way, and is not perfectly correlated with the share price, no risk-free hedge between the equity and the option exists. Additional securities (such as long- and short-term bonds or other options on the same equity) may be needed to generate this hedge, and the Black–Scholes formula would have to be modified accordingly. However, for most short-term options, the modification to the option's value due to unpredictable changes in interest rates is a negligible one.

Example 8.8

Computing Black–Scholes Warrant Values for BP

Use the normal distribution table (Table A.5 in Appendix A) at the end of the book (or a spreadsheet function such as NORM.S.DIST in Microsoft Excel 2010) to calculate the fair market value of a three-month BP in-the-money option that is listed on Eurex. For the purposes of calculation, we shall need to provide hypothetical estimates for some of the variables in this example. Assume that: (1) the price of BP shares is £6.16 today; (2) BP's historical annualized share price return volatility, σ, is 16 per cent per year (which is 0.16 in decimal form); (3) the risk-free rate is 4.78 per cent per year (annually compounded); (4) the options are American options, but no dividends are expected to be paid over the life of the option (it is thus possible to value the options as European options); (5) the options expire in exactly three months; and (6) the strike price is £6.20.

Answer: The present value of the strike price is £6.20/1.0478$^{0.25}$ = £6.1280. The volatility times the square root of time to maturity is the product of 0.16 and the square root of 0.25, or 0.08. The Black–Scholes equation gives that the value of the call is therefore

$$c_0 = £6.16N(d_1) - £6.1280N(d_1 - 0.08)$$

where

$$d_1 = \frac{\ln(£6.16/£6.1280)}{0.08} + \frac{1}{2}(0.08) = 0.1050$$

The normal distribution values for d_1 (= 0.1050) and d_1 − 0.08 (= 0.0250) in Table A.5 in Appendix A indicate that the probability of a standard normal variable being less than 0.1050 is 0.5418, and the probability of it being less than 0.0250 is 0.5100. Thus the no-arbitrage call value is

$$£6.16(0.5418) - £6.1280(0.5100) = £0.21$$

Dividends and the Black–Scholes Model

It is especially important with continuous-time modelling to model the path of the share price when stripped of its dividend rights, if dividends are paid before the expiration date of the option. For example, the Black–Scholes model assumes that the logarithm of the return on the underlying equity is normally distributed. This means that, in any finite amount of time, the share price may be close to zero, albeit with low probability. Subtracting a finite dividend from this low value would result in a negative ex-dividend share price. Hence, unless one is willing to describe the dividend for each of an infinite number of share price outcomes in this type of continuous price model, it is important to model the process for the equity stripped of its right to the dividend. This was illustrated with the binomial model earlier, but it is more imperative here.[17]

8.7 Estimating Volatility

The only parameter that requires estimation in the Black–Scholes model is the volatility, σ. This volatility estimate also may be of use in estimating u and d in a binomial model (see Chapter 7).

There are a number of ways to estimate *s*, assuming it is constant. One method is to use historical data, as shown in Exhibit 8.9. We now analyse this issue.

[17] A numerical example illustrating the Black–Scholes valuation of a European option on a dividend-paying equity appears later in this chapter. In terms of the above formula, one merely substitutes the value of the equity stripped of the present value of the dividends to expiration for S_0 in equation (8.3) to arrive at a correct answer. This is simply the current share price less the risk-free discounted value of the dividend payment.

Exhibit 8.9 Computation of the Volatility Estimate for the Black–Scholes Model Using Historical Return Data on Adidas AG.

Date	Price	Return	Gross Return	ln(Gross Return)
Apr 2021	153.15			
May 2021	181.43	18.47%	1.18	0.1695
Jun 2021	186.77	2.94%	1.03	0.0290
Jul 2021	182.05	−2.53%	0.97	−0.0256
Aug 2021	177.50	−2.50%	0.98	−0.0253
Sep 2021	158.11	−10.92%	0.89	−0.1157
Oct 2021	163.71	3.54%	1.04	0.0348
Nov 2021	144.60	−11.67%	0.88	−0.1241
Dec 2021	144.00	−0.41%	1.00	−0.0042
Jan 2022	136.52	−5.19%	0.95	−0.0533
Feb 2022	117.83	−13.69%	0.86	−0.1472
Mar 2022	117.80	−0.03%	1.00	−0.0003
Apr 2022	119.66	1.58%	1.02	0.0157

Using Historical Data

The appropriate volatility computation for the *s* in the Black–Scholes model is based on the volatility of instantaneous returns.

1. Obtain historical returns for the equity the option is written on.
2. Convert the returns to gross returns (100 per cent plus the rate of return in percentage form, 1 plus the return in decimal form).
3. Take the natural logarithm of the decimal version of the gross return: thus, before taking the log, divide by 100 if the gross return is in percentage form.
4. Compute the unbiased sample standard deviation of the logged return series and annualize it by multiplying it by the square root of the ratio of 365 to the number of days in the return interval (for example, for monthly returns multiply by the square root of 12, and for quarterly returns multiply by the square root of 4).

Using Spreadsheets to Compute the Volatility

Spreadsheet standard deviation functions typically provide the unbiased estimate of the standard deviation.[18] Remember to annualize the standard deviation obtained from the spreadsheet, because the spreadsheet does not know whether the returns were taken weekly, monthly, daily, and so on. In Exhibit 8.9, which reports monthly returns, this adjustment amounts to multiplying the output from the spreadsheet by 3.4641, which is the square root of 12.

In the Adidas example in Exhibit 8.9, the standard deviation is calculated as 0.0856 or 8.56 per cent per month. The annualized standard deviation is 0.2964, or 29.64 per cent.

Frequency Choice

Exhibit 8.9 uses monthly data to estimate the volatility of Adidas. Statistical theory suggests that one should use returns that are sampled more frequently to obtain more precise volatility estimates; our preference is weekly data. The use of daily data may be inferior, because the bid–ask spread tends to make volatility estimates overstate the true volatility of returns.

[18] For example, STDEV in Excel.

Improving the Volatility Estimate

Procedures similar to those designed to improve beta estimation for the Capital Asset Pricing Model can improve the volatility estimate. Consider the spectrum of historical estimates of σ for a large number of securities. Those securities with the highest (lowest) estimated volatilities from historical data are more likely to have overestimates (underestimates) of the true volatility because of sampling error. This information can be used to improve volatility estimates. In particular, an improved volatility estimate can be derived by taking a weighting of the average estimated volatility over a large group of securities and the historical volatility estimate for a single security.

The Implied Volatility Approach

An alternative approach for estimating volatility in a security is to look at other options on the same security. If market values for the options exist, there is a unique **implied volatility** that makes the Black–Scholes model consistent with the market price for a particular option.

Exhibit 8.10 illustrates this concept. The *s* at point A, the intersection of the horizontal line (representing the £5 market price of the call option) and the upward-sloping line (representing the Black–Scholes value), is the implied volatility. In this graph, it is about 19 per cent.

Averaging the implied volatilities of other options on the same security is a common approach to obtaining the volatility necessary for obtaining the Black–Scholes valuation of an option. Since the implied volatilities of the other options are obtained from the Black–Scholes model, this method implicitly assumes that the other options are priced correctly by that model.

Implied volatility is a concept that is commonly used in options markets, particularly the over-the-counter markets. For example, price quotes are often given to sophisticated customers in terms of implied volatilities, because these volatilities change much less frequently than the equity and option prices. A customer or a trader can consider an implied volatility quote and know that tomorrow the same quote is likely to be valid, even though the price of the option will be different because the price of the underlying asset has changed. Implied volatility quotes help the investor who is comparison-shopping among dealers for the best option price.

Exhibit 8.10 The Value of a Call Option as a Function of Its Volatility

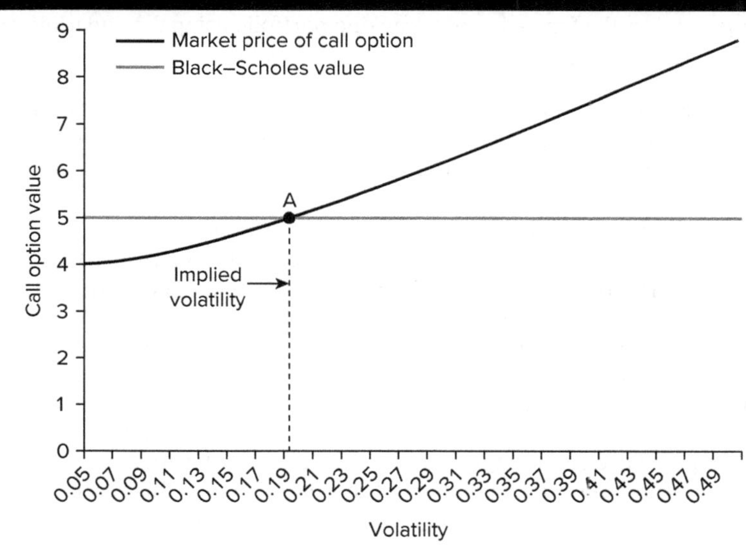

If options of the same maturity but different strike prices have different implied volatilities, arbitrage is possible. This arbitrage requires purchase of the low implied volatility option and writing of the high implied volatility option. The next section explores the arbitrage of mispriced options in more depth.

8.8 Black–Scholes Price Sensitivity to Share Price, Volatility, Interest Rates and Expiration Time

This section develops some intuition for the Black–Scholes model by examining whether the call option value in the formula, equation (8.3), increases or decreases as various parameters in the formula change. These parameters are the current share price S_0, the share price return volatility σ, the risk-free interest rate r_f, and the time to maturity T.

Delta: The Sensitivity to Share Price Changes

The Greek letter delta (Δ) is commonly used in mathematics to represent a change in something. In finance, **delta** is the change in the value of the derivative security with respect to movements in the share price, holding everything else constant. The delta of the option is the derivative of the option's price with respect to the share price: $\partial c_0/\partial S_0$ for a call, $\partial p_0/\partial S_0$ for a put. The derivative of the right-hand side of the Black–Scholes formula, equation (8.3), with respect to S_0, the delta of the call option, is $N(d_1)$ (see exercise 8.4).

Delta as the Number of Shares of Equity in a Tracking Portfolio

Delta has many uses. One is in the formation of a tracking portfolio. Delta can be viewed as the number of shares of equity needed in the tracking portfolio. Let x be the number of shares in the tracking portfolio. For a given change in s_0, ds_0, the change in the tracking portfolio is xds_0. Hence, unless x equals $\partial c_0/\partial s_0$ for a call or $\partial p_0/\partial s_0$ for a put, xds_0 will not be the same as the change in the call or put value, and the tracking of the option pay-off with a portfolio of the underlying equity and a risk-free bond will not be perfect.

Because $N(d_1)$ is a probability, the number of shares needed to track the option lies between zero and one. In addition, as time elapses and the share price changes, d_1 changes, implying that the number of shares in the tracking portfolio needs to change continuously. Thus the tracking of the option using the Black–Scholes model, like that for the binomial model, requires dynamically changing the quantities of the equity and risk-free bond in the tracking portfolio. However, these changes require no additional financing.

Delta and Arbitrage Strategies

If the market prices of options differ from their theoretical prices, it is possible to design an arbitrage. Once set up, the arbitrage is self-financing until the arbitrage position is closed out.

As always, arbitrage requires the formation of a tracking portfolio using the underlying asset and a risk-free security. One goes long in the tracking portfolio and short in the option, or vice versa, to achieve arbitrage (see exercise 8.3).

In the design of the arbitrage, the ratio of the underlying asset position to the option position must be the negative of the partial derivative of the *theoretical* option price with respect to the price of the underlying security. For a call option that is priced by the Black–Scholes formula, this partial derivative is $N(d_1)$, the option's delta.

Delta and the Interpretation of the Black–Scholes Formula

Viewing $N(d_1)$ as the number of shares of equity in the tracking portfolio lends a nice interpretation to the Black–Scholes call option formula. The first part of the Black–Scholes formula in equation (8.3), $S_0N(d_1)$, is the cost of the shares needed in the tracking portfolio. The second term, $\text{PV}(K)N(d_1 - \sigma\sqrt{T})$, represents the amount of cash borrowed at the risk-free rate. The difference between the two terms is the cost of the tracking portfolio. Hence the Black–Scholes formula is simply an arbitrage relationship. The left-hand side of the equation, c_0, is the value of the option. The right-hand side represents the market price of the tracking portfolio.

An examination of the tracking portfolio reveals that call options on equity are equivalent to leveraged positions in equity. When you focus on the capital market line, the more leverage you have, the greater the beta, standard deviation and expected return, as pointed out in Chapter 5. For this reason, call options per unit of cash invested are always riskier than the underlying equity per unit of cash invested.

Black–Scholes Option Values and Equity Volatility

One can use the Black–Scholes formula, equation (8.3), to show that an option's value is increasing in σs, the volatility of the underlying equity. (Refer again to the Black–Scholes call value in Exhibit 8.10, which has a positive slope, and see exercise 8.5.)

Results

Result 8.9

As the volatility of the share price increases, the values of both put and call options written on the equity increase.

Result 8.9 is a general property of options, holding true for calls and puts and both American and European options. It has a number of implications for the financial behaviour of both corporate finance executives and portfolio managers, and is a source of equity holder–debt holder conflicts.[19]

The intuition for this result is that increased volatility spreads the distribution of the future share price, fattening up both tails of the distribution, as shown in Exhibit 8.11. Good things are happening for a call (put) option when the right (left) tail of the distribution is more likely to occur. It is not good when the left (right) tail of the distribution is more likely to occur, but exercise of the option does *not* take place in this region of outcomes, so it is not so bad either. After a certain point, a fatter tail on the left (right) of the distribution can hurt the investor much less than a fat tail on the right (left) of the distribution can help. The worst that can happen is that an option expires worthless.

Exhibit 8.11 Effect of Increasing Volatility

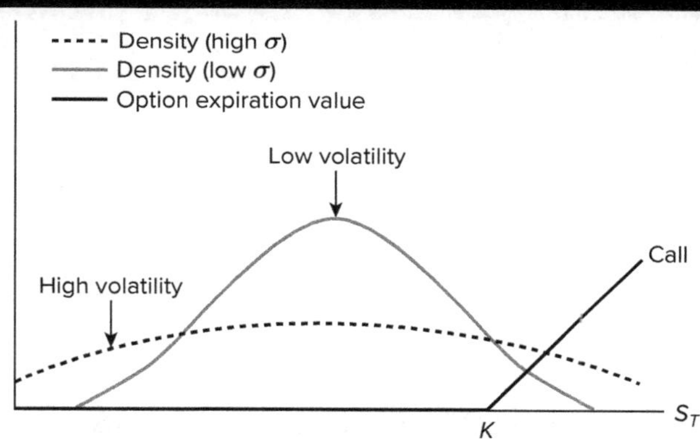

Option Values and Time to Option Expiration

European calls on equities that pay no dividends are more valuable the longer the time to expiration, other things being equal, for two reasons. First, the terminal share price is more uncertain, the longer the time to expiration. Uncertainty, described in our discussion of *s*, makes options more valuable. Moreover, given the same strike price, the longer the time to maturity, the lower is the present value of the strike price paid by the holder of a call option.

In contrast, the discounting of the strike price makes European puts less valuable. Thus the combination of the effects of uncertainty and discounting leaves an ambiguous result. European puts can increase or decrease in value, the longer the time to expiration. American puts and calls, incidentally, have an unambiguous sensitivity to expiration time. These options have all the rights of their shorter-maturity cousins in addition to the rights of exercise for an even longer period. Hence the longer the time to expiration, the more valuable are American call and put options, even for dividend-paying equities.

Option Values and the Risk-Free Interest Rate

The Black–Scholes call option value is increasing in the interest rate r (see exercise 8.6) because the payment of K for the share of equity whose call option is in the money costs less in today's money (that is, it has a lower

[19] These conflicts are discussed in Chapter 16.

discounted value) when the interest rate is higher. The opposite is true for a European put. Since one receives cash, puts are less valuable when the interest rate is higher. As noted earlier in this chapter, the timing of equity delivery is irrelevant as long as there are no dividends. Only the present value of the cash payment upon option exercise and whether this cash is paid out (call) or received (put) determine the effect of interest rates on the option value. Once again, this is a general result that holds for European and American options, and works the same in the binomial model and the Black–Scholes model.

A Summary of the Effects of the Parameter Changes

Exhibit 8.12 summarizes the results in this section, and includes the impact on the value of a long forward contract (equivalent to a call less a put). These exercises hold constant all the other factors determining option value, except the one in the relevant row.

An increase in strike price K or an increase in the dividend paid, although not listed in the exhibit, will have the opposite effect of an increase in the share price. It also is interesting to observe what has not been included in Exhibit 8.12 because it has no effect. In particular, risk aversion and the expected growth rate of the share price have no effect on option values, which are determined solely by the no-arbitrage relation between the option and its tracking portfolio (as Chapter 7 emphasized). When tracking is impossible (for example, executive share options), option values are not tied to tracking portfolios. In such cases, considerations such as risk aversion or share price growth rates may play a role in option valuation.

Exhibit 8.12 Determinants of Current Option and Forward Prices: Effect of a Parameter Increase

Parameter increased	Long forward	American call	American put	European call	European put
S_0	↑	↑	↓	↑	↓
T	↑	↑	↑	↑	Ambiguous
σ	No effect	↑	↑	↑	↑
r_f	↑	↑	↓	↑	↓

8.9 Valuing Options on More Complex Assets

Options exist on many assets. For example, corporations use currency options to hedge their foreign currency exposure. They also use swap options, which are valued in exactly the same manner as bond options, to hedge interest rate risk associated with a callable bond issued in conjunction with interest rate swaps. Option markets exist for semiconductors, agricultural commodities, precious metals and oil. There are even options on futures contracts for a host of assets underlying the futures contracts.

These options trade on many organized exchanges and over the counter. For example, currency options are traded on Eurex, but large currency option transactions tend to be over the counter, with a bank as one of the parties. Clearly, an understanding of how to value some of these options is important for many finance practitioners.

The Forward Price Version of the Black–Scholes Model

To value options on more complex assets such as currencies, it is important to recognize that the Black–Scholes model is a special case of a more general model having arguments that depend on (zero-cost) forward prices instead of spot prices. Once you know how to compute the forward price of an underlying asset, it is possible to determine the Black–Scholes value for a European call on the underlying asset.

To transform the Black–Scholes formula into a more general formula that uses forward prices, substitute the no-arbitrage relationship from Chapter 7, $S_0 = F_0/(1 + r_f)^T$, where F_0 is the forward price of an underlying asset in a forward contract maturing at the option expiration date, into the original Black–Scholes formula, equation (8.3). The Black–Scholes equation can then be rewritten as

$$c_0 = \text{PV}[F_0 N(d_1) - KN(d_1 - \sigma\sqrt{T})$$

where

$$d_1 = \frac{\ln[F_0/K]}{\sigma\sqrt{T}} + \frac{\sigma\sqrt{T}}{2}$$

and where PV is the risk-free discounted value of the expression inside the brackets. This equation looks a bit simpler than the original Black–Scholes formula.

Investors and financial analysts can apply this simpler, more general version of the Black–Scholes formula to value European call options on currencies, bonds,[20] dividend-paying equities and commodities.

Computing Forward Prices from Spot Prices

In applying the forward price version of the Black–Scholes formula, it is critical to use the appropriate forward price for the underlying asset. The appropriate forward price F_0 represents the price one agrees to today, but pays at the option expiration date, to acquire one unit of the underlying asset at that expiration date.

The following are a few rules of thumb for calculating forward prices for various underlying assets.

- *Foreign currency.* Multiply the present spot foreign currency rate, expressed as *home currency/foreign currency* (for example, R/$ for a South African firm and £/€ for a British firm) by the *present value* of a riskless unit of foreign currency paid at the forward maturity date (where the discounting is at the foreign riskless interest rate). Multiply this value by the *future value* (at the maturity date) of one unit of currency paid today: that is, multiply by $(1 + r_f)^T$, where T represents the years to maturity and r_f is the domestic riskless interest rate. Chapter 7 describes forward currency rate computations in detail when currencies are expressed as *foreign currency/home currency.*
- *Riskless coupon bond.* Find the present value of the bond when stripped of its coupon rights until maturity: that is, current bond price less PV(coupons). Multiply this value by the future value (at the maturity date) of one unit of currency paid today. (Depending on how the bond price is quoted, an adjustment to add accrued interest to the quoted price of the bond to obtain the full price may also need to be made, as described in Chapter 2.)
- *Stock with dividend payments.* Find the present value of the equity when stripped of its dividend rights until maturity: that is, current share price less PV(dividends). Multiply this value by the future value (at the maturity date) of one unit of currency paid today.
- *Commodity.* Add the present value of the storage costs until maturity to the current price of the commodity. Subtract the present value of the benefits, known as the *convenience yield,* associated with holding an inventory of the commodity to maturity.[21] Multiply this value by the future value, at the maturity date, of one unit of currency paid today.

Note that all forward prices multiply some adjusted market value of the underlying investment by $(1 + r_f)^T$, where r_f is the riskless rate of interest. Multiplying by 1 plus the risk-free rate of interest accounts for the cost of holding the investment until maturity. The cost is the lost interest on the money spent to acquire the investment. For example, with an equity that pays no dividends, the present value of having the equity in one's possession today as opposed to some future date is the same. However, the longer the investor can postpone paying a pre-specified amount for the equity, the better off he or she is. The difference between the forward price and the share price thus reflects interest to the party with the short position in the forward contract, who is essentially holding the equity for the benefit of the party holding the long position in the forward contract.

The difference between the forward price and the share price also depends on the benefits and any costs of having the investment in one's possession until forward maturity. With equity, the benefit is the payment of dividends; with bonds, the payment of coupons; with foreign currency, the interest earned in a foreign bank when that currency is deposited; with commodities, the convenience of having an inventory of the commodity less the cost of storage.

Applications of the Forward Price Version of the Black–Scholes Formula

Example 8.9 demonstrates the use of the generalized Black–Scholes formula to value European call options having these more complex underlying assets.

[20] The Black–Scholes formula assumes that the volatility of the bond price is constant over the life of the option. Since bond volatilities diminish at the approach of the bond's maturity, the formula provides only a decent approximation to the fair market value of an option that is relatively short-lived compared with the maturity of the bond.

[21] See Chapter 22 for a more detailed discussion of convenience yields.

American Options

The forward price version of the Black–Scholes model also has implications for American options. For example, the reason why American call options on equities that pay no dividends sell for the same price as comparable European call options is that the risk-free discounted value of the forward price at expiration is never less than the current share price, no matter how much time has elapsed since the purchase of the option. If a discrete dividend is about to be paid and the equity is relatively close to expiration, the current cum-dividend price of the equity exceeds the discounted value of the forward price, and premature exercise may be worthwhile. If one can be certain that this will not be the case, waiting is worthwhile. One can generalize this result as follows.

Example 8.9

Pricing Securities with the Forward Price Version of the Black–Scholes Model

The UK sterling risk-free rate is assumed to be 6 per cent per year, and all σs are assumed to be 25 per cent per year. Use the forward price version of the Black–Scholes model to compute the value of a European call option to purchase one year from now.

a €1 at a strike price of £0.75. The current spot exchange rate is £0.70/€ and the one-year risk-free rate is 4 per cent in France.

b A 30-year bond with an 8 per cent semi-annual coupon at a strike price of £100 (full price). The bond is currently selling at a full price of £102 (which includes accrued interest) per £100 of face value, and has two scheduled coupons of £4 before option expiration, to be paid six months and one year from now. (At the forward maturity date, the second coupon payment has just been made.)

c A FTSE 100 contract with a strike price of £6,800. The FTSE 100 has a current price of £6,609 and a present value of next year's dividends of £165.

d A barrel of oil with a strike price of £46.57 ($95 a barrel at an exchange rate of $2.04/£). A barrel of oil currently sells for £43.62 ($89 a barrel). The present value of next year's storage costs is £1, and the present value of the convenience of having a barrel of oil available over the next year (for example, if there are long gas lines owing to an oil embargo and extremely bad weather in the Gulf region) is £1.

Answer: The forward prices are, respectively:

a $\frac{£0.70(1.06)}{1.04} = £0.7134$

b $£102(1.06) - £4\sqrt{1.06} - £4 = £100.0017$

c $(£6{,}609 - £165)(1.06) = £6{,}830.64$

d $(£43.62 + £1 - £1)(1.06) = £46.24$

Plugging these values into the forward price version of the Black–Scholes model yields

a $$c_0 = \frac{£0.7134N(d_1) - 0.75N(d_1 - 0.25)}{1.06}$$

where

$$d_1 = \frac{\ln(0.7134/0.75)}{0.25} + 0.125 = -0.751$$

Thus c_0 is approximately £0.0528.

b $$c_0 = \frac{£100.0017N(d_1) - £100N(d_1 - 0.25)}{1.06}$$

where

$$\mathrm{d}_1 = \frac{\ln(100.0017/100)}{0.25} + 0.125 = 0.13$$

Thus c_0 is approximately £9.39.

c $$c_0 = \frac{£6,830.64N(d_1) - £6,800N(d_1 - 0.25)}{1.06}$$

where

$$d_1 = \frac{\ln(6,830.64/6,800)}{0.25} + 0.125 = 0.1430$$

Thus c_0 is approximately £654.14.

d $$c_0 = \frac{£46,24N(d_1) - £46,57N(d_1 - 0.25)}{1.06}$$

where

$$d_1 = \frac{\ln(46,24/46,57)}{0.25} + 0.125 = 0.966$$

Thus c_0 is approximately £4.20 (or $8.57 a barrel).

Results

Result 8.10

An American call (put) option should not be prematurely exercised if the value of the forward price of the underlying asset at expiration, discounted back to the present at the risk-free rate, either equals or exceeds (is less than) the current price of the underlying asset. As a consequence, if one is certain that over the life of the option this will be the case, American and European options should sell for the same price if there is no arbitrage.

There are several implications of Result 8.10. With call options on the FTSE 100 where dividends of different equities pay off on different days so that the overall dividend stream resembles a continuous flow, American and European call options should sell for the same price if the risk-free rate to expiration exceeds the dividend yield. Also, with bonds where the risk-free rate to option expiration is greater (less) than the coupon yield of the risk-free bond, American and European call (put) options should sell for the same amount as their European counterparts if the option strike price is adjusted for accrued interest (as it usually is, unlike in Example 8.9) so that the coupon stream on the bond is like a continuous flow. This suggests that when the term structure of interest rates (see Chapter 10) is steeply upward (downward) sloping, puts (calls) of the European and American varieties are likely to have the same value.

American Call and Put Currency Options

Result 8.10 also has implications for American currency options on both calls and puts. These implications are given in Result 8.11.

Results

Result 8.11

If the domestic interest rate is greater (less) than the foreign interest rate, the American option to buy (sell) domestic currency in exchange for foreign currency should sell for the same price as the European option to do the same.

8.10 Empirical Biases in the Black–Scholes Formula

The Black–Scholes model is particularly impressive in the general thrust of its implications about option pricing. Option prices tend to be higher in environments with high interest rates and high volatility. Moreover, you find remarkable similarities when comparing the values of many options, even American options, with the results given by the Black–Scholes model.

However, after a close look at the prices in the newspaper, it is easy to see that the Black–Scholes formula tends to underestimate the market values of some kinds of option and overestimate others. MacBeth and Merville (1979) used daily closing prices to study actively traded options on six equities in 1976. Their technique examined the implied volatilities of various options on the same securities, and found these volatilities to be inversely related to the strike prices of the options. This meant that the Black–Scholes value, on average, was too high for deep out-of-the-money calls and too low for in-the-money calls. These biases grew larger, the further the option was from expiration.

A similar but more rigorous set of tests was conducted by Rubinstein (1985). Using transaction data, he first paired options with similar characteristics. For example, a pairing might consist of two call options on the same equity with two different strike prices, but the same expiration date, that traded within a small interval of time (for example, 15 minutes). With these pairings, 50 per cent of the members of the pair with low strike prices should have higher implied volatilities than their counterparts with high strike prices. Rubinstein also used pairings in which the only difference was the time to expiration. He then evaluated the pairings and found that shorter times to expiration led to higher implied volatility for out-of-the-money calls. This would suggest that the Black–Scholes formula tends to underestimate the values of call options close to expiration relative to call options with longer times to expiration.

Rubinstein also found a strike price bias that was dependent on the period examined. From August 1976 to October 1977, lower strike prices meant higher implied volatility. In this period, the Black–Scholes model underestimated the values of in-the-money call options and overestimated the values of out-of-the-money call options, which is consistent with the findings of MacBeth and Merville. However, for the period from October 1977 to August 1978, Rubinstein found the opposite result, except for out-of-the-money call options that were close to expiration.

Although these biases were highly statistically significant, Rubinstein concluded that they had little economic significance. In general, Rubinstein found that the biases in the Black–Scholes model were of the order of a 2 per cent deviation from Black–Scholes pricing. Hence a fairly typical €2 Black–Scholes price would coincide with a €2.04 market price. *This means that the Black–Scholes model, despite its biases, is still a fairly accurate estimator of the actual prices found in options markets.*

Since these studies were completed, many traders have referred to what is known as the **smile effect** (see Exhibit 8.13). If one plots the implied volatility of an option against its strike price, the graph of implied volatility looks like a 'smile'. This formation suggests that the Black–Scholes model underprices both deep in-the-money and deep out-of-the-money options relative to near at-the-money options.

Exhibit 8.13 Implied Volatility versus Strike Price

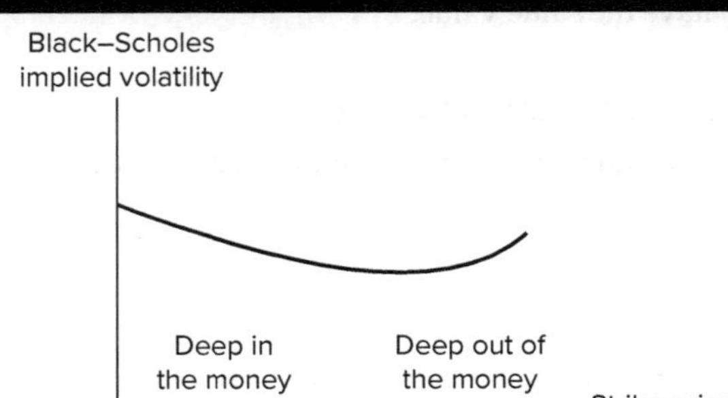

8.11 Summary and Conclusions

This chapter developed the put–call parity formula, relating the prices of European calls to those of European puts, and used it to generate insights into minimum call values, premature exercise policy for American calls and the relative valuation of American and European calls. The put–call parity formula also provided insights into corporate securities and portfolio insurance.

This chapter also applied the results on derivative securities valuation from Chapter 7 to price options, using two approaches: the binomial approach and the Black–Scholes approach. The results on European call pricing with these two approaches can be extended to European puts. The put–call parity formula provides a method for translating the pricing results with these models into pricing results for European puts.

The pricing of both American calls on dividend-paying equities and American puts cannot be derived from European call pricing formulae, because it is sometimes optimal to exercise these securities prematurely. This chapter used the binomial method to show how to price these more complicated types of option.

This chapter also discussed various issues relating to the implementation of the theory, including: (1) the estimation of volatility and its relationship with the concept of an implied volatility; (2) extending the pricing formulae to complex underlying securities; and (3) the known empirical biases in option pricing formulae. Despite a few biases in the Black–Scholes option pricing formula, it appears that the formulae work reasonably well when properly implemented.

Key Concepts

Result 8.1: (*The put–call parity formula.*) If no dividends are paid to holders of the underlying equity prior to expiration, then, assuming no arbitrage,

$$c_0 - p_0 = S_0 - \text{PV}(K)$$

That is, a long position in a call and a short position in a put sells for the current share price less the strike price discounted at the risk-free rate.

Result 8.2: It never pays to exercise an American call option prematurely on an equity that pays no dividends before expiration.

Result 8.3: An investor does not capture the full value of an American call option by exercising between ex-dividend or (in the case of a bond option) ex-coupon dates.

Result 8.4: If the underlying equity pays no dividends before expiration, then the no-arbitrage values of American and European call options with the same features are the same.

Result 8.5: (*Put–call parity formula generalized.*) $c_0 - p_0 = S_0 - \text{PV}(K) - \text{PV}(\text{div})$. The difference between the no-arbitrage values of a European call and a European put with the same features is the current share price less the sum of the present value of the strike price and the present value of all dividends to expiration.

Result 8.6: It is possible to view equity as a call option on the assets of the firm and to view risky corporate debt as riskless debt worth PV(K) plus a short position in a put option on the assets of the firm ($-p_0$) with a strike price of K.

Result 8.7: (*The binomial formula.*) The value of a European call option with a strike price of K and N periods to expiration on an equity with no dividends to expiration and a current value of S_0 is

$$c_0 = \frac{1}{(1+r_f)^N} \sum_{j=0}^{N} \frac{N!}{j!(N-j)!} \pi^j (1-\pi)^{N-j} \max(0, u^j d^{N-j} S_0 - K)$$

where

r_f = risk-free return per period

π = risk-neutral probability of an up move
u = ratio of the share price to the prior share price, given that the up state has occurred over a binomial step
d = ratio of the share price to the prior share price, given that the down state has occurred over a binomial step.

Result 8.8: (*The Black–Scholes formula.*) If an equity that pays no dividends before the expiration of an option has a return that is lognormally distributed, can be continuously traded in frictionless markets and has a constant variance, then, for a constant risk-free rate, the value of a European call option on that equity with a strike price of K and T years to expiration is given by

$$c_0 = S_0 N(d_1) - \text{PV}(K) N(d_1 - \sigma\sqrt{T})$$

where

$$d_1 = \frac{\ln[S_0/\text{PV}(K)]}{\sigma\sqrt{T}} + \frac{\sigma\sqrt{T}}{2}$$

The Greek letter σ is the annualized standard deviation of the natural logarithm of the stock return, ln( ) represents the natural logarithm, and $N(z)$ is the probability that a normally distributed variable with a mean of zero and variance of 1 is less than z.

Result 8.9: As the volatility of the share price increases, the values of both put and call options written on the equity increase.

Result 8.10: An American call (put) option should not be prematurely exercised if the value of the forward price of the underlying asset at expiration, discounted back to the present at the risk-free rate, either equals or exceeds (is less than) the current price of the underlying asset. As a consequence, if one is certain that over the life of the option this will be the case, American and European options should sell for the same price if there is no arbitrage.

Result 8.11: If the domestic interest rate is greater (less) than the foreign interest rate, the American option to buy (sell) domestic currency in exchange for foreign currency should sell for the same price as the European option to do the same.

Key Terms

Exercises

8.1 T-bills currently yield 2.1 per cent and the Man Group plc share price is £0.97. There is no possibility that the equity will be worth less than £0.50 per share in one year.

a What is the value of a call option with a £0.97 exercise price? What is the intrinsic value?

b What is the value of a call option with a £0.70 exercise price? What is the intrinsic value?

c What is the value of a put option with a £1.10 exercise price? What is the intrinsic value?

8.2 The share price of ABC plc will be either £2 or £1.5 at the end of the year. Call options are available with one year to expiration. UK government bond yields are currently at 3 per cent.

a Suppose the current share price of ABC plc is £1.74. What is the value of the call option if the exercise price is £1.75 per share?

b Suppose the exercise price is £1.9 in part *a*. What is the value of the call option now?

8.3 The price of National Bank of Greece shares will be either €1.74 or €1.43 at the end of the year. Call options are available with one year to expiration. T-bills currently yield 7 per cent.

a Suppose the current price of National Bank of Greece shares is €1.68. What is the value of the call option if the exercise price is €1.50 per share?

b Suppose the exercise price is €1.68 in part *a*. What is the value of the call option now?

8.4 Ken is interested in buying a European call option written on Southeastern Airlines plc, a non-dividend-paying equity, with a strike price of £110 and one year until expiration. Currently, Southeastern's equity sells for £100 per share. In one year Ken, knows that Southeastern's shares will be trading at either £125 per share or £80 per share. Ken is able to borrow and lend at the risk-free EAR of 2.5 per cent.

a What should the call option sell for today?

b If no options currently trade on the equity, is there a way to create a synthetic call option with identical payoffs to the call option just described? If there is, how would you do it?

c How much does the synthetic call option cost? Is this greater than, less than or equal to what the actual call option costs? Does this make sense?

8.5 Maverick Manufacturing plc must purchase gold in three months for use in its operations. Maverick's management has estimated that if the price of gold were to rise above $875 per ounce, the firm would go bankrupt. The current price of gold is $850 per ounce. The firm's chief financial officer believes that the price of gold will either rise to $900 per ounce or fall to $825 per ounce over the next three months. Management wishes to eliminate any risk of the firm going bankrupt. Maverick can borrow and lend at the risk-free APR of 16.99 per cent.

a Should the company buy a call option or a put option on gold? To avoid bankruptcy, what strike price and time to expiration would the company like this option to have?

b How much should such an option sell for in the open market?

c If no options currently trade on gold, is there a way for the company to create a synthetic option with identical payoffs to the option just described? If there is, how would the firm do it?

d How much does the synthetic option cost? Is this greater than, less than or equal to what the actual option costs? Does this make sense?

8.6 You hold an American call option with a £30 strike price on an equity that sells at £35. The option sells for £5 one year before expiration. Compare the cash flows at expiration from: (1) exercising the option now, and putting the £5 proceeds in a bank account until the expiration date; and (2) holding on to the option until expiration, selling short the equity, and placing the £35 you receive into the same bank account.

8.7 Combine the Black–Scholes formula with the put–call parity formula to derive the Black–Scholes formula for European puts.

8.8 HSBC Holdings equity has a volatility of $\sigma = 0.25$ and a price of £9.25 a share. A European call option on HSBC stock with a strike price of £10 and an expiration time of one year has a price of £1. Using the Black–Scholes model, describe how you would construct an arbitrage portfolio, assuming that the present value of the strike price is £9.43. Would the arbitrage portfolio increase or decrease its position in HSBC if shortly thereafter the share price of HSBC rose to £9.30 a share?

8.9 Take the partial derivative of the Black–Scholes value of a call option with respect to the underlying security's price, S_0. Show that this derivative is positive and equal to $N(d_1)$. *Hint:* first show that $S_0N'(d_1) - \text{PV}(K)N'(d_1 - \sigma\sqrt{T})$ equals zero by using the fact that the derivative of N with respect to d_1, $N'(d_1)$, equals $1\ \sqrt{2\pi}\,[\exp^{(-0.5d_1^2)}]$.

8.10 Take the partial derivative of the Black–Scholes value of a call option with respect to the volatility parameter. Show that this derivative is positive and equal to $S_0\sqrt{T}N'(d_1)$.

8.11 If PV(K) = $K/[(1 + r)^T]$, take the partial derivative of the Black–Scholes value of a call option with respect to the interest rate r_f. Show that this derivative is positive and equal to $T \times \text{PV}(K) N(d_1 - \sigma\sqrt{T})/(1 + r_f)$.

8.12 Suppose you observe a European call option on an asset that is priced at less than the value of S_0 – PV(K) – PV(div). What type of transaction should you execute to achieve arbitrage? (Be specific with respect to amounts, and avoid using puts in this arbitrage.)

8.13 Consider a position of two purchased calls (BASF, three months, K = €96) and one written put (BASF, three months, K = €96). What position in BASF equity will show the same sensitivity to price changes in BASF equity as the option position described above? Express your answer algebraically as a function of d_1 from the Black–Scholes model.

8.14 The share price of Strategy AB is €50. The equity follows a binomial process where each period the share price either goes up by 10 per cent or down by 10 per cent. Compute the fair market value of an American put option on Strategy AB equity with a strike price of €50 and two periods to expiration. Assume that Strategy AB pays no dividends over the next two periods. The risk-free rate is 2 per cent per period.

8.15 Steady plc has a share value of £50. At-the-money American call options on Steady plc with nine months to expiration are trading at £3. Sure plc also has a share value of £50. At-the-money American call options on Sure plc with nine months to expiration are trading at £3. Suddenly, a merger is announced. Each share in both corporations is exchanged for one share in the combined corporation, 'Sure & Steady'. After the merger, options formerly on one share of either Sure plc or Steady plc were converted to options on one share of Sure & Steady. The only change is the difference in the underlying asset. Analyse the likely impact of the merger on the values of the two options before and after the merger. Extend this analysis to the effect of mergers on the equity of firms with debt financing.

8.16 FSA is a privately held firm. As an analyst trying to determine the value of FSA's ordinary equity and bonds, you have estimated the market value of the firm's assets to be €1 million and the standard deviation of the asset return to be 0.3. The debt of FSA, which consists of zero-coupon bank loans, will come due one year from now at its face value of €1 million. Assuming that the risk-free rate is 5 per cent, use the Black–Scholes model to estimate the value of the firm's equity and debt.

8.17 Describe what happens to the amount of equity held in the tracking portfolio for a call (put) as the share price goes up (down). *Hint:* prove this by looking at delta.

8.18 Callable bonds appear to have market values that are determined as though the issuing corporation optimally exercises the call option implicit in the bond. You know, however, that these options tend to get exercised past the optimal point. Write up a non-technical presentation for your boss, the portfolio manager, explaining why arbitrage exists, and how to take advantage of it with this investment opportunity.

8.19 The following tree diagram outlines the share price of a company over the next two periods:

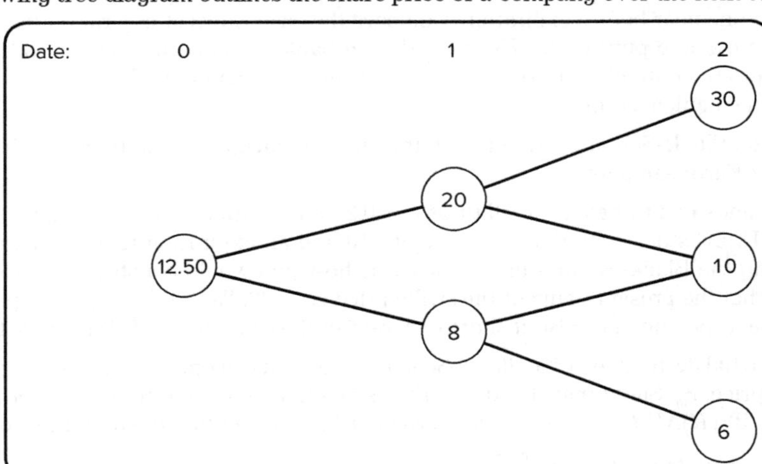

The risk-free rate is 12 per cent from date 0 to date 1, and 15 per cent from date 1 to date 2. A European call on this equity (1) expires in period 2, and (2) has a strike price of £8.

8.20 Calculate the risk-neutral probabilities implied by the binomial tree.

8.21 Calculate the pay-offs of the call option at each of three nodes at date 2.

8.22 Compute the value of the call at date 0.

8.23 A non-dividend-paying equity has a current price of £30 and a volatility of 20 per cent per year.

8.24 Use the Black–Scholes equation to value a European call option on the equity above with a strike price that has a present value of £28 and time to maturity of three months.

8.25 Without performing calculations, state whether this price would be higher if the call were American. Why?

8.26 Suppose the equity pays dividends. Are otherwise identical American and European options likely to have the same value? Why?

References and Additional Reading

Black, F. (1976) The pricing of commodity contracts *Journal of Financial Economics,* 3(1/2): 167–179.

Black, F. and Scholes, M. (1973) The pricing of options and corporate liabilities *Journal of Political Economy,* 81(3): 637–659.

Cox, J.C. and Rubinstein, M. (1985) *Options Markets.* Englewood Cliffs, NJ Prentice Hall.

Cox, J.C. Ross, S.A., and Rubinstein, M. (1979) Option pricing: a simplified approach *Journal of Financial Economics,* 7(3): 229–263.

Galai, D., and Masulis, R. (1976) The option pricing model and the risk factor of stock *Journal of Financial Economics,* 3(1/2): 53–81.

Garman, M. and Kohlhagen, S. (1983) Foreign currency option values *Journal of International Money and Finance,* 2(3): 231–237.

Geske, R. (1979) The valuation of compound options *Journal of Financial Economics,* 7(1): 63–82.

Geske, R. and Johnson, H. (1984) The American put option valued analytically *The Journal of Finance,* 39(5): 1511–1524.

Grabbe, J.O. (1983) The pricing of call and put options on foreign exchange *Journal of International Money and Finance,* 2(3): 239–253.

Hull, J.C. (1997) *Options, Futures, and Other Derivatives,* 3rd edn. Upper Saddle River, NJ: Prentice Hall

MacBeth, J.D. and Merville, L.J., (1979) An empirical examination of the Black–Scholes call option pricing model *The Journal of Finance,* 34(4): 1173–1186.

Merton, R.C. (1973) Theory of rational option pricing *Bell Journal of Economics and Management Science,* 4(1): 141–183.

Ramaswamy, K. and Sundaresan, S. (1985) The valuation of options on futures contracts *The Journal of Finance,* 40(5): 1319–1340.

Rendelman, R.J. Jr and Bartter, B.J. (1979) Two-state option pricing *The Journal of Finance,* 34(5): 1093–1110.

Rubinstein, M. (1985) Nonparametric tests of alternative option pricing models using all reported trades and quotes on the 30 most active CBOE option classes from August 23, 1976 through August 31, 1978 *The Journal of Finance,* 40(2): 455–480.

Rubinstein, M. (1994) Presidential address: implied binomial trees *Journal of Finance,* 4(3): 771–818.

Smith, C. (1976) Option pricing: a review *Journal of Financial Economics,* 3(1/2): 3–51.

Stoll, H. (1969) The relationship between put and call option prices *The Journal of Finance,* 24(5): 801–824.

Whaley, R. (1981) On the valuation of American call options on equities with known dividends *Journal of Financial Economics,* 9(2): 207–211.

Practical Insights for Part II

Allocating Capital for Real Investment

- Mean-variance analysis can help determine the risk implications of product mixes, mergers and acquisitions, and carve-outs. This requires thinking about the mix of real assets as a portfolio. (Section 4.6)
- Theories to value real assets identify the types of risk that determine discount rates. Most valuation problems will use either the CAPM or APT, which identify market risk and factor risk, respectively, as the relevant risk attributes. (Sections 5.8, 6.10)
- An investment's covariance with other investments is a more important determinant of its discount rate than is the variance of the investment's return. (Section 5.7)
- The CAPM and the APT both suggest that the rate of return required to induce investors to hold an investment is determined by how the investment's return covaries with well-diversified portfolios. However, existing evidence suggests that most of the well-diversified portfolios that have traditionally been used, in either a single-factor or a multiple-factor implementation, do a poor job of explaining the historical returns of ordinary equities. Although multifactor models do better than single-factor models, all model implementations have difficulty (to varying degrees) explaining the historical returns of investments with extreme size, market-to-book ratios and momentum. These shortcomings need to be accounted for when allocating capital to real investments that fit into these anomalous categories. (Sections 5.11, 6.12)

Financing the Firm

- When issuing debt or equity, the CAPM and APT can provide guidelines about whether the issue is priced fairly. (Sections 5.8, 6.10)
- Because equity can be viewed as a call option on the assets of the firm when there is risky debt financing, the equity of firms with debt is riskier than the equity of firms with no debt. (Sections 8.3, 8.8)
- Derivative valuation theory can be used to value risky debt and equity in relation to one another. (Section 8.3)

Knowing Whether and How to Hedge Risk

- The fair market values, not the actual market values, determine appropriate ratios for hedging. These are usually computed from the valuation models for derivatives. (Section 8.8)
- Portfolio mathematics can enable the investor to understand the risk attributes of any mix of real assets, financial assets and liabilities. (Section 4.6)
- Forward currency rates can be inferred from domestic and foreign interest rates. (Section 7.2)

Allocating Funds for Financial Investments

- Portfolios generally dominate individual securities as desirable investment positions. (Section 5.2)
- Per unit of cash invested, leveraged positions are riskier than unleveraged positions. (Section 4.7)
- There is a unique optimal risky portfolio when a risk-free asset exists. The task of an investor is to identify this portfolio. (Section 5.4)
- Mean-variance analysis is frequently used as a tool for allocating funds between broad-based portfolios. Because of estimation problems, mean-variance analysis is difficult to use for determining allocations between individual securities. (Section 5.6)

- If the CAPM is true, the optimal portfolio to hold is a broad-based market index. (Section 5.8)
- If the APT is true, the optimal portfolio to hold is a weighted average of the factor portfolios. (Section 6.10)
- Since derivatives are priced relative to other investments, opinions about cash flows do not matter when determining their values. With perfect tracking possible here, mastery of the theories is essential if one wants to earn arbitrage profits from these investments. (Section 7.3)
- Apparent arbitrage profits, if they exist, must arise from market frictions. Hence, to obtain arbitrage profits from derivative investments, one must be cleverer than competitors at overcoming the frictions that allow apparent arbitrage to exist. (Section 7.6)
- Derivatives can be used to insure a portfolio's value. (Section 8.3)
- The somewhat disappointing empirical evidence for the CAPM and APT may imply an opportunity for portfolio managers to beat aggregate market indices and other benchmarks they are measured against. (Sections 5.8, 6.10, 6.12)
- Per unit of investment, call options are riskier than the underlying asset. (Section 8.8)

Executive Perspective

Myron S. Scholes

For large financial institutions, financial models are critical to their continuing success. Since they are liability managers as well as asset managers, models are crucial in pricing and evaluating investment choices, and in managing the risk of their positions. Indeed, financial models, similar to those developed in Part II of this text, are in everyday use in these firms.

The mean-variance model, developed in Chapters 4 and 5, is one example of a model that we use in our activities. We use it and stress management technology to optimize the expected returns on our portfolio subject to risk, concentration and liquidity constraints. The mean-variance approach has influenced financial institutions in determining risk limits and measuring the sensitivity of their profit and loss to systematic exposures.

The risk–expected return models presented in Part II, such as the CAPM and the APT, represent another set of useful tools for money management and portfolio optimization. These models have profoundly affected the way in which investment funds are managed, and the way in which individuals invest and assess performance. For example, passively managed funds, which generally buy and hold a proxy for the market portfolio, have grown dramatically, accounting for more than 20 per cent of institutional investment. This has occurred, in part, because of academic writings on the CAPM and, in part, because performance evaluation using these models has shown that professional money managers as a group do not systematically outperform these alternative investment strategies. Investment banks use both debt and equity factor models – extremely important tools – to determine appropriate hedges to mitigate factor risks. For example, my former employer, Salomon Brothers, uses factor models to determine the appropriate hedges for its equity and debt positions.

All this pales, of course, with the impact of derivatives valuation models, starting with the Black–Scholes option-pricing model that I developed with Fischer Black in the early 1970s. Using the option-pricing technology, investment banks have been able to produce products that customers want. An entire field called financial engineering has emerged in recent years to support these developments. Investment banks use option-pricing technology to price sophisticated contracts and to determine the appropriate hedges to mitigate the underlying risks of producing these contracts. Without the option-pricing technology, presented in Chapters 7 and 8, the global financial picture would be far different. In the old world, banks were underwriters, matching those who wanted to buy with those who wanted to offer coarse contracts such as loans, bonds and equities. Derivatives have reduced the costs to provide financial services and products that are more finely tuned to the needs of investors and corporations around the world.

Mr Scholes is the chairman of the Board of Economic Advisors at Stamos Capital and the Frank E. Buck Professor of Finance Emeritus, Stanford University Graduate School of Business. Mr. Scholes is a recipient of the 1997 Nobel Prize in Economics.

PART 3

Valuing Real Assets

Part contents

Part II focused on how to value financial assets in relation to one another. We learned that the future cash flows of financial assets, like derivatives and equity, can be tracked (nearly perfectly or imperfectly) by a portfolio of some other financial assets. This tracking relationship allowed us to derive risk – expected return equations such as the CAPM and the APT, as well as describe the no-arbitrage price of a derivative, given the value of its underlying financial asset.

The lessons learned from studying valuation in the financial markets carry over to the valuation of real assets, such as factories and machines. There is a tight connection between the theory of financial asset valuation and corporate finance. Although corporate managers employ a variety of techniques to value and evaluate corporate investment projects, all these techniques essentially require tracking of the real asset's cash flows with a portfolio of financial assets.

The correct application and appropriateness of real asset valuation techniques depend largely on how well the corporate manager understands the linkage between these techniques and the principles used to value financial assets in Part II. When these techniques are viewed as black boxes – formulae that provide cut-off values that the manager blindly uses to adopt or reject projects – major errors in project assessment are likely to arise.

The first issue to address when valuing real assets is what to value. By analogy with our previous discussion of financial assets, we know that we should be evaluating the future cash flows that are generated from the asset that is being valued. As we shall emphasize in Chapter 9, cash flows and earnings are two different things, and it is the cash flows, not the earnings, that are the relevant inputs to be used to value the assets. Hence the ability to translate projections of accounting numbers into cash flows, also considered in Chapter 9, is critical. Chapter 9 also devotes considerable space to the simple mechanics of discounting, which is critical for obtaining the values of future cash flows with many of the project evaluation techniques discussed in Part III.

Chapter 10 focuses on projects where the future cash flows are known with certainty. Although this is not the typical setting faced by corporate managers, it is ideal for gaining an understanding of the merits and appropriate application of various project evaluation techniques. In this simplified setting, one can perfectly track the future cash flows of projects with investments in financial assets. We learn from this setting that two techniques, the discounted cash flow (DCF) and the internal rate of return (IRR) approaches, can generally be appropriately used to evaluate projects. However, there are several pitfalls to watch out for, particularly with the IRR. In many cases, even the DCF method has to be modified to fit the constraints imposed on project selection.

Andor et al. (2015),[1] surveyed firms on the practices used to evaluate investments in real assets. The most striking insight from their research was the significant variation across countries in the techniques used by firms. Whereas Graham and Harvey (2001)[2] found that the two most popular techniques in the US were the NPV and the IRR approaches, many European firms also use both techniques to evaluate their real investment projects, but other approaches are also regularly utilised. For example, a popular investment method in Europe is payback period – a very simple metric that measures the time it takes for an initial investment to be recouped (see Chapter 10). Necessary modifications of the DCF approach – for example, the profitability index approach – are also used by some firms (12 per cent) where situations call for them. (This approach is also analysed in Chapter 10.)

Another project evaluation technique is the accounting rate of return method (commonly used in the UK, Singapore, Poland and Germany). Chapter 10 discusses the pitfalls that are likely to arise if one employs the accounting rate of return and payback period techniques to evaluate projects. Although payback and accounting rate of return are popular, as the practice of corporate finance becomes more sophisticated these more traditional approaches will most likely give way to the DCF and IRR approaches.

Of course, one typically applies real asset valuation techniques to value risky future cash flows. This raises a host of issues, discussed in Chapter 11. Here the principle of tracking is still applied to value real assets and make appropriate decisions about corporate projects. However, in contrast to Chapter 10, the tracking portfolios for risky projects do not perfectly track the project's cash flows. Hence appropriate techniques are designed to ensure that the tracking error risk carries no risk premium, and thus carries no value.

Managers also use other techniques besides DCF, IRR, payback and accounting rate of return methods to evaluate projects. For example, Brounen et al. (2004) report that many firms use ratio comparison approaches, such as price to earnings multiples, and in France real options approaches, which are based on the derivative

[1] Andor, G., Mohanty, S.K. and Toth, T. (2015) Capital Budgeting Practices: A Survey of Central and Eastern European Firms, *Emerging Markets Review*, 23: 148–172.

[2] Graham, J. and Harvey, C.R. (2001) The theory and practice of corporate finance: evidence from the field, *Journal of Financial Economics*, 60(2–3): 187–243.

valuation techniques presented in Chapters 7 and 8, are the most common form of investment appraisal technique. These approaches and their proper use are discussed in Chapter 12. This chapter also shows how these techniques can be used as tools for evaluating strategies as well as capital expenditures on projects. For example, a major oil firm would not consider in isolation the opportunity to develop a natural gas field in Thailand. Instead, the firm would be thinking about the strategic implications of an increased presence in Asia, with the natural gas field as only one aspect of that strategy. Chapter 12 discusses how to estimate the value created by these strategic implications, and provides broad principles that apply even to cases where quantitative estimation is difficult.

Finally, Chapter 13 introduces corporate tax deductions for debt financing, and discusses how the financing of a project may affect its value to the firm. This sets the stage for Part IV, where the focus is chiefly on the optimal financial structure of a corporation.

Chapter 9

Discounting and Valuation

Learning Objectives

After reading this chapter, you should be able to:

- Understand what a present value is.
- Know how to define, compute and forecast the unlevered cash flows used for valuation.
- Compute incremental cash flows for projects.
- Mechanically compute present values and future values for single cash flows and specially patterned cash flow streams, such as annuities and perpetuities, in both level and growing forms.
- Apply the principle of value additivity to simplify present value calculations.
- Translate interest rates from one compounding frequency into another.
- Understand the role that opportunity cost plays in the time value of money.

The fifth wealthiest man in the world as of 2022, Warren Buffett, is universally regarded as an investment guru who is always worth listening to, in addition to being one of the most successful investors in history. His average rate of return on investments is more than 20 per cent over his full career, and his greatest success was the purchase of Coca-Cola in 1988, which netted him an 800 per cent return over 12 years. Buffett's philosophy is simple: invest only in firms whose intrinsic value is greater than their cost to purchase. Similarly, firms should invest only in real assets whose value is greater than their cost.

Corporations create value for their shareholders by making good real investment decisions. **Real investments** are expenditures that generate cash in the future and, as opposed to financial investments such as equities and bonds, are not financial instruments that trade in the financial markets. Although one typically thinks about expenditures on plant and equipment as real investment decisions, in reality almost all corporate decisions, including those involving personnel and marketing, can be viewed as real investment decisions. For example, hiring new employees can be viewed as an investment, since the cost of the employees in the initial months exceeds the benefits they provide to their employer; however, over time, as they acquire skills, they provide positive net benefits. Similarly, when a firm increases its advertising expenditures, it is sacrificing current profits in the hope of generating more sales and future profits.

One of the major thrusts of this text is that financial managers should use a market-based approach to value assets, whether valuing financial assets, such as equities and bonds, or real assets, such as factories and machines. To value these real assets, corporate managers must apply the valuation principles developed in Part II. There, we used portfolios to track investments, and compared the expected returns (or costs) of the tracking portfolios with the expected returns (or costs) of the financial assets we wanted to value. This allowed us to value the tracked investment in relation to its tracking portfolio. Models such as the CAPM, the APT and the binomial derivative pricing model were used to determine relevant tracking portfolios.

The techniques developed in Part III largely piggyback onto these models and principles. The chapters in Part III show how to combine the prices available in financial markets into a single number that managers can compare with investment costs to evaluate whether a real investment increases or diminishes a firm's value. This number is the **present value (PV)**,[1] which is the market price of a portfolio of traded securities that tracks the future **cash flows** of the proposed project (the free cash that a project generates). Essentially, a project creates value for a corporation if the cost of investing in it is less than the cost of investing in a portfolio of financial assets that track the project's future cash flows.

Thus the PV measures the worth of a project's future cash flows at the present time by looking at the market price of identical, or nearly identical, future cash flows obtained from investing in the financial markets. To obtain a PV, you typically discount (a process introduced in Chapter 7) the estimated future cash flows of a project at the rate of return of the appropriate tracking portfolio of financial assets. This rate of return is known as the **discount rate.** As the name implies, *discounting* future cash flows to the present generally reduces them. Such discounting is a critical element of Warren Buffett's philosophy, as described in this chapter's opening vignette.

The mechanics of discounting are the focus of this chapter. There are two aspects to the mechanics of discounting cash flows:

1 understanding how to compute future cash flows, and
2 applying the formulae that derive present values by applying discount rates to future cash flows.

In the conclusion to this chapter, we briefly touch on the issue of why we discount to obtain present values. More insight into this issue, including the issue of which discount rate to use, is explored in Chapters 10 and 11.

9.1 Cash Flows of Real Assets

An ability to understand the cash flows of real assets is an essential skill for the analysis of a real investment decision. The cash flows of an asset are represented as numbers attached to dates in time, with date **0** generally referring to the current date. The sign of the cash flow tells the analyst whether the cash flow is an inflow or an outflow. For example, the date 0 purchase of a factory for £10 million is a cash flow to the purchaser of –£10 million and thus an outflow. The sale of the same factory at date 1 for £15 million represents a cash flow to the seller of £15 million, and is thus an inflow to him. The difference of £5 million is the profit or capital gain on the factory.

Of course, in lieu of selling the factory, cash flows at date 1 could be generated from sales of products that the factory produces. In this case, the date 1 cash flow would be increased by cash receipts generated from sales, and reduced by cash expenses and any necessary cash reinvestment needed to keep the factory running. The cash flow numbers can be obtained from pro-forma cash flow statements or derived from earnings, as we describe below.

The cash flows of projects or firms can come directly from the real assets of the project or firm, or indirectly, via financing subsidies that the project or firm manages to garner, notably the tax subsidy associated with debt financing, relocation or other subsidies (a good example is the reimbursable launch investment that Airbus receives from the European Union each time it successfully delivers a new aeroplane). It will not be until Chapter 13 that we have to consider the effect of these financing-related subsidies on valuation. These subsidies are ultimately important. However, for now, we consider only how to compute the cash flow component that arises directly from the real assets.

[1] Present value is a concept first developed in Part II's discussion of derivatives and tracking portfolios, where the present value was the cost of the portfolio, consisting of the underlying asset and a risk-free asset that tracked the derivative or a component of one of its future cash flows, like a future cash payout or receipt. It means much the same thing here, except that the 'underlying' financial assets track a real asset rather than a derivative or a component of one of the derivative's future cash flows.

Unlevered Cash Flows

When evaluating a project, one must first identify the project's **unlevered cash flows** – that is, cash flows generated directly from the real assets of the project or firm. In a hypothetical world where financing does not affect the operations of a project – for example, by altering relationships with customers, employers and suppliers, or by generating bankruptcy costs – unlevered cash flows are the cash flows from the project's (or firm's) assets under the assumption that the project (or firm) is all-equity financed – hence the name 'unlevered'. The unlevered cash flows, generated entirely by real assets, like a power plant, are not affected by and should not be confused with any **financing cash flows**, which are associated with (1) issuance or retirement of debt and equity, (2) interest or dividend payments, and (3) any interest-based tax deductions that stem from debt financing. One derives unlevered cash flows from forecasts of cash flow statements or, more often, from forecasts of **earnings before interest and taxes**, more commonly known as **EBIT**.

Deriving Unlevered Cash Flows from the Accounting Cash Flow Statement

The increase (or decrease) in cash reported near the bottom of a firm's cash flow statement represents the difference in the cash (plus cash equivalents) position of the firm for two consecutive balance sheets. This **accounting cash flow** is a type of cash flow, but it is not the same as the unlevered cash flow that is discounted for valuation purposes. The accounting cash flow includes cash flows arising from the financing of the firm, including interest and dividends. Moreover, because debt interest usually reduces the tax liability of the firm, the reduction in cash flow due to taxes on the cash flow statement is too conservative.

Accounting cash flow statements break up the cash flow into the sum of operating cash flows, investing cash flows and financing cash flows. As we shall learn, these distinctions are often arbitrary, artificial and ambiguous. Moreover, different accounting standards can make the process of calculating unlevered cash flows even more difficult. There are two main accounting standards, and which one you deal with depends on the country in which the firm is incorporated or listed. US firms use what is known as Generally Accepted Accounting Principles (GAAP), whereas companies incorporated or listed in the UK, European Union and Australia use International Financial Reporting Standard (IFRS). Foreign firms cross-listed in the USA need to report both GAAP and their local accounting standards.

As a rule of thumb, the detailed cash flow statement should be examined when estimating unlevered cash flows. Under IFRS, the cash flow statement is separated into three distinct sections relating to the net cash flow arising from operating activities, investing activities and financing activities. When accountants refer to operating cash flows, they are referring to cash flows that stem directly from operations. Investing cash flows normally relate to the capital expenditure and income the firm incurs during the financial year. Finally, financing cash flows involve any cash that comes from the financing of the project. It is this last component that can cause problems when calculating unlevered cash flows.

Unlike IFRS, US GAAP includes interest payments in the operating section of the cash flow statement, and this needs to be adjusted. If the firm was financed entirely with equity, interest payments would not exist. Hence operating cash flow, under US GAAP, does not account properly for cash flows that stem directly from the firm's operations. Unfortunately, many US finance textbooks use the terminology 'operating cash flows' to refer to 'unlevered cash flows', often confusing students schooled in accounting. To obtain unlevered cash flows from the cash flow statement under US GAAP, you must add the operating and investing cash flow, add interest, and then subtract the tax subsidy provided by debt interest, as the following result indicates. With IFRS, the estimation of unlevered cash flows is much simpler, since all financing activities are included under the financing section, and only the debt interest tax subsidy (to be discussed later) needs to be estimated.

Results

Result 9.1

Under US GAAP: Unlevered cash flow = operating cash inflow
+ investing cash inflow (which is usually negative)
+ debt interest – debt interest tax subsidy

Under IFRS: Unlevered cash flow = net cash flow from operating activities
+ net cash flow from investing activities (which is usually negative)
– debt interest tax subsidy

Fast-growing companies tend to have negative unlevered cash flows, even when they are very profitable. Technology firms and new start-ups require investment in capital expenditure in order to grow, and this normally drains any cash that is earned from existing projects. When growth opportunities diminish, firms may become what some people refer to as a 'cash cow', generating more cash than they invest. Apple was an example of a cash cow. Between 2012 and 2014, the company paid extraordinarily high dividends, because it couldn't find worthwhile projects in which to invest. Ignoring this cash cow stage would result in significant undervaluation of technology firms.

The cash flow statements of financial services companies or companies with substantial financial services subsidiaries also tend to have negative unlevered cash flow, despite high profitability. This is because a large proportion or nearly all of their investment activities are in marketable securities through providing leases, selling commercial paper, trading securities for profit, and so on. The wealth creation of financial firms comes principally from financing activities, which a direct application of our unlevered cash flow valuation methodology ignores. Hence our basic methodology would not be appropriate for valuing financing businesses.

To value assets, it is important to value only those cash flows that are generated by the assets. Since financing takes place on the right-hand side rather than on the left-hand (asset) side of the balance sheet, counting financing cash flows in addition to asset cash flows would involve double-counting cash flows. As financing activities *per se* play no role in increasing or decreasing the cash flows generated by the assets of the project, counting them in an asset valuation would be inappropriate. A notable exception arises when there is an obvious and easily measured subsidy associated with financing, such as a tax subsidy, which can be ascribed to the asset being valued. In this case, because the asset being valued is responsible for the financing-related subsidy, we need to find ways to account for this subsidy. Two commonly used ways in which to do this are discussed in Chapter 13. Another exception, noted above, arises with financing companies and financial intermediaries, where the assets themselves are the financing activities. However, since the wealth creation associated with the activities of these companies is virtually impossible to measure, we are wary about applying the valuation methodology described in Part III of this text to analyse companies or projects for which the cash generated comes largely from the financing activities.

Example 9.1

Computing Unlevered Cash Flow

Compute the unlevered cash flow for a hypothetical firm with all figures in millions of euros.

Consolidated statements of cash flows (million €)	2022	2021
Net income	1,410	2,912
Depreciation and amortization of intangible assets, property, plant and equipment and financial assets	3,740	3,180
Changes in inventories	1,094	136
Changes in receivables	2,065	(739)
Changes in operating liabilities, pension provisions, defined benefit assets and other non-cash items	(2,039)	(466)
Cash provided by operating activities	**6,270**	**5,023**
Payments related to intangible assets and property, plant and equipment	(2,507)	(2,521)
Payments related to financial assets and securities	(641)	(976)
Payments related to acquisitions	(1,509)	(637)
Proceeds from divestitures	62	73
Proceeds from the disposal of long-term assets and securities	513	601
Cash used in investing activities	**(4,082)**	**(3.460)**

Consolidated statements of cash flows (million €)	2022	2021
Capital increases/repayments and other equity transactions	(134)	45
Share repurchases	–	(1,618)
Proceeds from the addition of financial liabilities	4,636	6,271
Repayment of financial liabilities	(5,546)	(2,082)
Dividends paid to shareholders	(2,089)	(2,157)
Cash provided by (used in) financing activities	**(3,133)**	**459**
Net changes in cash and cash equivalents	**(945)**	**2,022**
Effects on cash and cash equivalents		
From foreign exchange rates	4	(31)
From changes in scope of consolidation	–	18
Cash and cash equivalents at the beginning of the year	**2,776**	**767**
Cash and cash equivalents at the end of the year	**1,835**	**2,776**

Answer: Assume the marginal tax rate is 30 per cent, and from its consolidated income statement, net interest for 2022 was €600 million. This means that interest expenses reduced the tax bill by 30 per cent of €600 million, which is €180 million. This needs to be subtracted from the net amount because, in effect, the €180 million is a cash inflow as a result of the financing decision. The firm's unlevered cash flow is therefore €2,008 million (= 6,270 – 4,082 – 180).

Deriving Unlevered Cash Flow from the Income Statement

To translate profit or EBIT into unlevered cash flow, note that profit before interest and taxes is:

- reduced by depreciation and amortization,[2] which affects earnings but not cash flow
- not affected by new investment in working capital,[3] which reduces cash flow
- not affected by purchases of capital assets (capital expenditures), which decrease cash flow, nor by sales of capital assets, which increase cash flow, except when such sales generate realized capital gains and losses
- computed before taxes, which reduce the unlevered cash flow.

Thus, to obtain the unlevered cash flow of a business or project from EBIT, one applies the formula given in Result 9.2.

Results

Result 9.2

Unlevered cash flow = profit before interest and taxes + depreciation and amortization
– change in working capital – capital expenditures
+ sales of capital assets – realized capital gains
+ realized capital losses – profit before interest and taxes × tax rate

[2] *Amortization* of real assets generally refers to depreciation of intangible assets. See Chapter 2 for a discussion of bond amortization.

[3] *Working capital* is current assets, typically trade receivables and inventory, less current liabilities, typically trade payables. Investment in working capital reduces cash. For example, a sale paid for by increasing trade receivables results in less cash than a cash sale and an inventory expansion paid with cash results in a cash outflow.

The last term translates the pre-tax cash flow to an unlevered (after-tax) cash flow. Thus unlevered cash flow is pre-tax cash flow less profit before interest and taxes × tax rate.[4]

Example 9.2

Computing Unlevered Cash Flow from Profit before Interest and Taxes

Consider a hypothetical investment decision facing Bayer Healthcare AG, the healthcare subsidiary of the German Bayer group. It wishes to purchase a magnetic resonance imaging system (MRI) for €500,000. For tax purposes, the MRI is straight-line-depreciated over five years; in reality it will last eight years, after which it has no salvage value. The MRI will be part-financed with €250,000 by an eight-year debt security, which pays interest of 10 per cent per year on an annual basis. Working capital, initially set at €80,000, will increase by €10,000 for each year of the eight-year period. For simplicity, let's assume that there are no capital expenditures or sales (and thus no realized gains or losses). The profit from operations of the MRI before interest and taxes is forecast to be €10,000 in each of the first five years, and €110,000 in years six to eight once the MRI has been fully depreciated. Compute the unlevered cash flows of the project, assuming a 40 per cent corporation tax rate.

Answer: Because there are no future sales or purchases of capital for this project, the project's pre-tax cash flows – unlevered cash flows plus EBIT × tax rate – of €100,000 per year are the same as **earnings before interest, taxes, depreciation and amortization (EBITDA)** less the 110,000 per year change in working capital. As Exhibit 9.1 shows, the unlevered cash flow is 196,000 in the first five years and 156,000 in the remaining years. The 140,000 difference arises from the lost depreciation tax shield.

Exhibit 9.1 Earnings and Cash Flows for Bayer Healthcare AG

Year	EBIT € (a)	Depreciation € (b)	EBITDA € (c)	Increase in working capital € (d)	Pre-tax cash flow € (e) = (c) – (d)	Taxes (at 40%) € (f) = (a) × (0.4)	Unlevered cash flow € (g) = (e) – (f)
1	10,000	100,000	110,000	10,000	100,000	4,000	96,000
2	10,000	100,000	110,000	10,000	100,000	4,000	96,000
3	10,000	100,000	110,000	10,000	100,000	4,000	96,000
4	10,000	100,000	110,000	10,000	100,000	4,000	96,000
5	10,000	100,000	110,000	10,000	100,000	4,000	96,000
6	110,000	0	110,000	10,000	100,000	44,000	56,000
7	110,000	0	110,000	10,000	100,000	44,000	56,000
8	110,000	0	110,000	10,000	100,000	44,000	56,000

Note that the €500,000 cost of acquiring the MRI is not listed in Exhibit 9.1, because it is not a *future* cash flow, and (except for its effect on depreciation and thus taxes) it does not affect the PV of the *future* cash flows of the project. Later in this chapter we shall learn how to compute the PV of the MRI's future cash flows.

Also, observe that the taxes associated with the unlevered cash flows in Exhibit 9.1 are not the true taxes paid, because the MRI is not all-equity financed. The debt interest tax deduction (40 per cent of €25,000 per year in interest) implies that the actual after-tax cash flows of the project will be higher than the unlevered cash flows computed for Bayer Healthcare AG in the previous example. One needs to account for this debt interest

[4] There are numerous additional minor adjustments that some consulting firms undertake to transform earnings (or net income) to cash flow. These are often related to minor pension accounting and inventory assumptions, and other esoteric adjustments that are beyond the scope of this text. We have also ignored the distinction between accrued debt interest and debt interest that is actually paid. Because these are so similar, most analysts tend to assume they are the same when making cash flow forecasts.

tax subsidy to obtain the true PV and net present value of any project that is partly financed with debt. We defer discussion of this important topic until Chapter 13.

In the project's first five years, its unlevered cash flows are its pre-tax cash flows less €4,000, because the depreciation tax shield eliminates €40,000 in taxes associated with the project's earnings. Once the depreciation tax shield is used, as in years 6 to 8, the tax bite goes up by €40,000. Accordingly, the unlevered cash flows are €40,000 lower in years 6 to 9. The computation of the unlevered cash flows in Exhibit 9.1 implicitly assumes that the acquisition of the MRI, were it financed entirely with equity, would increase the tax bill of Bayer Healthcare AG. If Bayer Healthcare AG were losing money on its existing projects, and consequently the tax bill was unaffected by acquiring the MRI, our calculations above would have to change. Since the existing projects of the firm can potentially alter the computed cash flows for Bayer Healthcare AG, the cash flows that we shall ultimately be discounting have to be the project's **incremental cash flows** – the cash flows of the firm with the project less the cash flows of the firm if the project were turned down.

Incremental Cash Flows

Thinking about the forecast cash flows for a project as incremental cash flows to the firm allows for all possible interactions that a project might have with the firm. The use of a key portion of a factory floor, for example, may preclude the production of another product that could generate positive cash flows. The lost cash flows of the other product need to be accounted for. (More on this in Chapter 10.) Alternatively, the project may enhance the cash flows of other projects that a firm has or is planning. For example, the design of the Honda Accord chassis leads not just to the cash flows of the American Honda Accord but to European and Japanese versions of the car. Thus the development of this Honda Accord chassis, while perhaps aimed primarily at the US sedan market, has an incremental effect on the cash flows of many other Honda vehicles across the world.

Example 9.3 provides a more concrete illustration of how to compute incremental cash flows.

We summarize the insight here as follows.

Results

Result 9.3

Projects should be valued by analysing their incremental cash flows to a firm.

Creating Pro-Forma Forecasts of Financial Statements

Cash flow forecasts are usually derived from forecasts of financial statements, although the forecasting of financial statements is useful for financial managers in its own right. For example, picturing what the future income statement, cash flow statements and balance sheet will look like under various assumptions allows you to answer the following questions.

- What will the firm's earnings per share look like under different financing alternatives?
- How much cash will the firm have at the end of the year?
- How much additional funding will the firm need to raise?
- What will the firm's debt to equity ratio look like next year?
- What effect would a share buyback have on the earnings per share and the times interest earned?

Example 9.3

Incremental Cash Flows: Cash Flow Differences in Two Scenarios

Flyaway Air is thinking of acquiring a fleet of new fuel-saving jets. The airline will have the following cash flows if it does not acquire the jets:

Cash flows (in € millions) at date			
0	1	2	3
100	140	120	100

If it does acquire the jets, its cash flows will be:

Cash flows (in € millions) at date			
0	1	2	3
80	180	110	130

What are the incremental cash flows of the project?

Answer: The incremental cash flows of the project are given by the difference between the two sets of cash flows:

Cash flows (in € millions) at date			
0	1	2	3
−20	40	−10	30

This subsection provides a few tips on constructing a usable forecasting model for a typical non-financial firm. Every financial forecast contains four major sections:

1 Assumptions
2 Income statement
3 Cash flow statement
4 Balance sheet.

Assumptions: Sales, Expenses, Financing, Dividends and Interest Rates

The most important number in your list of assumptions is the sales forecast, since this will drive many of the other items on the income statement and the balance sheet. There is no one method of sales forecasting that is right for all firms. A good analyst not only looks at trends based on past performance, but also examines the firm's plans for future products, the competitive position of the firm relative to its competitors, and general trends affecting the industry, such as the attraction of substitute products.

Expense items are typically forecast as a percentage of sales. This is because the cost of goods sold and the level of inventory are often direct functions of sales. The assumed percentages can be derived from past experience. If you are doing multiple scenarios, you should remember to change your expense assumptions along with your sales assumptions in the different scenarios.

An important consideration in designing a forecasting model is the fraction of the firm's expenses that is fixed and the fraction that is variable, since you may wish to use your forecasting model to investigate scenarios with very different levels of sales. In the long run, most expenses are variable, and a percentage of sales is probably a good way to forecast the expenses. In the short run, however, most expenses are fixed, so a 'more of the same' approach may result in a better forecast.

The firm's decisions on financing will have a major effect on the financial statements. Thus the net amounts of debt and equity that the firm will issue are major assumptions. If you are unsure about what amounts to assume, start with zero. If the firm's cash level drops too low or becomes negative, then additional financing is necessary. Since equity offerings are perceived as quite costly, firms will usually choose debt to meet funding needs unless further debt financing would result in too much debt.

Your interest rate forecast should reflect the average interest rate that you expect the firm to be paying on its indebtedness during the forecast period. If you want to be extremely precise, you can use separate interest rate assumptions for long-term debt and short-term debt to reflect the cost differences between the two different types of debt.

Income Statement: Cost of Sales, EBIT, Interest, Taxes and Other Items

First, the cost of sales is calculated by applying the percentage cost assumption to your sales forecast assumption. This allows us to calculate EBIT, an extremely important number for analysis, since it represents the income from the operations of the firm before other claimants, such as tax collectors, lenders and shareholders, are paid. It thus is a measure of the operating profitability of the firm. Calculate EBIT directly by subtracting the cost of sales from the sales forecast.

To obtain earnings from EBIT, we must first subtract interest, which leaves us with **earnings before taxes**. Interest expense is a function of the expected future average interest rate and the expected future debt outstanding. Apply the interest rate forecast only to debt that accrues interest, including short- and long-term debt, and notes payable. Accruals such as trade payables and deferred taxes usually do not incur explicit interest payments. Using a percentage of sales to forecast interest expense is usually a poor forecasting method.

Finally, earnings after taxes simply subtracts taxes from earnings before taxes. Estimate taxes by multiplying the tax rate that you are forecasting for the year in question by the earnings before taxes.

Often, financial statements are filled with unusual line items with such illustrative titles as 'Other-net'. Forecasting these for the future may be difficult, since the nature of the transactions that give rise to the item may not be clear from published financial reports. If the item is small, then it is not worth spending much time attempting to forecast. Any method will do, since it will have a negligible effect on the important numbers in the forecast. If a number is large ('material' in accounting-speak), then you should go back and attempt to understand the economic forces that are driving the number. If you expect the item's influence to grow with the size of the firm, then percentage of sales is a useful forecasting method. If the unusual item is not expected to grow with the firm, then keeping it the same or reducing it may make sense.

Cash Flow Statement

Recall that the cash flow statement has three components: net cash flow from operating activities, net cash flow from investing activities, and net cash flow from financing activities. Under IFRS, the net cash flow from operations would have already been adjusted from the net profit figure.

The first item in operating cash flows is profit before taxation, which comes straight from the income statement. To this, we add back depreciation. Since the accountants have subtracted it in determining net income, it needs to be added back. The same is true for amortization of goodwill and other intangibles, as well as non-cash charges used to create reserves, such as during restructurings. Investment in working capital is then subtracted, because it costs the firm money to increase its working capital. Increases in inventories, trade receivables and other current assets (except cash) are cash outflows for the firm, and are thus subtracted. Money that the company spends on plant and equipment, or buying other companies, is an investment cash outflow. Note that the investing cash flows should tie to the balance sheet items, particularly property, plant and equipment (PPE). Observe that

$$\text{new PPE (net)} = \text{old PPE} + \text{capital investments} - \text{depreciation-sales of assets}$$

If we assume that sales of assets are negligible, a reasonable assumption for a growing firm is that

$$\text{capital investments} = (\text{new PPE} - \text{old PPE} + \text{depreciation})$$

Consequently, if you forecast net PPE directly in your spreadsheet, then you should use (new PPE − old PPE + depreciation) as your cash outflow in the investing cash flow section. Note that, since this is a cash outflow, the depreciation here exactly offsets the depreciation used above in the operating cash flow section. Thus your assumption about the depreciation expense is irrelevant as far as the total change in cash position is concerned.

Finally, we turn to the financing cash flows. Paying off debt represents a cash outflow, and borrowing represents a cash inflow. For forecasting purposes, you may wish to look only at the net change in debt. Payment of dividends represents a cash outflow, sale of equity is an inflow, and buying equity back is an outflow.

Balance Sheet Assets: Cash, Trade Receivables and Inventories, PPE and Other Items

Cash comes directly from the cash flow statement. When you are forecasting, this number may be negative, indicating a need to obtain additional financing or to scale back asset needs. Many firms prefer to have a minimum of 15 to 30 days' worth of sales around in cash and cash equivalents. This cash is needed to facilitate transactions and provide a buffer for short-term differences between making and receiving payments. Companies may prefer to hold larger cash reserves in anticipation of spending it later on planned projects, as a reserve against future downturns, or to take advantage of future opportunities that might arise. Exhibit 9.2 presents a typical balance sheet (or Statement of Financial Position). Notice that the balance sheet is split into current and non-current liabilities and assets, as well as shareholders' equity.

Exhibit 9.2 Statement of Financial Position as at 31 December 2022

	31 December 2022		31 December 2021	
	€ millions	%	€ millions	%
Assets				
Intangible assets	10,449	20.4	9,889	19.4
Property, plant and equipment	16,285	31.8	15,032	29.6
Investments accounted for using the equity method	1,340	2.6	1,146	2.3
Other financial assets	1,619	3.2	1,947	3.8
Deferred taxes	1,042	2.0	930	1.8
Other receivables and miscellaneous long-term assets	946	1.8	642	1.3
Long-term assets	**31,681**	**61.8**	**29,586**	**58.2**
Inventories	6,776	13.2	6,763	13.3
Accounts receivable, trade	7,738	15.1	7,752	15.2
Other receivables and miscellaneous long-term assets	3,223	6.3	3,948	7.8
Marketable securities	15	.	35	0.1
Cash and cash equivalents	1,835	3.6	2,776	5.4
Short-term assets	**19,587**	**38.2**	**21,274**	**41.8**
Total assets	**51,268**	**100.0**	**50,860**	**100.0**
Shareholders' equity and liabilities				
Subscribed capital	4,405	8.6	4,417	8.7
Retained earnings	12,916	25.2	13,250	26.0
Other comprehensive income	156	0.3	(96)	(0.2)
Minority interests	1,132	2.2	1,151	2.3
Shareholders' equity	**18,609**	**36.3**	**18,722**	**36.8**
Provisions for pensions and similar obligations	2,255	4.4	1,712	3.4
Other provisions	3,289	6.4	2,757	5.4
Deferred taxes	2,093	4.1	2,167	4.3
Financial indebtedness	12,444	24.3	8,290	16.3
Other liabilities	898	1.7	917	1.8
Long-term liabilities	**20,979**	**40.9**	**15,843**	**31.2**
Accounts payable, trade	2,786	5.4	2,734	5.4
Provisions	3,276	6.4	3,043	6.0
Tax liabilities	1,003	2.0	860	1.7
Financial indebtedness	2,375	4.6	6,224	12.2
Other liabilities	2,240	4.4	3,434	6.7
Short-term liabilities	**11,680**	**22.8**	**16,295**	**32.0**
Total shareholders' equity and liabilities	**51,268**	**100.0**	**50,860**	**100.0**

After cash, the next most common items on the balance sheet are trade receivables and inventories. The need for both receivables and inventories is influenced by the level of sales. Thus using a percentage of sales technique usually results in an accurate forecast.

To forecast PPE, there are several choices.

1 *Direct method:* If you can forecast capital expenditures and asset sales directly, then you can forecast PPE using the accounting relationships. Just add the forecast expenditures to the old PPE, and then subtract your estimate of the next year's depreciation expense and equipment sales. (Note here that we are talking about the depreciation expense for the year. Take care not to confuse this with the total depreciation reserve, which affects the balance sheet.)
2 *More of the same method:* If the firm has substantial excess capacity, and is not planning on adding capacity, then the previous method simplifies: the new PPE is just the old PPE less depreciation expense for the coming year.
3 *Percentage of sales:* Since the need for PPE usually rises with the level of sales, using a percentage of sales is usually pretty accurate if more precise information is not available.

Finally, other assets represents other long-term assets such as goodwill (often referred to as 'excess of cost over the market value of net assets acquired') and other intangibles. The best way to forecast these is determined by the nature of the assets. Since goodwill is usually amortized, one would forecast such an item to decline in the future, unless you expect the company to continue making acquisitions that result in good-will. If the nature of the 'other assets' is not clear, then use percentage of sales.

Balance Sheet Liabilities: Borrowings, Current Liabilities, Deferred Taxes and Other Items

The new amounts for the long- and short-term debt will be the old debt numbers plus new debt that you are assuming the firm will issue.

Current liabilities, such as trade and other payables, and other accrued expenses, are directly related to sales, and are best forecast by using a percentage of sales.

Deferred taxes arise from timing differences between when the company reports taxes on its financial statements and when those payments are actually made to the tax collectors. These usually arise from the differences between book and tax depreciation, but may also arise from differences in the timing of revenue recognition. Since the bulk of deferred taxes arise from depreciation differences, and depreciation is tied to investment in PPE, it makes sense to forecast the deferred taxes as a function of your forecast of PPE.

Many firms have a large portion of 'other liabilities' that do not accrue interest. These 'other liabilities' are not debt in the conventional sense. The best method for forecasting these depends on the nature of the transactions that give rise to them. For example, a firm that takes a large charge against earnings for a restructuring may establish a large reserve for the estimated payments that it will make in the future. Such a reserve would be expected to decline as the firm actually makes the payments, unless the firm undertakes more restructurings. The other liabilities may also be reserves for damages for which the company is liable, such as accidents or environmental liabilities. Use your best judgement in forecasting these items. When in doubt, use the percentage-of-sales method.

Balance Sheet Equity

The number of interest here is the total equity. One usually does not forecast the components (for example, paid-in capital and owner's equity) separately. The forecast equity is the old owner's equity from before plus any increases that occur during the year from net income and new equity sales minus the amounts paid in equity buybacks and cash dividends. The accountants allow some items, such as foreign exchange translation gains, to be entered directly into owner's equity. Since such items are difficult to forecast, one usually forecasts no change in them.

9.2 Using Discount Rates to Obtain Present Values

Having learned how to obtain cash flows from standard accounting items, and how to forecast various accounting statements, it is now time to learn how to discount cash flows to obtain present values. At the beginning of this chapter, we learned that the discount rates used are simply rates of return.

Single-Period Returns and Their Interpretation

Over a single period, a return is simply profit over initial investment. Algebraically, this is

$$r = \frac{P_1 - P_0}{P_0} \tag{9.1a}$$

where

P_1 = date 1 investment value (plus any cash distributed, such as dividends or coupons)
P_0 = date 0 investment value.

Hence an investment of €1 that grows to €1.08 has a rate of return of 0.08 (or 8 per cent) over the period.

There is a close relationship between interest on a bank account and the bank account's rate of return. A bank account that pays 8 per cent interest returns €1 in principal plus €0.08 in interest per euro invested. In short, the investment value grows from €1 to €1.08 over the period. Hence the interest rate paid is another way of expressing the rate of return on the bank account. However, as Chapter 2 noted, interest is not always so highly linked to the rate of return. For example, certain types of traded bond, known as *discount bonds*, pay less in legal interest than their promised rate of return, which is sometimes referred to as their *yield to maturity*. Interest, in this case, is something of a misnomer. The appreciation in the price of the bond is a form of implicit interest that is not counted in the legal calculation of interest.

Equation (9.1a) makes it appear as though prices determine rates of return. Rearranging equation (9.1a), however, implies that:

$$P_0 = \frac{P_1}{1 + r} \tag{9.1b}$$

or

$$P_1 = P_0(1 + r) \tag{9.1c}$$

Equation (9.1b) indicates that the current or *present value* of the investment is determined by the rate of return. Hence, to earn a rate of return of 8 per cent over the period, an investment worth €1.08 at date 1 requires that €1.00 be invested at date 0. Similarly, an investment worth €1 at date 1 requires that €1.00/1.08 (or approximately €0.926) be invested at date 0 to earn the 8 per cent return. This suggests that a rate of return is a discount rate that translates future values into their date 0 equivalents. Equation (9.1c) makes it seem as though the future value of the investment is determined by the rate of return. Of course, all these equations and interpretations of r are correct and state the same thing. Any two of the three variables in equations (9.1) determine the third. Which equation you use depends on which variable you don't know.

Rates of Return in a Multi-Period Setting

Exhibit 9.3 illustrates what happens to an investment of P_0 after t periods if it earns a rate of return of r per period, and all profit (interest) is reinvested.

Exhibit 9.3 indicates that, when r is the interest rate (or rate of return per period) and all interest (profit) is reinvested, an investment of P_0 at date 0 has a *future value* at date t of:

$$P_t = P_0(1 + r)^t \tag{9.2}$$

The date 0 value of an amount P_t, paid at date t, also known as the *present value* or *discounted value*, comes from rearranging this formula, so that P_0 is on the left-hand side: that is,

$$P_0 = \frac{P_t}{(1 + r)^t} \tag{9.3}$$

If r is positive, equation (9.3) states that P_0 is smaller the larger t is, other things being equal. Hence a euro in the future is worth less than a euro today. Cash received early is better than cash received late, because the earlier one receives money, the greater the interest (profit) that can be earned on it.

Equations (9.2) and (9.3) have added a fourth variable, t, to the present value and future value equations. It can be an unknown in a finance problem, too, as the following example illustrates.

Example 9.4

Computing the Time to Double Your Money

How many periods will it take your money to double if the rate of return per period is 4 per cent?

Answer: Using equation (9.2), find the t that solves:

$$2P_0 = P_0(1 + 0.04)^t$$

which is solved by

$$t = \frac{\ln(2)}{\ln(1.04)} = 17.673 \text{ (periods)}$$

Exhibit 9.3 The Value of an Investment over Multiple Periods When Interest (Profit) Is Reinvested

Beginning-of-period date	End-of-period date	Initial principal balance	Interest (profit) earned over period	End-of-period value
0	1	P_0	$P_0 r$	$P_0 + P_0 r = P_0(1 + r)$
1	2	$P_0(1 + r)$	$P_0(1 + r)r$	$P_0(1 + r) + P_0(1 + r)r = P_0(1 + r)^2$
2	3	$P_0(1 + r)^2$	$P_0(1 + r)^2 r$	$P_0(1 + r)^2 + P_0(1 + r)^2 r = P_0(1 + r)^3$
–	–	–	–	–
–	–	–	–	–
–	–	–	–	–
$t - 1$	t	$P_0(1 + r)^{t-1}$	$P_0(1 + r)^{t-1} r$	$P_0(1 + r)^{t-1} + P_0(1 + r)^{t-1} r = P_0(1 + r)^t$

The answer to Example 9.4 is approximated as 70 divided by the percentage rate of interest (4 per cent in this case). This **rule of 70** provides a rough guide to doubling time without the need to compute logarithms. For example, at a 5 per cent rate of return, doubling would occur approximately every 14 periods, because 14 = 70/5. The more precise answer is ln(2)/ln(1.05) = 14.207 periods.

Generalizing the Present Value and Future Value Formulae

The present value and future value formulae generalize to any pair of dates t_1 and t_2 that are t periods apart: that is, $t_2 - t_1 = t$. Equation (9.2) represents the value of the date t_1 cash flow at date t_2, and equation (9.3) represents the value of the date t_2 cash flow at t_1 if the two dates are t periods apart. Hence, if $t_1 = 3$ and $t_2 = 8$, equation (9.2), with $t = 5$, would give the value at date 8 of an investment of P_0 at date 3. In addition, t, t_1 or t_2 need not be whole numbers. In other words, t could be 0.5, 3.8, $\frac{1}{3}$, or even some irrational number such as π. Thus, if $t_1 = 2.6$ and $t_2 = 7.1$, equation (9.3) with $t = 4.5$ (= 7.1 – 2.6) represents the value at date 2.6 of an amount, P_1, paid at date 7.1.

Explicit versus Implicit Interest and Compounding

The discussion for Exhibit 9.3 reads as though we are examining a bank account that earns compound interest. Compound interest rates reflect the interest that is earned on interest. Compound interest arises whenever interest earnings are reinvested in the account to increase the principal balance on which the investor earns future interest. But what about securities that never explicitly pay interest, and thus have no interest or profit to reinvest? We can also use the compound interest formulae to refer to the yield or rate of return of these securities.

To see how to apply these formulae when interest (or profit) cannot be reinvested, consider a zero-coupon bond, which (as Chapter 2 noted) is a bond that promises a single payment (known as its face value) at a future date. With a date 0 price of P_0 and a promise to pay a face value of 100 at date T and nothing prior to date T, the yield (or rate of return) on the bond can still be quoted in compound interest terms. This yield on the bond is the number r that makes

$$100 = P_0(1 + r)^T$$

which implies that

$$r = \left(\frac{100}{P_0}\right)^{\frac{1}{T}} - 1 \tag{9.4}$$

Thus r makes 100 equal to what the initial principal on the bond would turn into by date T if the bond appreciates at a rate of r per period, and if all profits from appreciation are reinvested in the bond itself.[5] Example 9.5 provides a numerical calculation of the yield of a zero-coupon bond.

Example 9.5

Determining the Yield on a Zero-Coupon Bond

Compute the per period yield of a zero-coupon bond with a face value of €100 at date 20 and a current price of €45.

Answer: Using the formula presented in equation (9.4),

$$r = \left(\frac{100}{45}\right)^{\frac{1}{20}} - 1 = 0.040733$$

or about 4.07 per cent per period.

Since a zero-coupon bond never pays interest, and thus provides nothing to reinvest, the process of quoting a compound interest rate for the bond is merely a convention – a different way of expressing its price. As in the case of the one-period investment, quoting a bond's price in terms of either its yield or its actual price is a matter of personal preference. Both, in some sense, are different ways of representing the same thing.

Investing versus Borrowing

Investing and borrowing are two sides of the same coin. For example, when a corporation issues a bond to one of its investors, it is in essence borrowing from that investor. The cash flows to the corporation are identical in magnitude but opposite in sign to those of the investor. The rate of return earned by the investor is viewed as a cost paid by the corporate borrower. Because investing and borrowing are opposite sides of the same transaction, the techniques used to analyse investing can also be used to analyse borrowing. For instance, in Example 9.5, a €45 loan paid back in one lump sum after 20 periods at a rate of interest of 4.0733 per cent per period would require payment of €100. Similarly, if you promise to pay back a loan with a €100 payment 20 periods from now at a loan rate of 4.0733 per cent per period, you are asking to borrow €45 today.

Results

Result 9.4

Let $C_1, C_2, \ldots, C_T$ denote cash flows at dates 1, 2, . . . , T, respectively. The present value of this cash flow stream is

$$\text{PV} = \frac{C_1}{(1+r)^1} + \frac{C_2}{(1+r)^2} + \cdots + \frac{C_T}{(1+r)^T} \tag{9.5}$$

if, for all horizons, the discount rate is r.

[5] While such profits are implicit if the bond is merely held to maturity, it is possible to make them explicit by selling a portion of the bond to realize the profits and then, redundantly, buying back the sold portion of the bond.

Example 9.6

Determining the Present Value of a Cash Flow Stream

Compute the present value of the unlevered cash flows of the MRI of Bayer Healthcare AG, computed in Exhibit 9.1. Recall that these cash flows were €96,000 at the end of each of the first five years and €56,000 at the end of years six to eight. Assume that the discount rate is 10 per cent per year.

Answer: The present value of the unlevered cash flows of the project is

$$PV = \frac{€96{,}000}{1.1} + \frac{€96{,}000}{1.1^2} + \frac{€96{,}000}{1.1^3} + \frac{€96{,}000}{1.1^4} + \frac{€96{,}000}{1.1^5} + \frac{€56{,}000}{1.1^6} + \frac{€56{,}000}{1.1^7} + \frac{€56{,}000}{1.1^8}$$
$$= €450{,}387$$

Value Additivity and Present Values of Cash Flow Streams

Present values (or discounted values), henceforth denoted as PV (rather than P_0), and future values obey the principle of **value additivity:** that is, the present (future) value of many cash flows combined is the sum of their individual present (future) values. This implies that the future value at date t of €14, for example, is the same as the sum of the future values at t of 14 €1 payments, each made at date 0, or $14(1 + r)^t$. Value additivity also implies that one can generalize equation (9.3) to value a stream of cash payments as follows.

Inflation

In the hypothetical example, Bayer Healthcare AG has pre-tax cash flows at €100,000 each year, which do not grow over time (see Exhibit 9.1). In an inflationary economic environment, however, one typically expects both revenues and costs, and thus cash flows, to increase over time. The **nominal discount rates** – that is, the rates obtained from observed rates of appreciation directly – apply to **nominal cash flows**, the observed cash flows, which grow with inflation. However, it is possible to forecast **inflation-adjusted cash flows**, often referred to as **real cash flows**, which take out the component of growth due to inflation.

When inflation-adjusted cash flow forecasts are employed, they need to be discounted at **real discount rates**, which are the nominal discount rates adjusted for appreciation due to inflation. If i is the rate of inflation per period, and $r_{nominal}$ is the appropriate nominal discount rate, the real discount rate per period is:

$$r_{real} = \frac{1 - r_{nominal}}{1 + i} - 1$$

To convert the date t nominal cash flow, C_t, to an inflation-adjusted cash flow, C_t^{IA}, use the formula:

$$C_t^{IA} = \frac{C_t}{(1 + i)^t}$$

The present value of the inflation-adjusted cash flow, using the real rate for discounting back t periods, is:

$$PV = \frac{C_t^{IA}}{(1 + r_{real})^t} = \frac{C_t/(1 + i)^t}{(1 + r_{real})^t} = \frac{C_t}{(1 + r_{nominal})^t}$$

The present value equality implies the following result.

Results

Result 9.5

Discounting nominal cash flows at nominal discount rates or inflation-adjusted cash flows at the appropriately computed real interest rates generates the same present value.

Annuities and Perpetuities

There are several special cases of the present value formula, equation (9.5), described earlier. When $C_1 = C_2 = \ldots C_T = C$, the stream of payments is known as a standard **annuity**. If T is infinite, it is a standard **perpetuity**. Standard annuities and perpetuities have payments that begin at date 1. The present values of standard annuities and perpetuities lend themselves to particularly simple equations. Less standard perpetuities and annuities can have any payment frequency, although it must be regular (for example, every half period).

Many financial securities have patterns to their cash flows that resemble annuities and perpetuities. For example, standard fixed-rate residential mortgages are annuities; straight-coupon bonds are the sum of an annuity and a zero-coupon bond (see Chapter 2). The dividend discount models used to value equity are based on a growing perpetuity formula.

Perpetuities

The algebraic representation of the infinite sum that is the present value of a perpetuity is

$$\text{PV} = \frac{C}{(1+r)} + \frac{C}{(1+r)^2} + \frac{C}{(1+r)^3} + \cdots \tag{9.6a}$$

A simple and easily memorized formula for PV is found by first multiplying both sides of equation (9.6a) by $1/(1 + r)$, which implies that

$$\frac{\text{PV}}{1+r} = \frac{C}{(1+r)^2} + \frac{C}{(1+r)^3} + \cdots \tag{9.6b}$$

Then subtract the corresponding sides of equation (9.6b) from equation (9.6a) to obtain

$$\text{PV} - \frac{\text{PV}}{1+r} = \frac{C}{1+r}$$

which is equivalent to

$$\text{PV} \times \frac{r}{1+r} = \frac{C}{1+r}$$

which simplifies to

$$\text{PV} = \frac{C}{T} \tag{9.7}$$

Results

Result 9.6

If r is the discount rate per period, the present value of a perpetuity with payments of C each period commencing at date 1 is C/r.

The next example illustrates this result.

Example 9.7

The Value of a Perpetuity

In 1752, the British government decided to consolidate all its debt into one perpetuity that paid a $3\frac{1}{2}$ per cent coupon. The bond, which is known as a consol, still exists today, except that its coupon has now changed to $2\frac{1}{2}$ per cent payable. Assuming that the discount rate on the bond is 5 per cent per annum, what is the value of the bond today?

Answer: Using Result 9.6, the value is

$$\text{PV} = £2.50/0.05 = £50$$

A perpetuity with payments of C commencing today is the sum of two types of cash flow: (1) a standard perpetuity, paying C every period beginning with a payment of C at date 1; and (2) a payment of C today. The standard perpetuity in item 1 has a present value of C/r. The payment of C today in item 2 has a present value of C. Add them to get the present value of the combined cash flows: $C + C/r$.

Note that the value for the 'backward-shifted' perpetuity described in the previous paragraph is also equal to $(1 + r)C/r$. This can be interpreted as the date 1 value of a payment of C/r at date 0. It should not be surprising that the date 1 value of a perpetuity that begins at date 1 is the same as the date 0 value of a perpetuity that begins at date 0. If we had begun our analysis with this insight, namely, that

$$\text{PV} \times (1 + r) = \text{PV} + C$$

we could have derived the perpetuity formula in equation (9.7), $\text{PV} = C/r$, by solving the equation immediately above for PV.

Deriving the perpetuity formula in this manner illustrates that value additivity, along with the ability to combine, separate and shift cash flow streams, is often useful for valuation insights. As the previous paragraph demonstrates, to obtain a formula for the present value of a complex cash flow, it is useful to first obtain a present value for a basic type of cash flow stream, and then derive the present value of the more complex cash flow stream from it. The ability to manipulate and match various cash flow streams, in whole or in part, is a basic skill that is valuable for financial analysis.

Example 9.8 illustrates how to apply this skill in valuing a complex perpetuity.

Example 9.8

Computing the Value of a Complex Perpetuity

What is the value of a perpetuity with payments of £2 every half-year commencing one-half-year from now if $r = 10$ per cent per year?

Answer: Examine the cash flows of the pay-offs, outlined in the following table:

Cash flow (in £) at year								
0.5	1	1.5	2	2.5	3	3.5	4	...
2	2	2	2	2	2	2	2	...

This can be viewed as the sum of two perpetuities with annual payments, outlined below:

	Cash flow (in £) at year								
	0.5	1	1.5	2	2.5	3	3.5	4	...
Perpetuity 1	2	0	2	0	2	0	2	0	...
Perpetuity 2	0	2	0	2	0	2	0	2	...

Perpetuity 2 is worth £2/r or £20. The first perpetuity is like the second perpetuity, except that each cash flow occurs one-half period earlier. Let us discount the pay-offs of perpetuity 1 to year 0.5 rather than to year 0. At year 0.5, the value of perpetuity 1 is £2 + £2/r, or £22. Discounting £22 back one half-year earlier, we find that its year 0 value is

$$£20.976 = \frac{£22}{(1.1)^{.5}}$$

Summing the year 0 values of the two perpetuities generates the date 0 value of the original perpetuity with semi-annual payments. This is

$$\frac{£2}{r} + \frac{£2 + 2/r}{(1 + r)^{.5}} = £20 + £20.976$$

The annuity formula derivation in the next subsection also demonstrates how useful it is to be able to manipulate cash flows in creative ways.

Annuities

A standard annuity with payments of C from date 1 to date T has the cash flows outlined in the following table:

Cash flow at date								
1	2	3	...	T	$T+1$	$T+2$	$T+3$	...
C	C	C	...	C	0	0	0	...

A standard annuity can thus be viewed as the difference between two perpetuities. The first perpetuity has cash flows outlined in the table below.

Cash flow at date							
1	2	3	...	$T+1$	$T+2$	$T+3$	...
C	C	C	...	C	0	0	...

The second perpetuity has cash flows that are identical to the first, except that they commence at date $T + 1$: that is, they are represented by:

Cash flow at date								
1	2	3	...	T	$T+1$	$T+2$	$T+3$	...
C	C	C	...	0	C	C	C	...

The first perpetuity has a date 0 value of C/r. The second perpetuity has a date T value of C/r, which implies a date 0 present value of:

$$\frac{C/r}{(1+r)^T}$$

The difference in these two perpetual cash flow streams has the same cash flows as the annuity. Hence the date 0 value of the annuity is the difference in the two date 0 values:

$$PV = \frac{C}{r} - \frac{C/r}{(1+r)^T}$$

This result is summarized as follows.

Results

Result 9.7

If r is the discount rate per period, the present value of an annuity with payments commencing at date 1 and ending at date T is

$$PV = \frac{C}{r}\left[1 - \frac{1}{(1+r)^T}\right] \tag{9.8}$$

Example 9.9

Computing Annuity Payments

Flavio has just borrowed £100,000 from his rich professor to pay for his doctoral studies. He has promised to make payments each year for the next 30 years to his professor at an interest rate of 10 per cent. What are his annual payments?

Answer: The present value of the payments has to equal the amount of the loan, £100,000. If r is 0.10, equation (9.8) indicates that the present value of £1 paid annually for 30 years is £9.427. To obtain a present value equal to £100,000, Flavio must pay:

$$\frac{£100{,}000}{9.427} = £10{,}608$$

at the end of each of the next 30 years.

Growing Perpetuities

A **growing perpetuity** is a perpetual cash flow stream that grows at a constant rate (denoted here as g) over time, as represented in the table below.

Cash flow at date				
1	2	3	4	...
C	$C(1+g)$	$C(1+g)^2$	$C(1+g)^3$	...

If $g < r$, the present value of this sum is finite and given by the formula

$$\text{PV} = \frac{C}{(1+r)} + \frac{C(1+g)}{(1+r)^2} + \frac{C(1+g)^2}{(1+r)^3} + \cdots \tag{9.9a}$$

A simpler formula for this present value is found by first multiplying both sides of equation (9.9a) by $(1+g)/(1+r)$, which yields

$$\text{PV} \times \frac{1+g}{1+r} = \frac{C(1+g)}{(1+r)^2} + \frac{C(1+g)^2}{(1+r)^3} + \cdots \tag{9.10}$$

Then, subtract the corresponding sides of equation (9.9b) from equation (9.9a) to obtain

$$\text{PV} - \frac{\text{PV} \times (1+g)}{1+r} = \frac{C}{1+r}$$

When rearranged, this implies the following result.

Results

Result 9.8

The value of a growing perpetuity with initial payment of an amount C one period from now is

$$\text{PV} = \frac{C}{r-g} \tag{9.11}$$

One of the most interesting applications of equation (9.10) is the valuation of equities. According to the **dividend discount model**, equities can be valued as the discounted value of their future dividend stream. A special case of this model arises when dividends are assumed to be growing at a constant rate, generating a share price per share of:

$$S_0 = \frac{\text{div}_1}{r - g}$$

where div_1 is next year's forecasted dividend per share, r is the discount rate and g is the dividend growth rate.

Example 9.10

Valuing a Share of Equity

Agfa-Gevaert NV (Agfa) is an imaging technology firm that is listed on NYSE Euronext and is a component of the Bel-20 index, an index of the 20 largest Belgian firms. For the last four years, it paid a gross dividend of €0.50 per year. Assume that next year Agfa will pay a dividend of €0.50, and that this will grow thereafter by 7 per cent per annum forever. If the relevant discount rate is 10 per cent, how much should you pay for Agfa stock?

Answer: Using equation (9.11), the share price is

$$\frac{€0.50}{0.10 - 0.07} = €16.67$$

Since no equities pay dividends that grow at a constant rate, the dividend discount formula, as represented in equation (9.11), is not a practical way to value companies. However, that does not by itself invalidate the premise that the fair value of an equity is the discounted value of its future dividend stream. After all, dividends are the only cash flow that the equity produces for its current and future shareholders, and thus represent the only basis on which to establish a fair valuation for the equity. This is true even for firms that do not currently pay dividends. Such no-dividend companies are not worthless – their current no-dividend policy does not imply that the company never will pay dividends. Moreover, the final cash payout to shareholders, whether it comes in the form of a liquidating dividend, or a cash payout by an acquiring firm, or a leveraged buyout, counts as a dividend in this model. Such terminal payouts are virtually impossible to estimate, and they suggest that there are numerous practical impediments to valuing firms with the dividend discount model.

Growing Annuities

A *growing annuity* is identical to a growing perpetuity except that the cash flows terminate at date T. It is possible to derive the present value of this perpetuity from equation (9.11). Applying the reasoning used to derive the annuity formula, we find that a growing annuity is like the difference between two growing perpetuities. One commences at date 1 and has a present value given by equation (9.11). The second perpetuity commences at date $T + 1$ and has a present value equal to:

$$\frac{C(1+g)^T}{(r-g)(1+r)^T}$$

The numerator, $C(1 + g)^T$, is the initial payment of the growing perpetuity, and thus replaces C in the equation. The second term in the denominator, $(1 + r)^T$, would not appear if we were valuing the perpetuity at date T. However, to find its value at date 0, we discount its date T value for an additional T periods. The difference between the date 0 values of the first and second perpetuities is given by

$$\text{PV} = \frac{C}{r-g}\left[1 - \frac{(1+g)^T}{(1+r)^T}\right] \tag{9.12}$$

which is the present value of a T-period growing annuity, with an initial cash flow of C, commencing one period from now and with a growth rate of g. Unlike perpetuities, growing annuities (with finite horizons) need not assume that $g < r$.

Simple Interest

The ability to handle compound interest calculations is essential for most of what we do throughout this text. Simple interest calculations are less important, but they are needed to compute accrued interest on bonds and certain financial contracts such as Eurodollar deposits and savings accounts (see Chapter 2). An investment that pays simple interest at a rate of r per period earns interest of rt at the end of t periods for every dollar invested today.

Time Horizons and Compounding Frequencies

This chapter has developed formulae for present values and future values of cash flows or cash flow streams based on knowing a compound interest rate (or rate of return or yield) per period. The various financial securities, however, define the length of this fundamental period differently. The fundamental time period for residential mortgages, for example, is one month, because mortgage payments are typically made monthly. The fundamental period for government bonds and notes and corporate bonds is six months, which is the length of time between coupon payments.

Annualized Rates

Finance practitioners long ago recognized that it is difficult to understand the relative profitability of two investments, where one investment states the amount of interest earned in one month whereas the other states it over six months. To facilitate such comparisons, interest rates on all investments tend to be quoted on an annualized basis. Thus the quoted rate quoted on a mortgage with monthly payments is 12 times the monthly interest paid per unit of principal. For the government bond with semi-annual coupons, the rate is twice the semi-annual coupon (interest) paid.

The annualization adjustment described is imperfect for making comparisons between investments, since it does not reflect the interest earned on reinvested interest. As a consequence, annualized quoted interest rates with the same r but different compounding frequencies mean different things. To make use of the formulae developed in the previous sections, where r is the interest earned over a single period per unit of cash invested at the beginning of the period, one has to translate the rates that are quoted for financial securities back into rates per period, and properly compute the number of periods over which the future value or present value is taken. Exhibit 9.4 does just this.

Exhibit 9.4 Translating Annualized Interest Rates with Different Compounding Frequencies into Interest Earned per Period

Annualized interest rate quotation basis	Interest per period	Length of a period
Annually compounded	r	1 year
Semi-annually compounded	$\frac{r}{2}$	6 months
Quarterly compounded	$\frac{r}{4}$	3 months
Monthly compounded	$\frac{r}{12}$	1 month
Weekly compounded	$\frac{r}{52}$	1 week
Daily compounded	$\frac{r}{365}$	1 day
Compounded m times a year	$\frac{r}{m}$	$\frac{1}{m}$ years

Equivalent Rates

A proper adjustment would convert each rate to the same compounding frequency. If the annualized interest rates for two investments are each translated into an annually compounded rate, the investment with the higher annually compounded rate is the more profitable investment, other things being equal.

Consider, for example, two 16 per cent rates: one compounded annually and the other semi-annually. A 16 per cent annually compounded rate means that £1.00 invested at the beginning of the year has a value of £1.16 at the end of the year. However, a 16 per cent rate compounded semi-annually becomes, according to the translation in Exhibit 9.4, an 8 per cent rate over a six-month period. At the end of six months, one could reinvest the £1.08 for another six months. With an 8 per cent return over the second six months, the £1.08 would have grown to £1.1664 by the end of the year. This 16.64 per cent rate, the *equivalent annually compounded rate,* would be a more appropriate number to use if comparing this investment with one that uses the annually compounded rate. In general, given the investment with the same interest rate, r, but different compounding frequencies, the more frequent the compounding, the faster the growth rate of the investment.

If the compounding frequency is m times a year and the annualized rate is r, the amount accumulated from an investment of PV after t years is:

$$P_t = \text{PV} \times \left(1 + \frac{r}{m}\right)^{mt} \tag{9.13}$$

Equation (9.13) is another version of equation (9.2), the future value formula, recognizing that the per period interest rate is r/m, and the number of periods in t years is mt.

If there is continuous compounding, so that m becomes infinite, this formula has the limiting value:

$$P_t = \text{PV} \times \text{e}^{rt} \tag{9.14}$$

where e is the base of natural logarithms, approximately 2.718.

Inverting equations (9.13) and (9.14) yields the corresponding present value formulae:

$$\text{PV} = \frac{P_t}{\left(1 + \frac{r}{m}\right)^{mt}} \tag{9.15}$$

$$\text{PV} = P_t \times \text{e}^{-rt} \tag{9.16}$$

To compute the equivalent rate using a different compounding frequency for the same investment, change m and find the new r that generates the same future value P_t in equation (9.15). Example 9.11 illustrates the procedure.

Residential mortgages are annuities based on monthly compounded interest. The monthly payment per £100,000 of a Y-year mortgage with interest rate r is the number x that satisfies the present value equation

$$£100{,}000 = \sum_{t=1}^{12Y} \frac{x}{\left(1 + \frac{r}{12}\right)^{t}}$$

Example 9.12 illustrates how to compute a monthly mortgage payment.

Example 9.11

Finding Equivalent Rates with Different Compounding Frequencies

An investment of £1.00 that grows to £1.10 at the end of one year is said to have a return of 10 per cent, annually compounded. What are the equivalent semi-annual and continuously compounded rates of growth for this investment?

Answer: Its semi-annual compounded rate is approximately 9.76 per cent, and its continuously compounded rate is approximately 9.53 per cent. These are found, respectively, by solving the following equations for r:

$$1.10 = \left(1 + \frac{r}{2}\right)^2$$

and

$$1.10 = \text{e}^{rt}$$

Example 9.12

Computing Monthly Mortgage Payments

Compute the monthly mortgage payment of a 25-year fixed-rate mortgage of £350,000 at 7 per cent.

Answer: The monthly unannualized interest rate is 0.07/12 or 0.0058. Hence the monthly payment x solves

$$£350{,}000 = \sum_{t=1}^{300} \frac{x}{1.0058^t}$$

which, after further simplification using the annuity formula from equation (9.8), gives

$$x = £2{,}464.80$$

Real-World Insights

Sustainability

An issue facing many sustainable investments is that it can take years for them to pay off, making these projects look unviable from a net present value perspective. Take, for example, a recyclable waste management system that takes fifty years to break down garbage or a forest that takes the same amount of time to be ready for harvest. If we use a discount rate of 6 per cent for a one-off cash flow of £10,000,000 fifty years from now, the present value of the project is only £203,212, which means that it would not be worth your while to invest if the initial cost was £1,000,000. Many economists argue that you should use a special low 'social discount rate' to reflect the social desirability of these societally improving investments. So, if we were to use a social discount rate of 1 per cent for the above project, a company could invest up to £6,080,388 in the same project for it to be deemed viable, nearly thirty times more than the initial estimate.

So, is a social discount rate appropriate? There is no consensus on whether firms should use a lower discount rate on long term sustainability projects. On one side, there doesn't seem to be an easy way to justify the cost of projects that have a climate/environment or a very long payback period. For example, how do you value an investment that improves the quality of life for future generations? Should we have a discount rate at all for sustainability projects? The other side of the argument is that a social discount rate is arbitrary and simply used to justify the cost of long-term projects. A more appropriate approach may be to identify all incremental cash flows (including side effects and real options) that may occur over the coming years because of making the decision to invest in a sustainability project.

As you can see, there is no simple answer. Hopefully, in the next edition of this text, we will have a better idea of how to appraise these projects!

9.3 Summary and Conclusions

Discounting simply reflects the time value of money. Investors with capital have investment alternatives that allow their money to appreciate over time. For these investors, €1 today is worth more than €1 in the future, because that euro today can earn a positive return. If you ask these same investors to commit capital to your project, they are going to require a return that is at least as high as they can obtain elsewhere before they commit that capital to you. This required return is the discount rate that we have used throughout this chapter to obtain present values.

The present value obtained with that discount rate represents what investors would be willing to commit to you today in exchange for those future cash flows. They are willing to do this because such an exchange earns these investors the required return that they can obtain elsewhere in the capital markets. In that sense, the present value represents a fair exchange price for the future cash flows that the project offers investors.

The alternatives that investors have to your project are blurred by risk. Generally, the alternatives investors have are many, ranging from bank accounts to mutual funds, to corporate bonds, to equities and bonds and options, each with differing risk–expected return profiles, as Part II of this text aptly pointed out. We have deliberately skirted this issue here, and leave a more adequate treatment of risk to later chapters in Part III. However, that does not obviate the need to offer investors a risk–expected return profile that is at least as good as what is currently available.

Before delving into this issue in more depth, we think it is best to learn the mechanics of obtaining present values. In this chapter, we learned that there were two aspects to this. One is learning how to compute and forecast cash flows from accounting statements. The second involves learning how to apply discount rates to cash flows to obtain present values.

To be skilled at discounting means that one is familiar with a few tricks. For example, we learned that the ability to take cash flows backwards and forwards in time is not tied to our present place in time. The value at year 6 of a cash flow paid at year 10 can sometimes be obtained more easily by placing ourselves at year 10 and going backwards in time four years. The cash received at year 10, discounted back four years, gives the value at year 6. Alternatively, the value at year 6 can sometimes be obtained more easily by discounting the year 10 cash back to year 0 and then figuring out the future value of this number six years in the future.

In combination with the value additivity principle, this ability to translate cash flows from any point in a timeline to any other point in time, in multiple ways, provides a great deal of flexibility in figuring out short and clever ways to value or to project cash flows. In particular, these principles can be applied to value perpetuities and annuities, which are building blocks for many of the types of cash flow stream observed in financial markets.

The principle of value additivity is useful not only for the same reasons but also because the theoretical results developed in modern finance, as well as many of the money-making schemes developed by practitioners, rely so much on this principle. It is closely tied to the no-arbitrage principle, which is one of the cornerstones on which modern finance theory is built, including the theory of valuation, as we shall learn in the next chapter.

Key Concepts

Result 9.1: Under US GAAP: Unlevered cash flow = operating cash inflow
+ investing cash inflow (which is usually negative)
+ debt interest – debt interest tax subsidy

Under IFRS: Unlevered cash flow = net cash flow from operating activities
+ net cash flow from investing activities (which is usually negative)
– debt interest tax subsidy

Result 9.2: Unlevered cash flow = profit before interest and taxes + depreciation and amortization
– change in working capital – capital expenditures
+ sales of capital assets – realized capital gains
+ realized capital losses – profit before interest and taxes × tax rate

Result 9.3: Projects should be valued by analysing their incremental cash flows to a firm.

Result 9.4: Let $C_1, C_2, \ldots, C_T$ denote cash flows at dates 1, 2, . . . , T, respectively. The present value of this cash flow stream is

$$PV = \frac{C_1}{(1+r)^1} + \frac{C_2}{(1+r)^2} + \cdots + \frac{C_T}{(1+r)^T}$$

if, for all horizons, the discount rate is r.

Result 9.5: Discounting nominal cash flows at nominal discount rates or inflation-adjusted cash flows at the appropriately computed real interest rates generates the same present value.

Result 9.6: If r is the discount rate per period, the present value of a perpetuity with payments of C each period commencing at date 1 is C/r.

Result 9.7: If r is the discount rate per period, the present value of an annuity with payments commencing at date 1 and ending at date T is

$$PV = \frac{C}{r}\left[1 - \frac{1}{(1+r)^T}\right]$$

Result 9.8: The value of a growing perpetuity with initial payment of an amount C one period from now is

$$PV = \frac{C}{t - g}$$

Key Terms

accounting cash flow 279
annuity 292
cash flow 278
discount rate 278
dividend discount model 296
earnings before interest and taxes (EBIT) 279
earnings before interest, taxes, depreciation and amortization (EBITDA) 279
earnings before taxes 285
financing cash flow 279
growing perpetuity 295
incremental cash flow 283
inflation-adjusted cash flow 291
nominal cash flow 291
nominal discount rate 291
perpetuity 292
present value (PV) 278
real cash flow 291
real discount rate 291
real investment 277
rule of 70 289
unlevered cash flow 279
value additivity 291

Exercises

9.1 Let PV be the present value of a growing perpetuity (the 'time 1 perpetuity') with an initial payment of C beginning one period from now and a growth rate of g. If we move all the cash flows back in time one period, the present value becomes PV × $(1 + r)$. Note that this is the present value of a growing perpetuity with an initial payment of C beginning today (the 'time 0 perpetuity').

a How do the cash flows of the time 1 perpetuity compare with those of the time 0 perpetuity from time 1 on?

b How do the present values of the cash flows discussed in part *a* compare with each other?

c How do the cash flows (and present values) for the two perpetuities described in part *a* compare?

d Write out a different value for the present value of the time 0 perpetuity in relation to the value of the time 1 perpetuity, based on your analysis in parts *b* and *c*.

e Solve for PV from the equation:

$$PV \times (1 + r) = \text{value from part } d$$

9.2 How long will it take your money to double at an annualized interest rate of 8 per cent compounded semi-annually? How does your answer change if the interest rate is compounded annually?

9.3 A 25-year fixed-rate mortgage has monthly payments of £717 per month and a mortgage interest rate of 6.14 per cent per year compounded monthly. If a buyer purchases a home with the cash proceeds of the mortgage loan plus an additional 20 per cent deposit, what is the purchase price of the home?

9.4 What is the annualized interest rate, compounded daily, that is equivalent to 10 per cent interest compounded semi-annually? What is the daily compounded rate that is equivalent to 10 per cent compounded continuously?

9.5 A woman who has just turned 24 wants to save for her retirement through a defined benefit employee pension scheme. She plans to retire on her 60th birthday and wants a monthly income, beginning the month after her 60th birthday, of £2,000 (after taxes) until she dies.

- She has budgeted conservatively, assuming that she will die at age 85.
- Assume that, until she reaches age 60, the pension scheme earns 8 per cent interest, compounded annually, which accumulates tax free.
- At age 60, assume that the interest accumulated in the pension pays a lump sum taxed at a rate of 30 per cent.
- Thereafter, assume that the investor is in a 0 per cent tax bracket and that the interest on her account earns 7 per cent interest, compounded monthly.

How much should the investor deposit annually in her pension, beginning on her 24th birthday and ending on her 60th birthday, to finance her retirement?

9.6 If r is the annually compounded interest rate, what is the present value of a deferred perpetuity with annual payments of C beginning t years from now?

9.7 An investor is comparing a 25-year fixed-rate mortgage with a 15-year fixed-rate mortgage. The 15-year mortgage has a considerably lower interest rate. If the annualized interest rate on the 25-year mortgage is 8 per cent, compounded monthly, what rate, compounded monthly on the 15-year mortgage, offers the same monthly payments?

9.8 Graph the relationship between the annually compounded interest rate and the present value of a zero-coupon bond paying €100 five years from today. Graph the relationship between present value and years to maturity of a zero-coupon bond with an interest rate of 8 per cent compounded annually.

9.9 The value of a share of stock is the present value of its future dividends. If the next dividend, occurring one year from now, is €2 per share, and dividends, paid annually, are expected to grow at 3 per cent per year, what is the value of a share of stock if the discount rate is 7 per cent?

9.10 A 24-year-old employee, who expected to work another 41 years, is injured in a plant accident and will never work again. His wages next year will be €40,000. A study of wages across the plant found that every additional year of seniority tends to add 1 per cent to the wages of a worker, other things held constant. Assuming a nominal discount rate of 10 per cent and an expected rate of inflation of 4 per cent per year over the next 40 years, what lump sum compensation should this worker receive for the lost wages due to the injury?

9.11 Iain invests £1,000 in a simple interest account. Thirty months later, he finds the account has accumulated to £1,212.50.

a Compute the annualized simple interest rate.

b Compute the equivalent annualized rate compounded (1) annually, (2) semi-annually, (3) quarterly, (4) monthly, and (5) continuously.

c Which rate in part *b* is largest? Why?

9.12 A nine-month T-bill with a face value of €100 currently sells for €96. Calculate the annualized simple interest rate.

9.13 Which of the following rates would you prefer: 8.50 per cent compounded annually, 8.33 per cent compounded semi-annually, 8.25 per cent compounded quarterly, or 8.16 per cent compounded continuously? Why?

9.14 The treasurer of Small Corp. is considering the purchase of a T-bill maturing in seven months. At a rate of 9 per cent compounded annually:

a Calculate the present value of the $10,000 face value T-bill.

b If you wanted to purchase a seven-month T-bill 30 months from now, what amount must you deposit today?

9.15 Helix, a third-year graduate student, is considering a delivery programme for a local grocery store to earn extra money for his studies. His idea is to buy a used car and deliver groceries after university and at weekends. He estimates the following revenues and expenses:

- start-up costs of £1,000 for the car and minor repairs
- weekly revenue of about £150
- ongoing maintenance and fuel costs of about £45 per week
- after nine months, replacement of the brake pads on the car for about £350
- sale of the car at year-end for about £450.

What is the difference between the PV of the venture (assuming a rate of 6 per cent compounded annually) and its start-up costs?

9.16 Consider a prospective project with the following future cash inflows: R9,000 at the end of year 1, R9,500 at the end of 15 months, R10,500 at the end of 30 months and R11,500 at the end of 38 months.

a What is the PV of these cash flows at 7.5 per cent compounded annually?

b How does the PV change if the discount rate is 7.5 per cent compounded semi-annually?

9.17 Suppose the future value of £10,000 today is £13,328, and the interest rate is 9 per cent compounded annually.

a What is the holding period t (in years)?

b How does t change if the interest rate is 9 per cent compounded semi-annually?

c How does t change if the interest rate is 11 per cent compounded annually?

9.18 You have just won the Lottery! As the winner, you have a choice of three pay-off programmes (assume that the interest rate is 9 per cent compounded annually): (1) a lump sum today of £350,000 plus a lump sum ten years from now of £25,000; (2) a 20-year annuity of £42,500 beginning next year; and (3) a £35,000 sum each year beginning next year paid to you and your descendants (assume that your family line will never die out).

a Which choice is the most favourable?

b How would your answer change if the interest rate assumption changes to 10 per cent?

c How would your answer change if the interest rate assumption changes to 11 per cent?

9.19 You need to insure your home over the next 20 years. You can either pay beginning-of-year premiums with today's premium of €5,000 and future premiums growing at 4 per cent per year, or prepay a lump sum of €67,500 for the entire 20 years of coverage.

a With a rate of 9 per cent compounded annually, which of the two choices would you prefer?

b How would your answer change if the rate were 10 per cent compounded annually?

c What is happening to the PV of the annuity as r increases?

9.20 Your rich uncle recently passed away and has left you an inheritance in the form of a varying perpetuity. You will receive £2,000 per year from year 3 to year 14, £5,000 per year from year 15 to year 22, and £3,000 per year thereafter. At a rate of 7 per cent compounded annually, what is the PV at the start of year 1 of your uncle's generosity?

9.21 You have just had a baby boy (congratulations!) and you want to ensure the funding of his college education. Tuition today costs £7,000, and is growing at 4 per cent per year. In 18 years, your son will enter a three-year undergraduate programme with tuition payments at the beginning of each year.

a At the rate of 7 per cent compounded annually, how much must you deposit today just to cover tuition expenses?

b What amount must you save at the end of each year over the next 18 years to cover these expenses?

9.22 Your financial planner has advised you to initiate a retirement account while you are still young. Today is your 35th birthday, and you are planning to retire at age 65. Actuarial tables show that individuals in your age group have a life expectancy of about 75. You want a £50,000 annuity beginning on your 66th birthday, which will grow at a rate of 4 per cent per year for ten years.

a What amount must you deposit at the end of each year through age 65 at a rate of 8 per cent compounded annually to fund your retirement account?

b How would your answer change if the rate is 9 per cent?

c After you have paid your last instalment on your 65th birthday, you learn that medical advances have shifted actuarial tables so that you are now expected to live to age 85. Determine the base-year annuity payment supportable under the 4 per cent growth plan with a 9 per cent interest rate.

9.23 You are considering a new business venture, and want to determine the present value of seasonal cash flows. Historical data suggest that quarterly flows will be €3,000 in quarter 1, €4,000 in quarter 2, €5,000 in quarter 3, and €6,000 in quarter 4. The annualized rate is 10 per cent, compounded annually.

a What is the PV if this quarterly pattern will continue into the future (that is, for ever)?

b How would your answer change if same quarter growth is 1 per cent per year in perpetuity?

c How would your answer change if this 1 per cent growth lasts only 10 years?

9.24 Assume that a homeowner takes on a 30-year, £100,000 floating-rate mortgage with monthly payments. Assume that the floating rate is 7.0 per cent at the initiation of the mortgage, 7.125 per cent is the reset rate at the end of the first month, and 7.25 per cent is the reset rate at the end of the second month. What are the first, second and third mortgage payments, respectively, made at the end of the first, second and third months? What is the breakdown between principal and interest for each of the first three payments? What is the principal balance at the end of the first, second and third months?

9.25 The Allied Corporation typically allocates expenses for CEO pay to each of its existing projects, with the percentage allocation based on the percentage of book assets that each project represents. Super-secret Project X, under consideration, will, if adopted, constitute 10 per cent of the company's book assets. As the CEO's salary amounts to £1 million per year, super-secret Project X will be allocated £100,000 in expenses. Does this £100,000 represent a reduction in the unlevered cash flows generated by your secret Project X?

9.26 Assume that the analyst who developed Exhibit 9.1 simply forgot about inflation. Redo Exhibit 9.1 assuming 2 per cent inflation per year and 2 per cent growth due to inflation in EBITDA, in column (c). Show how columns (a)–(g) change, and explain why column (b) does not change.

9.27 Find the present value of the MRI's unlevered cash flows for the revised exhibit you constructed in exercise 9.26. Assume a discount rate of 10 per cent.

9.28 Using the assumptions of exercise 9.26, provide inflation-adjusted figures for Exhibit 9.1.

a Compute the real discount rate if the nominal discount rate is 10 per cent.

b Discount the inflation-adjusted unlevered cash flows of the MRI at the real discount rate to obtain their present value.

9.29 Compute TomTom's unlevered cash flow from its most recent financial statements. TomTom is a Dutch manufacturer of satellite navigation systems (www.tomtom.com).

References and Additional Reading

Graham, J. and Harvey, C.R. (2001) The theory and practice of corporate finance: evidence from the field, *Journal of Financial Economics*, 60(2–3): 187–243.

Ross, S., Westerfield, R. and Jordan, B. (1998) *Fundamentals of Corporate Finance*, 4th edn, Burr Ridge, IL: Irwin/McGraw-Hill.

Chapter 10

Investing in Risk-Free Projects

Learning Objectives

After reading this chapter, you should be able to:

- Comprehend why sunk costs do not affect the incremental cash flows for projects.
- Apply the net present value (NPV) criterion to evaluate riskless projects, both when there are no constraints and when there are constraints that make projects mutually exclusive.
- Understand how value additivity relates to the proper application of NPV for project evaluation when projects are mutually exclusive.
- Understand the concept of Economic Value Added (EVA), and the relation between EVA and the NPV criterion.
- Compute hurdle rates for the internal rate of return (IRR) criterion when bond interest rates vary according to bond maturity.
- Apply the IRR criterion to evaluate projects, and be able to distinguish cases for which it is possible to obtain appropriate evaluations with the IRR criterion from those that preclude proper IRR-based evaluations.

A *Fortune* magazine cover story, 'The real key to creating wealth', discusses a technique known as Economic Value Added (or EVA™). 'Managers who run their businesses according to EVA have hugely increased the value of their companies,' the article reports. Companies that have benefited from EVA include CSX, Briggs & Stratton and Coca-Cola, all of which have witnessed dramatic increases in their stock prices since the adoption of EVA.

Source: Fortune, 20 September 1993

Real investments range in magnitude from the very small to the very large. A relatively small investment might be the addition of a kitchen in the office of a corporation in order to decrease ongoing catering expenses. A major investment decision would be Fiat's launching of a new division to build a new line of automobiles.

Of course, corporations think quite differently about adding a kitchen than they do about launching a division. There are no strategic implications associated with adding the kitchen, and while uncertainty is associated with the future savings on catering bills, that uncertainty can be safely ignored in most cases. However, the risks and strategic implications linked to launching a division are considerable: thus major projects need to be evaluated with more sophisticated valuation procedures[1] that properly account for the effect of uncertainty on the project's value.

To be able to evaluate major strategic investments, the manager first needs to master the basic tools of project evaluation. Skill at using these tools comes from learning how to evaluate the more mundane projects, such as the kitchen, where the uncertainty about the project's future cash flows can be safely ignored without catastrophic consequences if this oversight leads to an incorrect decision. Later chapters in Part III develop the more sophisticated methods for evaluating strategic investments under uncertainty.

How can a manager determine whether adopting a project creates value for the company's shareholders? For riskless cash flows, this is quite straightforward. The manager simply examines whether the investment project offers an arbitrage opportunity. In essence, the **net present value (NPV) criterion**, our preferred evaluation technique, measures the arbitrage profits associated with an investment project, and recommends projects for which arbitrage profits are positive. A riskless project has future cash flows that are perfectly tracked by a portfolio of riskless bonds of various maturities. Hence arbitrage profits can be created whenever the project's start-up cost is less than the cost of acquiring the tracking portfolio of riskless bonds.

This chapter focuses on riskless cash flows exclusively, because they illustrate some of the same basic principles required for valuing risky cash flows, while keeping the analysis simple. After developing a consistent intuition for real asset valuation, this chapter focuses on complex problems in valuation that arise because of the multi-period nature of cash flows. One problem arises when discount rates vary with the date of cash flow payment.[2] Another problem is the effect of a variety of constraints, such as limited capital and **mutually exclusive projects** (which occur whenever taking one project excludes the possibility of taking any of the other projects).

One of the insights in this chapter is that, with riskless cash flows, the net present value method is equivalent to the **discounted cash flow (DCF) method**, which obtains the NPV by discounting *all* cash flows at the rate(s) of return prevalent in the securities markets and adding the discounted cash flows together.

The NPV/DCF method has been around for a long time. Under sexier names, however, it seems to be rediscovered periodically. One version is **Economic Value Added (EVA™)**, described in the opening vignette, which is a trademarked product marketed by the consulting firm Stern Stewart & Company. EVA is a measure of a company's true economic profitability. Consulting firms such as McKinsey and the Boston Consulting Group have similar products that also are being implemented by a vast number of companies, apparently with substantial success.[3] Part of the success of EVA is due to its use as a tool for managerial performance evaluation.[4] However, an additional benefit is that EVA steers managers away from some of the less appropriate methods of evaluating real investments and towards the adoption of projects with positive NPVs.

10.1 Cash Flows

The most important inputs for evaluating a real investment are the incremental cash flows that can be attributed to the investment. Chapter 9 discussed these in detail. The critical lesson learned is to use incremental cash flows: the firm's cash flows with the investment project less its cash flows without the project. Such a view

---

[1] **Capital budgeting** procedures, as these valuation procedures are sometimes called, are the decision-making rules used to evaluate real investments. The name derives from the fact that each project adopted by a firm requires that some *capital* be assigned or *budgeted* to the project.

[2] The **term structure of interest rates** – also known as the **yield curve** – is the pattern of yields on riskless bonds, based on their maturity. The term structure is 'flat' when riskless bonds of all maturities have the same yield to maturity. See the appendix to this chapter for further discussion.

[3] McKinsey calls its measure *Economic Profits,* and BCG employs three measures, which it calls *Cash Value Added (CVA), Cash Flow Return on Investment (CFROI)* and *Total Shareholder Return* or *Total Business Return* (*TSR* or *TBR*). The methods can differ in the way in which they calculate cash flows, as well as in how the cost of capital is calculated.

[4] See Chapter 18.

of a project's cash flows necessarily excludes sunk costs (sunk costs are incurred whether or not the project is adopted). It also allows for synergies and other interactions between a new project and the firm's existing projects. These additional cash flows need to be accounted for when one values a project.[5]

10.2 Net Present Value

The **net present value (NPV)** of an investment project is the difference between the project's *present value* (*PV*), the value of a portfolio of financial instruments that track the project's future cash flows, and the cost of implementing the project. Projects that create value are those whose PVs exceed their costs, and thus represent situations where a future cash flow pattern can be produced more cheaply, internally, within the firm, than externally, by investing in financial assets. These are called *positive NPV* investments.

In some cases, such as those associated with riskless projects discussed in this chapter, the tracking portfolio will perfectly track the future cash flows of the project. When perfect tracking is possible, the value created by real asset investment is a pure arbitrage gain achievable by taking the project along with an associated short position in the tracking portfolio. Since shorting the project's tracking portfolio from the financial markets offsets the project's future cash flows, a comparison between the date 0 cash flows of the project and the tracking portfolio is the only determinant of arbitrage. Value is created if there is arbitrage, as indicated by a positive NPV, and value is destroyed if there is a negative NPV.[6] The financial assets in the tracking portfolio are thus the zero point on the NPV measuring stick, as the real assets are always measured in relation to them.

The perspective we provide here on the valuation of real assets is one that allows corporations to create value for their shareholders by generating arbitrage opportunities between the markets for *real assets* and *financial assets*. In other words, by making all financial assets zero-NPV investments we are implicitly assuming that it is impossible to make money, for example, by buying BP shares and short-selling Vodafone shares. However, Vodafone may be able to make money by investing in a new operating system and financing it by selling its own equity. In an informationally efficient financial market (defined in Chapter 3), financial securities are always fairly priced – but bargains can and do exist in the market for real assets, even when the financial markets are informationally efficient. Because of its special abilities or circumstances, Vodafone can develop and market a new operating system better than its competitors and, as a result, can create value for its shareholders.

Discounted Cash Flow and Net Present Value

When the cash flows of a project are riskless, they can be tracked perfectly with a combination of default-free bonds. For convenience, this chapter uses zero-coupon bonds, which are bonds that pay cash only at their maturity dates (see Chapter 2) as the securities in the tracking portfolio. This subsection shows that the NPV is the same as the discounted value of the project's cash flows.[7] The discount rates are the yields to maturity of these zero-coupon bonds.

Yield to Maturity of a Zero-Coupon Bond: The Discount Rate[8]

The per-period *yield to maturity* of a zero-coupon bond is the discount rate (compounded once per period) that makes the discounted value of its face amount (the bond's payment on its maturity date) equal to the current market price of the bond: that is, the r_t that makes

$$P = \frac{\text{FV}}{(1 + r_t)^t}$$

[5] One cannot ignore project financing when considering the possibility that the firm can create value from its financing decisions by altering the firm's tax liabilities. For this reason, Chapter 13, which focuses on taxes and valuation, considers both cash flows and the tax effect of the financing cash flows.

[6] This is true even if financial assets are not fairly valued: that is, even if the financial markets are not informationally efficient.

[7] Although this is also true for risky cash flows, in many of these cases we would not discount cash flows to compute the NPV of a risky cash flow stream. See Chapter 12 for further detail.

[8] See Chapter 2 for more on yield to maturity.

where

P = current bond price per £1 payment at maturity

t = number of periods to the maturity date of the bond

FV = face value of the bond to be paid at the maturity date.

When markets are frictionless, a concept defined in Chapter 5, and if there is no arbitrage, the yields to maturity of all zero-coupon bonds of a given maturity are the same.

A Formula for the Discounted Cash Flow

We now formally define the discounted cash flow (DCF) of a riskless project. A project has riskless cash flows:

$$C_0, C_1, C_2, \ldots, C_T$$

where

C_t = the (positive or negative) cash flow at date t. Positive numbers represent *cash inflows* (for example, when a sale is made) and negative numbers represent *cash outflows* (for example, when salaries are paid), which are positive costs.

The **discounted cash flow** of the project is

$$\text{DCF} = C_0 + \frac{C_1}{1 + r_1} + \frac{C_2}{(1 + r_2)^2} + \cdots + \frac{C_T}{(1 + r_T)^T} \tag{10.1}$$

where

r_t = the per-period yield to maturity of a default-free zero-coupon bond maturing at date t.

A project's DCF is the sum of all of the discounted future cash flows plus today's cash flow, which is usually negative, since it represents the initial expenditure needed to start the project. The 'discounted *future* cash flow stream', equation (10.1) with C_0 omitted on the right-hand side, is often used inter-changeably with the term 'present value of the project's future cash flows' or simply 'project present value'. Similarly, the sum of the present value of the future cash flows plus today's cash flow, referred to as 'the net present value of the project', is then used interchangeably with the term 'discounted cash flow stream'.

Using Different Discount Rates at Different Maturities

Many formulae compute PVs (and NPVs) using the same discount rate for cash flows that occur at different times. This simplification makes many formulae appear elegant and simple. However, if default-free bond yields vary as the maturity of the bond changes, the correct approach must use discount rates that vary depending on the timing of the cash flows. These discount rates, often referred to as the **costs of capital** (or costs of financing), are the yields to maturity of default-free zero-coupon bonds.

Project Evaluation with the Net Present Value Rule

This subsection shows why the NPV rule, 'adopt the project when NPV is positive', is sensible. Below, we show that the NPV rule is consistent with the creation of wealth through arbitrage.

Arbitrage and NPV

Adopting a project at a cost less than the PV of its future cash flows (that is, positive NPV) means that financing the project by short-selling this tracking portfolio leaves surplus cash in the firm today. Since the future cash that needs to be paid out on the shorted tracking portfolio matches the cash flows coming in from the project, the firm that adopts the positive-NPV project creates wealth risklessly. In short, adopting a riskless project with a positive NPV and financing it in this manner is an arbitrage opportunity for the firm.

Hence, when there are no project selection constraints, NPV offers a simple and correct procedure for evaluating real investments:

Results

Result 10.1

The wealth-maximizing NPV criterion is that:

- All projects with positive NPVs should be accepted.
- All projects with negative NPVs should be rejected.

The Relation between Arbitrage, NPV and DCF

Below, we use a riskless project tracked by a portfolio of zero-coupon bonds to illustrate the relationship between NPV and arbitrage. This illustration points out – at least for riskless projects – that NPV and DCF are the same. Begin by looking at a project with cash flows at two dates, 0 (today) and 1 (one period from now). The algebraic representation of the cash flows of such a project is given in the first row below the following timeline:

	Cash flows at date	
	0	1
Algebra	C_0	C_1
Numbers	–£10 million	£12 million

The second row of the timeline is a numerical example of the cash flows at the same two dates. Inspection of the timeline suggests that default-free zero-coupon bonds, maturing at date 1, with aggregated promised date 1 payments of C_1 (£12 million), perfectly track the *future* cash flows of this project. Let

P = the current market value of these tracking bonds = $C_1/(1 + r)$, where

r = yield to maturity of these tracking bonds (an equivalent way of expressing each bond's price) = $(C_1/P) - 1$.

For example, if each zero-coupon bond is selling for £0.93 per £1.00 of face value, then P = £0.93 and r = 7.5 per cent (approximately). Since, by the definition of the yield to maturity, $P = 1/(1 + r)$, the issuance of these tracking bonds, in a face amount of C_1, results in a date 0 cash flow of

$$P = C_1/(1 + r), \text{ or numerically } £12 \text{ million}/1.075$$

and a cash flow of $-C_1$, or –£12 million, at date 1.

Hence a firm that adopts the project and issues C_1 (£12 million) in face value of these bonds has cash flows at dates 0 and 1 summarized by the timeline below.

	Cash flows at date	
	0	1
Algebra	$C_0+C_1/(1+r)$	0
Numbers	$-£10 \text{ million} + \dfrac{£12 \text{ million}}{1.075}$	

Since the date 1 cash flow from the combination of project adoption and zero-coupon bond financing is zero, the firm achieves arbitrage if $C_0 + C_1/(1 + r)$, the value under date 0, is positive, which is the case here.

The algebraic symbol or number under date 0 above, the project's NPV, is the sum of the DCFs of the project, including the (undiscounted) cash flow at date 0. It also represents the difference between the cost of buying the tracking investment for the project's *future* cash flows, $C_1/(1 + r)$ (or £12,000,000/1.075), and the cost of initiating the project, $-C_0$ (£10 million). If this difference, $C_0 + C_1/(1 + r)$ (or −£10 million + 12 million/1.075), is positive, the future cash flows of the project can be generated more cheaply by adopting the project (at a cost of $-C_0$) than by investing in the project's tracking investment at a cost of $C_1/(1 + r)$. Example 10.1 extends this idea to multiple periods.

Example 10.1

The Relationship between Arbitrage and NPV

Consider the cash flows below.

Cash flows (in £ millions) at date			
0	1	2	3
−20	40	−10	30

Explain how to finance the project so that the combined future cash flows from the project and its financing are zero. What determines whether this is a good or a bad project?

Answer: The cash flows from the project at dates 1, 2 and 3 can be offset by:

- issuing – that is, selling – short, zero-coupon bonds maturing at date 1 with a face value of £40 million
- purchasing zero-coupon bonds maturing at date 2 with a face value of £10 million
- short-selling zero-coupon bonds maturing at date 3 with a face value of £30 million.

The cash flows from this bond portfolio in combination with the project are shown below.

Cash flows at date			
0	1	2	3
V	0	0	0

where V represents the cost of the tracking portfolio less the £20 million initial cost of the project, and thus is the project's NPV. Clearly, if V is positive, the project is good because it represents an arbitrage opportunity. If V is negative, it represents a bad project.

All riskless projects can have their future cash flows tracked with a portfolio of zero-coupon bonds. Shorting the tracking portfolio thus offsets the future cash flows of the project. To see this, let $C_1, C_2, \ldots, C_T$ denote the project's cash flows at dates 1, 2, . . . , T, respectively. A short position in a zero-coupon bond maturing at date 1 with a face value of C_1 offsets the first cash flow; shorting a zero-coupon bond with a face value of C_2 paid at date 2 offsets the second cash flow; and so forth. A portfolio that is short by these amounts creates a cash flow pattern similar to that in Example 10.1, with zero cash flows at future dates and, possibly, a non-zero cash flow at date 0.

The logic of the NPV criterion for riskless projects and the equivalence between NPV and DCF follows immediately. Result 10.2 summarizes our discussion of this issue.

Results

Result 10.2

For a project with riskless cash flows, the NPV – that is, the market value of the project's tracking portfolio less the cost of initiating the project – is the same as the discounted value of all present and future cash flows of the project.

Financing Versus Tracking the Real Asset's Cash Flows

With frictionless markets, a firm can in fact realize arbitrage profits if it finances a positive-NPV real asset by issuing the securities that track its cash flow. However, our analysis does not require the firm to finance the project in this way. In Chapter 14, we show that, with frictionless markets, if the cash flow pattern is unaffected, the financing choice does not affect values.

Present Values and Net Present Values Have the Value Additivity Property

A consequence of no arbitrage is that two future cash flow streams, when combined, have a value that is the sum of the PVs of the separate cash flow streams. An arbitrage opportunity exists when an investor can purchase two cash flow streams separately, put them together, and sell the combined cash flow stream for more than the sum of the purchase prices of each of them. Arbitrage is also achieved if it is possible to purchase a cash flow stream and break it up into two or more cash flow streams (as in equity carve-outs), and to sell them for more than the original purchase price. Chapter 9 noted that the PV from combining two (or more) cash flow streams is the sum of the PVs of each cash flow stream. In this section, we are learning that this *value additivity* property is closely linked to the principle of no arbitrage.

The NPV, which, as seen earlier, is also so closely linked to the principle of no arbitrage in financial markets, possesses the value additivity property. NPV value additivity is apparent from the DCF formula, equation (10.1). If project A has cash flows $C_{A0}, C_{A1}, \ldots, C_{AT}$ and project B has cash flows $C_{B0}, C_{B1}, \ldots, C_{BT}$, then, because cash flows appear only in the numerator terms of equation (10.1), NPV$(C_{A0} + C_{B0}, C_{A1} + C_{B1}, \ldots, C_{AT} + C_{BT})$ is the sum of NPV$(C_{A0}, C_{A1}, \ldots C_{AT})$ and NPV$(C_{B0}, C_{B1}, \ldots C_{BT})$.

Implications of Value Additivity for Project Adoption and Cancellation

Value additivity implies that the value of a firm after project adoption is the PV of the firm's cash flows from existing projects, plus cash for future investment, plus the NPV of the adopted project's cash flows. (If one is careful to define the cash flows of the project as incremental cash flows, this is true even when synergies exist between the firm's current projects and the new project.) Value additivity also works in reverse. Thus, if the NPV of a project is negative, a firm that has just adopted the project would find that its incremental cash flow pattern for cancelling the project and acquiring the tracking bonds is the stream given in the table below, which has a positive value under date 0.

Cash flows at date	
0	1
$-C_0 - \frac{C_1}{1+r}$	0

This table demonstrates that a negative NPV for adoption of the project implies a positive NPV for cancelling the project, once adopted, and vice versa.

Implications of Value Additivity When Evaluating Mutually Exclusive Projects

The value additivity property makes it easy to understand how to properly select the best project from among a group of projects that are mutually exclusive. For example, a firm may choose to configure a manufacturing plant to produce either tractors or trucks, but it cannot use the plant for both. Value additivity implies that the best of these mutually exclusive projects is the one with the largest positive NPV.

Results

Result 10.3

The wealth-maximizing NPV criterion is that:

Given a set of investment projects, each with positive NPV, one should select the project with the largest positive NPV if allowed to adopt only one of the projects.

One way to understand this is to recognize that adopting the project with the cash flows that have the largest NPV generates the largest net present value of the firm's aggregated cash flows. This is because value additivity implies that the NPV of the firm, a collection of projects, is the sum of the NPV of the firm without the adoption of any of the proposed projects plus the NPV of the incremental cash flows of whichever project is adopted.

Another way to understand that the project with the largest NPV is the best is that the cost of adopting one of two mutually exclusive projects, each with positive NPV, is the forgone cash flows of the other project, not a zero-NPV investment in the financial markets. Recall that the concept of incremental cash flows compares the cash flows of the firm with the project with the cash flows of the firm without the project. With mutual exclusivity, not adopting a particular project means that the firm adopts its next-best alternative project, provided that the latter has positive NPV. Thus the true incremental cash flows of a particular project are the difference between the cash flows of the project and those of the forgone alternative. By value additivity, or more precisely 'subtractivity', the NPV of this differenced cash flow stream is the difference between the NPVs of the two projects. Example 10.2 illustrates this point.

Example 10.2

Mutually Exclusive Projects and NPV

The law firm of Jacob & Meyer is small, and has the resources to take on only one of four cases. The cash flows for each of the four legal projects and their NPVs discounted at the rate of 10 per cent per period are given below.

Which is the best project?

	Cash flows (in £000s) at date			NPV (in £000s)
	0	1	2	
Project A	−7	11	12.1	13
Project B	−1	22	−12.1	9
Project C	−5	44	−24.2	15
Project D	−1	11	0	9

Answer: These cash flows are calculated as the cash flows of the firm with the project less the cash flows of the firm without any of the four projects. Clearly, project C has the highest NPV and should be adopted.

It is possible to calculate the cash flows differently. With mutual exclusivity, the cost of adopting one of the projects is the loss of the others. Hence computation of the cash flows relative to the best alternative should provide an equally valid calculation. The best alternative to projects A, B and D is project C. The best alternative to project C is project A. The appropriate cash flow calculation subtracts the cash flows of the best alternative, and is described with the *pairwise project comparisons* below.

	Cash flows (in £000s) at date			NPV (in £000s)
	0	1	2	
Project A (less C)	−2	−33	36.3	−2
Project B (less C)	4	−22	12.1	−6
Project C (less A)	2	33	−36.3	2
Project D (less C)	4	−33	24.2	−6

Only project C has a positive NPV. Thus selecting the project with the largest positive NPV, as in the first set of NPV calculations, is equivalent to picking the only positive-NPV project, when cash flows are computed relative to the best alternative.

We have assumed here that mutual exclusivity implies that only one project can be selected. Example 10.3 discusses how we might generalize this.

Example 10.3

Ranking Projects

Suppose that it is possible to adopt any two of the four positive NPV projects from Example 10.2. Which two should be selected?

Answer: Projects A and C have the two largest positive NPVs and thus should be adopted.

Using NPV with Capital Constraints

The last subsection considered the possibility of having mutually exclusive projects because of physical constraints. Among those was the possibility that some important input was in short supply, perhaps land available for building a manufacturing facility, or managerial time.

This subsection considers the possibility that the amount of capital the firm can devote to new investments is limited. For truly riskless projects, these **capital constraints** are unlikely to be important, because it is almost always possible to obtain outside financing for profitable riskless projects. However, the cash flows of most major projects are uncertain, and their probability distributions are difficult to verify, so the availability of outside capital for these projects may be constrained.

Profitability Index

We are concerned here with how a corporation, constrained in its choice because of a limited supply of capital, should allocate the capital that it can raise.[9] Specifically, this subsection introduces an extension of the NPV rule known as the **profitability index**, which is the present value of the project's *future* cash flows divided by $-C_0$, the negative of the initial cash flow, which is the initial cost of the project. In the absence of a capital constraint, the value-maximizing rule with the profitability index is one that adopts projects with a profitability index greater than 1 if C_0 is negative. (If C_0 is positive, a firm should adopt projects with a profitability index of less than 1.) This is simply another form of the NPV rule. For example, with annual cash flows, denote:

$$\text{PV} = \frac{C_1}{1+r_1} + \frac{C_2}{(1+r_2)^2} + \cdots + \frac{C_T}{(1+r_T)^T}$$

The NPV rule says that one should select projects for which

$$C_0 + \text{PV} > 0$$

or, equivalently,

$$\text{PV} > -C_0$$

or

$$\frac{\text{PV}}{-C_0} > 1 \text{ if } C_0 < 0 \text{ and } \frac{\text{PV}}{-C_0} < 1 \text{ if } C_0 > 0$$

The profitability index can be particularly useful if C_0 is negative for all projects under consideration and if there is a capital constraint in the initial period. If the projects under consideration can be scaled up or down to any degree, the project with the largest profitability index exceeding 1 is the best. This point is demonstrated in Example 10.4.

[9] Parts IV and V of the text explain why these capital constraints exist.

Example 10.4

The Profitability Index

There is a capital constraint of £10,000 in the initial period. The two scalable projects available for investment are projects B and C from Example 10.2. The cash flows, NPVs at 10 per cent, and profitability indices are given below.

	Cash flow (in £000s) at date			NPVs (in £000s)	Profitability index
	0	1	2		
Project B	−1	22	−12.1	9	10
Project C	−5	44	−24.2	15	4

Which is the better project?

Answer: Project B is the best, because it gives the biggest 'bang per buck'. For the maximum initial expenditure of £10,000, it is possible to run ten B projects, but only two C projects. The old NPV rule calculation is deceiving here, because it reflects the benefit of adopting only one project. But adopting ten B projects would yield an NPV of £90,000, which exceeds £30,000, the NPV from two C projects. The profitability index reflects this, because it represents the PV of future cash flows per pound invested.

Net Profitability Rate

Perhaps a better representation of the relative profitability of two investments is offered by the **net profitability rate**, where

$$\text{net profitability rate} = (1 + \text{risk-free rate}) \times (\text{profitability index}) - 1$$

If C_0 is negative, the net profitability rate represents the additional value next period of all future cash flows per unit of cash invested in the initial period. It is, in essence, the NPV translated into a rate of return.[10]

Using NPV to Evaluate Projects That Can Be Repeated Over Time

Capital allocation takes place in the presence of many different kinds of constraint, so it is often inappropriate to look at projects in isolation. One type of constraint is a space constraint, which would exist, for example, if there was space for only one piece of equipment on the shopfloor. Here, the mere fact that projects have different lives may affect the choice of project. Longer-lived projects use space, the scarce input, to a greater degree and should be penalized in some fashion. Example 10.5 demonstrates how to solve a capital allocation problem with a space constraint.

Example 10.5 points out the value of being able to repeat a project over time. One makes an appropriate comparison between repeatable mutually exclusive projects only after finding a common date where, after repeating in time, both projects have lived out their full lives. This date is the least common multiple of the terminal dates of the projects under consideration.

Example 10.5

Evaluating Projects with Different Lives

Two types of canning machine, denoted A and B, can be placed only in the same corner of a factory. Machine A, the old technology, has a life of two periods. Machine B costs more to purchase but cans products faster. However, machine B wears out more quickly and has a life of only one period. The delivery

[10] The net profitability rate amortizes the project's net present value over the first period of the project's life. It can be used to make decisions about the economic profitability of both riskless and risky projects.

and set-up of each machine takes place one period after initially paying for it. Immediately upon the set-up of either machine, positive cash flows begin to be produced. The cash flows from each machine and the NPVs of their cash flows at a discount rate of 10 per cent are as follows.

	Cash flow (in £ millions) at date			NPV (in £ millions)
	0	1	2	
Machine A	−0.8	1.1	1.21	1.2
Machine B	−1.9	3.30		1.1

It appears that machine A is a better choice. Is this true?

Answer: A second picture tells a different story.

	Cash flow (in £ millions) at date			NPV (in £ millions)
	0	1	2	
Machine A	−0.8	1.1	1.21	1.2
First machine B	−1.9	3.3		1.1
Second machine B		−1.9	3.30	1.0
Sum of the two B machines	−1.9	1.4	3.30	2.1

Over the life of machine A, one could have adopted machine B, used it to the end of its useful life, purchased a second machine B, and let it live out its useful life as well. In this case, machine B seems to dominate.

Two other approaches can also help in the selection between repeatable, mutually exclusive projects with different lives. One of these approaches repeats the project in time infinitely. It values the project's cash flows as the sum of the PVs of perpetuities. The other approach computes the project's **equivalent annual benefit**: that is, the periodic payment for an annuity that ends at the same date and has the same NPV as the project. The project with the largest equivalent annual benefit is the best project.

At a 10 percent discount rate, the cash flows at dates 0, 1 and 2 of machine A from Example 10.5 (respectively, £0.8 million, £1.1 million and £1.21 million) have the same PV (as cash flows of £0.63 million at date 1 and £0.63 million at date 2). The equivalent annual benefit of machine A is thus £0.63 million. Similarly, the cash flows at dates 0 and 1 of machine B from Example 10.5 (respectively, £1.9 million and £3.3 million) have the same PV as a cash flow of £1.21 million at date 1. The equivalent annual benefit of machine B is thus £1.21 million. Since the equivalent annual benefit of machine B exceeds the equivalent annual benefit of machine A, machine B is the better project, given the factory space constraint described in Example 10.5.

10.3 Economic Value Added (EVA)

This chapter's opening vignette, which described one of the most reprinted articles in the history of *Fortune* magazine, demonstrates that corporations are wild about EVA and the related measures of true Economic Value Added (EVA) profitability introduced by other consulting firms. EVA was originally conceived as an adjustment to accounting earnings that better measures how firms are performing.[11] However, as this section shows, one of the keys to EVA's success is that its implementation provides a system in which managers are encouraged to take on positive-NPV investment projects.

[11] The discussion of the accounting rate of return in Section 10.6 illustrates how accounting earnings can mislead corporate managers.

EVA is simply a way of accounting for the cost of using capital in computing profit. In contrast to accounting earnings, which charge only for the interest paid on debt capital, EVA imposes a charge on both debt and equity capital. Also, while EVA prefers cash flow to accounting earnings, it recognizes that changes in capital affect cash flow. When initiating a project, for example, the project's initial cash flow C_0 is probably negative because of a large capital expenditure on items such as machines, land and a factory. Similarly, at the termination date of a project, the capital is returned to the firm's investors in the form of cash as the depreciated capital assets are sold for their salvage value. This reduction in capital tends to make the terminal cash flow C_T large, even when the project may not be very profitable in its final year. Along the way there also may be additional capital expenditures, sales of capital equipment or reductions in the value of the capital due to economic depreciation. By **economic depreciation**, we mean the reduction in the salvage value of the capital, estimated by what the market is willing to pay for the project's capital assets at the end of a period compared with their value when the project is initiated.

One advantage of accounting earnings over cash flow is that the former tends to smooth out the abrupt changes in cash flow due to changes in capital, and to present a more stable year-to-year picture of operating profitability. Proponents of EVA advocate that the smoothing (or, to use accounting terminology, *amortization*) of capital expenditures over the life of the project can be achieved in a more economically sensible way.

Specifically, EVA attempts to account for the cash flow impact of capital. To understand how EVA is computed, let I_t = the date t book value, adjusted for economic depreciation, of the project's capital assets. (Special cases: at $t = 0$, it is the purchase price; at $t = -1$, the date before the project begins, and at $t = T$, the terminal date at which the assets are sold, $I_t = 0$.)

The date t cash flow, C_t, is broken into the sum of three components:

$I_{t-1} - I_t$ = the reduction in capital from $t - 1$ to t[12]
$I_{t-1}r$ = a fair charge for the use of capital from $t - 1$ to t
EVA_t = a measure of the project's true economic profitability from $t - 1$ to t.

Since EVA_t is defined as whatever is left over after accounting for the first two components, the date t EVA of the cash flow stream is

$$\text{EVA}_t = C_t - (I_{t-1} - I_t) - I_{t-1}r \tag{10.2a}$$

Note that if one groups the I_{t-1} terms in equation (10.2a) together, then

$$\text{EVA}_t = C_t + I_t - I_{t-1}(1 + r) \tag{10.2b}$$

There are two special cases. At beginning date 0 (as capital did not exist prior to date 0), there is no charge for capital. Hence, at date 0, equation (10.2b) states that

$$\text{EVA}_0 = C_0 + I_0$$

At the terminal date T, equation (10.2b) implies that

$$\text{EVA}_T = C_T - I_{T-1}(1 + r)$$

because all the capital is liquidated at the terminal date, which implies that $I_T = 0$.

Now discount the EVA stream from date 0 through to date T, generating

$$\text{Discounted EVA stream} = \text{EVA}_0 + \frac{\text{EVA}_1}{1 + r} + \frac{\text{EVA}_2}{(1 + r)^2} + \cdots + \frac{\text{EVA}_{T-1}}{(1 + r)^{T-1}} + \frac{\text{EVA}_T}{(1 + r)^T}$$

Substituting equation (10.2b) into this formula implies

$$\begin{aligned}\text{Discounted EVA stream} &= C_0 + I_0 + \frac{C_1 + I_1 - I_0(1 + r)}{1 + r} + \frac{C_2 + I_2 - I_1(1 + r)}{(1 + r)^2} + \cdots \\ &\quad + \frac{C_{T-1} + I_{T-1} - I_{T-2}(1 + r)}{(1 + r)^{T-1}} + \frac{C_T - I_{T-1}(1 + r)}{(1 + r)^T} \\ &= C_0 + \frac{C_1}{1 + r} + \frac{C_2}{(1 + r)^2} + \cdots + \frac{C_{T-1}}{(1 + r)^{T-1}} + \frac{C_T}{(1 + r)^T}\end{aligned}$$

[12] Reduction in capital includes the sale of capital assets as well as economic depreciation. Increases in capital arise from capital expenditures and economic appreciation in the salvage value of a capital asset

Because the I_t terms, representing capital, cancel one another in the expression for the discounted EVA stream, the discounted EVA stream is the same as the NPV of the project!

Example 10.6 illustrates this point numerically.

Example 10.6

Computing EVAs

Assume that NASA is allowed to select one of three commercial projects for the next space shuttle mission. Each of these projects has industrial spin-offs that will generate cash for NASA over the next two periods. The cash flows and NPVs of the projects are described below.

	Cash flow (in \$ millions) at date			NPV at 2% (in \$ millions)
	0	1	2	
Project A	−17.0	12	9	3.42
Project B	−16.8	10	11	3.58
Project C	−16.9	11	10	3.50

What are the EVAs and the discounted values of the EVA streams of the three projects? Assume a discount rate of 2 per cent per period and, for simplicity, no changes in capital at date 1. Also assume that the negative cash flow at date 0 is entirely a capital expenditure, implying that $EVA_0 = 0$.

Answer: The EVAs of the three projects occur only at dates 1 and 2. The following table gives the six EVAs and their present values for each project.

	EVA_1 (in \$ millions)	EVA_2 (in \$ millions)	$PV(EVA_1) + PV(EVA_2)$ at 2% (in \$ millions)
Project A	11.660 = 12 − 17.0(0.02)	−8.34 = 9 − 17.0(0.02) − 17.0	3.42
Project B	9.664 = 10 − 16.8(0.02)	−6.14 = 11 − 16.8(0.02) − 16.8	3.58
Project C	10.662 = 11 − 16.9(0.02)	−7.24 = 10 − 16.9(0.02) − 16.9	3.50

Note, as suggested earlier, that the summed discounted values of EVA_1 and EVA_2 for the three projects in Example 10.6 (which assumes $EVA_0 = 0$) are the same as their respective NPVs. Result 10.4 states this formally.

Results

Result 10.4

The discounted value of the stream of EVAs of a project is the same as the NPV of the project.

Real World Insight

Sustainable Value Added

In this section, we considered using the EVA model to estimate the value of an investment. The methodology is flexible enough to extend the concept to other societal objectives, such as climate change and environmental impact. Sustainable Value Added (SVA) is one attempt to modify the EVA model to incorporate these other objectives. In addition to economic value added, there are two main components to any sustainable investment: the sustainability reward from the project and sustainability cost of the project.

Take, for example, the decision to install a new offshore windfarm, A, with improved energy technology that will greatly enhance the energy efficiency of existing models. The offshore windfarm will create value but it will also have environmental impacts tied to where it is placed in relation to the local community, marine life, and economic infrastructure (such as fishing rights). Assume that the value added by the project is €10 billion but the environmental impact has four key components: Climate Change (kg CO_2 eq/kWh), Ecotoxicity (kg 1.4-DB eq/kWh), Urban Land Occupation (m^2a/kWh), Metal Depletion (kg Fe eq/kWh).

For the purposes of this case, we will only consider one dimension, ecotoxicity, but it is straightforward to extend to other factors. Assume that toxicity from the new windfarm will be approximately 2 kg CO_2 eq/kWh. Standard offshore windfarms, B, have less toxicity of 1.6 kg CO_2 eq/kWh but also less value added, €4 billion.

The Sustainable Value Added is calculated as

$$\text{SVA} = \left(\frac{\text{value added}_A}{\text{economic impact}_A} - \frac{\text{value added}_B}{\text{economic impact}_B}\right) \times \text{economic impact}_A$$

And for the new offshore windfarm, the SVA is

$$\text{SVA} = \left(\frac{\text{€10 billion}}{2 \text{ kg } CO_2 \text{ eq/kWh}} - \frac{\text{€4 billion}}{1.6 \text{ kg } CO_2 \text{ eq/kWh}}\right) \times 2 \text{ kg } CO_2 \text{ eq/kWh} = \text{€5 billion}$$

To have a complete view of the sustainability of the project, we would carry out the above exercise for all key environmental measures.

10.4 Using NPV for Other Corporate Decisions

Although the techniques examined in this chapter have typically been applied only to the evaluation of capital investments, the introduction of EVA has had the effect of getting managers to think about other uses for the NPV rule. These could include flexible employment strategies, pricing strategies, product development strategies, and so forth. To illustrate this point, this section considers two examples. The first, Example 10.7, analyses an employment decision.

Example 10.7

Laying off Workers as an Investment Decision

Ace Farm Equipment is currently suffering from a slowdown in sales, and temporary overstaffing.

The company can save €600,000 at the end of each of the next three years if it cuts its workforce by 25 individuals. In four years, however, it expects that its market will improve, and that it will have to hire replacements for the 25 individuals who were laid off. Ace estimates that the cost of hiring and training workers is €100,000 per employee, or €2.5 million for the 25 employees. If the discount rate is 10 per cent per year, should Ace temporarily cut its workforce?

Answer: The incremental cash flows associated with the layoffs are as follows.

Cash flow (in € millions) at end of year			
1	2	3	4
0.6	0.6	0.6	2.5

$$\text{NPV} = -€215 \text{ million} \left(= \frac{€0.6 \text{ million}}{1.1} + \frac{€0.6 \text{ million}}{1.1^2} + \frac{€0.6 \text{ million}}{1.1^3} + \frac{€2.5 \text{ million}}{1.1^4} \right)$$

The negative NPV implies that layoffs destroy shareholder wealth.

Example 10.8 analyses a project pricing decision.

Example 10.8

Cutting Product Price as an Investment Decision

Assume that Local Beers Ltd currently sells about 10,000 cases of beer per month in the UK, which is 15 per cent of the beer market. Management at Local Beers is considering a temporary price cut to attract a larger share of the market. If management chooses to lower beer prices from £4.00 to £3.80 a case, Local Beers will expand its market by 50 per cent. Dr Kaka, the CFO, estimates that the beer costs £3.50 per case, so that the company would be making £5,000 per month with the higher price but only £4,500 per month with the lower price. However, the company plans to stick with the lower price for two years, and then raise the price to £3.90 per case. Management believes that, at this higher price, it still will be able to keep its new customers for the subsequent two years, allowing Local Beers to generate a monthly cash flow of £6,000 per month in years 3 and 4. If the discount rate is 1 per cent per month, should prices be lowered?

Answer: The incremental cash flows are as follows.

Cash flow at the end of month								
1	2	. . .	24	25	26	. . .	48
−£500	−£500	. . .	−£500	£1,000	£1,000	. . .	£1,000

$$\text{NPV} = £6.109 = \frac{-£500}{1.01} + \frac{-£500}{1.01^2} + \cdots + \frac{-£500}{1.01^{24}} + \frac{-€1,000}{1.01^{25}} + \frac{-£1,000}{1.01^{26}} + \cdots + \frac{-£1,000}{1.01^{48}}$$

The positive NPV means that cutting prices is worthwhile.

10.5 Evaluating Real Investments with the Internal Rate of Return

Deriving the NPV with the DCF is the most popular method for evaluating investment projects. Almost as many corporate managers, however, base their real investment decisions on the **internal rate of return (IRR)** of their investments. For this reason, we analyse this approach in depth.

The IRR for a cash flow stream $C_0, C_1, \ldots, C_T$ at dates 0, 1, . . . , T, respectively, is the interest rate y that makes the NPV of a project equal zero: that is, the y that solves:

$$0 = C_0 + \frac{C_1}{1+y} + \frac{C_2}{(1+y)^2} + \cdots + \frac{C_r}{(1+y)^T} \tag{10.3}$$

Since internal rates of return cannot be less than −100 per cent, $1 + y$ is positive.

Intuition for the IRR Method

The **internal rate of return method** for evaluating investment projects compares the IRR of a project with a **hurdle rate** to determine whether the project should be taken. In this chapter, where cash flows are riskless, the hurdle rate is always the risk-free rate of interest. For risky projects, the hurdle rate, which is the project's cost of capital (see Chapter 11), may reflect a risk premium.

Projects have several kinds of cash flow pattern. A **later cash flow stream** starts at date 0 with a negative cash flow and then, at some future date, begins to experience positive cash flows for the remaining life of the project. It has this name because all the positive cash flows of the project come later, after a period when the firm has pumped money into the project. A later cash flow stream can be thought of as the cash flow pattern for investing. When investing, high rates of return are good. Thus a project with a later cash flow stream enables the firm to realize arbitrage profits by taking on the project and shorting the tracking portfolio whenever the project's IRR (its multi-period rate of return) exceeds the appropriate hurdle rate (which is the multi-period rate of return for the tracking portfolio). Projects with internal rates of return less than the hurdle rates have low rates of return, and are rejected.

The reverse cash flow pattern, when all positive cash flows occur first and all negative cash flows occur only after the last positive cash flow, is known as an **early cash flow stream**. This cash flow pattern resembles borrowing; when borrowing, it is better to have a low rate (IRR) than a high rate. Hence the IRR rule for this cash flow pattern is to reject projects that have an IRR exceeding the hurdle rate, and to accept those for which the hurdle rate exceeds the IRR.

Some cash flow patterns, however, are more problematic, because they resemble both investing and borrowing, including those that start out negative, become positive, and then become negative again. Such cash flow patterns create problems for the IRR method, as we shall see shortly.

Numerical Iteration of the IRR

The computation of the IRR is usually performed using a technique known as **numerical iteration**, which can be viewed as an intelligent 'trial-and-error' procedure. Iterative procedures begin with an initial guess at a solution for the interest rate y. They then compute the discounted value of the cash flow stream given on the right-hand side of equation (10.3) with that y, and then increase or decrease y depending on whether the right-hand side of equation (10.3) is positive or negative. The procedure generally stops when the discounted value of the present and future cash flows is close enough to zero to satisfy the analyst. Most electronic spreadsheets and financial calculators have built-in programs that compute internal rates of return.

Formulae for computing the IRR directly (that is, without numerical iteration) exist only in rare cases, such as when a project has cash flows at only a few equally spaced dates. For example, if a project has cash flows only at year 0 and year 1, we can multiply both sides of equation (10.3) by $1 + y$ and solve for y. The resulting equation, $0 = C_0(1 + y) + C_1$, has the solution:

$$y = -\frac{C_1}{C_0} - 1$$

If there are cash flows exactly zero, one and two periods from now, multiplying both sides of equation (10.3) by $(1 + y)^2$ results in a quadratic equation. This can be solved with the quadratic formula. Most of the time, however, projects have cash flows that occur at more than three dates, or are timed more irregularly. In this case, numerical iteration is used to find the IRR.

NPV and Examples of IRR

This subsection works through several examples to illustrate the relation between NPV and IRR.[13]

Examples with One IRR

Examples 10.9 and 10.10 are simple cases having only one IRR.

Example 10.9

An IRR Calculation and a Comparison with NPV

Clacher's Snooker Emporium is considering whether to re-cover its snooker tables, which will generate additional business. The project's cash flows, which occur at dates 0, 1, 2 and 3, are assumed to be riskless, and are described by the following table.

[13] As we discuss later, there are more problematic examples of cash flow streams with multiple IRRs.

Cash flows (in £000s) at date			
0	1	2	3
–9	4	5	3

If the yields of riskless zero-coupon bonds maturing at years 1, 2 and 3 are 8 per cent, 5 per cent and 6 per cent per period, respectively, find the NPV and the IRR of the cash flows.

Answer: The NPV, obtained by discounting the cash flows at the zero-coupon yields, is

$$-£9,000 + \frac{£4,000}{1.08} + \frac{£5,000}{1.05^2} + \frac{£3,000}{1.06^3} = £1,758$$

The IRR is approximately 16.6 per cent per period: that is,

$$-£9,000 + \frac{£4,000}{1.166} + \frac{£5,000}{1.166^2} + \frac{£3,000}{1.166^3} = 0$$

In Example 10.9, the IRR of the project exceeds the rate of return of all the bonds used to track the project's cash flow. In this case, it is not surprising that the NPV is positive. In Example 10.10, the IRR is negative.

Example 10.10

NPV and IRR with Irregular Periods

A contractor is considering whether to take on a renovation project that will take two and a half years to complete. Under the proposed deal, the contractor has to initially spend more money to pay workers and acquire material than he receives from the customer to start the project. After the initial phase is completed, there is a partial payment for the renovation. A second phase then begins. When the company completes the second phase, the customer makes the final payment. The cash flows of the project are described by the following table.

Years from now:	0	0.5	1.25	2.5
Cash flows (in €000s):	–10	5	–15	18

The respective annualized zero-coupon rates are shown below.

Years to maturity:	0.5	1.25	2.5
Yield (% year):	6	6	8

Find the NPV and IRR of the project.

Answer: The NPV of the project is

$$-€10,000 + \frac{€5,000}{1.06^{0.5}} - \frac{€15,000}{1.061^{1.25}} + \frac{€18,000}{1.08^{2.5}} = -€4.240$$

This is a negative number. The IRR is approximately –6.10 per cent per year.

In Example 10.10, the negative IRR was below the yield on each of the zero-coupon bonds used in the project's tracking portfolio, and the NPV was negative.

An Example with Multiple IRRs

One reason why it was easy to compare the conclusions derived from the NPV and IRR in Examples 10.9 and 10.10 is that both examples had only one IRR. Whenever the cash flows have only one IRR, the internal rate of return method and the NPV method will usually result in the same decision. However, the project in Example 10.11, for instance, has multiple internal rates of return, making comparisons between the two methods rather difficult.

Example 10.11

Multiple Internal Rates of Return

Strip Mine, Inc., is considering a project with the cash flows described in the following table.

Cash flows (in $ millions) at date			
0	1	2	3
−10	41	−30	−1

Compute the IRR of this project.

Answer: This project has two internal rates of return, 213.19 per cent and 0 per cent, determined by making different initial guesses in the IRR program of a financial calculator or spreadsheet.

Exhibit 10.1 outlines the NPV of the project in Example 10.11 as a function of various hypothetical discount rates. The exhibit shows two discount rates at which the NPV is zero.

Multiple internal rates of return can (but do not have to, as Example 10.10 illustrates) arise when there is more than one sign reversal in the cash flow pattern. To understand this concept better, let us use the plus sign (+) if the cash flow is positive, and the minus sign (−) if the cash flow is negative. In Example 10.11, the sign pattern is − + − −, which has two sign reversals: one sign reversal occurs between dates 0 and 1, when the cash flow sign switches from negative to positive; and the other occurs between dates 1 and 2, when the cash flow sign switches from positive to negative.

In Example 10.11, it is obvious that 0 per cent is an IRR, because the sum of the cash flows is zero. As the interest rate increases to slightly above zero, the future cash flows have a PV that exceeds $10 million because a small positive discount rate has a larger effect on the negative cash flows at $t = 2$ and $t = 3$ than it does at $t = 1$. With very high interest rates, however, even the cash flow at $t = 1$ is greatly diminished after discounting; and subsequently higher discount rates lower the PV of the future cash flows. Thus, as the interest rate increases, eventually there will be a discount rate that results in an NPV of zero. This rate is 213.19 per cent.

Exhibit 10.1 NPV for Cash Flows in Example 10.11 as a Function of Discount Rates

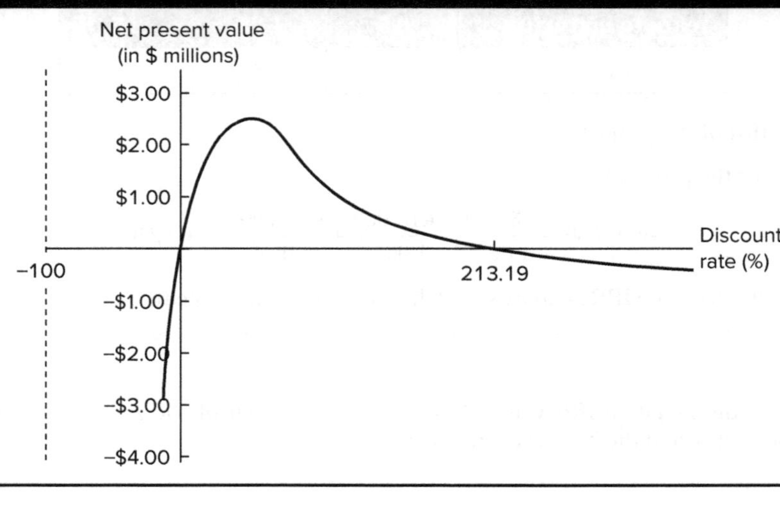

An Example with No IRR

It is also possible to have no IRR, as Example 10.12 illustrates.

Example 10.12

An Example Where No IRR Exists

Some statisticians are thinking of taking two years' leave from their academic positions to form a consulting firm for analysing survey data from polls in political campaigns. The project has the cash flows described by the following table.

Cash flows (in $000s) at date		
0	1	2
10	−30	35

Compute its IRR.

Answer: This project has no IRR. As Exhibit 10.2 illustrates, all positive and negative discount rates (above −100 per cent) make the DCF stream from the project positive.

Because the NPV is positive at every discount rate, the project in Example 10.12 is a very good project indeed! However, this does not mean that the absence of an IRR implies that one has a positive-NPV project. If the signs on the cash flows of Example 10.12's project were reversed, all positive and negative discount rates would make the NPV of this project negative. However, there is still no IRR. Thus the lack of an IRR does not indicate whether a project creates or destroys firm value.

Exhibit 10.2 NPV for Cash Flows in Example 10.12 as a Function of Discount Rates

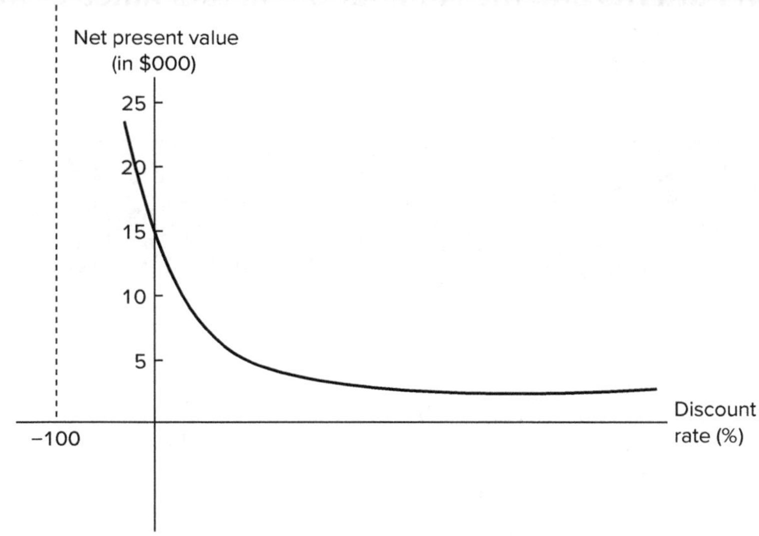

Term Structure Issues

The previous material illustrated problems that arise with the IRR method because of multiple internal rates of return in some cases and none in others. Additional problems exist when the term structure of riskless interest rates is not flat. In this case, there is ambiguity about what the appropriate hurdle rate should be. In general, long-maturity riskless bonds have different yields to maturity than short-maturity riskless bonds, implying that the appropriate hurdle rate should be different for evaluating riskless cash flows occurring at different time periods. Although this creates no problem for the NPV method, it does create difficulties when the IRR method is applied.

Most businesses, confused about what the appropriate IRR hurdle rate should be, take a coupon bond of similar maturity to the project and use its yield to maturity as the hurdle rate. This kind of bond has a yield that is a weighted average of the zero-coupon yields attached to each of the bond's cash flows. Although this may provide a reasonable approximation of the appropriate hurdle rate in a few instances, using the yield of a single-coupon bond as the hurdle rate for the IRR comparison generally will not provide the same decision criteria as the NPV method. Result 10.5 outlines a technique for computing a hurdle rate that makes the NPV method and the internal rate of return method equivalent in cases where the IRR is applicable, even when the term structure of interest rates is not flat.

Results

Result 10.5

The appropriate hurdle rate for comparison with the IRR is that which makes the sum of the discounted *future* cash flows of the project equal to the selling price of the tracking portfolio of the *future* cash flows.

Although the hurdle rate in Result 10.5 generates the same IRR-based decision as the NPV method, it requires additional computations. Indeed, an analyst has to compute the PV of the project in order to compute the appropriate hurdle rate. Because of the additional work – as well as other pitfalls in its use that will shortly be discussed – we generally do not recommend the IRR as an approach for evaluating an investment project. However, in some circumstances the IRR method may be useful for communicating the value created by taking on an investment project. An assistant treasurer, communicating his or her analysis to the CFO, may have more luck communicating the value of taking on a project by comparing the project's IRR with the rate of return of a comparable portfolio of bonds, rather than by presenting the project's NPV.

Example 10.13 illustrates a case that makes this comparison.

Cash Flow Sign Patterns and the Number of Internal Rates of Return

Adopting a project only when the IRR exceeds the hurdle rate is consistent with the NPV rule as long as the pattern of cash flows has *one sign reversal*, and *cash outflows precede cash inflows*. One example of this is the later cash flow sign pattern (of pluses and minuses) seen below for cash flows at six consecutive dates.

Date 0–5 timeline					
Cash flow sign at date					
0	1	2	3	4	5
–	–	+	+	+	+

Later Cash Flow Streams

While the illustration above has two negative cash flows followed by four positive ones, a later cash flow stream can have an arbitrary number of both negative and positive cash flows. Having only *one* sign reversal, however, means that a later cash flow stream can have only one IRR.

The uniqueness of the IRR in a later cash flow stream is best demonstrated by looking at the value of the cash flow stream at the date when the sign of the cash flow has just changed. If, for some discount rate, the value of the entire cash flow stream discounted to that date is zero, then that discount rate corresponds to an IRR. Let's look at the date 2 value of the cash flow stream in the timeline above. Date 2 is where the cash flow sign has changed from negative to positive. If the date 2 value of the entire stream of the six cash flows is zero for discount rate r, then the value of the stream at date 0 is simply the date 2 value divided by $(1 + r)^2$. Thus, if the date 2 value of the six cash flows in the date 0–5 timeline is zero, their value at date 0 is also zero, which makes r, by definition, an IRR.

Example 10.13

Term Structure Issues and the IRR

Assume the following for a project: zero-coupon bonds maturing at date 1 have a 6 per cent yield to maturity, those maturing at date 2 have an 8 per cent yield, and cash flows are given in the table below.

Cash flows (in \$000s) at date		
0	1	2
10	–30	35

The NPV of the project is £602.79, which is positive, indicating a good project. The IRR of the project is 7.92 per cent. Does the IRR also indicate that it is a good project?

Answer: There is ambiguity about which number the IRR must be compared with. If one compares the IRR with 6 per cent, it appears to be a good project, but it is a bad project if compared with a hurdle rate of 8 per cent.

The appropriate comparison is with some weighted average of 6 per cent and 8 per cent. That number is another IRR: the yield to maturity of a bond portfolio with payments of £40,000 at date 1 and £50,000 at date 2. In a market with no arbitrage, this bond should sell for its PV, £80,602.79, because

$$\frac{£40,000}{1.06} + \frac{£50,000}{(1.08)^2} = £80,602.79$$

Its yield to maturity is the number y that makes

$$-£80,602.79 + \frac{£40,000}{1+y} + \frac{£50,000}{(1+y)^2} = £0$$

which is 7.39 per cent. Since the project's internal rate of return, 7.92 per cent, exceeds the 7.39 per cent IRR (or yield to maturity) of the portfolio of zero-coupon bonds that track the future cash flows of the project, it should be accepted.

Without assigning actual numbers to these cash flows, it is possible to analyse the date 2 values of the positive and negative cash flows separately as the discount rate changes. The date 2 value of the four positive cash flows in the timeline always diminishes as the discount rate increases. Moreover, for a very large discount rate, their date 2 value is close to zero. For a very small discount rate (that is, close to –100 per cent), their date 2 value becomes large.

Now, consider the value at date 2 of the two negative cash flows at dates 0 and 1. Their negative date 2 value is becoming more negative as the discount rate increases. For a very small discount rate (close to –100 per cent), the value is close to zero. For a very large discount rate, the date 2 value of the cash flows at dates 0 and 1 is extremely negative. Hence, summing the date 2 values of the positive and negative cash flows, one finds that at low discount rates the sum is large and positive and close to the date 2 value of the four positive cash flows, while at high interest rates it is negative and close to the date 2 value of the two negative cash flows. Moreover, as one increases the discount rate, the sum of the date 2 values of the positive and negative cash flow streams decreases. Thus, because the IRR coincides with the discount rate where the date 2 values of the stream's positive and negative cash flows just offset each other, there always is a unique internal rate of return for a later cash flow stream. Moreover, if discounting *all cash flows* (present and future) with the hurdle rate yields a positive NPV, then the IRR is larger than the hurdle rate. In other words, only a larger discount rate achieves a zero discounted value. Conversely, a negative NPV implies that the IRR lies to the left of the hurdle rate.

Early Cash Flow Streams

Examples 10.14 and 10.15 illustrate the intuition developed earlier about how to apply the IRR method, depending on whether the positive portion of the cash flow stream is later or earlier.

Example 10.14

Implementing the IRR Rule for Investing

Refer to the Clacher's Snooker Emporium project in Example 10.9, where the cash flows (in £000s) at dates 0, 1, 2 and 3 were $C_0 = -9$, $C_1 = 4$, $C_2 = 5$ and $C_3 = 3$, respectively, with associated zero coupon yields of 8 per cent, 5 per cent and 6 per cent at maturity dates 1, 2 and 3, respectively. How does the IRR compare with the hurdle rate for the project?

Answer: The yield to maturity (or IRR), y, of the bond portfolio that tracks the future cash flows of the project satisfies the equation

$$\frac{£4,000}{1.08} + \frac{£5,000}{1.05^2} + \frac{£3,000}{1.06^3} = \frac{£4,000}{(1+y)} + \frac{£5,000}{(1+y)^2} + \frac{£3,000}{(1+y)^3}$$

The left-hand side, which equals £10,758, is the PV of the *future* cash flows from the project (which is why the –£9,000 initial cash flow does not appear). It is the project's NPV less its initial cash flow. It also represents the price of the portfolio of bonds that tracks the future cash flows of the project. The IRR, or y, on the portfolio of bonds is the constant discount rate that makes the portfolio a zero-NPV investment. This number, about 5.92 per cent, represents the hurdle rate for the project. Since the project's IRR, the 16.6 per cent found in Example 10.9, exceeds the hurdle rate, one should adopt the project.

Example 10.15

Implementing the IRR Rule for Borrowing Needs

Consider the cancellation of the project in Example 10.14, immediately after Clacher's Snooker Emporium made the adoption decision. In other words, the decision was made not to re-cover the snooker tables, following the earlier decision to re-cover them. What are the cash flows from cancelling the project? How does the IRR compare with the hurdle rate in this case?

Answer: The relevant incremental cash flows for the cancellation decision (a project in its own right) are found by subtracting the cash flow position of the snooker emporium when it adopted the table re-covering project from its cash flow position without the project. These cash flows are simply the negatives of the cash flows in Example 10.3: £9,000 at $t = 0$, –£4,000 at $t = 1$, –£5,000 at $t = 2$, and –£3,000 at $t = 3$. The NPV calculation is

$$£9,000 - \frac{£4,000}{1.08} - \frac{£5,000}{1.05^2} - \frac{£3,000}{1.06^3} = -£1,758$$

The IRR and the hurdle rate are still the same, approximately 16.6 per cent and 5.92 per cent, respectively. Reversing signs does not change the IRR calculation! Thus, as in Example 10.14, the IRR exceeds the hurdle rate.

In Example 10.15, the NPV rule says that cancelling the project, once adopted, is a bad decision. This makes sense, because Example 10.14 determined that adopting the project was a good decision. From the standpoint of the IRR, it also makes sense. The pattern of cash flows from the cancellation of the project has signs that can be described by the early cash flow pattern + – – –. Like the later cash flows, this pattern has only one sign change, and thus has only one IRR. Because this cash flow sign pattern is more like borrowing than investing, the appropriate IRR-based investment evaluation rule is to *accept* a project when the IRR is *lower* than the hurdle rate, and reject it otherwise (as in this case).

The Correct Hurdle Rate with Multiple Hurdle Rates

The IRR is unique when a cash flow sign pattern exhibits the pattern of an early cash flow stream or a later cash flow stream. Even in these cases, however, there may still be multiple hurdle rates if the term structure of interest rates is not flat. The point of this subsection is that no one should worry about these cases.

For a later cash flow stream where the PVs of the *future* cash flows of the project are negative (which can happen only if the stream starts off with two or more negative cash flows), two interest rates can be candidates for the hurdle rate, if hurdle rates are computed with the procedure suggested in Result 10.5.[14] A negative PV and a negative initial cash flow imply a negative NPV. Clearly, the correct hurdle rate is one that results in rejection. Fortunately, both of these hurdle rates will exceed the IRR, which thus tells us to reject the project, as Example 10.16 illustrates.[15]

Example 10.16

Multiple Hurdle Rates

The following timeline describes the cash flows of a bad project. The appropriate discount rates for riskless cash flows of various maturities are given below the cash flows.

Cash flows and discount rates for date			
0	1	2	3
−€5	−€10	€5	€5
	4%	5%	6%

Compute the IRR and the two hurdle rates for the project.

Answer: The unique IRR is −19.81 per cent. The hurdle rates are found by first discounting the cash flows from years 1–3, which gives a PV of −€0.882. The cash flows of the (zero NPV) bond portfolio that tracks the *future* cash flows of the project are therefore as follows.

Tracking portfolio cash flows at date			
0	1	2	3
€0.882	−€10	€5	€5

Note that, in contrast to the cash flows of the project, the cash flows of the tracking portfolio have two sign changes, and thus may have more than one IRR. The two hurdle rates of the four cash flows of the tracking portfolio are 6.86 per cent and 976.04 per cent. Both hurdle rates exceed the IRR, implying the project should be rejected.

These considerations suggest the following IRR adoption rule for projects with later and early cash flow streams.

Results

Result 10.6

(*The appropriate IRR rule.*) In the absence of constraints, a project with a later cash flow stream should be adopted only if its IRR exceeds the hurdle rate(s). A project with an early cash flow stream should be adopted only if the hurdle rate(s) exceed the IRR of the project.

[14] As we demonstrate shortly, the reason why two hurdle rates may sometimes arise is that the hurdle rates are themselves internal rates of return of a portfolio of zero-coupon bonds. If this bond portfolio has a cash flow pattern with more than one sign reversal (implying both long and short positions in zero-coupon bonds), it is possible for two internal rates of return to exist. In the following sections, the existence and implications of multiple internal rates of return are described in greater detail.

[15] A similar problem arises with an early cash flow stream when the present value of its future cash flows is positive. In this case, the project has a positive NPV. If the project has two hurdle rates because of this, both will exceed the IRR, and indicate that the project should be adopted. Since a project has a positive NPV when it has an early cash flow stream with future cash flows that have a positive present value, the internal rate of return rule in this case makes the correct decision, regardless of which of the two hurdle rates is used.

Sign Reversals and Multiple Internal Rates of Return

The previous subsection noted that multiple internal rates of return for the bond portfolio that tracks the project, and thus determines the hurdle rates, do not prevent us from using the IRR to determine whether projects with later or early cash flow streams should be adopted. By contrast, the existence of multiple internal rates of return for the project's cash flows has a major impact on one's ability to use the IRR for evaluating investments.[16]

A project could have more than one IRR if its cash flows exhibit more than one sign reversal. These multiple sign reversals can arise for many reasons. For example, environmental regulations may require the owner of a strip mine to restore the land to a pristine state after the mine is exhausted. Or the tax authorities may not require a firm to pay the corporate income tax on the sale of a profitable product until one year after the profit is earned. In this case, the last cash flow for the project is merely the tax paid on the last year the project earned profits. The next section illustrates how mutually exclusive projects can create sign reversals, even when the cash flows of the projects *per se* do not exhibit multiple sign reversals.

In the event of multiple sign reversals, many practitioners employ very complicated and often *ad hoc* adjustments to the IRR calculation. In principle (although rarely in practice), these adjustments can ensure that the IRR rule yields the same decisions as the NPV rule. However, it makes little sense to bother with these troublesome procedures when the NPV rule gives the correct answer and is easier to implement.

Mutually Exclusive Projects and the Internal Rate of Return

When selecting one project from a group of alternatives, the NPV rule indicates that the project with the largest positive net present value is the best project.

Do Not Select the Project with the Largest IRR

It is easy, but foolhardy, to think that one should extend this idea to the internal rate of return criterion and adopt the project with the largest IRR. Even if all the projects under consideration are riskless and have the later cash flow stream pattern, each project might have different hurdle rates if the term structure of interest rates is not flat. If the project with a large IRR also has a larger hurdle rate than the other projects, how does one decide? Is it then more appropriate to look at the difference between the IRR and the cost of capital or the ratio? Fortunately, it is unnecessary to answer this question, because even if all the projects have the same hurdle rate, the largest IRR project is not the best, as Example 10.17 illustrates.

Example 10.17

Mutually Exclusive Projects and the IRR

Consider a firm with two projects, each with a discount rate of 2 per cent per period. The following table describes their cash flows, NPVs and internal rates of return.

	Cash flows at date			NPV at 2% (in € millions)	IRR (%)
	0	1	2		
Project A	−10	−16	30	3.149	10.79
Project B	−10	2	11	2.534	15.36

Given that the firm must select only one project, should it choose A or B?

Answer: The NPV of project A, about 13.149 million, is higher than the net present value of B, about 12.534 million. Thus project A is better than project B, even though it has a lower IRR.

[16] However, Cantor and Lippman (1983) have shown that multiple internal rates of return can have useful interpretations. Specifically, when lending is possible at a rate of r but borrowing is not possible, and projects are repeated in time because cash from the first run of the project is needed to fund the second project, and so on, then if discounting at r yields a positive NPV for the project, the smallest IRR above r represents the growth rate of the project if the project is repeated in perpetuity.

The appropriate IRR-based procedure for evaluating mutually exclusive projects is similar to that used for the NPV rule: subtract the cash flows of the next best alternative. If one is lucky, and the difference in the cash flow streams of the two projects has an early or later sign pattern, one can choose which of the two projects is better. In Example 10.17, the cash flows of project A less those of project B can be described by the following table.

	Cash flows at date			NPV at 2% (in € millions)	IRR (%)
	0	1	2		
Project A – B	0	−18	19	0.615	5.56

There is only one sign reversal and a later cash flow. The implication is that project A is better than project B, because the 5.56 per cent IRR is higher than the 2 per cent hurdle rate.

How Multiple Internal Rates of Return Arise from Mutually Exclusive Projects

The last subsection showed how differencing the cash flows of two projects might lead to a correct IRR-based rule for evaluating mutually exclusive projects. The key concept is that the comparison of the pair leads to a differenced cash flow that has only one sign reversal. If there are many projects, a large number of comparisons of two projects like those described in the last subsection must be made. As Example 10.18 demonstrates, it is highly likely that some of the differenced cash flows will have more than one sign reversal, even if all the projects have later or early cash flow sign patterns.

The NPV criterion tells us to adopt the project with the largest positive NPV. The appropriateness of this rule follows from the value additivity property of the NPV formula. However, the value additivity property does not apply to the IRR. We can summarize the implications of this as follows.

Results

Result 10.7

The project with the largest IRR is generally not the project with the highest NPV, and thus is not the best among a set of mutually exclusive projects.

Example 10.18

Multiple IRRs from Mutually Exclusive Projects

Reconsider Example 10.6, where NASA must select one of three commercial projects for the next space shuttle mission. Each of these projects has industrial spin-offs that will pay off in the next two years. The cash flows, NPVs and internal rates of return of the projects are described below.

	Cash flows at date			NPV at 2% (in $ millions)	IRR (%)
	0	1	2		
Project A	−17.0	12	9	3.415	16.16
Project B	−16.8	10	11	3.577	15.98
Project C	−16.9	11	10	3.496	16.07

Which project should NASA select?

Answer: The NPV criterion indicates that project B is the best project, even though it has the *lowest IRR*. The IRR criterion fails, because the differences in the cash flows of various pairs of projects have multiple internal rates of return. In this case, there are three pairs of cash flow differences.

	Cash flows at date			NPV at 2% (in $ millions)	IRR (%)
	0	1	2		
Project A – B	−0.2	2	−2	−0.162	12.7 and 787.3
Project A – C	−0.1	1	−1	−0.081	12.7 and 787.3
Project B – C	0.1	−1	1	0.081	12.7 and 787.3

The multiple internal rates of return arise from the two sign reversals in the cash flow differences. The pair of IRRs are identical for all three differences, and thus cannot provide information about the best project.

However, the net present value, based on cash flow differences, selects project B, which was the project with the highest NPV without cash flow differencing. The reason why cash flow differences alone tell us that project B is the best of the three projects is twofold:

- The difference between the cash flows of projects A and B has a negative NPV, indicating that A is worse than B.
- The difference between the cash flows of projects B and C has a positive NPV, indicating that B is better than C.

Modified Internal Rate of Return

Both IRR and NPV assumes that cash flows earned in the future are reinvested at the same rate as the internal rate of return. However, in many cases, this will not be true, and the firm may need to reinvest future investment cash flows in another part of the business or project with a different discount rate.

As an example, consider a firm with a project that generates the following cash flows. The company's discount rate is 10 per cent:

Year	0	1	2	3	4
Cash flow	−1,000	400	400	300	300

The IRR of this project is 16 per cent.

If the company were to reinvest the project cash flows elsewhere in the business, the reinvestment rate of the future cash flows would be the company's discount rate of 10 per cent. When the reinvestment rate is different from the IRR, we must calculate the modified internal rate of return (MIRR). The first step is to calculate the terminal value of the project cash flows using the reinvestment rate. In this example, the reinvestment rate is 10 per cent and the IRR is 16 per cent.

Year	0	1	2	3	4
Cash flow	−1,000	400	400	300	300
Year 1 cash flow of 400 compounded 3 years at 10 per cent					532.4
Year 2 cash flow of 400 compounded 2 years at 10 per cent					484
Year 3 cash flow of 300 compounded 1 year at 10 per cent					330
Cash flows	−1,000	400	400	300	1 646.4

We have now converted the project to two cash flows: the initial outlay of 1,000 and the terminal value in year 4 of 1,646.4. We calculate the MIRR as follows:

$$\text{MIRR} = \sqrt[n]{\frac{\text{terminal cash flow}}{\text{initial investment}}} - 1$$

In the example above, the MIRR is

$$\text{MIRR} = \sqrt[4]{\frac{1646.4}{1,000}} - 1 = 0.1327 = 13.27\%$$

Note how the MIRR of 13.27 per cent is less than the IRR of 16 per cent. This is because the reinvestment rate of 10 per cent is lower than the IRR.

The MIRR method is sometimes viewed to be more realistic than IRR because it assumes project cash flows will be reinvested elsewhere in the firm rather than a similar project to the investment. That is, both IRR and NPV assume project cash flows will be reinvested in the exact same project, which might not be possible.

10.6 Other Popular Procedures for Evaluating Real Investments

Other evaluation methods besides NPV and IRR exist, including ratio comparisons, exemplified by the price to earnings multiple and the competitive strategies approach.[17]

This section briefly discusses two popular rules of thumb used by many managers to evaluate investment projects: the *payback* method and the *accounting rate of return* method.

The Payback Method

The **payback method** evaluates projects based on the number of years needed to recover the initial capital outlay for a project. For example, an investment that costs £1 million and returns £250,000 per year would have a payback of four years. By the payback criterion, this investment would be preferred to a £1 million investment that returned £200,000 per year and thus had a payback of five years.

A major problem with the payback method is that it ignores cash flows that occur after the project is paid off. For example, most of us would prefer the second project over the first if the second project generated £200,000 per year for the next 20 years and the first project generated £250,000 per year for only five years, and nothing thereafter. There is no reason to ignore cash flows after the payback period, except that the payback method provides a simple rule of thumb that may help managers make quick decisions on relatively minor projects.[18] Experienced managers do not need a financial calculator to tell them that a routine minor project with a one-year payback has a positive NPV; they know this is almost always the case.

The Accounting Rate of Return Criterion

The **accounting rate of return** criterion evaluates projects by comparing the project's **return on assets**, which is the accounting profit earned on the project divided by the amount invested to acquire the project's assets. The accounting rate of return is then compared with some hurdle rate in the same manner as the IRR decision rule.

Our principal objection to this criterion is that accounting profits are often very different from the cash flows generated by a project. When making a comparison between a project and its tracking portfolio, we understand why it would be inappropriate to use earnings in such a calculation.

The wealth creation associated with the NPV rule is based on the date 0 arbitrage profits from a long position in the project and a short position in the project's tracking portfolio. This combined position is supposed to eliminate all future cash flows, to allow a comparison between the date 0 cost of the investment strategy in real assets and the date 0 cost of the tracking portfolio's financial assets as the basis for deciding whether value is created or destroyed. However, all future cash flows are not eliminated in attempting to match the project's earnings with a tracking portfolio. Paying the cash flows on the tracking portfolio to some outside investor requires actual cash, which is not balanced by the reported earnings generated by the project. Earnings differ from cash flows for a number of reasons, including, notably, depreciation.

---

[17] See Chapter 12.

[18] Variations of the payback method, such as discounted payback, also exist. This method suffers from a similar deficiency of ignoring cash flows after the payback period.

10.7 Summary and Conclusions

This chapter focused on the project selection decision. Since projects have cash flows that occur in the future, it is important to have a selection technique that accounts for the greater interest-earning capability of cash that arrives sooner. The best way of taking the time value of money into account is to study carefully how investors value existing portfolios of securities with cash flows that are similar to the cash flows of the project.

In assessing investment projects, the NPV rule properly accounts for the time value of money, and is easy to implement when the future cash flows are riskless. The NPV rule is also useful for evaluating risky cash flows, as will be seen in later chapters, and it is easily modified to account for various capital constraints. The IRR rule, the other major alternative, also accounts for the time value of money, but is too fraught with ambiguities to be used appropriately, except in special circumstances.

Despite this, the IRR rule is still widely used. We have no good explanation for this. It may be that practitioners prefer to think about rates of return rather than about PVs when making decisions. However, the net profitability rate, a variation on the NPV rule, is couched in terms of the rate of return, and is not as popular as the IRR.

Many businesses, aware of the problems inherent in multiple internal rates of return, have adopted procedures that 'correct' the flaws in the IRR-based capital allocation criterion. One correction of this type is to compute an IRR by first computing the sum of the discounted future negative cash flows at the hurdle rate, and then adding this to the initial cash flow. The adjusted IRR is then computed as the rate that makes this sum, plus the discounted value of all future positive cash flows (discounted at the adjusted IRR), equal to zero. Another correction finds the 'IRR' for the project as if only two cash flows existed: an initial cash flow, and a cash flow at the terminal date of the project that is equivalent in value to the future cash flows of the project.

These methods are not really IRR methods, but merely variations of the net profitability rate (a different way of expressing the NPV criterion). These adaptations work fine in the absence of particular constraints; however, it is easy to misuse these methods when such constraints exist. For example, the method that computes the value of future cash flows at the project's terminal date essentially spreads the rate of return from the net profitability rate over the life of the project. However, if capital is constrained only in the early stages of a project, this method is unfairly biased towards shorter-term projects.

It may be that firms tend to be overly optimistic about the cash flows that stem from a project. In this case, firms using the NPV rule would favour longer-term projects more than firms using the IRR rule or its adaptations. The bias of the NPV rule in favouring longer-term projects occurs because each additional year of overly optimistic cash flows would increase the net present value. However, we think that using an inappropriate rule is a poor way to correct the tendency of a firm's employees to exaggerate cash flow estimates.

Firms use other rules and rules of thumb to evaluate investments. In contrast to the IRR method, which can be justified under some circumstances, the payback and accounting rate of return methods are not sound decision criteria. Specifically, payback and accounting rates of return are based on accounting concepts. Unlike the IRR and NPV rules, they do not adjust for the time value of money. As a result, they are being used less and less for evaluating major investments. That obviously inferior rules, such as payback and accounting rate of return, are used at all for major decision-making suggests to us that the commonly used IRR rule contains no hidden virtue that makes it superior to NPV. We suspect that IRR rules, like the accounting-based rules, persist because of habits or ignorance, and over time we expect to see the use of IRR diminish.

Key Concepts

Result 10.1: The wealth-maximizing NPV criterion is that:

- All projects with positive NPVs should be accepted.
- All projects with negative NPVs should be rejected.

Result 10.2: For a project with riskless cash flows, the NPV – that is, the market value of the project's tracking portfolio less the cost of initiating the project – is the same as the discounted value of all present and future cash flows of the project.

Result 10.3: Given a set of investment projects, each with positive NPV, one should select the project with the largest positive NPV if allowed to adopt only one of the projects.

Result 10.4: The discounted value of the stream of EVAs of a project is the same as the NPV of the project.

Result 10.5: The appropriate hurdle rate for comparison with the IRR is that which makes the sum of the discounted *future* cash flows of the project equal to the selling price of the tracking portfolio of the *future* cash flows.

Result 10.6: (*The appropriate IRR rule.*) In the absence of constraints, a project with a later cash flow stream should be adopted only if its IRR exceeds the hurdle rate(s). A project with an early cash flow stream should be adopted only if the hurdle rate(s) exceed the IRR of the project.

Result 10.7: The project with the largest IRR is generally not the project with the highest NPV, and thus is not the best among a set of mutually exclusive projects.

Key Terms

Exercises

10.1 Your firm has recently reached an expansion phase and is seeking possible new geographic regions to market the newly patented chemical compound Glupto. The five regional projections are as follows.

Years from now:	Cash flows (in € millions)					
	0	1	2	3	4	5
Germany	–95	15	20	25	30	30
France	–75	15	20	20	25	30
Italy	–60	10	15	20	20	25
Ireland	–35	5	10	10	15	15
Spain	–20	5	5	6	6	10
Zero-coupon yields (%)		6.5	7	7	7.5	8

a Which countries would be profitable to the firm? Which of the five is the most profitable?

b If current budgeting can support a €100 million expenditure in year 0, what combination of regions is optimal?

c Assume now that you can expand without regional saturation. With the budget constraint in part *b*, which region is optimal?

10.2 Consider the purchase of a new milling machine. What purchase price makes the NPV of the project zero? Base your analysis on the following facts.

- The new milling machine will reduce operating expenses by exactly £20,000 per year for 10 years. Each of these cash flow reductions takes place at the end of the year.
- The old milling machine is now 5 years old, and has 10 years of scheduled life remaining.
- The old milling machine was purchased for £45,000, and has a current market value of £20,000.
- There are no taxes or inflation.
- The risk-free rate is 6 per cent.

Exercises 10.3–10.6 make use of the following information.

Your company is investigating a possible new project, Project X, which would affect corporate cash flow as follows.

Cash flows (in €000s) without Project X in year					
0	1	2	3	4	5
150	175	185	185	195	200

Cash flows (in €000s) with Project X in year					
0	1	2	3	4	5
110	165	200	205	210	213

10.3 Respond to parts *a* to *d*.

a What are the incremental cash flows associated with undertaking Project X? Are these inflows or outflows, costs or revenue?

b What is the PV of Project X under a flat term structure of 8 per cent, compounded annually, irrespective of maturity?

c Under these assumptions, what is the hurdle rate? Without further calculation, determine whether the IRR for Project X is higher or lower than the hurdle rate. (*Hint:* Use part *b*.)

d Why might a flat rate structure be unrealistic?

10.4 Describe the equivalent tracking portfolio for Project X, giving long and short positions and amounts, under a flat term structure of 8 per cent, compounded annually. Conceptually, why are we interested in tracking Project X's cash flows with a portfolio of marketable securities?

10.5 Let B_t = price per €100 of face value of a zero-coupon bond maturing at year *t*. Let B_1 = €94.00, B_2 = €88.20, B_3 = €81.50, B_4 = €76.00 and B_5 = €73.00, implying that the term structure of interest rates is no longer flat.

a Determine zero-coupon rates for years 1–5 to the nearest 0.01 per cent.

b Reconsider the tracking portfolio in exercise 10.4. What is the cost or revenue associated with such a tracking portfolio at date 0 under the new term structure?

c What is the NPV of Project X under the new term structure?

d How are your answers to parts *b* and *c* related?

10.6 Consider the cash flows associated with undertaking Project X.

a Is this an early or later cash flow stream?

b Based on the term structure of interest rates in exercise 10.5, what is the hurdle rate?

What does such a hurdle rate represent?

c Calculate the IRR for Project X.

d Based on the hurdle rate calculated and a comparison with the IRR, should you undertake the project?

e If the sign of each cash flow were reversed, how would the hurdle rate and project IRR change? How would your decision change? Why?

10.7 As a regional managing director of Finco, an Italy-based investment company, your mandate is to scour Europe in search of promising investment opportunities, and to recommend *one project* to corporate headquarters in Milan. Your analysts have screened thousands of prospective ventures, and have passed on the following four projects for your final review.

	Cash flows (in € millions)					
Years from now:	**0**	**1**	**2**	**3**	**4**	**5**
Project 1	–40	10	10	15	15	20
Project 2	–25	5	5	10	15	15
Project 3	–20	5	5	5	10	15
Project 4	–15	3	3	6	6	13
Zero-coupon yields (%)	–	5	5	6	6	5

a Calculate the NPV, hurdle rate and IRR for each project. Which project appears most promising?

b Determine NPVs using pairwise project comparisons to verify your decision from part *a*.

c How would your answer change if all projects could be scaled and you have a year 0 budget constraint of €50 million? (*Hint:* Calculate profitability indices.)

10.8 ABC Metalworks wants to determine which model sheetcutter to purchase. Three choices are available: machine 1 costs the least, but must be replaced the most frequently; machine 2 has average cost and average lifespan; machine 3 costs the most, but needs only infrequent replacement. Assume that all three machines meet production quality and volume standards; that annual maintenance is inversely proportional to the purchase price (that is, the cheaper machine requires higher maintenance); and that machine replacement, being instantaneous, will not disrupt production.

	Machine 1	Machine 2	Machine 3
Initial cost	£2,000	£3,200	£4,500
Annual maintenance	£400	£300	£200
Lifespan	2 years	3 years	4 years

a Under a flat discount rate assumption of 5 per cent per year, calculate the NPV for each machine.

b Which machine makes the most sense for cost-efficient production?

c How does your answer to part *b* change under a flat 6 per cent discount rate assumption? Why?

10.9 Investco, a South African research company, must decide on the level of computer technology it will buy for its analysis department. Package A, a mid-level technology, would cost R15 million for firmwide installation, whereas package B, a higher-level technology, would cost R21 million. Equipped with level A technology, the firm could generate a cash flow of R9 million for two years before the technology would require replacement; with level B technology, the firm could generate a cash flow of R10.2 million for three years, after which the technology would require replacement. Investco is interested in a six-year planning horizon. Assume the following about discount rates:

Zero-coupon yields for year					
1	2	3	4	5	6
5%	5.5%	6%	6%	6.5%	7%

a What is the nearest terminal date that is concurrent for both packages? What are the associated cash flows for each package or sequence of packages?

b What is the optimal decision, given Investco's planning horizon?

c At approximately what alternative package B price would Investco be indifferent between the two packages?

10.10 Marielle Machinery Works is considering a project that has an initial investment of £10,000 and expected cash flows of £0 in year 1, £7,500 in year 2 and £8,500 in year 3. The company uses the IRR rule to accept or reject projects, and has asked for your assessment on what to do if the required rate of return is 12 per cent. A colleague suggests that, since the firm can only reinvest the cash flows at the the firm's discount rate of 12 per cent, you should use the MIRR method instead. What is the project's MIRR and how does it compare to the IRR? Which method should you use?

References and Additional Reading

Cantor, D.G. and Lippman, S.A. (1983) Investment selection with imperfect capital markets, *Econometrica*, 51(4): 1121–1144.

Hillier, D., Ross, S., Westerfield, R. and Jaffe, J. (2009) *Corporate Finance: European Edition*, 1st edn. Maidenhead: McGraw-Hill.

Hirshleifer, J. (1970) *Investment, Interest, and Capital*, Englewood Cliffs, NJ: Prentice Hall.

Pindyck, R.S. and Rubinfeld, D.L. (1991) *Econometric Models and Economic Forecasts*, 3rd edn. New York: McGraw-Hill.

Appendix 10A The Term Structure of Interest Rates

The term structure of interest rates, or yield curve, mentioned earlier in the chapter, is the pattern of yields to maturity for riskless bonds of all maturities. Usually, the yields from zero-coupon Treasury securities define the term structure. Although Treasury securities of all maturities do not always exist, the concept of a term structure is so important to corporate finance and investment management that rates are computed between the existing maturities by interpolating the rates.

10A.1 Term Structure Varieties

There are a variety of term structures. The **par yield curve** represents the yields and interpolated yields of on-the-run coupon-paying Treasury securities of various maturities (see Chapter 2). The **annuity term structure** represents the yields to maturity of riskless bonds with level payments. There also is the **spot term structure,** which represents the yields to maturity of zero-coupon bonds of various maturities.

Uses of Spot Yields and Where They Come From

The DCF approach, as exhibited in equation (10.1), makes use of the spot (or zero-coupon) yield curve. Generally, one obtains a more accurate picture of spot yields by looking at the implied zero-coupon yields of par (straight coupon) bonds than by looking at the yields of zero-coupon bonds.

Forces Driving the Term Structure of Interest Rates

Historically, the yield curve has had many shapes. Moreover, yield curves for different countries can have different shapes at the same time. Sometimes it is upward sloping, sometimes downward sloping, sometimes nearly flat, and sometimes it has bumps in it, particularly at the short end. Exhibit 10A.1 shows graphs of nominal yield curves for the UK and Eurozone in 2022.

The activities of central banks (for example, the Federal Reserve System in the United States, or the European Central Bank) generally determine the rates at the short end of the yield curve. Attempts to slow down the economy generally drive up short-term rates, while expansionary monetary policy tends to lower short-term rates. Often these policies have an opposite effect at the long end of the yield curve, because inflationary expectations tend to drive the long end of the yield curve. A contractionary monetary policy is often intended to reduce inflation, which reduces long-term yields while simultaneously driving short-term yields upwards.

Rates at the short end of the yield curve are generally 30–40 per cent more volatile than rates at the long end, probably because monetary policy acts primarily at the short end of the curve and is counter-cyclical. Hence, if long-term prospects are in some sense an average of short-term prospects, and if subsequent short-term prospects tend to reverse mistakes in previous policies or eliminate shocks, then long-term rates will be more stable.

10A.2 Spot Rates, Annuity Rates and Par Rates

This subsection discusses how to convert par rates to spot rates and annuity rates, and *vice versa*. First, it provides a general rule for comparing the three types of term structure, which are graphed in Exhibit 10A.2.

If the term structure of one of the three yield curves (spot, annuity or par) is consistently upward or downward sloping, the other two yields will slope in the same direction. The spot yield curve will have the

Exhibit 10A.1 Nominal Yield Curves (0 to 30 Years) for the UK and Eurozone in 2022

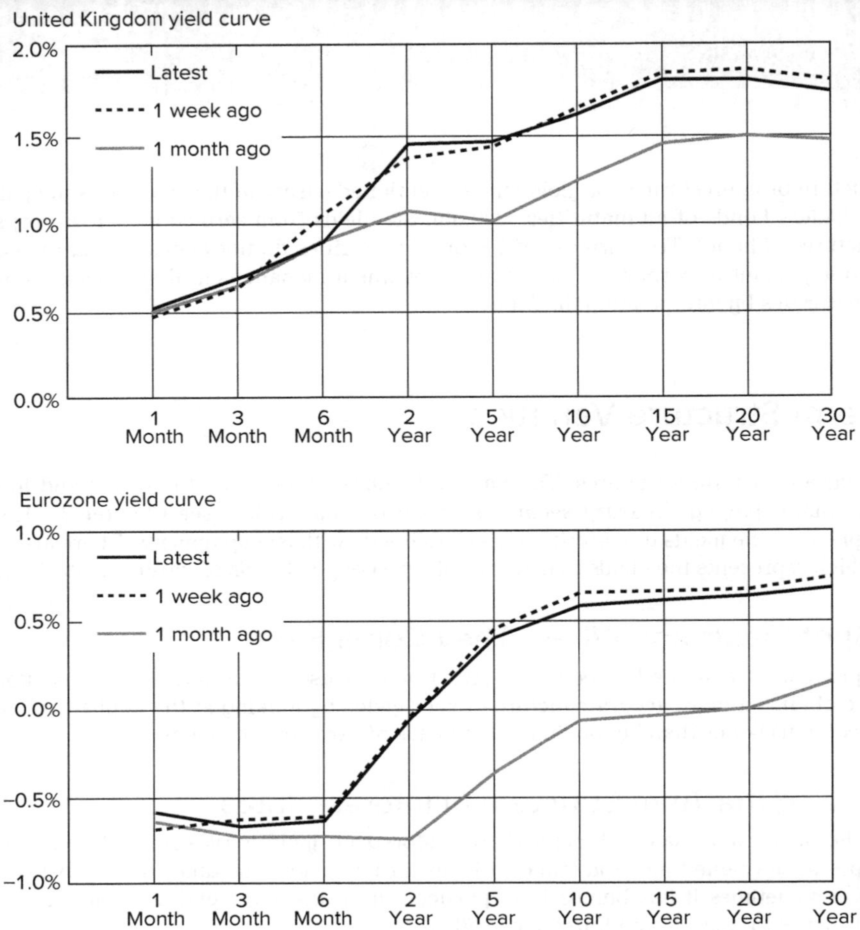

Source: FT.com, 5 April 2022. The Financial Times LTD 2022

steepest slope, the par curve will have the second steepest slope, and the annuity yield curve will have the gentlest slope. If the yield curve is flat, all three yield curves will be identical.[19]

To simplify the analysis of how to translate one type of yield into another, assume that the yields are compounded annually and computed only at years 1, . . . , T. Use interpolation to generate approximate yields for fractional years (for example, 1.5 years or 2.3 years).

Using Spot Yields to Compute Annuity Yields and Par Yields

Computing annuity yields from spot yields is relatively straightforward. The annuity yield for year t is found by assuming a cash payment of a fixed amount for years 1, 2, . . . , t: for example, £1 is paid at each of those years. This is like a portfolio of t zero-coupon bonds, each with a £1 face value. Using spot yields, compute the PV of each zero-coupon bond, and sum up the t present values. If the present value is P, find the IRR for the cash flows: $-P$, 1, 1, . . . , 1. This is the annuity yield to maturity for date t. Repeat this process for $t = 1$, $t = 2$, $t = 3$, . . . , and $t = T$.

[19] This relationship between the slopes is due to the different timing and size of the cash flows (see Chapter 23) of the three types of bond.

Exhibit 10A.2 Three Types of Yield Curve

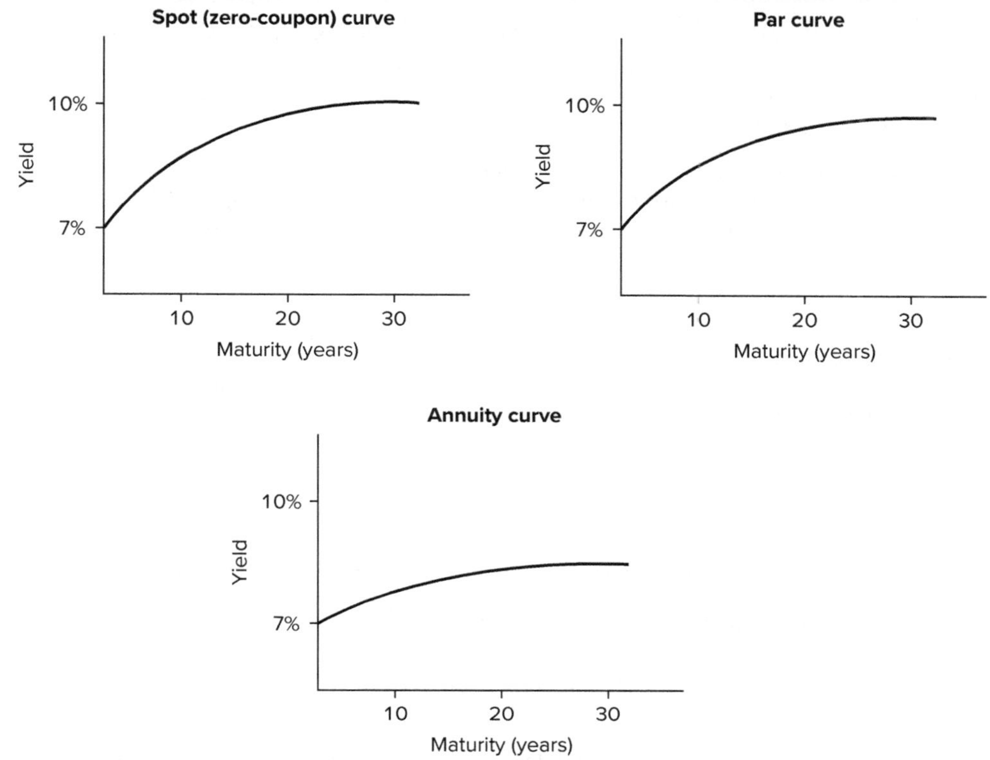

To compute par yields from spot yields, strip off £100, the principal, from the final payment of the par bond, assumed for purposes of illustration to have a face value of £100. This leaves an annuity with a maturity identical to the par bond and a cash flow equal to the bond's coupon. For a £100 bond, this coupon is the coupon rate on a par bond in percentage terms. To identify this coupon, note that the annuity's PV equals £100, the present value of the par bond, less the present value of £100 paid at maturity, discounted with the zero-coupon rate for that maturity. Thus the bond's coupon is the ratio of the PV of this annuity to the present value of a £1 annuity of the same maturity. Since, for par bonds, the coupon rate and yield to maturity are the same on coupon payment dates (see Chapter 2), this ratio is the par yield to maturity, in percentage terms.

Example 10A.1 demonstrates how to compute annuity yields and par yields from spot yields.

Computing Spot Yields from Par Yields and Annuity Yields

There are many ways to compute the spot yield curve from the par yield curve. Perhaps the easiest way to proceed is to move sequentially from the shortest maturity to the longest. With annual compounding and annual coupons, the par bond with the earliest maturity is a zero-coupon bond. The spot yield is identical to the par yield in this case. The two-year spot yield is computed from a long position in the two-year par bond and a short position in the one-year par bond. Because the one-year par bond is a zero-coupon bond, it is possible to form a portfolio that looks like a zero-coupon bond with two years' maturity by weighting the two par bonds properly. The yield of this properly weighted portfolio is the spot yield for two years' maturity. Given the one- and two-year spot rates, it is possible to form a portfolio consisting of a long position in a three-year par bond and short positions in one- and two-year zero-coupon bonds that look like a three-year zero-coupon bond. The yield of this bond is the three-year spot rate. Proceed sequentially in this manner as far out into time as necessary.

Example 10A.1

Computing Annuity Yields and Par Yields from Spot Yields

Assume that spot yields in the UK, compounded annually, are 7 per cent, 8 per cent and 9 per cent for years 1, 2 and 3, respectively. Compute (1) the annuity yields and (2) par yields for years 1, 2 and 3, assuming annual cash flows for these bonds.

Answer: (1) The annuity yield for year 1 is 7 per cent, because a one-year annuity with annual payments has only one payment, and thus behaves like a zero-coupon bond. The annuity yield for year 2 is found by first computing the PV of a two-year annuity. With £1 payments, such a bond has a value of

$$\frac{£1}{1.07}+\frac{£1}{1.08^2}=£1.7919$$

The yield to maturity of a bond with a cost of £1.7919 and payments of £1 at year 1 and 2 is 7.65 per cent. This is the point on the annuity yield curve for year 2. The annuity yield for year 3 is the yield to maturity of a bond with payments of £1 in years 1, 2 and 3, and a cost of

$$\frac{£1}{1.07}+\frac{£1}{1.08^2}+\frac{£1}{1.09^3}=£2.5641$$

This is 8.28 per cent.

(2) The one-year par yield is the same as the zero-coupon yield, because its cash flows are the same as that of a zero-coupon bond. To compute the two-year par yield, assume a face value of £100. Stripping the principal off the end of the bond leaves an annuity with a PV of

$$£100-\frac{£100}{1.08^2}=£14.266118$$

Since a £1 annuity of two years' maturity has a PV of £1.7919, both the coupon rate and the yield to maturity (in per cent) of the two-year par bond must be

$$\frac{£14.266118}{£1.7919}=7.96\%$$

Repeating the process for stripping £100 off the last payment of the three-year par bond leaves a PV of

$$£100-\frac{£100}{1.09^3}=£22.781652$$

Dividing this by the PV of a £1 annuity with a maturity of three years gives the coupon and yield to maturity of the three-year par bond in percentage terms:

$$\frac{£22.781652}{£2.5641}=8.88\%$$

Example 10A.2 illustrates the procedure described above.

Example 10A.2

Computing Spot Yields from Par Yields

Compute the spot yield curve for Ireland, assuming annually compounded yields, for years 1, 2 and 3, given par curve yields as follows.

	Maturity in years		
	1	2	3
Par yield	9%	8%	7%

All par yields assume coupons paid annually and all yields are compounded annually.

Answer: The one-year spot yield is 9 per cent, because the one-year par bond is the same as a zero-coupon bond.

The two-year par bond has an 8 per cent coupon paid at year 1. As a par bond, its face value is the same as its market value. Assume a face value of €100, although any value will do. The cash flows of this bond are €8 at year 1 and €108 at year 2. The one-year par bond has a cash flow of €109 at year 1. A long position in the two-year €100 par bond and a short position in 8/109 of the one-year €100 par bond has a future cash flow at year 2 in the amount of €108 and no future cash flows at other dates. Thus the position is equivalent to a two-year zero-coupon bond and, since it has a value of €92.66055 (=€100 – (8/109) €100), the yield of this bond, *r*, satisfies the equation

$$\frac{€108}{(1+r)^2} = €92.66055$$

which implies that $r = 7.96$ per cent. Alternatively, knowing that the appropriate discount rate for the €8 coupon of the par bond at year 1 is 9 per cent, stripping that coupon leaves a bond with a value of €100 – €8/1.09 = €92.66055, which, as seen above, implies a 7.96 per cent yield.

To find the year 3 spot rate, strip the two €7 coupons at years 1 and 2 from the par bond. This leaves a bond with a value of

$$€100 - \frac{€7}{1.09} - \frac{€7}{(1.0796)^2} = €87.5722$$

With a future pay-off at year 3 in the amount of €107, and no future cash flows at other dates, the stripped bond now has the pay-off of a zero-coupon bond with a three-year spot yield *r* that solves

$$\frac{€107}{(1+r)^3} = €87.5722$$

which implies that $r = 6.91$ per cent.

To compute zero-coupon yields from annuity yields, strip all payments from the annuity except the last one. If the annuity yields are known, the PV of the stripped cash flows and the original annuity is known. This leaves a single future cash flow. The yield to maturity of this cash flow is the spot yield for that maturity.

Example 10A.3 illustrates how to compute spot yields from annuity yields.

Example 10A.3

Computing Spot Yields from Annuity Yields

If the annuity yields in Spain are 7 per cent, 7 per cent and 8 per cent for years 1, 2 and 3, respectively, compute the spot yields. Assume annual cash flows and annual compounding.

Answer: The first two spot yields are both 7 per cent. The first is 7 per cent because the annuity is a zero-coupon bond. The second is 7 per cent because the annuity yield would be higher (lower) than 7 per cent if the spot yield was higher (lower) than 7 per cent. (You can prove this with the method we now use.)

The PV of the two-year annuity at 7 per cent, using €1 cash flows, is about €1.81. The PV of the three-year annuity at 8 per cent is about €2.58. The difference between the values of the two- and three-year annuities is €0.77. For the PV of €1 paid in three years to be €0.77, the three-year spot yield has to be about 9.15 per cent.

Why Spot Yields Should Be Computed from Par Yields

The term structure of risk-free interest rates given by the Treasury yield curve is generally computed from on-the-run Treasury bonds. You can think of on-the-run bonds as newborns. They become slightly less interesting to many investors as they become toddlers, and traders begin to lose interest in them as they become children and young adults. As these bonds age, many of them get tucked away into pension accounts and insurance funds to pay off future liabilities. As the actively traded supply of these bonds begins to diminish, it becomes more difficult to use the bonds for short sales. Moreover, the lack of active trading means that investors are never sure whether the price they pay is fair, because the last trading price they observe is often stale.

For this reason, it is useful to focus on the on-the-run bonds to compute a Treasury yield. The prices are fresh, the trading is active, and the opinions of many bond market participants have gone into determining their yields. Even though many zero-coupon Treasury bonds – they are known as *Treasury strips* – are available, it is still better to infer spot yields from on-the-run par bonds than to compute them directly from the Treasury strips.

While we generally agree with this approach, there is one major caveat. On-the-run Treasury securities do not exist at every maturity. In some markets, governments issue five or six different denominated bonds (e.g. 90-day, 180-day, one-year, two-year, three-year, five-year, seven-year and ten-year bonds). What about years 6, 8, 9 and 11–29? A similar problem arises if one needs a zero-coupon rate for a fractional horizon such as 3.5 years.

The general procedure to use when maturities for on-the-run securities are missing is to interpolate par yields for the missing maturities, and to compute spot rates from the interpolated par yields. Traditional practice typically uses linear interpolation to fill in the missing date, but clearly superior non-linear interpolation procedures also exist that make the yield curve appear to be smooth. These techniques are beyond the scope of this text. In every case, the first place one should look for government bond yields is the country's central bank website, where the yields for on-the-run bonds are usually published.

Key Terms

Exercises

10A.1 A zero-coupon bond maturing two years from now has a yield to maturity of 8 per cent (annual compounding). Another zero-coupon bond with the same maturity date has a yield to maturity of 10 per cent (annual compounding). Both bonds have a face value of $100.

- a What are the prices of the zero-coupon bonds?
- b Describe the cash flows to a long position in the 10 per cent zero-coupon bond and a short position in the 8 per cent zero-coupon bond.
- c Are the cash flows in part *b* indicative of arbitrage?
- d Suppose the 10 per cent bond matured in three years rather than two years. Is there arbitrage now?

10A.2 Compute annuity yields and par yields for years 1, 2 and 3 if spot yields for years 1, 2 and 3 are, respectively, 4.5 per cent, 5 per cent and 5.25 per cent. Assume annual compounding for all rates and annual payments for all bonds.

10A.3 Compute spot yields and annuity yields for years 1, 2, 3 and 4 if par yields for years 1, 2, 3 and 4 are, respectively, 4.5 per cent, 5 per cent, 5.25 per cent and 5.25 per cent. Assume annual compounding for all rates and annual payments for all bonds.

References and Additional Reading

Duffie, D. (1996) Special repo rates, *The Journal of Finance*, 51(2): 493–526.

Grinblatt, M. (2001) An analytic solution for interest rate swap spreads, *Review of International Finance*, 2(3): 113–149.

Chapter

11

Investing in Risky Projects

Learning Objectives

After reading this chapter, you should be able to:

- Estimate the cost of capital with the CAPM, APT and dividend discount models.
- Understand how to implement the comparison approach with the risk-adjusted discount rate method, and know its shortcomings.
- Understand when to use comparison firms and when to use scenarios to obtain present values.
- Discount expected future cash flows at a risk-adjusted rate, and know when to discount the certainty equivalent at a risk-free rate.
- Identify the certainty equivalent of a risky cash flow, using equilibrium models, risk-free scenarios and forward prices.

Thermo Fisher Scientific (http://www.thermofisher.com), a general science firm listed on NYSE, has followed the general strategy of starting or acquiring new lines of business and turning them into independent public companies with their own publicly traded shares. Thermo Fisher Scientific benefits from this strategy in two ways. First, by taking its projects public, it learns how financial market participants value its investment projects, which helps the company's managers make better capital allocation decisions. Second, since the compensation of the managers who run the various divisions is based on the share price of the division, they are highly motivated to make decisions that maximize share price.

In the previous two chapters, we emphasized that a manager should adopt a project if the cost of investing in it is less than the cost of a portfolio of financial assets that produces approximately the same future cash flow stream. With any purchase a firm makes, value is enhanced by buying from the cheapest sources. Capital investments are no different. Managers should buy their future cash flow streams from the cheapest source–whether it is the real asset or the financial markets.

This approach to project evaluation is also equivalent to asking how the cash flows of a corporate project would be valued by a competitive capital market if the project could be spun off and sold as a separate entity.

If the separate entity has its own traded equity, it is easy to understand how to choose value-creating real investments: the firm creates value by taking all real investment projects that cost less than the amount the project can generate from the sale of equity in the project. In this simple world, where all investment projects are sold to the capital markets, the criterion for accepting an investment project is the same as that used with any other product a firm might sell. Dell would not sell a computer if the costs were higher than the selling price. Likewise, the company would not create a new division if the costs of doing so were greater than the expected proceeds from taking the division public with a new issue.

Thermo Fisher Scientific, described in this chapter's opening vignette, obviously views the benefits of its approach to real asset investment as exceeding the costs of taking each of its divisions public, which can be substantial (see Chapter 3). However, they are unusual in this regard, and we are unaware of any other firm that follows this strategy.[1] Other firms attempting to address the question 'How much would the financial markets pay for the future cash flows of this investment project?' must recognize that, since the sale of equity in the project is only hypothetical, answering this question is much more difficult than it is for Thermo Fisher Scientific. How to answer this question, in a practical way, without selling your project or division, is the subject of this chapter.

In most firms, managers value risky investments in much the same way that they value riskless investments. First, the manager *forecasts* the future cash flows of the investment and then discounts them at some discount rate. This task, however, is much more difficult for risky investments because: (1) the manager needs to know what it means to forecast cash flows when they are risky; and (2) identifying the appropriate discount rate is more complex when cash flows are risky.

One of the lessons of this chapter is that the way one forecasts cash flows determines the discount rate used to obtain present values. This chapter considers two ways to 'forecast' a cash flow:

1 Forecast the expected cash flow.

2 Forecast the cash flow adjusted for risk (defined shortly).

First, consider the case (see point 1) where the manager forecasts a stream of expected cash flows for the proposed project. Each **expected cash flow**, generated as the probability-weighted sum of the cash flow in each of a variety of scenarios, could then be discounted with a risk-adjusted discount rate determined by a risk-return model such as the CAPM or the APT. Obtaining PVs in this fashion is known as the **risk-adjusted discount rate method**.

An outline of a traditional valuation with this approach is to:

- estimate the expected future cash flows of the asset
- obtain a risk-adjusted discount rate and discount just as we did in the previous chapter to find the present value.

Since the expected cash flows are generated by assets that we are trying to value, it is important to find their present values by discounting them at the expected returns of *assets* that are comparable to the assets being valued. These typically are the assets of publicly traded firms in the same line of business as the asset being valued. The problem is that even the assets of publicly traded firms–for example, their factories and machines–are rarely traded. Instead, financial markets trade claims on the cash flows of these assets. Examples of these claims are the debt and equity of publicly traded firms. Hence one has to start with the debt and equity claims on assets and somehow convert them to an asset expected return to obtain the appropriate risk-adjusted discount rate. The first step is to identify the betas of these claims. Then one typically:

a uses a formula to convert the equity and debt betas of comparable publicly traded firms to asset betas to undo the confounding effect of leverage on equity betas (this process is known as *unlevering the beta*)

b applies an asset pricing model to convert the asset beta to an asset expected return, which is then used as the risk-adjusted discount rate.

Alternatively, one can:

a use an asset pricing model to convert the equity beta to an equity expected return

b use a formula to convert the equity expected return (and sometimes the debt return) of comparable publicly traded firms to asset expected returns to undo the confounding effect of leverage on equity betas (this process is typically known as *unlevering the equity return*); the asset expected return is then used as the risk-adjusted discount rate.

---

[1] Other firms undertake the same type of equity carve-outs described for Thermo Fisher Scientific, but none does it with the same frequency or the same intent.

(These steps become even more complex in the presence of corporate taxes, a topic we refer to in Chapter 13.)

As noted above (see point 2), there is another case where managerial forecasts of cash flows are adjusted for risk. As we shall see, this does not necessarily present problems when managers are fully aware of the way they are forecasting, and understand its implications for the discount rate. However, managers are often unaware of what they are forecasting, or how they are adjusting for risk. For example, managers often think they are forecasting expected cash flows when, in reality, their forecasts are not true expectations, because they ignore possible events that potentially can make the cash flows zero.

As an illustration of this, consider the billions of euros (€9.5 billion) invested by Uniper, Wintershall Dea, OMV, Engie, Gazprom and Royal Dutch Shell in the gas pipeline, Nord Stream 2, knowing there was a very small chance of losing the entire investment in the event of a Russian invasion of Ukraine. The managers of these firms would have recognized this threat when they calculated the expected cash flows. They may also have arbitrarily increased the discount rate to reflect the higher risk. However, instead of employing this *ad hoc* adjustment to the discount rate, one should adjust the expected cash flows to reflect the possibility of the unfortunate outcome, and discount expected cash flows at the appropriate risk-adjusted rate.

In other situations, managers account for the riskiness of a cash flow by reporting a conservative 'expected cash flow' – that is, they place too much weight on the bad outcomes and too little on the good ones. This procedure, while generally misapplied, has some merit. In some instances, the conservative forecasted cash flow can be viewed as a **certainty equivalent**, or hypothetical riskless cash flow that occurs at the same time and has the same present value as the risky cash flow being analysed.[2] Valuing a stream of certainty equivalents with the **certainty equivalent method** involves discounting at the risk-free rate. Thus, for valuation purposes, certainty equivalent cash flows can be treated as if they are certain.

The choice of whether to obtain a present value by discounting an expected cash flow at a risk-adjusted discount rate or by discounting a certainty equivalent cash flow at a risk-free rate depends largely on the information available to value the project. If traded securities exist for companies that have the same line of business as the project, then the beta risk of these comparison securities can be used to identify the appropriate discount rate for the project's expected cash flows. In this case, if the expected cash flows are easier to identify than the certainty equivalents of the cash flows, discounting expected cash flows will be the preferred method.

If it is not possible to identify the beta risk of comparison securities (for example, because securities in the same line of business are non-existent), then beta risk needs to be identified from scenarios that allow a statistician to estimate it. In the latter setting, the certainty equivalent method is generally more convenient. In addition, it is sometimes easier to identify certainty equivalent cash flows than expected cash flows, particularly when forward or futures prices exist for commodities that are fundamental to the profitability of the project: in this case, discounting certainty equivalents at a riskless rate of interest would be the preferred method of identifying the present values of real assets.

When applied properly, discounting expected cash flows at a risk-adjusted discount rate and certainty equivalent cash flows at a risk-free discount rate provide the same value for the project's future cash flows. They are equivalent because both methods are applications of the general valuation principle used throughout the text: identify a tracking portfolio and use its value as an estimate of the value of the asset's future cash flows. Real asset investment should be undertaken only in situations where the financial investments that track the future cash flows of the real asset have a value that exceeds the project's cost.

The approach to valuing risky real assets presented in this chapter is eminently practical. For example, numerous corporations and banks use the two valuation methodologies. Moreover, the chapter analyses in depth a great number of implementation issues and obstacles.[3]

11.1 Tracking Portfolios and Real Asset Valuation

The discounted cash flow valuation formula is founded on the tracking portfolio approach. The formula is a statement that the market price of a combination of financial investments that track the future cash flows of the project should be the same as the value of the project's future cash flows.

[2] Chapter 7 introduced forward prices for zero-cost financial contracts. The certainty equivalent can be thought of as the preferred terminology for the forward prices of real asset cash flows.

[3] However, one practical issue of great importance, of which the reader needs to be aware, is not addressed in this chapter: the issue of how corporate taxes affect the valuation of projects financed with debt. Unless the reader is valuing only equity-financed projects or projects with no corporate tax implications, we urge the study of Chapter 13, which addresses this topic.

Although this method is fairly straightforward with riskless cash flows, it is much more difficult to apply it to risky projects. A portfolio that perfectly tracks the cash flows of a risky project exists only in special circumstances. One case might be an oil well whose cash flows can be perfectly tracked by a portfolio of forward contracts on oil and some investment in risk-free bonds. Another case is a copper mine, which can be perfectly tracked by a portfolio of copper forward contracts and a risk-free investment.[4] In most cases, however, there will be some *tracking error:* that is, a difference between the cash flows of the tracking portfolio and the cash flows of the project. The analyst who wants to value a project in these cases needs to employ a theory that describes how to generate tracking portfolios for which the tracking error has a present value of zero. The next section elaborates on this point.

Asset Pricing Models and the Tracking Portfolio Approach

When tracking error exists, the analyst generally must turn to asset pricing models, such as the Capital Asset Pricing Model (CAPM) and the arbitrage pricing theory (APT), to derive a project's present value. Specifically, imperfect tracking portfolios can be used for valuation purposes if the tracking error has zero present value, which is the case only when the tracking error consists entirely of unsystematic or firm-specific risks.

An Example of How to Use Tracking Portfolios for Valuation

Consider the cash flows from the following hypothetical project, which, for simplicity, we initially assume can be perfectly tracked by a mix of the market portfolio and the risk-free asset: faced with the possibility of legalized onshore gambling in the USA, the senior management of Hilton Hotels wants to evaluate the prospects for a hotel/casino. To simplify the analysis, focus only on the valuation of a single risky cash flow from the casino to be received by Hilton one year from now. Assume, further, that this cash flow can take on one of only three values:

1 $12.3 million in the good state (40 per cent probability)

2 $11.3 million in the average state (40 per cent probability)

3 $9.3 million in the bad state (20 per cent probability).

The table below attaches to these states the future values of the market portfolio per dollar invested.

State	Probability	Cash flow next year of	
		Hilton hotel/casino (in $ millions)	Market portfolio (per $1 invested)
Good state	0.4	12.3	1.40
Average state	0.4	11.3	1.20
Bad state	0.2	9.3	0.80

Given the state probabilities, the expected cash flow of the casino next year is $11.3 million. If the risk-free rate is 6 per cent, the future cash flow of the Hilton hotel/casino can be perfectly tracked by a $10 million investment:

- $5 million in a risk-free asset (worth $5.3 million one year from now), and
- $5 million in the market portfolio (worth $6 million one year from now).

Since a portfolio of financial assets worth $10 million tracks the cash flow of the casino, the present value of the casino's future cash flow is $10 million.

Note that if one were discounting the casino's expected cash flow to obtain a present value, the appropriate discount rate must equal the discount rate for the tracking portfolio's expected cash flow, namely, the expected return of the tracking portfolio. This is a weighted average of the expected return of the market portfolio and the risk-free return, where the weights correspond to the respective portfolio weights on the market (β) and risk-free asset ($1 - \beta$) in the tracking portfolio.[5] Here, it turned out that β equals 0.5.

---

[4] See Chapter 12.

[5] Discounting the expected cash flow at the tracking portfolio's expected return generates the present value *only if the present value is of the same sign (positive or negative) as the expected cash flow, and both the present value and expected cash flow are non-zero.* For example, as either the present value or the expected cash flow (but not both) approaches zero, the expected return (i.e. the discount rate) approaches (plus or minus) infinity. In such cases, we have to abandon the risk-adjusted discount rate method, and instead use the certainty equivalent method (discussed later in the chapter) to generate present values.

Tracking Error and Present Values

The perfect tracking seen above arises because we constructed an example where the return on the market portfolio is perfectly correlated with the casino cash flow. Changing any one of the three casino cash flows or three market portfolio cash flows eliminates this perfect correlation. In this case, we would find, at best, that only imperfect tracking is possible.

With imperfect tracking, the mix of the market portfolio and the risk-free asset that best tracks the Hilton cash flow is one that minimizes the variance of the tracking error. Much of this chapter is devoted to illustrating how to obtain this mix. For now, simply assume that the portfolio that best tracks the casino cash flow, in the sense of minimizing the variance of tracking error, is one that contains $5 million of the market portfolio and $5 million of the risk-free asset.

As noted above, since the tracking portfolio has a $10 million value, the value of the casino cash flow should also be $10 million. As Chapter 10 illustrated, this is obvious when there is perfect tracking, given the assumption of no arbitrage. It is useful to review why this is also the case with imperfect tracking. First, valuation requires a tracking portfolio with the same expected future cash flow as that of the real asset it tracks. This implies that the tracking error, measured as the difference between the tracking portfolio's future value and the casino's cash flow, has an expected value of zero. Moreover, the tracking error from a properly designed tracking portfolio represents unsystematic (or diversifiable) risk. Whenever tracking error has no systematic (or factor) risk and has zero expected value, it has zero present value and can be ignored. Thus we can often use a tracking portfolio's market value as a fair representation of what a cash flow is worth, even when it tracks the cash flow imperfectly.

The following result generalizes this.

Results

Result 11.1

Whenever a tracking portfolio for the future cash flows of a project generates tracking error with zero systematic (or factor) risk and zero expected value, the market value of the tracking portfolio is the present value of the project's future cash flows.

Implementing the Tracking Portfolio Approach

If the financial manager identifies a tracking portfolio that is mean-variance efficient, valuation is a straightforward task. For example, if the CAPM holds, simply knowing the $5 million (market portfolio) and $5 million (risk-free asset) composition of the Hilton casino tracking portfolio indicates that the project's present value is $10 million. The manager does not need to know the expected return of the market, the risk-free return, or even the expected cash flow of Hilton to compute this present value.

This situation is rare, however. For example, we might be able to look at traded casino equities and compute their average beta as 0.5, but how would we know that $5 million is the correct investment in the market portfolio without first estimating the expected future cash flow and the expected return of the market portfolio?

Estimating Tracking Portfolios Without Expected Cash Flows or Returns

There are a few ways to estimate a tracking portfolio without knowing expected returns or expected cash flows. One way arises when there is perfect or almost perfect tracking. Because tracking error that is zero or close to zero can be ignored, perfect or almost perfect tracking has a further advantage: a financial manager can use any combination of financial assets to track the investment, including those that are not mean-variance efficient. This approach is clearly superior to the CAPM/APT approaches, which generate substantial tracking error because of the restrictive composition of their tracking portfolios, but nevertheless imply that the tracking error has zero present value. As a first pass, a manager should try to identify a tracking portfolio with minimum tracking error variance, and only when this variance is large turn to asset pricing models that specify a tangency portfolio as the critical tracking instrument.

Using the Market Portfolio or Factor Portfolios in Computing the Tracking Portfolio

In most cases, the existence of tracking error necessitates the use of a market portfolio or a set of factor portfolios, combined with a risk-free asset, to track a project. However, the specification of the appropriate mix of financial assets in the tracking portfolio can be complicated.

Linking Financial Asset Tracking to Real Asset Valuation with the SML

Despite this complexity, it is very important to determine, as best as one can, the proper mix of assets in the tracking portfolio, especially when there is tracking error. In this subsection we use the securities market line to illustrate why being careless about this estimation can be costly.

The returns of risky zero-NPV investments, such as financial assets, can be graphed as lying on the securities market line. This line (see Exhibit 11.1) is based on the risk–expected return relation developed from the tangency portfolio discussion in Chapter 5. Having a cash flow with return beta of β– computed with respect to the tangency portfolio–means that we can track the cash flow per unit of present value with a portfolio that has a weight of β on the tangency portfolio and a weight of $1 - \beta$ on the risk-free asset. In the Hilton example, the β of the project return and thus the weight on the market portfolio is $\frac{1}{2}$.

Exhibit 11.1 Real Assets and the Securities Market

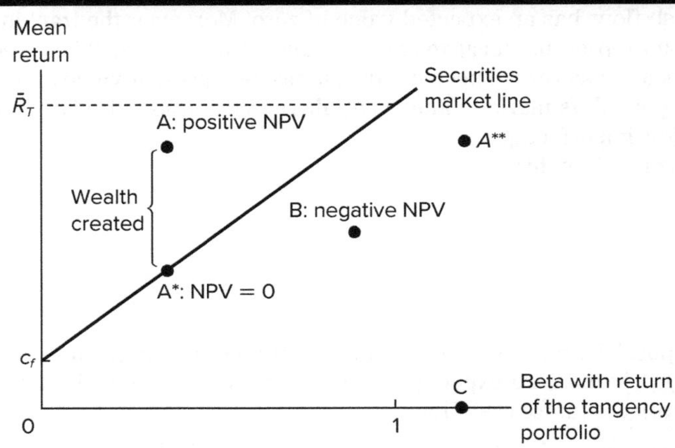

Positive-NPV projects plot above the securities market line at, for example, point A. Conversely, negative-NPV projects plot below the securities market line at point B. Expected returns on the projects in Exhibit 11.1 are computed *using the cost of initiating the project as the base price.* Since these costs can be either above or below the present value of the project's future cash flows, the expected returns calculated in this manner can plot above or below the securities market line. When a project's future cash flows are sold to the financial markets, as in the Thermo Fisher Scientific discussion in the opening vignette, returns are computed with the present value as the base price. Hence a positive-NPV project, such as point A in Exhibit 11.1, when spun off to the financial markets, would lie at point A*. The movement from A to its counterpart A* on the securities market line signifies that wealth is created by adopting the project and spinning it off to the securities markets. This wealth arises because the firm can sell those future cash flows for more than it costs to produce them.

The key to recognizing a positive-NPV project is to know the project's beta. If beta is overestimated – for example, if the project at point A is assumed to have a beta at point C and thus is erroneously interpreted as being at point A** – a positive-NPV project can mistakenly appear to have a negative NPV. It is also possible to underestimate the betas of negative-NPV projects, which could lead to adoptions of bad projects. Thus it is very important to understand how to best identify the project's beta. The next section discusses this issue at great length.

11.2 The Risk-Adjusted Discount Rate Method

This section discusses what is perhaps the most popular method for obtaining the present value of the future cash flows of a real asset. The method discounts the expected future cash flows at a rate known as the project's *cost of capital.* The cost of capital of a project is the expected return that investors require for holding an investment with the same risk as the project. To employ this method, one has to estimate the expected cash flow, the expected return of the market (or factor portfolios), and the CAPM beta (or factor betas) of the project return.[6]

Defining and Implementing the Risk-Adjusted Discount Rate Method with Given Betas

The method of discounting expected cash flows at a risk-adjusted discount rate, the *risk-adjusted discount rate method*, is used primarily in cases where there is a comparison firm or set of firms in the same line of business as the project. Managers who use this valuation method are assuming that the returns of the traded equity of the comparison firm or set of firms have the same beta as the returns of the project. As shown below, using the risk-adjusted discount rate method generally provides present values that are consistent with the tracking portfolio approach.

For simplicity, we begin our analysis by assuming a single cash flow that is generated in the next period. The following result describes how to calculate present values with the risk-adjusted discount rate method.

Results

Result 11.2

To find the present value of next period's cash flow using the risk-adjusted discount rate method:

1. Compute the expected future cash flow next period, $E(\widetilde{C})$.
2. Compute the beta of the return of the project, β.
3. Compute the expected return of the project by substituting the beta calculated in step 2 into the tangency portfolio risk–expected return equation.
4. Divide the expected future cash flow in step 1 by one plus the expected return from step 3. In algebraic terms:

$$\text{PV} = \frac{E(\widetilde{C})}{1 + r_f + \beta(\overline{R}_T - r_f)} \tag{11.1}$$

Example 11.1 illustrates how to implement the risk-adjusted discount rate method.[7]

Example 11.1

Using the Cost of Capital to Value a Non-Traded Subsidiary

Assume that BA Cityflyer, which is a wholly owned subsidiary of International Airlines Group (created when BA merged with Iberia), has a β of 1.2 when computed against the tangency portfolio. One year from now, BA Cityflyer has a 0.9 probability of being worth £5 per share and a 0.1 probability of being worth £4 per share. The risk-free rate is 6 per cent per year. The tangency portfolio has an expected return of 14 per cent per year. What is the present value of a share of BA Cityflyer, assuming no dividend payments are made in the coming year?

Answer:

$$0.9(£5) + 0.1(£4) = £4.90$$

[6]Also, as noted in an earlier footnote, the expected cash flow and present value have to be either both positive or both negative.

[7] Example 11.1 is used to value an entire subsidiary, which is a collection of projects. The risk-adjusted discount rate method also can be used to value a single project.

According to the tangency portfolio risk-expected return equation, the appropriate discount rate for BA Cityflyer is

$$0.06 + 1.2(0.14 - 0.06) = 15.6\,\% \text{ per year}$$

BA Cityflyer's present value per share is the share's expected future value divided by 1 plus the appropriate discount rate, or approximately

$$\frac{\pounds 4.90 \text{ per share}}{1.156} = \pounds 4.24 \text{ per share}$$

The β in Example 11.1 was given to us. In general, the hallmark of the risk-adjusted discount rate method is that it is implemented with a **comparison approach**, which provides an estimate of the appropriate beta for the project by analysing the betas of traded comparison securities. In Example 11.1, the comparison approach would have identified the project β of 1.2 by estimating the betas of the traded equities of comparison firms in the airline industry and using some average of their betas as a proxy for BA Cityflyer's β. Implicitly, this comparison approach assumes that the present value is not negative or zero.

The Tracking Portfolio Method is Implicit in the Risk-Adjusted Discount Rate Method

To understand the relationship between the risk-adjusted discount rate method and tracking, assume that the CAPM is applied to value the Hilton casino cash flow considered in the last section. To do this, we discount the expected cash flow, assumed to be \$11.3 million, at the discount rate implied by the CAPM.

The average of the betas of the traded equity of a group of comparison casinos is estimated to be 0.5. Thus the Hilton casino cash flow is tracked by a portfolio that is invested:

- 50 per cent in the market portfolio, and
- 50 per cent in the risk-free asset.

If the expected return on the market is 20 per cent and the risk-free rate is 6 per cent, the appropriate discount rate is

$$0.06 + 0.5(0.20 - 0.06) = 0.13$$

Hence the present value of the expected future cash flow is

$$\$11.3 \text{ million}/1.13 = \$10 \text{ million}$$

The 13 per cent used to discount the \$11.3 million expected future cash flow from the Hilton casino is the expected return of the tracking portfolio. Hence, if one buys enough of the tracking portfolio to have an expected future value of \$11.3 million, the tracking portfolio will cost \$10 million today. This tracking portfolio consists of \$5 million in the market portfolio (50 per cent) and \$5 million in the riskfree asset (50 per cent). Thus the discounted (or present) value of the expected future cash flow is nothing more than the cost of acquiring the tracking portfolio's cash flows (\$10 million), while the CAPM beta (0.5) represents the proportion of the tracking portfolio allocated to the market portfolio, which is assumed to be the tangency portfolio.

11.3 The Effect of Leverage on Comparisons

Since the risk-adjusted discount rate method uses the traded equities of comparison firms to estimate the betas of projects, it is important that the beta risk of the equity of the comparison firms be truly comparable. However, it is not enough merely to use firms in the same line of business as the project. Since the amount of debt financing a firm takes on can dramatically affect equity betas, it is necessary to adjust for differing amounts of debt financing in order to make appropriate beta risk comparisons.

In this section, we explore the effect of debt financing, also known as leverage, on the beta and standard deviation of a firm's equity. We begin by performing a financing experiment in which a firm issues risk-free debt, but does not alter the operations of the firm. Hence the proceeds of the debt issue are used to retire outstanding equity, while sales, EBIT, marketing, production and so forth remain the same.

The Balance Sheet for an All-Equity-Financed Firm

Begin with an all-equity-financed firm. Exhibit 11.2 illustrates the familiar accounting balance sheet in T-account form. The left-hand side reflects the assets of the firm, and the right-hand side reflects the debt (liabilities) and equity. In contrast to an accounting balance sheet, which reflects book values, the T-account in Exhibit 11.2 describes market values. Hence A represents the market value of the firm's assets and E the market value of the firm's equity. In the absence of leverage, A equals E, because the two sides of the balance sheet add up to the same number: that is, they *balance*. This identity implies that the *risk* of A and E in the all-equity-financed firm must be the same, whether risk is measured as standard deviation (in which case $\sigma_A = \sigma_E$), or as beta risk (in which case $\beta_A = \beta_E$).

Exhibit 11.2 Balance Sheet for an All-Equity-Financed Firm

Assets	Liabilities and equity
A	Debt 0 (i.e. $D = 0$)
	Equity E

The Balance Sheet for a Firm Partially Financed with Debt

Now, let us introduce debt. In this case, the balance sheet looks like the T-account depicted in Exhibit 11.3. Because the two sides of the balance sheet must balance,

$$A = D + E$$

Exhibit 11.3 Balance Sheet for a Firm with Leverage

Assets	Liabilities and equity
A	Debt D ($D > 0$)
	Equity E

In other words, the market value of the assets of the firm must equal the sum of the market values of the debt and equity. This makes sense. All the future cash flows from the assets of the firm must at some point flow to the cash flow claimants. An investor who buys up all the debt and equity of the firm has a right to all the cash flows produced by the assets. Hence the sum of the market values of the debt and equity must be the same as the market value of the firm's assets.

The Right-Hand Side of the Balance Sheet as a Portfolio

Now, view the right-hand side of the balance sheet in Exhibit 11.3 as a portfolio of investments, with the weight on debt as $D/(D + E)$, and the weight on equity as $E/(D + E)$.

To understand the relationship between asset risk and equity risk, we now use the portfolio mathematics developed in Chapters 4 and 5 to analyse risk measures of each of the components, A, D and E. With risk-free debt, all of the risk is borne by the equity holders. In this case, σ_D and β_D are both zero for risk-free debt, implied by the portfolio formulae developed earlier,

$$\sigma_A = \left(\frac{D}{D+E}\right)0 + \left(\frac{E}{D+E}\right)\sigma_E$$

and

$$\beta_A = \left(\frac{D}{D+E}\right)0 + \left(\frac{E}{D+E}\right)\beta_E \qquad (11.2a)$$

Inverting these equations to place the equity risk measures on the left-hand side results in

$$\sigma_E = \left(1 + \frac{D}{E}\right)\sigma_A$$

and

$$\beta_E = \left(1 + \frac{D}{E}\right)\beta_A \qquad (11.2b)$$

Recall that the experiment performed is one in which altering the mix of financing between debt and equity does not change *A*, the operating assets of the firm. Hence equation (11.2b) and the equation above it imply the following result.

Results

Result 11.3

Increasing the firm's debt (raising *D* and reducing *E*) increases the (beta and standard deviation) risk per unit of equity investment. It will increase linearly in the *D/E* ratio if the debt is risk free.

Result 11.3 stems from the equivalence of the assets of the firm to a portfolio of the firm's debt and equity, with respective positive portfolio weights of $D/(D + E)$ and $E/(D + E)$. Thus

$$\tilde{r}_A = \left(\frac{D}{D+E}\right)\tilde{r}_D + \left(\frac{E}{D+E}\right)\tilde{r}_E \qquad (11.3a)$$

This also means that each unit of equity can be thought of as a portfolio-weighted average of the firm's assets and debt, with a long position in the assets and a short position in debt. Here the respective portfolio weights are $(1 + D/E)$ on the assets and $-D/E$ on the debt: that is, upon rearranging equation (11.3a) to place $\tilde{r}_E$ on the left-hand side, we obtain

$$\tilde{r}_E = \left(1 + \frac{D}{E}\right)\tilde{r}_A - \left(\frac{D}{E}\right)\tilde{r}_D \qquad (11.3b)$$

Distinguishing Risk-Free Debt from Default-Free Debt

In the previous subsection, we assumed that the debt of the firm was risk-free. Risk-free debt is necessarily default-free debt, but the reverse is not necessarily true. There are two sources of risk associated with debt. One is interest rate risk, which is associated with general changes in long-term interest rates, and the other is credit risk, which is associated with the possibility of default. All long-term debt, even if it is default-free, will see its value move inversely with long-term interest rates (bond yields), as Chapter 2 observed. Asset values, however, also tend to move inversely with long-term interest rates, which means that long-term debt, even if it is default-free, tends to have a positive beta (typically around 0.2, when computed with respect to broad-based stock portfolios such as the FTSE 100 or S&P 500). Risk-free debt is necessarily short term because it cannot have its value altered by changes in long-term interest rates. Short-term default-free debt tends to have a beta near zero and, for our purposes, can also be regarded as risk-free debt.

The main goal of this section is to analyse the effect of debt on beta and expected return. In particular, and as the next section illustrates, it is useful to isolate the impact of credit risk on bond and equity betas for high-leverage ratios. To avoid confounding the effect of interest rate risk and credit risk, we have deliberately chosen to analyse risk-free debt, which has a beta of zero.

It is straightforward to modify the analysis of the effect of leverage when debt has a positive beta. Again, viewing the firm as a portfolio, equation (11.2a) would generalize to

$$\beta_A = \left(\frac{D}{D+E}\right)\beta_D + \left(\frac{E}{D+E}\right)\beta_E$$

implying that equation (11.2b) generalizes to

$$\beta_E = \left(1 + \frac{D}{E}\right)\beta_A - \left(\frac{D}{E}\right)\beta_D$$

Equation (11.3b) remains unchanged.

Graphs and Numerical Illustrations of the Effect of Debt on Risk

Exhibit 11.4 illustrates the beta of equity as a function of the **leverage ratio**, *D/E*. When the debt is default free, the firm's equity holders bear all the risk from swings in asset values. By equation (11.2b), the beta of equity as a function of *D/E* should graph as a straight line in this case. When debt default is possible, debt holders bear part of the risk, implying that equity holders bear less risk. As a result, the beta risk of equity becomes a curved line.

Exhibit 11.4 Equity Beta as a Function of the Firm's Leverage Ratio

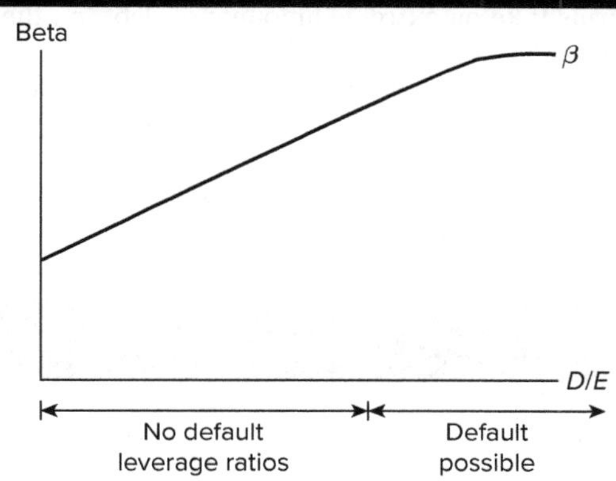

To explore Result 11.3 further, we illustrate numerically why equity holder (beta or standard deviation) risk per unit of money invested increases with leverage. First, note that if a firm's total cash flows are independent of its **capital structure** – that is, its mix of debt and equity financing – the total risk borne by the aggregation of the investors of a firm, debt holders plus equity holders, does not change when the firm changes its capital structure. Thus an all-equity-financed firm with assets that change from a value of €100 million in 2022 to €110 million in 2023, and then to €88 million in 2024, has equity that experiences the same value changes. For each euro invested, such equity holders experience value changes amounting to a 10 per cent increase from 2022 to 2023, and a 20 per cent decrease from 2023 to 2024.

However, if the same assets had been financed with €75 million in risk-free debt, implying an initial debt-to-equity ratio of 3, the equity jumps from €25 million (= €100 million – €75 million) in 2022 to €35 million (= €110 million – €75 million) in 2023. The equity increase of 40 per cent (€25 million to €35 million) is four times larger for each euro invested than the 10 per cent equity increase of the all-equity firm (€100 million to €110 million). Thus leverage benefits the firm's shareholders when asset values appreciate, but, from 2023 to 2024, when the assets drop from €110 million to €88 million (a 20 per cent decrease), the equity of the levered firm goes from €35 million in 2023 to €13 million in 2024, a 63 per cent decrease.[8]

The Cost of Equity, Cost of Debt and Cost of Capital as a Function of the Leverage Ratio

The **cost of equity** for a firm is the expected return required by investors to induce them to hold the equity. Since the firm's equity beta increases linearly as the amount of default-free debt financing increases, it should not be surprising that the firm's cost of equity capital also increases linearly as a function of the leverage ratio, *D/E*. Specifically, taking expectations of equation (11.3b) and grouping terms yields the following result.

[8] The 63 per cent decrease for the leveraged firm is not quite four times the 20 per cent decrease experienced by the assets, because the debt–equity ratio is smaller than 3 to 1 in 2024.

Results

Result 11.4

The cost of equity,

$$\bar{r}_E = \bar{r}_A + \left(\frac{D}{E}\right)(\bar{r}_A - \bar{r}_D)$$

increases as the firm's leverage ratio *D/E* increases. It will increase linearly in the ratio *d/e* if the debt is default free and if $\bar{r}_A$, the expected return of the firm's assets, does not change as the leverage ratio increases.[9]

In Result 11.4, the expected (and actual) return of a firm's debt $\bar{r}_D$, its **cost of debt**, equals r_f for moderate leverage ratios. As long as the firm's debt is default free, the cost of equity capital increases linearly in the firm's leverage ratio. However, when firms take on extreme amounts of debt, $\bar{r}_D$, the expected return on risky debt, rises as *D/E* increases. Since debt holders share part of the risk in this case, the cost of equity increases more slowly as *D/E* rises than it does with default-free debt. Again, the risks of the assets are shared by both debt holders and equity holders when default is possible, but they are borne only by equity holders when default is not possible.

Exhibit 11.5 summarizes the findings of this section. It plots the cost of equity, $\bar{r}_E$, the cost of debt, $\bar{r}_D$, and the cost of capital, $\bar{r}_A$, as functions of the leverage ratio *D/E*.

Exhibit 11.5 Cost of Debt, Cost of Equity and Cost of Capital as Functions of *D/E*

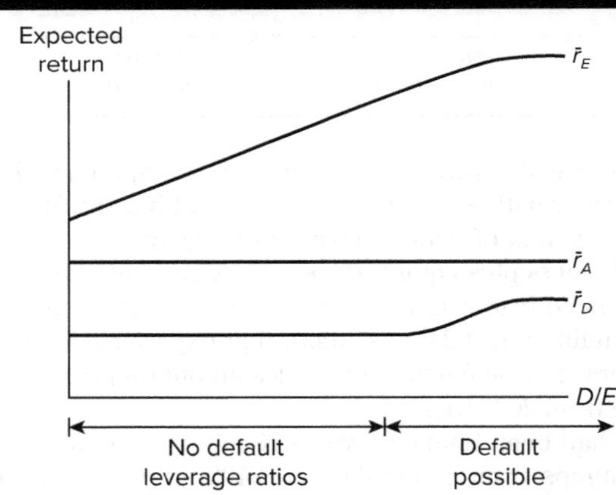

11.4 Implementing the Risk-Adjusted Discount Rate Formula with Comparison Firms

Suppose that the CAPM is correct. Going back to Example 11.1, BA Cityflyer has operations similar to those of Ryanair and easyJet, which are airline companies with similar destinations and comparable business models. Ryanair and easyJet are traded on the London Stock Exchange, whereas BA Cityflyer, since it is a wholly owned subsidiary of International Airlines Group, is not traded. In this case, it might be possible to use Ryanair and easyJet's beta – computed by regressing Ryanair and easyJet's past equity returns on the returns of a

[9] Result 11.4 also applies when expected returns are determined by factor betas in a multifactor setting. In this vein, note that interest rate risk, discussed earlier in this chapter, may make the beta of default-free fixed-rate debt non-zero, but only default risk can generate the curvature seen in Exhibits 11.4 and 11.5.

market proxy – to determine beta, and thus the expected return, for BA Cityflyer. However, one needs to be cautious about drawing this connection, because the way in which a firm is financed can affect its equity beta, as indicated in Section 11.3. It is important not only for Ryanair, easyJet and BA Cityflyer to have similar lines of business, but also for both to have similar leverage ratios. It would not be appropriate in this case to use International Airlines Group, the parent company, as the comparison firm, since it follows a different business model and flies to many more destinations across the world.

The CAPM, the Comparison Method and Adjusting for Leverage

If an acquisition (or project) and its comparison firm(s) are financed differently, it may be possible to adjust the comparison firm's beta for the difference in leverage ratios. However, making this type of adjustment can be tricky, especially when one takes corporate taxes into account. We shall discuss beta adjustments in the absence of taxes below, and will examine how these adjustments are affected by taxes in Chapter 13. (In the absence of taxes, the *weighted average cost of capital* and the *unlevered cost of capital*, terms commonly used in the financial services industry, are identical to the expected return on assets, $\bar{r}_A$).

An Illustration of the Necessary Leverage Adjustment without Taxes

Example 11.2 illustrates the simpler task of how to adjust for leverage differences in the absence of taxes.

Example 11.2

Using the Comparison Approach to Obtain Beta and Cost of Capital

Returning to the BA Cityflyer example (Example 11.1), we must identify comparison firms that have similar business models and operations. BA Cityflyer is a British company and operates from the UK, so, where possible, we must choose comparison firms from the same country. As of 2022, there were five British airlines that could be used as comparisons. These are easyJet, Flypop, Jet2.com, Ryanair and Wizzair. Assume that easyJet is the closest comparator to BA Cityflyer and it has an equity beta of 0.71, a market capitalization of equity (E) equal to £2.62 billion and book value of debt (D) equal to £0.46 billion.

Assume also that the risk-free rate is 6 per cent per year, the risk premium on the market portfolio is 8.4 per cent per year, the CAPM holds, and the debt of easyJet is risk free. Estimate the cost of capital for BA Cityflyer.

Answer: Using equation (11.2a), we first find easyJet's asset beta:

$$\beta_A = \left(\frac{E}{D+E}\right)\beta_E = \left(\frac{2.62}{2.62+0.46}\right)0.71 = 0.604$$

Applying the CAPM risk-expected return equation, using the 0.604 estimate of easyJet's asset beta, gives BA Cityflyer's cost of capital, 11.07 per cent per year:

$$0.06 + 0.604(0.084) = 0.1107$$

In Example 11.2, β_E, the equity beta, determines the cost of equity capital. Recall from the previous section that if β_E is positive, then this beta and the associated expected return on the equity increase as the leverage of the firm increases. The cash flows that are discounted by the risk-adjusted discount rate method are the cash flows from the project's assets, which do not have debt interest payments subtracted from them. Hence it is inappropriate to discount these cash flows at a rate used for discounting the cash flows that belong to the leveraged equity of comparison firms.

By multiplying the betas by $E/(D + E)$, Example 11.2 identifies the beta of the portfolio of debt and equity of the comparison firms (with $\beta_D = 0$). Since assets equal debt plus equity, this portfolio beta is indeed the asset beta that generates an appropriate discount rate for the cash flows of the assets.

As an alternative to the process of unlevering the betas described in Example 11.2, one can compute the CAPM-based expected returns of the equity of comparison firms. Use the equation

$$\tilde{r}_A = \left(\frac{D}{D+E}\right)\tilde{r}_D + \left(\frac{E}{D+E}\right)\tilde{r}_E$$

(obtained from the expected values of both sides of equation (11.3a)) to unlever the equity expected returns and obtain the expected asset return of the comparable firms.

Weighting the Betas of Comparison Firms

Note that in Example 11.2 we used only one beta estimate (easyJet's). If we wish to use more comparison firms, we would average the betas to estimate the beta of BA Cityflyer's assets. This averaging is appropriate if each comparison firm provides an equally valid estimate of the BA Cityflyer asset beta. However, if some firms provide better comparisons than others, their betas should be weighted more than those of the less closely matched firms. For example, assume that we also decide to use the asset beta of Ryanair. Given that it operates out of Dublin, we may argue that it is a less appropriate match than easyJet. We might therefore give the asset beta of Ryanair a lower weight than the beta of easyJet.

Obtaining a Cost of Capital from the Arbitrage Pricing Theory

Earlier, we learned that when the tangency portfolio is the market portfolio, the cost of capital – that is, the discount rate in the denominator of the present value formula, equation (11.1) – is obtained from the Capital Asset Pricing Model. An alternative to the CAPM is the arbitrage pricing theory (APT), developed in Chapter 6, which is the correct theory to use when a combination of factor portfolios, instead of the market portfolio, is the tangency portfolio.

The Multifactor APT Version of the Risk-Adjusted Discount Rate Formula

When computing costs of capital using the expected returns generated by the APT, the present value of the project's future cash flow is

$$\text{PV} = \frac{E(\tilde{C})}{1 + r_f + \lambda_1\beta_1 + \lambda_2\beta_2 + \cdots + \lambda_K\beta_K} \tag{11.4}$$

The project's net present value is computed by subtracting the project's initial cost from this present value.

The discount rates provided by the APT generally differ from those of the CAPM. Thus, they can generate different capital allocation decisions. If the APT is correct and the CAPM is incorrect, firms would be missing out on some good projects and opting for poor ones by using the wrong discount rate from the CAPM. As the following case study illustrates, such differences in the cost of capital between the two models are not uncommon.

Case Study

Arbitrage Pricing Theory versus Capital Asset Pricing Model

Consider the following hypothetical example. A consulting firm provides its clients with the costs of equity capital and costs of capital for a variety of firms using both the CAPM and the APT. There are many versions of the APT, and the version that the firm uses is based on a five-factor model, where the five pre-specified factors are changes in:

- short-term inflation (SINF)
- long-term inflation (LINF)
- the level of short-term interest rates (INT)
- the premium for default risk (PREM)
- the monthly gross domestic product (GDP).

Exhibit 11.6 presents the hypothetical equity expected returns from both the CAPM and APT, as well as the CAPM beta, for six well-known Swedish firms.

Exhibit 11.6 Cost of Equity Capital

CAPM			APT					
				Premiums from sensitivity to five factors				
Firm	Equity beta	Equity expected returns (%)	Equity expected returns (%)	SINF	LINF	INT	PREM	GDP
Ericsson	1.03	11.42	12.61	0.83	1.25	1.39	0.95	1.22
Nordea	0.60	9.57	10.41	0.52	0.76	0.86	0.56	0.74
SHB	1.24	12.34	11.89	0.57	1.13	1.24	0.82	1.15
Skandia	1.52	13.56	11.79	0.39	1.16	1.31	0.69	1.26
Telia	1.05	11.53	8.95	–0.03	0.54	0.61	0.22	0.64
H&M	0.98	11.19	8.54	–0.07	0.45	0.49	0.17	0.52

For each row, the sum of the numbers in the five right-hand columns in Exhibit 11.6 represent the APT risk premiums. APT equity expected returns (the costs of equity capital) are computed as the sum of these risk premiums plus the risk-free rate of 6.98 per cent.

With adjustments for risky debt and taxes, these numbers translate into Exhibit 11.7's comparative costs of capital for the typical existing project of these firms.[10] The difference in the cost of capital computed with the CAPM and APT in Exhibit 11.7 is as large as 2.58 per cent per year, as you'll note in the case of H&M (2.58% = 11 53% – 8.95%). Many projects that are similar to the existing projects of Telia, a telecommunications firm, typically have large investments in the early years – primarily wages for programmers and expenses for advertising and promotion – and substantial revenues from sales that are not likely to occur until much later, perhaps 5 to 15 years after the initial investment. Therefore adoption decisions about any prospective project that resembles Telia's existing collection of projects will be greatly affected by whether one selects the CAPM or the APT to compute Telia's discount rate.

Exhibit 11.7 CAPM and APT Costs of Capital with Leverage Ratios (*D/E*) for Six Firms

Firm	Debt-to-equity ratio (%)	CAPM cost of capital (%)	APT cost of capital (%)	Difference between APT and CAPM cost of capital (%)
Ericsson	6.36	11.02	12.14	1.12
Nordea	46.90	7.93	8.51	0.58
SHB	51.31	9.85	9.55	–0.30
Skandia	778.74	5.65	5.45	–0.20
Telia	0.00	11.53	8.95	–2.58
H&M	27.50	10.12	8.04	–2.08

[10] Adjustments for taxes are discussed in Chapter 13.

Costs of Capital Computed with Alternatives to CAPM and APT: Dividend Discount Models

The CAPM and the APT are the two most popular models for determining risk-adjusted discount rates. Although both models are applied in practice, their applications have been criticized because of the difficulties associated with estimating their essential inputs.

Impediments to Using the CAPM and APT

Specifically, the CAPM requires knowledge of not only the covariance (or beta) of the return of an investment with the return of the market portfolio, but also an estimate of the expected return of the market portfolio. The APT requires multiple factor sensitivities and the corresponding expected returns on multiple factor portfolios.

The Dividend Discount Model

A number of financial analysts estimate required rates of return using analysts' forecasts of future earnings with a special case of what Chapter 9 referred to as the *dividend discount model.* This special case, where dividends grow at a constant rate, is sometimes known as the **Gordon growth model**, because it was first developed by Gordon (1962). According to this model, the equity of a firm with a dividend stream growing at a constant rate can be valued as follows:

$$S_0 = \frac{\text{div}_1}{\bar{r}_E - g} \tag{11.5}$$

where

S_0 = the firm's current share price
div_1 = the expected dividend per share one year from now
$\bar{r}_E$ = the market required rate of return of the firm's equity (its cost of equity capital)
g = the expected growth rate of dividends.

Equation (11.5a) is an application of the growing perpetuity formula developed in Chapter 9. By rearranging this equation, one sees that the expected rate of return on an equity can be expressed as the sum of the growth rate and the dividend yield:

$$\bar{r}_E = g + \frac{\text{div}_1}{S_0} \tag{11.5b}$$

Using Analyst Forecasts to Estimate the Expected Dividend Growth Rate

To compute the risk-adjusted discount rate for equity from this equation, only g, the expected rate of growth of the firm's dividends, and div_1/S_0, the firm's dividend yield, need to be estimated.[11] Analysts' forecasts of the growth rate of a firm's earnings provide one estimate for g. Under the assumption that a firm pays a fixed percentage of its earnings as dividends, the expected growth rate in dividends equals the forecast growth rate in earnings. This growth rate can then be added to the existing dividend yield to derive the expected return on the firm's equity.[12]

For example, at the beginning of 2022, analysts expected the earnings of Barclays plc (a multinational bank) to grow by 9.73 per cent between 2022 and 2023 (source: Yahoo! Finance). The firm paid dividends in 2022 with a dividend yield of 4.15 per cent, and so the expected rate of return on Barclays shares was 13.88 per cent. To obtain a cost of capital for a Barclays-like project, it is necessary to adjust this 13.88 per cent rate of return for debt in Barclays' capital structure. For example, in the risk-free debt, no taxes case of Section 11.2, one can obtain $\bar{r}_A$ by multiplying by $E/(D + E)$.

[11] A historical average of the ratio of dividend per share to prior year share price, sometimes over a period of five years, can be used if the coming year's dividend payout is expected to be unusual.

[12] Note that using the current dividend yield in equation (11.5b) gives the wrong answer. The formula requires next year's expected dividend in the numerator. Multiplying the current dividend per share by $1 + g$ and dividing by the current share price gives the appropriate dividend yield estimate.

Using the Retention Ratio Formula to Estimate the Expected Dividend Growth Rate

An alternative method for estimating g, the growth rate in dividends, employs accounting data. This method estimates the growth rate as:

$$g = b \times \text{ROE} \tag{11.6}$$

where

b = the **ploughback ratio** or **retention ratio**, the fraction of earnings retained in the firm

ROE = **book return on equity**–that is, earnings divided by last year's (mid-year) book equity.[13]

The intuition for the **retention ratio formula**, given in equation (11.6), is that the book return on equity (ROE) represents the rate of growth of capital invested in the firm. When a firm has an ROE of 10 per cent, every £1 invested in the firm returns £1.00 of equity capital and £0.10 of earnings next year, or £1.10. If this £1.10 is entirely reinvested, it will grow another 10 per cent to £1.21 one year later. However, if 75 per cent of the earnings are paid out in the form of dividends, implying a retention ratio of 0.25, the capital will only grow at a rate of (1 – 0.75)(£0.10) – that is, at 25 per cent of the 10 per cent growth rate, or 2.5 per cent. In this case, at the end of the first year, 75 per cent of £0.10 would be paid out in dividends, implying that only £1.025 [= £1.10 – 0.75(£0.10)] is left in the firm for reinvestment. This would grow to £1.025(1.1), but if 75 per cent of the amount over £1.025 (the earnings) is paid out as a dividend, the amount to be reinvested is just £1.025(1.1) – 0.75(£1.025)(0.1) = £1.025^2. Thus paying out a fixed proportion of a company's earnings as dividends slows the growth rate of the funds available for reinvestment. Moreover, since earnings and dividends are a constant proportion of the reinvestment amount, their growth rates will be the same as the growth rate of the funds available for investment in the firm.

Assumptions and Pitfalls of the Dividend Discount Model

The retention ratio formula, equation (11.6), uses the book return on equity in lieu of the return on new investment, the return that theoretically should be used but which is more difficult to measure accurately. If old assets and new assets have different returns, ROE in the retention ratio formula should be the *book return of equity for new asset investment.* If the project is a positive-NPV project, the appropriate book return of equity will exceed the project's cost of capital.

The implicit assumptions of the dividend discount model's estimate of the cost of capital are as follows.

- The earnings growth forecasts, whether from analysts or from equation (11.6), are unbiased: that is, they do not tend to systematically underestimate or overestimate the earnings growth rate.
- The earnings growth forecasts are based on the same information that investors use to value the firm's equity.
- The firm's earnings and dividends grow at the same constant rate, for ever.

To the extent that these assumptions are valid, the dividend discount model may provide a better estimate of the expected rate of return on a firm's equity or project than either the CAPM or the APT, because it does not require estimates of beta or estimates of the expected return of the market portfolio or of factor portfolios. However, these assumptions, particularly that of a constant growth rate, are stringent, and may not apply to many of the firms or projects that an analyst wants to value.

What if No Pure Comparison Firm Exists?

Many firms are large, diversified entities that have many lines of business. In this instance, the equity returns of potential comparison firms are distorted by other lines of business and cannot easily be used as comparison firms for projects that represent only a single line of business. Unfortunately, in many situations there is no appropriate comparison firm with a single line of business. A financial manager in this situation still may be able to obtain an appropriate comparison by forming portfolios of firms that generate a 'pure' line of business. The mathematics behind the approach taken in Example 11.3, which illustrates how to create comparison investments in a pure line of business when none initially exists, is similar in spirit to the formation of pure factor portfolios in Chapter 6.

[13] Alternatively, it is possible to use forecasts of next year's earnings divided by this year's (mid-year) book equity.

The procedure used in Example 11.3 is based on the idea that portfolio betas are portfolio-weighted averages of the betas of individual securities. If we view firms with multiple lines of business as portfolios of lines of business, it may be possible to infer the betas of the individual lines of business by solving systems of linear equations.

When valuing a potential acquisition, it may be possible to identify an appropriate comparison portfolio using accounting numbers. For example, regression coefficients from a regression of the historical sales numbers of the acquisition target on the comparable sales figures of a group of tracking firms generate a portfolio of these tracking firms that best tracks the historical sales figure of the acquisition target. If one thought that the critical accounting value to target was an equal weighting of sales, earnings, assets and book/market ratio, then regressing this equal weighting of the historical accounting numbers from the target firm on the historical values from an equal weighting of the accounting numbers from a group of tracking firms would also generate an appropriate weighting of these tracking firms. Such a portfolio is the one that, in a statistical sense, has best tracked the acquisition in the relevant accounting dimensions.

11.5 Pitfalls in Using the Comparison Method

As the discussion below indicates, there are a number of pitfalls to watch for when implementing the comparison approach.

Example 11.3

Finding a Comparison Firm from a Portfolio of Firms

Assume that WarnerMedia is interested in acquiring the ABC television network from Disney. It has estimated the expected incremental future cash flows from acquiring ABC, and desires an appropriate beta in order to compute a discount rate to value those cash flows. However, the two major networks that are most comparable, NBC and Fox, are owned by Comcast and Fox Entertainment Group–, respectively–, which have substantial cash flows from other sources. For these comparison firms, the table below presents hypothetical equity betas, debt to asset ratios, and the ratios of the market values of the network assets to all assets.

	β_E	$\frac{D}{D+E}$	$\frac{\text{Network assets}}{\text{All assets}} = \frac{N}{A}$
Comcast	1.1	0.1	0.25
Fox Entertainment Group	1.3	0.4	0.50

Estimate the appropriate beta for the ABC acquisition. Assume that the debt of each of the two comparison firms is risk-free. Also assume that the non-network assets of Comcast and Fox Entertainment Group are substantially similar, and thus have the same beta.

Answer: Using equation (11.2a), $\beta_A = [E/(D+E)]\,\beta_E$, first find the asset betas of the two comparison firms. For the two firms, these are, respectively,

	β_A
Comcast	$0.99 = (0.9)(1.1)$
Fox Entertainment Group	$0.78 = (0.6)(1.3)$

Viewing the comparison firms as portfolios of network and non-network assets, and recognizing that the beta of a portfolio is a portfolio-weighted average of the betas of the portfolio components, implies the following equation:

$$\beta_A = \frac{N}{A} \times (\text{network assets' beta}) + \frac{A - N}{A} \times (\text{on-network assets' beta})$$

For the two comparison firms this equation is represented as

Comcast:	$0.99 = (0.25)\beta_{NETWORK} + (0.75)\beta_{NON\text{-}NETWORK}$
Fox Entertainment Group:	$0.78 = (0.5)\beta_{NETWORK} + (0.5)\beta_{NON\text{-}NETWORK}$

Multiplying both sides of the second equation (Fox Entertainment Group) by 1.5, subtracting it from the first equation (Comcast), and solving for $\beta_{NETWORK}$ yields $\beta_{NETWORK} = 0.36$, which is used for the ABC acquisition.

Project Betas are Not the Same as Firm Betas

Most firms use their own cost of capital as a discount rate for evaluating specific investment projects. This could be appropriate, for example, if the analyst is estimating the value of one new Marks & Spencer outlet: each Marks & Spencer store is largely a clone of the others, and its risk probably closely matches the overall risk of Marks & Spencer plc, which is basically a collection of these cloned stores. Hence the cost of capital for Marks & Spencer as a whole is probably a good discount rate for evaluating the profitability of opening up a Marks & Spencer store in a new location.

In most cases, however, using the firm's cost of capital as the discount rate for a new project is inappropriate. For example, new projects may have higher beta risk than the firm's mature projects. This would tend to occur if the project has more R&D investment in its early years, has more **operating leverage**, the ratio of fixed to variable costs, or more options associated with it than the firm as a whole. Alternatively, a project may be less risky than the firm's existing projects, or it may support a higher percentage of debt than the firm as a whole.[14] This would argue for using a lower cost of capital for the project than that experienced by the firm. Most importantly, however, and especially in newer industries, a firm's market value is determined both by its existing projects and by the firm's perceived ability to develop new profitable projects, even projects that are not yet 'on the drawing board'. There is no reason to believe that the discount rate for a firm's perceived ability should be the discount rate for any of its projects.

Growth Opportunities are Usually the Source of High Betas

The previous subsection observed that when a firm's value is generated largely by its perceived ability to develop new profitable projects – more commonly referred to as **growth opportunities** or **growth options** – one must be cautious about using it as a comparison firm for a project, even one of its own. Consider Tesco, for example. The value of this firm's assets can be regarded as the value of the existing Tesco outlets in addition to the value of any outlets that Tesco may open in the future. The option to open new stores is known as a *growth option*. Because growth options tend to be most valuable in good times and have implicit leverage (as Chapter 8 noted for call options in general), which tends to increase beta, they contain a great deal of systematic risk. Hence individual projects can differ in their risk from the firm as a whole because they lack the growth options that are embedded in the firm's share price.

Marks & Spencer plc, however, has gone through a difficult time in recent years, so the growth option is probably small, indicating that Marks & Spencer's cost of capital may be appropriate for valuing a Marks & Spencer store.[15] On the other hand, Tesco, which has been exceptionally successful with its online shopping, may have most of its value generated by growth options. An individual Tesco store thus has assets that look quite different from the assets of Tesco plc, which consist of the relatively low-risk existing stores and high-risk growth options in online shopping. One would be exaggerating the systematic risk of an individual Tesco store by using the risk of Tesco's equity as the appropriate comparison.

There is no good rule of thumb for adjusting the risk of comparison firms for growth options. Usually, but not always, growing franchises like Just Eat, promising biotech and Internet firms – which have high price – earnings

[14] See Chapter 13.

[15] One must be cautious with this example, because Marks & Spencer plc is currently experiencing a modest turnaround and may soon experience the same comparison problems as Tesco.

ratios – or firms with high ratios of market value of equity to book value of equity have valuable growth options. However, the systematic risk of these growth options, which is the risk that is relevant for discounting, depends on how strongly the growth is tied to the health of the economy. The stronger the tie to the health of the economy, the riskier the growth option.

Mineral exploration and discovery companies, whose success depends largely on the successful discovery of commercially viable mineral veins, have growth options that are tied less directly to the health of the economy. For this reason, the beta of these firms' growth options may be low. On the other hand, the potential advertising and subscription revenues of Google, or the willingness of individuals to regularly pay for home deliveries through Just East, are probably tied to the health of the economy – implying relatively high betas for the growth options of Google and Just Eat. Reaching conclusions with casual observations like this is deceiving, however. Despite the observations above, mineral exploration firm betas can be quite high.

Case study

Amgen's Beta and the Discount Rate for Its Projects: The Perils of Negative Cash Flows

Amgen Inc. is a biotechnology company. In 2022, it was selling twenty drugs and had an equity market capitalization of about $133.7 billion. Each of Amgen's projects requires substantial R&D that is not expected to generate profits for many years. A typical project tends to generate substantial negative cash flows in its initial years after inception, and significant positive cash flows in the far-distant future as the drug developed from the project's R&D efforts is sold. Although the positive cash flows depend on the success of early research and clinical trials, assume for the moment that these cash flows are certain. In this case, the future cash flows of any one of Amgen's projects can be tracked by a short position in short-term debt, which has a beta close to zero, and a long position in long-term default-free debt, such as government-backed zero-coupon bonds with maturities from 10 to 30 years. Such long-term bonds have positive but modest betas, as discussed earlier in this chapter. It is useful to think of the negative cash flows that arise early in the life of the project as leverage generated by short-term debt, and the positive cash flows – even though they are assumed to be certain – as risky assets with a modest amount of beta risk. As a leveraged position in positive-beta long-term debt, the combination of these long and short positions results in a beta for the project's value, and ultimately for the firm's value, that is quite high.

As Amgen has matured, its R&D efforts have started to bear fruit. Amgen now generates $6.85 billion in revenue from its twenty drug products. The profit margin on these products is very high, because the heavy expense phase for these drugs is now past. Amgen also has a host of drugs 'in the pipeline'. These projects have passed through much of their large negative cash flow stage, and are now much closer to the prospect of generating significant profits. The positive cash flows of these 'old' and 'middle-aged' projects will arrive soon or have already arrived. This implies that the *values of their positive cash flows,* even if riskless, have lower betas than if they were expected in the distant future. Moreover, these successful projects are leveraged less than a project just starting out (that is, they do not have a series of many early years with substantial negative cash flows). This also contributes to a much lower beta. As a result of mixing these more mature projects with Amgen's usual portfolio of start-up projects, there has been a steady drop in Amgen's beta over time. Amgen's year 2022 beta was 0.58 down from 0.79 in 2007, 1.3 in 2001 and 2 at the beginning of the 1990s.

Although Amgen's beta, and hence the firm's overall cost of capital, dropped considerably during this time period, the risk of the projects it has been implementing has not changed appreciably. Hence the discount rate used to value Amgen projects should not have changed. Indeed, the discount rates used to value Amgen projects may have nothing to do with Amgen's beta, which is tied to Amgen's rate of return (a return made riskier because of the leverage discussed above). Recall that the typical Amgen product has negative cash flows in its early years, and positive cash flows far down the road. Although this creates a high beta for the return on the value of projects in their early years, and consequently for the return of Amgen stock, that value, like the equity in a leveraged firm, is the difference between the value of the long-term positive cash flows and the implicit cost of financing those positive cash flows (in the form of the present value of the costs represented by the negative near-term cash flows). That difference is relatively small, but bears all the risk from the high value long-term positive cash flows.

Clearly, one cannot track both the expected negative cash flows (occurring early on) and the expected positive cash flows (occurring later on) of a start-up Amgen project with the same tracking portfolio. A tracking portfolio with a fixed expected rate of return cannot generate both a positive expected value at one horizon and a negative expected value at another horizon. If separate tracking portfolios are used for the near-term and distant cash flows, one with long positions in securities to track the positive cash flows, and the other with short positions in securities to track the negative cash flows, it is likely that both tracking portfolios would have modest and perhaps negligible betas. The negative early cash flows of a typical Amgen project are largely predetermined. If they vary, it is because there is a need for more or less R&D and testing of the product. Thus the typical negative cash flow is unlikely to have any systematic risk, and has a tracking portfolio consisting of a *short position* in a short-term risk-free asset. The long-term cash flows that are forecast to be positive have positive betas, both because of their horizon (long-term bonds have betas of around 0.2) and because the demand for drugs and drug reimbursement rates from health maintenance organizations and the government are likely to be modestly tied to the health of the economy. However, the betas of the typical long-term cash flow are probably small, say, 0.4, as most of its risk is due to the success of clinical trials and medical needs, not the economy. Such a tracking portfolio would have *positive* weights of 0.4 on both the market portfolio and a short-term risk-free asset.

In conclusion, given the unsystematic nature of the risk associated with the cash flows from most of Amgen's projects, if one were to use a single discount rate for the cash flows of its projects, it would have to be relatively low.

Multi-Period Risk-Adjusted Discount Rates

Virtually all projects have cash flows over multiple periods. Traditionally, multi-period valuation problems have been viewed as simple extensions of the one-period analysis.

The Approach Used by Practitioners

To value the multi-period cash flow *stream* from a project, practitioners typically use the following approach.

1. Estimate the equity beta from a comparison firm using historical data, typically of weekly or monthly frequency. Usually, the comparison firm is the firm doing the project.
2. Compute the expected return using the risk–expected return formula of choice (CAPM or APT) with parameters estimated from historical data.
3. Adjust for leverage and taxes[16] to obtain a cost of capital.
4. Use the cost of capital as a single discount rate for each period in the way that we used the risk-free rate (assuming a flat term structure) in Chapter 10 to discount multi-period cash flows.

Example 11.4 illustrates this approach.

Example 11.4

Applying a One-Period Cost of Capital to Multi-Year Cash Flows

Example 11.2 identified easyJet as a comparison firm for BA Cityflyer, and from this estimated 11.07 per cent per year as the cost of capital for BA Cityflyer. Assume that BA Cityflyer is expected to produce £25 million in cash flows at the end of this year, and that this number will grow by 5 per cent per year for ever. At what price would International Airlines Group be willing to sell BA Cityflyer?

[16] See Chapter 13.

Answer: The present value, using a risk-adjusted discount rate of 11.07 per cent per year, is

$$PV = \frac{£25 \text{ million}}{1.1107} + \frac{£25 \text{ million } (1.05)}{1.1107^2} + \frac{£25 \text{ million } (1.05)^2}{1.1107^3} + \cdots$$

Recognizing this as a growing perpetuity (see equation (9.10)), BA Cityflyer's value would be

$$PV = \frac{£25 \text{ million}}{0.1107 - 0.05} = £411.86 \text{ million}$$

Pitfalls in Using the Practitioner Approach

Using a single cost of capital to discount each of the expected future cash flows – the approach taken in Example 11.4 – is popular with analysts, because it is simpler than using a different discount rate for each individual cash flow. However, in many cases a single cost of capital tends to misvalue cash flows.

This can be true even when cash flows are riskless. Chapter 10 emphasized that analysts should discount the cash flows in different years at different discount rates. For example, if the rate on a default-free zero-coupon bond maturing in the year 2025 is 7 per cent, then a certain cash flow occurring in 2025 must be discounted at a 7 per cent rate. Similarly, if the rate on a default-free zero-coupon bond maturing in 2029 is 9 per cent, then cash flows occurring in 2029 also must be discounted at 9 per cent. Hence, if analysts used a single discount rate of 8 per cent, the near-term cash flows would be undervalued and the cash flows in the more distant future would be overvalued.[17] Misvaluation will be extreme if some future cash flows are negative and others are positive, as the Amgen case aptly illustrated.

The same lesson applies to risky projects. In seeking a comparison firm for the cash flows of BA Cityflyer, International Airlines Group can use the 11.07 per cent expected rate of return of comparison equities only if the cash flows of BA Cityflyer, at each horizon, have expected values and market (or factor) risk identical to those of the tracking portfolio. For example, if the expected cash flows of easyJet have faster growth rates than the cash flows of BA Cityflyer, then they represent an inappropriate comparison, and should not be used in the tracking portfolio.

Long-Term Risk-Free Rate or Short-Term Risk-Free Rate?

The expected rate of return of the firms comparable to BA Cityflyer (easyJet, Ryanair and Whizz Air, for example) are based on risk–expected return models such as the CAPM and APT. A portfolio of these comparison firms would be assumed to track the BA Cityflyer cash flows. In turn, the cost of capital for a given comparison firm is a statement that the firm is tracked by a weighted average of the risk-free asset and the market portfolio (or factor portfolios). For these risk–expected return formulae, *there is no theoretical reason to select a short-term risk-free rate over a long-term risk-free rate, or vice versa.* Moreover, the decision about which horizon to use for the risk-free return in these formulae is not at all tied to the horizon of the cash flow one is trying to value.

In general, the use of the long-term versus the short-term risk-free rate in the CAPM or APT risk–expected return relation depends on practical considerations, not on the horizon of the cash flow. As an illustration, consider the valuation of a long-horizon certain cash flow. It is very clear that the yield of a default-free zero-coupon bond of matched horizon provides the appropriate rate for discounting the certain cash flow. As Chapter 10 emphasized, this discounting is equivalent to finding a tracking portfolio, comprised entirely of a default-free zero-coupon bond, that *perfectly tracks the certain cash flow. For practical reasons,* valuation with perfect tracking is generally more accurate than valuation using the market portfolio or factor portfolios.

Thus, for a long horizon, the beta of the certain cash flow, measured over long horizons, is zero, and the risk-free rate is the long-term riskless rate. However, if one believes the CAPM is correct, it is also appropriate to track a long-horizon certain cash flow with *short-horizon* riskless bonds and the market portfolio.

Since, over short intervals of time, the values of both the certain cash flow and the market portfolio tend to decrease when expected inflation increases, and *vice versa*, the certain cash flow is likely to have a positive

[17] With a riskless cash flow stream, it is possible that all of the overvaluations and undervaluations would cancel out if the single 8 per cent discount rate were used. However, this would be true only if (1) the project's cash flows were identical to those of the tracking portfolio and (2) the internal rate of return of the tracking portfolio was 8 per cent.

beta when measured against the short-term return of the market portfolio. Indeed, as this chapter noted earlier, a typical default-free long-term zero-coupon bond has a beta, measured over short horizons, of about 0.2. With a market risk premium of 8 per cent per year, this generates a reasonable forecast of the typical 1.5 to 2 per cent higher yield of default-free long-term bonds over short-term bonds. Thus the beta of 0.2 obtained from regressions using short-horizon returns suggests that the long-horizon certain cash flow of the long-term bond, and by extension the long-term certain cash flow of any real asset, is tracked by a portfolio that is 20 per cent invested in the market portfolio and 80 per cent invested in a rollover position in short-term riskless bonds.

Note that the beta of the cash flow of the long-term bond above depends on the maturity of the debt used in the tracking portfolio. The bond cash flow's short-horizon CAPM beta of 0.2 identifies the best mix of the market portfolio and a short-term risk-free asset that, with rollovers in the position, tracks the long-horizon certain cash flow. However, the weights of 0.2 on the market portfolio and 0.8 on the short-term risk-free asset change to 0 and 1, respectively, when the market portfolio is combined with a long-term risk-free asset.

Although technically correct, the short-horizon CAPM-based method of valuing a riskless long-horizon cash flow has substantial tracking error. Because of the difference in tracking error with the two approaches, it is preferable to use a long-horizon riskless bond as the sole instrument in the tracking portfolio for a long-term riskless cash flow, and to avoid the CAPM-based approach altogether.

The same considerations apply when evaluating a risky long-horizon cash flow. Whether it is better to include a long-term risk-free bond or a short-term risk-free bond in the tracking portfolio depends on which bond generates a better tracking portfolio. The better tracking portfolio is the one that generates the tracking error with a present value that is closest to zero. The outcome of this horse race will be determined partly by the amount of tracking error and partly by how closely the risk–expected return relationship described by the tracking portfolio approximates reality.

In contrast with a riskless cash flow, the decision about using a long-term or a short-term risk-free rate in valuing a risky cash flow that cannot be perfectly tracked is less clear-cut. In this case, which of the two imperfect tracking portfolios to use – market portfolio and short-term risk-free investment or market portfolio and long-term risk-free investment (*with a different mix of the two in each pairing*) – is an empirical issue best left to the analyst's judgement. Given our ambivalence on this topic, we are fortunate to be able to present a compromise position: the two-factor APT allows the tracking of a future cash flow with a short-term risk-free investment, a long-term risk-free investment and a proxy for the market portfolio – if these are indeed the appropriate factors. If including each one of these three financial assets improves the tracking ability of the overall tracking portfolio, then such a tracking portfolio would be superior to one that leaves out either of the two risk-free investments.

Cash Flow Horizon and Beta Risk

The previous subsection illustrated that the horizon of the returns used in the tracking portfolio may affect the computed beta for a cash flow of a given horizon. This subsection considers whether beta risk depends on the horizon of the cash flow. In practice, financial analysts who implement the risk-adjusted discount rate method almost always use the same beta for every cash flow in a cash flow stream. Below, we argue that in many cases this practical shortcut leads to major valuation errors.

The prices of comparison equities represent the present values of the cash flow streams. Unless the cash flow pattern of the comparison stream matches well with the stream of cash flows being valued, the beta risk of comparison firms may not provide an appropriate discount rate for the project.[18] Moreover, as we saw with Amgen, when the cash flows of a project at some horizons are expected to be negative and those at other horizons are expected be positive, comparison firm betas, even in the case of a good match of the cash flow streams, tend to be too high for both the positive and the negative cash flows.

Such cautions about using comparison firms apply doubly to individual cash flows. A single cash flow, 10 years out, is unlikely to have the same beta risk as a firm in the same line of business. The risk of the comparison firm depends on the risk of each of its future cash flows. Hence the beta of the comparison firm is, in essence, a blend of the betas of each of the cash flows in its cash flow stream. These cash flows occur at many different horizons.

There are no hard-and-fast rules for how betas vary with the cash flow horizon. For some projects, the initial cash flows are relatively safe, but the cash flows in the future depend much more on market returns. In this case, other things being equal, it is best to use a lower discount rate for the shorter-horizon cash flows. In other

[18] This remains an issue whether we believe that an appropriate tracking portfolio (that is, a tracking portfolio with zero-PV tracking error) is composed of a long-horizon riskless bond and the market portfolio (or factor portfolios), or whether it is composed of a short-horizon riskless bond rolled over each period and the market portfolio (or factor portfolios).

cases, long-horizon cash flows tend to have less systematic risk than similar cash flows of short horizons, because many cash flows are highly correlated with the contemporaneous returns of traded securities and the health of the economy at the time the cash flow is produced, but are not significantly correlated with cumulative past returns.

For example, the cash flows of a brokerage firm such as Merrill (previously known as Merrill Lynch) are determined primarily by same-year and prior-year transaction volume, which is highly correlated with the market return. This would imply that the returns of the market over the next 8 years probably have little impact on Merrill's brokerage cash flows 10 years from now. As a consequence, Merrill's year 10 cash flow should be discounted back to year 8 at a risky rate of interest, and from year 8 to date 0 discounted at a much lower rate of interest, perhaps even the risk-free rate.

To understand this, consider the case where the risk-free rate over all horizons was 8 per cent per year and the risky rate was 15 per cent per year. The per year discount rate for the year 10 cash flow should be the geometric mean of eight years of 8 per cent returns and two years of 15 per cent returns, or:

$$[(1.08)^8(1.15)^2]^{1/10} - 1$$

More generally, the geometric mean of T returns, $\tilde{r}_1, \tilde{r}_2, \cdots \tilde{r}_T$, is

$$[(1 + \tilde{r}_1) \times (1 + \tilde{r}_2) \times \cdots \times (1 + \tilde{r}_T)]^{1/T} - 1$$

This is the short-horizon rate of return that, when compounded, gives the return over the long horizon.

Competitive considerations also suggest that long-horizon cash flows contain relatively little systematic (or factor) risk. When market returns are high, business is often good. However, good times often encourage entry into the market by competitors, who can erode profits in subsequent years. Hence, if the economy is doing well in year 5 and Tesla is selling a record number of electric cars in that year, Nissan, BMW and other competitors also might decide to expand their electric car line. By the time year 10 rolls around, the competitors' products will be eroding Tesla's profits in this line of vehicles. This means that although the year 5 market return is positively correlated with the year 5 cash flow for the Tesla project, it may actually be negatively correlated with the year 10 cash flow. Hence the year 10 cash flow may not be highly sensitive to the cumulative 10-year return of the market portfolio.

Empirical Failures of the CAPM and APT

The tracking portfolio metaphor applies even if one questions the validity of the CAPM and APT. If, after reading the empirical evidence in Chapters 5 and 6, one believes that market-to-book ratios and firm size are better determinants of an equity's *future* expected rate of return than market betas or factor betas, then the expected return of each comparison firm is identical to that of a portfolio of firms with similar firm size and market-to-book ratios. In the case of BA Cityflyer, this means that the average historical returns of firm size and market-to-book matched portfolios would be good estimates for the expected returns of easyJet.

In 2022, for example, easyJet had a market-to-book ratio of 1.65 and market capitalization of about £4.35 billion. If the average historical return of a portfolio of firms with this same market-to-book ratio and market capitalization is 15 per cent per year, then the appropriate required return for projects with the same risk as easyJet's is 15 per cent per year. Because this is only an estimate of the project's cost of capital, we may want to do the same computation for other comparison firms, averaging their required rates of return with easyJet's 15 per cent per year estimate to obtain a more statistically precise estimate of the cost of capital for BA City flyer.[19]

However, if one believes that the empirical evidence from the past is the result of a psychological fad, a statistical accident, poor research or some other anomaly that is unlikely to repeat in the future, then one should be more cautious in discarding CAPM or APT-based expected return estimates.

What if No Comparable Line of Business Exists?

Using comparisons to identify beta risk is fine if portfolios of traded assets exist. However, for some real assets there is no suitable comparison line of business in which to search for the components of a tracking portfolio. In 2022, for example, Facebook changed its name to Meta and announced that it would focus on VR technologies and the Metaverse. To value investments in the metaverse (which has still fully to be defined) either from the perspective of Meta or any companies wishing to create new products for the company, one would need to

[19] For simplicity, we have ignored the usual adjustments for leverage that need to be made.

estimate beta risk, yet no comparison firm to Meta exists that has the same size or reach. In instances like this, beta risk can be computed by estimating the project's cash flows in each of many scenarios. Each scenario is associated with a particular realization of the return of the tangency portfolio.

Using Scenarios to Estimate Betas for the Risk-Adjusted Discount Rate Method

Example 11.5 illustrates one way to estimate betas with scenarios. As we shall see shortly, there are some pitfalls to this approach.

In Example 11.5, adoption of the new computer system is a negative-NPV project because the €100,000 cost exceeds the benefit of €82,311. These calculations were based on beta estimates that generate the correct project adoption/rejection decision in simple cases. However, these betas are not really correct. As discussed below, the *true* beta in Example 11.5 is actually lower than the beta *of the return of the project.*

Example 11.5

Estimating Betas with Scenarios

The Flashy Travel Agency wishes to estimate the present value of next year's cash flow from the purchase of 10 new airline reservation computers, at a cost of €10,000 per computer. The new computers, which are faster than the current ones at the agency, are expected to increase the number of reservations that each agent can handle. For simplicity, assume that the additional cash flows associated with the increase in booking capacity are all received one year from now. The size of the increase is tied to the state of the economy. Over the next year, three possible economic scenarios, described in the following table, are considered.

Outcome	Probability	Market return (%)	Incremental cash flow in one year (€)	Return on computers
Recovery	$\frac{3}{4}$	25	150,000	$50\% = \frac{€150{,}000 - €100{,}000}{€100{,}000}$
Recession	$\frac{3}{16}$	−1	35,000	$-65\% = \frac{€35{,}000 - €100{,}000}{€100{,}000}$
Depression	$\frac{1}{16}$	−15	5,000	$-95\% = \frac{€5{,}000 - €100{,}000}{€100{,}000}$

What is the present value of the additional cash flow one year from now if the risk-free return over the next year is 8.625 per cent, and the CAPM determines the expected returns of traded securities?

Answer: The market portfolio's expected return is

$$\frac{3}{4}(25\%) + \frac{3}{16}(-1\%) + \frac{1}{16}(-15\%) = 17.625\,\%$$

The variance of the market return is

$$\frac{3}{4}(25 - 0.17625)^2 + \frac{3}{16}(-0.01 - 0.17625)^2 + \frac{1}{16}(-0.15 - 0.17625)^2 = 0.017236$$

The expected return of the incremental cash flow is

$$\frac{3}{4}(50\%) + \frac{3}{16}(-65\,\%) + \frac{1}{16}(-95\%) = 19.375\%$$

The covariance of the cash flow return with the return of the market portfolio is

$$\frac{3}{4}(0.5 - 0.19375)(0.25 - 0.17625) + \frac{3}{16}(-0.65 - 0.19375)(-0.01 - 0.17625) = 0.0697$$

$$+ \frac{1}{16}(-0.95 - 0.19375)(-0.15 - 0.17625) = 19.375\%$$

This yields a return beta (β) of

$$\frac{0.0697}{0.017236} = 4.045$$

With a cost of €100,000 and a return of 19.375 per cent, the expected cash flow, $E(\widetilde{C})$, is

$$€100,000(1+0.19375)=€119,375$$

Thus, by the risk-adjusted discount rate formula,

$$PV=\frac{€119,375}{1+0.08625+4.045(0.17625-0.08625)}=€82,311$$

Exhibit 11.8 Gross Returns of the Project and its Tracking Portfolio for Example 11.5

Outcome	Probability	Project return + 100%	Tracking portfolio return + 100%
Recovery	$\frac{3}{4}$	$150\%=\frac{€150,000}{€100,000}$	$\frac{€150,000}{PV}$
Recession	$\frac{3}{16}$	$35\%=\frac{€35,000}{€100,000}$	$\frac{€35,000}{PV}$
Depression	$\frac{1}{16}$	$5\%=\frac{€5,000}{€100,000}$	$\frac{€5,000}{PV}$

Why Betas of Returns are not the Correct Betas for the Project

The beta computed in Example 11.5 is not the true beta, because the project returns used have a base price of €100,000 instead of a base price equal to the project's present value, which is lower than €100,000. The securities market line relation between beta and expected return holds for the returns of financial assets, which are zero-NPV investments and, by extension, all real asset investments that are zero NPV.

Suppose that, instead of computing beta with scenarios for project returns, we computed scenarios for a portfolio of financial securities that perfectly track the cash flow of the Flashy Travel Agency project. Example 11.5 resorted to the scenario computation of beta because a comparison firm, needed to generate a tracking portfolio, did not exist. However, it is instructive to examine what the beta computation would be if a comparison-based tracking portfolio did exist.

The Flashy Travel Agency project has a negative NPV, but the hypothetical comparison-based tracking portfolio has a zero NPV. To indicate that the project has a negative NPV, the cost of the tracking portfolio (that is, the project's PV) has to be *smaller* than €100,000. Hence, in each of the three scenarios of Example 11.5, the tracking portfolio's **gross return**, which is the return plus 100 per cent, would be larger than the gross return of the project.

Exhibit 11.8, along with the observation in the Flashy example that $-C_0$ = €100,000, demonstrates that the gross return of the project in each of the three scenarios is:

$$\frac{\text{PV}}{-C_0}\times\left(\text{the gross return of the tracking portfolio}\right)$$

Recall from Chapter 10 that PV/($-C_0$) is the profitability index. Since, in this example, the profitability index is less than 1, the gross returns of the hypothetical tracking portfolio are of larger scale, and thus have a larger beta, than the project's gross returns.[20] More generally, we have the following result.

Results

Result 11.5

The betas of the actual returns of projects equal the project's profitability index times the appropriate beta needed to compute the true present value of the project. Since the profitability index exceeds 1 for positive-NPV projects and is below 1 for negative-NPV projects, this error in beta computation does not affect project selection in the absence of project selection constraints.

[20] We know from Chapter 4 that the covariance of a constant times the return of security i with the return of security j is the constant times the covariance of the returns of securities i and j.

One can take only momentary comfort in the fact that the erroneous beta and, consequently, the erroneous present value computed from project returns do not alter the decision about whether a real investment should be accepted or rejected. The discussion below points out that incorrect capital allocation decisions will be made with mutually exclusive projects if one does not make corrections for return betas of negative-NPV projects that are too low and those of positive-NPV projects that are too high.

Properties of the Correct Beta and Correct Present Value

How one computes a correct beta and present value is not immediately obvious. For example, it is tempting to think that one could do this for Example 11.5 by using the calculated PV of €82,311 as the base number for computing returns and their betas. However, since this PV is still higher than the true PV of the project, it too is inappropriate as a base number. Also, the profitability index that, at least in theory, could be used as a divisor to generate the correct beta and thus the correct PV requires that the analyst first knows the correct PV. While correct in theory, the adjustment implied by Result 11.5 obviously is impractical.

The correct PV has the following property: if the analyst made a lucky guess and selected the correct PV number, the returns (generated by using that PV as a base number) would have a beta and an associated discount rate from the CAPM or APT that would generate the original PV as the discounted expected future cash flow. A general formula for identifying this PV appears in Section 11.6 on the certainty equivalent method, where the formula identifying the PV does not use a risk-adjusted discount rate.

Mutually Exclusive Projects

If no comparison firms exist in the same line of business, forcing the use of scenarios to compute the betas for the risk-adjusted discount rate formula, Result 11.5 points out that the project's return betas will be misestimated by a factor equal to the project's profitability index, $PV/(-C_0)$. This can lead to the wrong choice among a set of mutually exclusive projects, as Example 11.6 demonstrates.

Example 11.6

Mutually Exclusive Projects – Pitfalls in Applying Risk-Adjusted Discount Rates with Scenarios

The Flashy Travel Agency, discussed in Example 11.5, has a choice between two new software reservation systems for its new computers: one is produced by International Airlines Group, the other by Air France-KLM. Both new reservation systems have positive net present values, and thus profitability indices above 1. The actual returns of International Airlines Group's system have a beta of 1, and the actual returns of Air France-KLM's system have a beta of 1.5. Both have an expected incremental future cash flow of €40,000 one year from now. The cost of initiating International Airlines Group's system is €17,679.56, whereas that of Air France-KLM's system is €16,555.43. Assume that the CAPM holds, that the one-year risk-free rate is 8.625 per cent, and that the one-year market risk premium is 9 per cent. Roger Flashman, the son of the owner and, more importantly, the graduate of a rather backward Master's programme that does not use this text, thinks that International Airlines Group's system has a higher net present value. He argues that the risk-adjusted discount rate formula implies that the net present value of International Airlines Group's system is about

$$\frac{€40,000}{1+0.08625+(1)0.09} - €17,679.56 = €16,327$$

The NPV of Air France-KLM's system is

$$\frac{€40,000}{1+0.08625+(1.5)0.09} - €16,555.43 = €16,198$$

which is smaller. Is Roger Flashman correct in his analysis?

Answer: Suppose that the International Airlines Group reservation computer system has a profitability index of 2.0 and the Air France-KLM system has a profitability index of 2.1. By Result 11.5, the betas computed for the International Airlines Group and Air France-KLM systems are too high. The true betas are thus 0.5 ($=\frac{1}{2}$) for the International Airlines Group system and 0.7143 (= 1.5/2.1) for the Air France-KLM system. Hence the true NPV of the International Airlines Group system (assuming the CAPM holds) is about

$$\frac{€40,000}{1+0.08625+(0.5)0.09} - €17,679.56 = €17,680$$

and that of Air France-KLM's system is

$$\frac{€40,000}{1+0.08625+(0.7143)0.09} - €16,555.43 = €18,211$$

Thus, in contrast to Mr Flashman's assertion, Air France-KLM's reservation system has the higher NPV if the profitability index assumptions are correct. However, note that the profitability indices of 2.0 and 2.1 are exactly the correct 'guesses' because they are consistent with what the true profitability indices turned out to be. Thus the profitability indices of 2.0 and 2.1 for International Airlines Group and Air France-KLM, respectively, are not really assumptions, but rather truths about the projects' profitabilities. Clearly, Roger Flashman is wrong and needs to read this text.

Chapter 10 emphasized that mutually exclusive projects should be chosen on the basis of the largest NPV, which is an arithmetic difference between the PV of the project's future cash flows and its initial cost. However, the way in which the PVs of positive-NPV projects are distorted – through the use of the project returns to compute betas for the risk-adjusted discounted rate formula – is a rather complicated function of the true PV and the project's initial cost. The distortion is certainly not an arithmetic difference. Hence it should not be surprising that it is possible to construct examples such as Example 11.6 where the naive manager may select the wrong project by using the risk-adjusted discount rate method.

11.6 Estimating Beta from Scenarios: The Certainty Equivalent Method

Hypothetical examples like Example 11.6 can illustrate the problem of using scenarios with the risk-adjusted discount rate method. In analysing a real-world project, however, financial managers face a significant challenge whenever projects are mutually exclusive and it is difficult to identify a comparison tracking portfolio. Managers do not know the true PV unless they know the beta computed using a base cost that makes the project a zero-NPV investment. However, they cannot know this true project return beta unless they know the true PV. This section suggests a way out of this quandary. The method introduced is also applicable in cases where the present value is not of the same sign as the expected cash flow.

Defining the Certainty Equivalent Method

As noted earlier, the certainty equivalent method is closely related to the risk-adjusted discount rate method. However, instead of discounting expected cash flows at risk-adjusted discount rates, certainty equivalent cash flows are discounted using risk-free interest rates.

To understand what a certainty equivalent cash flow is, consider a project that pays off either €100, €200 or €300 next year, depending on the state of the economy. If these three states of the economy are equally likely, the expected cash flow is €200. Because of risk aversion, however, a project that paid €200 for certain would be preferred to this project. In other words, the certainty equivalent cash flow for this hypothetical project is less than €200 – the project's expected cash flow. On the other hand, we know that this risky project is more valuable than a project with a guaranteed pay-off of €100, the project's lowest cash flow. The certainty equivalent cash flow is thus some certain amount between €100 and €200 that would make the manager indifferent between taking the certain cash flow and taking the risky cash flow.[21] Specifically, the certainty equivalent of a risky cash flow paid at future date t is the riskless cash flow paid at date t that has the same present value as the risky cash flow.

Finding the present value of a stream of certainty equivalent cash flows is straightforward. Simply discount the certainty equivalent cash flows at the relevant risk-free rates, exactly as riskless cash flows were discounted

[21] In rare cases, specifically projects with negative betas, the certainty equivalent may exceed the expected cash flow.

in Chapter 10. The *certainty equivalent method* first obtains the certainty equivalent of the future cash flow. It then discounts the certainty equivalent back to date 0 at the risk-free rate.

The difference between the risk-adjusted discount rate method and the certainty equivalent method is simply a matter of where the risk adjustment occurs. Recall that the present value of a cash flow can be expressed as the ratio of the projected cash flow to 1 plus the discount rate. *With the certainty equivalent method, the numerator of that ratio, the certainty equivalent cash flow, is adjusted for risk and discounted at a risk-free interest rate in the ratio's denominator. By contrast, the risk-adjusted discount rate method places the expected cash flow in the numerator and discounts it in the ratio's denominator at a risk-adjusted interest rate.* Either method is theoretically acceptable; it is appropriate to risk-adjust in either the numerator or the denominator of the present value expression. The preferred method depends on the practical considerations emphasized throughout the chapter.

Identifying the Certainty Equivalent from Models of Risk and Return

Denote $\text{CE}(\tilde{C})$ as the certainty equivalent of uncertain future cash flow $\tilde{C}$ and $E(\tilde{C})$ as the cash flow mean. Result 11.6 describes how to compute certainty equivalents from a risk-expected return model.

Results

Result 11.6

To obtain a certainty equivalent, subtract the product of the cash flow beta and the tangency portfolio risk premium from the expected cash flow: that is,

$$\text{CE}(\tilde{C}) = E(\tilde{C}) - b(\bar{R}_T - r_f)$$

where

$$b = \frac{\text{cov}(\tilde{C}, \tilde{R}_T)}{\sigma_T^2}$$

The Cash Flow Beta and Its Interpretation

Result 11.6 adjusts for risk with the cash flow beta, denoted as b. The **cash flow beta** is the covariance of the *future cash flow* (not the return on the cash flow) with the return of the tangency portfolio, divided by the variance of the return of the tangency portfolio: that is,

$$b = \frac{\text{cov}(\tilde{C}, \tilde{R}_T)}{\sigma_T^2}$$

This risk measure is the amount of the tangency portfolio that must be held to track, as best as possible, the future cash flow. In contrast to the return beta (β), which is used with the risk-adjusted discount rate method, the cash flow beta (b) can be computed directly after forming scenarios, as we shall illustrate shortly. Since obtaining this cash flow beta does not require prior knowledge of the present value, *the certainty equivalent is a superior vehicle for identifying present values when return and cash flow estimation in scenarios is the only method available for generating risk measures.*

The Certainty Equivalent Present Value Formula and Its Interpretation

To obtain the present value, discount the certainty equivalent at the risk-free rate. Combining this finding with Result 11.6 generates the following result.

Results

Result 11.7

(*The certainty equivalent present value formula.*) PV, the present value of next period's cash flow, can be found by: (1) computing $E(\tilde{C})$, the expected future cash flow and the beta of the future cash flow;

(2) subtracting the product of this beta and the risk premium of the tangency portfolio from the expected future cash flow; and (3) dividing by (1 + the risk-free return): that is,

$$\text{PV} = \frac{E(\widetilde{C}) - b(\overline{R}_T - r_f)}{1 + r_f}$$

Thus the certainty equivalent present value formula adjusts first for the risk-premium component and then for the time value of money. To compute the net present value, subtract the initial cost of the project, $-C_0$, from this present value.

One interpretation of the certainty equivalent formula in Result 11.6 comes from recognizing that b, the cash flow beta, is the tracking portfolio's monetary investment in the tangency portfolio. The tangency portfolio earns an extra expected return (that is, a risk premium) because of risk. Specifically, $\overline{R}_T - r_f$ is the future additional amount earned per unit invested in the tangency portfolio because of the tangency portfolio's systematic (or factor) risk. For an investment of b (e.g. euros) in the tangency portfolio, the additional expected cash flow (in euros) from the project's systematic (or factor) risk is thus

$$b(\overline{R}_T - r_f)$$

Hence subtracting $b(\overline{R}_T - r_f)$ from the expected cash flow $E(\widetilde{C})$ yields

$$E(\widetilde{C}) - b(\overline{R}_T - r_f)$$

This represents the cash flow that would be generated if the project had a cash flow beta of zero or, alternatively, if the future cash flow were risk free.

An Illustration of a Present Value Computation When the Cash Flow Beta is Given

Example 11.7 illustrates how to compute present values, given cash flow betas.

Example 11.7

Computing the Cost of Capital

Each share of BA Cityflyer, a wholly owned subsidiary of International Airlines Group plc, first seen in Example 11.1, has a cash flow beta (b) of £5.125 when computed against the tangency portfolio. One year from now, this subsidiary has a 0.9 probability of being worth £5 per share and a 0.1 probability of being worth £4 per share. The risk-free rate is 6 per cent per year. The tangency portfolio has an expected return of 14 per cent per year. What is the present value of BA Cityflyer, assuming no dividend payments to the parent firm in the coming year?

Answer: The expected value of BA Cityflyer one year from now is

$$0.9(\pounds5) + 0.1(\pounds4) = \pounds4.90 \text{ per share}$$

The numerator in the certainty equivalent formula, the certainty equivalent, is thus

$$\pounds4.90 - \pounds5.125(0.14 - 0.06) = \pounds4.49$$

The subsidiary's present value is its certainty equivalent divided by 1 plus the risk-free rate, or approximately

$$\frac{\pounds4.49 \text{ per share}}{1.06} = \pounds4.24 \text{ per share}$$

Cash Flow Betas and Return Betas

The answer in Example 11.7 is identical to the answer given in Example 11.1, because Example 11.7 uses a cash flow beta consistent with the return beta from Example 11.1. Note that, in Example 11.1, β is the beta of a comparison financial security, which is a zero-NPV investment. The cash flow beta b = £4.24: that is, the ratio of the cash flow beta to the return beta (as computed for a cost of £4.24) equals the project's present value:

$$PV = \frac{b}{\beta}$$

This equation is not valid if PV ≤ 0 (and expected cash flow is non-negative).

The CAPM, Scenarios and the Certainty Equivalent Method

The previous subsection suggested that scenarios provide one way to identify cash flow betas and present values with the certainty equivalent method. Example 11.8 illustrates how to implement this scenario method, assuming that the market portfolio is the tangency portfolio.

Example 11.8 is based on the same numbers as Example 11.5, where, using the risk-adjusted discount rate method, we computed an erroneous present value for the Flashy Travel computer cash flow of €82,311. The latter number was too high, because negative-NPV projects have underestimated return betas.

Example 11.8 demonstrates that the certainty equivalent method gives the true present value of €76,379. The last section and Example 11.6, using the same travel agency, emphasized the importance of knowing this true present value for mutually exclusive projects.

Example 11.8

Present Values with the Certainty Equivalent Method

The Flashy Travel Agency, examined in Examples 11.5 and 11.6, wishes to estimate the present value of the cash flow from purchasing 10 new airline reservation computers. The new computers, which are faster than the current ones in place at the agency, are expected to increase the number of reservations each agent can handle. For simplicity, assume that all the additional cash flows associated with the increase in booking capacity are received one year from now. The size of the increase is tied to the state of the economy. Over the next year, three possible economic scenarios are considered, which are described in the following table, taken from Example 11.5.

Outcome	Probability	Market return (%)	Incremental cash in one year (€)
Recovery	$\frac{3}{4}$	25	150,000
Recession	$\frac{3}{16}$	−1	35,000
Depression	$\frac{1}{16}$	−15	5,000

What is the present value of the additional cash flow one year from now if the risk-free return over the next year is 8.625 per cent, and the CAPM determines the expected returns of traded securities?

Answer: The risk premium of the market portfolio is

$$\bar{R}_M - r_f = \frac{3}{4}(0.25) + \frac{3}{16}(-0.01) + \frac{1}{16}(-0.15) - 0.08625 = 0.09$$

while the variance of the market return (computed in Example 11.5) is 0.017236.

The expected incremental cash flow is

$$\frac{3}{4}(€150,000) + \frac{3}{16}(€35,000) + \frac{1}{16}(€5,000) = €119,375$$

The covariance of the cash flow with the return of the market portfolio is

$$\begin{aligned}\text{cov}(\widetilde{C}_r, \widetilde{R}_{\text{m}}) &= \frac{3}{4}(0.25 - 0.17625)(€150{,}000 - €119{,}375) \\ &+ \frac{3}{16}(-0.01 - 0.17625)(€35{,}000 - €119{,}375) \\ &+ \frac{1}{16}(-0.15 - 0.17625)(€5{,}000 - €119{,}375) \\ &= €6{,}972.656\end{aligned}$$

which generates a cash flow beta of €6,972.656/0.017236. Substituting these values into the certainty equivalent formula leaves a present value of approximately

$$\text{PV} = \frac{€119{,}375 - (€6{,}972.656/0.017236)(0.09)}{1 + 0.08625} = €76{,}379$$

The APT and the Certainty Equivalent Method

To obtain the certainty equivalent in the one-factor APT, subtract from the expected future cash flow the product of:

1 the factor loading of the future cash flow, and
2 the risk premium of the factor.

If there is more than one factor, sum these products over all factors and then subtract.[22] Then discount this certainty equivalent at the risk-free rate to obtain the present value: that is,

$$\text{PV} = \frac{E(\widetilde{C}) - (\lambda_1 b_1 + \lambda_2 b_2 + \cdots + \lambda_K b_K)}{1 + r_f}$$

where b_j ($j = 1, \ldots, K$) is the factor loading of the *future cash flow* (not the cash flow return) on the jth factor. The symbol b_j represents the amount of money invested in the jth factor portfolio that best tracks the cash flow of the project. The amount subtracted from $E(\widetilde{C})$ in the numerator of this ratio is thus the additional expected cash flow arising from the factor risk of the project.

The Relationship between the Certainty Equivalent Formula and the Tracking Portfolio Approach

Recall the Hilton casino illustration from Sections 11.1 and 11.2, which ascribed a present value of $10.0 million to an expected cash flow of $11.3 million from gambling in the US. Hilton's tracking portfolio for the casino consisted of $5 million invested in the market portfolio, which has a risk premium of 14 per cent (= 20 per cent – 6 per cent), and $5 million invested in a risk-free asset, which has a return of 6 per cent. As suggested in the previous subsection, the amount invested in the tangency portfolio (in this case, the market portfolio) is the cash flow beta (b). Hence the Hilton casino cash flow beta is $5 million. Using this cash flow beta in the certainty equivalent formula (see Result 11.6) yields a certainty equivalent (the numerator) of

$$\$11.3 \text{ million} - \$5.0 \text{ million} \times 0.14 = \$10.6 \text{ million}$$

and thus a present value (see Result 10.7) of

$$\$10.6 \text{ million}/1.06 = \$10 \text{ million}$$

In practice, one first obtains the cash flow beta, $5 million, from scenarios, and only then is it possible to recognize this as the amount of the tracking portfolio invested in the market portfolio. To keep the tracking as

[22] In the multifactor case, the cash flow factor loading will be its multiple regression coefficient against the factor, and it will be its covariance with the factor divided by the factor variance only if the factors are uncorrelated.

close as possible, the expected cash flow from the tracking portfolio of financial securities must be the same as the expected cash flow from the casino. (Can you explain why?) Hence, in deriving this tracking portfolio, it is important to know that the expected cash flow from the casino was \$11.3 million. Then, solving for the risk-free investment, x, in combination with a \$5 million investment in the market portfolio, yields an expected future cash flow of \$11.3 million, which pins down the risk-free investment. Algebraically, x solves

$$x(1.06) + \$5{,}000{,}000(1.2) = \$11{,}300{,}000 \text{ giving } x = \$5{,}000{,}000$$

The certainty equivalent method gives the same present values as the tracking portfolio approach used earlier. Indeed, the certainty equivalent is derived from the tracking portfolio approach, as evidenced by the fact that cash flow beta b is the tracking portfolio's expenditure on the market (or tangency) portfolio.

11.7 Obtaining Certainty Equivalents with Risk-Free Scenarios

The CAPM and APT implementations of the certainty equivalent method require knowledge of the composition of a portfolio that tracks the evaluated investment's cash flow. Moreover, to obtain the certainty equivalent of the cash flow, the manager must:

1. compute two items: the expected cash flow, and its adjustment for risk, based on the cash flow's covariance with the return of the tangency portfolio multiplied by the risk premium of the tangency portfolio
2. obtain the difference between these two items.

In this section, we present an alternative approach for computing certainty equivalents.

A Description of the Risk-Free Scenario Method

An alternative computational approach to the certainty equivalent, which we call the **risk-free scenario method**, provides the manager with a simple way to estimate the certainty equivalent cash flow. The risk-free scenario method generates the certainty equivalent with a typically conservative cash flow forecast under a scenario where all assets are expected to appreciate at the risk-free rate. In other words, the certainty equivalent cash flow is assumed to be the expected cash flow in situations where the tangency portfolio return equals the risk-free rate.

Distributions for Which the Risk-Free Scenario Method Works

This method works when the returns of the tangency portfolio and the future cash flows of the project have specific distributions. Specifically, it must be a distribution where the expectation of the future cash flow, given the return of a mean-variance efficient portfolio, is a linear function of the return of the tangency portfolio. Algebraically, this can be expressed as

$$E(\widetilde{C} \mid \text{given the return } R_T) = a + bR_T$$

The values of a and b, the intercept and cash flow beta, respectively, do not change for different outcomes of the return of the tangency portfolio. This is basically the assumption of linear regression, and it is satisfied by, among other distributions, the normal distribution. The key feature of this distributional assumption is that the error in the cash flow forecast is distributed independently of the tangency portfolio's return.

Inputs for the Risk-Free Scenario Method

The risk-free scenario method uses as its input an estimate of the project's cash flows, assuming that the return of the tangency portfolio, and thus the tracking portfolio, equals the risk-free return. In other words, instead of asking the engineers and marketing research managers to estimate the expected cash flows of a project, the analyst asks them to come up with what they think the cash flows would be in a scenario where the tracking portfolio (a combination of the market portfolio and a risk-free asset if the CAPM holds) has a return that equals the risk-free rate. As shown below, eliciting this kind of information is useful because, under the conditions noted above, these **conditional expected cash flows** – that is, expected cash flows conditional on the tracking portfolio return equalling the risk-free return – can be viewed as the cash flow's certainty equivalent. To see this, regress the *actual* excess returns of any zero-NPV investment (return $\tilde{r}$ less the risk-free rate) on the actual excess return of the tangency portfolio. The resulting equation is

$$\tilde{r} - r_f = \alpha + \beta(\widetilde{R}_T - r_f) + \tilde{\varepsilon}$$

where (for each particular outcome of the return of the tangency portfolio)

$$E(\tilde{\varepsilon}) = 0$$

Equation (11.7) indicates that high-beta investments are expected to outperform low-beta investments in scenarios where the tangency portfolio return exceeds the risk-free return. The opposite is true in scenarios where the risk-free return exceeds the tangency portfolio's return. However, when the tangency portfolio return equals the risk-free return, the expected returns of all zero-NPV investments are equal to α (alpha), irrespective of their betas. Moreover, it is possible to show that the intercept (α) is 0 in equation (11.7) by first calculating the expected values of both sides of the equation and noting, from the familiar risk–expected return equation first developed in Chapter 5, that

$$\bar{r} = r_f + \beta(\overline{R}_T - r_f) \tag{11.8}$$

Hence, letting $\alpha = 0$, as implied by equation (11.8), the expectation of the left-hand side of equation (11.7) in the risk-free scenario is 0, and thus

$$E(\tilde{r} \mid \text{given } \widetilde{R}_T = r_f) = r_f$$

Obtaining PVs with the Risk-Free Scenario Method

This analysis demonstrates that when the return of the tangency portfolio equals the risk-free return, all zero-NPV investments are expected to appreciate at the risk-free rate. In this risk-free scenario, a project's expected future value is

$$E(\widetilde{C} \mid \text{given risk-free scenario}) = (1 + r_f) \times \text{PV}$$

Thus, once the product $(1 + r_f) \times \text{PV}$ is estimated, the analyst can determine the PV by discounting the expected cash flow for the risk-free scenario,

$$E(\widetilde{C} \mid \text{given risk-free scenario})$$

at the risk-free rate.

Results

Result 11.8

(*Estimating the certainty equivalent with a risk-free scenario.*) If it is possible to estimate the expected future cash flow of an investment or project under a scenario where all securities are expected to appreciate at the risk-free return, then the present value of the cash flow is computed by discounting the expected cash flow for the risk-free scenario at the risk-free rate.

There is no need to estimate betas or to identify the tangency portfolio used in the tracking portfolio if it is possible to forecast the future cash flow under a scenario where all securities are expected to appreciate at the risk-free rate. Moreover, the task of estimating the cash flows for all possible scenarios and weighting by the probabilities of the scenarios is eliminated with the risk-free scenario method. The only scenario where cash flow forecasts are needed is one in which all securities are expected to earn the risk-free return. Because the tangency portfolio return equals its expected return in the average scenario, and the tangency portfolio's expected return is larger than the risk-free return, the risk-free scenario is more pessimistic than the average scenario.

An Illustration of How to Implement the Risk-Free Scenario Method

Example 11.9 illustrates how to implement the risk-free scenario method.

Example 11.9

Valuation with the Risk-Free Scenario Method

You are asked to evaluate a project with a one-year life that has an uncertain cash flow at the end of the first year. Your managers estimate that the project will generate a cash flow of €100,000 at the end of year 1 under a scenario where all securities are expected to earn the risk-free return of 5 per cent per year. What is the present value of this risky project? For what costs should the project be accepted or rejected?

Answer: €100,000 is the certainty equivalent of the future cash flow. Discounting this at a rate of 5 per cent yields €100,000/1.05 or €95,238. Therefore, if the project costs less than €95,328, your managers should accept it. If it costs more than €95,328, they should reject it.

Advantages of the Risk-Free Scenario Method

As a practical matter, the advantage of employing the risk-free scenario method is obvious. In the risk-free scenario, investors expect the equity held by shareholders in the manager's own firm and the equity in all other firms in the industry to appreciate at the risk-free rate (with dividends reinvested). For this moderately pessimistic scenario, the manager may find it easier to estimate the future cash flow of the project than to estimate both its expected value over all scenarios and its covariance with the tangency portfolio, assuming that it is possible to even identify the tangency portfolio.

In theory, the present value obtained with the risk-free scenario method should be the same as that obtained with the traditional certainty equivalent method. In practice, however, there is no reason for these methods to generate either identical certainty equivalents or identical present values, because the estimates of cash flows for risk-free scenarios and estimates of cash flow betas for traditional certainty equivalent approaches are imperfect.[23]

Implementing the Risk-Free Scenario Method in a Multi-Period Setting

The risk-free scenario method avoids many of the problems faced by more traditional methods in a multiperiod setting (see Section 11.5). To illustrate the multi-period use of the risk-free scenario method, assume that yields on one-year, five-year and ten-year risk-free zero-coupon bonds are respectively 5, 6 and 7 per cent. Consider a computer operating system designed by Microsoft; it has a life of 10 years and will have three major versions: Fox 1 (sold at the end of 1), Fox 2 (sold at the end of year 5) and Fox 3 (sold at the end of year 10). For simplicity, assume that so much software pirating is going on between these major revisions of the software product that the cash flows between revisions are essentially zero.

To obtain the present value of the three future cash flows, it is necessary to obtain estimates of the year 1, year 5 and year 10 cash flows under their respective risk-free scenarios. These cash flow estimates are not easily obtained but, as we show below, are probably no more difficult to obtain than estimates of the year 1, year 5 and year 10 *expected* cash flows.

To obtain the risk-free scenario estimate for year 1, envisage an estimate of the cash flow under a scenario in which all assets, with dividends reinvested, are expected to appreciate by 5 per cent, the one-year risk-free rate. The present value of the year 1 cash flow is that estimate discounted back one year at a rate of 5 per cent. To obtain the risk-free scenario estimate for year 5, envisage what the year 5 cash flow would be if all assets, with dividends reinvested, are expected to appreciate at a rate of 6 per cent per year for these five years, the yield on a five-year risk-free bond. The present value of the year 5 cash flow is that estimate discounted back five years at a rate of 6 per cent. To obtain the risk-free scenario estimate for year 10, envision what the year 10 cash flow would be if all assets, with dividends reinvested, are expected to appreciate at a rate of 7 per cent

[23] The major drawback to the risk-free scenario method is that it will provide the true present value only if the distribution of the return of the tangency portfolio and the cash flow belong to certain families of distributions, including the bivariate normal distribution. If the distribution of the cash flow and the return of the tangency portfolio is one in which the conditional expectation is non-linear, then the forecast under this scenario is not the same as the certainty equivalent.

per year for these 10 years, the yield on a 10-year risk-free bond. The present value is this estimate, discounted back 10 years at a rate of 7 per cent per year.

When the mean-variance efficient (that is, tangency) portfolio appreciates at the risk-free rate, all securities are expected to appreciate at the risk-free rate, including the equity of Microsoft. Thus a reasonable procedure for estimating the cash flows for the risk-free scenarios at the three horizons is to forecast the cash flow as a multiple of Microsoft's future share price, and compute what the price of Microsoft's equity and the project cash flow would be when Microsoft's share price appreciates at a risk-free rate.[24]

This forecast will be the true certainty equivalent if the error in the cash flow forecast is distributed independently of the return of the mean-variance efficient portfolio for that horizon. For simplicity, assume that Microsoft will not pay any dividends over the next 10 years. For companies that pay dividends, forecast the equity value with all dividends reinvested.

If Microsoft is currently trading at \$100 a share, it will trade at \$105 a share one year from now in a risk-free scenario, given a risk-free rate of 5 per cent per year. Over a five-year period, Microsoft will trade at \$133.82 if it appreciates at the five-year risk-free rate, 6 per cent per year. In 10 years, it will trade at \$196.72 if it appreciates at the 10-year risk-free rate, 7 per cent per year.

Assume that Microsoft's managers believe the operating system is expected to generate cash equal to 10 million times Microsoft's share price. Hence the new operating system is expected to generate \$1.05 billion at the end of year 1 if Microsoft equity with dividends reinvested is then selling at \$105 a share, \$1.3382 billion at the end of year 5 if Microsoft equity sells for \$133.82 a share at that point, and \$1.9672 billion at the end of year 10 if Microsoft equity sells for \$196.72 at that point.

The present value of the operating system is then

$$\begin{aligned} PV &= \frac{\$1.05 \text{ billion}}{1.05} + \frac{\$1.3382 \text{ billion}}{(1.06)^5} + \frac{\$1.9672 \text{ billion}}{(1.07)^{10}} \\ &= \frac{\$1.05 \text{ billion}}{1.05} + \frac{\$1.3382 \text{ billion}}{1.3382} + \frac{\$1.9672 \text{ billion}}{1.9672} = \$3 \text{ billion} \end{aligned}$$

Example 11.10 presents another illustration of the risk-free scenario method.

Example 11.10

Multi-Period Valuation with the Risk-Free Scenario Method

Cardigan, a game software company, wants to value the cash flows of its new *Haw-Haw* game at years 5 and 10. Assume the following:

- Cash flow forecast errors are noisy: that is, they are distributed independently of everything.
- The year 5 cash flow of *Haw-Haw* has an expected value of £39 million if its five-year equity return, with dividends reinvested in Cardigan, is 30 per cent over the five years.
- The year 10 cash flow of *Haw-Haw* has an expected value of £80 million if an investment in its equity (with all dividends reinvested) doubles over 10 years.
- At date 0, £1.00 buys £1.30 in face value of a risk-free, five-year zero-coupon bond.
- At date 0, £1.00 buys £2.00 in face value of a risk-free, 10-year zero-coupon bond.

What are the present values of the two cash flows?

Answer: Applying the certainty equivalent formula, the present value of the year 5 cash flow is

$$\frac{\pounds 39 \text{ million}}{1.30} = \pounds 30 \text{ million}$$

and the year 10 cash flow's present value is

$$\frac{\pounds 80 \text{ million}}{2.00} = \pounds 40 \text{ million}$$

[24] This multiple could differ for different horizons, but, in the example, we shall assume that it does not change with the horizon.

The cash flow estimate in Example 11.10 is trickier than it may seem at first. The long-term appreciation in the share price is assumed to equal the appreciation of a risk-free security. This does not mean that the equity has to appreciate year by year at the same rate as the risk-free security. Like the tortoise and the hare, the equity can start off faster than the risk-free security, then slow down, or *vice versa*, just as long as they end up in the same place at the same time. In a risk-free scenario, the manager knows that the geometric mean of the equity return is the risk-free rate, but he or she does not know the pattern of short-horizon returns by which that geometric mean is achieved. Each pattern could generate a different project cash flow. In this case, it is important to analyse and weigh the likelihood of paths in order to arrive at the expected cash flow under the scenarios in which the equity's geometric mean return is the risk-free rate.

The firm's own share price is not the only candidate to use for a risk-free scenario; other traded securities or portfolios of securities are perfectly adequate substitutes. Generally, using more securities and portfolios makes it more likely that the cash flow forecast error will be distributed independently of the return of the mean-variance efficient portfolio.

The ease with which the risk-free scenario method is applied in a multi-period setting gives it a major advantage over the risk-adjusted discount rate method or the traditional certainty equivalent method. When it can be applied, we believe that the risk-free scenario method generates better approximations to the true present values than those estimated with more traditional methods.

Providing Certainty Equivalents without Knowing It

In many instances, the cash flow for the risk-free scenario is provided unwittingly by analysts or managers. This situation usually arises when the manager wants to be conservative in his or her forecast, knowing that the cash flow is risky and the forecast imprecise.

For example, consider a financial analyst working at a hypothetical company that we shall call Kato Hand Tools. The engineers have designed a new hand drill, and have calculated the costs of setting up a plant to manufacture this product. After the engineers calculate the manufacturing costs per unit, the market research department estimates a projected selling price and the number of units that they think Kato Hand Tools can sell. Based on all this information, the financial analyst forecasts a stream of future cash flows and then evaluates whether the company should go through with the project.

To discount the cash flow stream, the financial analyst has to know a bit about how the cash flows were estimated. If the engineers and marketing researchers decide to give conservative estimates because the cash flows are risky, then the cash flow stream may be better thought of as a certainty equivalent that should be discounted at the risk-free rate. The analyst would not want to discount such risk-adjusted cash flows at a risk-adjusted discount rate. However, the analyst must also be aware that the conservative estimates of the engineers and marketing researchers are unlikely to be the precise certainty equivalent.[25]

Real World Insight

Valuing Long-Term Risky Assets

With climate change already having tangible impact on business operations because of drought, flooding, and temperature fluctuations, analysts have begun to investigate ways in which long-term projects incorporate future climate change risks. An additional issue is whether prices and valuations incorporate climate change risks now. An very insightful study by Bernstein et al. (2019) examined the valuation effect of sea level rises on properties exposed to a future risk of flooding and worse. They found that building exposed to the risk of sea levels rising (for example, those on coastlines) are priced at an average of a 6.6 per cent discount relative to comparable properties with no or little exposure. However, this discount increases to 14.7 per cent for the most exposed properties. This type of analysis helps policy makers calculate the overall impact of climate change and also guides investment in initiatives to mitigate its impact.

[25] The analyst, however, might also want to consider the possibility that the managers may have a tendency to be overly optimistic. This could offset the bias towards conservative estimates and justify a higher discount rate.

11.8 Computing Certainty Equivalents from Prices in Financial Markets

In some cases, prices from financial markets provide information that analysts can use to project future cash flows.

Forward Prices

Forward prices are related to estimates of the future spot prices of different currencies and commodities. As Chapter 7 pointed out, the forward price represents the certainty equivalent of the uncertain future price rather than its expected value. Whenever forward prices are available for future cash flows, use the certainty equivalent method for valuation. Such forward prices effectively translate data from the complex world of risky cash flows to the much simpler world of riskless cash flows, which were considered in Chapter 10.

Example 11.11 illustrates how to value zinc using this method.

Example 11.11

Present Values with Certainty Equivalents from Futures Prices

This example is a common issue for mining and extraction firms. Lers Strang plc have the rights to extract zinc from a mine in Greenland. After extraction, the zinc ore needs to be transported to another location or company for refining. Assume that your company is considering the purchase of 100,000 tonnes of unrefined zinc ore from Lers Strang in order to refine and sell it on. Only 14 per cent of the ore can usefully be extracted to become usable zinc. The asking price for the zinc ore is £19.5 million, and it will cost £80,000 to arrange for transport and security while in transit. In addition, the refining process will cost £420,000. The (unannualized) risk-free interest rate over this six-month period is 3 per cent, and the only source of uncertainty associated with this transaction is the future market price of zinc. However, on the New York Mercantile Exchange (NYMEX), we observe a six-month forward price for zinc of £1,500 per tonne (converted from dollars). Should your company purchase the zinc ore?

Answer: Only 14 per cent of the ore (14,000 tonnes) can be extracted into zinc. Therefore £21 million (= £1,500 × 14,000 tonnes) is the certainty equivalent for the zinc revenue produced by your company in six months. A comparison of the present value of that amount, £20.388 million (= £21 million/1.03), with the cost of the zinc ore, the transit, security and refining, £20 million (= £19.5 million + £80,000 + £420,000), implies that your company should purchase the zinc ore from Lers Strang, because the project has a positive NPV of £0.388 million.

Tracking Portfolios that Contain Forward Contracts

It would be difficult to calculate an expected cash flow and to apply the risk-adjusted discount rate approach in Example 11.11. In this case, the tracking portfolio approach provides an equivalent answer; the appropriate tracking portfolio would be a forward contract to sell 14,000 tons of zinc ore along with £21 million/1.03 in a risk-free investment with a return of 3 per cent. Since the forward contract has zero value (see Chapter 7), the value of that tracking portfolio is £21 million/1.03, which is the present value of the future cash flows.[26]

[26] Chapter 12 further examines how to identify present values from futures and forward prices.

11.9 Summary and Conclusions

This chapter analysed the rules for computing the market values of the future cash flows of risky investment projects. Academics often recommend and practitioners implement two equivalent discounted cash flow methods – the risk-adjusted discount rate method and the certainty equivalent method – to value future cash flows. As a simple practical approach, we also recommend a particular implementation of the certainty equivalent method – the risk-free scenario method.

The major theme of this chapter is that practical rather than theoretical considerations dictate which valuation approach to use and how to implement it. The risk-adjusted discount rate method, which obtains the discount rate (that is, the cost of capital) from commonly used theories of risk and return, such as the CAPM and APT, is impractical when the betas of comparison firms are hard to estimate. Also, a variety of nuances require adjustments to the beta estimates. These adjustments can make this seemingly simple valuation method extremely complicated. In cases where comparison firms do not exist, and scenarios are required to estimate risk, practical considerations dictate that the certainty equivalent method is the better valuation method to use. Once the cash flow's certainty equivalent is obtained, there are no further nuances and complications to watch out for. Hence, whenever observable forward prices or internal estimation procedures lead to certainty equivalents, the certainty equivalent is the preferred valuation method.

Despite a thorough treatment of real asset valuation in the last two chapters, our coverage of this important topic remains incomplete; several additional issues that have a major impact on the capital allocation decision remain. Chapter 12 studies the impact of growth options and other strategic options. It also explores an alternative valuation approach that is quite popular in a number of practical settings: the ratio comparison approach. Chapters 13–15 analyse financing and dividend policies, and their impact on corporate tax liabilities in deciding between projects. The effect of capital structure and dividend policy on incentives for choosing positive-NPV projects, as well as bankruptcy costs, are studied in the latter half of Part IV. Managerial incentives and information asymmetries are dealt with in Part V of the text.

Key Concepts

Result 11.1: Whenever a tracking portfolio for the future cash flows of a project generates tracking error with zero systematic (or factor) risk and zero expected value, the market value of the tracking portfolio is the present value of the project's future cash flows.

Result 11.2: To find the present value of next period's cash flow using the risk-adjusted discount rate method:

1. Compute the expected future cash flow next period, $E(\tilde{C})$.
2. Compute the beta of the return of the project, β.
3. Compute the expected return of the project by substituting the beta calculated in step 2 into the tangency portfolio risk–expected return equation.
4. Divide the expected future cash flow in step 1 by one plus the expected return from step 3. In algebraic terms:

$$\text{PV} = \frac{E(\tilde{C})}{1 + r_f + \beta(\bar{R}_T - r_f)}$$

Result 11.3: Increasing the firm's debt (raising D and reducing E) increases the (beta and standard deviation) risk per unit of equity investment. It will increase linearly in the D/E ratio if the debt is risk free.

Result 11.4: The cost of equity,

$$\bar{r}_E = \bar{r}_A + \left(\frac{D}{E}\right)(\bar{r}_A - \bar{r}_D)$$

increases as the firm's leverage ratio D/E increases. It will increase linearly in the ratio D/E if the debt is default free and if $\bar{r}_A$, the expected return of the firm's assets, does not change as the leverage ratio increases.

Result 11.5: The betas of the actual returns of projects equal the project's profitability index times the appropriate beta needed to compute the true present value of the project. Since the profitability index exceeds 1 for positive-NPV projects and is below 1 for negative-NPV projects, this error in beta computation does not affect project selection in the absence of project selection constraints.

Result 11.6: To obtain a certainty equivalent, subtract the product of the cash flow beta and the tangency portfolio risk premium from the expected cash flow: that is,

$$\text{CE}(\widetilde{C}) = E(\widetilde{C}) - b(\overline{R}_T - r_f)$$

where

$$b = \frac{\text{cov}(\widetilde{C}, \overline{R}_T)}{\sigma_T^2}$$

Result 11.7: (The certainty equivalent present value formula.) PV, the present value of next period's cash flow, can be found by: (1) computing $E(\widetilde{C})$, the expected future cash flow and the beta of the future cash flow; (2) subtracting the product of this beta and the risk premium of the tangency portfolio from the expected future cash flow; and (3) dividing by (1 + the risk-free return): that is,

$$\text{PV} = \frac{E(\widetilde{C}) - b(\overline{R}_T - r_f)}{1 + r_f}$$

Result 11.8: (Estimating the certainty equivalent with a risk-free scenario.) If it is possible to estimate the expected future cash flow of an investment or project under a scenario where all securities are expected to appreciate at the risk-free return, then the present value of the cash flow is computed by discounting the expected cash flow for the risk-free scenario at the risk-free rate.

Key Terms

Exercises

11.1 A project has an expected cash flow of €1 million one year from now. The standard deviation of this cash flow is €250,000. If the expected return of the market portfolio is 10 per cent, the risk-free rate is 5 per cent, the standard deviation of the market return is 5 per cent, and the correlation between this future cash flow and the return on the market is 0.5, what is the present value of the cash flow? Assume the CAPM holds. (Hint: Use the certainty equivalent method.)

Exercises 11.2–11.6 make use of the following information.

Assume that BA Cityflyer has the following joint distribution with the market return:

Market scenario	Probability	Market return (%)	Year 1 cash flow forecast (£)
Bad	0.25	−15	20 million
Good	0.50	5	25 million
Great	0.25	25	30 million

Assume also that the CAPM holds.

11.2 Compute the expected year 1 cash flow for BA Cityflyer.

11.3 Find the covariance of the cash flow with the market return and its cash flow beta.

11.4 Assuming that historical data suggest that the market risk premium is 8.4 per cent per year and the market standard deviation is 40 per cent per year, find the certainty equivalent of the year 1 cash flow. What are the advantages and disadvantages of using such historical data for market inputs as opposed to inputs from a set of scenarios, such as those given in the table above exercise 11.2?

11.5 Discount your answer in exercise 11.4 at a risk-free rate of 4 per cent per year to obtain the present value.

11.6 Explain why the answer to exercise 11.5 differs from the answer in Example 11.2.

11.7 Start with the risk-adjusted discount rate formula. Derive the certainty equivalent formula by rearranging terms and noting that $b = \beta = \text{PV}$.

11.8 In Section 11.3's illustration, asset values increased 10 per cent from 2012 to 2013, from €100 million to €110 million.

a Compute the percentage increase in the value of equity if the firm is financed with 150 million in debt.

b Compute the leverage ratio of this firm in 2013.

11.9 Explain intuitively why the certainty equivalent of a cash flow with a negative beta exceeds the cash flow's expected value.

Exercises 11.10–11.14 make use of the following data.

Assume that your firm, Smith plc, is evaluating the acquisition of its main supplier, Benefit Participation, which is privately held. Recognizing that the appropriate discount rate for the projected cash flows of Benefit Participation is different from your own cost of capital, you assume that Benefit Participation has approximately the same risk as two listed suppliers, Assembly plc and Genesis plc, which deals in the same products. Specifically, assume the following inputs.

Comparison	β_E	*D/E*
Smith	1.20	0.40
Assembly	0.90	0.90
Genesis	0.85	0.70

Target *D/E* for Benefit Participation's acquisition = 1
Benefit Participation's expected cash flow next year = £300 million
Growth rate of Benefit Participation's cash flows = 5 per cent per year
Appropriate discount rate on debt (riskless = rate) 8 per cent
Expected return of the tangency portfolio = 14 per cent

11.10 Analyse the Benefit Participation acquisition by first computing the betas of the comparison firms, Assembly and Genesis, as if they were all equity financed. Assume no taxes.

11.11 Compute the beta of the assets of the Benefit Participation acquisition, assuming no taxes, by taking the average of the asset betas of Assembly and Genesis.

11.12 Compute the cost of capital for the Benefit Participation acquisition, assuming no taxes.

11.13 Compute the value of Benefit Participation with the cost of capital estimated in exercise 11.12.

11.14 Compute the value of Benefit Participation if your firm's cost of capital is used as a discount rate instead of the cost of capital computed from the comparison firms.

11.15 In a two-factor APT model, easyJet has a factor beta of 1.15 on the first factor portfolio, which is highly correlated with the change in GDP, and a factor beta of −0.3 on the second factor portfolio, which is highly correlated with interest rate changes. Suppose the risk-free rate is 5 per cent per year, the first factor portfolio has a risk premium of 2 per cent per year, and the second has a risk premium of −0.5 per cent per year.

a Compute the cost of capital for the BA Cityflyer project that uses easyJet as the appropriate comparison firm. Assume no taxes and no need for leverage adjustments.

b What is the present value of an expected £1 million BA Cityflyer cash flow one year from now, assuming that easyJet is the appropriate comparison? Assume no taxes and no need for leverage adjustments.

c What are the cash flow beta and the certainty equivalent for the BA Cityflyer project?

11.16 Risk-free rates at horizons of one year, two years and three years are 6.00 per cent per year, 6.25 per cent per year and 6.75 per cent per year, respectively. A firm forecasts respective cash flows of $200 million, $250 million and $300 million for these three years under the risk-free scenario. Value each of these cash flows separately.

References and Additional Reading

Some important recent articles on valuation and discount rates include:

Abudy, M., Benninga, S. and Shust, E. (2016) The cost of equity for private firms, *Journal of Corporate Finance*, 37, 431–443.

Bekaert, G., Harvey, C.R., Lundblad, C.T. and Siegel, S. (2016) Political risk and international valuation. *Journal of Corporate Finance*, 37, 1–23.

Cochrane, J.H. (2011) Presidential address: Discount rates. *The Journal of finance*, 66(4): 1047–1108.

Dessaint, O., Olivier, J., Otto, C.A. and Thesmar, D. (2021) CAPM-based company (mis) valuations, *The Review of Financial Studies*, 34(1): 1–66.

Jagannathan, R., Matsa, D.A., Meier, I. and Tarhan, V. (2016) Why do firms use high discount rates?, *Journal of Financial Economics*, 120(3): 445–463.

Van Binsbergen, J. H., Diamond, W. F. and Grotteria, M. (2021) Risk-free interest rates, *Journal of Financial Economics*.

Other references:

Bernstein, A., Gustafson, M.T. and Lewis, R. (2019) Disaster on the horizon: The price effect of sea level rise, *Journal of financial economics*, 134(2): 253–272.

Brennan, M. (1997) The term structure of discount rates *Financial Management*, 26(1): 81–90.

Copeland, T., Koller, T. and Murrin, J. (1994) *Valuation: Measuring and Managing the Value of Companies*. New York: John Wiley.

Cornell, B. (1993) *Corporate Valuation: Tools for Effective Appraisal and Decision Making*. Burr Ridge, IL: Business One Irwin.

Cornell, B., and Cheng, S. (1995) Using the DCF approach to analyze cross-sectional variation in expected returns Working paper, University of California, Los Angeles.

Damodoran, A. (1996) *Investment Valuation*. New York: John Wiley.

Elton, E., Gruber, M. and Mei, J. (1994) Cost of capital using arbitrage pricing theory: a case study of nine New York utilities *Financial Markets, Institutions, and Instruments*, 3(3): 46–73.

Gordon, M. (1962) *The Investment Financing and Valuation of the Corporation*. Richard D. Irwin Burr Ridge, IL: Richard D. Irwin.

Harris, R. (1986) Using analysts' growth forecasts to estimate shareholder required rate of return *Financial Management*, 15(1): 58–67.

Rappaport, A. (1986) *Creating Shareholder Value: The New Standard for Business Performance*. New York: Free Press.

Ross, S.A. (1978) Mutual fund separation in financial theory: the separating distributions *Journal of Economic Theory*, 17(2): 254–286.

Ruback, R. (1992) Marriott Corporation: the cost of capital Harvard Case Study 289-047, in W. Fruhan et al. (eds), *Case Problems in Finance* Burr Ridge, IL: Richard D. Irwin.

Rubinstein, M. (1973) A mean-variance synthesis of corporate financial theory *Journal of Finance*, 28(1): 167–181.

Shapiro, A. (1995) Creating shareholder value Working paper, University of Southern California.

Appendix 11A Statistical Issues in Estimating the Cost of Capital for the Risk-Adjusted Discount Rate Method

The implementation of the risk-adjusted discount rate method uses an estimate of the cost of capital. Error in the cost-of-capital estimate can arise from several sources, including:

- having the wrong comparison firm (or portfolio) for computing beta
- using historical data to estimate beta, which does not estimate beta perfectly
- adjusting for leverage with estimated leverage ratios instead of true leverage ratios[27]
- knowing that inherent flaws are in the model of how to adjust equity risk for leverage (for reasons discussed in Chapter 12 and Part IV of the text)
- having an improper model of how risk relates to return.

The mere fact that errors exist in the cost-of-capital estimate means that the process of estimation itself leads the firm to reject good projects and to accept bad projects. In the presence of such cost of capital estimation error, it would be desirable to have a valuation procedure that leads to an unbiased estimate of the present value, implying that the expected NPV of an estimated positive-NPV project is still positive, and that the expected NPV of a negative-NPV project is negative. However, an estimation procedure that yields unbiased estimates of the cost of capital is a procedure that generates biased present values.

11A.1 Estimation Error and Denominator-Based Biases in Present Value Estimates

Assume that the true cost of capital is $\bar{r}$ and the estimated cost of capital is $\bar{r} + \tilde{e}$, the true cost of capital plus an error where the expected error $E(\tilde{e}) = 0$. Then the expected present value estimate for the cash flow is

$$E(\mathrm{PV}) = E\left[\frac{E(\tilde{C})}{1+\bar{r}+\tilde{e}}\right]$$

This is approximately equal to the sum of the true present value, $E(\tilde{C})/(1 + \bar{r})$, and the product of the discounted expected cash flow and the discounted variance of the discount rate estimation error, $[E(\tilde{C})/(1 + \bar{r})]\ [\mathrm{var}(\tilde{e})/(1 + \bar{r})]$, which generates an expected present value estimate of

$$E(\mathrm{PV}) = \left[\frac{E(\tilde{C})}{1+\bar{r}}\right]\left[1+\frac{\mathrm{var}(\tilde{e})}{1+\bar{r}}\right]$$

Since the first factor in brackets, $E(\tilde{C})/(1 + \bar{r})$, is the true present value, and the second factor, $1+[\mathrm{var}(\tilde{e})/(1 + \bar{r})]$, is greater than 1 , the expected present value estimate is larger than the true present value.

The upward bias in the present value estimate arises because the denominator of a ratio is estimated with error, and the numerator tends to be positive. An upward adjustment to the discount rate can eliminate the

---

[27] For example, data on the market value of debt are not readily available.

upward bias in the present value estimate. The degree of the adjustment depends on one's (admittedly ballpark) estimate for var($\tilde{e}$), the estimation error variance of the cost of capital.

The recommended bias correction is to increase the estimated discount rate by an amount equal to the estimated variance of the error divided by 1 plus the estimated discount rate: that is, var($\tilde{e}$)/(1 + $\tilde{r}$ + $\tilde{e}$). The estimate of present value of the cash flow would then be:

$$\frac{E(\tilde{C})}{1+\tilde{r}+\tilde{e}+\dfrac{\mathrm{var}(\tilde{e})}{1+\tilde{r}+\tilde{e}}}$$

Example 11A.1 illustrates the procedure.

Example 11A.1

Obtaining Unbiased PVs from an Unbiased Cost-of-Capital Estimate

In Example 11.2, the comparison firm (easyJet) for BA Cityflyer was used to generate 11.07 per cent as the subsidiary's cost of capital. Assume that this cost-of-capital estimate has a standard deviation of 3 per cent per year. What is the best discount rate to use for a six-month cash flow for BA Cityflyer?

Answer: If the standard deviation is 0.03 per year, the variance is 0.0009. Hence it is appropriate to increase the estimated discount rate from 11.07 per cent to

$$11.07\% + \frac{0.0009}{1.1107} = 11.15\%$$

For reasons that will be explained in the next subsection, one should implement this upward adjustment to the cost of capital adjustment only for short-horizon cash flows.

11A.2 Geometric versus Arithmetic Means and the Compounding-Based Bias

The previous subsection demonstrated that, on average, estimated present values tend to be higher than true present values. To correct for this bias, one should increase the estimate of the cost of capital. In a multi-period setting, estimated present values tend to be too low rather than too high. This occurs because, as Section 11.5 noted, the financial manager generally compounds an imprecise cost of capital to discount a long-horizon cash flow in a multi-period setting. The size of this overestimate depends on the number of times the estimated discount rate is compounded. The bias also depends on the size of the estimation error.

The type of bias described in this subsection does not arise if the discount rate is not compounded. There is no compounding of the discount rate whenever the cash flow has the same horizon as the returns used to estimate beta. Hence, in Example 11A.1, a financial manager using six-month returns as the basis for estimating the cost of capital for BA Cityflyer needs only to adjust the cost of capital upward for the denominator-based bias described in the last subsection. The opposite bias, from compounding the cost of capital, does not exist in this case.

However (see Example 11A.1), if BA Cityflyer's financial manager uses monthly returns to estimate the monthly cost of capital as 0.8788 per cent per month (= $1.1107^{1/12} - 1$), a present value would be obtained by first compounding the monthly rate six times (that is, 1.008788^6) and then discounting the six-month expected cash flow $E(\tilde{C})$ with the formula

$$PV = \frac{E(\tilde{C})}{1.008788^6} = \frac{E(\tilde{C})}{1.1107^{1/2}}$$

Exhibit 11A.1 The Bias in Compounded Average Returns

Date	FTSE 100	DAX	CAC 40	DJIA
1991	12.99798	26.18551	7.114396	18.12397
1992	25.03615	29.28394	25.74178	25.8281
1993	−29.4262	−36.6826	−38.9312	−36.7539
1994	−5.21191	0.922654	−13.1683	0.227149
1995	7.6871	19.64982	13.34522	16.16984
1996	18.71278	33.35723	26.42774	3.574091
1997	10.51313	4.835411	7.565055	0.01783
1998	23.07843	47.702	23.84577	30.22495
1999	−30.9286	−46.2013	−34.1559	−18.8124
2000	−17.9865	−24.8344	−25.6168	−8.88517
2001	0.462631	−0.5919	5.983946	−0.48599
2002	6.317843	32.4739	33.11562	16.90062
2003	8.015022	16.14992	34.03739	18.36881
2004	27.66032	46.36597	26.04705	16.04867
2005	13.73926	22.87762	24.52251	26.27824
2006	25.66185	22.20353	12.40892	40.36151
2007	−14.325	−7.17336	−22.9824	−3.38079
2008	24.38729	38.52662	31.72328	20.19106
2009	9.178594	−6.85037	−5.49779	2.687853
2010	18.4721	18.82966	18.68987	17.79717
Arithmetic average (%)	6.70	11.85	7.51	9.22
20-year compound return from arithmetic averages (%)	265.98	839.37	325.64	483.94
Geometric average (%)	5.09	8.36	4.76	7.62
Total actual return (%)	170.14	398.38	153.51	334.58

Source: *ychoo! Finance.* © 2011 Yahoo! Inc.

In this case, if the compounding-based bias just balances or is larger than the opposite, denominator-based bias, there may be no need to adjust the cost of capital at all – or, possibly, the cost of capital may require a downward adjustment to correct for the stronger bias generated by compounding.

To understand the rough magnitude of the compounding-based bias, assume that expected returns do not change with the horizon of the cash flow: for example, if the expected one-year return on an investment is 10 per cent per year, its expected 10-year return is $1.1^{10} - 1$. Although this seems to suggest that it is sufficient to collect data that estimate annual mean returns and to adjust the mean for the appropriate horizon with the standard compound interest formula, it would be the wrong thing to do. Why is this the case?

One statistical estimate of the annual mean return is the **arithmetic sample mean,** which looks at annual returns and then averages them. Exhibit 11A.1 illustrates the annual arithmetic mean returns for four major equity indices (the FTSE 100 (UK), DAX (Germany), CAC 40 (France) and the Dow Jones Industrial Average (US)) over 20 years between 1991 and 2010. Below the annual returns are average arithmetic annual returns for each index. Next, is presented the 20-year compound return that has been calculated from the arithmetic average. For example, the 20-year compound return of the FTSE 100 Index is calculated as $(1.0670)^{20} - 1$. Compare this with the actual return on the index over the 20 years and note that the actual 20-year return is always less than the compounded return computed from the arithmetic averages.

A general property of the arithmetic sample mean is that, when compounded, it always overestimates the true return. Hence, although the arithmetic sample mean is a good estimate of the one-period mean return, errors in the estimate are greatly magnified when the analyst compounds the sample mean to produce an estimate of the long-horizon mean. A little algebra illustrates this bias with greater generality. Suppose that an asset has returns in two consecutive years denoted as B_1 and B_2. One unit of cash invested over two years in the asset would earn

$$(1+\tilde{r}_1)(1+\tilde{r}_2)=\left(1+\frac{\tilde{r}_1+\tilde{r}_2}{2}+\frac{\tilde{r}_1-\tilde{r}_2}{2}\right)\left(1+\frac{\tilde{r}_1+\tilde{r}_2}{2}-\frac{\tilde{r}_1-\tilde{r}_2}{2}\right)=\left(1+\frac{\tilde{r}_1+\tilde{r}_2}{2}\right)^2-\left(\frac{\tilde{r}_1-\tilde{r}_2}{2}\right)^2$$

Taking the one-period sample mean, $(\tilde{r}_1+\tilde{r}_2)/2$, and compounding it over two periods indicates that one unit of cash earns

$$\left(1+\frac{\tilde{r}_1+\tilde{r}_2}{2}\right)^2$$

which exceeds the actual amount earned over the two periods by $[(\tilde{r}_1+\tilde{r}_2)/2]2$. This overestimate of the long-run return occurs because any positive deviations of the sample mean from the true mean are exacerbated more than negative deviations, as a result of compounding. Thus it may be important to reduce the estimated cost of capital to eliminate the bias.

The cost of capital adjustment that achieves unbiased present values depends on the frequency with which means are estimated, the length of time over which data are available, and the horizon of the cash flow. If the horizon of the cash flow is fairly long, it may be better to estimate the per-period mean as the geometric mean (discussed earlier in this chapter), instead of the arithmetic mean. For short-horizon returns, the arithmetic mean may provide a better estimate. Blume (1974) argued that there is an appropriate weighting of the arithmetic mean and the geometric mean that provides the correct estimate of the long-run mean return on a comparison investment. The following considerations determine the weights.

- If pairs of consecutive returns are negatively correlated, more weight should be placed on the geometric mean.
- If a great number of small-return horizons are averaged to obtain the arithmetic mean (for example, a day, a week), more weight should be placed on the geometric mean.
- If the horizon of the cash flow is long term, more weight should be placed on the geometric mean.

These insights apply even when the short-horizon expected return is obtained with an equilibrium model that relates expected return to beta risk. For example, the three considerations concerning the appropriate weighting of arithmetic and geometric means still apply when estimating the expected return of the tangency portfolio. Moreover, because of error in estimating beta along with the expected return of the tangency portfolio, the short-horizon cost of capital of an equity is estimated with error. As a result, adjustments need to be made to the cost of capital to correct for the compounding-based bias in present values.

The compounding-based bias is avoided only if one estimates returns by averaging (or estimating a risk-return model such as the CAPM) over periods of the same length as the cash flow horizon. For example, if the horizon of the cash flow is five years, an estimate of the five-year expected return of an investment, obtained by averaging the five-year returns during 1998–2002, 2003–2007, 2008–2012, and so on, is not subject to the compounding-based bias. Hence an unbiased present value estimate of a cash flow five years out in this case requires an upward adjustment to the cost-of-capital estimate to compensate for the denominator-based bias, but it would not require an adjustment for the bias induced by compounding.

Key Terms

Reference

Blume, M.E. (1974) Unbiased estimators of long-run expected rates of return *Journal of the American Statistical Association*, 69(347): 634–638.

Chapter 12

Allocating Capital and Corporate Strategy

Learning Objectives

After reading this chapter, you should be able to:

- Identify the sources of positive net present value.
- Implement the real options approach to value projects, know the options inherent in mines and vacant land, and the options to wait or to expand a project.
- Know the effect of these options on a firm's choice to diversify and select different production techniques from its competitors.
- Use the ratio comparison approach to value real assets and, in the case of price/earnings ratios, know how to adjust the ratio to make appropriate comparisons between firms with different leverage ratios.
- Compare the virtues and pitfalls of the competitive analysis approach to evaluate real investments, and know how to apply it.

My father and I started a cosmetic cream factory in the late 1940s. At the time, no company could supply us with plastic caps of adequate quality for cream jars, so we had to start a plastic business. Plastic caps alone were not sufficient to run the plastic-moulding plant, so we added combs, toothbrushes and soap boxes. This plastic business also led us to manufacture electric fan blades and telephone cases, which in turn led us to manufacture electrical and electronic products and telecommunication equipment. The plastics business also took us into oil refining, which needed a tanker-shipping company. The oil-refining company alone was paying an insurance premium amounting to more than half the total revenue of the then largest insurance company in Korea. Thus an insurance company was started. This natural step-by-step evolution through related businesses resulted in the Lucky-Goldstar group as we see it today. For the future, we shall base our growth primarily on chemicals, energy and electronics. Our chemical business will continue to expand towards fine chemicals and genetic engineering, while the electronics business will grow in the direction of semiconductor manufacturing, fibre-optic tele-communications and, eventually, satellite telecommunications.'

Source: Koo Cha-kyung, former CEO, LG Group (Chaebol)

Chapters 10 and 11 examined the traditional discounted cash flow (DCF) method for valuing real assets. DCF is useful in many cases, but it does not get to the heart of how intimately capital allocation is linked to long-term corporate strategy. This chapter's opening vignette, a quotation from the CEO of the LG Group in Korea, illustrates the way in which past investment projects generate future as well as current opportunities – an important consideration that DCF rarely takes into account.

This chapter presents a variety of advanced valuation techniques that remedy some of the deficiencies inherent in traditional DCF. The main emphasis will be on techniques that emphasize the role that the adoption of projects plays in the overall long-term strategy of a corporation. Among these advanced techniques are:

- a **real options approach**, which refers to the application of the derivatives valuation methodology introduced in Chapters 7 and 8 to value real assets
- a **ratio comparison approach**, which values an investment at approximately the same ratio of value to a salient economic variable as an existing comparable investment for which the same ratio is observable
- a **competitive analysis approach**, which attributes positive net present value to any project of a firm that can identify its competitive advantages and a negative NPV (net present value) to any project where competitors have the advantages.

These valuation approaches are not, in any way, inconsistent with the traditional DCF approach for valuing real investments. The real options approach and the ratio comparison approach, however, both recognize that financial market information can be useful for determining the expected cash flows of a project, as well as the appropriate discount rate, and can thus provide more accurate estimates of value. For example, the futures price for copper, used to value a copper mine with the real options approach, provides information about the expected future profits of a copper mine, and can be used to compute the certainty equivalent of a copper mine's cash flows. Or the ratio of Apple's share price to current earnings – used with the ratio comparison approach – may provide information about how the market assesses the future potential of the smartphone business.

Some of these advanced techniques, particularly the real options approach, also make an explicit attempt to value new opportunities typically missed in the direct cash flow forecasts of traditional valuation methods. These opportunities, which arise as a result of undertaking the project, are often referred to as **strategic options**.

The value of strategic options, and the real options approach used in their valuation, is attracting considerable attention. The valuation technique has been discussed in considerable detail in the financial press, and has been picked up by many of the leading management consulting firms. There are also websites specifically devoted to the latest real options methodology (see, for example, www.real-options.org).

In a few industries, and in some strategic arenas, these advanced valuation techniques have had a major impact on the way projects are evaluated. The real options approach, for example, has taken the energy industry by storm, and the ratio comparison approach has been common in the real estate sector for a while. In valuing potential acquisitions, the competitive analysis approach now plays a major role.

12.1 Sources of Positive Net Present Value

It is worthwhile to step back and ask where positive-NPV projects come from. To a large extent, firms are in a position to generate positive-NPV projects because of situations arising from prior investments. For example, Apple exploited its dominant position with its iPod range to compete with Nokia, Sony Ericsson, Motorola and Samsung in the highly lucrative mobile phone market with the iPhone. Apple then used the knowledge gained by the iPhone to launch the iPad, Apple Watch and AirPods.

In valuing potential investment projects, most firms do not adequately recognize that the adoption of an investment project generates future investment opportunities that often are quite valuable. Firms typically evaluate projects by discounting only the cash flows directly tied to the project under consideration, thereby underestimating the project's total value. However, the most successful corporations, such as Apple, grow and prosper as a result of new opportunities serendipitously arising from the company's past investment decisions.

Results

Result 12.1

New opportunities for a firm often arise as a result of information and relationships developed in its past investment projects. Therefore firms should evaluate investment projects on the basis of their potential to generate valuable information and to develop important relationships, as well as on the basis of the direct cash flows they generate.

Sources of Competitive Advantage

In general, the ability to generate profits in a competitive market is due to the advantages one firm has over its competitors.[1] These competitive advantages arise for a variety of reasons. First, there may be **barriers to entry**, or obstacles, that prevent competition by other firms from eroding profits. Consider AstraZeneca, one of the first firms in the world to develop a Covid vaccine, which gave the company a temporary monopoly on the production and sale of the vaccine in many countries. There may also be **economies of scale**, which arise when per-unit production costs decline with the scale of production, and thus make producers of large quantities of a good more efficient than small producers. Economies of scale give firms with a large market share a sustainable advantage. There are also **economies of scope**, which arise when a certain product or service can be supplied more efficiently by a firm that makes a related product. Economies of scope manifest themselves in the superior knowledge, marketing system or production technology that is acquired only by first producing a related product. In AstraZeneca's case, it could be argued that it benefits from both economies of scale and economies of scope, as a result of its size and variety of operations in the pharmaceutical sector.

Economies of Scope, DCF and Options

Much of the discussion in this chapter focuses on economies of scope, because they are the most important source of competitive advantage for a firm. If some of the positive cash flows that firms achieve from projects are positive only because of the economies of scope generated by earlier investments, then these positive cash flows should have been attributed to the earlier related investments. In evaluating the earlier investments, however, we noted earlier that most firms unnecessarily limit their analysis to the investment's direct cash flows, and rarely consider the indirect cash flows that might subsequently follow.

An implication of this limited analysis is that the DCF method leads to bad decisions. As currently implemented, DCF is biased against long-term projects, because it ignores many aspects of long-term investment projects that cannot easily be quantified.[2] Managers who use the DCF method tend to focus on what can easily be quantified, and thus tend to ignore the indirect cash flows.[3]

Take the case of Meta, formerly known as Facebook, and its decision to rebrand and enter fully into the VR/AR market. It may be possible to arrive at some estimate of this strategic change on Meta's cash flows, but the biggest value comes from future opportunities not yet identified. Because these future opportunities may subsequently prove to be valuable, they must be considered when calculating the cash flows of an original investment project. However, making a precise calculation of the value of subsequent opportunities is a heroic task. This chapter develops a real options approach, based on the derivatives valuation methodology, which at least can provide rules of thumb about when subsequent opportunities are likely to significantly enhance a project's value, and may even provide 'ballpark quantitative estimates' of the degree of this enhancement.

---

[1] For a detailed description of these advantages and a plethora of real-world illustrations, see Shapiro (1985).

[2] Hayes and Abernathy (1980) present the details of this argument.

[3] It is wrong, however, to assert that the discounted cash flow method is flawed as a result of this short-term focus, because the method itself does not tell us to ignore indirect long-term cash flows that stem from a project. It is simply the case that most managers do not consider indirect long-term cash flows.

Option Pricing Theory as a Tool for Quantifying Economies of Scope

Because subsequent opportunities will be pursued further only if they prove to be valuable, they are options that the firm possesses. Most investment projects include an option-like component. In addition to the option to pursue additional projects, financial managers also need to recognize that the adoption of almost any project contains other important options – among them, options to cancel, downsize or expand the project. The decision about exercising these types of option at a later date can be viewed as an investment project in the same way that Meta's potential future projects are considered separate projects.

The analysis of whether to 'exercise the option' and enter into these new projects will depend on underlying economic variables such as the demand for the products, the level of interest rates, the health of the economy, the success of competitors, the political climate and so forth. These underlying variables affect the values of many traded securities, including the company's own equity. Hence, if it is possible to model how the project and other traded securities are affected by underlying economic variables, it is possible to use real options techniques to value the indirect cash flows. Even in cases where the modelling is very crude, and one can obtain only a few guiding rules of thumb about the nature of the strategic option, it is important to consider such options when valuing an investment project. These options contribute to the value of any investment project in which management has flexibility in future implementation.

12.2 Valuing Strategic Options with the Real Options Methodology

The term *strategic options* is an appropriate label for the opportunities that arise from the ability to alter a project mid-course, or to enter into new projects as a result of some investment. There are two reasons for this. First, strategic options represent strategies that the firm has an option to pursue only by taking on the earlier project: that is, unless the firm undertakes the earlier project, there is no possibility of obtaining the cash flows from the strategic option. Second, strategic options are valued with the same option pricing methodology developed in Chapter 7 (and applied to options in Chapter 8). This section analyses the application of this pricing methodology for the valuation of real assets.

We indicated in Chapter 7 that a derivative is an investment whose value is determined by the value of another investment. One example is an equity option, which has a value determined by the price of the underlying equity. Another example is a forward contract to purchase copper for a specific price at a specific date in the future. The techniques used to value derivatives can also be used to value projects in relation to some underlying financial asset(s). In the following sections, we shall illustrate the use of the real options methodology to value:

- a mine with no strategic options
- a mine with an abandonment option
- vacant land
- the option to delay the start of a project
- the option to expand capacity
- flexibility in production technology.

Valuing a Mine with no Strategic Options

The valuation of natural resource investments (for example, oil wells and copper mines) illustrates how to implement the real options approach developed in this chapter. This subsection focuses on a copper mine. The choice of a mine stems from the unambiguous connection to an underlying asset, a forward contract on a metal, and the popularity, in practice, of the real options approach among natural resource firms. This subsection first examines how to use real options techniques to value a copper mine when no strategic options exist. In the absence of strategic options, the approach to mine valuation is identical to the certainty equivalent method discussed in Chapter 11.

The cash flows of a copper mine can be tracked by financial assets, since the mine's value is determined largely by the price of copper. Suppose that some of the copper in the mine will be extracted at date 1, and the remainder at date 2. If the extraction costs are known, or can be contracted for in advance, then the cash flows from this mine are contingent only on the price of copper.

The date 1 and date 2 cash flows from the mine, C_1 and C_2, respectively, can be expressed as

$$C_1 = p_1 Q_1 - K_1 C_2$$
$$C_2 = p_2 Q_2 - K_2$$

where

p_1 = date 1 copper price
p_2 = date 2 copper price
Q_1 = date 1 quantity of copper extracted
Q_2 = date 2 quantity of copper extracted
K_1 = date 1 cost of extraction
K_2 = date 2 cost of extraction.

Only p_1 and p_2 are assumed to be unknown at the adoption decision time, date 0.

Profits from holding a forward contract on copper also are determined only by the price of copper. Exhibit 12.1 illustrates the cash flows of forward contracts to exchange Q_t units of copper for cash at future date t.[4]

Exhibit 12.1 Cash Flows of Forward Contracts to Exchange Q_t Units of Copper for Cash at Future Date t

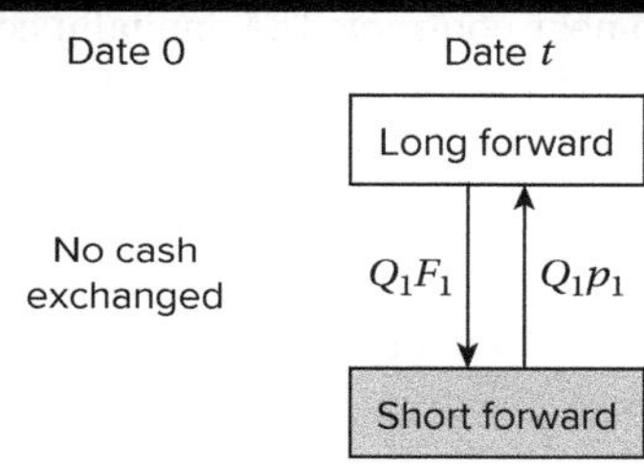

F_1 = Forward price agreed upon at date 0 (certain)
p_1 = Price of copper at date t (uncertain)
$Q_1 (p_1 - F_1)$ = Incremental cash flow

It is possible to use the forward prices from copper forward contracts maturing at dates 1 and 2 to value the copper mine. To see this, note that the respective cash flows at dates 1 and 2 from operating the mine, $p_1Q_1 - K_1$ and $p_2Q_2 - K_2$, are exactly the same as the future cash flows incurred by holding the following tracking portfolio. These are:

1 a forward contract to purchase Q_1 units of copper at date 1 at the current forward price of F_1 per unit, and a second forward contract to purchase Q_2 units of copper at date 2 at the current forward price of F_2 per unit
2 a risk-free zero-coupon bond paying $F_1Q_1 - K_1$ in year 1, and a second risk-free zero-coupon bond paying $F_2Q_2 - K_2$ at date 2.

We see this because, in year 1, the incremental cash flow from the forward contract is $Q_1(p_1 - F_1)$ and in year 2 it is $Q_2(p_2 - F_2)$. The risk-free bond pays out $F_1Q_1 - K_1$ in year 1, and $F_2Q_2 - K_2$ in year 2. The net cash flows are thus as follows:

$$\text{Year 1:} Q_1(p_1 - F_1) + F_1 Q_1 - K_1 = p_1 Q_1 - K_1$$
$$\text{Year 2:} Q_2(p_2 - F_2) + F_2 Q_2 - K_2 = p_2 Q_2 - K_2$$

Since F_1 and F_2 represent the current forward prices, the contracts have zero value at date 0, and thus item 1 in the tracking portfolio (see above) costs nothing. The present value of the uncertain cash flows from the mine equals the present value of the zero-coupon bonds in item 2. The value of the mine is thus given by

$$\text{PV} = \frac{F_1 Q_1 - K_1}{1 + r_1} + \frac{F_2 Q_2 - K_2}{(1 + r_2)^2}$$

[4] The absence of a cash flow at the initiation of these contracts is another way of saying that the future exchange price of these contracts is set to a value that makes the contracts have zero present value.

where

r_t = the yield to maturity of zero-coupon bonds maturing at date t ($t = 1, 2$)

$F_tQ_t - K_t$ = the future payment of the zero-coupon bond maturing at date t ($t = 1, 2$).

Example 12.1 implements this valuation procedure numerically.

Example 12.1

Valuing a Gold Mine

AngloGold Ashanti, a South African mining firm, owns the Geita Gold Mine in the north of Tanzania. The mine has a total 8.474 million ounces of gold (source: AngloGold Ashanti Tanzania Report). Although in a normal year between 300,000 and 600,000 ounces are extracted, for the purposes of this example assume that all the gold will be extracted in year 1 (2.474 million ounces) and year 2 (6 million ounces). The most recent year's extraction costs were \$497/oz, but this is exceptionally high because of an unusual combination of drought followed by extremely heavy rains in the Mwanza region of Tanzania where the Geita Gold Mine is situated. A more appropriate estimate of extraction costs is \$275/oz. The current forward prices are \$851/oz for a one-year contract and \$900/oz for a two-year contract. The annually compounded risk-free rates are 3.75 per cent for one-year zero-coupon bonds and 4 per cent for two-year zero-coupon bonds.

What is the present value of the cash flows from the mine, assuming that payments for the mined gold are received at the end of each year?

Answer:

$$\text{Mine value} = \frac{\$851(2.474 \text{ million}) - \$275(2.474 \text{ million})}{1 + 0.0375} + \frac{\$900(4 \text{ million}) - \$275(6 \text{ million})}{(1 + 0.04)^2}$$

$$= \$4.841 \text{ billion}$$

The valuation of the Geita Gold Mine in Example 12.1 is based on identifying the cost of a combination of investments traded in the financial market that *perfectly* track the mine's future cash flows at the end of the first and second years. As Exhibit 12.2 illustrates, the forward contracts (items a and b), in combination with a series of zero-coupon bonds maturing at two different dates (items c and d), produce future cash flows (bottom row, two right-hand columns) identical to those of the gold mine. The tracking portfolio costs approximately \$4.841 billion, which is the value attributed to the identical future cash flows of the gold mine.[5]

Valuing a Mine with an Abandonment Option

The analysis of mine valuation assumed that the amount of gold to be extracted was known with certainty, and was not controllable. In other words, the owner of the mine would not, or could not, alter the production decision as economic conditions changed.

In the real world, gold mine owners close their mines when the price of gold becomes too low or the costs of mining become too high to make mining profitable. Alternatively, mining firms may speed up production when gold prices are unusually high or the costs of extraction fall. The opportunity to alter production in this way is an example of a strategic option that enhances the value of the mine.

[5] This analysis assumes that gold production takes place on the dates when forward contracts mature. In reality, gold production is a continuous process, spread out over an entire period. To obtain a reasonable approximation of the value of a continuous mining process, assume that the present value of these spread-out cash flows is the same as the present value computed as though all production takes place at the 'average date'. For example, to compute the present value of all cash flows in the first year, assume that all first-year cash flows take place six months from now. Similarly, all second-year cash flows occur 18 months from now.

When forward contracts that settle 6 months and 18 months from now do not exist, the hypothetical forward price – found from linearly interpolating the forward prices that surround the target extraction date – generates a satisfactory mine value with the tracking procedure described above. For example, given four-month and eight-month forward contracts, with respective forward prices of \$820/oz and \$870/oz, it would be reasonable to assume that a six-month forward contract, if one existed, would have a forward price of about \$845/oz.

Exhibit 12.2 Future Cash Flows and Current Costs of Geita Gold Mine versus Portfolio of Forward Contracts and Zero-Coupon Bonds

F_1 = year 1 forward price \$851 per ounce			
F_2 = year 2 forward price \$900 per ounce			
Investment	**Cost beginning of first year**	**Cash flow end of first year**	**Cash flow end of second year**
Geita Gold Mine	PV unknown	$2.474(p_1 - \$275)$	$6(p_2 - \$275)$
a. Forward contract to buy 2.474 million ounces of gold at beginning of year 1	\$0	$2.474(p_1 - \$851)$	\$0
b. Forward contract to buy 6 million ounces of gold at beginning of year 2	\$0	\$0	$6(p_2 - \$900)$
c. Buy zero-coupon bonds; maturity = year 1 face amount = \$2.474(851 – 275)	$\frac{\$2.474(851-275)}{1.0375}$	\$2.474(851 – 275)	\$0
d. Buy zero-coupon bonds; maturity = year 2 face amount = \$6(900 – 275)	$\frac{\$6(900-275)}{1.04^2}$	\$0	\$6(900 – 275)
Total: $a + b + c + d$	\$4.841 billion	$\$2.474(p_1 - \$275)$	$\$6(p_2 - \$275)$

A Binomial Illustration of the Brennan–Schwartz Method

Consider a gold mine that generates a cash flow equal to the maximum of 0 and $(p_1Q_1 - K_1)$ in year 1 and nothing thereafter. In this case, the mine owner is in effect willing to buy gold at its extraction cost as long as this cost is less than the value of the gold. This is an option that is exercised (that is, mine the gold) or not exercised (that is, shut down the mine), depending upon whether the price of the gold, p_1, is sufficiently high to cover the cost of extraction. Indeed, the cash flows from the mine are exactly equal to the cash flows of an option to purchase Q_1 units of gold at an exercise price of K_1. If it were possible to observe the value of a call option to purchase gold, one would know the value of the mine. In most investments of this type, unfortunately, the type of traded option that tracks the real investment does not exist.

Brennan and Schwartz (1985) developed a method for valuing mines that takes into account the owner's options to reduce and increase production, which does not require the observation of the market price of an option to purchase the mineral being mined. The inputs used in their valuation method are the current forward price of the mineral, the volatility of the price of the mineral, and the risk-free rate of interest.

Although the Brennan and Schwartz method is complex, it can be approximated with the binomial approach developed in Chapters 7 and 8. This technique, used in valuing derivative assets, assumes that the future price movements of the underlying asset (for example, gold) follow a binomial process in which the price of the asset takes on one of only two possible values after one time period: a high value or a low value. The derivative asset – in this case, the gold mine – also takes on only one of two possible values at the end of the time period. Thus the future value of the gold mine can be tracked by a portfolio of two traded investments, which, according to the no-arbitrage assumption, implies that the value of the mine is simply the cost of the tracking portfolio. Example 12.2 illustrates how to compare the tracking portfolio with the mine to derive the mine's value.

Example 12.2

Valuing a Gold Mine with a Shutdown Option

Let's return to the Geita Gold Mine example (Example 12.1). Assume now that if economic conditions are favourable, it will produce 8.474 million ounces of gold one year from now. Assume two possible outcomes for gold prices then: \$551 per ounce and \$900 per ounce. The year 1 forward price is currently \$851 per ounce, implying that a forward contract has a negative future cash flow of $300 per ounce next year if gold prices are $500, and a positive future cash flow of $49 per ounce if gold is $900 per ounce. The risk-free one-year interest rate is 3.75 per cent. The extraction costs are $275 per pound, so if gold prices fall, AngloGold Ashanti will shut down the mine. What is the value of this mine?

Answer: Exhibit 12.3 illustrates the pay-offs from the mine in two scenarios, and can be used to find the portfolio of forward contracts and risk-free zero-coupon bonds that tracks the mine's future cash flows in either gold price scenario.

Exhibit 12.3 Pay-offs of a Gold Mine with a Shutdown Option

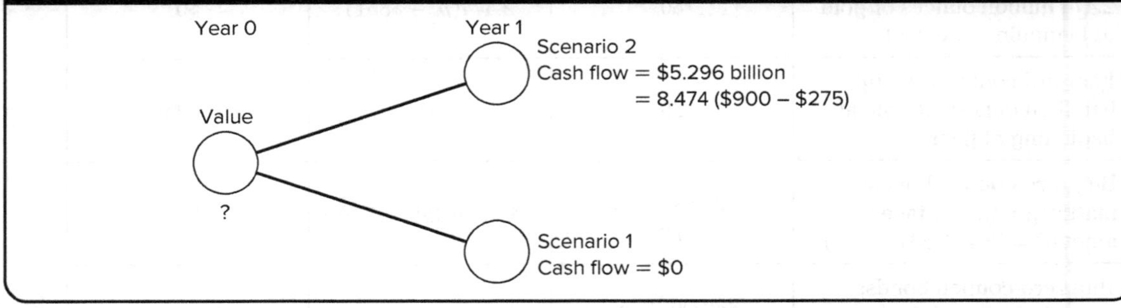

Scenario 1 (low gold price = $551 per ounce): in this scenario, the gold mine will shut down and be worth zero. The equation when the tracking portfolio is worth zero in the event that gold prices are low is

$$x(\$300 - \$851) + y(1.0375) = \$0$$

where

x = ounces of gold purchased forward
y = dollars invested in zero-coupon bonds today that mature in one year.

Scenario 2 (high gold price = $900 per ounce): in this scenario, the gold mine will be profitable. It will earn $49 per ounce of gold mined, and it thus pays to produce at maximum capacity. The cash flow in this scenario is $5.296 billion = 8.474($900 – $275).

The equation when the same tracking portfolio also yields $5.296 billion if gold prices are high is

$$x(\$900 - \$851) + y(1.0375) = \$5.296 \text{ billion}$$

Simultaneously solving the equations for scenarios 1 and 2 gives the tracking portfolio:

x = 15,175,501 ounces of gold received from a one-year forward contract
y = $4.388 billion invested in zero-coupon bonds.

The value of this tracking portfolio is $4.388 billion. Therefore the gold mine must also have a value of $4.388 billion.

Practical Considerations

Example 12.2 is useful for showing how to value a real asset with an option, but it contains simplifications that make mine valuation simpler than it is in the real world. First, it assumes that if the gold is not extracted at the end of the period, it cannot be extracted in the future. More realistic mine valuations should not limit the mining to a specific date by which the mineral or commodity must be extracted. There are procedures for valuing mines in this case, where the option to extract is perpetual.

Risk-Neutral Valuation

Chapter 7 indicated that the tracking portfolio approach to valuation is equivalent to valuation with 'risk-neutral' probabilities. Applying risk-neutral probabilities to the cash flows of the mine and discounting the risk-neutral expected cash flow at the risk-free rate would have yielded the same answer. These risk-neutral probabilities are implicitly given by the prices of traded investments. Exercise 12.7 at the end of the chapter asks you to compute the risk-neutral probabilities that make the forward price equal the 'expected' future spot price. (To illustrate the use of the risk-neutral valuation technique, the next section values land.)

Exchange Options and Volatility

Another practical consideration in valuing a mine is that the extraction cost, as well as the price of the commodity, is generally uncertain. The mine is thus analogous to an **exchange option**, which is the option to exchange one item (an asset, liability or commodity) for another. Margrabe (1978) first valued this type of option by noting that the underlying price for the option value was the ratio of the prices of the two items being exchanged. In this case, AngloGold Ashanti has the option to exchange the extraction costs for the gold; the relevant variable that determines the value of the gold mine in the Margrabe model is the ratio of the gold price to the extraction costs. As the volatility of this ratio increases, the value of the mine increases. Result 12.2 summarizes this discussion.

Results

Result 12.2

A mine can be viewed as an option to extract (or purchase) minerals at a strike price equal to the cost of extraction. Like an equity option, the option to extract the minerals has a value that increases with both the volatility of the mineral price and the volatility of the extraction cost.

Generalizing the Real Options Approach to Other Industries

The valuation of a mine is a particularly fruitful area for applying the real options approach, chiefly because the mine's future value is so closely related to the value of a traded financial asset, in this case a forward contract on the gold being mined. For most companies, however, the valuation of a typical project is not so closely linked to any single financial asset.

For example, a proposed line of HP laptop computers may have future cash flows that are related to the prices of long-term futures contracts on semiconductors, but the cash flows also are related to the health of the economy, Hewlett Packard's reputation, interest rates, the strength of competition, technological advances, advances in production efficiency, and consumer tastes.

Some of these determinants of cash flow are closely tied to a financial asset or a group of financial assets, which certainly belong in the tracking portfolio. For example, a proxy for Hewlett Packard's reputation such as its share price, a proxy for the health of the US economy such as the value of the S&P, a proxy for the health of the computer industry such as the value of a portfolio of computer hardware firm equities, and a host of interest rate futures contracts are possible candidates for the Hewlett Packard project's tracking portfolio.

In contrast to the tracking of the mine, however, the HP laptop line's tracking portfolio probably generates substantial tracking error. This is partly because some important cash flow determinants of the laptop line are not properly captured by the prices of any financial assets, and partly because estimating the weights of the various financial assets in the tracking portfolio is more complex than it was in the mine valuation case.

These obstacles to implementing the real options approach in more general cases do not imply that the financial analyst should not attempt the implementation. Even when the quantitative estimates are imprecise, important lessons can be learned from such an exercise. Illustrations of these lessons are provided throughout the remainder of this chapter.

Valuing Vacant Land

Vacant land has value, because it represents an option to turn it into developed land. For example, a particular plot of land may be developed into an apartment block, an office building or a shopping centre. In the future, the developer will have an incentive to develop the property for the use that maximizes the difference between the value of the project's future revenues and its construction costs. However, the best possible future use for the land may not be known at present.

The real options approach can be used to determine the worth of an option to construct one of a number of possible buildings with strike prices equal to the building's construction costs. One can value this option, and thus the land, by first computing the risk-neutral probabilities associated with various outcomes. Example 12.3

uses the binomial approach to obtain the risk-neutral probabilities necessary to value vacant land. One derives these probabilities from the observed market prices of traded investments (for example, the price of existing apartments and the risk-free rate of interest).

Example 12.3

Valuing Vacant Land

Consider an exploration and mining company that owns exploration and mining rights for several undeveloped sites in Australia, Greenland and Brazil. The company commissioned an extensive feasibility study of one of its sites, which reported that there were 995,000 tonnes of proven zinc ore in the area. The proven reserves would allow the extraction of 17.1 per cent of pure zinc from the ore as well as 3.1 per cent of pure lead. At the time of the feasibility study, the prices of zinc and lead were $1,900/tonne and $1,100/tonne, respectively.

If the firm were to set up mining facilities and install new extraction equipment, the net expected capital expenditure and extraction costs are estimated to be $38 million. The company has the choice of seeking funding to develop the mine immediately at current market prices or waiting a year. If market conditions are favourable next year, the prices of zinc and lead would be $2,700/tonne and $3,600/tonne, respectively. If conditions are unfavourable, the prices of zinc and lead would be $1,400/tonne and $800/tonne, respectively. In either scenario, the extraction costs would be $38 million. If the risk-free rate is 6 per cent per year, and all the zinc and lead could be extracted in one year, what is the value of the zinc site?

Answer: Before analysing the choice facing the mining company, it is important to estimate the actual amount of zinc and lead that can be extracted from the site.

$$\text{The amount of zinc} = 995{,}000 - 17.1\% = 170{,}145 \text{ tonnes}$$
$$\text{The amount of lead} = 995{,}000 - 3.1\% = 30{,}845 \text{ tonnes}$$

Now consider the profit that the firm would make if it starts operations immediately.

$$\text{Profit} = [(170{,}145 \times \$1{,}900) + (30{,}845 \times \$1{,}100)] - 38 \text{ million} = \$319{,}205{,}000$$

If the company decides to wait for one year and start operations then, it will receive the pay-offs illustrated in panel A of Exhibit 12.4. This shows that, by waiting a year and constructing a mine if market conditions are favourable, the company will realize a total profit of $532,433,500. It will construct a mine and realize a total profit of $224,879,000 if unfavourable market conditions prevail. If the present value of this pair of cash flows is larger than the $319,205,000 profit from building the mine now, waiting is the best alternative. Assuming that the company waits, the value of the site is computed by valuing the two possible cash flow outcomes: $532,433,500 (favourable conditions) and $224,879,000 (unfavourable conditions).

To calculate the present value of this cash flow pair, first compute the risk-neutral probabilities, π and $(1 - \pi)$, associated with the two states. As the binomial tree in panel B of Exhibit 12.4 shows, investing in 1 tonne of zinc and lead today (Year 0) would cost $3,000 (= $1,900 + $1,100), which would lead to a year-end (Year 1) value of either $6,300 (= $2,700 + $3,600) or $2,200 (= $1,400 + $800), depending on market conditions. This implies that the risk-neutral probabilities must satisfy

$$\frac{\pi\$6{,}300 + (1 - \pi)\$2{,}200}{1.06} = \$3{,}000$$

which is solved by $\pi = 0.239$.

Discounting next year's expected cash flows at the risk-free rate of 6 per cent, seen in panel C, with expectations computed using the risk-neutral 'probabilities', gives the current value of the land under the assumption that it will remain vacant until next year. This current value is

$$\frac{(0.239)\$532{,}433{,}500 + (0.761)\$224{,}879{,}000}{1.06} = \$281{,}494{,}835$$

Since $281,494,835 is less than the $319,205,000 profit that would be realized by developing the mine immediately, it is better to invest now. The value of the undeveloped site is approximately $281.5 million.

Exhibit 12.4 Binomial Trees for Land Valuation

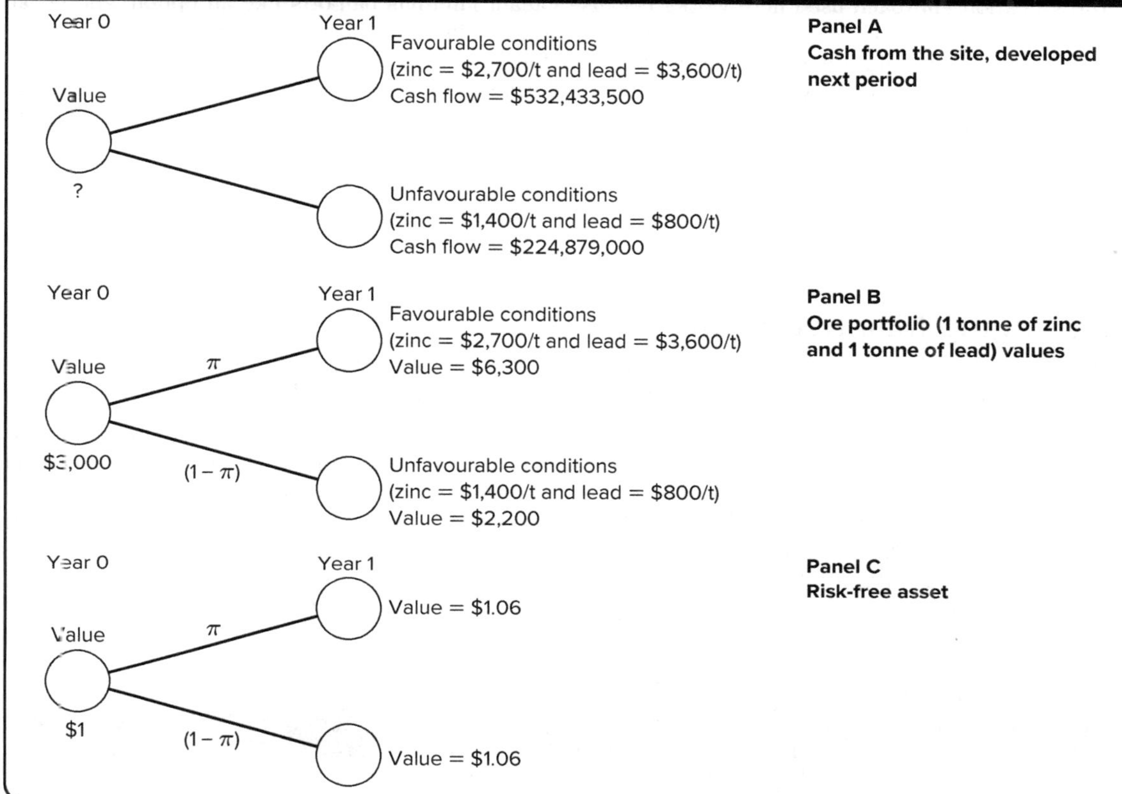

Calculating these risk-neutral probabilities requires solving for probabilities that generate expected cash flows for traded assets that equal their certainty equivalent cash flows. In other words, with the correct risk-neutral probabilities, the expected cash flows of traded assets, discounted at the risk-free rate, will equal the observed market price of the traded asset. These same risk-neutral probabilities can then be applied to the cash flows of the investment being valued to calculate the risk-neutral (or certainty equivalent) cash flows, which are then discounted at the risk-free rate. Example 12.3 illustrates how this procedure can be followed to value vacant land as an option to build a mine depending on market conditions. How realistic is this? Chapter 8 indicated that option values are increasing in the volatility of the underlying asset – in this case, developed land. In a study of commercial properties in the Chicago area, Quigg (1993) found that land was indeed more valuable with greater uncertainty. Result 12.3 summarizes this view.

Results

Result 12.3

Vacant land can be viewed as an option to purchase developed land where the exercise price is the cost of developing a building on the land. Like equity options, this more complicated type of option has a value that is increasing in the degree of uncertainty about the value (and type) of development.

Titman (1985) shows that development restrictions, such as ceilings on building height or density, may reduce uncertainty, leading to both a lower value for vacant land and a greater desire to exercise the option – that is, to develop the land. This curious phenomenon – that development restrictions may lead to more development – arises because the benefit of waiting is the greatest force keeping vacant landholders from exercising the development option. The benefit of waiting is greater when the degree of uncertainty about the option's terminal value is greater, as noted in Chapter 8.

The valuation approach used here works because vacant land has pay-offs like an option, and because the possibility of arbitrage keeps prices in line. Example 12.4 illustrates how to achieve arbitrage if the real estate market places a different price on the value of the land than on the price derived from risk-neutral valuation. The investment in Example 12.4 yields a risk-free gain of $37,703,088. Because this kind of gain cannot exist in equilibrium, investors will bid down the price of the land from $319,205,000 to its equilibrium value of $281,494,835.

Example 12.4

Arbitraging Mispriced Land

Assume that the mining firm is offered $319,205,000 for the zinc site today: show how investors can earn arbitrage profits by purchasing the land and hedging the risk by selling short the zinc and lead.

Answer: One achieves risk-free arbitrage by short-selling the land, buying a comparable amount of zinc and lead, and buying $59,849,756/1.06 of risk-free, zero-coupon bonds maturing in one year. The present value of 75,013.29 tonnes of zinc and lead completely hedges the risk from owning the vacant land since the difference between the value of the units in the favourable and unfavourable states, $307,554,500 (= 75,013.29 × ($6,300 – $2,200)), exactly offsets the difference in land values in the two states ($532,433,500 – $224,879,000). Note that the determination of the amount invested in the zero-coupon bond and the amount of tonnes of zinc and lead required can easily be calculated using simultaneous equations.

The arbitrage opportunity is summarized as follows.

Investment	Cash inflow today ($)	Cash in favourable state next year ($)	Cash in unfavourable state next year ($)
Buy 75,013.29 tonnes of lead and zinc	–225,039,878	472,583,744	165,029,244
Short sell vacant land	319,205,000	–532,433,500	–224,879,000
Buy risk-free bonds	–59,849,756/1.06	59,849,756	59,849,756
Total	37,703,088	0	0

It is tempting to argue that arbitrage is impossible in the situation described in Example 12.4, because it is impossible to sell short vacant land. However, someone who already owns similar mines could sell them, and buy both the lead and zinc and the risk-free asset. At the margin, this looks like an arbitrage opportunity, because the change in cash flows associated with this decision is riskless and yields positive cash today.

Valuing the Option to Delay the Start of a Manufacturing Project

Strategic options affect a variety of investment decisions. The zinc mine example in the last subsection illustrated the value of delay, which permitted some flexibility in the adoption of the mine development. Delay has value, because it provides the developer with more time to determine the optimal mine development. In practice, the lead and zinc extraction decision would be assessed separately, and would depend on the prices of lead and zinc in the financial markets. In addition, the firm (not explored in the example) could extract the metals slowly over time, in an attempt to capture future price dynamics of the metal. Ultimately, the optimal decision cannot be known until economic conditions unfold over time.

Delay also allows the firm more time to decide whether to adopt a project. When a firm accepts a project, it exercises an option, and hence loses the value from waiting longer. The value of waiting makes it imprudent to exercise an American call option on a non-dividend-paying equity before the option's expiration date (see

Chapter 8). This lesson should not be forgotten when dealing with the strategic options of a real asset. Although the future cash flows of a real asset may not exactly mimic the future cash flows of an American call option, the generic lesson is the same: for the call option, delay exercise until the last possible moment; for the real asset, it is often better to delay accepting a project, even when the project currently has a positive NPV, as computed by discounting its direct cash flows. In the zinc mine example, the optimal decision was to start mining immediately, because of the danger of metal price collapse. However, a multi-period analysis may actually change the decision as future metal prices are modelled more accurately.

To understand why value from delay arises, think about each project as a combination of two or more mutually exclusive investments that are defined by the time they are first implemented. For example, investment 1 might be to initiate the project immediately, while investment 2 is to wait one year and then initiate the project only if economic conditions are favourable. Initiating the project immediately may be a positive-NPV investment, but the NPV of waiting one year may be even higher.[6]

Viewed from this perspective, it might make sense to turn down positive-NPV projects, at least temporarily, as Example 12.5 illustrates. In this example, it pays to turn down the positive-NPV project at year 0, and in year 1 adopt the project if the good state occurs, and reject the project if the bad state occurs.

Example 12.5

Creating Value by Rejecting a 'Positive-NPV Project'

Clacher Industries is considering building a cider brewery. After an initial investment of £100 million, the brewery will be completed in one year and then have the series of annual cash flows shown in Exhibit 12.5. Clacher's managers can decide to invest the £100 million immediately, or they can wait until next year to decide whether to build or not.

Exhibit 12.5 Cash Flows for Clacher's Brewery Timing Decision

	Year 0	Year 1	Year 2	Years 3, 4, 5
Panel A: do not wait:	£100 million	£10 million Good	£15 million	£15 million per year for ever
		£10 million Bad	£2.5 million	£2.5 million per year for ever
Panel B: wait one year and initiate only in good state	£0	–£100 million Good	£15 million	£15 million per year for ever
		£0 Bad	£0	£0 per year for ever

If the project is built immediately, panel A in Exhibit 12.5 shows that after a year of start-up procedures, next year's cash flow will be £10 million, but a perpetual annual cash flow stream of either £15 million or £2.5 million will occur each year thereafter, depending on whether the economy is good or bad one year from now. If the project is delayed, panel B of Exhibit 12.5 shows that the first year's initial £10 million cash flow will be lost. Only the perpetual cash flow stream of £2.5 million or £15 million, beginning two years hence, will be captured, depending on the state of the economy in year 1. Assuming that the risk-free interest rate is 5 per cent per year, and that £1.00 invested in the market portfolio today will be worth either £1.30 (if the economy does well) or £0.80 (if the economy does poorly), compute the NPV of the project, and decide whether or not it pays to wait.

[6] Ingersoll and Ross (1992) note that, even if the manager knows that cash flows will not change as a result of waiting to invest, the present values of cash flows will change, because interest rates are always changing. Hence every project can be viewed as an option on interest rates.

Answer: View the decision to wait or build now as two mutually exclusive projects, with the higher-NPV project winning out. Each of the two projects can be valued as a derivative using the binomial option valuation methodology. First, compute the value of the plant if Clacher builds it immediately.

If the market return is good, the brewery has a year 1 value of £10 million plus the value of the perpetuity: that is,

$$\text{£10 million} + \frac{\text{£15 million}}{0.05} = \text{£310 million}$$

If the market return is bad, the year 1 value is

$$\text{£10 million} + \frac{\text{£2.5 million}}{0.05} = \text{£60 million}$$

To compute the present value, calculate the risk-neutral probabilities, π and $1-\pi$, associated with the valuation of the market portfolio. These solve

$$\text{£1.00} = \frac{\pi(\text{£1.30}) + (1-\pi)(\text{£0.80})}{1.05}$$

implying that $\pi = 0.5$. Applying the probabilities π and $1-\pi$ to the relevant values in the two states yields a present value for the brewery of

$$\frac{(0.5)\,\text{£310 million} + (0.5)\,\text{£60 million}}{1.05} = \text{£176.19 million}$$

Since this is greater than the £100 million cost of building the brewery, the project has a positive NPV of £76.19 million (= £176.19 million – £100 million).

The alternative of waiting one year and then investing in the brewery only if the favourable outcome occurs results in an NPV of

$$0.5 \times \frac{\text{£15 million}/0.05 - \text{£100 million}}{105} = \text{£95.24 million}$$

Since £95.24 million exceeds £76.19 million, the alternative of waiting is preferred.

Results

Result 12.4

Most projects can be viewed as a set of mutually exclusive projects. For example, taking the project today is one project, waiting to take the project next year is another project, and waiting three years is yet another project. Firms may pass up the first project, that is, forgo the capital investment immediately, even if doing so has a positive NPV. They will do so if the mutually exclusive alternative, waiting to invest, has a higher NPV.

Valuing the Option to Expand Capacity

Perhaps the most important application of the real options approach is assessing the importance of flexibility in the design of investment projects. In an uncertain environment, flexibility – such as the ability to take a project already initiated and expand it, reduce its scale (perhaps liquidating some of its assets), or completely abandon it–is an option, and each option available enhances the project's value.

One example of flexibility is the abandonment option seen earlier in this chapter when we discussed the valuation of the Geita Gold Mine. There, AngloGold Ashanti simply stopped mining gold at no cost. This is probably unrealistic, as flexibility generally imposes some costs on the firm. For example, scaling down or scaling up the capacity of a project already started often requires additional cash–for example, severance payments or shutdown costs with scaling down, and additional machinery or employees with scaling up. It is therefore important to value the option to be flexible and compare it with the cost of acquiring that flexibility. Example 12.6 demonstrates how to use the binomial approach to value investment projects that have this more complex flexibility.

Example 12.6

Valuing the Option to Increase a Brewery's Capacity

Clacher Industries is considering building another cider brewery. The brewery will generate cash flows two years from now, as described in Exhibit 12.6. The cash flows from the brewery will be £200 million following two good years (point D), £150 million following one good and one bad year (point E), and £100 million (point F) following two bad years. The initial cost of the plant is £140 million (point A). After one year, however, if the state of the economy looks good, the firm has the option to double the plant's capacity by investing another £140 million.

Exhibit 12.6 Cash Flows if There is No Capacity Change at Year 1

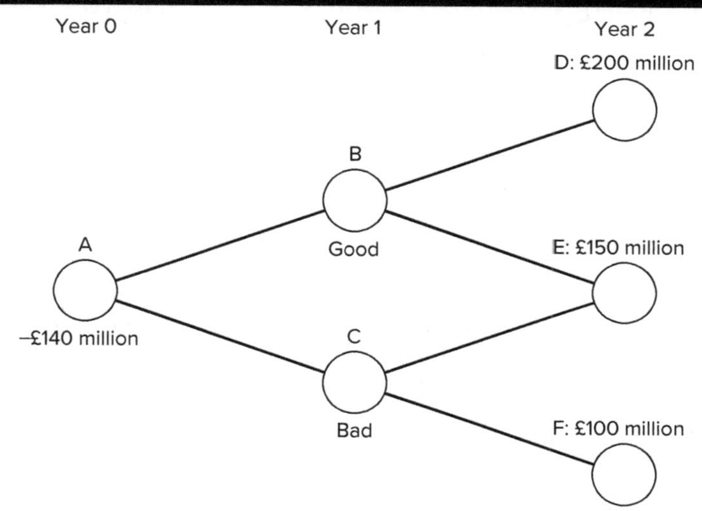

Exhibit 12.7 shows that doubling the brewery's capacity will have the effect of doubling the cash flows to either £400 million or £300 million in its final year (compare the two point Ds and points E and E1 in

Exhibit 12.7 Cash Flows if Plant Capacity Is Doubled at Good Node in Year 1

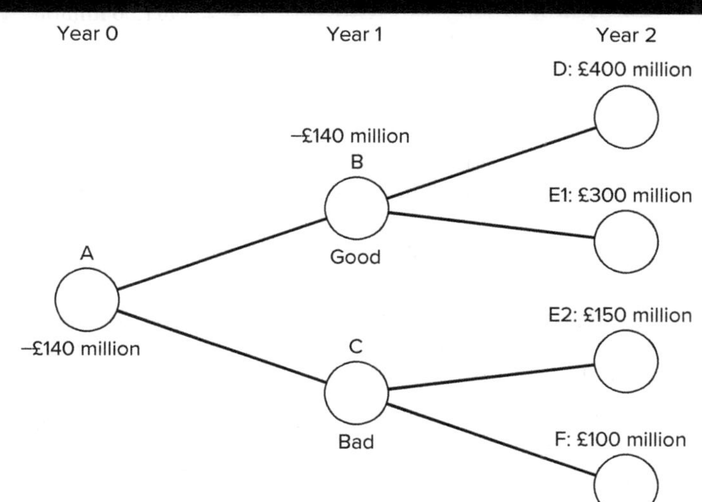

Exhibit 12.8 Market Portfolio Pay-offs for Determining Risk-Neutral Probabilities

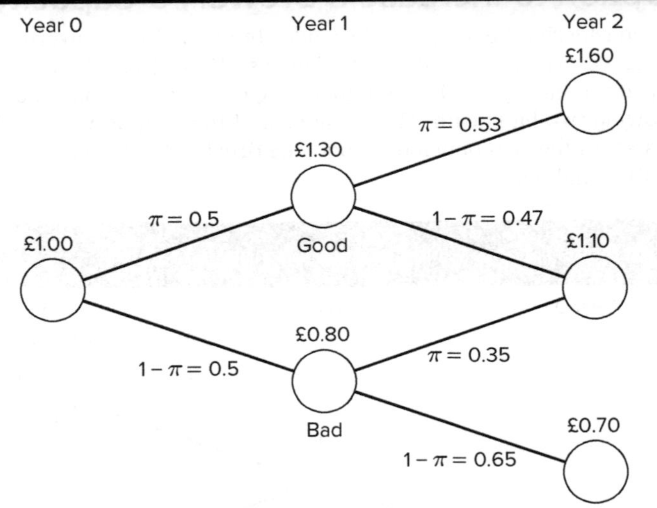

Exhibits 12.6 and 12.7). Assume a risk-free rate of 5 per cent per year, and that £1.00 invested in the market portfolio today yields future values, depending on the state of the economy, shown by the tree diagram in Exhibit 12.8. The corresponding risk-neutral probabilities, π and $1 - \pi$, attached to the nodes in the tree have been computed to be consistent with these market portfolio values, and appear next to the branches in the tree diagram in Exhibit 12.8.

Compute the value of building a plant under two scenarios: in scenario 1, the option to double the brewery's capacity is ignored; in scenario 2, it is not ignored.

Answer: *Scenario 1:* applying the risk-neutral probabilities, π and $1-\pi$, from Exhibit 12.8 to compute expectations and discounting at the 5 per cent per year risk-free rate implies that the value of the brewery at point B (the good node) in Exhibit 12.6 is

$$\frac{(0.53)\ £200 \text{ million} + (0.47)£150 \text{ million}}{1.05} = £168.10 \text{ million}$$

The value of the brewery at point C (the bad node) in Exhibit 12.6 is

$$\frac{(0.35)£150 \text{ million} + (0.65)£100 \text{ million}}{1.05} = £111.90 \text{ million}$$

The value of the brewery at point A (the initial node) is thus

$$\frac{(0.5)£168.10 \text{ million} + (0.5)£111.90 \text{ million}}{1.05} = £133.33 \text{ million}$$

which yields an NPV of – £6.67 million = £133.33 million – £140 million.

Scenario 2: using the risk-neutral probabilities from Exhibit 12.8, the value of the brewery at point B (the good node) in Exhibit 12.7 is

$$-£140 \text{ million} + \frac{(0.53)£400 \text{ million} + (0.47)£300 \text{ million}}{1.05} = £196.19 \text{ million}$$

The –£140 million appears in this equation because, at point B, the firm takes advantage of the option to double the brewery's capacity by spending an additional £140 million. The point C value is the same as in scenario 1. Thus the value of the brewery at date 0 is

$$\frac{(0.5)£196.19 \text{ million} + (0.5)£111.90 \text{ million}}{1.05} = £146.71 \text{ million}$$

which yields an NPV of £6.71 million = £146.71 million – £140 million.

Ignoring the option to increase the brewery's capacity (scenario 1 in Example 12.6) results in a £140 million cost that exceeds the present value of its future cash flows (£133.33 million). Thus a naive forecast of the cash flows of the brewery makes it appear as though building the brewery destroys value. However, unless Clacher builds the plant at year 0, it can never take advantage of the option to increase capacity. Scenario 2 in Example 12.6 shows that this flexibility option enhances the value of building the brewery by more than £13 million, which is enough to turn an apparent negative-NPV project into a positive-NPV one.

Valuing Flexibility in Production Technology: The Advantage of Being Different

Using what we have learned about strategic options, particularly the option to expand, it is possible to demonstrate that in many instances a firm can gain a competitive advantage by being different from its competitors. This subsection shows that firms that have the option to vary their output levels may want to choose a method of production that differs from that of their competitors. By doing this the firm increases risk, thereby increasing the value of its flexibility option.

Consider, for example, a firm that produces and sells refined sugar in a market with a large number of competitors. It must decide whether to purchase equipment that allows it to produce the sugar from sugar cane or from sugar beet. The other sugar producers in its market use sugar cane as their input for refined sugar production. As a result, the price of refined sugar immediately reflects any increases in the price of sugar cane. However, because the competing firms currently do not use sugar beet as an input, fluctuations in the price of sugar beet are not as tied to the price of refined sugar as is the price of sugar cane.

A firm that lacks flexibility about how much sugar it will be producing will want to design its facilities to use the input with the lowest present value of its costs. However, as Example 12.7 shows, if the firm has a plant that gives it the option to increase production, the added uncertainty linked to using an input (sugar beet) that differs from the inputs used by competitors (sugar cane) can be valuable.

Example 12.7

The Effect of Capacity Expansion on the Choice to be Different

The tree diagram in panel A of Exhibit 12.9 illustrates some of our assumptions:

- In a good economy, the cost of producing refined sugar with sugar cane is €0.60 per pound and the cost of using sugar beet is €0.54 per pound.
- In a bad economy, the cost of producing refined sugar with sugar cane falls to €0.40 per pound; however, the demand for sugar beet is somewhat less cyclical than that for sugar cane, because it is not generally used to produce refined sugar. Thus the cost of producing refined sugar with sugar beet falls somewhat less, to €0.50 per pound.
- The risk-neutral probabilities associated with each of these two states of the economy (seen next to the branches of the tree diagram in panel A of Exhibit 12.9) are assumed to be 0.5.
- The price of refined sugar is always €0.03 per pound greater than the cost of production using sugar cane, which is reasonable, because virtually all producers use sugar cane as their input.

Assuming that the fixed cost of building a sugar cane plant and a sugar beet plant are the same, which method of producing refined sugar is better when (a) capacity is fixed, or (b) capacity is flexible in that the firm is committed to producing at least 1 million pounds of refined sugar in the plant but, at a cost of €40,000, the firm can double capacity to 2 million pounds upon discovering the state of the economy?

Answer: (a) Capacity is fixed. Using the risk-neutral probabilities of 0.5 and 0.5 to compute expectations, the expected production costs, from panel A in Exhibit 12.9, are €0.50 per pound [= 0.5(€0.60/lb) + 0.5(€0.40/lb)] for sugar cane and €0.52 per pound [= 0.5(€0.54/lb) + 0.5(€0.50/lb)] for sugar beet. Hence sugar cane is the better input.

(b) Capacity can be doubled. If the firm uses sugar cane as its input, then it will earn €30,000 from selling 1 million pounds of sugar in both the good and bad economies, as seen in panel C of Exhibit 12.9. Since the cost of additional capacity, €40,000, exceeds the profit from expanded capacity, €30,000, a firm

Exhibit 12.9 Production of Refined Sugar

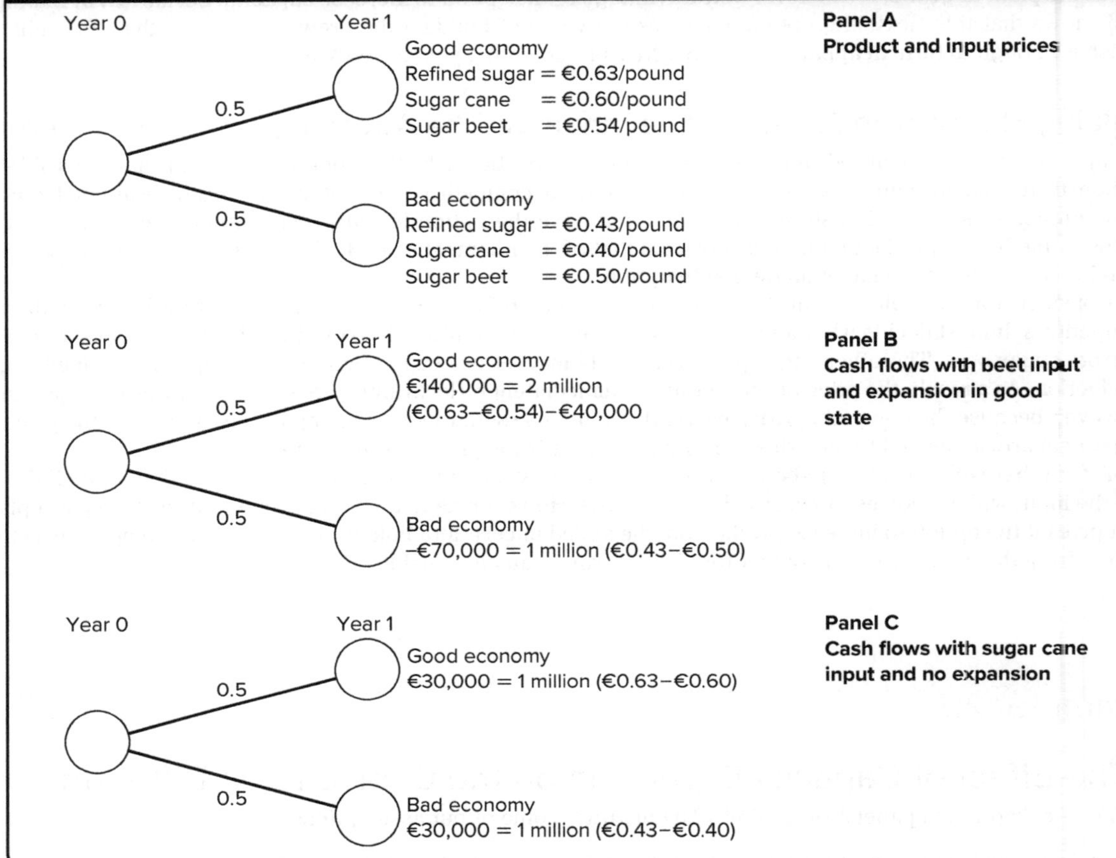

using sugar cane will choose not to exercise its option to double capacity. However, if the firm chooses to use sugar beet as its input, it will earn €0.09 per pound if the good state of the economy occurs, because the price of refined sugar in this state of the economy is €0.63 per pound while production costs are €0.54 per pound. The firm will therefore make €90,000 on the first 1 million pounds of production. By exercising its option to double production, the firm makes €90,000 – €40,000 = €50,000 on the second 1 million pounds of production. Hence, as seen in panel B of Exhibit 12.9, the total profit in the good economy is €140,000. In the bad economy, the firm using the sugar beet input loses €70,000 at the lower refined sugar price of €0.43 per pound. Despite this loss, however, the firm's expected profit using sugar beet is €35,000, which exceeds the €30,000 in expected profits it achieves using sugar cane as its input (panel C). Thus, with the capacity to expand, sugar beet represents the superior raw input for production of refined sugar.

What is the intuition for the conclusion in Example 12.7 that sugar beet is a better raw input than sugar cane, despite being the more expensive input, on average? For the sugar beet input, the lower output price in the bad economy reflects the drop in the price of sugar cane, the dominant raw material for producing refined sugar. Because output prices are correlated with the price of the dominant input, sugar producers who use *sugar cane* as the raw input generate profits that are partly insured against swings in the economy. However, producers who use *sugar beet* as the raw input in the production of refined sugar experience only a small decline in their input price when prices for refined sugar and sugar cane drop dramatically. Refined sugar production using *sugar beet* as the raw input is thus subject to wild swings in profit – earning €140,000 in the good economy and losing €70,000 in the bad economy. While this might seem like a disadvantage, it can be turned into an advantage if options such as the option to expand capacity exist. This is simply an application of the principle learned in Chapter 8 that options become more valuable when there is more volatility in the underlying asset.[7]

It is important to emphasize that the benefits of being different are not a principle, only a possibility. Had the numbers in Example 12.7 been different, one could easily have concluded that sugar cane manufacturing was still the cheaper method, despite the option to increase capacity. Irrespective of which production method in the last example is cheap, one always would conclude that the advantage associated with being different is greater when there is more uncertainty, and when the firm has greater flexibility to expand.

Real Option Valuation When There is Uncertainty about the Effect of Past Events

Real option methods predict the future to model the impact of potential shocks in the production process. However, another form of uncertainty is the permanent or transitory effect of production shocks that have occurred in the past. Standard real option theory models all shocks as permanent, but this is not necessarily the case with every event or shock, and firms may not know whether it will lead to a permanent cash flow change or whether it will be transitory. For example, when BP experienced the catastrophic oil spill in the US Gulf, managers were uncertain as to whether the political backlash that could have led to BP being restricted from further activity in the region would be permanent or transitory. This was only understood with greater certainty as time passed. Grenadier and Malenko (2010) consider this issue, and specifically the option to wait until there is greater clarity on the impact of past shocks. They argue that ignoring this very salient aspect of managerial decision-making may lead to erroneous investment decisions and sub-optimal performance. They also show that the timing of cash flows arising from a project can have a critical effect on the value of the option to wait to obtain clarity about previous shocks.[8] Clearly, then, managers must be careful to model all sources of uncertainty when undertaking real asset valuations.

Real-World Insights

Real option valuation methods are ideal for assessing the viability of sustainability projects. While a single project may not, on its own, appear viable, only once potential options arising from an endeavour are incorporated into an investment appraisal can its true value be understood. Take, for example, natural resource investment in woodlands, peatlands, wetlands, and coastline projects. When considering investments of this type, a conventional discounted cash flow analysis will lead to project undervaluation because regulatory constraints will reduce net present value. In addition, real options are ignored. A more appropriate approach to sustainable investments is to accept regulatory constraints (which will reduce project cash flows) but to incorporate, as standard, all real options embedded in the potential project. A real option checklist for analysts is as follows:

1. **Real options tied to project life.** Sustainable investment is, by its nature, long-term. Whereas a standard corporate investment will last up to ten years before obsolescence or competition brings a natural end to a project, a sustainable investment could last up to one hundred years or even longer. This gives a firm two real options to consider: (a) an option when to make the investment, and (b) an option on the length of project operations. Having a fifty or one hundred year time-frame means a firm can decide the optimal time to start operations and the optimal length of operations to maximise value.
2. **Understand project cash flow volatility.** One of the factors that affect option values is volatility of the underlying asset. This means that more volatile cash flows can increase the real option value of an investment. With long-term horizons and climate change uncertainty, understanding the volatility of future cash flows arising from weather extremes can create significant value.
3. **Project stage-gating.** All investments can be thought of as a series of decisions based on possible sequential events during the project's life. Over a five or ten-year horizon, there will be a small number of nodal periods when operations can be abandoned or continued, scaled up or scaled down, and

[7] The risk-free return is not mentioned in Example 12.7 because it does not affect any of the conclusions. The production method with the largest risk-neutral expected profit is also the method with the largest present value.

[8] Related literature that considers cash flow and parameter uncertainty includes Décamps, Mariotti and Villeneuve (2005), Gorbenko and Strebulaev (2010), Klein (2007, 2009), and Miao and Wang (2007).

extended or modified. With a much longer project life, the opportunity to embed decision points is substantially greater and this creates considerable value for a project.

4. **Options on options.** Many decision points might lead to different options. Future paths will have their own options, creating value through options on options. This is known as a compound option and can be valued accordingly.
5. **Technology options.** The long-term nature of sustainable investments means that over the lifetime of a project, new technology is very likely to be introduced that will improve the efficiency of operations and reduce the risk of future cash flows. Technology options can be easily embedded into a long-term project and create value for the investment.

This checklist of five potential option types should form the basis for sustainable project investment appraisal, particularly related to natural resources where project lives are normally much longer than a standard corporate investment.

12.3 The Ratio Comparison Approach

A popular way in which investment bankers and analysts value firms, projects or assets is to compare them with other traded firms, projects or assets. One of the best examples of this occurs in the field of real estate. The standard DCF method is often used to value real estate, but it is not the principal method. For example, most commercial property is valued relative to comparable property that sold recently. A building should sell for £20 million if it has twice the annual cash flow (rent revenues less maintenance costs) as a building across the street that recently sold for £10 million. The implicit assumption is that the cash flows of the two buildings will grow at the same rate, so that twice the cash flows of the comparable building tracks the future cash flows of the subject building.

Although the current annual cash flows of the building being valued may be twice those of the comparable building, this method is reasonable only if all future cash flows of the subject building are going to be twice as large as those of the comparable building. When this is not a reasonable assumption, other variables besides current cash flows might better summarize all future cash flows, and thus serve as better proxies for generating the tracking investment.

For example, investment bankers consider a multiple of the forecast annual earnings of comparison firms when valuing the initial public offering (IPO) of a company's ordinary equity.[9] Earnings are often smoothed proxies for long-run cash flows, and may work better as proxies than the current cash flow in determining the tracking portfolio. In some cases, these comparisons are based on book values or replacement values. For example, it is common to describe the prices of **real estate investment trusts (REITs)**, which are property portfolios that list and trade like shares of equity on an exchange, as a percentage of the book values of their assets. Other variables besides cash flow, earnings and book value are also used in valuation. For example, a multiple of the number of subscribers is typically used to estimate the prices of non-traded cable television companies. Equity analysts value money management firms as a fraction of the amount of assets they have under management. Newspapers, magazines and internet portals are valued relative to their advertising revenue and circulation.

These approaches to valuation assume that a new investment should sell at approximately the same ratio of price to some salient economic variable as an existing investment with an observable ratio, which is why this approach is called the *ratio comparison approach.* This section illustrates the ratio comparison approach by using the ratio of price to earnings, P/NI, where NI stands for net income (that is, earnings) on the accounting income statement.[10] However, the examples above show that it is possible to use alternative numbers for earnings – sales revenue, book value, subscribers, monthly rents, advertising lines, website visitors or cash flow – as the denominator for this comparison.

[9] To price a firm that is going public, the firm's investment bankers will generally try to project the earnings of the firm and then come up with an earnings multiple by analysing the price/earnings ratios of comparison firms. This provides an initial estimate of the firm's value, which is likely to be adjusted for any specific risks of the IPO and unusual market conditions.

[10] This is sometimes referred to as the P/E ratio, but we often use the variable E in the text to represent the market value of equity, so we employ P/NI.

The Price/Earnings Ratio Method

With the **price/earnings ratio method**, one obtains the present value of a project's future cash flows as follows.

Results

Result 12.5

(*The price/earnings ratio method.*) The present value of the future cash flows of a project can be found by (1) obtaining the appropriate price/earnings ratio for the project from a comparison investment for which this ratio is known, and (2) multiplying the price/earnings ratio from the comparison investment by the first year's net income of the project. In a similar vein, a company should adopt a project when the ratio of its initial cost-to-earnings is lower than the price to earnings ratio of the comparison investment. (Alternative ratio comparison methods simply substitute a different economic variable for earnings.)

Subtracting the cost of initiating the project from this present value (PV) yields the NPV. A company should adopt a project whenever the project's NPV is positive, which occurs when the project produces the future cash flow stream more cheaply than the comparable investment. Expressed another way, if the cost-to-earnings ratio of the project is less than the price/earnings ratio of a comparison investment, the project is a bargain, since it generates a unit of earnings at a lower cost than the comparable investment.

Keep in mind that the market price of an investment incorporates both the appropriate discount rate as well as the appropriate earnings growth rate. As a result, the price/earnings ratio method may avoid some of the difficulties in estimating either discount rates or growth rates. The price/earnings ratio method assumes, however, that the comparison investment on which the price/earnings multiple is based has the same discount rate and earnings growth as the project being valued. This is a safe assumption in some settings, but it may be inappropriate in others.

When Comparison Investments are Hidden in Multi-Business Firms

Finding an investment with an observable value that is comparable to, for example, a speciality steel plant is more difficult than finding something comparable to an office building. Therefore it may be necessary to examine combinations of the traded securities of a number of firms to identify an appropriate comparison investment. This approach is similar to the identification of beta risk when the betas of comparison firms are generated by multiple lines of business. (See Chapter 11, Example 11.3.) When using price/earnings ratios to value projects, it may be necessary to use Result 12.6.

Results

Result 12.6

The price/earnings ratio of a portfolio of equities 1 and 2 is a weighted average of the price/earnings ratios of equities 1 and 2, where the weights are the fraction of earnings generated, respectively, by equities 1 and 2. Algebraically, this is

$$\frac{P}{\mathrm{NI}} = w_1 \frac{P_1}{\mathrm{NI}_1} + w_2 \frac{P_2}{\mathrm{NI}_2}$$

where

P/NI = price/earnings ratio of the portfolio
P_i/NI_i = price/earnings ratio of equity i (i = 1 or 2)
w_i = fraction of portfolio earnings from equity i.[11]

---

[11] This result is derived by noting that

$$P = P_1 + P_2 = \left(\frac{\mathrm{NI}_1}{\mathrm{NI}}\right)\left(\frac{P_1}{\mathrm{NI}_1}\right)\mathrm{NI} + \left(\frac{\mathrm{NI}_2}{\mathrm{NI}}\right)\left(\frac{P_2}{\mathrm{NI}_2}\right)\mathrm{NI}$$

which implies that

$$\frac{P}{\mathrm{NI}} = \left(\frac{\mathrm{NI}_1}{\mathrm{NI}}\right)\left(\frac{P_1}{\mathrm{NI}_1}\right) + \left(\frac{\mathrm{NI}_2}{\mathrm{NI}}\right)\left(\frac{P_2}{\mathrm{NI}_2}\right) = w_1\left(\frac{P_1}{\mathrm{NI}_1}\right) + w_2\left(\frac{P_2}{\mathrm{NI}_2}\right)$$

To apply this result to the speciality steel plant, consider a situation where the only potential comparison firm producing speciality steel is also in the oil business. How does an analyst filter out the impact of the oil business on the price/earnings ratio of the comparison firm?

Result 12.6 implies that the comparison firm, in combination with a firm producing similar oil-related products, might be a pure speciality steel portfolio, which can be used to determine the appropriate price/earnings ratio for valuing the speciality steel division. Example 12.8 illustrates how to do this when the line of business is the production of passenger buses (rather than speciality steel).

Example 12.8

Price/Earnings Ratio Comparisons with Multiple Lines of Business

Ford is considering the opportunity to enter the European passenger bus market. Assume that General Motors (GM) currently produces similar buses, from which it realizes 10 per cent of its earnings. The rest of GM's cash flows come from automobile lines that are essentially the same as Ford's.

If GM's price/earnings ratio is 11.07, and if the price/earnings ratio of its automobile division is (as seems reasonable) assumed to be the same as the price/earnings ratio of Ford, which is 11.2, what is the implied price/earnings ratio for the bus division?

Answer: 90 per cent of GM's earnings have a price/earnings ratio of 11.2, 10 per cent of the earnings have a price/earnings ratio of x, and the total GM value is 11.07 times the company's total earnings. Viewing GM as a portfolio of a pure automobile business and a pure bus business, and applying Result 12.6, implies that x must solve

$$0.9(11.2) + 0.1x = 11.07$$

Thus $x = 9.9$.

If the cost of the bus plant in Example 12.8 is less than 9.9 times the initial earnings of the plant, and if it is realistic to assume that those earnings will grow at the same rate and have the same risk as the General Motors bus plant, then Ford should accept the project.

The Effect of Earnings Growth and Accounting Methodology on Price/ Earnings Ratios

The price/earnings ratio method is useful in many circumstances, but it has drawbacks. As mentioned earlier, the earnings of the project and the comparison portfolio must have similar growth rates. For example, if the earnings of the comparison portfolio are growing at a faster rate than those of the project, the price/earnings ratio method is invalid, because the value of the comparison portfolio will be enhanced by the faster growth rate. Even if the project costs little to initiate, and seems to have a favourable cost-to-earnings ratio compared with the price/earnings ratios available from similar investments, the project could destroy value if the low cost does not make up for the project's low earnings growth rate.

Analysts who use the price/earnings ratio method also must be especially careful that the earnings calculations reflect the true economic earnings of the firm. Different accounting standards, such as IFRS or US GAAP, can lead to different earnings estimates, and it is important for the analyst to be aware of the relevant financial reporting standards, especially those regarding Fair Value Accounting. Accounting changes, such as one-time write-downs or accounting for bad debts, can dramatically affect the reported earnings of firms without affecting their cash flows or their market values. Companies can also artificially inflate reported earnings through creative accounting techniques such as discretionary accruals, 'sale and leaseback' transactions, extraordinary items and different depreciation estimates. Analysts who naively use reported earnings to calculate the appropriate value of a project will substantially misvalue the project. For this reason, some analysts who employ the price/earnings ratio method use EVA or similar measures of adjusted earnings in lieu of earnings *per se.*

In general, the valuation expert must be aware of how accounting earnings differ from true economic earnings; specifically, how accrual accounting, working capital changes and depreciation affect reported earnings. To address these concerns, some analysts use the price-to-cash-flow ratio in lieu of the price/ earnings ratio. However, it is also easy to distort the comparison with the price-to-cash-flow ratio. For example, a comparison firm may find itself cash rich simply because a major customer decides to obtain an income tax deduction by paying its bill at the end of the current year instead of at the beginning of the new year. Customers who speed up the payment of their bills by a few days have a negligible effect on the comparison firm's PV, but they may substantially increase the reported cash flow in the relevant fiscal year, and reduce the cash flow in the year after.

The Effect of Leverage on Price/Earnings Ratios

To use the price/earnings ratio method to make capital allocation decisions, it also is important to understand how leverage affects a firm's net income per share (EPS) and, consequently, its price/earnings ratio. As this chapter will demonstrate shortly, an increase in leverage, holding the firm's operations and total value constant, will increase or decrease the firm's net income per share and price/earnings ratio, depending on the relative sizes of the price/earnings ratio and the reciprocal of the yield on debt borrowing.

When Leverage Decreases the Price/Earnings Ratio

Example 12.9 illustrates a hypothetical case where leverage decreases the *P*/NI ratio of GlaxoSmithKline plc.

Example 12.9

A Case Where Leverage Decreases the Price/Earnings Ratio

Consider the financial data of a hypothetical firm given below.

Assets (book value)	£25.553 billion
Liabilities (book value)	£15.905 billion
Equity (book value)	£9.648 billion
Equity market value	£67.633 billion
Number of shares outstanding	5.548 billion
Equity book value (BE) per share	$£1.74 = \frac{€9.648}{5.548}$
Share price	$£12.19 = \frac{£67.633}{5.548}$
Net income (year 0)	£5.389 billion
Earnings per share (year 0)	£0.971
5-year earnings growth rate	5.11%
Expected EPS (year 1)	£1.02 = £0.971(1 + 0.0511)
$\frac{P}{\text{NI}}$	$11.95 = \frac{£12.19}{1.02}$
ROE (year 1)	$58.71\% = \frac{\text{NI}}{\text{BE}} = \frac{£5.389(1.0511)}{£9.648}$

Assume that the firm issues £5 billion in debt at the beginning of the fiscal year at a rate of 6 per cent, and that equity is decreased by the same amount through a repurchase of 410,172,272 shares at £12.19 each. Assuming no taxes and thus no response in share price per share to the increase in leverage, how does the debt issue affect the firm's balance sheet account and expected financial performance for the year?

Answer: As a result of the debt issuance, resulting in a £5 billion increase in liabilities and a £5 billion decrease in equity, the balance sheet accounts and expected financial performance for the year will be as follows.

Assets (book value)	£25.553 billion
Liabilities (book value)	£20.905 billion
Equity (market value) pre-debt issue	£67.633 billion
Number of shares outstanding	5.138 billion
Equity book value (BE) per share pre-debt issue	$€1.74 = \frac{€9.648}{5.548}$
Equity (book value) post-debt issue	£8.940 billion = £1.74 (5.138 billion)
Equity (market value) post-debt issue	£62.633 billion = £67.633 – £5
Share price	$£12.19 = \frac{£62.633}{5.138}$
Net income (year 0)	£5.389 billion
Earnings per share (year 0)	£0.971
5-year earnings growth rate	5.11%
Expected EPS (year 1) pre-debt issue	$£1.02 = \frac{£5.389(1+0.0511)}{5.548}$
Expected EPS (year 1) post-debt issue	$£1.04 = \frac{£5.389(1+0.0511) - £5(0.06)}{5.138}$
$\frac{P}{\text{NI}}$	$11.72 = \frac{£12.19}{£1.04}$
ROE (year 1)	$60.0\% = \frac{\text{NI}}{\text{BE}} = \frac{5.389(1+0.0511) - £5(0.06)}{8.940}$

What Determines Whether Leverage Increases or Decreases the Price/Earnings Ratio?

The general principle is formally stated as follows.

Results

Result 12.7

Assume that the market value of the firm's assets is unaffected by its leverage ratio. Also assume that all debt is risk free. If the ratio of price to earnings of an all-equity firm is larger than $1/r_D$, where r_D is the interest rate on the firm's (assumed) risk-free perpetual debt, then an increase in leverage increases the price/earnings ratio. If the price/earnings ratio of an all-equity firm is less than $1/r_D$, then the increase in leverage lowers the price/earnings ratio of the firm.

To prove Result 12.7, simply write out the price/earnings ratio, assuming risk-free perpetual debt, where

A = the market value of the assets

X = unlevered earnings

A/X = the price/earnings ratio of an all-equity firm.

The ratio of the market value of equity to the firm's total net income (assuming zero taxes) is

$$\frac{\text{Price}}{\text{Earnings}} = \frac{A - D}{X - r_D D} = \frac{1}{r_D}\left[\frac{\left(\frac{A/X}{1/r_D}\right)X - r_D D}{X - r_D D}\right] \tag{12.1}$$

Note that the expression in brackets in the equation above is either larger or smaller than 1, depending on the relative size of A/X and $1/r_D$. An increase in D, which moves the expression in brackets closer to 1, decreases the price/earnings ratio when $A/X < 1/r_D$ and increases it otherwise.

Adjusting for Leverage Differences

If one uses a comparison firm's price/earnings ratio to value a particular project, it is important to value the project with the **unleveraged price/earnings ratio**, which is the ratio that would exist if the comparison investment were all-equity financed, rather than the leveraged price/earnings ratio that one observes. One values the project as the product of the **unlevered earnings** of the project and the unleveraged price/earnings ratio of the comparison: that is,

$$PV_{\text{project}} = \left(\frac{A}{X}\right)_{\text{comparison}} \times (X)_{\text{project}}$$

To 'unlever' a price/earnings ratio, use equation (12.1) in reverse. First, substitute the measured price/earnings ratio on the left-hand side and then solve for the A/X, the unleveraged price/earnings ratio, that makes equation (12.1) hold.[12] With corporate taxes, multiply the denominator expression in brackets, $X-r_D D$, by (1 – corporate tax rate) before solving for A/X.

12.4 The Competitive Analysis Approach

We previously discussed how financial analysis tools can be used to clarify the thinking of a corporation's long-run strategic planners. This section turns the tables somewhat by discussing how issues typically considered by strategic planners can be used to analyse the value created by specific projects.

Determining a Division's Contribution to Firm Value

In many cases, it is impossible to unravel the contribution of a particular division to a firm's value. For example, trying to obtain the appropriate price/earnings ratio for an investment in toothpaste production by examining the financial statements of multiproduct companies such as Procter & Gamble or Wyeth is pointless; their toothpaste divisions account for only a small part of the performance reported in their consolidated financial statements. However, with a great deal of confidence, one can assert that toothpaste is a product that will continue to be used in the future. In addition, it is likely that a firm probably has a positive-NPV project if it can either produce toothpaste more cheaply or sell it more effectively than its competitors. If this is not the case, the project's NPV is probably negative. In other words, the NPV of a project is ultimately determined by a firm's advantages relative to those of its competition. A firm that can accurately assess its competitive advantages may find that this is the best method of assessing the NPV of a project.

Results

Result 12.8

(*The competitive analysis approach.*) Firms in a competitive market should realize that they can achieve a positive NPV from a project only if they have some advantage over their competitors. When other firms have competitive advantages, the project has a negative NPV.

[12] See exercise 12.11 for an algebraic solution to this problem.

Disadvantages of the Competitive Analysis Approach

The competitive analysis approach, like the other valuation methods, has its pitfalls. Prior to the global covid pandemic, for example, most oil firms were spending more to explore for oil than the oil was worth. Because the competitive analysis approach implicitly assumes value-maximizing competitors, it could lead a value-maximizing firm astray when this assumption is false. A manager of a firm with non-value-maximizing competitors might accurately project the demand for oil in the foreseeable future, and correctly ascertain that it has a competitive advantage in its production (for example, lower costs). The manager might assume that, even if oil prices declined, less efficient competitors would stop production before the price level dropped to a point where the firm started to incur losses. Given these assumptions, the competitive analysis approach suggests that oil exploration is a good investment. However, if other firms are in the oil business for reasons other than value maximization (for instance, company pride), the manager may find that, as oil prices decline, competitors do not exit, or possibly even increase production, believing that they can survive a 'price war' and drive prices even lower. This type of market would be unattractive, even for the lowest-cost firm.

12.5 When to Use the Different Approaches

Part III of the text has discussed various different approaches to real asset valuation. The approaches in Chapters 10 and 11 include DCF, using the risk-adjusted discount rate and certainty equivalent approaches, and internal rate of return. This chapter has discussed the real options, ratio comparison and competitive analysis approaches. Which approach or set of approaches should a manager use?

Can These Approaches be Implemented?

Some of these approaches may be difficult to apply in practice. For instance, the intuition gained from the examples that employ the real options approach in this chapter is always going to be useful, but this advanced valuation technique is not always applied easily. For example, the strategic options associated with many investment projects are difficult to specify before the project is actually initiated. Moreover, it is frequently impossible to estimate the random process (for example, the binomial tree) that generates the future asset prices that determine the investment's PV. This makes it difficult to apply the real options approach literally. It is also difficult in many cases to estimate the expected or certainty equivalent cash flows of an investment, so the DCF method may also be difficult to implement reliably.

Valuing Asset Classes versus Specific Assets

In addition, when asking questions like 'Is property a good investment?', the real options and the ratio comparison approaches cannot be used. These approaches are based on a comparison between highly similar investments, and reveal little about the relative pricing of widely disparate classes of assets, so they are not effective for identifying whether broad asset classes are mispriced.

To determine the attractiveness of property investments as a group, one would have to determine the risk of a broad-based portfolio of property investments, and assess whether the financial markets are appropriately pricing that risk. Therefore it is best for this purpose to use a model – either the CAPM or the APT – that makes statements about the risk–return relationship across asset classes. In contrast, given the empirical shortcomings of the CAPM and APT (see Chapters 5 and 6), one should look to alternatives in more specific cases when they are available. For example, it would be inappropriate to use the CAPM and APT to value an office building when a suitable comparable office building exists.

Tracking Error Considerations

The tracking portfolio metaphor may be useful in determining the best valuation approach. The CAPM argues that every investment should be tracked with a weighted average of the market portfolio and a risk-free asset. Tracking with the CAPM has to be highly imperfect, considering the dissimilarities between a particular office building and the market portfolio. Financial analysts who use the CAPM to value a real asset rely on the insight that the CAPM-based tracking error has a zero PV to conclude that the valuation is correct. If the CAPM as a theory is untrue in certain circumstances, then this conclusion is unwarranted. We already know that the tracking error does not have zero PV for equities with low market-to-book ratios, small market capitalizations and high past returns. Thus there is no reason to have similar confidence in the tracking error for any particular investment project.

In contrast, the cash flows from a portfolio composed of a comparable office building and the risk-free asset tracks the evaluated building's cash flows more closely than a combination of the market portfolio and a risk-free asset. In either case, there is no theoretical reason to believe that the tracking error will have zero PV. However, one obtains a better PV by using the comparable office building in a ratio comparison than by using the CAPM if the tracking error with the comparable office building is so small as to be negligible.

Other Considerations

While the ratio comparison approach and the competitive analysis approach seem easy to implement, and implicitly account for the strategic options embedded in most projects, they are limited by the degree to which the comparison investments and firms exhibit rationality, either in their pricing (for example, in the price/earnings approach)[13] or in their behaviour (for example, in the competitive analysis approach). Moreover, it may be difficult to ensure that the comparison investment (or firm) is truly an appropriate comparison, or to take into account all factors for which there are differences between the comparison entity and the project.

The practical focus we emphasize here suggests that using any single approach discussed in this chapter need not preclude a manager from also valuing a project with a second method when it is practical to apply an alternative. Indeed, it probably makes sense to value major investment projects using two or three approaches.

12.6 Summary and Conclusions

A good portion of this chapter focused on using the real options approach to value projects with strategic options. This approach requires making a number of simplifying assumptions that may not be particularly realistic (for example, the assumption that cash flows evolve along a binomial tree). As a result, one should consider the calculated values as rough estimates rather than exact quantities. Nevertheless, although the pricing of strategic options is still an inexact science, the methods described in this chapter provide useful intuition about the kinds of project that are likely to be more valuable, or to have large components of value missed by the DCF method.

Among the intuitive lessons to remember are those listed below.

- Strategic options exist whenever management has any flexibility regarding the implementation of a project.
- Options to change the scale of a project, abandon it or drastically change its implementation in the future need to be considered. The more different a firm is from its competitors, the more valuable the options (for example, the option to expand).
- The existence of these options improves the value of an investment project. If management ignores such options, the project will be undervalued. Hence a manager who computes a zero or slightly negative NPV for a project with the standard DCF method can feel confident about adopting the project. The cash flows arising from strategic options that were missed because of their indirect nature will push the NPV of the project well into the positive range.
- The values of most options increase with the maturity of the option. This suggests that strategic options are generally more valuable for longer-term projects. Standard DCF methods, which tend to ignore such options, may underestimate the value of long-term projects more than they underestimate the value of short-term projects. If decision-makers ignore such options in their valuation analysis, long-term projects will be undervalued more than short-term projects.
- The greater the uncertainty about the future value of the underlying investment, the greater the option's value. This suggests that strategic options are more valuable the higher the risk of the project, indicating that it is probably beneficial to build more flexibility into projects with more uncertain future cash flows. Traditional DCF methods that ignore strategic options are likely to undervalue high-risk projects more than low-risk projects, so it is important for decision-makers to be careful before rejecting high-risk projects.

In addition to the real options approach, this chapter studied two other methods for analysing capital allocation: the ratio comparison approach and the competitive analysis approach.

[13] For example, the purchaser of the comparison office building across the street might have paid too much for the property.

All three valuation methods, like nearly every valuation method for valuing financial assets or real assets studied in this text, are based on comparisons between assets. Each asset is tracked, sometimes approximately, by a portfolio of other assets. Financial valuation is simply a way of connecting the value of an asset that has a known price to the asset being valued.

What if the manager believes that the market is incorrect? For example, if managers think that the comparable office building is undervalued, or the underlying gold price is too low, should they use their superior information and accept investment projects that the market incorrectly undervalues but which are overvalued relative to their tracking portfolios? Generally, the answer to this question is no. If the cost of a prospective investment exceeds the cost of its tracking portfolio, it is clearly better to buy the tracking portfolio than to take the investment. This is true regardless of the market's assessment – correct or incorrect – of the value of the tracking portfolio.

In summary, the advantages of this chapter's valuation methods over the standard DCF method largely have to do with deficiencies in the way in which the standard DCF method is implemented. Two general rules often ignored by practitioners who use the standard DCF method should be emphasized:

1 Because decision-makers are ultimately trying to evaluate the market value of a project, financial managers should use observable market prices as much as possible. Don't rely on estimated market values when actual market prices can be observed.
2 Managers should think in terms of investment strategies instead of isolated individual investment projects. Most projects are flexible in their implementation, and often provide the firm with additional profitable investment opportunities in the future. Consider these options, which add value to an investment strategy, when evaluating investment projects.

Key Concepts

Result 12.1: New opportunities for a firm often arise as a result of information and relationships developed in its past investment projects. Therefore firms should evaluate investment projects on the basis of their potential to generate valuable information and to develop important relationships, as well as on the basis of the direct cash flows they generate.

Result 12.2: A mine can be viewed as an option to extract (or purchase) minerals at a strike price equal to the cost of extraction. Like an equity option, the option to extract the minerals has a value that increases with both the volatility of the mineral price and the volatility of the extraction cost.

Result 12.3: Vacant land can be viewed as an option to purchase developed land where the exercise price is the cost of developing a building on the land. Like equity options, this more complicated type of option has a value that is increasing in the degree of uncertainty about the value (and type) of development.

Result 12.4: Most projects can be viewed as a set of mutually exclusive projects. For example, taking the project today is one project, waiting to take the project next year is another project, and waiting three years is yet another project. Firms may pass up the first project, that is, forgo the capital investment immediately, even if doing so has a positive NPV. They will do so if the mutually exclusive alternative, waiting to invest, has a higher NPV.

Result 12.5: (*The price/earnings ratio method.*) The present value of the future cash flows of a project can be found by (1) obtaining the appropriate price/earnings ratio for the project from a comparison investment for which this ratio is known and (2) multiplying the price/earnings ratio from the comparison investment by the first year's net income of the project. In a similar vein, a company should adopt a project when the ratio of its initial cost-to-earnings is lower than the price to earnings ratio of the comparison investment. (Alternative ratio comparison methods simply substitute a different economic variable for earnings.)

Result 12.6: The price/earnings ratio of a portfolio of equities 1 and 2 is a weighted average of the price/earnings ratios of equities 1 and 2, where the weights are the fraction of earnings generated, respectively, by equities 1 and 2. Algebraically, this is

$$\frac{P}{\text{NI}} = w_1\frac{P_1}{\text{NI}_1} + w_2\frac{P_2}{\text{NI}_2}$$

where

P/NI = price/earnings ratio of the portfolio
P/NI_i = price/earnings ratio of equity i ($i = 1$ or 2)
w_i = fraction of portfolio earnings from equity i.

Result 12.7: Assume that the market value of the firm's assets is unaffected by its leverage ratio. Also assume that all debt is risk free. Then, if the ratio of price to earnings of an all-equity firm is larger than $1/r_D$, where r_D is the interest rate on the firm's (assumed) risk-free perpetual debt, then an increase in leverage increases the price/earnings ratio. If the price/earnings ratio of an all-equity firm is less than $1/r_D$, then the increase in leverage lowers the price/earnings ratio of the firm.

Result 12.8: (*The competitive analysis approach.*) Firms in a competitive market should realize that they can achieve a positive NPV from a project only if they have some advantage over their competitors. When other firms have competitive advantages, the project has a negative NPV.

Key Terms

Exercises

12.1 Assume that company A merges with company B. Assume that A's price/earnings ratio is 20 and B's is 15. If A accounts for 60 per cent of the earnings of the merged firm, and if there are no synergies between the two merged firms, what is the price/earnings ratio of the merged firm?

12.2 The XYZ firm can invest in a new chip factory for $425 million. The factory, which must be invested in today, has cash flows two years from now that depend on the state of the economy. The cash flows when the factory is running at full capacity are described by the following tree diagram.

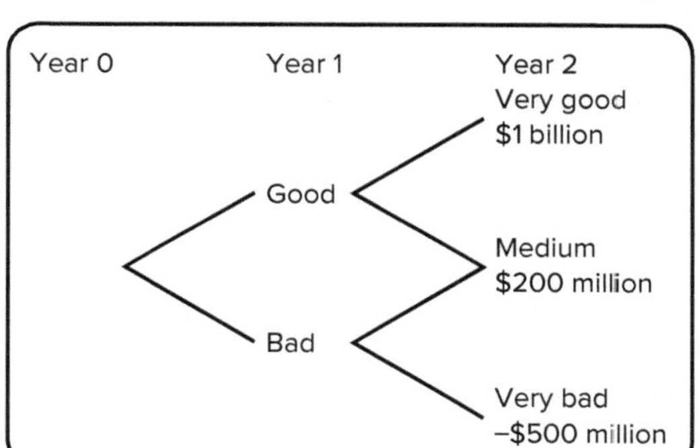

In year 1, the firm has the option of running the plant at less than full capacity. In this case, workers are laid off, production of memory chips is scaled down, and the subsequent cash flows are half of what they would be when the plant was running at full capacity.

An alternative use for the firm's funds is investment in the market portfolio. In the states that correspond to the branches of the tree above, \$1 invested in the market portfolio grows as follows.

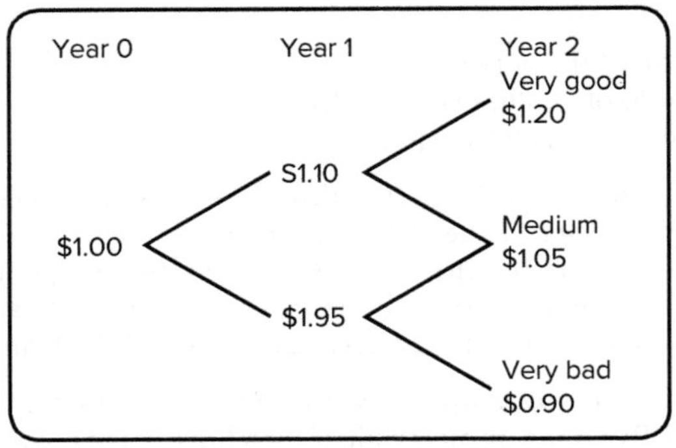

Assume that the risk-free rate is 5 per cent per year, compounded annually. Compute the project's PV (a) with the option to scale down and (b) without the option to scale down. Compute the difference between these two values, which is the value of the option.

12.3 Vacant land has been zoned for either one 10,000-square-foot five-unit apartment block or two single-family homes, each with 3,000 square feet. The cost of constructing the single-family homes is £100 per square foot and the cost of constructing the apartments is £120 per square foot. If the property market does well next year, the homes can be sold for £300 per square foot and the apartments for £230 per square foot. If the market performs poorly, the homes can be sold for £200 per square foot and the apartments for £140 per square foot. Today, comparable homes could be sold for £225 per square foot and comparable apartments for £180 per square foot. First-year rental rates (paid at the end of the year) on the comparable apartments and homes are 20 per cent and 10 per cent, respectively, of today's sales prices.

a What is the implied risk-free rate, assuming that short selling is allowed?

b What is the value of the vacant land, assuming that building construction will take place immediately or one year from now? Which is the best building alternative?

12.4 A silver mine has reserves of 25,000 troy ounces of silver. For simplicity, assume the following schedule for extraction, ore purification and sale of the silver ore:

Extraction and sale date	Troy ounces
Today	10,000
One year from now	10,000
Two years from now	5,000

Also assume the following:

- The mine, which will exhaust its supply of silver ore in two years, is assumed to have no salvage value.
- There is no option to shut down the mine prematurely.
- The current price of silver is £7.53 per troy ounce.
- Today's forward price for silver settled one year from now is £7.32 per troy ounce.
- Today's forward price for silver settled two years from now is £7.75 per troy ounce.
- The cost of extraction, ore purification and selling is £1 per troy ounce now and at any point over the next two years.
- The risk-free return is 6 per cent per year.

What is the value of the silver mine?

12.5 Widget production and sales take place over a one-year cycle. For simplicity, assume that all costs are paid and all revenues are received at the end of the one-year cycle. A factory with a life of three years (from today) has a capacity to produce 1 million widgets each year (which are to be sold at the end of each year of production). Widgets produced within the last year have just been sold. Each year, production costs can either rise or decline by 50 per cent from the previous year's cost. Over the coming year, widgets will be produced at a cost of €2 per widget. Unlike production costs, which vary from year to year, the revenue from selling widgets is stable. Assume that in the coming year and in all future years the widget selling price is €4 per widget. The performance of a portfolio of equities in the widget industry depends entirely on expected future production costs. When widget production costs increase by 50 per cent from date t to date $t + 1$, the return on the industry portfolio over the same interval of time is assumed to be – 30 per cent. If the production costs decline by 50 per cent, then the industry portfolio return is assumed to be 40 per cent over that time period.

Assume that the factory producing the widgets is to be closed down and sold for its salvage value whenever the cost of extraction per widget exceeds the selling price of a widget. This closure occurs at the beginning of the production year. Value the factory, assuming that its salvage value is zero and that the risk-free return is 4 per cent per year.

12.6 Assume that the futures closing prices on the New York Mercantile Exchange at the end of August 2023 specify that futures prices per barrel for light sweet crude oil delivered monthly from mid-October 2023 through to mid-December 2025 are, respectively, \$101.56, \$101.08, \$100.63, \$100.23, \$99.88, \$99.55, \$99.26, \$99.00, \$98.76, \$98.58, \$98.41, \$98.25, \$98.09, \$97.93, \$97.83, \$97.77, \$97.71, \$97.66, \$97.61, \$97.56, \$97.52, \$97.48, \$97.46, \$97.46, \$97.46, \$97.47 and \$97.48. Compute the 27 August 2023 value of an oil well that produces 1,000 barrels of light sweet crude oil per month for the months October 2023 through to December 2025, after which the well will be dry. Assume that there are no options to increase or decrease production, and that the cost of producing each barrel of oil and shipping it to market is \$10.00 per barrel. Also assume that the risk-free return is 4 per cent per year, compounded annually.

12.7 Compute the risk-neutral probabilities attached to the two states – high demand and low demand – in Example 12.2. Show that applying these probabilities to value the mine provides the same answer for valuing the outcomes in scenarios 1 and 2, as given in Example 12.2.

12.8 Although there is no empirical evidence to strongly support this hypothesis, some financial journalists have claimed that British managers are short-sighted and overly risk averse, preferring to take on relatively safe projects that pay off quickly instead of taking on longer-term projects with less certain pay-offs. Assume that the journalists are correct.

a Explain why managers who use a single discount rate for valuing projects are likely to have a systematic bias against longer-term projects if the systematic risk of the cash flows of many long-term investment projects declines over time.

b Discuss how the presence of strategic investment options affects the decisions to adopt long-term rather than short-term investments.

12.9 Example 12.9 illustrates how an increase in leverage can affect GlaxoSmithKline's price/earnings ratio. If the interest rate on the new debt was 12 per cent rather than 6 per cent, would the firm's price/earnings ratio increase or decrease?

12.10 It has been argued that firms may want to overinvest in production capacity to show a commitment to maintain their market share to competitors. In their model, excess plant capacity would not be a positive-NPV project if the cash flow calculations take the competitors' actions as given. However, since competitors are less likely to enter a market when the incumbent firm has excess capacity, the added capacity may be worthwhile even if it is never used. Comment on whether this strategic consideration should be taken into account when analysing an investment project.

12.11 Solve the unlevered price/earnings ratio, A/X, by rearranging equation (12.1).

References and Additional Reading

Aguilar, F. and Cho, D.-S. (1985) *Gold Star Co. Ltd,* Case 9-385-264, Harvard Business School.

Amram, M. and Kulatilaka, N. (1998) *Real Options: Managing Strategic Investment in an Uncertain World.* Cambridge, MA: Harvard Business School Press.

Brennan, M. and Schwartz, E. (1985) Evaluating natural resource investments *Journal of Business* 58(2): 135–157.

Brounen, D. de Jong, A., and Koedijk, K. (2004) Corporate finance in Europe: confronting theory with practice *Financial Management,* 33(4): 77–101.

Copeland, T. and Antikarov, V. (2001) *Real Options: A Practitioner's Guide.* Boston, MA: Texere Monitor Group.

Décamps, J.-P. Mariotti, T. and Villeneuve, S. (2005) Investment timing under incomplete information *Mathematics of Operations Research* 30(2): 472–500.

Dixit, A., and Pindyck, R. (1994) *Investment under Uncertainty* Princeton University Press, Princeton, NJ.

Ekern, S. (1985) An option pricing approach to evaluating petroleum projects *Energy Economics,* 10(2): 91–99.

Elder, J. and Serletis, A. (2010) Oil price uncertainty *Journal of Money, Credit and Banking,* 42(6): 1137–1159.

Fine, C.H. and Freund, R.M. (1990) Optimal investment in product-flexible manufacturing capacity *Management Science,* 36(4): 449–466.

Gorbenko, A.S. and Strebulaev, I.A. (2010) Temporary versus permanent shocks: explaining corporate financial policies *The Review of Financial Studies,* 23(7): 2591–2647.

Grenadier, S.R. and Malenko, A. (2010) A Bayesian approach to real options: the case of distinguishing between temporary and permanent shocks *The Journal of Finance,* 65(5): 1949–1986.

Hayes, R., and Abernathy, W. (1980) Managing our way to economic decline *Harvard Business Review,* 58(July–August): 67–77.

Ingersoll, J.E. and Ross, S.A. (1992) Waiting to invest: investment and uncertainty *Journal of Business,* 65(1): 1–29.

Jacoby, H.D. and Laughton, D.G. (1992) Project evaluation: a practical asset pricing method *Energy Journal,* 13(2): 19–47.

Klein, M. (2007) Irreversible investment under incomplete information Working Paper, INSEAD.

Klein, M. (2009) Comment on investment timing under incomplete information *Mathematics of Operations Research,* 35: 249–254.

Kogut, B. and Kulatilaka, N. (1993) Operating flexibility, global manufacturing, and the option value of a multinational network *Management Science,* 40(1): 123–139.

Kulatilaka, N. and Marcus, A.J. (1988) General formulation of corporate real options in *Research in Finance,* vol. 7, A Chen (ed.). Greenwich, CT: JAI Press, 183–199.

Lerner, E. and Rappaport, A. (1968) Limit DCF in capital budgeting *Harvard Business Review,* 46(Sept.–Oct.): 133–139.

Lohrenz, J. and Dickens, R.N. (1993) Option theory for evaluation of oil and gas assets: the upsides and downsides *Proceedings of the Society of Petroleum Engineers Hydrocarbon Economics and Evaluation Symposium,* Dallas, TX, 179–188.

Majd, S. and Pindyck, R.S. (1987) Time to build, option value, and investment decisions *Journal of Financial Economics,* 18(1): 7–27.

Margrabe, W. (1978) The value of an option to exchange one asset for another *The Journal of Finance,* 33(1): 177–186.

McDonald, R. and Siegel, D. (1985) Investment and the valuation of firms when there is an option to shut down *International Economic Review,* 26(2): 331–349.

Miao, J. and Wang, N. (2007) Experimentation under uninsurable idiosyncratic risk: an application to entrepreneurial survival Working paper, Boston University.

Milgrom, P. and Roberts, J. (1992) *Economics, Organization and Management.* Englewood Cliffs, NJ: Prentice Hall.

Myers, S.C. (1977) Determinants of corporate borrowing *Journal of Financial Economics,* 5(2): 147–175.

Paddock, J.L. Siegel, D.R., and Smith, J.L. (1988) Option valuation of claims on real assets: the case of offshore petroleum leases *Quarterly Journal of Economics,* 103(3): 479–508.

Pakes, A. (1986) Patents as options: some estimates of the value of holding European patent stocks *Econometrica,* 54(4): 755–784.

Porter, M.E. and Spence, A.M. (1982) The capacity expansion process in a growing oligopoly: the case of corn wet milling in John McCall (ed.) *The Economics of Information and Uncertainty* Chicago: University of Chicago Press, 259–316.

Quigg, L. (1993) Empirical testing of real option-pricing models *The Journal of Finance,* 48(2): 621–640.

Rappaport, A. (1992) Forging a common framework *Harvard Business Review,* 70(May–June): 84–91

Schwartz, E. and Moon, M. (2000) Rational pricing of Internet companies *Financial Analysts Journal,* 56(3): 62–75.

Schwartz, E. and Trigeorgis, L. (eds) (2000) *Real Options and Investment Under Uncertainty.* Cambridge, MA: MIT Press.

Shapiro, A. (1985) Corporate strategy and the capital budgeting decision *Midland Corporate Finance Journal,* 3(1): 22–36.

Stibolt, R.D. and Lehman. J. (1993) The value of a seismic option *Proceedings of the Society of Petroleum Engineers Hydrocarbon Economics and Evaluation Symposium,* Dallas, TX, 25–32.

Titman, S. (1985) Urban land prices under uncertainty *American Economic Review,* 75(3): 505–514.

Triantis, A.J. and Hodder, J.E. (1990) Valuing flexibility as a complex option *The Journal of Finance,* 45(2): 549–565.

Trigeorgis, L. (1996) *Real Options.* Cambridge, MA: MIT Press.

Chapter 13

Corporate Taxes and the Impact of Financing on Real Asset Valuation

Learning Objectives

After reading this chapter, you should be able to:

- Understand the effect of leverage on the cost of equity and the beta of the firm when there is a corporate tax deduction for interest payments.
- Apply the adjusted present value method (apv) to value real assets.
- Understand the weighted average cost of capital (wacc), and the effect of leverage on the wacc when there is a corporate tax deduction for interest payments.
- Understand how debt affects the pay-offs of projects to equity holders.

The Airbus–Boeing trade dispute, which was resolved in 2021, has been one of the major business stories of the last 20 years. Both firms alleged that their competitor received illegal subsidies in one form or another that allowed it to improve the commercial viability of its aeroplane manufacturing business. In 2019, the WTO declared that the EU illegally supported Airbus. This was followed in 2020 with the WTO finding that the US illegally supported Boeing. The support from the EU and the US was in the form of subsidies, tax breaks, indirect funding, preferred bidder status and loans with below-market interest rates. All governments offer inducements to encourage foreign direct investment in their country and these can take similar forms to those offered to Airbus and Boeing by their respective governments. It is the manager's responsibility to value these support packages and incorporate them into capital budgeting decisions.

Up to this point in the text, we have assumed that firms can create value only on the asset (left-hand) side of their balance sheets. In reality, however, firms also create value on the liability (right-hand) side, because the design of the financing of investment projects can create value for the firm. The best example of this is that debt interest payments are tax deductible, implying that debt financing is somewhat cheaper than equity financing if additional debt does not add substantial financial distress costs. Another example would be subsidized loans, such as those received by Airbus. This chapter takes as given the mix of debt and equity financing for a project, and asks how to value investments, taking into account the way in which they are financed.[1]

Two valuation methods, both extensions of the methods discussed in Chapter 11, can be used to account for the additional cash flows that arise from the project's debt financing. The first method, the **adjusted present value (APV) method,** introduced in Myers (1974), calculates present values that account for the debt interest tax shield and other loan subsidies by:

1 forecasting a project's unlevered cash flows
2 valuing the cash flows in step 1, assuming that the project is financed entirely with equity (any method of computing present values (pvs) discussed in the last three chapters can be used for this step)
3 adding to the value obtained in step 2 the value generated as a result of the tax shield and other subsidies from the project's debt financing.

The second method, known as the **weighted average cost of capital (WACC) method,** is an adaptation of the risk-adjusted discount rate method, designed to account for the cost of debt and equity financing from the firm's perspective. It generates PVs by:

1 estimating a project's expected unlevered cash flows
2 valuing the expected cash flows in step 1 by discounting them at a single risk-adjusted discount rate that varies with the degree of debt financing that can be attributed to the project.

The WACC approach thus combines steps 2 and 3 of the APV method into one step by adjusting the discount rate.

The result below summarizes these points formally.

Results

Result 13.1

Analysts use two popular methods to evaluate capital investment projects: the APV method and the WACC method. Both methods use as their starting point the unlevered cash flows generated by the project, assuming that the project is financed entirely by equity. The APV method calculates the net present value (NPV) of the all-equity-financed project and adds the value of the tax (and any other) benefits of debt. The WACC method accounts for any benefits of debt by adjusting the discount rate.

Although corporations use the WACC method more than the APV method, most academics believe that the APV method is the better approach for evaluating most capital investments, and that the APV approach will grow in popularity over time. The advantage of the APV method is that it calculates separately the value created by the project and the value created by the financing. For this reason, it is often referred to as **valuation by components.** It also fits in nicely with the alternative approaches discussed in Chapter 12, such as the real options approach and the ratio comparison approach. Moreover, the APV method is much easier to use when debt levels or tax rates change over time.

The WACC method may be conceptually easier to understand, because it discounts only one set of cash flows, whereas the APV method discounts separately the cash flows of the project and the cash flows of the tax savings or other debt subsidies. In addition, the WACC method is used more widely, so that analysts presenting a WACC-based valuation will be able to communicate their analysis to others more easily. It is important to understand both approaches – the APV method because it is a superior, more flexible approach, and the WACC method because it is more widely used and understood.

The business decisions of Airbus and Boeing, discussed in this chapter's opening vignette, are driven by huge enticements, including packages of subsidized loans, tax breaks and preferential bidding terms. A financial analyst needs to value the subsidies received by Airbus and Boeing, and determine whether the present value of the subsidies exceeds the net additional value of undertaking other, possibly more lucrative, investments.

[1] Part IV addresses the implications of this observation for the optimal financial structure of a firm.

Although we are unfamiliar with the methods used by the chief financial officers of Airbus and Boeing, the APV method provides the best way to account for these subsidies. The APV method accounts for all subsidies by discounting their cash flows at the discount rate that is appropriate for the risk of the cash flows, *irrespective of where they come from.* For example, the APV method would treat the cash flows from the tax breaks in a similar manner to the incremental cash flows that are generated by subsidized loans. By contrast, the WACC method draws a distinction between subsidies that are related to the project's financing and those that are not related to financing. Thus, with the WACC method, the loan subsidies offered to Airbus would affect the discount rate applied to the remaining cash flows, but would not affect the size of what is discounted.

To simplify the analysis, this chapter ignores personal taxes.[2] It is also important to emphasize that this chapter considers as given the amount of new debt financing the firm will add when taking the project, which we call the project's **debt capacity.**[3]

13.1 Corporate Taxes and the Evaluation of Equity-Financed Capital Expenditures

The starting point for both the APV and WACC approaches is the determination of the unlevered cash flows of the firm or project that is being evaluated, defined first in Chapter 9. Until we get to Chapter 15, we shall assume that the unlevered cash flows – that is, the after-tax cash flows generated directly by the real assets of the project or firm – are unaffected by the amount of debt financing the firm uses. Because of this assumption, we can compute the unlevered cash flow as the after-tax cash flows of the project or firm under the assumption that the project or firm is financed entirely with equity (hence the term 'unlevered'). Having estimated the future unlevered cash flows of the project or firm in this manner, we then need to estimate the appropriate cost of capital or discount rate for these cash flows.

The Cost of Capital

Distinguishing the Unlevered Cost of Capital from the WACC

For an all-equity-financed, or 'unlevered', firm, the appropriate risk-adjusted discount rate for a project's future cash flow when the cash flow has the same risk as the overall firm is the firm's cost of capital. This required rate of return on the firm's assets is the same as the expected rate of return on the unlevered firm's equity, as described in Chapter 11. In the presence of corporate tax deductions for interest payments, we need to be concerned with two costs of capital. The **unlevered cost of capital,** denoted $\bar{r}_{UA}$, is the expected return on the equity of the firm if the firm is financed entirely with equity. Because there is no debt tax shield for a firm that is financed entirely with equity, and because the two sides of the balance sheet 'balance', the unlevered cost of capital is also the required rate of return on the firm's unlevered assets. The *weighted average cost of capital* or *WACC* is a weighted average of the after-tax expected return paid by the firm on its debt and equity. In the absence of a debt tax shield, debt subsidy or other market frictions that favour one form of financing over another, the WACC is the expected return of the firm's assets. In this case, the WACC and the unlevered cost of capital are the same. However, we need to distinguish the two cost of capital concepts whenever there is a debt tax shield.

Note that the expected return paid by the firm to its equity holders is the same as the expected return received by the equity holders. This point – that the expected rate of return the firm pays for the use of the capital is the same as the expected rate of return the investor receives for providing the capital – is not true, in general. When a third party, such as the government taxing authority, favours one form of financing over another, the cost of the favoured form of financing will differ from the expected return to investors. For example, the tax deductibility of interest implies that the cost of debt financing to a corporation (as measured by the after-tax return paid by the corporation) may be less than the rate of return on a firm's debt received by the firm's debt holders. Because of this, the WACC differs from the unlevered cost of capital when there is a debt tax shield.

---

[2] Personal taxes are discussed in Chapters 14 and 15.

[3] The analysis of debt capacity is discussed in Parts IV and V.

Why it is Important to Calculate the Unlevered Cost of Capital for a Levered Firm

If, as is generally assumed, cash flow horizon does not affect the discount rate, then valuing an equity-financed project that is a scale replication of a comparison all-equity firm is straightforward. In this case, the project is a miniaturized version of the comparison firm's equity, implying that the project's cost of capital is the expected rate of return on the comparison firm's equity. Chapter 11 described a variety of techniques for estimating this expected rate of return. For example, measuring the comparison firm's market beta and using this beta in the CAPM risk–expected return formula is one way to generate the project's cost of capital.

However, the inclusion of debt financing complicates this analysis. To value an all-equity-financed project when the comparison firm has debt financing, it is necessary to calculate the required rate of return on the comparison firm's equity in the hypothetical case of a comparison firm that is all-equity financed. Moreover, when the project adds to the ability of the firm adopting the project to take on tax-advantaged debt, it is necessary to understand how shifting the comparison firm's debt affects the risk of the comparison firm's equity. Chapter 11 studied this issue in the absence of taxes, but a real-world application of the valuation techniques developed in this text requires us to account for the effect of taxes.

The Risk of the Components of the Firm's Balance Sheet with Tax-Deductible Debt Interest

A financial manager who employs either the WACC or the APV method needs to understand how debt financing and taxes affect the risks of various components of the firm's balance sheet. To develop this understanding, we return to the simplified balance sheet of Chapter 11. Exhibit 13.1, which is a development of Exhibit 11.3, Chapter 11's balance sheet exhibit, presents the two sides of the balance sheet of a firm for which there is a corporate tax deduction for debt interest payments, but no personal taxes. Exhibit 13.1 illustrates that, typically, the assets of the firm contain two components, one associated directly with the firm's operations and the other an indirect asset associated with a financing subsidy. The former component, the **unlevered assets (UA),** is defined as the present value of the unlevered cash flows; the other component, the **debt tax shield (TX),** is the present value of the financing subsidy (that is, the present value of the debt interest deduction for all corporate profits taxes: federal, state and city, where applicable). The more debt the firm has, the bigger this tax shield. Note that the two sides of the balance sheet must add up to the same number – that is, must balance – implying that the value of the UA can be viewed as the sum of the debt and equity, $D + E$, less the value of the debt tax shield.[4]

Exhibit 13.1 Balance Sheet for a Firm with Leverage When Debt Interest is Corporate Tax Deductible

Assets	Liabilities and equity
Debt tax shield (TX) $T_C D$	Debt D
Unlevered assets (UA) $D + E - T_C D$	Equity E

Viewing the assets of the firm with value A as a portfolio of unlevered assets with value UA and debt tax shields with value TX implies that the beta (or expected return) of the assets is the portfolio-weighted average of the betas (or expected returns) of the unlevered assets and debt tax shields: that is,

$$\beta_A = \left(\frac{\text{UA}}{D+E}\right)\beta_{\text{UA}} + \left(\frac{\text{TX}}{D+E}\right)\beta_{\text{TX}} \tag{13.1a}$$

and

$$\bar{r}_A = \left(\frac{\text{UA}}{D+E}\right)\bar{r}_{\text{UA}} + \left(\frac{\text{TX}}{D+E}\right)\bar{r}_{\text{TX}} \tag{13.1b}$$

where:

β_{UA} = beta risk of the unlevered assets
β_{TX} = beta risk of the debt tax shield
$\bar{r}_{\text{UA}}$ = expected return of the unlevered assets
$\bar{r}_{\text{TX}}$ = expected return of the debt tax shield.

[4] More generally, TX can be viewed as the present value of *any* debt financing subsidy.

Static Perpetual Risk-Free Debt

Let T_C denote the effective corporate tax rate. Exhibit 13.1 has the firm's debt tax shield expressed as

$$\text{TX} = T_C D \tag{13.2}$$

and thus

$$\text{UA} = D + E - T_C D \tag{13.3}$$

The values for TX and UA, both in Exhibit 13.1 and in equations (13.2) and (13.3), are developed in a model by Hamada (1972). If the firm issues default-free perpetual debt (that is, debt that never matures) with aggregate face amount of D and interest payments equal to the risk-free rate, each interest payment of Dr_f saves $T_C Dr_f$ in taxes in the year it is paid. The present value of the tax savings from the interest payments (see Chapter 9 for the formula for the present value of a perpetuity) is

$$T_C D = \frac{T_C D r_f}{r_f}$$

The same present value is also achieved when the risk-free rate changes over time and the firm rolls over one-period risk-free debt.

The Hamada model assumes that the tax shield is riskless, and thus each period's tax deduction arising from an interest payment should be discounted back to date 0 at the risk-free rate. This implies that the beta of the debt tax shield in the Hamada model is zero. Using this observation, and substituting equations (13.2) and (13.3) into equation (13.1a), yields

$$\beta_A = \left(\frac{D + E - T_C D}{D + E}\right)\beta_{\text{UA}} \tag{13.4}$$

In the typical case where the beta of the unlevered assets of the firm, β_{UA}, is positive, equation (13.4) states that the beta of the combination of the unlevered assets and the debt tax shield assets, β_A, must decline with an increase in leverage to reflect the addition of the risk-free tax savings. To see this, note that the portfolio weight on β_{UA}, $(D + E - T_C D)/(D + E)$, which equals $1 - [T_C D/(D + E)]$, declines as the leverage ratio $D/(D + E)$ increases, reflecting the fact that risk-free debt tax shields constitute a larger proportion of the firm's assets as leverage increases.

The key assumptions that lead to this result are as follows.

1 The debt is perpetual: in other words, it is either a perpetuity or consists of rolled-over short-term debt positions.

2 The debt is default-free and pays the risk-free rate.

3 The face value of the debt and the tax rate do not change over time.

The third assumption distinguishes the Hamada model from other models that will be discussed later in this chapter.

Equity Betas and Asset Betas

Equity betas are also affected by taxes. Chapter 11 indicated that (assuming risk-free debt) the equity beta is

$$\beta_E = \left(1 + \frac{D}{E}\right)\beta_A \tag{13.5}$$

Substituting the right-hand side of equation (13.4) for β_A in equation (13.5) gives

$$\beta_E = \left(1 + \frac{D}{E}\right)\left[\frac{D + E - T_C D}{D + E}\right]\beta_{\text{UA}}$$

With a little simplification, this equation, which is based on the Hamada model, becomes

$$\beta_E = \left[1 + (1 - T_C)\frac{D}{E}\right]\beta_{\text{UA}} \tag{13.6}$$

Assuming that β_{UA} does not change with leverage,[5] equation (13.6) states that, for a given debt increase, the beta of the firm's equity increases less the larger is the corporate tax rate, and increases the most when there are no taxes. Reversing this equation also allows us to identify β_{UA} from β_E, which is often a necessary step when using the discounted cash flow method for valuation when debt tax shields exist.

[5] Chapters 16–19 discuss situations where this may not be the case.

Identifying the Unlevered Cost of Capital

Chapter 11 examined how one could value a project using a risk-adjusted discount rate estimated from the equity returns of comparison firms.[6] These risk-adjusted discount rates required an adjustment for the effect of leverage. However, the unlevering procedure described in Chapter 11 assumed no taxes. With corporate tax deductions for interest, the procedure for identifying a project's unlevered cost of capital is very similar to the procedure used in Chapter 11. However, the formula for unlevering the betas must be modified whenever the betas of the debt tax shields differ from the betas of unlevered assets.

The formula for unlevering the equity betas of comparison firms in the presence of corporate taxes is embedded in equation (13.6) which, when reversed, reads

$$\beta_{UA} = \frac{\beta_E}{1 + (1 - T_C)D/E} \qquad (13.7)$$

Since β_{UA} is the same as the beta of the firm (as well as the beta of its equity) assuming that the firm is all-equity financed, substituting β_{UA} into a risk–expected return formula gives the desired unlevered cost of capital.

The BA Cityflyer Example Revisited

Valuations with the risk-adjusted discount rate method typically use comparisons with traded securities. When debt tax shields exist, it is the betas and required rates of return of the *unlevered assets* of comparison firms, and not their *assets*, that are perceived as being similar to those of the project being valued. For this reason, equation (13.7) and related equations that generate β_{UA} or $\bar{r}_{UA}$ from observable statistics such as β_E are central to the risk-adjusted discount rate method. To illustrate this point, Example 13.1 reworks Example 11.2 to account for corporate taxes.

Example 13.1

Using the Comparison Method to Obtain Beta and $\bar{r}$ with Taxes

Recall from Example 11.2 that International Airlines Group identified easyJet as the comparison firm for BA Cityflyer. For this comparison firm, the equity beta estimate (β_E), book value of debt (D), and market value of equity (E) have been identified as follows:

Comparison firm	β_E	D (in £ billions)	E (in £ billions)
easyJet	0.71	0.46	2.62

Estimate the unlevered cost of capital for BA Cityflyer. Assume that the risk-free rate is 6 per cent per year, the risk premium on the market portfolio is 8.4 per cent per year, the corporate tax rate is 28 per cent, the CAPM holds, the debt of easyJet is risk free and it is a good comparison for BA Cityflyer.

Answer: Using equation (13.7), find the unlevered asset beta of easyJet.

Comparison firm	β_{UA}
easyJet	$0.63 = \dfrac{0.71}{1 + 0.72(0.46/2.62)}$

Applying the CAPM risk–expected return equation using this estimate of BA Cityflyer's unlevered asset beta gives BA Cityflyer's unlevered cost of capital, 11.29 per cent per year, since

$$0.06 + 0.63(0.084) = 0.1129$$

[6] This comparison firm can be the firm adopting the project if the project's cash flow and the firm have similar unlevered asset betas.

Example 13.1, using the same comparison firm as Example 11.2, concludes that $\beta_{UA} = 0.63$, and that the unlevered cost of capital is 11.29 per cent. These are larger than the respective unlevered beta and cost of capital in Example 11.2, namely, 0.604 and 11.07 per cent. The reason is that the risk-free tax savings from debt mitigate the increase in equity betas that is generated by the leverage of easyJet. Thus the reduction in beta arising from the unleveraging equation is not as great here as it was in the absence of taxes.

The Hamada Formula is not Always Correct

If the firm uses debt in a flexible manner, the Hamada formulae for leveraging and unleveraging equity betas, represented in equations (13.6) and (13.7), are not correct. For example, if the firm issues debt as the value of the unlevered assets rises, and retires debt as the value of the unlevered assets falls, then equity betas will move more in response to leverage changes than equation (13.6) suggests they should. As this chapter later shows, in the extreme case where the issuance and retirement of debt is perfectly positively correlated with the value of the unlevered assets, the correct formula for leveraging and unleveraging equity betas is the same as in the no-tax case. However, if firms tend to retire debt when they are doing well, then the Hamada formula overstates the impact of leverage on equity betas. The tendency of firms to retire debt when they do well, which is especially common following leveraged recapitalizations, is consistent with Kaplan and Stein's (1990) observation that equity betas are less sensitive to changes in leverage than predicted by equation (13.6).

13.2 The Adjusted Present Value Method

Our recommended approach for valuing investment projects is the adjusted present value (APV) method. The left-hand side of Exhibit 13.1 can be used to describe the APV method in a setting with corporate tax deductions for interest payments. First, one values the lower left-hand side of the T-account, the unlevered assets. One way of doing this is to discount expected unlevered cash flows at $\bar{r}_{UA}$, the required rate of return for equity financing with risk equal to β_{UA}. Then one values the upper half of the left-hand side of the T-account, the debt tax shield, with what typically is a different discount rate. For example, in Exhibit 13.1, where such assets are assumed to be risk free, the risk-free rate would be the appropriate discount rate. Finally, the two PVs, those of the unlevered assets and the debt tax shield, are added together to generate the project's present value.

Three Sources of Value Creation for Shareholders

Exhibit 13.2 depicts three sources of value to the shareholders of a firm that adopts an investment project:

1. The PV of the project's unlevered cash flows
2. The PV of subsidies due to the financing of the project, such as the debt tax shield
3. Transfers to shareholders from existing debt holders due to the financing of the project.

The sum of these three sources of value must be compared with the cost of initiating the project to assess whether the project has a positive NPV.

Exhibit 13.2 Sources of Shareholder Value

Total increase in shareholder value		
Present value of unlevered cash flows (after-tax cash flows assuming all-equity financing)	Present value of financing subsidies (such as debt tax shields)	Transfers to or from existing debt holders (can be positive or negative)

Present Value of Unlevered Cash Flows

The main source of value from an investment project is the unlevered assets, portrayed in the left-hand box of Exhibit 13.2. To obtain this value, compute the present value of the unlevered cash flows from the project.

Present Value of Financing Subsidies

The middle box in Exhibit 13.2 illustrates that the project's financing can create value for the firm. Although the reduction in corporate taxes linked to debt financing may be the most important source of value created by financing (as measured relative to the all-equity financing case), it is not the only source. For example, many governments have attractive debt financing schemes to entice foreign companies to set up operations in their country, or in underprivileged areas within their dominion. There are also grant funding opportunities available from government-funded organizations. One example is the UK Foreign, Commonwealth and Development Office (CFDO), which provides grant funding and discounted debt schemes to eligible British firms across the world.

In addition to direct debt subsidies, small market inefficiencies (arising perhaps from regulations) can generate financing bargains. For example, consider a group of investors with a taste for highly leveraged positions in certain equities. If regulations preclude these investors from borrowing sufficient funds to buy such equities, it might be possible for a firm to create value by issuing overpriced warrants to these investors. Also, it is important to emphasize that these subsidies should not be counted if they can be earned without undertaking the project.

Transfers from Existing Debt Holders

The third source of value to shareholders, illustrated in the right-hand box of Exhibit 13.2, is transfers of wealth from existing debt holders to equity holders. For example, the selection of high-risk projects can benefit equity holders at the expense of debt holders, and the selection of safe projects can do the reverse (as the discussion towards the end of this chapter points out). In addition, new debt financing can sometimes reduce the value of existing debt financing, to the benefit of equity holders, an issue we shall examine in detail in Chapter 16. Although the APV method was not originally designed to account for such transfers, it can be used to take them into account.

Debt Capacity

The notion that the debt tax shield creates value suggests, holding all else equal, that firms should be financed with enough debt to eliminate their tax liabilities. However, there are limits to the amount of debt that firms can issue, and costs that offset the tax benefits of debt financing. Some of these limits and costs arise because the probability of bankruptcy increases if a firm uses more debt financing and bankruptcy can be costly. Other limits to debt financing may arise because of frictions in the capital markets. For the moment, we need to know only that each firm has a specific debt capacity, which is the amount of debt that management decides is in the firm's best interest. A project's debt capacity is the marginal amount by which a firm's debt capacity increases as a direct result of taking on the project.

Dynamic versus Static Debt Capacity

In general, we would expect debt capacity to be dynamic – that is, to change over time, depending on the profitability of the firm or the project. Thus a project may initially be financed entirely with internal funds but become debt-financed at a later date when the firm finds it more convenient or less costly to issue debt. In such instances, this dynamic sequence of debt financing must be taken into account in determining the corporate tax subsidy. As we shall see, this is much easier to do with the APV method than with the WACC method.

What Determines Debt Capacity?

Debt capacity is determined by management's view of the difference between the present value of the benefits of debt (for example, tax-advantaged interest deductions) and the present value of the disadvantages of debt (for example, bankruptcy costs). The debt capacity of a project may depend on both the characteristics of the project and the characteristics of the firm.[7]

The APV Method is Versatile and Usable with Many Valuation Techniques

The APV method can be used in conjunction with any valuation technique that generates a present value for the unlevered cash flows. Hence the APV method is appropriate to consider in conjunction with the risk-adjusted discount rate method, the certainty equivalent method, the real options approach or the ratio comparison approach.

The APV and the Risk-Adjusted Discount Rate Method in Complicated Tax Situations

The APV method is also ideally suited to complicated tax situations. Consider, for example, a project that initially has a great deal of non-debt tax deductions because of accelerated depreciation write-offs or tax credits for research and development expenses. For a firm that is marginally profitable, such a project might

---

[7] The issues important for determining a firm's optimal debt capacity are discussed in later chapters.

initially add little to the firm's ability to employ debt financing. Later, however, when cash flows materialize, there is a substantial increase in the amount of debt that the project can support. The changes in the financing of the project cause its cost of capital to change over time, which makes calculating the project's NPV with the WACC method somewhat tedious, and perhaps impossible. However, it is fairly straightforward to value such a project with the APV method, as Example 13.2 illustrates.

Example 13.2

Applying the APV Method to Value a Project

United Technologies (UT) is considering a project that has a cost of capital of 14 per cent if it is financed entirely with equity. The project is expected to generate unlevered cash flows in the next four years as follows.

Cash flows (in € millions) at end of			
Year 1	Year 2	Year 3	Year 4
€100	€100	€1,000	€1,000

Since the project generates large tax deductions in the first two years, UT will initially finance the project exclusively with equity. However, at the start of year 3 the firm will repurchase some of its equity and borrow €2 billion to finance the project for the last two years of its life. The borrowing (and discount) rate at this time will be 8 per cent per year, and the corporate tax rate will be 34 per cent. What is the present value of the project, given this plan for debt financing?

Answer: To value this project, first calculate the present value of the unlevered cash flow stream:

$$
\begin{aligned}
\text{PV(unlevered cash flows)} &= \frac{€100 \text{ million}}{1.14} + \frac{€100 \text{ million}}{1.14^2} + \frac{€1,000 \text{ million}}{1.14^3} + \frac{€1,000 \text{ million}}{1.14^4} \\
&= €87.72 \text{ million} + €76.95 \text{ million} + €674.97 \text{ million} + €592.08 \text{ million} \\
&= €1,431.72 \text{ million}
\end{aligned}
$$

To this amount, add the present value of the debt tax shields generated by the debt financing:

$$
\text{PV(debt tax shields)} = \frac{0.34(0.08 \times €2 \text{ billion})}{1.08^3} + \frac{0.34(0.08 \times €2 \text{ billion})}{1.08^4} = €83.17 \text{ million}
$$

Thus the present value of the levered project is

$$
\begin{aligned}
\text{PV(unlevered cash flow and debt tax shields)} &= €1,431.72 \text{ million} + €83.17 \text{ million} \\
&= €1,514.89 \text{ million}
\end{aligned}
$$

The Discount Rate for Risky Debt Tax Shields

Most applications of the APV assume that the debt tax savings can be discounted at the risk-free rate. However, the tax savings from debt will not be risk free, and should not be discounted at the risk-free rate if the firm's financing plans are flexible, or if there is a chance that the firm may not be able to generate cash flows large enough to take full advantage of the interest tax shield.[8]

[8] Country tax laws can be quite different from each other, especially in the degree to which earnings losses can be carried forwards or backwards into different tax years to offset profits and reduce taxes. The ability to transfer losses through time allows firms to utilize debt tax shields better, but rarely to the full extent, because: (1) there are limits to the numbers of years a loss can be carried forwards or backwards; (2) it is always possible that all the tax years to which the loss can be transferred have insufficient profits to offset the loss; and (3) the time value of money is not properly adjusted for in these transfers of losses. For example, deferring a loss generated by a debt interest payment to a future profitable year implies that interest payments realize only the present value of a future tax deduction, which is less than the tax impact of the interest payment if the company had been profitable in the tax year the interest payment was incurred.

Example 13.3

Computing NPVs When the Debt Tax Shield is Risky

The managers of the Engoleum plc are considering the possibility of buying new moulding equipment at a cost of £100 million. The equipment is expected to generate unlevered cash flows of £20 million per year for the next 10 years. Analysts estimate that the beta of these cash flows, β_{UA}, is close to 1, and that the expected return on the market is 13 per cent. Although the risk-free rate is 5 per cent, the firm's borrowing rate is 8 per cent. Assume that the project adds £80 million to the firm's debt capacity for the life of the project, and that the corporate tax rate is 28 per cent. To calculate the present value of the debt tax shield associated with the project, the analyst must account for the spread that exists between the risk-free rate and the firm's promised debt yield. The spread between the risk-free rate and the firm's borrowing rate reflects the debt holders' belief that the debt might not be paid in full, which implies that the debt tax shield may not be fully utilized. Assuming that the company will use, on average, only 75 per cent of the debt interest tax shields, and that the beta of the firm's debt is 0.25, calculate the project's NPV.

Answer: The present value of the firm's unlevered cash flows is

$$\frac{\pounds 20 \text{ million}}{1.13} + \frac{\pounds 20 \text{ million}}{1.13^2} + \cdots + \frac{\pounds 20 \text{ million}}{1.13^{10}} = \pounds 108.52 \text{ million}$$

The debt interest tax shield adds £1.792 million (= 0.08 × 0.28 × £80 million) to cash flows each year if it is fully utilized, and thus is expected to add 75 per cent of this amount or £1.344 million per year. We conjecture that the beta of these tax savings is somewhat less than the beta of the firm's unlevered cash flows, and probably resembles the beta of the firm's debt, 0.25. Thus the required rate of return on the tax shields is given by the CAPM formula:

$$0.05 + 0.25 \times (0.13 - 0.05) + 0.07$$

This implies a present value for the tax shields of

$$\frac{\pounds 1.344 \text{ million}}{1.07} + \frac{\pounds 1.344 \text{ million}}{1.07^2} + \cdots + \frac{\pounds 1.344 \text{ million}}{1.07^{10}} = \pounds 9.44 \text{ million}$$

Adding the two PVs and subtracting the £100 million cost leaves an NPV of

$$\text{NPV} = \pounds 108.52 \text{ million} + \pounds 9.44 \text{ million} - \pounds 100 \text{ million} = \pounds 17.96 \text{ million}$$

Example 13.3 illustrates how to use such a discount rate to implement the APV method.

As Example 13.3 illustrates, calculating the present value of debt tax shields may be complex when there is uncertainty about the extent to which the firm will utilize them. As the Manchester United case study suggests below, uncertainty about the evolution over time of the debt capacity of the project or the firm can increase this complexity even more.

Real World Insights

Malcolm Glazer, Manchester United and Debt Tax Shields

Malcolm Glazer, the American businessman and sports team owner, was ever present in the news in 2005 when he bought Manchester United, the top English football team, through his company Red Football Ltd. The buyout itself was not an issue; the main concern for Manchester United fans was that the financing for the purchase was backed by debt. The total cost of the takeover was £790 million, and this was made up of three main funding streams. Glazer himself used £272 million of his own capital. A syndicate of banks, led by J.P. Morgan Chase & Co, made a loan to Glazer to the amount of £265 million, which was immediately transferred to the balance sheet of Manchester United and secured against the club's assets. The third source of funding, preference shares, also came from the bank consortium and amounted to £275 million.

The difference between the £812 million (£272 + £265 + £275) raised by Glazer and the £790 million paid for Manchester United went in transaction costs and funding for the promised expansion of Old Trafford, the home of the club.

In cases like Manchester United, the tax savings from debt were uncertain. If Manchester United had performed poorly, it would not have paid down its debt, and its debt tax shield would have been larger than if it had performed well. Thus debt tax shields increase when a firm performs poorly, at least for many leveraged buy-out (LBO) financed firms. Because performance is tied partly to the overall health of the economy (football merchandising income rises and falls with disposable income), debt tax shields in this kind of situation tend to have negative betas, implying that the tax shields should be discounted at a rate less than the risk-free rate. However, if Manchester United had performed poorly, it would not have had sufficient earnings to utilize its debt tax shields, which would have reduced its tax savings. This loss of debt tax shields tends to increase the beta of the debt tax shields.

Without a careful analysis of Manchester United's future unlevered cash flows and financing plans, it is impossible to determine which of the two effects dominates: the tendency to pay down debt after performing well, or the inability to use debt tax shields fully when earnings are negative. When the debt level of the project is fixed but the utilization of the debt tax shield is uncertain, the underutilized tax shields, which generate positive betas, are the only consideration. In this case, it would be appropriate to discount the expected tax shields at a rate somewhere between the cost of capital used to discount the firm's unlevered cash flows and the risk-free rate. The expected return derived from the beta of the debt financing is a reasonable proxy for this discount rate.

The APV and the Certainty Equivalent Method

Combined with the APV method, the certainty equivalent method provides perhaps the simplest method for evaluating risky projects, at least in cases where the debt tax shields are certain. When the debt tax shields are certain, one simply adds the debt tax shields to the certainty equivalent cash flows of the project and discounts the sum at the risk-free rate. Example 13.4 illustrates this method.

When the tax shields are uncertain, the financial analyst also must calculate their certainty equivalents. The certainty equivalent tax savings in this case should be somewhat less than the tax savings achieved from debt interest when the firm is highly profitable, to account for the firm's inability to use all of the debt interest expense as a tax deduction in the most unfavourable states of the economy. However, we would not recommend using the risk-free scenario method, a novel procedure developed in Chapter 11, for computing the certainty equivalent of an uncertain tax shield. This method assumes that the distribution of outcomes is symmetrical, but the distribution of tax savings is rarely so, because, for a given amount of debt, tax savings pay-offs are capped at a maximum value.

Combining the APV and the Real Options Approaches

It should now be apparent that most major investment projects involve strategic future choices that are not easy to evaluate using traditional valuation methods. As the discussion above indicates, the financing choice is also a strategic variable in many cases, because firms have the option to increase or decrease their reliance on debt financing. Although this strategic tax-related option creates value for the firm, valuation of the interest tax shield is complex. Fortunately, the APV method works extremely well with the real options approach, as Example 13.5 illustrates.

Example 13.4

Using the APV Method with the Certainty Equivalent Method

Lufthansa, a German airline, is considering the purchase of a new online air ticket purchasing system. The system costs €150,000 and lasts five years, after which it will be made obsolete by more advanced systems that will be in place at that time. Analysts estimate the expected incremental unlevered cash flows to be

€50,000 per year for the next five years and zero thereafter. The certainty equivalent cash flows, which tend to decline with the horizon when the expected cash flows are constant, are given in the table below.

Cash flows (in €000s) at end of				
Year 1	Year 2	Year 3	Year 4	Year 5
€45	€40	€35	€30	€25

The purchasing system adds €100,000 to the firm's debt capacity in years 1 and 2, €50,000 in years 3 and 4 and zero in year 5. If Lufthansa has a borrowing rate of 6 per cent and a tax rate of 29.8 per cent, and will use its tax shields with certainty, what is the NPV of this investment if the risk-free rate is 5 per cent?

Answer: Add the certain tax savings associated with debt financing to the certainty equivalents of the unlevered cash flows. These savings will be €1,788 (= €100,000 × 0.06 × 0.298) in years 1 and 2 and €894 (= €50,000 × 0.06 × 0.298) in years 3 and 4. Hence the total certainty equivalent cash flows for the project's unlevered assets and debt tax shield are shown in the table below.

Cash flows (in €000s) at end of				
Year 1	Year 2	Year 3	Year 4	Year 5
€46.788	€41.788	€35.894	€30.894	€25.0

Discounting these certainty equivalent cash flows at the risk-free rate of 5 per cent generates the present value of the project:

$$PV = \frac{€46,788}{1.05} + \frac{€41,788}{1.05^2} + \frac{€35,894}{1.05^3} + \frac{€30,894}{1.05^4} + \frac{€25,000}{1.05^5} = €158,474$$

and

$$NPV = -€150,000 + €158,474 = €8,474$$

Example 13.5

Using the APV Method with the Real Options Approach

Reconsider Example 12.6, which featured Clacher Industries, a company with the option to expand its brewery's capacity during good times. The initial cost of the plant was £140 million, and the cost of the expansion was an additional £140 million. The risk-free rate was 5 per cent per period. Assume the following.

- For tax purposes, Clacher will expense at year 2 (when the project's income is realized) both the £140 million initial cost and, provided it expands capacity, the additional £140 million in expansion costs.
- Clacher is generating plenty of taxable earnings over the next few years, and will be able to take advantage of any tax losses if the project turns out to be unprofitable.
- Clacher is financed initially with £100 million in debt, but it can issue an additional £200 million in debt if the good state of the economy occurs and the firm expands capacity.
- The interest rate on the debt is 10 per cent and the marginal tax rate is 28 per cent.

What is the value of the project? How much of that value can be attributed to the firm's debt capacity?

Answer: The unlevered cash flows and the debt tax shields are given in Exhibit 13.3. Recall that the risk-neutral probabilities at the two branches emanating from the 'good' node were 0.53 and 0.47, respectively, and the two corresponding bad node probabilities were 0.35 and 0.65. From year 0, both risk-neutral probabilities were 0.5. Hence the project's unlevered asset value is computed as follows.

Exhibit 13.3 The Unlevered Cash Flows and Debt Tax Shields for Clacher Industries

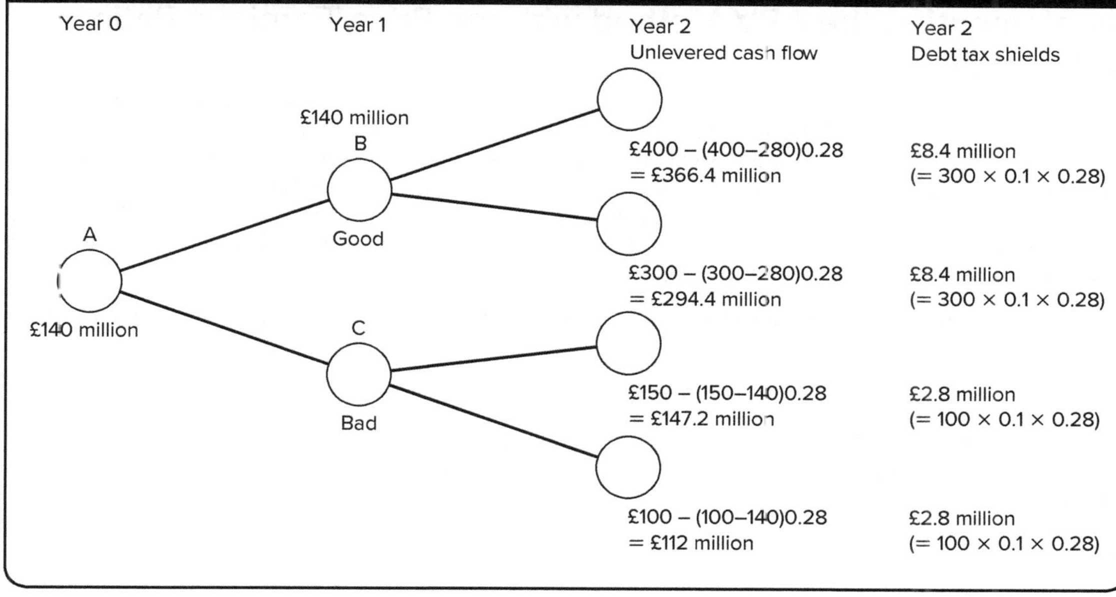

The unlevered value of the project at the 'good' node is

$$-140 + \frac{(0.53)366.4 + (0.47)294.4}{1.05} = £176.72 \text{ million}$$

The unlevered value of the project at the 'bad' node is

$$\frac{(0.35)147.2 + (0.65)111.2}{1.05} = £117.90 \text{ million}$$

The unlevered present value of the project at the initial node is therefore

$$\frac{(0.5)176.72 + (0.5)117.90}{1.05} - 140 = £0.30 \text{ million}$$

Hence the NPV of the project is approximately zero under the assumption that the project adds nothing to the firm's debt capacity. However, the present value of the project's debt tax shields is

$$\frac{£5.6 \text{ million}}{(1.05)(1.05)} = £5.08 \text{ million}$$

because, with equal risk-neutral probabilities emanating from the initial node, the £8.4 million debt tax shield outcomes are as likely as the £2.8 million debt tax shield outcomes. This makes the risk-neutral expected tax shield the average of £8.4 million and £2.8 million, or £5.6 million. The NPV of the project calculated with the APV method is £5.38 million.

The APV and the Ratio Comparison Approach

Chapter 12 noted that investment bankers and analysts often value firms and projects by examining various ratios for comparison firms or other investments. Popular ratios for the comparison include price to earnings, price to book value, price to cash flow and price to sales revenue.

The APV method is well suited for use along with any of the ratio comparison approaches. If the project being evaluated supports a higher debt level than that used by the comparison firm, then the value of the additional tax shields is an important component of the project's value. The APV method adds or subtracts the value associated with the difference between the tax benefits of the project and the comparison firm. Example 13.6 illustrates this point.

Example 13.6

Implementing the APV Method with the Price/Earnings Ratio Approach

Assume that Hewlett-Packard is thinking about developing a new business desktop workstation. It projects the cost of development will be $100 million, and the expected earnings in the first year of the project will be $15 million. Thereafter, the earnings will grow at about the same rate as those of Oracle, which currently produces a similar workstation. Assume that Oracle is almost exclusively financed with equity and has a current price to earnings ratio of 6.5. Is the project acceptable if there is no debt financing of the project? If not, assume that Hewlett-Packard's managers believe the project has substantial debt capacity. How large must the debt tax shield be to warrant project adoption?

Answer: If the project were financed almost exclusively with equity, as Oracle is, then the present value of the project's cash flows would be

$$\$15 \text{ million} \times 6.5 = \$97.5 \text{ million}$$

If this were the case, Hewlett-Packard should reject the project, since the NPV is −$2.5 million. If the present value of the tax benefits from debt financing exceeds $2.5 million, Hewlett-Packard should accept the project.

Summary of the Applicability of the APV Method

Result 13.2 summarizes this section.

Results

Result 13.2

Firms can easily use the APV method with a variety of valuation methods, including those that make use of risk-adjusted discount rates, certainty equivalents, ratio comparisons and real option approaches.

13.3 The Weighted Average Cost of Capital

In contrast to the APV method, the WACC method computes only unlevered cash flows, and accounts for the debt tax subsidy by adjusting the discount rate that is applied to the unlevered cash flows. The adjusted discount rate, which is applied to the expected unlevered cash flows, is the weighted average cost of capital of the project, to be explained shortly. Most large firms use some variant of the *firm's* WACC to evaluate their capital expenditures. There are practical reasons for doing so. In any given year, a large corporation may evaluate hundreds of different projects from various divisions, and it would be costly to come up with a different discount rate for each project. Using the firm's WACC, however, is inappropriate for valuing projects with different risks and different debt capacities from those of the firm as a whole. As the subsection below indicates, obtaining a WACC to discount the cash flows of an entire business is generally simpler than obtaining a WACC for an individual project.

Valuing a Business with the WACC Method When a Debt Tax Shield Exists

Consider the case of ExMart, currently an all-equity firm. Flavio Veronesi is interested in purchasing ExMart, financing 50 per cent of the purchase with debt and the remaining 50 per cent with equity. To value ExMart, it is necessary to estimate its expected future unlevered cash flows, and discount them at the appropriate WACC. This discount rate reflects Veronesi's various sources of capital. Mathematically this can be expressed as

$$\text{WACC} = w_E \bar{r}_E + w_D(1 - T_C)\bar{r}_D \quad (13.8)$$

where

WACC = weighted average cost of capital

$w_E = E/(D + E)$ = market value of equity over market value of all financing

$w_D = D/(D + E)$ = market value of debt over market value of all financing

T_C = marginal corporate tax rate if interest is fully tax deductible (or, more generally, the debt-financing subsidy in percentage terms).

The costs of the financing components are

$\bar{r}_E$ = the expected return on equity to investors

$\bar{r}_D$ = the expected return on debt to investors.

The two expected returns, $\bar{r}_E$ and $\bar{r}_D$, represent the expected rates of return that investors require as compensation for the riskiness of the firm's equity and debt securities, respectively. The term $\bar{r}_D(1 - T_C)$, the expected after-tax *cost of debt* to the firm, differs from $\bar{r}_D$ because every unit of interest paid to the debt holders represents a deduction on the corporate income tax statement that would not be available with equity financing.

Example 13.7 provides an illustrative calculation of the WACC.

Example 13.7

Computing a Weighted Average Cost of Capital

Mr Veronesi believes that the required rate of return on ExMart equity when it is 50 per cent levered will be 12 per cent per year. Since ExMart is a very stable business, it will be able to borrow at the risk-free rate of 6 per cent per year. If the marginal corporate tax rate is 28 per cent, what is the WACC for ExMart?

Answer: WACC = 0.5(0.12) + 0.5(1 – 0.28)(0.06) = 0.06 + 0.0216 = 0.0816 = 8.16%

WACC Components: The Cost of Equity Financing

One input for calculating the WACC is $\bar{r}_E$, the required expected rate of return on the equity (see Chapter 11), which also is known as the *cost of equity* financing. This rate of return can be determined in many ways. Typically, one uses expected return formulae from the Capital Asset Pricing Model, the arbitrage pricing theory or the dividend discount model to compute $\bar{r}_E$. With the CAPM and APT, equity betas estimated from historical return data are generally used in the formulae. Note that the expected rate of return of a firm's equity obtained with these methods is the relevant cost of equity financing, whether or not there are tax advantages to debt financing.

WACC Components: The Cost of Debt Financing

The methods used to estimate $\bar{r}_D$, the firm's pre-tax cost of debt, which is the other major input in the WACC formula, are generally not the same as those used to calculate the cost of equity capital.

Default-Free Debt

Practitioners typically assume that the firm's pre-tax cost of debt is the yield to maturity of the firm's debt. (The yield to maturity, being certain, lacks the bar over r_D in contrast to the expected value of an uncertain return, $\bar{r}_D$.) The yield to maturity provides a fairly accurate estimate of a firm's pre-tax cost of debt when the debt is highly rated, and not callable or convertible. (Chapter 2 notes that default rates on investment-grade debt are negligible.) Example 13.8 illustrates how to use the CAPM to calculate the WACC of a firm with debt of this type.

Example 13.8

Computing the After-Tax Cost of Debt and WACC When Default is Unlikely

The financing of United Technologies (UT) consists of 20 per cent debt and 80 per cent equity. With so little debt, the firm is able to borrow at the risk-free rate of 6 per cent per year. The interest expense is tax deductible, and the corporate tax rate is 28 per cent. Assuming that the CAPM holds, the expected return of the market portfolio is 14 per cent and the beta of the firm's equity is 1.2, what is the WACC of UT?

Answer: Using the CAPM, UT's cost of equity is

$$\bar{r}_E = 6\% + 1.2(14\% - 6\%) = 24.4\%$$

The firm's cost of debt in this case is

$$r_D(1 - T_C) = 6\%(1 - 0.28) = 4.32\%$$

Therefore

$$\text{WACC} = w_E r_E + w_D r_D(1 - T_C) = 0.8 \times 24.4\% + 0.2 \times 4.32\% = 20.38\%$$

Risky Debt

Using the *promised yield* times *one minus the corporate tax rate* as the cost of debt may be appropriate for relatively risk-free debt. Generally, however, this after-tax yield is not the cost of debt capital for highly levered firms. For firms with risky debt, the promised return on the debt (that is, the yield to maturity) is larger than the debt's expected return, because of the possibility of default.

Expected rather than promised debt returns are the WACC inputs because the WACC method, as a debt- and tax-based generalization of the risk-adjusted discount rate method, is designed to discount *expected* cash flows. As Chapter 11 noted, the risk-adjusted discount rate method requires that *expected* cash flows be discounted at *expected* rates of return.

The yield to maturity, a promised rather than an expected return for debt, overstates the pre-tax cost of any debt financing with non-negligible default risk. Partially offsetting this, however, is the observation that the tax shields of highly levered firms go unused when firms have insufficient taxable earnings. This makes the marginal corporate tax rate overstate the appropriate input for T_C (and one less than tax rate understates the appropriate input for $1 - T_C$). Despite the fact that it would be a remarkable coincidence if these two biases just offset one another, some practitioners use this insight to rationalize the promised yield on debt and the corporate tax rate as WACC inputs for firms with risky debt.

Let's assume, however, that you are not this foolish, and are using the expected return on debt, rather than its promised yield, as your WACC input. In this instance, the appropriate value to use for T_C in the WACC formula may be higher or lower than the corporate tax rate, depending on the relationship between the promised yield of the debt, the expected return of the debt, the frequency with which the firm is unprofitable and the likely timing of default.

In simple cases where the debt interest tax deduction is either fully used or fully unused, and where the probability of full use is the same at any point in time *in perpetuity*, the T_C input for the WACC is given by the equation:

$$T_C = \frac{\text{corporate tax rate} \times \text{probability of utilization} \times \text{promised yield to maturity}}{\bar{r}_D} \qquad (13.9)$$

The tax gain variable, T_C, is thus higher than the corporate tax rate if the product of the probability of utilization and the promised yield to maturity exceeds $\bar{r}_D$, and is lower otherwise. In these instances, one needs only to compute the numerator in the preceding formula, which equals $\bar{r}_D T_C$, and subtract it from $\bar{r}_D$ to obtain the after-tax cost of debt, $\bar{r}_D(1 - T_C)$.

For example, suppose the promised and expected yield on the debt is 14 per cent and the corporate tax rate is 28 per cent. With a probability of 0.75 the firm enjoys the full tax benefit of the 14 per cent debt interest payment, and with a probability of 0.25 it enjoys no tax benefit from debt interest payments. In this case, each unit of debt has an expected tax benefit of 2.94 per cent [= 0.75(0.28)14%]. Subtracting 2.94 per cent from $\bar{r}_D$ yields the after-tax cost of debt to the firm, $\bar{r}_D(1 - T_C)$. When $\bar{r}_D$ exceeds 11.06 per cent, T_C is less than the corporate tax rate of 28 per cent, and if $\bar{r}_D$ is less than 11.06 per cent, T_C is greater than the corporate tax rate.

In cases where the probability of utilizing the tax shield changes over time, T_C may differ from the value given in equation (13.9). To illustrate this point, consider high-yield debt. Firms that issue high-yield debt tend to have low default rates in the early years after the debt is issued. In these early years, the tax deduction for profitable firms issuing high-yield debt is based on the actual debt interest payments, which early on are likely to be larger than the promised interest payments of firms issuing safer debt. Default for firms issuing high-yield debt reduces or even reverses the tax advantages of debt (because of a possible taxable capital gain to the firm), but tends to occur many years after issuance, and typically at a time when the firm's tax bracket is zero. Thus, for firms issuing high-yield debt, events that are relatively tax disadvantageous tend to be deferred, and the tax benefit of paying high coupons on the high-yield debt tends to be immediate. The favourable timing of the debt tax benefit suggests that the appropriate T_C for the WACC formula is greater than the T_C given in equation (13.9).

Of course, one also can generate cases for which the opposite is true. The complexity of adjusting the WACC method to account for the timing of taxation punctuates our reasons for preferring the APV method to analyse the debt tax shield in complicated scenarios.

Computing the Expected Return of Risky Debt

Let us return now to the issue of computing $\bar{r}_D$, the expected return on debt, which the WACC method requires as the pre-tax cost of debt. Two popular methods are used to identify expected returns on risky debt, and they tend to give similar values for $\bar{r}_D$. The first method subtracts expected losses due to default from the promised yield (weighted by the no-default probability) to generate the pre-tax cost of debt financing. For example, the promised yield on a high-yield bond may be 14 per cent; however, if 4 per cent of these bonds default in a given year with the bondholders recovering about 60 per cent of their original investment (the 60 per cent is known as the **recovery rate**), and thus losing 40 per cent, the expected return on the bonds is

$$0.96(14\%) + 0.04(-40\%) = 11.84\%$$

The second method uses either the CAPM or APT to calculate the expected return of the debt. Estimated betas for junk debt range from about 0.3 to about 0.5.[9] Assuming a 6 per cent risk premium on the market, the CAPM would project a 1.8 per cent (= 0.3 × 6%) to 3 per cent (= 0.5 × 6%) spread between the expected returns of a junk bond and a default-free bond.

Example 13.9 provides an estimate of the cost of debt capital that accounts for default and the loss of tax benefits arising from negative net income and default.

Example 13.9

Calculating the Cost of Debt for Highly Levered Firms

Assume that 3i Group plc, a UK venture capital and private equity firm, has issued high-yield bonds to finance a leveraged buy-out. Assume that the outstanding bonds currently have a 14 per cent per year yield to maturity, a beta of 0.5 and interest payments that are tax deductible with a probability of 0.75. If the risk-free rate is 6 per cent per year, the expected return of the market portfolio is 10 per cent and the corporate tax rate is 28 per cent, what is the after-tax cost of debt to 3i Group?

Answer: Using the CAPM, the expected return on the 3i Group bonds is

$$6\% + 0.5(10\% - 6\%) = 8\%$$

(To check whether this estimated default premium of 6 per cent (14% – 8%) is sensible, see whether the product of the expected default rate and the recovery rate is 6 per cent.)

[9] In contrast, investment-grade debt typically has a beta of about 0.2.

To calculate the after-tax cost of debt, note that when 3i Group has sufficient income to take advantage of the tax shield, it enjoys tax savings of 3.92 per cent (= 14% × 0.28). With 0.75 as the probability of utilization, the expected tax savings per pound of debt equals 2.94 per cent (= 3.92% × 0.75), so 3i Group's after-tax cost of debt is 5.06 per cent (= 8% × 2.94%).

Determining the Costs of Debt and Equity When the Project is Adopted

For a firm, the relevant pre-tax cost of debt capital $\bar{r}_D$ or the cost of equity capital $\bar{r}_E$ is the expected rate of return of the respective sources of capital at the time the firm decides to adopt the project, rather than the actual cost that the firm incurred to obtain the funds. Example 13.10 illustrates this distinction.

Example 13.10

Cost of Capital is Based on Forgone Financial Market Investments

Suppose that the CFO of Celtron, in anticipation of future capital requirements, decided in December 2022 to float a AAA €100 million, 20-year bond at an annual interest rate of 9 per cent. By April 2023, interest rates on 20-year AAA bonds had increased to 10 per cent. What is Celtron's pre-tax cost of debt capital?

Answer: In April 2023, Celtron would not want to take a risk-free project yielding 9.5 per cent, even though it had previously borrowed at 9 per cent. It could do better by repurchasing its outstanding bonds. Given the increase in interest rates, the bonds would have fallen to a level that provides investors with a 10 per cent return, which is Celtron's pre-tax cost of debt capital.

The Effect of Leverage on a Firm's WACC when there are No Taxes

In determining the relevant discount rate for a firm's expected unlevered cash flows, a manager needs to know how leverage affects the firm's WACC. A naive manager might note that the cost of debt is typically less than the cost of equity, so that an increase in the proportion of debt financing would reduce its WACC. However, this logic ignores the fact that an increase in a firm's debt level also increases the risk of its equity and (usually also its) debt, and therefore raises the required return of each source of financing. In the absence of taxes, the increase in the risk of the two sources of capital is exactly offset by a shift in the WACC formula's weights towards the cheaper source of financing, leaving the WACC unchanged. Result 13.3 states this formally.

Results

Result 13.3

In the absence of taxes and other market frictions, the WACC of a firm is independent of how it is financed.

Result 13.3 implies what this chapter suggested earlier: in the absence of taxes, the WACC is the same as the unlevered cost of capital, as a consequence of both being identical to the expected return of assets (in the no-tax case). Thus Result 13.3, despite being at the heart of modern corporate finance, is an insight derived from portfolio theory. Because the assets of the firm are identical to a portfolio of equity and debt, their expected return is

$$\bar{r}_A = \left(\frac{E}{D+E}\right)\bar{r}_E + \left(\frac{D}{D+E}\right)\bar{r}_D \tag{13.10}$$

The WACC equation (13.8), with $T_C = 0$, is identical to the right-hand side of equation (13.10). Hence, as long as the firm's leverage ratio, D/E, does not affect $\bar{r}_A$, it will not affect the WACC.

The *Modigliani–Miller theorem* (examined in detail in Chapter 14) says that, in the absence of taxes and other frictions that might alter either $\bar{r}_A$ or expected future cash flows, the financing mix is irrelevant for valuation. It should not be surprising that early versions of this theorem were presented in the language of Result 13.3.

Example 13.11

The Effect of Debt on the WACC without Corporate Taxes

Ivo Technologies has no debt financing and has an equity beta of 1.2. Assume that the risk-free rate is 4 per cent, the CAPM holds, the expected rate of return of the market portfolio is 10 per cent and there are no corporate taxes. If the firm can repurchase one-third of its outstanding shares and finance the repurchase by issuing risk-free debt carrying a 4 per cent interest rate, what will be the effect of a debt-financed share repurchase on its WACC and cost of equity?

Answer: The cost of capital of Ivo Technologies before issuing risk-free debt is its cost of equity:

$$4\% + 1.2(10\% - 4\%) = 11.2\%$$

After the repurchase, Ivo Technologies has a 1 to 2 debt to equity ratio, but the same WACC = 11.2 per cent. The WACC's $\left(\frac{2}{3}, \frac{1}{3}\right)$ weighted average of the cost of equity and the 4 per cent cost of debt can only be 11.2 per cent if the cost of equity increased to 14.8 per cent. (Equation (13.5) could also have been used here.)

Exhibit 13.4 graphs the WACC, the cost of equity capital, and the cost of debt capital as a function of the leverage ratio, *D/E*, based on the figures given for Ivo Technologies in Example 13.11. The WACC is a weighted average of the cost of equity, the upwardly sloping line beginning at 11.2 per cent, and the cost of debt, the horizontal line, at 4 per cent. The WACC line is horizontal because, as *D/E* increases, the WACC weight, $D/(D + E)$, on the 4 per cent horizontal line, r_D, increases while the complementary weight on the upward-sloping cost of equity line decreases.

Exhibit 13.4 WACC, Cost of Equity and Cost of Debt vs. *D/E* with No Taxes

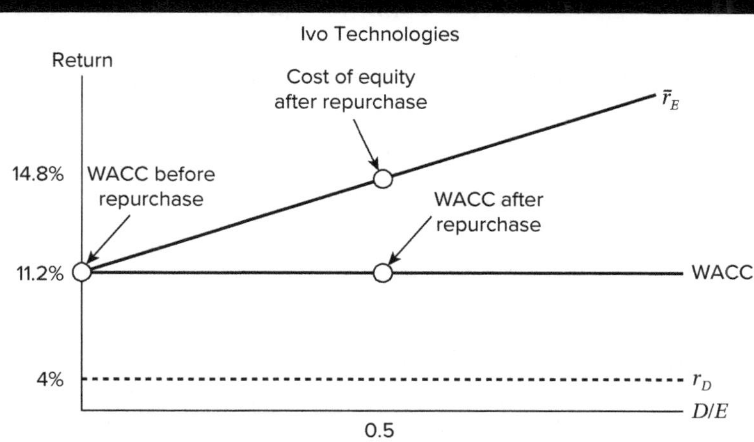

If the cost of equity did not increase as leverage increases, the WACC would decline as leverage increases. However, as *D/E* increases, which means a movement to the right on the graph, the increase in $\bar{r}_E$ exactly offsets the effect from placing greater weight on the lower cost of debt line, resulting in a horizontal line for the WACC. *When the WACC line is horizontal, it means that the WACC is unaffected by leverage.*

The Effect of Leverage on a Firm's WACC with a Debt Interest Corporate Tax Deduction

The picture of the WACC in Exhibit 13.4 changes when a tax gain is associated with leverage. With corporate taxes, the WACC declines with an increase in debt because, relative to all-equity financing, part of the cost of financing is borne by the government. To analyse this issue, note that equation (13.10) is valid even when there are taxes. Rearranging this equation to obtain the equity term in the WACC equation, $[E/(D+E)]\bar{r}_E$, we get:

$$\left(\frac{E}{D+E}\right)\bar{r}_E = \bar{r}_A - \left(\frac{D}{D+E}\right)\bar{r}_D$$

Substituting this into the WACC equation (13.8) yields:

$$\text{WACC} = \bar{r}_A - \left(\frac{D}{D+E}\right)T_C\bar{r}_D$$

Recall, now, that earlier in this chapter we learned that the expected return on assets is a portfolio-weighted average of the expected returns of the unlevered assets and the debt tax shield. As leverage increases, the portfolio weight on the debt tax shield increases. It would be extremely aberrational to have a debt tax shield with higher beta risk than the unlevered assets. Because of this, it is safe to conclude that the expected return on assets does not increase as leverage increases.

Equation (13.11)[10] thus implies the following result.

Results

Result 13.4

When debt interest is tax deductible, the WACC will decline as the firm's leverage ratio, D/E, increases.

The Adjusted Cost of Capital Formula

In the Hamada model, with static perpetual debt, both debt and its tax shield are risk-free, which implies that $\bar{r}_D = r_f$, $\beta_{\text{TX}} = 0$ and $\text{TX} = T_C D$. In this case, the portfolio-weighted average of the expected returns of the unlevered assets and the debt tax shield, given in equation (13.1b), simplifies to

$$\bar{r}_A = \left(1 - \frac{T_C D}{D+E}\right)\bar{r}_{\text{UA}} + \frac{T_C D}{D+E}\bar{r}_D$$

If we substitute this equation into equation (13.11), equation (13.11) reduces to Modigliani and Miller's (1963) **adjusted cost of capital formula,** which gives the firm's WACC as a function of its debt to value ratio that is.

$$\text{WACC} = \bar{r}_{\text{UA}}\left[1 - T_C\left(\frac{D}{D+E}\right)\right]$$

An application of this formula is provided in Example 13.12.

Example 13.12

The Effect of Leverage on the WACC with Corporate Taxes

Example 13.8 found that United Technologies (UT), with liabilities consisting of 20 per cent debt and 80 per cent equity, had a WACC of 20.38 per cent when the corporate tax rate was 28 per cent. In a financial restructuring designed to raise to 40 per cent the proportion of UT financed with debt, UT issues debt and buys back its equity with the proceeds. Compute the firm's new WACC given the assumptions of the Hamada model.

---

[10] Equation (13.11) applies to risky debt as long as one adjusts T_C to account for non-use of the tax shields, as discussed earlier in the chapter.

Answer: To calculate the firm's new cost of capital, first estimate UT's unlevered cost of capital. From the adjusted cost of capital formula, a WACC of 20.38 per cent with 20 per cent debt financing corresponds to an $\bar{r}_{UA}$ that satisfies

$$0.2038 = \bar{r}_{UA}[1 - (0.28)(0.20)]$$

Therefore $\bar{r}_{UA} = 0.2159$. Plugging this value into the adjusted cost of capital formula at a 40 per cent $D/(D + E)$ ratio leaves a WACC satisfying

$$\text{WACC} = 0.2159[1 - (0.28)(0.4)] = 0.1917$$

Therefore the new WACC is 19.17 per cent.

Graphing the WACC, Cost of Debt and Cost of Equity with Corporate Taxes

Exhibit 13.5 graphs United Technologies' WACC, cost of equity capital and cost of debt capital as a function of the leverage ratio, D/E, when the corporate tax rate is 28 per cent, based on the figures in Example 13.12. Note, as suggested earlier, that as D/E increases, more weight is placed on the bottom horizontal line, $\bar{r}_D(1 - T_C)$, in the computation of the WACC. However, in contrast to the no-tax case, the increase in $\bar{r}_E$ as D/E increases is insufficient to offset the additional weight on the lower debt cost $\bar{r}_D(1 - T_C)$. Hence, unlike the pattern shown in Exhibit 13.4, the WACC in Exhibit 13.5 declines from the starting point of 21.59 per cent = $\bar{r}_{UA}$ as D/E increases. The WACC continues to decline as D/E increases, up to the point where the firm eliminates all corporate taxes. Thereafter the WACC is flat.

Exhibit 13.5 WACC, Cost of Equity, and Cost of Debt vs. D/E with Corporate Taxes

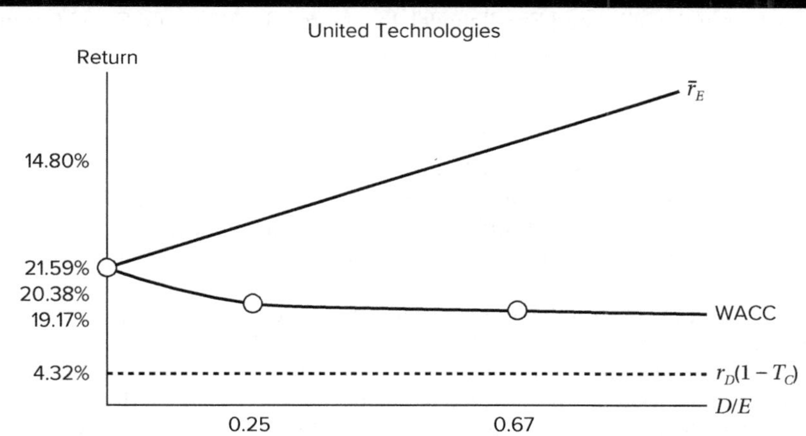

Dynamic Perpetual Risk-Free Debt

Up to this point we have assumed that the firm has a fixed amount of debt outstanding. Alternatively, if the firm wants to maintain a given ratio of debt to equity, it will need to issue new debt and repurchase equity as the firm's (or project's) value rises, and issue equity to retire debt as the value of the firm (or project) falls.

In the Miles and Ezzell (1980, 1985) model, D is perfectly correlated with the value of the unlevered assets of the firm, and thus the tax savings from debt issuance are perfectly correlated with the prior period's value of the unlevered assets. This implies that, at least approximately,

$$\beta_{TX} = \beta_{UA}$$

implying that the expected returns of assets, unlevered assets and the debt tax shield are about the same. As periods become arbitrarily short, this equality between the expected returns of the assets and the unlevered assets holds exactly, rather than approximately, in which case equation (13.11) reduces to

$$\text{WACC} = \bar{r}_{\text{UA}} - \left(\frac{D}{D+E}\right) T_C \bar{r}_D$$

Dynamic updating of debt to maintain a constant leverage ratio has implications for both the WACC and the APV methods, because it affects asset betas, and thus the formulae for leveraging and unleveraging equity betas. The Miles and Ezzell model, for example, which assumes risk-free debt, implies that only the tax shield associated with the first interest payment, which has a present value of $T_C D_{rf}/(1 + r_f)$ is certain, and the remainder of the tax shield has the same beta risk as the unlevered assets. Thus the beta of all the assets is a portfolio-weighted average of 0 and β_{UA}, with the portfolio weight on 0 being $T_C D r_f/(1 + r_f)$ and the portfolio weight on β_{UA} being $(1 - T_C) D r_f/(1 + r_f)$. This implies that the β of the assets can be expressed as

$$\beta_A = \left[1 - \left(\frac{T_C D}{D+E}\right)\left(\frac{r_f}{1+r_f}\right)\right]\beta_{\text{UA}}$$

When the updating interval is short, the term in brackets is very close to 1, and thus this formula says that, with dynamic updating of debt, the beta of the assets and the beta of the unlevered assets are approximately the same. As periods become arbitrarily short, the value of the first debt interest payment becomes infinitesimal, and the two betas become exactly the same. As suggested earlier, this implies that the no-tax versions of equations (13.6) and (13.7) can be used to adjust equity betas for leverage when taxes exist, provided that the firm dynamically maintains a constant ratio of D to E.

One-Period Projects

If a project lasts for only one period, there is only a single interest payment. In this case, the present value of the tax shield, $T_C D r_f/(1 + r_f)$, is the same as the present value of the riskless component of the tax shield in the Miles and Ezzell model. Thus the beta of the assets when there is debt that lasts only a single period has the same formula as that in the Miles and Ezzell model. In general, the Miles and Ezzell formulae for the WACC and the beta of equity apply to one-period projects. This is because the fraction of the assets that is risk-free is identical in the two cases.

Which Set of Formulae Should Be Used?

If the unlevered assets of the firm have a significant risk premium, the models of Hamada and Miles/Ezzell generate different adjusted cost of capital formulae, as well as different formulae for leverage adjustments of equity betas. Dynamic updating of debt and equity to maintain a constant leverage ratio, as in Miles and Ezzell, tends to generate larger WACC changes for a given leverage change than the Hamada model, which assumes that the amount of debt does not change.

Many firms, particularly those with low to moderate amounts of leverage, try to maintain a target debt to equity ratio, but update rather slowly, perhaps because the cost of frequently issuing and repurchasing debt and equity is prohibitive. For such firms, truth lies somewhere between the models of Hamada and Miles/Ezzell. The weighting of the two models depends on which behavioural assumption the firm conforms to better. Large firms, firms with existing shelf registrations and those with a history of repurchasing equity are likely to be more active in dynamically updating. Also, for projects with short lives, truth is probably closer to that given by the Miles and Ezzell formulae (with the caveat that comparison firms are perpetual).

However, we noted earlier that for many highly leveraged firms it is possible that the debt tax shield has a negative beta. For firms and projects with this property, it is important to use even a lower WACC and lower equity beta adjustments for leverage than those suggested by the Hamada model.

Finally, it is important to recognize that the field of corporate finance has yet to develop formulae for how leverage changes affect the WACC, equity betas, and the expected returns of assets, unlevered assets, debt tax shields and equity in many realistic situations. Foremost among these is the case of the growing firm with debt tied to its growth and reinvestment. This kind of problem, however, can often be analysed by a skilled practitioner using the APV method. For this reason, we are still puzzled by the overwhelming popularity of the WACC method as a tool for valuation.

Evaluating Individual Projects with the WACC Method

The appropriate discount rate for a particular project must reflect the risk and debt capacity of the project, rather than the risk and debt capacity of the firm as a whole. Although the tracking portfolio analysis in Chapter 11 emphasized this in great detail, some financial managers believe that they are losing money whenever a project returns less than the firm's WACC. Examples 13.13 and 13.14 provide an additional perspective on why this line of thinking is fallacious, by examining an extreme case where a risky firm is evaluating a project that has no risk.

Example 13.13

Adopting Projects that Have Rates of Return Below Your Cost of Capital

Although Aircharter.com is a real company, the following example is hypothetical.

Aircharter.com, with a 20 per cent CAPM-based WACC, leases private corporate jets to a variety of clients. For a Gulfstream jet, it charges $500,000 per year on its 10-year lease, payable at the end of each year. The cash flows associated with such leases are risk-free, and once the lease is signed, it is not possible to get out of it. Aircharter.com is in the process of closing a deal with the management of AMD (Advanced Micro Devices) on one of these jets. AMD, which has an equity beta of 1 and a cost of capital equal to 12 per cent, suddenly makes an intriguing offer. AMD offers to lease the jet for 10 years, but with an upfront payment of $3 million in lieu of the 10 separate annual payments of $500,000. What discount rate should Aircharter.com use to decide whether to accept the offer if the corporate tax rate is 50 per cent and the risk-free rate is 6 per cent?

Answer: This is clearly a project that can be evaluated with the DCF method. If Aircharter.com maintains the status quo, it is, in essence, forgoing a cash flow of $3 million at date 0 in exchange for $500,000 per year in annual pre-tax cash flows at the end of years 1–10. Note that if Aircharter.com uses its 20 per cent cost of capital to discount the after-tax cash flows of 10 annual payments, it computes the present value of the after-tax lease payments as $1.048 million, which would make it think that AMD was offering it a good deal at $3 million (even though half of it must be paid in taxes to the government). However, using the risk-free rate of 6 per cent generates a present value for the ten payments (after tax) equal to $1.84 million, which exceeds the $1.5 million it would otherwise receive after taxes from the initial $3 million payment. In this case, AMD would be obtaining a good deal, but Aircharter.com would be obtaining a bad deal if it accepts the upfront payment. It should be clear that the risk-free rate of 6 per cent, rather than Aircharter.com's 20 per cent cost of capital, is the appropriate discount rate here, and that it should reject the offer. If Aircharter.com were to take the upfront payment, pay taxes on it, and buy a 10-year annuity with the remaining cash, the payments on the annuity would be computed at the 6 per cent rate. It would generate only $203,801 a year, less than the $250,000 it would earn after taxes from the $500,000 per year lease.

Riskless Project, Riskless Financing

In Example 13.13, the project has riskless cash flows. The project's financing is also riskless, consisting of debt with tax-deductible interest payments. In this case, analysts can evaluate the project directly by comparing the project's proceeds with its financing costs. In contrast to the analysis of riskless projects in Chapter 10, however, the analyst now has to account for the debt tax shield.

Riskless Project, Risky Equity Financing

Example 13.14 is more difficult to analyse, because the risk-free project is financed by an equity offering. The expected cost of new equity financing is higher than the expected return of the project. However, as we shall see in this example, the risk-free rate is still the appropriate marginal, or incremental, cost of raising capital for the project.

The relevant measure for the cost of capital of a project is the firm's **marginal cost of capital,** or the amount by which the firm's total cost of financing will increase if it raises an additional amount of capital to finance the project. In Example 13.13 this amount was apparent, because even though the firm's original capital was composed entirely of equity, risk-free debt could be used to finance the lease payments. However, Example 13.14 shows that even if the company funds a new investment with equity, the same concept applies: *the marginal cost of capital for the project reflects the risk of the project and not the risk of the firm as a whole.*

Example 13.14 illustrates that the marginal cost of capital – that is, the project's WACC – provides the appropriate hurdle rate for determining whether a project should be selected. We also know from the value additivity concept, discussed in Chapter 10, that the value created by an investment project equals the NPV of the project, calculated here by discounting the project's cash flows at the *project's* WACC and subtracting from this value the initial expenditure on the project.

Example 13.14

The Marginal WACC

Assume that Gration Technologies (GT) is an all-equity firm that has a market value of £1 billion and a beta of 2. Given that the expected rate of return on the market of 11 per cent and the risk-free rate of 6 per cent, its cost of capital is 16 per cent. The firm is considering a project that costs £1 billion, but is risk free. Since GT generates no taxable income, it finances the project by issuing additional equity. How does the company determine whether to accept or reject the project? To simplify the example, assume that both existing projects and the new project have perpetual cash flows with expected values that do not change with the cash flow horizon.

Answer: Discount the project's cash flows at the 6 per cent return and see whether the discounted value exceeds £1 billion. This is equivalent to valuing the firm's cash flows, both with and without the project, using the appropriate WACC in each case.

To understand this point, note that at a 16 per cent return, shareholders expect to earn £160 million per year from GT's existing projects on the £1 billion invested in the firm. Assume, for the moment, that the new project is a zero-NPV project. If management decides to go forward with the project, the total risk of GT will decline as its risk falls from a beta of 2 to a beta of 1, which is the average of the betas of the firm's existing assets and the beta of the new project. With a beta of 1, GT's cost of capital would then be 11 per cent, the same as the market portfolio's expected return. With this return, shareholders expect to earn £220 million per year on the £2 billion invested in the firm. This is indeed what GT's shareholders will receive if the incremental cash flows from the new project are £60 million per year. Thus GT's shareholders are indifferent about whether to adopt the project if it provides exactly £60 million per year in incremental expected cash flow. Note that discounting the £60 million per year at 6 per cent results in a £1 billion present value and a zero NPV. Thus 6 per cent is the correct discount rate to use for the project's incremental cash flows.

If the project's expected cash flows exceed £60 million per year, implying that GT's investors prefer project adoption, then the 6 per cent discount rate will indicate that GT's project has a positive NPV. Analogously, if the expected cash flows are less than £60 million per year, the 6 per cent discount rate will indicate a negative-NPV project.

The Importance of Using a Marginal WACC

In Examples 13.13 and 13.14, shareholders gain from selecting risk-free projects whose rates of return exceed the risk-free rate, but which return less than the firm's WACC. In Example 13.13, the project could be financed by risk-free borrowing, so that accepting the project represented an arbitrage gain. The increase in cash flows from the project exceeded the cash outflow from the financing. In Example 13.14, an all-equity-financed firm used additional equity financing to fund the project. In this case, the project created value for the firm by lowering its risk and thus the required WACC. Managers who think that firms cannot create value by accepting safe projects that yield 8 per cent returns when the firm as a whole has a cost of capital of 12 per cent are forgetting to consider how the firm's risk, and hence its cost of capital, is affected by adopting the project.

Computing a Project WACC from Comparison Firms

The last two examples illustrate that the WACC of a firm is the relevant discount rate for the *incremental* cash flows of one of its projects only when the project has exactly the same risk profile as the entire firm. In other words, the project must (1) have the same beta and (2) contribute the same proportion as the entire firm to the firm's debt capacity. If these conditions do not hold, firms can apply the WACC method by finding another firm with the same risk profile as the project being valued and using the WACC of the comparison firm to discount the expected real asset cash flows of the project. Example 13.15 illustrates how this can be done.

Example 13.15

Adjusting Comparison Firm WACCs for Leverage

This extends Example 13.1, where the unlevered cost of capital for BA Cityflyer was found to be 11.29 per cent per year when the corporate tax rate is 28 per cent. Compute the WACC for BA Cityflyer, assuming that BA Cityflyer's debt capacity implies a target $D/E = 0.4$ and static perpetual risk-free debt, as in the Hamada model.

Answer: There are two ways to solve this problem. This example uses the Modigliani–Miller adjusted cost of capital formula. Exercise 13.8 focuses on applying the WACC formula, equation (13.8), directly after releveraging the equity. Note that:

$$\frac{D}{D+E} = \frac{D/E}{1+D/E}$$

Hence

$$\frac{D}{D+E} = \frac{0.4}{1+0.4} = 0.2857$$

Substituting this into the Modigliani–Miller adjusted cost of capital formula at the target $D/(D+E)$ of 0.2857 yields a WACC of:

$$0.1129[1 - 0.28(0.2857)] = 10.39\%$$

This chapter's computation of the risk- and tax-adjusted discount rate for BA Cityflyer, being fairly typical, serves as a blueprint for many of the project valuations you may do in a practitioner setting. Here is a detailed summary of how we ended up with the WACC above.

- We recognized that BA Cityflyer was not traded, and that analysis of International Airlines Group, which does have traded equity, would not generate an appropriate discount rate, because its risk is affected by the other operations of International Airlines Group, notably long-haul flights.
- We identified traded securities for firms that, as a consequence of their line of business, had unlevered assets that were comparable to those of BA Cityflyer. We recognized that, for an 'apples-with-apples comparison', only the unlevered assets of comparison firms provide discount rates that are relevant to BA Cityflyer. This is because taxes and leverage alter the risk of the comparison firms' assets and equity.
- To address these points, we estimated the equity beta of easyJet with comparable unlevered assets; then Example 13.1 unlevered the equity beta with a formula, equation (13.7).[11] We would have preferred to have more companies as comparisons, but unfortunately there were no other appropriate firms.

[11] Alternatively, we could have: (a) used a formula that substitutes the risk premiums of levered and unlevered assets for betas in equation (13.7) to unlever the equity expected return associated with easyJet's equity betas; or (b) used the Modigliani–Miller adjusted cost of capital formula to unlever easyJet's WACC, as computed from equation (13.8) with the risk-free rate as the input for the cost of debt. These two approaches give the same answer as the procedure described in the text, although it is important to recognize that both equation (13.1) and the adjusted cost-of-capital formula assume risk-free debt. Hence, if any portion of the estimation does not use the risk-free rate for the cost of debt, it will appear as though the methods are providing different answers, when they are simply being applied incorrectly.

- To obtain the BA Cityflyer WACC, Example 13.15 converted the unlevered cost of capital, obtained from easyJet, into a levered WACC with a formula – the Modigliani–Miller adjusted cost of capital formula – using the division's target debt ratio for $D/(D + E)$. The resulting WACC, used to discount the unlevered cash flows of BA Cityflyer, generates the value of the assets of BA Cityflyer (including the asset component generated by the debt tax shield).[12]

13.4 Discounting Cash Flows to Equity Holders

The valuation approaches discussed up to this point value the cash flows of real assets, which accrue to the debt holders as well as to the equity holders. Because these cash flows do not account for transfers between debt and equity holders, the decision rules that arise from their valuation select projects that maximize the total value of the firm's outstanding claims: that is, the value of its debt plus the value of its equity. In some instances, this decision rule conflicts with the objective of maximizing the value of the firm's equity.

Positive-NPV Projects Can Reduce Share Prices When Transfers to Debt Holders Occur

The last section examined two risk-free projects, and showed that discounting their cash flows at a risk-free rate was appropriate. This approach is correct as long as the objective is to maximize firm value. However, maximizing firm value is not always the same as maximizing the firm's share price. The adoption of a positive-NPV project can transfer wealth from equity holders to debt holders, which adversely affects share prices. Example 13.16 points out that, when these conflicts exist, discounting cash flows at a risk-free rate may not be consistent with maximizing the firm's share price.

Example 13.16

When Discounting Riskless Cash Flows at a Risk-Free Rate Is Wrong

Sheyma Al-Betty, a recent graduate, is evaluating a project for Glastron that is virtually riskless and returns 12 per cent per year. Given that the risk-free borrowing rate is currently at 10 per cent, she recommends to her supervisor that the company undertake the project, because its return exceeds the cost of capital for a riskless project. Her supervisor, Kevin Hudson, thinks that the company should reject the project. He notes that Glastron, which is highly levered, has a BBB debt rating and cannot borrow at the 10 per cent rate assumed in Al-Betty's analysis. How can Glastron make money, he asks, if it borrows at 13 per cent to fund an investment that yields only 12 per cent? Al-Betty finds it difficult to answer this question. On the one hand, she has been taught that risk-free projects should be discounted at the risk-free rate. However, when taking the project's financing mix into account, the project generates negative cash flows to the firm's equity holders. Who is right?

Answer: Hudson is correct if you believe that the firm's goal is to maximize its share price. However, to maximize the value of the firm, as would be the case if the firm was also beholden to bankers and other debt holders, Al-Betty's point is correct.

In the last example, the cash flows from the Glastron project that accrue to the equity holders are negative with certainty. This implies that the value to the equity holders must necessarily be negative. However, since these certain returns of the project exceed the risk-free return, the project must create value for someone. In this example, the project creates value for existing debt holders. The addition of a riskless project reduces the

[12] If we were using the APV method, we would use the unlevered cost of capital, estimated from easyJet, to obtain the value of the unlevered assets of BA Cityflyer by discounting its unlevered future cash flows. We would then add the present value of BA Cityflyer's debt tax shield to obtain the value of BA Cityflyer's assets.

overall risk of the firm, which, in turn, increases the amount that the debt holders expect to recover in the event of default.[13]

Example 13.16 illustrates that it is not enough to ask whether a project generates a value that exceeds its cost. Instead, the analyst has to ask whether the value created accrues to the firm's equity holders or its debt holders. In Example 13.14, where Gration Technologies had no debt, the marginal WACC generated a project selection rule that maximized share price. It is important to emphasize that the shareholders of Gration Technologies would have profited even if their project had been financed with new debt. However, when a firm is already partly financed with debt, as in Example 13.16, discounting expected unlevered cash flows with the marginal WACC measures a value that accrues to existing debt holders as well as equity holders.

Computing Cash Flows to Equity Holders

For the firm as a whole, **cash flow to equity holders** is the pre-tax unlevered cash flow, less payments to debt holders, less taxes. Computing a project's incremental cash flows to equity holders is similar to the computation of incremental real asset cash flows described in Chapter 10. First, compute the cash flows that equity holders receive (from all of the firm's existing projects) if the new project is not adopted; then subtract this from the cash flows to the *same* shareholders, assuming that the project is adopted. This difference is the project's incremental cash flow to equity holders.

Although it is easy to state how to compute incremental cash flows, it is not simple to implement this computation in practice. Analysts typically avoid the complexities by computing the cash flow to equity holders as the difference between the incremental unlevered cash flows of the project and the after-tax interest payments associated with the project's debt financing. This approach is correct with **non-recourse debt,** also called **project financing,** which is debt with claims only to the project's cash flows. However, it should be noted that, with non-recourse debt, the cash flows that accrue to the equity holders from a project can never be negative, and thus have option-like properties. When a firm finances a project with corporate debt (with claims on all corporate assets), one must take into account that the cash flows to equity holders can be negative. In addition, as we shall discuss in more detail in Chapter 16, the incremental cash flows to equity holders, in this case, will also be determined by the correlation between the new project returns and the returns on existing projects. When the correlation is very low, the new project decreases the overall risk of the firm (through the diversification effect), and thus a large portion of the value created by the project accrues to the firm's debt holders. When the project is very risky, and highly correlated with existing projects, the cash flows to equity holders will often be higher, and the implementation of the project might hurt the debt holders.

Valuing Cash Flow to Equity Holders

To calculate the NPV *of a project to equity holders,* the analyst must determine the appropriate discount rate for the cash flow to equity holders. Since these cash flows are often highly levered, they probably have betas that are substantially larger than those used to discount unlevered cash flows. In addition, given the option-like pay-offs of these equity holder claims, it is very cumbersome to use a CAPM- or APT-based risk-adjusted discount rate approach to value these pay-offs. In our view, the real options approach would be the preferred valuation approach whenever these options are likely to affect the valuation to a significant degree.

Example 13.17 illustrates how the real options approach can be used for this application.

Example 13.17

Valuing Cash Flow to Equity Holders with Real Options

In a two-date binomial model, assume that Glastron, from Example 13.16, has existing projects that generate a firm worth €110 million at date 1 if the up state occurs and €71.5 million if the down state occurs. Assuming no taxes, a risk-free rate of 10 per cent, and risk-neutral probabilities of $\frac{1}{2}$ attached to each of the two states, Glastron's date 0 value is €82.5 million (= [0.5(€110 million) + 0.5(€71.5 million)]/1.1). Glastron currently has debt maturing at date 1 with a face value of €77 million and a date 0 market value of €67.5

[13] Chapter 16 will discuss this in detail. As Chapter 16 points out, the opposite is also true: for equity holders, high-risk projects are more attractive than comparable NPV low-risk projects when the firm's debt is risky.

million (= [0.5(€77 million) + 0.5(€71.5 million)]/1.1) and equity with a date 0 market value of €15 million (= [0.5(€110 million – €77 million) + 0.5(€0)]/1.1).

Sheyma Al-Betty identifies a riskless project that will cost Glastron €28.23 million and produce a cash flow of €31.62 million at date 1, providing a 12 per cent return. The project will be financed entirely with debt that is equal in seniority to Glastron's existing debt. Compute the effect of the adoption of this project on the value of Glastron's existing debt, and on the value of its equity.

Answer: After adopting the project, Glastron's date 1 cash flows will be €141.62 million (= €110 million + €31.62 million) in the up state and €103.12 million (= €71.5 million + €31.62 million) in the down state. This generates a new firm value of €111.25 million (= [0.5(€141.62 million) + 0.5(€103.12 million)]/1.1). Since the new debt holders' payment of €28.23 million is a fair market price for their debt, the existing debt and equity holders now have claims worth €83.02 million. The additional €0.52 million in value for the existing debt and equity holders (€83.02 million versus €82.5 million) is simply the NPV of the project (= –€28.23 million + €31.62 million/1.1).

For €28.23 million to be the fair market price of the new debt, the promised payments on the new debt, F, which capture the fraction $F/(F + \$77 \text{ million})$ of the firm's assets in default, must satisfy

$$\left[0.5F - 0.5\left(\frac{F}{F + €77 \text{ million}}\right)(€103.12 \text{ million})\right]/1.1 = €28.23 \text{ million}$$

which implies that F = €31.90 million, and a debt yield (for both old and new debt) of 13 per cent (= [€31.90 million – €28.23 million]/€28.23 million).

However, with promised payments to debt holders at €108.90 million (= €77 million + €31.90 million) if the project is adopted, the value of the shares of the equity holders is only €14.87 million (= [0.5(€141.62 million – €108.90 million) + 0.5(€0)]/1.1).

Thus the adoption of the project destroys €0.13 million in equity value. This €0.13 million is transferred to the existing debt holders along with the €0.52 million positive NPV.

The loss in equity value, seen in Example 13.17, occurs whether the project is financed with debt or with equity, or with any mix of the two. The NPV to equity holders criterion rejects the project, whereas the NPV to the firm criterion says adopt the project, because it accounts for the fact that the project enhances the value of the firm's *existing* debt.

Real Options versus the Risk-Adjusted Discount Rate Method

Example 13.17 illustrates the importance of using the real options approach when wealth transfers, generated by debt default, are significant considerations in project evaluation. It is true that traditional approaches, such as the risk-adjusted discount rate method, can easily be applied to value cash flows to equity holders when the options arising because of default play a negligible role in valuation. However, as the next result points out, project PVs computed with the WACC method and those computed by discounting cash flows to equity holders are identical, in the absence of such default considerations.

Results

Result 13.5

In the absence of default, the present value of a project's future unlevered cash flows, discounted at the WACC, is identical to the present value of cash flows to equity holders discounted at the cost of equity. Hence, in the absence of default, the NPVs generated with both present value calculations select and reject the same projects. When debt default is a significant consideration, projects that increase firm value may not increase the values of the shares held by equity holders, and *vice versa*. However, in these cases, it is more appropriate to analyse the values of cash flows with the real options approach.

13.5 Summary and Conclusions

Previous chapters examined how risk affects a firm's cost of capital and its capital allocation decisions in the absence of taxes. This chapter showed how taxes and financing choices can also have an important effect. Two methods of accounting for the valuation effect of debt and taxes were introduced: the weighted average cost of capital (WACC) method and the adjusted present value (APV) method. Some analysts prefer the WACC method to the APV approach, since it is the more commonly used approach. However, the WACC method is appropriate only in limited circumstances. For example, if the debt capacity of a project changes over time, the WACC method is difficult to apply. In addition, in contrast to the APV framework, the WACC method cannot easily be adapted to evaluate investments with real options. For this reason, the APV method should be implemented for all major investments, although corporations may want to be aware of their WACC and use that method to evaluate smaller projects.

The discussion up to this point has indicated that the financing and the risk of an investment project determine its value. We discussed how different projects generate cash flows with different levels of risk, but provided little discussion about why different projects add more or less to a firm's debt capacity. At this point, one might conclude that firms should use as much debt as possible, since doing so creates value. However, there are costs associated with debt financing that offset these tax advantages, which is the subject of Part IV.

Key Concepts

Result 13.1: Analysts use two popular methods to evaluate capital investment projects: the APV method and the WACC method. Both methods use as their starting point the unlevered cash flows generated by the project, assuming that the project is financed entirely by equity. The APV method calculates the net present value (NPV) of the all-equity-financed project and adds the value of the tax (and any other) benefits of debt. The WACC method accounts for any benefits of debt by adjusting the discount rate.

Result 13.2: Firms can easily use the APV method with a variety of valuation methods, including those that make use of risk-adjusted discount rates, certainty equivalents, ratio comparisons and real options approaches.

Result 13.3: In the absence of taxes and other market frictions, the WACC of a firm is independent of how it is financed.

Result 13.4: When debt interest is tax deductible, the WACC will decline as the firm's leverage ratio, *D/E*, increases.

Result 13.5: In the absence of default, the present value of a project's future unlevered cash flows, discounted at the WACC, is identical to the present value of cash flows to equity holders discounted at the cost of equity. Hence, in the absence of default, the NPVs generated with both present value calculations select and reject the same projects. When debt default is a significant consideration, projects that increase firm value may not increase the values of the shares held by equity holders, and *vice versa*. However, in these cases, it is more appropriate to analyse the values of cash flows with the real options approach.

Key Terms

Exercises

Exercises 13.1–13.7 make use of the following data.

As an automobile manufacturer, Brown Motors, you are evaluating the acquisition of Kyrie Technologies to have access to ita electrical lithium-ion batteries. Recognizing that the appropriate WACC for discounting the projected cash flows for Kyrie Technologies is different from your own firm's WACC, you have assumed that Kyrie Technologies is of approximately the same risk as Echion Technologies and Envia Systems, which currently produce lithium-ion batteries similar to those of Kyrie Technologies. Specifically, assume the Hamada model of debt interest tax shields and the inputs in the table.

13.1 Analyse the Kyrie Technologies acquisition by first computing the betas of the comparison firms, Echion Technologies and Envia Systems, as if they were all equity financed. (*Hint:* use equation (13.7) to obtain β_{UA} from β_{E}.)

13.2 Compute β_{UA}, the beta of the unlevered assets of the Kyrie Technologies acquisition, by taking the average of the betas of the unlevered assets of Echion Technologies and Envia Systems.

Comparison firm	β_E	D/E
Brown Motors	1.20	0.40
Echion Technologies	0.90	0.90
Envia Systems	0.85	0.70
Target D/E for acquisition of Kyrie Technologies = 1		
Kyrie Technologies' expected unlevered cash flow next year = $300 million		
Growth rate of cash flows for Kyrie Technologies = 5% per year		
Marginal corporate tax rate = 34%		
Appropriate discount rate on debt: riskless rate = 8%		
Expected return of the tangency portfolio = 14%		

13.3 Compute the β_E for the Kyrie Technologies acquisition at the target debt level.

13.4 Compute the WACC for the Kyrie Technologies acquisition.

13.5 Compute the value of Kyrie Technologies with the WACC from exercise 13.4.

13.6 Compute the value of Kyrie Technologies if the WACC of Brown Motors at its existing leverage ratio is used instead of the WACC computed from the comparison firms (see exercise 13.4).

13.7 Apply the APV method. First, compute the value of the unlevered assets of the Kyrie Technologies acquisition. Next, compute the present value of the tax shield. Finally, add the two numbers.

13.8 Compute the WACC of BA Cityflyer in Example 13.15 by doing the following.

a Compute the β_E of BA Cityflyer using equation (13.6).

b Apply the CAPM's risk–expected return equation to obtain BA Cityflyer's $\bar{r}_E$, assuming a risk-free rate of 6 per cent and a market risk premium of 8.4 per cent.

c Estimate the WACC, using equation (13.8).

d Compare this WACC with the WACC in Example 13.15. If they are not the same, you have made a mistake.

13.9 GT Associates have plans to start a widget company financed with 60 per cent debt and 40 per cent equity. Other widget companies are financed with 25 per cent debt and 75 per cent equity, and have equity betas of 1.5. GT's borrowing costs will be 14 per cent, the risk-free rate is 6 per cent and the expected rate of return on the market is 10 per cent. The tax rate is 28 per cent. Compute the equity beta and WACC for GT Associates.

13.10 The HTT Company is considering a new product. The new product has a five-year life. Sales and net income after taxes for the new product are estimated in the following table.

Year	Net sales (in €000s)	Net income after taxes (in €000s)
1	1,000	40
2	2,000	75
3	4,000	155
4	6,000	310
5	2,000	75

The equipment to produce the new product costs €500,000. The €500,000 would be borrowed at a risk-free interest rate of 5 per cent. However, the $\bar{r}_E$ machine adds only €300,000 to the firm's debt capacity in years 1, 2 and 3, and only €200,000 in years 4 and 5.

Although net income includes the depreciation deduction, it does not include the interest deduction (that is, it assumes that the equipment is financed with equity). The equipment can be depreciated on a straight-line basis over a five-year life at €100,000 per year. The equipment is expected to be sold for €100,000 in five years.

Net working capital (NWC) required to support the new product is estimated to be equal to 10 per cent of net sales of the new product. The NWC will be needed at the start of the year. This means that if sales were €1 in year 1, the NWC needed to support this one euro of sales would be committed at the beginning of year 1. The company's discount rate for the unlevered cash flows associated with this new product is 18 per cent, and the tax rate is 37.3 per cent.

What is the NPV of this project?

13.11 Compute the NPV of the online air ticket purchasing scheme in Example 13.4, assuming that the debt capacity of the project is zero.

13.12 Use the risk-neutral valuation method to directly show that the risk-neutral discounted value of the existing debt of Glastron is €636,000 higher if the project in Example 13.17 is adopted.

13.13 Applied Micro Devices (AMD) currently spends £213,333 a year leasing office space in Leeds, UK. Because lease payments are tax deductible at a 28 per cent corporate tax rate, the firm spends about £153,600 per year [= £213,333(1 – 0.28)] on an after-tax basis to lease the building. The firm has no debt, and has an equity beta of 2. Assuming an expected market return of 12 per cent and a risk-free rate of 6 per cent, its CAPM-based cost of capital is 18 per cent. Suppose that AMD has the opportunity to buy its office space for £1 million. The office building is a relatively risk-free investment. The firm can finance 100 per cent of the purchase with tax-deductible mortgage payments. The mortgage rate is only slightly higher than the risk-free rate. How does AMD determine whether to buy the building or continue to lease it?

13.14 SL is currently an all-equity-firm with a beta of equity of 1. The risk-free rate is 6 per cent and the market risk premium is 11 per cent. Assume the CAPM is true, and that there are no taxes. What is the company's WACC? If management levers the company at a debt to equity ratio of 5 to 1, using perpetual riskless debt, what will the WACC become? How would your WACC answer change if the government raised the tax rate from zero to 28 per cent?

13.15 Akron plc consists of £50 million in perpetual riskless debt and £50 million in equity. The current market value of its assets is £100 million and the beta of its equity return is 1.2. Assume the risk-free rate is 6 per cent, the expected return of the market portfolio is 13 per cent per year and the CAPM is true. Compute the expected return of Akron's equity and its WACC assuming a 28 per cent corporate tax rate.

13.16 Akron, from the last example, is considering an exchange offer where half of Akron's outstanding debt (£25 million) is retired. The purchase of this debt would be financed by issuing £25 million in equity to the debt holders of Akron. Assuming debt policy that is consistent with the Hamada model, what will Akron's new WACC be after the exchange offer?

References and Additional Reading

Benninga, S. and Sarig, O. (1997) *Corporate Finance: A Valuation Approach.* New York: Mc Graw-Hill.

Copeland, T., Koller, T. and Murrin, J. (1994) *Valuation: Measuring and Managing the Value of Companies.* New York: John Wiley.

Cornell, B. (1993) *Corporate Valuation: Tools for Effective Appraisal and Decision Making.* Burr Ridge, IL: Business One Irwin.

Damodoran, A. (1996) *Investment Valuation.* New York: John Wiley.

Hamada, R. (1972) The effect of a firm's capital structure on the systematic risk of common stocks *The Journal of Finance,* 27(2): 435–452.

Kaplan, S. and Stein, J. (1990) How risky is the debt of highly leveraged transactions? *Journal of Financial Economics,* 27(1): 215–246.

Kuwahara, H. and Marsh, T. (1992) The pricing of Japanese equity warrants *Management Science,* 38(11): 1610–1641.

Miles, J. and Ezzell, J. (1980) The weighted average cost of capital, perfect capital markets, and project life: a clarification *Journal of Financial and Quantitative Analysis,* 15(3): 719–730.

Miles, J. and Ezzell, J. (1985) Reformulating tax shield valuation: a note *The Journal of Finance,* 40(5): 1485–1492.

Miller, M.H. (1977) Debt and taxes *The Journal of Finance,* 32(2): 261–275.

Modigliani, F. and Miller, M. (1958) The cost of capital, corporation finance and the theory of investment *American Economic Review,* 48(3): 261–297.

Modigliani, F. and Miller, M. (1963) Corporate income taxes and the cost of capital: a correction *American Economic Review,* 53(3): 433–443.

Myers, S.C. (1974) Interactions of corporate financing and investment decisions: implications for capital budgeting *The Journal of Finance,* 29(1): 1–25.

Practical Insights for Part III

Allocating Capital for Real Investment

- Firms create value by implementing real investment projects that generate returns that are tracked by combinations of financial instruments with values that exceed the project's costs. (Introduction to Chapter 10, 10.2, 11.1)
- The expected return of a project's tracking portfolio is the appropriate discount rate to use to value the project. (Sections 10.2, 11.1, and 11.2)
- When choosing between mutually exclusive investments, pick the project with the highest NPV, which is rarely the one with the highest IRR. (Section 10.2)
- EVA™ is a concept that allocates NPV to the dates at which future cash flows occur. (Section 10.3)
- Unlevered cash flows, which can be obtained from forecast earnings or cash flow statements, are critical for valuation. (Section 9.1 and Introduction to Chapter 13)
- The NPV rule is useful for evaluating many different corporate decisions in addition to capital investments. (Section 10.4)
- The internal rate of return (or IRR) is a useful concept for projects that can be described as consisting of an initial negative cash flow, the cost of the project, and a subsequent series of positive cash flows. In this case, projects with internal rates of return that exceed the expected rate of return on an appropriate tracking portfolio create value for the firm. (Section 10.5)
- Projects with future cash flows that alternate between positive and negative values may have more than one IRR. For these projects, the IRR generally is not a useful concept. (Section 10.5)
- IRRs are not very useful when choosing between mutually exclusive projects. (Section 10.5)
- Generally, a project with a negative present value (PV) cannot be valued with the risk-adjusted discount rate method. (Sections 11.1 and 11.2)
- Analysts often examine the return characteristics of publicly traded firms with real investments that are similar to the real investments being evaluated to determine the appropriate tracking portfolio and discount rate. (Sections 11.2 and 11.4)
- The APT and the CAPM require knowledge of betas and the expected returns on the relevant tracking portfolios. Analysts without good estimates for these inputs sometimes use a dividend discount model to compute discount rates. (Section 11.4)
- A common mistake made by many firms is to use the firm's own cost of capital rather than the expected return of the appropriate tracking portfolio to value the cash flows of a project. (Sections 11.5 and 13.3)
- Publicly traded firms consist of assets in place and growth opportunities. Their betas are weighted averages of the risks associated with these two sources of value. Growth opportunities generally have much higher betas than do assets in place. Therefore the beta of a growth firm is likely to be substantially higher than the betas of their assets in place. Analysts should consider this when using the comparison firm approach to estimate the cost of capital for a project. (Section 11.5)
- Financial analysts tend to use a single discount rate to evaluate an investment, to simplify their analysis. However, more accurate valuations can be achieved by accounting for the fact that cash flows at different horizons should be discounted at different rates. (Section 11.5)
- A single discount rate obtained from comparison firms is often far too large for the cash streams of firms with some negative low beta cash flows. (Section 11.5)
- If a project's cash flows tend to decline over time following unusually large cash flow increases, and vice versa, then expected cash flows generated far in the future should be discounted at lower rates than the cash flows occurring in the near future. (Section 11.5)
- It is often easier to evaluate projects by discounting certainty equivalent cash flows at risk-free rates than by discounting expected cash flows at risk-adjusted discount rates. (Section 11.6)
- For projects that generate cash flows over many years, the estimate of the cash flows in a risk-free scenario may be the best way to obtain their certainty equivalents and their PVs. (Section 11.7)

- Positive-NPV investment opportunities often arise as a result of past investments. When evaluating prospective investments, consider the fact that additional investment opportunities may be created as a result of this investment. Option pricing theory may be useful for evaluating these potential opportunities. (Section 12.1)
- Option pricing theory has proved to be especially useful for evaluating natural resource investments, such as copper mines and oil fields. (Section 12.2)
- Most real investments contain options. Firms have the option to delay the project's initiation date, expand the project, downsize it, or liquidate the project. Option pricing models are useful for evaluating all of these options. (Section 12.2)
- More flexible manufacturing processes provide the firm with more options. These options are more valuable in more uncertain environments. (Section 12.2)
- Information from the option markets and the forward and futures markets often provides useful information for evaluating investment projects. (Sections 11.8 and 12.2)
- When future cash flows are difficult to estimate, the financial ratios of comparable firms, such as price/earnings ratios and market/book ratios, may be the best way to value an investment project. Price/earnings ratios are often used to evaluate real estate investments, and to value IPOs. (Section 12.3)
- When interest payments are tax deductible, the value of an investment project depends in part on its debt capacity. (Section 13.1)
- Both the APV and the WACC methods account for the debt tax shield when they value a project. Although the WACC method is currently more popular, the APV method is the superior method. (Sections 13.2 and 13.3)
- The APV method can be combined with every approach for valuing real assets. The WACC method can be used only when discounting expected cash flows at risk-adjusted discount rates. (Sections 13.2 and 13.3)
- A common mistake is to use the yield on a risky bond as the cost of debt capital. The appropriate cost of debt, the expected return on the bond, is generally less than the yield on a risky bond. (Section 13.3)
- The APV and WACC methods assume that the manager wishes to maximize the combined value of the firm's outstanding debt and equity. For highly levered firms, projects that improve the value of the firm may negatively affect the value of the firm's stock. Analysts may therefore want to evaluate the project cash flows that accrue to the firm's equity holders when such a possibility exists. However, this is sometimes difficult to do with traditional discounting methods. (Section 13.4)

Financing the Firm

- National and local governments often subsidize debt financing, either indirectly through the tax system or directly by giving cheap financing to attract investments that they view favourably. Firms should take advantage of these financing bargains, and account for them when valuing investment projects. (Sections 13.1, 13.2, 13.3)
- When debt is tax deductible, the firm's WACC is reduced if the firm uses more debt financing. (Section 13.3)

PART 4

Capital Structure

Part contents

Firms raise investment funds in various ways. They can borrow from banks and other financial institutions, or they can issue various kinds of debt, preference shares, warrants and ordinary equity. A firm's mix of these different sources of capital is referred to as its *capital structure.*

Part 3 pointed out that the capital structure of a corporation can affect capital allocation decisions. In that part of the text, a firm's capital structure and the financing mix of its investment projects were taken as given. Part 4 examines how corporate capital structures are determined.

If a firm's capital structure includes a great deal of debt, then the firm is said to be highly leveraged. The term *leverage* is used because a high debt ratio allows a relatively small percentage change in a firm's earnings before interest, taxes, depreciation and amortization (EBITDA) to translate into a large percentage change in the firm's net income.

The extent to which a firm is leveraged is measured in several different ways (see Exhibit 14.1). The first two *debt-to-value ratios* measure the portion of a firm's capitalization financed with debt. The market value of debt is often difficult to calculate, since a large percentage of corporate debt takes the form of either privately placed bonds or bank loans, which do not generally trade. As a result, the amount of debt in a firm's capital structure – the numerators in these expressions – is generally measured at its book value. The denominator in these expressions represents book debt plus either the market value (row 1) or the book value (row 2) of the firm's equity.[1] Because the market value of equity measures the firm's discounted *future* cash flows, ratios with market values in the denominator are good measures of the firm's future ability to meet its interest payments. Because the book value of equity is determined by how well the firm has done in the past, the ratio of debt to the book value of equity is not as reliable an indicator of the firm's ability to meet its interest payments. However, it does indicate how a firm has historically financed its new investments.

An additional measure of leverage is the firm's *interest coverage ratio,* which is the ratio of EBITDA to interest payments. The interest coverage ratio is an indicator of a firm's *current* ability to meet its interest payments.

Exhibit IV.2 provides the financial ratios described in Exhibit IV.1 for a sample of well-known corporations from around the world, and from different industries. It shows that high-tech companies such as Microsoft and TomTom tend to rely little on debt financing; their zero debt-to-value ratios indicate no reliance whatsoever on debt. The most highly leveraged companies on this list are in industries that require significant levels of fixed assets. One of the requirements of most debt issues is the use of collateral, which is normally non-current assets, such as property, plant and equipment. These can be sold on if the firm goes into default, and so firms with high levels of fixed capital are more attractive to providers of debt. There are also differences within industries. Consider Avenir Telecom, Nokia and Telefonica, which, although all in telecommunications, have substantial differences in leverage. In contrast to Avenir Telecom and Telefonica, which have a large component of their revenues in fixed-line telecommunications, Nokia's main focus is mobile phone technology. This means that it is closer in operations to Microsoft, and thus has less reliance on debt.

Part 4 will explain more fully why firms such as Boeing and PetroChina choose to be highly levered, whereas firms such as Microsoft and Siemens use little debt financing. The starting point for this discussion is the *Modigliani–Miller theorem,* which states that, in the absence of taxes and other market frictions (for example, transaction costs and bankruptcy costs), the capital structure choice does not affect firm values. According to this theorem, managers should put all their effort into making the real investment decisions described in Part 3; how these real investments are actually financed is a matter of indifference.

Of course, the real world is very different from the frictionless markets model set forth by Modigliani and Miller; in reality, managers can create value for their corporations by making astute financing decisions. Chapters 14 and 15 discuss how taxes affect financing choices. The key insight is that when interest payments, but not dividends, are tax deductible, debt is a less expensive form of financing than equity. However, the corporate tax advantage of debt can be somewhat mitigated by the personal tax advantages of equity financing. In particular, the returns that accrue to equity holders are often treated as capital gains, which tend to be more lightly taxed than the interest income paid to the firm's debt holders. In addition, because equity holders must pay personal taxes on dividend income, they may be better off if the firm finances its investments with retained earnings instead of paying a dividend and financing new investment with borrowing.

Chapters 16 and 17 describe how contracting and transactions costs can affect the capital structure choice. In the world of Modigliani and Miller, a firm that goes bankrupt has its assets transferred costlessly from equity holders to debt holders. Their model also assumes that the real investment and operating decisions of the firm

[1] Debt-to-equity ratios, D/E, are also frequently observed, with E measured either as a market value or as a book value.

can be made independently of this potential transfer of ownership, which is likely to be the case in the absence of contracting and transaction costs. In reality, however, legal costs are associated with this transfer. Perhaps more importantly, managerial incentives in a firm close to bankruptcy will change in ways that can create substantial costs to the firm. Because of these potential costs, firms tend to limit their use of debt financing despite its tax advantages.

Exhibit IV.1 Common Leverage Measures

Leverage measure	What is measured
Debt/(Debt + Market value of equity)	Measures long-term ability to meet interest payments
Debt/Total book assets	Measures historical financing of investments
EBITDA/Interest	Measures ability to meet current interest payments

Exhibit IV.2 Financial Ratios of Selected Corporations, 2021

Company name	Country	Industry	Debt/Debt + Market equity	Debt/Total Book Assets	EBITDA/ Interest
Microsoft	USA	Software	2.72%	21.64%	36.29
McDonald's	USA	Restaurants	15.14%	69.17%	10.07
Boeing	USA	Aerospace/defence	32.89%	41.96%	−0.08
Kingfisher	UK	Home improvement	30.10%	20.60%	8.13
Marks & Spencer	UK	Retail	57.58%	46.86%	2.75
Celtic	UK	Football	7.35%	6.12%	4.18
PetroChina	China	Oil/gas	34.36%	18.89%	24.38
Siam Cement	Thailand	Cement	39.55%	35.39%	11.18
Glanbia	Ireland	Cheese/meat production	21.28%	26.31%	17.66
Siemens	Germany	Conglomerate	0.29%	1.24%	128.25
Avenir Telecom	France	Telecommunications	31.63%	13.89%	−14.85
Nokia	Finland	Telecommunications	15.27%	14.60%	15.67
Neways Electronics Int.	Netherlands	ICT/electronics	29.44%	25.15%	20.04
Telefónica	Spain	Telecommunications	71.95%	53.79%	12.21
Atlantia	Italy	Aerospace	71.29%	44.92%	3.14
Distell Group	South Africa	Distillers	11.32%	18.25%	10.48

Our goal in Part 4 is to provide guidelines for managers in situations where all parties have a shared objective to maximize the wealth of shareholders. However, the maximization of shareholder wealth may not be the objective of all managers, because of the transaction and contracting costs alluded to above. Part 5 examines how financial decisions are made when managers have differing objectives from those of shareholders, which will complete the analysis of capital structure.

Chapter 14

How Taxes Affect Financing Choices

Learning Objectives

After reading this chapter, you should be able to:

- Understand that in the absence of taxes, transaction costs, and other market frictions, capital structure can affect firm values *only* when the debt–equity choice affects cash flows (the Modigliani–Miller theorem).
- Explain how corporate taxes provide incentives for firms to use debt financing, as well as how they affect the decision to buy or lease capital assets.
- Understand why personal taxes provide an incentive for firms to use equity financing.
- Explain how non-debt tax shields, such as depreciation deductions and R&D expenses, affect the capital structure choice.
- Use the yields on municipal bonds to quantify the total tax gain associated with a leverage change.
- Understand how inflation affects the capital structure choice.

After the Second World War, the US airline industry expanded, and some airlines issued additional equity to fund their expansions. Jack Frye, then CEO of TWA, thought that TWA should also issue equity to fund its expansion. However, Howard Hughes, TWA's largest shareholder, disagreed. Partly because of this disagreement, Frye was replaced as CEO.

In a Civil Aeronautics Board hearing in 1959 concerning Howard Hughes' control of TWA, Hughes explained his position at the earlier time: 'My position was [that]... debt financing was very attractive. Interest rates were low, and interest could be paid out of basic earnings before taxation. Equity financing, to leave a satisfied [share]holder, probably should have returned something between 7 and 10 per cent, and that would have been required to be paid out of earnings after taxation.'[1]

[1] Robert W. Rummel, *Howard Hughes and TWA*. Washington, DC: Smithsonian Institution Press, 1991, p. 128.

Chapter 13 discussed how taxes and a firm's financial structure can interact to affect its real investment decisions. This chapter and the one that follows it take one step backwards and examine how taxes affect the proportions of debt and equity used to finance a firm. To understand how taxes affect a firm's financing choices, one must first understand what financing choices would be like without taxes. Hence the springboard for discussion of this topic is the no-tax capital structure irrelevance theorem offered by Franco Modigliani and Merton Miller.

The **Modigliani–Miller theorem,** which was largely responsible for both authors winning Nobel Prizes in Economics, states that if the capital structure decision has no effect on the total cash flows that a firm can distribute to its debt and equity holders, then the decision also will have no effect – in the absence of transaction costs – on the total value of the firm's debt and equity. This means that a manager who is contemplating whether it is cheaper to finance the firm primarily with junk bonds (that is, very high-yield, high-risk debt) or with equity and perhaps a small amount of high-quality debt should stop worrying: neither financing decision is superior to the other!

The premise of the Modigliani–Miller theorem, that capital structure has no effect on cash flows, is not true in the real world. Because the interest on debt is tax deductible, the after-tax cash flows of firms increase when they include more debt in their capital structures, leading firms to favour debt over equity financing. However, the capital structure choice becomes more complicated when one considers personal as well as corporate taxes. Personal taxes tend to favour the use of equity in a firm's capital structure, since a large portion of the returns on equity are taxed at the capital gains rate, which is generally more favourable than the ordinary tax rate that applies to interest income.

It is worthwhile at this point to look at the different tax rates and regimes in different countries, since this will have a major impact on what actually happens. Tax systems are notoriously complex, and managers should be familiar with their own country's situation when considering the effect of financing on firm value. Exhibit 14.1 presents, in a very brief fashion, the corporation, income and capital gains tax rates of countries around the world. It should be noted that, in most countries, all tax rates have levies and other adjustments, and the figures in Exhibit 14.1 should be taken as benchmarks and not exact figures. In addition, country tax systems and rates change from year to year. However, as a rule of thumb, capital gains tax rates will be less than income tax rates.

Exhibit 14.1 Tax Rates Around the World, 2022

Country	Corporation tax	Country	Corporation tax
Australia	30%	New Zealand	30%
Austria	25%	Norway	28%
Belgium	33.99%	Pakistan	35%
Brazil	15%	Poland	19%
Canada	16.50%	Portugal	25%
China	33%	Russia	20–24%
Denmark	25%	Saudi Arabia	20%
Finland	26%	South Africa	28%
France	33.30%	Spain	30%
Germany	30–33%	Sweden	26.30%
Greece	23%	Switzerland	10.7–24.5%
India	33.66–41.82%	Taiwan	25%
Ireland	12.50%	Tanzania	30%
Italy	27.50%	Thailand	30%
Japan	30%	Turkey	20%
Malaysia	25%	United Kingdom	28%
Netherlands	20%/23.5%/25.5%	United States	40%

14.1 The Modigliani–Miller Theorem

The first step in understanding the firm's capital structure choice is the Modigliani–Miller theorem. Much of the rest of this chapter – indeed, much of the rest of this text – will build results based on this theorem. First, we shall examine the issue of capital structure, ignoring the impact of taxes, and then reintroduce it later in the section.

Slicing the Cash Flows of the Firm

Exhibit 14.2 illustrates the total cash flows generated by a firm as a pie chart, and the various claims on those cash flows as slices of the pie. Pie 1 illustrates the case in which all of the cash flows accrue to debt holders and equity holders; the way that the pie is sliced does not affect the total cash flows available. This is the assumption of the Modigliani–Miller theorem.

Pies 2 and 3 illustrate how a firm's capital structure affects the total cash flows to its debt and equity holders. Pie 2 has a piece removed for tax payments to the government. Again, how the pie is sliced does not affect its total size. However, the owners of the firm are not interested in the total size of the pie. They are interested only in those cash flows that they can sell to security holders – that is, the debt and equity portions. Hence the owners would like to minimize the size of the slice going to the government, which they cannot sell. When more of the pie is allocated to the debt holders, less is allocated to the government, which implies that the combined debt and equity slices increase.

Exhibit 14.2 Slicing the Cash Flows of the Firm

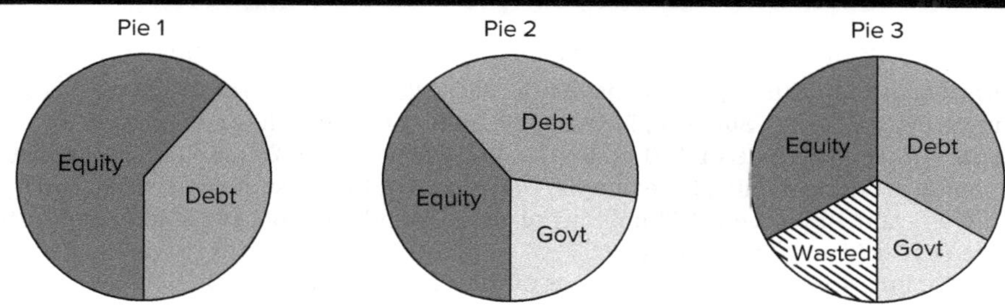

Slicing the pie doesn't affect the total amount available to debt holders and equity holders

The size of the debt slice can affect the size of the slice going to government

The size of the debt slice can affect the size of the wasted slice

Finally, pie 3 includes an additional piece that reflects the possibility that part of the pie is wasted. In other words, a slice of the pie is lost because of inefficiency, lost opportunities or avoidable costs. Chapters 16 to 19 describe various reasons why the size of this wasted slice may be determined partly by how a firm is financed.

This section, and the two sections that follow it, consider the case illustrated by pie 1, where the total *future* cash flows that the firm generates for its debt and equity holders are unaffected by the debt–equity mix. As we shall show, if the total cash flows are unaffected by the debt–equity mix, the total *value* of a firm's debt and equity also is unaffected by their mix.

The remainder of this chapter focuses on pie 2. Here, again, the total cash flows generated by the firm's assets are unaffected by the debt– equity mix. However, in contrast to pie 1, the corporate profits tax, studied in Section 14.4, and the personal income and capital gains taxes, studied in Section 14.5, claim a portion of these cash flows, and the size of these government claims depends on the debt–equity mix.

Proof of the Modigliani–Miller Theorem

Modigliani and Miller (1958) proved the irrelevance theorem by showing that if two firms are identical except for their capital structures, then an opportunity to earn arbitrage profits exists if the total values of the two firms are not the same. To illustrate this, assume that two firms exist for one year, produce identical pre-tax cash flows ($\widetilde{X}$) at the end of that year, and then liquidate. However, the firms are financed differently: company U is unleveraged (that is, it has no debt) and company L is leveraged (that is, it has some debt in its capital structure).

Exhibit 14.3 presents the cash flows of companies U and L, the split of the cash flows between debt and equity, and the present values of the cash flows. Since company U has no debt, its uncertain cash flow, J, is split only among the firm's equity holders. Thus the current value of company U, or V_U, is the same as the value of its equity. Company L, in contrast, has a debt obligation in one year of $(1 + r_D)D$ pounds. If, for simplicity, we assume that the debt is riskless, and r_D is equal to the riskless rate, company L's debt holders will receive $(1 + r_D)D$ at the end of the year, and its equity holders will receive the remaining $\tilde{X} - (1 + r_D)D$ pounds. The current value of company L, or V_L, is the current value of its outstanding debt D plus its equity E_L.

Exhibit 14.3 Liability Cash Flows and Their Market Values for Two Firms with Different Capital Structures

	Company U		Company L	
	Future cash flow	Current value	Future cash flow	Current value
Debt	0	0	$(1 + r_D)D$	D
Equity	$\tilde{X}$	V_U	$\tilde{X} - (1 + r_D)D$	E_L
Total	$\tilde{X}$	V_U	$\tilde{X}$	$V_L = D + E_L$

According to the Modigliani–Miller Theorem, V_U must equal $D + E_L$, which can be seen by applying the tracking approach to valuation introduced in Part 2. Since company U's equity is perfectly tracked in the future by company L's debt plus equity, the value of company U's equity must equal the combined value of company L's debt plus equity. If these values are unequal, an opportunity to earn arbitrage profits exists.

Earning Arbitrage Profits When the Modigliani–Miller Theorem Fails to Hold

To illustrate this arbitrage opportunity, first consider the case where the value of company U is greater than the value of company L ($V_U > D + E_L$). Suppose, for example, that company U has an equity value of £100 million, and company L has an equity value of £60 million and a debt value of £30 million. If this were the case, a shrewd investor could profit by buying, for example, 10 per cent of the outstanding shares (equity) of company L (costing £6 million) and 10 per cent (£3 million) of its outstanding debt, and selling short 10 per cent (or £10 million) of the shares (equity) of company U.

Assuming that the investor receives the proceeds of the short sale, this transaction yields a net cash inflow of £1 million [£10 million – (£6 million + £3 million)]. However, when cash flows are realized at year-end, the investor will receive

$$0.1\left[\tilde{X} - (1 + r_D)D\right] + 0.1(1 + r_D)D$$

in cash from company L's equity and bonds, and must pay out $0.1\tilde{X}$ to cover the short sale of company U's equity. Thus the net combined future cash flow from these transactions is

$$0.1\left[\tilde{X} - (1 + r_D)D\right] + 0.1(1 + r_D)D - 0.1\tilde{X}$$

which is zero, regardless of the future value that J realizes. In other words, the transaction generates cash for the investor at the beginning of the period, but requires nothing from the investor at the end of the period. Similar opportunities for arbitrage exist if company U has a lower value than company L, that is, $V_U < D + E_L$. Since we assume that such arbitrage opportunities cannot exist, the total value of the two firms must be the same, regardless of how they are financed.

Example 14.1 illustrates this type of arbitrage opportunity in a simple case where the firm's cash flows can take on one of only two possible values.

Example 14.1

An Arbitrage Opportunity if the Modigliani–Miller Theorem is False

Assume the following:

- Company U is financed totally with equity and is worth €100 million.

- An otherwise identical company L is financed with €40 million in equity plus €50 million (market value) in riskless debt that offers a 10 per cent interest rate: thus the bonds pay €55 million (= €5 million in interest plus €50 million in principal) at the end of the year.
- If the economy is weak, cash flows for each company will be €80 million; if the economy is strong, cash flows for each company will be €200 million.

Show how a shrewd investor, able to purchase or short up to €10 million in any security, would profit from this violation of the Modigliani–Miller theorem.

Answer: The shrewd investor can profit by purchasing 10 per cent of company L's equity (€4 million) and 10 per cent of its outstanding debt (€5 million) while selling short 10 per cent of the shares of company U. The investor would then realize an immediate cash inflow of €1 million (= 0.10 (€100 million – €40 million – €50 million)). However, as the following table shows, the investor would have no net obligations at the end of the year, so the initial €1 million inflow can be considered a risk-free profit.

	Cash flow to investor (in € millions) at		
	Beginning of year	End of year	
		Weak economy	Strong economy
Short sale of U equity	10	–8.0	–20.0
Purchase of L equity	–4	2.5	14.5
Purchase of L debt	–5	5.5	5.5
Net cash inflow	1	0.0	0.0

The year-end equity figures for company L are, by definition, the total cash flows for company L less the principal and interest payments to debt holders.

Stating the Modigliani–Miller Theorem Explicitly

Example 14.1 illustrated how a shrewd investor can realize arbitrage profits when the Modigliani–Miller theorem is violated. Result 14.1 states explicitly the assumptions and the implications of this theorem.

Results

Result 14.1

(*The Modigliani–Miller theorem.*) Assume: (1) a firm's total cash flows to its debt and equity holders are not affected by how it is financed; (2) there are no transaction costs; and (3) no arbitrage opportunities exist in the economy. Then the total market value of the firm, which is the same as the sum of the market values of the items on the right-hand side of the balance sheet (that is, its debt and equity), is not affected by how it is financed.

Assumptions of the Modigliani–Miller Theorem

Result 14.1 indicates that the capital structure irrelevance theorem holds only under some restrictive assumptions. The Modigliani–Miller theorem is important, though, because it provides a framework that allows managers to focus on those factors that are important determinants of the optimal capital structure choice. Examining the different assumptions of the theorem provides important insights into how the capital structure decision affects firm values.

The Key Assumption

The first assumption of the Modigliani–Miller theorem – that the sum of all future cash flows distributed to the firm's debt and equity investors is unaffected by capital structure – is really the key, and it will be the focus of much of the remainder of this text. In reality, capital structure can affect a firm's cash flows for a number of reasons. This chapter focuses on how capital structure can affect a firm's total cash flows by altering its tax liabilities.[2]

The Importance of Transaction Costs

The second assumption, no transaction costs, was used throughout Parts 2 and 3 of the text. However, transaction costs play a special role here that requires some additional discussion. In the absence of transaction costs, the cash flows to investors from any new security that a firm issues can be tracked by other securities that already exist in the market.[3] This means that the issuing firm is not really offering the investing public a pattern of returns that they could not otherwise obtain. However, transaction costs limit the availability of return patterns that can be obtained in the market, and sometimes provide firms with an opportunity to improve their value by issuing special securities that investors desire.

The Absence of Arbitrage

The final Modigliani–Miller assumption, no arbitrage, is made throughout the text. Analysing any sort of decision that affects a corporation's value requires some framework for determining valuation. The Modigliani–Miller theorem is consistent with all pricing models that satisfy the most basic assumption in asset pricing: equilibrium prices cannot provide opportunities for riskless arbitrage profits.

14.2 How an Individual Investor Can 'Undo' a Firm's Capital Structure Choice

The proof of the Modigliani–Miller Theorem described in the last section implicitly assumes that firms with identical cash flows but different capital structures exist. An alternative interpretation of the Modigliani–Miller Theorem is that, under its assumptions, a firm's shareholders are indifferent to a change in its capital structure. This is illustrated in Example 14.2.

Example 14.2

Undoing Elco's Capital Structure Change

Elco is considering a change in its capital structure. Before the change, the firm's equity sells for €100 per share, and the firm has 1,000 shares outstanding. The firm is also financed with riskless zero-coupon debt maturing in one year, and having a current market value of $D = €10{,}000$.

Suzy Iniko currently owns 100 shares of Elco equity (10 per cent of its equity). In the absence of a capital structure change, Suzy's pay-off next year will equal

$$0.1\left[\tilde{X} - (1 + r_D)€10{,}000\right] = 0.1\tilde{X} - (1 + r_D)€1{,}000$$

Here X is the firm's cash flows and r_D is the risk-free interest rate to be paid to debt holders, so that the firm's future debt service obligation is $(1 + r_D)€10{,}000$. The firm plans to repurchase 500 shares of its outstanding equity for €50,000, and will finance the equity repurchase by issuing €50,000 in risk-free debt.

First, show what Suzy's pay-off will be if she does nothing to counteract the firm's actions. Then show how she, as an individual investor, can alter her personal portfolio to undo the effect of any change in the firm's leverage, so that she attains the same cash flows she would have received without the leverage change.

---

[2] Chapters 16–19 examine how the financing mix affects a firm's investment choices and the efficiency of its operations.

[3] This tracking does not have to be perfect. For example, if the CAPM holds, the Modigliani–Miller theorem still applies. The key is that investors cannot be made better off by the issuance of a new security.

Answer: If Suzy chooses not to alter her portfolio, her share of Elco's cash flow next period will be

$$0.2\left[\widetilde{X} - (1 + r_D)€60{,}000\right]$$

because she would own 20 per cent (= 100/500) of the firm's outstanding shares if half of the shares were repurchased. She would then have a riskier investment than she held previously, which she may or may not prefer.

However, if Suzy sells 50 shares of her equity, using the proceeds to buy €5,000 in bonds, she will once again own 10 per cent (= 50/500) of the firm's shares, and will realize a return equal to

$$0.1\left[\widetilde{X} - (1 + r_D)€60{,}000\right] + (1 + r_D)€5{,}000 = 0.1\widetilde{X} - (1 + r_D)€1{,}000$$

Example 14.2 illustrates how shareholders can undo the effect of a change in a firm's capital structure by making offsetting changes to their own portfolio. The shareholder can achieve the same cash flow pattern and continue to control the same percentage of the firm's shares. Thus, without transaction costs, the shareholder is indifferent to changes in the firm's capital structure.

14.3 How Risky Debt Affects the Modigliani–Miller Theorem

Up to this point, we have assumed that all debt is riskless: that is, there is no bankruptcy. This section discusses situations in which firms can go bankrupt, which thus makes their debt risky.

The Modigliani–Miller Theorem with Costless Bankruptcy

The assumptions of the Modigliani–Miller theorem permit bankruptcy, but no bankruptcy costs. In other words, the theorem assumes that if a firm is unable to meet its debt obligations and goes bankrupt, then the ownership and control of the firm's assets move costlessly from the equity holders to the debt holders.[4]

To understand what we mean by costless bankruptcy, return to Example 14.2, in which the pay-off to Suzy Iniko, who owns 10 per cent of Elco's shares, is 10 per cent of the cash flow less Elco's debt obligations:

$$0.1\left[\widetilde{X} - (1 + r_{DS})€10{,}000\right]$$

where r_{DS} is the promised interest rate to be paid to the original or senior debt holders.

If the debt in Example 14.2 had been risky, then the cash flow described in the above expression would be the pay-off to Suzy *only if this quantity is positive*. Because shareholders enjoy limited liability, they receive nothing if the debt obligation exceeds the cash flows for the period; in this case, debt holders receive the entire cash flow $\widetilde{X}$ of the firm, assuming no bankruptcy costs. The debt is risky because, in these instances, the entire cash flow can still be considerably less than the promised debt payment.

Leverage Increases and Wealth Transfers

When bankruptcy can occur, we must be more explicit about what we mean when we say that the capital structure decision is irrelevant. The possibility of bankruptcy implies that capital structure changes can result in transfers of wealth between the firm's equity holders and its debt holders. Hence a change in a firm's debt–equity mix can affect its share price even if the change does not affect the sum of the firm's debt and equity values.

The potential for wealth transfers from existing debt holders to the firm's equity holders depends on whether the new debt must be subordinated. In bankruptcy proceedings, *subordinated* or *junior debt* (see Chapter 2) has a claim to the assets of the firm only after the debt with higher priority has been fully paid off.

[4] Of course, this assumption is unrealistic. Lawyers are very much involved in the bankruptcy process, and they are expensive. The various costs of bankruptcy are discussed in detail in Chapter 16.

As we shall show, if a new debt issue is not subordinated to the old debt, the new debt can generate a transfer of wealth from the existing debt holders to the equity holders. However, if the debt is subordinated, shareholders will continue to be indifferent to a capital structure change that does not affect the assets of the firm.

The Effect of Leverage Changes When New Debt is Subordinated to Existing Debt

To understand the effect of a capital structure change when debt is risky, consider again the possibility that Elco issues €50,000 in new debt and uses the proceeds to repurchase 500 shares. Assume initially that the new debt is junior to existing debt (€10,000 face amount) in the event of bankruptcy, and, as a consequence, its coupon rate, r_{DJ}, is greater than r_{DS}, the promised rate on senior debt.

Exhibit 14.4 illustrates that Miss Iniko can, in effect, undo the effects of additional risky debt in Elco's capital structure by buying €5,000 of the new debt and selling 50 shares. This leaves her with 50 shares (100 shares less the 50 sold) and €5,000 of the new junior debt.

Note that, in each scenario of Exhibit 14.4, the cash flow is identical to what Miss Iniko would have received as a shareholder, given the firm's original capital structure. In scenarios A and B – where the firm has sufficient cash to pay off its obligations to senior debt holders – the investor receives the same cash flow he or she would have received as an equity holder, given the firm's original capital structure – that is, $0.1[\tilde{X} - (1 + r_{DS})€10{,}000]$. In scenario C, the state in which the firm generates insufficient cash flows to pay off its senior debt, an equity holder would have received nothing, even in the absence of a new debt issue. Now the investor still receives nothing as an investor holding both equity and junior debt.

Exhibit 14.4 Undoing the Effects of Additional Risky Debt When New Debt is Junior to Old Debt

	Cash flows		
	Scenario A	**Scenario B**	**Scenario C**
Investment	Cash flow exceeds all debt obligations: $\tilde{X} > (1 + r_{DS})€10{,}000 + (1 + r_{DS})€50{,}000$	Cash flow exceeds senior but not junior debt obligation: $(1 + r_{DS})€50{,}000 > \tilde{X} - (1 + r_{DS})€10{,}000 > 0$	Senior debt obligation exceeds cash flow: $\tilde{X} < (1 + r_{DS})€10{,}000$
50 shares of equity	$0.1[\tilde{X} - (1 + r_{DS})€10{,}000] - 0.1[(1 + r_{DS})€50{,}000]$	0	0
€5,000 of new debt	$0.1[(1 + r_{DS})€50{,}000]$	$0.1[\tilde{X} - (1 + r_{DS})€10{,}000]$	0
Total	$0.1[\tilde{X} - (1 + r_{DS})€10{,}000]$	$0.1[\tilde{x} - (1 + r_{DS})€10{,}000]$	0

Note: r_{DS} *represents the promised interest rate on the senior debt and* r_{DJ} *is the promised interest rate on the junior debt.*

Result 14.2 summarizes the main points about how capital structure changes affect debt and equity holders when new debt is subordinated to existing debt.

Results

Result 14.2

Assume: (1) a firm's total cash flows to its debt and equity holders are unaffected by how it is financed; (2) there are no transaction costs; and (3) no arbitrage opportunities exist in the economy. Then, if a firm's existing debt holders have a senior claim in the event of bankruptcy, both the firm's share price per share and the value of its existing senior debt claims are unaffected by changes in the firm's capital structure.

What Occurs When New Debt is not Subordinated to Old Debt?

When firms issue junior debt, its promised yield must exceed r_{DS}, the promised yield on the existing senior debt, to compensate for the greater default risk borne by the junior debt holders. If a new debt issue is not junior, but rather has the same priority as existing debt, both new and existing debt holders proportionately share the assets of the bankrupt firm. The new debt holders' greater claim to bankrupt assets makes the existing debt holders worse off, but it allows the new debt issue to attract investors with a lower promised yield than if it were junior to the existing debt.

This cost to the existing debt holders benefits the shareholders. To understand this, consider again the case analysed in Exhibit 14.4, except now assume that the new debt is *not* subordinated. Assume again that the investor undoes the capital structure increase by selling 50 shares of equity and buying €5,000 of new debt. In scenario A, the investor still receives the same cash flow that would have been achieved under the original capital structure. Under scenarios B and C where the firm is bankrupt, however, the investor receives greater cash flows than Exhibit 14.4 specifies, because the new debt that the investor holds now receives a proportional share of the bankruptcy proceeds.

Results

Result 14.3

If a firm's existing debt holders do not have a senior claim in the event of bankruptcy, a new debt issue can decrease the value of existing debt. Under the assumptions listed in Result 14.1, however, the loss to the old debt holders would be offset by a gain to the equity holders, leaving the total value of the firm unaltered by this type of capital structure change.

During the last few years, several firms increased their debt ratios substantially, most dramatically in leveraged buyout transactions that took public companies private. In a number of these transactions, the transfer of wealth from the original debt holders to the equity holders was quite large.[5]

14.4 How Corporate Taxes Affect the Capital Structure Choice

Financial managers spend a great deal of time making decisions about their firms' capital structures. In addition, share prices react dramatically when firms make major changes in their capital structures.[6] This suggests that it probably would be unwise to stick with the conclusion that the capital structure decision is irrelevant.

The apparent relevance of the capital structure decision suggests that some of the assumptions underlying the Modigliani–Miller theorem are unrealistic, and that relaxing them may have important implications for the firm's capital structure choice. The most obviously unrealistic assumption is that of no taxes. Taxes have a major effect on the cash flows of firms and, as a result, strongly influence their capital structure decisions. Indeed, in a study of European CFOs, Brounen et al. (2004) found that approximately 27 per cent of those surveyed agreed that tax considerations played either an important or a very important role in their capital structure choices. The preceding two sections indicated that, in the absence of taxes, a firm's value does not depend on its capital structure. It follows that, in the absence of other market frictions, minimizing the amount paid in taxes maximizes the cash flows to the firm's equity holders and debt holders, thereby maximizing the firm's total value.

In most countries, the existence of corporate taxes favours debt financing. This is because interest tends to be a tax-deductible corporate expense. However, since dividends are viewed as distributions of profits rather than expenses of doing business, they are not tax deductible.[7]

---

[5] Studies by Asquith and Wizman (1990) and Warga and Welch (1993) indicate that bondholders lost money in several other leveraged buyouts as well.

[6] Share price reactions to corporate events such as capital structure changes are discussed in Chapter 19.

[7] In many countries, a firm can carry back the net losses in its current year as far as two years. When there is not enough income in the previous two years to allow the loss carryback, the firm may carry forward those losses for some years to offset future taxable profits. Hence the corporate tax advantage of debt financing applies even to firms that are temporarily unprofitable, although the debt tax shield is used less efficiently if it must be carried forward.

Howard Hughes' perceptive analysis of the tax benefits of debt financing, described in this chapter's opening vignette, pre-dated the academic discussion of debt and taxes by several years. This section explores the types of tax benefit he mentioned in more detail, specifically considering situations in which there are (1) corporate taxes, (2) tax-deductible interest expenses, and (3) no personal taxes. In the next section and in Chapter 15 we shall explore the effects of personal taxes.

How Debt Affects After-Tax Cash Flows

If the corporate tax rate is T_C, a firm with pre-tax cash flows of $\widetilde{X}$, which we shall assume for simplicity is EBIT (earnings before interest and taxes), and interest payments of r_D, then D has taxable income of $\widetilde{X} - r_D D$ and pays a corporate tax of $(\widetilde{X} - r_D D)T_C$. Since interest expense is tax deductible, a firm can reduce its tax liabilities and thus increase the amount it distributes to its security holders by issuing additional debt. Therefore, in the absence of personal taxes, transaction costs and bankruptcy costs, and if the pre-tax cash flow generated by the firm is held constant, the value-maximizing capital structure includes enough debt to eliminate the firm's tax liabilities.

To examine how debt affects firm values in the presence of corporate taxes, assume that the firm is financed with a combination of equity and a risk-free perpetuity bond (see Chapter 2), which pays interest at a fixed rate of r_D for ever. The year t sum of the after-(corporate) tax payments to its debt and equity holders is expressed in the following equation:

$$\widetilde{C}_t = (\widetilde{X}_t - r_D D)(1 - T_C) + r_D D \tag{14.1}$$

By rearranging terms, the firm's cash flows to its debt and equity holders can be expressed as the sum of the cash flows that the firm would have generated if it were an all-equity firm – its unlevered cash flows – plus the additional cash flows it generates because of the tax gain from debt:

$$\widetilde{C}_t = \widetilde{X}_t(1 - T_C) + r_D D T_C \tag{14.2}$$

How Debt Affects the Value of the Firm

As Chapter 13 showed, the value of the firm is the present value of the stream of future cash flows generated by the unlevered cash flows and tax savings expressed in equation (14.2). To determine how the value of the firm changes with a change in leverage, note that $\widetilde{X}_t(1 - T_C)$ is the year t cash flow that would be achieved by an unlevered firm. Therefore the present value of this series of cash flows, $\widetilde{X}_1(1 - T_C), \widetilde{X}_2(1 - T_C), \ldots$, must equal the value of the firm had it been unlevered (V_U). In addition, recall that, with static perpetual debt, the present value of the firm's yearly tax savings $r_D T_C D$ is $T_C D$. This implies the following result.

Results

Result 14.4

Assume that the pre-tax cash flows of the firm are unaffected by a change in a firm's capital structure, and that there are no transaction costs or opportunities for arbitrage. With corporate taxes at the rate T_C, but no personal taxes, the value of a levered firm with static risk-free perpetual debt is the value of an otherwise equivalent unlevered firm plus the product of the corporate tax rate and the market value of the firm's debt: that is,

$$V_L = V_U + T_C D \tag{14.3}$$

As equation (14.3) illustrates, the value of the firm increases with leverage by the amount $T_C D$, which is the tax gain from leverage.

To illustrate how tax-deductible debt can increase the cash flows to shareholders as well as increase firm value, Example 14.3 recalculates the answer to Example 14.2, assuming that there are corporate taxes.

Example 14.3

The Effect of Corporate Taxes on Cash Flows to Equity and Debt Holders

Recall from Example 14.2 that Suzy Iniko held 10 per cent of the firm's equity, and that the firm was increasing its debt level from €10,000 to €60,000. In this example, the firm uses perpetuity bonds instead of zero-coupon bonds for debt financing, and retires €50,000 in equity with the proceeds.

Compute Suzy's cash flow (1) in the original low-leverage scenario and (2) in the high-leverage scenario in which the investor attempts to undo the firm's capital structure change by selling €5,000 of her shares and using the proceeds to buy €5,000 in bonds. Assume that there is a corporate tax on earnings at a rate of T_C

Answer: The cash flow to Suzy, given the initial low level of debt, is

$$\tilde{C}_{\text{low lev}} = 0.1(\tilde{X} - r_D €10{,}000)(1 - T_C)$$

A leverage increase of €50,000 that is offset by a change in Suzy's portfolio will now yield cash flows to Suzy of

$$\tilde{C}_{\text{high lev}} = 0.1(\tilde{X} - r_D €60{,}000)(1 - T_C) + r_D €5{,}000 = 0.1(\tilde{X} - r_D €10{,}000)(1 - T_C) + r_D T_C €5{,}000$$

A firm that increases its debt level by issuing, as in Example 14.3, an additional €50,000 in bonds and buying back €50,000 in equity is doing its shareholders a favour. In this case, a 10 per cent equity investor in the firm, like Suzy, who sells €5,000 in equity and uses the proceeds to buy €5,000 in bonds, increases her cash flow by $r_D T_C$ €5,000 while restoring the rest of her portfolio to where it was before the firm increased its leverage. This insight generalizes to every shareholder, irrespective of their percentage ownership in the firm, and to every debt issuance, with more debt generating a larger benefit to the shareholder. This implies the following result.

Results

Result 14.5

Assume that the pre-tax cash flows of the firm are unaffected by a change in a firm's capital structure, and that there are no transaction costs or opportunities for arbitrage. With corporate taxes but no personal taxes, a firm's optimal capital structure will include enough debt to completely eliminate the firm's tax liabilities.

Example 14.4 illustrates the tax gains associated with leverage for a hypothetical leverage increase.

Example 14.4

Recapitalizing

Assume that a company earns £2,159 million before interest and taxes, out of which £64 million is paid out in interest and £678 million in taxes. These are net figures, which include interest income and expenditure. Suppose the firm chooses to recapitalize by distributing to its *shareholders* £5 billion in 9.4 per cent notes, requiring £470 million in annual interest payments. Assuming that the investment choice and the pre-tax cash flows (and EBIT) of the firm are unchanged, how would this additional £470 million affect the cash flows to a tax-exempt shareholder?

Answer: From the company's annual report, we compute the following:

	(£millions)	Recapitalization (in £millions)
EBIT	2,159	2,159.0
– Net interest expenses	−64	– 534.0
EBT	2,095	1,625.0
– Taxes (rate = 32.4%)	−678	−526.5
Net income	1,417	1,098.5
Gain from extraordinary item	314	314.0
Net profits (a)	1,731	1,412.5
Net investment (b)	874	874.0
Dividends [(a) – (b)]	857	538.5
CF to shareholders (from equity and bonds)	857	1008.5
	(£0.33/share)	(£0.39/share)

The difference in the cash flows between the two scenarios, £151.5 million (= £1,008.5 – £857) equals the tax savings from the debt, 0.324 × 0.094 × £5 billion.

Real-World Insights

Green Taxes

The tax rates discussed in this chapter are baseline marginal corporate tax rates that apply to all companies in a country. However, governments have a wide range of tax incentives to encourage firms to pursue more sustainable operations. These incentives and levies can change the attractiveness of new investments and the degree to which debt is more attractive than equity in a firm's capital structure. Examples of green tax incentives in the UK include:

- Climate Change Levy: The Climate Change Levy is an environmental tax that all companies pay on the energy they use. Firms can reduce the amount they spend on the levy if they have entered into a Climate Change Agreement with the UK Environment Agency. Firms committing to sustainability targets can receive a reduction of 90 per cent on the levy for electricity and 65 per cent for gas usage.
- Capital Allowances on energy-efficient items: Firms can claim up to 100% depreciation in the same year of purchase for energy-efficient items, such as electric cars. This depreciation allowance reduces the firm's tax, and thus incentivized the purchase of sustainable assets.
- Landfill Taxes: Firms must pay an additional tax if they use landfill sites to remove industrial waste.
- Aggregates Levy: Firms that import, dig or dredge sand, rock or gravel from the ground must pay a levy for every tonne removed. As of 2022, this levy is £2 per tonne.

14.5 How Personal Taxes Affect Capital Structure

A tax-exempt shareholder, such as a pension fund, is indifferent about whether the cash flows of a firm come in the form of interest on debt, dividends on equity or capital gains on equity, as long as the form of the payment does not affect the magnitude of the payment. Since the total cash flows to the equity and debt holders of firms are larger when cash flows are paid out in the form of debt interest payments instead of retained or paid as dividends, tax-exempt shareholders will prefer firms to have high leverage. However, investors who pay personal taxes prefer to receive income in the form of capital gains, because capital gains can often be deferred and, in many countries, are taxed at lower rates than interest or dividend income.[8] As a result, the average tax rate on equity income T_E, which generally has a capital gains component, is normally less but no more than the average tax rate on debt income T_D, which is taxed as ordinary income: that is, $T_E < T_D$. This preference for capital gains income can lead some taxable shareholders to prefer firms with less leverage.

The Effect of Personal Taxes on Debt and Equity Rates of Return

We first examine how personal taxes affect the expected rates of return required to induce investors to hold debt securities instead of equity securities. In general, debt is less risky than equity, and thus requires a lower expected rate of return. To simplify this analysis, we assume that debt is risk-free with a promised coupon and return of r_D. We also assume that investors are risk neutral, so that the expected return on equity, $\bar{r}_E$, which more generally can be viewed as a pre-tax zero-beta expected return, differs from r_D only because of taxes. (Our results apply to positive beta equity with risk-averse investors if we first adjust expected returns downwards by their risk premiums in the formulae we present here.)

Which Investors Prefer Debt and Which Prefer Equity?

In the absence of taxes and other market frictions, the expected return of zero-beta equity equals the return on riskless debt (see Chapter 5). With personal taxes, however, it is necessary to account for the fact that the returns to equity, which often come in the form of capital gains, are generally taxed less heavily than the returns to debt. To compensate taxable investors for its relative tax disadvantage, the pre-tax return on debt should exceed the pre-tax zero-beta expected return on equity.

This pre-tax return difference leads tax-exempt investors to prefer debt to equity. However, if the return difference is not too large, investors in the highest tax brackets should prefer equity to debt. There will also be investors who are indifferent between holding debt and equity. The personal tax rates on debt and equity of these indifferent investors satisfy the following condition:

$$r_D(1 - T_D) = \bar{r}_E(1 - T_E) \tag{14.4}$$

so that the after-tax expected return is the same for each security. In general, if $r_D(1-T_D) > \bar{r}_E(1-T_E)$ for a particular investor incurring tax rates of T_D and T_E – that is, the after-tax return to debt exceeds the after-tax expected return to equity – the investor will prefer debt to equity. If the inequality is reversed, the investor will prefer equity to debt. Example 14.5 explores this further.

Example 14.5

Personal Tax Preferences for Holding Debt versus Equity Securities

Assume that the expected rates of return on debt and zero-beta equity securities are as follows:

$$r_D = 7\%$$
$$\bar{r}_E = 6\%$$

Iain has a tax rate on debt income of 40 per cent, and Charlie has a tax rate on debt income of 20 per cent. Both individuals are subject to the same marginal tax rate on equity income, the capital gains rate, which is 20 per cent. Which investor prefers the debt security and which prefers the equity?

Answer: For Iain, the after-tax rate of return on debt is 4.2 per cent, which is less than his after-tax expected rate of return on zero-beta equity, which is 4.8 per cent. However, Charlie receives an after-tax rate of return on debt of 5.6 per cent, which exceeds his after-tax rate of return on the equity security of 4.8 per cent. Hence Iain prefers the equity investment, and Charlie prefers the debt investment.

---

[8] We would advise managers to examine the tax rates that apply in their country, since tax regimes are very complex, and companies can qualify for many tax breaks, incentives and levies that will affect their marginal tax rate. Similarly, many countries have incremental tax bands for individuals, which are dependent on an individual's annual income.

The Analysis When Investors Have Identical Tax Rates

To understand how personal taxes affect the choice between issuing debt and issuing equity, consider the total cash flows distributed to the firm's debt and equity investors. For simplicity, assume that the personal tax rates, T_D and T_E, do not differ across investors. The after-tax cash flow C that these investors receive is determined by corporate taxes, personal taxes and the way in which the firm is financed. Exhibit 14.5 illustrates this as a stream of cash that starts with all the firm's realized pre-tax cash flows X, and branches out into smaller streams that reflect the cash distributed to debt and equity holders, and to the government in the form of taxes. To keep this illustration simple, Exhibit 14.5 assumes that the firm pays out all its earnings, and that its EBIT exceed its promised interest payment, $r_D D$.

Exhibit 14.5 The Earnings Stream

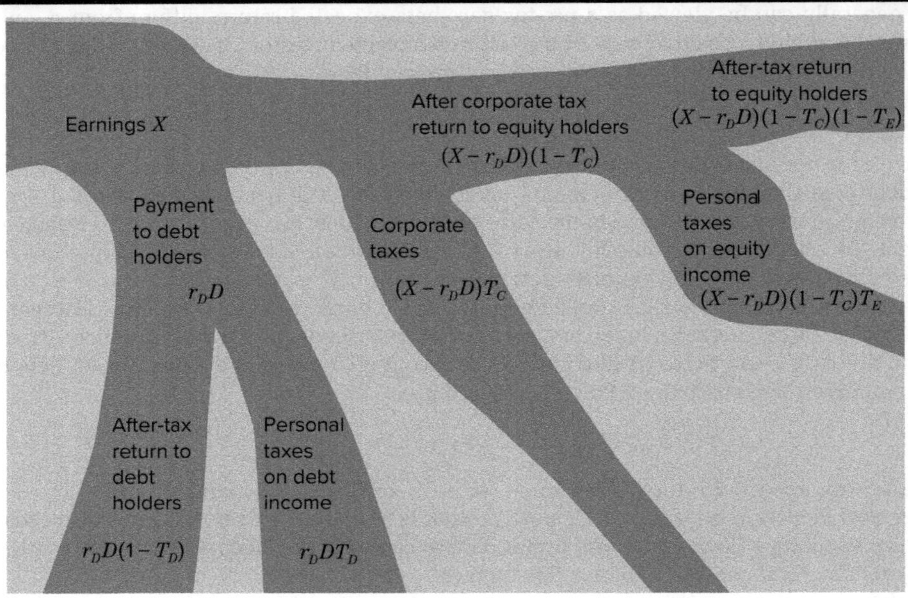

As Exhibit 14.5 illustrates, some of the cash, $r_D D$, is diverted into a branch of the stream labelled 'Payment to debt holders'. This branch of the stream reaches a fork where some of the cash flows go to the government in the form of personal taxes on the debt interest payments, while the rest goes to the debt holders as an after-tax return.

The upper branch of the stream carries the pre-tax cash that flows to the equity holders. Part of this cash, $(X - r_D D)T_C$, is diverted to the government in the form of corporate taxes. The remainder of the firm's cash flows, $(X - r_D D)(1 - T_C)$, flow to the firm's equity holders, where $(X - r_D D)(1 - T_C)T_E$ is diverted to the branch labelled 'Personal taxes on equity income', with the rest going to equity holders as an after-tax return.

By summing the branches labelled 'After-tax return to debt holders' (bottom left) and 'After-tax return to equity holders' (top right), we derive the total after-tax cash flow stream flowing to the debt and equity holders:

$$C = (X - r_D D)(1 - T_C)(1 - T_E) + r_D D(1 - T_D) \tag{14.5a}$$

By rearranging terms, equation (14.5a) can be rewritten as

$$C = (X - T_C)(1 - T_E) + r_D D[(1 - T_D) - (1 - T_C)(1 - T_E)] \tag{14.5b}$$

where the last part of equation (14.5b), $r_D D[(1 - T_D) - (1 - T_C)(1 - T_E)]$, represents the tax gain from leverage.

If the level of debt is permanently fixed, this tax gain can be viewed as a perpetuity that accrues tax free to the firm's debt and equity investors. It can be valued by discounting the perpetuity payments at the after-(personal) tax rate on debt $r_D(1 - T_D)$ or, equivalently, at the after-(personal) tax return on equity (see equation (14.4)). The present value of this perpetual stream of tax savings, obtained by dividing the right-hand side of equation (14.5b) by $r_D(1 - T_D)$, is $T_g D$, where T_g is given by

$$T_g = 1 - \frac{(1 - T_C)(1 - T_E)}{1 - T_D} \tag{14.6}$$

This generalizes Result 14.4 to include the effect of personal taxes.

Results

Result 14.6

Assume that the pre-tax cash flows of the firm are unaffected by a change in a firm's capital structure, and that there are no transaction costs or opportunities for arbitrage. If investors all have personal tax rates on debt and equity income of T_D and T_E, respectively, and if the corporate tax rate is T_C, then the value of a levered firm exceeds the value of an otherwise equivalent unlevered firm by $T_g D$: that is,

$$V_L = V_U + T_g D$$

where

$$T_g = 1 - \frac{(1 - T_C)(1 - T_E)}{1 - T_D}$$

If T_g in equation (14.6) is positive, firms will want to issue enough debt to eliminate their tax liability; if T_g is negative, firms will want to include no debt in their capital structures. Firms will be indifferent about their debt level if T_g is zero, which is the case when the following equality holds:

$$(1 - T_D) = (1 - T_C)(1 - T_E) \tag{14.7}$$

When this equality holds, each investor pays directly in personal taxes and indirectly through the corporate tax the same amount in taxes for every pre-tax unit of cash that the firm earns. This holds regardless of whether the earnings are distributed in the form of interest payments to debt holders or accrue as capital gains to shareholders. Thus the investor and firm are indifferent about the capital structure choice the firm makes when equation (14.7) holds. Note that this condition is different from the condition that makes the same investor indifferent about holding debt versus equity, equation (14.4).

The preceding example demonstrates that personal taxes can significantly reduce the tax advantage of debt. T_g will be further reduced if one accounts for the fact that capital gains can be deferred as well as taxed at a rate lower than the ordinary income tax rate.

As shown in Example 14.6, the zero-beta firm's after-tax cost of capital will be the same for debt and equity if equation (14.7) applies, and if its investors are indifferent between holding debt or equity.

To prove this, combine equation (14.7), which provides the condition for the firm to be indifferent between debt and equity, with equation (14.4), which provides the condition for an investor to be indifferent between holding debt or equity, to yield

$$r_D(1 - T_C) = \bar{r}_E \tag{14.8}$$

The left-hand side of the equation is the firm's after-(corporate) tax cost of debt; the right-hand side its after-tax (and pre-tax) cost of equity. Thus equation (14.8) states that the after-tax cost of capital (adjusted for risk premiums) is the same for debt and equity whenever the personal tax rates of the firm's investors make them indifferent about debt versus equity financing. Note, also, that if the left-hand side of equation (14.8) is larger than the right-hand side, firms will find equity financing to be cheaper ($T_g < 0$) if their investors are indifferent, and vice versa.

Example 14.6

The Effect of Corporate Taxes and Personal Taxes on the Tax Gain from Leverage

In 2022 in the UK, the maximum personal income tax rate was 45 per cent, the maximum corporate tax rate was 19 per cent, and the rate on capital gains was 20 per cent. Using these tax rates, what is the tax gain or loss from leverage in the UK?

Answer: From equation (14.6), $T_g = 1 - [(0.81 \times 0.80)/0.55] = -0.178 = -17.8\%$

Since $T_g < 0$, equity financing is cheaper than debt financing in the UK.

Capital Structure Choices When Taxable Earnings Can Be Negative

Up to this point, we have assumed that firms can always utilize their interest tax shields. However, this is unrealistic for many firms. Many firms have extremely low taxable earnings, even before taking the interest tax deduction into account. For example, many start-up firms with substantial **non-debt tax shields,** such as R&D and depreciation deductions, and very little current revenues, have no taxable earnings. This fact will allow us to develop a theory of optimal capital structure, based solely on taxes, in which different firms, each with 'indifferent investors' as discussed above, have different optimal mixes of debt and equity financing.

Since firms with low taxable earnings will not always be able to take advantage of the tax gain associated with leverage, they will prefer equity financing if the returns on equity and debt satisfy equation (14.8) for those firms that will be paying corporate taxes with certainty: that is, $\bar{r}_E = (1 - T_C)r_D$, where T_C (throughout this subsection) is the corporate tax rate for those firms that will be paying the full corporate tax rate. In other words, firms that are indifferent between debt and equity when they are assured of using the debt tax deduction will prefer equity financing when they are uncertain about being able to use the tax deduction. For such firms to issue debt, (1) the after-tax cost of debt (adjusted for its risk premium) must be less than the (risk-premium-adjusted) cost of equity when the firm can use the debt tax shield.[9] In addition, if firms are to include equity in their capital structures, (2) the cost of debt financing must be greater than the cost of equity financing when the firm cannot take advantage of the interest tax deduction. Statements (1) and (2) imply that

$$r_D > \bar{r}_E > (1 - T_C)r_D \tag{14.9}$$

The inequality $\bar{r}_E > (1 - T_C)r_D$ implies that a firm that has positive taxable income ($X > r_D D$) would have achieved a lower cost of capital if it had issued more debt. However, the inequality $r_D > \bar{r}_E$ implies that a firm with negative taxable income ($X > r_D D$), which cannot take advantage of the interest tax deduction, would have achieved a lower cost of capital had it issued more equity.

If the inequalities in equation (14.9) are satisfied, firms will have an optimal capital structure consisting of both debt and equity. Under certainty, the optimal capital structure includes just enough debt to eliminate the firm's taxable earnings ($X = r_D D$). When firms are uncertain about their taxable earnings, their optimal debt levels can be determined by weighing the costs associated with using higher-cost debt in situations where the firm cannot use the interest tax shield against the benefit of having a lower after-tax cost of debt, and hence lower weighted average cost of capital in situations where the firm can use the full debt tax shield.

This point is illustrated in the case study.

[9] See DeAngelo and Masulis (1980) for a discussion of this point. We have presented this theory under the assumption that all investors have the same personal tax rates, and that these tax rates make them indifferent about holding debt and equity. We recognize that some investors are not taxed, and that personal tax rates will differ between investors when there are graduated income tax rates. However, as the appendix to this chapter indicates, firms may care most about investors who have personal tax rates that make them indifferent about holding debt or equity. In equilibrium, the costs of debt and equity may be set so that the most reluctant investor in the firm's debt is one who is indifferent between debt and equity.

Real-World Insight

Prodist and Pharmcorp

Consider two firms that initially have equal amounts of debt.

- The first firm, Prodist, is engaged primarily in production and distribution; the second firm, Pharmcorp, is a pharmaceutical company with high depreciation deductions.
- Assume that each firm currently has equal EBITDA, and wishes to raise €14 million in new capital with either debt or equity. (For simplicity, rule out the possibility of a debt–equity mix.)
- Assume that Pharmcorp's EBITD is negative, because the firm has high depreciation deductions. However, Prodist has no non-debt tax shields, and positive taxable income.

When evaluating whether to issue debt or equity, the firms take into account the following information:

$$r_D = 12\%$$
$$\bar{r}_E = 10\%$$
$$\text{Capital to be raised} = €14{,}000{,}000$$
$$T_C = 34\%$$

Therefore $r_D(12\%) > \bar{r}_E(10\%) > (1 - T_C)r_D(7.92\%)$.

Exhibit 14.6 illustrates how the capital structure choices of Prodist and Pharmcorp affect the cash flows to the original shareholders of each firm, assuming that the firms held no previous debt. Exhibit 14.6 shows the after-tax cash flows available to the equity holders when the two firms issue debt and when they issue equity. In this scenario, Pharmcorp equity holders are better off if the firm issues equity, because they receive €54,600,000 instead of €54,320,000, whereas Prodist's shareholders are better off if the firm issues debt, because they receive €35,851,000 instead of €35,560,000. The companies make different decisions, because Prodist can use the tax shield benefit of debt and Pharmcorp cannot.

Exhibit 14.6 assumes that Pharmcorp's negative taxable earnings and Prodist's positive taxable earnings are certain. Of course, earnings are likely to be uncertain in the real world. Nevertheless, since Pharmcorp has high depreciation deductions at any given debt level, the possibility of its having negative taxable income during some period is much more likely than it would be for Prodist. As a result, Pharmcorp's optimal capital structure is likely to include less debt than that of Prodist.

Exhibit 14.6 Debt–Equity Trade-Offs for a Distribution Company and a Pharmaceutical Company

Item	Prodist (distribution company)		Pharmcorp (pharmaceutical company)	
	Debt (€000s)	Equity (€000s)	Debt (€000s)	Equity (€000s)
EBITDA	56,000	56,000	56,000	56,000
– Non-debt tax shields	0	0	–58,000	–58,000
EBIT	56,000	56,000	–2,000	–2,000
– Interest expense	–1,680	0	–1,680	0
Taxable income	54,320	56,000	–3,680	–2,000
– Corporate tax (T_c = 34%)	–18,469	–19,040	0	0
Net income	35,851	36,960	–3,680	–2,000
Return to new shareholders (10% of €14,000)	0	–1,400	0	–1,400
Tax shields subtracted earlier for tax purposes			58,000	58,000
Cash flows available to original shareholders	35,851	35,560	54,320	54,600

Given that firms with non-debt tax shields, such as large depreciation and research and development expenditures, are more likely to have negative taxable income at any given debt level, they should have lower debt levels than firms without non-debt tax shields. Non-debt tax shields are probably an important determinant of the capital structures of biotech firms, which may have substantial value but very little taxable earnings in the near future.[10] However, non-debt tax shields are probably not relevant to the capital structure choice of a firm such as BT Group, a British telecommunications firm, with a long history of positive taxable earnings. If BT were to realize negative taxable income in the present year, it could defer them to offset future earnings. Thus it would be extremely unlikely for BT to lose the tax benefits associated with debt financing. Hence, from a pure tax standpoint, BT may be better off issuing debt to fund its new investment. However, start-up firms with large depreciation write-offs and R&D expenditures may have negative or only slightly positive taxable incomes for a long period of time. Since these firms may not be able to take advantage of available tax credits even if they can be deferred for many years, they will be better off financing their investments with equity rather than debt.

Result 14.7 summarizes the implications of the preceding discussion.

Results

Result 14.7

Assume that there is a tax gain from leverage, but the taxable earnings of firms are low relative to their present values.

- With riskless future cash flows, firms will want to use debt financing up to the point where they eliminate their entire corporate tax liabilities, but they will not want to borrow beyond that point.
- With uncertainty, firms will pick the debt ratio that weighs the benefits associated with the debt tax shield when it can be used against the higher cost of debt in cases where the debt tax shield cannot be used.
- Firms with more non-debt tax shields are likely to use less debt financing.

The *marginal tax rate* on a corporation's profits, which is the extra tax paid per additional cash unit of profit, is often less than the statutory tax rate. Because firms frequently employ various tax shields to defer their tax liabilities, the actual rate companies pay is regularly below the published marginal tax rate. For example, although Amazon earned more than $35 billion in profit in 2021, it's effective tax rate was only 6 per cent and not the 21 per cent it should have paid if there were no tax shields. As Exhibit 14.6 illustrated, corporations with a high effective tax rate have a significant tax gain associated with leverage. However, for most smaller corporations, the tax gain associated with leverage is likely to be quite small. In addition, high-tech firms are less able to have debt and therefore debt tax shields, whereas large firms and industries with high concentrations of fixed assets will tend to benefit from debt tax shields.

14.6 Taxes and Preference Shares

Chapter 3 noted that preference shares (or preferred equity) are similar to a bond because they have a fixed payout. In contrast to bonds, however, preference shareholders cannot force the firm into bankruptcy if it fails to meet its dividend obligation. Although the claims of a preference shareholder are always junior to the claims of the firm's debt holders in the event of bankruptcy, such claims are senior to the claims of the firm's ordinary shareholders. The ordinary shareholders cannot receive a dividend until the preferred dividends (including all past dividends) are paid. In addition, preference shareholders, unlike debt holders, may have voting rights.

[10] Taxable earnings are often very different from reported earnings. There are a number of high-tech companies with positive reported earnings that have negative taxable earnings.

Preference shares sometimes have attractive tax properties in some countries. For example, in many countries, dividends of preference shares are not tax deductible, whereas the coupon payments of a bond are. This has led some analysts to conclude that subordinated bonds provide cheaper financing than preferred equity.

14.7 The Effect of Inflation on the Tax Gain from Leverage

Recall that the last part of equation (14.5b) had an expression for the yearly savings associated with increased leverage. Note that $r_D D[(1-T_D)-(1-T_C)(1-T_E)]$, the tax gain, increases as the interest rate on corporate debt increases. Although interest rates for corporate borrowers can change for various reasons, the most notable cause is a change in the expected rate of inflation. If investors expect inflation to be high, nominal borrowing costs will also be high, reflecting the decreased purchasing power of the cash used to repay the loans.

Fisher's (1930) well-known theory of interest rate changes postulates a one-to-one relation between interest rates and expected inflation: that is, if inflation is expected to be one percentage point higher, the nominal interest rate also increases by approximately one percentage point.[11] This suggests that an increase in inflation increases the tax gain associated with leverage for firms that will be able to use the interest tax deductions. Higher rates of inflation imply higher nominal borrowing costs, which, in turn, create higher tax deductions. Example 14.7 illustrates how increases in inflation can reduce taxable income and hence reduce taxes.

Example 14.7

The Effect of Inflation on Prodist's Corporate Taxes

Prodist (see Exhibit 14.6) has a large amount of taxable income. It raised €14 million with 12 per cent notes. Show the impact of a 4 per cent increase in inflation, assuming that this increases the rate on the notes to 16 per cent, and that the inflation-adjusted cash flows are unchanged.

Answer: The assumed inflation increases Prodist's tax shield from €1.68 million to €2.24 million, as shown below.

	Cash flows (€millions) given		
	Low inflation	High inflation	Difference
Inflation-adjusted cash flows	56.00	56.00	–
– Interest expense (= tax shields)	–1.68	–2.24	+0.56
Taxable income	54.32	53.76	–0.56
Corporate tax (34%)	35.85	35.48	–0.37

In this case, the increase in inflation of 4 per cent leads to a €0.56 million increase in tax shields for the same amount of debt. Although this suggests that inflation encourages higher leverage ratios, this is true only when a firm can take advantage of all of its tax shields. By increasing the magnitude of the tax deduction for each euro of debt, inflation reduces the amount of debt needed to eliminate the firm's taxable income. Since firms have no tax incentive to borrow beyond this point, firms that previously had little taxable income may reduce their leverage ratios when inflation increases.

[11] See Chapter 9.

14.8 The Empirical Implications of the Analysis of Debt and Taxes

We have suggested in this chapter that taxes play an important role in determining the debt–equity mix of corporations. Firms that are generating substantial taxable EBIT should use a substantial amount of debt financing to take advantage of the tax deductibility of the interest payments. However, firms with substantial amounts of other tax shields, such as depreciation deductions and R&D expenses, are likely to have much lower EBIT relative to their values, and would thus choose lower debt–equity ratios. Hence, in a comparison across firms, there should be a negative correlation between a firm's non-debt tax shields and its debt ratio.

Do Firms with More Taxable Earnings Use More Debt Financing?

In reality, we do not observe a positive cross-sectional relation between EBIT and debt ratios. Indeed, those firms that generate the largest amount of taxable earnings tend to have the lowest debt ratios, which is the opposite of what we might expect from the analysis in this chapter (Graham 2000; Faulkender and Petersen 2006; Kayhan and Titman 2007; Goyal and Murray 2010). This negative correlation between EBIT and debt–equity ratios probably arises because firms only rarely issue new equity, which implies the following.[12]

- Non-debt tax shields and the use of debt financing are positively correlated, because firms tend to finance most major capital expenditures, which generate investment tax credits and depreciation deductions, with debt.
- Firms that perform poorly (that is, have low or negative EBIT) tend to accumulate debt to meet their expenses.
- Firms with less access to public debt markets will have less leverage. Faulkender and Petersen (2006) showed that companies with credit ratings were more able to take on debt than firms who could rely only on active lenders, such as banks.

The preceding observations, however, do not rule out the possibility that firms take taxes into account when they consider whether or not to issue equity. Indeed, a study by MacKie-Mason (1990) found that firms do consider the tax benefits when they decide between issuing substantial amounts of either new debt or new equity. Firms that are unable to use their interest deductions are much more likely to issue equity than debt. In contrast, firms that have significant taxable earnings are more likely to issue debt. In a more recent study, which calculates the **effective marginal tax rates** discussed previously, Graham (1996) found that firms with high marginal tax rates are more likely to increase leverage than firms with low marginal tax rates.

An additional issue that managers must consider is the impact of the tax regime under which their company is operating. In countries such as the United Kingdom and Australia an imputation system is in effect, where investors receive tax credits for corporation tax that has already been paid by the firm. This means that, to an investor, there are no tax benefits of debt, and personal taxation has a different effect in this regime from that of a classical tax system (Faff et al. 2000). Dividend policy is discussed in detail in Chapter 16.

For a full review of the impact of tax on capital structure (and other areas including dividend policy), read Graham (2008), who reviews the theoretical and empirical literature on tax effects. Evidence from other countries outside the USA is very light, and consequently there isn't much evidence on whether European, Asian or African managers view debt in a similar way. Moreover, given the heterogeneity of tax codes and regimes across the world, it would be extremely difficult to carry out a comparative cross-country analysis that was meaningful. Relevant research includes Wald (1999), Ozkan (UK 2001), Miguel and Pindado (Spain 2001) and Gaud et al. (Switzerland 2005).

14.9 Are There Tax Advantages to Leasing?

Up to this point, we have assumed that firms finance their capital assets by raising either debt or equity capital. This section considers the tax advantages and disadvantages associated with a third financing possibility: leasing the capital assets.

[12] There are personal tax, as well as information, explanations for this behaviour. See Chapters 15, 17 and 19.

Operating Leases and Capital Leases

As Chapter 2 discussed, an **operating lease** is an agreement to obtain the services of an asset for a period that generally represents only a small part of the asset's useful life. For example, one might lease a car for three years. At the end of this period, the lease may or may not be extended. In a **financial lease** (also known as a **capital lease**), the lease agreement extends over most of the asset's useful life.

The decision to enter into an operating lease generally relates to the transaction costs associated with buying and selling the assets. For example, leasing rather than buying a car makes sense if you need a car for only two months. Other issues relevant to the 'lease versus buy' decision include information about the resale value of an asset, potential renegotiation problems at the end of the lease (for example, you might want to keep the asset longer), and incentive problems (for example, you might be likely to drive a car differently if you leased rather than bought it).

The above considerations are much less relevant for financial leases, which should be considered more or less as a financing alternative that is equivalent to buying the asset with borrowed funds. The major difference between buying an asset with borrowed funds and leasing the equipment relates to the timing of payments, which, in turn, affects the tax treatment of the two alternatives.

The After-Tax Costs of Leasing and Buying Capital Assets

Under previous accounting standards (IAS 17), it was possible to create value from leases if the **lessee** had a different corporate tax rate from the **lessor.** However, since the introduction of IFRS 16, the taxation benefits of leases to a lessee have effectively disappeared. This is because the lease now appears on the balance sheet instead of the income statement. With leased assets treated for tax considerations in the exact same way as bought assets, a firm cannot create value from choosing to lease instead of buying an asset, since the after-tax costs will be the same. The lesson is as follows.

Results

Result 14.8

Firms should be indifferent between buying an asset and leasing it.

14.10 Summary and Conclusions

This chapter analysed how taxes affect the capital structures of firms. In the absence of taxes and other market imperfections, the value of a firm is independent of how it is financed. However, the interest tax deduction makes debt financing less expensive than equity financing, which implies that, in the absence of personal taxes and other market frictions, firms should use sufficient debt to eliminate their entire corporate tax liabilities.

Personal taxes somewhat offset the tax advantage of debt financing. Because equity returns (often taxed as capital gains) are taxed at a more favourable personal rate than debt, the pre-tax (zero-beta) expected rate of return on equity may be lower than the pre-tax (zero-beta) expected rate of return on debt. When considering personal as well as corporate taxes, it is possible that the after-tax costs of zero-beta debt and equity are equal. However, current tax rates along with the observed gap between the rates on taxable corporate bonds suggest that, in reality, there is still a tax advantage to debt financing.

Although the analysis up to this point presents a fairly complete discussion of the corporate tax advantages of debt financing, the discussion of personal taxes remains incomplete. Chapter 15, which completes our analysis of taxes, analyses how personal taxes affect a firm's dividend policy. The effect of taxes on dividend policy can have an important effect on its capital structure, because earnings that are not distributed to shareholders are retained within the firm, and add to its equity base. Indeed, most new equity on corporate balance sheets comes from retained earnings rather than new equity issues. Hence no discussion of the effect of taxes on capital structure is complete without considering the effect of taxes on dividend policy.

Of course, taxes are only one aspect of a corporation's capital structure choice. Corporate executives often express concerns about the ability of their firms to meet debt obligations, and about how debt financing affects their firms' access to investment capital in the future. More recently, executives have started to consider the beneficial role that debt has on management incentives, and the information conveyed to shareholders by their financing decisions. These and other topics are discussed in future chapters.

Key Concepts

Result 14.1: (*The Modigliani–Miller theorem.*) Assume: (1) a firm's total cash flows to its debt and equity holders are not affected by how it is financed; (2) there are no transaction costs; and (3) no arbitrage opportunities exist in the economy. Then the total market value of the firm, which is the same as the sum of the market values of the items on the right-hand side of the balance sheet (that is, its debt and equity), is not affected by how it is financed.

Result 14.2: Assume: (1) a firm's total cash flows to its debt and equity holders are unaffected by how it is financed; (2) there are no transaction costs; and (3) no arbitrage opportunities exist in the economy. Then, if a firm's existing debt holders have a senior claim in the event of bankruptcy, both the firm's share price per share and the value of its existing senior debt claims are unaffected by changes in the firm's capital structure.

Result 14.3: If a firm's existing debt holders do not have a senior claim in the event of bankruptcy, a new debt issue can decrease the value of existing debt. Under the assumptions listed in Result 14.1, however, the loss of the old debt holders would be offset by a gain to the equity holders, leaving the total value of the firm unaltered by this type of capital structure change.

Result 14.4: Assume that the pre-tax cash flows of the firm are unaffected by a change in a firm's capital structure, and that there are no transaction costs or opportunities for arbitrage. With corporate taxes at the rate T_C, but no personal taxes, the value of a levered firm with static risk-free perpetual debt is the value of an otherwise equivalent unlevered firm plus the product of the corporate tax rate and the market value of the firm's debt: that is,

$$V_L = V_U + T_C D$$

Result 14.5: Assume that the pre-tax cash flows of the firm are unaffected by a change in a firm's capital structure, and that there are no transaction costs or opportunities for arbitrage. With corporate taxes but no personal taxes, a firm's optimal capital structure will include enough debt to completely eliminate the firm's tax liabilities.

Result 14.6: Assume that the pre-tax cash flows of the firm are unaffected by a change in a firm's capital structure, and that there are no transaction costs or opportunities for arbitrage. If investors all have personal tax rates on debt and equity income of T_D and T_E, respectively, and if the corporate tax rate is T_C, then the value of a levered firm exceeds the value of an otherwise equivalent unlevered firm by $T_g D$: that is,

$$V_L = V_U + T_g D$$

where

$$T_g = 1 - \frac{(1 - T_C)(1 - T_E)}{1 - T_D}$$

Result 14.7: Assume that there is a tax gain from leverage, but the taxable earnings of firms are low relative to their present values.

- With riskless future cash flows, firms will want to use debt financing up to the point where they eliminate their entire corporate tax liabilities, but they will not want to borrow beyond that point.
- With uncertainty, firms will pick the debt ratio that weighs the benefits associated with the debt tax shield when it can be used against the higher cost of debt in cases where the debt tax shield cannot be used.
- Firms with more non-debt tax shields are likely to use less debt financing.

Result 14.8: Firms should be indifferent between buying an asset and leasing it.

Key Terms

Exercises

14.1 Suppose $r_D = 12\%$, $\bar{r}_E = 10\%$, $T_C = 33\%$, $T_D = 20\%$.

a What is the marginal tax rate on equity income, T_E, that would make an investor indifferent in terms of after-tax returns between holding equity or bonds? Assume that all betas are zero.

b What is the probability that a firm will not utilize its tax shield if, on the margin, the firm is indifferent between issuing a little more debt or equity?

14.2 Consider a single-period binomial setting where the riskless interest rate is zero, and there are no taxes. A firm consists of a machine that will produce cash flows of £210 if the economy is good and £80 if the economy is bad. The good and bad states occur with equal risk-neutral probability. Initially, the firm has 100 shares outstanding and debt with a face value of £50 due at the end of the period. What is the share price of the firm?

14.3 Suppose the firm in exercise 14.2 unexpectedly announces that it will issue additional debt, with the same seniority as existing debt and a face value of £50. The firm will use the entire proceeds to repurchase some of the outstanding shares.

a What is the market price of the new debt?

b Just after the announcement, what will the price of a share jump to?

c Show how a shareholder with 20 per cent of the shares outstanding is better off as a result of this transaction when he or she undoes the leverage change.

d Show that the Modigliani–Miller theorem still holds.

14.4 Assume that the real riskless interest rate is zero and the corporate tax rate is 12.5 per cent. TAL Industries can borrow at the riskless interest rate. It will have an inflation-adjusted EBIT next year of €200 million. It would like to borrow €50 million today. Its only deductions will be interest payments (if any).

a What are its interest payments, taxable income, tax payments and income left for shareholders in a no-inflation environment?

b Suppose there is inflation of 10 per cent per year, but the real interest rate stays at zero. This means that investors now will require a sure payment of €1.10 next year for each €1.00 loaned today. Repeat part *a*, assuming that EBIT is affected by inflation.

c In which environment is the inflation-adjusted income left for shareholders higher? Why?

14.5 As owner of 10 per cent of ABC Industries, you have control of its capital structure decision. The current corporate tax rate is 25 per cent, and your personal tax rate is 20 per cent. Assume that the returns to shareholders accrue as non-taxable capital gains. ABC currently has no debt, and can finance the repurchase of 10 per cent of its outstanding shares by borrowing $100 million at the risk-free rate of 10 per cent. The long-term government bond rate is 8 per cent. If you hold your 10 per cent of the firm constant and buy the long-term government bonds, what is your annual after-tax gain from this transaction?

14.6 Explain how inflation affects the capital structure decision. Does inflation affect the capital structure choice differently for different firms?

14.7 Assume that the corporate tax rate is 50 per cent, AAA corporate bonds are trading at a yield of 9 per cent and long-term government bonds are trading at a yield of 6 per cent. How can the shareholders of an AAA-rated firm gain by increasing the leverage of their firm without increasing the leverage of their personal portfolio? Assume that the probability of bankruptcy is zero.

14.8 New start-up airlines will normally lease used commercial aeroplanes, whereas older, more established airline firms will tend to buy new aeroplanes. Explain why.

14.9 Restaurant chains such as McDonald's sometimes franchise their restaurants and sometimes own them outright. The franchised restaurants are usually owned by individuals who hold them as sole ownership firms or partnerships, which pass income through directly to the owners. There is no corporate tax on this income, but the owner must pay personal taxes on the income.

a From the perspective of the owner of the franchise, is there a tax advantage to debt financing?

b Which organizational form is better from the perspective of tax minimization: corporate ownership of the individual restaurants or franchises?

14.10 REITs are companies set up to manage investment properties such as office buildings and apartment houses. They are not subject to corporate taxes. How do we expect taxes to affect the capital structure choice of REITs?

14.11 X-Tex Industries has large depreciation tax deductions, and can thus eliminate all of its taxable income with a relatively small amount of debt. In contrast, Unique Scientific Equipment Corporation is generating a substantial amount of taxable income. Despite the tax advantage of debt, Unique uses only a modest amount of debt financing, because the nature of its products would make financial distress very costly. Suppose the rate of inflation increased from 3 per cent to 6 per cent, increasing borrowing rates from 6 per cent to 9 per cent. How would this affect the optimal capital structures of these two firms?

14.12 Helix started an Internet company, Survey-Partner.com, which, unlike others in the industry, generated taxable earnings almost immediately. Helix owns 10 per cent of the shares, and the rest of the shares are held by tax-exempt institutions. The firm needs to raise £100 million in new capital. Helix would like to see the firm issue equity, and would be willing to purchase £10 million of the new equity to keep his ownership stake constant. However, the institutions would like to see the firm raise the capital through debt. Explain how part of this disagreement might be related to taxes

14.13 ABC GmbH, financed with both equity and €10 million in perpetual debt, has pre-tax cash flow estimates for the current year as follows:

Probability	Pre-tax cash flow
0.3	€1.5 million
0.5	€2 million
0.2	€4 million

The corporate tax rate is 38.36 per cent, the effective personal tax rate on equity is 0 per cent, and the interest rate on the perpetual debt is 10 per cent. If the expected after-tax cash flows to the debt holders, as a group, are the same as the expected after-tax cash flows to the equity holders, as a group, what is the personal tax rate on debt?

14.14 B&D Builders Ltd is financed entirely with equity, and has grown very quickly over the past eight years. The firm has hired the consulting firm of M&P Ltd to analyse the firm's financing. The consulting firm recommends that the firm borrow £100 million (face value) in perpetual riskless debt at the current market interest rate of 10 per cent and buy back £100 million in equity. The founders, a team of brothers who know how to build houses very well, but not finance, explain that taking on debt would reduce the earnings available to equity each year by the amount of the interest, and thus reduce the value of the equity's claim, Therefore it would not benefit the shareholders, most of whom are family. Analyse the founders' argument, and compute the value of the debt tax shield proposed by M&P Ltd, assuming that $T_E = 0.18$, $T_D = 0.40$ and $T_C = 0.28$.

References and Additional Reading

Asquith, P. and Wizman, T. (1990) Event risk, covenants, and bondholder returns in leveraged buyouts, *Journal of Financial Economics*, 27(1): 195–213.

Brounen, D., de Jong, A. and Koedjik, C.G. (2004) Corporate finance in Europe: confronting theory with practice, *Financial Management*, 33: 71–101.

DeAngelo, H. and Masulis, R. (1980) Optimal capital structure under corporate and personal taxes, *Journal of Financial Economics*, 8(1): 3–29.

Faff, R., Hillier, D. and Wood, J. (2000) Beta and return: implications of Australia's dividend imputation system, *Australian Journal of Management*, 25(3): 245–260.

Faulkender, M. and Petersen, M.A. (2006) Does the source of capital affect capital structure?, *The Review of Financial Studies*, 19(1): 45–79.

Fisher, I. (1930) *The Theory of Interest*. Reprint (1965). New York: Augustus Kelly.

Gaud, P., Jani, E., Hoesli, M. and Bender, A. (2005) The capital structure of Swiss companies: an empirical analysis using dynamic panel data, *European Financial Management*, 11(1): 51–69.

Givoly, D., Hayn, C., Ofer, A. and Sarig, O. (1992) Taxes and capital structure: evidence from firms' response to the Tax Reform Act of 1986, *The Review of Financial Studies*, 5(2): 331–355.

Goyal, V and Murray, F. (2010) Capital structure decisions: which factors are reliably important?, *Financial Management*, 38(1): 1–37.

Graham, J. (1996) Debt and the marginal tax rate, *Journal of Financial Economics*, 41(1): 41–73.

Graham, J. (2000) How big are the tax benefits of debt?, *The Journal of Finance*, 55(5): 1901–1941.

Graham, J. (2008) Taxes and corporate finance, in B.E. Eckbo (ed.), *Handbook of Corporate Finance: Empirical Corporate Finance*. Amsterdam: Elsevier Science.

Graham, J. and Harvey, C. (2001) The theory and practice of corporate finance: evidence from the field, *Journal of Financial Economics*, 60(2–3): 187–243.

Graham, J., Michael Lemmon, M. and Schallheim, J. (1998) Debt, leases, taxes, and the endogeneity of corporate tax status, *The Journal of Finance*, 53(1): 131–162.

Kayhan, A. and Titman, S. (2007) Firms' histories and their capital structures, *Journal of Financial Economics*, 83(1): 1–32.

MacKie-Mason, J.K. (1990) Do taxes affect corporate financing decisions?, *The Journal of Finance*, 45(5): 1471–1493.

Miguel, A. de and Pindado J. (2001) Determinants of capital structure: new evidence from Spanish panel data, *Journal of Corporate Governance*, 7(1): 77–99.

Miller, M.H. (1977) Debt and taxes, *The Journal of Finance*, 32(2): 261–275.

Modigliani, F. and Miller, M.H. (1958) The cost of capital, corporation finance, and the theory of investment, *American Economic Review*, 48(3): 261–297.

Ozkan, A. (2001) Determinants of capital structure and adjustment to long run target: evidence from UK company panel data, *Journal of Business Finance and Accounting*, 28(1–2): 175–198.

Titman, S. and Wessels, R. (1988) The determinants of capital structure choice, *The Journal of Finance*, 43(1): 1–19.

Wald, J.K. (1999) How firm characteristics affect capital structure: an international comparison, *Journal of Financial Research*, 22(2): 161–187.

Warga, A. and Welch, I. (1993) Bondholder losses in leveraged buyouts, *The Review of Financial Studies*, 6(4): 959–982.

Appendix 14A: How Personal Taxes Affect the Capital Structure Choice: The Miller Equilibrium

In his 1976 presidential address to the American Finance Association, 'Debt and taxes', Merton Miller presented a model where, in equilibrium, firms are indifferent between financing their new investments by issuing debt or issuing equity. This model is called the **Miller equilibrium**. In the Miller equilibrium, equation (14.8) holds, so that the after-tax cost of debt equals the cost of equity financing.

To understand Miller's argument, we shall look first at the demand by investors for debt and equity instruments. We then consider the incentive of firms to supply these instruments. The equilibrium in this market is determined at the point where the amount of debt and equity supplied by firms equals the amount of each instrument demanded by investors at the instruments' equilibrium rates of return.

Recall that if the pre-tax costs of debt and equity (adjusted for risk premiums) are equal, then debt is cheaper on an after-corporate tax basis. This is the case considered in Chapter 13, where a firm's weighted average cost of capital was shown to decline as the firm added debt to its capital structure. In this case, if there are no offsetting costs associated with debt financing, firms have an incentive to increase their debt levels, and will do so by issuing debt to repurchase their own shares.

As Exhibit 14A.1 illustrates, the Miller equilibrium assumes that the supply curve for debt, the light line, is flat. Since Miller assumes that there are no costs associated with debt financing (for example, no bankruptcy costs), firms will use debt financing exclusively if the cost of debt, $r_D(1 - T_C)$, is less than the cost of equity, $\bar{r}_E$, and they will use equity financing exclusively otherwise.

Tax-exempt investors are willing to invest their entire portfolio in debt as long as its zero-beta expected rate of return exceeds the expected rate of return of zero-beta equity. The demand curve for debt, the dark line, would then be flat up to the point where the supply of funds from tax-exempt investors is exhausted. To induce taxable investors to hold debt instruments, a return premium must be offered, because debt is a tax-disadvantaged instrument from their perspective. Hence the demand curve slopes upwards after the point at

Exhibit 14A.1 Miller Equilibrium

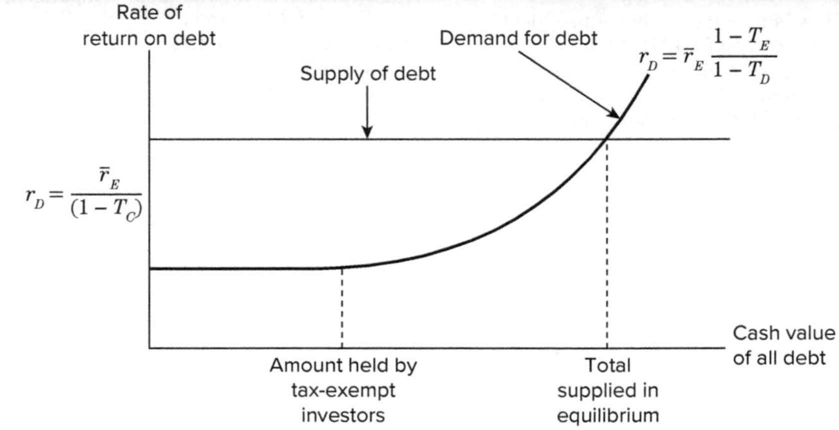

which the tax-exempt investors are fully invested, which reflects the fact that investors in higher tax brackets require increasingly higher debt returns to hold debt instead of equity.

To understand the Miller equilibrium, consider first the case where the pre-tax returns on zero-beta debt and equity are the same. In this case, firms have an incentive to increase leverage, and will continue to replace equity with debt financing, moving up the demand curve by increasing the return they offer as a group to debt investors until the after-tax cost of zero-beta debt equals the cost of zero-beta equity. This point is reached at the intersection of the supply and demand curves in Exhibit 14A.1.

In this equilibrium, the investor who is indifferent between holding debt and equity must have tax rates that satisfy equation (14.4),

$$r_D(1 - T_D) = \bar{r}_E(1 - T_E)$$

and the equilibrium rates from the supply curve

$$r_D(1 - T_C) = \bar{r}_E$$

must be satisfied. By combining the above equations, we see that the tax rates for the indifferent investor satisfy

$$1 - T_D = (1 - T_C)(1 - T_E)$$

which makes T_g zero. In other words, at the personal tax rates of the investor who is indifferent between holding debt and equity, there is no tax gain from leverage for the firm.

The conditions that must be satisfied for the existence of the equilibrium described above are described in Result 14A.1.

Results

Results 14A.1

(*The Miller equilibrium.*) If the following assumptions hold:

- the interest deduction for debt always reduces taxes at the margin – that is, firms experience positive earnings after paying interest,
- $(1 - T_D)$ is less than $(1 - T_C)(1 - T_E)$ for some investors – that is, investors who prefer equity to debt,
- there are no costs such as bankruptcy costs associated with increasing debt levels,

then, in equilibrium, $T_g = 0$: that is, $(1 - T_D) = (1 - T_C)(1 - T_E)$ and $r_D(1 - T_C) = \bar{r}_E$. This implies that firms should be indifferent about leverage when both corporate taxes and personal taxes are taken into account.

Discussion of the Miller Equilibrium

In the Miller equilibrium, the total supply of debt in the economy is determined at the intersection of the supply and demand curves illustrated in Exhibit 14A.1. However, the amount of debt supplied by each firm is a matter of indifference.

That such an important decision is a matter of indifference is not unusual in economics. Consider a group of farmers who can produce either apples or oranges. If competition eliminates economic rents from both products, the farmers will be indifferent about which product to produce. However, consumer tastes will determine the mix of apples and oranges produced in the entire economy. Similarly, in the Miller equilibrium, competition implies that the relative advantages associated with issuing debt and equity securities vanish, making firms ultimately indifferent about which to issue. Again, consumer tastes – in this case, investor tastes for receiving ordinary income instead of capital gains – determine the mix of debt and equity in the economy as a whole.

Key Term

Chapter 15

How Taxes Affect Dividends and Share Repurchases

Learning Objectives

After reading this chapter, you should be able to:

- Explain why, in the absence of personal taxes, there is an equivalence between dividends and share repurchases, and why tax-paying investors prefer a share repurchase to a dividend payment.
- Provide reasons why firms pay taxed dividends instead of repurchasing shares.
- Understand the difference between the classical tax system and the imputation system, and how these differences affect capital structures and dividend policies.
- Understand empirical evidence about how expected equity returns relate to dividend yields.
- Describe how personal taxes on dividend distributions can lead to distortions in both investment and financing decisions.

In June 2022, Polar Capital plc, a financial services fund that manages a range of investment trusts, announced a 15 per cent increase in its annual dividend. However, at the same time, the company announced that its profit before tax fell by 18 per cent, despite its total income increasing by 7.6 per cent over the same period. To make matters more complex, core operating profit grew by 35 per cent, but performance fee profits fell by 78.9 per cent. Shares rose 1.5 per cent following the announcement. So what drove the share price movement? Was it performance, or was it due to an increase in the dividend? This chapter will consider this question in detail, drawing on recent research findings.

Dividend policy, which specifies a firm's policy on the distribution of cash to its shareholders, is perhaps the topic that financial economists have the most trouble discussing with corporate managers. Academics cite the **Miller–Modigliani dividend irrelevancy theorem,** which states that, except for tax and transaction cost considerations, dividend policy is irrelevant. Corporate managers, however, who sometimes spend long hours considering their dividend choices, think that this irrelevance proposition is crazy. This difference of opinion persists despite numerous articles on the subject in professional and academic journals, as well as academic forums that bring together participants from both academia and business.

The communication gap between financial economists and corporate managers stems, at least in part, from the fact that the two groups often consider different issues when they think about dividend policy. When corporate managers talk about optimal dividend policies, they are to a large extent really discussing the investment and cash payout policies of their firms. Managers are asking whether earnings could be better invested within the firm rather than outside the firm. They also think about how dividend policies affect their leverage ratios, and about the trade-offs between financing new investments with internally generated equity versus increasing dividends and funding the new investments with debt.

Financial economists view the dividend choice from a narrower perspective, stressing that a firm's dividend choice need not be related to either its investment decisions or its leverage decision. Financial economists believe that any analysis of a firm's dividend policy should hold the firm's investment decisions and its capital structure choice constant.

As this chapter later shows, when investment choices and leverage ratios are held constant, the only alternative to paying a dividend is for the firm to use the funds to repurchase shares. Hence most of the academic literature on dividend policy considers the pros and cons of paying dividends versus repurchasing shares. For example, the Miller–Modigliani dividend irrelevancy theorem does not say that the choice between paying dividends and retaining the earnings to either pay off debt or to fund new investment is a matter of indifference. Rather, it merely says that, in the absence of tax and transaction cost considerations, the way in which the earnings are distributed to shareholders – that is, the choice between paying a dividend and repurchasing shares – does not affect shareholders.

This chapter analyses how taxes and transaction costs affect the way firms distribute cash to their shareholders. It shows that share repurchases are the better alternative for most investors who must pay personal taxes. However, some tax-exempt investors may prefer to receive cash distributions in the form of dividends because of their lower transaction costs. The chapter also examines how personal taxes and transaction costs can make internally generated funds less expensive than externally generated funds. As a result, personal taxes and transaction costs affect how firms are financed, as well as how investment choices are made.[1]

15.1 How Much of Corporate Earnings is Distributed to Shareholders?

Aggregate Dividend Payouts

Exhibit 15.1 summarizes dividend payout data for a sample of countries in 2021, and represents the percentage of firms on Worldscope, a financial database, that paid dividends during that year. A caveat to the results is that the data for international firms on Worldscope is incomplete, and may give an unrepresentative picture for some countries. The exhibit reveals that the percentage of firms that pay dividends is extremely varied across countries. Moreover, the location or financial development of the country does not seem to be a factor in which countries pay dividends.

One of the aspects of payout policy is that share repurchases can substitute for dividend payments. Indeed, this appears to be one of the reasons why there are significant differences across countries in Exhibit 15.1. Von Eije and Megginson (2008) show for fifteen European Union countries, and Skinner (2008) shows for the USA, that share repurchases have become a more common method of payout to shareholders than dividends. For example, in the EU, share repurchases accounted for more than half of the dividends paid by firms (von Eije and Megginson 2008).

Dividend Policies of Selected Firms

Exhibit 15.2 provides a representative sample of well-known corporations and their **dividend yields,** the ratio of the dividend per share to the price per share, and **dividend payout ratios,** the ratio of the dividend per share to the earnings per share (income before extraordinary items) for 2021. The exhibit reveals major

[1] In addition, as Chapter 21 discusses, the taxes and transaction costs associated with distributing cash also provide an important motive for why firms hedge their cash flows.

Exhibit 15.1 Percentage of Firms that Pay Dividends

Country	% firms that pay dividends	Country	% firms that pay dividends
Australia	21.97%	New Zealand	51.89%
Austria	66.67%	Norway	43.28%
Belgium	68.13%	Portugal	50.00%
Canada	10.63%	Singapore	53.02%
Denmark	41.06%	South Africa	61.76%
Finland	58.52%	South Korea	44.97%
France	46.14%	Spain	50.61%
Germany	54.04%	Sweden	30.47%
Hong Kong	36.95%	Switzerland	69.85%
Ireland	51.61%	Thailand	64.51%
Italy	63.16%	Turkey	35.08%
Japan	76.75%	United Kingdom	48.78%
Malaysia	46.62%	United States	29.23%
Netherlands	54.17%		

Source: Worldscope (2022)

Exhibit 15.2 Selected Dividend Yields and Payout Ratios, 2010–2021

Company name	Country	Industry	Dividend yield (%)	Payout ratio (%)
Microsoft	USA	Software	0.70	27.81
McDonald's	USA	Restaurants	1.96	52.31
Boeing	USA	Aerospace/defence	0.00	0.00
Kingfisher	UK	Home improvement	2.97	30.77
Marks & Spencer	UK	Retail	0.00	0.00
Celtic	UK	Football	0.00	0.00
PetroChina	China	Oil/gas	4.62	45.00
Siam Cement	Thailand	Cement	4.79	47.06
Glanbia	Ireland	Cheese/meat prod.	2.38	50.86
Siemens	Germany	Conglomerate	0.38	26.13
Avenir Telecom	France	Telecommunications	0.00	0.00
Nokia	Finland	Telecommunications	0.00	0.00
Neways Electronics	Netherlands	ICT/electronics	9.47	188.73
Telefonica	Spain	Telecommunications	7.24	20.26
Atlantia	Italy	Aerospace	4.24	96.79
Distell Group	South Africa	Distillers	0.00	0.00

Source: Worldscope (2022)

differences in the dividend policies of various types of firm. Normally, high-tech growth firms have both low dividend yields and low payout ratios. Nokia is a good example of this. Microsoft is also interesting, since it has a payout ratio of 27.81 per cent. The reason for this is that the market for Windows products is saturated and, as a result, Microsoft has found it difficult to identify good investments. As a result, it has a much higher payout ratio than would be expected for a high-tech firm. It is notable that many firms in Exhibit 15.2 paid no dividends in 2021 as a result of the global disruption cause by the pandemic restrictions around the world at the time. Another interesting aspect of Exhibit 15.2 is that Alitalia paid out nearly 100 per cent of its earnings and Neways Electronics paid out over 100 per cent of its earnings. Payout ratios over 100 per cent are most likely due to dividend smoothing, where the board makes a decision to keep dividends at a specific level even though earnings figures have fallen suddenly. Finally, if we were to carry out a historical analysis, dividend yields and payout ratios would have fallen for most firms. This is partly due to the continuing trend of firms substituting share repurchases for dividends (von Eije and Megginson 2008).

15.2 Distribution Policy in Frictionless Markets

As we discuss later in this chapter, the dividend choice is closely related to the capital structure choice, and, like the capital structure choice, is strongly influenced by market frictions such as taxes and transaction costs. Before considering how market frictions affect dividend policy, we examine a simple case where there are no transaction costs and no taxes, and where the dividend choice conveys no information to investors.[2] An analysis of this case serves as a useful benchmark for understanding the more realistic settings examined later. We shall start with the case in which the firm knows how much cash it would like to distribute, but has not decided whether to distribute the cash by paying a dividend or by repurchasing shares.

The Miller–Modigliani Dividend Irrelevancy Theorem

In their classic article, Miller and Modigliani (1961) examined a firm that wanted to distribute a fixed amount of cash to its shareholders either by repurchasing shares or by paying a cash dividend. The authors assumed that the choice between these two alternatives would affect neither the firm's investment decisions nor its operations. Given these assumptions, they demonstrated that, in the absence of personal taxes and transaction costs, the choice between paying a dividend and repurchasing shares is a matter of indifference. Shareholders are indifferent, and firm values are unaffected by which of the two methods is used. Result 15.1 summarizes the Miller–Modigliani dividend irrelevancy theorem.

Results

Result 15.1

(*The Miller–Modigliani dividend irrelevancy theorem.*) Consider the choice between paying a dividend and using an equivalent amount of money to repurchase shares. Assume that:

- there are no tax considerations
- there are no transaction costs
- the investment, financing and operating policies of the firm are held fixed.

Then the choice between paying dividends and repurchasing shares is a matter of indifference to shareholders.

[2] Chapter 19 examines how information considerations affect dividend policy.

A Proof of the Miller–Modigliani Theorem

To understand Result 15.1, consider two similar equity-financed biotech firms with different dividend policies.

- One firm, Signetics, has announced that it will pay a £1 million dividend next year.
- The other firm, Comgen, has announced that it will repurchase £1 million in outstanding shares.
- At the end of the year, the firms will each be worth the same amount, X (after paying dividends or repurchasing shares), which lies somewhere between £10 million and £20 million, depending on industry conditions.
- Each firm initially has 1 million shares outstanding.

These assumptions imply that a share of Signetics will sell for one-millionth of $\widetilde{X}$ at the end of the year: hence, if $\widetilde{X}$ is £15 million, each share will be worth £15. Calculating the year-end value of Comgen equity is slightly more complicated. Comgen will repurchase N shares for £1 million, which implies that

$$\text{share price} \times N = £1 \text{ million} \tag{15.1}$$

Since the year-end value of Comgen equals $\widetilde{X}$, its share price must satisfy

$$\text{share price} = \frac{\widetilde{X}}{1 \text{ million} - N} \tag{15.2}$$

For example, if $\widetilde{X}$ is £15 million, then equations (15.1) and (15.2), two equations with two unknown variables, can be solved for both N and the share price. With $\widetilde{X}$ equal to £15 million, Comgen will repurchase 62,500 shares at a price of £16 per share. In this case, a tax-exempt investor who holds 100 shares of Signetics equity receives a dividend of £100 (£1 dividend per share), and holds shares worth £1,500 (£15 per share). If this same investor holds 100 shares of Comgen equity, he receives no dividends at the end of the year. However, his shares will be worth £1,600. In both cases, the value of the shares plus the cash dividend (for Signetics) is the same.

Although the above example assumes that the year-end value was £15 million for both Signetics and Comgen, the equivalence between dividends and share repurchases holds regardless of the firms' year-end values, as long as they are the same for the two firms. The future values of these two corporations are assumed to track each other perfectly, regardless of their dividend policies. Thus the two firms, which differ only in their dividend policies, should sell for the same initial price. If Signetics and Comgen shares sell for different prices, then there will be an arbitrage opportunity, as Example 15.1 illustrates.

Example 15.1

Arbitrage Opportunities that Arise when the Miller–Modigliani Theorem Does Not Hold

Suppose that Signetics equity is currently selling at £13 a share and Comgen is selling at £12.80 a share. What can an investor do to realize an arbitrage gain?

Answer: An investor who buys 100 shares of Comgen for £12.80 a share and sells short 100 shares of Signetics at £13 a share will realize an initial £20 cash inflow. This £20 is free money; there will be no net cash outflow at the end of the year.

For example, assume that both companies are going to be worth either £10 million or £20 million next year. The Comgen shares will then be worth either £20 per share or £10 per share, depending on industry conditions. The Signetics shares will be worth either £9 per share or £19 per share, depending on the state of the economy, plus a dividend of £1 per share. Hence the year-end value of this arbitrage portfolio is zero, regardless of the state of the economy.

Example 15.1 shows that if two firms are equivalent except for their dividend policies, their values should be the same in the absence of taxes and transaction costs. If the values are not the same, then smart investors can realize arbitrage profits.

Real-World Insights

Merck

Consider the German pharmaceutical firm Merck. On 30 April, the company paid out a dividend of €1.05 per share. Given that it had 51.3 million shares, this amounted to a total of €53.865 million. Exhibit 15.3 compares the effects on the value of Merck if it had repurchased €53.865 million of its own equity instead. Ignoring taxes and transaction costs, investors would be indifferent between the two alternatives.[3]

Exhibit 15.3 Merck's Choice: Dividends or Share Repurchase

	Before transaction (in millions)	Pay €53.865 million in dividends (in millions)	Repurchase €53.865 million of equity (in millions)
Share price at 30 April	€100	€100	€100
No. of shares	51.3	51.3	51.3
Market capitalization	€5,100.3	€5,100.3	€5,100.3
Dividends		€53.865	
Market cap after dividends		€5,046.435	
Shares repurchased			0.538650
Market cap after repurchase			€5,046.435
Shares outstanding	51.3	51.3	50.76135
Equity value per share	€100	€98.37105	€99.41491
Dividends per share		€1.05	
Investors proceeds from selling shares			€53.865
Investor portfolio value (in € millions)	€5,100.3	€5,100.3	€5,100.3

Optimal Payout Policy in the Absence of Taxes and Transaction Costs

Let's now consider the trade-off between distributing earnings to shareholders, either by paying a dividend or repurchasing shares, and retaining the earnings to increase internal investment. The previous subsections indicated that, in the absence of taxes and transaction costs, dividends and share repurchases are equivalent. Therefore a distinction between the two methods of distribution at this point is unnecessary.

Result 15.2 specifies the assumptions made up to this point, along with their implications for the corporation's choice between distributing or retaining the earnings.

[3] Accounting considerations also may lead firms to prefer share repurchases over dividends. Compared with dividends, share repurchases generally increase both earnings per share and return on shareholder's equity.

Results

Result 15.2

Consider the choice between paying out earnings to shareholders versus retaining the earnings for investment. Assume that:

- there are no tax considerations
- there are no transaction costs
- the choice between paying a dividend and retaining the earnings for reinvestment within the firm does not convey any information to shareholders.

Then a dividend payout will either increase or decrease the firm's value, depending on whether there are positive net present value (NPV) investments that could be funded by retaining the money within the firm. If there are no positive-NPV investments, then the money should be paid out.

Result 15.2 restates the more fundamental point discussed in Part 3 of this text. With frictionless capital markets, firms should accept all positive-NPV projects and reject all negative ones. However, as we see below, this will not necessarily be the case when taxes and transaction costs are present.

15.3 The Effect of Taxes and Transaction Costs on Distribution Policy

One of the major differences in corporate finance across the world is the way in which taxes are charged on dividends. There are two main approaches to charging tax: the classical tax system and the imputation tax system. We'll deal first with the classical tax system, which taxes profits at the corporate tax rate and then taxes dividends at the personal income tax rate. This is, in effect, a double taxation of corporate profits. In many countries, such as the USA and Netherlands, corporations first pay corporate taxes on their earnings, and shareholders pay tax again on the distributed profits. Example 15.2 shows that, from a shareholder's perspective, the effective tax on corporations that operate in a classical tax system can be considerable.

Example 15.2

The Effective Tax Rate on Walt Disney's Profits

Walt Disney Company earned \$2.56 billion in pre-tax profits in 2021. Assume that its corporate tax rate was 28 per cent and that Bob Chapek, the chief executive, owns 10 per cent of the firm's shares, and has a personal marginal tax rate of 37 per cent. From Chapek's perspective, what is the effective tax rate on Walt Disney's profits if its entire after-tax profits are distributed as a dividend and it operates under a classical tax system?

Answer: Walt Disney will pay \$716.8 million in corporate taxes and distribute \$1.843 billion to shareholders in the form of a dividend. Chapek thus receives \$184.3 million in dividends and pays \$68.1984 million in personal taxes, leaving him with \$116.1216 million after taxes from his \$256 million share of the firm's pre-tax profits. From Chapek's perspective, the effective tax rate on corporate profits is 54.64 per cent [= 1 – (\$116.1216 million/\$256 million)].

A Comparison of the Classical and Imputation Tax Systems

Several countries have changed their tax systems to eliminate the double taxation of corporate profits. Greece and Norway, for example, allow dividends to be deducted from corporate taxes, and thus treat dividends and interest payments symmetrically. Australia has an **imputation system** and the UK has a partial imputation system, under which investors who receive taxable dividends get a tax credit for part or all of the taxes paid by the corporation. This tax credit at least partly offsets the personal taxes these investors must pay on dividend income.

All textbooks that are written in the United States for an American readership will focus on the **classical tax system.** In a classical tax system, dividends are taxed as ordinary income, and capital gains are generally taxed at a lower rate than ordinary income. Shareholders do not receive tax credits, offsetting the taxes paid by corporations, which implies that the classical tax system effectively double-taxes corporate profits. In 2022, dividend income is taxed at 20 per cent in the USA for most people but low-income individuals pay no tax on dividends received. In many other countries, the classical tax system has been replaced by an imputation system, so much of what is written in US textbooks may not be appropriate.

Financial economists and policymakers have expressed concern about the adverse consequences of the classical tax system, and have suggested that countries move to an imputation system. In particular, under the classical system, the cost of funding investments through retained earnings is lower than the cost of funding investment by issuing new equity. As a result, new firms with promising opportunities but insufficient amounts of internally generated cash will find it more expensive to fund their investment needs than more mature firms with less promising opportunities.

The Tax System in the United Kingdom

Tax systems and tax rates change continually. As of 2022, dividends in the United Kingdom are taxed at three different rates, depending on the investor's annual income. If an individual earns less than £50,270 in a year, their tax rate on dividends is 8.75 per cent, and if they earn up to £150,000 (but above £50,270) they must pay 33.75 per cent. Individuals in the highest tax bracket (income above £150,000) must pay 39.35 per cent. The United Kingdom has a partial imputation tax system, and a tax-free dividend allowance of £2,000 per annum is applied to dividends before any tax is charged.

Other Tax Systems

To cover all the details and intricacies of each country's tax codes is far beyond the remit of this text. Readers should refer to their country's tax authorities for the most up-to-date guidance on dividend taxes and any possible exemptions or discounts.

How Taxes Affect Dividend Policy

Personal taxes on dividends can profoundly affect a firm's choice between paying dividends and repurchasing shares. Because the pre-tax proceeds from the two strategies are equal, the only difference between the two methods of cash distribution is the amount of the tax liability generated by each. Switzerland is a good case study to understand the effect of taxes on dividend policy. Corporate tax reform in 2011 led to a subset of Swiss companies being able to pay tax-exempt dividends. After the tax cut, companies able to take advantage of zero tax rates on dividends increased their payouts by 30 per cent, which strongly suggests that tax is an important factor in dividend policy (Isakov et al. 2021).

The Tax Disadvantage of Dividends

Exhibit 15.4 details the immediate tax consequences for an individual investor if a firm chooses to distribute £100 million in the form of a dividend versus distributing £100 million as a share repurchase. It assumes that the investor currently owns 10 per cent of the outstanding shares, and plans on maintaining the 10 per cent

Exhibit 15.4 Tax Consequences: Dividend versus Share Repurchase (in £ millions)

Dividend alternative	
Dividend	£100.0
Tax rate	× 22.5%
Immediate tax liability	£22.50
Share repurchase alternative	
Proceeds from sale of 20 million shares	£100.0
Less original cost (at £3.80/share)	−76.0
Taxable capital gain	£24.0
Tax rate	× 18%
Immediate tax liability	£4.32

ownership. It also assumes that the shares, if repurchased, will be repurchased at a price of £5.00 a share, and that they were originally purchased at a price of £3.80 a share. It uses 22.5 per cent as the tax rate on dividends and 18 per cent as the tax rate on capital gains.

Although the *immediate* tax liability is considerably higher with the dividend alternative, the *future* tax liability incurred by shareholders when their shares are eventually sold is higher when shares are repurchased. This is because the share prices drop by the amount of the dividend when a dividend is paid, making the future capital gains lower for shareholders who purchased equity prior to the dividend. However, the total amount paid in taxes (and its present value) is still considerably lower with the repurchase alternative.

Results

Result 15.3

In many countries, taxes favour share repurchases over dividends. The gain associated with a share repurchase over a cash dividend depends on:

- the difference between the capital gains rate and the tax rate on ordinary income
- the tax basis of the shares – that is, the price at which the shares were purchased
- the timing of the sale of the shares (if soon, the gain is less, but if too soon, the gain may not qualify for the long-term capital gains rate).

Can Individual Investors Avoid the Dividend Tax?

Miller and Scholes (1978) claimed that individual investors should be indifferent between repurchases and dividends, because they can avoid the tax on dividends. Their dividend tax avoidance scheme is quite simple: an individual borrows money and invests in tax-deferred or tax-free savings accounts. The interest on the loan is tax deductible, and can offset the taxable dividend income but not the individual's labour income. These transactions are illustrated in Example 15.3.

Example 15.3

Deferring the Dividend Tax

Ronald Simpson has £12,000 in dividend income. How can he defer the taxes on this dividend if he can borrow at 6 per cent, and tax-free savings accounts pay an interest rate of 6 per cent?

Answer: Ronald should borrow £200,000 at 6 per cent and invest the proceeds in a tax-deferred insurance annuity. By doing this, the tax on the £12,000 dividend is deferred (since the dividend is offset by the £12,000 interest payment) until the money is withdrawn from the insurance annuity.

In reality, individual investors rarely avoid the dividend tax in the way that Miller and Scholes suggest. Indeed, Feenberg (1981) found that individual investors in the USA paid over $8 billion in taxes on dividend income in 1977. Similar findings by Peterson et al. (1985) indicated that individual tax returns included more than $33 billion of dividend income in 1979, which was slightly more than two-thirds of the total amount of dividends paid by US corporations. Thus, since shareholders seem unable to avoid taxes on dividends, the argument of Miller and Scholes fails to explain why corporations continue to pay dividends, given the tax advantages of share repurchases.

The Miller and Scholes insights may be useful for individuals wishing to reduce their own taxes. However, deferring taxes may be more difficult in practice than in theory. It requires, for example, that investors be able to borrow on the same terms that they invest in the tax-free savings account, matching investment horizon as well as rates. It also assumes that there are no costs associated with such transactions.

Dividend Clienteles

The tax advantages of a share repurchase do not apply to all investors. A large percentage of investors are tax exempt (for example, pension funds and university endowments). As previously demonstrated, these investors are indifferent between receiving dividends or having the firm repurchase shares when there are no transaction costs. In reality, however, transaction costs *do* exist. Shareholders and the firm must pay brokerage fees as part of a share repurchase. Also, shares repurchased with a tender offer usually carry underwriting fees and registration costs. Although these transaction costs are small relative to the tax gains enjoyed by taxable investors with repurchases, they might lead tax-exempt investors to prefer dividends.

Some authors (Allen et al. 2000; Baker and Wurgler 2004; Graham and Kumar 2006; Li and Lie 2006, Korkeamaki et al. 2009, Jiang et al. 2013) have suggested that firms have different dividend payout ratios to appeal to different **investor clienteles** – that is, the different groups of investors with different tastes for receiving dividend income. Firms that pay no dividends are likely to attract individual investors in high tax brackets, whereas firms that pay large dividends are likely to attract tax-exempt institutions, individual investors in low marginal tax brackets and corporations attracted by the dividend tax preference. In relation to this, Brown et al. (2007) showed that dividend policy varied with the shareholdings of managers rather than individuals.

Tax reform in Finland in 2004 allowed Korkeamaki et al. (2010) to study dividend clienteles when the country moved from an imputation system to a partial classical tax system of double taxation on corporate income. Korkeamaki et al. (2010) found that Finnish firms changed their dividend policy to reflect the impact of the new tax regime on their largest shareholders. Empirical tests by Pettit (1977), Lewellen et al. (1978), and Desai and Lin (2011) provide further evidence that the dividend yields of investors' portfolios are related to their marginal tax rates. Investors with high marginal tax rates tend to select equities with low dividend yields, and investors with low or zero marginal tax rates tend to select equities with high dividend yields.

Why do Corporations Pay Out so Much in Taxed Dividends?

The previous subsection suggested that some investors prefer dividends to share repurchases, while others prefer share repurchases to dividends. However, the dividend tax borne by the taxable investor is likely to be larger than the transaction costs associated with a repurchase, suggesting that corporate values would probably increase if firms cut their dividends and repurchased shares instead. Total payout behaviour has also changed massively. Kahle and Stulz (2020) report that aggregate payouts (dividends plus share repurchases) have tripled during the 2000–2019 period compared with the thirty-year period between 1970 and 1999. This has led some financial economists to suggest that the dividend policy of some firms is something of a puzzle.[4] To understand why dividend policy is so puzzling, consider the situation in the United States during the 1960s and 1970s. Most investors during this period were individual investors, many of whom paid taxes at marginal tax rates as high as 70 per cent. For these investors the tax advantage of a share repurchase over a dividend was very large, but repurchases were uncommon at that time. While we can only speculate on why US firms paid out so much in tax-disadvantaged dividends at that time, our best guess is that the decisions of financial managers at that time were simply wrong, and that most shareholders would have been better off if corporations had cut dividends and, instead, repurchased shares.

The explosion in repurchase activity that began in the 1980s supports the hypothesis that most managers previously had misunderstood the relationship between dividends and share repurchases, and were changing their behaviour to reflect their improved understanding of the tax advantage of share repurchases. Of course, other changes may have been taking place in the 1980s that would have made repurchases more attractive than dividends. However, the tax law changes in 1982 and 1986, which substantially decreased the tax disadvantage of dividends, should have had the opposite effect. In addition, the percentage of equity held by tax-exempt institutions greatly increased over this period, increasing the percentage of shareholders who might prefer dividends to share repurchases. These two changes had the effect of making dividends a relatively more attractive vehicle for paying out corporate cash than they previously were. Yet, share repurchases were, and still are, becoming increasingly popular.

Brav et al. (2005) surveyed 384 US financial executives to investigate their decisions and views regarding dividend policy. The survey provided some interesting insights: notably, the flexibility of share repurchases in timing market movements to the firm's benefit and increasing earnings per share were cited as the major

[4] See Black (1976) for an early discussion of this dividend puzzle.

reasons why share repurchases were preferred to dividends. In addition, the executives did not believe that there exist investor clienteles for dividend-paying equities, nor did they feel that tax considerations were particularly important. The Brav et al. (2005) results were subsequently contradicted by Becker et al. (2011), who found that firms headquartered in areas with more elderly investors were more likely to have higher dividend yields. The striking difference between academic research and executive perceptions is startling and raises more questions than answers.

15.4 How Dividend Policy Affects Expected Equity Returns

We have asserted that share repurchases provide a better method of distributing cash than dividends because most investors prefer capital gains income to an equivalent dividend taxed at a higher rate. Equities with higher dividend yields, to compensate investors for their tax disadvantage, should thus offer higher expected returns than similar equities with lower dividend yields. Firms with higher dividend yields, but equivalent cash flows, should then have lower values, reflecting the higher discount rates that apply to their cash flows.

Researchers have taken two approaches to evaluate the effect of dividend yield on expected equity returns. The first approach measures equity returns around the date that the equity trades ex-dividend. Recall from Chapter 8 that the *ex-dividend date* (or the ex-date) is the first date on which purchasers of new shares will not be entitled to receive the forthcoming dividend. For example, a dividend paid on 15 February may have an ex-dividend date of 5 February, which means that purchasers of equity on and after 5 February will not receive the dividend. Since investors who purchase the equity before the ex-dividend date (4 February or earlier in this example) receive the dividend, whereas those who purchase equity on or after this date do not, the decline in the share price on the ex-dividend date provides a measure of how much the market values the dividend. The second approach measures how dividend yield affects expected returns cross-sectionally.

Ex-Dividend Share Price Movements

Consider Example 15.4, which assumes that a dividend is taxed at an investor's personal income tax rate, and that capital gains are not taxed at all.

Example 15.4

The Decision to Purchase Equity Before or After the Ex-Dividend Date

Trevtex plans to pay a dividend of €1 per share. Tomorrow is the ex-dividend date, so investors who purchase the equity tomorrow will not receive the dividend. Assume that Trevtex is selling for €20.00 per share today, and is expected to sell for €19.20 per share tomorrow. Should an investor with a 33 per cent marginal tax rate, who is not taxed on capital gains, purchase the equity today and receive the dividend, or should the investor wait one day and purchase it without the dividend?

Answer: The net cost per share of buying the equity with the dividend is €20 minus €1 for the dividend plus the tax the investor must pay on the imminent dividend. For an investor with a 33 per cent marginal tax rate, this net cost is €19.33 per share. Hence purchasing the equity ex-dividend for €19.20 per share would be preferred to purchasing the equity for €20 per share just prior to the ex-dividend date, which has a net cost of €19.33. However, a tax-exempt investor would prefer to purchase the equity prior to the ex-dividend date, since the net cost per share is €19 (= €20 – €1).

Example 15.4 shows that a €1 dividend may be worth less than €1 because of personal taxes that investors must pay on the dividends. As a result, share prices will drop by less than the amount of the dividend on the ex-dividend date. For instance, the share price would fall by €0.67 after the payment of a €1.00 dividend if the marginal investor, who would be indifferent between buying either before or after the ex-dividend date, had a 33 per cent tax rate on dividends, assuming that there is no tax on capital gains.

Empirical Evidence on Price Drops on Ex-Dividend Dates

Elton and Gruber (1970) examined the price movements around the ex-dividend dates of listed equities from April 1966 to the end of March 1967. They found that, on average, the share price decline was 77.7 per cent of the dividend, which implies that shareholders place a value of only slightly more than $0.77 on a dividend of $1.00. The authors also found that the percentage price drop was related to the size of the dividend. For dividends greater than 5 per cent of the share price, the price drop on the ex-dividend date exceeded, on average, 90 per cent of the dividend. For the smallest dividends, however, the price drop on the ex-dividend date was closer to 50 per cent of the dividend.

Elton and Gruber interpreted the differential price drop as evidence of the investor clientele effect. Because the marginal investor in an equity with a high dividend yield is likely to have a low marginal tax rate, the after-tax value of the dividend should be relatively close to the amount of the payout. However, the marginal buyer of an equity with a low dividend yield is likely to have a high marginal tax rate and thus will place a much lower value on the dividends.

Non-Tax-Based Explanations for the Magnitudes of the Ex-Dividend Date Price Drops

A second explanation for the differential price drop was suggested by Kalay (1982). To understand this explanation, consider first the case where there are no transaction costs. In this case, if the share price drop was not close to the amount of the dividend, traders would have an opportunity to earn arbitrage profits. In Example 15.4, traders could buy the equity at €20.00, receive the €1.00 dividend, and sell the equity the next day for €19.20. Because the capital loss from the price drop is fully tax deductible at the personal income tax rate for short-term traders, this transaction yields an after-tax as well as a pre-tax gain. This arbitrage gain will exist as long as the price does not drop by the full amount of the dividend.

Consider next the case where there is a €0.10 per share transaction cost. In this case, the price need not drop the full €1.00, but it must drop at least €0.90, or 90 per cent of the dividend, to preclude arbitrage. However, on a €0.40 dividend, the price needs to drop only €0.30, or 75 per cent of the dividend, to preclude arbitrage. Hence, for smaller dividends, smaller price drops as a percentage of the dividend are needed to preclude arbitrage, which is exactly what Elton and Gruber observed. Consistent with this, if prices are set to preclude arbitrage, then returns on the ex-date that include the dividend should be independent of the amount of the dividend. This means that, on the margin, a 1 cent increase in the dividend should lead to a 1 cent increase in the price drop. A study by Boyd and Jagannathan (1994) found that this was indeed the case.

Other evidence leads us to suspect that the observed behaviour of share prices on ex-dividend dates may have nothing to do with taxes. First, the kind of behaviour observed on the ex-dividend date in the United States seems to be an international phenomenon, even where dividends are not tax disadvantaged. Frank and Jagannathan (1998) observed that, in Hong Kong, where dividends are not taxed, share price changes on ex-dividend dates are similar to those observed in the United States. This finding may have been due to an inefficient share registration system, which Hong Kong fixed in 1993, as share price drops on ex-dividend dates since 1993 have averaged about 100 per cent of the dividend. In addition, share prices also fall by much less than the amount of the dividend on the ex-dividend dates of equity dividends. Since equity dividends are not taxed, one cannot use a tax-based story to explain the share price behaviour around the time of ex-dividend dates for equity dividends.[5]

Since the original Elton and Gruber (1970) paper, many studies have been written that have tried to determine whether the tax explanation was true for other countries (see, for example, Menyah 1993; Michaely and Murgio 1995; McDonald 2001). Elton et al. (2005) revisited the original topic and, accepting the research that took place during the intervening period, carried out a similar study on a sample of taxable and non-taxable closed-end mutual funds for the period 1988 to 2001. Their findings reconfirmed the validity of the tax hypothesis. This is further supported by Graham et al. (2003) and Whitworth and Rao (2010).

The Cross-Sectional Relationship Between Dividend Yields and Equity Returns

If a firm's dividend policy is determined independently of its investment and operating decisions, the firm's future cash flows are also independent of its dividend policy. In this case, dividend policy can affect the value of a firm only by affecting the expected returns that investors use to discount those cash flows. For example, if dividends are taxed more heavily than capital gains, then, as noted earlier, investors must be compensated for this added tax by obtaining higher pre-tax returns on high-dividend-yielding equities. (They would not hold shares in such equities, and supply would not equal demand, if this were not true.)

[5] Studies by Eades et al. (1984) and Grinblatt et al. (1984) document positive returns on ex-dates for equity dividends and equity splits.

Equities with high dividend yields do, in fact, have higher returns, on average, than equities with low dividend yields. However, Blume (1980) recorded that the relationship between returns and dividend yield is actually U-shaped. Equities with zero dividend yields have substantially higher expected returns than equities with low dividend yields, but for equities that do pay dividends, expected returns increase with dividend yields. This finding is consistent with the idea that equities with zero dividend yields are extremely risky, but for firms that pay dividends, higher dividends require higher expected returns because of their tax disadvantage.

To test whether a return premium is associated with high-yield equities, several studies estimate cross-sectional regressions of the following general form:[6]

$$R_j = a + \gamma_1 \beta_j + \gamma_2 \text{ Divyld}_j + \varepsilon_j \tag{15.3}$$

where

β_j = the firm's beta

Divyld_j = the firm's expected dividend yield[7]

ε_j = the error term.

The hypothesis is that γ_2, which measures the effect of dividend yield on required returns, is positive to reflect the tax disadvantage of dividend payments, and that γ_1, the coefficient of beta, is positive to reflect the effect of systematic risk on returns. Most of these studies found that the coefficient of the expected dividend yield was positive, which they interpreted as evidence favouring a tax effect.

These interpretations assume that the beta estimates used as independent variables in the regression in equation (15.3) provide an adequate estimate of the equities' risks. However, as discussed in Chapter 5, finance academics find weak support for the idea that market betas provide a good measure of the kind of risk that investors wish to avoid. Distinguishing between tax and risk effects is further compounded by the relationship of the dividend yield to other firm characteristics that are likely to be related to risk and expected returns. For example, Keim (1985) showed that both firms paying no dividends and firms paying large dividends were primarily small firms. This suggests that the expected dividend yield may be acting as a proxy for firm size in the regression shown in equation (15.3). In addition to being related to firm size, dividend yield is correlated with a firm's expected future investment needs and its profitability – both attributes that are likely to affect the riskiness of a firm's equity.

In a slightly different approach, Baker and Wurgler (2006) considered the role of investor sentiment in the cross-section of equity returns. They found that investor sentiment has a larger effect on securities whose values are most subjectively calculated. Thus small, young, non-dividend-paying, high-growth or financially distressed firms will have high returns in the future when investor sentiment is high. In contrast, when market sentiment is high, these equities have relatively low returns. The rationale behind their results is that mispriced securities are those that experience an uninformed price shock in the existence of arbitrage constraints. Securities that are most difficult to value will be more sensitive to uninformed demand, and will thus react differently to investor sentiment.

Results

Result 15.4

Equities with high dividend yields are fundamentally different from equities with low dividend yields in terms of their characteristics and their risk profiles. Therefore it is nearly impossible to assess whether the relationship between dividend yield and expected returns is due to taxes, risk or other factors such as investor sentiment.

[6] The first study to test this specification was Brennan (1970), who concluded that there was a return premium associated with equities that have high dividend yields.

[7] The expected dividend yield, rather than the actual dividend yield, must be used in these regressions because of the information content of the dividend choice. For example, a firm that pays a high dividend in a given year is likely to have a high return in that year because of the favourable information conveyed by the dividend increase (which we shall discuss in detail in Chapter 19). Miller and Scholes (1982) pointed out that this information effect was ignored in the early studies on this topic, and, as a result, the purported finding of a tax effect was spurious.

However, Litzenberger and Ramaswamy (1982) measured an expected dividend yield, using information available prior to the time the returns were measured, and found the coefficient of the expected dividend yield to be positive and statistically significant, supporting the hypothesis of a tax-related preference for capital gains.

Since it may be impossible to detect whether paying dividends increases a firm's required expected rate of return, one cannot be certain that a policy of substituting share repurchases for dividends will have a lasting positive effect on the firm's share price. Although some articles by finance academics claim that dividends increase an equity's required rate of return, these studies are open to interpretation.

15.5 How Dividend Taxes Affect Financing and Investment Choices

Although it is very difficult to determine whether the taxation of dividends is reflected in equity returns, it is true that some investors incur a tax penalty when they receive dividends. In addition, firms impose taxes and transaction costs on their shareholders when they distribute excess cash by repurchasing shares. These taxes and transaction costs can distort investment and financing choices.

Dividends, Taxes and Financing Choices

This subsection re-examines the capital structure decision from the perspective of a firm that subjects its shareholders to personal tax liabilities when it distributes a portion of its earnings to them. Recall from Chapter 14 that most countries' tax systems bias firms towards issuing debt rather than equity financing. However, the analysis there largely ignored the distinction between internally generated and externally generated equity. This distinction is quite important, however, if distributed earnings are taxed at high personal rates.

Dividends, Taxes and Investment Distortions

The personal tax on dividends affects a firm's choice between paying out earnings and retaining them for internal investment. This section shows that shareholders who are taxed differently on their dividend income favour different investment policies for their firms.

The Investment Policy Favoured by Tax-Paying Shareholders

Assume that you own shares in Continental Corporation and have a marginal tax rate on personal dividend income of 22.5 per cent and 40 per cent on all other income. Suppose that Continental Corporation must decide whether to pay out an additional £1 million in dividends or to retain the earnings for internal investment. As the holder of 10 per cent of the outstanding shares, you have a major say in the decision, and need to consider the possibilities seriously. Your advisers calculate that, over the next five years, the firm will earn 6 per cent after corporate taxes with certainty on the £1 million, and that these earnings will be distributed to the shareholders in addition to the dividends they would have received otherwise. At the end of the five years, the £1 million retained this year will be distributed to shareholders. In essence, the choice for shareholders is whether to defer the £1 million dividend for five years and receive, as compensation for this deferral, additional annual dividends of £60,000 per year (= £1 million × 0.06) in the interim period. Deferral does not seem particularly attractive at first glance, because the rate of return on five-year UK Treasury bonds is 7 per cent, which is where you would invest the dividend if it was paid now.

Your tax advisers, however, urge you to compare the after-tax cash flows from these alternatives, which appear in Exhibit 15.5. They suggest that, given your 22.5 per cent marginal tax rate on personal income, you are better off if the money is retained within the corporation. After taxes, the immediate £100,000 dividend (10 per cent of the £1 million distribution) would be worth only £77,500, which, according to Alternative 1 in Exhibit 15.5, generates only £3,255 per year after taxes if invested at 7 per cent.

The after-tax cash flows on the internally invested retained earnings, Alternative 2 in Exhibit 15.5, are higher than those on the distributed dividends, Alternative 1. A return is earned on the *entire* £1 million of earnings kept within the firm rather than on *77.5 per cent* of this amount, as is the case for Alternative 1, because the earnings are distributed. As a result, tax-paying investors tend to prefer retaining the earnings within the firm rather than receiving a cash dividend.

The Investment Policy Favoured by Tax-Exempt Shareholders

Tax-exempt institutions would evaluate these alternatives quite differently. From their perspective, assuming the same 10 per cent ownership of the outstanding shares, cash flows would be as specified in Exhibit 15.6. Thus, from the perspective of a tax-exempt institution, a cash dividend, Alternative 1, would be preferred.

The tax rate on the distribution is irrelevant, because the cash must eventually be distributed, either now or later, and the tax rate on the distribution is assumed to be the same in either case. However, if there are expected to be changes in the tax rate on the distribution, such changes could affect the payout/reinvestment decision. If, for example, tax rates on distributions are expected to increase, there will be an increased incentive to pay out cash flows now (when the tax on distributions is low), rather than later (when the tax rate on distributions is higher). Similarly, a corporation will have an incentive to delay distributions if it believes that the tax on distributions is going to decline.

Exhibit 15.5 After-Tax Cash Flows for a Taxable Investor

Alternative 1: Investment of after-tax dividend of £77,500 in Treasury bonds.					
Coupon payment is 7% of £77,500 = £5,425.					
After-tax cash flow is (1 – 40%) of £5,425 = £3,255					
After-tax cash flows					
Year 1	**Year 2**	**Year 3**	**Year 4**	**Year 5**	**Principal payment**
£3,255	£3,255	£3,255	£3,255	£3,255	£77,500
Alternative 2: Retain earnings and invest internally for five years, which returns 6 per cent to shareholders per year with a final dividend in year 5.					
Pre-tax dividend payment is 6% of 10% of £1,000,000 = £6,000					
After-tax dividend is (1 – 22.5%) of £6,000 = £4,650					
Deferred dividend is (1 – 22.5%) of £100,000 = £77,500					
After-tax cash flows					
Year 1	**Year 2**	**Year 3**	**Year 4**	**Year 5**	**Deferred dividend**
£4,650	£4,650	£4,650	£4,650	£4,650	£77,500

Exhibit 15.6 Cash Flows for a Tax-Exempt Investor

Alternative 1: Investment of £100,000 dividend in Treasury bonds.					
Cash flows					
Year 1	**Year 2**	**Year 3**	**Year 4**	**Year 5**	**Principal payment**
£7,000	£7,000	£7,000	£7,000	£7,000	£100,000
Alternative 2: Retain earnings and invest internally for five years, which returns 6 per cent to shareholders per year with a final dividend in year 5.					
Cash flows					
Year 1	**Year 2**	**Year 3**	**Year 4**	**Year 5**	**Deferred dividend**
£6,000	£6,000	£6,000	£6,000	£6,000	£100,000

These considerations suggest that a corporation, investing on behalf of taxable investors, may find that investment from retained cash is subject to a less stringent criterion than investment financed with outside equity. To understand this point, consider Example 15.5.

Example 15.5

The Effect of Personal Taxes on Corporate Investments

GT Associates can earn 15 per cent before taxes on its investments. However, being taxed at a 33.33 per cent rate on corporate income, it earns only 10 per cent after taxes. Equity investments that exactly track the future cash flows of GT's projects have a pre-tax rate of return of 10 per cent, and are taxed at a 20 per cent personal capital gains tax rate at the time the gain is realized. The 10 per cent return on the tracking portfolio is GT's cost of capital (see Chapters 11 and 13), as it represents the financial market's alternative to an investment in the real assets of GT. GT has an investment opportunity that costs €125 million and earns 10 per cent, after taking out corporate taxes, which is exactly the firm's cost of capital. Describe how GT would assess the profitability of this project: (1) in the case where GT must raise outside equity to fund the project; and (2) where it has internally generated cash that it would otherwise distribute to its shareholders.

Answer: (1) Observe that the project, with an after-corporate tax return equal to the 10 per cent cost of capital, has a zero NPV. Hence, if funding the project requires outside equity, the firm should be indifferent about taking on the project. To understand this point in the presence of personal taxes, we first need to recognize that the capital gains rate in this case is irrelevant for assessing whether GT makes money, loses money, or breaks even on internal investments funded by external equity. As an alternative to its investors' tracking portfolio, GT can raise €125 million externally by issuing additional equity. In its zero-NPV project, the €125 million grows to €137.5 million in the next year.

What happens if the €137.5 million in cash from the project is returned to GT's investors? Repurchasing the previously issued equity after one year provides GT's investors with €137.5 million in cash, minus a €2.5 million capital gains tax (20 per cent of the €12.5 million gain), for a total after-tax payout of €135 million. This is *exactly* what GT's investors would have received after capital gains taxes by acquiring the tracking portfolio for €125 million, watching it appreciate over the year and liquidating it at the end of the year. This is not surprising, since zero-NPV investments are, by definition, those that do not create or destroy wealth for a firm's investors relative to the alternatives available to them in the financial markets.

(2) Now suppose that GT has €125 million of internally generated cash. Let's compare the consequences of either paying out the €125 million to GT's shareholders by repurchasing shares immediately, or investing it internally at the after-tax rate of 10 per cent and repurchasing shares one year later. If it pays out the €125 million immediately, GT's investors will receive €100 million after paying the capital gains tax, which they can invest in the financial markets to receive €108 million after capital gains taxes one year later. However, if GT invests the €125 million internally in a project that earns 10 per cent after taxes, it will have €137.5 million to distribute to its shareholders the following year. Under this alternative, and after paying the 20 per cent capital gains tax on the €137.5 million capital gain, the investors will be left with €110 million. This amount exceeds the €108 million they would have earned had GT distributed the €125 million in cash in the previous year. In this sense, the project, despite being a zero-NPV project when financed with outside equity, creates €2 million in wealth at the end of the period for GT's shareholders when funded with internal cash. This €2 million in wealth is the benefit of deferring the €25 million in taxes on unrealized capital gains of €125 million for an additional year at the 8 per cent after personal tax rate of return.

Summary of How Personal Taxes Influence Investment Choices

In general, investors prefer retained earnings over a cash dividend (or share repurchase) if expected returns, adjusted for their premiums due to risk, satisfy

$$(1 - T_C) \times (\text{pre-tax return within the corporation}) > (\text{after personal tax return outside the corporation}) \quad (15.4)$$

otherwise, investors prefer the cash dividend (or share repurchase).

Note that the entire left-hand side of the inequality is simply the project's return, computed as is usually done from after-corporate tax cash flows, whereas the right-hand side is the product of the return of the tracking portfolio (that is, the project's cost of capital) and (1 – personal tax rate on the distribution). Hence inequality (15.4) can be contrasted with the NPV requirement discussed in Chapter 13 – that investment projects funded with externally raised equity must earn an after-tax rate of return that exceeds the pre-tax rate of return that investors can earn in the financial markets from the project's tracking portfolio:

$$(1 - T_C) \times (\text{pre-tax return within the corporation}) > (\text{pre-tax return outside the corporation}) \qquad (15.5)$$

A comparison of expressions (15.4) and (15.5) reveals that, for tax-exempt shareholders, the two expressions are identical. Hence a tax-exempt investor will want the corporation to make the same real investment choices, regardless of whether the investment is funded from retained earnings, which would otherwise be paid out as a dividend, or with a new equity issue. These expressions, however, are not equivalent for investors who are subject to personal taxes on dividend distributions or share repurchases. These investors will require a lower rate of return on investments that the corporation funds from retained earnings, if the alternative is a taxed distribution.

The above discussion is summarized in Result 15.5.

Results

Result 15.5

Tax-exempt and tax-paying shareholders agree about which projects a firm should fund from external equity issues, but they may disagree about which projects should be financed from retained earnings. In particular:

- Tax-exempt shareholders require the same expected return for internally financed projects as they do for externally financed projects.
- Tax-paying shareholders prefer that firms use lower required rates of return for internally financed projects, if the alternative is paying taxable dividends or repurchasing their shares.

To summarize, the discussion in this section suggests that the investment policies preferred by shareholders, who are subject to personal taxes, may differ from the policies described in Chapter 14 for firms that are generating significant amounts of cash. The hurdle rate required by the firm with cash on hand should be lower than the hurdle rate required of a corporation that must raise equity to fund the investment. This does not mean, however, that a corporation with cash should be taking on projects with very negative NPVs. The opportunity cost of a project is still the rate of return that can be earned by investing in equivalent investments in the financial markets. This return can be viewed, on an after-corporate-tax basis, as an alternative to what the firm can earn from investing in real assets.

Real-World Insight

Disagreements at Apple

Consider a corporation such like Apple, which by 2022 had accumulated about $51.511 billion in *excess* cash (that is, cash not currently needed for debt repayment or investment). Equation (15.5) suggests that tax-exempt institutional investors prefer the firm to pay out the cash as a dividend. However, equation (15.4) suggests that Tim Cook, Apple's CEO, and other shareholders with higher marginal tax rates than the corporation, prefer to have the corporation retain the earnings and invest the money in Treasury bonds. Shareholders with the same marginal tax rate as the corporation will be indifferent between the two alternatives.

Although companies like Apple sometimes invest excess cash in government bonds and equivalent instruments, Tim Cook may prefer alternative uses for these funds. For example, he may prefer to diversify his portfolio by using Apple to buy another company's equity instead of buying the equity with his personal money. Since US corporations are taxed on only 50 per cent of the dividend income they receive from other corporations, they can often earn a higher after-tax rate of return by buying the ordinary or preferred shares of other companies than they can earn from holding debt instruments such as T-bonds.

15.6 Personal Taxes, Payout Policy and Capital Structure

Recall that, in Chapter 14, we argued that, given reasonable assumptions about corporate and personal tax rates on debt and equity, most countries' tax laws favoured debt over external equity financing. However, in the previous section we also showed that financing projects with retained earnings, by paying corporate rather than personal taxes on their returns, provides an added benefit to shareholders with higher personal tax rates on their investment returns than the corporation pays. With the Tim Cook example, we showed that these same investors may even want the firm to use retained earnings to invest in financial assets, including debt, on their behalf.

Corporations must recognize that the incentives associated with payout policy also have implications for capital structure. A firm that pays out retained earnings to its shareholders, by reducing the amount of equity outstanding, increases its leverage ratio. Such a firm also increases the total amount of debt financing relative to using those same retained earnings as 'internal equity financing' for new investment. This is because the external financing that makes up for the payout is more likely to be in the form of debt, given its tax advantage over external equity.

The arguments in the last section can be extended to show that the firm will want to fund new investment with retained earnings rather than debt if the firm's shareholders' personal tax rate on debt exceeds the corporate tax rate. This can be seen if we view the investment illustrated in Exhibit 15.5 as paying off some of the firm's debt or, equivalently, as using the internally generated capital so that the firm does not have to take on additional debt.[8] If Tim Cook prefers that Microsoft use its retained earnings to invest in debt on his behalf, this debt may just as well be the firm's debt as any other source of debt that would ultimately be netted against the firm's liabilities.

Given that the tax preference for debt financing versus internal equity financing depends on the personal tax rates of shareholders, it follows that shareholders with different marginal tax rates may not agree about capital structure policy. This disagreement is illustrated in the following case study.

Real-World Insight

Should Apple Increase its Leverage?

Tim Cook, CEO of Apple, recognizes that there is a tax gain from debt financing, and that Apple can increase the firm's leverage, either by repurchasing shares or by paying a dividend, and funding more of the firm's investment needs from debt securities without running any significant risk of bankruptcy. This would increase firm value by lowering its corporate tax bite.

Assume that Apple currently owns about 4 per cent of the company's shares. Assume that he would like to retain this percentage of ownership. The US corporate tax rate is currently 21 per cent, and Cook's personal tax rate is 37 per cent on ordinary income and 20 per cent on capital gains. Different shareholders may have different opinions about whether the firm should pay a large dividend, repurchase shares or continue with its policy of retaining most of its earnings to fund its investments internally. For example, tax-exempt institutions definitely would prefer that the firm repurchase shares or pay a dividend to increase its debt, at least to the point where there is some risk of bankruptcy. However, Tim Cook may personally prefer to keep the firm underleveraged. If the firm uses a large dividend to distribute its retained earnings, Cook will have to pay 37 per cent of the distribution in taxes. Because of the lower capital gains tax, he would prefer a share repurchase over a dividend. However, if Tim Cook is going to keep his percentage ownership of the firm constant, he will have to sell some of his shares, forcing him to realize the capital gains on his shares. As we showed in the last section, Cook's incentive to have Apple distribute cash depends on the difference between his personal rate and Apple's corporate tax rate. If the corporate tax rate is less than the personal rate, he will prefer retaining the earnings rather than distributing them.

[8] As long as the tax cost associated with distributing capital to shareholders (for example, the capital gains rate that is triggered by a share repurchase) is constant, the actual rate is irrelevant. However, if the rate is changing over time, corporations may find it in their interests to time their distribution choices optimally to correspond to situations where the tax cost of the distribution is minimized.

Consistent with Result 15.6, an in-depth study of large corporations by Gordon Donaldson (1961) found that managers prefer funding investment first with retained earnings, second, after the supply of retained earnings has been exhausted, with debt, and finally, when it is imprudent for the firm to borrow additional amounts, by issuing outside equity. This financing hierarchy is known as the **pecking order of financing choices**.[9]

Results

Result 15.6

The combination of the corporate tax deductibility of interest payments and the personal taxes on dividends (and share repurchases) implies that:

- tax systems favour debt financing over financing investments by issuing equity
- for taxable shareholders, the tax preference for debt over internally generated equity (that is, retained earnings) is less than the tax preference for debt over newly issued equity; indeed, individual investors with sufficiently high personal tax rates have a tax preference for financing new investment with retained earnings, rather than paying out the earnings and financing new investment with debt.

Real-World Insights

Sustainability

Shareholders will rarely block a dividend, but that is what happened with the Russian oil giant Gazprom, in 2022. In 2019, Gazprom introduced a new dividend policy to pay out at least 50 per cent of its earnings each year. As a result of record gas prices, profits hit a record-breaking $36.4 billion despite the widespread sanctions on the firm, meaning that shareholders would have received around $21.8 billion.

The company's biggest shareholders are the Russian government (38 per cent) and two other state firms (12 per cent), giving the Russian state control over the firm's decisions. Why did the government block the dividend? There are several possible reasons. One is that the government wanted to preserve cash in case sanctions worsened. Liquidity would be required to support new investments and pipelines. Another explanation is that although profits are excellent, this has been because of the price of gas rather than the sales the firm made during the year, which fell by 30 per cent.

On the announcement that the proposed dividend had been blocked, Gazprom's share price collapsed by 25 per cent causing trading in the company's shares to halt on the Moscow Stock Exchange.

15.7 Summary and Conclusions

This chapter analysed two methods by which firms distribute earnings to their shareholders: dividends and share repurchases. In the absence of taxes and transaction costs, the two methods of distributing cash are virtually identical. However, taxable investors would normally prefer share repurchases.

The chapter presented a few hypotheses that might explain why corporations have paid out so much in tax-disadvantaged dividends instead of repurchasing their shares, yet none of the explanations is entirely convincing. We are still puzzled by the significant amount of dividends that corporations pay. We believe that tax-paying shareholders would be better off if firms increased their share repurchase programmes and simultaneously cut their dividends. Firms may continue to pay dividends because managers observe

[9] Non-tax-based explanations for this pecking order behaviour are described in Chapters 17 and 19.

an increase in their share prices when they announce dividend increases. However, we do not believe that the positive share price response to dividend increases provides a good rationale for paying a dividend.[10]

Other inexplicable puzzles also relate to dividend policy and taxes. First, a number of US firms implemented share repurchase programmes in the 1980s. This occurred even as US tax laws were changing to lessen the tax disadvantage of dividends relative to share repurchases. Second, there are large differences across countries in both the tax treatment of dividends and the ability of firms to repurchase shares. However, we do not observe systematic differences in dividend yields across countries that correspond to these tax and institutional differences.

Our analysis of the payout of dividends and taxes suggests that equities with high dividend yields should offer higher expected returns to attract tax-paying investors. Unfortunately, testing this proposition has turned out to be difficult. Historically, equities with high dividend yields have had higher returns than equities with low dividend yields, but we cannot conclude that the return premium represents compensation for taxes. Since dividend policies are highly correlated with investment policies cross-sectionally, it also is likely that dividend policies are highly correlated with systematic risk. Therefore it may be impossible to distinguish whether equities with high dividend yields require higher rates of return because they are tax disadvantaged or whether they receive higher rates of return because they are in some ways riskier. As Chapter 5 discussed, most recent empirical tests of asset pricing have failed to document a relationship between systematic risk and expected returns, which makes us less sanguine about the possibility of determining how dividends affect expected returns.

Key Concepts

Result 15.1: (*The Miller–Modigliani dividend irrelevancy theorem.*) Consider the choice between paying a dividend and using an equivalent amount of money to repurchase shares. Assume that:

- there are no tax considerations
- there are no transaction costs
- the investment, financing and operating policies of the firm are held fixed.

Then the choice between paying dividends and repurchasing shares is a matter of indifference to shareholders.

Result 15.2: Consider the choice between paying out earnings to shareholders versus retaining the earnings for investment. Assume that:

- there are no tax considerations
- there are no transaction costs
- the choice between paying a dividend and retaining the earnings for reinvestment within the firm does not convey any information to shareholders.

Then a dividend payout will either increase or decrease a firm's value, depending on whether there are positive net present value (NPV) investments that could be funded by retaining the money within the firm. If there are no positive-NPV investments, the money should be paid out.

Result 15.3: In many countries, taxes favour share repurchases over dividends. The gain associated with a share repurchase over a cash dividend depends on:

- the difference between the capital gains rate and the tax rate on ordinary income
- the tax basis of the shares – that is, the price at which the shares were purchased
- the timing of the sale of the shares (if soon, the gain is less, but if too soon, the gain may not qualify for the long-term capital gains rate).

[10] This topic is discussed in Chapter 19.

Result 15.4: Equities with high dividend yields are fundamentally different from equities with low dividend yields in terms of their characteristics and their risk profiles. Therefore it is nearly impossible to assess whether the relationship between dividend yield and expected returns is due to taxes, risk or other factors such as investor sentiment.

Result 15.5: Tax-exempt and tax-paying shareholders agree about which projects a firm should fund from external equity issues, but they may disagree about which projects should be financed from retained earnings. In particular:

- Tax-exempt shareholders require the same expected return for internally financed projects as they do for externally financed projects.
- Tax-paying shareholders prefer that firms use lower required rates of return for internally financed projects if the alternative is paying taxable dividends or repurchasing their shares.

Result 15.6: The combination of the corporate tax deductibility of interest payments and the personal taxes on dividends (and share repurchases) implies that:

- tax systems favour debt financing over financing investments by issuing equity
- for taxable shareholders, the tax preference for debt over internally generated equity (that is, retained earnings) is less than the tax preference for debt over newly issued equity; indeed, individual investors with sufficiently high personal tax rates have a tax preference for financing new investment with retained earnings, rather than paying out the earnings and financing new investment with debt

Key Terms

classical tax system 493
dividend payout ratio 487
dividend policy 486
dividend yield 487
imputation system 492
investor clientele 495
Miller–Modigliani dividend irrelevancy theorem 486
pecking order of financing choices 504

Exercises

15.1 Explain why the proportion of earnings distributed in the form of a share repurchase has increased substantially over the past 50 years.

15.2 Explain why the aggregate payout (dividends plus share repurchases) has tripled in the period 2000–2019 compared to the period 1970–1999.

15.3 You are considering buying shares in AMEC plc, which is trading today at £12.31 a share. AMEC is going ex-dividend tomorrow, paying out £2.00 per share. If you believe the equity will drop to £11 following the dividend, should you buy the equity before or after the dividend payment? Explain how your answer depends on the tax rate on ordinary income, capital gains and your expected holding period.

15.4 Acidnet Ltd is issuing equity for the first time and needs to determine an initial proportion of debt and equity. In its first years, the firm will have substantial tax write-offs as it amortizes the uranium in the mine. In later years, however, it will have high taxable earnings. Make a proposal regarding the firm's optimal capital structure and future payout policy.

15.5 Suppose you are a manager who wants to retain as much as possible of the firm's earnings in order to increase the size of the firm. How would you react to proposals to repurchase shares that would make it less costly to distribute cash to shareholders? How does your reaction relate to your answer in exercise 15.1?

15.6 Hunter Industries has generated £1 million in excess of its investment needs. The firm can invest the excess cash in Treasury bonds at 8 per cent or distribute the cash to shareholders as a dividend. Assume that the corporate tax rate is 28 per cent and that the firm is owned by three different kinds of taxpayer: the first type is tax exempt, the second type has a 25 per cent marginal tax rate and the third type has a 40 per cent marginal tax rate. Describe the decision preferred by the three different investors, indicating the reasons for the decision and providing calculations to show your conclusions. Next, consider the possibility that the firm can invest in preferred equity that pays 7 per cent per year. Describe how this would affect Hunter's decision, given the 70 per cent dividend exclusion for corporate investors.

15.7 Suppose that the capital gains tax rate in the USA is expected to increase in three years. How would this affect Tim Cook's decision on whether Apple should use some of the company's excess cash to repurchase shares?

15.8 The XYZ Corporation has an expected dividend of €4 one period from now. This dividend is expected to grow by 2 per cent per period.

a What is the value of a share of equity, assuming that the appropriate discount rate for expected future dividends (e.g. the expected rate of appreciation in the share price of XYZ between dividends) is 10 per cent per period? For your answer, assume that the effective personal tax rate on dividends is 20 per cent and the effective personal tax rate on capital gains and share repurchases is zero.

b The XYZ Corporation announces that it will stop paying dividends. Instead, the company will engage in an equity repurchase plan under which future cash that would previously have been earmarked for dividend payments will now be used exclusively for equity repurchases. Assuming no information effects, what should the new price of a share of XYZ equity be when market participants first learn of this announcement?

15.8 Alpha Corporation earned £150 million in before-tax profits. Its corporate tax rate is 28 per cent. Con Daniels, who owns 20 per cent of the firm's shares, has a personal marginal tax rate of 22.5 per cent on dividend income. From Daniels' perspective, what is the effective tax rate on Alpha's profits if its entire after-tax profits are distributed as a dividend?

15.9 You are engineering an LBO of Suntharee Industries, an industrial bottle maker. After the LBO, the firm will be financed 90 per cent with debt and 10 per cent with equity. Maria Benjamin, the CEO, will own 30 per cent of the shares. Maria thinks the proposed capital structure is too highly levered, and points out that, in the first few years, the firm will not be able to use all its debt tax shields. Initially, the interest payments are €400 million per year and EBIT is only €300 million per year. However, EBIT is projected to increase by 20 per cent per year for the next five years.

Give Maria a pure tax argument that supports the high level of debt. Take into account her personal taxes as well as corporate taxes. Does your tax argument depend on whether Maria wants to dilute her ownership of the company in the future?

References and Additional Reading

Acharya, V.V., Myers, S.C. and Rajan, R.G. (2011) The internal governance of firms, *The Journal of Finance*, 66(3) 689–720.

Aharony J. and Swary, I. (1980) Quarterly dividend and earnings announcements and shareholders' returns: an empirical analysis, *The Journal of Finance*, 35(1): 1–12.

Allen, F. and Michaely, R. (1995) Dividend policy, Chapter 25 in *Handbooks in Operations Research and Management Science: Volume 9, Finance*, Jarrow, R., Maksimovic, V. and Ziemba, W. (eds), Elsevier Science, Amsterdam.

Allen, F., Bernardo, A.E. and Welch, I. (2000) A theory of dividends based on tax clienteles, *The Journal of Finance* 55(6): 2499–2536.

Almeida, H., Fos, V. and Kronlund, M. (2016) The real effects of share repurchases, *Journal of Financial Economics*, 119(1): 168–185.

Bagwell, L.S. and Shoven, J. (1989) Cash distributions to shareholders, *Journal of Economic Perspectives*, 3(3): 129–140.

Baker, M. and Wurgler, J. (2004) A catering theory of dividends, *The Journal of Finance*, 59(3): 1125–1165.

Baker, M. and Wurgler, J. (2006) Investor sentiment and the cross-section of equity returns, *The Journal of Finance*, 61(4): 1645–1680.

Barrot, J.N., Loualiche, E. and Sauvagnat, J. (2019) The globalization risk premium, *The Journal of Finance*, 74(5): 2391–2439.

Becker, B., Ivković, Z. and Weisbenner, S. (2011) Local dividend clienteles, *The Journal of Finance*, 66(2): 655–683.

Bhattacharya, U. and E. Jacobsen, S. (2016) The share repurchase announcement puzzle: Theory and evidence, *Review of Finance*, 20(2): 725–758.

Black, F. (1976) The dividend puzzle, *Journal of Portfolio Management*, 2, 5–8.

Black, F. and Scholes, M. (1974) The effects of dividend yield and dividend policy on common share prices and returns, *Journal of Financial Economics*, 1(1): 1–22.

Blume, M.E. (1980) Stock returns and dividend yields: some more evidence, *Review of Economics and Statistics*, 62(4): 567–577.

Boyd, J. and Jagannathan, R. (1994) Ex-dividend day behavior of common equities, *The Review of Financial Studies*, 7(4): 711–741.

Brav, A., Graham, J.R., Harvey, C.R. and Michaely, R. (2005) Payout policy in the 21st century, *Journal of Financial Economics*, 77(3): 483–527.

Brennan, M. (1970) Taxes, market valuation, and corporate financial policy, *National Tax Journal*, 23(4): 417–427.

Brown, J.R., Liang, N. and Weisbenner, S. (2007) Executive financial incentives and payout policy: firm responses to the 2003 dividend tax cut, *The Journal of Finance*, 62(4): 1935–1965.

Chemmanur, T.J., He, J., Hu, G. and Liu, H. (2010) Is dividend smoothing universal?: New insights from a comparative study of dividend policies in Hong Kong and the US, *Journal of Corporate Finance*, 16(4): 413–430.

Chen, N., Grundy, B. and Stambaugh, R.F. (1990) Changing risk, changing risk premiums, and dividend yield effects, *Journal of Business*, 63(1): S51–S70.

Chen, J., Leung, W. S. and Goergen, M. (2017) The impact of board gender composition on dividend payouts, *Journal of Corporate finance*, 43, 86–105.

Crane, A. D., Michenaud, S. and Weston, J. P. (2016) The effect of institutional ownership on payout policy: Evidence from index thresholds, *The Review of Financial Studies*, 29(6): 1377–1408.

Denis, D.J. and Obosov, I. (2008) Why do firms pay dividends? International evidence on the determinants of dividend payout policy, *Journal of Financial Economics*, 89(1): 62–82.

Desai, M.A. and Jin, L. (2011) Institutional tax clienteles and payout policy, *Journal of Financial Economics*, 100(1): 68–84.

Donaldson, G. (1961) *Corporate Debt Capacity: A Study of Corporate Debt Policy and the Determination of Corporate Debt Capacity*. Boston, MA: Harvard Graduate School of Business Administration.

Dunsby, A. (1993) *Share Repurchases and Corporate Distributions: An Empirical Study*. Working paper. Philadelphia, PA: University of Pennsylvania.

Eades, K., Hess, P. and Kim, H. (1984) On interpreting security returns during the ex-dividend period, *Journal of Financial Economics*, 13(1): 3–34.

Elton, E. and Gruber, M. (1970) Marginal shareholders' tax rates and the clientele effect, *Review of Economics and Statistics*, 52(1): 68–74.

Elton, E., Gruber, M. and Blake, C. (2005) Marginal shareholder tax effects and ex-dividend-day price behavior: evidence from taxable versus nontaxable closed-end funds, *Review of Economics and Statistics*, 87(3): 579–586.

Fama, E.F. and Babiak, H. (1968) Dividend policy: an empirical analysis, *Journal of the American Statistical Association*, 63(324): 1132–1161.

Feenberg, D. (1981) Does the investment interest limitation explain the existence of dividends?, *Journal of Financial Economics*, 9(3): 265–270.

Frank, M. and Jagannathan, R. (1998) Why do share prices drop by less than the value of the dividend? Evidence from a country without taxes, *Journal of Financial Economics*, 47(2): 161–188.

Fuller, K.P. and Goldstein, M.A. (2011) Do dividends matter more in declining markets?, *Journal of Corporate Finance*, 17(3): 457–473.

Ginglinger, E., Megginson, W. and Waxin, T. (2011) Employee ownership, board representation, and corporate financial policies, *Journal of corporate finance*, 17(4): 868–887.

Graham, J.R. and Kumar, A. (2006) Do dividend clienteles exist? Evidence on dividend preferences of retail investors, *The Journal of Finance*, 61(3): 1305–1336.

Graham, J.R., Michaely, R. and Roberts, M. (2003) Do price discreteness and transaction costs affect equity returns? Comparing ex-dividend pricing before and after decimalization, *The Journal of Finance*, 58(6): 2611–2636.

Grinblatt, M., Masulis, R. and Titman, S. (1984) The valuation effects of equity splits and equity dividends, *Journal of Financial Economics*, 13(4): 461–490.

Hanlon, M. and Heitzman, S. (2010) A review of tax research, *Journal of Accounting and Economics*, 50(2–3): 127–178.

Hartzmark, S.M. and Solomon, D.H. (2019) The dividend disconnect, *The Journal of Finance*, 74(5): 2153–2199.

Hoberg, G., Phillips, G. and Prabhala, N. (2014) Product market threats, payouts, and financial flexibility, *The Journal of Finance*, 69(1): 293–324.

Hubbard, J. and Michaely, R. (1997) Do investors ignore dividend taxation? A reexamination of the Citizens Utilities case, *Journal of Financial and Quantitative Analysis*, 32(1): 117–135.

Isakov, D., Pérignon, C. and Weisskopf, J. P. (2021) What if dividends were tax-exempt? Evidence from a natural experiment, *The Review of Financial Studies*, 34(12): 5756–5795.

Jensen, G.R., Lundstrum, L.L. and Miller, R.E. (2010) What do dividend reductions signal?, *Journal of Corporate Finance*, 16(5): 736–747.

Jiang, Z., Kim, K. A., Lie, E. and Yang, S. (2013) Share repurchases, catering, and dividend substitution, *Journal of Corporate Finance*, 21, 36–50.

John, K. and Williams, J. (1985) Dividends, dilution and taxes, *The Journal of Finance*, 40(4): 1053–1070.

John, K., Knyazeva, A. and Knyazeva, D. (2011) Does geography matter? Firm location and corporate payout policy, *Journal of Financial Economics*, 101(3) 533–551.

Kahle, K. and Stulz, R.M. (2020) *Why are Corporate Payouts so High in the 2000s?* (No. w26958). National Bureau of Economic Research.

Kalay, A. (1982) Shareholder–bondholder conflict and dividend constraints, *Journal of Financial Economics*, 10(2): 211–233.

Keim, D. (1985) Dividend yields and equity returns: implications of abnormal January returns, *Journal of Financial Economics*, 14(3): 473–489.

Korkeamaki, T., Liljeblom, E. and D. Pasternack (2009) Tax reform and payout policy: do shareholder clienteles or payout policy adjust?, *Journal of Corporate Finance*, 16, 572–587.

Korkeamaki, T., Liljeblom, E. and Pasternack, D. (2010) Tax reform and payout policy: Do shareholder clienteles or payout policy adjust?, *Journal of Corporate Finance,* 16(4): 572–587.

Kumar, A., Lei, Z. and Zhang, C. (2022) Dividend sentiment, catering incentives, and return predictability, *Journal of Corporate Finance,* 72, 102128.

Leary, M.T. and Michaely, R. (2011) Determinants of dividend smoothing: Empirical evidence, *The Review of Financial Studies,* 24(10): 3197–3249.

Lewellen W., Stanley, K., Lease, R. and Schlarbaum, G. (1978) Some direct evidence on the dividend clientele phenomenon, *The Journal of Finance,* 33(5): 1385–1399.

Li, W. and Lie, E. (2006) Dividend changes and catering incentives, *Journal of Financial Economics,* 80(2): 293–308.

Litzenberger, R. and Ramaswamy, K. (1982) The effects of dividends on common share prices: tax effects or information effects?, *The Journal of Finance,* 37(2): 429–443.

Long, J.B., Jr. (1978) The market valuation of cash dividends: a case to consider, *Journal of Financial Economics,* 6(2/3): 235–264.

McDonald, R.L. (2001) Cross-border investing with tax arbitrage: the case of German dividend tax credits, *Review of Financial Studies,* 14(3): 617–657.

Menyah, K. (1993) Ex-dividend equity pricing under UK tax regimes, *Journal of Business Finance and Accounting,* 20(1): 61–82.

Michaely, R. (1991) Ex-dividend day share price behavior: the case of the 1986 Tax Reform Act, *The Journal of Finance,* 46(3): 845–859.

Michaely, R. and Murgio, M. (1995) The effect of tax heterogeneity on prices and volume around the ex-dividend day: evidence from the Milan Equity Exchange, *Review of Financial Studies,* 8(2): 369–399.

Michaely, R. and Roberts, M.R. (2012) Corporate dividend policies: Lessons from private firms, *The Review of Financial Studies,* 25(3): 711–746.

Michaely, R. and Moin, A. (2021) Disappearing and reappearing dividends, *Journal of Financial Economics.*

Miller, M.H. and Modigliani, F. (1961) Dividend policy, growth, and the value of shares, *Journal of Business,* 34(4): 411–433.

Miller, M. and Scholes, M. (1978) Dividends and taxes, *Journal of Financial Economics,* 6(4): 333–364.

Miller, M.H. and Scholes, M.S. (1982) Dividends and taxes: some empirical evidence, *The Journal of Political Economy,* 90(6): 1118–1141.

Peterson, P.P., Peterson, D.R. and Ang, J.S. (1985) Direct evidence on the marginal rate of taxation on dividend income, *Journal of Financial Economics,* 14(2): 267–282.

Pettit, R. (1977) Taxes, transaction costs and the clientele effect of dividends, *Journal of Financial Economics* 5(3): 419–36.

Poterba, J. (1986) The market valuation of cash dividends: the Citizens Utilities case reconsidered, *Journal of Financial Economics,* 15(3): 395–405.

Sharma, V. (2011) Independent directors and the propensity to pay dividends, *Journal of Corporate finance,* 17(4): 1001–1015.

Sheikh, S. (2022) CEO power and the likelihood of paying dividends: Effect of profitability and cash flow volatility, *Journal of Corporate Finance,* 73, 102186.

Skinner, D. (2008) The evolving relation between earnings, dividends, and stock repurchases, *Journal of Financial Economics,* 87(3): 582–609.

Von Eije, H. and Megginson, W. (2008) Dividends and share repurchases in the European Union, *Journal of Financial Economics,* 89(2): 347–374.

Whitworth, J. and Rao, R.P. (2010) Do tax law changes influence ex-dividend stock price behavior? Evidence from 1926 to 2005, *Financial Management,* 39(1): 419–445.

Chapter 16

Bankruptcy Costs and Debt Holder–Equity Holder Conflicts

Learning Objectives

After reading this chapter, you should be able to:

- Understand the effect of direct bankruptcy costs on borrowing rates and capital structure choices.
- Describe the factors contributing to the conflicts of interest between debt holders and equity holders.
- Explain how debt can cause equity holders to take on projects that are too risky and to pass up positive-NPV projects.
- Identify various situations in which debt holders and equity holders may disagree on the liquidation decision.
- Understand how bond covenants, bank loans, privately placed debt, project finance and convertible bonds can mitigate some of these debt holder–equity holder conflicts.
- Describe how conflicts between debt holders and equity holders affect capital structure choices.

In 2018, one of the UK's largest firms, Carillion plc, filed for bankruptcy. There have been many reasons provided for the company's collapse, but another interesting facet of the case was how management attempted to address the impending default. One particular approach was the use of an invoice factoring early payment facility (EPF), where the firm used what was, in effect, very expensive short-term loans, to avoid taking out further bank loans. An EPF is a scheme where banks pay supplier invoices early (120 days in Carillion's case) in return for a percentage of the invoice value (2 per cent for Carillion). At the due date of the invoice, Carillion would receive the cash from its suppliers and pass this directly to the lending bank.

According to Frank Field, the head of the subsequent UK government inquiry, Carillion, '. . . used its suppliers as a line of credit to shore up its fragile balance sheet, then in another of its accounting tricks 'reclassified' this borrowing to hide the true extent of its massive debt.'

When Carillion collapsed, the firm owed £7 billion to its supplier, lenders and pension fund.

Up to this point, we have examined the firm's capital structure decision within a simplified setting that either ruled out the possibility of bankruptcy or, alternatively, assumed that if bankruptcy occurs, the assets of the corporation would transfer costlessly from equity holders to debt holders. This chapter moves beyond these simplifying assumptions and examines the capital structure choice in a world where bankruptcy imposes costs on the firm.

Treasurers of bankrupt firms who saw their firm's share price fall almost to zero might claim that bankruptcy is extremely costly. However, while debt financing may have contributed significantly to the bankruptcy, most of the loss in firm value leading up to the bankruptcy cannot be attributed to debt financing *per se* but to misfortunes affecting the firm's actual business operations. Only those lost revenues or increased operating costs attributed either directly or indirectly to the event of bankruptcy or, more generally, to the threat of bankruptcy are relevant to a firm's capital structure decision. Therefore, as long as bankruptcy or the threat of bankruptcy does not affect the cash flows available to the firm's debt and equity holders, the possibility of bankruptcy is irrelevant to a firm's capital structure decision.

The extent to which bankruptcy reduces the cash flows of firms has been debated extensively in the academic literature. The reductions in cash flows related to bankruptcy or the threat of bankruptcy are generally classified as either direct bankruptcy costs or indirect bankruptcy costs. **Direct bankruptcy costs** relate to the legal process involved in reorganizing a bankrupt firm. **Indirect bankruptcy costs** are not directly related to the reorganization and can arise among **financially distressed firms**, or those firms that are close to bankruptcy, but which may never actually go bankrupt. As shown later in this chapter and in Chapter 17, most indirect bankruptcy costs arise because financial distress creates a tendency for firms to engage in actions that are harmful to their debt holders and **non-financial stake-holders** such as customers, employees and suppliers. As a result of these harmful actions, a financially distressed firm may find it difficult to obtain credit, and may find it more costly in other ways to efficiently carry out its day-to-day business.

This chapter focuses on the conflicts of interest that can arise between a firm's debt holders and equity holders. In this chapter's opening vignette, for example, Carillion tried to protect its share price at the expense of suppliers and lenders. In fact, the Carillion management continually avoided issuing new equity, which would have harmed the share price through dilution, to raise money via debt.

When these conflicts exist, the net present value (NPV) of a project, calculated by discounting the cash flows to equity holders, can be substantially different from the NPV calculated with either the APV or WACC method. For example, Chapter 13 showed how the NPV of the equity holders' cash flows from a relatively safe investment project could be negative, even though the NPV of the total cash flows to both debt holders and equity holders is positive. In other words, firms that operate solely in the interests of their equity holders, thereby ignoring the interests of their debt holders, may pass up value-creating projects. In addition, these firms may take on excessively risky projects that benefit equity holders but lower the value of the firm's debt.

This chapter argues that the equity holders of a firm ultimately can be hurt by the firm's tendency to ignore the interests of its debt holders. This tendency may result in a firm's inability to obtain debt financing at attractive terms, and in some cases it may prevent a firm from obtaining any debt financing at all. One solution to this problem (discussed later in the chapter) is to design the debt so that it minimizes the potential for conflict. This can be accomplished through convertibility features and debt covenants (see Chapter 2), which are terms included in many debt contracts to limit a firm's investment and financing choices. Because these solutions are imperfect, however, firms generally will want to limit the amount of debt in their capital structure, even when there are substantial tax benefits to debt financing.

Most of the key issues in this chapter are developed with a set of relatively simple numerical examples. Unless specified otherwise, valuation in these examples assumes risk neutrality, no direct bankruptcy costs, no taxes and a risk-free rate of zero.

16.1 Bankruptcy

Bankruptcy codes around the world are beginning to converge in substance as a result of the global integration of the world's economies. However, there are important country-level differences. The European Union introduced its bankruptcy regulation in 2002, *Regulation on Insolvency Proceedings,* which is followed by all EU countries, with the exception of Denmark. This was updated in 2019 to accommodate early restructuring should a firm get into financial difficulty. Essentially, whenever firms find themselves in difficulty, they now have the opportunity to restructure operations during a protected period.

Bankruptcy in the United Kingdom

Brexit means that EU bankruptcy codes no longer apply in the UK. Firms in the UK that are unable to make the required payments to their creditors can be voluntarily or compulsorily **wound up**. This is also known as becoming *dissolved* or *liquidated*. The process leads to the liquidation of the firm's assets in the settlement of creditors' claims. Alternatively, the firm can appoint an **administrator**, which allows the firm to restructure its debt and equity claims, restore the company as a going concern or sell it on to other parties. In all cases, an administrator's objective is to continue the firm's operations.

Liquidation

In a liquidation or insolvency, a court issues a winding-up order after it has been petitioned by a creditor, the company, its directors or shareholders. Within two or three days of the order an official receiver is appointed, who liquidates the assets of the firm and distributes the proceeds to the debt holders. Any proceeds from the liquidation that remain after settling the debt holders' claims are then distributed to the company's shareholders. These proceeds are divided among the claim holders according to the **absolute priority rule**, which states that debt holders must be paid in full before equity holders receive any proceeds of the bankruptcy. The rule also states that secured debt holders must be paid before unsecured debt holders, and that the more senior of the unsecured debt holders must be paid in full before the more junior debt holders.

Administration

Going into administration is much more complicated than going into insolvency. Under administration, the claims of debt and equity holders cannot be settled with cash realized from the liquidation of assets. Rather, the debt and equity holders receive new financial claims in exchange for their existing claims. For example, debt holders often end up with equity in the newly reorganized firm that emerges from administration.

Almost all bankruptcies of large corporations start out with the firm going into administration, and insolvency occurs only when the various claimants fail to agree on a **company voluntary agreement (CVA)**, which specifies how the new financial claims are to be distributed among the claim holders. If creditors reject the offer, or the corporation fails to submit a CVA, the judge overseeing the bankruptcy case can give the corporation an extension during which it must come up with an acceptable plan, or ask the creditors to come up with their own **reorganization plan**. In most cases, at least one extension is granted.

To determine the acceptability of the CVA, each class of **impaired creditors** – the creditors who will not be paid in full – as well as the equity holders must vote on it. For a CVA to be accepted, 75 per cent of the claimants must vote for the plan. If the plan is accepted, it is binding on all creditors who were entitled to vote.

Bankruptcy in Other Countries

Most countries have an approach to bankruptcy that is very similar to that of the United Kingdom. The US equivalent to administration is filing for **Chapter 11 bankruptcy**, and the equivalent to insolvency is filing for **Chapter 7 bankruptcy**. All other aspects of the system are practically the same. European Union members follow the same principles as enshrined in the *Regulation on Insolvency Proceedings* (2015) and the *Restructuring and Insolvency Directive* (2019). However, there are notable differences. Ireland's bankruptcy law is almost identical to that of the UK. Spain is governed by its Insolvency Law of 2020, which presents a single process for bankruptcy. Under this system, a creditors' meeting is organized at which an agreement is sought on ways to maintain the firm as a going concern (similar to a CVA in the UK). If this is not possible, the firm will be wound up. In France, there is a three-stage process, beginning with pre-insolvency hearings. These can occur if the firm's auditor has material concerns about the solvency of the firm. If the auditor is not happy with the response, and dialogue cannot present a solution, they can submit the case to the commercial court. In France, any interested party can submit a case to the commercial court. A firm may at this point request a three-month window to secure an agreement to restructure its debt (similar to a CVA) through an amicable settlement. If this is unsuccessful, the firm will be wound up. In Italy, insolvency is defined not as a legal process, but as the situation where companies are unable to pay their obligations. The outcome of being insolvent may be bankruptcy or winding-up. However, Italy follows the same approach as other European countries in that pre-insolvency proceedings are carried out, followed by some form of CVA, finalized by a winding-up if all else fails.[1]

[1] The principles upon which European Union members' bankruptcy codes are based are similar, but the details are quite different. Interested European readers should visit the European Commission's website on bankruptcy.

China's bankruptcy regulations are very similar to those of other developed countries, and they follow the US system most closely. With China's move away from a communist economy, its bankruptcy code has changed from its previous incarnation. The biggest change is that of absolute priority. Under the new system, priority is given to debt holders and then to shareholders, as in all Western capitalist countries. This is in contrast to the old Chinese bankruptcy code, which gave the firm's workers first call on any of the company's assets. The South African bankruptcy system is similar to British bankruptcy law. There are significant differences, however. South Africa does not have an equivalent to the administration process that is common in the United Kingdom. Creditors, shareholders, or the company itself may apply to the High Court to place the firm in liquidation. The process is then worked through the system, and restructuring or winding-up may be an outcome of this process.

The Direct Costs of Bankruptcy

If the bankruptcy process is relatively costless, the possibility of bankruptcy does not affect a firm's capital structure decision. Recall from Chapter 14 of this text that the Modigliani–Miller theorem does not require that there be no bankruptcy, only that the bankruptcy be costless.

There are, however, various costs directly related to bankruptcy, including the time spent dealing with creditors, and the additional time creditors spend with the managers of a bankrupt firm. Legal expenses, court costs and advisory fees also are direct costs of bankruptcy. For example, legal costs for the Carillion bankruptcy are likely to total at least £150 million.

Estimates of the Direct Costs of Bankruptcy

Warner (1977) estimated that the direct costs of bankruptcy for large railways, although substantial in magnitude, are quite small relative to the size of the firms, averaging only 5.3 per cent of their (already diminished) debt and equity values just before the bankruptcy filings. A study of bankruptcies of large firms by Weiss (1990) determined that direct costs averaged about 3.1 per cent of the total value of the debt and equity of the bankrupt firms. LoPucki and Doherty (2004) reported that professional fees were 1.4 per cent of total assets. Finally, Bris et al. (2006) estimated direct costs for Chapter 7 bankruptcy to be 8.1 per cent of pre-bankruptcy assets.

Because most of the direct costs of bankruptcy are the same for both small and large firms, the bankruptcy costs of small firms, as a proportion of the value of their assets, are much larger. For small firms, these costs may be fairly large, perhaps 20–25 per cent of a firm's value.[2] However, even these high percentages suggest that the direct costs of bankruptcy add very little to a firm's borrowing costs, except in cases where bankruptcy is quite likely. This is because these costs (1) are percentages of an already diminished firm value, and (2) must be multiplied by the probability of bankruptcy, and then discounted, to determine their impact on borrowing costs.

Who Bears the Bankruptcy Costs?

Under the absolute priority rule, most of a firm's value in the event of bankruptcy is transferred to its debt holders. Since the direct costs of bankruptcy diminish the value of the firm, most direct bankruptcy costs are thus ultimately borne by the firm's debt holders.

Why should managers, who represent the interests of the firm's equity holders, be concerned about the costs borne by debt holders? Although equity holders are not directly concerned with costs that may be imposed on their firm's lenders, they are concerned about the rates at which the firm can borrow. Since lenders realize they will be bearing costs in the event of bankruptcy, they will demand a *default premium* on the interest rate they charge the firm. The **default premium**, the difference between the promised yield to the bond's lenders and the yield on a bond with no default, reflects the probability and cost of the firm's bankruptcy. In paying this default premium, shareholders are, in effect, paying the expected bankruptcy costs whenever they issue risky debt. Therefore they must consider that at least a portion of the premium (that due to the cost of bankruptcy) reflects a cost that may offset other advantages associated with debt financing.

[2] See Ang et al. (1982) and Altman (1984).

Example 16.1

How Bankruptcy Affects Borrowing Costs

Westlake plc would like to borrow £1 million for one year. There is a 90 per cent chance that the loan will be repaid in full, and a 10 per cent chance that the firm will be bankrupt at the end of the year. In the event that the firm is bankrupt, its assets can be sold for £600,000. However, the legal costs of seizing Westlake's assets will cost the bank £100,000. How much will a bank charge for the loan, if it prices loans to companies like Westlake to earn, on average, 10 per cent? How is the interest rate charged on the loan affected by the potential bankruptcy costs?

Answer: To realize its 10 per cent expected return, the bank needs to receive, on average, £1.1 million at the end of the year. If Westlake is bankrupt, the bank will receive only £500,000. Hence, to receive £1.1 million, on average, it must receive £1.167 million if the firm is not bankrupt (since $0.1 \times$ £0.5 million + $0.9 \times$ £1.167 million = £1.1 million). In other words, the bank must charge 16.7 per cent on the loan. If there were no costs associated with bankruptcy, the bank would recover £600,000 instead of £500,000 in the event of bankruptcy, and it would then need to charge only 15.6 per cent on the loan.

The general principle to remember from Example 16.1 is that lenders are likely to anticipate future events and thus require compensation for the costs they expect to bear.

Results

Result 16.1

Debt holders charge an interest premium that reflects the expected costs they must bear in the event of default. Therefore equity holders indirectly bear the expected costs of bankruptcy and must consider these costs when choosing their optimal capital structures.

16.2 Debt Holder–Equity Holder Conflicts: An Indirect Bankruptcy Cost

If direct bankruptcy costs were the only costs associated with debt financing, it would be difficult to justify the relatively low debt ratios of firms such as Microsoft and Nokia that have long histories of generating taxable earnings and could presumably lower their costs of capital by increasing their leverage. The expected present value of the direct costs of bankruptcy is incorporated into the firm's borrowing costs. Therefore these direct costs cannot exceed the present value of the yearly difference between the firm's borrowing rate and the comparable default-free rates of interest (for example, the rates on Treasury bonds). The difference between Microsoft's borrowing rate and the default-free interest rate on government bonds is small – about 0.5 to 1.0 per cent. This suggests that the direct costs of bankruptcy should have a trivial effect on Microsoft's capital structure decision. Moreover, a large part of the difference in borrowing rates may be due to the favourable tax treatment and greater liquidity of government bonds.

To justify why many firms continue to use more costly equity financing, one must consider the indirect costs of bankruptcy. Indirect costs often arise because of the threat of bankruptcy, and are relevant even if the firm never defaults on its obligations. Because of this, we often refer to them as **financial distress costs**. The threat of bankruptcy affects a firm's relationships with its lenders, and in other ways affects its ability to operate efficiently. While Part 4 contains a comprehensive treatment of these bankruptcy-related inefficiencies, this chapter focuses exclusively on the operating inefficiencies generated by bankruptcy-induced distortions in the relationship between debt holders and equity holders.[3]

[3] Indirect bankruptcy costs that arise for other reasons are examined in Chapter 17.

Equity Holder Incentives

The incentives of equity holders to maximize the value of their shares are not necessarily consistent with the incentive to maximize the total value of the firm's debt and equity. Indeed, shareholders of a levered firm often have an incentive to implement investment strategies that reduce the value of the firm's outstanding debt. To understand this concept, remember that the total value of a firm equals the value of its debt plus the value of its equity. Therefore strategies that decrease the value of a firm's debt without reducing its total value increase the firm's share price. Equity holders have an incentive to carry out these kinds of strategies if permitted to do so. Similarly, they may also implement strategies that *reduce* the total value of the firm's debt and equity claims, if these strategies transfer a sufficient amount from the debt holders to the equity holders. The implications of this point are summarized in Result 16.2.

Results

Result 16.2

Firms acting to maximize their share prices make different decisions when they have debt in their capital structures than when they are financed completely with equity.

Who Bears the Costs of the Incentive Problem?

Before considering specific strategies that enable equity holders to gain at the expense of debt holders, note that sophisticated lenders will anticipate the equity holders' incentives to implement strategies of self-interest, and will determine the interest rates they charge on their loans accordingly. A lender who anticipates that equity holders will take actions in the future that reduce the value of the lender's claims will charge higher interest rates. In this way, the equity holders bear the expected costs of their future adverse incentives in the form of higher interest rates at the time they borrow. As a result, firms have an incentive to convince their lenders that they will not engage in such behaviour, and that they will instead act to maximize the total value of the firm: the value of their debt plus the value of their equity. However, firms may have difficulty committing credibly to a policy of maximizing the firm's total value rather than the value of their shares.

How Equity Holders Can Expropriate Debt Holder Wealth

The firm's equity holders can expropriate wealth from its debt holders in various ways. For example, they could instruct the firm's managers to sell off all its assets and pay the proceeds of this liquidation as a dividend to the shareholders, leaving the debt holders with valueless paper. Debt holders, aware that equity holders might implement this type of action, demand covenants, which are contracts between the borrower and lender that preclude such actions.[4] However, as we shall discuss in Section 16.3, debt covenants cannot solve all potential conflicts that can arise between equity holders and debt holders.

The various distortions in investment strategies that might arise because of conflicts of interest between equity holders and debt holders can be placed into one of the following categories.

- The **debt overhang problem**: equity holders may *underinvest* – that is, pass up profitable (positive-NPV) investments because the firm's existing debt captures most of the project's benefits; this is sometimes referred to as the **underinvestment problem**.
- The **asset substitution problem**: equity holders have a tendency to take on overly risky projects, even when they have negative NPV.
- The **short-sighted investment problem**: equity holders will have a tendency to pass up profitable investment projects that pay off over a long time horizon in favour of less profitable (lower-NPV) projects that pay off more quickly.
- The **reluctance to liquidate problem**: equity holders may want to keep a firm operating when its liquidation value exceeds its operating value.

Each of these possibilities will be considered in the following subsections.

[4] In reality, regulations exist in most countries to prevent a firm from expropriating wealth from the firm's debt holders by paying out all its cash as a liquidating dividend. However, lenders must still be aware of the incentive of equity holders to pay out excessive amounts of cash.

The Debt Overhang Problem

Chapter 13 noted that, with risky debt, the NPV calculated by discounting the total cash flows generated by a project at the project's WACC can substantially differ from the NPV of the cash flows to equity holders. Recall from Example 13.16 that Glastron had a riskless project that yielded 12 per cent per year. Hence, if the risk-free rate is 10 per cent per year, Glastron can create value by taking this project, because it generates cash flows that exceed those of another investment, the risk-free asset, which costs the same and perfectly tracks the project. However, this value is realized by Glastron's shareholders only when the firm can borrow at the risk-free rate. Since Example 13.16 assumed that Glastron's borrowing rate was 13 per cent, Glastron shareholders would be worse off if the project was selected. By taking the project, Glastron shareholders would realize a cash inflow of 12 per cent per year, which would be financed by a cash outflow of 13 per cent per year. Thus Glastron's shareholders would lose 1 per cent of this project's cost in every period.

Discounting Cash Flows to Equity Holders versus Discounting Total Cash Flows

The Glastron project was a positive-NPV project as traditionally defined. However, the cash flows to the firm's shareholders, after financing the project, are always negative, so it follows that the NPV of the project must be negative from the shareholders' perspective. This example illustrates that it is important to distinguish between NPVs to the firm and the NPV of the project that accrues to the firm's shareholders.

Results

Result 16.3

Selecting projects with positive NPVs can at times reduce the value of a levered firm's equity.

In the Glastron example, the risk-free project will create value, as the traditional NPV rule indicates. However, the project creates value for the firm's debt holders rather than its equity holders. By adding the safe project, the firm becomes somewhat less risky, and if the firm does go bankrupt, debt holders are likely to have more assets to divide up. Hence debt holders would like the firm to take the project, but equity holders would like the firm to pass it up.

Underinvestment as a Consequence of Debt Overhang

Glastron exemplifies the underinvestment that is generated by *debt overhang*.[5] This problem arises when a firm's existing debt load causes it to pass up positive-NPV projects because borrowing is too costly, or, as in the following illustration, impossible.

To examine the debt overhang problem in more depth, consider Lily Pharmaceuticals Research, a recent start-up firm shown in Exhibit 16.1. Lily recently spent €100 million to undertake research on a new drug to

Exhibit 16.1 Lily Pharmaceuticals Research

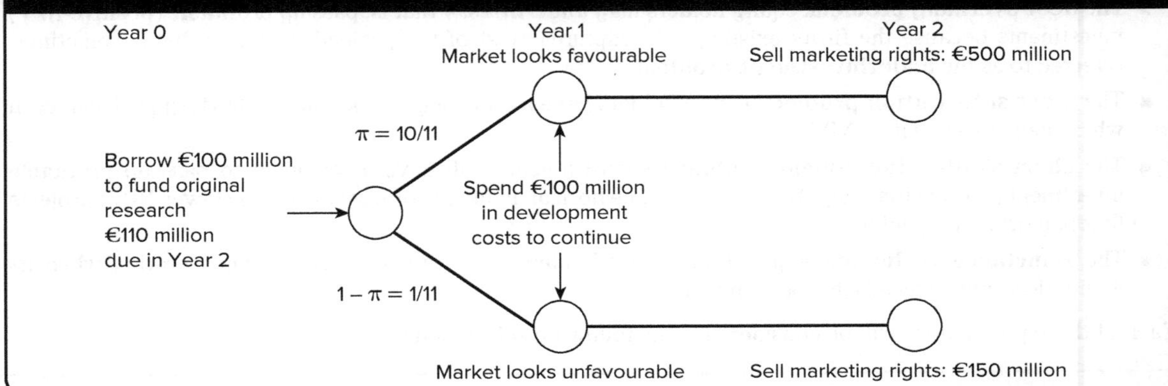

[5] Myers (1977) originally described this underinvestment problem.

prevent facial wrinkles. Assume that if the market for this drug looks favourable (see the upper branch of Exhibit 16.1), the firm can spend an additional €100 million to develop the drug further, receive regulatory approval and bring it to market. If this happens, which we assume will happen 10 out of 11 times, Lily, one year later, can sell the marketing rights to the drug for €500 million. However, if the market looks less favourable (see the lower branch of the exhibit – 1 out of 11 times), then the company will have a drug with marketing rights worth only €150 million, provided that it spends the additional €100 million for development in year 1.

To finance this research, Lily issued a bond with a covenant specifying that any additional debt the firm issues must have lower priority in the event of bankruptcy. To simplify this example, assume that investors are risk neutral and that the appropriate expected rate of return on bonds is zero. However, as shown below, the firm will default on this obligation and pay nothing when the market is unfavourable, which occurs 1 in 11 times. Therefore, to raise the €100 million, Lily must promise to pay €110 million in the future to compensate investors for the possibility that they may not be paid.

In the less favourable situation, continuing with the project is still a positive-NPV investment, because it costs €100 million and returns €150 million. The initial €100 million research investment, which has already been spent, is a sunk cost that should not affect the calculation of the NPV of this project. However, given the firm's €110 million senior debt obligation, new investors with subordinated claims would be unwilling to provide more than €40 million – the difference between the €150 million in value and the €110 million senior claim – to fund the project. As a result, the firm will be unable to obtain year 1 financing when the project is less successful, and it will therefore default on the original loan if this situation arises.

Results

Result 16.4

Firms that have existing senior debt obligations may not be able to obtain financing for positive-NPV investments.

Underinvestment and the Free-Rider Problem

The original lenders at Lily would have been better off if it had been possible, as a group, to put up the year 1 money needed to fund the project. Given that they would otherwise lose their original €100 million investment, it would pay them to invest the additional €100 million, even if the pay-off on the new loan is only €40 million. However, if the original debt is held by a diffuse group of lenders, it would be difficult to persuade them to invest additional funds, because the new debt would achieve below market returns. The situation creates what is known as a free-rider problem. In this **free-rider problem**, the collective interest of the original lenders is to provide additional funds to the firm, but it is not in the interest of any of the individual lenders to do the same. Each individual lender would like to free-ride on the decision of other lenders to bail out the firm.[6]

How the Seniority Structure of Debt Affects the Debt Overhang Problem

The debt overhang problem in the Lily example arose because Lily's existing debt had protective covenants that prevented the company from issuing new debt that was senior to the existing debt. Financing the R&D with unprotected debt would have allowed the firm to finance the additional investment with new debt that would be senior to the original debt.[7] If existing debt is unprotected, new debt can be issued to fund the project, as long as the project's value exceeds the new debt obligation. If Lily's original debt financing was not senior, a new riskless senior debt obligation of €100 million could be issued to fund the €100 million investment, leaving €50 million for the original debt holders when the senior obligation is paid.

Unfortunately, although using unprotected debt solves the underinvestment problem analysed in the Lily example, it can cause additional problems that are likely to make this alternative unattractive. In particular, it provides firms with an incentive to raise additional senior debt when they do not really need it. In addition, unprotected debt increases the incentive for firms to take on overly risky projects, as we discuss later in this chapter. A related but better alternative, which we consider in more detail later in the chapter, is project

[6] Later in this chapter, when discussing how to resolve incentive conflicts between debt holders and equity holders, we analyse how a banking relation may help a firm solve this free-rider problem and mitigate the effect of debt overhang.

[7] The relevance of debt seniority rules for the debt overhang problem is considered in Stulz and Johnson (1985).

financing, which can be used in cases where the cash flows of the project can be separated from the cash flows of the rest of the firm.

How the Debt Overhang Problem Affects Dividend Policy

The Lily example assumed that the firm needs to raise money from external sources. However, most firms have internally generated funds available for investments, and often must address the relevant decision of whether to distribute the funds to shareholders as a dividend or a share repurchase or, alternatively, use the money to fund additional investment. When an investment is financed from a firm's retained earnings, the tendency to underinvest becomes even more clear, as the next example illustrates.

Real World Insight

Debtholder–Equityholder Conflicts in a Financially Risky Firm

Consider Con Partners Ltd, which has purchased a £100 million office building. The company provided a down payment on the building of £20 million, and financed the rest with a 10-year fixed coupon bond with a coupon rate of 10 per cent. The bond required annual payments of £8 million per year for 10 years with £80 million in principal due at the end of 10 years. At the time of purchase, Con Partners knew that the building was going to generate £12 million in annual rent and require £3 million a year in maintenance to maintain its value.

Two years after Con Partners bought the building, the Glasgow office market suffered a serious decline, and the building's value fell to £70 million. Fortunately, the firm had long-term leases, so their rental income was not seriously affected. However, the group's incentive to pay out the rental income as cash to the partners rather than use the cash to maintain the building was affected by this downturn. Since the partners believed that the group was quite likely to default on the final £80 million repayment of principal, they had an incentive to distribute (to the partners) as much cash as possible before the final repayment date, without regard for how their actions would affect the building's value.

The partners discussed cutting their annual maintenance budget from £3 million to £2 million, which would increase the amount distributed to the partners by £1 million per year. Cutting the maintenance budget would also lower the building's value by £18 million at the time of the final mortgage payment, due in eight years. Under most circumstances the partners generally would not consider saving £1 million per year over an eight-year period, if it meant reducing the building's value by £18 million. However, the £1 million annual savings would be distributed directly to the partners, so if the market for office buildings failed to turn around, the £18 million loss in value would be borne by the holders of the mortgage. As a result, maintaining the building properly – clearly a positive-NPV project when considering the interests of debt as well as equity claimants – was an option that was rejected by the partners. Apparently, the decision was made without regard for the lenders.

This case study illustrates the following point.

Results

Result 16.5

With risky debt, equity holders have an incentive to pass up internally financed positive-NPV projects when the funds can be paid out to equity holders as a dividend.

Using Loan Covenants to Mitigate the Underinvestment Problem

Most commercial mortgages contain covenants that protect the lender from the kind of behaviour described in the Con Partners Real World Insight case. The covenants can be written in one of two ways. The first specifies that the partners maintain the building appropriately. The second eliminates the incentive to cut maintenance by restricting the payout to the partners. This second approach works because the partners have no incentive to underinvest in maintenance if they are unable to immediately pass on the cost savings to themselves.

The first alternative is impractical, because it is very difficult to specify in most corporate loan contracts exactly what kinds of investment a firm must undertake. As a result, most corporate loans and privately placed bonds have restrictions on the amount of funds the firm can pay out in dividends or, equivalently, the monetary value of shares that can be repurchased per year. This is also true for most public bonds that are not investment grade.

Typically, bond and loan covenants specify dividend restrictions as a function of a firm's earnings. For example, a corporation may be required to retain at least 50 per cent of its earnings. The disadvantage of this kind of covenant is that it provides an incentive for firms to inflate their earnings artificially so that they can pay out more in dividends. In the Con Partners case, for example, a reduction in building maintenance services would lead to an increase in reported earnings, since maintenance is generally expensed. This would allow the firm to pay out more in dividends. Hence dividend restrictions tied to corporate earnings may not keep firms from cutting back on items such as maintenance and service; these may be good investments for the firm, but they have the effect of initially reducing reported income.

Empirical Evidence on Dividends and Investment Distortions

Although dividend distortions of this kind seem to be important in theory, there is no empirical evidence suggesting that investment distortions of this kind are prevalent.[8] This may be because the tendency to increase payouts and underinvest is not particularly important when the probability of bankruptcy is low, or because covenants are effective at limiting these distortions. With respect to the latter hypothesis, there is empirical evidence that, for firms in financial distress, dividend covenants seem to be effective in forcing dividend cuts.[9]

The Short-Sighted Investment Problem

A popular topic for financial journalists is the perceived short-sightedness of British and American businesses. A common claim was that short-sightedness was worsened by the increased use of debt financing by some firms; highly levered firms prefer projects that pay off quickly, since short-term projects allow them to meet their near-term debt obligations more easily. An alternative view, which is discussed in later chapters, is that the short-term horizons of investors encourage managers to make myopic investment decisions.

By extending the analysis in the preceding subsection, we can see how future debt obligations can make firms short-sighted; in other words, debt can lead firms to favour lower-NPV investment projects that pay off quickly over higher-NPV projects with lower initial cash flows. The intuition for this is rooted in the debt overhang problem. Firms with large debt obligations need to pay high borrowing rates on new subordinated debt used to refinance the portion of their existing debt that is maturing. Thus firms have an incentive to generate cash quickly to minimize the amount of debt that they will need to refinance at high rates.

To illustrate this possibility, consider the case of Applied Textronics, which has debt obligations that are due both next year and in two years. The firm has a debt obligation of €100 million due next year and €40 million due the following year. The firm is considering two equally costly mutually exclusive projects:

1. a short-term project that generates positive cash flows next year and zero cash flows thereafter
2. a long-term project with positive cash flows next year and the following year.

The year 1 (and only) cash flow for the short-term project is €50 million, whereas cash flows are €20 million in year 1 and €40 million in year 2 for the long-term project (see Exhibit 16.2).

Assume that the risk-free rate of interest is zero and both cash flows are certain, implying that the present value of the long-term project exceeds the present value of the short-term project. The firm can also forecast with certainty the €50 million in cash flows from its existing investment projects next year.

However, the firm's cash flows from its existing investments in year 2 are uncertain. The cash flow is €60 million in the favourable state of the economy and €10 million in the unfavourable state of the economy. The probability of each state of the economy is 50 per cent.

If Applied Textronics selects the short-term project, it will be able to meet its €100 million debt obligation next year; its year 1 cash flows of €50 million from its existing assets plus the €50 million from the new investment equals the size of the year 1 debt obligation. If the firm takes the long-term project, however, it will generate total cash flows of only €70 million (= €50 million + €20 million) in year 1, and will thus require an

---

[8] Long et al. (1994) found no evidence that firms increase their dividends significantly following an increase in their outstanding debt. However, there is some evidence that bond prices react negatively when firms announce large increases in their dividends. See Dhillon and Johnson (1994). Maxwell and Stephens (2003) find that bond prices fall and credit ratings are likely to be downgraded after share repurchases.

[9] This issue was examined in a study of financially distressed firms by DeAngelo and DeAngelo (1990).

Exhibit 16.2 Applied Textronics Cash Flows

	Debt due	From existing assets	From short-term projects	From long-term project
Year 1	€100 million	€50 million	€50 million	€50 million
Year 2	€40 million	€60 million in favourable state €10 million in unfavourable state	€0 million	€40 million

additional €30 million in new debt to meet its year 1 debt obligation. If this new debt is subordinated to the old debt, the firm must offer to pay the new lenders €50 million at the end of the following year in order to raise the €30 million. This is because the lenders will receive, on average, only €30 million if €50 million is promised: €50 million as promised in the favourable state, but only €10 million in the unfavourable state (the €50 million in cash from existing assets and the long-term project less the €40 million senior debt obligation).

The amounts given in Exhibit 16.2 indicate that Applied Textronics will be unable to meet its year 2 debt obligation if the unfavourable state of the economy occurs, regardless of whether the firm chooses the long-term or short-term project. If the short-term project is selected, the firm has only €10 million in cash and a €40 million obligation. If the long-term project is selected, the firm has €50 million in cash, but a €90 million obligation (the existing €40 million obligation plus the new €50 million obligation). In either case, the firm's equity will be worth zero in the unfavourable state of the economy.

If the firm takes the long-term project, the firm's equity will be worth €10 million in the favourable state of the economy [€40 million + €60 million – (€40 million + €50 million)]. If the firm takes the short-term project, its equity value in the favourable state of the economy will be €20 million (€60 million – €40 million). Hence the firm's equity holders are better off selecting the short-term project, even though it has a lower NPV.

How do the shareholders benefit from taking the lower-NPV investment? Since the firm's existing debt holders are made worse off when the firm selects the short-term project, the gain to the equity holders comes at the expense of the original debt holders, whose debt is due at the end of year 2. These debt holders are paid in full in the unfavourable state of the economy if the firm takes the long-term project, but they receive only €10 million of their €40 million obligation in the unfavourable state of the economy when the short-term project is selected. This insight is summarized below.

Results

Result 16.6

Firms with large amounts of debt tend to pass up high-NPV projects in favour of lower-NPV projects that pay off sooner.

The Asset Substitution Problem

This subsection describes an additional problem that might arise when firms are financed with debt. Debt provides an incentive for firms to take on unnecessary risk, substituting riskier investment projects for less risky projects. We call this the *asset substitution problem.*[10]

Option pricing theory provides one way to think about the asset substitution problem. Recall from Chapter 8 that the pay-off to equity holders is similar to the pay-off from a call option on the firm's assets. Equity holders can realize an unlimited upside, but in the event of an unfavourable outcome, they can do no worse than lose their entire investment because they have limited liability. Hence the pay-off to the equity holders will be either the firm's cash flows less its debt obligation (when cash flows from assets exceed the debt obligation) or zero (when the debt obligation exceeds the cash flows).

[10] A large body of academic literature discusses the asset substitution problem. Jensen and Meckling (1976) and Galai and Masulis (1976) were the original contributors to the literature.

The implication of the option pricing model – that option values increase with increases in the volatility of the underlying equity – can thus be applied to show that a firm's equity will be more valuable if the firm's managers select more risky investments. However, a firm's debt, which can be viewed as the combination of the firm's assets along with a short position in a call option on those assets, becomes less valuable if the firm's investments become riskier. Hence increasing a firm's risk transfers wealth from the firm's debt holders to its equity holders.

The Incentives of a Firm to Take Higher Risks: The Case of Unistar

Consider Unistar, a start-up firm that plans to manufacture memory chips, and has borrowed the money to build a factory. Unistar's managers now have to decide on one of two designs for the production process. Although the two processes look nearly identical to the firm's bankers, and each costs £70 million, Unistar's management knows that process 2 involves much more risk than process 1.

Debt holders are aware of the two alternatives, and can forecast the possible pay-offs of each, but they cannot observe which process the firm will decide upon until after they lend the money. To simplify the analysis, assume as before that investors are all risk neutral, and thus want to maximize expected returns. Also assume that the risk-free interest rate is zero. Thus the present values of the projects are their expected pay-offs. The projects have different pay-offs, depending on whether the state of the economy is favourable or unfavourable. These pay-offs, which are equally likely to occur, are given in Exhibit 16.3.

Exhibit 16.3 Unistar's Alternative Pay-offs

	Cash flow if state of the economy is		
	Unfavourable ($\pi = 0.5$)	Favourable ($1 - \pi = 0.5$)	Expected value
Process 1	£50 million	£100 million	£75 million
Process 2	£25 million	£115 million	£70 million

From the perspective of an all-equity firm, process 1 is the better alternative. It achieves a £5 million NPV, the £75 million expected value minus the £70 million cost, whereas process 2 achieves zero NPV, since the costs and expected values are both £70 million.

Assume that the firm uses debt to finance £40 million of the £70 million to be invested, and raises the other £30 million from internal sources. These internal funds can be viewed as the equity holders' contribution. Exhibit 16.4 presents a summary of the pay-offs to the firm's equity holders *after repayment of the £40 million debt obligation.*

Exhibit 16.4 Unistar's Pay-offs to Equity Holders When the Debt Obligation Is £40 Million

	Cash flow if state of the economy is		
	Unfavourable ($\pi = 0.5$)	Favourable ($1 - \pi = 0.5$)	Expected value
Process 1	£10 million	£60 million	£35.0 million
Process 2	£0 million	£75 million	£37.5 million

The pay-offs shown in Exhibit 16.4 equal the pay-offs in Exhibit 16.3 less the £40 million debt obligation, with one important exception. The equity holders' pay-off in the unfavourable state of the economy for process 2 is given as 0 instead of –£15 million (= £25 million – £40 million) because limited liability implies that equity holders can do no worse than receive zero. Given these pay-offs, the equity holders' expected pay-off of £37.5 million from process 2 exceeds their pay-off of £35.0 million from process 1. Result 16.7 summarizes the concept illustrated by this example.

Results

Result 16.7

The equity holders of a levered firm may prefer a high-risk, low-NPV (or even negative-NPV) project to a low-risk, high-NPV project.

How Do Debt Holders Respond to Shareholder Incentives?

If debt holders naively believe that process 1 (the higher-NPV project described in Exhibit 16.3) will be selected, they will provide the debt financing assumed above. However, sophisticated debt holders should understand Unistar's incentives to take the riskier project, process 2, and realize that in this situation they would not be making a sensible loan. Specifically, if debt holders anticipate that Unistar will select the high-risk project when it has a £40 million loan obligation, they will realize that their loan would have default risk, and that they will receive only £25 million of the £40 million promised debt payment if the bad state of the economy occurs. Thus their loan has an expected value of only £32.5 million (0.5 × £25 million + 0.5 × £40 million), which implies that the debt holders would be unwilling to provide £40 million today for the uncertain promise of obtaining £40 million in the future.

If debt holders contribute only £32.5 million now for £40 million promised in the future, the firm's equity holders would have to contribute £37.5 million to fund the project. However, as shown in Exhibit 16.4, equity holders would receive only £35.0 million, on average, when process 1 is selected, so they would expect to lose money in this case. Exhibit 16.4 shows that process 2 provides equity holders with £37.5 million, on average, which exactly equals their costs. Thus Unistar fails to gain from the high-risk, low-NPV project, and is unable to realize the gain from the positive-NPV project.

If the equity holders were able to commit to taking process 1, debt holders would be willing to contribute £40 million for the £40 million obligation, because (with the lowest cash flow from process 1 being £50 million) they would be repaid with certainty. Equity holders would then need to put up only the remaining £30 million needed, creating for them a £5 million surplus (= £35 million – £30 million). However, if debt holders find it difficult to monitor a firm's investments, it may not be easy for Unistar to include loan covenants that allow it to commit credibly to process 1. The debt holders would realize that Unistar's equity holders will try to convince them that they (the equity holders) will select process 1. But if this process cannot be verified, the equity holders have an incentive to adopt process 2 after debt holders and the company finalize the terms of the loan. Hence the terms of the loan will reflect the risks associated with process 2, not process 1, and the equity holders ultimately bear the costs associated with their distorted incentives.

Results

Result 16.8

With sophisticated debt holders, equity holders must bear the costs that arise because of their tendency to substitute high-risk, low-NPV projects for low-risk, high-NPV projects.

The Unistar example points out that if the firm raised £32.5 million by issuing a bond with a face value of £40.0 million, then the zero-NPV project would be taken, and the equity holders could not realize the gains from the positive-NPV project. This can be considered a cost of having risky debt. If Unistar had instead raised only £25 million in debt, it would have had no problem. Debt holders would be willing to lend this amount, because no matter which project Unistar chooses, debt holders would receive their £25 million with certainty. If the company chose process 1, equity holders would receive an expected pay-off of £50 million [0.5 × (£50 million – £25 million) + 0.5 × (£100 million – £25 million)]. If the company chose process 2, equity holders would have an expected pay-off of £45 million [= 0.5 × (£0) + 0.5 × (£115 million – £25 million)]. Since equity holders would have contributed £45 million in either case, they would prefer process 1 and would capture its £5 million NPV. These issues are illustrated in Example 16.2.

Example 16.2

The Cost Associated with the Asset Substitution Problem

Unoit Industries has two mutually exclusive €50 million investment opportunities, R and S, which it plans to fund with debt. Project S pays off €60 million for certain, and project R pays off only €20 million when the economy is poor and €90 million when the economy is good. For simplicity, assume that investors are risk neutral.

a What is the NPV of each project, assuming that the economy is equally likely to be favourable or unfavourable, and the discount rate is 0 per cent?

Suppose Unoit can raise the £50 million by issuing a bond with a face value of £50 million (because the lender naively believes the company will take the safe project).

b Which project will Unoit shareholders prefer?

c What is the expected pay-off to the naive lenders?

Now suppose that the debt holders are sophisticated.

d What must the debt holders be promised, which project will the company select, and what do the shareholders gain?

Answer:

a $NPV_S = 0.5(£60 \text{ million}) + 0.5(£60 \text{ million}) - £50 \text{ million} = £10 \text{ million}$

$NPV_R = 0.5(£20 \text{ million}) + 0.5(£90 \text{ million}) - £50 \text{ million} = £5 \text{ million}$

b With naive debt holders, the pay-off to equity holders with project S is

$0.5(£60 \text{ million} - £50 \text{ million}) + 0.5(£60 \text{ million} - £50 \text{ million}) = £10 \text{ million}$

The pay-off to equity holders with project R is

$0.5(£0) + 0.5(£90 \text{ million} - £50 \text{ million}) = £20 \text{ million}$

Thus, if the firm's managers act in the interest of shareholders, they will choose project R.

c Given that project R is chosen, the naive debt holders do not receive full payment in the poor state of the economy. On average, they receive only 0.5(£20 million) + 0.5(£50 million) = £35 million.

d Sophisticated lenders, aware of both projects, will realize that equity holders have an incentive to invest in the riskier project. For the £50 million loan, they will require a promised future payment of £80 million. With the selection of project R, they receive an expected pay-off of 0.5(£20 million) + 0.5(£80 million) = £50 million, so on average they recover their investment. In this situation, the pay-off to equity holders selecting project R is 0.5(0) + 0.5(£90 million – £80 million) = £5 million. The pay-off is zero if project S is selected, because in neither state of the economy can the £80 million obligation be met. Thus equity holders will select project R despite its lower NPV. If they had been able to commit to taking project S, equity holders would have created and been able to capture £10 million instead of £5 million in NPV.

Asset Substitution in the Banking Sector

The fact that debt can lead firms to select extremely risky projects does not by itself create a cost of debt financing. Indeed, in the early 2000s, a number of banks initially created value for their shareholders by investing in high-risk mortgages and other risky ventures that may not have had positive NPVs. These investments were funded with debt that was raised in the form of insured deposits. The shareholders would have received large gains if the investments had turned out well. However, when the global financial crisis erupted in 2008, some of the losses that occurred when the investments turned bad were shared by the government, which essentially insured the deposits.

Taking added risks was especially attractive to the banks because of deposit insurance and, as a result, the borrowing costs of the banks did not accurately reflect the risks that the banks were taking with subprime mortgages.

Credit Rationing

The tendency to increase risk when a firm's debt obligations increase also implies that an increase in interest rates adversely affects a firm's project choice. Some economists have argued that, because of the tendency to increase risk, some banks ration credit rather than increase borrowing rates when credit conditions tighten.[11] In 2008, this hypothesis became all too real when the subprime mortgage credit crisis led to a global credit squeeze, and credit effectively dried up. This was so severe that Northern Rock plc, a British bank, was unable to roll over short-term credit and had to apply to the Bank of England for emergency funding. As happened to Northern Rock, in such situations, lenders may choose not to lend to certain firms, regardless of the rate of

[11] See, for example, Stiglitz and Weiss (1981).

interest the firms are willing to pay. The choice not to lend stems from the lenders' belief that firms will respond to higher interest obligations by choosing riskier investments. The following discussion illustrates how a firm that is able to obtain credit when interest rates are low may be denied credit when interest rates are high.

The Multi-Universal Corporation has an opportunity to take on one of two €100 million projects that the firm's debt holders cannot distinguish from each another. For simplicity, again assume that investors are risk neutral, and the risk-free rate of interest is initially zero per cent. The pay-offs and probabilities of these two mutually exclusive projects are summarized in Exhibit 16.5. The pay-offs for the two projects are the same if a bad outcome is realized (€50 million), but the pay-off is higher with a good outcome if the company takes on project B (€150 million) rather than project A (€130 million). The probability of a good outcome is only 20 per cent if the company selects project B, but it is 80 per cent if it selects project A.

Exhibit 16.5 Multi-Universal's Project Pay-offs

	Cash flow if state of the economy is		Probability of good	Expected value
	Good	Bad		
Project A	€130 million	€50 million	0.8	€114 million
Project B	€150 million	€50 million	0.2	€70 million

The NPV of project A is €14 million (= €114 million – €100 million). The NPV of project B is –€30 million (= €70 million – €100 million). If the firm can convince the lender that it will take project A, then it will be able to obtain the required €100 million financing by issuing a zero-coupon bond that pays €112.5 million at year-end when the pay-offs are realized. As the following equation shows, a zero-coupon bond that promises €112.5 million provides the lender with the expectation of

$$0.8 \times €112.5 \text{ million} + 0.2 \times €50.0 \text{ million} = €100.0 \text{ million}$$

With a zero discount rate, the firm will select the less risky project (project A), because the expected pay-off to the firm's shareholders from taking project A is

$$0.8 \times (€130 \text{ million} - €112.5 \text{ million}) = €14 \text{ million}$$

The expected pay-off from taking project B is

$$0.2 \times (€150 \text{ million} - €112.5 \text{ million}) = €7.5 \text{ million}$$

Now consider what happens if the risk-free rate of interest increases to 12 per cent and the pay-offs of the projects remain the same. Lenders who believe that the company will take the safe project (project A) will now demand a €127.5 million promised payment for a €100.0 million loan, because a €127.5 million promised payment is required for the lender to receive the €112.0 million needed, on average, to achieve a 12 per cent expected rate of return: that is,

$$0.8 \times €127.5 \text{ million} + 0.2 \times €50 \text{ million} = €112 \text{ million}$$

However, as seen below, with a promised payment of this magnitude, the firm will prefer project B, the more risky project, because it provides a higher return for the equity holders.

With a €127.5 million promised payment to debt holders, the expected pay-off to the equity holders from selecting project A is

$$0.8 \times (€130 \text{ million} - €127.5 \text{ million}) = €2.0 \text{ million}$$

The expected pay-off from project B is

$$0.2 \times (€150 \text{ million} - €127.5 \text{ million}) = €4.5 \text{ million}$$

Realizing that the company will select the more risky project in these circumstances, the lender would not be willing to offer a €100.0 million loan for a €127.5 million promised payment, since it will not, on average, achieve the 12 per cent expected return on its investment. In this case, there is no promised interest payment that will induce the bank to lend money to the firm, because even the maximum debt obligation that the firm can possibly pay, €150 million, is insufficient to yield the lender an expected 12 per cent return. This example illustrates the following result.

Results

Result 16.9

Firms with the potential to select high-risk projects may be unable to obtain debt financing at any borrowing rate when risk-free interest rates are high.

The effect of the level of interest rates on the ability of firms to obtain debt financing is further illustrated in Example 16.3.

Example 16.3

Interest Rate Changes, Risk Incentives and Credit Rationing

The Red Lagoon is choosing between project M, which introduces a mass-produced deep-fried Mars bar and project K, which introduces a healthy, low-fat kangaroo burger. Project M costs £100 million – used for marketing, training of cooks, and so forth – and yields cash flows for the next year of £115 million with certainty. Project K also costs £100 million but, because of the controversial nature of the meat, has only a limited probability of success. The marketing experts at Red Lagoon estimate that there is only a 1 in 3 chance that kangaroo meat will be accepted and the project will be successful. If project K is successful, it will yield cash flows over the next year of £142 million. If it fails, cash flows will only be £60 million. The table summarizes the projects available to Red Lagoon.

	Project cost	Success pay-off	Failure pay-off	Success probability
Project M	£ 100 million	£115 million	–	1
Project K	£ 100 million	£ 142 million	£ 60 million	$\frac{1}{3}$

a Suppose the discount rate is zero. What is the NPV of each project?

b Could Red Lagoon obtain £100 million in debt financing by issuing a zero-coupon bond with a face value of £100 million? Which project would Red Lagoon take if it can issue such a bond?

c Suppose the risk-free discount rate is 10 per cent, so that lenders require a zero-coupon bond with a face value of £110 million to make a riskless loan of £100 million. Would rational lenders make such a loan to Red Lagoon?

d What would the bond's face value need to be in order for debt holders to receive a fair return?

Answer:

a $NPV_M = £115 \text{ million} - £100 \text{ million} = £15 \text{ million}$

$$NPV_K = \frac{1}{3}(£142 \text{ million}) + \frac{2}{3}(£60 \text{ million}) - £100 \text{ million} = -£12.667 \text{ million}$$

b With such a bond, the expected pay-off to equity holders from project M is

$$£115 \text{ million} - £100 \text{ million} = £15 \text{ million}$$

and the expected pay-off to equity holders if Red Lagoon chooses project K is

$$\frac{1}{3}(£142 \text{ million} - £100 \text{ million}) + \frac{2}{3}(£0) = £14 \text{ million}$$

Thus equity holders would choose project M. When the company selects project M, debt holders receive their £100 million for sure, and thus are willing to pay £100 million for the bond. With zero interest rates, Red Lagoon can realize the gains from the positive-NPV project.

c With a bond having a face value of £110 million, the expected pay-off to equity holders from project M is

$$\text{£115 million} - \text{£110 million} = \text{£5 million}$$

The expected pay-off to equity holders if the company selects project K is

$$\frac{1}{3}(\text{£142 million} - \text{£110 million}) + \frac{2}{3}(\text{£0}) = \text{£10.667 million}$$

Thus equity holders would select project K. If they select project K, the debt holders expect to receive only

$$\frac{1}{3}(\text{£110 million}) + \frac{2}{3}(\text{£60 million}) = \text{£.76.667 million}$$

which is less than the £110 million they require for the loan of £100 million, so rational lenders will not provide £100 million in debt financing for a £110 million debt obligation from Red Lagoon.

d Given that project K is chosen, the lender will require a payment of F in the good state for £100 million in debt financing, where F solves

$$\frac{1}{3}(F) + \frac{2}{3}(\text{£60 million}) = \text{£110 million}$$

Solving this yields F = £210 million. But such a large promised payment is not feasible. With a £210 million debt obligation, Red Lagoon would always default, and equity would receive nothing. Thus neither project will be taken. Because of the increase in interest rates, Red Lagoon cannot profit from the positive-NPV project.

The Reluctance to Liquidate Problem

One of the most difficult decisions a firm must make is whether to remain in business. It must decide whether to continue to operate or to dismantle the business and sell its property and equipment for its liquidation value. Like the investment decision, the liquidation decision is affected by how much debt the firm has outstanding. In addition, the decision to liquidate can be affected by the firm's bankruptcy status.

Liquidation Costs versus Bankruptcy Costs

Liquidation costs are the difference between the firm's **going concern value** – the present value of the future cash flows that the firm's assets would generate if it were to continue operating – and its **liquidation value**, which is what the firm could collect by liquidating its assets and selling them. Because bankruptcy and liquidation often occur together, liquidation costs are sometimes considered a direct cost of bankruptcy. This makes them an important determinant of a firm's capital structure. However, as we pointed out at the beginning of this chapter, bankruptcy does not necessarily imply liquidation. Indeed, in many bankruptcies, firms are reorganized and continue operating.

Generally, it is in the interests of both debt holders and equity holders to reorganize and to continue operating a bankrupt firm if its going concern value exceeds its liquidation value. As a result, firms that liquidate in bankruptcy tend to do so because the net proceeds from liquidation exceed the present value of the future cash flows that the firm would generate if it were to continue operating. Given that bankruptcy is likely to lead firms to liquidate when it is optimal to do so, liquidation costs should not be viewed as a relevant bankruptcy cost in determining the firm's optimal capital structure.[12]

How Capital Structure Affects Liquidation Policy

Although bankruptcy need not cause a firm to liquidate when it is worth more as a going concern, capital structure can still affect liquidation policy. Managers of financially sound firms, as representatives of their

[12] See Haugen and Senbet (1978) for further elaboration of this point.

equity holders, have an incentive to continue operating their firm, even when the liquidation values of the firm exceed its going concern value.[13] To understand this point, remember that equity holders, as the firm's most junior claimants, receive proceeds from the liquidation only after all other claimants have been satisfied. Therefore, if the face value of a firm's debt exceeds the firm's liquidation value, equity holders are likely to receive nothing in a liquidation. In addition, compared with the pay-off from continuing to operate, liquidation provides a relatively safe pay-off. Therefore liquidation will be less attractive to equity holders than the riskier alternative of continuing to operate. This is analogous to the decision not to exercise an out-of-the-money option, again viewing equity as a call option on the value of the firm: the option is worth nothing if exercised, but it still might pay off in the future.

Managers, of course, have a direct interest in keeping the firm operating, even when the firm's liquidation value exceeds its operating value, because they are likely to lose their jobs if the firm liquidates. Hence they have a strong incentive to continue operating as long as they control the firm. In the event of bankruptcy, managers and equity holders lose much of their control to representatives of debt holders who have an interest in liquidating the firm if doing so enhances the firm's value. As a result, whether a firm liquidates depends on who has the power to make that decision.

The Financial Distress of Energy Distribution Companies in the UK

Consider the problem faced by energy distribution companies in the UK in late 2021. During the summer of 2021, during the global covid restrictions, the price of gas was around £0.55/therm. Within a few months of lockdowns being lifted, followed by the Russian invasion of Ukraine, the price had increased tenfold to £5.50/therm. The UK has a price cap on all retail bills and so from about August 2021, energy companies had to trade at a loss on all retail business. The higher the wholesale liquid gas price became, the bigger the energy companies loss. Most energy distribution companies had debt, so assume that a hypothetical firm had a £50 million debt obligation, and that its going concern value would be worth £60 million if business opportunities recovered (a 50 per cent probability in late 2021), but the company would be forced to liquidate and receive proceeds of only £20 million if poor business conditions continued. Alternatively, it could liquidate immediately and receive £48 million.

The firm's equity holders would clearly prefer to keep the company going in this situation, since there would be nothing left for them in a liquidation once debt holders were paid off. However, if the firm could keep going until the liquid gas price fell back to normal levels, equity holders would realize a value of £10 million (£60 million – £50 million). The debt holders, however, prefer to have the energy firm liquidate its assets immediately! Debt holders realize that there is a 50 per cent chance that they will be paid in full if the gas price falls. However, there also is a 50 per cent chance that most of the liquidation value will be dissipated if the debt holders wait to liquidate, leaving them with only £20 million. Result 16.10 illustrates the point.

Results

Result 16.10

Since debt holders have priority in the event of liquidation, they have a stronger interest in liquidating the assets of a distressed firm than the firm's equity holders, who profit from the possible upside benefits that may be realized if the firm continues to operate. As a result, a firm's financial structure partially determines the conditions under which it liquidates.

Bankruptcy and Liquidation Decisions of Firms with More Than One Class of Debt

When a firm has more than one class of debt (for example, junior and senior debt), the determinants of its bankruptcy and liquidation decisions become considerably more complicated. For the purpose of this discussion, assume that a firm will go bankrupt if:

- it has insufficient cash flow to meet its debt obligations
- it is unable to borrow a sufficient amount to meet its debt obligations.

One might think that the preceding conditions imply that a firm would be bankrupt if it were not generating sufficient cash flow to meet its current debt obligations, and if it were not expecting improvements in the future.

---

[13] See Titman (1984) and Gertner and Sharfstein (1991) for further discussion of this point.

As shown below, however, this is not necessarily true, and such a firm might continue to operate as a going concern, even when its liquidation value greatly exceeds its going concern value.

To understand how a firm can remain in business under these conditions, consider the differing incentives of the firm's equity holders and debt holders in the event of a financial crisis. Equity holders have an incentive to delay bankruptcy, and an even greater incentive to delay liquidation. The value of the equity holders' claims, with their option-like characteristics, increases as its time to maturity lengthens. For this reason, management, when acting in the equity holders' interests, will want to avoid defaulting on the company's debt obligations. Defaulting would make all the firm's current obligations come due immediately, which in effect would eliminate the option value of the equity claims.

For similar reasons, junior creditors may also be reluctant to force a firm into bankruptcy, since their claims also have option-like features.[14] In many cases, these junior creditors may find it in their interest to lend additional money to a firm in financial distress to keep it from going bankrupt. Thus a lender may be willing to make a new loan – which by itself is not a good investment – if doing so increases the value of its past loans to the firm.

Consider, for example, the case of Emruss Holdings, which has no cash flow in the current period, but will have cash flows of £1.5 million next year if the economy is favourable and £0.5 million if the economy is unfavourable. Assuming risk neutrality, a zero discount rate and equal probabilities of the two events, the going concern value of the firm is £1.0 million. Also assume that if the firm were liquidated immediately, it would generate £1.2 million in proceeds. Hence, if the firm were financed entirely with equity, equity holders would choose to have the firm liquidated immediately.

Emruss's capital structure consists of both debt and equity. The debt, described in Exhibit 16.6, includes a £1,000,000 senior debt obligation due next year, with a £150,000 coupon payment due immediately. In addition, Emruss has borrowed money from a venture capitalist to whom it owes £200,000, which is due next year. The debt to the venture capitalist is junior to the £1 million senior debt.

Exhibit 16.6 Emruss's Debt Obligations

	Debt obligations	
	Immediate	Next year
Senior debt holders	£150,000	£1,000,000
Venture capitalist	£0	£200,000

Emruss will be forced into bankruptcy if it cannot meet its £150,000 current senior obligation. If this happens, all its debt obligations become due immediately, and the debt holders will take control of the firm. Exhibit 16.7 shows that senior debt holders will choose to liquidate the firm in this situation, because in an immediate liquidation they are paid in full. However, if the firm does liquidate, the equity holders receive nothing from the liquidation proceeds, and only £50,000 of the venture capitalist's *junior claim* is paid (the £1,200,000 liquidation value less the senior £1,150,000 debt obligation).

Exhibit 16.7 Liquidation Proceeds for Emruss

Pay-off in the event of liquidation	
Senior debt holders	£1,150,000
Venture capitalist	£50,000
Equity holders	£0

Both Emruss's equity holders and its venture capitalist have an incentive to keep the firm going, even though the firm's total value is maximized by liquidating its assets immediately. Given its weak condition, Emruss is willing to promise to pay the venture capitalist £100,000 in interest for a one-year loan that provides an additional £150,000 in financing. Although the 67 per cent *promised* interest rate sounds outrageous, the venture capitalist will be repaid only half of the time, so the expected rate of return on the new loan is actually

[14] See Bulow and Shoven (1978) for further discussion.

negative. However, the venture capitalist cannot view this loan in isolation. By making the loan, the venture capitalist has a 50 per cent chance of being paid the £200,000 owed on the original loan (in the favourable state of the economy) rather than receiving £50,000 immediately from the liquidation proceeds.

Exhibit 16.8 illustrates the pay-offs to the senior debt holders, the venture capitalist and the equity holders if the venture capitalist provides the needed cash infusion. Consider first the incentives of the venture capitalist. The exhibit, which combines the two loans from the venture capitalist as a single package, shows that offering the new loan entails an immediate outlay of £150,000 and a pay-off of £450,000 in the favourable state of the economy, and nothing in the unfavourable state. Comparing this pay-off stream with the alternative of receiving the £50,000 liquidation pay-off immediately, we see that the net cost of offering the loan rather than allowing the firm to liquidate is £200,000 (£150,000 in new financing plus £50,000 in forgone liquidation proceeds). Since a 50 per cent chance of receiving £450,000 is worth more than the £200,000 investment, the venture capitalist would find it worthwhile to make the loan.

Exhibit 16.8 Pay-offs in the Event of a Cash Infusion

	Immediate	Next year states of the economy	
		Favourable	Unfavourable
Senior debt holders	£150,000	£1,000,000	£500,000
Venture capitalist	– £150,000	£450,000	£0
Equity holders	£0	£50,000	£0

Note that the senior debt holders in the Emruss example are made worse off when the more junior venture capitalist injects additional capital into the firm, even though the additional capital has a junior claim. The debt holders receive only £500,000 next year if the firm continues to operate and the unfavourable state of the economy occurs. However, they would have been paid in full had the firm liquidated. Emruss was able to obtain this cash infusion more easily since it had a venture capitalist with an incentive to keep the firm going, just like its equity holders. However, the firm also could have kept going, at least in theory, to the detriment of its senior lenders, by issuing new equity. Example 16.4 illustrates this idea.

Example 16.4

The Incentive to Issue Equity to Avoid Liquidation

Consider Emruss Holdings' financial condition, as described in Exhibit 16.6. Now assume that it does not have the loan obligation to the venture capitalist. Assuming risk neutrality, interest rates of zero and frictionless capital markets, will Emruss issue equity to meet the immediate debt obligation?

Answer: If Emruss does not meet the debt obligation, its equity will have a value of zero. If Emruss raises the £150,000 to meet the coupon payment, its equity will be worth zero if the unfavourable state of the economy is realized and £500,000 (£1,500,000 – £1,000,000) if the favourable state of the economy is realized. The value of the firm's equity is thus worth £250,000 if the firm obtains a £150,000 equity infusion. Therefore the firm can issue equity worth £150,000, making its existing equity worth £100,000.

Note that equity holders and other junior claimants have claims resembling options, which may be virtually worthless if bankruptcy occurs. They thus have an incentive to put more money into the firm if it allows them to extend the life of their claims, in the hope that the claims will eventually have value. This is especially true when asset values are highly volatile. Because of this incentive to keep its options alive, the firm described in Example 16.4 was able to raise funds to continue operating despite having a liquidation value that exceeded its going concern value. Equity holders benefited from this at the expense of the firm's senior debt holders.

16.3 How the Administration Process Mitigates Debt Holder–Equity Holder Incentive Problems

This section discusses how some of the problems that arise because of the debt holder–equity holder conflict can be mitigated by firms going into administration. It is important to remember that countries have different approaches to administration. For example, in the USA, firms declare Chapter 11 bankruptcy. In many countries, bankrupt firms are given a window within which they can attempt to restructure their debt. For the purposes of consistency (not necessarily correctness), we shall call this process 'administration'. However, it should be clear that the term administration is a uniquely British term, and does not exactly apply to other countries.

Consider again Lily Pharmaceuticals, described in Exhibit 16.1, which passed up a positive-NPV investment because of the debt overhang problem. Recall that firms suffer from debt overhang when they have a substantial amount of existing debt with protective covenants that prevent them from issuing additional debt that is senior to the existing debt.

By going into administration, a firm like Lily may be able to obtain additional financing that is senior to existing debt. The new debt obtained under administration allows a bankrupt corporation to raise the money necessary to fund investments that are required for its continued operation. In other words, through negotiation with their creditors, firms may obtain permission to violate the debt covenant that otherwise would keep the firm from obtaining additional funds.

The Lily example provides some insights into why bankruptcy codes allow for a protective window. The original lenders to Lily are actually better off, because the weakening of their seniority allows the firm to make a good investment. Of course, the firm could have avoided going into administration if its original debt was unprotected. However, debt holders would not want to grant the firm an unrestricted ability to issue new senior debt. By allowing the firm to issue senior claims only under extreme situations, administration can create some of the advantages of unprotected debt while avoiding some of the disadvantages. Of course, these advantages have to be weighed against the efficiency losses and legal costs of going through the bankruptcy process.

Some of the efficiency losses in bankruptcy arise because the ability to raise new financing through a company voluntary agreement (CVA) can allow a firm to continue operating when it would be better off liquidating. As the last section showed, junior creditors have an incentive to keep a distressed firm operating if they stand to receive little from the firm's liquidation. If the senior debt has covenants that keep the firm from borrowing an additional amount, the distressed firm is likely to be forced into bankruptcy. However, once the firm has gone into administration, it will seek financing that allows the firm to continue operating. This buys time, and benefits the more junior claimants, but it may keep alive a dying firm that would be worth more if it were liquidated.

Results

Result 16.11

By going into administration, firms may be able to obtain more financing. To some extent, this mitigates the debt overhang/underinvestment problem. However, the provision also may allow some firms to continue operating when they would be better off liquidating.

16.4 How Can Firms Minimize Debt Holder–Equity Holder Incentive Problems?

Going into administration may lessen some of the costs associated with conflicts between debt holders and equity holders, but bankruptcy would probably not be a manager's preferred way to deal with the problem. This section examines other solutions to these incentive problems. As discussed earlier, equity holders should be motivated to control their incentive problems, since ultimately they must bear the costs that such problems create.

The simplest solution to debt holder–equity holder incentive problems is to eliminate the debt holders. The problems are of course eliminated if the firm is all equity financed. However, there are offsetting advantages to the inclusion of debt in a firm's capital structure. Some of these benefits of debt (for example, tax advantages) were discussed in earlier chapters. Other benefits will be discussed in Chapters 17, 18 and 19. Therefore firms have incentives to include debt in their capital structures, and to design their debt in ways that minimize the potential conflicts between borrowers and lenders.

The following discussion briefly describes six ways in which owners of a firm can minimize the incentive costs associated with debt financing. These are:

1 protective covenants
2 bank and privately placed debt
3 the use of short-term instead of long-term debt
4 security design
5 project financing
6 management compensation contracts.

Protective Covenants

Earlier, this chapter discussed protective covenants that specify the seniority of the debt, as well as covenants that specify the amount that firms can distribute to shareholders as a dividend or repurchase. In addition, covenants that require the firm to satisfy restrictions on various accounting ratios, such as the debt/equity ratio, interest coverage and working capital, are often observed. Other covenants restrict the sale of assets. Firms that violate these covenants are in **technical default**, which means that debt holders can demand repayment even if the firm has not missed an interest payment. (See Chapter 2 for additional detail.)

What Covenants Do We Observe?

In their study of bond covenants, Smith and Warner (1979) reported that about 90 per cent of a sample of bonds issued in 1974 and 1975 restricted the issuance of additional debt, 23 per cent restricted dividends, 39 per cent placed constraints on merger activity, and about 35 per cent placed restrictions on how a firm can sell its assets. These covenants provide some protection to the original debt holders against the tendency of a firm's management to undertake high-risk investment projects in the future. Junior debt holders, who have the lowest priority of repayment if a firm defaults, would have an incentive to withhold financing if they think the firm is likely to be taking on excessively risky projects. However, the covenants are much weaker than might be expected, given the potential conflicts described earlier in this chapter.

Covenants that directly limit the types of project that firms can undertake are less common. For example, in a study of bonds issued by large US corporations, McDaniel (1986) found almost no restrictions on the ability of firms to increase their risk. This is because it is very difficult to specify in a contract the exact types of investment that are allowed over the 20- to 30-year life of a bond. In many cases, subtle changes in a production technology (for example, making the plant more labour intensive) can lead to important changes in risk. Even if it were possible to write contracts to prevent such changes, firms may find that the costs of limiting management's flexibility would exceed the benefits of limiting the bondholders' risk.

Nash et al. (2003) examined changes in bond covenants between 1989 and 1996, and reported some surprising patterns. The percentage of firms that had dividend restrictions fell from 39.7 to 20.8 per cent over the seven-year period. Limitations on the amount of new debt issued by firms fell from 40 to 27.4 per cent. While the more traditional use of debt and dividend restrictions fell, constraints on the use of sale and leaseback activity surged from 11.2 to 54.8 per cent, and negative restrictions, which stop firms from certain actions, also grew from 50.1 to 78.6 per cent of all firms. Most firms (around 90 per cent) had some restrictions on mergers and acquisition activities, and 13 per cent of firms had constraints on asset sales.

Covenants on Investment-Grade versus Non-Investment-Grade Debt

The studies mentioned above focused mainly on the bonds of major companies with high credit ratings. Since these firms have relatively low leverage, the debt holder–equity holder conflicts described in this chapter are unlikely to be severe. For this reason, investment-grade bonds generally have relatively weak covenants.

Nash et al. (2003) examined differences in bond covenants between firms with high and low growth opportunities. Firms with low growth opportunities are more likely to become financially distressed, and, as a result, the use of dividend and debt restrictions is much higher for these firms. For example, 28.5 per cent of low-growth firms had dividend restrictions, compared with 11.3 per cent of their high-growth counterparts. Similarly, additional debt constraints were in place for 33.3 per cent of low-growth firms compared with 15 per cent of high-growth firms.

Cineworld, the global cinema chain, is an excellent case study to understand the use of covenants for financially distressed firms. After getting into financial difficulty in 2021 because of the global covid restrictions, the firm renegotiated its debt and financial covenants. The covenants addressed a number of issues, including:

- borrowing limits
- minimum liquidity levels
- cash flow restrictions
- leverage ratio constraints
- minimum tangible net worth and net income
- minimum financial accounting ratios
- dividend restrictions
- capital expenditure restrictions
- minimum levels of collateral.

Covenants Cannot Solve all Problems

Some of the incentive problems would be especially difficult to eliminate with contractual provisions. At the outset, for example, the debt overhang problem leads firms to pass up positive-NPV investments. Although it is plausible that contracts can be written to preclude certain projects, we don't believe it is possible to include debt covenants that prevent firms from turning down positive-NPV projects that lower the value of the firm's common stock. A second potential conflict concerns how an infusion of equity can help the original equity holders by allowing the firm to keep operating at the expense of the debt holders, who prefer the firm to liquidate. In this case, the gain to the equity holders is less than the loss to the debt holders, which suggests that it would be beneficial to prevent an equity infusion of this type. In reality, however, firms would not want to rule out equity infusions, because, generally, equity issues that fund positive-NPV projects benefit both debt holders and equity holders.

McDaniel (1986) argued that the covenants of bonds issued in the 1960s, 1970s and early 1980s were entirely inadequate, because they were written at a time when actions such as levered recapitalizations were far less common. The author argued that, in many cases, bondholders had implicit agreements with management that subsequently were violated. If McDaniel is correct, one might expect to find that bonds issued more recently are better protected. Indeed, Lehn and Poulsen (1992) found that about 30 per cent of a sample of bonds issued in 1989 included covenants that explicitly protected bondholders from the risks of takeovers and recapitalizations. This increased to nearly 90 per cent for a sample studied in 1996 (Nash et al. 2003).

It should be noted that, although debt covenants may solve some incentive problems, they come with costs. They can be costly to write and enforce, and they can limit a firm's flexibility. Thus publicly traded investment-grade debt rarely has covenants that could trigger a technical default. However, covenants of this type are observed in private debt, such as the Cineworld example, whose holders can more easily monitor covenant compliance, and in non-investment-grade debt, which is more subject to the kinds of concerns discussed in this chapter.

Bank and Privately Placed Debt

Recall that debt financing can cause either debt overhang or asset substitution, depending upon the circumstances. Bond covenants that affect the firm's ability to issue debt that is senior to existing debt can affect the firm's tendency to experience these problems. As noted in Section 16.2, the ability to issue debt that is senior to existing debt eliminates the debt overhang problem, but it also increases the asset substitution problem.

The use of bank debt may be advantageous, because it solves the free-rider problem that contributes to the debt overhang problem. Recall the situation described in Section 16.2, in which the debt holders as a group benefit from infusing new capital into a corporation, but individual debt holders do not find it in their interests to provide capital by themselves. The problem arises because the new debt by itself is not a good investment, but the capital infusion increases the value of the existing debt. It is possible to eliminate this free-rider problem if the firm has only one lender, such as a bank, which can take into account how its new loans affect the value of its existing loans.

Bank debt and, to a lesser extent, debt that is privately placed with insurance companies and pension funds have additional advantages over publicly traded bonds when the incentives to increase risk are most severe. Banks and other private providers of debt capital are better able to monitor the investment decisions of firms and enforce protective covenants. In addition, more stringent covenants can be imposed on private debt, because it is much easier to renegotiate and to enforce a covenant with a bank than with a group of bondholders. Consequently, bank loan covenants limit flexibility far less than equivalent bond covenants.

Several articles have argued that the conflict between debt holders and equity holders in Japan and Germany is less of a problem than it is in the United Kingdom and United States, because large banks not only provide most of the debt financing for firms but also own large holdings of the firms' shares (see Chapter 1). These articles argue that because the banks in these countries own both debt and equity claims, they have incentives to preclude policies that promote inefficient investment for the sake of transferring wealth between claim holders.

However, despite the advantages of bank debt, the importance of banks has been diminishing over time throughout the world. Increasingly, since the global banking crisis of 2008, firms throughout the world have been going to the bond and commercial paper markets to raise debt capital. Firms raising their debt capital through the public markets instead of through banks are primarily the larger, higher-quality, less risky firms, which are less likely to be subject to the types of financial distress costs discussed in this chapter. For these firms, the benefits of bank debt are insufficient to justify the added costs associated with bank loans – costs that are passed on to the borrower in the form of higher interest payments.

There are costs associated with bank debt that firms may be able to avoid by going directly to the bond or commercial paper market. The first is what we would call a pure intermediation cost that arises because banks require buildings and labour, and are unable to lend out all their funds because of reserve requirements. A second cost has to do with potential incentive problems within banks that arise because loan officers may extend additional credit to marginal borrowers, either because they don't want to reveal that their initial loan to the firm was bad, or because they don't want to face the unpleasant task of forcing a client into bankruptcy. For the reasons discussed earlier, the costs associated with a bank's suboptimal actions may need to be passed on to the firm borrowing from it. Finally, there may exist what is known as a hold-up problem that makes bank debt less attractive for some borrowers. A **hold-up problem** occurs if a firm relies too much on any single bank, and the bank takes advantage of this reliance and charges the firm above-market rates on its subsequent loans. In such a situation, the firm may find it difficult to access capital from other, potentially cheaper, sources, since the firm's inability to raise the capital from its bank could be viewed as a signal that the bank believes the firm's prospects are not favourable.[15]

The Use of Short-Term versus Long-Term Debt

Most of the debt holder–equity holder conflicts discussed in this chapter are more severe when firms use long-term rather than short-term debt financing. To understand why this is true, recall that these conflicts arise because equity holders have an incentive to implement investment strategies that are advantageous to them by lowering the value of the firm's outstanding debt. Hence, since the value of short-term debt is much less sensitive to changes in a firm's investment strategy than the value of long-term debt, conflicts are lower for firms financed with short-term debt.

Mitigating the Debt Overhang Problem

Myers (1977) noted that it is possible to eliminate the debt overhang problem if the firm's existing debt matures before the time when it must raise additional debt to fund a new project. To understand this, consider again the example of Glastron, which had a risk-free project yielding 12 per cent when the risk-free rate was 10 per cent. The firm passed up the project, because its borrowing costs were high enough to exceed the project's return. If the firm's debt was all short term, there would have been no debt overhang problem. In this case, the interest payment on all the firm's debt would have been renegotiated simultaneously with the selection of the new project. Thus the addition of a risk-free project, which would lower the overall risk of the firm, would also lower the firm's borrowing costs, making it attractive for the firm to accept the project.

Mitigating the Asset Substitution Problem

The use of short-term debt also makes it more difficult for equity holders to gain at the expense of debt holders by selecting riskier projects. Consider the case of a firm that must decide whether to design its production facilities so that the process is more or less risky. The equity holders of a highly levered firm may prefer the risky project, because the upside potential is higher, and they share any downside risk with the debt holders. However, if the firm's debt is primarily short term, the incentive to increase asset risk diminishes. With short-term financing, the lending rate is renegotiated after completion of the production process, which largely eliminates a firm's ability to gain at the expense of its lenders.

---

[15] See Diamond and Rajan (2000) and Rajan (1992) for a discussion of the hold-up problem.

Disadvantages of Short-Term Debt

Of course, there is also a downside to funding long-term projects with short-term debt. With short-term financing, unexpected increases in interest rates or liquidity squeezes could potentially bankrupt a highly levered firm. This is exactly what happened to Northern Rock plc, a British bank, in 2007, which funded 25-year mortgages with 30-day T-bills. This extremely risky strategy eventually caught up with the firm when the global credit markets contracted because of the subprime mortgage crisis in the United States. It should be emphasized that the Northern Rock example is an exceptional case and not a normal example. Short-term borrowing coupled with hedging interest rate risk in the futures and swap markets is a possibility, which would reduce the risk of borrowing short-term.[16]

The Use of Project Financing

Project financing is capital to finance an investment project for which both the project's assets and the liabilities attached to its financing can effectively be separated from the rest of the firm. For example, most major oil companies structure at least some of their foreign operations as separate operating units with their own financing. Similarly, power-generating plants are often structured as independently financed units of electrical utilities. In most cases, the parent company provides equity for the project (in many cases along with a joint venture partner), which appears on the firm's balance sheet. However, the parent is not responsible for the project's debt (that is, the project is financed with what is called **non-recourse debt**), which implies that the debt need not appear on the parent firm's balance sheet. Moreover, the project's debt has a senior claim on the cash flows generated by the project.

The use of project financing can mitigate the debt holder–equity holder conflicts in a number of ways. Recall the case of Lily Pharmaceuticals, considered earlier, where a positive-NPV project was passed up because the wealth transferred from equity holders to debt holders exceeded the project's NPV. In this case, if project financing were used, there would be substantially less of a wealth transfer from equity holders to debt holders, because the project's debt would have the senior claim on the project's cash flows. Moreover, since project financing is tied to a specific project, there is generally less scope for the kind of asset substitution problems discussed in Section 16.2.

Of course, project financing is not a panacea that solves all debt holder–equity holder conflicts. In many cases, it is difficult to define a firm's project in a way that allows it to be financed as a separate entity. Suppose, for example, that Fiat can upgrade its domestic manufacturing facilities at a cost of €3 billion. Since the manufacturing facilities are already owned by Fiat, financing their renovation would be difficult to structure as a separate project.

In addition, although project financing, when it can be used, generally mitigates the underinvestment problem, it can often exacerbate the asset substitution problem. To understand why project financing can exacerbate the asset substitution problem, consider the behaviour of an entrepreneur with 10 diverse investment projects that can be financed either as 10 independent projects or together as one firm. If each of the 10 projects is financed with non-recourse debt, the incentive to increase the risk of any specific project may be quite high, since the entrepreneur will capture all the upside benefits associated with the more favourable outcomes, while the debt holders bear the increased downside costs associated with the unfavourable outcomes. However, if the projects are all financed under the umbrella of one corporation, with conventional debt financing, part of the gain associated with the favourable outcomes in any given project benefits the debt holders, since it might offset an unfavourable outcome from another project. Put differently, because of diversification, the value of debt is not particularly sensitive to the fortunes or misfortunes of any one project, since most of the project-specific risk has been diversified away.

Management Compensation Contracts

Up to this point, we have assumed that managers make investment choices that maximize their firm's share price. However, managers often have other objectives.[17] For example, sometimes they are under more pressure to please their debt holders than their equity holders. This can be seen in some highly levered firms, which depend on banks to finance their day-to-day operations, and in countries such as Germany and Japan, where the banks have greater influence over managers.

[16] These issues are discussed in greater detail in Chapter 21.

[17] These will be discussed extensively in Chapter 18.

In addition, some of the natural tendencies of managers are more aligned with the interests of debt holders than of equity holders. First, relative to other equity holders, managers generally have a much larger portion of their wealth tied up in the firms they manage, and thus are likely to act as though they are more risk averse. This would increase their tendency to take on less risky and diversifying investments that might counteract the incentive to take on too much risk. Second, prestige and power go hand in hand with operating a growing firm, providing an incentive for managers to overinvest. The incentive to overinvest probably counteracts the equity-controlled firm's incentive to underinvest, which derives from the debt overhang problem. Thus managers may make choices that benefit debt holders at the expense of equity holders.

It is worth emphasizing that it is not in the equity holders' best long-term interests to have managers who act purely in the interests of either debt holders or equity holders. To maximize the firm's current value, a firm must commit its managers to make future choices that are in the combined best interests of all claimants, maximizing the combined value of the firm's debt and equity. A firm will be able to borrow at more attractive rates if the manager can assure the lender that the interests of the debt holders as well as those of the equity holders will be considered when investment choices are made. This means that firms have an incentive to compensate managers in ways that make them sensitive to the welfare of both debt holders and equity holders.

The results of this section are summarized as follows.

Results

Result 16.12

The adverse effects of debt financing on a firm's unlevered cash flows arising from debt holder–equity holder conflicts may be mitigated by using:

- protective covenants
- bank debt and privately placed debt
- short-term debt instead of long-term debt
- convertible bonds
- project financing
- properly designed management compensation contracts.

However, many of these remedies have downsides to them as well.

16.5 Empirical Implications for Financing Choices

The preceding discussion contains important insights about which firms should have high leverage and which should have low leverage. This section reviews empirical evidence about the extent to which the issues described in this chapter affect observed capital structure choices.

How Investment Opportunities Influence Financing Choices

Since debt financing distorts investment incentives, firms with substantial investment opportunities should be more conservative in their use of debt financing. Existing cross-sectional empirical studies tend to support this hypothesis. The variables used to measure future investment opportunities include, among other things, research and development expenditures, because the point of most research is to develop new opportunities, and the ratio of the firm's market value to its book value, because market value measures the combined value of a firm's existing assets and future opportunities whereas book value measures only the value of existing assets.

Consistent with the discussion in this chapter, both of these variables are negatively related to the amount of debt included in a firm's capital structure.[18] Firms that have high R&D expenditures and high market values

[18] See Bradley et al. (1984), Long and Malitz (1985), Titman and Wessels (1988), Smith and Watts (1992), Baker and Wurgler (2002), Hovakimian, Hovakimian and Tehranian (2004), Flannery and Rangan (2006) and Hillier et al. (2010).

relative to their book values tend to include little debt in their capital structures.[19] Consistent with the discussion in Section 16.4, empirical studies find that firms with good future opportunities tend to prefer short-term rather than long-term debt.[20]

How Financing Choices Influence Investment Choices

A second type of study examines whether financing constraints affect investment choices. Malmendier and Tate (2005) examine this issue in the context of managerial overconfidence. They conclude that managers invest when they have internal funds at their disposal, but cut back on investment when external financing is required. This relationship is even more striking when managers are overconfident of their abilities. Almeida and Campello (2007) find that firms with tangible (and therefore pledgeable) assets are better able to obtain debt financing for projects that require more pledgeable assets. This implies that investment by financially constrained firms, which require external capital, is more sensitive to cash flow when their assets are tangible. Lang et al. (1996) showed that more highly levered firms tend to invest less than firms with lower leverage ratios. The authors argued that this reflects the fact that firms with poor investment opportunities choose to be highly levered, as well as the fact that debt inhibits a firm's ability to invest. In other words, poor investment opportunities can cause firms to be more highly levered, and high leverage might cause firms to invest less.

Direct evidence about how debt financing leads firms to invest less comes from the study's analysis of the investment behaviour of the non-core business segments of diversified firms. The basic idea is that a company such as Mobil Oil would select its debt ratio based on the fundamentals of the oil industry. However, the firm's debt ratio could have inadvertently affected the investment choices of Montgomery Ward, a retail firm that used to be owned by Mobil. The Lang et al. (1996) study found that, on average, the level of investment in the non-core business segments of diversified firms decreased when the overall leverage of the firms increased, supporting the idea that debt causes firms to invest less.[21]

Firm Size and Financing Choices

The following two reasons explain why the debt holder–equity holder conflict may be worse for small firms.

1 Small firms may be more flexible and thus better able to increase the risk of their investment projects.

2 The top managers of small firms are more likely to be major shareholders, which gives them a greater incentive to make choices that benefit equity holders at the expense of debt holders.

These arguments suggest that small firms should exhibit lower debt ratios, which does not seem to be the case. However, small firms do tend to choose debt instruments that minimize conflicts between debt holders and equity holders. In particular, their long-term debt is more likely to be convertible, and a greater proportion of their total debt financing tends to be short-term debt.[22] Faulkender and Petersen (2006) examined the source of capital and found that firms with access to the public debt markets and which also have a credit rating are more likely to have debt. Given that small firms rarely have strong credit ratings, they are less likely to have debt. Kisgen (2006) also reported that firms that are close to a ratings upgrade or downgrade are less likely to issue debt because of the discrete costs of issuing debt when the yield on bonds is likely to change as a result of the ratings change.

Small firms may also avoid long-term debt because of the transaction costs of issuing long-term bonds in relatively small amounts. As shown in Chapter 1 (see Exhibit 1.7), the transaction costs of a $500 million bond issue averages about 1.64 per cent of the total dollar amount, whereas a $10 million bond issue may entail transaction costs of about 4.39 per cent of the total. As a result, smaller firms may opt for less expensive loans from banks, which have lower fixed transaction costs than bond issues, but which tend to provide only short-term financing.

[19] Other explanations for these findings are discussed in Chapter 17.

[20] See, for example, Barclay and Smith (1995), Guedes and Opler (1996), Stohs and Mauer (1996), Johnson (2003) and Berger et al. (2005).

[21] Lamont (1997) examined similar issues, using detailed data on the investment choices within the oil industry, and arrived at similar conclusions.

[22] See Titman and Wessels (1988).

Evidence from Bank-Based Economies

As noted earlier, the debt holder–equity holder conflicts are not likely to be as severe in continental Europe, Scandinavia and Japan as they are in the United Kingdom and United States.[23] In bank-based systems, banks play a much greater role in the financing of corporations. They hold both corporate debt and stock in the companies to which they lend, and their representatives typically sit on corporate boards of directors. Thus debt holders have more control of the day-to-day operations of companies in these environments, and, with bank debt more prevalent, free-rider problems have less relevance. This suggests that variables such as R&D expenditures, which serve as a proxy for future investment opportunities, may be less related to financial leverage ratios in bank-based systems than in countries that have strong capital markets. Prowse (1990) found that the negative relationship between R&D expenditures and leverage is weak in Japan, a bank-based country. These findings stand in sharp contrast to those in market-based countries.

A study by Flath (1993) provides further evidence about how Japanese banks mitigate the debt holder–equity holder conflicts. He found that Japanese growth firms, which potentially have the greatest conflicts, are generally less highly levered than other Japanese firms. However, Japanese growth firms that have a close banking relationship, characterized by the bank's holding of a significant fraction of the firm's stock, tend to be more levered than their counterparts without a banking relationship of this type. His evidence suggests that because banks are able to exercise more control when they hold more shares, they can better protect their interests and can thus offer greater amounts of debt financing in situations where potential conflict exists.

16.6 Summary and Conclusions

This chapter discussed some of the costs a firm might bear in the event that it becomes too highly levered. We began with a brief discussion of the direct legal and administrative costs of bankruptcy, which are likely to be a relatively small proportion of the assets of most large corporations. The chapter's main focus was on the indirect costs of financial distress that arise because of conflicts of interest between debt holders and equity holders. These conflicts of interest create the following investment distortions.

- Highly levered firms tend to pass up positive-NPV investment projects.
- Debt creates an incentive for firms to increase risk.
- Debt creates an incentive for firms to take on projects that pay off quickly, leading them to pass up projects with higher NPVs that take longer to pay off.
- Debt creates an incentive for equity holders to keep a firm operating when it might be worth more if it were liquidated.

To the extent that lenders anticipate how debt distorts investment incentives, equity holders will bear the costs of the investment distortions caused by their firm's financial structure. A firm with an incentive to make investment decisions that reduce the value of its debt will be subject to higher borrowing costs, and may at times be unable to obtain debt financing. Given this, firms have an incentive to design their financial structures and in other ways position themselves to minimize these investment distortions.

This chapter provided the following suggestions for firms wanting to minimize the costs associated with investment distortions that arise from debt financing.

- Use debt covenants that limit dividend payouts, the amount of new debt financing and investments substantially outside the firm's main line of business.
- Use short-term debt instead of long-term debt.
- Use bank debt (or private placements) instead of public bonds.
- Use convertible debt or bonds with attached warrants.
- Design management compensation contracts that eliminate the incentives of managers to distort investments.

[23] See Chapter 1 for more detail on the different financial systems.

The last suggestion requires further elaboration. Lenders may be more concerned about the preferences of managers than of shareholders. Therefore the underinvestment problem may not be significant if managers have a preference to overinvest to maximize the growth rates of their firms. Chapter 18, which takes a more careful look at large management-run firms, concludes that the kinds of distortion created by debt financing can sometimes be beneficial rather than costly.

Key Concepts

Result 16.1: Debt holders charge an interest premium that reflects the expected costs they must bear in the event of default. Therefore equity holders indirectly bear the expected costs of bankruptcy, and must consider these costs when choosing their optimal capital structures.

Result 16.2: Firms acting to maximize their share prices make different decisions when they have debt in their capital structures than when they are financed completely with equity.

Result 16.3: Selecting projects with positive NPVs can at times reduce the value of a levered firm's equity.

Result 16.4: Firms that have existing senior debt obligations may not be able to obtain financing for positive-NPV investments.

Result 16.5: With risky debt, equity holders have an incentive to pass up internally financed positive-NPV projects when the funds can be paid out to equity holders as a dividend.

Result 16.6: Firms with large amounts of debt tend to pass up high-NPV projects in favour of lower-NPV projects that pay off sooner.

Result 16.7: The equity holders of a levered firm may prefer a high-risk, low (or even negative)-NPV project to a low-risk, high-NPV project.

Result 16.8: With sophisticated debt holders, equity holders must bear the costs that arise because of their tendency to substitute high-risk, low-NPV projects for low-risk, high-NPV projects.

Result 16.9: Firms with the potential to select high-risk projects may be unable to obtain debt financing at any borrowing rate when risk-free interest rates are high.

Result 16.10: Since debt holders have priority in the event of liquidation, they have a stronger interest in liquidating the assets of a distressed firm than the firm's equity holders, who profit from the possible upside benefits that may be realized if the firm continues to operate. As a result, a firm's financial structure partially determines the conditions under which it liquidates.

Result 16.11: By going into administration, firms may be able to obtain more financing. To some extent, this mitigates the debt overhang/underinvestment problem. However, the provision also may allow some firms to continue operating when they would be better off liquidating.

Result 16.12: The adverse effects of debt financing on a firm's unlevered cash flows arising from debt holder–equity holder conflicts may be mitigated by using:

- protective covenants
- bank debt and privately placed debt
- short-term debt instead of long-term debt
- convertible bonds
- project financing
- properly designed management compensation contracts.

However, many of these remedies have downsides to them as well.

Key Terms

Exercises

16.1 A firm has £100 million in cash on hand, and a debt obligation of £100 million due in the next period. With this cash, it can take on one of two projects – A or B – which cost £100 million each. Assume that the firm cannot raise any additional outside funds. If the economy is favourable, project A will pay £120 million and project B will pay £101 million. If the economy is unfavourable, project A will pay £60 million and project B will pay £101 million. Assume that investors are risk neutral, there are no taxes or direct costs of bankruptcy, the riskless interest rate is zero and the probability of each state is 0.5.

a What is the NPV of each project?

b Which project will equity holders want the managers to take? Why?

16.2 Neneh Buffalos can invest in pastures for grass fed beef. The firm will have cash flows next period of €210 if the economy is favourable, and €66 if the economy is unfavourable. One-third of these proceeds must be paid out in taxes if the firm is all equity financed; however, because of the tax advantage of debt, Neneh Buffalos saves €0.05 in taxes for every €1.00 of debt financing the firm uses. Assume that investors are risk neutral, the riskless rate is 10 per cent per period, and the probability of each state is 0.5. Also assume that if Neneh Buffalos goes bankrupt and debt holders take over, the legal fees and other bankruptcy costs total €20.

a If the firm is all equity financed, what will it be worth?

b Suppose Neneh Buffalos sold a zero-coupon bond worth €144 at maturity next period. How much would the firm receive for the debt?

c With the debt level above, how much would the equity be worth?

d How much would the firm be worth?

e Would the firm be worth more if it had a debt obligation of 170 next period?

16.3 A firm has a senior bond obligation of €20 due this period and €100 next period. It also has a subordinated loan of €40 owed to Jack and Jill and due next period. It has no projects to provide cash flows this period. Therefore, if the firm cannot get a loan of €20, it must liquidate. The firm has a current liquidation value of €120. If the firm does not liquidate, it can take one of two projects with no additional investment. If it takes project A, it will receive cash flows of €135 next period, for sure. If the firm takes project B, it will receive cash flows of either €161 or €69 with equal probability. Assume risk neutrality, a zero interest rate, no direct bankruptcy costs and no taxes.

a Which has a higher PV: liquidating, project A or project B?

b Should Jack and Jill agree to lend the firm the €20 it needs to stay operating if they receive a (subordinated) bond with a face value of €20.50?

c If the firm does receive the loan from Jack and Jill, which project will the managers choose if they act in the interest of the equity holders?

16.4 Larsson Fashion Corporation (LFC) can pursue either project Dress or project Cosmetic, with possible pay-offs at year-end as follows.

	Bad economy (prob. = 30%) (in SKr millions)	Good economy (prob. = 70%) (in SKr millions)
Project Dress	20	90
Project Cosmetic	70	60

Each project costs SKr60 million at the beginning of the year. Assume that there are no taxes, there are no direct bankruptcy costs, all investors are risk neutral and the risk-free interest rate is zero.

a Which project should LFC pursue if it is all equity financed? Why?

b If LFC has a SKr50 million bond obligation at the end of the year, which project would its equity holders want to pursue? Why?

16.5 Sigma Design, a computer interface start-up firm with no tangible assets, has invested R500, 000 in R&D. The success of the R&D effort as well as the state of the economy will be observed in one year. If the R&D is successful (prob. = 90%), Sigma requires a R530, 000 investment to start manufacturing. If the economy is favourable (prob. = 90%), the project is worth R1,530, 000 and, if it is unfavourable, the project will have a value of R610,000. Demonstrate how the value of Sigma is affected by whether or not it was originally financed with debt or with equity. Assume no taxes, no direct bankruptcy costs, all investors are risk neutral and the risk-free interest rate is zero.

16.6 In Germany, financial institutions hold significant equity interests in the borrowing firms. How does this affect the costs of financial distress and bankruptcy?

16.7 Describe the relationship between the zero-beta expected return on common stock and the zero-beta expected return on corporate bonds in an economy where stock returns are taxed more favourably than bond returns, interest payments are tax deductible and bankruptcy costs are important determinants of a firm's capital structure choice.

16.8 ABC plc, which currently has no assets, is considering two projects that each cost £100. Project A pays off £120 next year in the good state of the economy and £90 in the bad state of the economy. Project B pays off £140 next year in the good state of the economy and £60 in the bad state of the economy. If the two states are equally likely, there are no taxes or direct bankruptcy costs, the risk-free rate of interest is zero and investors are all risk neutral, which project would equity holders prefer if the firm is 100 per cent equity financed? Which project would equity holders prefer if the firm has an £85 bond obligation due next year?

16.9 Suppose you are hired as a consultant for Tailways, just after a recapitalization that increased the firm's debt-to-assets ratio to 80 per cent. The firm has the opportunity to take on a risk-free project yielding 10 per cent, which you must analyse. You note that the risk-free rate is 8 per cent, and apply what you learned in Chapter 11 about taking positive-NPV projects: that is, accept those projects that generate expected returns that exceed the appropriate risk-adjusted discount rate of the project. You recommend that Tailways takes the project.

Unfortunately, your client is not impressed with your recommendation. Because Tailways is highly levered and is in risk of default, its borrowing rate is 4 per cent greater than the risk-free rate. After reviewing your recommendation, the company CEO has asked you to explain how this 'positive-NPV project' can make him money when he is forced to borrow at 12 per cent to fund a project yielding 10 per cent. You wonder how you bungled an assignment as simple as evaluating a risk-free project. What have you done wrong?

16.10 In the event of bankruptcy, the control of a firm passes from the equity holders to the debt holders. Describe differences in the preferences of the equity holders and debt holders, and how decisions following bankruptcy proceedings are likely to change.

16.11 Why are debt holder–equity holder incentive problems less severe for firms that borrow short term rather than long term?

16.12 Consider the case of Ajax Manufacturing, which was just completed an R&D project on satellite navigation that required a €70 million bond obligation. The R&D effort resulted in an investment opportunity that will cost €75 million and generate cash flows of €85 million in the event of a recession (prob. = 20%) and €150 million if economic conditions are favourable (prob. = 80%). What is the NPV of the project assuming no taxes, no direct bankruptcy costs, risk neutrality and a risk-free interest rate of zero? Can the firm fund the project if the original debt is a senior obligation that doesn't allow the firm to issue additional debt?

16.13 Assume now that if Ajax Manufacturing (see exercise 16.12) uses a more capital-intensive manufacturing process, it can produce a greater number of satellite navigation tools at a lower variable cost. Given the greater fixed costs, the cash flows are only €5 million in an unfavourable economy with the capital-intensive process but are €170 million in a favourable economy. Hence equity holders would receive €100 million in the good state of the economy (€170 million – €70 million) and zero in a recession, because €5 million is less than the €70 million debt obligation. Can the firm issue equity to fund the project?

16.14 When firms go into administration, they may be able to obtain additional amounts of debt that is senior to the firm's existing debt. Explain how the firm's existing debt holders can benefit from this.

16.15 You have been hired as a bond analyst. A highly levered firm, Emax, has switched to a more flexible management process that enables it to change its investment strategy more quickly. How do you expect this change in the management process to affect bond values?

16.16 Atways is involved in two similar mining projects. The Tanzania project was financed through the firm's internal cash flows, and appears as an asset on its balance sheet. The Zambia project was set up as a wholly owned subsidiary of Atways. The subsidiary was financed 20 per cent with equity provided by Atways and 80 per cent with non-recourse debt.

How do the different ways in which these projects were originally financed and structured affect future investment and operating decisions?

References and Additional Reading

Almamy, J., Aston, J. and Ngwa, L.N. (2016) An evaluation of Altman's Z-score using cash flow ratio to predict corporate failure amid the recent financial crisis: Evidence from the UK, *Journal of Corporate Finance,* 36, 278–285.

Almeida, H. and Campello, M. (2007) Financial constraints, asset tangibility and corporate investment, *Review of Financial Studies,* 20(5): 1429–1460.

Altman, E. (1984) A further empirical investigation of the bankruptcy cost question, *The Journal of Finance,* 39(€): 1067–1089.

Ang, J., Chua, J. and McConnell, J. (1982) The administrative costs of bankruptcy: a note, *The Journal of Finance,* 37(1): 219–226.

Azizpour, S., Giesecke, K. and Schwenkler, G. (2018) Exploring the sources of default clustering, *Journal of Financial Economics,* 129(1): 154–183.

Baker, M. and Wurgler, J. (2002) Market timing and capital structure, *The Journal of Finance,* 62(1): 1–32.

Barclay, M. and Smith, C. (1995) The maturity structure of corporate debt, *The Journal of Finance,* 50(2): 609–631.

Benmelech, E. and Bergman, N.K. (2011) Bankruptcy and the collateral channel, *The Journal of Finance,* 66(2): 337–378.

Berger, A., Espinosa-Vega, M., Frame, W.S. and Miller, N. (2005) Debt maturity, risk and asymmetric information, *The Journal of Finance,* 60(6): 2895–2922.

Berk, J.B., Stanton, R. and Zechner, J. (2010) Human capital, bankruptcy and capital structure, *The Journal of Finance,* 65(3): 891–926.

Bernstein, S., Colonnelli, E. and Iverson, B. (2019) Asset allocation in bankruptcy, *The Journal of Finance,* 74(1): 5–53.

Bradley, M., Jarrell, G. and Kim, E.H. (1984) On the existence of an optimal capital structure: theory and evidence', *The Journal of Finance,* 39(3): 857–878.

Brennan, M. and Schwartz, E. (1981) The case for convertibles, *Chase Financial Quarterly,* 1(3): 27–46.

Bris, A., Welch, I. and Zhu, N. (2006) The costs of bankruptcy: Chapter 7 liquidation versus Chapter 11 reorganization, *The Journal of Finance,* 61(3): 1253–1303.

Bulow, J. and Shoven, J. (1978) The bankruptcy decision, *Bell Journal of Economics,* 9(3): 437–456.

Cole, R., Johan, S. and Schweizer, D. (2021) Corporate failures: Declines, collapses and scandals, *Journal of Corporate Finance,* 67, 101872.

DeAngelo, H. and DeAngelo, L. (1990) Dividend policy and financial distress: an empirical investigation of troubled NYSE firms, *The Journal of Finance,* 45(5): 1415–1432.

DeAngelo, H., DeAngelo, L. and Wruck, K. (2002) Asset liquidity, debt covenants and managerial discretion in financial distress: the collapse of LA Gear, *Journal of Financial Economics,* 64(1): 3–34.

Dhillon, U.S. and Johnson, H. (1994) The effect of dividend changes on stock and bond prices, *The Journal of Finance*, 49(1): 281–289.

Diamond, D. and Rajan, R. (2000) A theory of bank capital, *The Journal of Finance*, 55(6): 2431–2465.

Faulkender, M. and Petersen, M.A. (2006) Does the source of capital affect capital structure?, *Review of Financial Studies*, 19(1): 45–79.

Finnerty, J. (1996) *Project Financing: Asset-Based Financial Engineering*. New York: Wiley.

Flannery, M.J. and Rangan, K.P. (2006) Partial adjustment toward target capital structures, *Journal of Financial Economics*, 79(3): 469–506.

Flath, D. (1993) Shareholding in keiretsu, Japan's financial groups, *Review of Economics and Statistics*, 75(2): 249–257.

Franks, J.R. and Torous, W.N. (1989) An empirical investigation of US firms in reorganization, *The Journal of Finance*, 44(3): 747–769.

Galai, D. and Masulis, R. (1976) The option pricing model and the risk factor of stock, *Journal of Financial Economics*, 3(1/2): 53–81.

Garlappi, L. and Yan, H. (2011) Financial distress and the cross-section of equity returns, *The Journal of Finance*, 66(3): 789–822.

Gertner, R. and Scharfstein, D. (1991) A theory of workouts and the effects of reorganization law, *The Journal of Finance*, 46(4): 1189–1222.

Green, R.C. (1984) Investment incentives, debt, and warrants, *Journal of Financial Economics*, 13(1): 115–136.

Greenwood, R., Hanson, S.G., Shleifer, A. and Sørensen, J.A. (2020) *Predictable financial crises* (No. w27396). National Bureau of Economic Research.

Guedes, J. and Opler, T. (1996) The determinants of the maturity of corporate debt issues, *The Journal of Finance*, 51(5): 1809–1833.

Haugen, R. and Lemma Senbet, L. (1978) The insignificance of bankruptcy costs to the theory of optimal capital structure, *The Journal of Finance*, 33(2): 383–393.

Hertzberg, A., Liberti, J.M. and Paravisini, D. (2011) Public information and coordination: evidence from a credit registry expansion, *The Journal of Finance*, 66(2): 379–412.

Hillier, D., Pindado, J., de Queiroz, V. and de la Torre, C. (2010) The impact of country-level corporate governance on research and development, *Journal of International Business Studies*, 42(1): 76–98.

Hoshi, T., Scharfstein, D. and Kashyap, A. (1993) *The choice between public and private debt: an analysis of post-deregulation corporate financing in Japan*. NBER Working Paper 4421, August.

Hotchkiss, E.S. (1995) Postbankruptcy performance and management turnover, *The Journal of Finance*, 50(1): 3–21.

Hovakimian, A., Hovakimian, G. and Tehranian, H. (2004) Determinants of target capital structure: the case of dual debt and equity issues, *Journal of Financial Economics*, 71(3): 517–540.

Jensen, M. and Meckling, W. (1976) Theory of the firm: managerial behavior, agency costs, and ownership structure, *Journal of Financial Economics*, 3(4): 305–360.

Johnson, S. (2003) Debt maturity and the effects of growth opportunities and liquidity risk on leverage, *Review of Financial Studies*, 16(1): 209–236.

Kensinger, J. and Martin, J. (1988) Project financing: raising money the old fashioned way, *Journal of Applied Corporate Finance*, 1(3): 69–81.

Kisgen, D. (2006) Credit ratings and capital structure, *The Journal of Finance*, 61(3): 1035–1072.

Koh, S., Durand, R.B., Dai, L. and Chang, M. (2015) Financial distress: Lifecycle and corporate restructuring, *Journal of Corporate Finance*, 33, 19–33.

Lamont, O. (1997) Cash flow and investment: evidence from internal capital markets, *The Journal of Finance*, 52(1): 83–109.

Lang, L., Ofek, E. and Stulz, R. (1996) Leverage, investment, and firm growth, *Journal of Financial Economics*, 40(1): 3–29.

Lehn, K. and Poulsen, A. (1992) Contractual resolution of bondholder–shareholder conflicts in leveraged buyouts, *Journal of Law and Economics*, 34(2, Part 2), 645–673.

Long, M.S. and Malitz, I.B. (1985a) Investment patterns and financial leverage, in Benjamin M. Friedman (ed.) *Corporate Capital Structure in the United States*. Chicago: University of Chicago Press, 325–352.

Long, M.S. and Malitz, I.B. (1985b) The investment–financing nexus: some empirical evidence, *Midland Finance Journal*, 3(3): 53–59.

Long, M.S., Malitz, I.B. and Sefcik, S.E. (1994) An empirical examination of dividend policy following debt issues, *Journal of Financial and Quantitative Analysis*, 29(1): 131–144.

LoPucki, L. and Doherty, J. (2004) The determinants of professional fees in large bankruptcy reorganization cases, *Journal of Empirical Legal Studies*, 1(1): 111–141.

Malmendier, U. and Tate, G (2005) CEO overconfidence and corporate investment, *The Journal of Finance*, 60(6): 2661–2700.

Maxwell, W.F. and Stephens, C.P. (2003) The wealth effects of repurchases on bondholders, *The Journal of Finance*, 58(2): 895–919.

McDaniel, M. (1986) Bondholders and corporate governance, *Business Lawyer*, 41, 413–60.

Mikkelson, W. (1981) Convertible calls and security returns, *Journal of Financial Economics*, 9(3): 237–264.

Myers, S. (1977) Interactions of corporate financing and investment decisions: implications for capital budgeting, *The Journal of Finance*, 29(1): 1–25.

Nakamura, M. (2002) Mixed ownership of industrial firms in Japan: debt financing, banks and vertical keiretsu groups, *Economic Systems*, 26(3): 231–247.

Nash, R.C., Netter, J.M. and Poulsen, A.B. (2003) Determinants of contractual relations between shareholders and bondholders: investment opportunities and restrictive covenants, *Journal of Corporate Finance*, 9(2): 201–232.

Prowse, S. (1990) Institutional investment patterns and corporate financial behavior in the United States and Japan, *Journal of Financial Economics*, 27(1): 43–66.

Rajan, R. (1992) Insiders and outsiders: the choice between informed and arm's length debt, *The Journal of Finance*, 47(4): 1367–1400.

Rajan, U., Seru, A. and Vig, V. (2015) The failure of models that predict failure: Distance, incentives, and defaults, *Journal of Financial Economics*, 115(2): 237–260.

Smith, C. and Warner, J. (1979) On financial contracting: an analysis of bond covenants, *Journal of Financial Economics*, 7(2): 117–162.

Smith, C. and Watts, R. (1992) The investment opportunity set and corporate financing, dividend, and compensation policies, *Journal of Financial Economics,* 32(3): 263–292.

Stiglitz, J. and Weiss, A. (1981) Credit rationing in markets with imperfect information, *American Economic Review,* 71(3): 393–410.

Stohs, M. and Mauer, D. (1996) The determinants of corporate debt maturity structure, *Journal of Business,* 69(3): 279–312.

Stulz, R.M. and Herb Johnson, H. (1985) An analysis of secured debt, *Journal of Financial Economics,* 14(4): 501–521.

Titman, S. (1984) The effect of capital structure on the firm's liquidation decision, *Journal of Financial Economics,* 13(1): 137–151.

Titman, S. and Roberto Wessels, R. (1988) The determinants of capital structure choice, *The Journal of Finance,* 43(1): 1–19.

Warner, J. (1977) Bankruptcy costs: some evidence, *The Journal of Finance,* 32(2): 337–347.

Weiss, Lawrence (1990) Bankruptcy resolution: direct costs and violation of priority of claims, *Journal of Financial Economics,* 27(2): 285–314.

Zhang, E. Q. (2022) Why are distressed firms acquisitive?, *Journal of Corporate Finance,* 72, 102126.

Chapter 17

Capital Structure and Corporate Strategy

Learning Objectives

After reading this chapter, you should be able to:

- Describe how a firm's financial situation is likely to affect its sales and its ability to attract employees and suppliers.
- Understand how financial distress can benefit some firms by inducing employees, suppliers and governments to make financial concessions to the firm.
- Explain how a firm's financial condition affects the way its competitors price their products.
- Describe how the past profitability of a firm affects its current capital structure.
- Understand empirical research relating a firm's characteristics to its capital structure choices.

Although the global financial crisis happened in 2007, the impact of the events around the time are still being felt fifteen years later. The low interest rates and high public debt levels that emerged in 2008 in response to the crisis remained and were the catalysts of the high inflation and cost of living crisis in 2022. Capital structure was at the centre of the reasons why banks collapsed and why liquidity disappeared across the world.

The basic business model of a bank is that it receives funds in the form of deposits and lends these out in the form of business or personal loans. The bank makes a profit on the spread between the deposit rate and the lending rate. One of the first banks to fall, Northern Rock, aggressively marketed loans and mortgages to risky borrowers at low margins. To fund the increase in its long-term loan portfolio, it borrowed in the short-term money markets under the assumption that liquidity would always be available. As long as Northern Rock paid back its short-term (in many cases 30-day paper) liabilities, it would be able to utilize this funding model. Essentially, the bank used short-term debt to fund long-term investments. It doesn't take an expert to see that this strategy is highly risky.

Chapter 16 discussed direct bankruptcy costs (for example, legal and administrative expenses) as well as the indirect bankruptcy costs that arise because of conflicts of interest between equity holders and debt holders. These indirect costs can occur whenever a firm faces financial difficulties, or what we have been calling financial distress, regardless of whether the firm eventually becomes bankrupt.

Financial distress costs that arise because of debt holder–equity holder conflicts may explain why emerging growth firms use so little debt. As the previous chapter illustrated, lenders are unlikely to provide significant amounts of debt capital to emerging growth firms at attractive terms, because of the way that debt distorts the firm's investment incentives. For most of the largest firms in the world, however, the indirect bankruptcy costs stemming from the conflicts between debt holders and equity holders do not appear to be a major deterrent to debt financing. Many of these large firms have access to eager lenders, willing to provide them with additional debt financing on reasonable terms.

This chapter builds on the framework developed in Chapter 16 and examines other financial distress costs that limit a corporation's desire to use debt financing. The financial distress costs examined in this chapter, in contrast to those considered in Chapter 16, explain why many firms choose to maintain low debt ratios even when lenders are willing to provide debt capital at attractive terms.

Since the continued low debt levels that began in 2007, debt in British and European firms has now grown substantially. Covid-19 restrictions in 2020 and 2021 led to further low-interest debt appearing on corporate balance sheets, so that firms were much more heavily levered by 2022. This will bring significant risks in future years when high inflationary periods will increase costs for most businesses, and, as we saw in Chapter 16, debt holder–equity holder conflicts will be exacerbated.

The ideas presented in the last three chapters suggest that a company could improve its value by increasing its leverage ratio. However, if a company chooses to be highly levered, it will face serious financial difficulties when inflation rates are high. We shall suggest in this chapter that financial distress is especially costly and highly levered firms have significant downside risk.

The first topic addressed here is how financial distress can affect the ability of a firm to operate its business profitably. Would a financially distressed firm lose customers because it is financially distressed? How would financial difficulties affect a firm's ability to attract and retain key employees? Would financial distress affect the quality of service provided by the firm's suppliers? How would competitors react to a financially distressed firm's difficulties?

To address these types of question, we present the 'stakeholder' theory of capital structure. **Non-financial stakeholders** are the associates of a firm, such as customers, employees, suppliers and the community in which the firm operates, who do not have debt or equity stakes in the firm, but nonetheless have a stake in the financial health of the firm. The **stakeholder theory** of capital structure suggests that the way in which a firm and its non-financial stakeholders interact is an important determinant of the firm's optimal capital structure. We argue that these non-financial stakeholders may be less willing to do business with a firm that is financially distressed; and that this is especially true for firms, such as airlines or technology businesses, whose service quality is difficult to evaluate, or whose products may need to be serviced in the future. Because of this, firms may choose to be conservatively financed, even when they can obtain substantial amounts of debt financing at attractive rates.

The interaction between how a corporation is financed and how it is viewed by its stakeholders suggests that the capital structure decision must be incorporated into the overall corporate strategy of the firm. For example, a firm that wants to project a reputation as a stable firm that produces quality products does not want to be too highly levered. Similarly, the way in which a firm interacts with its suppliers and employees and how it competes within its industry, determine its capital structure choice.

This chapter also analyses dynamic aspects of the capital structure decision, such as how a firm's history affects its current capital structure. Finally, the chapter analyses the empirical evidence on the theories of capital structure presented in this part of the text. We conclude that the empirical evidence is largely supportive of these theories.

17.1 The Stakeholder Theory of Capital Structure

Previous chapters examined the firm as a collection of different investments that need to be financed. The analysis largely ignored the nature of the investments and the overall environment in which the firm must operate. This chapter takes that environment more seriously, and considers how a firm's financial decisions interact with the design of its products, its employment policy and other strategic choices of the firm.

Exhibit 17.1 illustrates how the environment in which a firm conducts business affects the firm's overall corporate strategy, which includes its capital structure choice. This environment includes the firm's non-financial stakeholders, who, one way or another, have business dealings with the firm, as well as the firm's competitors. This section and the next examine how the non-financial stakeholders affect the firm's capital structure choice. Section 17.3 examines how the competitive environment affects capital structure choices.

Exhibit 17.1 Firm Environment and Corporate Strategy

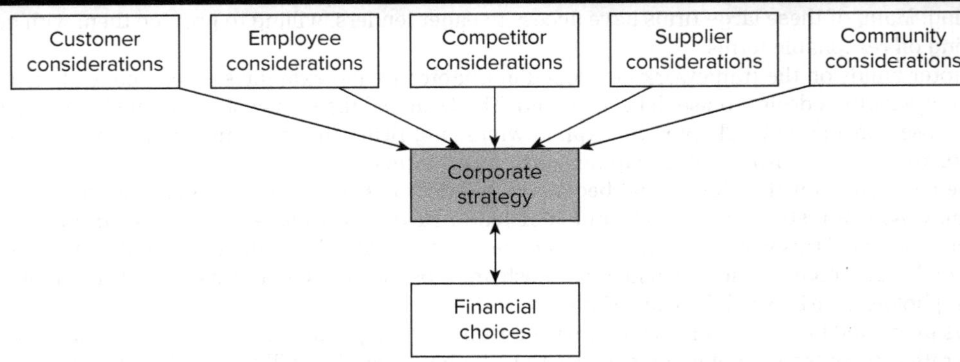

Non-Financial Stakeholders

As defined earlier, the non-financial stakeholders of a firm include those parties other than the debt and equity holders who have a stake in the financial health of the firm. These include:

- the firm's customers
- the firm's suppliers
- the firm's employees
- the overall community in which the firm operates.

These stakeholders can be hurt by a firm's financial difficulties, examples of which are described below. Customers may receive inferior products that are difficult to service, suppliers may lose business, employees may lose jobs, and the economies of entire communities can be disrupted.

Because of the costs they potentially bear in the event of a firm's financial distress, non-financial stakeholders will be less interested, all else being equal, in doing business with a firm having financial difficulties. This understandable reluctance to do business with a distressed firm creates a cost that can deter a firm from undertaking excessive debt financing, even when lenders are willing to provide it on favourable terms.

How the Costs Imposed on Stakeholders Affect the Capital Structure Choice

To understand why non-financial stakeholders are concerned about a firm's financial health, it is first important to understand why there might be a connection between the firm's financial health and the decisions a firm might make that affect its stakeholders.[1] Consider first the firm's liquidation decision.

The Connection between Bankruptcy and Liquidation

Recall from Chapter 16 that when equity holders, the last to get paid in a liquidation, control a levered firm, they may not want the firm to liquidate its assets, even if the firm's liquidation value exceeds its going concern value. Furthermore, managers who fear losing their jobs often resist liquidations, even those that are in the interests of equity holders.[2] However, the bias in favour of keeping a bankrupt firm operating is not as great when the

[1] The arguments in this subsection are based on the theoretical work in Titman (1984).

[2] This topic will be discussed in more detail in Chapter 18.

lenders share in the decision process. Indeed, because lenders get paid first from liquidation proceeds, they tend to prefer a liquidation. This means that a financially distressed firm, given its high probability of bankruptcy, is much more likely to liquidate in the future than is a financially healthy firm.

Liquidation Costs Imposed on Stakeholders

The connection between a firm's financial structure and its liquidation choice is important, because frequently there are spillover costs imposed on the non-financial stakeholders of a firm that goes out of business. Consider the costs that were imposed on the stakeholders of Carillion, the UK's largest construction and facilities management firm, when the company became insolvent in 2018. More than 450 public projects (including schools and hospitals) in which Carillion was lead contractor quickly got into difficulty themselves. Similarly, 3,000 employees and 75,000 suppliers with specific human or physical capital also found the firm's liquidation costly because of the loss of jobs.

The more sophisticated stakeholders anticipate the costs of doing business with a firm that may subsequently liquidate. To avoid any potential costs to them from a firm's liquidation, these stakeholders will avoid doing business with a firm that is experiencing financial distress. Customers will not be willing to pay as much for the products of such a firm, and in some cases will avoid purchasing from it altogether. Indeed, airlines that are in financial distress find new ticket sales drop because travellers are worried the airline is either less safe or won't be around when they actually travel. Northern Rock, discussed in this chapter's opening vignette, lost many customers who were afraid that they wouldn't be able to withdraw their deposits if the bank went into administration. Similarly, employees and suppliers will be less willing to do business with such a firm, and therefore will demand higher wages and charge higher prices. As a result, the revenues of a distressed firm are likely to decline, while its costs are likely to increase. Example 17.1 shows that such considerations may lead firms to choose equity financing over debt financing, even when there is a large tax advantage associated with using debt.

Example 17.1

The Trade-Off between Tax Gains and the Effect of Debt on Product Prices

Suppose that Dell produces computers at a cost of €1,000 and sells them for €1,200. This €200 profit margin on each computer generates large taxable earnings for Dell. Dell is considering a large increase in financial leverage that will increase the firm's probability of bankruptcy from zero to 10 per cent, but will save the firm €29 million per year in taxes as a result of the interest tax deduction, given its 12.5 per cent corporate tax rate.

Although this is a financial decision, the financial managers decide to consult with the firm's marketing department prior to increasing Dell's leverage. The marketing managers argue that it will be more difficult to sell computers if consumers believe that bankruptcy is even a remote possibility. Each computer can be sold for €1,200 if customers can be assured of Dell's continued support of upgrades and new software in the future, but for only €600 if Dell's future bankruptcy is perceived as certain. Hence, if customers thought the probability of bankruptcy was 10 per cent, and valued computers as probability-weighted averages of their values when Dell, respectively, was solvent and bankrupt, then they would be willing to pay only €1,140 for the computers [€1,140 = 0.9(€1,200) + 0.1(€600)]. If Dell expects to sell 1 million computers per year, should it take on this added leverage?

Answer: The added leverage will save Dell €29 million per year in taxes. However, the company's pre-tax profits on its computers will be reduced by €60 million per year, because the added debt reduces the firm's revenues and profits. With a marginal tax rate of 12.5 per cent, the firm is better off not taking on the added debt. The €29 million in annual tax savings is more than offset by the €52.5 million loss of annual after-tax cash flow arising from the lower selling price of its computers.

Estimating the Financial Distress Costs

Example 17.1 illustrates how Dell Computer might have incorporated the costs of financial distress into the calculations of its optimal debt ratio. In reality, quantifying these costs is extremely difficult, and depends on rough estimates. Example 17.2 provides an insight into how to calculate a rough estimate of financial distress costs.

Example 17.2

Estimating Financial Distress Costs

A common strategy for firms in financial distress is to offer rebates or discounts on their goods or services. This is a strategy to encourage sales to customers who are hesitant in dealing with a struggling business. Downside risks to the customer are that there may be little or no after-sales service. Replacement parts and maintenance may also be affected by financial distress. The upside to the customer is it gets to access the goods or services at a discount.

Consider a financially distressed automobile firm that is offering rebates on its cars and trucks to attract customers. A rough estimate of part of the cost of the firm's financial distress can be obtained by multiplying the average rebate times the number of cars sold. Assuming that the company sells 1,438,000 cars and trucks, and that a €300 rebate, on average, is given for each car and truck sold, estimate a minimum value for the cost of financial distress to the automobile manufacturer.

Answer: Multiplying the 1,438,000 cars sold by the €300 loss per car amounts to a minimum total loss of €431 million due to financial distress.

In the preceding example, the operating loss attributable to financial distress is likely to be much larger than any direct costs of bankruptcy. However, the financial distress costs estimated in Example 17.2 still underestimate the total costs, because they do not take into account the lost sales due to customer concerns.

Real World Insight

Quantifying Financial Distress Costs

In the 1980s, Texaco and Pennzoil became involved in a prolonged legal dispute involving the takeover of Getty Oil. Texaco had purchased a large block of Getty Oil equity, despite an existing agreement for Getty Oil to be acquired by Pennzoil. The case eventually led to Texaco being asked to pay Pennzoil $3 billion. Thus the gain to Pennzoil ($3 billion) should have approximately equalled the loss to Texaco ($3 billion).

This case provides a unique way to gauge the combined direct and indirect expected costs of bankruptcy. If the market expected that there would be no bankruptcy costs, then Pennzoil's equity should have increased in value at the time of the award announcement by an amount approximately equal to the amount by which Texaco's equity declined. For example, if investors thought that Texaco would ultimately pay Pennzoil $3 billion dollars, we would expect the value of Pennzoil to increase by $3 billion dollars and the value of Texaco to decrease by $3 billion dollars.

Cutler and Summers (1988) studied the changes in market value of the two firms through the course of the legal battle, and found that Pennzoil equity gained much less than Texaco's equity declined, implying that the combined values of the two firms declined. The net loss in combined market values of the two companies was more than $3 billion, which one might view as the market's assessment of the expected cost of Texaco's bankruptcy.

The $3 billion decline in combined shareholder value is too large to be attributed to the direct costs of bankruptcy. We believe that the drop in the combined value of the two firms reflected two factors. The first is the costs of financial distress discussed in this chapter. Second, the market may have been concerned about how wisely Pennzoil would invest its cash windfall. When managers receive cash windfalls, they tend to increase their level of investment beyond what would be considered optimal.[3]

Financial Distress and Reputation[4]

Non-financial stakeholders may be concerned about a firm's financial health even when liquidation is unlikely. Chapter 16 discussed how high leverage ratios can make a firm pass up investments it would otherwise make. What concerns a firm's non-financial stakeholders in this regard is how debt affects the firm's incentive to

[3] This topic will be discussed in more detail in Chapter 18.

[4] The arguments in this subsection are based on the theoretical work in Maksimovic and Titman (1991); see also the discussions in Shapiro and Titman (1985) and Cornell and Shapiro (1987).

continue to invest in upholding its reputation for dealing honestly with employees and suppliers, for providing quality products to its customers and for its overall integrity.

In normal circumstances, firms have an incentive to maintain a good reputation to ensure their long-run profitability. However, the incentive to be short-term oriented in times of financial distress applies to investments in reputation as well as in physical assets. Under financial distress, the long-run value of a good reputation may be less important to managers than the short-run need to generate enough cash to avoid bankruptcy. For this reason, a firm may lower the quality of its products, or cut corners in other ways, to raise cash to meet its immediate debt obligations. Example 17.3 illustrates this kind of situation.

Example 17.3

Borrowing Costs and Product Quality

Handy Andy Langoustines has earned a reputation for exporting the best langoustines in the world and, as a result, is able to charge a premium price. The value of maintaining this reputation is clear. Lowering quality will save the firm money and boost profits by £20 million next year, but in later years, as the company's reputation erodes, profits will fall dramatically. Andy calculates that if the firm loses its reputation, it will lose £4 million per year over a nine-year period before it can regain its reputation. Based on these calculations, Andy concludes that, under normal circumstances, the firm is better off exporting high-quality langoustines. However, Handy Andy is currently having financial difficulties, and will need to raise £20 million 'in some way' before the end of the year.

Because of the firm's financial difficulties, its borrowing rate will be 16 per cent instead of the usual 10 per cent. How do the financial difficulties affect Handy Andy Langoustines' quality choice?

Answer: Exporting a high-quality product can be considered an investment that costs £20 million and yields £4 million per year for nine years. The internal rate of return of that investment is 13.7 per cent. Under normal circumstances, Andy would export high-quality langoustines, since the rate of return from doing so exceeds the firm's 10 per cent cost of capital. However, if borrowing costs increase to 16 per cent, shareholders will be better off if the firm exports low-quality langoustines.

Real World Insight

Budget Airlines

The criticisms of budget airlines in recent years offer some of the best examples of alleged quality-cutting by firms in financial distress. Year on year, reports have come out from whistleblowers about poor training, reduced fuel loads to save flight costs, and other measures that may have an impact on flight safety. Budget airlines require planes to be in the air as much as possible because their margins are so low, and, frequently, landing and take-off turnaround can be as little as 30 minutes. Examples of cost-cutting abound: during the Covid-19 pandemic restrictions, despite significant government support, many airlines (including easyJet) were alleged to have made many staff redundant to save costs. However, when travel rebounded in 2022 after restrictions were lifted, the airlines were caught out and thousands of flights were cancelled in the UK alone. The impact this had on budget airline revenues was significant and entirely avoidable.

Unfortunately for those airlines that cut too many costs, the ramifications can be deadly. Rational customers understand the budget airlines' incentives, and thus will not pay as much for, or will completely avoid, the products of firms facing financial distress.

As these cases illustrate, being close to bankruptcy can make it very difficult for some firms to carry out their business. However, there are other firms that need to be even more vigilant about maintaining a pristine credit rating.

Who Would You Rather Work For?

Although we mentioned briefly that employees are important non-financial stakeholders, our examples up to this point have analysed the effect of debt and financial distress on a firm's customers. However, many readers of this text will probably be looking for a job soon, and may want to consider how career prospects at a prospective employer relate to that employer's financial structure. Perhaps these readers already work harder to get interviews with firms that appear to be financially strong, and avoid those firms that appear to be having financial difficulties. They now should have a better understanding of why this strategy makes sense.

As discussed earlier in this chapter, a highly levered firm is more likely to go into administration, and such a firm is more likely to liquidate. However, this is only one reason – and probably not the most important reason – why a highly levered firm may be a less attractive employer. Because of the debt overhang problem (see Chapter 16), firms that are more highly levered tend to invest less, which means they may be less willing to take on new opportunities, and thus may offer their employees less opportunity for advancement.

In addition, more highly levered firms have a greater tendency to lay off workers and reduce employment in response to a short-term reduction in demand. A firm with less onerous debt obligations may be willing to maintain high employment when times are bad, in order to reduce the future costs of hiring and retraining workers when demand increases. However, a more highly levered firm may be forced to cut costs by laying off workers to meet its debt obligations. Empirical studies by Sharpe (1995), Hanka (1998) and Hillier et al. (2007) provide evidence that suggests that a firm's debt ratio does in fact affect employment. Specifically, Hillier et al. (2007) found that, holding all else constant, firms with higher debt ratios are more likely to lay off employees. Bae et al. (2011) report that employee-friendly firms have lower debt levels. Sharpe examined employment growth rates and found that the cyclical nature of the size of a firm's labour force was positively related to its financial leverage. In other words, firms with less debt were more likely to maintain a larger workforce through a recession than were firms with higher debt ratios. The more highly levered firms were more likely to reduce their workforce in response to modest declines in demand.

The success of a corporation depends largely on the quality of management that it attracts, and many of the best managers choose to work for a company that provides better future opportunities over one that pays more but offers fewer opportunities for advancement. Because of this, a high debt ratio may be very costly for a firm that is trying to attract the best talent. However, as we discuss in the next section, a firm that is not planning on attracting a large number of new managers in the future may find it advantageous to have a relatively high debt ratio.

Summary of the Stakeholder Theory

The discussion in this section suggests that financial distress can be costly for a firm because it affects how the firm is viewed by its customers, employees, suppliers and any other firms or individuals that in some way have a stake in its success. The stakeholders' views are especially important for firms whose products need future servicing, such as automobiles and computers, or whose product quality is important but difficult to observe, such as prescription drugs. Financial distress will also be costly for firms that require their employees and suppliers to invest in product-specific training and physical capital. On the other hand, firms that produce non-durable goods, such as agricultural products, or provide services that are not particularly specialized, such as hotel rooms, probably have low financial distress costs. The main results in this section are summarized below.

Results

Result 17.1

A firm's liquidation choice and its decisions relating to the quality of its product and fairness to employees and suppliers depend on its financial condition. As a result, a firm's financial condition can affect how it is perceived in terms of being a reliable supplier, customer and employer.

Financial distress is especially costly for firms with:

- products with quality that is important yet unobservable
- products that require future servicing
- employees and suppliers who require specialized capital or training.

These types of firm should have relatively less debt in their capital structure.

Financial distress should be less costly for firms that sell non-durable goods and services, that are less specialized, and whose quality can easily be assessed. These firms should have relatively more debt in their capital structures.

The stakeholder theory explains why some firms choose not to borrow when lenders are willing to provide debt financing at attractive terms. The presence of debt reduces the firm's profits even if bankruptcy never occurs. Indeed, some firms cannot be viable if their probability of bankruptcy becomes too high. In such cases, the stakeholders' fear that the firm may ultimately fail can actually *cause* the firm to fail.

17.2 The Benefits of Financial Distress with Committed Stakeholders

The last section emphasized that when stakeholders commit resources to doing business with a firm, they are effectively betting on the long-term viability of that firm. If the firm does well, the stakeholders will do well; if the firm does poorly, the stakeholders are likely to be hurt financially. Hence, in a competitive market, the terms of trade between the firm and the stakeholders are determined in part by the viability of the firm's future prospects.

This section examines how debt affects the relationship between a firm and its stakeholders in situations where the parties are not transacting in a competitive market. For example, the firm might be dealing with a union or a monopoly supplier. Alternatively, the firm might be dealing with an ongoing supplier, or with employees who have invested in specialized equipment or developed specialized human capital. After specialized investments in human or physical capital have been made, the relationships between customers and suppliers, employees and employers, and governments and corporations develop into bilateral monopoly relationships. In **bilateral monopolies** the terms of trade (for example, prices and wages) between the parties are open to negotiation. In such cases, the financial distress of a firm may provide it with a negotiating advantage, because suppliers and employees must then consider how their wage and price demands affect the firm's future viability.

Bargaining with Unions

One of the best examples of the influence of debt on bargaining outcomes is the relationship between a large firm and the union representing the firm's employees. By increasing leverage, the firm can reduce its employees' demands by exploiting their fear that a wage increase will push the firm towards bankruptcy. Without attractive alternative sources of employment, unionized employees gain less from achieving higher wages if the higher wages substantially increase the probability that the firm will become bankrupt. Hence high debt ratios may effectively facilitate employee concessions during business downturns.[5] On the other hand, when it costs more to fire employees, which happens when unions are strong, debt levels tend to be lower, possibly as a result of high financial distress costs (Serfling 2016).

Example 17.4 illustrates how debt financing can affect the way in which a firm bargains with its unions.

Example 17.4

Debt and Bargaining Power

Nakamura Auto will be renegotiating its wage contracts within 12 months. The union is aggressive, and would like to increase wages from £15 per hour to £22 per hour. Management recognizes that an increase in wages of this magnitude will lower profits from £80 million to £30 million. How can Nakamura increase its bargaining power so that the union will not demand more than £20 per hour, which lowers profits only to £35 million?

Answer: One solution would be for Nakamura to issue enough debt and repurchase shares with the proceeds, so that the increased debt requires £35 million in additional interest payments. Profits will then decline to £45 million prior to the renegotiated loan contract. The union recognizes that with this additional debt the firm will be unable to meet its debt payments if forced to pay £22 per hour, and the firm will be put in a fairly unstable position – that is, zero profit – if forced to pay £20 per hour. Any wage demand above £20 per hour generates losses, and would not be sustainable in the long run.

[5] Bronars and Deere (1991), Dasgupta and Sengupta (1993), Perotti and Spier (1994) and Spier and Sykes (1998) describe how leverage can be used to improve bargaining outcomes.

Results

Result 17.2

Financial distress can benefit some firms by improving their bargaining positions with their stakeholders.

Real World Insight

Airline Bankruptcies and Reorganizations after 11 September 2001

Many commentators have suggested that the airline industry used the 11 September 2001 attacks as a justification for drastic and unpopular restructuring, when it was in great need of doing so anyway. After the terrorist attacks on the Twin Towers in the USA, many airlines publicly argued that the downturn in air travel meant that they were no longer able to sustain the same level of employees and benefits. As a result, several airlines went into administration or Chapter 11 bankruptcy. United Airlines made probably the most drastic cuts, including laying off tens of thousands of staff, cancelling several routes, closing all its ticket offices in the USA and killing off some major hubs. The most heavily criticized cuts, however, were the abolition of its employee pension plan and significant pay cuts for its pilots and mechanics. At the same time, however, it was investing in new products, including its budget airline, Ted, and a completely new business-class service. The strategy wasn't just confined to US airlines. British Airways, KLM, Air France and ITA have all cut costs in recent years along the same lines as their American counterparts.

Bargaining with the Government

Both local and national communities can sometimes be thought of as stakeholders that can be hurt in the event of the demise of a major corporation. The UK government gave an estimated £410 billion during 2020 and 2021 in support of businesses during the Covid pandemic. Most of this funding was to keep businesses afloat during the lockdown restrictions in place for more than a year. Other examples exist for specific industries. The banking crisis in the late 2000s had a negative ripple effect throughout many communities in the UK and Europe, affecting cinemas, retailers, restaurants and many other local establishments that had no direct links to these industries. Because of these spillover costs, both national and local governments have provided subsidies, such as loan guarantees, to many distressed firms to keep them from failing. In both cases, the financial distress was beneficial to the firms, because it allowed them to obtain below-market financing that they otherwise would not have obtained.

In our opinion, the costs of financial distress for most firms outweigh the benefits of government subsidies. However, the potential government subsidy is definitely a consideration that will tilt firms towards using more debt financing. It should be stressed that governments subsidize failing firms not because of their concern for the firm's debt holders, but because of their concern for non-financial stakeholders such as organized union employees who may have political importance. Since the combined political power of the stakeholders of relatively small firms is not likely to be great, only the largest firms should expect government subsidies in the event of financial distress.

17.3 Capital Structure and Competitive Strategy

Having explored how a firm's interactions with its customers, suppliers, employees and the government affect its financing, we now introduce another player into our analysis: the firm's competitors. This section describes how leverage can affect the competitiveness of an industry, and how this, in turn, is taken into account by firms selecting their leverage ratios.

Chapter 16 discussed how leverage affects a firm's incentives to take on risky projects and to liquidate its business. If these investment and exit decisions influence the actions of a firm's competitors, then the firm's leverage choice may be a strategic tool that allows it to achieve a competitive advantage.

To understand the strategic role of the capital structure choice, it is necessary to understand the importance of a firm's ability to commit to a strategy that it might later want to change. An excellent example of this is a market leader's commitment to maintain an 80 per cent market share. Carrying out such a commitment would be costly if one of its competitors chose to contest the market leader and capture a larger share of the market for itself. In this case, a price war is likely to result, creating losses for the market leader and its competitor.

A competitor that believes the market leader will fight to keep its market share will be reluctant to expand its own market share aggressively. Hence the market leader can capture a strategic advantage if it credibly commits to protecting its market share aggressively. However, the competitor may not believe that the market leader's commitment is credible, and may believe instead that, faced with an aggressive competitor, the market leader will acquiesce and give up market share rather than struggle through a costly price war. As we discuss below, a firm's capital structure choice can play an important role in determining how these strategic issues evolve.

Does Debt Make Firms More or Less Aggressive Competitors?

Firms can sometimes benefit from debt if high debt ratios allow them to commit to an aggressive output policy that they otherwise would not be able to carry out.[6] For example, a firm may wish to send a message to its competitors that it plans to increase its production. If the competitors ignore this message, the added production is likely to reduce the price of the output, and thus reduce profits for both the firm and its competitors. However, if the message is credible, the competitor may accommodate the firm by reducing its output instead of engaging in a price war. In this case, the aggressive policy does increase the firm's profits.

How does a high debt ratio help a firm to send a credible message that will convince competitors that it will indeed increase output? To understand this, first note that when aggregate demand for a product is highly uncertain, higher output generally increases risk. Higher output increases risk because it leads to higher profits when product demand turns out to be high, but lower profits when demand turns out to be low. Hence, since higher leverage increases a firm's appetite for risk (see the discussion of the asset substitution problem in Chapter 16), the greater a firm's leverage, the greater its incentive to produce at a high level of output. Competitors, observing a firm's high leverage ratio, will realize that the firm is going to produce at a high level. Not wishing to drive the price down to the point where no firm profits, the competitors may accommodate the firm's high output by producing at a lower level.

Will debt always make a firm act more aggressively? Not necessarily. Although limited liability increases the probability that a firm will act aggressively, if debt contracts are designed with this in mind, higher financing costs are likely to reduce this behaviour (Faure-Grimaud 2000). Povel and Raith (2004) show that financial constraints can also have an impact on firm behaviour. Firms with internal financing constraints have high bankruptcy costs compared with firms with low financial constraints. As a result, managers in constrained firms will be less inclined to pursue aggressive product market strategies.

Recall from Chapter 16 that debt financing can lead firms to reduce their level of investment, which can make them act less aggressively. Consider, for example, a firm that can increase its market share by either lowering its price or increasing its advertising. The firm is likely to suffer reduced profits in the short run by carrying out either strategy, but it should realize greater profits in the long run from gaining a higher market share. Gaining market share with either of these approaches is thus an investment that becomes more or less attractive as the relevant discount rate increases or decreases. As we discussed in Chapter 16, because of the debt overhang problem, more highly levered firms use higher discount rates to evaluate investments. This implies that they will compete less aggressively to increase their market share.[7]

Example 17.5 illustrates how a firm's capital structure choice can affect a firm's borrowing costs and thereby affect its incentive to price aggressively to obtain greater market share.

Example 17.5

Montaña's Pricing Choice

Montaña, a small supermarket chain in Spain, is considering lowering prices in one of its markets to attract more customers. Its managers have estimated that the firm will initially make less money from the lower-price strategy, since it reduces its margins on existing customers and it will take a while before it attracts

[6] See Brander and Lewis (1986), Maksimovic (1986) and Kovenock and Philips (1995).

[7] This argument is based on models developed by Chevalier and Scharfstein (1996) and Dasgupta and Titman (1998).

new customers. Within a year, however, it will have attracted enough new customers that its cash flows will be higher than they were prior to the price reduction.

Although Montaña's total cash flows are quite risky, its director of marketing believes that the incremental cash flows associated with a more aggressive pricing strategy can be estimated with virtual certainty. Based on this assumption, he has made the following projections.

	Year 1 cash flows	Year 2 cash flows
Low price strategy	€100,000	€147,000
High price strategy	€120,000	€125,000

Montaña's assistant treasurer is asked to give his opinion of the strategies under two scenarios. Under the first scenario, the *differences* in the cash flows between the low and high price strategies, being risk free, are evaluated given the firm's current borrowing rate of 8 per cent, which corresponds to the risk-free rate. He is also asked to consider how the strategy would be affected under a second scenario in which the firm has substantially more debt, and thus must pay an interest rate of 12 per cent on additional debt. Will the change in leverage affect his recommendation?

Answer: First, calculate the difference between the low and the high price cash flows.

Year 1 difference	Year 2 difference
−€20,000	€22,000

Hence the low-price strategy is a positive-NPV investment as long as its cash flows are discounted at a rate that is less than 10 per cent. If the strategy is evaluated by discounting the cash flows to the equity holders, the low-price strategy is an attractive strategy when the firm has a low leverage ratio and an 8 per cent borrowing rate, but not if it has a high leverage ratio and a 12 per cent borrowing rate.

The preceding example illustrates how increased debt can make firms less aggressive competitors. However, as we discussed above, there are other situations where increased debt can make firms more aggressive. We summarize this discussion as follows.

Results

Result 17.3

Leverage affects the competitive dynamics of an industry. In some situations, leverage makes firms more aggressive competitors, in others less aggressive.

Debt and Predation

A firm's leverage ratio will also affect the strategies of its competitors. Specifically, a highly levered firm might be especially vulnerable to **predation** from more conservatively financed competitors.[8] In other words, a competitor might purposely lower its prices in an attempt to drive the highly levered firm out of business. This could be to the competitor's advantage in the long run, if doing so bankrupts its more highly levered rival, forcing it to exit the market.

[8] Bolton and Scharfstein (1990) consider a model where a less levered firm prices aggressively to drive a more levered firm from the market.

The predatory policy of the conservatively financed firm is especially effective in industries where customers and other stakeholders are concerned about the long-term viability of the firms with which they do business. For example, a producer of specialized computer equipment might be driven from the market more easily by an aggressive competitor than a producer of a breakfast cereal. If the computer equipment producer's customers believe that the firm is likely to go bankrupt and might not be able to service its products, these customers will stop purchasing the products, making the belief self-fulfilling. It would be much more difficult to scare off the customers of a company making breakfast cereal, so predatory pricing to force out highly levered firms in this industry is likely to be less effective.

An alternative form of predation is stealing trade secrets or top staff from competitor firms, which can massively affect firm value of both the aggressor and victim. Klasa et al. (2018) find that firms exposed to predatory attacks will have lower debt levels to avoid financial distress risks.

Empirical Studies of the Relationship between Debt Financing and Market Share

Although some theoretical arguments suggest that highly levered firms can become more aggressive, leading them to increase market share, the empirical evidence more strongly supports the idea that high leverage tends to generate losses in market share. For example, Opler and Titman (1994) found that highly levered firms lose market share to their more conservatively financed rivals during industry downturns, when high leverage is likely to lead to financial distress.

There are at least three reasons why high debt ratios might cause firms to lose market share.

1. The financially distressed firm faces debt overhang, and, as a result, may invest less and be forced to sell off assets and reduce its selling efforts in other ways.
2. Because of concerns about its long-term viability and the quality of its products, a highly levered firm may find it difficult to retain and attract customers.
3. Rivals may view a highly levered firm as a less formidable competitor, and seize the opportunity to steal its customers and perhaps eliminate it.

Evidence on Why Distressed Firms Lose Market Share

There is evidence to support all three of these reasons. First, distressed firms tend to sell off assets and cut back on their level of investment.[9] Second, the more highly levered firms with high R&D expenditures have the greatest tendency to lose market share during industry downturns.[10] High-R&D firms tend to produce more specialized products, and, as a result, their customers are more concerned about their long-term viability. Hence the correlation between R&D expenditures and the tendency of highly levered firms to lose market share supports the stakeholder theory.

Real World Insight

Alitalia

Before Alitalia, the Italian airline, ceased operations in 2021, it attempted different strategies to turn around its operations. The international restrictions on travel during 2020 hammered the final nail in the company's coffin and the Italian government ended up selling the firm to a newly created carrier, ATA, in late 2021.

Our analysis of stakeholder costs, along with the incentive distortions created by highly levered firms, provides some insights into the issues raised by airline collapses, like Alitalia's. Recall, for example, the discussion regarding passenger concerns about the quality of service on a financially distressed airline. Because of these concerns, a financially distressed airline would have to charge significantly lower prices to attract customers than a financially healthy airline could charge. The executives of healthy airlines could claim that they were forced to match those price cuts, which probably is not completely true, because

[9] See studies by Asquith et al. (1994), Lang et al. (1995) and Pulvino (1998).

[10] See Opler and Titman (1994) and Andrade and Kaplan (1998).

most passengers prefer healthy airlines, even if their prices are somewhat higher. Nevertheless, the pricing behaviour of the distressed airlines probably did contribute to a downward pressure on prices.

Neither equity holders nor management has an incentive to shut down a financially distressed airline, because the proceeds of a liquidation would go almost entirely to the firm's debt holders, particularly the most senior creditors. In addition, the airlines would have an incentive to keep prices low to increase the number of seats they fill for each flight, because it would be difficult to justify to the bankruptcy judge that the airline should remain in operation if the planes were flying with most of their seats empty.

There is also evidence to suggest that the third reason is relevant. For example, Opler and Titman (1994) found that the tendency of highly levered firms to lose market share during industry downturns is related to the number of competitors in the industry. In industries with few competitors, the highly levered firms lose the most market share, which supports the idea that a firm with a significant market share will attract predators when it is financially weakened. In the more competitive industries, individual firms have fairly small market shares and do not present such inviting targets when they are financially distressed.

Zingales (1998) found that US trucking companies with high leverage found it difficult to cope with increased competition after deregulation of the industry. The underinvestment problem associated with high debt and high financial leverage were the major factors contributing to the poor performance.

Changes in Market Share Following Substantial Leverage Increases

Although modest amounts of debt probably affect competition only during industry downturns, extremely large increases in debt can have an almost immediate effect. To explore this possibility, Phillips (1995) and Chevalier (1995a, 1995b) examined how large capital structure changes affect the competitive dynamics of an industry. Phillips examined four different industries in which one or more of the largest firms substantially increased its leverage. In three of the four industries, the leverage increase led to corresponding decreases in industry output and increases in prices. In these cases, the industries became less competitive. In the fourth case, the leverage increase resulted in greater industry output and lower prices.

Chevalier examined in great detail one industry, retail supermarkets, a particularly interesting industry to study for two reasons. First, several supermarket chains initiated levered buyouts (LBOs) in the 1980s, substantially increasing their leverage, while others remained conservatively financed. In addition, the widespread use of electronic checkout scanners has made data for individual product prices at individual stores readily available. The study of the entry, exit and expansion behaviour of supermarket chains in 85 metropolitan areas (Chevalier, 1995a) demonstrated that rival firms are more likely to enter and expand in a local market if a large share of the incumbent firms have undertaken LBOs. In other words, highly levered stores are viewed as less formidable competitive rivals.

In her other study, Chevalier (1995b) found that supermarket prices tend to rise in cities in which the dominant firm or firms restructure in ways that substantially increase their leverage. This increase is substantially mitigated, however, and perhaps reversed, in cities that include a relatively large rival with a large market share. In addition, she found that in the 1990s, subsequent to the restructurings, the firms that increased leverage tended to charge higher prices. This evidence supports the idea that increased leverage makes firms less aggressive competitors, but in some situations an increase in leverage also can make a firm's competitors more aggressive.

Other interesting industry studies include (again) Zingales (1998) and Khanna and Tice's (2000) study of how discount department stores responded to the expansion of Walmart into their markets. Zingales found that in the sector of the trucking industry, where service is more important, the more highly levered firms tended to charge lower prices and were less likely to survive. This evidence is consistent with the idea that customers are reluctant to do business with a firm that could potentially be financially distressed. The Khanna and Tice study found that leverage made department stores that were owned by large publicly traded firms less aggressive in their response to Walmart. In addition, the publicly held department stores responded more aggressively than the privately owned stores, and stores owned by public firms with more inside ownership responded less aggressively.[11]

[11] See Chevalier and Scharfstein (1996) and Campello (2003).

17.4 Dynamic Capital Structure Considerations

Up to this point, we have discussed the capital structure decision within a simple, static context. The discussion assumed that firms initially would choose their preferred capital structure, and later would bear the consequences. If the firm's overall business subsequently did well, the managers who took on a large amount of debt would be pleased with this decision, because the firm would enjoy the tax benefits of debt and probably would avoid the negative aspects of debt financing. However, if the firm's business did very poorly, its managers, unable to use the tax benefits of debt, and faced with the financial distress costs of debt, would regret being highly levered. According to the **static capital structure theory**, which assumes that capital structures are optimized period by period, firms weigh the costs of having too much debt when they are doing poorly against the tax benefits of debt when they are doing well to arrive at their optimal capital structures.

Section 17.5 presents some empirical evidence that supports the various static theories of capital structure presented up to this point in the text. Before these tests can be discussed, however, we must consider that managers do not, in reality, optimize their capital structures period by period as these theories suggest, but determine their capital structures as the result of a dynamic process that accounts for the costs associated with capital structure adjustments. Hence, at any given point in time, a firm may deviate from its long-term optimal or target debt ratio.

There are two main views regarding dynamic capital structure. The first is pecking order theory, where there is a natural hierarchy of preferred financing routes for managers wishing to raise funds. If a preferred financing source is not available, the firm will try to raise funding through the next preferred choice. This goes on until there are no financing sources left. The alternative view concerns the market-timing behaviour of managers. Firms raise funding through the equity markets during periods of high market valuations, and through debt at other times. The observed capital structure of firms is a path-dependent function of financing choices throughout the life of the firm.

The debate as to the most appropriate explanation has reignited since Baker and Wurgler (2002) introduced the market-timing hypothesis. We shall first discuss the pecking order theory, and then market timing, before reviewing the empirical literature comparing the two theories.

The Pecking Order of Financing Choices

Dynamic capital structure theory, the dynamic process that governs the capital structure choice, is still not well understood by financial economists. As a starting point in our explanation of what is understood, consider again (see also Chapter 15) what Donaldson (1961) called the pecking order of financing choices, which describes how managers make their financing decisions. A summary of this pecking order includes the following observations.

1 Firms prefer to finance investments with retained earnings rather than external sources of funds.

2 Because of their preference to finance investment from retained earnings, firms adapt their dividend policies to reflect their anticipated investment needs.

3 Because of firms' reluctance to change their dividend policy substantially, and because of fluctuations in their cash flows and investment requirements, retained earnings may be more or less than a firm's investment needs. If the firm has excess cash, it will tend to pay off its debt prior to repurchasing shares. If external financing is required, firms tend to issue the safest security first. They begin with straight debt, next issue convertible bonds, and issue equity only as a last resort.

A substantial amount of empirical evidence verifies Donaldson's behavioural description. Most notably, extremely profitable firms tend to use a substantial amount of their excess profits to pay down debt rather than to repurchase equity. In addition, less profitable firms that need outside capital tend to use debt to fund their investment needs. As a result, firms that were profitable in the past have relatively low debt ratios, whereas those that were relatively less profitable in the past have relatively high debt ratios. The main difference between what one might expect to observe from the static trade-off models and what is actually observed is that firms generally do not issue equity when they are having financial difficulties. The reluctance of firms to issue equity, as Donaldson observed, appears to be greatest when firms need the equity capital the most.

Various explanations are offered for this pecking order behaviour, including those listed below.

1 Taxes and transaction costs favour funding new investment with retained earnings and debt over issuing new equity (see Chapter 15).

2 Managers generally can raise debt capital without the approval of the board of directors. However, issuing equity generally requires board approval and hence more outside scrutiny (see Chapter 18).

3 Issuing equity conveys negative information to investors (see Chapter 19).

4 A firm having financial difficulties may want to maintain a high leverage ratio in the hope of gaining concessions from its employees and suppliers (see Section 17.2).

5 The debt overhang problem makes equity issues less attractive for a financially distressed firm (see Chapter 16).

We believe that a combination of all of the preceding reasons explains this observed pecking order behaviour. The first reason was discussed in detail in Chapter 15; the others are described in more detail below.

An Explanation Based on Management Incentives

The second reason is based on the idea that managers personally benefit from having their firms relatively unlevered. As discussed earlier, one reason why managers might prefer lower debt ratios is that less levered firms can raise investment capital more easily than highly levered firms can, creating greater opportunities for the managers. This need for flexibility is even more important during favourable macroeconomic conditions, and empirical evidence supports the view that financially unconstrained managers time their issues to specifically exploit these windows of opportunity (Korajczyk and Levy 2003).Therefore managers prefer to retain rather than pay out earnings, and probably would prefer to issue equity as well, except that an equity issue requires the approval of the board of directors and thus leads to more scrutiny.[12]

An Explanation Based on Managers Having More Information than Investors

The third explanation of Donaldson's observation of the pecking order is based on Myers and Majluf's (1984) information-based model. The basic idea is that managers are reluctant to issue equity when they believe their shares are undervalued.[13] Because of this, investors often see an equity issue as an indication that managers believe the company's equity is overvalued, which in turn implies that the share price will fall when the company announces it will issue new shares. The negative equity market reaction to an equity issue may deter firms from issuing equity, even when they believe the market's perception that the firm's equity is overvalued is incorrect.

An Explanation Based on the Stakeholder Theory

In general, most non-financial stakeholders are pleased to see the firm issue equity. For example, employees will find their jobs more secure and their bargaining power improved if the firm has less leverage. However, that does not necessarily mean that the shareholders will find that issuing equity is in their interest. More profitable firms may anticipate expanding and, as a result, will want to maintain low debt ratios to attract the best employees, and to appear as attractive as possible to potential strategic partners. Less profitable firms may plan on shrinking in size, and could do so more efficiently with a higher leverage ratio. When a firm is shrinking, it might want to renegotiate contracts with suppliers and employees; and, as discussed earlier, the firm may be in a better position to ask for concessions if it is highly levered and is having financial difficulties.

An Explanation Based on Debt Holder–Equity Holder Conflicts

The firm's financial claimants (that is, debt holders and equity holders) may also disagree about the attractiveness of issuing equity. Chapter 16 noted that a firm with a substantial amount of long-term debt may have little incentive to issue equity after a series of losses. If bankruptcy costs are borne primarily by the firm's debt holders, the equity holders benefit little from an infusion of new equity. Indeed, share prices will decline when firms replace debt with equity, because decreasing the firm's leverage increases the value of existing debt, and transfers wealth from the equity holders to the debt holders. An exception to this general rule occurs when reducing leverage significantly cuts the costs of financial distress, and thus significantly increases the total value of the firm. We discuss this possibility in more detail below.

In extreme cases, a financially distressed firm may be unable to raise equity capital. For example, when gas prices exploded in late 2020, many UK energy companies were forced to buy gas at a much higher price than they could sell to customers because of a price cap in place to protect domestic consumers. Companies like Bulb Energy saw the value of its assets fall by 80 per cent. In cases like this, the firm cannot get out of financial distress simply by issuing equity. As Example 17.6 illustrates, avoiding financial distress requires that the lenders either forgive some of their debt or provide the firm with an additional infusion of cash.

---

[12] Zweibel (1996) presents a theoretical argument similar to this discussion.

[13] This topic is explained in detail in Chapter 19.

Example 17.6

Can Financially Distressed Firms Issue Equity?

Darnel plc is having financial difficulties, and although it has not yet defaulted, its bonds are selling at 50 per cent of their face value. The current value of the firm is £600 million, which consists of £50 million in equity and £550 million (market value) in zero-coupon bonds. These bonds have an aggregate face value of £1.1 billion, with one class of bonds, having a face value of £100 million, due in six months and another class with £1 billion due in two years. Can Darnel issue equity within the next six months to raise the funds needed to meet its £100 million near-term debt obligation, assuming that the aggregate value of all classes of bonds would increase by 10 per cent as a result of this equity infusion?

Answer: Probably not. Although Darnel is close to bankruptcy, its equity still retains some value, because investors believe that there is a slight chance that the firm can be turned around. In this case, the equity should be thought of as an out-of-the-money option that will probably expire worthless. While there is a sizeable upside if the firm does manage to survive for the next two years, this does not mean that the firm can issue new equity at the current share price.

The £100 million equity infusion, which would pay the near-term debt obligation, increases the value of the firm by £100 million, since paying off debt is a zero-NPV investment. This infusion makes the bonds more valuable, because it increases the likelihood that they will be repaid in full. Since the bonds gain £55 million in value as a result of this infusion, the post-issue value of all of the firm's equity must be only £95 million. Hence investors will not be willing to put up an additional £100 million in equity.

Example 17.6 describes a firm that is unable to issue new equity because debt holders capture a large part of the gain associated with the recapitalization. If the recapitalization does not make the firm more valuable, then an equity infusion hurts equity holders by transferring value from them to the debt holders. In many cases, however, a financially distressed firm does become more valuable after a recapitalization, in which case both equity holders and debt holders can benefit. This will happen, for example, when a firm is unable to sell its products, or is losing key employees because of its financial difficulties. Since financial distress reduces the current cash flows to equity holders, it provides an incentive for a firm to issue new equity, which can increase the value of the firm's existing equity as well as its debt. Example 17.7 Illustrates this point.

Example 17.7

Issuing Equity to Improve Customer Confidence

Consider again the case of Darnel plc, but now assume that one reason for its low value is that its customers have lost faith in the firm's ability to produce quality products because of its financial distress. Although the assets of the firm are currently valued at £600 million, the equity infusion will restore customer confidence, and Darnel's asset value (before the £100 million debt payment) will increase to £900 million. Under this scenario, is it possible for the firm to issue £100 million in equity?

Answer: Yes. The proceeds from the issue are not fully dissipated by an improvement in the value of the firm's debt. If the debt increases in value by less than £200 million as a result of the equity infusion and restored customer confidence, it follows that the post-issue equity value of the firm will exceed £150 million, implying that the equity can be issued, and that the original shareholders will benefit from the recapitalization.

Example 17.6 shows that when there are high costs associated with financial distress, equity holders have an incentive to recapitalize. However, if it is costly to repurchase or issue debt or equity, firms that have relatively low financial distress costs will have their leverage ratios determined to a large extent by their past history. That is, we expect a firm's current debt-to-equity ratio to be low if its past earnings were high, and its leverage ratio to be substantially higher if its past earnings were negative. This argument suggests the following result.

Results

Result 17.4

If the costs of changing a firm's capital structure are sufficiently high, a firm's capital structure is determined in part by its past history. This means that:

- very profitable firms are likely to experience increased equity values and thus lower leverage ratios
- unprofitable firms may experience lower equity values and perhaps increased debt, and thus higher leverage ratios.

Market-Timing Behaviour of Managers

Baker and Wurgler (2002) argued that the dynamic capital structure of firms was not determined by a pecking order of financing choices, but rather by the outcome of repeated attempts by management to time the markets. Companies tend to issue equity when market valuations are high relative to book valuations, and issue debt when market-to-book ratios are low (corresponding to the view that managers feel their equity is undervalued). Therefore firms will tend to have more equity after good performance, and more debt after bad performance.

The market-timing theory of capital structure has some fairly major ramifications for corporate finance. Conventional wisdom derived from theory is that each firm will have an optimal capital structure, and firms will aim over the long term to converge to that capital structure. Baker and Wurgler (2002) argue, on the other hand, that there is no optimal capital structure. Instead, observed capital structures are driven from historical valuations and managers' market-timing behaviour. Managers do not have a target capital structure. Instead, they take advantage of market conditions to derive the maximum market value from financing.

17.5 Empirical Evidence on the Capital Structure Choice

Chapters 14 to 17 discuss a variety of theories about the costs and benefits of debt financing. Taken together, these theories help to explain why firms select the capital structures that they do. In summary, the theories suggest a trade-off between the tax benefits of debt and a variety of costs, as well as some benefits of incurring financial distress. This section examines some of the empirical tests of these theories.

One of the earliest empirical findings was that firms in the same industry tend to choose similar capital structures (Leary and Roberts 2013; Grieser et al. 2022). Capital structures also tend to be unstable with debt levels varying over time from the same firms (DeAngelo and Roll 2015). These findings provide evidence that the optimal capital structures of firms vary from industry to industry, reflecting the differential costs and benefits of debt, which presumably are related to a firm's line of business. This evidence, however, is consistent with any theory that proposes a trade-off between the costs and benefits of debt financing, and it may even be consistent with capital structure irrelevance. In essence, the evidence may simply indicate that firms like to use industry norms to select their debt ratios. Because the use of industry norms is not harmful to firm value if capital structure is irrelevant, there is no reason to rule it out. In an international study of capital structure over 37 countries, Gungoraydinoglu and Öztekin (2011) report that one third of the variation in capital structure across firms is caused by country-level factors (e.g. regulatory or legal), and at the firm-level both trade-off and pecking order theories are supported by the data. Similarly, Öztekin and Flannery (2012) report that country-level legal and financial factors drive target adjustment speed, and strong creditor rights are strongly associated with lower debt levels (Cho et al. (2014). DeAngelo et al. (2011) showed that firms have target leverage ratios but purposely deviate from the target for a transitory period to fund new investments, subsequently allowing debt levels to revert to the target over a period.

Various empirical studies have documented evidence more supportive of the trade-off theories.[14] The evidence indicates that debt ratios are systematically linked to variables related to the costs of bankruptcy

[14] See Bradley et al. (1984), Long and Malitz (1985) and Titman and Wessels (1988). International evidence is presented by Rajan and Zingales (1995).

and financial distress (see Exhibit 17.2). Past research finds that observed debt ratios are negatively related to the firms' past profitability, research and development expenditures, and advertising and selling expenses. In addition, firms in industries that produce durable goods, such as machines and equipment, are usually less levered than firms that produce non-durables; and more unionized firms are usually more levered than less unionized firms. Small firms use about the same amount of long-term debt as larger firms, but small firms use significantly more short-term debt.

Exhibit 17.2 Summary of Empirical Evidence on the Capital Structure Choice

Variable	Relation to leverage ratio	Explanation
EBIT/total assets (profitability)	Strong negative relation	Pecking order description
R&D/sales	Strong negative relation	Tax reasons
Selling expenses/sales Market value/book value		Specialized assets and products imply greater stakeholder costs and potentially more conflicts between debt holders and equity holders
Machines and equipment producers (dummy variable)	Less highly levered	Customer avoidance of purchasing durable goods of distressed firms
Unionization[a]	Highly unionized industries are more levered	Leverage increases the firm's bargaining power
Size	Small firms use more short-term debt	Transaction costs of issuing long-term debt Adverse incentive costs associated with long-term debt[b]

[a] See Bronars and Deere (1991).

[b] This explanation was discussed in Chapter 16.

The negative relationship between operating profit and leverage is found in numerous countries.[15] This relationship reflects the pecking order of financing behaviour. When firms generate substantial amounts of cash from their operations, they tend to pay down debt before paying out dividends and repurchasing shares. When firms generate insufficient cash to cover investment needs, they tend to borrow rather than issue equity to cover the shortfall.

There are several explanations for the negative relationship of R&D and selling expenses to leverage. First, firms with large R&D and selling expenses may have little in the way of taxable earnings, and hence may be able to utilize debt tax shields only rarely, if at all (see Chapter 14). In addition, firms with high R&D and selling expenses are likely to be growth firms that produce specialized products. To the extent that these are indeed growth firms, they are not likely to have access to sizeable amounts of debt financing, because of the debt holder–equity holder conflicts described in Chapter 16. The tendency of these growth firms to borrow short term provides further support for this idea, because short-term debt creates fewer conflicts than long-term debt. Moreover, since firms with high R&D and selling expenses produce more specialized products, their non-financial stakeholders are more likely to require investments in specialized human and physical capital. Hence the stakeholder theory also suggests that these firms should have low leverage ratios. For similar reasons, firms that produce machines and equipment requiring future maintenance tend to have relatively low leverage ratios.

The fact that unionized firms are more highly levered relates to our earlier discussion (see Section 17.2) about how committed stakeholders generate an environment of bilateral monopoly, characterized by negotiation. As we discussed earlier, unionized firms may prefer to take on more debt, because it allows them to bargain more effectively with their unions.

Market Timing versus Pecking Order

The empirical findings of Baker and Wurgler (2002) have been supported to a large extent by a number of subsequent papers. Fama and French (2002) found that leverage ratios take a very long time to move towards their long-run mean after exogenous market shocks. Over the short term, it will appear that there is no optimal

[15] See Rajan and Zingales (1995).

capital structure. Welch (2004) similarly reported that the capital structure of firms tends to move in line with market valuations, and there appeared to be no effort to correct market-driven changes in leverage ratios. Huang and Ritter (2005) also found that equity issues increase when expected equity risk premiums are lower, issue date returns are expected to be higher and market-to-book ratios are higher.

Although the papers cited in the previous paragraph suggest that external market forces drive capital structure, they do implicitly assume that changes in leverage are costless. Leary and Roberts (2005) found that when adjustment costs are incorporated into the analysis of dynamic capital structure, firms appear to have an optimal capital structure range. When leverage ratios are outside this range, firms actively rebalance their capital structure to return to the optimal band.

Flannery and Rangan (2006) argued that previous research into the trade-off, pecking order and market timing theories of capital structure uses inappropriate econometric methods to model adjustment to target leverage ratios. They employed a more sophisticated methodology and found that firms *do* adjust their capital structure ratios to an optimal level. Their estimation was that a typical firm converges to its target debt ratio by about 33 per cent each year.

Finally, Kayhan and Titman (2007) examined the relationship between what has happened to the firm in the past and the level of capital structure. They found that capital structure is influenced by past share price levels and the level of external financing that has been raised by the firm. However, over the longer term, these trends tend to be reversed, suggesting that there is indeed some type of optimal capital structure that firms aim towards. This is suggestive of the trade-off theory of capital structure.

As is clear, opinions on the best explanation for firm capital structures are still very much divided. For example, Shyam-Sunder and Myers (1999) and Lemmon and Zender (2007) supported the pecking order theory, whereas Leary and Roberts (2010) found no such evidence to make them believe that it is valid. Going deeper, Chang et al. (2006) report that the level of information quality relating to a firm has a big effect on whether managers wish to time the market. Specifically, firms with strong analyst following time the market less.

To date, almost all research on market timing has studied US firms, with very little work on other countries. Ownership structures, financial, economic and legal development differ across countries. It is to be hoped that future research in this area will deliver different insights.

17.6 Summary and Conclusions

The previous chapters examined a variety of costs and benefits of debt financing that firms must consider when they make their financing decisions. The discussion has suggested which firms should be financed more heavily with debt, and which should include very little debt in their capital structures. For example, producers of non-durable goods (for example, tobacco or chocolate bars) that do little research and development generally have relatively high debt ratios. These firms are likely to have low costs associated with financial distress, because their customers and other stakeholders are not likely to be especially concerned about their long-run viability. The potential for such firms to increase the risk of their investments substantially is also limited, so that borrowers are willing to lend to them at attractive terms. Such firms are also likely to generate high taxable earnings, because they usually have minimal tax shields, and as a result can fully utilize their interest tax deductions.

Producers of high-technology durable goods (for example, computers and other scientific equipment) generally are not highly levered. These firms have the highest costs associated with financial distress, because their stakeholders are very concerned about their long-term viability. In addition, the potential for taking on risky projects is present for such firms, making lenders reluctant to supply large amounts of debt capital. These firms also have lower taxable earnings, relative to their values, and hence can utilize only limited amounts of debt tax shields.

Although the types of product a firm sells and other aspects of its overall strategy have an important influence on its financial structure, a firm's capital structure is also determined by its history. Firms that are profitable often use some of their profit to repay debt, and as a result reduce their leverage ratio over time. In contrast, firms that suffer substantial losses generally accumulate debt; as a result, they become highly levered.

Bankruptcy rates would be substantially lower if firms issued equity instead of debt subsequent to incurring substantial losses. This chapter has provided several explanations for why firms do not do this. For example, issuing equity in these situations can result in a substantial transfer of wealth from the firm's equity holders to its debt holders. In addition, issuing equity might make it more difficult for the firm to bargain effectively with its employees and suppliers; perhaps by keeping the threat of bankruptcy high, employees and suppliers will make concessions that make the firm more competitive. Additional explanations based on managerial incentives and information considerations will be discussed in more detail in Part 5.

This chapter completes Part 4, which was devoted exclusively to issues of capital structure and dividend policy. The chapters in this part provided a fairly thorough discussion of how financial managers make capital structure choices in an ideal world where shareholders and managers are equally informed about the prospects of their firms, and agree that the objective of the firm is to maximize shareholder value. This provides a useful framework for thinking about how one should choose the optimal financing mix for a firm, but it provides an incomplete description of how these decisions are made in practice.

In reality, top managers may have an incentive to finance their firms in ways that do not maximize the value of their equity. For example, managers may choose conservative financial structures because of personal aversions to placing their firms in financial distress. In other cases, managers may choose high debt ratios to convey favourable information to their shareholders: that is, they signal their confidence in the firm's ability to generate sufficient earnings to repay the debt. These issues are addressed in Part 5.

Key Concepts

Result 17.1: A firm's liquidation choice and its decisions relating to the quality of its product and fairness to employees and suppliers depend on its financial condition. As a result, a firm's financial condition can affect how it is perceived in terms of being a reliable supplier, customer and employer.

Financial distress is especially costly for firms with:

- products with quality that is important yet unobservable
- products that require future servicing
- employees and suppliers who require specialized capital or training.

These types of firm should have relatively less debt in their capital structures.

Financial distress should be less costly for firms that sell non-durable goods and services, that are less specialized, and whose quality can easily be assessed. These firms should have relatively more debt in their capital structures.

Result 17.2: Financial distress can benefit some firms by improving their bargaining positions with their stakeholders.

Result 17.3: Leverage affects the competitive dynamics of an industry. In some situations, leverage makes firms more aggressive competitors, in others less aggressive.

Result 17.4: If the costs of changing a firm's capital structure are sufficiently high, a firm's capital structure is determined in part by its past history. This means that:

- very profitable firms are likely to experience increased equity values and thus lower leverage ratios
- unprofitable firms may experience lower equity values and perhaps increased debt, and thus higher leverage ratios.

Key Terms

bilateral monopoly 551
dynamic capital structure theory 557
non-financial stakeholders 545
predation 554
stakeholder theory 545
static capital structure theory 557

Exercises

17.1 What are the differences between direct and indirect bankruptcy costs? Who bears these costs? Explain your answer by referring to a real situation from the recent past.

17.2 As a potential employee, why might you be interested in the employer's capital structure?

17.3 Compare qualitatively the indirect bankruptcy costs of operating a franchised hotel with those of running a high-tech start-up computer firm.

17.4 You are the manager of a company that produces motor vehicles. A union contract will come up for renegotiation in two months, and you wish to increase your firm's bargaining power prior to hearing the union's initial demands. The union is likely to ask for a 25 per cent increase from existing wage levels of €20 per hour for the 1,000 workers at your company. Workers typically work 2,000 hours per year. The firm has €100 million of debt outstanding at an interest rate of 10 per cent annually, and an equity market value of €200 million. Income before interest is €20 million per year. Assume no taxes. What specific financing strategies would you implement, and why?

17.5 BCD Manufacturing is considering repurchasing 40 per cent of its equity. Management estimates the tax savings from such a move to be £33.6 million, based on the addition of £1 billion of debt at a rate of 12 per cent with a 28 per cent marginal tax rate. However, the company's suppliers are unhappy with the decision, and are threatening to revoke the company's net-30 day credit terms, which will cost the firm an additional 2 per cent on its £1.5 billion inventory. Should management go ahead with the repurchase? Why or why not?

17.6 FagEnd and DeathBreath, two cigarette producers of comparable size, are struggling for market share in a declining market. FagEnd has just undergone a levered buyout, and is able to meet its fixed expenses with its existing market share, but it may be forced into bankruptcy if it loses market share. As a manager of DeathBreath, how would you establish your pricing policy? If FagEnd enters bankruptcy, it would (a) be forced to liquidate, (b) lose market share because of customer concerns, or (c) emerge recapitalized with no harm to market share. How would these three possibilities affect your decision?

17.7 Comparing the indirect costs of bankruptcy, explain why the technology wearables firm, Garmin, includes very little debt in its capital structure whereas the automobile manufacturer, Volkswagen, uses a fairly large amount of debt.

17.8 Describe the trade-offs involved when firms decide how to price their products. What are the costs and benefits of raising prices? How do interest rates affect the decision? How do leverage ratios affect the decision?

17.9 Weston Trattore is a cyclical business that is forced to lay off workers during downturns. The CEO estimates that they saved €50 million during the last recession by laying off excess labour. However, the company had additional expenses of €70 million three years later when it had to retrain the new workers. The firm is currently facing a similar situation. The risk-free rate is 4 per cent, but Weston's current borrowing rate is 10 per cent. Should Weston lay off the workers? If Weston was less highly levered, it would be able to borrow at 6 per cent. How would this affect the firm's decision? Discuss how a prospective employee would react on learning that Weston was increasing its leverage substantially.

17.10 Compass Computers has suffered an unexpected loss and is currently having financial difficulties. Explain why Compass may choose not to issue equity to solve its financial problems. If Compass does not issue equity, should it change its product market strategy to account for the firm's weaker financial health?

17.11 As the CEO, which do you prefer: a competitor with high leverage or one with low leverage? Under what conditions will you act more or less aggressively if your competitor is highly levered?

17.12 Compton Holdings currently has 2 million shares outstanding at £3 per share. Because the company is having financial difficulties, it also has £50 million in face value of long-term outstanding debt that is selling at only 60 per cent of its face value. As Compton's CEO, you estimate that you will need a cash inflow of £10 million within six months to meet your payroll. Since covenants in the existing debt preclude further debt financing, you are forced to consider an equity offering. Is such an offering possible, assuming the equity issue would result in a 20 per cent increase in the value of the debt? Explain why.

17.13 You have been hired by Garmin, the Swiss wearables firm, to advise it on its capital structure. This €869 million company would like to raise an additional €250 million to acquire the assets of one of its competitors. It currently has very little debt, but it is considering borrowing the entire €250 million. In order to make your recommendation, you have asked the following questions.

a Is the CEO, who is a major shareholder, planning on reducing his stake in the business?

b Does Garmin require specially trained Garmin technicians for servicing, or can the service be acquired from a variety of sources?

c Does Garmin expect to be generating significant amounts of cash in excess of its investment needs in the future, or is it likely to require additional external capital in the future?

Explain how the answers to these questions would affect your advice.

17.14 Your company has close to $10 billion in cash on its balance sheet invested in short-term securities. Your largest shareholder wants to use the cash to buy back shares. At the very least, the shareholder wants the cash, which yields about 4 per cent, to be used to repurchase the company's outstanding bonds, which yield 7 per cent. How can you justify holding cash yielding 4 per cent when the firm has bonds that can be retired that yield 7 per cent?

17.15 Explain why grocery store prices tended to increase in markets where one or more of the main competitors initiated an LBO. (*Hint:* think of market share as an investment.)

17.16 Over the past 30 years, the transaction costs associated with issuing and repurchasing debt and equity securities have declined. What effect do you think this change has had on capital structure choices?

References and Additional Reading

Admati, A.R., DeMarzo, P.M., Hellwig, M.F. and Pfleiderer, P. (2018) The leverage ratchet effect, *The Journal of Finance*, 73(1): 145–198.

Andrade, G. and Kaplan, S. (1998) How costly is financial (not economic) distress? Evidence from highly leveraged transactions that became distressed, *The Journal of Finance*, 53(5): 1443–1493.

Asquith P., Gertner, R. and Scharfstein, D. (1994) Anatomy of financial distress: an examination of junk-bond issuers, *Quarterly Journal of Economics*, 109(3): 625–658.

Bae, K. H., Kang, J. K. and Wang, J. (2011) Employee treatment and firm leverage: A test of the stakeholder theory of capital structure, *Journal of Financial Economics*, 100(1): 130–153.

Baker, M. and Wurgler, J. (2002) Market timing and capital structure, *The Journal of Finance*, 62(1): 1–32.

Barclay, M.J. and Smith, C.W. Jr. (1995) The maturity structure of corporate debt, *The Journal of Finance*, 50(2): 609–631.

Bessler, W., Drobetz, W., Haller, R. and Meier, I. (2013) The international zero-leverage phenomenon, *Journal of Corporate Finance*, 23, 196–221.

Blouin, J., Core, J.E. and Guay, W. (2010) Have the tax benefits of debt been overestimated?, *Journal of Financial Economics*, 98(2): 195–213.

Bolton, P. and Scharfstein, D. (1990) A theory of predation based on agency problems in financial contracting, *American Economic Review*, 80(1): 93–106.

Bradley, M., Jarrell, G. and Kim, E.H. (1984) On the existence of an optimal capital structure: theory and evidence, *The Journal of Finance*, 39(3): 857–878.

Brander, J.A. and Lewis, T.R. (1986) Oligopoly and financial structure: the limited liability effect, *American Economic Review*, 76(5): 956–970.

Bronars, S.G. and Deere, D.R. (1991) The threat of unionization, the use of debt, and the preservation of shareholder wealth, *Quarterly Journal of Economics*, 106(1): 231–254.

Campello, M. (2003) Capital structure and product markets interactions: evidence from business cycles, *Journal of Financial Economics*, 68(3): 353–378.

Chang, X., Dasgupta, S. and Hillary, G. (2006) Analyst coverage and financing decisions, *The Journal of Finance*, 61, 3009–3048.

Chevalier, J.A. (1995a) Capital structure and product market competition: an empirical study of supermarket LBOs, *American Economic Review*, 85, 206–256.

Chevalier, J.A. (1995b) Do LBO supermarkets charge more? An empirical analysis of the effects of LBOs on supermarket pricing, *The Journal of Finance*, 50(4): 1095–1112.

Chevalier, J. and Scharfstein, D. (1996) Capital markets, imperfections and countercyclical markups: theory and evidence, *American Economic Review,* 86, 703–726.

Cho, S.S., El Ghoul, S., Guedhami, O. and Suh, J. (2014) Creditor rights and capital structure: Evidence from international data, *Journal of Corporate Finance,* 25, 40–60.

Cook, D.O. and Tang, T. (2010) Macroeconomic conditions and capital structure adjustment speed, *Journal of Corporate Finance,* 16(1): 73–87.

Cornell, B. and Shapiro, A. (1987) Corporate stakeholders and corporate finance, *Financial Management,* 16(1): 5–14.

Cutler, D.M. and Summers, L.H. (1988) The costs of conflict resolution and financial distress: evidence from the Texaco–Pennzoil litigation, *Rand Journal of Economics,* 19(2): 157–172.

Dasgupta, S. and Sengupta, K. (1993) Sunk investment, bargaining, and choice of capital structure, *International Economic Review,* 34(1): 203–220.

Dasgupta, S. and Titman, S. (1998) Pricing strategy and financial policy, *The Review of Financial Studies,* 11(4): 705–737.

DeAngelo, H., DeAngelo, L. and Whited, T.M. (2011) Capital structure dynamics and transitory debt, *Journal of Financial Economics,* 99(2): 235–261.

DeAngelo, H. and Roll, R. (2015) How stable are corporate capital structures?, *The Journal of Finance,* 70(1): 373–418.

Devos, E., Dhillon, U., Jagannathan, M. and Krishnamurthy, S. (2012) Why are firms unlevered?, *Journal of Corporate Finance,* 18(3): 664–682.

Donaldson, G. (1961) *Corporate Debt Capacity: A Study of Corporate Debt Policy and the Determination of Corporate Debt Capacity,* Harvard Graduate School of Business Administration, Boston, MA.

Fama, E. and French, K. (2002) Testing trade-off and pecking order predictions about dividends and debt, *Review of Financial Studies,* 15(1): 1–33.

Faure-Grimaud, A. (2000) Product market competition and optimal debt contracts: the limited liability effect revisited, *European Economic Review,* 44(10): 1823–1840.

Fischer, E.O., Heinkel, R. and Zechner, J. (1989) Dynamic capital structure choice: theory and tests, *The Journal of Finance,* 44(1): 19–40.

Flannery, M. and Rangan, K. (2006) Partial adjustment towards target capital structures, *Journal of Financial Economics,* 79(3): 469–506.

Gomes, J.F. and Schmid, L. (2010) Levered returns, *The Journal of Finance,* 65(2): 467–494.

Greenwood, R., Hanson, S. and Stein, J.C. (2010) A gap-filling theory of corporate debt maturity choice, *The Journal of Finance,* 65(3): 993–1028.

Grieser, W., Hadlock, C., LeSage, J. and Zekhnini, M. (2022) Network effects in corporate financial policies, *Journal of Financial Economics,* 144(1): 247–272.

Gungoraydinoglu, A. and Öztekin, Ö. (2011) Firm-and country-level determinants of corporate leverage: Some new international evidence, *Journal of Corporate Finance,* 17(5): 1457–1474.

Hanka, G. (1998) Debt and the terms of employment, *Journal of Financial Economics,* 48(3): 245–282.

Harris, M. and Raviv, A. (1991) The theory of capital structure, *The Journal of Finance,* 46(1): 297–355.

Harris, M. and Raviv, A. (2010) Control of corporate decisions: Shareholders vs. management, *The Review of Financial Studies,* 23(11): 4115–4147.

Hillier, D., Marshall, A., McColgan, P. and Werema, S. (2007) Employee layoffs, shareholder wealth and firm performance: evidence from the UK, *Journal of Business Finance and Accounting,* 34(3–4): 467–494.

Hovakimian, A. and Li, G. (2011) In search of conclusive evidence: How to test for adjustment to target capital structure, *Journal of Corporate Finance,* 17(1): 33–44.

Huang, R. and Ritter, J. (2005) Testing the market timing theory of capital structure, *Journal of Financial and Quantitative Analysis,* 1(2): 221–246.

Jensen, M. and Meckling, W. (1976) The theory of the firm: managerial behavior, agency costs and ownership structure, *Journal of Financial Economics,* 3(4): 305–360.

Kayhan, A. and Titman, S. (2007) Firms' histories and their capital structures, *Journal of Financial Economics,* 83(1): 1–32.

Khanna, N. and Tice, S. (2000) Strategic responses of incumbents to new entry: the effect of ownership structure, capital structure and focus, *The Review of Financial Studies,* 13(3): 749–779.

Klasa, S., Ortiz-Molina, H., Serfling, M. and Srinivasan, S. (2018) Protection of trade secrets and capital structure decisions, *Journal of Financial Economics,* 128(2): 266–286.

Kovenock, D. and Phillips, G. (1995) Capital structure and product-market rivalry: how do we reconcile theory and evidence?, *The American Economic Review,* 85(2): 403–408.

Korajczyk, R. and Levy, A. (2003) Capital structure choice: macroeconomic conditions and financial constraints, *Journal of Financial Economics,* 68(1): 75–109.

Korteweg, A. (2010) The net benefits to leverage, *The Journal of Finance,* 65(6): 2137–2170.

Lang, L.H., Poulsen, A. and Stulz, R.M. (1995) Asset sales, firm performance, and the agency costs of managerial discretion, *Journal of Financial Economics,* 37(1): 3–37.

Leary, M. and Roberts, M. (2005) Do firms rebalance their capital structures?, *The Journal of Finance,* 60(6): 2575–2619.

Leary, M.T. and M.R. Roberts (2010) The pecking order, debt capacity, and information asymmetry, *Journal of Financial Economics,* 95, 332–355.

Leary, M.T. and Roberts, M.R. (2013) Do peer firms affect corporate financial policy?, *The Journal of Finance,* 69(1): 139–178.

Lemmon, M. and Zender, J. (2004) Debt capacity and tests of capital structure theories. Unpublished working paper, University of Utah.

Long, M. and Malitz, I. (1985) The investment-financing nexus: some empirical evidence, *Midland Corporate Finance Journal,* 3, 53–59.

Mackie-Mason, J.K. (1990) Do taxes affect corporate financing decisions?, *The Journal of Finance,* 45(5): 1471–1495.

Maksimovic, V. (1986) *Optimal Capital Structure in Oligopolies,* PhD dissertation, Harvard University.

Maksimovic, V. and Titman, S. (1991) Financial policy and reputation for product quality, *The Review of Financial Studies,* 4(1): 175–200.

Matsa, D.A. (2010) Capital structure as a strategic variable: Evidence from collective bargaining, *The Journal of Finance*, 65(3): 1197–1232.

Miller, M.H. (1977) Debt and taxes, *The Journal of Finance*, 32(2): 261–275.

Myers, S.C. (1984) The capital structure puzzle, *The Journal of Finance*, 39(3): 575–592.

Myers, S.C. and Majluf, N. (1984) Corporate financing and investment decisions when firms have information that investors do not have, *Journal of Financial Economics*, 13(2): 187–221.

Opler, T. and Titman, S. (1994) Financial distress and corporate performance, *The Journal of Finance*, 49(3): 1015–1040.

Öztekin, Ö. and Flannery, M.J. (2012) Institutional determinants of capital structure adjustment speeds, *Journal of Financial Economics*, 103(1): 88–112.

Perotti, E. and Kathy E. Spier, K.E. (1994) Capital structure as a bargaining tool: the role of leverage in contract renegotiation, *American Economic Review*, 83(5): 1131–1141.

Phillips, G.M. (1995) Increased debt and industry product markets, *Journal of Financial Economics*, 37(2): 189–238.

Povel, P. and Raith, M. (2004) Financial constraints and product market competition: ex ante vs ex post incentives, *International Journal of Industrial Organization*, 22(7): 917–949.

Pulvino, T. (1998) Do asset fire sales exist? An empirical investigation of commercial aircraft transactions, *Journal of Finance*, 53(3): 939–978.

Rajan, R.G. and Zingales, L. (1995) What do we know about capital structure? Some evidence from international data, *The Journal of Finance*, 50(5): 1421–1460.

Rampini, A.A. and Viswanathan, S. (2013) Collateral and capital structure, *Journal of Financial Economics*, 109(2): 466–492.

Rauh, J.D and Sufi, A. (2012) Explaining corporate capital structure: Product markets, leases, and asset similarity, *Review of Finance*, 16(1): 115–155.

Robb, A.M. and Robinson, D.T. (2014) The capital structure decisions of new firms, *The Review of Financial Studies*, 27(1): 153–179.

Robinson, J.E. (1992) *Freefall: The Needless Destruction of Eastern Airlines and the Valiant Struggle to Save It.* New York: HarperCollins.

Serfling, M. (2016) Firing costs and capital structure decisions, *The Journal of Finance*, 71(5): 2239–2286.

Shapiro, A. and Titman, S. (1985) An integrated approach to corporate risk management, *Midland Corporate Finance Journal*, 3(2): 41–56.

Sharpe, S. (1995) Financial market imperfections, firm leverage, and the cyclicality of employment, *American Economic Review*, 84(4): 1060–1074.

Shyam-Sunder, L. and S. Myers (1999) Testing static tradeoff against pecking order models of capital structure, *Journal of Financial Economics*, 51, 219–244.

Spier, K. and Sykes, A. (1998) Capital structure, priority rules, and the settlement of civil claims, *International Review of Law and Economics*, 18(2): 187– 200.

Strebulaev, I.A. and Yang, B. (2013) The mystery of zero-leverage firms, *Journal of Financial Economics*, 109(1): 1–23.

Titman, S. (1984) The effect of capital structure on the firm's liquidation decision, *Journal of Financial Economics*, 13(1): 137– 152.

Titman, S. and Wessels, R. (1988) The determinants of capital structure choice, *The Journal of Finance*, 43(1): 1–19.

Welch, I. (2004) Capital structure and stock returns, *Journal of Political Economy*, 112(1): 106–131.

Zingales, L. (1998) Survival of the fittest or fattest: exit and financing in the trucking industry, *The Journal of Finance*, 53(3): 905–938.

Zweibel, J. (1996) Dynamic capital structure under managerial entrenchment, *American Economic Review*, 86(5): 1197–1215.

PART 5

Incentives, Information and Corporate Control

Part contents

Up to this point, we have explored financial strategies that firms can employ to enhance the value of their shares. In reality, however, financial managers do not always make the decisions that maximize the share prices of their firms. To understand how financial decisions are actually made, we have to understand how managerial incentives can differ from shareholder incentives.

Part V takes a closer look at how managers actually make financial decisions. Chapter 18 examines managerial incentives in detail, paying particular attention to the general belief among managers that they must satisfy a broad constituency that includes shareholders as only one of many relevant players. For example, managers generally view their employees as important constituents, so typically they are somewhat averse to making decisions that jeopardize their employees' jobs. They are also interested in their own job security and future prospects; as a result, managers may take on negative-NPV investments that allow their firms to grow, and may also include less than the optimal amount of debt in their capital structures.

Although these incentive issues probably cannot be eliminated, financial markets have evolved in recent years in ways that lessen the more significant problems. In most companies, for example, the debt– equity choice is a decision made at the board of directors' level. Hence firms with active outside board members – that is, members of the board of directors who are not employees of the company – can force managers to select a debt ratio higher than that which the managers would personally prefer. In addition, outside board members might want to see the firm more highly levered than would be optimal in the absence of managerial incentive problems, since the added debt burden may mitigate the incentives of managers to overinvest.

A more direct way to align the incentives of managers and shareholders, which is also examined in Chapter 18, is to make the pay of managers more sensitive to the performance of their share prices. The threat of outside takeovers, examined in Chapter 20, also helps to align the interests of managers and shareholders. As Chapter 19 notes, however, many types of performance-based compensation, such as executive share options and the threat of outside takeovers, can make managers overly concerned about the current share prices of their firms. When this is the case, managers may take actions that convey favourable information to investors that temporarily boost share prices at the expense of lowering the intrinsic or long-term values of their firms.

The incentives of managers to make financial decisions that convey favourable information to investors are examined in Chapter 19. We argue, for example, that managers may want to distribute cash to shareholders, in the form of either dividends or share repurchases, because cash distributions signal that firms are generating cash, thus resulting in favourable share price responses. Similarly, leverage increases signal that managers are confident that they can take advantage of the debt tax shield, and are not overly concerned about incurring the costs of financial distress. Hence, when firms announce an increase in their debt ratios, share prices generally respond favourably.

An important lesson of Chapter 19 is that the share price response to the announcement of a financial decision may provide misleading information about how investors view the particular decision. For example, managers may believe that shareholders prefer higher dividends because share prices react favourably to dividend increases. In reality, however, shareholders may react favourably to dividend increases because of the favourable information the decision conveys, even though investors dislike the tax consequences of the higher dividends. A second important lesson of this chapter is that there may be negative consequences associated with making managers overly concerned about boosting the current share price of their firm.

Chapter 20, which examines mergers and acquisitions and their effect on the control of firms, applies the material used throughout this text. For example, an understanding of the incentive and information issues examined in Chapters 18 and 19 is particularly important for individuals who evaluate mergers and acquisitions. In some cases, mergers and acquisitions mitigate the incentive and information problems; in other cases, however, mergers can worsen these problems. In addition, many of the tax issues discussed in Chapters 13 to 15, and the valuation techniques developed in Part III, prove to be important in the evaluation and structuring of merger and acquisition deals.

Both risk aversion and the time value of money, which were central to our analysis of asset pricing in the first half of this text, provide an unnecessary layer of complication to the analysis of how information and incentive problems affect corporate behaviour. Hence, unless specified otherwise, the discussion and examples in Part V assume that investors are risk neutral and the interest rate is zero or, equivalently, that the present value of a future cash flow equals its expected future value.

Chapter 18

How Managerial Incentives Affect Financial Decisions

Learning Objectives

After reading this chapter, you should be able to:

- Distinguish between managerial incentives and shareholder incentives.
- Understand how the differences between manager and shareholder incentives affect the ownership structure, capital structure and investment policies of firms.
- Describe ways to design compensation contracts that minimize manager–shareholder incentive problems.

Chief executives and other directors regularly get criticized for excessive pay and rewards, despite only satisfactory performance. For example, the Institute of Policy Studies reported that CEO pay in US firms was 670 times higher than the average worker in 2021. The UK pay-gap ratio is lower at 86 times, with median CEO pay around £2.7 million.

However, there are also cases where CEOs voluntarily take pay cuts because of poor performance or not hitting targets. For example, Yves Guillemot, the CEO of French games firm, Ubisoft, chose to take a thirty per cent pay cut because his firm did not meet financial targets during the global pandemic in 2021. Operating profit was down 14 per cent and the company's share price was down fifty per cent from the year before. However, the company hit other targets such as gender equality (25 per cent of total workforce were women) and carbon emissions (down 14 per cent in one year). Many CEOs would argue that their performance should be seen across all domains, not just financial, and that their salary is appropriate for their level, irrespective of how well their company does during the year. Yves Guillemot, on the other hand, took personal responsibility and reflected the financial performance in his own salary.

Up to this point, we have presented a fairly simplistic view of how corporate decisions are made. The previous chapters considered financial decisions within the context of a firm whose shareholders know as much about the business as the managers, and whose managers act in the interests of shareholders. In most cases, these assumptions provide a useful framework for understanding how investment and financing decisions *should* be made to create value for shareholders. However, given the conflicts of interest between managers and shareholders, this framework does not provide a good general description of how these financial decisions are *actually* made.

This chapter has two purposes. The first is to provide a more realistic picture of how financial decisions are *actually made* by firms, taking into account the potential incentive problems that can exist between managers and shareholders. The second purpose is to re-examine how financial decisions *should be made* in this more realistic setting, accounting for inherent manager–shareholder conflicts.

One can take two views as to why management decisions might deviate from those that maximize firm values. The first, more cynical, view is that managers take advantage of their positions and engage in actions that allow them to benefit personally at the expense of shareholders. Although the popular press has emphasized this cynical view of the management–shareholder conflict, we emphasize a different view: that managers view their positions as serving a broader constituency than just shareholders.

The most important source of conflict between managers and shareholders arises from the sense of loyalty most managers feel towards their employees and other stakeholders. For example, managers generally find it unpleasant to lay off employees and, similarly, find it rewarding to offer their employees good career opportunities. Indeed, many people believe that taking care of employees – not maximizing share prices – should be the primary goal of corporations.

Perhaps the most important implication of both the cynical view and the stakeholder view is that managers may choose investment and financing strategies that do not maximize the firm's value. For example, to enhance their own opportunities as well as those of their employees, managers may bias their investment and financing decisions in ways that reduce risk and increase the firm's growth rate. To accomplish these goals, a manager may accept negative-NPV projects that increase the size and diversity of the firm and use less than the value-maximizing level of debt financing.

Since managers and shareholders do not always have the same interests, financial decisions can be viewed from different perspectives. For example, the previous chapters viewed financial decisions from the perspective of a firm run by value-maximizing managers. This chapter views the financial decisions from two different perspectives: (1) from the perspective of a manager who has complete control of the firm and who may, for personal reasons, want less risk and more growth than shareholders; and (2) from the perspective of a large shareholder, or perhaps a board member, who can influence the firm's overall strategy but cannot control the day-to-day decisions made by the firm's managers. These large outside shareholders may influence a firm's capital structure decision, since they can readily observe the capital structure choice, but they may not be able to influence the firm's investment choices.

This chapter addresses the question of how outside shareholders should exert their influence on the capital structure choice in order to *indirectly* influence the manager's investment choice. This chapter also examines ways of compensating managers so that these incentive problems are minimized.[1]

18.1 The Separation of Ownership and Control

Most large corporations are effectively controlled by managers who hold a relatively small amount of their firm's shares. To borrow from the influential book by Berle and Means (1932), there is a separation between ownership and control in large corporations. This separation causes problems, because the interests of managers are not generally aligned with those of shareholders.

Whom Do Managers Represent?

Equity holders are interested in maximizing the value of their shares. Managers, however, generally see equity holders as just one of many potential constituents. Donaldson and Lorsch (1983) suggested that top executives see themselves as representatives of three separate constituencies, including both financial and non-financial stakeholders:

1 investors (for example, the company's equity holders and debt holders)
2 customers and suppliers
3 employees.

[1] Later chapters examine how incentive issues affect both merger and acquisition strategies (Chapter 20) and risk management strategies (Chapter 21).

In making decisions, managers tend to trade off the interests of all three groups, rather than simply maximize shareholder value. Of course, when decisions do not affect the well-being of a firm's customers, suppliers and employees, there is no conflict. In reality, however, this is rarely ever the case.

The tendency of managers to consider the interests of all the firm's stakeholders is somewhat natural, given that executives spend most of their typical day dealing with customers, suppliers and employees, and building personal relationships with these individuals. They spend much less time interacting with equity holders, although the time spent with institutional shareholders is certainly increasing.

What Factors Influence Managerial Incentives?

Several factors influence the extent to which managers act in the interests of shareholders. For example, as the length of time a CEO stays in the job increases, the loyalty to the individuals with whom he or she must deal on a day-to-day basis also increases. This makes it more difficult for the executive to make tough decisions that might improve the firm's share price at the expense of customers and employees.

Imagine, for example, the dilemma faced by an executive who has the opportunity to substantially improve her firm's value by restructuring the firm. Should she act in the interests of the institutional shareholders who bought the equity last month and plan to sell it after the restructuring is completed, or should she act in the interests of the employees with whom she has worked for many years, and who may be forced into early retirement if the restructuring is implemented?

The proportion of the company's equity owned by managers also determines the extent to which management's interests deviate from those of equity holders. Jensen and Meckling (1976) provided an intuitive explanation of why a manager who owns more shares will act more in the interests of equity holders. If the manager owns only 5 per cent of the firm's shares, each dollar of perquisites, or unnecessary expenditures that benefit the manager personally, costs him or her only \$0.05, with the other \$0.95 borne by other shareholders. For example, a £1 million corporate jet will, in essence, have a personal cost to the manager of only £50,000. Because of this, the manager is likely to use corporate resources inefficiently, consuming in ways that would not occur if the cost of the consumed resources were paid from the manager's personal funds.

While providing some insight into the pecuniary benefits that can accrue to a manager with low shareholdings, the example doesn't capture the full complexity of the relationship between managerial behaviour and their ownership in the firm. Davies et al. (2005) presented a highly non-linear relationship, and argued that the trade-off managers face between following their own personal agendas and following that of shareholders changes as ownership levels increase.

At very low levels of ownership, external and internal control structures are likely to dominate managerial objectives (Fama 1980; Hart 1983; Jensen and Ruback 1983). As managerial shareholdings become greater, their interests will converge with those of shareholders. However, at the same time, managers also become more powerful because of their voting rights. This increase in power within the firm is likely to be a stronger motivation for personal wealth accumulation rather than shareholder wealth maximization, and as a result is likely to see managers pursue their own objectives. It is natural that, as managerial shareholding grows, their objectives will become congruent with shareholders, and their behaviour and investment decisions will favour those of external shareholders. This will be the case until managerial shareholdings reach approximately 50 per cent and external discipline collapses when managers take control of the firm. At this point, managers may pursue their own objectives again. Finally, at very high levels of shareholdings (above 70 per cent), managers effectively become shareholders and act in shareholders' interests.

Results

Result 18.1

Management interests are likely to deviate from shareholder interests in various ways. The extent of this deviation is likely to be related to the amount of time the managers have spent on the job and the number of shares they own.

How Management Incentive Problems Hurt Shareholder Value

Articles in news magazines and papers provide several examples of firms that experienced large price run-ups subsequent to the deaths of their CEOs (Quigley et al. 2017). For similar reasons, unexpected retirements can also lead to a positive share price response. For example, Hillier and McColgan (2008) found that widely held UK companies experienced *excess* returns of 1.16 per cent over a six-month period when their CEO resigned. Family firms had even higher returns of 3.42 per cent. When CEO turnover is forced (that is, involuntary), share prices respond much more, with excess returns of greater than 15 per cent over a six-month period for family firms.

One interpretation of the positive share price reactions to CEO retirements and deaths is that investors believe that a new CEO, with fewer ties to the firm's other managers, may be more willing to make the kind of tough decisions that might be required to improve share values. In 2016, for example, the price of Tootsie Roll Industries' equity increased by 13 per cent upon the sudden death of its CEO, Melvin Gordon. Moreover, this wasn't a one-off. Quigley et al. (2017) found that over the twenty-year period, 1990–2009, share prices rose by 9 per cent on average following an unexpected CEO death.

Why Shareholders Cannot Control Managers

Given the large anticipated gains in share prices linked to changing the policies of entrenched managers, it is surprising that shareholders are unable to force them to act in ways that maximize the firm's share prices, or force them to resign earlier. Jensen and Murphy (1990b) reported that, in 1986, the median percentage of inside shareholdings for 746 CEOs in the *Forbes* compensation survey was 0.25 per cent, with 80 per cent of this sample holding less than 1.4 per cent of the shares in their firms. In the UK, boards, as a whole, held approximately 10 per cent of their company's equity (Hillier and McColgan 2008).

As a group, outside shareholders generally cannot force managers to maximize share prices, because their ownership is too diffuse. This creates the kind of free-rider problem described in Chapter 16. In this case, the *free-rider problem* arises because it is not in the interest of any individual shareholder to take actions that discipline a non-value-maximizing manager, even though it is in the interests of all shareholders as a group to have this manager removed.

Shareholders who want to challenge the policies of management must stage **proxy fights**, which require organizing shareholders to oust the incumbent board of directors by electing a new board that supports an alternative policy. Proxy fights are very expensive, and outsiders who attempt to organize outside shareholders to vote against incumbent management usually don't win them. Carl Icahn, for example, spent millions in 2022 on his unsuccessful proxy fight to force McDonalds to use more humane methods in treating pigs. This doesn't mean that all proxy contests are unsuccessful, however. For example, in 2008, the same Carl Icahn spent over $2 billion building up a stake in Motorola before winning his proxy fight to open the board to more external representation. Although the aggregate benefits to all shareholders involved in such a proxy fight may very well exceed their costs, the individual bearing the costs usually receives only a fraction of the benefits. The remainder of the benefiting shareholders are thus free riders. Hence it isn't surprising that proxy fights rarely occur.

Why is Ownership So Diffuse if It Leads to Less Efficient Management?

Chapters 4 and 5 noted that investors have an incentive to hold diversified portfolios. Indeed, the Capital Asset Pricing Model suggests that all investors hold the same market portfolio, implying that an investor's shareholdings in any individual firm must be extremely small. However, the preceding discussion suggests the possibility of an inherent conflict between the desire to hold diversified portfolios and the ability of shareholders to control management.

An individual investor who wishes to obtain enough shares to control management would generally have to hold an undiversified portfolio. Although the investor would benefit by getting management to make value-maximizing decisions, he or she would bear significant costs by holding an undiversified portfolio. Hence investors face a trade-off between diversification and control. The undiversified investor, however, shares the benefits of control (the higher share price) with other shareholders, but must bear alone the cost of having an undiversified portfolio, as Example 18.1 illustrates.

Example 18.1

The Trade-Off Between Diversification and Improved Monitoring

Marco Bajo believes that he can take control of Osov SpA and improve its value by €60 million over the next five years. He can do this by investing his entire wealth of €60 million to purchase 20 per cent of Osov's outstanding shares. Osov's equity has a standard deviation of about 40 per cent per year, which is about twice the standard deviation of the market portfolio. Should Marco go ahead with this investment?

Answer: Osov realizes the €60 million increase in value in five years if Marco gains control. For a €300 million company, this is equivalent to an additional 20 per cent return over five years, which is less than 4 per cent per year. It's likely that Marco could realize a much higher expected return with the same level of total risk with a levered position in the market portfolio. The gains from increased monitoring that arise from holding a large stake, therefore, are not enough to offset the costs of having an undiversified portfolio.

How does this marry with the situation in most countries around the world? In most economies, except the UK and USA, concentrated ownership is the norm (La Porta et al. 1999; Faccio and Lang 2002; Bortolotti and Faccio 2009). The main reason is that firms in these countries have always been closely held, and the benefits of control outweigh the disadvantages of undiversified holdings. Environments with poor shareholder rights are more likely to lead to concentrated ownership patterns, because the protection of external equity holders is not strong enough to encourage diversified but low shareholdings (Burkart and Panunzi 2006). Moreover, in recent years, the UK and USA have seen a concerted move towards private equity, where firms are bought over and delisted to be sold a few years later. In this situation, the acquiring management requires control of the firm to introduce changes in management and business structure. The expected excess returns that accrue as a result of the corporate restructuring more than offset any disadvantage from being undiversified.

Results

Result 18.2

Firms with concentrated ownership are likely to be better *monitored* and thus better managed. However, shareholders who take large equity stakes may be inadequately diversified. All shareholders benefit from better management; however, the costs of having a less diversified portfolio are borne only by the large shareholders. Because of the costs of bearing firm-specific risk, ownership is likely to be less concentrated than it would be if management efficiency were the only consideration.

Can Financial Institutions Mitigate the Free-Rider Problem?

The importance of holding a diversified portfolio explains why individual investors rarely choose to take positions that are large enough to allow them to adequately monitor and control management. However, the diversification motive does not explain why institutions do not arise to provide such monitoring services. For example, one can imagine an economy in which investors pool their money and buy into large, relatively diversified mutual funds. Given their large size, these mutual funds could in theory take individual positions that were large enough to influence management, yet still remain reasonably diversified. For example, a £5 billion mutual fund, such as the large cap Fidelity Europe Fund, might put £1 billion into each of five different European shares. If a number of different funds formed portfolios in such a way and communicated with one another, as a group they would be able to monitor management effectively.

As noted in Chapter 1, in the UK and USA, large shareholdings are not very common, especially among the largest firms. This is in contrast to the situation in other countries, such as Germany and Japan, where banks hold significant amounts of equity, and exert control over managers. Pension funds, the other major institutional holders of ordinary equity, have recently begun to exert more influence on corporate behaviour. Corporate pension funds, however, are still reluctant to exert significant influence on corporate managers, which is not surprising. For example, the managers of Vodafone would not like to see the company's pension fund second-guessing the management of another firm. Doing so might set a precedent that would give the pension funds at other corporations the idea that they should meddle in Vodafone's affairs. However, pension funds for public employees have no similar disincentive keeping them from acting as active monitors of management. Indeed, some large pension funds – most notably CALPERS, the large pension fund for California's public employees, and the NAPF, the National Association of Pension Funds in the UK – have recently taken on a more active role in their relationship with corporate management. As we discuss below, there has recently been much more pressure on managers to act in the interests of their shareholders, partly because of the growing importance of public pension funds.

Whether institutional shareholder activism is successful in improving the performance of firms is still an open question. Mutual and pension fund managers have been found to have no real performance impact when they choose to become involved in the affairs of companies (see Black 1998; Gillan and Starks 2007). However, Brav et al. (2008) reported that hedge fund managers may be much more successful at influencing managerial behaviour to improve corporate performance. Brav et al. (2008) propose several reasons why hedge funds, but not mutual or pension funds, can be effective monitors. One, the incentive of hedge fund managers is much stronger than in other financial institutions. Because the hedge fund industry is subject to little regulation compared with other financial services industries, managers are able to invest large proportions of their portfolios in a small number of firms. Moreover, they are able to use debt and derivatives to increase their holdings in firms beyond their actual cash investment capacity. Interestingly, and contrary to public perception, hedge fund managers are not confrontational (less than 30 per cent undertake hostile activities such as lawsuits or public campaigns), nor do they attempt to take control of companies. Clearly, more research is required in this area.

International Corporate Governance Codes

Corporate governance codes across the world are regularly updated to reflect changes in the external market environment and economy. However, there are commonalities across governance codes that focus on country-level governance, shareholder and stakeholder rights, the role of financial institutions in the governance of a firm, financial reporting quality and the performance of corporate boards.

Exhibit 18.1 presents the main codes for a selection of developing and emerging countries. Whereas there are differences across countries, almost all the codes follow the main principles of corporate governance that were published by the G20/OECD in 2015. Interested readers should visit the website of the European Corporate Governance Institute (www.ecgi.global), which presents the full documentation of many countries' corporate governance codes.

Do Corporate Governance Problems Differ Across Countries?

One of the reasons why each country has its own corporate governance code is that corporate governance problems differ across countries as well as over time. In some countries, most notably the USA, the UK and former British colonies, there is relatively strong legal protection for outside shareholders. Other countries, however, provide much less legal protection for outside shareholders. For example, Russia started moves in 2022 to allow the nationalization of companies operating in Russia that belong to 'unfriendly countries'. This means that if a company were to leave Russia because of international sanctions, the Russian government would seize the company's assets and auction them to the highest bidder.

As one might expect, countries with the strongest protection for outside shareholders have the largest and the most active equity markets. Countries with weaker protection for outside shareholders have smaller equity markets, and many fewer new companies going public. Recent evidence suggests that there are clear advantages associated with the increased equity market activity and higher market valuations that are associated with greater investor protection.[2]

Of course, changes that improve investor protection and create more active equity markets are not necessarily easy to implement. In particular, there may be intense opposition from politically connected families who control the large corporations in those countries where investor protection is the weakest. Such reforms are likely to reduce the degree to which these families control their businesses, and the reforms are likely to make it easier for potential competitors to raise cash and challenge their dominance.

The global financial crisis in 2008 raised new questions as to the real effectiveness of corporate governance. This was because many of the world's best-governed banks were found to have undertaken exceptionally risky business practices, and governance had no impact in reducing the prevalence of this. As a result, most countries have now introduced new corporate governance codes that promote accountability and proactive shareholder engagement (see Exhibit 18.1 for the most recent codes).

[2] See, for example, Aggarwal et al. (2010), Leuz et al. (2010), Doidge et al. (2004, 2007), Klapper and Love (2004), La Porta et al. (2000, 2002) and Levine and Zervos (1998).

Exhibit 18.1 Country and Regional Codes of Corporate Governance

Country	Code
Australia	*Corporate Governance Principles and Recommendations* (2019)
Austria	*Austrian Corporate Governance Code* (2021)
Bahrain	*Corporate Governance Code Kingdom of Bahrain* (2010)
Belgium	*Belgian Code on Corporate Governance* (2020)
China	*Code of Corporate Governance for Listed Companies* (2018)
Denmark	*Recommendations for Corporate Governance* (2017)
EU	*EVCA Corporate Governance Guidelines* (2005)
Finland	*Finnish Corporate Governance Code* (2020)
France	*Corporate Governance Code of Listed Corporations* (2020)
Germany	*German Corporate Governance Code* (2022)
Greece	*Hellenic Corporate Governance Code* (2021)
India	*Corporate Governance Voluntary Guidelines* (2009)
Ireland	Follows *The UK Corporate Governance Code* (2019)
Italy	*Italian Corporate Governance Code* (2020)
Malaysia	*Malaysian Code on Corporate Governance* (2021)
Netherlands	*Dutch Corporate Governance Code* (2016)
Norway	*The Norwegian Code of Practice for Corporate Governance* (2018)
OECD	*G20/OECD Principles of Corporate Governance* (2015)
Oman	*Code of Corporate Governance for Public Listed Companies* (2016)
Pakistan	*Code of Corporate Governance* (2012)
Poland	*Code of Best Practice for WSE Companies* (2012)
Portugal	*Corporate Governance Code* (2020)
Saudi Arabia	*Corporate Governance Regulations in the Kingdom of Saudi Arabia* (2017)
Singapore	*Code of Corporate Governance* (2018)
South Africa	*King Report on Corporate Governance for South Africa* (2016)
Spain	*Code of Good Governance of Listed Companies* (2020)
Sweden	*Swedish Code of Corporate Governance* (2016)
Switzerland	*Swiss Code of Best Practice for Corporate Governance* (2014)
UAE	*Corporate Governance Code for Small and Medium Enterprises Dubai* (2011) *Ministerial Resolution No. (518) of 2009 Concerning Governance Rules and Corporate Discipline Standards* (2009)
UK	*The UK Corporate Governance Code* (2018)
US	*Corporate Governance Principles For US Listed Companies* (2017)

18.2 Management Shareholdings and Market Value

Despite the diversification motive suggested by portfolio theory, the ownership of shares in corporations in most countries is actually quite concentrated. La Porta et al. (1999) recorded that, for many countries, a large individual shareholder or an institution owns a significant percentage of the outstanding shares. Many of the large shareholders are the company's founders. Notable examples of company founders maintaining large shareholdings are Sergey Brin and Larry Page of Alphabet, and Mark Zuckerburg of Meta. As one might expect from the discussion in the previous subsection, concentrated shareholdings are especially common in countries that have the weakest legal protection for outside shareholders.

The Effect of Management Shareholdings on Share Prices

As Chapter 15 discussed, tax reasons might explain why Steve Ballmer may choose not to sell his Microsoft equity to diversify his portfolio. An entrepreneur like Steve Ballmer may also be concerned about how the sale of his equity would affect the firm's share price. By selling shares, an entrepreneur may be indirectly communicating unfavourable information to the firm's shareholders. Holding a large number of shares tells investors that the entrepreneur is confident about the firm's prospects, and that he or she plans on implementing a strategy that maximizes the value of the company's shares.[3]

Demsetz and Lehn (1985) suggested that executives in industries with the greatest potential for incentive problems retain the largest share of ownership in their firms. For example, the CEOs of media companies (such as Rupert Murdoch), which are likely to be fraught with incentive problems, typically hold a relatively large fraction of the firms that they manage. In contrast, the top managers of companies that are monitored more easily are likely to own a smaller fraction of the firms they work for.

Example 18.2 illustrates the trade-off between the benefits of retaining shares to improve incentives and the diversification benefits of selling shares.

Example 18.2

Inside Ownership and Firm Value

Bates Productions is owned exclusively by John Bates, who would like to sell a significant fraction of the firm in an IPO. Bates' investment bankers have asserted that the value of Bates Productions is tied very closely to the efforts of John Bates. They believe the firm is worth £100 million, based on the way it is currently operating. They also believe that if Bates sells over 50 per cent of the shares in the IPO, they will value the company at only £80 million, because investors will not be assured that Bates will put in the same effort that he had been expending in the past. However, if Bates retains two-thirds of the shares, the investment bankers believe they can price the firm at about £90 million. What should John Bates do?

Answer: If John Bates sells half of the firm, he will end up with £40 million in cash and shares worth £40 million. However, if he sells one-third of the firm, he will end up with £30 million in cash and shares worth £60 million. The amount he should sell depends not only on the value of his cash and shares but also on his aversion to effort (we are assuming that he will put in less effort if he owns less equity) and his aversion to risk.

Results

Result 18.3

Entrepreneurs may obtain a better price for their shares if they commit to holding a larger fraction of the firm's outstanding shares. The entrepreneur's incentive to hold shares is higher for those firms with the largest incentive to 'consume on the job'. The incentive to hold shares is also related to risk aversion.

---

[3] See Chapter 19 for more discussion of this issue.

Empirical studies by Downes and Heinkel (1982) and Ritter (1984) provide evidence that, when entrepreneurs retain a higher stake in their firms when they go public, they do indeed get higher prices for the shares they sell. The following subsection reviews a number of empirical studies that examine the relationship between management ownership stakes and firm values for larger, more established firms.

Management Shareholdings and Firm Value: The Empirical Evidence

Davies et al. (2005) examined the relationship between market values and management shareholdings in a sample of FTSE All Share firms. They found that, for relatively small shareholdings, firms with higher concentrations of management ownership have higher market values relative to their book values. However, as management's holdings rise above 5 per cent, the firms become less valuable. This suggests that as the managers' holdings become too large, managers become entrenched, allowing them more freedom to pursue their own agendas in lieu of value-maximizing policies. Firms increase in value relative to their book values again until shareholdings are around 50 per cent, at which point external market discipline collapses, because firms are effectively controlled by management. This results in market valuations falling again until very high shareholdings when the managers become shareholders, and maximizing shareholder wealth becomes their main objective.[4]

Unfortunately, it is difficult to interpret the evidence on the relationship between value creation and ownership concentration, because the ratio of a firm's market value to its book value, which is used in these studies as a measure of value creation, measures more than how well the firm is managed. For example, firms with substantial intangible assets, such as patents and brand names, may have high market-to-book ratios even if they are poorly managed. Similarly, well-managed firms may have relatively low market-to-book ratios because they own few intangible assets. Perhaps management ownership is related to market-to-book ratios because there are more benefits attached to the control of intangible assets. We would expect, for instance, that it would be a great deal more fun to own a controlling interest in a football team, such as Glasgow Celtic, or a movie studio, such as Paramount, where most assets are intangible, than a copper mine, where most assets are tangible.

Measuring the value created by managers is much easier in the case of **closed-end mutual funds**, which are publicly traded mutual funds with a fixed number of shares that can be bought and sold on the open market rather than bought and redeemed directly from the fund at their net asset values, as is the case for **open-end mutual funds**. The ratio of the share price of the closed-end mutual fund to the net asset value per share of the portfolio it holds provides an excellent measure of the value created by the fund's managers, since the net asset value of the fund provides a good measure of the market value that could be achieved without the manager (for example, if the fund were liquidated). If investors believe a fund is badly managed, or that it generates excessive expenses, they will not be willing to pay the full net asset value of the shares. Indeed, there have been many cases of closed-end funds selling at more than a 25 per cent discount.

Barclay et al. (1993) found that the average discount was 14.2 per cent for closed-end funds with a large shareholder, but only 4.1 per cent for funds without a large shareholder. This evidence indicates that large shareholders tend to depress values, suggesting that the negative effects of management ownership in this case outweighed the positive benefits.[5]

18.3 How Management Control Distorts Investment Decisions

Analysing the separation between the ownership and control of corporations provides a great deal of insight into how a firm makes investment decisions. This section examines a firm's investment policies in two situations:

- when a self-interested manager controls most of the firm's investment decisions
- when a large outside shareholder has influence over the firm's strategy for investing, but only indirect control over specific investment choices.

[4] Morck et al. (1988), McConnell and Servaes (1990), Hermalin and Weisbach (1991), Kole (1995) and Short and Keasey (1999) provide further evidence that share prices increase with the concentration of management holdings, but, beyond a certain point, increased management ownership can depress firm values.

[5] The authors of this study noted that, in many cases, individuals purchase large blocks of shares in closed-end funds and improve the fund's value either by forcing managers to liquidate the funds or, alternatively, by turning the fund into an open-end fund. Since those cases where large shareholders improve value will not exist in a sample of existing closed-end funds, one should not conclude from the evidence in this study that large shareholders always diminish the value of closed-end funds.

The Investment Choices Managers Prefer

An important premise of this chapter is that there are significant benefits associated with controlling a large corporation, and that top executives prefer investments that enhance and preserve those benefits. As discussed below, a firm's investment choice can affect control benefits in a number of ways.

Making Investments that Fit the Manager's Expertise

If the benefits from controlling a corporation are sufficiently large, a CEO's desire to remain on the job will also be very large, providing the CEO with an incentive to bias financing and investment decisions in a manner that makes it more difficult to replace him in the future (see Shleifer and Vishny 1989; Scharfstein and Stein 2000). To become entrenched, managers may choose to make irreversible investments in projects for which they have a particular expertise, so that they will not become expendable in the future. For this reason, oil firms may have continued to invest in oil exploration in the early 1980s, despite falling oil prices.

Managers may also wish to rely on implicit contracts and personal relationships in their business dealings to make it more difficult for potential replacements to complete the deals that they have initiated. Consider, for example, the threat by Steven Spielberg in the late 1980s to stop making movies with Warner Brothers if its CEO back then, Stephen Ross, left the company. This of course made Ross's job much more secure, and probably allowed him to extract greater perquisites than he might otherwise have obtained.

Making Investments in Visible/Fun Industries

Most of us would probably prefer managing a media company to a chemical company. There are clearly more opportunities for doing interesting things and meeting interesting people at a movie studio than at a refinery. Although we have no reason to believe that Todd Boehly's purchase of Chelsea Football Club in 2022 was not for financial reasons, he, probably at least subconsciously, must have considered the personal benefits associated with being in the football business when he made the acquisition.

Making Investments that Pay Off Early

An additional consideration is that managers may want to make investments that help the current share price of the firm, even when they hurt it in the long run. Having favourable financial results in the short run may allow a manager to raise capital at more favourable rates and, perhaps, both increase his compensation and reduce the chance that he will lose his job. Chapter 19 describes how these advantages create a tendency for managers to select projects with a short payback period over higher-NPV investments that require a longer payback period.

Making Investments that Minimize the Manager's Risk and Increase the Scope of the Firm

The high personal cost of a firm's bankruptcy provides an additional bias to the investment and financing choices of managers. Gilson (1990) reported that only 43 per cent of the chief executive officers and 46 per cent of the directors keep their jobs subsequent to the bankruptcy of their firms. Kang and Shivdasani (1997) found that US firms reduced director salaries less than 2 per cent of the time that firms experienced large performance declines compared with 13 per cent of Japanese firms. In the UK, Hillier and McColgan (2007) found that 20 per cent of companies changed their CEOs, with just over 8 per cent forcibly removing their chief executive.

The fear of bankruptcy may explain why managers prefer large empires to small empires, and hence often choose to expand their companies faster than they should, investing more of the company's earnings and distributing less in dividends than is optimal for value maximization. Managers may also have a tendency to be more risk averse in their choice of investments than they should be, especially in terms of their treatment of those risks that shareholders can avoid through diversification. Only systematic risk matters to shareholders. From the manager's perspective, however, unsystematic risk as well as systematic risk may be of importance, because both affect the probability of the firm getting into financial trouble and ultimately the probability of the manager retaining his or her job. This same logic suggests that managers also may prefer less than the value-maximizing level of debt in their capital structures.

Of course, the reduction of risk is not the only reason that explains why managers want to increase the size of their companies. There is added prestige associated with being the chief executive of a larger company. In addition, it is easier to justify higher salaries for individuals managing larger organizations. Indeed, compensation consultants include the size of a manager's organization as a key input in making compensation recommendations.

The tendency of managers to overinvest the firm's internally generated cash can be illustrated by the situation at RJR Nabisco before its levered buyout (LBO) in 1988. About one and a half years before its LBO,

RJR Nabisco's baking unit devised a plan to completely revamp and modernize its baking facilities, at a cost of \$2.8 billion. The annual savings from this modernization would have been only \$148 million, providing a pre-tax return of only about 5 per cent.[6] After the LBO, which substantially cut the resources available for investment, the modernization plan was scaled back considerably.

Summarizing Management Investment Distortions

Result 18.4 summarizes the preceding discussion about the ways in which investments chosen by managers may differ from investments selected purely on the basis of value maximization.

Results

Result 18.4

Managers may prefer investments that enhance their own human capital and minimize risk. This implies that:

- managers may prefer larger, more diversified firms
- managers may prefer investments that pay off more quickly to those that would maximize the value of their shares.

Outside Shareholders and Managerial Discretion

Up to this point, we have assumed that managers control the investment choice. However, large *outside* shareholders, knowing that managers have a tendency to skew decisions in directions that benefit them personally, have an incentive to reduce management's discretion. These outside shareholders may favour investments in fixed assets and other technologies that limit the manager's future discretion.

Real World Insight

Academic Industries

Consider the hypothetical example of Academic Industries, a university spin-out company, run by academics. The founders have invented a new machine to measure the radius of blood vessels immediately after a drug has been injected into them, and have received venture capital funding to take the firm into production. The venture capitalist, Academic Industries' major shareholder, must meet with the academic founders to discuss the future of the company. The academics are clearly a good choice to manage the company, because they understand the new machinery better than anyone in the world. As a champion of quality, they represent a commitment to customers that Academic Industries' machinery will be the best on the market.

Unfortunately, the academics' commitment to quality is also their biggest weakness. The venture capitalist is worried that the academics will spend too much money to produce the 'perfect' machine when an 'almost perfect' machine would still be the best on the market.

Before completely turning over the division to the academics, the venture capitalist must decide between two production processes: a labour-intensive process and a capital-intensive process. The labour-intensive process requires more upfront training costs, but the yearly cost of the capital-intensive process is actually the higher of the two processes, given the high maintenance costs of the machinery. The academics would certainly prefer the labour-intensive process if they were running the company themselves. In addition to its lower costs, the labour-intensive process provides the flexibility to improve the quality of the product by increasing costs. However, since the venture capitalist wishes to delegate all future decisions to the academics, it believes that the capital-intensive technology will be the better alternative, because it does not wish to give the academics too much discretion in choosing the quality of the product.

[6] *Wall Street Journal*, 14 March 1989.

Trading Off the Benefits and Costs of Discretion

The Academic Industries example illustrates a negative aspect of flexibility. However, as Chapter 12 noted, under uncertainty, flexible investment designs can add value to a firm, since flexibility increases a firm's operating options. The value of that flexibility is greater, the greater is the uncertainty. Hence the cost associated with having to limit flexibility because of incentive problems is greater, the greater the level of uncertainty. With sufficient uncertainty, it is better for the outside shareholders to expend more effort monitoring management but also to allow managers greater flexibility and discretion (Harris and Raviv 2010). However, when there is very little uncertainty, the outside shareholders may want to limit the managers' flexibility. In summary, we have the following result.

Results

Result 18.5

Allowing management discretion has benefits as well as costs.

- The benefits of discretion are greater in more uncertain environments.
- The costs of discretion are greater when the interests of managers and shareholders do not coincide.

Therefore we might expect to find more concentrated ownership and more managerial discretion in firms facing more uncertain environments.

18.4 Capital Structure and Managerial Control

As noted earlier, a manager may prefer less than the optimal level of debt, because additional debt increases the risk of bankruptcy and limits a manager's discretion. In some circumstances, however, outside shareholders might view these factors as advantages. The added debt may prevent a manager from expanding the firm more rapidly than would be optimal. Moreover, since higher debt ratios increase the threat of bankruptcy, which managers are anxious to avoid, increased debt can induce management to avoid policies they might personally prefer, but which reduce firm value.[7]

The basic idea is that the fear of losing one's job is a good motivator. Therefore the shareholders of a firm that is run by 'self-interested' management may prefer a higher leverage ratio than one would find in firms that are managed in the shareholders' interest.

The Relationship between Shareholder Control and Leverage

Mehran (1992) provided evidence supporting the idea that control by outside shareholders affects how firms are financed. In his sample of 124 manufacturing firms, Mehran found a positive relationship between a firm's leverage ratio and:

- the percentage of total executive compensation tied to performance
- the percentage of equity owned by managers
- the percentage of investment bankers on the board of directors
- the percentage of equity owned by large individual investors.

In other words, firms tend to be more highly levered if they are managed by individuals with a strong interest in improving current share prices, or if they are monitored by board members or large shareholders who have those interests. However, Moh'd et al. (1998) showed that when changes in insider and institutional ownership are investigated, debt ratios fall as insiders and institutions increase their stake in the company. This result can be interpreted in two ways. First, managers decrease debt ratios to reduce their personal risk as their wealth becomes increasingly tied to the firm. Alternatively, insider and institutional ownership concentration may substitute for the disciplinary effects of debt. In evidence for Spanish firms, Pindado and de la Torre (2006)

[7] This argument was made by Grossman and Hart (1982).

look on the issue in a different way. Their main hypothesis is that capital structure determines insider ownership rather than the opposite causality, which tends to dominate in earlier research. Consistent with Moh'd et al. (1998), they argue that managers reduce their holdings in response to high leverage and its associated risks.

Results

Result 18.6

Shareholders prefer a higher leverage ratio than that preferred by management. As a result, firms that are more strongly influenced by shareholders have higher leverage ratios.

How Leverage Affects the Level of Investment

Chapter 16 discussed how debt financing could limit the amount that a firm invests. However, if management has a tendency to overinvest, then limiting management's ability to invest may enhance firm value.[8]

Real World Insight

Gordon and Gary's Victorian Building Development: Using Debt to Limit Future Investments

To understand why an investor might want to use debt to limit a firm's investment opportunities, consider the case of Gordon and Gary, former university flatmates. One afternoon Gordon, who had become an architect, called Gary, an investment banker, with a proposal to buy an old Victorian house to convert into apartments. Gordon estimated that the total cost of the house and the renovations would be about £200,000. As the project's architect, Gordon would receive a small fee from the profits, and he would have complete control over the project once it was financed. Gary was asked to come up with the best financing alternatives.

Gary carefully calculated the project's net present value. After considering several possible scenarios, he concluded that Gordon's assessment of the project's potential was reasonably accurate. Gary then considered financing alternatives, and settled on a fixed-rate mortgage as the best alternative. The next question was to determine how much to borrow, and how much of their own money to invest in the project.

Both Gordon and Gary have £25,000 to invest in the project. Gordon would prefer to invest his entire £25,000, since his alternative is to put the money in a bank savings account paying 5.5 per cent interest, and the mortgage rate would be 7 per cent. Gary has no good alternatives for his £25,000, but he has one reservation about putting up such a large down-payment on the house. With a large down-payment, the monthly payments would be much lower, so Gordon would face much less pressure to cut costs and increase cash flows. With a large equity investment, Gary also could easily secure an additional loan to make further renovations. Although Gary trusts Gordon completely, he realizes that Gordon has a tendency to make his projects perfect, regardless of costs. For this reason, Gary believes that the project should have a smaller down-payment and a larger loan.

This example illustrates one very important point:

Results

Result 18.7

A large debt obligation limits management's ability to use corporate resources in ways that do not benefit investors.

[8] See Jensen (1986), Stulz (1990) and Rauh (2006).

Selecting the Debt Ratio that Allows a Firm to Invest Optimally

Chapter 16 discussed how too much debt may force a firm to pass up some positive-NPV projects. The *debt overhang problem* indicates that a firm that chooses a high debt ratio will find the costs of obtaining additional funds high, reducing the amount that equity holders will want the firm to invest. The analysis in this section suggests that outside shareholders may be able to use this debt overhang problem to their advantage. When managers have a tendency to overinvest, debt financing can be used to mitigate that tendency.[9] Example 18.3 illustrates how this can be done.

Example 18.3

Selecting the Debt Ratio that Leads to the Optimal Investment Strategy

Consider a firm that is financed with an initial investment of €100 million. In exactly one year it must decide whether to go ahead with a project that requires an additional €100 million investment. The present values (at the end of the first year) of the pay-offs from taking or not taking the additional investment in three future states of the economy are given in the following table.

	Value (in € millions) when state of the economy is		
	Good	Medium	Bad
Value with investment	250	175	125
Value without investment	50	50	50
Internal cash flow	100	25	100

One year from now, if in either the good or medium states, the additional investment has a positive NPV – that is, it creates more than €100 million in value in the good and medium states. In the bad state, however, where only €75 million (€125 million – €50 million) is created by taking the investment, the additional investment has a negative NPV.

Assume that, when financing the investment at the beginning of year 1, the original entrepreneurs understand that the manager they hire will want to fund the new investment at the end of year 1, even if it has a negative NPV. How should they finance the original investment to ensure that the firm can raise sufficient funds only when the additional investment has a positive NPV at the end of year 1?

Answer: If the original €100 million investment is financed completely with equity, the additional investment can be funded by issuing debt even in the bad state of the economy. To keep the managers from funding the additional investment in the bad state of the economy, the firm can finance *part* of the original investment with senior debt that requires additional debt to be of lower priority. Note that if the original investment at the beginning of year 1 is financed *completely* with senior debt, the firm will be unable to finance the additional €100 million investment in the medium state of the economy. (Since the original €100 million investment must be paid first in the medium state of the economy, only €75 million is left to pay the new investors.) In this case, a positive-NPV project is passed up. However, if the firm issues more than €25 million in senior debt but less than €75 million, it will be able to finance the project in the good and medium states of the economy but not in the bad state of the economy.

The outside shareholders in Example 18.3 were able to induce the firm's managers to invest exactly the right amount by selecting the appropriate debt ratio. In reality, however, things may not work out as nicely. For one thing, Example 18.3 ignores the possibility that the firm also has internally generated funds to invest in the project. This does not necessarily cause a problem if the firm generates cash in those states of the economy in which it has positive-NPV investments. However, as Example 18.4 illustrates, if the firm generates a substantial

[9] These ideas were developed in Jensen (1986), Stulz (1990) and Hart and Moore (1995).

amount of cash when its investments have negative NPVs, it may not be possible to induce managers to invest the optimal amount in every state of the economy by simply selecting the appropriate capital structure.

Example 18.4

Can Financing Choices Always be Used to Achieve the Optimal Investment Strategy?

Consider, again, Example 18.3 with the added assumption that the firm also generates funds internally. The cash flows and pay-offs in the different states of the economy are described below.

	Value (in € millions) when state of the economy is		
	Good	**Medium**	**Bad**
Value with investment	250	175	125
Value without investment	50	50	50
Internal cash flow	100	25	100

Is it possible for the firm to select a debt ratio that allows it to fund the investment in the medium and good state of the economy but not in the bad state of the economy?

Answer: It is not possible. The firm can be kept from financing what would be a negative-NPV project in the bad state of the economy by taking on:

(a) a €100 million short-term debt obligation due when the initial cash flows are realized, and
(b) an additional €26 million in senior debt (or any amount above €25 million) due in the following year.

These debt obligations, which prevent the firm from borrowing additional amounts in the bad state of the economy, also prevent the firm from investing in the medium state of the economy even though doing so is a positive-NPV investment. If the debt obligations are lowered to allow the firm to finance its investments in the medium state of the economy, then the firm will also be able to finance its operations in the bad state of the economy.

Results

Result 18.8

A firm's debt level is a determinant of how much the firm will invest in the future, and it can be used to move the firm towards investing the appropriate amount. In general, however, capital structure cannot by itself induce managers to invest optimally.

A Monitoring Role for Banks

Examples 18.3 and 18.4 assumed that the firm's debt could not be renegotiated, which is a reasonable assumption if the firm's debt is held by diffuse debt holders. In this regard, bank debt may have an advantage over public bonds, since it is possible for the firm to reduce free-rider and information problems if it is dealing with one banker instead of a large number of bondholders. Therefore a banker may be able to mitigate the overinvestment–underinvestment problems described in the examples above by evaluating the firm's projects and deciding selectively whether to offer additional credit.

In Example 18.4, an underinvestment problem in the medium state of the economy will arise if the firm issues €100 million in short-term debt as well as €26 million in senior debt. The assumption made in this example was that the debt could not be renegotiated, even though debt holders would be better off in the medium state of the economy if they forgave a portion of the firm's debt obligation. However, if a bank owns the debt, it will have an incentive to renegotiate the loan in the medium state of the economy; otherwise, the firm will go bankrupt and lose a positive-NPV project, which would increase the value of the bank's claim. The problem considered in Example 18.4 can thus be solved by having the firm take on enough bank debt to prevent it from taking on the negative-NPV project in the bad state of the economy, and by allowing the firm to renegotiate the debt obligation in the medium state of the economy.

Bank financing also may be beneficial when it is necessary to monitor management. The free-rider problem that keeps individual shareholders from monitoring the firm also probably keeps individual debt holders from doing much monitoring. This is especially true for firms with low leverage ratios, since in this case the debt holders are likely to be paid in full, even if management does poorly. However, if a firm is highly levered and bankruptcy appears likely, the debt holders will have an incentive to monitor management, especially if they have concentrated holdings.

Bank lending is particularly suited to serve this function, since financial institutions have the resources to hold a large fraction of a firm's debt and are capable of monitoring management. Delegating the monitoring of management to their *fixed* claimants (debt holders) rather than their residual claimants (equity holders) also reduces the asset substitution problem discussed in Chapter 16 (that is, the incentive of a firm's management to choose risky projects that transfer wealth from debt holders to equity holders). However, if debt holders have more influence over management than equity holders, then managers, acting in the interests of their debt holders, may be too conservative in their investment choices.

Another advantage of borrowing through a commercial bank arises for firms with proprietary information. For example, a firm may be able to exploit favourable market conditions only if competitors remain unaware of the situation. Hence a public debt offering, which reveals this information, places a firm at a competitive disadvantage. However, if this information can be revealed confidentially to the lender, a firm can obtain funds at attractive terms without revealing its information to competitors.

A Monitoring Role for Private Equity

Suppliers of private equity, such as venture capital firms and levered buyout sponsors, may provide monitoring services that are similar to those that banks provide. These suppliers of private equity capital are likely to provide more monitoring of management, for at least three reasons. First, they generally take substantial equity stakes in the businesses that they invest in. Second, their shares cannot be sold as easily, giving the private equity holders a greater stake in the long-term profitability of the firms they invest in. Finally, they have personnel with the kind of expertise that can help the firms in which they invest to create value for their shareholders. In other words, the private equity and venture capital firms provide advice and consulting as well as monitoring.

The downside to monitoring is that it can disincentivize firms from innovating or taking risks. Intensive monitoring has two main downsides: weaker strategic advising and greater managerial myopia (Faleye et al. 2011). In particularly intense monitoring, the negative effect of the downsides actually outweighs the benefits of monitoring, particularly when acquisitions and innovation are significant value drivers for the firm.

18.5 Executive Compensation

Economists describe the relationship between owners and management as a **principal–agent relationship**, with shareholders considered the **principals** and management as the **agents** hired by the principals to take actions on their behalf. To solve the **agency problem** that arises from the conflicting interests of agents and principals, economists have considered various ways to compensate agents in order to motivate them to work for the benefit of the principals.

The Agency Problem

Perhaps the earliest discussions of agency problems involved the relationship between a farm manager (the agent), whose effort cannot be directly observed, and the owner of the farm (the principal). To motivate the farm manager to work hard, the amount of compensation must be tied to the farm's output. However, because the crop yield is determined by unobservable soil conditions and unexpected weather, as well as by the farmer's effort, tying the farmer's compensation too strongly to the farm's output may not be optimal. Doing so would expose the farmer to uncontrollable risks that can be borne more efficiently by the owner of the farm because he may be able to diversify away much of this risk. As a result, there is a trade-off between the incentive benefits of tying compensation to output and the disadvantages of subjecting the farm manager to excessive risk over which the manager has no control.

Two Components of an Agency Problem

The farm manager discussion above illustrates the two essential features of an agency problem: uncertainty that the agent cannot control, and a lack of information on the part of the principal. If the principal were able to observe the actions of the agent, and if there were no free-rider problem, there would be no incentive problems. The principal could simply force the agent to work in his or her interests. The agent who refused could be fired. In addition, if the agent were not averse to bearing the risk of a particular project or, alternatively, if there were no risk that the agent could not control, the principal could motivate the agent to make value-maximizing choices by having the agent bear all of the risks associated with his or her actions. In short, if a manager were not averse to risk and had the capital, the best situation would be one in which the manager owned all the firm's equity.

Measuring Inputs versus Measuring Outputs

The agency problem can be substantially alleviated if the principal can accurately observe the agent's actions. The principal can do this in one of two ways: (1) closely monitor the agent to ensure that he or she works the specified number of hours at the required level of intensity – that is, measure the agent's labour *input;* or (2) indirectly measure the agent's actions by observing the agent's *output.*

Before the mid-1980s, most large corporations tried to solve the agency problem by measuring inputs. Systems were put in place to monitor managers, to make sure that they were doing their jobs appropriately. However, although it may be possible to evaluate the quantity of a manager's effort, it is difficult to evaluate the quality of that effort – in other words, the extent to which the manager's effort creates value for the firm. Moreover, even if the quantity and the quality of a manager's effort could be evaluated, it would be extremely difficult, contractually, to specify a bonus that was tied to such a vague concept. As a result, there has been a worldwide trend towards evaluating and compensating managers based on outputs (for example, profits) rather than inputs. In other words, there is an increased tendency of firms to tie employees' pay to performance.

Designing Optimal Incentive Contracts

A firm's profits are determined by several factors. Some of these are under the manager's control, but others are not. In general, well-designed compensation contracts minimize the extent to which managers can be penalized by factors outside their control. For example, the farm manager should be penalized less for exhibiting low output in years of little rainfall than for poor performance in years of abundant rainfall. Hence information about rainfall can be used to reduce the agent's risk and improve the relationship between the tenant farmer and the landowner.

In applying this logic to management compensation contracts, one would conclude that a manager's compensation should not be tied simply to the firm's share price or earnings performance, but to the amount by which the firm's equity return or earnings exceed the return on the market in general, or the performance of other firms in the industry.[10]

Edmans and Liu (2011) discussed the use of inside debt in addition to equity in designing optimal managerial incentive contracts. Inside debt incentivizes managers to avoid liquidation because the value of the debt is dependent on both the likelihood of default and the expected value of the firm in default.

Minimizing Agency Costs

Agency costs represent the difference between the value of an actual firm and the value of a hypothetical firm that would exist in a more perfect world where management and shareholder incentives are perfectly aligned. The discussion in this subsection provides ways in which firms can minimize agency costs. These are summarized in Result 18.9.

Results

Result 18.9

Agency problems partly arise because of imperfect information and risk aversion. Agency costs can thus be reduced by improving the flow of information and by reducing risk. To minimize the risk borne by managers, optimal compensation contracts should eliminate as much extraneous risk (or risk unrelated to the manager's efforts) as possible.

---

[10] This point was made in Diamond and Verrechia (1982).

Is Executive Pay Closely Tied to Performance?

Executives receive compensation from various sources. Part of their pay is fixed, part is contingent on corporate profits, and part is contingent on improvements in the share price of their companies. Anecdotal evidence suggests that executive pay became much more tied to firm performance during the 1980s and 1990s. However, there is some disagreement about how sensitive CEO compensation is to performance.

The Jensen and Murphy Evidence

In their *Harvard Business Review* article, Michael Jensen and Kevin Murphy (1990a) argued that executive compensation is not nearly as performance sensitive as it should be. They examined the compensation and share ownership of 2,505 CEOs from 1974 to 1988, and calculated how much the compensation of the CEOs increased with each $1,000 increase in the value of their companies. They concluded that the pay-for-performance sensitivity of most CEO's compensation is surprisingly low, and that most CEOs are not given sufficient monetary incentives to cut costs and create value for their shareholders. For example, the Jensen and Murphy estimates suggest that if an executive at a large US corporation purchased an extra $10 million jet for his or her personal use, he or she would be penalized only about $30,000 in lost compensation.

More Recent Evidence

Subsequent evidence by Boschen and Smith (1995) and Hall and Liebman (1998) suggests that Jensen and Murphy may have underestimated average pay-for-performance sensitivities, and that these sensitivities have been increasing over time. Boschen and Smith (1995) examined how the equity returns of a company affect the future as well as the current compensation of its CEO. This study concluded that the Jensen and Murphy evidence substantially underestimates the sensitivity of CEO pay to performance.

To understand why it is important to consider the CEO's future compensation, consider a CEO who was promised a bonus in each of the next five years equal to 30 per cent of the amount by which the company's earnings exceeded a certain level. If the CEO took actions that doubled earnings in his or her first year, the share price would probably increase substantially upon the announcement of the higher earnings, reflecting not only this year's earnings but also the higher earnings predicted in the future. In this case, one would observe only a weak relationship between the CEO's compensation in a given year and the firm's equity return in that year. In the first year of the contract, the firm's share price would increase substantially, and the CEO would receive a bonus reflecting the higher earnings in that year. In subsequent years, however, one would not expect the firm's share price to respond to favourable earnings, since the expectation of good earnings was already reflected in the share price at the end of the first year. However, the CEO would continue to receive the same bonus he or she received in the first year. Hence the correlation between the firm's equity returns in a given year and the CEO's compensation in that year would not be particularly strong. However, if one looked across firms, one might find a relationship between equity returns and compensation levels cumulated over many years. Boschen and Smith (1995) found that the cumulative response of pay to performance is about 10 times as large as the pay-to-performance sensitivity found by comparing equity returns and compensation levels in individual years.

Corporate governance can also have an impact on the relationship between executive pay and firm performance. Core et al. (1999) found that companies with ineffective governance structures are affected by higher agency costs, and part of this is higher executive compensation and poorer performance. Jenter and Lewellen (2021) found that up to 55 per cent of CEO turnover events are induced by performance concerns.

Cross-Sectional Differences in Pay-for-Performance Sensitivities

The Jensen and Murphy (1990a) study, along with more evidence in Murphy (1999), reveals that the pay-for-performance sensitivities differ substantially across firms. For example, the CEOs of media companies generally have compensation contracts with substantial pay-for-performance sensitivities, whereas the compensation contracts of regulated utility company CEOs exhibit very little in the way of pay-for-performance sensitivities. This difference probably reflects the fact that the CEOs of media companies have many more opportunities to 'consume on the job', and are more difficult to monitor than an executive at a regulated utility.

It is also the case that CEOs of small firms have much higher pay-for-performance sensitivities than the CEOs of large firms. This is not particularly surprising, given the way Jensen and Murphy (1990a) calculate pay-for-performance sensitivities. For example, suppose that the CEO of a £100 billion company had a pay-for-performance sensitivity of 1 per cent, meaning that he or she would receive an extra £10 in compensation for every £1,000 in value improvement. With such a compensation contract, the CEO would be given a bonus of more than £100 million for increasing the value of the firm by just 10 per cent. While a 1 per cent pay-for-performance sensitivity is probably not feasible at a company as large as £100 billion, far larger sensitivities are often observed at much smaller companies. In addition, because the CEOs of growth companies generally have more discretion than the CEOs of more mature companies, several authors have argued that the compensation of growth company CEOs should be more closely tied to their companies' performance. However, the empirical evidence on this is somewhat mixed.[11]

One reason why growth firm executives may not have higher pay-for-performance sensitivity is that these firms tend to be very risky. Recall that the most important cost of increasing performance-based pay is the added risk that must be borne by managers. This implies that, holding all else equal, we expect more risky firms to employ less performance-based compensation. A study by Aggarwal and Samwick (1999) of the pay-for-performance sensitivities of the top executives of large US firms found that this is indeed true. In general, executives working for companies with less volatile share prices have higher pay-for-performance sensitivity than executives who work for companies with more volatile share prices. However, once size is controlled for in the analysis, the picture becomes less clear. Dee et al. (2005) looked at internet firms during the 1997–1999 industry growth period, and found that the sensitivity of pay to performance actually increases once the size of firms is taken into account.

How Does Firm Value Relate to the Use of Performance-Based Pay?

If performance-based compensation improves incentives, then firms that implement incentive compensation programmes should realize higher values. Empirical studies that have documented the positive reaction of share prices to the adoption of performance-based executive compensation plans tend to support this hypothesis. For example, Tehranian and Waegelein (1985) examined equity returns at the time of the adoption of 42 performance-based compensation plans during the 1970s. They found that share prices increased about 20 per cent, on average, from seven months before the announcement of the adoption of the plans until the adoption date. Mehran (1995) looked cross-sectionally at the relationship between the ratio of the market-to-book value of a firm's shares and the extent of performance-based compensation for top management. He found that these two variables are positively correlated, indicating that, on average, firms using more performance-based compensation have higher share prices.

Unfortunately, it is difficult to infer causality from these studies. Performance-based compensation is associated with higher share prices; however, it is difficult to tell whether this compensation causes share prices to be higher or, alternatively, whether managers are more willing to adopt performance contracts after observing increases in their share prices. Perhaps it would be easier to sell managers on the idea of adopting performance-based compensation if the managers would have made more money in the recent past had the plan been adopted earlier. In addition, managers are more willing to adopt performance-based compensation plans when they have special information suggesting that the firm may be undervalued.

Example 18.5 illustrates why the adoption of a performance-based compensation plan conveys information to investors.

Example 18.5

The Information Conveyed from Adopting a Performance-Based Compensation Plan

Consider the CEOs of two firms, Gordon and Ally. The two firms currently have shares priced at £20 per share. Gordon has favourable proprietary information that leads him to believe that his firm's equity is really worth £30 per share. Ally has unfavourable proprietary information that leads her to believe that her firm's equity is worth only £15 per share. Both CEOs are considering proposals that would lower their fixed salary in exchange for equity options exercisable in one year at £20 per share. Which manager would be more inclined to accept such an offer? How would agreeing to a performance-based incentive plan affect the company's share price?

[11] Clinch (1991), Smith and Watts (1992) and Gaver and extensively in the compensation of executives in growth firms. However, Bizjak et al. (1993) and Gaver and Gaver (1995) found no significant relationship between growth opportunities and compensation in their samples. Gaver (1993) found that equity and options are used more extensively in the compensation of executives in growth firms. However, Bizjak et al. (1993) and Gaver and Gaver (1995) found no significant relationship between growth opportunities and compensation in their samples.

Answer: Gordon is more willing than Ally to adopt the performance plan because his proprietary information implies that the expected value of the options on his firm is higher. If investors understand these incentives, they will view Gordon's acceptance of the performance plan as good news, and bid up the price of his firm's equity.

As Example 18.5 illustrates, share prices may react positively to the adoption of a performance-based compensation plan, even if the plan has no effect on the managers' productivity.

Is Executive Compensation Tied to Relative Performance?

Recall from Result 18.9 that compensation contracts should be designed to eliminate as much extraneous risk as possible. One way to eliminate extraneous risk is with a **relative performance contract**, which determines executive compensation according to how well the executive's firm performs relative to some benchmark, such as the performance of the firm's competitors. The relative performance contract would thus have the desired feature of reducing the effect of risk elements that affect all industry participants, which probably are not within the CEO's control, while rewarding the executive only when he or she beats the relevant competition.

By far the largest fraction of performance-based pay comes from equity options. Although these options could, in theory, be indexed to industry share price movements, in practice they are not, implying that relative performance does not have a major effect on pay. For some firms, however, annual bonuses are tied to relative performance. Murphy (1999) reported that in a 1997 survey of 177 large US firms by the consulting firm Towers Perrin, 21 per cent of the 125 industrial companies tied their annual bonuses to their firm's performance relative to their industry peers. The survey indicated that the percentage of financial firms that do this is 57 per cent, and the percentage of utilities that base their executives' bonuses on relative performance is 42 per cent. Aggarwal and Samwick (1999) found that relative performance evaluation is more likely in highly competitive industries.

Oyer (2004) theoretically put forward the view that relative performance evaluation is not common because CEOs have outside employment opportunities. When the market is doing well, demand for good chief executives is much higher, and firms must pay more to retain their loyalties. Therefore awarding compensation based on total, and not relative, performance is the optimal strategy. Rajgopal et al. (2006) presented empirical evidence that supports this theory. Moreover, they found that chief executive employment opportunities are positively related to the amount of financial press visibility and the firm's industry-adjusted return on assets.

Another reason why few industrial firms have embraced relative performance-based pay may be the fact that these contracts can adversely affect the competitive environment within an industry. The disadvantage of this type of contract is its undesirable side effect of providing the CEO with an incentive to take actions that reduce its competitor's profits, even if doing so doesn't help his or her own firm. For example, a firm that utilizes a relative performance contract may compete more aggressively for market share, since the costs imposed on competitors from being aggressive improve the CEO's compensation, even if the gain in market share does not improve profits. The consequences are that if all industry participants instituted relative performance contracts of this type, industry competition would be more aggressive, and profits would probably be lower for all firms in the industry. Perhaps this is one reason why we do not observe explicit relative performance compensation contracts.

The only case where firms embrace relative metrics is in identifying peers to justify executive pay metrics. Faulkender and Yang (2010) and Bizjak et al. (2011) report that firms select highly paid peers to assess market pay levels, and that the effect is stronger when the CEO is also the chair of the firm. Morse et al. (2011) further finds that powerful CEOs induce boards to choose performance metrics that make their company look better.

Results

Result 18.10

Relative performance contracts, which reward managers for performing better than either the entire market or, alternatively, the firms in their industry, have an advantage and a disadvantage.

- The advantage is that the contracts eliminate the effect of some of the risks that are beyond the manager's control.
- The disadvantage is that the contracts may cause firms to compete too aggressively, which would reduce industry profits.

Equity-Based versus Earnings-Based Performance Pay

Performance-based compensation contracts come in two distinct forms: *equity-based compensation contracts,* which include executive share options (see Chapter 8) and other contracts that provide an executive with a pay-off tied directly to the firm's share price, and *earnings or cash flow-based compensation contracts,* based on non-market variables such as earnings, cash flow and adjusted cash flow numbers such as Stern Stewart's Economic Value Added (EVA™), discussed in Chapter 10.

Equity-Based Compensation

The advantage of equity-based compensation is that it motivates the manager to improve share prices, which is exactly what shareholders would like the manager to do. However, there also are disadvantages associated with equity-based compensation, which lead us to believe that earnings-based or cash-flow-based compensation might be preferred in many cases.

The first disadvantage of equity-based compensation is that share prices change from day to day, for reasons outside the control of top managers (for example, changes in interest rates). The second disadvantage is that share prices move because of changes in expectations as well as realizations. This second disadvantage is illustrated in Example 18.6.

Example 18.6

Using Equity Returns to Evaluate Management Quality

Consider two CEOs, Gary and Walter, who are hired at the same time to manage competing toy companies. Investors initially have an extremely favourable opinion of Gary, and expect his company, the Coy Toy Company, to do well. However, investors initially are extremely sceptical about Walter's qualifications and the prospects of his company, Toyco. How will the equity market react over the next few years if the two toy companies do equally well?

Answer: If both companies do equally well, Coy Toy will have performed worse than expected and Toyco will have performed better than expected. Hence Toyco's share price will perform much better, merely because of the improved opinion of Toyco's future.

In general, companies would like to compensate managers based on how much they contribute to shareholder value. As Example 18.6 shows, however, share prices reflect how well the managers did relative to expectations. Hence with equity-based compensation plans managers are penalized when investors have favourable expectations, and are helped when investors have unfavourable expectations.

Earnings-Based Compensation

The principal advantage of compensating managers on the basis of earnings and cash flows is that the numbers are generally available for the individual business units of a firm, as well as for non-traded companies that cannot easily base compensation on an observable share price. However, compensating managers based on earnings and cash flows also has its drawbacks. First, it is difficult to calculate the cash flow number that would be appropriate to use for evaluating performance. For example, one cannot simply base the executive's compensation on total earnings or cash flows, because this will provide an incentive to increase the *scale* of the corporation's operations, even if doing so requires the firm to take on negative-NPV projects. Hence there is a need to adjust the cash flows for the amount of capital employed, which is likely to change from period to period. In addition, both cash flow and earnings numbers that can be pulled easily from a firm's income statements are accounting numbers that include various adjustments for inventory valuation methods, pension fund liabilities, and so forth, and might not provide a very reliable measure of a firm's performance.

Dangers of Performance-Related Compensation

Société Générale provides an interesting case study of how performance-related compensation contracts can encourage suboptimal behaviour. Jérôme Kerviel was a junior trader at the bank's programme trading division, which dealt in quantitative trading systems using derivative securities such as swaps and futures. Driven by the promise of an exceptional performance-based bonus, he was convicted of hacking into colleagues' trading accounts to take extremely large positions in index derivatives. According to a report published by the bank's independent directors, Kerviel received a bonus of €60,000 in 2006, and expected a bonus of €600,000 (he actually received €300,000) in 2007. These bonuses were directly linked to his trading performance in the previous years, and reflected the profit he had made for Société Générale. When the fraudulent activities were uncovered, the bank reported a loss of €4.9 billion, although the trader's net exposure was significantly higher at €49.9 billion, much larger than the market value of Société Générale itself. It is important to emphasize that Jérôme Kerviel did not, at any time, make money for himself from the trading activities. His objective was to make money for his employer so that he could maximize his performance-related annual bonus.

Value-Based Management

The idea that managers in individual business units should be compensated according to the contribution of their units to overall firm value has attracted substantial attention. Consultants such as Stern Stewart and Boston Consulting Group have developed what they call **value-based management** methods to transform accounting cash flows into economic cash flows so that they more accurately measure the economic cash flows that are most useful in compensating managers.[12] Each of the preceding methods shares the insight that managers create value by making positive-NPV choices, and rewards managers for making such choices. As discussed in Chapter 10, these methods calculate the value created by a particular business unit by subtracting a charge for the amount of capital employed from the cash flows of each unit. The methods can differ in the way that cash flows and the cost of capital are calculated.

The advantage of a value-based management compensation method over equity-based compensation methods is summarized below.

Results

Result 18.11

Equity-based compensation has the advantage that it motivates managers to improve share prices. However, share prices change for reasons outside a manager's control, and only partially reflect the efforts of a manager who heads an individual business unit in a diversified corporation. A cash flow-based compensation plan that adjusts appropriately for capital costs may provide the best method for motivating managers in these cases.

Compensation Issues, Mergers and Divestitures

The discussion in the last subsection suggests that although equity-based compensation contracts might prove useful for motivating top management, they are less useful as a device for motivating the head of a business unit who has little influence on the firm's overall profitability. For example, the efforts of Garmin's CEO are better reflected in the price of the company's equity than the efforts of his counterpart in the wearables division of a multidivisional firm such as Apple. This puts Apple at a comparative disadvantage to Garmin in motivating the managers in its wearables group, because their compensation cannot be structured as easily to reflect the results of their efforts. This is especially true when the economic cash flows of the individual business units are hard to measure.

Spin-Offs and Carve-Outs

Schipper and Smith (1986), Aron (1991) and Chemmanur and Yan (2004), among others, have argued that these motivational issues are one reason why firms sometimes choose to **spin off** a division – transforming the division into a new company by distributing shares of the new company to the firm's existing shareholders – or **carve out** a division – that is, do an IPO of the division, making it an independent operating firm. Announcements of spin-offs and carve-outs usually lead to a favourable reaction in share prices. In a sample of 93 spin-off announcements between 1963 and 1981, Schipper and Smith (1986) found that share prices increased 2.84 per cent, on average, when the spin-offs were announced.

Chemmanur and Yan (2004) proposed the idea that, in multidivisional firms, incumbent managers are more likely to lose their jobs to a more able rival if the company undertakes a spin-off or carve-out. In this scenario, an incumbent manager will work harder to ensure his or her position, thereby improving firm performance.

[12] Chapter 10 discusses the products offered by various consultants.

Alternatively, the incumbent will lose control, and the division will then be run by a more able manager, improving performance again.

Cusatis et al. (1994) described the case of Quaker Oats spinning off Fisher Price, its toy subsidiary, in 1991. Fisher Price reported losses of $37.3 million and $33.6 million in the two years before the spin-off, but in its first two years as a public company Fisher Price showed profits of $17.3 million and $41.3 million, respectively. The authors attributed at least part of the strong operating performance of the new company to the financial incentives of the officers and directors, 14 of whom held 6.2 per cent of the outstanding shares as of 23 March 1993. Although these individuals might have held equity in Quaker Oats prior to the spin-off, the connection between their efforts and the resulting pay-off would have been much less direct, so the incentive effects would have been substantially reduced.

Mergers

Divestitures of corporate divisions – achieved via spin-offs, carve-outs or direct sales to a third party – are the opposite of mergers, which combine separate firms into a single entity. Indeed, many divestitures often reverse prior *conglomerate mergers*, which occur when the combining entities are in unrelated lines of business. The discussion above implies that such mergers may adversely affect managerial incentives. Specifically, the CEO of an independent firm with publicly traded equity is likely to find that his or her incentive to maximize shareholder value weakens when the firm becomes a division of a much larger entity, particularly when that entity combines many disparate businesses.

Chapter 20 describes various operating synergies that offset the incentive problems that arise from combining firms in a merger. In cases where both the synergies and the incentive problems are large, a partial takeover may be warranted. In a partial takeover, the acquiring firm buys a controlling interest in the target, possibly to take advantage of synergies, but it leaves a number of shares outstanding on the market. These remaining shares make it possible to compensate the partially owned subsidiary's management more efficiently. Partial takeovers of this kind are common in many countries.

We summarize the discussion here as follows.

Results

Result 18.12

Improved management incentives provide one motivation for corporate spin-offs and carve-outs. Similarly, conglomerate mergers may weaken the incentives of executives at the various divisions.

18.6 Summary and Conclusions

This chapter examined why the financial decisions of managers often deviate from those predicted by the theories presented in Parts 3 and 4. We first described the types of conflict that are likely to arise between the interests of shareholders and managers. Some of these conflicts arise because managers simply prefer more pleasant to less pleasant tasks. Other conflicts arise because managers have an incentive to steer their firms in directions that enhance their own career opportunities and limit their risks. Finally, top executives are likely to develop more of a loyalty to their employees, suppliers and customers, with whom they interact on a day-to-day basis, than to their investors, with whom they are in much less frequent contact.

Since the 1980s, various changes have reduced these incentive problems, and have thus improved the profitability of major corporations. One innovation was the greater use of executive share options and other contracts contingent on share price, which link the pay of top executives directly to the performance of their companies' equity. Another change was the increased use of debt financing, which creates pressure on managers to improve productivity, while reducing their ability to initiate wasteful investments. A third change was the greater participation of institutional investors. A final change was a more active takeover market, which made it more difficult for underperforming managers to keep control of their firms.

We should emphasize that the agency models of management behaviour are somewhat cynical, and do not entirely capture management behaviour. Brennan (1994) and others have expressed concern that the way we teach students about self-interested managers may in fact be self-fulfilling, convincing students that self-interested behaviour is the appropriate norm. Indeed, Frank et al. (1993) reviewed experiments that implied that undergraduate students who trained as economists are much less likely than other students to co-operate for the common good. Moreover, Frank and Schulze (2000) compared economics students with other individuals and found them to be significantly more corrupt.

The fact that the interests of managers and shareholders differ doesn't mean that managers are purely self-interested or greedy. Indeed, the greatest source of management–shareholder conflict probably arises from the loyalty of managers to their employees. Most managers will try to keep a sick or disabled employee on the payroll – at the expense of the firm's shareholders – out of concern for the employee and his or her family, rather than because of any personal benefit to the manager. Clearly, there are notable exceptions, but we have no reason to suspect that management incentives are anything but noble. However, when evaluating financial decisions, we must take into account that these incentives are not always aligned with those of shareholders.

Key Concepts

Result 18.1: Management interests are likely to deviate from shareholder interests in various ways. The extent of this deviation is likely to be related to the amount of time the managers have spent on the job and the number of shares they own.

Result 18.2: Firms with concentrated ownership are likely to be better *monitored* and thus better managed. However, shareholders who take large equity stakes may be inadequately diversified. All shareholders benefit from better management; however, the costs of having a less diversified portfolio are borne only by the large shareholders. Because of the cost of bearing firm-specific risk, ownership is likely to be less concentrated than it would be if management efficiency were the only consideration.

Result 18.3: Entrepreneurs may obtain a better price for their shares if they commit to holding a larger fraction of the firm's outstanding shares. The entrepreneur's incentive to hold shares is higher for those firms with the largest incentive to 'consume on the job'. The incentive to hold shares is also related to risk aversion.

Result 18.4: Managers may prefer investments that enhance their own human capital and minimize risk. This implies that:

- managers may prefer larger, more diversified firms
- managers may prefer investments that pay off more quickly to those that would maximize the value of their shares.

Result 18.5: Allowing management discretion has benefits as well as costs.

- The benefits of discretion are greater in more uncertain environments.
- The costs of discretion are greater when the interests of managers and shareholders do not coincide.

Therefore we might expect to find more concentrated ownership and more managerial discretion in firms facing more uncertain environments.

Result 18.6: Shareholders prefer a higher leverage ratio than that preferred by management. As a result, firms that are more strongly influenced by shareholders have higher leverage ratios.

Result 18.7: A large debt obligation limits management's ability to use corporate resources in ways that do not benefit investors.

Result 18.8: A firm's debt level is a determinant of how much the firm will invest in the future, and it can be used to move the firm towards investing the appropriate amount. In general, however, capital structure cannot by itself induce managers to invest optimally.

Result 18.9: Agency problems partly arise because of imperfect information and risk aversion. Agency costs can thus be reduced by improving the flow of information, and by reducing risk. To minimize the risk borne by managers, optimal compensation contracts should eliminate as much extraneous risk (or risk unrelated to the manager's efforts) as possible.

Result 18.10: Relative performance contracts, which reward managers for performing better than either the entire market or, alternatively, the firms in their industry, have an advantage and a disadvantage.

- The advantage is that the contracts eliminate the effect of some of the risks that are beyond the manager's control.
- The disadvantage is that the contracts may cause firms to compete too aggressively, which would reduce industry profits.

Result 18.11: Equity-based compensation has the advantage that it motivates managers to improve share prices. However, share prices change for reasons outside a manager's control, and only partially reflect the efforts of a manager who heads an individual business unit in a diversified corporation. A cash flow-based compensation plan that adjusts appropriately for capital costs may provide the best method for motivating managers in these cases.

Result 18.12: Improved management incentives provide one motivation for corporate spin-offs and carve-outs. Similarly, conglomerate mergers may weaken the incentives of executives at the various divisions.

Key Terms

agency costs 587
agency problem 586
agent 586
carve out 592
closed-end mutual fund 579
open-end mutual fund 579
principal 586
principal–agent relationship 586
proxy fight 574
relative performance contract 590
spin off 592
value-based management 592

Exercises

18.1 Discuss why managers might tend to want their organizations to grow.

18.2 Discuss the factors that determine whether firms are likely to have large ownership concentrations.

18.3 Jimmy Johnstone, the CEO of High Tech Industries, owns 51 per cent of the shares of his £50 million company. The firm is starting a new project that requires £25 million in new equity capital. Johnstone is considering two ways to fund the project. The first is to issue £25 million in new equity. The second is to form a partially owned subsidiary of High Tech, which would be called Super Tech, and have the subsidiary issue the equity. Under the second proposal, Super Tech would be 55 per cent owned by High Tech and 45 per cent owned by new shareholders. Describe how the incentives of the managers of the new business and Jimmy Johnstone are likely to be affected by the two proposals.

18.4 Consider three similar firms that differ only in the extent to which they are controlled by their boards of directors. In firm 1, the board has complete control of the investment decisions, operating decisions and financing choices. In firm 2, the board is unable to monitor investment and operating decisions, but does control financing decisions. In firm 3, the board has very little control over either investment, operating or financing decisions. Describe how debt ratios are likely to differ in the three firms.

18.5 As a policy analyst, you are asked to comment on a proposed law that would make it more difficult for large outside shareholders to extract private benefits from the partial control they can exert over management. How would such a law affect the incentives of outside shareholders to monitor management?

18.6 You are a member of the compensation committee of the board of directors for both Fiat and BP. How should the compensation contracts for the CEOs of these two companies differ?

18.7 The tendency of firms to use equity-based compensation is higher for firms with higher market-to-book ratios. Provide two explanations for this empirical observation.

18.8 Cybertex's management currently owns 1 per cent of the firm's outstanding shares. The firm is currently financed with 50 per cent debt and 50 per cent equity, but is planning to increase its leverage ratio to 80 per cent debt by borrowing and using the funds to repurchase shares. Management has decided not to participate in the repurchase, so their percentage ownership of the firm will increase.

Explain how managers' investment incentives are likely to change after the recapitalization.

Specifically, discuss their incentives to take:

- negative-NPV projects that benefit them personally
- risky projects
- long-term projects that take more than 10 years to provide an adequate return to capital.

18.9 Suppose that you are designing the compensation contract for England's football coach. Two main alternatives are possible. In (a) you will design his bonus based on the total number of wins during the year and the team's success during the World Cup qualification campaign, and will ignore any specific decisions made by the manager. In (b) you will consider the specific measures taken by the manager, and, perhaps with the help of independent outside experts, will base the compensation on the quality of those decisions but ignore the number of wins during the World Cup qualification campaign. Explain the advantages and disadvantages of the two compensation contracts.

References and Additional Reading

Aggarwal, R.K. and Samwick, A.A. (1999) The other side of the trade-off: the impact of risk on executive compensation, *Journal of Political Economy*, 107(1): 65–105.

Aggarwal, R., Erel, I., Stulz, R. and Williamson, R. (2009) Differences in governance practices between US and foreign firms: Measurement, causes, and consequences, *The Review of Financial Studies*, 22(8): 3131–3169.

Armstrong, C.S. and Vashishtha, R. (2012) Executive stock options, differential risk-taking incentives, and firm value, *Journal of Financial Economics*, 104(1): 70–88.

Aron, D. (1991) Using the capital market as a monitor: corporate spin-offs in an agency framework, *Rand Journal of Economics*, 22(4): 505–518.

Bacon, J. (1989) *Members and Organization of Corporate Boards*, Research Report No. 940. New York: The Conference Board, Inc.

Barclay, M., Holderness, C. and Pontiff, J. (1993) Private benefits from block ownership and discounts on closed-end funds, *Journal of Financial Economics*, 33(3): 263–291.

Bebchuk, L.A., Grinstein, Y. and Peyer, U. (2010) Lucky CEOs and lucky directors, *The Journal of Finance*, 65(6): 2363–2401.

Bebchuk, L.A. and Weisbach, M.S. (2010) The state of corporate governance research, *The Review of Financial Studies*, 23(3): 939–961.

Bennedsen, M., Pérez-González, F. and Wolfenzon, D. (2020) Do CEOs matter? Evidence from hospitalization events, *The Journal of Finance*, 75(4): 1877–1911.

Berle, A., Jr and Means, G. (1932) *The Modern Corporation and Private Property*. New York: Macmillan.

Bizjak, J., Brickley, J. and Coles, J. (1993) Stock-based incentive compensation and investment behavior, *Journal of Accounting and Economics*, 16(1–3): 349–372.

Bizjak, J., Lemmon, M. and Nguyen, T. (2011) Are all CEOs above average? An empirical analysis of compensation peer groups and pay design, *Journal of Financial Economics*, *100*(3): 538–555.

Black, B. (1998) Shareholder activism and corporate governance in the United States, in Peter Newman (ed.) *The New Palgrave Dictionary of Economics and the Law*. Basingstoke: Palgrave Macmillan.

Borghesi, R., Houston, J.F. and Naranjo, A. (2014). Corporate socially responsible investments: CEO altruism, reputation, and shareholder interests, *Journal of Corporate Finance*, 26, 164–181.

Bortolotti, B. and Faccio, M. (2009) Government control of privatized firms, *The Review of Financial Studies*, 22(8): 2907–2938.

Boschen, J. and Smith, K. (1995) You can pay me now and you can pay me later: the dynamic response of executive compensation to firm performance, *Journal of Business*, 68(4): 577–608.

Boycko, M., Shleifer, A. and Vishny, R.W. (1994) Voucher privatization, *Journal of Financial Economics*, 35(2): 249–266.

Brav, A., Jiang, W., Partnoy, F. and Thomas, R. (2008) Hedge fund activism, corporate governance, and firm performance, *The Journal of Finance*, 63(4): 1729–1775.

Brennan, M. (1994) Incentives, rationality, and society, *Journal of Applied Corporate Finance*, 7(2): 31–39.

Burkart, M. and Panunzi, F. (2006) Agency conflicts, ownership concentration, and legal shareholder protection, *Journal of Financial Intermediation*, 15(1): 1–31.

Chava, S. and Purnanandam, A. (2010) CEOs versus CFOs: Incentives and corporate policies, *Journal of Financial Economics*, 97(2): 263–278.

Chemmanur, T. and Yan, A. (2004) A theory of corporate spin-offs, *Journal of Financial Economics*, 72(2): 259–290.

Clinch, G. (1991) Employee compensation and firms' research and development activity, *Journal of Accounting Research*, 29(1): 59–78.

Conyon, M.J., Core, J.E. and Guay, W.R. (2011). Are US CEOs paid more than UK CEOs? Inferences from risk-adjusted pay, *The Review of Financial Studies*, 24(2): 402–438.

Core, J., Holthausen, R. and Larcker, D. (1999) Corporate governance, chief executive officer compensation, and firm performance, *Journal of Financial Economics*, 51(3): 371–406.

Cronqvist, H., Makhija, A.K. and Yonker, S.E. (2012) Behavioral consistency in corporate finance: CEO personal and corporate leverage *Journal of Financial Economics*, 103(1): 20–40.

Cusatis, P., Miles, J.A. and Woolridge, J.R. (1994) Some new evidence that spinoffs create value, *Journal of Applied Corporate Finance*, 7(2): 100–107.

Dahya, J., McConnell, J. and Travlos, N. (2002) The Cadbury Committee, corporate performance, and top management turnover, *The Journal of Finance*, 57(1): 461–483.

Davies, J.R., Hillier, D. and McColgan, P. (2005) Ownership structure, managerial behavior and corporate value, *Journal of Corporate Finance*, 11(4): 645–660.

Dee, C.C., Lulseged, A. and Nowlin, T. (2005) Executive compensation and risk: the case of Internet firms, *Journal of Corporate Finance*, 12(1): 80–96.

Demsetz, H. and Lehn, K. (1985) The structure of corporate ownership, *Journal of Political Economy*, 93(6): 1155–1177.

Diamond, D. and Verrechia, R. (1982) Optimal managerial contracts and equilibrium security prices, *The Journal of Finance*, 37(2): 275–287.

Doidge, C.G., Karolyi, A. and Stultz, R. (2004) Why are foreign firms listed in the US worth more?, *Journal of Financial Economics*, 71(2): 205–238.

Doidge, C., Karolyi, C.A. and Stulz, R.M. (2007) Why do countries matter so much for corporate governance?, *Journal of Financial Economics*, 86(1): 1–39.

Donaldson, G. and Lorsch, J. (1983) *Decision Making at the Top: The Shaping of Strategic Direction*. New York: Basic Books.

Downes, D. and Heinkel, R. (1982) Signaling and the valuation of unseasoned new issues, *The Journal of Finance*, 37(1): 1–10.

Edmans, A. and Liu, Q. (2011) Inside debt, *Review of Finance*, 15(1): 75–102.

Ertimur, Y., Ferri, F. and Muslu, V. (2011) Shareholder activism and CEO pay, *The Review of Financial Studies*, 24(2): 535–592.

Faccio, M. and Lang, L. (2002) The ultimate ownership of Western European corporations, *Journal of Financial Economics*, 65(3): 365–395.

Faccio, M., Marchica, M.T. and Mura, R. (2011) Large shareholder diversification and corporate risk-taking, *The Review of Financial Studies*, 24(11): 3601–3641.

Fahlenbrach, R., Minton, B.A. and Pan, C.H. (2011) Former CEO directors: lingering CEOs or valuable resources?, *The Review of Financial Studies*, 24(10): 3486–3518.

Faleye, O., Hoitash, R. and Hoitash, U. (2011) The costs of intense board monitoring, *Journal of Financial Economics*, 101(1): 160–181.

Fama, E. (1980) Agency problems and the theory of the firm, *Journal of Political Economy*, 88(2): 288–307.

Faulkender, M. and Yang, J. (2010) Inside the black box: The role and composition of compensation peer groups, *Journal of Financial Economics*, 96(2): 257–270.

Field, L., Lowry, M. and Mkrtchyan, A. (2013) Are busy boards detrimental?, *Journal of Financial Economics*, 109(1): 63–82.

Frank, B. and Schulze, G. (2000) Does economics make citizens corrupt?, *Journal of Economic Behavior & Organization*, 43(1): 101–113.

Frank, R.H., Gilovich, T. and Regan, D.T. (1993) Does studying economics inhibit co-operation?, *Journal of Economic Perspectives*, 7(2): 159–171.

Gaver, J.J. and Gaver, K.M. (1993) Additional evidence on the association between the investment opportunity set and corporate financing, dividend, and compensation policies, *Journal of Accounting and Economics*, 16 (1–3): 125–160.

Gaver, J.J. and Gaver, K.M. (1995) Compensation policy and the investment opportunity set, *Financial Management*, 24(1): 19–32.

Gervais, S., Heaton, J.B. and Odean, T. (2011) Overconfidence, compensation contracts, and capital budgeting, *The Journal of Finance*, 66(5): 1735–1777.

Goergen, M. and Renneboog, L. (2011) Managerial compensation, *Journal of Corporate Finance*, 17(4): 1068–1077.

Gillan, S. and Starks, L. (2007) The evolution of shareholder activism in the United States, *Journal of Applied Corporate Finance*, 19(1): 55–73.

Gilson, S. (1989) Management turnover and financial distress, *Journal of Financial Economics*, 25(2): 241–262.

Gilson, S. (1990) Bankruptcy, boards, banks and blockholders: evidence on changes in corporate ownership and control when firms default, *Journal of Financial Economics*, 27(2): 355–387.

Giroud, X. and Mueller, H.M. (2011) Corporate governance, product market competition, and equity prices, *The Journal of Finance*, 66(2): 563–600.

Gompers, P.A., Ishii, J. and Metrick, A. (2010) Extreme governance: An analysis of dual-class firms in the United States, *The Review of Financial Studies*, 23(3): 1051–1088.

Gopalan, R., Milbourn, T. and Song, F. (2010) Strategic flexibility and the optimality of pay for sector performance, *The Review of Financial Studies*, 23(5): 2060–2098.

Graham, J.R., Harvey, C.R. and Puri, M. (2013) Managerial attitudes and corporate actions, *Journal of Financial Economics,* 109(1): 103–121.

Graham, J.R., Li, S. and Qiu, J. (2012) Managerial attributes and executive compensation, *The Review of Financial Studies,* 25(1): 144–186.

Grossman, S. and Hart, O. (1982) Corporate financial structure and managerial incentives, in John MCall (ed.) *The Economics of Information and Uncertainty.* Chicago: University of Chicago Press, 107–140.

Guiso, L., Sapienza, P. and Zingales, L. (2015) The value of corporate culture, *Journal of Financial Economics,* 117(1): 60–76.

Hall, B.J. and Liebman, J.B. (1998) Are CEOs really paid like bureaucrats?, *Quarterly Journal of Economics,* 113(3): 653–691.

Harris, M. and Raviv, A. (2010) Control of corporate decisions: Shareholders vs. management, *The Review of Financial Studies,* 23(11): 4115–4147.

Hart, O. (1983) The market mechanism as an incentive scheme, *Bell Journal of Economics,* 14(2): 366–382.

Hart, O. and Moore, J. (1995) Debt and seniority: an analysis of the role of hard claims in constraining management, *American Economic Review,* 85(3): 567–585.

Hermalin, B. and Weisbach, M. (1991) The effects of board compensation and direct incentives on firm performance, *Financial Management,* 20(4): 101–112.

Hillier, D. and McColgan, P. (2006) An analysis of changes in board structure during corporate governance reforms, *European Financial Management,* 12(4): 575–607.

Hillier, D. and McColgan, P. (2007) *Corporate responses to performance declines: evidence from the UK.* Working paper, Leeds University Business School.

Hillier, D. and McColgan, P. (2009) Firm performance and managerial succession in family managed firms, *Journal of Business Finance & Accounting,* 36(3–4): 461–484.

Hirshleifer, D., Low, A. and Teoh, S.H. (2012) Are overconfident CEOs better innovators?, *The Journal of Finance, 67*(4): 1457–1498.

Holderness, C.G. and Sheehan, D.P. (1988) The role of majority shareholders in publicly held corporations, *Journal of Financial Economics,* 20(1–2): 317–346.

Hoshi, T., Kashyap, A. and Scharfstein, D. (1991) The role of banks in reducing the costs of financial distress in Japan, *Quarterly Journal of Economics,* 106(1): 33–60.

Huang, J. and Kisgen, D.J. (2013) Gender and corporate finance: Are male executives overconfident relative to female executives?, *Journal of Financial Economics,* 108(3): 822–839.

Huson, M.R., Parrino, R. and Starks, L. (2001) Internal monitoring mechanisms and CEO turnover: a long-term perspective, *The Journal of Finance,* 56(6): 2265–2297.

Jensen, M. (1986) Agency cost of free cash flow, corporate finance and takeovers, *American Economic Review,* 76(2): 323–339.

Jensen, M.C. and Meckling, W.H. (1976) Theory of the firm: managerial behavior, agency costs and ownership structure, *Journal of Financial Economics,* 3(4): 305–360.

Jensen, M.C. and Murphy, K.J. (1990a) CEO incentives–it's not how much you pay, but how, *Harvard Business Review,* 90(3): 138–153.

Jensen, M.C. and Murphy, K.J. (1990b) Performance pay and top-management incentives, *Journal of Political Economics,* 98(2): 225–264.

Jensen, M.C. and Ruback, R.S. (1983) The market for corporate control: the scientific evidence, *Journal of Financial Economics,* 11(1–4): 5–50.

Jenter, D. and Lewellen, K. (2021) Performance-induced CEO turnover, *The Review of Financial Studies,* 34(2): 569–617.

Johnson, W.B., Magee, R.P., Nagarajan, N.J. and Newman, H.A. (1985) An analysis of the share price reaction to sudden executive deaths: implications for the managerial labor market, *Journal of Accounting,* 7(1–3): 151–174.

Kang, J.-K and Shivdasani, A. (1997) Corporate restructuring during performance declines in Japan, *Journal of Financial Economics,* 46(1): 29–65.

Kaplan, S.N., Klebanov, M.M. and Sorensen, M. (2012) Which CEO characteristics and abilities matter?, *The Journal of Finance,* 67(3): 973–1007.

Kim, J.B., Li, Y. and Zhang, L. (2011) CFOs versus CEOs: Equity incentives and crashes, *Journal of Financial Economics,* 101(3): 713–730.

Klapper, L. and Love, I. (2004) Corporate governance, investor protection, and performance in emerging markets, *Journal of Corporate Finance,* 10(5): 703–728.

Kole, S.R. (1995) Measuring managerial equity ownership: a comparison of sources of ownership data, *Journal of Corporate Finance,* 1(3–4): 413–435.

Lambert, R.A. and D.F. Larker (1986) Golden parachutes, executive decision-making and shareholder wealth, *Journal of Accounting and Economics,* 7(1–3): 179–203.

La Porta, R., Lopez-de-Silanes, F. and Shleifer, A. (1999) Corporate ownership around the world, *Journal of Finance,* 54(2): 471–517.

La Porta, R., Lopez-de-Silanes, F. Shleifer, A. and Vishny, R. (2000) *Investor Protection: Origins, Consequences, Reform,* NBER working paper.

La Porta, R., Lopez-de-Silanes, F., Shleifer, A. and Vishny, R. (2002) Investor protection and corporate valuation, *The Journal of Finance,* 57, 1147–1170.

Leuz, C., Lins, K.V. and Warnock, F.E. (2010) Do foreigners invest less in poorly governed firms?, *The Review of Financial Studies,* 22(8): 3245–3285.

Levine, R. and Zervos, S. (1998) Equity markets, banks, and economic growth, *American Economic Review,* 88(3): 537–558.

Liu, Y. and Mauer, D.C. (2011) Corporate cash holdings and CEO compensation incentives, *Journal of Financial Economics,* 102(1): 183–198.

Manso, G. (2011) Motivating innovation, *The Journal of Finance,* 66(5): 1823–1860.

Masulis, R.W. and Mobbs, S. (2011) Are all inside directors the same? Evidence from the external directorship market, *The Journal of Finance,* 66(3): 823–872.

Masulis, R.W. and Mobbs, S. (2014) Independent director incentives: Where do talented directors spend their limited time and energy?, *Journal of Financial Economics,* 111(2): 406–429.

McConnell, J.J. and Servaes, H. (1990) Additional evidence on equity ownership and corporate value, *Journal of Financial Economics,* 27(2): 595–612.

Mehran, H. (1992) Executive incentive plans, corporate control, and capital structure, *Journal of Financial and Quantitative Analysis,* 27(4): 539–560.

Mehran, H. (1995) Executive compensation structure, ownership and firm performance, *Journal of Financial Economics,* 38, 163–184.

Moh'd, M., Perry, L. and Rimbey, J (1998) The impact of ownership structure on corporate debt policy: a time-series cross-sectional analysis, *The Financial Review,* 33(3): 85–98.

Morck, R., Shleifer, A. and Vishny, R. (1988) Management ownership and market valuation: an empirical analysis, *Journal of Financial Economics,* 20(1–2): 293–316.

Morse, A., Nanda, V. and Seru, A. (2011) Are incentive contracts rigged by powerful CEOs?, *The Journal of Finance,* 66(5): 1779–1821.

Murphy, K.J. (1999) Executive compensation, Chapter 38 in Ashenfelter, O. and Caed, D. (eds) *Handbook of Labor Economics.* Amsterdam: Elsevier Science.

Oyer, P. (2004) Why do firms use incentives that have no incentive effects?, *The Journal of Finance,* 59(4): 1619–1650.

Pindado, J. and de la Torre, C. (2006) The role of investment, financing and dividend decisions in explaining corporate ownership structure: empirical evidence from Spain, *European Financial Management,* 12(5): 661–687.

Prowse, S. (1990) Institutional investment patterns and corporate financial behavior in the United States and Japan, *Journal of Financial Economics,* 27(1): 43–66.

Quigley, T.J., Crossland, C. and Campbell, R.J. (2017) Shareholder perceptions of the changing impact of CEOs: Market reactions to unexpected CEO deaths, 1950–2009, *Strategic Management Journal,* 38(4): 939–949.

Rajgopal, S., Shevlin, T. and Zamora, V. (2006) CEOs' outside employment opportunities and the lack of relative performance evaluation in compensation contracts, *The Journal of Finance,* 61(4): 1813–1844.

Rauh, J. (2006) Investment and financing constraints: evidence from the funding of corporate pension plans, *The Journal of Finance,* 61(1): 33–71.

Ravina, E. and Sapienza, P. (2010) What do independent directors know? Evidence from their trading, *The Review of Financial Studies,* 23(3): 962–1003.

Ritter, J. (1984) Signaling and the valuation of unseasoned new issues: a comment, *The Journal of Finance,* 39(4): 1231–1237.

Roe, M. (1994) *Strong Managers, Weak Owners: The Political Roots of American Corporate Finance.* Princeton, NJ: Princeton University Press.

Scharfstein, D. and Stein, J. (2000) The dark side of internal capital markets: divisional rent-seeking and inefficient investment, *The Journal of Finance,* 55(6): 2537–2564.

Schipper, K. and Smith, A. (1986) A comparison of equity carve-outs and seasoned equity offerings: share price effects and corporate restructuring, *Journal of Financial Economics,* 15(1–2): 153–186.

Shleifer, A. and Vishny, R.W. (1989) Management entrenchment: the case of manager-specific investments, *Journal of Financial Economics,* 25(1): 123–139.

Short, H. and Keasey, K. (1999) Managerial ownership and the performance of firms: evidence from the UK, *Journal of Corporate Finance,* 5(1): 79–101.

Smith, C.W., Jr and Watts, R.L. (1992) The investment opportunity set and corporate financing, dividend, and compensation policies, *Journal of Financial Economics,* 32(3): 263–292.

Stulz, R.M. (1990) Managerial discretion and optimal financing policies, *Journal of Financial Economics,* 26(1): 3–27.

Sunder, J., Sunder, S.V. and Zhang, J. (2017). Pilot CEOs and corporate innovation, *Journal of Financial Economics,* 123(1): 209–224.

Tehranian, H. and Waegelein, J.F. (1985) Market reaction to short-term executive compensation plan adoption, *Journal of Accounting and Economics,* 7(1–3): 131–144.

Chapter 19

The Information Conveyed by Financial Decisions

Learning Objectives

After reading this chapter, you should be able to:

- Understand how financial decisions are affected by managers who are better informed than outside shareholders about firm values.
- Identify situations in which managers have an incentive to distort accounting information.
- Explain how financial decisions about the firm's dividend choice, capital structure and real investments affect share prices.
- Interpret the empirical evidence about the reaction of share prices to various financing and investing decisions.

In July 2022, the UK motor insurer, Sabre, surprised investors by announcing a large fall in expected profits from £18 million to £3.5 million. Share prices collapsed by 35 per cent on the day of the announcement. Media stories were awash that the company's dividends were likely to be cut by a significant amount. This followed a year when dividends had already been cut from £0.085 to £0.047. Given the confounding signal, it was unclear whether the share price drop was primarily because of the profit warning or about the change in dividend expectations.

The example of Sabre is characteristic of what happens when a firm announces a dividend decrease, as normally a dividend change will impact upon the market value of a company. Share prices often move 10 to 15 per cent when firms announce changes in their investment, dividend or financing choices, which implies that decisions like these convey information to investors that causes them to re-evaluate, and thus revalue, the firm. Although Sabre did not announce a dividend cut in July 2022, investors may have anticipated a change in dividend policy and acted immediately on the information. This would have resulted in a share price fall.

This chapter provides a framework that will help you to decipher the messages conveyed by financial events such as Sabre's, and to understand how information considerations affect financial decisions. The discussion in this chapter is based on the premise that top managers have proprietary information that enables them to derive more accurate internal valuations of their companies than the investor valuations determined in the market. In other words, managers may have information, which cannot be directly disclosed, about whether the firm's equity is either undervalued or overvalued.

Managers may not be able to disclose their information to the firm's shareholders for a variety of reasons.

- The information may be valuable to the firm's competitors.
- Firms run the risk of being sued by investors if they make forecasts that later turn out to be inaccurate.
- Managers may prefer not to disclose unfavourable information.
- The information may be difficult to quantify or substantiate.

Direct disclosures provide imperfect and incomplete information, but investors will incorporate indirect evidence into their evaluations. In particular, they will attempt to decipher the information content of observable management decisions. These information-revealing decisions, or **signals**, might include decisions related to the firm's capital expenditures, financing choices, dividends and equity splits, as well as managers' decisions to acquire or sell shares for their personal account. For example, a decrease in company shareholdings by Sabre's top executives might signal that management is pessimistic about the firm's prospects. In fact, two months earlier, Sabre's Chief Risk Officer sold 8,924 shares worth approximately £20,000 (there is no suggestion that this was illegal, because the firm signed off on the transaction beforehand). In many instances, an indirect signal of this type can provide more credible information than a direct disclosure. As is often said, 'Actions speak louder than words.'

It is natural to assume that managers take the market's expected reaction into account when making major decisions.[1] This is especially true when the ability of managers to keep their jobs, maintain their autonomy and increase their pay depends, in part, on the performance of their firm's equity. If managers have a strong incentive to increase the current share prices of their firms, they will bias their decisions towards actions that reveal the most favourable information to investors. As we shall demonstrate, these actions will not, in general, maximize the *intrinsic* (or long-term) value of the firm. In particular, managers may sometimes make value-reducing decisions because they convey favourable information.

When taken to the extreme, this behaviour can lead to catastrophic results, and the series of corporate scandals that involved companies around the world are a testament to this. Enron (USA, 2001), Worldcom (USA, 2002), Royal Ahold (Netherlands, 2003), Parmalat (Italy, 2003) and HealthSouth (USA, 2003) are good examples of companies manipulating their financial accounts to present a much rosier picture to investors. In recent years the level of scandals involving accounting fraud has dropped significantly. This is partly due to the beneficial impacts of increased regulatory scrutiny, concomitant with the exceptionally strong punishments that have been meted out to transgressors.

An important lesson of this chapter is that a distinction must be made between management decisions that *create* value and decisions that simply signal or convey favourable information to shareholders. In many cases, value-creating decisions signal unfavourable information and result in share price declines, and value-destroying decisions signal favourable information and result in share price increases. For example, if Sabre chose to increase its dividend, it may have been considered value destroying if the extra cash payments could have been used instead to maintain liquidity in the firm. However, as this chapter discusses, the dividend increase might signal favourable information about the firm's ability to generate cash from its existing operations.

If bad decisions sometimes convey favourable information, one must be careful when interpreting share price reactions to corporate announcements. For example, a company might think that its shareholders prefer higher dividends, because its share price always reacts favourably when a dividend increase is announced. However, as shown later in the chapter, share prices can respond favourably to a dividend increase because the increase conveys favourable information, even when most shareholders actually prefer the lower dividend.

19.1 Management Incentives When Managers Have Better Information than Shareholders

Most of the discussion in this text assumes that managers act to maximize their firm's share price. However, if there is a difference between what managers believe their firm's shares are worth and the market price of those shares then the appropriate goal of the managers needs further elaboration. Should managers act to maximize

---

[1] See Subrahmanyam and Titman (1999), Van Bommel and Vermaelen (2003) and Hill and Hillier (2009).

the current market price of the firm's shares, which reflects only public information, or should they act to maximize what they believe is the present value of the firm's future cash flows, which reflects the managers' private information?

In some cases there is no conflict between these two objectives, even when there is a difference between the firm's full information value, which we refer to as the **intrinsic value**, and its current market value. However, as shown later in this chapter, when a decision conveys information that analysts use to value a firm's equity, decisions that maximize the firm's current share price may not be in the best long-term interests of shareholders. When this is the case, different shareholders will not necessarily agree on how managers should choose between these conflicting objectives.

Shareholders who plan to hold on to their shares for a long time will capture the intrinsic value, even if they eventually sell their shares, because the share price at the time of the sale will reflect the manager's private information about future cash flows that the investor has not yet directly captured. Hence long-term shareholders prefer managers to make decisions that maximize the intrinsic value of the shares. This of course assumes that managers correctly assess the firm's intrinsic value, and are not, for example, overly optimistic. However, shareholders who plan to sell their shares in the near future prefer managers to take actions that improve the firm's current or short-term share price, irrespective of how this affects the firm's intrinsic or long-run value. Thus there is an inherent conflict between the interests of long-term and short-term shareholders.

As in many of the previous chapters, our examples here are simplified by assuming that investors are risk neutral, and the discount rate is zero. In this case, current share prices are equal to expected share prices at any near-term horizon where the cash flow implications of the manager's actions are not yet fully known to investors. However, even with risk aversion and positive discount rates, short-term share prices tend to be higher when current share prices are higher. Hence short-term shareholders prefer that the managers take actions that immediately or shortly *signal* good information and *conceal* bad information about the firm's cash flows, even if the manager privately knows that those actions are detrimental to the firm's long-term future cash flows.

Conflicts between Short-Term and Long-Term Share Price Maximization

Exhibit 19.1 shows that managers have several competing pressures that determine how a firm's current share price and its intrinsic value enter the decision criteria. If a manager expects to be a long-term player at the firm, and intends to continue to hold equity and options in the firm, then he or she is likely to want to maximize the firm's intrinsic value. However, most managers are also concerned about the firm's current share price.

Exhibit 19.1 Conflicting Incentives that Motivate Management

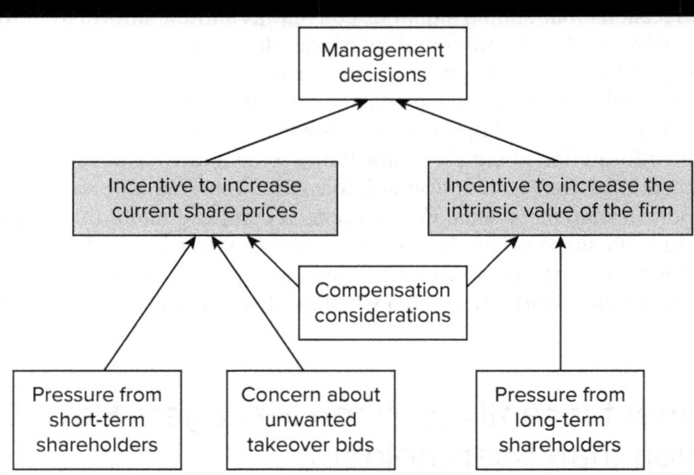

The concern for current share prices can arise for several reasons.

- Managers may plan to issue additional equity or sell some of their own equity in the near future.
- Managers may be concerned about the acquisition of the firm by an outsider at a price that is less than the firm's intrinsic value.

- Managerial compensation may be directly or indirectly tied to the current share price of the firm.
- The ability to attract customers and other outside stakeholders may be related to outsiders' perceptions of the firm's value.

Although managers usually have an incentive to increase the firm's current share price, the degree to which they are willing to sacrifice intrinsic value varies. Indeed, managers might also want to temporarily lower the current share price of their firms, as we illustrate in the next section.

Given these inevitable conflicting incentives, we might best view a manager's objective function as one of maximizing a weighted average of the firm's current share price and intrinsic value. Result 19.1 summarizes this discussion.

Results

Result 19.1

Management incentives are influenced by a desire to increase both the firm's current share price and its intrinsic value. The weight that managers place on these potentially conflicting incentives is determined by, among other things, the manager's compensation and the security of the manager's job.

Example 19.1 illustrates how the weights on current and intrinsic value are determined.

Example 19.1

The Trade-Off between Current Value and Intrinsic Value

Ben Williams, CEO of Tremont plc, has just exercised 10,000 equity options and now owns 20,000 shares of Tremont equity. He plans on selling the 10,000 shares within the next month, and will hold the remaining 10,000 shares indefinitely. Assuming that his salary is fixed, and that Mr Williams is entrenched in his job and is unconcerned about outside takeover threats, describe how his objective function would weight current value and intrinsic value.

Answer: Mr Williams would weight current value and intrinsic value equally. In other words, he would be willing to make a decision that reduces Tremont's intrinsic share price by £1 per share if it increased its current share price by more than £1 per share.

If Mr Williams, in the previous example, was concerned about takeover threats or about losing his job for other reasons, his decisions would be further biased towards those choices that enhance the current value of his firm's shares. As we show in the following case, the weight that managers place on current share prices versus the firm's intrinsic value can have an important effect on the decisions that they make.

Real World Insight

The Joint Venture of Virgin Media O2 and Telefonica

The 2022 joint venture between Virgin Media O2 (the company) and Telefonica to collaborate in providing high speed fibre optic broadband across the UK provides an example of how corporate decisions can provide information that is potentially relevant for pricing a firm's equity. On the announcement of such a venture, analysts and investors would have attempted to assess whether the joint venture was a good decision, and whether it would be successful. For example, if they believed the decision was good for the company, there would have been upward pressure on the price of Virgin Media O2's equity. On the other hand, if they believed it was a bad decision, there would have been downward pressure on the price of the company's equity. In addition, the market reaction to the announcement would have reflected new information about the company that was signalled indirectly by the announcement.

This new information might have had almost nothing to do with the merits of the particular transaction. For example, the joint venture could have been viewed as a favourable signal about the company's future prospects, because it showed that it was confident about its ability to fund a major new investment. Alternatively, such an investment might be viewed as a negative signal if the analysts' interpretation was that the company had unfavourable prospects in the UK high speed broadband market, and the company was not confident about its ability to develop new business on its own. If this negative information was sufficiently important, then the company's share price would have dropped on the announcement of the joint venture, even if the venture was believed to be a good decision.

Virgin Media O2's managers were thus faced with a dilemma in making such a choice. If they were concerned about the firm's current share price and they anticipated an unfavourable share price reaction, then they might have chosen to pass up the joint venture, even if the project itself made economic sense.

Results

Result 19.2

Good decisions can reveal unfavourable information, and bad decisions can reveal favourable information. This means that:

- share price reactions are sometimes poor indicators of whether a decision has a positive or a negative effect on a firm's intrinsic value
- managers who are concerned about the current or short-term share prices of their firms may bias their decisions in ways that reduce the intrinsic values of their firms.

19.2 Earnings Manipulation

The focus of this chapter is on how information considerations affect financing and investing choices. However, it is instructive to look first at how these considerations affect the earnings reported by firms.

Recent accounting research suggests that managers sometimes manipulate the earnings numbers of their firms in ways that increase reported income in the current year at the expense of reporting lower earnings in the future. Managers have some discretion over the firm's accounting methods, which allows them to shift reported income from the future to the current year, and *vice versa*. For example, managers have discretion in coming up with a number of estimates, including the service lives and salvage values of depreciable assets, the lives of intangibles, the uncollectible rate on accounts receivable, the cost of warranty plans, the degree of completion when the percentage-of-completion method is used for certain assets, the actuarial cost basis for a pension plan, and the interest rates for capitalized leases and pension accounting.

Incentives to Manipulate Accounting Figures

Firms show the greatest tendency to artificially inflate accounting earnings when managers have the most to gain from increasing share prices. For example, Teoh et al. (1998a, 1998b) found that firms make discretionary accounting choices that temporarily increase reported earnings before both initial and seasoned public offerings of equity. In these cases, managers are especially interested in improving the firm's current share price, because they want to maximize the proceeds from the equity issues. Unfortunately for managers, Shivakumar (2000) found that investors appear to disentangle the manipulations and inferred the correct implications of earnings figures.

Regulatory requirements can also induce managers to manipulate their accounting figures. For example, in China, firms were required to have a return on equity of greater than 10 per cent for each of the three years prior to issuing new shares. Chen and Yuan (2004) reported that there was a clustering of firms with return on equity just above the required minimum. Similarly, Australian credit unions arbitrarily reallocated their assets into lower risk categories in response to increased capital adequacy requirements that were introduced by the Australian Securities and Investments Commission (Hillier et al. 2008).

Occasionally, managers also manipulate their earnings downwards when they want their firms to appear weaker than they really are. Liberty and Zimmerman (1986) found that some firms manipulated their earnings downwards before union negotiations, and Jones (1991) found strong evidence of managers manipulating their company's earnings downwards prior to appealing to the government for help against foreign competitors. The severity of financial misreporting can potentially be caused by the short-horizon objectives of financial institutional shareholders. Short-term investors are less likely to engage in costly monitoring because it is of limited use in the short-term. Burns et al. (2010) find that although misreporting is higher when firms have a lot of short-horizon institutional investors, it is lessened when the shareholdings become more concentrated, suggesting that higher proportional shareholdings are associated with stronger monitoring.

19.3 Short-Sighted Investment Choices

Savvy investors and analysts, understanding the incentives of firms to manipulate their earnings numbers, are generally reluctant to take the reported earnings numbers at face value. Some analysts have a preference for evaluating firms based on cash flow rather than earnings numbers, since it is less subject to accounting manipulation. However, firms also make real investment and operating decisions that affect the cash flow numbers, as well as earnings, and managers may be motivated to bias these decisions in ways that make the firm look better in the short run, but which hurt the firm in the long run.

Management's Reluctance to Undertake Long-Term Investments

Some financial economists have argued that the incentive for managers to generate short-term share price performance makes them reluctant to take on long-term investment projects that generate low initial cash flows.[2] The reluctance to take on long-term projects arises because investors understand that managers have an incentive to falsely claim that their investment projects have substantial pay-offs several years down the road. However, investors have no way of knowing whether the managers are telling the truth about future pay-offs, or whether they are simply making long-term promises to cover up their current poor performance. As a result, the market price of a firm's equity tends to react negatively to poor performance in the current period, generally ignoring management claims of big pay-offs in the future. This is not a problem for managers who are interested only in the intrinsic value of their shares, but it creates problems for other managers who have incentives to keep their current share prices high. This problem is illustrated in Example 19.2.

Example 19.2

The Incentive to Choose Projects that Pay Off More Quickly

Micro Industries has two long-term investment strategies and a short-term strategy available to it. The cash flows, which are retained in the firm, and their present values (assuming a discount rate of zero) are described below.

	Cash flows (in € millions)		
	Year 1	Years 2–11 (annual cash flow)	Present value
1. Good long-term strategy	40	80	840
2. Short-term strategy	60	50	560
3. Bad long-term strategy	40	40	440

[2] Management's incentive to be short-sighted in making investment choices is analysed in Narayanan (1985), Stein (1989) and Brennan (1990).

Micro Industries is not considering the third strategy, because its present value of €440 million is obviously an inferior choice. This third strategy creates a problem for Micro, however, because investors are aware of this strategy, and in the absence of further proof do not believe that Micro can generate the kind of returns reflected in strategies 1 and 2 described above. As a result, if the good long-term strategy is selected, Micro's market price at the end of year 1 will be only €440 million, reflecting the market's belief that the cash flows of the third strategy will be realized. However, the market price will rise to €840 million the following year when the year 2 cash flow of €80 million is observed. If the short-term strategy is selected, investors will realize its potential when the year 1 cash flow of €60 million is observed, and they will value the firm at €560 million. Which project should management select?

Answer: If management is concerned only with maximizing the firm's intrinsic value, it should select the good long-term strategy. However, if managers place sufficient weight on having a high share price in year 1, they should take the short-term strategy, because the market price after one year will then be €560 million rather than €440 million.

In Example 19.2, management may be reluctant to select the superior long-term strategy, because the first-year cash flows lead investors to believe that the company's future profits will be much lower than they will be in reality. However, by choosing the lower-valued short-term strategy, investors quickly recognize the firm's ability to generate better-than-expected cash flows and reward it by boosting its share price. The insights of this example are summarized in the following result.

Results

Result 19.3

Managers will select projects that pay off quickly over possibly higher-NPV projects that pay out over longer periods if they place significant weight on increasing their firm's short-term share price.

What Determines a Manager's Incentive to be Short-Sighted?

The tendency of managers to implement strategies with better long-term pay-offs increases as the weight that they place on maximizing the current or near-term share price declines. To understand this, consider again Example 19.2, and assume that management places a 75 per cent weight on the year 1 value of the firm and a 25 per cent weight on its intrinsic value, implying that the weighted average pay-off from the long-term strategy (0.75 × €440 million + 0.25 × €840 million) is €540 million, which is less than the €560 million pay-off from picking the short-term strategy. However, if management weights intrinsic value and next year's share prices equally, then the long-term strategy will be selected because the weighted average value from the strategy is €640 million (0.5 × €440 million + 0.5 × €840 million), which exceeds the value of the short-term strategy.

Some policymakers and journalists have argued that the incentive to be short-sighted, as Example 19.2 illustrates, applies more to managers in market-based economies, such as the UK and USA, than to bank-based economies, such as continental Europe and Japan, because the former countries place greater weight on the current share prices of their firms. The basic argument for this tendency is that market-focused managers are monitored more closely by institutional investors, are more subject to takeover threats and have a larger part of their compensation tied to the short-term performance of their firms. Some writers have claimed that these factors have tended to make firms in market-based systems less willing to make long-term investments that ensure their long-term competitiveness.[3]

[3] Kaplan (1994) provides evidence at odds with this basic belief. He suggests that Japanese managers (bank-based) also may be strongly motivated to improve the short-term performance of the firms they manage.

19.4 The Information Content of Dividend and Share Repurchase Announcements

This section examines the information conveyed by dividend and share repurchase announcements. As this chapter's opening vignette illustrates, dividend changes can lead to dramatic changes in share prices.

Empirical Evidence on Equity Returns at the Time of Dividend Announcements

When firms announce dividend increases, their share prices generally increase by about 2 per cent (see Aharony and Swary 1980). Announcements of the initiation of dividend payouts by firms that previously paid no dividends generate even larger share price reactions (see Asquith and Mullins 1983; Healy and Palepu 1988; Michaely et al. 1995). Moreover, share prices generally experience similar declines when firms announce dividend decreases or omissions, falling about 9.5 per cent, on average, at the announcement of an omission (Healy and Palepu 1988).

An interesting study by Conroy et al. (2000) examined simultaneous dividend and earnings announcements, as well as next year's dividend and earnings predictions, for Japanese companies. They found that earnings surprises caused significant changes in share prices, but the effect of dividend changes was only marginal. Although the evidence is supportive of Miller and Modigliani's dividend irrelevance theorem, it also indicates that dividends are taken as signals of the future earnings power of firms. When earnings predictions are released at the same time, dividends lose their predictive power and signalling content. This finding was also reported for Chinese firms by Chen et al. (2002).

Results

Result 19.4

Share prices increase, on average, when firms increase dividends, and decrease, on average, when they decrease dividends. Dividend signals are strongly related to future earnings predictions.

As a corporate executive, you might interpret a positive share price reaction to an announced dividend increase as evidence that investors consider the dividend increase to be a good decision. This evidence, however, does not necessarily imply that dividend increases improve the intrinsic value of firms. Financial decisions that convey favourable information to the market tend to increase share prices, even when the decisions are bad for the firm's future profitability. As shown below, dividend increases can diminish intrinsic values, but still generate positive share price responses because they signal favourable information.

A Dividend Signalling Model

Although finance researchers have proposed various signalling-based explanations for the positive share price response to dividend increases, we shall describe only one model.[4] This model, which we believe is the most intuitive, is based on an analysis of what an all-equity-financed firm does with the operating cash flow produced by its assets. The sources and uses of funds equation

$$\text{operating cash flow} = \text{investment expenditures} - \text{change in equity} + \text{dividends}$$

suggests that the cash flows produced by the assets of the firm (after taxes) have either to be retained within the firm for investment expenditures (for example, for maintenance of assets or expansion of assets) or be paid out to equity holders as either a share repurchase or a dividend.

Information Observed by Investors

The following argument assumes that investors cannot observe the operating cash flows of the firm, perhaps because managers can manipulate the relevant accounting numbers. In addition, outside investors cannot

[4] This discussion is based on Miller and Rock (1985).

observe all the items that constitute the firm's investment expenditures, such as equipment maintenance and expenditures to update its customer database. We shall assume, however, that investors know how much the firm *should* invest to maximize shareholder value. In addition, the investors do, of course, observe the dividends that they receive, as well as the amount of capital the firm either raises (for example, through an equity offering) from the capital markets or retires (for example, by repurchasing shares).

The Information Content of a Dividend Change

The dividends and changes in outstanding equity provide investors with information about the firm's operating cash flows as well as the level of investment expenditures. However, investors cannot decipher the meaning of an unexpected change in dividends. For example, a dividend increase may reflect the fact that the firm's operating cash flow was higher than expected, which would be good news, since this would suggest that the firm is more profitable than was originally believed. On the other hand, the firm may have generated the cash for the higher dividend by cutting back investment, which would be bad news, because it implies that the firm is sacrificing *future* operating cash flows to generate higher dividends. To understand the information content of dividends we shall first examine Example 19.3, which considers the case where investors observe the level of investment expenditures.

Example 19.3

The Information Content of Dividend Payouts

Analysts observe that Johnson Haulage, an all-equity firm, has not issued or repurchased shares over the past year. They have also observed that Johnson has paid out £10 million in dividends over the past year, and they believe that the firm has invested £15 million of its operating cash flow back into the business. From this information, what do the analysts infer about the firm's operating cash flows?

Answer: Since the level of equity financing has not changed, the level of dividends plus investment must equal the operating cash flow. The analysts would thus infer that Johnson's operating cash flows were £25 million.

Example 19.3 suggests that an increase in dividends from £10 million to £15 million would imply that Johnson Haulage's operating cash flow increased from £25 million to £30 million. This would be considered good news by shareholders, and would result in an increase in the firm's share price. Hence a dividend change may convey important information to shareholders, even if managers are not explicitly trying to use dividends as a signalling tool.

Dividend Signalling and Underinvestment

A manager faced with the situation in Example 19.3 would choose the optimal level of investment if he or she was interested solely in maximizing the intrinsic value of the firm. However, as suggested above, a manager who has an incentive to boost share prices temporarily may want to cut back on unobserved investment expenditures and use the proceeds to increase the distribution to shareholders. Hence an incentive to convey favourable information to shareholders will generally lead to observable payouts that are too high, and unobservable investment expenditures that are too low. Example 19.4 illustrates this possibility.

Example 19.4

Dividend Signalling and Underinvestment

Johnson Haulage is deciding whether to pay out £10 million (option 1), £15 million (option 2) or £20 million (option 3) in dividends. As in Example 19.3, a £10 million dividend, which allows investment of £15 million, will maximize the intrinsic value of the equity. Higher dividends, on the other hand, will result in an immediate share price increase but, because of the cut in investment expenditures, will reduce the firm's intrinsic value. The following table provides the firm's intrinsic values and current market values associated with the different dividend alternatives.

	Option 1	Option 2	Option 3
	£10 million dividend	£15 million dividend	£20 million dividend
	£15 million invested	£10 million invested	£5 million invested
Intrinsic value	£220 million	£210 million	£200 million
Current value	£190 million	£210 million	£215 million

If managers want to maximize an equally weighted average of the firm's current market value and intrinsic value, what are they likely to decide?

Answer: The £15 million dividend (option 2) is the best option, given the managers' preferences. However, if they place significantly more weight on intrinsic value, they will prefer the lower dividend; if they place more weight on current market value, they will prefer the higher dividend.

Example 19.4 shows that Johnson Haulage's market value and intrinsic values are equal when the firm pays out £15 million in dividends (option 2), suggesting that the market correctly inferred that the firm would invest only £10 million and correctly priced the equity. In other words, the £15 million dividend signals the firm's value, because analysts and investors correctly infer management's incentive to increase the firm's current market value at the expense of its intrinsic value. If the firm had paid out more dividends and invested less than analysts expected, there would have been a deviation between the firm's current share price and its intrinsic value.

To understand this point, consider what would happen if analysts view managers as having little incentive to increase the firm's current share price at the expense of its intrinsic value when, in reality, their incentive to increase the share price (perhaps because of a takeover threat) was quite large. In such a case, a large dividend would be incorrectly interpreted as evidence of increased operating cash flow when, in reality, the cash for the dividend was generated by decreasing investment expenditures.

Do Positive Share Price Responses Imply that a Decision Creates Value?

In Example 19.4, the higher dividends (options 2 and 3) use funds that could have been used more productively within the firm. However, analysts still view the higher dividend payments as good news, because they reveal that the firm has more cash – and perhaps greater earnings potential – than the analysts had previously believed. In this case, the share price will react favourably to a dividend increase because of the information it conveys, even though it is a bad decision. Similarly, share prices may react unfavourably to good decisions. If a firm is experiencing a cash shortfall, it may be in the firm's best interests to cut its dividend payout. However, the announcement of a dividend cut would reveal the firm's difficulties, so the market is likely to react negatively to the announcement.

Results

Result 19.5

An increased dividend implies, holding all else constant, higher cash flows and hence higher share prices. By cutting investment expenditures on items that cannot readily be observed by analysts, firms can increase reported earnings and dividends, thereby increasing their current share prices. A manager's incentive to temporarily boost the firm's share price may thus lead the firm to pass up positive-NPV investments.

Result 19.5 indicates that share price increases that occur when firms announce dividend increases do not imply that investors like the higher dividend payout. Although the dividend increase conveys favourable information, it doesn't necessarily create value for shareholders. Hence the observed share price response to dividend increases is a misguided rationale for increasing dividends.

Share Repurchases versus Dividends

Chapter 15 indicates that, in the absence of taxes and transaction costs, dividends and share repurchases are essentially identical. A share repurchase should also convey the same information as a dividend because, in both cases, cash is distributed to shareholders, revealing to investors that the firm has generated a sizeable operating cash flow.

Indeed, Dann (1981), Vermaelen (1981), Rees (1996) for the UK, Hatakeda and Isagawa (2004) for Japan and Hackethal and Zdantchouk (2006) for Germany all documented impressive share price responses to share repurchase announcements, suggesting that the repurchase alternative conveys the same favourable information to investors as a dividend payment. Dann found that, on average, firms that repurchase shares with tender offers experience about a 16 per cent return on the announcement date. In his sample, the tender offers were made at a premium that averaged about 22 per cent above the share price just before the offer. The number of shares repurchased averaged about 15 per cent of the outstanding shares, taking the premium into account, which represented, on average, 19 per cent of the outstanding equity of these firms.

Given the large number of shares repurchased in these tender offers, it is not surprising that the share price reaction to a share repurchase of this kind is much greater than the price reaction to a dividend increase. When firms want to repurchase smaller amounts of their equity (for example, 3 to 7 per cent of their outstanding shares), they usually buy the shares on the open market. The equity returns at the time of the announcements of open market repurchase announcements are about 3 per cent, which is comparable to the returns from the initiation of a new dividend. The exception is Germany, where the announcement date return is significantly higher at 12 per cent. As Example 19.5 illustrates, this is not the only explanation for why share prices do not react as much to open market repurchases as they do to tender offers.

Example 19.5

Share Price Response to an Open Market Repurchase

Rogerston plc announces that it will repurchase up to 15 per cent of its outstanding shares in the open market. The equity reacts by increasing from €17 to €18 per share. While the price increase was somewhat higher than the average increase for an open market repurchase, the number of shares Rogerston plans to repurchase is substantially higher than the average. Indeed, the planned repurchase is about as large as the typical tender offer repurchase in which share prices generally have a much greater reaction. Why didn't Rogerston's share price react more?

Answer: While various explanations can be offered about why Rogerston's share price didn't react more favourably to the repurchase announcement, we emphasize the following.

- The announcement of an intention to repurchase a quantity of shares on the open market is not a firm commitment. Rogerston could repurchase fewer shares.
- In a tender offer, management offers to repurchase shares at a price substantially above the prevailing share price. This provides an additional signal of the equity's value, since the firm would be substantially overpaying for its equity if the current price was not substantially below the equity's intrinsic value. In open market repurchases, no premium is offered.

Real World Insight

Whittaker and FPL: Simultaneous Dividend Cuts and Share Repurchases

For tax reasons, it makes sense to substitute a share repurchase for a dividend. In theory, such a transaction should not convey information to investors if the amount of the repurchase is identical to the amount of the dividend cut. However, the market may view the dividend cut positively if investors place a value upon receiving income in the form of more lightly taxed capital gains. Alternatively, share prices may react negatively if the market views the share repurchase as a one-time event and the dividend cut as permanent.

Unfortunately, there are few examples of firms substituting share repurchases for dividend payments. However, Woolridge and Ghosh (1985) reported that, on 24 July 1984, Whittaker Corporation announced a cut in its cash dividend from $0.40 to $0.15 per share and, at the same time, instigated a share repurchase plan. On the announcement, the share price increased by $0.125 to $18.625, suggesting that a dividend cut packaged with a share repurchase is not necessarily bad news.

Similarly, Soter et al. (1996) reported that, on 9 May 1994, Florida Power and Light (FPL) announced a 32 per cent dividend reduction along with its intention to repurchase up to 10 million shares over the next three years. In adopting this change in dividend policy, the company noted the personal tax advantages of the substitution of share repurchases for dividend payments. On the day of the announcement, the company's share price fell from $31.88 to $27.50, a drop of almost 14 per cent. However, the drop in share prices was quickly reversed; Soter et al. reported that 'as analysts digested the news and considered the reasons for the reduction, they concluded that the action was not a signal of financial distress'. On 31 May, FPL's equity closed at $32.17.

Results

Result 19.6

It is unlikely that signalling considerations explain why firms pay dividends rather than repurchase shares.

Dividend Policy and Investment Incentives

The argument in the last subsection assumed that investors could correctly infer the firm's investment expenditures, even though the investments are not directly observable. This assumption requires that investors understand the investment opportunities of the firm, as well as the degree of emphasis that managers place on maximizing the firm's current share price versus maximizing the firm's intrinsic value. If investors know management's incentives and understand the firm's investment opportunities, they can accurately infer how much the firm will invest. The only unobservable factor in the all-equity firm's sources and uses of funds equation would then be operating cash flow, which can be inferred from the observed dividends and changes in equity financing. (For firms with debt and equity financing, operating cash flow could be inferred by additionally observing interest payments and changes in debt financing.)

In reality, investors and analysts are usually unable to make accurate inferences about a firm's investment opportunities or how much managers want to invest. As a result, the dividend choice conveys information about both the opportunities and incentives to invest as well as the firm's operating cash flows. This implies that a firm's unanticipated dividend cut could provide a mixed signal. A dividend cut could mean that the firm was less profitable; alternatively, the cut could mean that the firm had good opportunities, and planned on investing more than investors had previously anticipated.

Can Dividend Cuts Signal Good News?

A dividend cut that is interpreted to mean that the firm has increased investment expenditures can be either good news or bad news, depending on whether investors believe that the firm will be investing in positive- or negative-NPV projects. Woolridge and Ghosh (1985) argued that if firms can effectively communicate to investors that an announced dividend cut is motivated by a desire to conserve cash to fund good investments, their share prices will react favourably. To illustrate this point, consider UBS, the Swiss bank. The subprime crisis in 2007 affected all banks, irrespective of whether they operated in the USA or other countries. On 12 December 2007, UBS announced that it would not be paying its dividend but replacing it with a SFr2 billion share issue. Several reasons were given. First, it stated that its provision for bad debts (due to the subprime mortgage crisis) would triple to $14.4 billion. It also warned that the company would report a loss for 2007. This extremely bad news was offset by an announcement that the Government of Singapore Investment Corporation (GIC) and an unnamed Middle Eastern investor would invest SFr13 billion in the bank.

Although existing shareholders would have their proportionate holdings diluted by 18 per cent, the news that the company was dealing with the challenges it was facing led to a share price increase of 2 per cent.[5]

Dividend Cuts and the Incentive to Overinvest

Arguing that a dividend cut is made to increase funds for investment will of course elicit a favourable price response only if shareholders believe that the firm will invest the money in positive-NPV projects. As Chapter 18 noted, managers may overinvest because they prefer to see their firms grow. Thus a signal indicating that management plans to increase investment can be considered both bad news and good news. As a result, share price responses to dividend increases and decreases should depend on the investment opportunities available to the firm. Investors would thus view a dividend increase more favourably when firms have poorer investment opportunities.

Results

Result 19.7

A dividend increase or decrease can provide information to investors about:

- the firm's cash flows
- management's investment intentions.

In the latter case, if investors believe that an increased level of investment associated with a dividend cut is motivated by improved prospects, they will view the dividend cut favourably. However, if investors believe that managers will make negative-NPV investments, they will interpret a dividend cut as bad news.

The findings in Lang and Litzenberger (1989) support the hypothesis that investors view dividend cuts more favourably when firms have better investment prospects, and view dividend increases more favourably when investment prospects are poorer.[6] They examined the share price reactions to announced dividend increases and decreases for shares that differed according to the relationship between their market values (MV) and their book values (BV). Firms with market values that *exceed* their book values are believed to have favourable investment opportunities, whereas those with market values that are *less than* their book values are believed to have unfavourable investment opportunities.

Lang and Litzenberger's sample was divided into four groups:

1. firms with MV > BV with dividend increases
2. firms with MV > BV with dividend decreases
3. firms with MV < BV with dividend increases
4. firms with MV < BV with dividend decreases.

As Exhibit 19.2 shows, a dividend increase created only a slight share price increase for firms believed to have favourable investment opportunities (that is, MV > BV). Likewise, a dividend decrease generated only a slight share price decrease for these firms. In contrast, dividend increases and decreases resulted in much larger share price responses for firms believed to have unfavourable investment opportunities (that is, MV < BV). This evidence suggests that dividend changes are viewed as signals of the firm's level of future investment.

Denis et al. (1994) provided an alternative interpretation of the observed differences in the share price reaction of high- and low-MV/BV firms to dividend changes. They pointed out that high-MV/BV firms generally have lower dividend yields and greater growth potential, which implies two things.

1. Increases in the dividends of high-MV/BV firms are less likely to be viewed as a surprise.
2. High-MV/BV firms are likely to attract investors who are less interested in dividends.

---

[5] The *Daily Telegraph,* 12 December 2007.

[6] Litzenberger and Lang's sample of daily returns consisted of 429 dividend change announcements that met two criteria: (1) the absolute value of the percentage dividend change was greater than 10 per cent; and (2) data on market and book values were available.

Exhibit 19.2 Average Daily Returns on Dividend Announcement Days, 1979–1984

	Dividend increase	Dividend decrease	Difference in absolute values for increases and decreases
MV > BV	0.003[a]	−0.003	0.000
MV < BV	0.008[a]	−0.027[a]	0.019[a]
Difference (row 2 −1)	0.005[a]	−0.024[a]	0.019[a]

[a]Statistically different from zero.

Source: Lang and Litzenberger (1989).

To understand the first point, recall from Chapter 11 that the Gordon growth model version of the dividend discount equation can be rearranged to show that the cost of capital is the sum of (1) the dividend yield and (2) the dividend growth rate. Hence holding the risk of the firm (and thus the cost of capital) constant, low dividend yields imply high dividend growth rates, and *vice versa*. The second point is an implication of dividend clienteles, discussed in Chapter 15. Both of these factors suggest that high-MV/BV firms will react less to dividend increases than low-MV/BV firms, even in the absence of the incentive problems discussed by Lang and Litzenberger.

Denis et al. (1994) demonstrated that after accounting for differences in dividend yields and the size of the dividend change, high- and low-MV/BV firms react similarly to dividend changes. In addition, they found that, following dividend increases, equity market analysts increase their earnings forecasts more for low-MV/BV firms than for high-MV/BV firms. Based on this evidence, they concluded that share prices respond to dividend changes because of the information the announcements convey about the firm's future earnings. Their evidence does not support the idea that share prices respond because dividend changes provide information about the firms' future investment choices.

Dividends Attract Attention

An additional possibility is that a firm's dividend increase or initiation results in a share price increase simply because it attracts attention to the firm. To understand why investors generally view decisions that attract attention as good news, one must consider the conditions under which the managers would put the firm under greater scrutiny. If the firm is undervalued, increased scrutiny is likely to lead to a positive adjustment in the firm's share price, but if the firm is overvalued, the increased scrutiny is likely to lead to a negative adjustment in the firm's share price. Hence the incentive to attract attention is greatest for those firms that are the most undervalued, which suggests that one might expect to see positive share price reactions to any announcements that attract considerable attention.

The positive share price reactions observed at the time when equity dividends and equity splits are announced support the idea that share prices respond to announcements of managerial decisions that do no more than attract attention to the firm. Unlike cash dividends, equity dividends and splits affect neither the firm's cash flows nor its investment alternatives. Yet observed equity returns at the time of equity dividend and equity split announcements are of approximately the same magnitude as the returns at the time when increases in cash dividends are announced.

Dividends Across Countries

In many countries, managers have concentrated shareholdings in their firm. Family firms, corporate groups and companies that have recently been founded by entrepreneurs are also common examples of companies with powerful shareholders. Chapter 16 reviewed the various types of conflict that can exist between debt and equity holders. When firms are owned as part of a corporate pyramid structure, or through a network of family or business contacts, it is easy for manager-shareholders to expropriate wealth from minority shareholders or debt holders. This can be done through various routes, most notably by undertaking unfair transactions between different firms in the network. Dividends are a good tool to mitigate this issue, because wealth is transferred from the company and insiders to external shareholders. La Porta et al. (2000) reported that firms in countries with strong minority shareholder rights pay higher dividends. Faccio et al. (2001) showed that companies that are indirectly owned by powerful investor families or corporate groups are also more likely to pay out higher dividends. There is a striking difference between companies in Europe and East Asia, however.

European organizations pay higher dividends, controlling for ownership and control rights, compared with East Asian firms. Faccio et al. (2001) therefore argue that 'in Europe, other large shareholders appear to help contain the controlling shareholder's expropriation of minority shareholders; in East Asia, they appear to collude in that expropriation'. Holding all else constant, countries with weak shareholder rights will experience much larger price increases on announcement of dividend increases.

19.5 The Information Content of the Debt–Equity Choice

This section examines the type of information conveyed to investors by a firm's debt–equity choice. The debt–equity choice conveys information to investors for two reasons. First, because of financial distress costs, managers will avoid increasing a firm's leverage ratio if they have information indicating that the firm could have future financial difficulties. Hence a debt issue can be viewed as a signal that managers are confident about the firm's ability to repay the debt. The second reason has to do with the reluctance of managers to issue what they believe are underpriced shares. Hence an equity issue might be viewed as a signal that the firm's shares are not underpriced, and therefore may be overpriced.

A Signalling Model Based on the Tax Gain/Financial Distress Cost Trade-Off

To understand why the debt–equity choice conveys information, assume, as a first approximation, that firms select their capital structures by trading off the tax benefits of debt financing (see Chapter 14) against the various costs of financial distress (see Chapters 16 and 17). In this setting, firms desire higher debt levels when expected cash flows are higher because they can better utilize the tax benefits of debt. In addition, for any given debt level, the probability of incurring the costs of financial distress is lower if expected cash flows are higher.

Because expected future cash flows determine the firm's optimal capital structure, the capital structure choice of better-informed managers is likely to convey information to shareholders. Whereas the information content of the capital structure decision would not affect the decisions of managers concerned only with intrinsic value, it would affect the decisions of managers who are also concerned about the current share prices of their firms. Indeed, managers whose objectives are heavily weighted towards the maximization of current share price are likely to avoid reducing leverage, even when doing so improves the intrinsic value of their shares but conveys information that reduces their current value. They may similarly choose to increase leverage beyond the point that maximizes intrinsic value.[7]

Results

Result 19.8

An increase in a firm's debt ratio is considered a favourable signal because it indicates that managers believe the firm will be generating taxable earnings in the future, and that they are not overly concerned about incurring financial distress costs. Managers understand that their firm's share price is likely to respond favourably to higher leverage ratios, and may thus have an incentive to select higher leverage ratios than they would otherwise prefer.

Real World Insight

CUC International Borrows to Pay a Special Dividend

In March 1989, CUC International's board of directors ratified a levered recapitalization plan that involved paying out a special dividend of $5 per share, financed in part by a loan from GE Capital. The total size of the dividend payment ($100 million) represented over half of the market value of CUC's equity prior to the

[7] Ross (1977) developed a theory of capital structure along these lines.

announcement. Walter Forbes, the company's chairman and CEO, admitted that part of the motivation for the recapitalization was the favourable signal of an increased debt ratio. Forbes said:

> We judged that borrowing a moderate amount of debt to finance the special dividend would add an appropriate amount of leverage to our capital structure as well as providing, through the repayment of the debt, a clear signal of CUC's ability to generate cash.

Source: This case study is based on Paul M. Healy and Krishna G. Palepu (1996) 'Using capital structure to communicate with investors: the case of CUC International, *Journal of Applied Corporate Finance*, 8(4), 30–44.

It is clear that one of CUC International's motivations for increasing its debt ratio was to send a signal to investors. However, an investor may question whether such a signal is credible, given that the motivation for the debt increase was to boost the firm's share price. The following result describes conditions under which a financial signal conveys favourable information credibly.

Results

Result 19.9

For a financial decision to convey favourable information credibly to investors, firms with poor prospects must find it costly to mimic the decisions made by firms with favourable prospects.

The Credibility of the Debt–Equity Signal

As Example 19.6 illustrates, issuing debt satisfies the requirement for a credible signal, as specified in Result 19.9, because additional debt is likely to have a much greater effect on the probability of bankruptcy for firms with unfavourable future prospects than for firms with favourable prospects.

Example 19.6

The Information Content of Leverage Changes

Analysts following Pesce Technologies are uncertain whether Pesce has successfully reduced its production costs. If it has been successful, Pesce's future earnings are expected to range from €50 million to €60 million per year. However, if the company has not been successful, its earnings will be in the range of €25 million to €30 million. Pesce announces a debt-for-equity swap that increases its interest payments to €40 million per year. What information is conveyed by this decision?

Answer: Analysts can infer that the cost reductions have been successful. Otherwise, such an increase in leverage would eventually expose the firm to substantial bankruptcy risk and the associated financial distress costs. Hence the market responds to the announcement by bidding up Pesce's share price. Since the firm is certain to have the cash flow to meet these interest payments, the signal did not reduce Pesce's long-term value.

Example 19.6 illustrates a situation in which a firm with favourable prospects is able to use debt financing to signal its value without risking bankruptcy. In more realistic cases, a firm that wishes to signal its value will have to take on much more debt than it otherwise would have found optimal.

Consider, for example, a firm whose managers have strong incentives to increase current share prices, and would be willing to take on a high debt level to achieve this goal. As a result, outside investors will not find moderately high leverage ratios to be credible signals of high values. Hence, if the firm does have favourable prospects, it will have to use much more debt financing than it would otherwise use in order to convince investors of its higher value. We illustrate this concept in Example 19.7.

Example 19.7

CEO Incentives and the Credibility of Financial Signals

Nollaig's CEO knows that the firm's assets are worth either €500 million, €400 million or €300 million, depending on the demand for their product. Because each possibility is equally likely, the average of these three numbers, €400 million, is the firm's intrinsic value. However, investors are not as optimistic about the firm's future earnings as the CEO, and believe that the firm will have respective values of €450 million, €350 million or €250 million in the three product demand scenarios given above, implying that the firm's current value is €350 million (assuming no financial distress costs). The €50 million discrepancy between the firm's intrinsic value and its current value presents a problem, because Nollaig's CEO plans to sell a large block of equity in the near future. As a consequence, before selling the equity, the CEO would like to signal to investors that Nollaig's value is €50 million higher than investors currently believe it is.

The CEO has announced his beliefs about Nollaig's prospects, and investors know that the only alternative to their own beliefs is the more optimistic beliefs of the CEO. However, the mere announcement of more optimistic beliefs is not a very credible signal to investors. They know the CEO would be delighted to engineer a temporary increase in Nollaig's share price before unloading his block of shares.

Assume that the CEO has announced his intention to sell half of his shares, and thus weights intrinsic value and current value equally. Also assume that financial distress costs reduce the value of the firm by €60 million in whichever product demand scenario such distress occurs. The CEO has concluded that he may be able to signal the more optimistic prospects credibly by issuing sufficient debt and using the proceeds to retire equity. From the CEO's perspective, the issuance of debt with a promised payment in excess of €400 million is precluded. There is no need to risk financial distress that reduces intrinsic value by more than one gains in current value (net of financial distress costs). Moreover, debt financing with a promised payment of less than €250 million would not be a very credible signal, in that – using either investor beliefs or the more optimistic CEO beliefs – financial distress never occurs.

Analyse what happens to investor beliefs if the CEO issues debt (and retires an equivalent amount of equity) with a promised payment (1) between €250 million and €350 million or (2) between €350 million and €400 million.

Answer: (1) Debt issuance between €250 million and €350 million is not a credible signal to investors that the higher firm values will be realized. Since Nollaig's CEO weights the current and intrinsic values of Nollaig equally, he would be willing to take on this amount of debt if doing so would signal the higher value, even if this signal were false. To see this, note that the CEO gains €50 million in current market value and loses only €20 million (1/3 × €60 million) in intrinsic value from being financially distressed in the lowest product demand scenario. Investors, aware of the incentive to be tricked by a CEO who sees cash flows as pessimistically as they do, will not believe that a debt signal of this magnitude is credible.

(2) A debt obligation between €350 million and €400 million would put the firm in financial distress 2/3 of the time if investor beliefs are correct but only 1/3 of the time if the more optimistic announced beliefs of the CEO were true. No CEO with pessimistic beliefs would take on this much debt, since, even if investors believe the CEO, the gain in current value (net of financial distress costs) is €30 million (€50 million less 1/3 of €60 million), while the loss in intrinsic value to the deceptive manager is €40 million (2/3 of €60 million). By contrast, the loss in intrinsic value to a manager who truly holds optimistic beliefs is €20 million (1/3 of €60 million). Thus the signal of debt is credible in this case, because managers with optimistic beliefs find it profitable to issue debt in amounts between €350 million and €400 million at the same time that managers with pessimistic beliefs find it unprofitable to signal by mimicking the same action.

The amount of debt financing a firm must use to credibly signal a high value depends on its managers' incentive to increase the firm's current share price. To understand this, consider two CEOs, Jane and Janet. Jane, who plans to retire soon and sell her holdings of her firm's equity, has a strong incentive to increase her firm's share price temporarily. Janet, on the other hand, plans to stay on as CEO at her firm for 10 years. She is also interested in boosting her firm's current share price, but she is much more concerned about the firm's long-term success, and, in addition, is worried about losing her job if the firm has trouble meeting future interest payments.

The interpretation of the signal offered by a leverage increase depends on whether the firm one is looking at is run by a CEO like Jane or a CEO like Janet. When Janet increases her firm's leverage, investors will infer that she is confident that the firm will be able to generate the cash flows to pay back the debt. They understand that she has little incentive to give a false signal, and she has a lot to lose if the firm subsequently fails to make the required interest payments. Investors are likely to react very differently to a leverage increase initiated by Jane. They understand that Jane has a strong incentive to appear optimistic, even when she isn't, and that the cost to her of overleveraging her firm is not substantial. Hence an equivalent leverage increase will result in a lower share price response to the leverage signal for Jane's firm than for Janet's.

Adverse Selection Theory

Consider a health insurance company offering two different policies. One policy is very expensive, but it pays 100 per cent of all of your medical bills. The second policy is much less expensive, but it pays only 80 per cent of your medical bills. How do you expect individuals to choose between the two policies?

Most economists predict that individuals will not *randomly select* between the policies. Rather, we shall observe what economists call adverse selection. In the health insurance example, **adverse selection** means that individuals will select their best actions based on their private information. Hence the more expensive policy will attract the least healthy individuals. An additional example of adverse selection, described in a seminal article by Akerlof (1970), is the 'lemons' problem connected with the sale of used cars. Akerlof argued that cars depreciate so much in their first year largely because people who have the most incentive to sell their cars after only one year are those with lemons, or faulty cars. Buyers, taking into account this adverse selection of used cars, are thus unwilling to pay as much for a used car as for a new car, which is less likely to be a lemon.

Adverse selection is also important when firms issue new equity. Managers have the greatest incentive to sell equity when the equity is a lemon. This means that the incentive to issue equity is highest when management believes that the firm's share price exceeds its intrinsic value. At these times, better-informed managers know that equity provides relatively inexpensive financing (that is, the expected return on equity is relatively low), and a new issue would thus increase the intrinsic value of existing shares. In contrast, issuing shares of equity at a price lower than management believes they are worth provides relatively expensive financing, and dilutes the intrinsic value of the firm's existing shares.

Adverse Selection Problems When Insiders Sell Shares

The incentive to retain rather than issue underpriced shares can be viewed within the context of an entrepreneur who is motivated to take his firm public in order to sell shares and diversify his portfolio.[8] To understand how an entrepreneur decides how many shares to sell, consider the situation faced by Mark Zuckerberg at the time of Facebook's (now Meta) initial public offering in 2012. In deciding whether or not to sell some of his own shares, Zuckerberg had to consider:

- the diversification benefits of selling shares
- the tax costs of selling shares (see Chapter 15)
- whether the shares are undervalued or overvalued.

If Zuckerberg values diversification, and the tax costs are not great, he will sell shares if he believes they are not substantially undervalued. Indeed, if he believes the shares are overvalued, he will sell them even if he places no value on diversification. Conversely, if Zuckerberg believes the shares are substantially undervalued, he will choose not to sell any shares, even if he is extremely risk averse.

Since investors understood Zuckerberg's incentives, they would have monitored his tendency to sell off shares when they valued Meta equity (both at the IPO and, subsequently, in the secondary market). If Zuckerberg were to sell off almost all of his shares, which he would do to diversify optimally, Meta's equity would probably fall substantially, because it would signal to investors that Zuckerberg no longer believed that Meta equity was an extraordinary investment. Zuckerberg thus faces a trade-off. By holding more shares, he provides a more favourable signal about Meta's prospects, which keeps the share price relatively high. However, this forces him to be less diversified than he would like to be.

[8] These issues were first addressed in Leland and Pyle (1977).

To understand the price effect of a sale of Meta shares by Zuckerberg, it is helpful to review the issues involved in buying a used car. If you know that the car's owner is moving overseas, you might think the adverse selection problem is minimal, and feel comfortable about buying the car. Similarly, if investors believe that Zuckerberg is extremely risk averse and therefore motivated to sell his shares, they will be less concerned about the adverse selection problem and be more willing to buy his shares. On the other hand, if investors believe that Zuckerberg is not very risk averse but is extremely averse to paying taxes, they will be much less willing to buy his shares.

Many decades ago, Howard Hughes sold a substantial fraction of his holdings in TWA equity. The share price of TWA did not plummet in response to the sale, because Hughes was able to credibly convince the market that he was selling TWA equity to remedy a 'cash crunch' that he was personally experiencing, and not because of any adverse information he held about TWA. More recently, high-tech billionaires, such as Michael Dell, founder of Dell Computer, and Bill Gates of Microsoft, have started to sell for diversification purposes without signalling poor prospects for their firms, by selling a relatively small fixed percentage of their outstanding shares every quarter. Because the sales are constant and anticipated, they do not adversely affect share prices.

Adverse Selection Problems When Firms Raise Money for New Investments[9]

As we discuss below, the adverse selection problem that creates problems for the seller of a used car can also make it costly for a firm to issue new equity. Firms often issue equity to raise capital to fund new investment. In the same way that it is easier to sell your car when you can convince would-be buyers that you are moving overseas, it is easier to convince investors that your equity is not overvalued if you can demonstrate that you are raising capital to fund an attractive investment project.

However, the adverse selection problem cannot always be solved by revealing the potential of a favourable investment. As a result, firms sometimes pass up good investments because of their reluctance to finance projects by issuing underpriced shares. The conditions under which a firm will pass up a positive-NPV investment are seen in the following equations, which compare the intrinsic values of a firm's shares with and without a new investment that is financed by issuing equity.

$$\text{Share value taking the project} = \frac{\text{PV of assets in place} + \text{PV of assets new investment}}{\text{number of original shares} + \text{number of new shares}}$$

$$\text{Share value not taking the project} = \frac{\text{PV of assets in place}}{\text{number of original shares}}$$

The preceding equations show that a firm may reduce the intrinsic value of its shares if the PV of the new investment is low relative to the number of shares it must issue. To understand this, consider a case where management believes the firm has assets worth £10 million with 1 million shares outstanding, suggesting that the firm's intrinsic value is £10 per share if it does not take any new investments. If this firm's shares are selling at only £7 per share, it will have to issue an additional 1 million shares to raise £7 million for a project that has a value of £9 million. The firm's intrinsic share value after taking the project would then be

$$\frac{£10\,\text{million} + £9\,\text{million}}{1\,\text{million} + 1\,\text{million}} = £9.50\,\text{per share}$$

Hence the firm reduces the intrinsic value of its shares by £0.50 per share by taking on a positive-NPV project. Although the project has a £2 million positive NPV, the financing for the project has a negative NPV of −£2.5 million, given what the firm's managers know about the value of the firm's existing assets. The −£2.5 million is the consequence of offering what managers know is a claim to £5 million in existing assets plus £4.5 million in assets from the new investment for the bargain price of £7 million. This possibility is illustrated further in Example 19.8.

[9] The discussion in this subsection is based on Myers and Majluf (1984).

Example 19.8

Issuing Equity When Managers Know More than Investors

Olympus GmbH is currently selling at €50 a share and has 1 million shares outstanding. The €50 share price reflects its current business, valued at €40 million, and an opportunity to take on an investment valued at €30 million, which costs only €20 million. The opportunity can be viewed as an asset with a €10 million NPV.

The management of Olympus has discovered a vast amount of oil, worth €50 million, on its property. This fact is unknown to shareholders, and thus is not reflected in Olympus's current share price. If information about this oil were known to shareholders, its shares would sell for €100 a share. Unfortunately, management has no way to reveal this information directly to the market, so expects that its shares will be undervalued for some time.

Suppose that the firm funds its new investment by issuing 400,000 shares at €50 a share. How will this affect the intrinsic value of the firm's existing shares?

Answer: If the firm passes up the project, its shares will ultimately be worth €90 each [(€40 million + €50 million)/1 million] when the information about the oil is revealed. However, if the project is taken and is financed with an equity issue, the firm's total intrinsic value will be €120 million (€40 million + €30 million + €50 million) and the total number of shares outstanding will be 1.4 million. The per share value will be €85.71 (€120 million ÷ 1.4 million) if Olympus issues shares and takes the project. Thus the firm will choose not to invest in the positive-NPV project if it requires issuing underpriced equity.

Using Debt Financing to Mitigate the Adverse Selection Problem

Example 19.8 illustrates why managers may choose not to issue equity when they believe that their firm's shares are underpriced. However, the example ignores the possibility that the firm can finance the project with debt. If the project can be financed with riskless debt, then the firm should take the project as long as it has a positive NPV. In this case, the share's intrinsic value will be equal to

$$\text{Share value: financing project with riskless debt} = \frac{\text{value of original assets} + \text{NPV of new project}}{\text{number of shares}}$$

This value clearly increases when the company commits to a positive-NPV project. However, the firm may still pass up the project if it is forced to issue risky debt that exposes it to the possibility of incurring financial distress costs. In this case, a firm must compare the costs of deviating from its optimal capital structure and the associated financial distress costs with the NPV of the particular investment project. Given this comparison, some positive-NPV investment projects will be passed up while others will be financed with debt, causing the firm to become at least temporarily overlevered.

Similarly, one could show that firms have an incentive to take on negative-NPV projects and become underlevered if it allows them to issue overpriced securities. Because of these incentives, issuing equity is considered to be an indication that a firm is overvalued. As a result, announcements of equity issues have a negative effect on a firm's share price, which has the effect of further reducing the incentive for firms to issue equity.

This discussion suggests that managers will prefer debt to equity financing when they have favourable private information. In Example 19.8, Olympus GmbH would have been able to realize a share price of €100 if it could have financed the investment with risk-free debt. If lenders are unwilling to lend the firm additional amounts (see Chapter 16), or if the firm is unwilling to borrow more because of the financial distress costs (see Chapter 17), then undervalued firms may choose to pass up positive-NPV investments.

Results

Result 19.10

A firm may pass up a positive-NPV investment project if it requires issuing underpriced equity. Since debt has a fixed claim on future cash flows, a firm's debt is less likely to be substantially undervalued. As a result, firms may prefer to finance new projects with debt rather than equity. With sufficiently high financial distress and adverse selection costs, however, firms may be better off passing up the positive-NPV investment.

Adverse Selection and the Use of Preference Shares

The dilution and financial distress problems that can arise when an underpriced firm finances a new project may be mitigated by issuing preference shares. Recall from Chapter 3 that preferred equity is similar to a bond, because it has a fixed payout. However, if a firm fails to meet its dividend obligation, preference shareholders cannot force it into bankruptcy. Hence preferred equity will not create the problems associated with financial distress. In addition, since preference shares offer a fixed claim, it is not likely to be as underpriced as ordinary equity, so the dilution costs of issuing underpriced shares are much less of a problem.

For these reasons, preference shares are good securities for firms to issue when they are having financial difficulties that they believe are temporary. If investors do not agree that the difficulties are temporary, the ordinary equity may be underpriced, so issuing ordinary equity may dilute the value of existing shares. In such a situation, the firm may not have taxable earnings, making debt financing less attractive. Furthermore, additional debt financing may lead to a drop in the firm's credit rating, which could create problems with the firm's non-financial stakeholders.

Preference shares may be the best financing alternative in this situation, because it is unlikely to be as undervalued as ordinary equity, given its senior status and fixed dividend, and it does not increase the risk of bankruptcy, as would happen when additional debt is issued.

Results

Result 19.11

When firms are experiencing financial difficulties, they prefer equity to debt financing for several reasons. In particular, the tax advantages of debt may be less and the potential for suffering financial distress costs may be greater. Issuing ordinary equity in these situations may be a problem, however, given the negative information conveyed by an equity offering. Hence a preference share issue may offer the best source of capital.

Empirical Implications of the Adverse Selection Theory

The adverse selection theory explains a number of observations about how firms externally finance themselves. First, the reluctance of managers to issue underpriced equity helps explain why share prices react unfavourably when firms announce their intention to issue equity. As we discuss in more detail in the section below, share prices drop about 2 per cent, on average, when firms announce the issue of new equity. The adverse selection theory also provides an explanation for Donaldson's pecking order of financing choices (see Chapters 15 and 17). Donaldson observed that firms prefer first to finance investment with retained earnings; then, when they need outside funding, they prefer to issue debt instead of equity. The adverse selection theory explains the reluctance of firms to issue equity, and, in addition, suggests that firms prefer to use their retained earnings to finance investment expenditures, because this allows them to retain the capacity to borrow in the future.

19.6 Empirical Evidence

Exhibit 19.3 gives a brief overview of three types of signalling theory that provide insights into financial decision-making and the reaction of share prices when firms make financing and dividend changes. This section discusses some of the empirical implications of those theories. We start by reviewing academic studies that measure the share price responses to these financial decisions. We shall then discuss the evidence on the information signalled by investment choices.

What is an Event Study?

Academic studies that examine share price responses to the announcements of particular information are generally referred to as **event studies**. For example, the event studies of dividend initiation announcements discussed previously were carried out as follows. The researchers first collected the dates when a sample of firms announced that they would be initiating new dividends. The equity returns on the announcement dates

Exhibit 19.3 Signalling Theories and Their Implications

Theory	Explanation	Empirical implications
Issuing equity dilutes current shareholders[a]	Management, representing existing shareholders, is reluctant to issue underpriced shares; this reluctance results in either underinvestment or excessive leverage	Selling shares to outside investors conveys unfavourable information and results in a share price decline; similarly, share repurchases result in share price increases
Distributing cash to outside investors reveals the firm's earnings capacity[b]	Cash outflows through dividends, repurchases or debt retirements reveal that the firm has been and is expected to continue generating sufficient cash flows	Dividends, repurchases and debt retirements convey favourable information and result in share price increases; equity and debt issues convey unfavourable information
The capital structure choice reveals management's assessment of the firm's future prospects[c]	Increased debt signals that firms are confident that they can meet higher interest payments, and that they have sufficient EBIT to use the interest tax shields	Increased leverage conveys favourable information, and is associated with positive share price responses

[a] See Leland and Pyle (1977) and Myers and Majluf (1984).

[b] See Miller and Rock (1985).

[c] See Ross (1977).

and the days immediately before and after the event were averaged across all firms in the sample. For example, researchers might find that the average return for a sample of shares on the day of a dividend initiation announcement in the press was 3.0 per cent, the average return on the day before the announcement was 1.2 per cent, and the average return on the day after the announcement was 0.2 per cent.

It is typical to find significant returns on the day(s) before a major announcement, because information sometimes leaks out early, or the press is slow to report the announcements. Therefore researchers sometimes add the returns from the day(s) immediately before the announcement to the return on the announcement date itself to gauge the event's total price impact. For example, one might say that the dividend initiation event led to an average return of 4.2 per cent, the 3.0 per cent return on the event date plus the 1.2 per cent return on the day prior to the announcement. With efficient markets, one expects to see only insignificant returns after the announcements. However, as discussed below, there is evidence that the market underreacts to some information events, and, consequently, some researchers also analyse returns on the days following the event.

In some event studies, researchers average market-adjusted excess returns instead of averaging total returns on the event dates. A **market-adjusted excess return** is the equity's return less the equity's beta times the market return on that date. For example, the market-adjusted excess return of an equity whose beta equalled 1 would be the return on the event day less the market return for that day. For relatively small samples, market adjustments are important because, by coincidence, particular announcements may be made on days when market returns are high. For large samples, however, it is unlikely that market returns will be either unusually high or unusually low on announcement dates, so that adjusting the returns for market movements makes little difference in these cases.

Event Study Evidence

Capital Structure Changes

Firms sometimes make capital structure changes that have no immediate effect on the asset side of their balance sheets. For example, a firm may issue equity and use the proceeds to pay down debt. Exhibit 19.4 summarizes some event studies that examined average share price movements around the time of the announcements of these pure capital structure changes.

The evidence summarized in Exhibit 19.4 indicates that leverage-increasing events tend to increase share prices, and leverage-decreasing events tend to decrease share prices. For example, Masulis (1983) found that at the time of the announcement of **exchange offers** (in which ordinary equity is retired and debt is issued), share prices increased about 14 per cent, on average. He also found that announcements of leverage-decreasing

Exhibit 19.4 Equity Market Response to Pure Capital Structure Changes

Type of transaction	Security issued	Security retired	Average sample size	Two-day announcement period return (%)
Leverage-increasing transactions:				
Equity repurchase[a]	Debt	Ordinary	45	21.9
Exchange offer[b]	Debt	Ordinary	52	14.0
Exchange offer[b]	Preference	Ordinary	9	8.3
Exchange offer[b]	Debt	Preference	24	2.2
Exchange offer[c]	Income bonds	Preference	24	2.2
Transactions with no change in leverage:				
Exchange offer[d]	Debt	Debt	36	0.6[o]
Security sale[e]	Debt	Debt	83	0.2[o]
Leverage-reducing transactions:				
Conversion-forcing call[e]	Ordinary	Convertible debt	57	0.4[o]
Conversion-forcing call[e]	Ordinary	Preference	113	2.1
Security sale[f]	Convertible debt	Convertible bond	15	2.4
Exchange offer[b]	Ordinary	Debt	30	2.6
Exchange offer[b]	Preference	Preference	9	7.7
Security sale[f]	Ordinary	Debt	12	4.2
Exchange offer[b]	Ordinary	Debt	20	9.9

Note: Exhibits 19.4 and 19.5 are slightly altered versions of tables reported in Smith (1986).

Sources:

[a]Masulis (1980).

[b]Masulis (1983). These returns include announcement days of both the original offer and, for about 40 per cent of the sample, a second announcement of specific terms of the exchange.

[c]McConnell and Schlarbaum (1981).

[d]Dietrich (1984).

[e]Mikkelson (1981).

[f]Eckbo (1986) and Mikkelson and Partch (1986).

[o]Not statistically different from zero.

exchange offers brought share prices down 9.9 per cent. This evidence supports the idea that higher leverage is a signal that managers are confident about their ability to meet the higher interest payments. Chaplinsky and Ramchand (2000) reported that companies that simultaneously issue equity in different countries experience a smaller negative reaction than when they issue equity only in their own market. The difference is small at 0.8 per cent, but significant within their analysis.

Issuing Securities

Exhibit 19.5 summarizes some event studies that examined share price reactions to the announcements of new security issues. It shows that raising capital is viewed as a negative signal. For example, when industrial firms issue ordinary equity their share prices decline, on average, about 13.1 per cent. This evidence supports the theory that firms seek outside equity when they think they can obtain cheap financing (that is, issue overpriced equity) as well as the theory that, by raising outside capital, firms reveal that they have generated insufficient capital internally.

Exhibit 19.5 Share Price Reactions to Security Sales

Type of announcement	Average sample size	Two-day announcement period return (%)
Security sales:		
Ordinary equity (industrial issuers)[a]	216	−3.1
Ordinary equity (utility issuers)[a]	424	−1.4
Preference shares[b]	102	−0.1[o]
Convertible preferred[c]	30	−1.4[o]
Straight debt[d]	221	−0.2
Convertible debt[d]	80	−2.1

Source:

[a]These figures are based on calculations by Eckbo and Masulis (1995). See also Pettway and Radcliff (1985), Asquith and Mullins (1986), Masulis and Korwar (1986), Mikkelson and Partch (1986) and Schipper and Smith (1986).
[b]Linn and Pinegar (1988) and Mikkelson and Partch (1986).
[c]Linn and Pinegar (1988).
[d]Dann and Mikkelson (1984), Eckbo (1986) and Mikkelson and Partch (1986).
[o]Not statistically different from zero.

In a sense, firms raising new debt are sending a mixed signal. They are seeking funds, which investors consider bad news, but they are increasing leverage, which investors believe is good news. As a result, when firms announce that they will issue straight bonds, their share prices generally react very little. However, issuing convertible bonds, an instrument that shares debt and equity characteristics, results in negative share price reactions.

Explanations for the Event Study Results

These empirical findings are consistent with the adverse selection theory, which states that firms are reluctant to issue ordinary equity when they believe their shares are underpriced. When firms do issue shares or, alternatively, exchange shares for bonds, management generally believes that the shares are probably either priced about right or overpriced. Analysts and investors observing the announcement of a share issue will then infer that management is not as optimistic as they had earlier thought, which is a bad signal about current share prices.

Since convertible bonds have a strong equity-like component, the adverse selection theory can also explain why the equity market generally reacts negatively when they are issued. On the other hand, short-term bank debt is least subject to adverse selection. Firms that believe that their equity is undervalued, and that their credit ratings will improve in the future, have the greatest incentive to borrow short term.[10] As a result, investors usually see short-term borrowing as a favourable signal and, as James (1987) showed, share prices generally respond favourably when firms increase their bank debt.

The adverse selection theory also explains the share price increases around the announcements of share repurchases and exchange offers that reduce the number of outstanding shares. Since management has the greatest incentive to reduce the total number of outstanding shares when the firm's equity is underpriced, these announcements convey favourable information to the market.

The discussion of taxes and financial distress costs provides an additional explanation for why share prices rise when firms increase their debt levels. Managers would be less willing to replace equity financing with debt if they thought that they were not going to generate sufficient income to utilize the tax benefits of the debt, or if they thought that repaying the debt would create problems. Thus, when firms increase their leverage, investors are likely to believe that management is unconcerned about either financial distress or having excess tax shields. Since this usually implies that managers are optimistic, leverage increases should be viewed as good news for shareholders.

The events considered in this section may also be signals of the intentions as well as the information of managers. For example, as Chapter 18 discussed, managers may have an incentive to overinvest, taking

[10] This idea is developed in much greater detail in Flannery (1986) and Diamond (1991).

negative-NPV projects that benefit them personally. Shareholders may see a distribution of cash or an increase in leverage as a signal that managers do not plan on initiating what the shareholders view as wasteful investment.

A Summary of the Event Study Findings

Result 19.12 provides a summary and interpretation of some of the more notable event study findings.

Results

Result 19.12

On average, share prices react favourably to:

- announcements that firms will be distributing cash to shareholders
- announcements that firms will increase their leverage.

Share prices react negatively, on average, to:

- announcements that firms will be raising cash
- announcements that firms will decrease their leverage.

These announcement returns can be explained by the information theories presented in this chapter and the incentive theories presented in Chapter 18.

Differential Announcement Date Returns

Recall from this chapter's discussion of adverse selection that the information conveyed by an equity or debt issue depends on the manager's perceived motivation for issuing the particular financial instrument. For example, if investors believe that a firm is already overlevered, and cannot easily finance new investments with debt, then they are likely to view an equity offer less negatively, and a debt offering as evidence that managers believe that their equity is undervalued. In contrast, investors are likely to view an equity offering as especially negative in cases where the firm could easily raise debt capital. In such instances investors may conclude that managers are issuing equity because they believe that their equity is overvalued.

To examine these possibilities, Bayless and Chaplinsky (1991) developed a model based on variables such as a firm's tax-paying status, its debt ratio relative to its historical average debt ratio and other firm characteristics, to predict which firms are the most likely to issue equity and which are the most likely to issue debt. They compared the equity market responses around the time that debt and equity issues are announced to determine how expectations regarding the financing instrument that the firm is likely to issue affect equity returns. Their evidence is consistent with the predictions of the theory of adverse selection. Equity returns around the time of equity issuance announcements are more negative for firms that are expected to use debt financing, and less negative for firms expected to issue equity.

Hadlock et al. (2001) examined this issue further by comparing the issue date returns of diversified firms with focused firms. The market appears to react less negatively to equity issues by diversified firms, which suggests that adverse selection risk is less in these types of company.

Post-Announcement Drift

The event studies described in this section assume that markets are efficient, and that share prices react fully to the information event under consideration. However, some studies have shown that, in a surprising number of cases, the market substantially underreacts to important information. This was first shown in the context of earnings announcements, where research indicates that share prices react favourably to announcements of unexpectedly good earnings, but tend to underreact to this information. As a result, investors can profit by buying shares immediately after the announcements of unexpected good earnings and selling the shares of firms whose earnings fall below expectations.[11]

[11] Studies that document these abnormal post-earnings-announcement returns include Foster et al. (1984), Bernard and Thomas (1989, 1990), Bartov et al. (2000), Liang (2003), Livnat and Mendenhall (2006) and Lerman et al. (2007).

Michaely et al. (1995) found that share prices underreact to the announcement of both dividend initiations and omissions. They found market-adjusted excess returns averaged about 15 per cent over the two years following a dividend initiation and about −15 per cent following a dividend omission. This means that, historically, the market has substantially underreacted to these dividend events.

Many studies, including Loughran and Ritter (1995), Ikenberry et al. (1995), Spiess and Affleck-Graves (1995) and Brav et al. (2000), have documented similar results for equity issues and share repurchases. Shares realize negative returns over the five years following an equity issue and positive returns over the four years following share repurchases. These results suggest that firms have historically been able to time the equity market successfully, issuing equity when it is overpriced and repurchasing equity when it is underpriced.

As in all empirical investigations, there is always the concern that the testing and models used in the analysis may be mis-specified. Eckbo et al. (2000) suggested that since equity offerings reduce leverage, new issuers have reduced exposure to inflation and default risk, which in turn reduces their expected return. The long-term underperformance is thus a result of the changing characteristics of issuing firms, something that wasn't captured by prior studies. Similarly, if managers time the market with equity issues, they will issue equity when market valuations are high. Schultz (2003) showed, using statistical simulations, that when the *ex ante* expected abnormal return is zero, *ex post* long-term abnormal returns will be significantly negative in event time (using event studies) but not calendar time. Again, methodological considerations and not investor beliefs may be driving the post-earnings announcement drift.

Results

Result 19.13

Empirical evidence suggests that the market underreacts to the information revealed by earnings reports and announcements of some financial decisions. In the past, investors could have generated substantial profits by buying shares following favourable announcements and selling shares following unfavourable announcements.

Behavioural Explanations

Many economists are sceptical about purported market inefficiencies, and argue that much managerial and investor decision-making can be rationalized through behavioural explanations. For example, a paper by Daniel et al. (1998) suggested that investors often underreact to information provided by managers because they tend to be overconfident about their knowledge of the firm before the disclosure. In particular, since these investors think they have a precise valuation of the firm before the announcement, they update their valuation very little when they receive new information. Hong and Stein (1999) tried to explain this underreaction by considering the way in which information spreads in a market. They argued that, if new information diffusion is gradual, there will be an underreaction to corporate news in the shorter term. However, this underreaction means that traders who implement simple buy-and-sell trading strategies based on past short-term price performance will cause prices to overreact in the longer term. Jegadeesh and Titman (2001) reported long-term empirical evidence that supports these ideas.

Grinblatt and Han (2005) argued that short-term momentum in prices may be caused by investors holding on to shares that are performing badly, while at the same time selling strongly performing shares. This behavioural interpretation is known as the *disposition effect,* and was first introduced by Odean (1998). However, one of the weaknesses of the behavioural studies is that they do not explicitly take into account the effect of taxes on investor behaviour. George and Hwang (2007) put forward the idea that much of the momentum and long-term price reversals seen in markets is more to do with the fact that investors in strongly performing shares wish to delay the capital gains tax costs incurred when they eventually sell their shares. If investors rationally lock in capital gains for a long time, so as to reduce the present value of capital gains tax payments, the short- and long-term price patterns can be explained without resorting to behavioural explanations.

These explanations imply that financial markets do not incorporate new information efficiently into share valuations. They also suggest that there can be profit opportunities available to savvy investors who exploit the tendency of share prices to underreact to information events. Of course, even a market that was inefficient in the past may not continue to be so in the future. We thus urge readers who plan to implement trading strategies that take advantage of these apparent inefficiencies to exercise caution.

How Does the Availability of Cash Affect Investment Expenditures?

According to the adverse selection theory, firms will sometimes choose not to issue equity, and will instead pass up positive-NPV investments when they are unable to borrow. Therefore the theory suggests that a firm's borrowing capacity and the availability of cash may be important determinants of its investment expenditures. The effect of the availability of cash on investment choices is illustrated in the following discussion with Dan Franchi, the assistant treasurer at Unocal. When asked how changes in cash flow affect Unocal's investment expenditures, Franchi replied:

> If oil prices were to drop $4 per barrel, Unocal would cut back funding for capital expenditures . . . because of the lack of available cash, not because the projects became considerably worse. The additional projects that are taken when cash flows are high are projects that would have been attractive anyway, but would have been delayed if we had insufficient internal funds.[12]

Unocal generally does not consider ordinary equity issuance to be an attractive alternative for raising investment capital in the event of a cash shortfall caused by a drop in oil prices. In addition, the company is generally unwilling to fund new investments with debt if it means lowering its credit rating. Franchi indicated that the company was concerned that a weakened credit rating would put Unocal at a competitive disadvantage in attracting business overseas:

> We feel that over the long term, we're going to be competing with companies overseas that tend to have A credit ratings. As a BBB company, we would be at a competitive disadvantage in the long term. Potentially, when a foreign government decides who they would like to have working on a project, they could be looking at the financial strengths of the company. And they would be more likely to want to work with a company that is more financially sound. For example, all else equal, the Chinese government would rather enter a long-term arrangement with a AAA company than a BBB company.[13]

Empirical Evidence

A substantial amount of empirical evidence suggests that there is a fairly widespread tendency of firms to determine their level of investment expenditures, at least partially, based on the availability of cash flow, as the adverse selection theory predicts. Many studies have recorded that year-to-year changes in firms' capital expenditures are highly correlated with changes in their cash flows, but are much less correlated with changes in their share prices.[14] Most papers have found that the tendency to link new investment expenditures to the availability of cash flows is greater for firms that are cash constrained.

19.7 Summary and Conclusions

Often, a firm's managers possess information that outside investors lack. This chapter examined how these differences in information influence financial decisions. It found that if managers' objectives place significant weight on the current share price, these information differences will distort financial decisions in important ways. For example, firms will tend to invest less and bias their investments towards projects that pay off more quickly. Firms also will pay out higher dividends and choose to be more highly levered than they would otherwise be.

Since the distortions that arise from these information differences are costly, managers have an incentive to take steps that minimize the distortions. One way to reduce these information-related costs is to increase the information available to analysts and investors, which thus decreases management's information advantage. Doing this reduces the extent to which outside investors must rely on indirect indicators of value, such as dividends and debt ratios, which management can manipulate to the firm's long-term detriment. One also could reduce the severity of the information problem by designing compensation packages that reduce a manager's incentive to increase the firm's current share price.

It is unrealistic, however, to think that the distortions caused by information differences can be eliminated completely. The competitive disadvantage of making too much information about the firm

[12] Dan Franchi, telephone conversation with one of the authors, 2 May 1995.

[13] Ibid.

[14] See Fazzari et al. (1988), Whited (1992), Bond and Meghir (1994), Love (2003), Allayannis and Mozumdar (2004), Almeida et al. (2004) and Agca and Mozumdar (2008).

public limits the amount that firms should disclose. Moreover, as Chapter 18 emphasized, offsetting incentive problems exist when managers are indifferent to their firm's current share price. In reality, firms need to strike a balance between the motivational benefits of having a fluid job market that requires compensation based on short-term performance and the costs associated with the potential short-sightedness that such compensation plans promote.

Key Concepts

Result 19.1: Management incentives are influenced by a desire to increase both the firm's current share price and its intrinsic value. The weight that managers place on these potentially conflicting incentives is determined by, among other things, the manager's compensation and the security of the manager's job.

Result 19.2: Good decisions can reveal unfavourable information, and bad decisions can reveal favourable information. This means that:

- share price reactions are sometimes poor indicators of whether a decision has a positive or a negative effect on a firm's intrinsic value
- managers who are concerned about the current share prices of their firms may bias their decisions in ways that reduce the intrinsic values of their firms.

Result 19.3: Managers will select projects that pay off quickly over possibly higher-NPV projects that pay out over longer periods if they place significant weight on increasing their firm's short-term share price.

Result 19.4: Share prices increase, on average, when firms increase dividends, and decrease, on average, when they decrease dividends. Dividend signals are strongly related to future earnings predictions.

Result 19.5: An increased dividend implies, holding all else constant, higher cash flows and hence higher share prices. By cutting investment expenditures on items that cannot readily be observed by analysts, firms can increase reported earnings and dividends, thereby increasing their current share prices. A manager's incentive to temporarily boost the firm's share price may thus lead the firm to pass up positive-NPV investments.

Result 19.6: It is unlikely that signalling considerations explain why firms pay dividends rather than repurchase shares.

Result 19.7: A dividend increase or decrease can provide information to investors about:

- the firm's cash flows
- management's investment intentions.

In the latter case, if investors believe that an increased level of investment associated with a dividend cut is motivated by improved prospects, they will view the dividend cut favourably. However, if investors believe that managers will make negative-NPV investments, they will interpret a dividend cut as bad news.

Result 19.8: An increase in a firm's debt ratio is considered a favourable signal, because it indicates that managers believe the firm will be generating taxable earnings in the future, and that they are not overly concerned about incurring financial distress costs. Managers understand that their firm's share price is likely to respond favourably to higher leverage ratios, and may thus have an incentive to select higher leverage ratios than they would otherwise prefer.

Result 19.9: For a financial decision to convey favourable information credibly to investors, firms with poor prospects must find it costly to mimic the decisions made by firms with favourable prospects.

Result 19.10: A firm may pass up a positive-NPV investment project if it requires issuing underpriced equity. Since debt has a fixed claim on future cash flows, a firm's debt is less likely to be substantially undervalued. As a result, firms may prefer to finance new projects with debt rather than equity. With sufficiently high financial distress and adverse selection costs, however, firms may be better off passing up the positive-NPV investment.

Result 19.11: When firms are experiencing financial difficulties, they prefer equity to debt financing for several reasons. In particular, the tax advantages of debt may be less and the potential for suffering financial distress costs may be greater. Issuing ordinary equity in these situations may be a problem, however, given the negative information conveyed by an equity offering. Hence a preference share issue may offer the best source of capital.

Result 19.12: On average, share prices react favourably to:

- announcements that firms will be distributing cash to shareholders
- announcements that firms will increase their leverage.

Share prices react negatively, on average, to:

- announcements that firms will be raising cash
- announcements that firms will decrease their leverage.

These announcement returns can be explained by the information theories presented in this chapter, and the incentive theories presented in Chapter 18.

Result 19.13: Empirical evidence suggests that the market underreacts to the information revealed by earnings reports and announcements of some financial decisions. In the past, investors could have generated substantial profits by buying shares following favourable announcements and selling shares following unfavourable announcements.

Key Terms

Exercises

19.1 Describe how a firm's investment decisions might be made differently if its management is highly concerned about the firm's current share price.

19.2 Why might a firm choose to increase its debt level in response to favourable information about its future prospects?

19.3 Exhibit 19.5 shows that share prices of industrial firms react more negatively to equity issues than do utilities. Why do you think this is the case?

19.4 Classical finance theory suggests that firms take projects with positive NPVs regardless of the amount of cash the firm has available. However, empirical evidence suggests that the amount that firms invest is heavily dependent on their available cash flows. Why might this be?

19.5 Why might a manager close to retirement select a higher debt ratio than a manager far from retirement?

19.6 ABC Industries is considering an investment that requires the firm to issue new equity. The project will cost £100, but will add £120 to the firm's value. Although management believes the firm's value is £1,000 without the new project, outside investors value the firm at £600 without the project. If the firm currently has 100 shares outstanding, how many new shares must it issue to finance the project? Now assume that the true value of the firm will become known to the market shortly after the new equity has been issued. What will the firm's share price be at this time if it chooses to finance this new investment? What will the share price be if it chooses to pass up the investment?

19.7 As economies develop, disclosure laws generally get tougher and accounting information becomes more informative. Briefly describe how such changes in the quality of information affect the incentives of firms to be financed by either debt or equity.

19.8 If it was known that management was selling shares at the same time as it was increasing leverage, how would this affect the credibility of the signal? Why? What other actions or motivations by management could affect the credibility of such a signal?

19.9 The following table describes management's view of Abracadabra plc's future cash flows, along with the consensus view of outside analysts.

	Cash flows (3)		
State of the economy:	**Low**	**Average**	**High**
Management's beliefs	400	500	600
Analysts' beliefs	300	400	500
Cost of distress	100	150	200

If the analysts can be convinced that management's beliefs are correct, the firm's value will increase by €200. Assume that there are no tax or other benefits from debt apart from the information the debt may convey. However, if the promised interest payments exceed the cash flows, the firm will lose €100, €150 or €200 because of financial distress, depending on the state of the economy. Assuming that management wants to maximize the intrinsic value of the firm, how much debt will the firm take on? Now consider the possibility that management's incentives place an equal weight on the firm's intrinsic value and its current value. How much debt must the firm take on to credibly convince the analysts that their cash flow estimates are wrong? (*Hint:* consider management's incentive to mislead analysts if the analysts' original projections are correct.)

19.10 Analysts project that Infotech, an information services company, will have the following financial data for equally probable high and low states.

	Value (€)	
State	**Low**	**High**
Cash	100	100
Fixed asset value	200	300
Growth opportunity NPV	100	100

The firm is currently financed entirely with equity. The growth opportunity consists of a positive-NPV project with a required initial investment of €200 and a value of €300. Management, knowing with 100 per cent certainty whether the firm is in the high or low state, has a choice of taking the project and issuing debt, taking the project and issuing equity, or not taking the project and doing nothing. Examine the pay-offs to current shareholders in the high and low states for each of these three decisions. What if management is unable to issue debt? (*Hint:* which beliefs of investors are self-fulfilling?)

19.11 Mr Chan and Mr Smith are the CEOs of similar textile manufacturing firms. Chan is 64 years old and plans to retire next year. Smith is 52 years old and expects to remain with the firm for some time. Both firms have just announced 10 per cent increases in their earnings. Which firm should expect the greatest share price increase? Explain.

19.12 Gordon Wu (the largest shareholder of Hopewell) has just announced that he is planning to issue out-of-the-money covered warrants on 10 per cent of Hopewell's outstanding equity. Does this announcement make you more or less optimistic about Hopewell's future profits? Does it affect your assessment of Hopewell's volatility?

19.13 When firms increase leverage with exchange offers, what generally happens to their share prices? Why might this be?

19.14 Innovative Technologies produces high-tech equipment for the agriculture industry. This is a very risky firm, because the technology is not completely established, and demand for farm equipment is very cyclical and interest-rate sensitive. As a new start-up, Innovative Tech cannot obtain long-term straight debt. However, it can issue equity, issue convertible debt or obtain funds from its bank. Devise a financing strategy for Innovative under the following assumptions.

a Management believes the firm is fairly priced.

b Management believes the firm is slightly undervalued.

c Management believes the firm is substantially undervalued.

19.15 Divided Industries recently announced a substantial increase in its dividend payout. Shareholders complained, because the increased dividend would place an added tax burden on them. Subsequent to the announcement, however, the share price of Divided Industries increased 10 per cent. Does this share price increase indicate that the market viewed the dividend increase as a good decision?

19.16 Explain why the threat of hostile takeovers can make firms more short-term orientated.

19.17 Show in Example 19.7 that it never pays to issue debt in excess of €400 million.

References and Additional Reading

Agca, S. and Mozumdar, A. (2008) The impact of capital market imperfections on investment-cash flow sensitivity, *Journal of Banking and Finance*, 32(2): 207–216.

Aharony, J. and Swary, I. (1980) Quarterly dividend and earnings announcements and shareholders returns: an empirical analysis', *The Journal of Finance*, 35(1): 1–12.

Akerlof, G.A. (1970) The market for 'lemons': quality uncertainty and the market mechanism, *Quarterly Journal of Economics*, 84(3): 488–500.

Allayannis, G. and Mozumdar, A. (2004) The investment-cash flow sensitivity puzzle: can negative cash flow observations explain it?, *Journal of Banking and Finance*, 28(5): 901–931.

Allen, F., Bernardo, A. and Welch, I. (2000) A theory of dividends based on tax clienteles, *The Journal of Finance*, 55(6): 2499–2536.

Almeida, H., Campello, M. and Weisbach, M. (2004) The cash flow sensitivity of cash, *The Journal of Finance*, 59(4): 1777–1804.

Asquith, P. and Mullins, D.W. Jr. (1983) The impact of initiating dividend payments on shareholders' wealth, *Journal of Business*, 56(1): 77–96.

Asquith, P. and Mullins, D.W. Jr. (1986) Equity issues and offerings dilution, *Journal of Financial Economics*, 15, 61–89.

Bartov, E., Radharkrishnan, S. and Krinsky, I. (2000) Investor sophistication and patterns in equity returns after earnings announcements, *The Accounting Review*, 75(1): 43–63.

Bayless, M. and Chaplinsky, S. (1991) Expectations of security types and the information content of debt and equity offers, *Journal of Financial Intermediation*, 1(3): 195–214.

Bernard, V.L. and Thomas, J.K. (1989) Post-earnings-announcement drift: delayed price response or risk premium?, *Journal of Accounting Research*, 27(supplement): 1–48.

Bernard, V.L. and Thomas, J.K. (1990) Evidence that stock prices do not fully reflect implications of current earnings for future earnings, *Journal of Accounting and Economics*, 13(4): 305–340.

Bhattacharya, S. (1979) Imperfect information, dividend policy, and "the bird-in-the-hand" fallacy, *Bell Journal of Economics*, 10(1): 259–270.

Bond, S. and Meghir, C. (1994) Dynamic investment models and the firm's financial policy, *The Review of Economic Studies*, 61(2): 197–222.

Brav, A., Gezcy, C. and Gompers, P. (2000) Is the abnormal return following equity issues anomalous?, *Journal of Financial Economics*, 56(2): 209–249.

Brennan, M. (1990) Latent assets, *The Journal of Finance*, 45(3): 709–730.

Brennan, M. and Hughes, P. (1991) Stock prices and the supply of information, *The Journal of Finance*, 46(5): 1665–1691.

Burns, N., Kedia, S. and Lipson, M. (2010). Institutional ownership and monitoring: Evidence from financial misreporting, *Journal of Corporate Finance*, 16(4): 443–455.

Chaplinsky, S. and Ramchand, L. (2000) The impact of global equity offerings, *The Journal of Finance*, 55(6): 2767–2789.

Charest, G. (1978) Dividend information, stock returns and market efficiency–II, *Journal of Financial Economics*, 6(2–3): 297–330.

Chen, G., Firth, M. and Gao, N. (2002) The information content of concurrently announced earnings, cash dividends, and equity dividends: an investigation of the Chinese equity market, *Journal of International Financial Management & Accounting*, 13(2): 101–124.

Chen, K. and Yuan, H. (2004) Earnings management and capital resource allocation: evidence from China's accounting-based regulation of rights issues, *The Accounting Review*, 79(3): 645–665.

Conroy, R., Eades, K. and Harris, R. (2000) A test of the relative pricing effects of dividends and earnings: evidence from simultaneous announcements in Japan, *Journal of Finance*, 55(3): 1199–1227.

Daniel, K., Hirshleifer, D. and Subrahmanyam, A. (1998) Investor psychology and security market under- and over-reactions, *The Journal of Finance*, 53(6): 1839–1885.

Dann, L.Y. (1981) Ordinary equity repurchases: an analysis of returns to bondholders and shareholders, *Journal of Financial Economics*, 9(2): 113–138.

Dann, L.Y. and Mikkelson, W.H. (1984) Convertible debt issuance, capital structure change and financing-related information: some new evidence, *Journal of Financial Economics*, 13(2): 157–186.

Denis, D.J., Denis, D.K. and Sarin, A. (1994) The information content of dividend changes: cash flow signaling, overinvestment, and dividend clienteles, *Journal of Financial and Quantitative Analysis*, 29(4): 567–587.

Diamond, D.W. (1991) Debt maturity structure and liquidity risk, *Quarterly Journal of Economics*, 106(3): 709–737.

Dietrich, J.R. (1984) Effects of early bond refunding: an empirical investigation of security returns, *Journal of Accounting and Economics*, 6(1): 67–96.

Donaldson, G. (1961) *Corporate Debt Capacity: A Study of Corporate Debt Policy and the Determination of Corporate Debt Capacity*. Boston, MA: Harvard Graduate School of Business Administration.

Eckbo, B.E. (1986) Valuation effects of corporate debt offerings, *Journal of Financial Economics*, 15(1–2): 119–151.

Eckbo, B.E. and Masulis, R. (1995) Seasoned equity offerings: a survey, Chapter 31 in *Handbooks in Operations Research and Management Science: Volume 9, Finance*, in Jarrow, R., Maksimovic, V., and Ziemba, W. (eds). Amsterdam, The Netherlands: Elsevier Science.

Eckbo, B.E. and Norli, Ø. (2005) Liquidity risk, leverage and long-run IPO returns, *Journal of Corporate Finance*, 11(1–2): 1–35.

Eckbo B.E., Masulis, R. and Norli, Ø. (2000) Seasoned public offerings: resolution of the 'new issues puzzle', *Journal of Financial Economics*, 56(2): 251–291.

Faccio, M., Lang, L. and Young, L. (2001) Dividends and expropriation, *American Economic Review*, 91(1): 54–78.

Fazzari, S., Hubbard, R.G. and Petersen, B. (1988) Financing constraints and corporate investment, *Brookings Papers on Economic Activity*, 19(1): 141–206.

Flannery, M.J. (1986) Asymmetric information and risky debt maturity choice, *The Journal of Finance*, 41(1): 19–37.

Foster, G., Olsen, C. and Shevlin, T. (1984) Earnings releases, anomalies, and the behavior of security returns, *The Accounting Review*, 59(4): 574–603.

George, T.J. and Hwang, C.-Y. (2007) Long-term return reversals: overreaction or taxes?, *The Journal of Finance*, 62(6): 2865–2896.

Grinblatt, M. and Han, B. (2005) Prospect theory, mental accounting, and momentum, *Journal of Financial Economics*, 78(2): 311–339.

Grinblatt, M., Masulis, R. and Titman, S. (1984) The valuation effects of equity splits and equity dividends, *Journal of Financial Economics*, 13(4): 461–490.

Hackethal, A. and Zdantchouk, A. (2006) Signalling power of open market share repurchases in Germany, *Financial Markets and Portfolio Management*, 20(2): 123–151.

Hadlock, C., Ryngaert, M. and Thomas, S. (2001) Corporate structure and equity offerings: are there benefits to diversification?, *Journal of Business*, 74(4): 613–635.

Hatakeda, T. and Isagawa, N. (2004) Share price behavior surrounding equity repurchase announcements: evidence from Japan, *Pacific Basin Finance Journal*, 12(3): 271–290.

Healy, P.M. and Palepu, K.G. (1988) Earnings information conveyed by dividend initiations and omissions, *Journal of Financial Economics*, 21(2): 149–175.

Hill, P. and Hillier, D. (2009) Market feedback, investment constraints, and managerial behavior, *European Financial Management*, 15(3): 584–605.

Hillier, D., Hodgson, A., Stevenson-Clarke, P. and Lhaopadchan, S. (2008) Accounting window dressing and template regulation: a case study of the Australian credit union industry, *Journal of Business Ethics*, 83(3): 579–593.

Hong, H. and Stein, J. (1999) A unified theory of underreaction, momentum trading, and overreaction in asset markets, *The Journal of Finance*, 54(6): 2143–2184.

Hoshi, T., Kashyap, A. and Scharfstein, D. (1991) Corporate structure, liquidity and investment: evidence from Japanese industrial groups, *Quarterly Journal of Economics*, 106(1): 33–60.

Ikenberry, D., Lakonishok, J. and Vermaelen, T. (1995) Market underreaction to open market share repurchases, *Journal of Financial Economics*, 39(2–3): 181–208.

James, C. (1987) Some evidence on the uniqueness of bank loans, *Journal of Financial Economics*, 19(2): 217–235.

Jegadeesh, N. and Titman, S. (2001) Profitability of momentum strategies: an evaluation of alternative explanations, *The Journal of Finance*, 56(2): 699–718.

Jones, J. (1991) Earnings management during import relief investigation, *Journal of Accounting Research*, 29(2): 193–228.

Kaplan, S. (1994) Top executive rewards and firm performance: a comparison of Japan and the United States, *Journal of Political Economy*, 102(3): 510–546.

Lambert, R.A., Leuz, C. and Verrecchia, R.E. (2012). Information asymmetry, information precision, and the cost of capital, *Review of Finance*, 16(1): 1-29.

La Porta, R., Lopez-de-Silanes, F., Shleifer, A. and Vishney, R. (2000) Agency problems and dividend policies around the world, *The Journal of Finance*, 55(1): 1–33.

Lang, L.H.P. and Litzenberger, R.H. (1989) Dividend announcements: cash flow signaling vs free cash flow hypothesis, *Journal of Financial Economics*, 24(1): 181–192.

Leland, H. and Pyle, D. (1977) Informational asymmetries, financial structure and financial intermediation, *The Journal of Finance*, 32(2): 317–387.

Lerman, A., Livnat, J. and Mendenhall, R. (2007) Double surprise into future returns, *Financial Analysts Journal*, 63(4): 63–71.

Liang, L. (2003) Post-earnings announcement drift and market participants information processing biases, *Review of Accounting Studies,* 8(2–3): 321–345.

Liberty, S. and Zimmerman, J. (1986) Labor union contract negotiations and accounting choices, *Accounting Review,* 61(4): 692–712.

Linn, S.C. and Pinegar, M.J. (1988) The effect of issuing preferred stock on common and preferred stockholder wealth, *Journal of Financial Economics,* 22(1): 155–184.

Livnat, J. and Mendenhall, R. (2006) Comparing the post-earnings announcement drift for surprises calculated from analyst and time-series forecasts, *Journal of Accounting Research,* 44(1): 177–205.

Loughran, T. and Ritter, J. (1995) The new issues puzzle, *The Journal of Finance,* 50(1): 23–52.

Love, I. (2003) Financial development and financial constraints: international evidence from the structural investment model, *The Review of Financial Studies,* 16(3): 765–791.

Masulis, R.W. (1980) The effects of capital structure change on security prices: a study of exchange offers, *Journal of Financial Economics,* 8(2): 139–177.

Masulis, R.W. (1983) The impact of capital structure change on firm value: some estimates, *The Journal of Finance,* 38(1): 107–126.

Masulis, R.W. and Korwar, A.N. (1986) Seasoned equity offerings: an empirical investigation, *Journal of Financial Economics,* 15(1–2): 91–118.

McConnell, J.J. and Schlarbaum, G.G. (1981) Evidence on the impact of exchange offers on security prices: the case of income bonds, *Journal of Business,* 54(1): 65–85.

Meyer, J.R. and Kuh, E. (1957) *The Investment Decision.* Cambridge, MA: Harvard University Press.

Michaely, R., Thaler, R. and Womack, K. (1995) Price reactions to dividend initiations and omissions: overreaction or drift?, *The Journal of Finance,* 50(2): 573–608.

Mikkelson, W.H. (1981) Convertible calls and security returns, *Journal of Financial Economics,* 9(3): 237–264.

Mikkelson, W.H. and Partch, M.M. (1986) Valuation effects of security offerings and the issuance process, *Journal of Financial Economics,* 15(1–2): 31–60.

Miller, M.H. and Rock, K. (1985) Dividend policy under asymmetric information, *The Journal of Finance,* 40(4): 1031–1051.

Myers, S.C. (1984) The capital structure puzzle, *The Journal of Finance,* 39(3): 575–592.

Myers, S.C. and Majluf, N.S. (1984) Corporate financing and investment decisions when firms have information that investors do not have, *Journal of Financial Economics,* 13(2): 187–221.

Narayanan, M.P. (1985) Managerial incentives for short-term results, *The Journal of Finance,* 40(5): 1469–1484.

Odean, T. (1998) Are investors reluctant to realize their losses?, *The Journal of Finance,* 53(5): 1775–1798.

Pettway, R.H. and Radcliff, R.C. (1985) Impacts of new equity sales upon electric utility share prices, *Financial Management,* 14(1): 16–25.

Rees, W. (1996) The impact of open market equity repurchases on UK equity prices, *European Journal of Finance,* 2(4): 353–370.

Ross, S. (1977) The determinants of financial structure: the incentive signalling approach, *Bell Journal of Economics,* 8(1): 23–40.

Schipper, K. and Smith, A. (1986) A comparison of equity carve-outs and seasoned equity offerings: share price effects and corporate restructuring, *Journal of Financial Economics,* 15(1–2): 153–186.

Schultz, P. (2003) Pseudo market timing and the long-run underperformance of IPOs, *The Journal of Finance,* 58(2): 483–518.

Seyhun, H.N. (1986) Insiders' profits, costs of trading, and market efficiency, *Journal of Financial Economics,* 16(2): 189–212.

Shivakumar, L. (2000) Do firms mislead investors by overstating earnings before seasoned equity offerings?, *Journal of Accounting and Economics,* 29(3): 339–371.

Smith, C.W., Jr. (1986) Raising capital: theory and evidence, *Midland Corporate Finance Journal,* 4(4): 4–22.

Soter, D., Brigham, E. and Evanson, P. (1996) The dividend cut "heard 'round the world": the case of FPL, *Journal of Applied Corporate Finance,* 9(1): 4–16.

Spence, M. (1973) Job market signalling, *Quarterly Journal of Economics,* 87(3): 355–374.

Spiess, D.K. and Affleck-Graves, J. (1995) Underperformance in long-run stock returns following seasoned equity offerings, *Journal of Financial Economics,* 38(3): 243–267.

Stein, J.C. (1989) Efficient capital markets, inefficient firms: a model of myopic corporate behavior, *Quarterly Journal of Economics,* 104(4): 655–669.

Subrahmanyam, A. and Titman S. (1999) The going-public decision and the development of financial markets, *The Journal of Finance,* 54(3): 1045–1082.

Teoh, S.H., Welch, I. and Wong, T.J. (1998a) Earnings management and the post-issue performance of seasoned equity offerings, *Journal of Financial Economics,* 50(1): 63–99.

Teoh, S.H., Welch, I. and Wong, T.J. (1998b) Earnings management and the long-term market performance of initial public offerings, *The Journal of Finance,* 53(6): 1935–1974.

Thomas, G. and Hwang, C.-Y. (2007) Long-term return reversals: overreaction or taxes?, *The Journal of Finance,* 62(6): 2865–2896.

Van Bommel, J. and Vermaelen, T. (2003) Post IPO capital expenditures and market feedback, *Journal of Banking and Finance,* 27(2): 275–305.

Vermaelen, T. (1981) Common stock repurchases and market signaling: an empirical study, *Journal of Financial Economics,* 9(2): 138–183.

Whited, T. (1992) Debt, liquidity constraints, and corporate investment: evidence from panel data, *The Journal of Finance,* 47(4): 1425–1460.

Woolridge, J.R. and Ghosh, C. (1985) Dividend cuts: do they always signal bad news?, *Midland Corporate Finance Journal,* 3(2): 20–32.

Chapter

20

Mergers and Acquisitions

Learning Objectives

After reading this chapter, you should be able to:

- Understand how taxes, operating synergies and management incentive conflicts provide motives for mergers and acquisitions.
- Discuss the advantages and disadvantages of corporate diversification.
- Know how and why the share prices of bidders and targets react around the time of acquisition announcements.
- Describe the empirical evidence regarding the gains from mergers and acquisitions.
- Apply the tools developed in Chapters 9–13 to value potential acquisitions, and the ideas developed in Chapters 14–19 to understand how such acquisitions should be financed.
- Describe how acquiring firms determine their bidding strategies, and how the targets of unwanted takeovers defend themselves.

In January 2022, Microsoft announced that it had acquired the game development and interactive content publisher, Activision Blizzard, inc. The purpose of the merger was to give Microsoft a strong foothold in the new metaverse environments, which Facebook (now Meta) embraced the year earlier. There were a number of uncertainties with this acquisition, common to others of the same type. First, the sector was different from the core business of Microsoft, which is a principally a software platform firm. Second, would the firm be able to take advantage of the joint strengths to create additional value for shareholders, where the two companies operating separately could not? What were the strategic strengths and weaknesses of the acquisition and were these identified fully beforehand? Whenever a firm undertakes a new investment decision, there is a lot that may or may not transpire as expected. This chapter provides insights into the main issues a manager must consider.

A **merger** is a transaction that combines two firms into one new firm. An **acquisition** is the purchase of one firm by another. In some cases, two organizations are combined into one, and two equities become one. In others, such as leveraged buyouts (LBOs), there is a transfer of ownership of a single firm. Despite the formal distinction we have drawn between a merger and an acquisition, the two terms are often used interchangeably.

From the Modigliani–Miller Theorem (see Chapter 14) we learned that, with perfect capital markets, value can neither be created nor destroyed by repackaging a firm's securities, as long as the repackaging leaves the total cash flows of the firms unchanged. Similarly, any merger or acquisition that has no effect on the after-tax cash flows of either firm will not create or destroy value. This means that, in order for a merger or acquisition to create value, the after-tax cash flows of the combined firm must exceed the sum of the after-tax cash flows of the individual firms before the merger.

Although sometimes one observes what is called a 'merger of equals', in most cases the parties in a merger can be classified as an **acquiring firm**, or bidder, which initiates the offer, and a **target firm**, or acquired firm, which receives the offer. In most cases, the acquiring firm offers to buy the target's shares at a substantial premium over the target's prevailing share price. For example, in the Microsoft–Activision Blizzard acquisition (in this chapter's opening vignette), Microsoft's offer was $95 per share, 45 per cent higher than Activision Blizzard's estimated value at the time of the transaction. Although this **takeover premium**, the difference between the prior share price and the amount offered, is somewhat larger than average, it is not unusually large. Takeover premiums generally range from 50 per cent to 100 per cent of the target firm's share price before the acquisition.

What motivates acquiring firms to offer such large premiums to acquire existing companies? Is it possible that a change in the ownership of a firm can create the kind of value implied by these takeover premiums? This chapter presents several potential ways in which value can be created by combining two firms. In addition, it is possible that the acquiring firm is willing to pay a premium for a target because the bidder's management believes the target is worth more than its current market value. For example, the bidder may have private information that the firm owns valuable assets that are not reported on its balance sheet. Large premiums may also reflect either managerial mistakes or non-value-maximizing incentives. For example, the bidder's management may want to buy the target because expanding or diversifying the firm may generate larger salaries, more perks and greater job security.

In addition to analysing what motivates mergers and acquisitions from both theoretical and empirical perspectives, it is important to understand mergers and acquisitions from an institutional perspective. This chapter therefore begins with a discussion of the history of mergers, and develops a taxonomy for classifying mergers and acquisitions.

20.1 A History of Mergers and Acquisitions

Global merger and acquisition (M&A) activity has increased substantially since the mid-1960s. In 1967, the total dollar value of all corporate mergers and acquisitions was under $20 billion; by 1984 this had grown to a total dollar volume of $100 billion; and by 2021 the dollar volume equalled $5.9 trillion.

Exhibit 20.1 graphs the total global market value of mergers and acquisitions completed in each year from 1985 to 2021. The exhibit shows that the size of M&A activity started to increase substantially around 1997. There are clear cycles in merger activity with peaks in 1999, 2007, 2015 and 2021.

The increased takeover activity that started in 1997 can be attributed to several factors, most notably the emergence of the high-technology industry. The temporary decline in M&A activity after 2001 and 2007 was caused by the bursting of the dotcom bubble and global financial crisis, respectively. It is more difficult to explain why mergers dropped after 2015, except that 2016 saw Donald Trump become President of the US and the UK voted to leave the European Union. This is supported by Bonaime et al. (2018), who suggest that merger and acquisition activity is negatively correlated with political uncertainty.

Exhibit 20.2 lists the largest M&A deals since 2000. There are two interesting things to note from this exhibit. The first is that most of the mergers are between companies in the same country. The second thing to note is most are horizontal mergers involving firms in the same industries. In particular, these large mergers created some of the largest oil, financial services and telecommunications companies in the world.

Finally, in many countries, M&A activity is uncommon. For example, in continental Europe there have been relatively few instances, in comparison with the United States and United Kingdom. This is because of the strength of anti-takeover legislation in many countries. For example, the hostile takeover of Mannesmann by Vodafone in 2000 was the very first in German corporate history. However, things are changing, because of the increase in shareholder activism and better corporate governance.

Exhibit 20.1 Dollar Volume ($billions) of Global Mergers and Acquisitions by Year

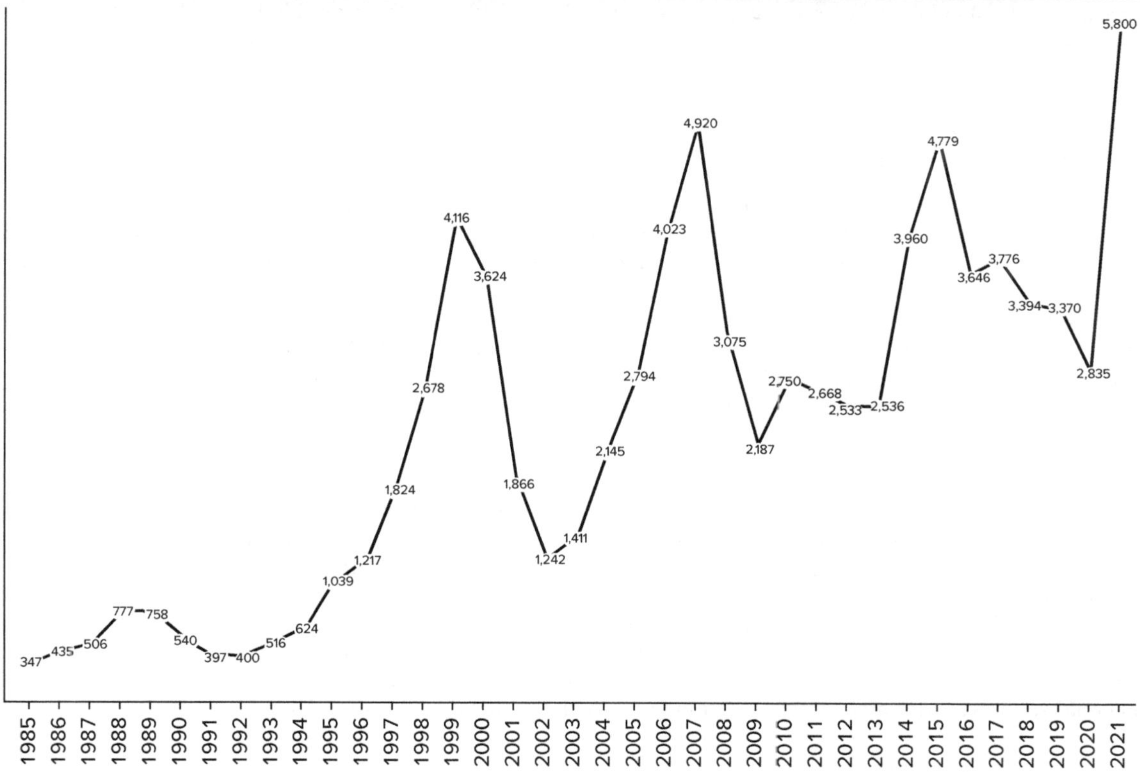

Source: Institute for Mergers, Acquisitions & Alliances.

Exhibit 20.2 Largest Mergers since 2000

Rank	Year	Acquirer	Target	Value ($billions)
1	2000	Vodafone Airtouch	Mannesmann	183.0
2	2001	America Online	Time Warner	182.0
3	2013	Verizon Communications	Vodafone Group	130
4	2015	Dow Chemical	E.I. du Pont de Nemours	130
5	2019	United Technologies	Raytheon	121
6	2015	AB InBev	SABMiller	107
7	2007	Gaz de France	Suez S.A.	107
8	2015	Heinz	Kraft	100
9	2001	GlaxoWellcome	SmithKline Beecham	78.7
10	2008	Gaz de France	Suez	75.2

Source: *Thomson Financial.* © 2022 Thomson Reuters

20.2 Types of Merger and Acquisition

There are probably almost as many types of merger and acquisition as there are bidders and targets. However, investment bankers find it useful to define three different categories of M&A transaction:

1. strategic acquisitions
2. financial acquisitions
3. conglomerate acquisitions.

Acquisitions are also often categorized as being friendly or hostile. An offer made directly to the firm's management or its board of directors is characterized as a **friendly takeover**. However, the managers of the target firm often object to being taken over, forcing the bidding firm to make a hostile offer for the target firm.

In a **hostile takeover**, the acquirer often bypasses the target's management and approaches the target company's shareholders directly with a tender offer for the purchase of their shares. A **tender offer** is an offer to purchase a certain number of shares at a specific price and on a specific date, generally for cash. Although a tender offer is usually associated with a hostile takeover, it also is used in friendly takeovers when the target's management approves the offer before it is presented to shareholders.

Strategic Acquisitions

In many cases, strategic mergers can be viewed as horizontal mergers. A **strategic acquisition** involves **operating synergies,** which means that the two firms are more profitable combined than separate. In the 1990s, strategic acquisitions became much more popular, and they are now the dominant form of acquisition.

The operating synergies in a strategic acquisition may occur because the combining firms were former competitors. Alternatively, one firm may have products or talents that fit well with those of another firm. For example, Microsoft's acquisition of Activision Blizzard for $68.7 billion would be considered a strategic acquisition, because it gave Microsoft access to the resources needed to exploit developments in the metaverse. You could say it was also a cheap way of competing with the metaverse leader, Meta.

Financial Acquisitions

Investment bankers generally classify an acquisition that includes no operating synergies as a **financial acquisition**. In a financial acquisition, the bidder usually believes that the price of the firm's equity is less than the value of the firm's assets. In contrast to strategic acquisitions, financial acquisitions have declined substantially since the late 1980s.

A financial acquisition is sometimes motivated by the tax gains associated with the acquisition. Alternatively, the acquirer may believe that the target firm's assets are undervalued because the equity market is ignoring important information. The most common motivation for a financial acquisition, however, is that the acquirer believes that the target firm is undervalued relative to its assets because it is badly managed. In most cases, a financial acquisition motivated by the acquirer's dismal view of target management is hostile. This type of acquisition is sometimes referred to as a **disciplinary takeover**.

For example, Ryanair, the budget airline carrier, made a bid for its domestic competitor, Aer Lingus, in 2008 on the basis that the Aer Lingus management had made the airline a marginal competitor in regional passenger business. However, the Aer Lingus management rebuffed the attempt, and argued that Ryanair was effectively attempting to get hold of its substantial cash reserves at an extremely low price. The Irish government, one of Aer Lingus' major shareholders, publicly stated that Ryanair had significantly undervalued Aer Lingus shares. Unsurprisingly, Ryanair failed in its takeover attempt.

Financial acquisitions are often structured as leveraged buyouts (LBOs). In most leveraged buyouts, an individual or a group, often led by a firm's own management, arranges to buy a public company and take it private. Thus all the publicly traded shares are purchased, and the firm ceases to be a public company. These are referred to as *leveraged* buyouts because the transactions are financed mainly with debt.

Because the acquirers in LBOs have no other assets, there are no potential synergies. Hence operating improvements must come from better management and improved incentives.

Conglomerate Acquisitions

A third type of acquisition, a **conglomerate (or diversifying) acquisition**, involves firms with no apparent potential for operating synergies. In this sense, the conglomerate acquisition is similar to the financial acquisition described above. However, conglomerate acquisitions are more likely to be motivated by **financial synergies**, which lower a firm's cost of capital, and thus create value even when the operations of merged firms do not benefit from the combination. As we shall discuss below, financial synergies can arise because of taxes as well as because of the information and incentive problems discussed in Chapters 16–19.

Most of the mergers that occurred in the United States during the 1950s, 1960s and 1970s were conglomerate mergers. A popular explanation for the predominance of conglomerate mergers during that time was that regulators would not approve most strategic combinations because of antitrust considerations. However, some authors have noted that conglomerate acquisitions have also been common in countries without strong antitrust regulations.[1] They have become much less common since then, reflecting either the loosening of antitrust rules that have allowed more strategic combinations or an increase in the efficiency of financial markets, which could have the effect of reducing the financial synergies associated with a merger.

Exhibit 20.3 presents a list of some of the world's largest conglomerates, together with their range of operations.

Summary of Mergers and Acquisitions

Exhibit 20.4 summarizes the three categories of acquisition discussed in this section. Note that individual acquisitions do not necessarily fit neatly into any one box. For example, Malcolm Glazer's acquisition of Manchester United would generally be categorized as a financial acquisition. However, Malcolm Glazer might have believed that an important source of value in the acquisition was the possible synergy between Manchester United and the American Football NFL team Tampa Bay Buccaneers, which he also owns. If this were the case, the acquisition could be categorized as a strategic acquisition.

Exhibit 20.3 Examples of Conglomerates

Conglomerate	Country	Industries
3M	US	Electronics, healthcare, optics, industrial chemicals
ABB	Switzerland	Power, automation, robotics
BAE Systems	United Kingdom	Aviation, electronics, munitions, defence
Bidvest	South Africa	Distribution, food, banking
Dassault Group	France	Aviation, media, real estate, football
Airbus Group	Europe	Aviation, military, space
Leonardo	Italy	Hi-tech, defence, space, transport, energy
Gazprom	Russia	Energy, finance, media, aviation
Impresa	Portugal	Media, TV, digital
Marfin Investment Group	Greece	Aviation, hotels, real estate, telecommunications
Maersk	Denmark	Transportation, energy, retail, energy
Norsk Hydro	Norway	Metals, hydro power, solar power
Philips	The Netherlands	Electronics, lighting, medical
Sandvik	Sweden	Hi-tech, metals, mining, construction
Siemens	Germany	Healthcare, energy, industry automation
Valmet	Finland	Machinery, aviation, transportation, military

[1] See, for example, Matsusaka (1996) and Comment and Jarrell (1995).

Exhibit 20.4 Types of Acquisition

Type of acquisition	Primary motivation	Hostile or friendly	Trend
Strategic	Operating synergies	Usually friendly	Increasing importance in recent years
Financial	Taxes, incentive improvements	Often hostile	Mainly a phenomenon of the 1980s
Conglomerate	Financial synergies, taxes and incentives	Hostile or friendly	Mainly a phenomenon of the 1960s and 1970s

20.3 Recent Trends in Takeover Activity

The volume of takeover activity has reached record levels since the turn of the century. However, the characteristics of recent takeovers are very different from those of the takeovers of the 1980s and 1990s. As we discuss below, in the last few years hostile takeovers have increased substantially.

The Fall and Rise of Hostile Takeovers

During the 1990s, the number of hostile takeovers and leveraged buyouts declined substantially. Andrade et al. (2001) reported that over 14 per cent of the bids in the 1980s were hostile, and about half of those were successful. In the 1990s, only about 4 per cent of the bids were hostile, and about one-third of these hostile bids failed. Holmstrom and Kaplan (2001) reported that leveraged buyout activity, which was often part of, or in response to, hostile offers, constituted close to 2 per cent of equity market value in the late 1980s but was virtually non-existent in the 1990s.

During periods of economic stress, companies tend to focus on less risky investments, and M&As are no different. In addition, the proliferation of hedge funds has introduced some interesting dynamics into the objectives of target shareholders. When hostile takeovers are announced, hedge funds quickly buy the target shares in order to earn a quick return from the subsequent price run-up. Since hedge funds have little loyalty to incumbent management groups, it is considerably easier for hostile takeovers to be successful.

Regionally, there are differences in merger and takeover trends, especially with respect to hostile takeovers. In the USA, *poison pills* are common. Poison pills are mechanisms that allow existing shareholders to purchase large amounts of unissued company equity when an investor acquires more than a minimum level of the company's shares. This defensive strategy clearly makes it more difficult for hostile takeovers to be successful. In Europe, poison pills are less common, and sometimes illegal. As a result, hostile takeover activity has been at its highest there.

20.4 Sources of Takeover Gains

Section 20.2 categorized takeovers according to the sources of takeover gains. This section examines the various sources in more detail. Result 20.1 summarizes the four main sources of takeover gains that were discussed briefly.

Results

Result 20.1

The main sources of takeover gains are:

- taxes
- operating synergies
- target incentive problems
- financial synergies.

We discuss each of these sources in turn.

Tax Motivations

Tax laws change substantially from year to year, and differ from country to country. As a result, we can provide only a brief overview of the relevant tax issues in this chapter. Taxation is governed by accounting rules, and the USA and the rest of the world have some differences in the way in which taxation for mergers and acquisitions is treated. Recently, there has been a drive towards greater convergence of tax rules, and the FASB (USA) and IASB (over 100 countries) have released a joint proposal to deal with mergers.

Acquiring Loss-Makers

One way to reduce the tax bill of a corporation is to acquire a firm that is unprofitable, and making a loss on operations. The combined firm will need to consolidate its accounts, and the taxable loss of the target will offset the taxable profit of the acquirer. Although this type of shopping activity will reduce the tax bill of the acquirer, which causes an increased value because of the higher tax shield, it is only worthwhile if ongoing synergies are found to increase the value of the combined firm in the future.

The Tax Gain from Leverage

Additional tax savings arise in cases where acquisitions are funded primarily with debt. The tax gain associated with these leverage-increasing combinations can be thought of as a financial synergy. As Chapter 14 discussed, a tax gain is associated with leverage because of the tax deductibility of debt interest payments. However, it is important to ask whether or not a takeover is required to accomplish this leverage increase before attributing this leverage-related tax gain to an acquisition.

The typical takeover results in increased leverage for several reasons. First, the combined firm is likely to be better diversified than the separate firms, and thus is less likely to have financial difficulties, or find itself with excess tax shields for any given level of debt financing. A second possibility is that the target and the bidder are underleveraged, and use the takeover as a means of increasing their combined debt-to-equity ratio. The firms may have been underleveraged because of the incentive reasons discussed in Chapter 18 or, as Chapter 15 discussed, because of the personal tax costs associated with increasing leverage.

Operating Synergies

In order for mergers to generate operating synergies, the uniting of two firms must either improve productivity or cut costs so that the unlevered cash flows of the combined firm exceed the combined unlevered cash flows of the individual firms. By definition, a target firm that provides such synergies is worth more to a potential acquirer than it is worth operating as an independent company.

Sources and Examples of Operating Synergies

There are several potential sources of operating synergy. For example, a **vertical merger** – that is, a merger between a supplier and a customer – can eliminate various co-ordination and bargaining problems between the supplier and the customer.[2] Oil companies are excellent examples of vertical integration. All the multinational oil corporations, such as BP, Shell and ExxonMobil, have operations spanning the exploration phase through to the final distribution phase. The gains from a **horizontal merger** – a merger between competitors – can include a less competitive product market as well as cost savings that occur when, for example, firms combine research and development facilities, combine sales forces, or dispose of underutilized computers and sales outlets.

Examining differences in innovation culture, Bena and Li (2013) report that combining innovation cultures in bidder and target firms can create value. Additional operating synergies arise when the merged firm can benefit from the ability to transfer resources from one division to another, and, as uncertainty increases, this option to transfer resources becomes increasingly valuable (see Chapter 12). Another explanation is that increases in cash flow uncertainty leads firms to pursue vertical mergers as an operational hedging strategy (Garfinkel and Hankins 2011).

Measuring Operating Synergies

Although there is substantial anecdotal evidence that operating synergies can be large, it is difficult to measure empirically the extent to which mergers have generated operating synergies, for reasons to be discussed shortly. Moreover, it is difficult to use the available empirical data to determine the extent to which value is created from operating synergies instead of other sources, such as tax savings or incentive improvements.

---

[2] For a discussion of these co-ordination and bargaining problems, see Klein et al. (1978) and Grossman and Hart (1986).

Management Incentive Issues and Takeovers

Chapter 18 described various ways in which the interests of managers can deviate from the interests of shareholders. Disciplinary takeovers are generally intended to correct these non-value-maximizing policies.

Disciplinary Takeovers and Leveraged Buyouts

Disciplinary takeovers are usually hostile, often lead to the break-up of large diversified corporations, and result in job losses for many of the target firm's top managers. For these reasons, disciplinary takeovers are more controversial than synergy-motivated strategic acquisitions. Disciplinary takeovers are particularly controversial when the acquirer, often referred to as the **raider,** is a relatively thinly capitalized individual or firm seeking to acquire a much bigger enterprise, using debt financing. These takeovers are generally structured as leveraged buyouts (LBOs).

LBO financing also has been used, albeit in a friendly way, by the top managers of firms who wish to buy their own firms and take them private. This type of LBO is often referred to as a **management buyout (MBO).** In contrast to the disciplinary takeover, the firm's top managers remain the same after an MBO.

In MBOs, as well as in hostile LBOs that do not involve management, we do not observe a union of two firms, so there can be no synergies. The gain from these takeovers then has to come from either tax savings or management improvements. Proponents of LBOs argue that firm value can still be improved by changing management incentives, even when the top managers are not replaced. These proponents argue that it is the change in ownership rather than the change in the actual managers that creates value in these transactions.

The changes in ownership structure can result in dramatic changes in management incentives following LBOs. Specifically, executives who had previously owned less than 1 per cent of the firm often find themselves owning more than 10 per cent; with additional equity options, they have the opportunity to accumulate substantially more equity in the event that the firm does well. Although the potential gain to executives is clearly greater following an LBO, there also is much less protection on the downside. Given the high leverage ratio of the post-LBO firm, the margin of error is much lower. If the firm is not successful, it will soon be bankrupt and the top executives will lose everything. Hence, following LBOs, executives have a much greater incentive to make the firm more profitable.

Incentives and Wealth Transfers

When firms are acquired, losers as well as winners emerge. For example, when TPG Capital took over Alltel in a leveraged buyout (see the opening vignette in Chapter 16), existing Alltel bonds were downgraded because of the perceived increase in the probability of their default. Employees, however, are often the more visible losers in takeovers. Critics of these takeovers have argued that a large part of the observed gain in many hostile takeovers comes at the expense of the target's employees, either through layoffs or through salary reductions.

The relationship between hostile takeovers and employee layoffs may simply reflect the need for a different type of manager at different stages of a corporation's growth. To build an effective organization, a growing firm requires managers who are good team players and who have a sincere interest in helping other individuals develop the skills needed to make the firm prosper. In most cases, however, the individuals best suited for nurturing and developing others are not particularly well suited to fire these same employees when downsizing is necessary. 'Nice guy', team-playing managers will find themselves recipients of unwanted takeover offers as a consequence of their reluctance to downsize their organizations. When these hostile bids are successful, 'more ruthless' managers are better suited to carry out the task of shrinking the organization.

Investors recognize that most managers are reluctant to cut jobs, and they bid up the share prices of firms that bring in CEOs with a reputation for cutting costs by cutting jobs. For example, when it was announced that Albert Dunlap was hired to be CEO of Sunbeam, Sunbeam's share price increased by almost 40 per cent. Dunlap earned the nickname 'Chainsaw' Dunlap for his ruthless job-cutting in eight different restructurings.

It should be noted, however, that policymakers and journalists may have overemphasized the relationship between takeovers and job losses. First, many takeovers resulted in more efficient organizations and increased employment. Second, the downsizing that occurred subsequently to many hostile takeovers also occurred at firms that were not taken over. Hence one should not necessarily view the takeovers as the cause of the job losses. Instead, takeovers should be viewed as one means by which inefficient organizations downsize.

Bidder Incentive Problems

Takeovers can be a symptom of as well as a cure for managerial incentive problems. Recall from Chapter 18 that managers often have the incentive to take on projects that benefit them personally, even when they do not improve share prices. For example, managers in declining industries may want to protect their jobs by acquiring firms in industries with better long-term prospects. In addition, some managers may simply want to manage bigger enterprises, and the takeover market may be the most expedient way to accomplish this goal. Examining the role of gender, Levi et al. (2014) report that female directors are less likely to make acquisitions and pay lower bid premiums.

Yim (2013) finds that CEO compensation permanently increases significantly after successful acquisitions. Lang et al. (1991) suggested that firms acquiring other firms for non-value-maximizing reasons are characterized by low share prices relative to their book values and cash flows. Such bidder firms are currently profitable, but their low market-to-book ratios (as well as related ratios) indicate that they are not expected to do particularly well in the future. Lang et al. (1991) found that when firms with these characteristics announce their intentions to acquire another firm, their share prices generally decline. They interpreted these share price declines to mean that the market considers the acquisitions to be either unwise or based on management incentives that are inconsistent with value maximization.

Mitchell and Lehn (1990) also examined what they called 'bad bidders', which they identified as firms that experience large share price declines when they announce plans for a major acquisition. They found that many of these bad bidders subsequently became targets of disciplinary takeovers. Mitchell and Lehn argued that one motivation for takeovers is to oust managers who have a tendency to make bad acquisitions. Bhagat et al. (1990) showed that the target in many of these disciplinary takeovers is broken up, and some of the former bad acquisitions are sold off.

Masulis et al. (2007) considered the corporate governance of acquirers and found that acquiring firms with strong anti-takeover provisions experience the worst response to takeover announcements. It appears that investors recognize that these firms are less likely to be taken over after poor performance, and their acquisition activity is driven more by empire building than by market discipline. In contrast, firms with strong governance structures experience the best announcement returns. In a similar vein, Wang and Xie (2009) found that when the acquirer has stronger governance than the target, greater synergies from an acquisition are created.

Financial Synergies

A common argument in support of diversification is that lowering the risk of a firm's equity increases its attractiveness to investors and thereby reduces the firm's cost of capital. However, both the Capital Asset Pricing Model (CAPM) and the arbitrage pricing theory (APT) suggest that investors are unlikely to be willing to pay a premium for the reduced risk of a diversified firm, since they can easily form a well-diversified portfolio on their own by holding the shares of several different firms in different industries (see Chapters 5 and 6). Hence, for a diversification strategy to increase the value of a firm's shares, it must do more than simply reduce risk. Diversification must create either operating synergies or financial synergies.

The discussion of optimal capital structure in the previous chapters provides some intuition about possible financial synergies. We have already discussed the financial synergies associated with the tax gains to leverage. Since diversification reduces the risk of bankruptcy for any given level of debt, it can increase the amount of debt in the firm's optimal capital structure, which in turn can lower the firm's cost of capital.

Financial synergies can also arise because of the personal taxes on cash distributions (see Chapter 15). Consider, for example, Marco's Pizza House, which is generating significant cash but has no investment opportunities, and Emanuele's Biotech, which has excellent investment opportunities but no internally generated cash. With perfect capital markets, capital will flow costlessly from Marco, who has only negative-NPV projects, to Emanuele, who has projects with high NPVs. Personal taxes, however, significantly impede this flow, since the dividends paid from Marco's profits are taxed before they are reinvested in Emanuele's Biotech. These personal taxes can be avoided if the two firms merge to form Emanuele and Marco's Biotech Pizza!

Information and incentive problems provide additional impediments to the flow of capital from Marco to Emanuele (see Chapters 18–19). Because of these problems, firms with investment requirements that significantly exceed internally generated funds may have to pass up positive-NPV projects, whereas cash-rich firms tend to overinvest, taking on negative-NPV projects. This suggests, at least in theory, that there is a potential to create value by combining the cash-rich firms having excess investment capital with the cash-starved firms that are underinvesting. This is illustrated in Example 20.1.

Example 20.1

The Advantage of Internal Capital Markets

TWT Technologies has an investment opportunity, based on proprietary technology, that requires it to raise £100 million in capital. TWT Technologies is currently priced at £22 per share. However, John Jacobs, its CEO and largest shareholder, believes that this technology will be very successful, and that the company's shares will be worth £40 per share when it demonstrates the technology publicly. Unfortunately, because competitors may attempt to clone the technology after seeing it demonstrated, TWT cannot demonstrate the technology prior to raising the capital. What are the company's financing options?

Answer: It clearly is unattractive to issue TWT equity at £22 a share if Jacobs believes the shares will soon be worth £40. However, the firm may be too risky to issue debt, and its ability to license the technology later will be more limited if the firm has difficulties meeting its debt obligations. Perhaps its best opportunity would be to find a cash-rich firm with which to merge.

Results

Result 20.2

Conglomerates can provide funding for investment projects that independent (smaller) firms would not have been able to fund using outside capital markets. To the extent that positive-NPV projects receive funding that they would not otherwise have received, conglomerates create value.

Example 20.1 and Result 20.2 suggest that the capital allocation process within a firm may be more efficient than outside capital markets when firms have proprietary information that they do not wish to disclose. TWT Technologies' possession of proprietary information suggests another advantage associated with diversification. An independent firm like TWT Technologies might be obligated to reveal information to its investors.[3] However, the disclosure of information to investors also reveals it to competitors, which could put the firm at a competitive disadvantage. Even if the proprietary information is not revealed directly, potential competitors can certainly observe the firm's financial performance, which entices them to become competitors when the performance of TWT is exceptional. This problem would be much less severe if TWT were a small division of a large conglomerate, where proprietary information can be more easily hidden.

Is an Acquisition Required to Realize Tax Gains, Operating Synergies, Incentive Gains or Diversification?

To evaluate the benefits of an acquisition, a financial analyst needs to do more than simply compare the costs and benefits of combining two firms with the current situation where the two firms have no relationship. The executives in the two companies also should investigate whether the gains from combining the firms can be achieved more efficiently in some other way. For example, to estimate the tax gains from the increased leverage associated with an acquisition, it is important to account for the possibility that the firm could increase leverage in another way, such as by repurchasing its shares.

Similarly, one must consider whether achieving operating synergies between two firms requires them to merge. For example, when Gillette and Duracell merged, the executives at both companies should have considered whether the benefits of having Duracell use Gillette's distributors outside the United States required a merger of the firms. A possible alternative might be some kind of joint marketing agreement that allows Gillette to sell batteries through its international distribution channels and to receive a commission on each battery sold.

[3] Managers may want to reveal information to investors even if their firms do not want to raise new capital. First, managerial compensation may be linked to the firm's share price. Second, managers can be sued for failing to reveal information.

Of course, writing a long-term joint marketing agreement can be complicated because of the large number of unforeseen circumstances that could arise in the future. The contract would have to specify what would happen if another company devised a better battery that Gillette also might want to sell. This would certainly hurt Duracell, but Gillette may not want to preclude such possibilities. Similarly, Gillette might be concerned that, after investing resources to promote Duracell batteries, Duracell may find that it can market its batteries without Gillette. To protect against this contingency, Gillette could insist on a long-term contract that makes it the exclusive marketing agent for Duracell. On the other hand, Duracell might be concerned about Gillette's incentive to expend the appropriate level of effort to market the batteries once Duracell has signed a contract that gives it no alternative.

In some cases, these incentive problems are best solved with a very explicit contract that specifies how both parties are to act under all relevant contingencies. In other cases, however, it is impossible to know all the relevant contingencies in advance, making it impossible to write a contract that satisfies the concerns of both parties. In such cases, a merger may be preferred.

We should stress that a merger does not necessarily solve all incentive problems. The Duracell people and the Gillette people may still bicker about who gets credit for battery sales in Norway after a Duracell/Gillette merger. Conflicts within a firm can create the same costs as conflicts that arise between firms.[4] In addition, as we shall discuss in the next two sections, additional costs and benefits associated with combining firms must also be taken into account.

20.5 The Disadvantages of Mergers and Acquisitions

The preceding section described various benefits associated with M&As, but there can also be offsetting disadvantages. The prevailing view of mergers has changed substantially over time. Investors and analysts have become more sceptical about potential gains from M&As, and more aware of the potential downside of combining two firms. This change in the prevailing view is especially true for the pure conglomerate acquisitions. In the 1960s, conglomerate acquisitions were in fashion, and acquiring firms were rewarded with rising share prices. The kind of logic illustrated in Example 20.1 was generally accepted by the market. However, for the reasons discussed below, diversifying takeovers have been viewed much more negatively since the 1980s.

Conglomerates Can Misallocate Capital

Combining two firms can destroy value if the managers of the combined firm use the added flexibility to transfer resources between the two firms to subsidize money-losing lines of business that would otherwise be shut down. Subsidization of this sort is likely to occur if the firm's top management is reluctant to cut jobs, or has other reasons to keep a losing business in operation. For example, the CEO may not want to admit that a past decision was a mistake. Hence the information asymmetries and incentive problems that can lead financial markets to allocate capital inefficiently also create even greater problems when managers allocate capital internally.

Mergers Can Reduce the Information Contained in Share Prices

When two firms combine, two different equity securities generally merge into one equity security. This can create a cost if share prices convey information that helps managers to allocate resources. For example, Starbucks may have interpreted the rise in its share price since 2008 as reflecting improving opportunities in the growing economies of China and Southeast Asia. This 'equity market opinion' might have led Starbucks to expand its efforts in that part of the world. However, if Starbucks were instead part of a large conglomerate, its executives would not have been able to observe market prices, and would have had to make their investment decisions based on more subjective information.

As Chapter 18 noted, the information from share prices is also useful for compensating and evaluating management. It is much easier to tie the compensation of Starbucks' CEO to his performance than it is to tie pay to performance for the head of Costa Coffee (owned by Coca-Cola), because there is no observable share price for Costa Coffee. In addition to providing motivation, Starbucks' share price provides a signal to shareholders of their CEO's effectiveness. In contrast, Coca-Cola's share price contains much less information about the success of any of its individual divisions, including Costa Coffee.

[4] See Grossman and Hart (1986) for further discussion along these lines.

A Summary of the Gains and Costs of Diversification

The past two sections have covered the advantages and disadvantages of purely diversifying takeovers. These are summarized in the following result.

Results

Result 20.3

The advantages of diversification can be described as follows.

- Diversification enhances the flexibility of the organization.
- The internal capital market avoids some of the information problems inherent in an external capital market.
- Diversification reduces the probability of bankruptcy for any given level of debt, and increases the firm's debt capacity.
- Competitors find it more difficult to uncover proprietary information from diversified firms.
- Diversification is advantageous if it allows the firm to utilize its organization more effectively.

The disadvantages of diversification can be described as follows.

- Diversification can eliminate a valuable source of information, and may, among other things, make it difficult to compensate the division heads of large diversified firms efficiently.
- Managers may find it difficult to cut back optimally on losing divisions when they can subsidize the losers out of the profits from their winners.

20.6 Empirical Evidence on Takeover Gains for Non-LBO Takeovers

Some academics and policymakers have asked whether, on average, mergers create value. In other words, are the various financial and operating synergies discussed in this chapter real, or are purported synergies merely a convenient rationale offered by managers attempting to expand their empires? This section reviews various studies that attempt to measure the value created by mergers.

Three types of study have sought to determine the extent to which non-LBO takeovers are value enhancing. The first type analyses equity returns around the time of the announcements of tender offers and merger offers, and it attributes the gains and losses in share prices to expected gains associated with combining the firms, improving management or identifying undervalued assets. The second type of study looks more specifically at whether diversified firms are either more or less valuable than non-diversified firms. The third type of study examines accounting data to determine the change, if any, in the profitability of the target firm's business after it has been absorbed by the bidder.

Equity Returns Around the Time of Takeover Announcements

Equity market studies look at the returns of both bidding firms and target firms. The sum of the two returns determines whether mergers create value.

Returns of Target Firms

Equity market evidence strongly indicates that target shareholders gain from a successful takeover. This is not surprising, given that target shareholders require a premium as an inducement to sell their shares to the acquiring firm. Jensen and Ruback (1983) reported that, on average, target shares increase in price from about 16 to 30 per cent around the date of the announcement of a tender offer. Evidence by Jarrell et al. (1988) found that these returns increased substantially during the 1980s to an average of about 53 per cent. Jensen and Ruback (1983) reported that the average return to target firms in negotiated merger offers is only about

10 per cent. Using data up to 2001, Moeller et al. (2004) reported that the average premium paid to US target firm shareholders was 68 per cent for large firms and 61 per cent for small firms. UK target firm shareholders receive on average a smaller, albeit large, premium of 45 per cent (Antoniou et al. 2008).

Returns of Bidder Firms

Returns to bidders around tender offer announcements are sometimes positive and sometimes negative, and the average returns vary considerably over time. Jarrell and Poulsen (1989) reported that the announcement return to bidders in tender offers dropped from a statistically significant 5 per cent gain in the 1960s to an insignificant 1 per cent loss in the 1980s. This finding can be attributed in part to regulations that are disadvantageous to the bidder, and perhaps to increased competition among bidders for specific targets. One also can interpret this finding as an indication that either the number of bad takeovers has been increasing or bidders have been paying too much in recent years.

Masulis et al. (2007) examined the target identity and type of payment to ascertain any differences in bidder returns. Publicly listed targets elicited the largest negative price reaction, as did older firms (Arikan and Stulz 2015), whereas target subsidiaries and private firms are associated with positive announcement abnormal returns. The form of payment was also important. Cash offers were rewarded with significant positive returns, whereas bids that included some equity were associated with significant negative returns for the acquirer.

In France, Chilkh and Filbien (2011) found that acquiring firms will cancel the deal if the market responds unfavourably, apart from when CEOs of the acquiring firm are heavily networked, which suggests that personal networks matter more than market reactions for highly connected CEOs. In another vein, when the target and bidder firms are connected by common directors, the acquirer will obtain higher announcement returns, principally because of lower takeover premiums (Cai and Sevilir 2012). Similarly, CEOs with strong business network connections improve acquirer returns (El-Khatib et al. (2015). Social connections between target and bidder directors, on the other hand, lead to significantly negative announcement and post-acquisition returns of the acquirer (Ishii and Xuan 2014).

Corporate social responsibility (CSR) is also an important factor in bidding firm returns. Deng et al. (2013) report that high CSR bidders experience higher announcement period returns and positive long-term returns. Deng et al.'s (2013) findings suggest a role for CSR in driving post-acquisition returns. Investing too much in CSR, however, can make a firm a stronger takeover target (Fairhurst and Greene 2022).

Summary of Bidder and Target Returns

Adding the bidder and target returns implies that, on average, there is a net gain to shareholders around the time of the merger announcement. Bradley et al. (1988) found that successful tender offers increased the combined values of the merging firms by an average of 7.4 per cent or $117 million (stated in 1984 dollars), which suggests that mergers are, on average, value enhancing.

Result 20.4 summarizes how share prices react at the time of takeover announcements.

Results

Result 20.4

Share price reactions to takeover bids can be described as follows.

- The share prices of target firms almost always react favourably to merger and tender offer bids.
- The bidder's share price sometimes goes up and sometimes goes down, depending on the circumstances.
- The combined market values of the shares of the target and bidder go up, on average, around the time of the announced bids.

Interpreting the Equity Return Evidence

As Chapter 19 discussed, the share price reaction on the announcement of a corporate decision cannot be attributed solely to how the decision affects the firm's profitability. The equity returns of the bidder at the time of the announcement of the bid may tell us more about how the market is reassessing the bidder's business than it does about the value of the acquisition. Indeed, share prices may react favourably to the announcement of an acquisition, even when investors believe that the acquisition harms shareholders.

For example, a tender offer, especially one for cash, may indicate that the bidding firm has been highly profitable in the past, given that it had accumulated the financial ability to make the offer. Hence the bidding firm's share price may increase even if the market views the acquisition as a negative-NPV project. Indeed, share prices react very favourably to a firm purchasing its own equity, because of the information this decision conveys, even though a share repurchase is a zero-NPV investment. Given that the share price reaction around the time of the announcement of an offer for another firm's equity is generally much weaker, one might conclude that the market, on average, views these acquisitions as negative-NPV investments.

Equity Returns and the Means of Payment

As discussed earlier in the chapter, the way in which a bidder pays for the target can have a major effect on how the bidder's equity reacts to the announced bid. Travlos (1987) and Franks et al. (1988) demonstrated that average bidder returns differ significantly, depending on whether the bidder offers cash or shares of its own equity in exchange for the target's shares. For example, Travlos (1987) found that in US acquisitions financed by an exchange of equity, the bidding firm's share price fell by 1.47 per cent, on average, on the two days around the offer's announcement. Franks et al. (1988) found a similar negative return for equity-financed bidders in both the United States and the United Kingdom. Both studies found that the market price of the bidder reacted favourably to announcements of cash acquisitions, but the returns, on average, were quite small. The returns on the two days around the announcement of a cash offer, as reported by Travlos, were only marginally different from zero (0.24 per cent), and the monthly returns around the announcements of cash offers reported in Franks et al. were 2.0 per cent in the United States and 0.7 per cent in the United Kingdom. These results are supported by the findings of other research, including Moeller et al. (2004) and Masulis et al. (2007).

Chapter 19 provides two explanations for why bidders who make cash offers experience higher returns. Bidders offer equity when they believe that their own equity is overvalued, but offer cash when they believe that their own equity is undervalued. In addition, a cash offer may signal that the bidder is able to obtain the financial backing of a bank or other financial institution. An equity offer may then signal that the banks refused to provide the bidder with financial backing, which reflects badly on the bidder's financial strength.

Results

Result 20.5

The bidder's share price reacts more favourably, on average, when the bidder makes a cash offer rather than an offer to exchange equity. This may reflect the relatively negative information about the bidder's existing business signalled by the offer to exchange equity.

Information Conveyed about the Target

A bidding firm does not only reveal information about itself when bidding for another company. If the financial markets believe that a bidder has special information about a target, then a bid is also likely to convey information to the market about the value of the target as a stand-alone company. One can obtain insights about the extent to which special information about a target is revealed by examining share price reactions when offers are terminated.

Share prices tend to decline subsequent to the failure of an initial bid, but the prices generally stay considerably above the share price for the target that existed before the bid (see Bradley 1980; Dodd 1980; Bradley et al. 1983). This evidence could indicate that the bidders have some special information, because, if the gains were all due to either improved management or synergies, the share price theoretically should drop back to its original level after a failed bid.

Bradley et al. (1983) suggested a different interpretation. They pointed out that the relatively small decline in share prices when initial bids fail may occur not because the initial bid signalled that the firm was undervalued, but because most failed targets do eventually get taken over. Indeed, a failed bid is often due to a better offer; therefore the share price may eventually exceed the price level attained after the initial acquisition announcement. The authors found that one to five years after the first price-raising bid, the average share prices of targets that were not subsequently acquired by any firm returned to the level that existed before the initial offer. This would suggest that the bidder generally had no special information, and that undervalued assets were not the motivation for the takeovers.

In the Bradley et al. (1983) sample, only 26 of 371 target firms (about 7 per cent) were not acquired once they were 'put into play', making it difficult to make strong inferences about the motivation of the initial bidders – whether the bidders felt that they could actually improve the value of the firms, or believed that the firms were undervalued.

In the 1980s there were substantially more takeover attempts that failed, and many were not subsequently taken over, making it easier to examine some of the hypotheses considered by Bradley et al. Safieddine and Titman (1999) examined 573 unsuccessful takeover attempts during the 1982–1991 period and found that, on average, target share prices declined 5.14 per cent on the termination date. This decline is smaller than the average increase when the takeover offers were originally announced, suggesting that either the takeover announcement conveyed information about the target's value or, alternatively, that the offer created value, even if the offer subsequently failed.

In contrast to Bradley et al.'s earlier sample, fewer than half of the targets of failed takeover bids in the 1982–1991 period were subsequently taken over. Moreover, more than two-thirds of the failed targets that stayed independent substantially increased their leverage ratios. Many of them implemented restructuring strategies that were similar to the strategies that would have been imposed on them by their hostile suitor. In particular, there was a tendency of the leverage-increasing failed targets to sell assets, reduce investment, reduce employment and increase focus. These firms subsequently performed quite well. This evidence suggests that value is often created by takeover offers even when they fail, and the firm is not subsequently taken over. Perhaps the threat of additional takeover attempts provides management with the incentives to cut wasteful spending and investment, and to take other steps that create value for their shareholders.

Empirical Evidence on the Gains from Diversification

Whether there are gains associated with takeovers depends, in part, on whether diversification helps or hurts firm values. Several empirical studies have examined whether diversification increases or decreases firm values. Lang and Stulz (1994) and Berger and Ofek (1995) found that the market places lower values on more diversified firms. Comment and Jarrell (1995), who examined changes in diversification during the 1980s, found that firms destroy value when they diversify, and create value when they sell off divisions and become more focused. Servaes (1996) found that the market's attitude towards diversification depends on the time period studied. In contrast with the earlier findings of diversification discounts in the 1980s, Servaes found no significant valuation penalty associated with diversification in the 1970s. However, he did find significant diversification penalties in the 1960s, as well as the 1980s. Denis et al. (1997) found that the tendency of firms to diversify is related to ownership structure. They found that firms managed by individuals who own more of the company's shares are less diversified. This finding supports the idea that the diversification discount at least partially reflects the tendency to diversify for managerial benefits when there are insufficient incentives to maximize share value. Rajan et al. (2000) argued that the diversification discount is caused by inefficient investment decisions. When there are large differences in power and resources within a diversified firm, funding will gravitate towards the most powerful divisions, and firm value will not be optimized.

The diversification discount may also be an empirical anomaly. Graham et al. (2002) examined firms that acquire other firms and reported that the diversification discount arises because takeover targets themselves tend to be discounted. This is supported by Campa and Kedia (2002), who showed that the relationship between diversification and firm value is an endogenous one. That is, low-value companies seek to diversify, and therefore diversification in itself does not destroy value. Using more accurate and precise business segment data, rather than the segmental data that is used in earlier research, Villalonga (2004) improved upon the measurement of diversification and actually found a diversification premium. This is robust to sample variations, business unit diversification, and different measures of excess value and diversification. Kuppuswamy and Villalonga (2010) investigated how well firms fared during the 2008 global financial crisis, and found that diversified firms actually increased in value relative to single-industry companies.

Lins and Servaes (1999) investigated the presence of a diversification discount in Germany, Japan and the United Kingdom. Interestingly, German firms did not exhibit any diversification discount, whereas Japanese and British firms had discounts of 10 and 15 per cent, respectively. Lins and Servaes explained the differences by different corporate governance systems across countries.

Accounting Studies

Because share price reactions reflect the information conveyed by an offer, it is difficult to use equity returns to draw inferences about the operating synergies or the economic efficiency generated by a merger. For this reason, some researchers have examined accounting data to draw inferences about the underlying economic impact of a merger.

Evidence of Negative Post-Merger Performance

In their comprehensive study, Ravenscraft and Scherer (1987) investigated more than 5,000 mergers occurring between 1950 and 1975. Using accounting data for each of the different lines of business in which the firms were involved, they calculated and compared the post-merger performance of acquired firms with the performance of non-acquired control groups in the same industry. On average, they found significant declines in the post-merger profitability of the acquired portions of those firms. Harford et al. (2012) find that entrenched managers destroy value by avoiding private targets, overpaying bid premiums and buying target firms with low operating synergies.

The Wealth Transfer Interpretation

The evidence in the Ravenscraft and Scherer study is inconsistent with the view that mergers create value. However, the interpretation of these results has been the subject of much disagreement. First, the validity of the results depends on the accuracy of the accounting numbers, which have been questioned by several authors. Second, the mergers may be creating value, even if the targets appear to be doing poorly after the takeover. This will be the case if enough wealth is transferred from the acquired firm to the acquirer. For example, Texas Air acquired Eastern Airlines for $600 million. Subsequent to the Eastern bankruptcy, some of Eastern's creditors suggested that wealth was transferred from Eastern to Texas Air. After only four months, Eastern sold a number of jumbo jets (at what some considered to be favourable prices) to Continental (also owned by Texas Air) and sold Eastern's reservation system to the parent firm. Finally, as Graham et al. (2002) suggest, the accounting performance of acquired firms will appear to be unfavourable if the targets are generally firms with poor prospects. Although these firms perform poorly subsequent to being taken over, they might have performed even worse had they remained independent.

Tobin's *q* and the Interpretation of Mediocre Accounting Performance

Hasbrouck (1985) offered support for the view that targets frequently are firms in decline. Hasbrouck assessed each firm's **Tobin's *q***, the ratio of the market value of the firm's assets to the replacement value of the assets, which can be viewed as a measure of managerial performance. Well-managed firms have a high Tobin's q value; poorly managed firms have a low Tobin's q. Hasbrouck found that target companies have relatively low values of Tobin's q; target shares are often selling at a value below their replacement cost. In addition, several studies (see, for example Asquith, 1983), have found that targets tend to experience lower returns than firms of comparable risk in the years before the merger. Hence, relative to either their past share prices or their replacement values, target share prices are low at the time of the initial offer, indicating that investors were somewhat pessimistic about the target's prospects as a stand-alone entity. This suggests that the subsequent mediocre post-merger accounting performance of firms might have occurred even if the acquisition had not taken place.

Evidence of Positive Post-Merger Performance

Healy et al. (1992) examined 50 large mergers between 1979 and 1983 and found improvements in both the sales and the profits of the combined firms following the mergers. This evidence suggests that the mergers of the early 1980s may have been quite different from those of the 1960s and 1970s examined by Ravenscraft and Scherer (1987). As mentioned earlier, the motivation for many of the mergers of the 1960s and 1970s was diversification, and there can be efficiency losses associated with diversification. However, diversification was a less important motivation for mergers in the 1980s, a decade in which many takeovers were motivated by the potential gains from improving managerial incentives. The Healy et al. (1992) evidence suggests that, in many cases, productivity did improve as a result of the takeovers.

A more comprehensive study by Andrade et al. (2001) examined approximately 2,000 mergers during the 1973 to 1998 period. Their results suggest that the combined target and acquirer operating margins improve by about 1 per cent subsequent to the merger.

20.7 Empirical Evidence on the Gains from Leveraged Buyouts (LBOs)

Many publicly traded firms have been taken over in highly leveraged transactions that transformed the public companies into privately held firms. The announcements of these LBOs generally resulted in dramatic increases in the share prices of the target firms, which suggests that LBOs create substantial value. However, because these LBOs did not involve the combination of two firms, the kind of synergies discussed previously do not apply. Most analysts point to improved management incentives as the motivation for LBOs.

How Leveraged Buyouts Affect Share Prices

A variety of studies have examined the premiums offered in LBOs, as well as the equity returns when the LBO transactions are first announced. These studies found that the average price paid in an LBO was 40 to 60 per cent above the market price of the shares one to two months before the offers. Around the time of the announcements of these offers, the share price increased by about 20 per cent, on average.

Characteristics of Higher Premium Targets

Lehn and Poulsen (1989) found that higher premiums were offered for firms with high cash flows, relatively low growth opportunities and high tax liabilities relative to their equity values. The higher premiums for the high-cash-flow/low-growth firms support the idea that there are larger gains associated with levering up firms with these characteristics (for example, leverage reduces their tendency to overinvest). The relationship between the tax liabilities and the premium suggests that part of the tax gain from the LBO transaction is passed along to the original shareholders.

Competing Bids

The presence of competing bids also affects the premium offered in LBOs. Lowenstein (1985) studied 28 LBOs, and found that those with fewer than three competing bids received an average premium of 50 per cent, whereas those with more than three competing bids received an average premium of 69 per cent.

Cash Flow Changes Following Leveraged Buyouts

A number of studies have analysed operating changes following LBOs. These studies, summarized in Exhibit 20.5, examined changes in several variables that provide insights into how LBOs affect a firm's performance.

The results summarized in Exhibit 20.5 indicate that the magnitude of the cash flow improvements following LBOs declined in the latter half of the 1980s. For example, Kaplan (1989) found that, from 1980 to 1986, cash flows increased, on average, by 20.1 per cent following an LBO. However, Opler (1993) found an average improvement in cash flows of only 8.8 per cent for LBOs initiated between 1986 and 1989. One explanation for this decline in the performance of LBOs is that the success of the earlier deals attracted new investors, resulting

Exhibit 20.5 Summary of Changes in Firm Operations after LBOs*

Variable	Kaplan (1989)	Muscarella and Vetsuypens (1990)	Opler (1993)	Smith (1990)
Cash flow/sales	20.1%	23.5%	8.8%	18%
Sales per employee	NA†	3.1%	16.7%	18%
Taxes	NA	NA	−90.5%	−80%
Investment/sales	−31.6%	−11.4%	−46.7%	−25%
Employees	0.9%	−0.6%	−0.7%	−22%
R&D/sales	NA	NA	0.0%	−75%
Time period studied	1980–86	1976–87	1986–89	1976–86
Number of LBOs	37	43	46	18
Window in years (before, after)	(−1, 2)	Variable	Variable	(−1, 2)

*Expressed as a percentage increase or decrease.
†NA means statistic not available or not computed.

in 'too much money chasing too few good deals', which, in turn, led to buyouts of firms with less potential for improvement.

Additional evidence suggests that LBOs occurring in later years were priced higher and were more highly leveraged, leading to much higher default rates on LBO debt. Kaplan and Stein (1993) found that *none* of the 24 LBOs in their sample initiated between 1980 and 1983 subsequently defaulted on its debt. However defaults claimed 46.7 per cent of the LBOs initiated in 1986, 30.0 per cent of those initiated in 1987, 16.1 per cent of those initiated in 1988 and 20.0 per cent of those initiated in 1989. Despite their high default rates, the firms that initiated these later LBOs still tended to show improvements in productivity. In many cases, however, the productivity gains were not sufficient to justify their high prices, and the firms did not generate sufficient cash flows to pay off the high levels of debt incurred in the LBOs.

Productivity Increases Following LBOs

Exhibit 20.5, which summarizes four LBO studies, provides evidence that at least part of the post-LBO increase in cash flows is due to increased productivity. The three studies that measured the average change in the value of sales per employee (labour productivity) found that labour productivity increases after LBOs. A study by Lichtenberg and Siegel (1990), using plant-level data, provides additional evidence about the sources of productivity improvements. They documented significant post-LBO reductions in the ratio of white-collar to blue-collar labour, reflecting perhaps a reduction in excess overhead. In addition, Smith (1990) found strong evidence that working capital is reduced after LBOs and Lerner et al. (2011) report that patents in LBO firms are more heavily cited, which suggests innovation improves after a firm has gone private. Similarly, Guo et al. (2011) report better operating performance and Boucly et al. (2011) report an improvement in profitability and increased capital expenditure in LBO firms.

The Direction of Causation for the LBO Cash Flow Improvement

The increase in cash flows following LBOs may not solely reflect improvements resulting from the LBOs. Perhaps firms that undergo leveraged buyouts would have shown similar improvements without the LBOs. Managers and LBO sponsors are unlikely to consider an LBO of a firm for which business prospects are forecast to be unfavourable. Therefore firms that undergo LBOs are likely to experience subsequent increases in their cash flows even without productivity improvements. In addition, some of the observed increase in the cash flows of LBOs can probably be explained by the selection process of LBO candidates. However, we are unaware of any convincing evidence on this.

Cost Deferral as an Explanation for the LBO Cash Flow Improvement

Another explanation for the observed increase in cash flows following LBOs is that higher leverage ratios provide managers with an incentive to increase cash flows in the short run at the expense of their long-run cash flows (see Chapter 16). Critics of leveraged buyouts say that, after initiating a leveraged buyout, firms improve their cash flows in the short run by deferring maintenance, cutting R&D, and reducing advertising and promotion budgets. If these actions were the prime cause of the observed increase in cash flows, then one would expect the increase to be reversed later. Although it is certainly plausible that some of the increase in cash flows can be explained by this possibility, we again are unaware of any convincing evidence suggesting that part of the short-term gain in cash flows comes at the expense of long-term cash flows.

Smith (1990), Lichtenberg and Siegel (1990) and Opler (1993) found that post-LBO research and development expenditures do not generally decline. However, this may not be particularly relevant, since most firms that have done LBOs belong to industries that conduct little R&D. Smith (1990) also found no significant reductions in advertising or maintenance following LBOs, but she is cautious about interpreting these results because of the limited size of her sample.

Results

Result 20.6

On average, cash flows of firms improve following leveraged buyouts. Three possible explanations for these improvements are:

1 productivity gains

2 initiation of LBOs by firms with improving prospects
3 the incentives of leveraged firms to accelerate cash flows, sometimes at the expense of long-run cash flows.

Although we expect all three factors to contribute to the observed increase in cash flows, existing empirical evidence suggests that a major part of the increase is due to productivity gains.

20.8 Valuing Acquisitions

Evaluating a potential merger candidate requires a great deal of care. These acquisitions are generally very large transactions that have important effects on the operating strategy and the financial structure of the acquiring firm.

Several firms have M&A departments devoted entirely to discovering and analysing acquisition candidates. Evaluating a potential acquisition is similar in most respects to analysing the NPV of any other investment project that a firm may be considering. Hence the techniques discussed in Chapters 9 to 13 also apply to evaluating acquisition candidates. There are some subtle differences, though. Most importantly, publicly traded acquisition candidates have an observable share price that provides an estimate of the market's evaluation of the present value of the firm's cash flows. This information allows the acquiring firm to estimate more accurately the present value of the cash flows from a potential acquisition than it can for most other investment projects.

Valuing Synergies

Obviously, an analyst cannot rely exclusively on a potential acquisition's current share price to determine the company's value. An acquiring firm will have to offer a premium over the target company's current share price to purchase the firm, implying that there has to be additional value created by combining the firms. In other words, there must be synergies that make the value of the target to the acquirer greater than the market value of the target on its own. The present value of the synergies must be added to the value of the firm's cash flows, given its current operations, to arrive at the present value of the acquisition.

In many cases, these synergies arise because of a reduction in the fixed costs of the combined firm. If these cost savings occur with certainty or, equivalently, are determined independently of the market portfolio's return (assuming the CAPM holds), then valuing the target is straightforward, as Example 20.2 illustrates.

Example 20.2

Valuing Isolated Industries

Isolated Industries is currently selling for €22 a share and has 1 million shares outstanding. Since, at present, analysts do not expect the firm to be a takeover target, €22 a share is also its current operating value. However, United Industries is considering the acquisition of Isolated Industries. It believes that by combining sales forces it can eliminate 10 salespeople at a saving of €500,000 per year. It expects this saving to be permanent and certain. If the discount rate is 10 per cent, how much is Isolated Industries worth to United Industries?

Answer: The present value of the perpetual savings from combining the sales forces is €5 million (= €500,000/0.1), or €5 per share. Hence United Industries would be willing to pay up to €27 per share for Isolated Industries.

Example 20.2 was simple, because it assumed that the synergies were certain and thus quite easy to value. The example also assumed that the firm's share price could be used to obtain a value for Isolated Industries as a stand-alone entity, which, in general, will not be the case. The target's share price will exceed the present value of the firm's future cash flows, given its current operating structure, if it reflects the possibility that the firm may eventually be taken over at a premium. Assuming risk neutrality and a zero discount rate, we can express the firm's current share price as

$$\text{current share price} = \text{current operating value} + \text{expected takeover premium} \times \text{takeover probability}$$

Equivalently, the current operating value of the firm can be expressed as

$$\text{current operating value} = \text{current share price} - \text{expected takeover premium} \times \text{takeover probability}$$

A Guide to the Valuation of Synergies

Valuing acquisitions draws upon the techniques for evaluating real investment projects described in Chapters 9 to 13. However, acquisitions tend to be much larger than the capital investments that firms typically undertake, so firms should go into more depth in their valuation. They should evaluate a variety of scenarios, and consider the various embedded options that exist in most firms (see Chapter 12). We suggest that acquiring firms take the following steps to evaluate prospective targets.

Step 1: Value the Target as a Stand-Alone Firm

Valuing the target as a stand-alone entity provides the analyst with a useful reality check for determining the value created by the acquisition. Such a valuation requires estimates of future cash flows and the appropriate rates for discounting the cash flows. The value obtained in this manner should be compared with the target firm's share price.

Step 2: Calibrate the Valuation Model

The analyst needs to explain any difference between the estimated value of the target and the target's pre-acquisition share price. As mentioned above, share prices may reflect takeover probabilities and takeover premiums, as well as the stand-alone value of the target. Also, share prices may not incorporate proprietary information that the acquiring firm's analysts may have obtained about the target's asset values during the course of their investigations. In many cases, especially in friendly takeovers, the acquiring firm has access to information that is unavailable to other investors. For example, the target's management may provide proprietary information when negotiating a selling price. The acquirer may also have come across new information in the course of its own investigation. When buying an entire company, the importance of collecting accurate information is greater than it is when buying even large numbers of shares. Hence it is plausible that the acquirer might value the target better than the financial markets.

If the acquiring firm's analysts believe they do not have superior information, and the difference between their estimated value of the target and the target share price cannot be explained by information about a possible takeover, they must conclude that their valuation is flawed. In other words, analysts are valuing the firm using assumptions about future cash flows and discount rates that differ from the assumptions implied by market prices. At this point, the analysts will have to revise their assumptions about cash flows and discount rates. Getting these assumptions right at this stage of the analysis is important, because these assumptions may also be used to value the synergies.

Step 3: Value the Synergies

To evaluate what the target is worth to the acquiring firm, analysts must value the synergies associated with combining the target and the acquirer. Doing this requires estimates of the cash flows generated by the synergies, along with the appropriate discount rates. To simplify the analysis, assume that some synergies are virtually certain while others are risky. For example, synergies that come from tax savings or reductions in fixed costs are often of a lower-risk category, whereas those related to increased sales or reductions in variable costs should be related to the risk of either the acquirer or the target, or perhaps both.

The future cash flows and the discount rates used in the stand-alone valuation model are likely to be used in valuing risky synergies. For example, to value a 10 per cent increase in the target's cash flows that will be generated for the first five years following a takeover requires both the pre-acquisition discount rate and the cash flows of the target. Valuing the synergies may also require an estimate of the acquiring firm's cost of capital and expected cash flows. Hence the acquiring firm will also want to use the procedures outlined in steps 1 and 2 to value its own equity and calibrate its cost of capital and cash flows.

As Example 20.3 illustrates, the synergies generated by a takeover should, in many cases, be discounted at a weighted average of the discount rates of the two merging organizations.

Example 20.3

Valuing the Marketing Synergies from Marks & Spencer and Wm. Morrison

Assume that, by combining sales forces, Marks & Spencer and Wm. Morrison Supermarkets both increase their pre-tax profits by 10 per cent per year. What discount rate should be used to value this synergy?

Answer: Since the gain in each year is proportional to the pre-acquisition cash flows of both firms, the appropriate discount rate is a weighted average of the two firms' costs of capital.

Example 20.3 illustrates a case with marketing synergies that affect both parties to the merger equally. However, this will not always be the case. In the Microsoft takeover of Activision Blizzard, the synergy was Microsoft's use of Activision Blizzard's gaming technology. If this is expected to result in a proportional increase in Microsoft's profits, but not Activision Blizzard's, then one would use Microsoft's cost of capital to value the synergy.

Because Microsoft's ability to enter new markets is the major gain from the acquisition, one might want to consider valuing the synergies as a strategic option, using the real options methodology, rather than the risk-adjusted discount rate method. Recall from Chapter 12 that strategic options exist whenever flexibility exists in the implementation of an investment. When a firm expands into a new market, it has the option to expand further if prospects turn out to be more favourable than originally anticipated, and to exit if the situation turns out to be unfavourable. In these situations, an investment may be substantially undervalued when such options are ignored.

Step 4: Value the Acquisition

The acquisition can be valued by simply adding the stand-alone value of the target to the synergies being produced. In general, we would suggest acquiring the target if it can be purchased for a price that is less than this sum. However, as discussed in Chapters 9–13, we also have to take into account mutually exclusive projects that may also have positive net present values, as well as a possible option to delay making the acquisition.

Valuing Conglomerates

Given the complex nature of conglomerates, it can be difficult to disaggregate the value components of a conglomerate firm. For example, 3M has divisions in electronics, healthcare and chemicals. One approach is to compare the divisions to stand-alone firms in the same industry as each division. However, this approach cannot capture the diversification benefits of internal capital markets in conglomerates. Boguth et al. (2022) suggest using divisional measures of value (Tobin's q) and propose a model to decompose a conglomerate's q measure into divisional qs.

Real World Insight

Hilton Buys Welch Hotels

Welch Hotels, a hypothetical company, is a relatively small chain with 23 hotels in Germany. Of the 2 million shares outstanding, more than 30 per cent are owned by the Welch family, who started the hotel chain. The remaining 70 per cent of Welch's shares trade on the Frankfurt Equity Exchange. On 3 October, Wolfgang Welch, the hotel chain's founder, announced that he wished to retire and would seek an international hotel company to buy the firm. Following this surprise announcement, the share price of Welch Hotels jumped from €60 to €72 per share, or €144 million for the entire chain, indicating that the market believed that an international hotel would place a higher value on the firm than its stand-alone value.

Hilton Worldwide hired Gordon Elliot, an investment banker, to evaluate this potential opportunity. Hilton executives believed that, with increasing tourism in continental Europe and the emerging markets in Eastern Europe, they would benefit from an increased presence in Germany. Since Hilton hotels are known internationally, Hilton's management believed that they can create value with such an acquisition. Specifically, they believe that Hilton is much better positioned to attract international business travellers, who value the Hilton name but know nothing about Welch. An added bonus of the acquisition would be increased recognition of Hilton hotels. By increasing its visibility within Germany, Hilton management hopes to increase the number of German business travellers who stay in their hotels when they travel outside Germany.

To value Welch Hotels, Elliot first values the chain as a stand-alone business. To this value, he adds the value created by its combination with Hilton. Elliot examines the projected cash flows of the corporation provided by Welch's top management and by the equity market analysts who follow the company. He finds that his cash flow forecasts, those of the analysts and those of Welch's management are pretty much the same. These estimates suggest that the unlevered cash flow that will accrue over the current year is €12 million, and that this value will increase, on average, at 2 per cent per year. Based on these projected cash flows and the company's value of €120 million before the proposed takeover, Elliot infers that if the company's pre-takeover value of €120 million does not capture an anticipated takeover premium, the WACC for Welch Hotels is 12 per cent – obtained by solving for the discount rate in the growing perpetuity formula (see Chapter 9), PV = $C/(r - g)$, where, for this illustration,

$$\begin{aligned} PV &= \text{firm value} = €120\,\text{million} \\ C &= \text{end of year expected unlevered cash flow} = €12\,\text{million} \\ g &= \text{growth rate of expected cash flow} = 2\% \\ r &= \text{WACC} = 12\% \end{aligned}$$

Elliot believes that this WACC is consistent with the hotels' risk, which supports his assumption that the value of the firm before the takeover represents the value of the hotel chain as a stand-alone business.

Elliot estimates that because of increased occupancy rates and more aggressive pricing generated as a result of Hilton's reputation and its worldwide reservation network, Welch Hotels will increase its expected unlevered cash flows more than the 2 per cent per year that it would have achieved as a stand-alone firm. He assumes that the expected unlevered cash flows will increase by 3 per cent in years 2 and 3, and 5 per cent thereafter. In other words, the expected unlevered cash flows after the takeover can be expressed as follows:

Unlevered cash flows (in € millions) at end of year			
1	2	3	4
12	12(1.03)	$12(1.03)^2$	$12(1.03)^2(1.05)$

The unlevered cash flows will increase by 5 per cent in each year past year 4.

Since the incremental cash flows depend on the state of the German economy, they have the same risk as the original cash flows, so the firm's cash flows after the takeover can be discounted at the 12 per cent WACC used to value the firm as a stand-alone business. This assumes that the tax effects on the WACC from both the financing mix and the cross-border transaction can be ignored.

To find the present value of this stream of cash flows, first calculate the end of year 4 value of the cash flows from year 4 on as

$$V_4 = €12\,(1.03)^2(1.05)\,\text{million} + \frac{€12\,(1.03)^2(1.05)^2\,\text{million}}{0.12 - 0.05} = €214\,\text{million}$$

The present value of the Welch Hotels is thus

$$\frac{€12\,\text{million}}{1.12} + \frac{€12\,(1.03)^2\,\text{million}}{1.12^3} + \frac{€12\,(1.03)^2\,\text{million}}{1.12^3} + \frac{€214\,\text{million}}{1.12^4} = €163\,\text{million}.$$

Valuing the spillover benefits that accrue to Hilton hotels outside Germany is somewhat more difficult. Elliot estimates that by buying the chain of Welch Hotels, 10,000 German individuals will come into contact with the Hilton name every day. He estimates that the cost of buying that sort of advertising would be about €500,000 per year, which he expects will remain fixed indefinitely. Since the benefits associated with that kind of publicity are determined by the demand for Hilton's hotels outside Germany, Elliot discounts the projected benefits of this publicity at Hilton's WACC, which is 10 per cent. Assuming that this €500,000 stream is perpetual, the value is €500,000/0.1 = €5 million. Adding this to the value of the hotels after the takeover provides a value of Welch Hotels to Hilton of €168 million. Given that this amount is substantially above the current market price of €144 million for Welch Hotels, Elliot recommends that Hilton proceed with an offer that is slightly higher than the current market price.

20.9 Financing Acquisitions

Major acquisitions are financed in a variety of ways. When the acquiring firm purchases the target with cash, it will usually have to borrow or issue new debt. Alternatively, the acquirer may purchase the target by offering target shareholders its own equity in exchange for the target's equity.

A study by Andrade et al. (2001) documented changes in the financing of mergers over the previous 20 years. They found that in the 1970s and 1980s fewer than half of the acquirers used any of their company's equity for acquisitions. However, in the 1990s, about 71 per cent of the acquisitions used some equity, and 58 per cent of the acquisitions were made exclusively with the acquiring firm's equity. Examining a different time period, 1990–2003, Moeller et al. (2004) reported that 46.5 per cent of all 3,333 mergers and takeovers that took place in the USA were all cash, compared with 53.5 per cent that involved some equity component.

In making the decision on how to finance an acquisition, managers should consider the:

- tax implications
- accounting implications
- capital structure implications
- information effects.

Tax Implications of the Financing of a Merger or an Acquisition

In a merger, the acquiring firm must decide whether to offer equity, cash, or a combination of the two for the shares of the target firm. The decision is often made because of tax considerations. Three tax considerations can affect the choice. These are:

1 the potential capital gains tax liability of the acquired firm's shareholders
2 the ability to write up the value of the purchased assets
3 the tax gains from leverage.

The Capital Gains Tax Liability

All else being equal, the target shareholders generally prefer an equity offer to cash for tax reasons, because they do not need to pay capital gains tax on the appreciation of their shares if they receive the acquirer's equity rather than cash for their shares. Moreover, they can still obtain cash by selling the shares received from the acquiring firms. In a cash offer they have no such option, and are forced to realize a taxable gain.

Since the shareholders of acquired firms may have a tax preference for equity-funded acquisitions, one might expect them to require lower premiums for equity-funded offers. The empirical evidence indicates that this is indeed true. Huang and Walkling (1987), Travlos (1987) and Franks et al. (1988) found that premiums in equity-exchange offers are much lower than in cases where the shareholders of the acquired firm are offered cash for their shares. Franks et al. (1988) reported that the differences in these premiums are reflected in a return to the acquired firm in the announcement month of 25.4 per cent for cash offers in the United States (30.2 per cent in the United Kingdom) and 11.1 per cent for equity offers in the United States (15.1 per cent in the United Kingdom).

Capital Structure Implications in the Financing of a Merger or an Acquisition

The financing of a takeover is partially determined by its effect on the firm's overall capital structure. As Chapter 17 discussed, firms that made profitable cash-generating investments in the past, but which have few profitable new investment opportunities, tend to use their cash to pay down debt and become underleveraged over time. Section 20.4 mentioned that firms in these situations often finance acquisitions with debt to move towards their long-run optimal debt ratio. However, firms that are overleveraged, perhaps because of previous debt-financed acquisitions, may have an incentive to finance new acquisitions by exchanging equity.

Information Effects from the Financing of a Merger or an Acquisition

When management believe that the shares of their own firm are underpriced, they are less likely to want to finance investments by issuing new equity (see Chapter 19). This logic applies to acquisitions of other companies as well as investment in capital equipment. Eckbo et al. (1990) suggested that uncertainty about the target's value also tends to lead firms to make equity offers rather than cash offers. Equity offers have the advantage that the acquiring firm ultimately pays less for the bad acquisitions, since the acquirer's share price is likely to perform worse after making a bad acquisition.

From the lender's perspective, firms with more tangible assets are less risky borrowers, because of the collateral that may be used for further debt financing in times of difficulty. In addition, larger firms are likely to be more diversified for a given leverage level, which also reduces the relative default risk of these companies. Faccio and Masulis (2005) showed that these factors influence the choice of financing in European mergers and acquisitions.

20.10 Bidding Strategies in Hostile Takeovers

In many hostile takeovers, the bidder initially attempts to buy less than 100 per cent of the target's shares. There are two reasons for this. First, the bidder might think that it is unnecessary to acquire all the outstanding shares to make the changes required to improve the firm's value. Second, some shareholders may not be willing to sell their shares at any price. For example, the target's managers are unlikely to sell their shares, if such a sale allows the firm to be taken over and the managers lose their jobs as a consequence.

The Free-Rider Problem

To simplify the following discussion, assume that the bidder can effectively take over a firm by accumulating over 50 per cent of the target firm's shares. We assume that the bidder buys the shares and uses the voting rights of those shares to appoint a new CEO, who implements the changes that increase the value of the bidder's original stake. By following this procedure, the bidder can, in theory, avoid the free-rider problem discussed in Chapter 18: that is, if shareholders are all small, none of them will find it in their interest to go to the expense of replacing a non-value-maximizing management team. However, if one of the smaller shareholders can accumulate enough shares to become a large shareholder, then this free-rider problem can be reduced.

Unfortunately, reducing the free-rider problem in this way is not always possible. We shall show that the bidder's ability to take over a target at a price that allows the bidder to offset his costs depends on how the bidder treats those shareholders who refuse to sell their shares. If the firm is able to force the bidder to offer non-tendering shareholders the post-takeover fair market value of their shares, then hostile takeovers may not be profitable.

Conditional Tender Offers

In recent years, many British football clubs have been targets of outside takeovers, sometimes hostile: Manchester United, Liverpool, Manchester City, Leeds United and Chelsea are examples. Suppose that John Douglas discovers that Southampton Football Club, currently selling for £20 a share, can be run more efficiently. Under Douglas's management, Southampton will be worth £30 a share. Douglas would like to buy enough shares to gain control of the firm and then make the improvements that will raise the firm's share price. Assume that Douglas offers to buy shares in a **conditional tender offer**, which is an offer to purchase a specific number of shares at a specific price. The offer is considered conditional because the buyer is not required to purchase any shares if the specific number of shares is not tendered.

Of course, what is rational for an individual shareholder may be bad for the shareholders as a group. If no one tenders, the shareholders are left with shares worth only £20 rather than the £25 (or £30) per share they would have received if more than half of them had tendered. This argument indicates that if most of the shareholders are small, tender offers will fail unless an offer equal to the target's post-takeover value is made. But, at this price, the bidder cannot make a profit unless the value of the shares to the bidder is greater than their value to the original shareholders after the takeover.[5] Again, we see that significant value improvements may fail to be implemented because of the small shareholders' incentives to free-ride on the efforts of others.

Results

Result 20.7

Small shareholders will not tender their shares if they are offered less than the post-takeover value of the shares. As a result, takeovers that could potentially lead to substantial value improvements may fail.

Example 20.4

The Success of a Conditional Tender Offer

Assume that Douglas chooses to make a conditional tender offer for 51 per cent of the outstanding shares at a price of £25 a share. He figures that he is giving the shareholders a good premium over their original £20 per share value, and that he will gain £5 per share after implementing his improvements. Would you expect target shareholders to tender their shares at this price?

Answer: To determine whether shareholders will tender their shares, the table below compares the value shareholders receive if they tender with the value they receive if they do not tender.

	Value if shareholder tenders	Value if shareholder doesn't tender
Bid succeeds	£25/share	£30/share
Bid fails	£20/share	£20/share

If the offer is successful, shareholders who tender their shares receive £25 a share. However, the shareholders realize that if Douglas is willing to pay £25 a share for the equity, it must be worth more than that after he gains control, so they are better off not tendering their shares. In this case, the shareholders who do not tender will have shares worth £30 a share, and will thus be better off than those shareholders who do tender. In the event that less than 51 per cent of the shares are tendered and the offer fails, shareholders will retain their shares whether or not they tendered, and all shares will be worth only £20. Hence small shareholders who believe that their decision has no effect on the outcome of the offer have an incentive *not* to tender their shares.

The above reasoning can be extended to situations where Douglas makes what is known as an **unconditional offer** or an **any-or-all offer**, which requires Douglas to purchase the tendered shares even if he fails to attract enough tendered shares to gain control of the firm.

Solutions to the Free-Rider Problem

In reality, acquiring firms find ways to get around the free-rider problem discussed in the last subsection. First, the acquiring firm may have secretly accumulated shares on the open market, and will profit on those shares when the target is taken over. Second, target shareholders may be induced to tender their shares if the bidder can convince them that they will not share in the profits that arise from the bidder's value improvements.

[5] The preceding argument was originally suggested in Grossman and Hart (1980).

Buying Shares on the Open Market

During the 1980s, many bidders secretly accumulated shares on the open market before making a bid. However, regulators in most countries now require purchasers to submit a report to the domestic equity exchange or regulator, in which they must state their intentions as soon as their holdings reach a certain threshold – usually between 3 and 5 per cent of the outstanding shares, depending on the country. At that point, the share price will reflect that the firm is a takeover target, and shareholders will again be unwilling to sell their shares for less than their value after the takeover. However, by purchasing some shares at £20 per share, Douglas may find it worthwhile to tender for a controlling block of additional shares, even if he must pay the value of the shares after the takeover. This strategy is illustrated in Example 20.5.

Example 20.5

Share-Tendering Strategies

Assume that Southampton Football Club has 10 million shares outstanding that are currently selling for £20 per share. Douglas believes that the shares will be worth £30 if he controls 51 per cent of the shares and implements some changes. The costs of mounting the takeover are expected to be £4 million. Can he take over Southampton profitably?

Answer: Douglas may be able to buy 5 per cent of the shares for £20 per share. However, after reaching the 3 per cent threshold for UK companies, he will have to make a tender offer for an additional 48 per cent of the shares for £30 per share. Although he will not gain on the shares purchased through the tender offer, he will realize a £10 per share profit on the 3 per cent of the shares he purchases on the open market. His total profits on these shares will be £3 million, which is less than his costs of £4 million, which implies that that a takeover will not be profitable.

In many cases, the potential gain on a bidder's original stake is not sufficient to compensate for the costs of making the bid. Douglas would be much more willing to bid if he could profit from the shares that he purchases in the tender offer as well as those that he secretly accumulates before the bid. To do this, he will have to induce shareholders to tender their shares at a price that is less than £30 a share. How can he do this?

Secret Share Accumulation by Risk Arbitrageurs as a Way to Resolve the Free-Rider Problem

Recall from Result 20.7 that only *small* shareholders will choose not to tender if the offer price is less than the value of the shares after the takeover. Large shareholders, who could affect the success or failure of the offer, may be willing to tender their shares at a price below their post-takeover value. This possibility is illustrated in Example 20.6.

Example 20.6

The Advantage of Accumulating Shares before a Tender Offer

Suppose that Joe Raider accumulated 15 per cent of Southampton equity following Douglas's tender offer to purchase shares for £26. Joe believes that the equity will be worth £30 per share if the offer succeeds, but only £20 per share if the offer fails. If Joe tenders his shares, the offer will succeed for sure. However, if he doesn't tender his shares, the offer has a 50 per cent probability of failure. Should Joe tender?

Answer: If Joe tenders his shares he will get £26 per share for sure. If he doesn't tender his shares, he will get $0.5 \times £20 + 0.5 \times £30 = £25$ per share, on average. He is better off tendering his shares.

Example 20.6 shows that so-called risk arbitrageurs like Joe Raider, who buy shares of prospective targets on the open market in the hope of profiting when the shares are tendered, can increase the likelihood of an offer. The presence of these individuals can allow the bidder to increase his profits by tendering for shares at a price below their post-takeover value.[6]

Shareholder Activism

Burkart and Lee (2022) suggest that shareholder activism may be more effective than takeovers at creating value in a target firm. When there is free-riding by dispersed shareholders, activism can be more profitable than hostile takeovers. Burkart and Lee (2022) propose that temporarily increasing shareholdings in a target to force changes in governance or strategy can be a better strategy than a direct hostile takeover attempt.

The Free-Rider Problem When There are Gains Captured Directly by the Bidder

Up to this point we have assumed that, following the takeover, the shares are worth the same amount to both the target shareholders and the bidder. If, however, the bidder values control of the firm, he or she may place a value on the acquired shares that exceeds their post-takeover value to target shareholders. This will occur when some of the gains from the takeover can be captured directly by the bidder and not by the target.

An alleged example of this occurred when Frank Lorenzo, the owner of Texas Air, took over Eastern Airlines. After the takeover, Eastern sold certain assets (most notably its reservation system) to Texas Air at what was alleged to be a reduced price. When transfers of this kind can be initiated, the bidder's value of the target's shares exceeds their post-takeover value in the equity market. Example 20.7 illustrates this possibility.

Example 20.7

How Wealth Transfers Facilitate Takeovers

Suppose that part of Douglas's £30 per share valuation of Southampton Football Club comes from the sale of its merchandising division to Southampton Merchandising Ltd, which Douglas also owns. Since the division will be sold to Southampton Merchandising at an attractive price, the post-takeover value of Southampton Football Club will be only £27 per share. In this case, can Douglas gain on the shares that are tendered?

Answer: Shareholders realize that their shares will be worth only £27 per share if the firm is taken over. Therefore they would be willing to tender their shares at £27 per share. As a result, Douglas will be able to earn a profit of £3 on each share that is tendered. The profit comes from the appreciation of his Southampton Merchandising equity, not from a gain on the Southampton Football Club equity that he purchases.

Two-Tiered Offers as a Way of Resolving the Free-Rider Problem

In most takeovers, the bidder expects to eventually purchase all the target's outstanding shares. This could create a substantial holdout problem if there was no way to force the remaining shareholders to sell their shares. In reality, however, if a sufficient number of target shareholders agree to merge the target firm with the bidding firm, the minority shareholders can be forced to sell their shares.[7]

In what has come to be known as a **two-tiered offer**, the bidder offers a price in the initial tender offer for a specified number of shares, and simultaneously announces plans to acquire the remaining shares at another price in what is known as a **follow-up merger**. In almost all cases, cash is used in the tender offer, but securities, worth less than the cash offered in the first-tier offer, are generally offered in the second tier. As a consequence, shareholders are induced to tender their shares to the bidder. Example 20.8 illustrates why these two-tiered offers are sometimes considered coercive.

[6] We should like to note, however, that the term *risk arbitrageur* is really misleading. As we discussed previously, an arbitrageur, by definition, makes money without taking risks: that is, he or she does not place bets. Individuals who are often referred to as risk arbitrageurs earn their living by placing bets on the outcomes of takeover battles. This activity certainly involves risks.

[7] In LBOs the bidding firm is a shell company, created for the purpose of merging with the target.

Example 20.8

Coercive Two-Tier Offers

Naimh plc has made a €25 per share tender offer for 51 per cent of SodaBread plc's shares. If the offer is successful, and at least 51 per cent of the shares are tendered, the firms will be merged. The shares not tendered in the first tier will receive a combination of bonds and preferred equity valued at €22 per share. As a shareholder, you believe the shares are actually worth as much as €30 per share, and would like the takeover to fail. Should you tender your shares?

Answer: We shall assume that you are a small shareholder and, as such, do not affect the success or failure of the offer. Your pay-offs in the event of the success or failure of the offer are given in the following table.

	Value if shareholder tenders	Value if shareholder doesn't tender
Bid succeeds	€25/share	€22/share
Bid fails	€30/share	€30/share

As the preceding numbers indicate, you should tender your shares regardless of what you think they are worth. If the bid succeeds, you are better off having tendered. If the bid fails, you are indifferent.

As Example 20.8 illustrates, two-tiered offers can be coercive, because they force some shareholders to tender their shares at prices they believe are inadequate. In theory, by making the second-tier offer sufficiently low, a bidder can successfully take over a firm at a price that all shareholders find unacceptable. There are, however, legal restrictions that limit how low the second-tier price can be. Although the bidder is not legally required to provide the target shareholders who do not tender with an amount that compensates them for all of the synergies brought about by the merger, the bidder is required to pay 'fair value' for the target shares in the follow-up merger.

In many takeovers that occurred in the 1980s, second-tier offers were substantially lower than first-tier offers. However, most companies currently have what is known as **fair price amendments** in their corporate charters, which require the second-tier price to be equal to the first-tier price. Most countries also have laws that require second-tier prices to be at least equal to first-tier prices.

20.11 Management Defences

Incumbent managers have come up with various defensive strategies to fight off unwanted takeover attempts. These include:

- paying **greenmail**, or buying back the bidder's equity at a substantial premium over its market price on condition that the bidder suspend his or her bid
- creating **staggered board terms** and **supermajority rules**, which can keep a bidder from taking over the firm even if he or she accumulates more than 50 per cent of the target firm's shares
- introducing **poison pills**, which provide valuable rights to target shareholders who choose not to tender their shares
- lobbying for anti-takeover legislation.

Greenmail

Greenmail was an activity that was popular in the US in the 1980s and 1990s. Hostile acquirers bought shares in a company and then asked for a premium on their holdings in order to go away (thereby reducing the likelihood of a hostile takeover). This premium was known as greenmail. Share prices generally drop when firms pay greenmail to large shareholders who are trying to take over the firm. In 1984, for example, David Murdoch, who owned about 5 per cent of Occidental Petroleum's equity, put pressure on Occidental's management to take actions to improve the value of its equity. Rather than change its policies, the firm bought Murdoch's shares at a substantial premium over their market price. It paid $40.10 for shares that had a market price of $28.75 just before the announcement of the purchase. In other words, it paid a premium of 42 per cent over the market price for Murdoch's shares, giving him a gain of over $56 million. On the announcement of the repurchase, the share price of Occidental dropped $0.875, indicating a reduction in the market value of the firm of more than $80 million. This $80 million loss underestimates the true drop in the firm's market value created by this buyout, since the price of Occidental's equity declined prior to the announcement of the buyback once shareholders began to anticipate not only that Murdoch might receive a $56 million gift but, more importantly, that he would be unsuccessful in getting the firm to change its policies.

Staggered Boards and Supermajority Rules

An acquirer does not necessarily gain control of a target firm after acquiring more than 50 per cent of its equity. Many corporations have supermajority rules that require shareholder approval by at least a two-thirds vote, and sometimes as much as 90 per cent of the shares, before a change in control can be implemented. In most cases, the board of directors can override the supermajority provision, but gaining control of the board can be difficult. Board members are often elected to three-year terms, which are generally staggered so that, in any given year, only one-third of the board members are elected.

Poison Pills

Poison pills, first introduced in the mid-1980s, are the most effective takeover defence, and thus warrant the most discussion. Poison pills are rights or securities that a firm issues to its shareholders, giving them valuable benefits in the event that a significant number of its shares are acquired. There are many varieties of poison pill, but all share the basic attribute that they involve a transfer from the bidder to shareholders who do not tender their shares, thereby increasing the cost of the acquisition and decreasing the incentives for target shareholders to tender at any given price.

Poison pills are illegal in many countries. For example, they are forbidden in the UK, where the supervisory authority, the Panel on Takeovers and Mergers, treats each takeover attempt on a case-by-case basis under the principles of the Takeover Code (2021). In Europe the situation is slightly different, because of the number of recently privatized companies and the political issues relating to takeovers by foreign investors. Many governments have **golden shares**, which are able to outvote all other shares in the case of a hostile bid. However, these have been ruled illegal by the European Commission in several cases, including BAA in the UK, and Telefonica, Repsol YPF and Endesa in Spain. Although explicit poison pills are uncommon in Europe, governments themselves can politically dissuade potential suitors from buying companies through implied regulatory sanctions and constraints, should a hostile bid be successful.

Flipover Rights Plans

The most popular poison pill defence is generally referred to as the **flipover rights plan**.[8] Under this plan, target shareholders receive the right to purchase the acquiring firm's equity at a substantial discount in the event of a merger. For example, if Alpha Corporation acquires Beta shares and then proceeds with a merger, existing Beta shareholders will receive rights to purchase Alphan equity at 50 per cent of its value in the event of the merger being consummated. This would make the merger prohibitively expensive for Alpha, which would be reluctant to proceed with the merger unless the poison pill was rescinded. In most cases, poison pills can be rescinded by the board of directors at a trivial cost to allow mergers that they believe are in the shareholders' interest to be implemented.

How Effective are Poison Pills?

Poison pills have been effective in allowing managers to delay unwanted takeovers, and to bargain more effectively with potential acquirers. However, they do not always make managers completely immune to unwanted takeovers. In many cases, bidders have taken target managers to court and have forced them to remove a poison pill. Comment and Schwert (1995) concluded that although poison pills have undoubtedly deterred some takeovers, these cases are relatively rare. Their evidence suggests that the decline in takeovers in the late 1980s and early 1990s was not due to poison pills and anti-takeover laws but to the demise of the junk

[8] For more information on poison pill defences, see Weston et al. (1990).

bond market and the credit crunch at commercial banks that occurred at about the same time. The boom in the takeover market in the 1990s, when credit markets recovered, provides further support for this claim. However, as we mentioned earlier, almost all the takeovers in this period were friendly.

Are Takeover Defences Good for Shareholders?

There has been an active debate about how good or bad these defensive actions are for shareholders. On the one hand, it is argued that takeover defences do no more than keep entrenched managers in power. A defensive action that prevents the success of an offer of £50 per share cannot be in the interests of shareholders if it results in the firm staying independent with a share price of £40. On the other hand, defensive actions sometimes result in the bidder making a higher offer, which of course benefits target shareholders. For example, a bidder who would otherwise bid £50 per share may be willing to raise his bid to £55 to prevent management resistance.

Evidence on the reaction of share prices to management defensive actions has been mixed. In some cases, share prices increase following the announcement of a defensive action, whereas in others the price decreases. Jarrell and Poulsen (1987) recorded that anti-takeover amendments, on average, lead to negative changes in the price of the target's equity. However, the share price reaction is not always negative, and is, on average, positive when a large percentage of the firm is held by institutional investors, who presumably are better able to block a proposed amendment that hurts shareholder value.

Humphery-Jenner and Powell (2011) considered Australian firms, where anti-takeover provisions are illegal. Unlike US takeovers, Australian takeovers create significant value for the acquirer's shareholders in terms of announcement returns and long-term productivity improvements. In contrast, Atanassov (2013) examines differences between states that have anti-takeover laws and those that don't. Atanassov (2013) finds that anti-takeover laws stifle innovation as measured by a fall in the number of patents and patent citations after the laws were introduced. This evidence is consistent with the hypothesis that most anti-takeover amendments hurt target shareholders, but on occasion their implementation may be in the shareholders' interests.

20.12 Summary and Conclusions

This chapter illustrates how the tools developed throughout this text can be used to analyse mergers and acquisitions. Acquisitions require the valuation of an existing business, which can be performed with the tools developed in Chapters 9–13. In addition, acquisitions need to be financed, so our analysis of the capital structure decisions in Chapters 14–19 is also applicable. The management incentive issues discussed in Chapter 18 are especially important for understanding the takeover market. Some acquisitions are motivated by value improvements created by correcting incentive problems. However, many bad acquisitions were motivated by bad incentives.

In summary, we suggest that managers consider the following checklist for evaluating a merger or acquisition proposal.

- Evaluate and quantify the real operating synergies of the acquisition. Is a merger the best way of achieving these synergies?
- Evaluate and quantify the tax benefits of the merger. Is a merger required to achieve these tax benefits?
- Evaluate how management incentives are affected by the merger. Will the acquisition correct an incentive problem, or will it create new incentive problems?

Based on an analysis of the empirical evidence, we cannot say whether mergers, on average, create value. Certainly, some mergers have created value, but others were either mistakes or bad decisions. Of course, many of the mistakes were due to unforeseen circumstances, and were unavoidable. However, we believe that other mergers and acquisitions were due to misguided notions about the value of diversification, misaligned incentives of the acquiring firm's management, or poor judgement. Fortunately, past experience has taught us a great deal about how mergers can create value, and we believe that firms can apply this knowledge to make sound acquisition decisions.

Key Concepts

Result 20.1: The main sources of takeover gains are:

- taxes
- operating synergies
- target incentive problems
- financial synergies.

Result 20.2: Conglomerates can provide funding for investment projects that independent (smaller) firms would not have been able to fund using outside capital markets. To the extent that positive-NPV projects receive funding they would not otherwise have received, conglomerates create value.

Result 20.3: The advantages of diversification can be described as follows.

- Diversification enhances the flexibility of the organization.
- The internal capital market avoids some of the information problems inherent in an external capital market.
- Diversification reduces the probability of bankruptcy for any given level of debt, and increases the firm's debt capacity.
- Competitors find it more difficult to uncover proprietary information from diversified firms.
- Diversification is advantageous if it allows the firm to utilize its organization more effectively.

The disadvantages of diversification can be described as follows.

- Diversification can eliminate a valuable source of information, and may, among other things, make it difficult to compensate the division heads of large diversified firms efficiently.
- Managers may find it difficult to cut back optimally on losing divisions when they can subsidize the losers out of the profits from their winners.

Result 20.4: Share price reactions to takeover bids can be described as follows.

- The share prices of target firms almost always react favourably to merger and tender offer bids.
- The bidder's share price sometimes goes up and sometimes goes down, depending on the circumstances.
- The combined market values of the shares of the target and bidder go up, on average, around the time of the announced bids.

Result 20.5: The bidder's share price reacts more favourably, on average, when the bidder makes a cash offer rather than an offer to exchange equity. This may reflect the relatively negative information about the bidder's existing business signalled by the offer to exchange equity.

Result 20.6: On average, cash flows of firms improve following leveraged buyouts. Three possible explanations for these improvements are:

1. productivity gains
2. initiation of LBOs by firms with improving prospects
3. the incentives of leveraged firms to accelerate cash flows, sometimes at the expense of long-run cash flows.

Although we expect all three factors to contribute to the observed increase in cash flows, existing empirical evidence suggests that a major part of the increase is due to productivity gains.

Result 20.7: Small shareholders will not tender their shares if they are offered less than the post-takeover value of the shares. As a result, takeovers that could potentially lead to substantial value improvements may fail.

Key Terms

acquiring firm 634
acquisition 633
any-or-all offer 657
conditional tender offer 656
conglomerate (or diversifying) acquisition 636
disciplinary takeover 636
fair price amendment 660
financial acquisition 636
financial synergies 637
flipover rights plan 661
follow-up merger 659
friendly takeover 636
golden shares 661
greenmail 660
horizontal merger 639
hostile takeover 636
management buyout (MBO) 640
merger 633
operating synergies 636
poison pill 660
raider 640
staggered board terms 660
strategic acquisition 636
supermajority rules 660
takeover premium 634
target firm 634
tender offer 636
Tobin's q 648
two-tiered offer 659
unconditional offer 657
vertical merger 639

Exercises

20.1 London Mitchell plc is currently selling for £25 a share, and pays a dividend of £2 a share per year. Analysts expect the earnings and dividends to grow at 4 per cent per year into the foreseeable future. The company has 1 million shares outstanding. Mark Mitchell, the CEO, would like to take the firm private in a leveraged buyout. Following the buyout, the firm is expected to cut operating costs, which will result in a 10 per cent improvement in earnings. In addition, the firm will cut administrative fixed costs by £200,000 per year and save £500,000 per year on taxes for the next 10 years. Assuming that the risk-free interest rate is 5 per cent, and that London Mitchell's cost of capital is 12 per cent per year, what value would you put on London Mitchell following the LBO?

20.2 Refer to exercise 20.1. Explain why Mark Mitchell is likely to make these changes following an LBO, but would not make the changes in the absence of an LBO.

20.3 What type of firm would you prefer to work for: a diversified firm or a very focused firm? What does your answer to this question tell you about one of the advantages or disadvantages of diversification?

20.4 Diversified Industries plc has made a bid to purchase Cigmatics plc, offering to exchange two Diversified shares for one share of Cigmatics. When this bid is announced, Diversified Industries' shares drop 5 per cent. The CEO has asked you to interpret what this decline in share prices means. Does it imply that Cigmatics is a bad acquisition?

20.5 Leveraged buyouts are observed mainly in industries with relatively stable cash flows and products that are not highly specialized. Explain why.

20.6 When a firm with an extremely high price/earnings ratio purchases a firm with a very low price/earnings ratio in an exchange of equity, its earnings per share will increase. Do you think firms are more likely to acquire other firms when it results in an increase in their earnings per share? Is it beneficial to shareholders to initiate a takeover for these reasons?

20.7 Tobacco companies have a large potential liability. In the future, they may be subject to extremely large product liability lawsuits. Discuss how this affects the incentives of tobacco companies to merge with food companies.

20.8 One of the stated benefits of a management buyout is the improvement in management incentives. In many cases, however, the top managers do not change after the buyout. Explain why.

References and Additional Reading

Ahern, K.R., Daminelli, D. and Fracassi, C. (2015) Lost in translation? The effect of cultural values on mergers around the world, *Journal of Financial Economics*, 117(1): 165–189.

Ahern, K.R. and Harford, J. (2014) The importance of industry links in merger waves, *The Journal of Finance*, 69(2): 527–576.

Aktas, N., Baros, A. and Croci, E. (2022) Corporate divestitures around acquisitions, *Journal of Corporate Finance*, 73, 102189.

Aktas, N., De Bodt, E. and Roll, R. (2011) Serial acquirer bidding: An empirical test of the learning hypothesis, *Journal of Corporate Finance*, 17(1): 18–32.

Almazan, A., De Motta, A., Titman, S. and Uysal, V. (2010) Financial structure, acquisition opportunities, and firm locations, *The Journal of Finance*, 65(2): 529–563.

Amihud, Y. and Lev, B. (1981) Risk reduction as a managerial motive for conglomerate mergers, *Bell Journal of Economics*, 12(2): 605–617.

Andrade, G., Mitchell, M. and Stafford, E. (2001) New evidence and perspectives on mergers, *Journal of Economic Perspectives*, 15(2): 103–120.

Anton, M., Azar, J., Gine, M. and Lin, L.X. (2022) Beyond the target: M&A decisions and rival ownership, *Journal of Financial Economics*, 144(1): 44–66.

Antoniou, A., Arbour, P. and Zhao, H. (2008) How much is too much? Are merger premiums too high?, *European Financial Management*, 14(2): 268–287.

Arikan, A.M. and Stulz, R.M. (2016) Corporate acquisitions, diversification, and the firm's life cycle, *The Journal of Finance*, 71(1): 139–194.

Asquith, P. (1983) Merger bids, uncertainty, and shareholder returns, *Journal of Financial Economics*, 11(1): 51–83.

Atanassov, J. (2013) Do hostile takeovers stifle innovation? Evidence from antitakeover legislation and corporate patenting, *The Journal of Finance*, 68(3): 1097–1131.

Baker, M., Pan, X. and Wurgler, J. (2012) The effect of reference point prices on mergers and acquisitions, *Journal of Financial Economics*, 106(1): 49–71.

Bena, J. and Li, K. (2014) Corporate innovations and mergers and acquisitions, *The Journal of Finance*, 69(5): 1923–1960.

Berger, P.G. and Ofek, E. (1995) Diversification's effect on firm value, *Journal of Financial Economics*, 37(1): 39–65.

Bhagat, S., Shleifer, A. and Vishny, R. (1990) Hostile takeovers in the 1980s: the return to corporate specialization, *Brookings Papers on Economic Activity: Microeconomics, Special Issue*, 1–72.

Bhide, A. (1990) Reversing corporate diversification, *Journal of Applied Corporate Finance*, 5(2): 70–81.

Boguth, O., Duchin, R. and Simutin, M. (2022) Dissecting Conglomerate Valuations, *The Journal of Finance*, 77(2): 1097–1131.

Bonaime, A., Gulen, H. and Ion, M. (2018) Does policy uncertainty affect mergers and acquisitions?, *Journal of Financial Economics*, 129(3): 531–558.

Boucly, Q., Sraer, D. and Thesmar, D. (2011) Growth lbos, *Journal of Financial Economics*, 102(2): 432–453.

Bradley, M. (1980) Interfirm tender offers and the market for corporate control, *Journal of Business*, 53(4): 345–376.

Bradley, M., Desai, A. and Kim, E.H. (1983) The rationale behind interfirm tender offers, *Journal of Financial Economics*, 11(1): 183–206.

Bradley, M., Desai, A. and Kim, E.H. (1988) Synergistic gains from corporate acquisitions and their division between the stockholders of target and acquiring firms, *Journal of Financial Economics*, 11(1): 3–40.

Burkart, M. and Lee, S. (2022) Activism and takeovers, *The Review of Financial Studies*, 35(4): 1868–1896.

Cai, Y. and Sevilir, M. (2012) Board connections and M&A transactions, *Journal of Financial Economics*, 103(2): 327–349.

Campa, J.M. and Kedia, S. (2002) Explaining the diversification discount, *The Journal of Finance*, 57(4): 1731–1762.

Chari, A., Ouimet, P.P. and Tesar, L.L. (2010) The value of control in emerging markets, *The Review of Financial Studies*, 23(4): 1741–1770.

Chikh, S. and Filbien, J.Y. (2011) Acquisitions and CEO power: Evidence from French networks, *Journal of Corporate Finance*, 17(5): 1221–1236.

Comment, R. and Jarrell, G.A. (1995) Corporate focus and stock returns, *Journal of Financial Economics*, 37(1): 67–87.

Comment, R. and Schwert, G.W. (1995) Poison or placebo? Evidence on the deterrence and wealth effects of modern antitakeover measures, *Journal of Financial Economics*, 39(1): 3–43.

Deng, X., Kang, J.K. and Low, B.S. (2013) Corporate social responsibility and stakeholder value maximization: Evidence from mergers, *Journal of Financial Economics*, 110(1): 87–109.

Denis, D.J., Denis, D.K. and Sarin, A. (1997) Agency problems, equity ownership and corporate diversifications, *The Journal of Finance*, 52(1): 135–160.

Dodd, P. (1980) Merger proposals, management discretion and shareholder wealth, *Journal of Financial Economics*, 8(2): 105–138.

Eckbo, B.E., Giammarino, R.M. and Heinkel, R.L. (1990) Asymmetric information and the medium of exchange in takeovers: theory and tests, *The Review of Financial Studies*, 3(4): 651–675.

El-Khatib, R., Fogel, K. and Jandik, T. (2015) CEO network centrality and merger performance, *Journal of Financial Economics*, 116(2): 349–382.

Erel, I., Liao, R.C. and Weisbach, M.S. (2012) Determinants of cross-border mergers and acquisitions, *The Journal of Finance*, 67(3): 1045–1082.

Faccio, M. and Masulis, R. (2005) The choice of payment method in European mergers and acquisitions, *Journal of Finance*, 60(3): 1345–1388.

Fairhurst, D.D. and Greene, D.T. (2022) Too much of a good thing? Corporate social responsibility and the takeover market, *Journal of Corporate Finance*, 73, 102172.

Ferreira, M.A., Massa, M. and Matos, P. (2010) Shareholders at the gate? Institutional investors and cross-border mergers and acquisitions, *The Review of Financial Studies*, 23(2): 601–644.

Franks, J.R., Harris, R.S. and Mayer, C. (1988) Means of payment in takeovers: results for the UK and US, in A.J. Auerbach (ed.) *Corporate Takeovers: Causes and Consequences*. Chicago: University of Chicago Press, 221–264.

Garfinkel, J.A. and Hankins, K.W. (2011) The role of risk management in mergers and merger waves, *Journal of Financial Economics*, 101(3): 515–532.

Graham, J., Lemmon, M. and Wolf, J. (2002) Does corporate diversification destroy value?, *The Journal of Finance*, 57(2): 695–720.

Grossman, S.J. and Hart, O.D. (1980) Takeover bids, the free-rider problem and the theory of the corporation, *Bell Journal of Economics*, 11(1): 42–64.

Grossman, S.J. and Hart, O.D. (1986) The costs and benefits of ownership: a theory of vertical and lateral integration, *Journal of Political Economy*, 94(4): 691–719.

Guo, S., Hotchkiss, E.S. and Song, W. (2011) Do buyouts (still) create value?, *The Journal of Finance*, 66(2): 479–517.

Harford, J., Humphery-Jenner, M. and Powell, R. (2012) The sources of value destruction in acquisitions by entrenched managers, *Journal of Financial Economics*, 106(2): 247–261.

Hasbrouck, J. (1985) The characteristics of takeover targets, *Journal of Banking and Finance*, 9(3): 351–362.

Healy, P., Palepu, K. and Ruback, R. (1992) Does corporate performance improve after mergers?, *Journal of Financial Economics*, 31(2): 135–175.

Hirshleifer, D. (1995) Mergers and acquisitions: strategic and informational issues, in *Handbooks in Operations Research and Management Science: Volume 9, Finance*, in Jarrow, R., Maksimovic, V., and Ziemba, W. (eds). Amsterdam: Elsevier Science, 839–885.

Holmstrom, B. and Kaplan, S. (2001) Corporate governance and merger activity in the United States: making sense of the 1980s and 1990s, *Journal of Economic Perspectives*, 15(2): 121–144.

Huang, Y.-S. and Walkling, R.A. (1987) Target abnormal returns associated with acquisition announcements: payment, acquisition form, and managerial resistance, *Journal of Financial Economics*, 19(2): 329–350.

Humphery-Jenner, M.L. and Powell, R.G. (2011) Firm size, takeover profitability, and the effectiveness of the market for corporate control: Does the absence of anti-takeover provisions make a difference?, *Journal of Corporate Finance*, 17(3): 418–437.

Ishii, J. and Xuan, Y. (2014) Acquirer-target social ties and merger outcomes, *Journal of Financial Economics*, 112(3): 344–363.

Jarrell, G.A. and Poulsen, A.B. (1987) Shark repellents and share prices: the effects of antitakeover amendments since 1980, *Journal of Financial Economics*, 19(1): 127–168.

Jarrell, G.A. and Poulsen, A.B. (1989) The returns to acquiring firms in tender offers: evidence from three decades, *Financial Management*, 18(3): 12–19.

Jarrell, G.A., Brickley, J. and Netter, J. (1988) The market for corporate control: the empirical evidence since 1980, *Journal of Economic Perspectives*, 2(1): 49–68.

Jensen, M.C. (1986) Agency costs of free cash flow, corporate finance, and takeovers, *American Economic Review*, 76(2): 323–329.

Jensen, M.C. and Ruback, R. (1983) The market for corporate control: the scientific evidence, *Journal of Financial Economics*, 11(1–4): 5–50.

John, K., Freund, S., Nguyen, D. and Vasudevan, G.K. (2010) Investor protection and cross-border acquisitions of private and public targets, *Journal of Corporate Finance*, 16(3): 259–275.

Kaplan, S.N. (1989) The effects of management buyouts on operating performance and value, *Journal of Financial Economics*, 24(2): 217–254.

Kaplan, S.N. and Stein, J. (1993) The evolution of buyout pricing and financial structure in the 1980s, *Quarterly Journal of Economics*, 108(2): 313–357.

Kaplan, S.N. and Weisbach, M.S. (1992) The success of acquisitions: evidence from divestitures, *The Journal of Finance*, 47(1): 107–138.

Klein, A. (1986) The timing and substance of divestiture announcements: individual, simultaneous and cumulative effects, *The Journal of Finance*, 41(3): 685–697.

Klein, B., Crawford, R.G. and Alchian, A.A. (1978) Vertical integration, appropriable rents and the competitive contracting process, *Journal of Law and Economics*, 21(2): 297–326.

Krüger, P., Landier, A. and Thesmar, D. (2015) The WACC fallacy: The real effects of using a unique discount rate, *The Journal of Finance*, 70(3): 1253–1285.

Kuppuswamy, V. and Villalonga, B. (2010) Does diversification create value in the presence of external financing constraints? Evidence from the 2008–2009 financial crisis, Working Paper, Harvard Business School.

Lang, L.H.P. and Stulz, R.M. (1994) Tobin's *q*, corporate diversification and firm performance, *Journal of Political Economy*, 102(6): 1248–1280.

Lang, L.H.P., Stulz, R.M. and Walkling, R.A. (1991) A test of the free cash flow hypothesis: the case of bidder returns, *Journal of Financial Economics*, 29(2): 315–336

Lehn, K. and Poulsen, A. (1989) Free cash flow and shareholder gains in going private transactions, *The Journal of Finance*, 44(3): 771–787.

Lerner, J., Sorensen, M. and Strömberg, P. (2011) Private equity and long-run investment: The case of innovation, *The Journal of Finance*, 66(2): 445–477.

Levi, M., Li, K. and Zhang, F. (2014) Director gender and mergers and acquisitions, *Journal of Corporate Finance*, 28, 185–200.

Lichtenberg, F.R. and Siegel, D. (1990) The effects of leveraged buyouts on productivity and related aspects of firm behavior, *Journal of Financial Economics*, 27(1): 165–194.

Lins, K. and Servaes, H. (1999) International evidence on the value of corporate diversification, *The Journal of Finance*, 54(6): 2215–2239.

Lowenstein, L. (1985) Management buyouts, *Columbia Law Review*, 85, 730–784.

Lys, T. and Vincent, L. (1995) An analysis of value destruction in AT&T's acquisition of NCR, *Journal of Financial Economics*, 39(2–3): 353–378.

Masulis, R., Wang, C. and Xie, F. (2007) Corporate governance and acquirer returns, *The Journal of Finance*, 62(4): 1851–1889.

Matsusaka, J.G. (1993) Takeover motives during the conglomerate merger wave, *Rand Journal of Economics*, 24(3): 357–379.

Matsusaka, J.G. (1996) Did tough antitrust enforcement cause the diversification of American corporations?, *Journal of Financial and Quantitative Analysis,* 31(2): 283–294.

Mitchell, M.L. and Lehn, K. (1990) Do bad bidders make good targets?, *Journal of Applied Corporate Finance,* 3(2): 60–69.

Moeller, S.B., Schlingemann, F.P. and Stulz, R.M. (2004) Firm size and the gains from acquisitions, *Journal of Financial Economics,* 73(2): 201–228.

Morck, R., Shleifer, A. and Vishny, R.W. (1990) Do managerial objectives drive bad acquisitions?, *Journal of Finance,* 45(1): 31–48.

Muscarella, C. and Vetsuypens, M. (1990) Efficiency and organizational change: a study of reverse LBOs, *The Journal of Finance,* 45(5): 1389–1413.

Opler, T.C. (1993) Operating performance in leveraged buyouts: evidence from 1985–1989, *Financial Management,* 21(1): 27–34.

Rajan, R., Servaes, H. and Zingales, L. (2000) The cost of diversity: the diversification discount and inefficient investment, *Journal of Finance,* 55(1): 35–80.

Ravenscraft, D.J. and Scherer, F.M. (1987) *Mergers, Selloffs, and Economic Efficiency.* Washington, DC: Brookings Institution.

Rock, K. (1984) *Gulf Oil Corporation–Takeover,* Harvard Case 9-285-053, Harvard Business Publishing.

Safieddine, A. and Titman, S. (1999) Leverage and corporate performance: evidence from unsuccessful takeovers, *The Journal of Finance,* 54(2): 547–580.

Sampson, A. (1973) *The Sovereign State of ITT.* New York: Stein & Day.

Serdar Dinc, I. and Erel, I. (2013) Economic nationalism in mergers and acquisitions, *The Journal of Finance,* 68(6): 2471–2514.

Servaes, H. (1996) The value of diversification during conglomerate merger waves, *The Journal of Finance,* 51(4): 1201–1225.

Shleifer, A. and Summers, L. (1988) Breach of trust in hostile takeovers, in *Corporate Takeovers: Causes and Consequences,* in A.J. Auerbach (ed.). Chicago: University of Chicago Press, 33–68.

Smith, A.J. (1990) Corporate ownership structure and performance: the case of management buyouts, *Journal of Financial Economics,* 27(1): 143–164.

Travlos, N.G. (1987) Corporate takeover bids, methods of payment, and bidding firms' equity returns, *The Journal of Finance,* 42(4): 943–963.

Tsang, A., Yang, N. and Zheng, L. (2021) Cross-listings, antitakeover defenses, and the insulation hypothesis, *Journal of Financial Economics,* 145(1): 259–276.

Villalonga, B. (2004) Diversification discount or premium? New evidence from the Business Information Tracking Series, *The Journal of Finance,* 59(2): 479–506.

Wang, C. and Xie, F. (2009) Corporate governance transfer and synergistic gains from mergers and acquisitions, *The Review of Financial Studies,* 22(2): 829–858.

Weston, J.F., Chung, K.S. and Hoag, S.E. (1990) *Mergers, Restructuring, and Corporate Control.* Englewood Cliffs, NJ: Prentice Hall.

Yim, S. (2013) The acquisitiveness of youth: CEO age and acquisition behavior, *Journal of Financial Economics,* 108(1): 250–273.

Practical Insights for Part V

Allocating Capital for Real Investment

- Managers, acting in their own interests, often invest more than shareholders would like. (Section 18.3)
- Managers and large shareholders sometimes prefer diversifying investments that reduce the probability of the firm going bankrupt over higher-NPV investments that provide less diversification. (Section 18.3)
- Managers may choose investment projects that pay off quickly over projects with higher NPVs that take longer to pay off if increasing the firm's current share price is an important consideration for them. (Section 19.3)
- Managers who wish to boost their share prices temporarily may underinvest in positive-NPV projects that cannot readily be observed by shareholders, and instead use the cash savings to pay a dividend or repurchase shares. (Section 19.4)
- Managers sometimes have information that indicates that their debt and equity is not fairly priced, which implies that their financing alternatives may not have zero NPVs. Managers may therefore pass up positive-NPV investments if they must be financed by negative-NPV instruments. (Section 19.5)
- Corporate takeovers can create value through tax savings, operating synergies and financial synergies, and by correcting incentive problems. (Section 20.4)
- Because of various capital market imperfections, conglomerates sometimes do better than the capital markets in allocating investment capital. However, markets allocate capital better when market prices contain useful information that managers do not have, and when there exist conflicts between managers' and shareholders' interests. (Section 20.4)

Financing the Firm

- In most major corporations, the debt–equity choice is made by the board of directors, but investment choices are made by management. If the board understands the tendency of management to overinvest, they might want to offset this tendency by increasing the firm's debt-to-equity ratio. (Sections 18.3, 18.4)
- Managers should not use share price reactions to corporate actions, such as dividend and leverage changes, to evaluate how the market views the decision. The market may be reacting to the information conveyed by the decision rather than to whether the decision is value enhancing. For example, the market may react positively to the announcement of a cash-financed acquisition if investors are surprised by the firm's ability to raise the cash for the acquisition. This may be the case even when the acquisition itself is a negative-NPV investment. (Section 19.1)
- If the firm's board of directors and its management believe that the firm is undervalued, they might choose to increase the firm's debt ratio to convince investors that its value is higher. Increasing leverage provides a favourable signal for two reasons. First, it demonstrates that managers (who personally find financial distress costly) are confident that they can generate the cash needed to meet the higher debt obligation. Second, the firm sends the signal that its shares are a 'good investment' when it increases its leverage by repurchasing shares. (Section 19.5)
- When a firm is doing poorly, there is generally a lot of uncertainty about its true value. A firm's share price would be likely to react very negatively in this situation if the firm issued equity. A manager might also consider debt financing very unattractive in this situation because of the threat of bankruptcy, and perhaps less need for the tax benefits of debt. For these reasons, we often observe firms issuing preferred equity in these situations. (Section 19.5)
- Firms often use their equity to finance major acquisitions. One previous advantage of this was that it allowed the firm to use pooling of interest accounting, which is no longer permitted. This financing option is also less attractive when the acquirer believes its own equity is undervalued. (Section 20.9)

Allocating Funds for Financial Investments

- Decisions that lead to higher leverage ratios generally result in higher share prices. Decisions that lead to lower leverage ratios generally result in lower share prices. (Section 19.6)
- Increased dividends and share repurchases generally result in higher share prices. Dividend cuts and equity issues generally result in lower share prices. (Section 19.6)
- Empirical evidence suggests that share prices underreact to some corporate announcements, such as dividend and capital structure changes. Investors may be able to profit by buying shares following announcements that convey positive information, and selling shares following announcements that convey negative information. (Section 19.6)

PART 6

Risk Management

Part contents

Risk management entails assessing and managing, through the use of financial derivatives, insurance and other activities, the corporation's exposure to various sources of risk. Hence risk management specialists need a sound understanding of derivative securities (see Chapters 7 and 8), tools for estimating the risk exposure of their firm (see Chapters 4–6) and an understanding of which risks should and should not be hedged.

Chapter 21, the first chapter in Part 6, describes the various motivations for firms to expend funds and human resources to reduce their exposures to various sources of risk. These hedging motivations relate closely to the issues examined in Parts 4 and 5: minimization of taxes, reducing financial distress costs, matching cash flows with investment needs and reducing incentive problems. We argue in this chapter that the motivation to hedge determines which risks the firms should hedge, as well as how firms should organize their hedging operations. In particular, Chapter 21 discusses the differences among firms in their motivations for hedging. Depending on these motivations, some firms seek to hedge cash flow (or earnings) risk, while others seek to hedge against changes in firm values.

Chapters 22 and 23 focus more on the implementation of risk management, analysing how firms can alter or eliminate their exposure to risk by acquiring various financial instruments. Chapter 22 is devoted largely to managing currency and commodity risk, and Chapter 23 focuses on interest rate risk. Interest rate risk deserves unique treatment because interest rates, as discount factors, affect the present values of cash flows, even when they do not affect the cash flows directly.

Risk management requires a firm to first estimate its risk exposure. For example, an oil firm might want to know how much its earnings will decline next year if oil prices drop $3 a barrel. A financial institution is similarly interested in how changes in interest rates affect the value of its loan portfolio. Both Chapters 22 and 23 discuss how such risk exposure is measured, using some familiar tools developed in previous chapters, including factor models, regression and theoretical derivative pricing relationships. The two chapters also introduce popular ways to measure risk, such as value at risk (VAR), and discuss various ways of measuring interest rate risk through concepts such as duration, DV01 and yield betas.

After estimating its risk exposure, the firm might want to consider various alternatives for eliminating the risk. If financial assets exist that track the risk exposure exactly, then risk can be eliminated or at least altered with offsetting positions in these assets. Both Chapters 22 and 23 discuss how to hedge with a variety of financial instruments that track a firm's risk.

Chapter

21

Risk Management and Corporate Strategy

Learning Objectives

After reading this chapter, you should be able to:

- Understand the different motivations for corporate hedging.
- Explain which firms should be the most interested in hedging.
- Understand which risks firms should hedge.
- Understand the different motivations for foreign currency and interest rate risk management.

BMW incurs most of its expenses in Germany, where it performs the bulk of its R&D and most of its manufacturing. However, the company generates revenues throughout the world. BMW is subject to substantial currency risk because of the relatively long time between its quotation of a price to a customer and the customer's payment for the purchased products. BMW's policy has been to actively hedge the currency exposures that arise in these situations.

Corporations throughout the world devote substantial resources to **risk management**. Risk management entails assessing and managing the corporation's exposure to various sources of risk through the use of financial derivatives, insurance and other activities.

Previous chapters assumed that a firm's **risk profile** – that is, the kinds of risks it is exposed to – is taken as given. This chapter moves back one step and examines how firms determine their risk profiles. For example, if BMW chooses not to **hedge**, or take offsetting positions, to eliminate the dollar exposure arising from its sales in the USA, its equity would probably show some sensitivity to movements in the dollar relative to the euro. By hedging that exposure, BMW's equity is less sensitive to those sorts of currency movement.

The idea that corporations should manage exposure to various sources of risk is becoming increasingly important. In contrast to the past, when the chief financial officer (CFO) of a corporation would spend a small portion of his time on hedging, many corporations now have entire departments devoted to hedging and risk management. A survey conducted for the G30 nations reported that more than 80 per cent of the surveyed corporations considered derivatives either very important (44 per cent) or imperative (37 per cent) in controlling risk. Of the respondents, 87 per cent used interest rate swaps, 64 per cent currency swaps, 78 per cent forward foreign exchange contracts, 40 per cent interest rate options and 31 per cent currency options.

Since the publication of the Group of Thirty study, derivative usage has continued to grow worldwide. For example, in a recent international study, Bartram (2017) showed that 60.5 per cent of firms use derivatives, with 45.5 per cent using currency derivatives, 33.1 per cent using interest rate derivatives and 9.8 per cent using commodity derivatives.

The trend towards greater attention to risk management is due to a number of factors, most notably the increased volatility of interest rates and exchange rates, and the increased importance of multinational corporations. In addition, the growing understanding of derivative instruments (see Chapters 7 and 8) has also contributed to their increased acceptance as tools for risk management.

The motivation for risk management comes from a variety of sources: taxes, financial distress costs, executive incentives and other important issues discussed in earlier chapters. Understanding these motives is important, because they provide insights into which risks should be hedged, and how a firm's hedging operations should be organized.

21.1 Risk Management and the Modigliani–Miller Theorem

Most financial innovations are associated with the markets for derivative securities, such as options, forward contracts, swap contracts and futures. These contracts provide relatively inexpensive and efficient ways for corporations and investors to bundle and unbundle various aspects of risk, allowing those who are least able to bear the risks to pass them off to others who can bear them more efficiently.

To understand this, return to the factor model introduced in Chapter 6 to re-examine the equity returns of firm i. We shall express those returns as

$$\tilde{r}_{\mathrm{ABC}} = \alpha_i + \beta_{i1}\tilde{F}_1 + \beta_{i2}\tilde{F}_2 + \cdots + \beta_{iK}\tilde{F}_K + \tilde{\varepsilon}_i \tag{21.1}$$

where

the $\tilde{F}$ represent macroeconomic factors such as interest rate movements, currency changes, oil price changes and changes in the aggregate economy

the β represent the equity's sensitivity to those factors, or factor betas

$\tilde{\varepsilon}$ is firm-specific risk.

An equity's sensitivity to factor risk as well as firm-specific risk is determined by the firm's capital expenditure and operating decisions (for example, whether to locate a plant in Belgium or Malaysia) and its financial decisions (for example, whether to borrow in dollars or euros).

Factor risk is generally not diversifiable, but often it can be hedged by taking offsetting positions in financial derivatives. *Firm-specific risk* is just the opposite; it is generally diversifiable, but cannot be hedged with derivative contracts. It is possible, however, to hedge many sources of firm-specific risk with insurance contracts. For example, a fire insurance contract provides a good hedge against the losses incurred as the result of a fire.

The Investor's Hedging Choice

Before analysing the hedging choice of firms, it is instructive to first consider the possibility that individual investors hedge on their own. Assume that an investor observes the factor sensitivities of the different investments available to them, and constructs a relatively balanced portfolio that diversifies away firm-specific risk and is weighted to give the investor their preferred exposure to the various sources of factor risk, as represented by a particular configuration of factor betas.

Recall that the betas or factor sensitivities of the portfolio are the weighted averages of the sensitivities of the different securities held in the portfolio. In addition to buying and selling equities and bonds with the appropriate risk profiles, the investor may use derivatives to alter more directly the portfolio's exposure to particular sources of systematic risk. For example, if $\tilde{F}_2$ in equation (21.1) represents uncertain movements in oil prices, investors can change the exposures of their portfolios to oil price movements directly by buying or selling oil price futures or forward contracts.

Derivatives such as forwards and futures are indeed used by many investors in exactly this manner. However the most important users of derivative instruments are corporations and financial institutions, such as banks that want to alter the risk profiles of their firms.

Implications of the Modigliani–Miller Theorem for Hedging

To understand why a firm like BMW would want to change its risk exposure, we must first return to the Modigliani–Miller theorem (see Chapter 14). This theorem states that, in the absence of taxes and other market frictions the capital structure decision is irrelevant. In other words, financial decisions cannot create value for a firm unless they in some way affect either the firm's ability to operate its business or its incentives to invest in the future.

The Modigliani–Miller theorem was applied initially to the analysis of the firm's debt–equity choice. However, the theorem is really much more general, and can be applied to the analysis of all aspects of the firm's financial strategy. This would include, for example, a firm's choice of borrowing at a fixed rate or a floating rate; issuing bonds with promised payments denominated in British pounds or US dollars; or issuing bonds with payments linked to the price of oil or some other commodity. In all cases, these choices affect firm values only when there are relevant market frictions such as taxes, transaction costs and financial distress costs. The Modigliani–Miller theorem also applies to other financial contracts and instruments. Firms can benefit from futures, forwards and swap contracts, but only in the presence of these same frictions.

The Modigliani–Miller theorem can be proved by showing that individual investors can use 'home-made' leverage on their own accounts to undo or duplicate any leverage choice made by the firms they own. It is also possible to apply this theorem to show that, in the absence of market frictions, shareholders are indifferent between hedging on their own accounts and having their firms do the hedging for them. For example, given frictionless markets, shareholders realize identical returns if BMW hedges its exposure to changes in the US dollar/euro exchange rate or if, alternatively, BMW chooses not to hedge, and the shareholders do the hedging in their personal accounts. In other words, investors can form portfolios with the same factor risk and the same expected returns, regardless of how firms hedge. As a result, in frictionless markets where the operations side of the firm is held fixed, investors gain nothing from the hedging choices of the firm.

Results

Result 21.1

If hedging choices do not affect cash flows from real assets, then, in the absence of taxes and transaction costs, hedging decisions do not affect firm values.

Relaxing the Modigliani–Miller Assumptions

To understand why firms hedge, we must re-evaluate the assumptions underlying the Modigliani–Miller Theorem, and ask which assumptions are likely to be unrealistic. Our method for understanding why firms hedge is thus similar to the method employed in Chapters 14–19 to understand the firm's capital structure choice, and we draw heavily from the analysis in those chapters.

The assumptions of the theorem imply that investors as well as corporations have access to hedging instruments with no transaction costs. In reality, corporations are often in a much better position than their shareholders to hedge certain risks. For example, most institutional and individual investors would find it costly to learn how to hedge a food company's exposure to changes in the price of palm oil, even though markets for such hedging instruments exist. In addition, corporate executives are much more knowledgeable than shareholders about their firm's risk exposures, and thus are in a better position to know how much to hedge.[1]

Nevertheless, the difficulties faced by shareholders who wish to hedge their portfolio are probably not a prime reason or motivation for why large firms, owned primarily by diversified investors, choose to hedge. Although these difficult-to-hedge risks may affect the volatilities of individual equities, most volatility is diversified away in large portfolios. Thus hedging is unlikely to reduce a firm's cost of capital significantly.

[1] Although hedging non-diversifiable risks, such as interest rate movements, can affect a firm's cost of capital, it should still have no effect on the firm's value. In this case, the reduction in the cost of capital should be offset exactly by the effect of the hedge on cash flows.

If hedging cannot reduce the discount rate a firm applies to value its cash flows, then hedging must increase expected cash flows if it is to improve the firm's value.

Results

Result 21.2

Hedging is unlikely to improve a firm's value if it does no more than reduce the variance of its future cash flows. To improve a firm's value, hedging must also increase expected cash flows.

21.2 Why Do Firms Hedge?

Shortly after Russia's invasion of Ukraine on 24 February 2022, the price of oil and gas went up substantially. Within months of the invasion, energy prices were at record levels and set to go even higher as Western sanctions caused Russia to cut gas supplies to Europe. Energy firms hedge against price fluctuations on a regular basis but after the Ukraine invasion, companies from all sectors started looking into hedging energy price risk.

A Simple Analogy

In our everyday life, individuals make choices that reduce risk. For example, when an executive wishes to travel from her home to the airport, she can choose between taking the car or the train. Most of the time she takes the car, because it is generally faster. However, travel time in the car varies considerably, depending on traffic conditions. Travelling on the motorway between 4:00 and 6:00 pm takes anywhere between 30 minutes and an hour, with an expected time of 40 minutes. With certainty, it takes 50 minutes to get to the airport on the train.

Even though, on average, it takes longer to go by train, the executive prefers this more certain route during rush hour, because the loss from getting a bad outcome on the risky route (for example, missing her plane) far outweighs the gain of getting a good outcome on this route (for example, having enough time to have a glass of wine before the flight leaves). Generally, it is this type of asymmetry between gains and losses that leads us to make choices that reduce risk.

As we shall show, similar asymmetries between losses and gains lead corporations to make choices that reduce their risks. This will be true even if the corporation is owned by shareholders who are risk neutral and thus prefer to maximize expected return. We describe the sources of these asymmetries below.

How Does Hedging Increase Expected Cash Flows?

The rest of this chapter will examine various ways in which firms can increase their expected cash flows by implementing risk management programmes. The primary benefits of hedging are related to taxes and to other market frictions discussed in Parts 4 and 5. Specifically, we shall discuss the following benefits associated with hedging.

1. Hedging can decrease a firm's expected tax payments.
2. Hedging can reduce the costs of financial distress.
3. Hedging allows firms to plan better for their future capital needs and reduce their need to gain access to outside capital markets.
4. Hedging can be used to improve the design of management compensation contracts, and it allows firms to evaluate their top executives more accurately.
5. Hedging can improve the quality of the investment and operating decisions.

The gain from hedging in items 1–3 arises because the loss in the corporation's value from receiving one pound less in profit is greater than the gain in value from one pound more in profit. For example, the third motivation is based on the idea that the cost of not having enough internal capital available to fund a corporation's investment needs is greater than the benefits of having more than enough capital. Example 21.1 illustrates how this asymmetry between gains and losses motivates firms to hedge. Note that this example, as well as other examples in this chapter (unless specified otherwise), assumes risk neutrality and a risk-free rate of zero. We use these assumptions not just for expositional simplicity, but to show that firms have incentives to reduce risk even when investors have no aversion to risk.

Example 21.1

How Hedging Creates Value

ScarpeItalia exports Italian-made shoes to the United Kingdom. Because of this, the firm's value is greater when the euro is more valuable relative to the British pound. Suppose that it is equally likely that the British pound will be worth €1.20, €1.30 or €1.40 next year. Under these scenarios, ScarpeItalia is worth €105 million, €140 million and €160 million, respectively. By purchasing British pounds in the forward market at the current forward price of €1.32 per British pound, the firm will realize for certain a value of €138 million next year. Should ScarpeItalia enter into the forward contract if its investors are risk neutral?

Answer: The €138 million realized by hedging exceeds the €135 million the firm would realize, on average, by not hedging. In this case, the firm benefits by hedging.

In Example 21.1, ScarpeItalia was willing to take an unfair bet, paying €1.32 for British pounds that would be worth only €1.30, on average, to reduce uncertainty. ScarpeItalia was willing to take this bet because movements in exchange rates that lower profits hurt the firm more than the firm is helped by equal-sized exchange rate changes in the opposite direction: that is, exchange rate uncertainty decreases ScarpeItalia's expected value. Thus the firm could improve its expected value by reducing this uncertainty.

In general, whenever a firm is hurt more by a negative realization of an economic variable (for example, an exchange rate change) than it is helped by a positive realization, the firm can increase its value by hedging. The following sections describe various situations where we might expect the costs of negative realizations to exceed the benefits of positive realizations. Each situation provides a motivation for why firms hedge.

How Hedging Reduces Taxes

Taxes play a key role in most financial decisions, and hedging is no different. Tax gains often accrue from hedging because of an asymmetry between the tax treatments of gains and losses. A British corporation that has earned £100 million will pay about £28 million in corporation tax. However, if that same corporation loses £100 million, the government will carry forward its share of the losses only up to the amount of taxes the firm paid in the prior three years. Hence the firm often loses more value from a £100 million pre-tax loss than it gains in value from a £100 million pre-tax gain. Example 21.2 illustrates how firms can gain from hedging risks in situations of this kind.[2]

Results

Result 21.3

Because of asymmetric treatment of gains and losses, firms may reduce their expected tax liabilities by hedging.

Hedging to Avoid Financial Distress Costs

Chapters 16 and 17 examined why financial distress can be costly. Distress costs include costs arising from conflicts between debt holders and equity holders, and those arising from the reluctance of many of the firm's most important stakeholders (for example, customers and suppliers) to do business with a firm having financial difficulties. By hedging its risks, a firm can increase its value by reducing its probability of facing financial distress in the future.

[2] Smith and Stulz (1985) discuss how hedging can be used by a corporation to reduce its expected tax liabilities.

Example 21.2

Taxes and Hedging

Cogen Pharmaceuticals sells a large fraction of its arthritis drugs in France, for which it receives payments in euros. Given that its costs are denominated in pounds, the firm's taxable earnings are subject to currency risk. Currency fluctuations are the firm's only source of risk, so the firm's pre-tax hedged and unhedged positions in two equally likely exchange rate scenarios can be described as shown in the table.

Pre-tax income for two equally likely scenarios (in £ millions)			
	Weak pound	Strong pound	Average
Unhedged	100	–20	40
Hedged	35	35	35

The firm will thus achieve higher average pre-tax profits if it chooses not to hedge. Assume, however, that there is a 40 per cent profits tax, but no tax deduction on losses. Show that the expected after-tax profits will be higher if the firm chooses to hedge.

Answer:

After-tax income for two equally likely scenarios (in £ millions)			
	Weak pound	Strong pound	Average
Unhedged	60	–20	20
Hedged	21	21	21

An Example Based on the Stakeholder Theory of Financial Distress

Consider, for example, Microtronics, a medium-sized Dublin-based manufacturer of scientific equipment, which needs to borrow €100 million to refinance an existing loan. Its operating value next year is assumed to depend on two factors: the health of the Irish economy and the dollar/euro exchange rate. Microtronics' value is highest when (1) the Irish economy is strong, since the demand for scientific equipment will then be strong, and (2) when the dollar is strong relative to the euro, which increases the euro costs of Microtronics' American competitors.

To evaluate Microtronics' loan application, the lender's analysts have calculated the firm's operating values under four scenarios. The analysts have assumed that the firm is unhedged, and that customers maintain their confidence in the firm. These operating values are described in Exhibit 21.1.

If the Irish economy is weak and the dollar is weak, the firm's value (€95 million) will be less than its debt obligation (€100 million). The bank is particularly concerned about the weak economy, because the €95 million value of the firm in this scenario assumes that customers maintain their confidence in the firm. As Chapter 17 noted, consumers of scientific equipment are reluctant to purchase from a firm with financial difficulties, because of potential problems in obtaining spare parts and service. Thus, if Microtronics is unable to meet its debt obligations, its value in this scenario will be considerably less than the €95 million it would be worth if the firm were solvent. If the firm loses its customer base because of its financial distress, the bank may find it difficult to recover even a small fraction of what it is owed on the loan.

Exhibit 21.1 Microtronics' Unhedged Value in Four Scenarios*

	Strong Irish economy	Weak Irish economy
Weak dollar	€150 million	€95 million
Strong dollar	€200 million	€125 million

*Assumes customer confidence is high.

Exhibit 21.2 Microtronics' Hedged Value in Four Scenarios

	Strong Irish economy	Weak Irish economy
Weak dollar	€165 million	€110 million
Strong dollar	€185 million	€110 million

By hedging some of its currency risk (that is, by selling forward or futures contracts on the dollar), Microtronics is betting that the dollar will weaken relative to the euro. Such a bet increases the firm's value in scenarios in which the dollar is weak relative to the euro and the firm is at a competitive disadvantage relative to its American competitors. Hedging currency risk, in effect, transfers value from the scenarios where the dollar is strong to scenarios where the dollar is weak.

If Microtronics hedges in a way that transfers €15 million from the strong-dollar scenario to the weak-dollar scenario, its values in the four scenarios would be as shown in Exhibit 21.2. If Microtronics is hedged in this way, the bank is assured of being paid back in all four scenarios, and the firm will not be exposed to the costs of bankruptcy. Hence, in the weak-dollar, weak-economy scenario, hedging has eliminated the discrepancy between the actual value of the firm and the value of the firm when customer confidence is maintained.

Exhibit 21.3, which plots the distribution of profits with and without hedging, illustrates the potential advantages of hedging. The firm illustrated in this exhibit has a debt obligation of $20 million, and will suffer financial distress costs if it cannot meet this obligation. The probability of not meeting the obligation is seen as the areas to the left of $20 million, under the two curves. Since this illustration assumes that hedging is costly, the mean of the unhedged distribution is greater than the mean of the hedged distribution. However, since the unhedged distribution has a larger variance, the area to the left of $20 million is greater than the corresponding area for the hedged distribution. In other words, hedging reduces the probability of financial distress.

Hedging does not always reduce the probability of financial distress. If the cost of hedging is sufficiently large, and if hedging reduces variance very little, then hedging may actually increase the probability of financial distress. Instances where this would occur are very unusual. However, if it is costly, then hedging may not be worthwhile for firms with very low financial distress costs.

Results

Result 21.4

Firms that are subject to high financial distress costs have greater incentives to hedge.

Exhibit 21.3 Distribution of Profits with and without Hedging

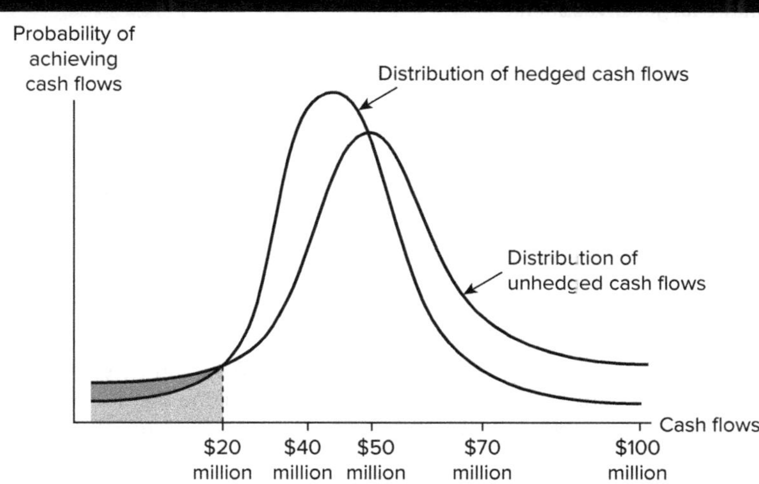

Hedging to Increase the Tax Shield from Debt Capacity

The Microtronics example suggests that hedging reduces the expected costs of financial distress for any given debt level. As hedging opportunities improve, however, firms can choose more highly leveraged capital structures, and take advantage of the tax and other advantages of debt financing (see Chapters 14–19). To understand why hedging allows a firm to take on more debt financing, consider again our analogy about the choice between taking the car or taking the train to the airport. Taking the car requires travellers to allow at least an hour to get to the airport, to be certain of catching the flight. However, when the slower but more certain option of taking the train is available, travellers can leave 10 minutes later, even though, on average, this route takes 10 minutes longer. Similarly, a firm that hedges its risks will be able to take on more debt while keeping its probability of financial distress at a reasonable level.

Hedging to Help Firms Plan for Their Capital Needs

Internal Financing, Underinvestment and Overinvestment

Previous chapters explained why corporations view internal sources of equity capital as cheaper than external sources. Recall that the lower costs of internal funds arise for information reasons, as well as because of taxes and transaction costs. Empirical evidence suggests that, because of the difference between the costs of internal and external capital, investment expenditures by firms correspond closely to their cash flows. Firms thus have a tendency to overinvest or underinvest, depending on the availability of internally generated cash flows. The reliance on internally generated cash can be especially costly for firms that need to plan their investments in advance but have highly variable cash flows. To the extent that hedging reduces this variability in cash flows, it can increase the value of the firm.[3]

Consistent with this view, Lewent and Kearney (1990) noted in their explanation of Merck's strategy of actively hedging foreign exchange risk that a key factor in deciding whether to hedge is the 'potential effect of cash flow volatility on our [Merck's] ability to execute our strategic plan – particularly, to make the investments in R&D that furnish the basis for future growth'. It is surprising that a firm like Merck, which has easy access to debt markets and can borrow at one of the lowest corporate borrowing rates available, would express such concerns. However, if Merck expresses concerns about funding its strategic plans, firms with weaker credit ratings must have even greater concerns.

Suppose, for example, that Carnival, the world's largest cruise operator, is planning to invest £100 million in modernizing equipment on its fleet of cruise ships next year, and that it can finance the investment from internally generated cash flows if sterling remains weak relative to the euro. However, if the pound strengthens, Carnival is likely to lose money on its European sales, and will thus have considerably less cash available for investment. The executives at Carnival believe that outside investors will become overly pessimistic about the firm's future prospects if the firm shows a loss next year because of currency fluctuations. In this case the firm may not be able to issue equity or borrow at attractive terms, and might be forced to pass up this positive-NPV project because of the negative NPV of its outside financing alternatives. By hedging its currency risk, Carnival ensures the availability of sufficient capital to fund this investment opportunity.

Perez-Gonzalez and Yun (2013) report that firms with active risk management policies have higher value and leverage, and make larger investments.

Results

Result 21.5

Firms that find it costly to delay or alter their investment plans, and which have limited access to outside financial markets, will benefit from hedging.

The Desirability of Partial Hedging

If either the investment requirements or the costs and benefits of obtaining external financing are determined by the risk factor the firm wishes to hedge, a firm may not want to hedge the risk completely. For example, an oil firm may want to increase its exploration budget when oil prices are high. If the firm can raise capital on

[3] This is discussed in more detail in Lessard (1991) and Froot et al. (1993).

more favourable terms after having shown increased earnings, it will want to maintain some exposure to the risks of oil price fluctuations, so that its earnings look good when there is a need for outside capital. Such a firm would not choose to eliminate its exposure to oil price movements completely, but it still would like to hedge risks to guarantee sufficient investment funds in the event of substantial oil price declines.

As Example 21.3 illustrates, the fact that oil companies have greater investment needs when oil prices are higher provides one explanation for why these companies generally hedge very little of their oil price risk. As we discuss in Chapter 22, this also provides a motivation for the use of options to hedge oil price risk, since they can be used to guarantee sufficient profits to avoid financial distress, while allowing the firm to benefit from very high oil prices.

Example 21.3

National Nickel's Partial Hedge

National Nickel currently has 3 million pounds of nickel in reserve that will be extracted within the next three years at a rate of 1 million pounds of nickel per year. Extraction costs are £6 per pound, and are expected to remain stable for the next three years. The current price of nickel is £22 per pound. Given current conditions, National is no longer exploring for new nickel, but the company plans to reassess the situation after three years. If nickel prices exceed £30 per pound, National will re-establish its exploration operations, which will require a capital investment of £35 million.

Forward contracts for the delivery of nickel in one, two and three years are available at a price of £24 per pound. National has overhead costs of about £3 million per year and interest obligations of £8 million per year. The firm will suffer significant financial distress-related costs if it cannot meet these fixed obligations should nickel prices fall significantly. How much should National hedge?

Answer: National would like to hedge its nickel price risk in a way that guarantees it will generate at least £11 million from its operations, so that it can cover its overhead costs and interest obligations. National can accomplish this by selling its entire supply of nickel on the forward markets, which would guarantee cash flows of £18 million in each year. However, if the firm is completely hedged, it will not accumulate enough internally generated capital to fund new exploration efforts if nickel prices exceed £30 per barrel. For this reason, National should hedge only enough to avoid financial distress, so that it has more money available if nickel prices rise. Using the forward markets to sell 17/24 of its extracted nickel annually is one way to achieve this.

How Hedging Improves Executive Compensation Contracts and Performance Evaluation

Chapter 18 discussed conflicts of interest between shareholders and management, and ways to design executive compensation contracts that minimize the costs of these conflicts. Recall that executive compensation should be designed to expose managers to the risk associated with factors they control (for example, success at cutting costs) while minimizing exposure to risks they do not control (for example, changes in interest rates). This suggests that a well-designed compensation package will not leave a risk-averse executive exposed to the risks of currency fluctuations, interest rate changes and other factors over which the executive has no control.

Consider, for example, an Irish electronics company that sells most of its products in the United States. Its costs are mainly in euros, but its revenues are predominantly in US dollars. If the dollar strengthens against the euro (that is, if the company receives more euros for every dollar it receives), then the company's profits increase, since its revenues improve while its costs (in euros) remain constant. Obviously, shareholders benefit from this, but it makes no sense to reward the company's top executives for this unexpected increase in profits, because the exchange rate change is completely outside their control. It also makes no sense to penalize the executives for a decline in profits due to a weakening of the dollar. The shareholders would like to eliminate risk that managers cannot control to the greatest extent possible, so that they can increase the managers' exposures to the risks they do control.

It is no doubt difficult to design a compensation package that eliminates a manager's exposure to all hedgeable risks. Doing this would create an excessively complicated contract, and would require prior knowledge of exactly how interest rates, currency movements and other hedgeable risks affect earnings and firm values, and how these relationships change over time. Corporations, however, may be better able to accomplish this objective with much simpler performance-based contracts if they allow their managers to hedge the appropriate risks, and compensate them in a way that gives them the incentive to hedge.

An additional, but related, advantage of implementing a hedging programme is that by requiring its managers to hedge, a firm will be able to evaluate its executives more accurately. Earnings become a more accurate indicator of managerial performance when extraneous noise in the earnings (that is, outside the managers' control) is eliminated. Unhedged risks provide managers with additional excuses when earnings are poor. A common excuse might be that 'the earnings would have been much better if the euro hadn't weakened'. Unhedged risks might also mask poor performance when managers are lucky enough to realize gains resulting from favourable currency or interest rate changes.

Real-World Insight

Evaluating the Management at International Chemicals

Despite being a relatively small British chemical company, International Chemicals (IC) is a true multinational. It has production facilities in France, the United Kingdom and Malaysia, and sells its products throughout the world. Despite IC's diversification, its earnings have been extremely volatile. Management explained the poor performance in one year, especially in the firm's European sales, as the result of the rapid decline in the US dollar, which fell by more than 20 per cent relative to the British pound. Because of the dollar's decline, IC was at a serious disadvantage relative to its most important competitor, which is located in the United States.

The board of directors of IC found management's explanation plausible. However, board members wondered how much of the record performance in earlier years could be attributed to favourable shifts in exchange rates, rather than to the hard work and clever decisions of the company's top managers. A senior director raised the following concern. 'How can we evaluate our top managers with such volatile currencies? When they do poorly, they can almost always point to losses due to currencies moving against them. When they do well, we shall always suspect that they were lucky, and that currencies moved in a favourable direction.'

In response to this concern, one of the directors made the following proposal. At the end of each year, the next year's earnings would be projected. The managers would receive a bonus if the earnings projection were exceeded, but there would be an even greater penalty for doing worse than the projection. The penalty for failure in meeting the projection would provide management with an incentive to use the futures market to hedge currency risks, so that unfavourable currency movements would not cause them to fall below their projections. The director making the proposal believed that by motivating management to hedge the effects of currency movements, it would be much easier to assess the quality of management's performance.

One of the newer board members questioned the wisdom of this hedging policy. Shouldn't the board encourage managers to take positions in currencies that are expected to appreciate? The response of the senior board member was quite forceful. 'We are in the chemical business, not the foreign exchange trading business. It is unlikely that our financial managers would have any better knowledge about currency movements than the bankers and professional speculators they would be "betting against" when executing such trades. In the absence of special information, a commodity or currency position is at best a zero net present value investment that should be avoided.'

The senior manager also provided an additional advantage of implementing the new corporate hedging policy: managers who are confident about their abilities will be attracted to firms that can evaluate their performance more accurately. Because a firm that chooses not to hedge its risks might be regarded as one that is less able to evaluate its managers, it may tend to attract managers who are less confident about their abilities, and prefer some noise in the evaluation process.[4]

[4] Theoretical articles by DeMarzo and Duffie (1995) and Breeden and Viswanathan (1996) explore how information issues affect hedging choices.

Results

Result 21.6

The gains from hedging are greater when it is more difficult to evaluate and monitor management.

How Hedging Improves Decision-Making

An active risk management programme can improve management's decision-making process by reducing the profit volatility of individual business units. Less volatile profits for a company's business units provide management at the firm's central headquarters with better information about where to allocate capital, and about which managers are the most deserving of promotions.

Using Futures Prices to Allocate Capital

Firms with sophisticated risk management groups have further advantages derived from their greater understanding of market prices, which they can utilize to make better capital allocation decisions. As Chapter 11 discussed, futures prices, viewed as certainty equivalents, provide an assessment of the current value of gold delivered in one year, enabling a gold miner to make intelligent decisions about whether to increase gold production. If the miner's costs are less than the futures price, he can increase his production and sell the futures contracts to lock in his gains. If the costs exceed the futures price, then the miner should probably cut his production.

Although we believe that futures markets generally lead managers to make better decisions, managers sometimes ignore new price information after hedging and, as a result, often make serious mistakes. This is what we call the *fallacy of sunk costs,* which Example 21.4 illustrates.

Example 21.4

Hedging and Production Choices: a Pitfall

Omega Chemicals sells a lemon-scented detergent base that is used by producers of both laundry detergent and dishwashing soap. Lemon oil is one of its most expensive ingredients, and its price is volatile. To hedge this price risk, Omega made a forward purchase of 300,000 pounds of lemon oil at €4.50 per pound for delivery over the next 12 months. Subsequent to this purchase, the price of lemon oil increased to €6.25 per pound because of political uncertainties in one of the major exporting countries. Omega's management views this as a prime opportunity to increase its market share aggressively, given its 'cost advantage' over its leading competitor, whose management chose not to hedge, and thus must pay €6.25 per pound for the lemon oil. Do you agree with management's logic?

Answer: Omega is much better off as a result of its forward purchase of lemon oil. However, the opportunity cost associated with the input of one pound of lemon oil is €6.25 rather than €4.50. Although it will be purchasing the lemon oil for €4.50 per pound, Omega could, if it wished, sell the lemon oil on the open market for €6.25. Hence, although the company made more than €500,000 on the forward purchase, its costs of using lemon oil have effectively increased just as much as those of its competitors.

When making pricing and other operating decisions, managers must rely on opportunity costs instead of historical costs. Managers who understand this should be able to greatly improve their operating and investment decisions when futures and forward markets exist for either their inputs or outputs.

Using Information from Insurance Premiums to Allocate Capital

One way to value the uncertain negative cash flows associated with adverse events is to use insurance premiums to obtain certainty equivalents. However, as the discussion below illustrates, there are risks that are best left uninsured.

Real-World Insights

BP's Insurance Choices

BP, recognizing that hedging risks can result in better decision-making, revised its corporate insurance strategy in a somewhat unconventional way. The conventional wisdom is that corporations should insure large risks but not small risks, because small risks should average out over time and can be diversified within the firm. BP, however, decided to take the opposite approach: to insure its small risks but not its large risks. The reason has absolutely nothing to do with the motivations for hedging described earlier. Instead, BP's rationale relates to how hedging affects decision-making.

To understand BP's rationale, consider the issues involved in deciding whether to spend £50 million on new refining capacity. There are various uncertain but insurable expenses associated with such an operation. For example, fires or natural disasters raise the potential for lawsuits, and on-the-job injuries might generate workers' compensation claims. If these uncertain costs were uninsured, the calculation of the NPV of the oil refining project would require BP's management to calculate the expected value of those uncertain losses as well as the corresponding discount rates.

The top executives of BP believe that insurance companies may be better able than BP management to calculate the present values of these insurable losses. One reason has to do with incentives. Conceivably, a situation might arise in which a manager may want to approve a marginal project, and thus might tend to understate the potential losses from fires and natural disasters. The second reason has to do with expertise. Insurance companies are probably in a better position to assess the expected losses from fires and other risks they insure as part of their regular business.

For more unusual and larger risks, BP probably has the better information. One might expect that it would have better information about the chances of incurring hundreds of millions of pounds in damages from an explosion in one of its oil tankers, caused by negligence. Because the oil giant can better assess these risks, it is difficult and expensive to insure against them. Insurance companies are concerned with the adverse selection problem (see Chapter 19), which in this context implies that firms have an incentive to insure those risks that insurance companies underprice. Understanding these incentives, insurance companies use extremely pessimistic assumptions in assessing risks when they are at an informational disadvantage compared with the firm's management. As a result, insurance quotes for these large risks are often unattractive to the firm.

Example 21.5 provides another example where the motivation for purchasing insurance relates to information rather than risk sharing.

Example 21.5

Hedging a Halftime Contest

At halftime during an exhibition match featuring Saracens and South Africa in 2009, Stuart Tinner, a job centre worker in Welwyn Garden City, punted a rugby ball 30 metres, hit the crossbar, and won £250,000 as part of a 'crossbar challenge'. As it turned out, Saracens, who were behind the contest, had hedged the risk associated with this contest by paying £10,000 to an insurance company, which was responsible for paying the £250,000. Why did Saracens, a prominent and wealthy sports outfit, choose to hedge such a small risk?

Answer: This hedge probably had more to do with information than risk. In doing the cost–benefit analysis of this halftime promotion, Saracens needed to gauge the probability of losing £250,000. This is a type of risk that Saracens knows nothing about. However, the insurance company is an expert at analysing such risks, and is thus in a better position to determine the expected cost of such a promotion.

The insights illustrated by the BP case study and Example 21.5 are summarized in Result 21.7.

Results

Result 21.7

Firms have an incentive to insure or hedge risks that insurance companies and markets cannot assess better. Doing this improves decision-making. Firms will absorb internally those risks over which they have the comparative advantage in evaluating.

21.3 The Motivation to Hedge Affects What is Hedged

The previous section noted that hedging can improve the values of firms for several reasons. In designing their risk management strategies, firms should consider each of the individual reasons for hedging. For example, firms would like to minimize taxes as well as the costs of financial distress, and they also would like a risk management system that improves the quality of their management. Unfortunately, it may be difficult to do all these things simultaneously. A firm's taxable income is not the same as the income that it reports to shareholders, so minimizing the volatility of its taxable income will not always minimize the volatility of its reported income. More importantly, a hedge that minimizes the volatility of a firm's earnings will not always effectively insure against longer-term changes in the firm's value, which is likely to be more important if there is concern about financial distress in the future.

Consider, for example, a Chinese textile firm that we shall call Beijing International. The firm manufactures a variety of shirts that it sells mainly in Europe. The firm is partially owned by one of China's wealthiest families, the Wangs, who also own a construction business and other small manufacturing firms. The Wang family fully delegates the management of Beijing International to a group of executives whom they have recently hired. The Wangs have let it be known, however, that the new managers will be replaced if they do not perform well within the next two years.

The Wang family can best assess their managers if they require them to hedge the firm's foreign exchange risk completely over the next two years. They would prefer to avoid replacing the managers because of poor performance if the problems were due entirely to unfavourable and unexpected movements in exchange rates. Likewise, they would not want to retain a poor-quality management team that was lucky enough to experience favourable movements in exchange rates. These objectives suggest that the Wangs should require their management team to minimize the volatility of the firm's *earnings* over the next two years.

Unfortunately, this objective may only partially solve a second concern of the Wang family. Beijing International is a highly levered firm, with a $100 million note due at the end of five years. To minimize the chances of default, which would greatly embarrass the family, the Wangs would like to instruct management to enter into forward contracts that minimize their chances of defaulting on this note. However, implementing a hedge that minimizes the chances of default will probably require larger positions in the forward and futures markets than would be required to minimize earnings uncertainty over the next two years, because the firm's *value* represents the discounted value of all future cash flows, not just the cash flows accruing in the next two years.

Results

Result 21.8

If a firm's main motivation for hedging is to better assess the quality of management, the firm will probably want to hedge its earnings or cash flows rather than its value. However, if the firm is hedging to avoid the costs of financial distress, it should implement a hedging strategy that takes into account both the variance of its value and the variance of its cash flows.

21.4 How Should Companies Organize Their Hedging Activities?

In addition to understanding whether to hedge and how to hedge, firms must consider the organization of their risk management activities. Should risk management be centralized, operating out of the firm's treasury department, or should hedging be performed at the level of the individual divisions? The answer to this question depends on the level of expertise in the various divisions, the availability of information about the divisions' exposures, the transaction costs of hedging, and the motivation for hedging.

At present, most risk management programmes are implemented at the corporate rather than the divisional level. One reason for this has to do with the costs of trading. In illiquid markets trading costs can be high, and it might make sense to consolidate trading. Consolidating allows the exposures of each of the business units to be netted against one another. Corporate managers then execute trades in the financial markets to hedge only the firm's aggregate exposure. A second reason has to do with the relative newness of the field of risk management, and the likelihood of limited expertise in it at the divisional level. A final reason is the fixed costs associated with setting up a risk management department.

As risk management expertise becomes more widespread, and the futures, forward and swap markets become more liquid, we expect to see hedging performed more at the divisional level. This is especially true when the principal motivation for hedging has to do with improving management incentives. Division heads, who have the best information about risk exposures in their divisions, ultimately should be responsible for hedging those risk exposures. Divisions may also want to hedge to assure themselves of investment funds if investment funds from corporate headquarters are tied in some way to the divisional profits. If, however, a firm's principal motivation for hedging has to do with either lowering expected tax liabilities or reducing the probability of bankruptcy, then most hedging should be carried out at the corporate level.

Results

Result 21.9

Corporations should organize their hedging in a way that reflects why they are hedging. Most hedging motivations suggest that hedging should be carried out at the corporate level. However, the improvement in management incentives that can be realized with a risk management programme is best achieved when the individual divisions are responsible for hedging.

21.5 Do Risk Management Departments Always Hedge?

Until now, our analysis has assumed that the purpose of a risk management department is to reduce the risks of a firm's cash flows. However, some corporations view risk management departments as 'profit centres', and have encouraged them to generate profits by speculating rather than hedging. Indeed, some firms have generated large profits by speculating in currencies and interest rates. We think that, in most cases, these efforts are seriously misguided. There have been some highly publicized cases where managers, thinking that they had special information, bet heavily in futures markets – and lost. For example, in 2006 Amaranth Advisors *gambled* that natural gas prices would rise in March 2007 and fall in April 2007, losing $6 billion on futures contracts.

Certainly, cases do arise where firms have special information that leads them to speculate instead of hedge. For example, Nestlé is one of the biggest buyers of cocoa in the world, and as a result it may have special information that allows the company to better predict cocoa prices. Although Nestlé will want to buy cocoa futures to hedge its anticipated future purchases, occasionally it will want to use its special information to speculate. Suppose, for example, that Nestlé anticipates that its needs will be less than normal over the next six months, resulting in a decline in cocoa prices. In this case, Nestlé might choose to sell rather than buy cocoa futures.

The above example is somewhat atypical, because only in exceptional cases do managers have superior information about future price changes. For example, we are very sceptical of corporate treasurers who claim to have superior information about foreign exchange, and use that information to speculate in those markets.

Results

Result 21.10

Managers have private information only in exceptional cases. Given this, they almost always should be hedging rather than speculating.

21.6 How Hedging Affects the Firm's Stakeholders

Up to this point, we have examined hedging from the perspective of managers who are trying to maximize total firm value (that is, the value of the debt plus the value of the equity). As Chapters 16 and 18 discussed, however, managers have competing pressures, and may not choose to maximize total firm value. Perhaps the instances where firms were observed to be speculating rather than hedging arose because management's objective was *not* to maximize total firm value. In this section, we explore the effect of hedging on the debt holders and equity holders separately, and how hedging can affect other stakeholders of the firm.

How Hedging Affects Debt Holders and Equity Holders

Previous chapters described how equity can be viewed as a call option on the firm's value. To the extent that hedging reduces volatility without increasing firm value, it reduces the value of this option, transferring value from equity holders to debt holders. From an equity holder's perspective, the value-maximizing benefits of hedging may be reduced, and possibly even reversed, by this transfer. The actions of managers to hedge in these circumstances certainly would not endear them to these equity holders. However, a firm's bankers and bondholders would certainly like the firm to hedge.

How Hedging Affects Employees and Customers

The interests of most of a firm's employees are closer to the interests of debt holders than of equity holders. Their jobs and reputations are at risk in the event of bankruptcy, and they may not realize substantial benefits if the firm does extremely well. Managers who look out for the interests of their employees would then have an incentive to hedge. Customers generally like to see a firm that will honour its warranties, supply replacement parts and generate additional products that will enhance the value of existing products. Since firms in financial distress are less likely to make choices that benefit their customers, hedging also benefits a firm's customers.

Hedging and Managerial Incentives

The discussion in the previous subsection suggests that managers who are loyal to their employees and customers may want to hedge more than the firm's shareholders would like them to. Managers' incentives to hedge differ from those of shareholders for several other reasons.

Managerial Incentives to Hedge

Consider the case of an entrepreneur such as Mark Zuckerberg at Meta, who starts a successful business and continues to hold a sizeable fraction of the firm's shares. Zuckerberg is probably more concerned than other shareholders about Meta's risk, because he is much less diversified than they are. As a result, Zuckerberg might want Meta to hedge to reduce his personal risks, even when doing so has no effect on the firm's expected cash flows. In this case, and in the absence of transaction costs, Zuckerberg is indifferent between hedging on his personal account and hedging through the corporation. However, it might be more efficient to have Meta, which has a trained staff of risk management experts, bear the transaction costs rather than bear these costs personally.

Managerial Incentives to Speculate

Managers may also have an incentive to speculate, even when the firm would be better off hedging. As noted in the previous section, this sometimes happens when managers have misguided notions that they possess superior information about future trends in currency and commodity prices. In addition, managers may have an incentive to speculate if they are compensated with executive equity options, which are worth more when share price volatility is higher. Longer-term considerations may provide managers with even more incentives to take speculative risks and choose not to hedge. Managers who realize a favourable outcome as a result of a risky strategy are likely to receive an attractive bonus and, in addition, be promoted and have many more opportunities in the future. As long as their upside potential exceeds their downside risk, managers will want to speculate rather than hedge.

The case of Jérôme Kerviel at Société Générale illustrates how perverse remuneration incentives, along with a lack of oversight, can lead to disaster. By making a series of enormous speculative bets on UK and European equity index futures, Kerviel managed to lose €4.9 billion for his firm, Société Générale. If these trades had been successful, and SocGen had earned instead of lost over €4.9 billion, Kerviel would have received a generous bonus and enjoyed increased opportunities and prestige within the firm. The upside associated with this risky strategy was clearly quite high. Perhaps Kerviel believed that all he had to lose in the event of a bad outcome was his job. Unfortunately, Kerviel not only lost his job but was charged with abuse of confidence and illegal access to computers.

Before concluding this section, we should stress that the Société Générale case, as well as the Metallgesellschaft case,[5] attracted a great deal of attention because of the huge losses created by the improper use of derivatives. However, these cases should not be viewed as typical. Our understanding is that most managers use derivative instruments to hedge rather than to speculate, and as a result add value to their corporations. Unfortunately, well-run corporations that use risk management tools effectively to benefit their shareholders are not nearly as newsworthy as their counterparts that take ill-advised positions that bankrupt their firms

21.7 The Motivation to Manage Interest Rate Risk

Until now, we have discussed the motivations for risk management in general terms, without reference to the particular sources of risk. In reality, however, a firm's motivation to hedge interest rate risk, which is closely tied to the capital structure choice, may be quite different from its incentive to hedge either commodity or foreign exchange risk.

Our earlier discussion of capital structure (Chapters 14–19) covered the issues surrounding the firm's choice between debt and equity financing in great detail. However, the choice between debt and equity financing is only the first step that firms must take when they determine the overall make-up of their liabilities. Because they affect who owns and controls the firm, decisions relating to the level of equity financing (for example, whether to issue new shares or repurchase existing shares) are important decisions, and are typically made at the highest levels of the corporation, generally the board of directors, which suggests that a treasurer's staff is unlikely to face these types of decision on a day-to-day basis. However, the nature of a firm's debt is something that the treasurer's staff faces on a continuing basis. This includes choosing whether to borrow at fixed or floating rates, or whether to roll over short-term commercial paper. In addition, they decide whether to borrow in the domestic currency, in a foreign currency or perhaps with commodity-linked bonds. These decisions all affect the firm's **liability stream**, which is the stream of interest costs that a firm will be paying in the future.

We can view all of the above as **liability management** decisions, because they affect the nature of the firm's liabilities. However, they can also be viewed as risk management choices, because the decisions affect the firm's exposure to various sources of risk. In general, when a firm determines its exposure to interest rates, commodities and foreign exchange through its borrowing choices without using derivatives, we think of these choices as *liability management* choices. When the firm alters these risk exposures with the aid of derivatives, we refer to this as *risk management.* However, since in many cases a firm might be close to being indifferent between, for example, (1) borrowing in euros and swapping the euro debt for a dollar obligation, and (2) simply borrowing in dollars, this distinction between liability management and risk management becomes largely irrelevant.

Alternative Liability Streams

It is useful to think about the different liability streams that a firm can create when it is restricted to borrowing only in its domestic currency. We further simplify this analysis by assuming that there are only two possible maturities for the debt: short term and long term. One might want to think of short-term debt as debt due in one year, and long-term debt as debt due in five years.

[5] Metallgesellschaft is discussed in Chapter 22.

Whether the firm is borrowing short term or long term, its cost of borrowing will consist of the sum of a risk-free component, r, which we can think of as a Treasury bond rate, and a default spread, d, which is determined by the firm's credit rating. As we shall see below, the firm can create four separate liability streams, depending on whether the firm borrows short term or long term, and whether it chooses to hedge its interest rate exposure.

If the firm chooses to roll over short-term debt, its liability stream can be described by the following equation:

$$i_{st} = r_{st} + d_{st} \tag{21.2}$$

where

i_{st} = the firm's short-term borrowing cost for period t, which consists of

r_{st} = the default-free short-term interest rate for period t, plus

d_{st} = the default spread for period t.

Note that the t subscripts indicate that short-term borrowing rates and the firm's credit rating change over time.

If the firm instead chooses to borrow long term at a fixed rate, then its liability stream can be described as

$$i_l = r_l + d_l \tag{21.3}$$

where

r_l = the long-term interest rate

d_l = the default premium.

Since these rates are fixed for the life of the loan, they do not have the t subscript.

The third approach involves a floating-rate loan. Firms may be able to obtain the floating-rate loans directly from their banks, or they can obtain the loans by borrowing long term and swapping a default-free fixed-rate obligation for a default-free floating-rate obligation (see Chapter 7). In either case, the floating-rate liability can be described by

$$i_{ft} = r_{st} + d_l \tag{21.4}$$

where

i_{ft} = firm's period t borrowing rate on the long-term floating-rate loan.

This liability stream subjects the firm to interest rate risk (that is, changes in r_{st}), but not to risk relating to changes in its credit rating.

The final possibility is a liability stream, i_{ht}, that hedges the risk of changing levels of the default-free interest rate, r_{st}, but leaves the firm exposed to changes in its credit rating or default spread:

$$i_{ht} = r_l + d_{st} \tag{21.5}$$

Firms were unable to create the liability stream described by equation (21.5) before the introduction of interest rate swaps and interest rate futures. Before the introduction of these instruments, borrowing short term implied exposure to interest rate risk and credit risk, whereas borrowing long term implied exposure to neither. Indeed, the principal advantage of these derivative instruments is that they allow firms to separate their exposures to interest rate risk from changes in their credit ratings. In particular, the liability stream described in equation (21.5) can be created by borrowing short term and swapping a floating for a fixed-rate obligation. Details on how to implement such a transaction are found in Chapter 22.

Results

Result 21.11

A firm's liability stream can be decomposed into two components: one that reflects default-free interest rates and one that reflects the firm's credit rating. When a firm borrows at a fixed rate, both components are fixed. When it rolls over short-term instruments, the liability streams fluctuate with both kinds of risk.

Derivative instruments allow firms to separate these two sources of risk: to create liability streams that are sensitive to interest rates but not their credit ratings, as described in equation (21.4); and to create liability streams that are sensitive to their credit ratings but not interest rates, as described in equation (21.5).

How Do Corporations Choose between Different Liability Streams?[6]

To understand how corporations decide between the various liability streams, consider the two components of their borrowing costs separately. We shall first think about how firms should structure their liabilities in terms of their exposure to changing levels of interest rate. Then we shall consider how firms decide on their exposure to changes in credit risk. To determine the optimal exposure of their liabilities to interest rate risk, firms must first think about the interest rate exposure they face on the asset side of their balance sheets. In other words, firms must ask whether their ability to make a profit is tied in any way to the prevailing interest rates in the economy.

Matching the Interest Rate Risk of Assets and Liabilities

Consider the following example, which provides a vivid illustration of the risks connected with ignoring interest rate exposure on the asset side of a firm's balance sheet. Massey-Ferguson, a manufacturer of tractors, was highly leveraged and had a substantial amount of short-term debt financing. When interest rates increased at the end of 1979, farmers found it difficult to buy and finance new tractors, causing Massey-Ferguson's sales and operating income to drop substantially.

In other words, the asset side of Massey-Ferguson's balance sheet was extremely sensitive to changes in interest rates, and as a result the interest rate sensitivities of the company's assets and liabilities were severely mismatched. An increase in interest rates, which made its short-term debt more expensive to service, coincided with a drop in the firm's unlevered cash flows, which compounded the problem and resulted in the firm facing severe financial distress. As a consequence of financial distress, Massey-Ferguson was forced to downsize, laying off thousands of employees. Perhaps those jobs could have been saved had Massey-Ferguson done a better job of matching the interest rate exposure of its assets and debt.

Decomposing Interest Rates into Real and Inflation Components

When thinking about a firm's interest rate exposure, recall that interest rates are composed of a real component and an expected inflation component, as Chapter 9 discussed. In many cases, a firm's cash flows are unaffected by changes in the real interest rate, but they are affected by changes in the inflation rate. For example, a manufacturer of furniture may see its nominal profits increase when the general price level in the economy increases if the prices that it charges and its labour costs increase at the overall rate of inflation. The furniture manufacturer might then prefer to have a floating-rate liability structure, because it does not want to run the risk of being locked into high long-term interest rates when inflation is reduced.

The experience many firms faced in 1982 provides a valuable lesson about the risks connected with locking in long-term interest rates when inflation is uncertain. In the early 1980s, interest rates were very high, and many firms were locked into fixed obligations with rates in excess of 15 per cent. The high rates did not seem excessive at the time, since inflation was running at well over 10 per cent per year. Firms were counting on paying back expensive loans with cheaper money in the future. However, policies to reduce inflation appeared to be successful by the middle of 1982, substantially increasing the real cost of existing fixed-rate loans. Short-term rates dropped substantially in 1982, so that firms with a substantial amount of floating-rate debt did much better than firms that were stuck with fixed-rate obligations.

Results

Result 21.12

If changes in interest rates reflect mainly changes in the rate of inflation, and if a firm's unlevered cash flows (and its EBIT) generally increase with the rate of inflation, then the firm will want its liabilities to be exposed to interest rate risk. If, however, interest rate changes are not due primarily to changes in inflation (that is, real interest rates change), and if the firm's unlevered cash flows are largely affected by the level of real interest rates, then the firm will want to minimize the exposure of its liabilities to interest rate changes.

---

[6] For more detailed analysis of the issues in this section, see Titman (1992).

Hedging Exposure to Credit Rate Changes

In addition to evaluating a firm's interest rate exposure, we must ask how exposed the firm is to changes in its own credit rating. In general, a firm would like to limit its exposure to changes in its own credit rating, since lenders almost always require larger default spreads when firms can least afford to pay the higher interest rates. Hence firms tend to prefer financing alternatives that keep their default spreads fixed, such as long-term fixed-rate loans or floating-rate loans. However, two factors offset this preference.

The first factor arises when there is disagreement about the firm's true financial condition. For example, the lender might believe that the firm will face financial difficulties in the future, but the borrower believes that its credit rating is likely to improve in the future. In this case, the borrower may not want to lock in what it considers an unfavourable default spread, preferring instead to borrow short term in the hope that its credit rating will improve in the future. The second factor arises because of the conflicts between debt holders and equity holders discussed in Chapter 16.

Recall that a lender who is concerned that the firm will take on excessively risky investments (that is, the asset substitution problem) is not willing to provide long-term financing on favourable terms. Both of these factors imply that the firm may borrow short term, taking on greater exposure to changes in its own credit rating than it would otherwise want, because the costs associated with long-term debt are simply too high. In these situations, firms often roll over short-term debt, and use interest rate swaps to insulate the firm's borrowing costs from the effect of changing interest rates, thereby creating the liability stream described in equation (21.5). We discuss how to do this in more detail in the next chapter.

21.8 Foreign Exchange Risk Management

Multinational corporations must pay particular attention to managing their currency risk. Changes in currency rates affect a firm's cash flows as well as its accounting profits. Currency rate changes also affect a company's market and book values.

Types of Foreign Exchange Risk

The various risks associated with changes in the value of currencies are generally divided into three categories: transaction risk, translation risk and economic risk, which Exhibit 21.4 defines.

Exhibit 21.4 Categories of Currency Risk

Risk category	Description	Example
Transaction risk	Associated with individual transactions denominated in foreign currencies: imports, exports, foreign assets and loans	A UK company imports parts from Japan; the UK company is exposed to the risk of the yen strengthening and, as a result, to the pound sterling price of parts increasing
Translation risk	Arising from the translation of balance sheets and income statements in foreign currencies to the currency of the parent company for financial reporting purposes	A UK enterprise has a German subsidiary; the UK enterprise is exposed to the risk of the euro weakening, and the value of the subsidiary's assets, liabilities and profit contributions decreasing in pound sterling terms in consolidated financial statements
Economic risk	Associated with losing competitive advantage due to exchange rate movements	A UK and a Japanese company are competing in Italy; if the yen weakens against the euro and the pound/euro exchange rate remains constant, the Japanese company can lower its prices in Italy without losing yen income, and thus obtain a competitive advantage over the UK company

Transaction Risk

To summarize, **transaction risk** represents only the immediate effect on cash flow of an exchange rate change. Exposure to transaction risk arises when a company buys or sells a good, priced in a foreign currency, on credit. Suppose, for example, that Dell sells computers to Nestlé, a Swiss company, for 10 million Swiss francs. Currently, the Swiss franc is worth US$0.90, with payment required in six months. If the Swiss franc depreciates in six months and is worth only US$0.80, Dell will receive the equivalent of US$8 million rather than the US$9 million it had originally expected to receive.

It is quite easy for firms to hedge against transaction risk. For example, Dell could simply require payment in US dollars, which effectively shifts the transaction risk onto Nestlé. Alternatively, Dell could enter into a forward contract to sell 10 million Swiss francs at a pre-specified dollar/Swiss franc exchange rate, with delivery in six months, to lock in the revenues from its sale in US dollars.

Hedges of this type are quite straightforward, and are commonly observed in businesses throughout the world. However, they control only the short-term implications of exchange rate changes. For example, Dell's profits in Switzerland are likely to decline if the Swiss franc weakens, unless the company raises the Swiss franc price of its computers to its Swiss customers. As a result, there are long-run implications of currency changes that are not hedged when risk management is restricted to individual transactions.

In the terminology described in Exhibit 21.4, the economic risk connected with currency changes is much larger than the transaction risk, because it takes into account the long-term consequences of the change in currency value.

Translation Risk

Translation risk occurs because a foreign subsidiary's financial statements must be translated into the home country's currency as part of the consolidated statements of the parent. For example, suppose Dell purchased a firm in the United Kingdom for £100 million when the pound was worth US$1.90. The British firm is then set up as a wholly owned subsidiary of Dell, with a book value of US$190 million. Subsequently, the dollar strengthens, so that the pound is worth US$1.60. Dell must now restate its balance sheet to account for this currency change, so that the book value of the subsidiary becomes US$160 million.[7]

Why is translation risk important? First, changes in value associated with exchange rate changes often reflect real economic changes that affect the future profitability of the firm. Translation risk may, however, be an important consideration, even when the firm's inflation-adjusted cash flows are unaffected by a change in the exchange rate, as long as the firm has contracts written with terms that are contingent on the firm's book value. For example, firms often have loan covenants that require them to keep their debt-to-book-value ratio above a certain level. In such cases, exchange rate changes that create a drop in the book value of a foreign subsidiary create violations of loan covenants, even when the exchange rate changes are driven by inflation. Since covenant violations can result in real costs, firms may find it beneficial to hedge against such possibilities.

Economic Risk

What are the determinants of **economic risk?** Or what are the factors that determine how changes in exchange rates affect the fundamentals of a firm's business? These factors include:

- differences between the location of the production facilities and where the product is sold
- the location of competitors
- determinants of input prices – are they determined in international markets or in local markets?

It is easy to see how a firm with a large percentage of its sales overseas is exposed to currency fluctuations. However, even firms that sell only in their domestic market are subject to currency risk if they import some of their supplies or have foreign competitors.

Why Do Exchange Rates Change?

To understand foreign exchange hedging in greater detail, it is important to think about why exchange rates change over time. Perhaps the most important contributor to exchange rate changes is the difference in the inflation rates of two countries. For example, suppose the euro is initially worth £0.75. If the inflation rate in

[7] The gain or loss on the translation of foreign currency in a firm's financial statements is not recognized in current net income, but is reported as a separate component of shareholders' equity. The amounts accumulated in this separate component of shareholders' equity are realized on the sale or liquidation of the investment in the foreign entity.

the Eurozone is 3 per cent over the next year, whereas the inflation rate in the United Kingdom is 0 per cent – and nothing else changes during this time period – then the euro is likely to fall in value by 3 per cent to £0.77. In this case the **nominal exchange rate**, which measures the British pounds price of euros, changes by 3 per cent, but the **real exchange rate**, which measures the relative price of British and Eurozone goods, remains unchanged. A French tourist in the United Kingdom will find British goods and services selling at the same price in terms of euros as they were selling for in the previous year.

The Case of No Real Effects

If you believe that differential inflation rates are the primary cause of exchange rate movements, would you need to hedge against unexpected changes? If your main concern is economic risk or transaction risk, there would be no need for your firm to hedge. The firm is subject to neither risk. This point is illustrated in Example 21.6.

Example 21.6

Currency Risk and Inflation

Pitsos, a Greek manufacturer of white goods (fridges, ovens and washing machines), will buy three million circuit boards from a small firm in Thailand in about one year. Each circuit board is currently priced at 160 baht, which is equivalent to about €3.569 at current exchange rates. Suppose Thailand has an uncertain monetary policy and could experience either inflation or deflation, which can cause currency movements of as much as 10 per cent. Is Pitsos exposed to currency risk?

Answer: If inflation is the only cause of exchange rate changes, then Pitsos is not exposed to currency risk. A 10 per cent increase in the Thai price level will result in a price increase of circuit boards to 176 baht. However, the inflation will simultaneously result in a drop in the value of the Thai baht to €0.020. The euro dollar price that Pitsos pays for the circuit boards is thus unchanged.

In Example 21.6, Pitsos was simply purchasing an item from a foreign company. Suppose now that Pitsos sets up a plant in Thailand to produce the circuit boards. In this case, an exchange rate change driven purely by inflation can have real effects, because it can affect how the firm's Thai assets are represented on its balance sheets, which could, in turn, affect bond covenants and other contracts.

Inflation Differences Tend to Generate Real Effects

Of course, it is rare when different inflation rates in two countries are not also generating real effects in the two countries. For example, when oil was discovered in the North Sea off Britain's coast, the British pound strengthened because, at the prevailing exchange rate, the United Kingdom was expected to have an excess of exports (especially oil) over imports. In this case, the strengthening of the pound did affect relative prices. A US tourist in the United Kingdom after the oil discovery would find that prices calculated in US dollars had increased. Since the real, or inflation-adjusted, exchange rate changed, a US firm that imported materials from the United Kingdom would see its costs increase. If the production costs of the British firm in British pounds stayed the same, the firm's price in pounds would also stay the same, which implies that US dollar prices would increase if the pound strengthened. A US firm would be exposed to currency risk in this case.

Results

Result 21.13

Exchange rate movements can be decomposed into those caused by differences in the inflation rates in the home country and the foreign country, and those caused by changes in real exchange rates. In most cases, the incentive is to hedge against real exchange rate changes rather than the component of exchange rate changes that is driven by inflation differences between the two countries.

Exhibit 21.5 Real and Nominal Exchange Rates in Three Countries*

Japan				
Consumer price indexes				
Year	**Yen exchange rate**	**Japan CPI**	**UK CPI**	**Real exchange rate 1990 yen/1990 pound**
1990	231.88	100.00	100.00	231.88
1995	155.35	109.08	128.69	183.28
2000	165.13	110.71	139.31	207.79
2005	196.51	108.22	149.78	271.98
2010	147.68	107.71	163.81	224.60
2015	178.19	111.01	185.26	297.37
2020	141.46	114.07	201.87	250.34

Source: Based on authors' calculations using data from Rateinflation.com.

Exhibit 21.5 documents both real and nominal exchange rate movements for the Japanese yen and British pound from 1990 to 2020. Note that nominal exchange rates changed dramatically over this time. However, the real exchange rates, which are more important for multinational firms, are somewhat less volatile over longer periods of time.

The exchange rates shown in Exhibit 21.5 represent the number of units of the local currency that can be exchanged for each British pound. For example, the 1990 exchange rate for the Japanese yen/British pound was 231.88, which means that 231.88 Japanese yen could have been exchanged for £1.00 on the spot market at the end of 1990. The consumer price index (CPI) for each year relates the price levels of each country to the price levels for 1990. An index value of 100 means that the price level is identical to the prices in that country in 1990. For example, the CPI of 114.07 for Japan in 2020 means that prices were 14.07 per cent higher in 2020 than they were in 1990.

The right-hand column summarizes the real exchange rate for each selected currency, or the equivalent purchasing power that must be exchanged from one currency to another. To determine the purchasing power being exchanged in the spot market, adjustments must be made for the rate of inflation in each evaluated country and in the United Kingdom. To accomplish this adjustment, the spot exchange rate is divided by the local CPI and multiplied by the UK CPI, resulting in the real exchange rate. Because all the local consumer price indexes and the UK CPI are stated with a 1990 basis, the real exchange rate reported is also relative to 1990 prices.

In 1990, for example, Japan's spot exchange rate was Y213.88 per British pound. To take into account the disparities in the inflation rates of the two countries, divide the 2020 spot rate of Y141.46 by the local CPI of 114.07 and multiply by the UK CPI of 201.87 to find the real exchange rate. In this case, the real exchange rate for 2020 is equivalent to Y250.34 per British pound. As you can see from Exhibit 21.5, the real exchange rate between Japan and the United Kingdom strengthened between 1995 and 2020. In other words, the UK pound cost of goods and services in Japan increased at a higher rate than the UK pound cost of goods and services in the United Kingdom.

Hedging When Both Inflation Differences and Real Effects Drive Exchange Rate Changes

Whenever exchange rates can change for purely monetary reasons as well as for real reasons, it is difficult to implement effective hedges. To understand this, consider again the case where a Spanish firm needs to purchase an input that will be priced in British pounds. By buying the pounds in the forward market, the firm effectively hedges against changes in the value of the pound that are unrelated to price level changes. However, if the pound fell 10 per cent in value because a monetary shift caused a 10 per cent increase in British prices, then the firm's loss on its foreign exchange contracts would not be offset by a decrease in the price of the inputs.

For the most part, short-term exchange rate changes are generated by real changes, indicating that short-term hedges should be effective. This follows from the fact that, over short intervals, exchange rates fluctuate more than inflation rates. Over long periods, however, inflation accounts for a large part of exchange rate movements. Perhaps this explains why firms tend to actively hedge short-term currency fluctuations, but tend to ignore the effect of long-term fluctuations.

Why Most Firms Do Not Hedge Economic Risk

Most major multinational firms hedge transaction and translation currency risk, at least partially. However, most firms do not hedge long-term economic risk. Hedging the long-term economic consequences of an exchange rate change is substantially more complicated than hedging either transaction or translation risk. The largest obstacle here is that it requires estimation of both the current and the long-term effects of exchange rate changes on the firm's cash flows.

Consider, for example, the case of a US firm such as Apple, which manufactures computers in the United States for sale in Europe. What is the effect of a change in the US dollar/euro exchange rate on Apple's long-term profitability? To answer this question, one must first ascertain whether the change in the euro can be attributed to a general change in price levels, so that the inflation-adjusted or real exchange rate remains constant. As mentioned above, if the real exchange rate remains constant, then a nominal exchange rate change is likely to have only a minor effect on Apple's cash flows. However, changes in real exchange rates can have a significant effect on these cash flows.

Consider what happens when the US dollar strengthens against the euro, making the computers more expensive in euros. If the euro weakened because of general inflation in Europe, so that the real exchange rate remained constant, then the price of computers in Europe, relative to other prices, would not have changed. In this case, demand for Apple computers would not be affected by the change in exchange rates. Contrast this case with one in which the real exchange rate does change, raising the relative price of Apple computers in Europe and lowering the demand for them. Apple's cash flows in Europe (calculated in US dollars) would probably decrease in this case, since it would either sell fewer computers at the same US dollar price or, alternatively, be forced by competitors to cut its US dollar price for computers.

As these arguments suggest, one of the major difficulties in assessing the effect of exchange rate changes on cash flows has to do with predicting the cause of the exchange rate movement. If we cannot predict whether future exchange rate fluctuations are associated with relative price changes, then forward and futures contracts provide imperfect hedges.

Results

Result 21.14

When exchange rate changes can be generated by both real and nominal changes, it may be impossible for firms to hedge their long-term economic exposures effectively.

When it is difficult to hedge in the derivatives markets, firms sometimes undertake what is known as *operational hedging*, which involves changing the structure of the firm's operations (see Chowdhry and Howe 1999, for details).

21.9 Which Firms Hedge? The Empirical Evidence

Various empirical studies have compared the characteristics of firms that use derivatives with those of firms that do not. Although research on this topic is still evolving, some patterns are worth considering.

Larger Firms are More Likely than Smaller Firms to Use Derivatives

Several studies have found that larger firms are more likely than smaller firms to use derivatives.[8] The fact that smaller firms are less likely than larger firms to use derivatives is inconsistent with the view that smaller firms generally face higher risks of bankruptcy, and thus have more to gain from hedging. However, the fixed

[8] See Dolde (1993), Nance et al. (1993), Geczy et al. (1997), Bodnar et al. (1998), Allayannis and Ofek (2001), Allayannis and Weston (2001) and Jin and Jorion (2006).

costs of setting up a hedging operation and their lower level of sophistication probably explains why smaller firms are less likely to hedge (Guay and Kothari 2003). Indeed, Dolde (1993) found that, among firms that have implemented hedging operations, the larger firms tend to hedge less completely than the smaller firms, leaving themselves more exposed to interest rate and currency risks. In other words, size is a barrier to setting up a hedging operation, but among firms that do hedge, smaller firms facing greater risks of bankruptcy hedge more completely.

Firms with More Growth Opportunities are More Likely to Use Derivatives

Nance et al. (1993), Geczy et al. (1997) and Allayannis and Ofek (2001) provided evidence that firms with greater growth opportunities are more likely to use derivatives. In particular, firms with higher R&D expenditures and higher market-to-book ratios are more likely to use derivatives than companies that spend less on R&D, have lower market-to-book ratios and, therefore, probably have fewer investment opportunities. This evidence is consistent with the idea that firms hedge to ensure that they have enough cash to fund their investment opportunities internally.

Various other reasons explain why R&D-intensive firms with high market-to-book ratios are more likely to use derivatives. As Chapter 17 discussed, firms with these characteristics generally have higher financial distress costs, suggesting that they should hedge to ensure that they will meet their debt obligations. Furthermore, because R&D expenditures are tax deductible, these firms are likely to have lower taxable earnings, which implies that the asymmetric tax treatment of gains and losses, a hedging motivation discussed earlier in this chapter, applies more to firms with high R&D expenditures.

Highly Levered Firms are More Likely to Use Derivatives

Block and Gallagher (1986), Wall and Pringle (1989) and Nance et al. (1993) found weak evidence that firms with more leveraged capital structures hedge more. The positive relationship between leverage ratios and the tendency to hedge is consistent with the view that firms hedge to avoid financial distress costs. However, the weakness of the evidence probably reflects the tendency of firms with high financial distress costs, which have the most to gain from hedging, to have the lowest leverage ratios. For example, as Chapter 17 discussed, high-R&D firms tend to use little debt, and also tend to hedge because of their potential costs of financial distress.

Geczy et al. (1997) found no significant relationship between the debt ratios of most firms and their tendency to use derivatives. However, among those firms with high R&D expenditures and high market-to-book ratios, firms with more leverage are more likely to hedge. This implies that firms that suffer the highest costs of financial distress are more likely to hedge when they are highly leveraged.

Graham and Rogers (2002) provided evidence that firms hedge so as to increase debt capacity. This results in a tax benefit of approximately 1.1 per cent of firm value, and is a much stronger factor than hedging because of tax asymmetries. Perez-Gonzalez and Yun (2013) report that firms with active risk management policies have higher value and leverage, and make larger investments.

Risk Management Practices in the Gold Mining Industry

The studies described above examined hedging choices across several different industries. A study by Tufano (1996) looked in greater detail at the risk management practices within a single industry: gold mining. Within a single industry, proxies for financial distress costs, financing constraints and investment opportunities will probably vary much less than they do across industries. Consequently, differences in the hedging strategies across firms within a single industry are likely to be related to differences in the incentives and tastes of the top executives.

The evidence described in the Tufano study indicates that management incentives and tastes do have an important effect on risk management practices in the gold mining industry. Specifically, managers who hold large amounts of their firm's equity tend to use forward and futures contracts to hedge more of their firm's gold price risk. Thus managers who are personally the most exposed to gold price risk choose to hedge more of the risk. However, those who own relatively more equity options tend to hedge less, which may reflect the greater value of the options when volatility is increased. Tufano also found that firms with CFOs hired more recently hedge a greater portion of their exposure than firms with CFOs who have been on the job longer.

Risk Management Practices in the Oil and Gas Industry

A study by Haushaulter (2000) examined hedging choices of firms in the oil and gas industry. His evidence suggests that most oil and gas producers hedge only a small percentage of their future production. Specifically, only a quarter of the firms in his sample hedge more than 28 per cent of their production. He also found that larger firms and firms that are more highly leveraged tend to hedge more, which is consistent with the studies mentioned earlier. Moreover, the evidence suggests that those firms whose production is located in regions where prices are highly correlated with the prices of exchange-traded futures contracts hedge more, which makes sense, since these firms can probably hedge more effectively. However, in contrast to Tufano's study of the gold industry, Haushalter did not find a strong relationship between the shareholdings and compensation of a firm's managers and the firm's risk management practices.

In recent years, gold, oil and gas have all seen massive growth in their prices. From 2003 until March 2011, gold had increased from $350/ounce to $1,430/ounce, oil had grown from just over $30 per barrel to $114 per barrel and gas had grown from $1.70 to $4.00 per gigajoule. Under these conditions, and expectations of continued energy and metal growth rates, it would be expected that producer firms would wish to leave themselves more exposed to the upward movements in value, while user firms would hedge to mitigate the price increases.

21.10 Summary and Conclusions

Although we believe, as a general guideline, that most firms can benefit by hedging, the gains from hedging differ across firms. Firms can gain from hedging that reduces their probability of being financially distressed, especially in those industries where financial distress costs are the highest. There are also tax reasons for distressed firms to hedge, and gains that come from the fact that a firm's reported cash flows and profits are more informative when the firm has hedged out extraneous risks.

This chapter also considered situations where firms should not hedge. When excellent investment opportunities tend to arise at times when existing assets (unhedged) are most profitable, they may be better off remaining unhedged, or only partially hedged. For example, an oil firm is likely to find more high-NPV exploration projects when oil prices and hence unhedged profits are the highest. An oil firm would not want to hedge away the variability in profits completely, because that would leave it short of funds when favourable investment opportunities exist.

In addition, firms may choose not to hedge those risks about which they have private information, or which they partially control. In this respect, firms are similar to individuals buying car insurance. The safest drivers choose to be underinsured, since they regard insurance as overpriced. Recognizing this tendency, insurance companies raise the rates for drivers wanting full insurance. In most cases these considerations do not affect whether firms hedge in derivatives markets, because firms are unlikely to have important private information about currency and commodity price movements. However, these considerations do affect whether firms insure against firm-specific risk, or choose liability streams that leave them exposed to changes in their own credit ratings. For the same reason that the safest drivers often choose to be underinsured, managers who believe that their firms are less risky than their credit rating reflects will choose to borrow short term, in the hope that their credit rating will improve in the future. In other words, the safest firms will be overexposed to the risks connected with changes in their credit rating.

Our discussion of both foreign exchange and liability risk management indicated that implementing a sound risk management strategy requires a good understanding of the relationships between interest rate changes, exchange rate changes and inflation. The appropriate interest rate hedging strategy depends on the extent to which interest rate volatility is due to changes in the rate of inflation. Similarly, the appropriate foreign exchange hedging strategy depends on the extent to which currency fluctuations are due to differences between domestic and foreign inflation rates.

This chapter presented our view of how firms can use risk management tools to maximize firm value, which may differ from current practice. This difference is partly due to the limited experience many managers have in dealing with derivatives markets and risk management problems, and partly due to potential incentive problems (see Chapter 18). For example, if managers get a large share of their compensation from equity options – to solve one kind of incentive problem – they may choose to speculate rather than hedge, since option values increase with risk.

Again, we must stress that risk management, like all corporate finance decisions, cannot be viewed in isolation. Corporations must view their risk management choices as part of an overall strategy that includes their choice of capital structure and executive compensation, as well as considerations of overall product market strategy.

Key Concepts

Result 21.1: If hedging choices do not affect cash flows from real assets, then, in the absence of taxes and transaction costs, hedging decisions do not affect firm values.

Result 21.2: Hedging is unlikely to improve a firm's value if it does no more than reduce the variance of its future cash flows. To improve a firm's value, hedging must also increase expected cash flows.

Result 21.3: Because of asymmetric treatment of gains and losses, firms may reduce their expected tax liabilities by hedging.

Result 21.4: Firms that are subject to high financial distress costs have greater incentives to hedge.

Result 21.5: Firms that find it costly to delay or alter their investment plans, and which have limited access to outside financial markets, will benefit from hedging.

Result 21.6: The gains from hedging are greater when it is more difficult to evaluate and monitor management.

Result 21.7: Firms have an incentive to insure or hedge risks that insurance companies and markets can better assess. Doing this improves decision-making. Firms will absorb internally those risks over which they have the comparative advantage in evaluating.

Result 21.8: If a firm's main motivation for hedging is to better assess the quality of management, the firm will probably want to hedge its earnings or cash flows rather than its value. However, if the firm is hedging to avoid the costs of financial distress, it should implement a hedging strategy that takes into account both the variance of its value and the variance of its cash flows.

Result 21.9: Corporations should organize their hedging in a way that reflects why they are hedging. Most hedging motivations suggest that hedging should be carried out at the corporate level. However, the improvement in management incentives that can be realized with a risk management programme are best achieved when the individual divisions are responsible for hedging.

Result 21.10: Managers have private information only in exceptional cases. Given this, they almost always should be hedging rather than speculating.

Result 21.11: A firm's liability stream can be decomposed into two components: one that reflects default-free interest rates, and one that reflects the firm's credit rating. When a firm borrows at a fixed rate, both components are fixed. When it rolls over short-term instruments, the liability streams fluctuate with both kinds of risk. Derivative instruments allow firms to separate these two sources of risk: to create liability streams that are sensitive to interest rates but not their credit ratings, as described in equation (21.4) and to create liability streams that are sensitive to their credit ratings but not interest rates, as described in equation (21.5).

Result 21.12: If changes in interest rates reflect mainly changes in the rate of inflation, and if a firm's unlevered cash flows (and its EBIT) generally increase with the rate of inflation, then the firm will want its liabilities to be exposed to interest rate risk. If, however, interest rate changes are not due primarily to changes in inflation (that is, real interest rates change), and if the firm's unlevered cash flows are largely affected by the level of real interest rates, then the firm will want to minimize the exposure of its liabilities to interest rate changes.

Result 21.13: Exchange rate movements can be decomposed into those caused by differences in the inflation rates in the home country and the foreign country, and those caused by changes in real exchange rates. In most cases, the incentive is to hedge against real exchange rate changes rather than the component of exchange rate changes that is driven by inflation differences between the two countries.

Result 21.14: When exchange rate changes can be generated by both real and nominal changes, it may be impossible for firms to hedge their long-term economic exposures effectively.

Key Terms

Exercises

21.1 Small firms currently hedge less than large firms. Why is this? Do you expect smaller firms to start hedging more in the future? Explain.

21.2 Why is it harder to hedge currency risks in countries with volatile inflation rates?

21.3 Piste Resorts is a Swiss ski resort based in the Alps. Discuss the resort's exposure to exchange rate risk.

21.4 It is now much easier to hedge risks than it was in the past. How should this affect a firm's optimal capital structure? Why?

21.5 The XYZ Corporation manufactures in both Indonesia and Japan for export to Germany. Japan has a stable monetary policy, and, as a result, its inflation is easy to predict. Monetary policy in Indonesia is much less predictable. In which of the two countries can XYZ more easily hedge against the risk that manufacturing costs, measured in euros, will become significantly more expensive? Why?

21.6 Purchasing power parity (PPP) implies that real exchange rates remain constant. If PPP holds, do firms need to hedge their long-term foreign exchange exposure? Explain.

21.7 Oil firms hedge only part of their exposure to oil price movements. Why might that be a good idea?

21.8 Harwood Outboard manufactures outboard motors for relatively inexpensive motor boats. The firm is optimistic about its long-term outlook, but its bond rating is only BB. Describe how you would manage Harwood's liability stream if you believed that within two years Harwood's credit rating would improve to A.

References and Additional Reading

Allayannis, G. and Ofek, E. (2001) Exchange rate exposure, hedging, and the use of foreign currency derivatives, *Journal of International Money and Finance*, 20(2): 273–296.

Allayannis, G. and Weston, J.P. (2001) The use of foreign currency derivatives and firm market value, *The Review of Financial Studies*, 14(1): 243–276.

Bartram, S.M., Brown, G.W. and Fehle, F.R. (2009) International evidence on financial derivatives usage, *Financial Management*, 38(1): 185–206.

Bartram, S.M., Brown, G.W. and Minton, B.A. (2010) Resolving the exposure puzzle: The many facets of exchange rate exposure, *Journal of Financial Economics*, 95(2): 148–173.

Bernile, G., Bhagwat, V. and Yonker, S. (2018) Board diversity, firm risk, and corporate policies, *Journal of Financial Economics*, 127(3): 588–612.

Biguri, K., Brownlees, C. and Ippolito, F. (2022) Corporate hedging and the variance of stock returns, *Journal of Corporate Finance*, 72, 102–147.

Block, S.B. and Gallagher, T.J. (1986) The use of interest rate futures and options by corporate financial managers, *Financial Management*, 15(3): 73–78.

Bodnar, G.M. and Gebhardt, G. (1999) Derivatives usage in risk management by US and German non-financial firms: a comparative survey, *Journal of International Financial Management and Accounting*, 10(3): 153–187.

Bodnar, G.M., Hayt, G.S. and Marston, R.C. (1998) Wharton 1998 survey of risk management by US non-financial firms, *Financial Management*, 27(4): 70–91.

Bolton, P. and Kacperczyk, M. (2021) Do investors care about carbon risk?, *Journal of Financial Economics*. 142(2): 517–549.

Breeden, D. and Vishwanathan, S. (1996) *Why do firms hedge? An asymmetric information model*. Working paper, Duke University.

Campbell, J.Y., Serfaty-De Medeiros, K. and Viceira, L.M. (2010) Global currency hedging, *The Journal of Finance*, 65(1): 87–121.

Chowdhry, B. and Howe, J.T.B. (1999) Corporate risk management for multinational corporations: financial and operational hedging policies, *European Finance Review*, 2(2): 229–246.

Cole, S., Giné, X. and Vickery, J. (2017) How does risk management influence production decisions? Evidence from a field experiment, *The Review of Financial Studies*, 30(6): 1935–1970.

DeMarzo, P. and Duffie, D. (1995) Corporate incentives for hedging and hedge accounting, *The Review of Financial Studies*, 8(3): 743–771.

Doherty, N. and Smith, C. (1993) Corporate insurance strategy: the case of British Petroleum, *Journal of Applied Corporate Finance*, 6(3): 4–15.

Dolde, W. (1993) *Use and effectiveness of foreign exchange and interest rate risk management in large firms*. Working paper, University of Connecticut.

Faccio, M., Marchica, M.T. and Mura, R. (2016) CEO gender, corporate risk-taking, and the efficiency of capital allocation, *Journal of Corporate Finance*, 39, 193–209.

Froot, K.A., Scharfstein, D.S. and Stein, J.C. (1993) Risk management: coordinating corporate investment and financing policies, *The Journal of Finance*, 48(5): 1629–1658.

Geczy, C., Minton, B. and Schrand, C. (1997) Why firms use currency derivatives, *The Journal of Finance*, 52(4): 1323–1354.

Graham, J. and Rogers, D. (2002) Do firms hedge in response to tax incentives?, *The Journal of Finance*, 57(2): 815–839.

Guay, W. and Kothari, S.P. (2003) How much do firms hedge with derivatives?, *Journal of Financial Economics*, 80(3): 423–461.

Haushalter, G.D. (2000) Financing policy, basic risk, and corporate hedging: evidence from oil and gas producers, *The Journal of Finance*, 55(1): 107–152.

Jin, Y. and Jorion, P. (2006) Firm value and hedging: evidence from US oil and gas producers, *The Journal of Finance*, 61(2): 893–919.

Kamiya, S., Kang, J.K., Kim, J., Milidonis, A. and Stulz, R.M. (2021) Risk management, firm reputation, and the impact of successful cyberattacks on target firms, *Journal of Financial Economics*, 139(3): 719–749.

Lessard, D.R. (1991) Global competition and corporate finance in the 1990s, *Journal of Applied Corporate Finance*, 3(4): 59–72.

Lewent, J.C. and Kearney, A.J. (1990) Identifying, measuring, and hedging currency risk at Merck, *Journal of Applied Corporate Finance*, 2(2): 19–28.

Li, K., Griffin, D., Yue, H. and Zhao, L. (2013) How does culture influence corporate risk-taking?, *Journal of Corporate Finance*, 23, 1–22.

Nance, D.R., Smith, C.W. and Smithson, C.W. (1993) On the determinants of corporate hedging, *The Journal of Finance*, 48(1): 267–284.

Pérez-González, F. and Yun, H. (2013) Risk management and firm value: Evidence from weather derivatives, *The Journal of Finance*, 68(5): 2143–2176.

Rawls, S.W. III and Smithson, C.W. (1990) Strategic risk management, *Journal of Applied Corporate Finance*, 2(4): 6–18.

Serfling, M.A. (2014) CEO age and the riskiness of corporate policies, *Journal of Corporate Finance*, 25, 251–273.

Shapiro, A. and Titman, S. (1985) An integrated approach to corporate risk management, *Midland Corporate Finance Journal*, 3(2): 41–56.

Sila, V., Gonzalez, A. and Hagendorff, J. (2016) Women on board: does boardroom gender diversity affect firm risk?, *Journal of Corporate Finance*, 36, 26–53.

Smith, C.W. and Stulz, R.M. (1985) The determinants of firms' hedging policies, *Journal of Financial and Quantitative Analysis*, 20(4): 391–405.

Titman, S. (1992) Interest rate swaps and corporate financing choices, *The Journal of Finance*, 47(4): 1503–1516.

Tufano, P. (1996) Who manages risk? An empirical examination of risk management practices in the gold mining industry, *The Journal of Finance*, 51(4): 1097–1137.

Wall, L.D. and Pringle, J. (1989) Alternative explanations of interest rate swaps: an empirical analysis, *Financial Management*, 18, 59–73.

Chapter 22

The Practice of Hedging

Learning Objectives

After reading this chapter, you should be able to:

- Describe the factor beta, standard deviation and value-at-risk methods of estimating risk exposure.
- Use forwards, futures, swaps and options to generate hedges.
- Apply the covered interest rate parity relation in foreign exchange markets to develop currency hedges.
- Understand why and how to tail a hedge with futures and forwards.
- Use regression and factor models to determine hedge ratios.
- Describe the relation between hedging with regression, minimum-variance hedging and mean-variance analysis.

In the 1990s, Metallgesellschaft AG, one of Germany's largest conglomerates, possessed considerable refinery capacity through a 51 per cent owned subsidiary. Promises to sell heating oil from its subsidiary's refineries to its customers at guaranteed prices over the subsequent 10 years exposed the company to considerable oil price risk. To offset the risk arising from these promises, management at Metallgesellschaft decided to purchase crude oil futures contracts on the New York Mercantile Exchange. In September 1993 oil prices dropped precipitously, and Metallgesellschaft began to receive margin calls on its futures contracts. The cash required to meet these margin calls soon exceeded the company's revenues from its sales of heating oil, and Metallgesellschaft was forced to liquidate much of its futures position, resulting in €880 million in capital losses. As a consequence of this hedging fiasco, senior management was replaced, and academics began to study what went wrong. The consensus was that Metallgesellschaft had the wrong hedge ratio – so wrong that its futures position increased rather than decreased the firm's exposure to oil price risk.

Hedging activity lowers the probability of negative events having a large enough impact to force a firm into financial distress. In general, competent hedgers incur lower loan interest rate premiums and have fewer capital expenditure restrictions in loan agreements (Campello et al., 2011). The risks a firm faces in its operations, often called its **exposures,** include, for example, exposures to interest rate risk, currency risk, business cycle risk, inflation risk, commodity price risk and industry risk. This chapter develops an understanding of how to reduce these risk exposures. As explored in earlier chapters, Société Générale, France's second largest bank, is an extreme example of a company exposed to risk. The company experienced €4.9 billion of losses as a result of one trader allegedly fraudulently speculating on equity market index futures. The net exposure of the bank was €30 billion on the pan-European Euro Stoxx index, €18 billion on the German Dax index, and €2 billion on the UK FTSE index. This was equivalent to France's aggregate budget deficit! Although the bank had risk measures in place to limit exposure to extremely risky positions, SocGen alleged that the trader illegally hacked into his colleagues' trading accounts to maximize his net exposure.

Risk exposures are closely tied to the factor betas in factor models. Most of the analysis of factor models in Chapter 6 focused on equity returns. In this context, **value hedging,** the acquisition of financial instruments that alter the factor betas of the firm's equity return in order to reduce the firm's equity return risks, is particularly pertinent. However, as Chapter 21 noted, some firms focus on the risk of their near-term cash flows rather than on the risk of their equity return. Reducing *cash flow risk exposure* requires **cash flow hedging,**[1] which is the acquisition of financial instruments to reduce the *cash flow factor betas* of the firm (see Chapter 11). To minimize risk exposure, one acquires financial instruments that, when packaged with the firm's assets, result in factor betas that are close to zero. Alternatively, targeting a risk exposure involves setting the factor beta to a **target beta** level.

Numerous financial instruments are used for hedging. These instruments include forward contracts, futures contracts, options, swaps and bonds. The size of the position per unit of the underlying asset or commodity that achieves minimum risk is known as the **hedge ratio.**[2] This ratio is often difficult to estimate. The proper instrument for hedging also may require complex analysis. In the Metallgesellschaft discussion in this chapter's opening vignette, for example, futures were ineffective instruments for hedging exposure to oil price risk. Metallgesellschaft's price guarantees to its customers, which generated its oil price risk exposure, were long-term contracts. Metallgesellschaft, however, hedged this long-term exposure by rolling over a series of short-term futures contracts. As this chapter later shows, it is not possible to perfectly hedge long-term oil price commitments by rolling over a series of short-term futures contracts. In principle, however, Metallgesellschaft could have hedged its price commitments better with more complex derivative securities or with a more sophisticated hedging strategy.

Although this chapter touches briefly on the topic of interest rate risk, it leaves the detailed analysis of interest rate risk to the next chapter. For the most part, we shall use commodity risk (risk exposure due to changing commodity prices) and currency risk (risk exposure due to changing exchange rates) as illustrative cases to address the basics of hedging.

The first part of the chapter discusses the measurement of risk exposure. The second part assumes that the firm has measured its risk exposure properly, and desires merely to find the proper hedge ratio to minimize its exposure.

22.1 Measuring Risk Exposure

Exposures are measured in a variety of ways, but as Chapter 21 and the discussion above noted, one can generally view an exposure as a factor beta, similar to the factor betas discussed in Chapter 6. This section discusses the measurement of risk exposure with factor models.

Assume that currency and interest rate uncertainty contribute to a firm's risk of doing business in Japan. The firm can measure the exposure of a future cash flow to these two factors by estimating a factor model. Assume that the estimation of the factor model generates the equation

$$\tilde{C} = 30 + 2\tilde{F}_{curr} - 4\tilde{F}_{int} + \tilde{\varepsilon}$$

where

$\tilde{C}$ = cash flow (in £ millions)
$\tilde{F}_{curr}$ = percentage change in the ¥/£ exchange rate over the coming year
$\tilde{F}_{int}$ = percentage change in the short-term UK interest rate over the coming year.

[1] As an alternative to cash flows, firms also focus on hedging the risk of their future earnings.

[2] While the analysis in Chapter 21 did not advocate that firms should minimize risk exposure, this chapter, for simplicity of exposition, focuses on how to implement hedging that minimizes exposure to risk factors. Our results can easily be generalized to target any desired set of risk exposures.

The +2 and −4 in the equation are the sensitivities of the cash flow to the exchange rate and interest rates, respectively, or the *cash flow's factor betas*. The $\tilde{\varepsilon}$ term represents the risks of the cash flow not captured by these two risk factors.

Using Regression to Estimate the Risk Exposure

The **regression method,** one of the most popular tools for analysing risk and developing hedges, examines how the unhedged cash flows of the firm performed historically in relation to a risk factor. Specifically, it estimates the factor betas as slope coefficients from regressions of historical returns or cash flows on the risk factors.

Measuring Risk Exposure with Simulations

The **simulation method** is a forward-looking method of estimating risk exposure. In rapidly changing industries, the simulation method is superior to regression estimation using historical data, which is back-ward looking.

Implementation with Scenarios

To implement the simulation method, a manager needs to forecast earnings or cash flows for a variety of factor realizations. With exchange rate risk, for example, a manager would implement this method by specifying a wide range of different exchange rate scenarios. Each scenario includes an estimate of the profits or cash flows that would occur under a variety of assumptions about industry demand, and about competitor and supplier responses.

Simulation versus Regression

Although simulations require much more judgement on the part of the analyst, they do not require that the past history of the firm provide the best estimate of the future. In reality, this can be very important in a changing environment. For example, one would not want to derive an estimate of the Dutch firm TomTom's British pound exposure solely from regressions that make use of data from the past 10 years. The satellite navigation industry is evolving rapidly, and competition from other satellite navigation firms such as Garmin is likely to become fiercer in the future. The firm's future exposure to the British pound will thus probably not be the same as its past exposure.

Modifying Initial Estimates Obtained from Regression

The simulation method for exchange rate risk simply asks the manager to estimate the firm's future costs and revenues under different exchange rate scenarios to obtain profit (or cash flow). Regression may provide useful inputs for these estimates, but the manager is not limited to the regression results for these estimates. He or she could also incorporate assumptions about the sensitivity of the demand for a product to its price, as well as expected competitor responses to exchange rate changes. In addition, the regression analysis specifies a linear relation between the determinants of profits (or cash flows) and exchange rate changes, which is unlikely to be true in reality. The manager will want to modify the regression-based estimates to account for any non-linearities in the statistical relationships.

For example, TomTom might assume that British satellite navigation firms will maintain the same British pound prices for their satnav equipment when faced with a small increase in the value of the pound, giving up some profit to maintain market share. If this is the case, TomTom would not benefit from a small increase in the value of the pound. However, if the pound strengthens significantly, British satnav producers may find it preferable to abandon certain European markets, an action that would greatly benefit TomTom.

Similar arguments can be made about a weakening of the British pound, which provides an advantage to British satellite navigation makers. A slight weakening may have no effect on the prices that European consumers pay for British satellite navigation systems, perhaps because British satnav firms are concerned about having to raise prices later if the pound subsequently strengthens. However, if the pound weakens considerably, giving British satnav firms a large cost advantage, they might exploit the opportunity to expand market share, which would significantly reduce TomTom's profits.

Pre-Specification of Factor Betas from Theoretical Relations

In some cases, factor betas can be pre-specified using knowledge of theory. For example, the commitments of Metallgesellschaft to sell heating oil at predetermined prices can be viewed as forward contracts. If the risk factor is the price of oil in 10 years, the factor beta of a 10-year forward contract for such a risk factor must equal 1.

Volatility as a Measure of Risk Exposure

Corporate managers often like to summarize risk exposure with a single number. For this reason, the standard deviation is often used to summarize the risk impact of a collection of factor betas. Extending the analysis of Chapter 6 to correlated factors, the formula for the variance of the factor risk of an investment is

$$\sigma^2 = \Sigma_{m=1}^{k} \Sigma_{n=1}^{k} \beta_m \beta_n \text{Cov}(\tilde{F}_m, \tilde{F}_n)$$

where

β_m = factor beta on factor m

β_n = factor beta on factor n.

The volatility (that is, standard deviation) of the cash flow or value owing to factor risk is the square root of this. Example 22.1 illustrates how to implement this formula.

Example 22.1

Computing Factor-Based Volatility for a Cash Flow

Assume that a firm has a cash flow one year from now (in £ millions) that follows the factor model

$$\tilde{C} = 30 + 2\tilde{F}_{curr} - 4\tilde{F}_{curr} + \tilde{\varepsilon}$$

where the currency factor, $\tilde{F}_{curr}$, is the percentage change in the ¥/£ exchange rate over the next year, and the interest rate factor, $\tilde{F}_{int}$, is the percentage change in three-month SONIA from now until one year from now. Assume that the variance of the currency factor is estimated to be 0.011, the variance of the interest rate factor is approximately 0.022, and the covariance between the two is 0.004. What is the factor-based volatility of the cash flow?

Answer: Using the variance formula above, the factor-based variance is

$$\sigma^2 = 4(0.011) - 8(0.004) - 8(0.004) + 16(0.022) = 0.332$$

The square root of this number, the volatility, is 0.576 (expressed in £ millions).

Clearly, the estimates of variances and covariances of the risk factors are critical for obtaining a good estimate of the volatility. One procedure for estimating the covariances and variances of risk factors is to compute historical variances and covariances. However, financial institutions that make use of volatility recognize that variances and covariances tend to change over time, so they have developed more sophisticated estimation procedures.

JPMorgan, for example, in its RiskMetrics covariance matrix (see http://www.jpmorgan.com), forecasts variances as weighted averages of the previous variance forecast and of the latest deviation from the forecast. This model is a special case of a procedure, Generalized Autoregressive Conditional Heteroskedastic (GARCH) estimation, developed in the economics statistics literature.[3]

Value at Risk as a Measure of Risk Exposure

Perhaps the most popular way to measure risk exposure today is **value at risk (VAR),** defined as the worst loss possible under *normal market conditions* for a given time horizon. For example, an investment position that loses a maximum of €100 million over the next year, no more than 1 per cent of the time, will be viewed by some managers as having a VAR of €100 million for the next year.

[3] However, until recently GARCH estimation was virtually impossible to implement when there are five or more risk factors.

Value at risk is determined by the time interval under consideration, as well as by what the manager regards as normal market conditions. A position with a VAR of €100 million over the next year will have considerably less VAR over a shorter horizon, say over the next month. Similarly, a manager who considers abnormally bad market conditions to be those that occur less than 5 per cent of the time will have less VAR than a manager who is willing to ignore only those losses that, because of their astonishing magnitude, occur less than 1 per cent of the time.

The importance of both the significance level (5 per cent or 1 per cent as the typical thresholds for determining abnormal market conditions) and the time horizon is illustrated when representing VAR in a diagram using the distribution of profits and losses. Exhibit 22.1 illustrates the VAR at the 5 per cent significance level for a transaction with zero expected profit. The time horizon affects the shape of the distribution curve. The longer the time horizon, the more uncertain the profits, and the more spread out is the normal distribution curve. This should shift point A – the boundary of the 5 per cent area under the curve's left tail – to the left, increasing VAR. The threshold for the area in the tail (5 per cent versus 1 per cent) matters, too, as a shift to a 1 per cent tail as the threshold moves point A to the left, thereby increasing VAR.

Exhibit 22.1 Probability Distribution and Value at Risk

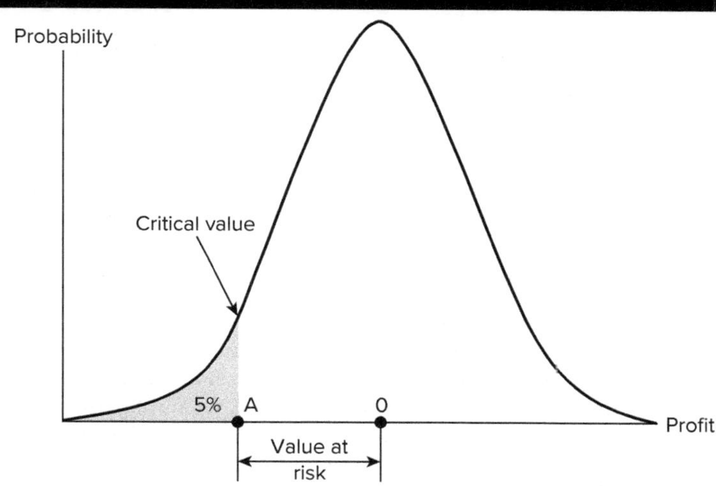

Value at risk is the standard methodology used for measuring the risk to the value of a portfolio of derivatives or other securities. An analogous methodology applied to cash flows, known as **cash flow at risk (CAR),** is becoming an increasingly important concept for corporations.

Estimating VAR and CAR from Standard Deviations

VAR and CAR are simple translations of the standard deviation if the value or cash flow is normally distributed. For example:

$$VAR(5\% \text{ significance level}) = 1.65\sigma$$

where σ is the standard deviation of the value. The same formula applies to CAR, except that σ is the standard deviation of the cash flow.

The 1.65 in the preceding equation is obtained from a normal distribution table, such as that found in Table A.5 in Appendix A at the end of this text. In particular, note that $N(-1.65)$ is approximately 0.05 in such a table. More generally, let x be the value or cash flow at which the probability that a normally distributed value or cash flow with a mean of zero and a standard deviation of σ is less than p per cent: that is, $N(x) = p\%$. Then VAR or CAR is $-x\sigma$.

Example 22.2 illustrates how to transform a σ to a CAR.

Example 22.2

Computing CAR from Standard Deviations Assuming a Normal Distribution

In Example 22.1, the standard deviation of the cash flow was approximately £576,200. What is the CAR at the 5 per cent significance level, assuming that the cash flow is normally distributed?

Answer: 1.65(£576,200) = £950,720.

Estimating VAR or CAR Using Simulation

When CAR is estimated, simulation is usually preferred to the standard deviation formula as an estimation procedure. Given pre-specified factor betas, the cash flow is then simulated from the factor equation for the factor values observed over a given historical period. The CAR is then the difference between the average cash flow and the fifth percentile outcome over the historical period.

22.2 Hedging Short-Term Commitments with Maturity-Matched Forward Contracts

Forward contracts are among the most popular tools for hedging. We begin with a review of forward contracts. Next, we analyse a firm, such as EDF Energy, which is exposed to gas price risk. We assume that it wants to minimize that risk by using forward contracts that mature on the same date as the obligation the company wishes to hedge.

Review of Forward Contracts

As discussed in Chapter 7, a *forward contract* is an agreement to buy or sell a security, currency or commodity at a pre-specified price, known as the *forward price,* at some future date. In contrast, the **spot market** for a commodity is the market for immediate delivery and payment. The amount paid for the commodity in the spot market is the *spot price* or, in the case of currencies, the *spot rate.* Generally, the forward price is set so that the contract is a zero present value (zero-PV) investment: thus no cash need exchange hands at the contract's inception. An exception to this takes place in what is known as an *off-market contract.* Generally, when a reference is made to the market's forward price, it is to the forward price of a generic zero-PV contract.

How Forward-Date Obligations Create Risk

EDF Energy would seek to mitigate gas price exposure from a series of forward contracts that, in essence, locked in the selling price at which its customers could purchase gas. Forward contracts are inherent in many business contracts, and have been around for hundreds of years. It is not surprising that EDF Energy would enter into forward contracts as part of its business strategy.

In the absence of these commitments, EDF Energy's profit is tied only to the spread between the prices of retail gas and wholesale liquid natural gas, because the company is a purchaser of liquid natural gas and a supplier of energy to households and businesses. However, by locking in its customers' gas prices, EDF Energy exposes itself to fluctuations in the price of liquid natural gas. These fluctuations are much more volatile than the spread between the retail gas and liquid natural gas prices. Hence, to minimize its gas price exposure, the company needs to lock in the liquid natural gas prices it pays to its suppliers. An additional series of liquid natural gas forward contracts is a natural vehicle by which EDF Energy could offset the effect of locking in the prices at which it sold its energy in the retail market.

Using Forwards to Eliminate the Liquid Natural Gas Price Risk of Forward Obligations

The future pay-off at date T of the long forward contract for liquid natural gas is the difference between an uncertain number $\tilde{S}_T$, the future spot price of liquid natural gas, and a certain number K, the forward price agreed on today.

Combining a Forward Commitment to Sell with the Acquisition of a Forward Contract

Consider a regasification plant that needs to buy liquid natural gas and, like EDF Energy, has locked in the price of its output. The operations of this business produce a constant gross revenue of G, but require the purchase of liquid natural gas at date T at the then prevailing oil price, $\tilde{S}_T$. The combination of the risk of this business operation, which has a cash inflow of $G - \tilde{S}_T$, and the forward contract, which at maturity has a cash inflow of $\tilde{S}_T - K$, eliminates the oil price risk. This is illustrated in Exhibit 22.2 by the horizontal line (with the height of $G - K$), which is the sum of cash flow from operations (line AB) and the cash flow from the forward (line CD). In this case, the firm can comfortably acquire liquid natural gas in the spot market at date T, and it knows that the price it pays, $\tilde{S}_T$, will be hedged by the gains or losses on the forward contract, as Example 22.3 indicates.[4]

Exhibit 22.2 Hedging Business Risk with a Forward Contract

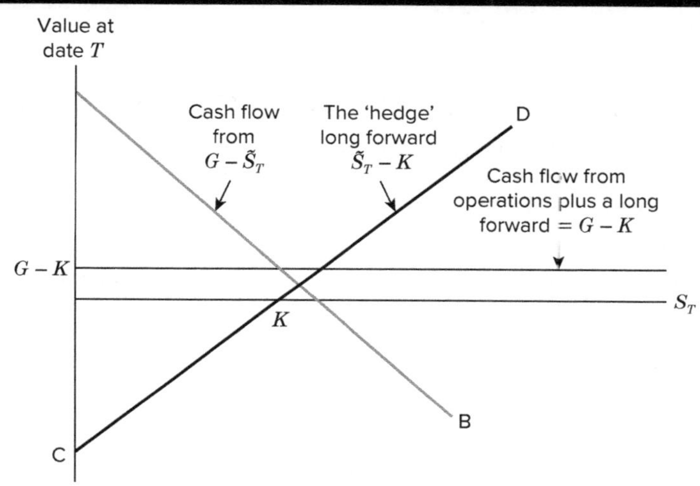

Example 22.3

Hedging Oil Price Risk with a Maturity-Matched Forward Contract

Assume that GEA Group has an obligation to deliver 1.25 million barrels of oil one year out at a fixed price of \$100 per barrel. How can it hedge this obligation in the forward market and eliminate its exposure to crude oil prices?

Answer: The cash needed to acquire the oil to meet this obligation is uncertain. GEA Group can eliminate the variability in its profit arising from this uncertainty by acquiring 1.25 million barrels of oil for forward delivery one year from now. If the date 0 forward price is less than \$100 per barrel, GEA Group will profit with certainty. If the forward price is greater than \$100 per barrel, it will lose money with certainty. In either case, its profit (or loss) from operations and hedging will be known at date 0.

[4] It is also possible to view a forward contract as simply locking in a price for gas needed for operations in the future. Obviously, this eliminates gas price risk. In many instances, however, the commodity delivered in the forward market is not precisely suited to the regasification plant's operations. Delivery might be at an inconvenient location, or the liquid natural gas might not be the right grade for the regasification plant's operations. In these cases the cash flow algebra used above tells us that if a slightly different product exists in the spot market, the forward contract described above will do a good job of hedging its price risk. The liquid natural gas received as a result of the maturation of the forward contract may be sold to a third party. The liquid natural gas needed for future operations, which may be slightly different in quality, delivery location, and so forth, can be bought in the spot market from a fourth party at approximately the same price. In this case the position in the forward contract still hedges oil price risk, albeit imperfectly. Further discussion of this topic is covered under cross-hedging in Section 22.9.

Using Forward Contracts to Hedge Currency Obligations

The last subsection illustrated how to use forward contracts to hedge commodity price risk – in that case, oil. Corporations and financial institutions also commonly use forward contracts to hedge currency risk. Lel (2012) reports that well-governed firms use currency hedging to lower the cost of external financing. Corporations generally enter into currency forward contracts with their commercial banker. Such contracts are customized for the amount and required maturity date, and can be purchased in almost all major currencies. Maturities can range from a few days to several years (long-dated forwards), although the average maturity is one year.

Because forward contracts are fairly simple and can be customized, they are the hedging tool most commonly used by corporate foreign exchange managers. Example 22.4 illustrates a typical foreign exchange hedge with currency forwards.

Example 22.4

Hedging Currency Risk with a Currency Forward Contract

Assume that BMW wants to hedge the currency risk associated with possible losses in the US over the next year. The expected loss is US$1 billion. How can BMW accomplish this, assuming that the current $/€ spot rate is US$1.47 per € and the forward rate for currency exchanged six months from now is US$1.49/€?

Answer: To approximate the 1 billion US dollar loss spread evenly over the entire year, assume that the entire loss occurs in six months. Thus, if BMW agrees to buy US$1 billion six months from now, it will have to pay €1 billion/1.49, or approximately €671.1 million. The €671.1 million is the locked-in loss. If the euro depreciates to US$1.35/€ six months from now, the US$1 billion loss becomes €740.8 million, but this is offset by a gain of €69.6 million on the forward contract:

$$\text{€}\frac{1\text{ billion}}{1.35} - \text{€}671.1\text{ million} = \text{€}69.6\text{ million}$$

Currency forward rates are determined by the ratios of the gross interest rates in the two countries. Specifically, we know from Chapter 7 that, in the absence of arbitrage, the forward currency rate F_0 (for example, US$/€) is related to the current exchange rate (or spot rate) S_0 by the covered interest parity equation:

$$\frac{F_0}{S_0} = \left(\frac{1 + r_{\text{foreign}}}{1 + r_{\text{domestic}}}\right)^T$$

where

T = years to forward settlement

r = annually compounded zero-coupon bond yield for a maturity of T.

Because forward rates are determined by the relative interest rates in the two countries, it should not be surprising that currency hedges can also be executed with positions in domestic and foreign debt instruments. A **money market hedge**, for example, involves borrowing one currency on a short-term basis and converting it to another currency immediately. In the absence of transaction costs and arbitrage, a money market hedge is exactly like a forward contract. Also, like a forward contract, it eliminates the uncertainty associated with exchange rate changes.[5] Example 22.5 explores this further.

[5] The equivalence of hedging with forward contracts and a money market hedge is known as the *covered interest parity relation*. See Chapter 7 for more detail.

Example 22.5

Hedging with a Money Market Hedge

How can BMW (see Example 22.4) use a money market hedge to ensure that the expected US$1 billion loss from its sales operations over the next year will not grow larger in euros as a consequence of a depreciating euro? Assume as before that the current spot rate is $1.47/€. To be consistent with the six-month forward rate of US$1.49/€, it is necessary to assume that six-month euro EURIBOR is 6 per cent per annum, that six-month dollar SOFR is 8.912 per cent per annum, and that six months is 182 days.

Answer: The money market hedge requires the following three steps.

1 Borrow euros in the EURIBOR market today for six months.
2 Exchange the euros for US dollars.
3 Invest the US dollars for six months in dollar SOFR deposits.

In six months, the maturing EURIBOR loan will require repayment in euros, and the maturing US$ SOFR investment will provide the necessary US dollars that the German company wanted to purchase. Hence, if the euros borrowed in step 1 are

$$€651.3 \text{ million} = \frac{\text{US\$1 billion}}{1.47\left[1 + 0.08912\left(\frac{182}{365}\right)\right]\text{US\$/€}}$$

exactly 1 billion US$ will be received in six months, and the EURIBOR loan in step 1 will require payment of

$$€671.1 \text{ million} = €651.3 \text{ million} \times \left[1 + 0.06\left(\frac{182}{365}\right)\right]$$

Note that the €671.1 million payout in six months is the same amount locked in as a loss with the forward rate, because the interest rates chosen were consistent with the covered interest parity relation.

22.3 Hedging Short-Term Commitments with Maturity-Matched Futures Contracts

This section investigates how to hedge obligations that generate risk exposure with futures contracts that mature on the same date as the obligation. As we shall see, there is an important difference between hedging with futures and hedging with forwards.

Review of Futures Contracts, Marking to Market and Futures Prices

In contrast to forward contracts, which can be tailored to the individual needs of the corporation, futures contracts are standardized. For example, the contracts on Euronext are limited to standard lot sizes, which differ between currencies, have standard maturity dates (quarterly), and involve only a selected number of major currencies.[6]

Recall that the essential distinction between a forward and a futures contract lies in the timing of their cash flows. With a futures contract, profit (or loss) is received (paid) on a daily basis, instead of being paid in one large sum at the maturity date, as is the case with a forward contract.

Because each party to a futures contract keeps a small amount of cash on deposit (that is, margin) with a broker to cover potential losses, brokers automatically execute the daily cash transfer, requiring only occasional notification to the two parties when margin funds are running low. If the futures price increases

[6] See www.euronext.com for a description of these standard features.

from the previous day's price, cash is taken from the accounts of investors who have short positions in the contract and placed in the accounts of those with long positions in the contract. If the futures price goes down, the reverse happens.

This procedure, known as *marking to market* (see Chapter 7), has a negligible effect on the fair market price of the futures relative to the forwards (with the notable exception of long-term interest rate contracts). This means that forwards and futures contracts can be treated the same, for the most part, for valuation purposes. Despite this valuation similarity, the next subsection points out that futures and forwards cannot be treated as if they are the same for hedging purposes.

Tailing the Futures Hedge

It is easy to become confused about how to hedge with futures because, as we shall see, futures hedges require *tailing* (defined shortly). The futures position in a tailed futures hedge is smaller than it is in a hedge that uses forward contracts, because it needs to account for the interest earned on the marked-to-market cash. The proper way to perform tailing on a hedge is a source of confusion for many practitioners, and it has caused grief for several corporations. Therefore we need to go through the logic of futures hedge tailing carefully.

No-Arbitrage Futures and Forward Prices

Assume that gold trades at $900 an ounce. To compute the futures price for gold, recall from Chapter 7 that, for an investment that pays no dividends, the no-arbitrage T-year forward price – and, because their values are approximately the same, the T-year futures price – is given by the equation:

$$F_0 = S_0(1 + r_f)^T$$

where:

F_0 = futures price

S_0 = today's spot price of the underlying investment

r_f = annually compounded yield on a T-year zero-coupon bond.

The futures price for gold delivered one year from now, with a risk-free interest rate of 10 per cent per year, would then be $990 [= $900(1.1)] per ounce of gold.

Creating a Perfect Futures Hedge

Suppose you own an ounce of gold that you wish to sell in one year. To fix the selling price today by selling futures contracts, it is necessary to *tail* your hedge – that is, you should sell less than one ounce in futures for each ounce that you plan to sell in one year.

Why is selling a futures contract on one ounce of gold overhedging in this case? Well, picture what would happen if the spot price of gold instantly changed today from $900 per ounce to $901 per ounce. According to the latest equation, the gold futures price would then change from $990 to $991.1 per ounce. Hence, as line *a* of Exhibit 22.3 illustrates, selling one futures contract to hedge the change in the price of gold would overhedge the gold price risk. As the gold price jumps from $900 to $901 per ounce, we gain $1 from holding one ounce of gold, but lose $1.10 from having sold a futures contract on one ounce of gold.

Selling less than one futures contract remedies this overhedging problem. Specifically, for a sale of 1/1.1 futures contracts, the loss on the futures contracts associated with the $1 gold price increase would be (1/1.1) × $1.10 or $1.00, which would exactly offset the $1.00 gain from holding one ounce of gold. This is shown in line *b* of Exhibit 22.3. The practice of selling less than one financial contract to hedge one unit of the spot asset is known as **tailing the hedge.**

Contrasting the Futures Hedge with the Forward Hedge

In our gold example, the no-arbitrage forward price, like the future price, is initially $990. This makes the forward contract, like the futures contract, a zero-PV investment. It seems curious that the minimum-risk hedge with the forward contract, where the hedge ratio is one-to-one, should *always* differ from the hedge ratio with the futures contract. Note, however, that the forward contract, in contrast with the futures contract, need not have a zero present value after the contract terms are set. This difference explains why futures hedges require tailing, but (maturity-matched) forward hedges do not.

Consider what happens to the present values of the two sides of the forward contract when the price of gold instantly jumps from $900 to $901 on the first day of the contract. The present value of the forward contract's

Exhibit 22.3 Hedging a Decline in the Price of Gold with Futures and Forwards

	(1)	(2)	(3)	(4)
Position	**Position value at initial gold price of \$900/oz (⇒ zero-PV forward and futures price = \$990)**	**Position value if gold price rises to £901/oz (⇒ zero-PV forward and futures price \$991.10)**	**Mark-to-market cash**	**Gain from position = (2) + (3) − (1)**
Hold 1 oz gold	\$900	\$901	\$0	\$1
Sell 1 futures contract	0	0	−1.1	−1.1
Sell 1/1.1 futures contracts	0	0	−1	−1
Sell 1 forward contract	0	$-1 = \frac{990}{1.1 - 901}$	0	−1
a. Hold 1 oz of gold and sell 1 futures contract	900	901	−1.1	−0.1
b. Hold 1 oz of gold and sell 1/1.1 futures contracts	900	901	−1	0
c. Hold 1 oz of gold and sell 1 forward contract	900	900 = 901 − 1	0	0

risk-free payment of \$990 at a 10 per cent discount rate remains the same (that is, \$900), but this payment is exchanged for gold that has a present value of \$901 after the \$1 price increase. Thus the forward contract's present value jumps from zero to \$1. In other words, instantaneous changes in the price of gold do not affect the present value of the cash payout of the forward contract, but they do affect the present value of the gold received, and hence the forward contract's value, on a one-for-one basis.

In other words, if the price of gold increases from \$900 to \$901 per ounce, the forward contract, formerly a zero-PV investment, becomes an investment with a positive PV of \$1. As line *c* of Exhibit 22.3 illustrates, immediately after the increase, the closing out of *one short position* in a forward contract, which loses \$1 in value, exactly offsets the \$1 gain from holding one ounce of gold.

Result 22.1 summarizes the distinction between hedging with futures and hedging with forwards.

Results

Result 22.1

Futures hedges must be tailed to account for the interest earned on the cash that is exchanged as a consequence of the futures mark-to-market feature. Such tailed hedges require holding less of the futures contract the further one is from the maturity date of the contract. The magnitude of the tail relative to an otherwise identical forward contract hedge depends on the amount of interest earned (on a dollar paid at the date of the hedge) to the maturity date of the futures contract.

22.4 Hedging and Convenience Yields

The forward price of gold is generally close to its spot price times one plus the risk-free return to the forward maturity date. In this respect, gold is very similar to an equity that pays no dividend.[7] Since the entire return from holding an equity that pays no dividend comes from capital appreciation, the present value of receiving a non-dividend-paying equity in the future must be the current price of the equity. As Chapter 8 noted, this is not true for equities that pay a dividend. The discounted value of the forward price of a dividend-paying equity is less than its current price by an amount equal to the present value of the dividends that will be paid between the current date and the maturity date of the forward contract.

From a valuation perspective, most commodities are like dividend-paying equity, because there is a benefit to owning them aside from their potential for price appreciation. The direct benefit from owning such commodities is called a convenience yield. The **convenience yield** is the benefit from holding an inventory of the commodity net of its direct storage costs, which arises because it is more convenient to have the inventory on hand than to have to purchase the commodity every time it is needed. For commodities with convenience yields, the number of the futures or forward contracts used to hedge the commodity would vary depending on the date of the future obligation.

When Convenience Yields Do Not Affect Hedge Ratios

Convenience yields do not affect forward or futures hedge ratios when the maturity of the future obligation one is trying to hedge matches the maturity of the futures or forward contract used as the hedging instrument. This point is an obvious one with forward hedges. Example 22.3, for instance, shows that a forward obligation is offset exactly with an opposite position in a maturity-matched forward contract with the same terms as the forward obligation. Example 22.3 is based on oil, a commodity that has long been known to have a convenience yield; Example 22.6 illustrates this point by showing how to hedge a forward obligation to deliver with a maturity-matched futures contract for oil.

Example 22.6

Hedging Oil Price Risk with a Futures Contract

Assume that GEA Group has an obligation to deliver 1.25 million barrels of oil one year out at a fixed price of $90 per barrel. How can it hedge this obligation in the futures market if the risk-free rate is 10 per cent per year?

Answer: Since forward contracts to buy 1.25 million barrels hedged this same obligation in Example 22.3, tailed positions in futures contracts to buy 1.25/1.1 million barrels would also hedge this obligation. The number of futures contracts would increase every day to reflect the shortening maturity of the contract.

Whenever the obligation is a forward contract, and risk is therefore eliminated with an offsetting opposite forward contract, the futures contract can generate the same perfect hedge provided that it is tailed for interest earned on the marked-to-market cash, just as in the gold illustration in Exhibit 22.3. When there is a mismatch in the maturity of the hedging instrument and the obligation to be hedged, the convenience yield affects the hedge ratio, whether the hedge is executed with forward contracts or with futures contracts. Before analysing this issue, it is important first to understand what determines convenience yields.

How Supply and Demand for Convenience Determine Convenience Yields

Consider the petrol that is used to fill up the tank in your car. When you go to the petrol station, you fill up your tank instead of pumping a single gallon of petrol or diesel into the tank, because it is convenient not to stop at

[7] There is some dispute about this among academics and practitioners. Central banks are willing to pay money to lease gold. This may imply that gold is more like an equity that pays dividends. Other researchers have argued that this lease value is tied to default risk.

a petrol station every 25 miles or risk running out of fuel. There is a small cost to this convenience: the petrol in the tank, on average, is not appreciating in value, whereas the money used to pay for the petrol might have earned interest (or you might have owed less interest on a credit card balance) if it had been in the bank instead of in the tank.

It would also be convenient to have even greater inventories of petrol. You would rarely have to stop at a petrol station if you could dig holes in your backyard and keep fuel storage tanks there, have extra storage tanks in your car, or have a fuel tanker truck follow you wherever you drive. You don't do this, because it would be prohibitively costly.

If storage of large amounts of petrol were free, you would probably choose to store the petrol. Note that *free* means not only free of the direct costs of storage, but also free in the sense that interest earned from holding fuel (in terms of its expected price appreciation, adjusted for systematic risk) would be comparable to that earned from cash deposited in the bank. Of course, this situation is not possible even if the direct costs of storage were zero. If everyone stored petrol to an unlimited degree, the price of petrol would be bid upwards, making its return smaller than the interest on cash deposited in the bank.

In essence, the demand for convenience and the supply of convenience, which depend on the cost of supplying convenience, determine the inventory of any commodity. For supply to equal demand, the difference between the expected price appreciation of the commodity and that of any other investment of identical risk must be the difference in their net convenience yields (the latter being the value of convenience less direct storage costs as a proportion of the commodity's price). For simplicity of exposition, we shall refer to the net convenience yield as the convenience yield.

Hedging the Risk from Holding Spot Positions in Commodities with Convenience Yields

Convenience yields tend to reduce the ratio of forward prices to spot prices. Consider, for example, the forward prices of crude oil. Refineries with oil inventories earn a convenience yield (which exceeds the cost of storage) because they avoid the risk of having to shut down the refinery if supplies are interrupted. Assume that crude oil has a convenience yield of 2 per cent per year. If oil is currently selling at \$90 a barrel and the risk-free rate is 10 per cent per year, then the no-arbitrage futures and forward price for oil delivered one year from now is

$$\$97.06 \text{ per barrel} = \frac{\$90(1.1)}{1.02}$$

More generally, if the commodity's convenience yield to the forward commitment's maturity date is y, and F_0 is the no-arbitrage forward price that would apply in the absence of a convenience yield, the forward price for the commodity should be

$$\frac{F_0}{1+y}$$

The division of F_0 by *one plus the convenience yield* affects hedge ratios when there is a mismatch between the maturity of the futures and the date of the position one is trying to hedge. For example, when trying to use forwards or futures to perfectly hedge the oil price risk from holding an inventory of oil, the convenience yield would affect the hedge ratio used. As Exhibit 22.4 shows, an increase in the current price of oil from \$90 per barrel in column (1) to \$100 per barrel in column (2) – which results in a zero-PV futures and forward price of \$107.84 – would be offset by a short position in 1.02/1.1 futures contracts (row *a*) or 1.02 forward contracts (row *b*).

Hence the 2 per cent convenience yield makes the hedge ratios for oil differ from those for gold, which we believe has very little or no convenience yield. In contrast with gold, the present value of the obligation to buy a barrel of oil one year from now is less volatile than the value of the purchase of a barrel of oil today. A purchase of oil one year from now is, in essence, equivalent to a purchase of 1/1.02 barrels of oil today, in terms of risk.

It is important to recognize that this risk comparison has been oversimplified by our assumption that the convenience yield of a commodity does not fluctuate with the commodity's price. For most commodities, convenience yields tend to increase as the price of the commodity increases, and decrease as the price of the commodity decreases. When this is the case, the forward price is even less volatile relative to the volatility of the spot price. This is discussed in detail in the next section.

Exhibit 22.4 Hedging a Decline in the Price of Oil with a 2 Per Cent Convenience Yield – Current Oil Position

	(1)	(2)	(3)	(4)
Position	**Position value at initial oil price of \$90/barrel (⇒ zero-PV forward and futures price \$97.06)**	**Position value if oil price rises to \$100/barrel (⇒ zero-PV forward and futures price \$107.84)**	**Mark-to-market cash**	**Gain from position = (2) + (3) − (1)**
Hold 1 barrel oil	\$90	\$100	\$0	\$10
Sell 1 futures contract	0	0	−10.78	−10.78
Sell 1.02/1.1 futures contracts	0	0	−10	−10
Sell 1 forward contract	0	$-9.80 = \frac{97.06 - 107.84}{1.1}$	0	−9.8
Sell 1.02 forward contracts	0	−10 = 1.02(9.8)	0	−10
Hold 1 barrel of oil and sell 1 futures contract	90	\$100	−10.78	− 0.78
Hold 1 barrel of oil and sell 1 forward contract	90	92.2 = 100 − 9.8	0	0.2
a. Hold 1 barrel of oil and sell 1.02/1.1 futures contracts	90	\$100	10	0
b. Hold 1 barrel of oil and sell 1.02 forward contracts	90	90 = 100 − 1.02(9.8)	0	0

22.5 Hedging Long-Dated Commitments with Short-Maturing Futures or Forward Contracts

A fundamental hedging problem faced by many corporations arises because most financial instruments, particularly futures, have relatively short maturities. Corporate commitments, in contrast, are often long term. Even when longer maturities exist for the desired hedging instruments, it is difficult to use them for sizeable hedging tasks, because very little trading takes place in the longer maturing financial instruments. The sheer market impact of a hedge would make hedging prohibitively costly. Corporations with long-dated obligations thus tend to hedge them by using the shorter-maturing futures or forwards.

As we show below, for the special case where convenience yields are constant, a perfect hedge can be implemented with short-term futures and forward contracts. This perfect hedging can be extended to the case where changes in the convenience yield are perfectly correlated with changes in the price of the commodity. However, because this assumption of perfect correlation is unrealistic, it is generally not possible to perfectly hedge a long-term obligation by rolling over a series of shorter-term forward or futures contracts.

Maturity, Risk and Hedging in the Presence of a Constant Convenience Yield

To understand the hedging of long-dated commitments with shorter-maturing futures and forwards, it is necessary to link the risk of each commitment and hedging instrument to the risk of holding the commodity. For example, assuming that oil has a convenience yield of 2 per cent per year, the forward commitment to buy a barrel of oil *10 years from now* is equivalent in risk to a position in $1/1.02^{10}$ barrels of oil purchased today. Similarly, a commitment to buy oil *one year from now* is equivalent in risk to a position in 1/1.02 barrels of oil purchased today. Hence, to perfectly hedge the obligation to buy a barrel of oil 10 years from now by selling a forward contract to purchase oil one year from now, sell forward contracts maturing one year from now:

$$\frac{1}{1.02^9} = \frac{1/1.02^{10}}{1/1.02} = 0.837$$

Rollovers at the Forward Maturity Date

As each day passes, it is unnecessary to alter the position in the one-year forward contract. For example, one-half year from now, the obligation to buy oil long term would be 9.5 years away, and the short-term forward would be 0.5 years from maturity. Hence the proper number of short-term forward contracts being sold would still be:

$$\frac{1}{1.02^9} = \frac{1/1.02^{9.5}}{1/1.02^{0.5}}$$

However, as the year elapses and the short-term forward contract matures, it is important to roll over the old contract and enter into a new one-year forward contract. For this new contract, the obligation would be nine years out. At this point, selling:

$$\frac{1}{1.02^8} = \frac{1/1.02^9}{1/1.02} = 0.853$$

of the new one-year forward contracts perfectly hedges the risk of the (now) nine-year-out obligation. Altering the number of offsetting forward contracts at the maturity date of the short-term hedging instrument is a form of tailing the hedge, similar to the tailing observed earlier with long-dated futures contracts.

Exhibit 22.5 illustrates the use of this tailed rollover strategy for hedging. The exhibit indicates that, at each annual rollover date of the series of short-term forward contracts, the number of forward contracts sold that would perfectly hedge the obligation increases, until in the final year – because of the matched maturity between the commitment and the hedging instrument – the perfect hedge involves selling exactly one forward contract.

Exhibit 22.5 Hedging a Long-Term Obligation with Short-Maturing Forwards Rolled Over at Maturity (Positive Convenience Yield)

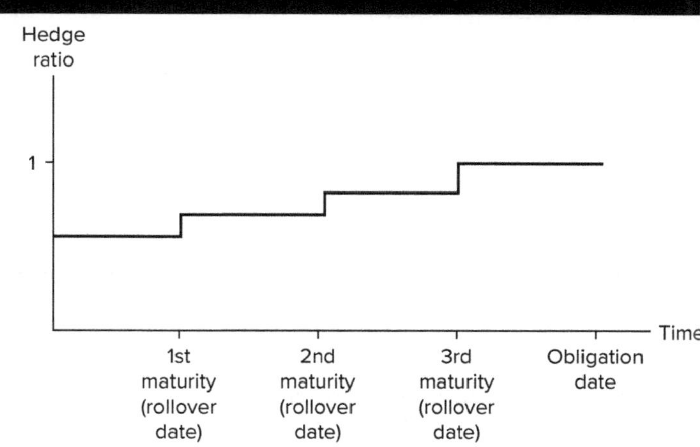

Futures Hedges

Earlier, we noted that a one-year futures contract is more risky than a one-year forward contract because of the mark-to-market feature of the futures. With a 10 per cent risk-free rate, each one-year futures contract is equivalent in risk to 1/1.1 one-year forward contracts. Hence, for the illustration above, a perfect futures hedge would involve selling:

$$\frac{1}{1.02^9(1.1)} = 0.761$$

one-year futures contracts at the outset. However, as each day elapses in that first year, it is necessary to tail the futures hedge, because it is getting closer to the forward contract in terms of its risk. For example, one half-year from now, the obligation to buy oil long term would be 9.5 years away, implying that the number of short-term futures contracts being sold would have to equal:

$$\frac{1}{1.02^9(1.1^5)} = \frac{1/1.02^{9.5}}{1/1.02^{0.5}} \div 1.1^{0.5} = 0.798$$

Thus, as Result 22.1 noted, the hedge ratio for a hedge involving a futures contract is always changing, both when there is and when there is not a convenience yield to holding the underlying commodity. Exhibit 22.6 illustrates the process of hedging with the futures rollover strategy. Note the difference between the hedge ratios from this exhibit and those in Exhibit 22.5; in particular, note the difference in the way the hedge ratios evolve between rollover dates.

Exhibit 22.6 Hedging a Long-Term Obligation with Short-Maturing Futures Rolled Over at Maturity (Positive Convenience Yield)

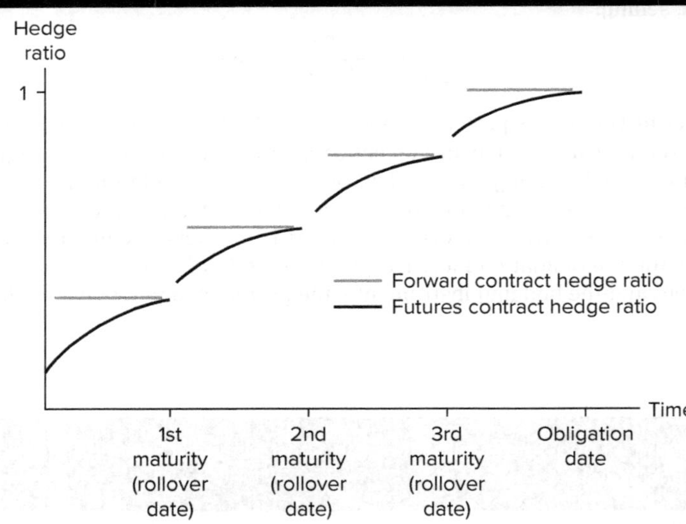

Example 22.7 applies these insights to a hypothetical hedging problem that is similar to the problem faced by Metallgesellschaft.

Example 22.7

Hedging Oil Price Risk with Short-Dated Futures and Forwards

Assume that GEA Group has an obligation to deliver 1.25 million barrels of oil one year from now at a fixed price of $90 per barrel.

a How can it hedge this obligation in the forward or futures markets, using forwards and futures maturing one month from now and then rolling over into new one-month forwards and futures as these mature? Assume that the convenience yield is 5 per cent per year and the risk-free interest rate is 10 per cent per year, both compounded annually.

b How would your answer change if you wanted to hedge against the change in value from owning 1.25 million barrels of oil?

Answer:

a The sum of 1 plus the one-month convenience yield per dollar invested is $1.05^{1/12}$. Hence the forward hedge would buy 1.25 million/$1.05^{11/12}$ barrels of oil one month forward. In the futures market, one would buy futures to acquire 1.25 million/$[(1.05^{11/12})(1.1^{1/12})]$ barrels of oil.

b The convenience yield makes the risk from holding 1.25 million barrels of oil greater than the risk associated with the present value of the obligation to receive 1.25 million barrels in one year. The risk-minimizing hedge would be to sell $1.05^{1/12} \times 1.25$ million barrels of oil for one-month-forward delivery. A futures position to sell $(1.05/1.1)^{1/12} \times 1.25$ million barrels of oil also eliminates the oil price risk.

Quantitative Estimates of the Oil Futures Stack Hedge Error

Mello and Parsons (1995) constructed a simulation model for GEA Group's hedging problem. Their model assumes that GEA Group has an obligation to deliver 1.25 million barrels of oil at a fixed price on a monthly basis for the next 10 years. This amounts to delivery obligations of 150 million barrels of oil at a fixed price. A possible strategy is to use what is known as a rolling stack of short-term futures contracts to undertake this hedge. With a **rolling stack,** the obligation to sell (buy) a commodity is offset with a series of short-term futures or forward contracts to buy (sell) the same amount of the commodity. GEA Group's commitment to sell 150 million barrels of oil at a preset price is hedged (albeit imperfectly) with a rolling stack that takes a position in short-term futures contracts to buy 150 million barrels of oil. As the futures contracts expire, they are replaced with futures contracts in amounts that maintain a one-to-one relation between the futures contracts to buy oil and the forward commitment to sell oil. Assume that the convenience yield of oil is 0.565 per cent per month and the risk-free rate is 0.565 per cent per month. Based on the analysis above, the obligation to sell 1.25 million barrels of oil at month t could be perfectly hedged by purchasing one-month futures contracts that are rolled over. If the convenience yield is constant, the number of futures contracts should be:

$$\frac{1.25 \text{ million}}{1.00565^t} = \frac{1.25 \text{ million}}{(1.00565^{t-1})(1.00565)}$$

For the obligation at each of the 120 months, the annuity formula gives a futures position (in barrels of oil) of

$$108.7 \text{ million} = \frac{1.25 \text{ million}}{1.00565} + \frac{1.25 \text{ million}}{1.00565^2} + \cdots + \frac{1.25 \text{ million}}{1.00565^t} + \cdots + \frac{1.25 \text{ million}}{1.00565^{120}}$$

Hence a rolling stack of 150 million barrels in futures positions overhedges the risky obligation of GEA Group by a considerable degree.

Intuition for Hedging with a Maturity Mismatch in the Presence of a Constant Convenience Yield

We summarize the results of this section as follows.

Results

Result 22.2

Long-dated obligations hedged with short-term forward agreements need to be tailed if the underlying commitment has a convenience yield. The degree of the tail depends on the convenience yield earned between the maturity date of the forward instrument used to hedge and the date of the long-term obligation. When hedging with futures, a greater degree of tailing is needed (see Result 22.1).

Result 22.2 derives from the fact that a convenience yield makes the receipt of a commodity at a future date less risky than receiving the same commodity now. Just as 50 per cent of an investor's risk disappears when he sells 50 per cent of his shares of equity in a company, or if the equity has a dividend equal to 50 per cent of its value, so does a 50 per cent convenience yield reduce the risk of a commodity received in the future by 50 per cent. Because y per cent of risk disappears with a y per cent convenience yield, eliminating the risk of a forward commitment by taking on a position in a (more risky) underlying (spot) commodity requires less than a one-to-one hedge ratio when the commodity has a convenience yield.

Perfect hedging of long-dated obligations with short-term forwards (or futures) has a less than one-to-one hedge ratio, because perfect hedging is a matter of matching up risks. The short-dated forward (or futures) contract is more like the underlying commodity, which has more risk than the long-term obligation. The closer the maturity date of the forward, the closer the hedge ratio (in a perfect hedge) is to the 'less-than-one' ratio for hedging the obligation by holding the underlying commodity. The longer the maturity of the forward contract, the more the forward contract looks like the forward commitment, and the closer the hedge ratio is to 1.

Convenience Yield Risk Generated by Correlation Between Spot Prices and Convenience Yields

The analysis up to this point has assumed that the convenience yield is constant. Generally, however, the convenience yield is uncertain, and correlated with the price of the commodity. This subsection examines the effect of the correlation on the hedge ratios.

It is not difficult to see that convenience yields are generally positively related to the price of the underlying commodity. In 2022, for example, oil prices rose by close to 50 per cent partially because of the Russian invasion of Ukraine and the associated sanctions imposed on each side of the conflict.

Earlier, we argued that petrol consumers fill up their tanks for the convenience of not having to stop again. However, when petrol prices rose in 2022, some motorists did not fill up their tanks when they were empty. Instead, they put in 20 litres at a time, hoping that in a few days the price of petrol would come down. Because petrol prices were *expected* to depreciate, the cost of convenience went up. After all, storing an inventory is not very profitable when the inventory value is declining. Note, however, that the convenience yield of oil also went up at this time, because the convenience benefit of that last litre in a 20-litre fill-up is a little higher than the convenience of the last litre in a 60-litre fill-up.[8]

Generally, the size of a commodity's convenience yield fluctuates inversely with the aggregate inventory of a commodity, which, in turn, is driven by supply and demand shocks. A necessary ingredient for a convenience yield – that is, for there to be a benefit from holding inventory – is that there must be some transaction cost, above and beyond the ordinary cost of the commodity, to acquire the commodity at certain times. A petrol station may pay the ordinary price for petrol when the supplier's tanker truck shows up on its weekly route. However, if between its regular deliveries the petrol station requires a special delivery of petrol because demand is exceptionally high, the supplier may impose a surcharge. This surcharge reflects the tanker truck driver's inability to deliver petrol using the most efficient route possible. At times of low aggregate inventory nationwide (for example, the summer driving season) the benefit of a large inventory of petrol (petrol's convenience yield) is high.

Hedge ratios are further reduced by convenience yields that tend to increase whenever the price of the commodity increases. The intuition for this insight, as with Result 22.2, is based on a comparison of the risk of the commodity's present value at different dates. In particular, the following result suggests that a convenience yield that increases a lot as spot prices increase tends to dampen the change in the long-term forward prices more than when the convenience yield exhibits only a mild increase in response to a spot price increase.

Results

Result 22.3

The greater the sensitivity of the convenience yield to the commodity's spot price, the less risky is the long-dated obligation to buy or sell a commodity.

[8] Some motorists of course continued to put as much petrol in their tanks as they had before the price increase. These motorists always place a high value on the convenience of petrol. However, these motorists were never the marginal investor in determining the convenience yield in the marketplace. Rather, it was the motorists who were willing to cut their inventory of petrol who determined the price of convenience in the marketplace.

The positive correlation between the convenience yield and the commodity's spot price means that the convenience yield acts as a partial hedge against spot price movements. Usually, the convenience yield is high when the commodity price is high, and low when it is low. Thus a more realistic picture of the convenience yield suggests that, in hedging long-dated commitments with short-term forwards or futures, the hedge ratio should be smaller than the ratio computed for a convenience yield that is assumed to be certain.

The exact computation of the hedge ratio in cases where the convenience yield changes depends on the process that generates the underlying commodity's spot price, which is tied to the fluctuating convenience yield.[9]

We summarize the results of this subsection as follows.

Results

Result 22.4

The greater the sensitivity of the convenience yield to the price of the underlying commodity, the lower is the hedge ratio when hedging long-dated obligations with short-term forward agreements. When hedging with futures, a further tail is needed (see Result 22.1).

In simple models, sensitivity as used in Results 22.3 and 22.4 can be thought of as the covariance between changes in the convenience yield and changes in the commodity's price. Alternatively, one can view sensitivity as the slope coefficient from regressing changes in the convenience yield on changes in the commodity's price.

Basis Risk

When hedging an obligation with a rollover position, there is an additional consideration known as basis risk. The **basis** at date t of a futures contract, B_t, is the difference between the futures (or forward) price and the spot price:

$$B_t = F_t - S_t$$

Basis risk is the degree to which fluctuations in the basis are unpredictable, given perfect foresight about the path the price takes in the future. Since the basis is simply the difference between the futures (or forward) price and the spot price, basis risk is also the degree to which the futures (or forward) price is unpredictable, given perfect foresight about the path the spot price will take.

Sources of Basis Risk

Basis risk may arise because investors are irrational, or face market frictions that prevent them from arbitraging a mispriced futures or forward contract. Basis risk may also arise because changes in interest rates are unpredictable. While this eliminates the ability to arbitrage any deviation from the futures–spot pricing relation, the effect on the pricing relation and on hedge ratios has to be negligible (see Grinblatt and Jegadeesh, 1996, for an example). Finally, basis risk may arise because of variability in convenience yields that is not determined by changes in the spot price of the commodity. Convenience yield risk of this type is unhedgeable, and eliminates not only the ability to perfectly hedge long-term obligations with short-term forwards, but also the ability to arbitrage deviations from the forward spot pricing relation. It is largely this unhedgeable convenience yield risk that the analyst needs to be concerned about when estimating hedge ratios.

How Unhedgeable Convenience Yield Risk Affects Hedge Ratios

Thinking about convenience yields in the same way one thinks about dividend yields aids in understanding the effect of unhedgeable convenience yield risk on the variance-minimizing hedge ratio. Recall from Chapter 11 that the share price is the present value of future dividends. Hence the share price 10 years in the future is the present value (PV) of the dividends from year 10 onwards, and the share price one year in the future is the PV of the dividends from year 1 onward. The difference is the PV of the dividends paid from years 1–10. Now, consider the hedge of a forward obligation to pay the year 10 share price offset with a one-year forward contract on the equity, and examine how variable the PVs of the two hedge components are over time. The variability of the PV of the one-year forward contract, which is due entirely to changes in PV of the share

[9] The interested reader is referred to Gibson and Schwartz (1990) and Ross (1997).

price one year in the future, exceeds the variability in the PV of the 10-year forward obligation, which stems entirely from the PV of the year 10 share price. The difference in variability is the variability in the PV of the dividends paid from years 1–10. There is a portion of this that cannot be hedged, because it is unrelated to the share price. As this chapter's prior and subsequent analysis shows (for example, Section 22.9), when the hedging instrument is more volatile than the obligation, the hedge ratio is generally lower, implying:

Results

Result 22.5

The greater the unhedgeable convenience yield risk, the lower is the hedge ratio for hedging a long-term obligation with a short-term forward or futures contract.

When hedging with a rollover strategy, the largest risk arises at the rollover dates of the short-term contracts. At these dates, the benefit of convenience embedded in the value of the hedging instrument drops abruptly as a result of the change in the forward maturity date. By contrast, the risk from changes in the convenience yield over small intervals of time between rollover dates is orders of magnitude smaller.

Situations Where Basis Risk Does Not Affect Hedge Ratios

Basis risk does not affect the size of the minimum variance hedge ratio when hedging a long-dated commitment with a comparably long-dated forward contract on the same underlying commodity or asset. In this case, the forward contract and the forward obligation are essentially the same investment, implying a hedge ratio of 1. As long as there is no arbitrage at the maturity date, $F_T = S_T$. Hence any basis risk before the maturity date is irrelevant.

22.6 Hedging with Swaps

The last section noted that many financial contracts have a shorter term than the commitments they try to hedge. The success of the swap market is due in part to swaps typically having longer-term maturities than the contracts offered in the futures and forward markets.

Review of Swaps

Swaps, discussed in detail in Chapter 7, are agreements to periodically exchange the cash flows of one security for the cash flows of another. In addition to specifying the terms of the exchange and the frequency with which exchanges take place, the swap contract specifies a notional amount of the swap. This amount represents the size of the principal on which the cash flow exchange takes place. The most common swaps are *interest rate swaps,* which exchange the cash flows of fixed- for floating-rate bonds, and *currency swaps,* which exchange the cash flows of bonds denominated in two different currencies.

Swaps can be used to hedge a variety of risks. For example, corporations often employ basket swaps to hedge currency risk. **Basket swaps** are currency swaps that exchange one currency for a basket of currencies. Typically, this basket of currencies is weighted to match the foreign currency exposure of the corporation.

Hedging with Interest Rate Swaps

Banc One's use of interest rate swaps, described by Backus et al. (1995), illustrates how swaps are used for risk management. According to a 1991 issue of *Bankers Magazine,* Banc One viewed itself as the McDonald's of retail banking. Banc One's franchises, which consisted originally of a set of acquired banks, grew in the 1980s and early 1990s to include banks in the west, south-west and east of America. All these 'franchises' have decentralized management whose decisions resulted in a situation in which the collective assets of the franchises are more short term than their liabilities. As a consequence, Banc One's liabilities are more sensitive to interest rate movements than its assets.[10]

[10] In contrast to Banc One, in the absence of hedging most large banks have income that increases when interest rates decrease.

Backus et al. computed that a 1 per cent decline in interest rates in the early 1990s resulted in an equity decline of about $180 million for Banc One. As a result of this interest rate sensitivity, headquarters management at Banc One assumed positions in interest rate derivatives in the 1990s, using mainly interest rate swaps with a notional amount of almost $40 billion. Banc One reported that a 1 per cent decline in interest rates decreased net income by 12.3 per cent without the swaps, but increased net income by 3.3 per cent with the swaps.

The Interest Rate Risk of an Interest Rate Swap

The key to interest rate hedging with interest rate swaps is that the present value of the floating side of the swap has virtually no sensitivity to interest rate risk, whereas the PV of the fixed side has the same kind of interest rate risk as a fixed-rate bond. Hence a swap to pay a fixed rate of interest and receive a floating rate of interest generates the same interest rate sensitivity as the issuance of a fixed-rate bond. Conversely, a swap to pay a floating interest rate and receive a fixed interest rate generates the same interest rate sensitivity as the purchase of a fixed-rate bond. As a result, an interest rate swap can effectively change positions in fixed-rate bonds into positions in floating-rate bonds, and vice versa. Ignoring credit risk considerations, rolled-over positions in short-term debt have the same risks as floating-rate debt. Thus interest rate swaps can also be thought of as vehicles for converting short-term debt into long-term debt, and vice versa.

Converting Fixed to Floating

If the present value of the assets of a firm is insensitive to interest rates, financing with a fixed-rate debt instrument creates interest rate exposure, increasing equity value when interest rates rise and decreasing equity value when interest rates fall. An interest rate swap can effectively convert the fixed-rate liability into a floating-rate liability, as Example 22.8 shows.

Example 22.8

Using Swaps to Convert a Fixed-Rate into a Floating-Rate Liability

Assume that Allied Irish Banks (AIB) has issued a five-year €1 million fixed-rate bond at the five-year Treasury rate + 200 basis points (bp), paid semi-annually, with principal due in five years. AIB would like to convert this into a floating-rate loan. How can it achieve this?

Answer: AIB should enter into a €1 million notional swap to receive a fixed rate equal to the five-year Treasury yield plus 200bp and pay EURIBOR plus a spread. The receipt of the Treasury yield plus 200bp effectively cancels out the fixed-rate payments on the AIB bond. The payment of the floating rate on the swap is all that remains.

The **swap spread** for a five-year swap is the number of basis points in excess of the five-year on-the-run Treasury yield that the payer of the fixed rate must pay in exchange for EURIBOR. Hence, in Example 22.8, if the swap spread for AIB is 50bp, the bank would convert a five-year fixed-rate loan at the five-year Treasury yield plus 200bp into a floating-rate loan at EURIBOR + 150bp (= 200bp – 50bp).

Converting Short-Term Debt to Long-Term Debt

If the assets of the firm are highly sensitive to interest rate risk, the firm might desire fixed-rate debt financing to offset this risk. However, as Chapter 21 discussed, a firm may expect its credit risk to improve, and thus prefer rolling over short-term debt. The firm could then use a swap to hedge the interest rate risk that arises with this strategy. This possibility is examined in Example 22.9.

Example 22.9

Hedging Interest Rate Risk

Assume that Fiat Chrysler needs to finance a project that requires €100 million for five years. The firm can obtain a fixed-rate loan for the five-year period with an interest rate of 10 per cent, which is three percentage points above the five-year Treasury note rate. Alternatively, Fiat Chrysler can roll over one-year bank loans to finance the project. Its current borrowing cost from such a loan is 9 per cent, which is three percentage points above the one-year Treasury note rate. The bank has also agreed to enter into a swap contract with Fiat Chrysler in which the bank pays Fiat Chrysler the interest rate on one-year Treasury notes, and Fiat Chrysler pays the bank 7.3 per cent, which is the interest rate on five-year Treasury notes plus 30 basis points. Fiat Chrysler is aware that the demand for automobiles is closely tied to changes in interest rates, and that it can ill afford to be exposed to interest rate risk. However, it also believes that its cost of long-term debt, 10 per cent, is much too high, given the firm's current prospects. It believes that, within a year, its credit rating will improve, and its borrowing costs will decline. What should Fiat Chrysler do, and what are the risks?

Answer: Fiat Chrysler does not want to be exposed to interest rate risk, but it does want to bet on its own credit rating. It can do this by rolling over short-term loans and entering into the interest rate swap with a notional amount of €100 million. With this combined transaction, the firm's initial borrowing cost will be 9% – 6% + 7.3% = 10.3%, which is slightly higher than the cost of borrowing with a fixed-rate loan. However, if Fiat Chrysler's credit rating does improve next year, so that its default spread is reduced from 3 per cent to 2 per cent, its borrowing cost will drop from 10.3 per cent to 9.3 per cent, and will not be subject to changes in default-free interest rates. Of course, Fiat Chrysler's projections may be wrong and its credit rating may not improve, in which case the firm would have been better off borrowing at a fixed rate.

Note that, in Example 22.9, Fiat is still exposed to interest rate risk on the asset side of its balance sheet. Because of this, its default spread may be correlated with changes in the interest rates. Specifically, Fiat might be concerned that a large increase in interest rates could lead to a drop in its sales, which in turn might cause its credit rating to decline. In this sense, the swap transaction described in the example does not totally insulate the firm's borrowing costs from the effect of changing interest rates.

Hedging with Currency Swaps

Currency swaps can be used to create foreign debt synthetically. As the last line of Exhibit 22.7 indicates, the cash outflows of foreign debt can be synthesized by combining domestic debt (outflows in row *a*) with a swap to pay foreign currency and receive domestic currency (net outflows as row *c* less row *b*).

Creating Synthetic Foreign Debt to Hedge Foreign Asset Cash Inflows

Allen (1987) suggested that Disney's profits from Tokyo Disneyland (net of its yen financing liabilities) created an exposure to yen currency risk for Disney in the mid-1980s. This yen-denominated cash inflow was estimated at 6 billion per year and growing. Disney could eliminate this yen exposure by issuing yen-denominated debt to a Japanese bank, but management saw this as prohibitively expensive. A comparable strategy, albeit not exactly the one Disney followed, would have the company issue US dollar-denominated debt and enter into a currency swap.

Exhibit 22.7 Creating Synthetic Foreign Debt

	Year					
	1	2	3	...	9	10
Net cash flows of £1 million UK £ debt						
a. Outflows (in £ millions)	0.09	0.09	0.09	...	0.09	1.09
Future cash flows from 10-year currency swap £1 million notional amount						
b. Inflows (in £ millions)	0.09	0.09	0.09	...	0.09	1.09
c. Outflows (in € millions)	0.13	0.13	0.13	...	0.13	1.13
Total outflows of domestic debt plus swap (in € millions) $a + c - b$						
	0.13	0.13	0.13	...	0.13	1.13

Creating Synthetic Domestic Debt to Save on Financing Costs

Sometimes, firms wish to issue domestic debt to hedge the interest rate risk of domestic assets. Example 22.10 shows that currency swaps can also be used to create domestic debt synthetically. If a company's debt issue is well received in a foreign country, the transaction can result in lower debt financing costs.

Example 22.10

Using Currency Swaps to Create Domestic Debt

Assume that Nokia can issue a 5 million Swiss franc five-year straight-coupon bond at a yield of 5 per cent. In Finland, its comparable euro straight-coupon debt issues are financed at 8 per cent. In the currency swap market, Nokia can swap the payments of 5 per cent Swiss franc bonds for those of 7 per cent euro bonds. How can Nokia get a €3.125 million loan synthetically at a yield of 7 per cent? Assume that the current exchange rate is 1.60 Swiss francs to the euro.

Answer:

1 Issue 5 million Swiss franc (SFr) notes at 5 per cent.

2 Enter into a five-year €3.125 million notional currency swap in which payments equivalent to the semi-annual payments from the 5 per cent Swiss franc notes (SFr125,000) are received. In exchange, Nokia pays 7 per cent in euros (€109,375 semi-annually) and an additional €3.125 million at the maturity of the swap. The cash received in Swiss francs on the swap funds the payment on the Swiss franc notes (interest and SFr5 million principal), leaving only the euro payments on one side of the swap as Nokia's obligation.

Example 22.10 shows that Nokia saves 100bp on its financing costs, or about €31,250 per year, because Swiss franc investors are treating Nokia relatively more favourably than Eurozone euro investors. There are a variety of explanations for this, but one reason is simply that Nokia may be offering Swiss investors a unique opportunity to diversify their bond portfolios. Because the number of Swiss companies issuing bonds (for example, Nestlé) is relatively small, and because the transaction costs of investing in bonds denominated in foreign currency (and then converting back to Swiss francs) may be prohibitively large, Swiss investors may be willing to pay a premium for Nokia bonds.

22.7 Hedging with Options

Options are used in two ways to hedge risk. In the first, a **covered option strategy,** one option is issued or bought per unit of the asset or liability generating the risk exposure. The resulting one-to-one hedge ratio places either a floor on losses or a cap on gains. With the alternative, **delta hedging,** one first computes the option's delta, where delta (Δ) is the number of units of the underlying asset in the option's tracking portfolio (see Chapter 7). Then options in the quantity $1/\Delta$ are issued or bought per unit of the asset or liability generating the risk exposure. Delta hedging can, at least theoretically, eliminate all risk. Such hedging typically has a greater than one-to-one hedge ratio, because Δ is generally between 0 and 1.

Why Option Hedging is Desirable

For a variety of reasons, the pay-off from an option hedge is sometimes preferred to the pay-off from hedged positions with futures or forwards. For example, a covered option hedge can be used when managers want to partake in some upside risk. Portfolio insurance (see Chapter 8), which offers this desirable pay-off, can be created by acquiring put options to partly offset the risk from holding assets.

Alternatively, options may be appropriate when the risk being hedged has some option-like component. For example, many companies purchase swap options when they enter into swaps that are designed to offset the interest rate risk of callable bonds issued by the firm. Once the bond is called by the issuing firm, the interest rate swap that formerly hedged the bond now hedges nothing. The interest rate swap now creates rather than mitigates interest rate risk. In such a case, the previously purchased swap option can be exercised when the bond is called to eliminate the risk from the interest rate swap.[11]

EDF Energy represents another case where option-based hedging might be useful. If retail energy prices declined substantially, EDF Energy might have had to deal with a set of irate customers who demanded renegotiation of their contracts to purchase gas at exorbitant prices. Faced with this option-like risk, EDF Energy find a more suitable hedge by issuing call options on gas instead of selling gas futures.

As Chapter 21 noted, options may be particularly useful in cases where firms would like to hedge to minimize the probability of financial distress, but do not want to eliminate all of the upside associated with favourable outcomes. For instance, in Example 21.3, National Nickel wanted to eliminate the possibility of financial distress, but also wished to have sufficient cash flow in the event of a nickel price increase to internally fund new exploration. Commodity options are particularly useful in such cases, because they place a floor on the company's commodity revenues while allowing them to generate higher revenues, and hence fund more exploration activity, as commodity prices rise above the strike price of the options.

Covered Option Hedging: Caps and Floors

The use of a single option in combination with a single position in the underlying asset (or liability) implicitly creates what is known as a *cap* or a *floor*, first discussed in Chapter 2. A floor, illustrated in panel A of Exhibit 22.8, can be thought of as a call option in combination with a risk-free security. It eliminates some downside risk – namely, all values below the floor value – so one generally pays more to acquire a floor-like position than a comparable pay-off without a floor. A cap, illustrated in panel B of Exhibit 22.8, can be thought of as a short position in a put option plus a risk-free security. It eliminates some upside volatility – eliminating all outcomes above the cap value – and thus costs less (or one is paid more) than the comparable pay-off without the cap.

Exhibit 22.8 Floors and Caps

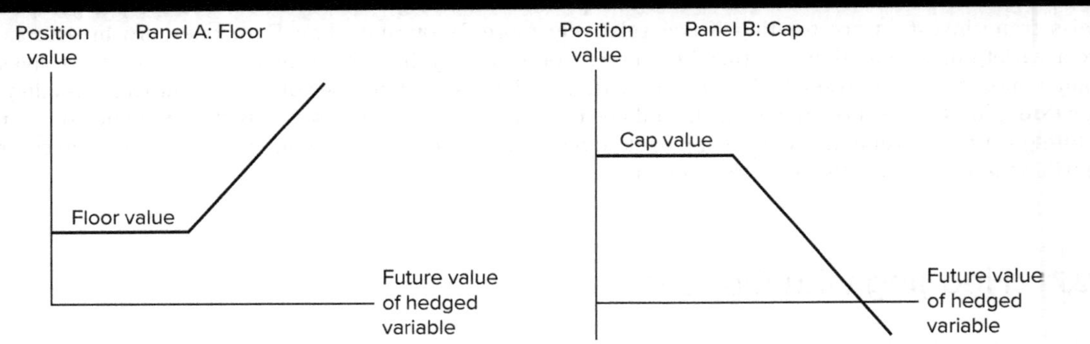

Put–Call Parity

The put–call parity relation discussed in Chapter 8 is useful for understanding the construction of caps and floors. A floor is created by buying an option on some underlying value or exposure of a firm. For example, if the value of the firm decreases when the price of oil declines, buying a put on oil prices creates insurance against the loss in the value of the firm that results from oil prices declining too much. If the value of the firm decreases when the price of oil increases (for example, when oil is a major input, not an output, in the production process), buying a call creates insurance against the loss in firm value that results from oil prices rising too much.

[11] In many cases, such option exercise is suboptimal. Chapter 8 indicated that there are correct rules for when to exercise an option early and when to defer exercise. The time at which the investor should optimally exercise a swap option often depends on interest rate risk alone, while the exercise of a call provision of a bond often occurs because the credit health of the company has improved. Hence the call of a bond by the issuing firm does not mean that the firm should exercise its swap option if it is trying to maximize the option's value.

Consider now a firm whose future value at date T, V_T, can be represented as a constant value a plus the product of a coefficient b and the price of oil S_T: that is,

$$V_T = a + bS_T \tag{22.1}$$

Then b is positive when there is a positive relation between oil prices and firm value, and is negative when there is a negative relation between oil prices and firm value. In Chapter 8's discussion of put–call parity we learned that the future difference between the date T value of a call and a put is

$$c_T - p_T = S_T - K$$

or

$$S_T = c_T - p_T + K \tag{22.2}$$

We now show how to create floor values or cap values that are related to the option strike price of K.

Creating Floors

Substituting equation (22.2) into equation (22.1) tells us that the firm's value at a given future date T is

$$V_T = a + bK + bc_T - bp_T \tag{22.3}$$

The expression $a + bK$ can be thought of as a risk-free bond. With a positive value for b, acquiring b puts at a cost of bp_0 converts the firm's date T value from that shown in equation (22.3) to

$$V_T^* = a + bK + bp_0(1 + r_f)^T + bc_T$$

where r_f denotes the risk-free interest rate per period.

This pay-off is like a call option plus a risk-free bond, where the risk-free bond has the pay-off

$$a + bK - bp_0(1 + r_f)^T$$

The floor value of $a + bK - bp_0(1 + r_f)^T$ is generated when S_T is small in this case. If b is negative, buying $-b$ calls, a positive number of calls, makes the firm value:

$$V_T^* = a + bK - bc_0(1 + r_f)^T + bp_T$$

Since b is negative, this is like having a risk-free bond plus a positive number of puts. In this case, the floor value of $a + bK + bc_0(1 + r_f)^T$ takes effect when S_T is large.

Example 22.11 provides a numerical illustration of how to create a floor by acquiring options.

Example 22.11

Using Options to Create Floors on Losses

Assume that GEA Group has an obligation to deliver 1.25 million barrels of oil one year from now at a fixed price of \$90 per barrel. If oil prices rise to \$110 a barrel, GEA Group loses \$20 per barrel on this promise. How can GEA Group insure itself against oil prices exceeding \$95 per barrel, yet profit if oil prices decline, as its analysts are forecasting?

Answer: Acquiring a call option to buy 1.25 million barrels of oil one year from now at \$95 per barrel will cap oil prices for GEA Group at \$95 per barrel, and put a floor on GEA Group's losses should oil prices rise.

Creating Caps

Caps are constructed by shorting options. Starting with the firm value shown in equation (22.3), shorting b calls when b is positive generates a new firm value of

$$V_T^* = a + bK + bc_0(1 + r_f)^T + bp_T$$

This has the pay-off of a risk-free bond and a short position in puts. This new value is capped at $a + bK + bc_0(1 + r_f)^T$ because the short put position can never have a positive value, and the remaining terms on the right-hand side of the equation, the cap value, are certain.

Similarly, with b negative, shorting $-b$ puts, a positive number of puts, creates a firm value of

$$V_T^* = a + bK - bp_0(1 + r_f)^T + bc_T$$

This has the pay-off of a risk-free bond and a short position in calls. The new firm value is now capped at $a + bK - bp_0(1 + r_f)^T$ because the short call position can never have a positive value, and the remaining terms on the right-hand side of the equation, the cap value, are certain.

Currency Caps and Floors

Multinational companies often use currency option contracts to hedge transaction exposure. Options and futures on currency are traded on organized exchanges, such as the Euronext. Options also trade over the counter through large commercial banks and other financial institutions.

Options on foreign currencies provide corporate foreign exchange managers with a unique hedging alternative to the forward or the futures contract. The purchase of options can create a floor. Selling options creates a cap. Options to buy a portfolio of currencies, known as **basket options,** are also popular because – with a diversified, and thus less volatile, basket of currencies underlying the option – they are less expensive than buying a portfolio of single currency options.

Example 22.12 illustrates how to use a single currency option to create a floor on foreign currency exposure.

Example 22.12

Using Currency Options to Create Floors on Losses

Return to the hypothetical case of BMW from Example 22.4: it needs to hedge the US$1 billion expected loss spread out over the next year. As the earlier example pointed out, this is similar to a US$1 billion loss six months from now. How can BMW use currency options to ensure that a six-month drop in the value of the euro below US$1.35 per € will not make the euro loss even larger?

Answer: Acquiring call options to buy US$1 billion with strike prices of €0.7407 per US$ (which is US$1.35 per €) creates a floor on the dollar loss. The option allows the firm to lock in the cost of purchasing US dollars for up to six months at a specified price (the strike price).

Contrast the option in Example 22.12 with a forward contract. If US$1 billion was purchased with a six-month forward contract at US$1.35 per €, and the value of the € increases from US$1.47 to US$1.60, the firm would be bound by the terms of the forward contract, and would not benefit from a dramatic rise in the euro *vis-à-vis* the dollar.

Assume that a six-month call option to buy US$1 billion at the forward price of €0.6803 per US$ costs €10,000 (or equivalently $14,700 at $1.47 per €). Such a call option insures against a drop in the euro below the forward rate of $1.35 per €. The option costs €10,000, which contrasts with the forward contract, which costs nothing, because it enables a company like BMW to earn additional dollar profits if the euro appreciates against the US dollar. This €10,000 cost must be weighed against the benefit of being able to partake in an increase in the value of the euro (versus the dollar).

It is interesting to note that the reference to calls or puts with currency options is discretionary: the right to *buy* British pounds in exchange for a pre-specified number of euros (a call) can also be viewed as the right to *sell* euros in exchange for a pre-specified number of British pounds (a put). While both views of the option are correct, this dual view raises the question of which risk-free interest rate to use for valuation: the domestic interest rate or the foreign rate? With foreign exchange options, the *interest rate differential* between the two countries ultimately determines option values. In addition, it is this differential that determines whether American-style currency options should be exercised prior to their maturity date.[12]

[12] The interested reader is referred to Margrabe (1978), who values exchange options. Subsequent researchers have pointed out that European-style options to buy currency can be viewed as a special case of exchange options.

Delta Hedging with Options

The caps and floors created above leave risk on one side – upside or downside risk. However, as Chapter 8 indicated, options are tracked by a dynamic portfolio of the underlying security and riskless bonds. The tracking portfolio's investment in the underlying security, the option's delta, referred to here as the **spot delta,** can be used in a dynamic trading strategy to eliminate all risk exposure from the underlying asset or liability.

Spot Delta versus Forward Delta

In the context of hedging currency or commodity risk associated with some future obligation, it is sometimes useful to think of options as a dynamic portfolio of forward contracts in the underlying security and riskless bonds. The **forward delta** represents the number of forward contracts that track the option. In the case of a non-dividend-paying equity, the forward delta and the spot delta of the option are the same. This means that if the option's equity-bond tracking portfolio contains two-thirds of a share of equity, the option's forward contract-bond tracking portfolio contains a forward contract to acquire two-thirds of a share of equity. However, if the equity pays dividends, or if the underlying asset is a commodity with a convenience yield or a currency with an interest rate that exceeds the interest rate on the currency with which the strike price is paid, then the forward delta generally exceeds the spot delta.

Delta Hedging with the Forward Delta

We now illustrate how to apply forward deltas to perfectly hedge risk. The use of forward deltas allows us to skirt the issue of how convenience yields affect delta hedging. Consider once again a firm with a future value of $a + bS_T$, where S_T is the uncertain future spot price of a barrel of oil at date T. If Δ (delta) represents the number of *forward* barrels of oil that track one option, and β is the number of risk-free dollars implicit in the option's tracking portfolio, then shorting b/Δ options creates a firm with a riskless future value of:

$$\begin{aligned} V_T^* &= a + (1 + r_f)^T \times (\text{option cost}) + bS_T - \left(\frac{b}{\Delta}\right)\Delta S_T - (1 + r_f)^T \times \left(\frac{\beta b}{\Delta}\right) \\ &= a + (1 + r_f)^T \times (\text{option cost}) - (1 + r_f)^T \times \left(\frac{\beta b}{\Delta}\right) \end{aligned}$$

The firm also may use options to alter the risk exposure from a commodity such as oil without completely eliminating the exposure. For the case above, shorting fewer than b/Δ options reduces but does not eliminate risk.

Example 22.13 assumes that GEA Group's b is 1.25 million, which is the number of barrels of oil generated by GEA Group's delivery agreement. It enters into option agreements to eliminate its exposure to oil price risk completely.

Example 22.13

Using an Option's Delta to Perfectly Hedge Oil Price Risk

Assume that GEA Group has an obligation to deliver 1.25 million barrels of oil one year from now at a fixed price of $90 per barrel. European options to buy oil in one year at a price of $95 per barrel have a forward delta (according to the Black–Scholes formula of Chapter 8) of 0.25. How many of these options should GEA Group buy to eliminate oil price risk generated by the delivery agreement?

Answer: Acquiring call options to buy 5 million barrels of oil one year from now at $95 a barrel eliminates oil price risk. Each option has the same sensitivity to oil price changes as one-fourth of a forward contract to deliver a barrel of oil. Thus the firm needs four times the number of options relative to forward contracts to perfectly hedge this risk.

Delta Hedges are Self-Financing

The option-hedging strategy in Example 22.13 is a dynamic strategy that hedges only instantaneous changes in oil prices. As oil prices change, the forward delta changes, implying that the number of options required for the hedge needs to change. While an increase in the delta implies that cash is needed to acquire additional options as the delta rises, the additional cash is balanced by the profit on the present value of the promise to deliver 1.25 million barrels of oil at \$90 a barrel. The reverse is true as well.

We summarize the results of this subsection as follows.

Results

Result 22.6

If a firm's exposure to a risk factor is eliminated by acquiring b forward contracts, then the firm also can eliminate that risk exposure by acquiring b/Δ options, where Δ represents the option's forward delta.

22.8 Factor-Based Hedging

This section discusses how the factor betas of commitments and financial instruments can be used for risk management.

Computing Factor Betas for Cash Flow Combinations

One of the most useful things about factor models is the additivity property of factor betas. To compute the aggregated factor sensitivities of combinations of cash flows, add their respective factor betas. Example 22.14 illustrates the computation.

Example 22.14

Computing Factor Loadings for Combinations of Cash Flows

Consider the following two-factor models for the cash flows of projects a, b and c, which are part of ABC plc. (Intercepts and coefficients are in millions of pounds.)

$$\tilde{C}_a = 3 + \tilde{F}_{curr} - 4\tilde{F}_{int} + \tilde{\varepsilon}_a$$
$$\tilde{C}_b = 5 - 3\tilde{F}_{curr} + 2\tilde{F}_{int} + \tilde{\varepsilon}_b$$
$$\tilde{C}_c = 10 - 1.5\tilde{F}_{cur} + 0\tilde{F}_{int} + \tilde{\varepsilon}_c$$

Write out the factor equations for (1) the combination of all three projects and (2) a super-project that involves doubling the size of project a and combining it with project b alone.

Answers:

$$(1)\ \alpha_p = 3 + 5 + 10 = 18$$
$$\beta_{p,\,curr} = 1 + 3 + 1.5 = 5.5$$
$$\beta_{p,\,int} = -4 + 2 = -2$$

So $\tilde{C}_p$ the cash flow of the collection of projects, satisfies the factor equation

$$\tilde{C}_p = 18 + 5.5\tilde{F}_{curr} + 2\tilde{F}_{int} + \tilde{\varepsilon}_p$$

where $\tilde{\varepsilon}_p$ is the sum of the three εs.

Thus:

$$(1)\ \alpha_p = 2(3) + 5 = 11$$
$$\beta_{p,\,curr} = 2(1) + 3 = 5.5$$
$$\beta_{p,\,int} = 2(-4) + 2 = -6$$
$$\tilde{C}_p = 11 + 5\tilde{F}_{curr} - 6\tilde{F}_{int} + \tilde{\varepsilon}_p$$

where

$$\tilde{\varepsilon}_p = 2\tilde{\varepsilon}_a + \tilde{\varepsilon}_b$$

The additivity property of factor models makes it easy to compute the risk impact of adding any financial instrument to a firm's cash flow. When combining the cash flow from a real asset with the cash flow from a financial instrument, add their respective betas together to obtain the impact on the risk of the firm.

Computing Hedge Ratios

The last subsection noted that the sum of the cash flow factor betas, factor by factor, yields the cash flow betas of the aggregated cash flows. This means that the quantities of various financial instruments that perfectly hedge the factor risk exposures have exactly the opposite sensitivity to the factors that the firm has. Therefore the computation of such quantities is generally a straightforward mathematical calculation, as Example 22.15 illustrates.

Example 22.15

Eliminating Factor Loadings with Portfolios of Factor Portfolios

Consider the following two-factor model, which describes, per euro of investment, how the cash flows of the projects of Dexys plc relate to the currency and interest rate factors:

$$\tilde{C}_s = 0.3 + \tilde{F}_{\text{curr}} - 4\tilde{F}_{\text{int}} + \tilde{\varepsilon}_s$$

Assume that pure factor portfolios can be constructed (see Chapter 6) that perfectly track the factors. How many euros need to be invested in the pure factor portfolio for currency (curr) and the pure factor portfolio for interest rates (int) to perfectly hedge the factor risk of Dexys?

Answer: Per euro of real investment, if Dexys sells short €1 of the pure factor portfolio for currency risk and buys €4 of the pure factor portfolio for interest rates, it will eliminate all factor sensitivity.

Results

Result 22.7

The factor risk of a cash flow is eliminated by acquiring a portfolio of financial instruments with factor betas exactly the opposite of the cash flow factor betas.

Direct Hedge Ratio Computations: Solving Systems of Equations

As Chapter 6 noted, pure factor portfolios must often be constructed from portfolios of more basic financial instruments. In this case, factor hedging can be implemented using the more basic financial instruments, as Example 22.16 illustrates.

Example 22.16

Eliminating Factor Loadings with Portfolios of Financial Instruments

Consider a two-factor model, where the two factors are interest rate movements and changes in inflation. Assume that Samara plc has a future cash flow with factor betas of 2.5 on the interest rate factor and 4.5 on the inflation factor. Samara would like to eliminate its sensitivity to both factors by acquiring financial securities, yet it does not wish to use its own cash to do this.

Samara contacts its bank and learns that it can (1) enter into a five-year interest rate swap contract, (2) purchase 30-year government bonds, and (3) acquire a sizeable chunk of shares in Desperate plc. Investment 1, the swap contract, has no upfront cost and, per contract, has a factor equation for its future value described by

$$\tilde{C}_1 = 5 - 5\tilde{F}_{\text{inflation}} - 3\tilde{F}_{\text{inflation}}$$

Investment 2, the 30-year government bond, per million pounds invested, has a factor equation for its future cash flow of

$$\tilde{C}_1 = 5 - 5\tilde{F}_{\text{inflation}} - 3\tilde{F}_{\text{inflation}}$$

Investment 3 is the equity of Desperate plc, which, per million pounds invested, has a factor equation for its end-of-period value of

$$\tilde{C}_3 = 0 + 1\tilde{F}_{\text{inflation}} + 1\tilde{F}_{\text{inflation}}$$

Design a proper hedge against inflation and interest rate movements in this environment.

Answer: To design a future cash flow that is insensitive to inflation or interest rate movements, we need to find a costless portfolio of financial investments with an interest rate sensitivity of –2.5 and an inflation sensitivity of –4.5. The three investments are denoted by

x_1 = the number of contracts in the costless swap investment
x_2 = millions of pounds in the 30-year government bonds
x_3 = millions of pounds in Desperate plc.

The portfolio of these three investments has a cost of $0x_1 + 1{,}000{,}000x_2 + 1{,}000{,}000x_3$. Its sensitivity to the interest rate factor is

$$-5x_1 - 5x_2 + 1x_3$$

Its sensitivity to the inflation factor is

$$-3x_1 - 1x_2 + 1x_3$$

Therefore the hedge portfolio is found by simultaneously solving

$$0x_1 + 1{,}000{,}000x_2 + 1{,}000{,}000x_3 = 0$$
$$-5x_1 - 5x_2 + 1x_3 = -2.5$$
$$-3x_1 - 1x_2 + 1x_3 = -4.5$$

Since the first equation says $x3 = -x2$, one can substitute for $x3$ in the other two equations, implying

$$-5x_1 - 6x_2 = -2.5$$

and

$$-3x_1 - 2x_2 = -4.5$$

Multiplying the first equation (of the two immediately above) by –0.6 and adding it to the second equation yields

$$1.6x_2 = -3$$

or

$$x_2 = -1.875$$

Plugging this back into either of the above equations yields $x_1 = 2.75$. Thus the solution is

1 Buy 2.75 swap contracts, representing £2.75 million in notional amount.
2 Short £1.875 million in 30-year government bonds.
3 Buy £1.875 million of Desperate plc.

22.9 Hedging with Regression

Regression provides a shortcut method for estimating a hedge ratio that minimizes risk exposure. By regressing the cash flow that one is trying to hedge against the value of the financial instrument used in the hedge, one derives a beta coefficient that determines the quantity of the hedging instrument that minimizes variance.[13]

Hedging a Cash Flow with a Single Financial Instrument

Consider a future cash flow $\tilde{C}$, which is random, and a financial instrument with a future value of $\tilde{P}$, also random, per unit bought. The variance of the combination of the cash flow and the short position in the financial instrument is

$$\text{var}(\tilde{C}) + \beta^2 \text{var}(\tilde{P}) - 2\beta \text{ cov}(\tilde{C}, \tilde{P}) \tag{22.4}$$

Hedge Ratios from Covariance Properties

Because covariance can be interpreted as the marginal variance, the combination of the cash flow and the hedge instrument that minimizes variance cannot have either a positive marginal variance or a negative marginal variance with the financial instrument. If it has a positive marginal variance, then a small reduction in the holdings of the financial instrument in the combination reduces variance. If it has a negative marginal variance, then a small increase in the holdings of the financial instrument reduces the variance of the combination. Only when the financial instrument has zero covariance with the combination of the financial instrument and the cash flow will the variance be minimized.

The covariance of the combination with the financial instrument's pay-off is:

$$\text{cov}(\tilde{C} - \beta\tilde{P}, \tilde{P}) = \text{cov}(\tilde{C}, \tilde{P}) - \beta \text{ cov}(\tilde{P}, \tilde{P}) = \beta \text{ cov}(\tilde{C}, \tilde{P}) - \beta \text{var}(\tilde{P})$$

This covariance is zero when:

$$\text{cov}(\tilde{C}, \tilde{P}) = \beta \text{var}(\tilde{P})$$

or when the number of units of the financial instrument that are sold satisfies:

$$\beta = \frac{\text{cov}(\tilde{C}, \tilde{P})}{\text{var}(\tilde{P})}$$

To show the same result with calculus, set the derivative with respect to *b* of the variance expression (equation (22.4)) to zero and solve for *b*. The resulting derivative,

$$2\beta \text{var}(\tilde{P}) 0 = 2 \text{ cov}(\tilde{C}, \tilde{P})$$

is zero when

$$\beta = \frac{\text{cov}(\tilde{C}, \tilde{P})}{\text{var}(\tilde{P})}$$

This is the same result that we achieved more intuitively above.

Note that the β that gives the minimum variance hedge is the regression coefficient (see Chapter 5). This suggests that the minimum variance hedge ratio can be found by using historical data to estimate regression coefficients. Example 22.17 illustrates how to use regression to determine hedge ratios after estimating slope coefficients from historical data.[14]

There are many things that can be learned from regression estimates. For example, commodities tend to have a term structure of volatilities much like the term structure of interest rates in Chapter 10. There are often regular patterns to these volatilities. The 10-year maturity oil forward price, for instance, when regressed against the one-year maturity oil forward price, has a regression coefficient of about 0.5, indicating that long-maturing oil forward prices are less volatile than short-maturing forwards. This reflects the fact that when oil prices have historically been high, they tend to decline and, when low, they tend to rise.

---

[13] The risk-free bond position in the two tracking portfolios always differs.

[14] Chapter 4 notes the conditions required for variance minimization and for the portfolio variance formulae used here.

Example 22.17

Using Regression to Determine the Hedge Ratio

Consider the problem of using one-month crude oil futures to hedge a heating oil contract to deliver 2.5 million barrels of heating oil one year from now at a pre-specified price. Historical data suggest that, for every $1.00 change in the one-month futures price of crude oil, the 'year ahead' heating oil prices change by $0.75. How many futures contracts should the heating oil company use to hedge the 2.5 million barrel heating oil obligation?

Answer: Since the regression coefficient is 0.75, and there are 2.5 million barrels for delivery, one should buy contracts to receive 1.875 million barrels (= 2.5 million × 75 barrels) of crude oil.

Cross-Hedging

Regression techniques also apply to **cross-hedging,** which is hedging across different commodities. Crude oil and heating oil are similar but not identical. Hence it is possible to find the best hedge of heating oil using crude oil futures, or to hedge the value of a lemon crop with orange juice futures, or whatever commodity one selects as the financial instrument for hedging.

Basis Risk

In addition, the regression method automatically takes account of basis risk in coming up with the variance-minimizing hedge. Generally, the more basis risk there is in the financial instrument, the smaller the hedge ratio.

Hedging with Multiple Regression

It is also possible to use two or more financial instruments to hedge a risk. For example, Neuberger (1999), studying long-dated oil price obligations from 1986 to 1994, used an elaboration of the regression technique to suggest that such obligations are best hedged, per barrel, by selling futures contracts to deliver 1.839 barrels of oil seven months ahead and buying contracts to deliver 0.84 barrels of oil six months ahead. He found that using futures contracts of multiple maturities in this way improves the variance reduction of the hedge dramatically.

Example 22.18 illustrates how to use multiple regression to determine hedge ratios for multiple hedging instruments.

Example 22.18

Using Multiple Regression to Determine the Hedge Ratios

Suppose we have estimated a regression equation for Vodafone in which the left-hand variable is the quarterly change in Vodafone's profits in millions of pounds and the right-hand variables are the quarterly change in the three-month €/£ exchange rate futures price (currently 1.14) and the quarterly change in the three-month FTSE All Share Index futures price (currently 4,000). The coefficient on the first right-hand variable is 7,000, and the coefficient on the second variable is 2. Interpret these coefficients in terms of risk exposures, and discuss their implications for the minimum variance hedge ratio.

Answer: The coefficient of 7,000 on the exchange rate implies that (holding the FTSE fixed) for each euro increase in the euro/sterling exchange rate (for example, the euro increases in value from 1.14 to 1.15 euro per £), Vodafone's quarterly profits increase by £70 million, on average. The coefficient of 2 on the FTSE All Share Index implies that (holding the €/£ exchange rate fixed) for each one-unit increase in the FTSE futures (for example, the three-month FTSE futures moves from 4,000 to 4,001), Vodafone's quarterly profits are expected to increase by £2 million. To hedge this risk with the two futures instruments, Vodafone should enter into futures contracts to sell €7 billion, as well as sell futures contracts on 2 million units of the FTSE All Share Index.

22.10 Minimum Variance Portfolios and Mean-Variance Analysis

So far, we have assumed that the real investments of the corporation are fixed, and have examined positions in derivative securities that minimize the corporation's risk. There are cases, however, where the corporation can alter the scale of its real investments as well as its derivatives position. In these cases, the variance-minimizing hedge ratio can differ from the hedge ratio identified with regression analysis. As we discuss below, the regression approach provides the variance-minimizing hedge ratio in instances where the hedging instrument is a contract, like a forward or a futures contract, which has zero value. However, when the hedging instrument is costly and the real investment can be scaled up or down in size, the relative weights in the *minimum variance* portfolio differ from the hedge ratio identified with regression analysis.

Hedging to Arrive at the Minimum Variance Portfolio

As Chapter 4 shows, the minimum variance portfolio of a set of equities is the portfolio with a return that has the same covariance with the returns of each of its component equities. This idea is easily extended to hedging a real asset with either a costly or a costless financial instrument that is used for hedging. In the case of a costless financial instrument, such as a swap or a forward contract, the hedge ratio provided by the minimum variance portfolio from mean-variance analysis is identical to the hedge ratio from regression. That is, *hedging with regression can be viewed as a special case of minimizing variance hedging when the hedging instrument is costless.*

There are situations, however, where the financial instrument is costly, and the corporation has flexibility in the size of its real asset. For example, a corporation that wishes to combine the purchase of oil refineries with oil-linked bonds would minimize the variance of that combination by forming a portfolio that has the same covariance with the return of oil refineries and the return of oil-linked bonds. The associated hedge ratio would be appropriate in cases where the size of the oil refinery position in the portfolio is variable. Similarly, a manufacturer of jet aeroplanes who wishes to hedge the sales price of these aeroplanes by acquiring equity in an airline company would use the same approach. As we show in Example 22.19, these minimum variance combinations will not generally be the same as the hedge positions obtained with regression analysis.

Example 22.19

Minimum Variance Hedge Ratios from Mean-Variance Analysis

Assume that Airbus is thinking about building a factory to manufacture its A350 line. The company has €1 billion to spend on the factory or on financial investments. The margin per A350 plane – that is, the selling price less variable costs – is an uncertain cash flow that will be captured five years from now. The fixed costs of building the factory, a cash outflow that occurs today, are proportionate to the output of the factory. With such a scalable production technology, the factory size required to produce 100Q planes costs €Q billion. This means that Airbus can purchase a factory for €1 billion that will produce 100 planes five years from now.

Alternatively, it can build a factory that will produce twice as many planes (200) at twice the fixed costs (€2 billion), half as many planes (50) at half the fixed costs (€500 million), 1 plane for €10 million in fixed costs, etc. After analysing the historical sales margin of an Airbus A350 plane against the return of Air France-KLM, Airbus's analysts find that the regression coefficient is – €20 million. This means that when Air France-KLM's share price increases by 1 per cent, the sales margin of each Airbus A350 declines by €200,000 on average. Assuming that each plane's sales margin five years from now has a standard deviation of €200,000 and the five-year variance of Air France-KLM's equity return is 0.75, identify the minimum variance portfolio combination of Air France-KLM equity and the factory, and interpret the result.

Answer: The covariance between Air France-KLM's (decimal) equity return and the Airbus A350 plane sales margin per euro invested is

$$-1.5 = \frac{-€20\text{ million}}{€10\text{ billion}} \times \text{var(Air France-KLM return)} = (-2)(0.75)$$

The variance of the sales price per €1 invested in the factory is

$$4 = \left(\frac{€20\text{ million} \times 100Q}{€Q\text{ billion}}\right)^2$$

The covariance of a minimum variance portfolio with the fraction x invested in the factory and the fraction $1 - x$ in Air France-KLM equity has x satisfying the equation that the covariance of the portfolio with the factory return and the Air France-KLM return is the same: that is,

$$4x - 1.5(1 - x) = 1.5x + 0.75(1 - x)$$

This is solved by $x = 0.29$, and it implies that if Airbus has €1 billion to spend and the factory is scalable, the minimum variance portfolio combination is achieved by making a factory that produces 29 planes at a cost of €290 million and buying €710 million of Air France-KLM equity.

The hedging solution in Example 22.19 differs from the regression solution. The regression solution has Airbus buy €2Q billion of Air France-KLM equity for each €Q billion spent on the factory (as a fixed cost) and results in a 2-to-1 hedge ratio instead of the 2.45-to-1 hedge ratio (710/290) of Example 22.19. The former ratio produces a cash flow that has no correlation with Air France-KLM's equity return, and makes any further reduction in variance impossible. This would be an appropriate hedge ratio if capital expenditures were not constrained by the investment in the hedging instrument. When costless financial instruments for hedging are not available, as in the case of Airbus's factory, managers need to think about downsizing the project as a hedging vehicle rather than using regression blindly. However, if the size of the position in the real asset is not alterable, then the hedge ratio provided by the mean-variance method is inappropriate.

Hedging to Arrive at the Tangency Portfolio

Managers implement real investments whenever they have higher mean returns than the financial instruments that track them. In the case of Airbus, €10 million in production costs per plane seems inexpensive compared with the cost of the Air France-KLM equity that tracks the future of an A350 series aircraft, which is usually obtained by analysing a regression coefficient such as the −2 that would be computed in Example 22.19. This is not an argument for regression-based hedge ratios as much as it is an argument for bringing mean returns into the picture. As in investment theory (see Chapter 5), managers trade off mean and variance in their project and hedging decisions. In many instances, the proper hedging goal should be the capital market line on the mean-standard deviation diagram instead of some minimum variance criterion.

Example 22.20 illustrates how to achieve a hedged position on the capital market line.

Example 22.20

Tangency Portfolios from Mean-Variance Analysis

Given the data in Example 22.19, $\sigma_{CC} = 4$, $\sigma_{CP} = -1.5$, and $\sigma_{PP} = 0.75$, where P represents the Air France-KLM investment and C represents an Airbus A350 factory, identify the tangency portfolio mix of factory and Air France-KLM equity if the expected sales margin of the 100 planes is €5.25 billion, the expected return of Air France-KLM equity over five years is 75 per cent, and the risk-free rate over five years is 25 per cent (or about 5 per cent per year).

Answer: Following the analysis in Chapter 5, the equations that solve for the tangency portfolio satisfy the property that the ratio of the covariances of the investment pair is equal to the ratio of the expected excess returns:

$$\frac{4x - 1.5(1 - x)}{-1.5x + 0.75(1 - x)} = \frac{5.25 - 1 - 0.25}{0.75 - 0.25}$$

This is solved by $x = 0.32$. Thus if Airbus has €1 billion to spend, and the factory is scalable, the mean-variance efficient combination of factory and Air France-KLM equity is a €320 million factory that produces 32 planes and a purchase of €680 million of Air France-KLM equity.

The *tangency portfolio hedge ratio* is based on the idea that capital is fixed, the financial instruments for hedging are given (for example, Air France-KLM equity), and the firm has a trade-off between mean and variance where it wishes to mix the financial instrument and the real investment in proportions that maximize the ratio of the expected excess return of the portfolio to its standard deviation.

The discussion in this section is summarized as follows.

Results

Result 22.8

Regression coefficients represent the hedge ratios that minimize variance given no capital expenditure constraints and no constraints on the use of costless financial instruments for hedging. Given flexibility in the scale of a real investment project, a cost to the hedging financial instrument and a capital expenditure constraint, the techniques of mean-variance analysis for finding the efficient portfolio or the global minimum variance portfolio may be more appropriate for finding a hedge ratio.

22.11 Summary and Conclusions

This chapter addressed the practice of hedging, examining how to use popular financial instruments such as forwards, futures, swaps and options for hedging. In addition, the discussion analysed a variety of tools to estimate risk exposure and hedge ratios, including factor models, regression, and mean-variance mathematics.

Although the analysis focused on the elimination of risk, risk elimination is not necessarily a desirable goal, because it often comes at a very high price. Rather, the focus of the manager should be on the management of risk. Once a target risk level for a risk exposure is identified, the manager can put the tools developed in this chapter to use. For example, a manager who estimates the firm's exchange rate exposure to be a £12 million decrease in profits for every 1 per cent increase in the £/€ exchange rate may target the optimal exchange rate risk exposure at '£7 million'. In this case, the manager's hedge is targeted to reduce the firm's exchange rate exposure from £12 million (per 1 per cent increase in the £/€ rate) to £7 million (per 1 per cent increase in the £/€ rate). This hedging would not be different from that of a manager who found himself with £5 million (= £12 million − £7 million) of exchange rate risk exposure and wanted to eliminate all of this exposure.

Before applying the tools of this chapter, managers need to analyse the firm's asset and liability picture from the broadest perspective possible. Even if they understand how to hedge, many managers may overhedge by failing to recognize the important message of Chapter 12; namely, that options are the key aspects to most projects and most firms. Many firms implement a hedge of their estimated cash flows without recognizing that the option to cancel, expand, downsize or fundamentally alter their projects may have important implications for hedge ratios. Indeed, these options in the projects often imply that options should be used in the hedging vehicles as well.

In short, straightforward answers and cookbook, albeit complex, formulae for almost any hedging problem can be found in the abundant literature on hedging. They are found in this chapter, too. However, the natural inclination to leave hedging to technicians is a foolish decision, no matter how mathematically skilled or competent such technicians are. Like the running of any major aspect of a business, hedging needs to be guided by artful, creative managers who are fairly skilled in the technical aspects of hedging so as not to be overly impressed by the recommendations of the technicians. Management needs to fully understand not only the motivations for hedging, but also the broader picture of what strategic considerations drive the firm's value and its risk.

Key Concepts

Result 22.1: Futures hedges must be tailed to account for the interest earned on the amount of cash that is exchanged as a consequence of the futures mark-to-market feature. Such tailed hedges require holding less of the futures contract the further one is from the maturity date of the contract. The magnitude of the tail relative to an otherwise identical forward contract hedge depends on the amount of interest earned (on a dollar paid at the date of the hedge) to the maturity date of the futures contract.

Result 22.2: Long-dated obligations hedged with short-term forward agreements need to be tailed if the underlying commodity has a convenience yield. The degree of the tail depends on the convenience yield earned between the maturity date of the forward instrument used to hedge, and the date of the long-term obligation. When hedging with futures, a greater degree of tailing is needed (see Result 22.1).

Result 22.3: The greater the sensitivity of the convenience yield to the commodity's spot price, the less risky is the long-dated obligation to buy or sell a commodity.

Result 22.4: The greater the sensitivity of the convenience yield to the price of the underlying commodity, the lower is the hedge ratio when hedging long-dated obligations with short-term forward agreements. When hedging with futures, a further tail is needed (see Result 22.1).

Result 22.5: The greater the unhedgeable convenience yield risk, the lower is the hedge ratio for hedging a long-term obligation with a short-term forward or futures contract.

Result 22.6: If a firm's exposure to a risk factor is eliminated by acquiring b forward contracts, then the firm can also eliminate that risk exposure by acquiring b/Δ options, where Δ represents the option's forward delta.

Result 22.7: The factor risk of a cash flow is eliminated by acquiring a portfolio of financial instruments with factor betas exactly the opposite of the cash flow factor betas.

Result 22.8: Regression coefficients represent the hedge ratios that minimize variance, given no capital expenditure constraints and no constraints on the use of costless financial instruments for hedging. Given flexibility in the scale of a real investment project, a cost to the hedging financial instrument and a capital expenditure constraint, the techniques of mean-variance analysis for finding the efficient portfolio or the global minimum variance portfolio may be more appropriate for finding a hedge ratio.

Key Terms

Basis 719
basis risk 719
basket option 726
basket swap 720
cash flow at risk (CAR) 705
cash flow hedging 702
convenience yield 712
covered option strategy 723
cross-hedging 732
delta hedging 723
exposures 702
forward delta 727
hedge ratio 702
money market hedge 708
regression method 703
rolling stack 717
simulation method 703
spot delta 727
spot market 706
swap spread 721
tailing the hedge 710
target beta 702
value at risk (VAR) 704
value hedging 702

Exercises

22.1 Consider, again, National Nickel from Example 21.3 in Chapter 21. In addition to the forward contracts described in Example 21.3, National Nickel can also buy (put) options that give it the right to sell nickel in one, two or three years at an exercise price of £20 per pound of nickel. The one-year option costs £2.00, the two-year option £3.00, and the three-year option £3.50 per pound of nickel. What should National Nickel do to eliminate the possibility of financial distress and still have money to fund new exploration in the event that nickel prices increase?

22.2 AB Cable, Wire & Fibre plans to open up a new factory three years from now, at which point it plans to purchase 1 million pounds of copper. Assume zero-coupon risk-free yields are going to remain at a constant 5 per cent (annually compounded rate) for all investment horizons, there is no basis risk in forwards or futures, storage of copper is costless, markets are frictionless, and forward spot parity holds. Copper has a 3 per cent per year (annual compounded rate) convenience yield.

a What should the relative magnitude of the futures and forward prices for copper be, assuming the contracts are of the same maturity? How should futures and forward prices change with contract maturity?

b Assume that one-year forwards are the only hedging instruments available. How many pounds of copper in forwards should be acquired today to maximally hedge the risk of the copper purchase three years from now? How does the hedge ratio change over time? Provide intuition and describe the rollover strategy at the forward maturity date.

c Assume that three-month futures are the only hedging instruments available. How many pounds of copper in futures can be acquired today to maximally hedge the risk of the copper purchase three years from now? How does the hedge ratio change over time? Provide intuition and describe the rollover strategy at the futures maturity date.

22.3 Assume a two-factor model for next year's profits of BP. The factors are one-year futures prices for oil and one-year futures prices for the £/US$ exchange rate. The relevant factor equation is

$$\text{Profit}_{BP} = \text{£}1 \text{ billion} + \text{£}10 \text{ million} \times \tilde{F}_{OIL} + \text{£}20 \text{ million } \tilde{F}_{\text{£}/\$} + \tilde{\varepsilon}_{BP}$$

Assume that each one-year oil futures contract purchased has the factor equation

$$\tilde{C}^1 = \text{£}10 \text{ million } \tilde{F}_{OIL}$$

Each one-year futures contract on the £/US$ exchange rate has the factor equation

$$\tilde{C}^1_{\text{£}/\$} = \text{£}100{,}000 \, \tilde{F}_{\text{£}/\$}$$

If BP wants to reduce its exposure to the two risk factors by half, how can it accomplish this by buying or selling futures contracts?

22.4 Assume that Fiat Chrysler is planning to acquire an automobile company in Sweden. The deal will probably be consummated within a year, provided that approval is granted by the proper regulatory authorities in Italy and Sweden. The two automakers have agreed upon the terms of the deal. Fiat Chrysler will pay SKr100 billion once the deal is consummated. Discuss the advantages and disadvantage of hedging the currency risk in this deal with forwards, options and swaps.

22.5 Assume that Natabrine, a drug manufacturer, has discovered that it is cheaper to manufacture one of its drugs in France than anywhere else. All revenues from the drug will be in the United Kingdom. The company estimates that the costs of manufacturing the drug will be €100 million per year, and that the factory has a life of 10 years. At the end of the 10 years, a balloon payment on the mortgage from the factory is due. Net of proceeds from salvage value, the company will have to pay €1 billion at the end of 10 years. How can the currency risk of this deal be eliminated with a currency swap?

22.6 Assume that Dell Computer, a worldwide manufacturer and mail-order retailer of personal computers, has estimated the following regression associated with its operations in Europe:

$$\text{European profits}_t = \$10 \text{ million} + \$8 \text{ million} \times (\$/€1 - \text{year forward exchange rate})_t + \tilde{\varepsilon}_t$$

a How should Dell Computer minimize variance associated with these European operations, using only forward contracts on the $/€ exchange rate? Is your answer affected by whether the European operations are fixed or scalable in size?

b Assuming that European profits are normally distributed, what is Dell's profit at risk at the 5 per cent significance level, assuming that the percentage change in the $/€ exchange rate is normally distributed and has a volatility of 10 per cent? Ignore risk for this calculation.

22.7 Your UK-based company has an opportunity to break into the German market, but your CEO is concerned about the currency risk of such a venture. You estimate that sales in Germany will be €2 million (worst-case scenario) or €5 million (best-case scenario) over the next 10 months. The likelihood that each of these scenarios will occur is equal. Your CEO wishes to hedge the expected value of these sales, but is not sure which hedging vehicle to use.

a You are given the following information, and are assigned the task of recommending the best method of hedging (that is, what is the highest pound sterling amount you can lock in today?):
current €/£ spot rate = €1.47/£
current forward rate for currency exchanged
10 months from today = €1.50/£
10-month UK£ SONIA is 3.5 per cent per annum
10-month EURIBOR is 5.7 per cent per annum.

b Is there an arbitrage opportunity here? If so, how would you exploit it?

22.8 Suppose you wish to hedge your exposure to oil prices by means of forwards and futures over the next year. You have the following information: the current price of oil is $90 per barrel, and the risk-free rate of interest is 10 per cent per year compounded annually. Assume that the spot price of oil changes instantaneously from $90 to $91 per barrel.

a Describe the necessary number of one-year forwards you must hold in order to perfectly hedge a long position in one barrel of oil. Then describe any changes in the perfectly hedged position of spot oil and forwards, including any cash that changes hands, when the spot price of oil instantaneously increases by $1.00.

b Repeat part *a* for a perfectly hedged position using futures contracts.

c Repeat parts *a* and *b*, assuming that you now want to hedge a short position of 5,000 barrels of oil.

22.9 Assume that EXCO has an obligation to deliver 1.5 million barrels of oil in nine months at a fixed price of $94 per barrel. Assume a constant convenience yield of 2 per cent per year and a risk-free rate of 9 per cent per annum, compounded annually.

a How can EXCO hedge all the risk of this obligation in the forward market, using only forwards maturing three months from now and then rolling over new three-month forwards?

b How can EXCO hedge all the risk of this obligation, using only three-month futures?

c Repeat parts *a* and *b*, assuming EXCO owns 1.5 million barrels of oil.

22.10 General Motors has an obligation to deliver 2 million barrels of oil in six months at a fixed price of $95 per barrel. European options exist to buy oil in six months at $98 per barrel. Assume the six-month annualized (continuously compounded) riskless rate is 5 per cent. Because of recent unrest in the Middle East, however, the volatility (that is, standard deviation) of the annualized percentage change in the price of oil has soared to an incredible 59.44 per cent (annualized).

Can General Motors eliminate its exposure to oil price risk generated by the delivery agreement using options, and if so, how many options will it have to buy or sell in order to do this? (*Hint:* The Black–Scholes option pricing equation is valid here.)

22.11 Disney wants to borrow €24 million for three years, and GEA Group wants to borrow US$20 million for three years. The spot exchange rate is currently €0.675/$. Suppose Disney and GEA Group can borrow euros and dollars from their domestic banks at the following (annual) fixed interest rates:

	US$	€
Disney	6.0%	9.7%
GEA Group	8.4%	10.0%

Design a currency swap agreement that will benefit both firms and also yield a 0.4 per cent profit for the bank acting as an intermediary for the swap.

22.12 Consider a two-factor model, where the factors are interest rate movements and changes in the exchange rate. Your company has a future cash flow with factor betas of 2 on the interest rate factor and 5 on the exchange rate factor. You would like to eliminate your sensitivity to both factors by means of financial securities, but do not wish to use any of the company's cash to do this.

The following investment opportunities are available to you.

- You can purchase 30-year government bonds.
- You can enter into a two-year interest rate swap agreement.
- You can invest in a foreign index fund.

The following factor equations, with the two factors being changes in interest rates and changes in exchange rates, correspond to the future values of the three investment opportunities, respectively.

$$\tilde{C}_1 = 4 - 4\tilde{F}_{int} \text{ (per £1 million invested)}$$
$$C_2 = 6 - 2\tilde{F}_{int} + 6\tilde{F}_{ex} \text{ (per £1 million invested)}$$
$$\tilde{C}_3 = 3 - 3\tilde{F}_{int} + 2\tilde{F}_{ex} \text{ (per £1 million invested)}$$

Design a proper hedge against interest rate movements and exchange rates in this environment.

22.13 Volkswagen is considering building a factory to produce its new Calzino model. The factory will cost €100 million and will produce 10,000 automobiles one year from now, but its cost and production can be scaled up or down. As an analyst at Volkswagen, you run a regression of the historical sales margin of 10,000 cars against the return of Volkswagen's equity. You find that the regression coefficient is – €130 million, that the sales margin of a Calzino one year from now has a standard deviation of €1,000, and that the volatility of Volkswagen's equity is 0.5. The risk-free rate over the coming year will be 10 per cent. You can assume that the return on the factory is the total sales margin from all cars produced by the factory divided by the cost of the factory, less one.

Your task is:

a to identify the minimum variance portfolio combination of Volkswagen equity and the factory, and to interpret the results

b to identify the tangency portfolio mix of factory and equity if the expected selling margin of the Calzino is €22,000 and the expected return of Fiat equity is 30 per cent over the next year.

References and Additional Reading

Allen, W. (1987) *The Walt Disney Company's Yen Financing,* Harvard Case 9-287-058, Harvard Business School Publishing.

Backus, D., Klapper, L. and Telmer, C. (1995) *Derivatives at Banc One (1994),* Case study, New York University, New York.

Brennan, M. and Crew, N. (1996) Hedging long maturity commodity commitments with short-dated futures contracts, in *Mathematics of Derivative Securities,* Michael Dempster and Stanley Pliska (eds), Cambridge University Press, Cambridge.

Campello, M., Lin, C., Ma, Y. and Zou, H. (2011) The real and financial implications of corporate hedging, *The journal of finance*, 66(5): 1615–1647.

Chowdhry, B., Grinblatt, M. and Levine, D (2001) Information aggregation, security design, and currency swaps, Working paper, UCLA.

Culp, C.L. and Miller, M.H. (1995) Metallgesellschaft and the economics of synthetic storage, *Journal of Applied Corporate Finance*, 7(4): 62–76.

Fama, E. and French, K. (1987) Commodity futures prices: some evidence on forecast power, premiums, and the theory of storage, *Journal of Business*, 60(1): 55–74.

Gibson, R. and Schwartz, E. (1990) Stochastic convenience yield and the pricing of oil contingent claims, *Journal of Finance*, 45(3): 959–976.

Grinblatt, M. and Jegadeesh, N. (1996) The relative pricing of Eurodollar futures and forward contracts, *Journal of Finance*, 51(4): 1499–1522.

Hoberg, G. and Moon, S. K. (2017) Offshore activities and financial vs operational hedging, *Journal of Financial Economics*, 125(2): 217–244.

Jorion, P. (1997) *Value at Risk*, Richard D. Irwin, Burr Ridge, IL.

Lel, U. (2012) Currency hedging and corporate governance: a cross-country analysis, *Journal of corporate finance*, 18(2): 221–237.

Lievenbrück, M. and Schmid, T. (2014) Why do firms (not) hedge?—Novel evidence on cultural influence, *Journal of Corporate Finance*, 25, 92–106.

Linsmeier, T.J. and Pearson, N.D. (1996) Risk measurement: an introduction to value at risk, Working paper, University of Illinois, Urbana-Champaign.

Margrabe, W. (1978) The value of an option to exchange one asset for another, *Journal of Finance*, 33(1): 177–186.

Mello, A. and Parsons, J. (1995) Maturity structure of a hedge matters, *Journal of Applied Corporate Finance*, 8(1): 106–121.

Neuberger, A. (1999) How well can you hedge long-term exposures with multiple short-term futures contracts?, *Review of Financial Studies*, 12(3): 429–459.

Opie, W. and Riddiough, S.J. (2020). Global currency hedging with common risk factors, *Journal of financial economics*, 136(3): 780–805.

Ross, S. (1997) Hedging long-run commitments: exercises in incomplete market pricing, *Economic Notes*, 2, 385–420.

Smithson, C., Smith, C. and Sykes Wilford, D. (1995) *Managing Financial Risk*, Richard D. Irwin Burr Ridge, IL.

Chapter 23

Interest Rate Risk Management

Learning Objectives

After reading this chapter, you should be able to:

- Describe the concept of PV01, the price value of a one-basis-point decrease (in original and term structure variations), and the concept of duration (in MacAuley, modified and present value variations).
- Understand the relation between duration and PV01, and the formulae needed to use either concept for hedging.
- Implement immunization and contingent immunization strategies, using both duration and PV01 explain the link between immunization and hedging, and how to use this link to manage the asset base and capital structure of financial institutions.
- Understand and compute convexity and know how to use it properly.

In 1995, Orange County, California, declared bankruptcy. This bankruptcy can be attributed to the investments of the county treasurer, Robert Citron. In late 1994, between one-third and one-half of Citron's investments were in 'inverse floaters', floating rate bonds with cash flows that decline as interest rates increase, and vice versa. The inverse floaters paid 17 per cent less twice the short-term interest rate, as long as this number was positive. The value of these esoteric notes was about three times more sensitive to interest rate movements than fixed-rate debt of comparable maturity. Moreover, Orange County leveraged these positions through repurchase agreements, making the positions three times larger in size than the cash spent on them, and therefore about nine times more sensitive to interest rate movements than an unleveraged position in fixed-rate debt of comparable maturity. It did not take a very large increase in interest rates to wipe out Orange County's pool of investable funds.[1]

[1] We are grateful to Richard Roll for providing us with some of the details of this bankruptcy.

Chapter 22 described how to hedge many of the sources of risk that corporations face. Here we complete the work in that chapter by analysing how to change the firm's exposure to an interest rate risk factor. Interest rate risk deserves special treatment because interest rates, in addition to their possible effect on future cash flows, generally affect the present values of cash flows, owing to their role in discounting. It is this latter role that makes interest rate risk unique.

In this chapter you will learn how interest rate risk is managed. The chapter abstracts from the influence of interest rates on future cash flows by assuming that future cash flows are certain. Hence the risk analysis here focuses only on the role of interest rates in determining present values.

The key to this analysis is understanding the relationship between the price of a financial instrument with riskless future cash flows (that is, a default-free bond) and its yield to maturity.[2] We introduce two important concepts that describe this relationship, *PV01* and *duration*, compare them with one another, and describe several important applications of each.

In addition to studying the use of these tools for measuring interest rate risk and designing hedges, the chapter examines **immunization,** which is the management of a portfolio of fixed-income investments so that they will have a riskless value at some future date, and the concept of **convexity,** which is a measure of the curvature in the price–yield relationship. Convexity is frequently used and misused in bond portfolio analysis and management. We shall try to understand the proper use of convexity as well as the pitfalls that lead to its misuse.

Obviously, bond portfolio managers and high-level financial managers in banks and other financial institutions should be familiar with the tools introduced in this chapter. However, it is also important for other individuals, such as corporate treasurers, to acquaint themselves with these tools. For example, the debt issued by a corporation is priced by the bond market. To analyse the firm's debt financing costs properly, it is essential for corporate treasurers to understand how interest rates affect bond prices. In addition, corporate treasurers often have to fund, manage or supervise the management of a corporate pension fund. Frequently, the assets in such funds are debt instruments. It would be difficult to meet the obligations of these pension funds without knowledge of the interest rate risk of both the obligations and the debt instruments held by the fund, as well as how to manage this risk. More generally, corporations typically target a maturity structure of their debt, measured as the debt's duration, which is tied to the interest rate sensitivity of the debt.[3] How to achieve that target is one subject of this chapter.

In much of this chapter we assume that there is a flat term structure of interest rates. Hence there is only one discount rate for risk-free cash flows of any maturity. Later in the chapter we relax this simplifying assumption, and discuss how to extend the analysis to deal with discount rates that vary with the maturity of the cash flow. The results obtained for hedge ratios and immunization strategies in this chapter work well in most realistic settings, despite being based on assumptions that, although virtuous for the simplicity they add, are not entirely realistic and may even be logically inconsistent.

23.1 The Value of a One-Basis-Point Decrease (PV01)

Once corporate managers have measured the interest rate risk exposure of a corporation or project, they can reduce the risk exposure of equity holders by acquiring or issuing bonds, the values of which move in an opposite direction to the value of the corporation or project as interest rates change. To implement a strategy like this, the financial manager needs to acquire familiarity with the tools of interest rate risk management.

One of the most important tools for understanding the relation between interest rates, as measured by a bond's yield to maturity, and bond prices is the *value of a one-basis-point (bp) decrease*, or **PV01,**[4] which is a measure of how much a bond's price will increase in response to a one-basis-point decline in a bond's yield to maturity. If the yield and interest rates are the same – as they would be if there was a flat term structure of interest rates – then PV01s will be useful for estimating interest rate risk. In this case, because high-PV01 bonds are more sensitive to interest rate movements than low-PV01 bonds, they also are more volatile than low-PV01 bonds. In a corporate setting, firms with values that have high PV01s are more exposed to interest rate risk.

[2] For expositional clarity, we shall often use the generic term *bond* to refer to all debt instruments. We recognize that there are important legal and economic distinctions between bonds, notes, bills and bank debt, but such distinctions are not critical for the analysis in this chapter.

[3] Chapters 16 and 21 broadly touched on the reasons why corporations might want short-term instead of long-term debt.

[4] PV01 is often referred to as the price value of a basis point (PVBP) or the dollar value of a basis point (DV01).

Hence, if a corporation measures the risk exposure of its stock as having a negative PV01 (for example, share prices go up when interest rates rise), then acquiring a bond position with a positive PV01 will reduce the interest rate exposure of the corporation's equity.

In reality, yields and interest rates differ because the term structure is not flat, making PV01 an inexact hedging tool. PV01, however, works remarkably well as a hedging tool despite this potential problem, as the introduction to this chapter noted.

Methods Used to Compute PV01 for Traded Bonds

The various ways to compute the PV01 of a bond are outlined below.

Method 1: Price at a Yield One Basis Point Below Existing Yield Less Price at Existing Yield

The method we shall generally use to compute a bond's PV01 is the negative of the change in its *full price*[5] for a one-basis-point *decrease* in its yield to maturity. One basis point is 1/100th of 1 per cent, implying, for example, that a one-basis-point decrease in a 10 per cent yield to maturity is a decrease from 10.00 per cent to 9.99 per cent. This is a very small decrease because PV01 is intended to approximate, in absolute magnitude, the derivative of the bond price movement with respect to the bond's *yield to maturity*. This derivative is the slope of the price–yield curve pictured in Exhibit 23.1.[6] PV01 is determined by a one-basis-point *decrease* in interest rates, so that the PV01 is positive for most bonds.[7]

Exhibit 23.1 Inverse Relation between Price and Yield

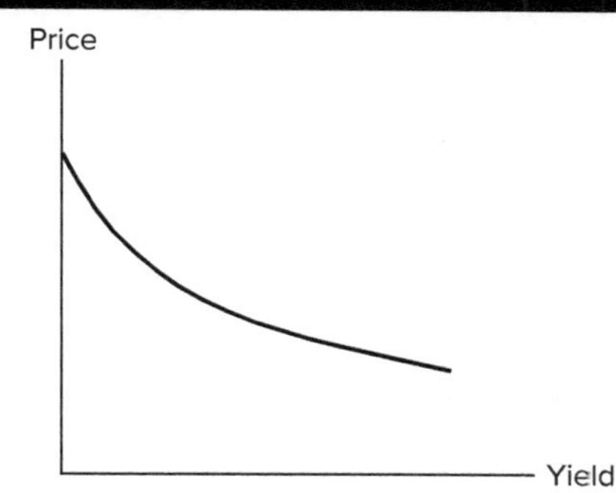

Method 2: Use Calculus to Compute the Derivative of the Price–Yield Relationship Directly

Some bond market participants use calculus to define the PV01 as the negative of the slope of the price– yield curve. In this case, the PV01 of a bond with a price of *P* is computed as:

$$\text{PV01} = -0.0001\frac{dP}{dr} \tag{23.1}$$

In equation (23.1), *r*, the bond yield, is given in decimal form. This gives a slightly different answer from method 1 because a one-basis-point decline, although small, is not infinitesimally small, as would be the case with the derivative calculation.

Method 3: Price at a Yield ½ Basis Point below Less Price at ½ Basis Point above Existing Yield

To approximate method 2's derivative calculation more accurately than method 1, some practitioners compute PV01 by subtracting the bond's present value at ½ basis point above the current yield to maturity from its

[5] See Chapter 2 for a description of full and flat bond prices.

[6] The derivative is negative because of the inverse relationship between price and yield.

[7] This avoids the awkwardness of always having to remember to place a minus sign in front.

present value at ½ basis point below the current yield. As with method 1, this definition of PV01 requires only a calculator for its computation, thus avoiding the use of calculus.

Using a Financial Calculator to Compute PV01 with Method 1

The differences between these versions of PV01 are negligible. We employ method 1 for most of the examples in this chapter, as in Example 23.1.

Example 23.1

Computing PV01

Compute the PV01 per £100 face value of a 20-year straight-coupon bond trading at par (see Chapter 2 for a definition) with a semi-annual coupon and an 8 per cent yield to maturity.

Answer: Using a financial calculator or computing the present value by hand, we find that at a discount rate of 7.99 per cent, the 8 per cent coupon bond should trade for approximately £100.10. At a discount rate of 8 per cent, it trades at £100. Thus the PV01 or difference is £0.10 per £100 of face value.

Using PV01 to Estimate Price Changes

One can use PV01 to estimate the price change of a bond or a bond portfolio for small changes in the level of interest rates, as measured by the bond's yield. To obtain the formula for this estimate, rearrange equation (23.1) as follows:

$$dP = -\text{PV01} \times 10{,}000 dr$$

Because $10{,}000\Delta r$ is the yield change in number of basis points, the non-calculus equivalent of this equation is

$$\Delta P = -\text{PV01} \times (\Delta \text{dp}) \tag{23.2}$$

where

ΔP = the change in the bond's price

Δbp = the interest rate change (in basis points).

Example 23.2 demonstrates how to use this formula to estimate bond price changes.

Example 23.2

Estimating Bond Price Changes with PV01

A bond position has a PV01 of €300. Its yield is currently 8.0 per cent. Estimate the change in the value of the bond position if the yield drops to 7.9 per cent.

Answer: Using equation (23.2), a drop of 10 basis points gives a price increase of

$$\Delta P = -€300 \times (-10) = €3{,}000$$

Note from equation (23.2) that if the PV01 is zero, the change in the price for a small change in yield is zero. We shall discuss how to use this insight for interest rate hedging shortly.

PV01s of Various Bond Types and Portfolios

Bonds with long maturities tend to have higher PV01s than short-maturity bonds with similar values. Zero-coupon bonds with long maturities tend to have low PV01s, because their prices are low. As a percentage of the price, however, the volatilities of these bonds tend to be high.

PV01s are proportional to the size of a bond position. The PV01 of a £1,000,000 position in a bond (face value or market value) is 10 times the PV01 of a £100,000 position in that same bond. To obtain the PV01 of a bond portfolio, add up the PV01s of all the components in that portfolio.

Practitioners often scale PV01 to be PV01 per £100 of face value or per £1 million of face value. This scaling makes it easy to compare individual bonds, but it is a minor inconvenience when determining the sensitivity of a bond portfolio's total value to yield changes. To overcome this inconvenience, first convert the PV01s per £100 or PV01s per £1 million into the PV01s of the total face values of each bond in the portfolio. Then add the PV01s of the components of the portfolio to obtain the PV01 of the portfolio itself. Keep in mind two helpful rules when computing the PV01 of a portfolio of bonds.

1 To convert a PV01 per £100 face value to a PV01 per actual face value, multiply the actual face value of the portfolio's position in the bond by the PV01 per £100 face value and then divide by £100.
2 To convert a PV01 per £1 million face value to a PV01 per actual face value, multiply the actual face value of the portfolio's position in the bond by the PV01 per £1 million face value and then divide by £1 million.

Example 23.3 uses the first of these two rules to compute the PV01 of a portfolio of bonds.

Example 23.3

The PV01 of a Portfolio of Bonds

Assume that the PV01 of a 30-year UK Treasury bond is £0.10 per £100 face amount, the PV01 of a 10-year UK Treasury note is £0.06 per £100 face amount, and the PV01 of a five-year UK Treasury note is £0.04 per £100 face amount. Compute the PV01 of a portfolio that has £5 million (face value) of 30-year bonds, £8 million (face value) of five-year notes, and (a short position) –£16 million (face value) of 10-year notes.

Answer: Sum the products of (a) the face amounts over £100 and (b) the corresponding PV01s per £100. The result is

$$\text{PV01} = \frac{\pounds 5 \text{ million}}{\pounds 100}(\pounds 0.10) + \frac{\pounds 8 \text{ million}}{\pounds 100}(\pounds 0.04) - \frac{\pounds 16 \text{ million}}{\pounds 100}(\pounds 0.06) = -\pounds 1.400$$

The negative PV01 means that the position's value increases when interest rates rise.

Using PV01s to Hedge Interest Rate Risk

PV01s are commonly used for interest rate hedging. This subsection discusses the hedging of interest rate risk in both investment management and corporate settings.

Hedging the Interest Rate Risk of a Bond Portfolio

A perfectly hedged bond portfolio is a portfolio with no sensitivity to interest rate movements. Result 23.1 characterizes such a portfolio in terms of PV01.

Results

Result 23.1

If the term structure of interest rates is flat, a bond portfolio with a PV01 of zero has no sensitivity to interest rate movements.

Example 23.4 illustrates how to construct a portfolio with a PV01 of zero.

Equation (23.2) suggests that, for the unhedged portfolio constructed in Example 23.3, a 10-basis-point decrease in interest rates (for example, rates decrease from 9.0 per cent to 8.9 per cent) would (approximately) result in a decline of £14,000 in the portfolio's value. However, after implementing the hedge in Example 23.4, the PV01 of the overall portfolio is zero, so the change in the hedged portfolio's value for a 10bp decrease in

Example 23.4

Using PV01s to Form Perfect Hedge Portfolios

Assume that changes in the yields of various maturity bonds are identical. How much of a seven-year bond, with a computed PV01 of £0.05 per £100 of face value, should be purchased to perfectly hedge the interest rate risk of the portfolio in Example 23.3, which has a PV01 of –£1,400?

Answer: The portfolio to be hedged has a PV01 of –£1,400. The PV01 of the portfolio if we buy £x face amount of the seven-year bond is

$$-£1{,}400 + \frac{£0.05x}{100}$$

This equals zero when x is £2.8 million. Thus a £2.8 million face amount of seven-year bonds hedges the portfolio against interest rate risk.

rates is zero (approximately). In this case, the £14,000 decline in the formerly unhedged portfolio is offset by a £14,000 increase in the £2.8 million of seven-year bonds.

Dynamically Updating the Hedge

The hedge in Example 23.4 needs to be constantly readjusted, because as time elapses or bond prices change, the PV01s of bonds change. Thus it will be necessary to sell or buy additional seven-year bonds as time elapses to maintain a PV01 of zero. In practice, to save on transaction costs, this updating usually involves waiting until a critical threshold of positive or negative PV01 for the 'hedged' portfolio is reached before rehedging. The size of the threshold depends on the size of the transaction costs for rehedging and the investor's aversion to interest rate risk.

Managing Corporate Interest Rate Risk Exposure

Hedging corporate exposure to interest rate risk is virtually identical to hedging the interest rate risk in a bond portfolio. If we estimate a corporation's interest rate risk exposure to be a PV01 of –£1,400, then £2.8 million of the seven-year bonds would perfectly hedge the corporation against interest rate risk.

It is also possible to use the mathematics of Example 23.4 to illustrate how to target an interest rate risk exposure that differs from zero.

How Compounding Frequency Affects the Stated PV01

The stated yield to maturity of a bond depends on the compounding frequency used for the yield.[8] Hence the meaning of a 1bp decline in yield and the size of the corresponding PV01 depend on whether annual, semi-annual or monthly compounding is used. The customary frequency for reporting PV01s and yields to maturity depends on the bond's coupon frequency. For example, PV01s for residential mortgages are typically based on monthly compounded 1bp declines. PV01s for corporate bonds are reported from semi-annually compounded 1bp declines.

Example 23.5

Using PV01s to Form Imperfect Hedges

The seven-year bond from the last example has a PV01 of £0.05 per £100 face value. Assuming that changes in the yields of bonds of various maturities are identical, how much of the seven-year bond should be bought to change the corporate risk exposure, measured currently as a PV01 of –£1,400, to a risk exposure with a PV01 of –£400?

[8] See Chapter 9.

Answer: Because portfolio PV01s are additive, if we buy £x face amount of the seven-year bond, the PV01 of the 'portfolio' consisting of the corporation and £x of the seven-year bonds is

$$-£1{,}400 + \frac{0.05x}{100}$$

The sum of these two terms is −£400 when x equals £2 million. Thus the £2 million face amount of seven-year bonds generates the target interest rate risk exposure.

For hedging purposes, the compounding frequency for the 1bp decline is irrelevant as long as the analyst consistently uses the same compounding frequency when computing PV01s for all the relevant investments. Maintaining this consistency might require some PV01 conversions. The PV01 conversions between compounding frequencies are given in the following result.

23.2 Duration

Duration is a concept that is closely related to PV01. The **duration** of a bond (or a bond portfolio or cash flow stream), denoted DUR, is a weighted average of the waiting times (measured in years) for receiving its promised future cash flows. The weight on each time is proportional to the discounted value of the cash flow to be paid at that time: that is, letting r denote the yield (or discount rate) for the bond, P denote the bond's market price, and C_t denote the cash flow at date t, the duration DUR of the bond is

$$\begin{aligned} DUR &= \frac{[C_1/(1+r)]1 + [C_2/(1+r)^2]2 + \cdots + [C_T/(1+r)^T]T}{C_1/(1+r) + C_2/(1+r)^2 + \cdots + C_T/(1+r)^T} \\ &= \sum_{t=1}^{T}\left[\frac{\text{PV}(C_t)}{P}\right]t \end{aligned} \qquad (23.3)$$

Note that the weights, $\text{PV}(C_t)/P$, always sum to 1.

We now explore some of the properties of duration.

The Duration of Zero-Coupon Bonds

The duration of a zero-coupon bond is the number of years to the maturity date of the bond. Since a zero-coupon bond has only one cash flow, paid at maturity, the weight on its maturity date is 1. Hence a 10-year zero-coupon bond has a duration of 10 years and a six-year zero-coupon bond has a duration of six years. A portfolio of a group of 10-year zero-coupon bonds would also have a duration of 10 years. All cash flows occur at year 10: hence the 10-year timing of these cash flows receives a weight of 1.

The Duration of Coupon Bonds

It is useful to view a bond with coupons as a portfolio of zero-coupon bonds. For example, a 10-year bond with a 5 per cent coupon paid annually and a €100 face value can be thought of as a 10-year zero-coupon bond with €105 face value – the principal plus the final coupon – plus nine other zero-coupon bonds, one for each of the first nine years, each with a face value of €5. A flat term structure of interest rates implies that the discount rate for each of the 10 cash flows is the same, and that duration is simply the (present value) weighted average of the durations of the cash flows that make up the bond, as Example 23.6 shows.

Durations of Discount and Premium-Coupon Bonds

Exhibit 23.2 illustrates the duration of a coupon bond, a weighted average of the times at which cash flows are paid, as the fulcrum (the black triangle) on the timescale where the *discounted values* of the cash flows (principal plus coupon) *balance*. As Exhibit 23.3 in comparison with Exhibit 23.2 indicates, the fulcrum in

Results

Result 23.2

Let r_n and r_m denote the annualized yield to maturity of the same bond computed with yields compounded n times a year and m times a year, respectively. The PV01 for a bond (or portfolio) using compounding of m times a year is $(1 + r_n/n)/(1 + r_m/m)$ times the PV01 of the bond using a compounding frequency of n times a year.[9]

Example 23.6

Computing the Duration of a Straight-Coupon Bond

Compute the duration of a semi-annual straight-coupon bond with a two-year maturity. The bond trades at par and has an 8 per cent annualized coupon. Assume the term structure of interest rates is flat.

---

[9] Here is a calculus proof of Result 23.2: equation (23.1) states that

$$\text{PV01 (for } r_m) = -0.00011\frac{dP}{dr_m}.$$

and

$$\text{PV01 (for } r_n) = -0.001\frac{dP}{dr_n}$$

where r_m and r_n are equivalent annualized rates of interest for compounding that occurs m times a year and n times a year, respectively. Dividing each side of the second equation into the corresponding sides of the first equation, we get

$$\frac{\text{PV01 (for } r_m)}{\text{PV01 (for } r_n)} = \frac{dr_n}{dr_m}$$

or

$$\text{PV01 (for } r_m) = \frac{dr_n}{dr_m}\text{PV01 (for } r_n)$$

To prove that

$$\frac{dr_n}{dr_m} = \frac{1 + \frac{r_n}{n}}{1 + \frac{r_m}{m}}$$

we refer the reader to Chapter 9. There we learned that two equivalent rates that compound m times a year and n times a year satisfy the condition that the future value of one unit of currency after one year must be the same: that is,

$$\left(1 + \frac{r_n}{n}\right)^n = \left(1 + \frac{r_m}{m}\right)^m$$

After taking the natural logarithm of both sides of this equation, this is equivalent to

$$n \ln\left(1 + \frac{r_n}{n}\right) = m \ln\left(1 + \frac{r_m}{m}\right)$$

Taking the derivative of both sides with respect to r_m yields

$$\left(\frac{1}{1 + \frac{r_n}{n}}\right)\frac{dr_n}{dr_m} = \frac{1}{1 + \frac{r_m}{m}}$$

When rearranged, this says

$$\frac{dr_n}{dr_m} = \frac{1 + \frac{r_n}{n}}{1 + \frac{r_m}{m}}$$

Answer: Since the bond trades at par and the term structure of interest rates is flat, the semi-annually compounded discount rate is 8 per cent. (See Result 2.2 in Chapter 2.)

- The first coupon of €4.00 paid six months from now has a present value of €3.846 at 8 per cent and thus a weight equal to 0.03846.
- The second coupon, one year from now, has a present value of €3.698 and a corresponding weight of 0.03698.
- The third coupon, 1.5 years from now, has a present value of €3.556 and a corresponding weight of 0.03556.
- The final cash flow, €104, has a present value of €88.900 and a weight of 0.889.

Hence duration, the weighted average of the times the cash flows are paid, is computed as

$$0.03846(0.5 \text{ years}) + 0.03698(1 \text{ year}) + 0.03556(1.5 \text{ years}) + 0.88900(2 \text{ years}) = 1.89 \text{ years}$$

Exhibit 23.2 needs to be shifted to the left to maintain a balance if the coupons increase, because such an increase would also increase their discounted values proportionately. Hence, other things being equal, premium bonds have lower durations, and discount bonds, being more like zero-coupon bonds, have higher durations.

Exhibit 23.2 Duration as a Fulcrum

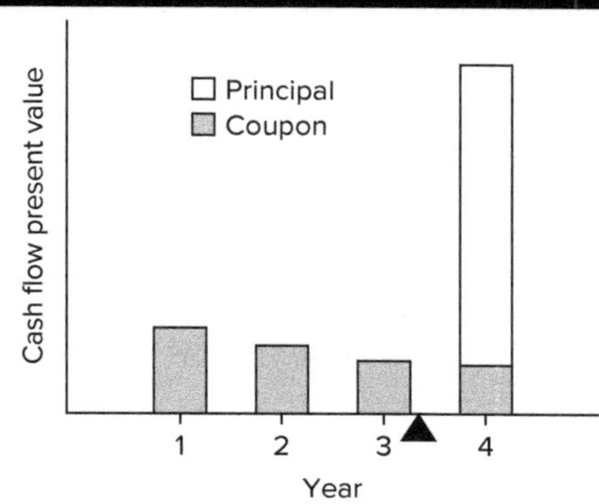

Exhibit 23.3 Duration as a Fulcrum (with Larger Coupons)

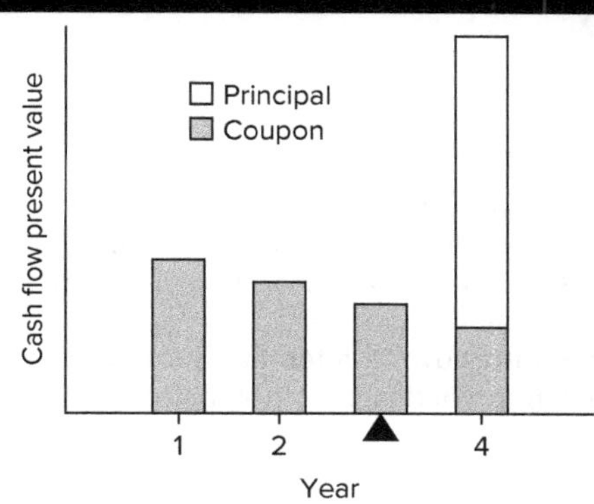

How Duration Changes as Time Elapses

Exhibit 23.4 shows the duration of a straight-coupon bond with semi-annual payments as time elapses, holding the yield to maturity constant. Note that, as time elapses, the bond's duration increases at coupon dates. As the coupon is paid, the weights on all the other cash flows are readjusted immediately. Between coupon dates, duration constantly decreases.

Exhibit 23.4 Duration as Time Elapses

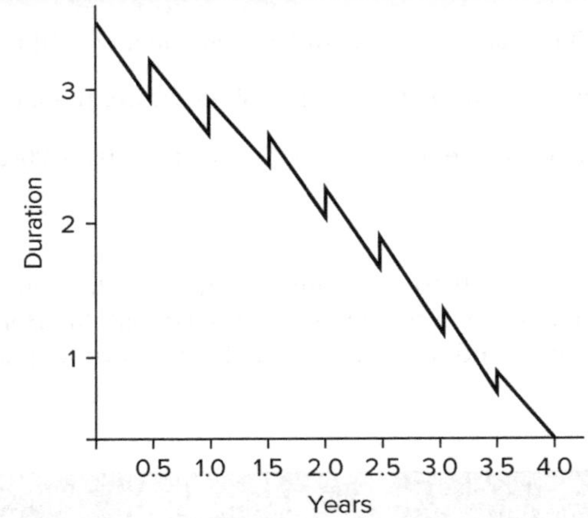

Durations of Bond Portfolios

The durations of bond portfolios are computed in the same manner as the durations of coupon bonds. If we were to hold both six-year zero-coupon bonds and eight-year zero-coupon bonds, the duration of the bond portfolio would lie somewhere between six and eight years. Suppose that the discounted value of the six-year and eight-year zero-coupon bonds is *1*10 million each. Then, since year 6 would have the same weight as year 8 and the weights add to 1, each weight would be 0.5 and the duration of the *1*20 million portfolio of the two bonds would be seven years [+ 0.5(6 years) + 0.5(8 years)]. This result can be generalized to any portfolio of bonds, as indicated below.

Results

Result 23.3

Assuming that the term structure of interest rates is flat, the duration of a portfolio of bonds is the portfolio-weighted average of the durations of the respective bonds in the portfolio.

How Duration Changes as Interest Rates Increase

Result 23.3 implies that an increase in the yield to maturity of the bond decreases duration (compare Exhibit 23.5 with Exhibit 23.4). If we think of a coupon-paying bond as a portfolio of zero-coupon bonds, then an increase in the bond's yield to maturity reduces the weight of the later cash flow payments proportionately more than it reduces the weight of the early cash flows.

Result 23.3 also provides insights into how to alter the duration of a corporation's debt. Example 23.7 demonstrates how this is achieved in a hypothetical situation involving Ryanair.

Exhibit 23.5 Duration as a Fulcrum (with a Higher Discount Rate)

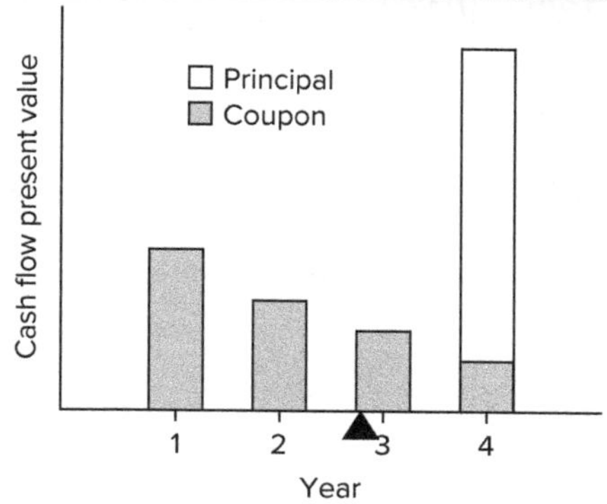

Example 23.7

Changing the Duration of Corporate Liabilities

Assume that Ryanair's debt obligations have a market value of €2 billion and a duration of five years. Half of this is a 10-year note with a duration of six years. The Ryanair treasurer has decided that the company should target a debt duration of four years instead of five. Assume that it is possible to issue four-year par straight-coupon notes, which have a duration of three years. If the proceeds from issuing these notes are used to retire 10-year notes, there will be a reduction in the duration of Ryanair's liabilities. Assuming a flat yield curve, how many euros of four-year notes should Ryanair issue?

Answer: Ryanair's existing liabilities consist of €1 billion in 10-year notes with a duration of six years and, by Result 23.3, €1 billion in other liabilities with a duration of four years. If Ryanair issues €x in notes with three years' duration, and uses the proceeds to retire the 10-year notes, the duration of its new liability structure will be:

$$\text{DUR} = \left[\frac{€x}{€2 \text{ billion}}\right] 3 \text{ years} + \left[\frac{€1 \text{ billion} - €x}{€2 \text{ billion}}\right] 6 \text{ years} + \left[\frac{€1 \text{ billion}}{€2 \text{ billion}}\right] 4 \text{ years}$$

DUR = 4 years when x = €2/3 billion. Thus issuing €666,666,667 in three-year notes and using the proceeds to retire two-thirds of the 10-year notes puts Ryanair at its target liability duration.

23.3 Linking Duration to PV01

This section develops formulae that link duration to PV01. First, it shows that the duration of a bond is related to the interest rate risk of the bond.

Duration as a Derivative

Duration is a useful tool for managing the interest rate risk of bond portfolios. This suggests that duration is related to the derivative of a bond's price with respect to interest rates. Such a derivative will also enable us to relate duration to PV01. To illustrate the relationship between duration and PV01, consider a two-year zero-coupon bond with a face value of £100 and a continuously compounded yield to maturity of r. The bond's price is $P = £100e^{-2}r$ and its duration is two years.

Using calculus, the percentage change in the bond's price, dP/P, for a change in the continuously compounded yield to maturity is

$$\frac{dP/P}{dr} = \frac{dP}{dr}\frac{1}{P} = £100(-2\,e^{-2r})\frac{1}{£100\,e^{-2r}} = -2 \qquad (23.4)$$

Thus −2, the negative of the bond's duration, is the percentage sensitivity of the bond's price to changes in the bond's continuously compounded yield.

This derivative property can be generalized. When the term structure of interest rates is flat, duration can always be viewed as minus the percentage change in the value of the bond (or portfolio) with respect to changes in its continuously compounded yield to maturity. For example, a bond maturing in T years, with cash flows of C_t at date t, $t = 1, \ldots, T$, has a price of

$$P = \sum_{t=1}^{T} C_t e^{-rt} \qquad (23.5)$$

if r is the bond's continuously compounded yield to maturity.

The percentage change in P with respect to the continuously compounded yield is

$$\frac{dP}{P/dR} = -\frac{1}{P}\left(\sum_{t=1}^{T} t C_t e^{-rt}\right) = -\text{DUR} \qquad (23.6)$$

This is the negative of duration, because the weight assigned to each relevant date (the ts) is the negative of the discounted value of the cash flow at that time divided by the discounted value of the entire bond P.

To alter equation (23.6) for different compounding frequencies, note the following formulae.

- If annually compounded yields had been used in place of continuously compounded yields for this analysis, the derivative corresponding to equation (23.6) would be

$$\frac{dP/P}{dr} = -\frac{1}{1+r}\left[\frac{1}{P}\left(\sum_{t=1}^{T} t\frac{C_t}{(1+r)^t}\right)\right] = \frac{\text{DUR}}{1+r}$$

  indicating that duration is the negative of $(1 + r)$ times the percentage price change for a small change in the yield.
- For semi-annually compounded yields, the derivative corresponding to equation (23.6) would be

$$\frac{dP/P}{dr} = -\frac{1}{1+r/2}\left\{\frac{1}{P}\left[\sum_{t=1}^{2T}\frac{t}{2}\frac{C_t}{(1+r/2)^t}\right]\right\}$$

  indicating that duration is the negative of $(1 + r/2)$ times the percentage price change for a small change in the yield.
- For monthly compounded yields, the derivative corresponding to equation (23.6) would be

$$\frac{dP}{dr/P} = -\frac{1}{1+r/12}\left\{\frac{1}{P}\left[\sum_{t=1}^{12T}\frac{t}{12}\frac{C_t}{(1+r/12)^t}\right]\right\} = \frac{\text{DUR}}{1+r/12}$$

  indicating that duration is the negative of $(1 + r/12)$ times the percentage price change for a small change in the yield.
- As the compounding frequency m becomes infinite, the denominator under DUR, $(1 + r/m)$, converges to 1, which leads to the formula in equation (23.6).

Formulae Relating Duration to PV01

The relation between duration and PV01 is straightforward if the 01 in PV01 is defined as a continuously compounded rate. In this case, PV01 is the product of −0.0001 and the derivative of the value of the bond with respect to a shift in the bond's continuously compounded yield: that is,

$$\text{PV01} = -0.0001\frac{dP}{dr}$$

Equation (23.6) implies that duration is the derivative of the percentage change in the value of the bond with respect to the (continuously compounded) yield to maturity: that is,

$$\text{DUR} = -\frac{1}{P}\frac{dP}{dr}$$

Solving either of the last two equations for dP/dr and substituting its equivalent value into the other equation gives an equation that relates PV01 to duration:

$$\text{PVO1} = \text{DUR} \times P \times 0.0001 \tag{23.7a}$$

Equation (23.7a) suggests the following result.

Results

Result 23.4

Because PV01 can be translated into duration, and vice versa, PV01 and duration are equivalent as tools both for measuring interest rate risk and for hedging.

Modified Duration

If PV01 is based on rates that are compounded m times a year instead of continuously, then the formula relating PV01 to duration is modified as follows:

$$\text{PV01} = \left(\frac{\text{DUR}}{1 + r/m}\right) \times P \times 0.0001 \tag{23.7b}$$

The term in brackets is known as **modified duration.**

Effective Duration for Assets and Liabilities with Risky Cash Flow Streams

Duration is more complicated to implement in a corporate setting without first linking duration to PV01. Because most corporate cash flows are risky, weighting the maturities of uncertain cash flows to come up with a measure of the future timing of cash flows makes little sense. However, duration, like PV01, is a measure of the interest rate sensitivity of a cash flow, which can alternatively be obtained from a factor model. Thus one can compute an **effective duration** of a corporate asset or liability with risk (generated both by the uncertain cash flow stream and by changes in the discount rate(s) for the cash flows in the stream) by first estimating its PV01 as an interest rate sensitivity in a factor model and then inverting equation (23.7b) to obtain DUR. This effective duration tells us that the corporate asset or liability is of the same sensitivity to interest rate risk per unit of currency invested as a riskless zero-coupon bond of maturity DUR.

Hedging with PV01s or Durations

The last section provided formulae that link PV01 directly to duration. Hence both duration and PV01 are equally good tools for hedging bond portfolios. Recall that a perfect hedge makes the new portfolio, including the hedge investment, have a PV01 of zero. To obtain a PV01 of zero, the ratio of the duration of the unhedged bond portfolio (DUR_B) to the duration of its hedged portfolio (DUR_H) must be inversely proportional to the ratio of the respective market values of the bonds:[10] that is,

$$\frac{\text{DUR}_H}{\text{DUR}_B} = \frac{P_B}{P_H}$$

If this property holds, the combination of the unhedged bond position and the short position in the hedge has a duration (and PV01) of zero.

When duration is based on non-continuously compounded yields, this relation is still valid, because the durations are both multiplied by the same constant. Of course, our caveat that perfect hedging with PV01s occurs only when the term structure of interest rates is flat applies here as well.

[10]From equation (23.7a), PV01 is zero when:

$$(\text{DUR}_B \times P_B \times 0.0001) - (\text{DUR}_H \times P_H \times 0.0001) = 0$$

This equation, when rearranged, proves the result.

Example 23.8 develops this point.

Example 23.8

Using Duration to Form a Riskless Hedge Position

Giuliola holds €1,000,000 (face value) of 10-year zero-coupon bonds with a yield to maturity of 8 per cent compounded semi-annually. How can she perfectly hedge this position with a short position in five-year zero-coupon bonds with a yield to maturity of 8 per cent (compounded semi-annually)?

Answer: The ratio of the durations of the two bonds is 10/5 = 2. The ratio of their market values should therefore be ½. The market value of the 10-year bonds is

$$\frac{€1{,}000{,}000}{1.04^{20}} = €456{,}386.95$$

The market value of the five-year bonds is

$$\frac{x}{1.04^{10}}$$

For the market value of the 10-year bond position to be half the value of the five-year position, x must solve

$$€456{,}386.95 = \frac{1}{2}\frac{x}{1.04^{10}}$$

or

$$x = €1{,}351{,}128.34$$

Hence selling short €1,351,128.34 (face value) of the five-year bonds hedges the 10-year bond position.

It is easy to compute what would have happened if the position in the 10-year zero-coupon bonds was left unhedged in the last example. When rearranged, equation (23.6) says

$$\frac{dP}{P} = -\text{DUR} \times dr$$

suggesting that a 10-basis-point increase in interest rates (for example, from 9 per cent to 9.1 per cent) would decrease the value of the bond portfolio by

$$0.001 \times \text{DUR} = 0.001 \times 10 = 0.01, \text{ or } 1\%$$

Hence the €1 million (face amount) bond investment in the last example, which cost €456,387, would decline by 1 per cent of €456,387, or €4,564, if left unhedged. Under this same interest rate change scenario, the €1.35 million (face value) of five-year zero-coupon bonds would also decline in value by €4,564. Hence Giuliola constructs a portfolio that has no interest rate sensitivity by selling short €1.35 million of the five-year bonds.

Duration targeting is often used to perfectly hedge pension fund liabilities. A pension that funds its liability for retirement obligations with default-free bonds would want the bonds to have the same interest rate sensitivity as the liabilities. An over-funded pension plan with this property guarantees that there will be no shortage of funds for the pension liabilities as a result of interest rate changes. Example 23.9 indicates how to target the duration of pension assets to hedge pension liabilities with this purpose in mind.

Example 23.9

Changing the Duration of Pension Fund Assets

As the new manager of a pension fund, assume that you have analysed the defined benefits of the plan and computed that the fund's liabilities amount to an £8 billion market value obligation with a duration of 12 years. Unfortunately, although the fund has £9 billion in assets, consisting largely of bonds, their duration is only eight years. This means that a steep decline in interest rates may increase the present value of the obligations by £1 billion more than such a decline increases the value of the fund's assets. While keeping a £1 billion surplus in the pension fund, how can a self-financing investment in five-year Treasury notes, with a duration of four years, and 30-year Treasury bonds, with a duration of 10 years, eliminate this problem?

Answer: If x denotes the amount invested in 30-year bonds, and an equivalent pound sterling amount of five-year bonds are sold short, the duration of the pension fund assets becomes

$$\text{DUR} = 8 \text{ years} + \left[\frac{x}{£9 \text{ billion}}\right] 10 \text{ years} + \left[\frac{x}{£9 \text{ billion}}\right] 4 \text{ years}$$

The ratio of the market values of the assets to the liabilities is 9/8. Hence the duration of the assets should be $10^{2/3}$ years, or 8/9 the 12-year duration of the liabilities to perfectly hedge interest risk. Solving for x above with DUR = $10^{2/3}$ years implies x = £4 billion. Thus buying £4 billion in 30-year bonds and selling short £4 billion in five-year bonds will result in the interest rate sensitivity of the pension fund assets matching that of the liabilities.

Example 23.9 points out how to eliminate interest rate sensitivity by matching assets and liabilities in a particular way. The next section examines how to carry this idea forward through time in order to fix an amount available for payment at some horizon date.

23.4 Immunization

Immunization is a technique for locking in the value of a portfolio at the end of a planning horizon. In a sense, immunization turns a portfolio into a zero-coupon bond.

Ordinary Immunization

Immunization was developed by F.M. Redington, an actuary, who showed that if the durations and market values of the assets and liabilities of a financial institution were equal, the equity of the institution would be insensitive to movements in interest rates.[11] We generalize this result here, allowing the ratios of the durations of the assets and liabilities to be inversely proportional to their market value ratios.

Applying Immunization Techniques to Stabilize the Future Value of a Bond Portfolio

Immunization techniques can be applied to reduce the interest rate sensitivity of the equity of financial institutions or the equity stake of a corporation in a defined benefit pension plan.[12] Today, however, immunization techniques are more often used to stabilize the value of a bond portfolio at the horizon date, which is the date at the end of some planning horizon.

For simplicity, assume that the term structure of interest rates is flat. In this case, the fundamental rule for immunizing a portfolio is to match the duration of the portfolio with the horizon date. For example, a manager with a horizon date of 1 January 2029 should, on 1 January 2023, have a portfolio duration of six years; on 1 January 2024, the portfolio duration should be five years; on 30 June 2027, it should be 1.5 years.

To implement the immunization strategy, it is important that all coupons, principal payments and other cash distributions received be reinvested in the portfolio. Maintaining a duration that is matched to the horizon date means that the rate at which these cash distributions are reinvested exactly offsets the gain or loss in the value of the portfolio as interest rates change.

Why Immunization Locks in a Value at the Horizon Date

To see why this strategy locks in the portfolio value at the horizon date, compare the portfolio with a zero-coupon bond of identical market value that has a maturity, and hence a duration, equal to the duration of the immunized portfolio. A long position in the portfolio and a short position in the zero-coupon bond has both a market value and a duration of zero.

[11] See Redington (1952).

[12] See Example 23.9.

When the duration of the combined long and short position is zero, its sensitivity to interest rate movements and hence its volatility is zero. For a brief instant, it is riskless. As time elapses, keeping it riskless requires adjusting the long position in the portfolio to have the same duration as the maturity of the zero-coupon bond by shortening the duration of the long position over time in order to maintain a duration of zero for the combination of the immunized portfolio (the long position) and the short position in the zero-coupon bond.

Since riskless self-financing investments do not appreciate or depreciate in value, the riskless self-financing combination of the immunized bond portfolio and the short position in the zero-coupon bond – if the former is properly updated over time – will have a value of zero at the maturity date of the zero-coupon bond. At the maturity date, this means that the immunized portfolio has to have a market value equal to the face value (and market value) of the zero-coupon bond.

Result 23.5 summarizes this procedure.

Results

Result 23.5

If the term structure of interest rates is flat, immunization 'guarantees' a fixed value for an immunized portfolio at a horizon date. The value obtained is the same as the face value of a zero-coupon bond with (1) the same market value as the original portfolio and (2) a maturity date equal to the horizon date selected as the target date to which the duration of the immunized portfolio is fixed.

Viewing the portfolio to be immunized as an asset, and the zero-coupon bond as a liability, we have done exactly what Redington suggested for financial institutions: matched the durations of assets and liabilities with the same market value. Of course, the zero-coupon bond was not actually sold short in order to immunize the portfolio. Rather, we merely pretended to sell short a zero-coupon bond to help clarify what to do to the portfolio to ensure a value at the horizon date.

Example 23.10 shows how to calculate the lock-in value at the horizon date.

Example 23.10

Computing the Lock-in Amount at Some Horizon Date

The current yield to maturity is 8 per cent compounded semi-annually for bonds of all maturities. A bond portfolio consists of €10 million (market value) of fixed-income securities. What amount will the portfolio manager be able to lock in three years from now?

Answer: The current market value of the portfolio is €10 million. At 8 per cent, the future value of the portfolio in three years is

$$1.04^6 \times €10 \text{ million} = €12.653 \text{ million}$$

Example 23.11 shows how to alter a portfolio to lock in its value.

Example 23.11

Using Immunization Techniques to Lock in a Pay-off

The €10 million portfolio in Example 23.10 is a pension portfolio, which currently has a duration of five years. Half the portfolio's market value consists of identical maturity zero-coupon bonds. The remainder consists of €5 million (market value) of the two-year straight-coupon bonds from Example 23.6. These bonds have a duration of 1.89 years and an 8 per cent yield, compounded semi-annually.

- a What is the maturity of the zero-coupon bonds in the portfolio?
- b How should the manager rebalance the portfolio between the two-year straight-coupon bonds and the zero-coupon bonds to immunize it at a three-year horizon date?

Answer:

a The zero-coupon bonds have to have a maturity of 8.11 years because this is the only maturity that makes an equal-weighted average of the two-year bonds' duration (1.89) and the zero-coupon bonds' duration equal five years.

b To immunize the portfolio for a horizon of three years, the duration of the portfolio has to be changed to three years. Find weights x and $1 - x$ that make the weighted average of the durations:

$$x(1.89) + (1 - x)8.11 = 3$$

The approximate solution is $x = 0.82154$. Hence €8.2154 million of the two-year straight-coupon bonds must be owned, which requires an additional purchase of €3.2154 million (face and market value) of these bonds. To finance the purchase, sell €3.2154 million (market value) of the zero-coupon bonds, which have an aggregate face value of about

$$€6.07 \text{ million} = €3.2154 \text{ million}(1.04)^{16.22}$$

Example 23.11 describes what the portfolio manager must do currently to immunize his portfolio for a horizon of three years. However, this manager cannot rest on his laurels. Every day, as time elapses and interest rates change, the immunized portfolio becomes non-immunized if the manager acts passively. To maintain the immunization, as Example 23.12 illustrates, it is important to constantly update the weighting of the zero-coupon bonds and the two-year straight-coupon bonds.

Example 23.12

Updating Portfolio Weights in an Immunized Portfolio

What must the portfolio manager do in the future to immunize the portfolio, particularly at the maturity date of the two-year straight-coupon bonds?

Answer: As each day elapses, the portfolio manager must shorten the duration by one day. Some of this shortening will happen even if the manager does nothing, since the duration of both bond types is diminishing as time elapses. However, it is unlikely that this natural shortening of duration will be exactly one day. Hence the manager must recompute duration periodically for the new interest rate and the time to payment of the cash flows, and adjust duration accordingly. This creates a problem after two years have elapsed. At that point, the manager would like the portfolio to have a one-year duration, but would have only zero-coupon bonds maturing in 6.11 years (and a duration of 6.11 years) once the straight-coupon bonds mature. This implies that the manager must begin to use a third security in the portfolio as the maturity date of the straight-coupon bonds nears.

The immunization strategy employed in Examples 23.10–23.12 was equivalent to designing a hypothetical portfolio with a duration of zero. This portfolio consists of the two-year straight-coupon bonds, 8.11-year zero-coupon bonds, and a short position in three-year zero-coupon bonds that finances the other two positions. If this hypothetical portfolio is managed so that it has a value of zero at the horizon date, the original immunized portfolio is managed so that it has a value equal to that of three-year zero-coupon bonds with an aggregate face value of €12.653 million.

The same insight can be used to understand Redington's result as it applies to financial institutions. If the assets and liabilities of the financial institution have unequal value, construct fictitious zero-coupon bonds with a market value equal to the market value of the institution's equity (assets minus liabilities) and a maturity equal to the horizon date at which the equity's value needs to be guaranteed. To immunize the equity in this fashion over time, manage a self-financing investment that is long the assets, short the liabilities and short the zero-coupon bonds, so that it maintains zero duration. This is equivalent to structuring the assets and liabilities of the institution so that they have a duration equal to the maturity of the zero-coupon bonds,[13] as Example 23.13 illustrates for a savings bank.

[13] The self-financing investment will continue to have a value of zero if the immunization procedure is followed, implying that the assets less the liabilities (which equals the equity) will have a value equal to the value of the fictitious zero-coupon bond.

Example 23.13

Using Immunization to Manage Savings Bank Assets

The assets of a savings bank consist of mortgages with a four-year duration and a present value of £10 billion. The bank's liabilities consist of customer deposits and CDs with a duration of two years and a present value of £5 billion. Interest rates are 8 per cent, compounded annually at all maturities. Assume that the bank's management wants to ensure that the bank has a fixed amount of equity capital at the time the bank's next regulatory examination is scheduled, in two years.

a How much equity value can it guarantee at the time of the next regulatory examination?

b Given that the savings bank can invest in commercial paper (which can be regarded as a short-term zero-coupon bond with a three-month maturity) and sell some or all of its mortgage assets, what should the bank do to lock in an equity value two years from now?

Answer:

a The current £5 billion in equity can have a 'lock-in' value in two years of

$$\text{£}5.832 \text{ billion } [= (1.08)^2 \times \text{£}5 \text{ billion }]$$

b To lock in this value, adjust the duration of the equity to two years, and then continually shorten the duration by one day as each day elapses. The current duration of the equity is a weighted average of the durations of the assets and liabilities. Since the assets are twice as large as the liabilities, the asset weight must be 2 and the liability weight must be −1 for the weights to sum to 1. This makes the current equity duration 2 × (4 years) −1 × (2 years) = 6 years. To shorten this to two years by changing the asset portfolio, the bank should sell some of the mortgage assets and buy commercial paper. This requires shortening the asset duration to a duration (DUR) that satisfies

$$2 \times \text{DUR} - 1 \times (2 \text{ years}) = 2 \text{ years}$$

Thus DUR = 2 years. The market value of mortgage assets x and commercial paper assets y that have a duration of two years satisfy

$$\frac{4x + 0.25y}{x + y} = 2$$

The market values of the mortgage position x and of the commercial paper position y must sum to £10 billion, the current value of the bank's assets. Thus x and y must also solve

$$x + y = \text{£}10 \text{ billion}$$

Substituting this into the previous equation yields:

$$\frac{4x + 0.25(\text{£}10 \text{ billion} - x)}{\text{£}10 \text{ billion}} = 2$$

This is solved by x = £4.67 billion, implying y = £5.33 billion. That is, sell £5.33 billion of the £10 billion in mortgage assets and use the proceeds to buy three-month commercial paper.

Immunization Using PV01

PV01-based techniques are just as appropriate as duration-based techniques for achieving immunization. If the duration of the portfolio matches the duration of a zero-coupon bond with (1) a maturity equal to the horizon date and (2) a price equal to that of the portfolio, then the PV01 of a long position in the portfolio and a short position in the bond is zero. Maintaining a PV01 of zero for this combined position also guarantees a fixed value portfolio at the horizon date.[14]

[14] We can easily extend this analysis to asset-liability management.

Practical Issues to Consider

Although immunization techniques are widely used in bond portfolio and asset-liability management, they cannot perfectly guarantee a value at the horizon date. First, transaction costs make it prohibitively expensive to continually rebalance the portfolio (or the assets and liabilities) to maintain the proper duration, which is constantly declining. For this reason, the necessary rebalancing is done only when the duration match is off by a critical amount. Second, immunization techniques assume that the term structure of interest rates is flat. This is rare even in an approximate sense and, when observed, tends to quickly evolve into upward- or (less frequently) downward-sloping or oddly shaped yield curves. In spite of these impediments, immunization seems to work well in most instances as a risk-reduction tool. As a consequence, it is popular despite its imperfection.

Contingent Immunization

Contingent immunization is the bond portfolio equivalent of portfolio insurance (which, as illustrated in Chapter 8, is generally used to insure equity portfolios). **Contingent immunization** sets a target value for the bond portfolio at the horizon date that is smaller than the face value of a zero-coupon bond with the same market value as the portfolio. This target value is regarded as a floor below which the future value of the bond portfolio should not fall. The bond portfolio is managed actively without regard for duration until its value falls to a critical level. From that point on, an immunization strategy is followed. In this sense, immunization is contingent on a decline in the bond portfolio to a pre-specified critical point.

We can regard the critical level in contingent immunization as the market value of a zero-coupon bond maturing on the horizon date with a face value equal to the floor value. Hence this critical value tends to rise over time, although it may fall when interest rates increase.

Immunization and Large Changes in Interest Rates

A €10,000 six-year 8 per cent straight-coupon bond with annual coupons trading at par has a duration of approximately five years. If the term structure of interest rates is flat, and the interest rate increases slightly, the reinvested coupons will have an increased value at year 5 that exactly counterbalances the decreased value of the bond in year 5 (that is, the year 5 value of its cash flows after year 5). The same is true when there is a small decline in interest rates.

It is important, however, to determine how well immunization strategies perform when there are substantial interest rate changes. Interest rates can sometimes jump by large amounts when important economic indicators are announced (for example, the monthly employment report or inflation rate changes). Moreover, even a series of small changes in interest rates can amount to a large effective change in interest rates if transaction costs lead investors to undertake a *lax immunization strategy* – failing to maintain the proper duration for the bond at all points in time.

One can be comforted that immunization strategies work 'pretty well' for the 8 per cent straight-coupon bond described above, and even for large interest rate changes such as 25 basis points in one day. A 25bp decline in interest rates, from 8 per cent to 7.75 per cent, makes the sum of the year 5 value of the bond and its reinvested coupons equal €14,693.14; in the absence of an interest rate shift, the bond's value is €14,693.28. This is a remarkably insignificant difference! Since a 25bp shift in the yield of a six-year bond would rarely occur over a single day, we can be fairly confident in stating that immunization in this case would not require exceptionally frequent rebalancing of the portfolio.

The next section discusses how to better quantify this degree of confidence.

23.5 Convexity

Convexity measures how much PV01 changes as the yield of a bond or bond portfolio changes. A portfolio with a PV01 of zero will be insensitive to small interest rate movements and less sensitive to large interest rate movements the smaller the convexity. In other words, the PV01 remains close to zero as interest rates change if convexity is close to zero.

Defining and Interpreting Convexity

Convexity is a measure that determines how secure an investor should feel about a 'perfectly hedged' portfolio (for example, whether an electronic feed of bond prices requires constant monitoring or whether the investor can relax and do other things). If the convexity of a hedged portfolio is zero, even fairly large changes in interest rates over a short time span should not alter the value of the portfolio drastically. If the convexity is large, constant monitoring of the bond prices might be a good idea.

Positive Convexity is More Typical

Most bonds have positive convexity, which expresses the type of curvature seen earlier in the price–yield curve (Exhibit 23.1). Exhibit 23.6 portrays price–yield curves for two bonds: one with a large amount of convexity and one with little convexity. In contrast to this picture, bond portfolios, with long and short positions in different bonds, can have positive or 'negative convexity'.[15]

Exhibit 23.6 Convexity

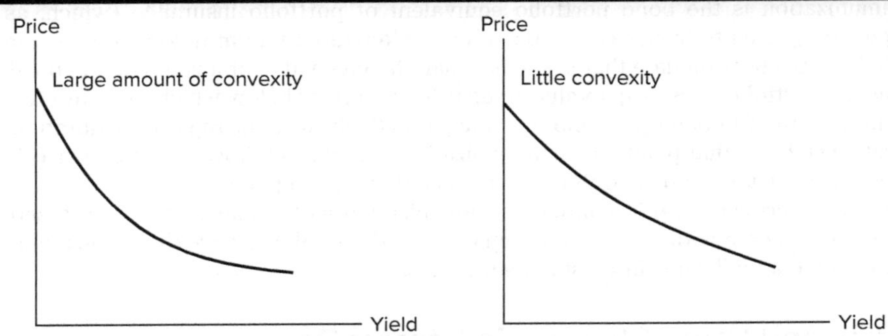

The Convexity Formula

At a single point on the price–yield curve for a bond or bond portfolio, the curvature, measured by convexity, is formally defined as follows: the convexity, CONV(r), of a bond or a bond portfolio at a yield to maturity of r is the product of (1) £1,000,000 divided by the bond price and (2) the difference between the current PV01 (of the entire bond position) and the PV01 (of the entire bond position) at a yield of $r + 0.0001$: that is,

$$\text{CONV}(r) = \left(\frac{£1 \text{ million}}{P}\right)[\text{PV01}(r) - \text{PV01}(r + 0.0001)]$$

PV01 can be viewed as a derivative of the bond price with respect to its yield to maturity. It differs from the derivative primarily in that PV01 multiplies the derivative by a constant. Convexity, CONV, is like the second derivative of the portfolio's price with respect to its yield in per cent (not its basis point shift). To obtain convexity, multiply the PV01 *difference* by 10,000 (the square of 100) to undo the PV01 convention of multiplying the derivative with respect to the percentage yield by 0.01 (100bps is 1 percentage point of interest). In addition, convexity is typically scaled per £100 of market value. Hence, after multiplying the difference between the PV01s at the two yields by 10,000, it is customary to multiply by £100 and divide by the bond price per £100 of face value. Example 23.14 illustrates the calculation.

Example 23.14

Computing Convexity

Compute the convexity of the 8 per cent two-year par straight-coupon bond analysed in Example 23.6.

Answer: The PV01 of this bond is 0.0181516 per €100 face value at an 8.00 per cent yield, since its price at 7.99 per cent is €100.0181516. At an 8.01 per cent yield, the PV01 is 0.0181473, the difference between the €100 price at 8.00 per cent and the price at 8.01 per cent, which is €99.9818527. The difference between the two PV01s is 4.3×10^{-6}. The convexity is 0.043, which is 1 million divided by 100 times this number.

---

[15] Despite its applications in science and mathematics, the word *concavity*, which is probably a better term than *negative convexity*, has yet to find a place in the vocabulary of the bond markets.

Implications of Convexity for Immunization Strategies

The last section indicated that immunizing a portfolio for a T-year horizon requires managing the portfolio, so that when it is combined with a hypothetical short position in a zero-coupon bond of T years maturity, the duration and value of the combined portfolio are zero. If the convexity of the *actual* portfolio is close to the convexity of the hypothetical T-year zero-coupon bond, the investor who is immunizing the portfolio does not have to constantly monitor bond prices. However, frequent rebalancing is needed to maintain the immunized position of the actual portfolio if its convexity differs substantially from that of the hypothetical portfolio. In the latter case, constant bond price monitoring is required.

Estimating Price Sensitivity to Yield

Investors often use convexity to improve upon the earlier (PV01 or duration-based) estimate of the change in the price of a bond portfolio for a given change in yield. Specifically, letting Δr denote the change in the yield to maturity (in per cent form) and P the starting price of the bond or bond portfolio, we can write[16]

$$\Delta P = -100\text{PV01}\Delta r + 0.5\frac{P}{100}\text{CONV}(\Delta r)^2 \qquad (23.8)$$

Example 23.15 illustrates how to apply the formula.

Example 23.15

Using Convexity for Accurate Estimates of Price Change

Compute the change in the price of a bond portfolio with a £200 market value for a 25-basis-point increase in yield. At the current yield to maturity, the bond has a PV01 of £0.15 and a convexity of 1.2 (convexity is computed per £100 of market value).

Answer: Using equation (23.8), the change in price is:

$$-100(\pounds 0.15)(0.25) + 0.5\frac{\pounds 200}{100}(1.2)(0.25^2) = -\pounds 3.675$$

Hence the new price will be £196.325.

One would estimate the change in price in Example 23.15 as –£3.75 using only PV01 to estimate the change. Using equation (23.8) thus improves the estimate of interest rate sensitivity by £0.075.

Convexity (unlike PV01, but like duration) is independent of the scale of the investment. Holding twice as many bonds of the same type does not change the convexity of the portfolio. Moreover, the convexity of a portfolio of bonds is the value-weighted average of the convexity of each bond in the portfolio.

Misuse of Convexity

Throughout this chapter, we have assumed that the term structure of interest rates is flat. This is the traditional approach taken in all but the most sophisticated bond portfolio analysis, and it is a good way to begin to understand the issues in bond portfolio management and interest rate hedging. However, we must express caution: not only is this assumption generally an incorrect portrait of realistic term structures, but it is fraught with several pitfalls that are based on inherent flaws in logic. A misguided application of convexity, discussed next, illuminates this point.

Convexity Appears to be Good

Equation (23.8) implies that the higher the convexity of a bond portfolio (holding market value and PV01 constant), the larger the value of the portfolio for both an increase and a decline in its yield to maturity. This seems to imply that convexity is a good thing to have in a portfolio and that, other things being equal, investments with a large amount of convexity are in some sense better than investments with little convexity or negative convexity. Exhibit 23.7 illustrates this point by plotting the price–yield curve for two default-free bonds, each

[16] This equation is derived from the second-order Taylor series expansion. See any elementary calculus text for details.

Exhibit 23.7 The Effects of Convexity for Similar Bonds

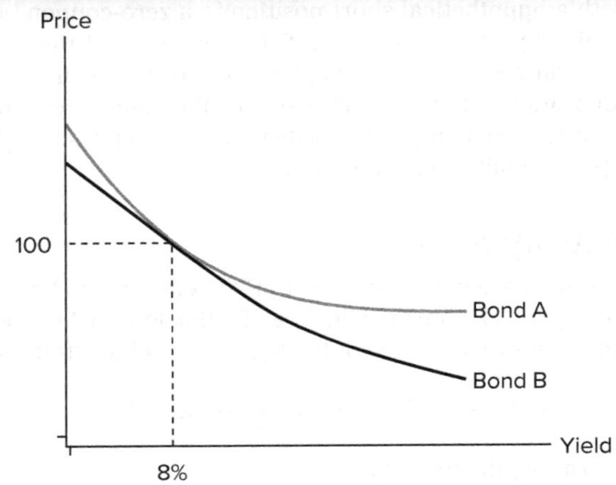

with the same market value and PV01 at a yield of 8 per cent. Note that, as yields change, irrespective of the direction of change, the price of bond A will be higher than that of bond B. Bond A thus appears to be the better bond because it has more convexity.

The flaw in this analysis is that the yields to maturity of the two bonds need not be the same. Unless the term structure of interest rates is flat, the two bonds need not have the same yields at the same time, and when one bond's yield moves up, the other's yield need not move up by the same amount. Comparing yields between two bonds is a comparison of apples and oranges.

Arbitrage Exists When the Term Structure of Interest Rates is Always Flat

What if the term structure of interest rates is always flat? Is it then possible to construct a pair of bond portfolio investments that look like bond A and bond B? Or is the construction of two such investments impossible? In the flat term structure scenario, it is always possible to create two portfolios with the same market value and the same PV01, but with different convexities. (They already have the same yield to maturity, by virtue of the assumption of a flat term structure of interest rates.) However, if one could find two bond portfolios with the characteristics of bonds A and B in Exhibit 23.7 there would be an arbitrage opportunity. By going long in the high-convexity portfolio and short in the low-convexity portfolio, one achieves an investment combination that is self-financing and – for any size move in the interest rate – has a positive value immediately after such move. What this means is that the relationships depicted in Exhibit 23.7 are unlikely to exist in reality.

Changing the Convexity of a Bond Portfolio

An easy way to increase convexity while holding PV01 and market value constant is to spread payments out around the duration.[17] For example, compare (1) a portfolio consisting of a single four-year zero-coupon bond worth €2 million, with (2) a €2 million bond portfolio with equal amounts invested in a three-year zero-coupon bond and a five-year zero-coupon bond. With a flat term structure curve, the duration of the two-bond portfolio is the value-weighted average of the durations of the three- and five-year bonds, or four years – just like the first zero-coupon bond. The PV01 of the two-bond portfolio is virtually identical to the PV01 of the one-bond portfolio[18] because the durations and market values of the two portfolios are the same.

If interest rates decline by 1bp, the initial effect on the values of the two portfolios will be about the same. However, since the five-year bond in the two-bond portfolio now carries relatively more weight, the duration of the two-bond portfolio will now be closer to five years than to three. For the next basis point decline in interest

[17] Note also that bond options, whether put or call options, have more convexity than the underlying bonds themselves. Similarly, floating-rate investments with caps and floors have more convexity than otherwise identical floating-rate investments without caps or floors.

[18] The derivative implementations of the two PV01s are exactly the same.

rates the price of the two-bond portfolio, which has a duration exceeding four years, will go up by more than the price of the one-bond portfolio, which has a duration of exactly four years. This would push the duration even closer to five years. With a higher price and a still higher duration, the PV01 of the two-bond portfolio would then exceed the PV01 of the one-bond portfolio by even more, and so on.

Consider the reverse situation. As interest rates increase, the duration of the three-year bond in the two-bond portfolio now carries greater weight. Hence, although the first basis-point increase has about the same effect on both portfolios, subsequent basis-point increases result in greater price declines for the one-bond portfolio because it has a larger duration. In this case, as interest rates move down from the original rate, the PV01 of the two-bond portfolio exceeds the PV01 of the one-bond portfolio by increasingly greater amounts. Since PV01s are proportional to the slopes in a price–yield graph, the price–yield graphs of the two portfolios look like those depicted in Exhibit 23.7, where the one-bond portfolio is bond B and the two-bond portfolio is bond A.

The previous discussion showed how to increase convexity by spreading payments around the duration of a bond, focusing on zero-coupon bonds. It is possible to generalize this procedure to coupon bonds. Panel A of Exhibit 23.8 plots the cash flows of an annuity bond against time. Panel B graphs the annuity bond's price–yield curve to illustrate the convexity of the bond. Panel C plots the cash flows of a portfolio of two zero-coupon bonds of different maturities. In panel D, the convexity of the two-bond portfolio is greater than the convexity of the annuity bond in panel B, seen as greater curvature in the former. Example 23.16 uses numerical computations to demonstrate this difference in convexity between an annuity bond and a portfolio of two zero-coupon bonds.

Exhibit 23.8 Spreading Cash Flow around the Duration of a Coupon Bond

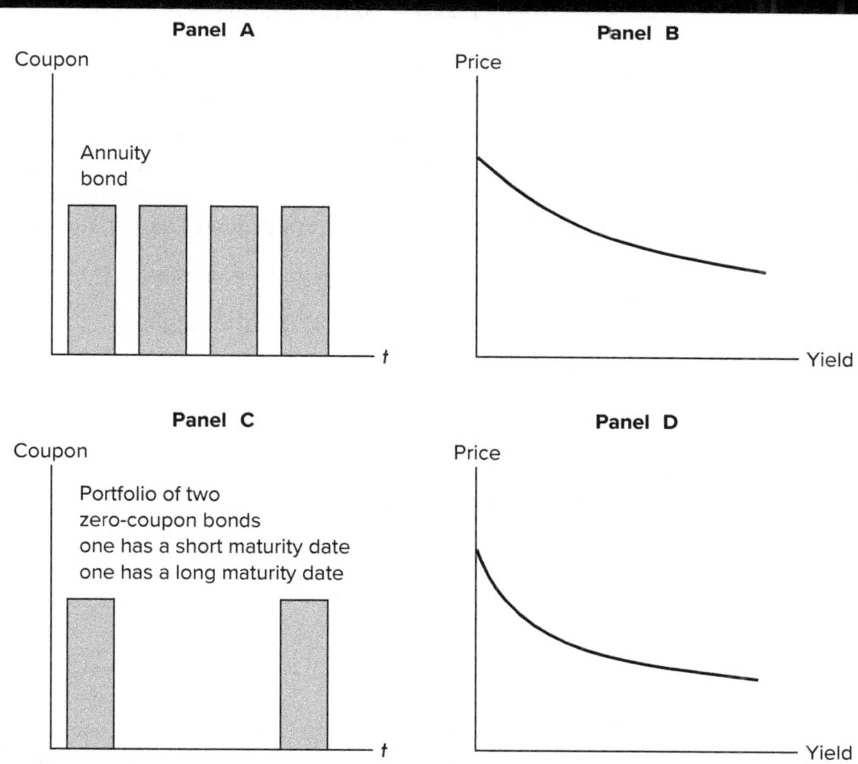

Example 23.16 illustrates how easy it is to increase convexity at no cost. Using equation (23.8), the difference in convexities for a 25bp shift upwards or downwards (to either 7.75 per cent or 8.25 per cent) implies that the portfolio of two zero-coupon bonds has a larger price than the annuity by the difference in the final terms in equation (23.8):

$$0.5\left(\frac{€1125.778}{100}\right)(2.487 - 1.510)(0.25^2) = €0.34$$

Example 23.16

Convexity of an Annuity Versus a Portfolio of Zero-Coupon Bonds

Consider a portfolio consisting of an annuity that pays €100 every year for the next 30 years. If 8 per cent compounded annually is the market interest rate at all maturities, then the present value of this annuity at 8 per cent is

$$€100\left(\frac{1}{0.80}\right)\left(1-\frac{1}{1.08^{30}}\right) = €1{,}125.7783$$

Its present values at 7.99 per cent and 8.01 per cent interest rates are, respectively,

$$€100\left(\frac{1}{0.0799}\right)\left(1-\frac{1}{1.0799^{30}}\right) = €1{,}126.8413$$

and

$$€100\left(\frac{1}{0.0801}\right)\left(1-\frac{1}{1.0801^{30}}\right) = €1{,}124.7170$$

The PV01s at 8.01 per cent and 8.00 per cent interest thus equal €1.0613 (€1,125.7783 – €1,124.7170) and €1.0630 (€1,126.8413 – €1,125.7783), respectively, implying that the annuity bond's convexity is

$$\frac{€1{,}000{,}000}{€1{,}125.7783}(1.0630 - 1.0613) = 1.510$$

Replacing this annuity with a portfolio consisting of zero-coupon bonds maturing at year 1 and year 30 can increase convexity while maintaining the same PV01 at 8 per cent interest. Find such a portfolio.

Answer: The problem requires finding a portfolio with face amounts x and y in the one-year and 30-year zero-coupon bonds, respectively. For a €1.00 face amount, note that a one-year zero-coupon bond has a PV01 of €.000085742, whereas a 30-year zero-coupon bond has a PV01 of €.000276445. Thus, to generate a portfolio with the same present value and PV01 as the annuity, x and y must satisfy the equations

$$\frac{x}{1.08} + \frac{x}{(1.08)^{30}} = €1{,}125.7783 \text{ (present value condition)}$$

$$0.000085742x + 0.000276445y = €1.0630 \text{ (PV01 condition)}$$

The first equation says $x = €1{,}125.7783(1.08) - y/(1.08)^{29}$. Substituting this into the second equation gives

$$y(0.000276445 - 0.000009202476147) = €0.958747165213$$

Thus $y = €3{,}587.60$ and $x = €830.80$ (approximately).

The PV01 of the portfolio of zero-coupon bonds is 1.0602 at an 8.01 per cent yield and 1.0630 at an 8.00 per cent yield. This makes convexity

$$\frac{€1{,}000{,}000}{€1{,}125.7783}(1.0630 - 1.0602)$$

or 2.487.

Hence going long in the portfolio of zero-coupon bonds and short in the annuity generates approximately a riskless €0.34 for a portfolio of this size.[19] Most portfolios would be much larger, particularly since this is a hedged portfolio. At 10,000 times the size, €3,400 is achieved without risk; at 100,000 times the size, €34,000 is achieved without risk.

It is difficult to believe that such arbitrage profits can be achieved. However, if the term structure of interest rates is always flat, there is no cost to forming a portfolio strategy in this manner. It is easy to prove that arbitrage profits also arise if the yield curve is not flat but only shifts in a parallel manner. If convexity is to come at a cost and if there is no arbitrage, term structure changes cannot be restricted to parallel shifts.

[19] This is only an approximation based on the Taylor series expansion. The actual arbitrage difference is closer to 10.37.

23.6 Interest Rate Hedging When the Term Structure is Not Flat

Our analysis of the price–yield relationship of a bond and its implications for interest rate hedging assumed that the term structure of interest rates is flat. We know that this assumption is unrealistic.

Consider Example 23.3, which computed the PV01 of a portfolio of 5-, 10- and 30-year bonds. This example illustrates a potential pitfall in using PV01s for hedging. Example 23.3 adds up the sensitivities of prices to yields to maturity, as if all three of the bonds had simultaneous 1bp declines in their yields to maturity. However, a 1bp decrease in the yield to maturity of a 30-year bond does not imply an identical decrease in the yield to maturity of the 10- and 5-year bonds. It does not even imply a decrease in the latter two yields. Therefore adding these PV01s together is like combining apples and oranges and peaches.

The Yield-Beta Solution

Fortunately, apples and oranges and peaches have something in common: all are fruits. And although the three bonds in Example 23.3 have yields that apply to different maturities, these yields are alike because they are all interest rates. When short-term interest rates go up, long-term rates also tend to go up, and vice versa, but not always and certainly not by exactly the same amount. For these reasons, perfect hedging can only be approximated with traditional PV01 methods.

Many practitioners have recognized this limitation of PV01 techniques. As a consequence, they have sought to improve the hedge with a variety of more sophisticated techniques. One of these employs the concept of a **yield beta,** which is the sensitivity of the hedge portfolio's yield to maturity to movements in the yield to maturity of the portfolio one is trying to hedge. The better hedge in this case is the hedge portfolio that makes the sum of

1 the PV01 of the portfolio that one is trying to hedge, and

2 the product of the PV01 of the hedge portfolio and its yield beta

equal to zero. If $PV01_H$ denotes the PV01 of the hedge portfolio, $PV01_P$ the PV01 of the original portfolio, and β the yield beta, then the hedge solution is represented algebraically by:

$$PVO1_P + PVO1_H\beta = 0$$

Example 23.17 illustrates how this works.

Example 23.17

Hedging with the Yield-Beta Method

Assume that the PV01 of BMW's liabilities is −€1 million from BMW's perspective. The PV01 of BMW's preferred hedging instrument, the euro futures contract traded on Euronext, is €100 per futures contract. For every one-basis-point increase in the yield of BMW's liabilities, the euro futures yield [which is computed as 1 − (euro futures price)/100] rises by 1.1 basis points (that is, the futures yield beta is 1.1). How many euro futures contracts should BMW buy or sell if it wants to target a PV01 of €100,000?

Answer: To obtain a PV01 of €100,000 with respect to the yield of its liabilities, BMW should buy x euro futures contracts, where x satisfies

$$€100{,}000 = -€1{,}000{,}000 + €100(1.1)x$$

Thus $x = 10{,}000$.

A limitation of the yield-beta method is that it leaves open the question of how to compute b. The usual approach to beta estimation in other contexts (for example, stock betas for the CAPM), running a regression of historical yields of the hedge portfolio on the yields of the hedged portfolio, is fraught with empirical pitfalls here. For example, the true yield beta tends to change as time elapses, suggesting that the true historical beta differs from the current yield beta. Moreover, slope coefficients estimated in this manner will differ radically, depending on the frequency of data used (for example, daily versus weekly) and the choice of investment used as the hedging instrument.

More precise hedging requires a sophisticated term structure model. Portfolio managers, corporate executives and traders who employ such models typically look at the price sensitivity to an interest rate factor in the model, and do not use PV01, the sensitivity to the yield to maturity. The relationship between the *price* sensitivity and *yield* sensitivity to a factor is given by the equation:

$$\Delta P = \frac{\Delta r}{\Delta f} \times \text{PV01} \tag{23.9}$$

where[20]

ΔP = the change in the value of the fixed-income security or portfolio

Δr = the change in its yield to maturity

Δf = the change in the interest rate factor that determines the term structure.

This equation states that the change in the value of the security is the product of (1) the change in the yield to maturity with respect to a change in the interest rate factor *and* (2) PV01.

The Parallel Term Structure Shift Solution: Term Structure PV01

It is possible to infer perfect hedge ratios from PV01s alone only if changes in yields to maturity for different maturity bonds are identical. This is an alternative between defining PV01 in terms of (1) the overly simplified 1bp shift in the yield to maturity of the portfolio or in terms of (2) the highly complicated 1bp shift in a factor that determines the term structure of interest rates in a sophisticated no-arbitrage model. This 'halfway' alternative defines PV01 as the change in value for a 1bp parallel shift in the entire term structure of interest rates, as Exhibit 23.9 shows. We call this a **term structure PV01.**

Exhibit 23.9 Parallel Shift in the Term Structure of Interest Rates by One Basis Point

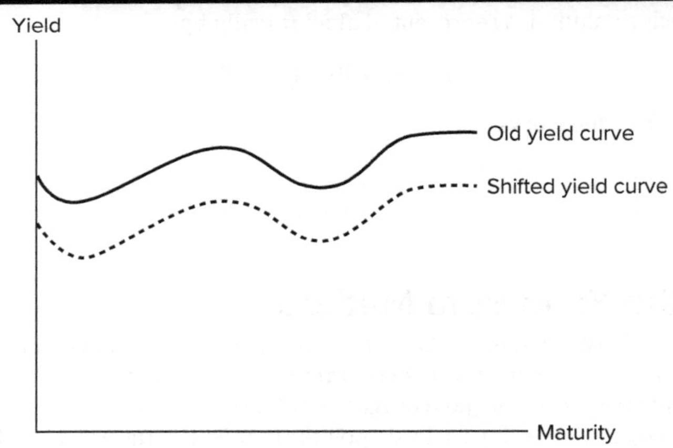

Hedging with term structure PV01 is identical to the yield-beta method when the yield beta is constrained to be 1. The method also implies that the term ($\Delta r/\Delta f$) in equation (23.9) is the same for different-maturity bonds. Despite its being more realistic than the flat term structure assumption, term structure PV01, like the flat term structure assumption, has an inconsistent logic to it. In particular, as the last section asserted, parallel term structure shifts imply arbitrage. Therefore be careful about reaching conclusions about profitable strategies using the ordinary PV01 approach or this term structure PV01 approach.

MacAuley Duration and Present Value Duration

When the term structure of interest rates is not flat, the definition of duration is somewhat ambiguous, because we do not know how to discount the cash flows to obtain the weights on cash flow maturities, as is necessary

---

[20] The Greek letter Δ implies that we look at the change in the variable to the right of it.

for a duration computation. One discount rate to consider is the yield to maturity of the bond. Duration computed using the bond's yield to maturity for discounting, known as the **MacAuley duration,** is the more traditional and common method for computing duration.[21] It is implicitly based on the assumption that yields for bonds of all maturities are identical.

An equally viable discounting alternative, however, is to discount cash flows at the yields to maturity of zero-coupon bonds that mature close to the dates when the cash flows are to be paid. The discount rates obtained from zero-coupon bonds will differ, depending on the cash flow maturity. For example, if long-term riskless bonds have higher yields to maturity than short-term bonds, the zero-coupon discount rates for riskless cash flows that occur far in the future will be larger than the discount rates for cash flows paid in the near future. Duration using weights on cash flow maturities obtained from discounting cash flows with zero-coupon bond yields is referred to as **present value duration.**

The two durations generally differ unless the bond is riskless and the yields to maturity of riskless cash flows of different maturities are the same. Example 23.18 illustrates the distinction in the way duration is computed, using each of the two duration methods.

Example 23.18

Computing MacAuley and Present Value Durations

Compute the MacAuley and present value durations for a portfolio of six- and eight-year zero-coupon bonds, assuming that the six-year bonds pay £18 million in six years and the eight-year bonds pay £20 million in eight years. Both bonds have market values of £10 million.

Answer: The yield to maturity of the portfolio, which solves

$$£20{,}000{,}000 = \frac{£18{,}000{,}000}{(1+r)^6} + \frac{£20{,}000{,}000}{(1+r)^8}$$

is approximately 9.593 per cent per year. This makes the discounted value of the year 6 cash flow (at 9.593 per cent) about £10.389 million and the discounted value of the year 8 cash flow (at 9.593 per cent) about £9.611 million. The MacAuley duration of the portfolio is therefore

$$\frac{10.389}{20}(6 \text{ years}) + \frac{9.611}{20}(8 \text{ years}) = 6.9611 \text{ years}$$

To find the present value duration, weight six years by the fraction of the bond portfolio's present value contributed by the six-year bonds (0.5 = £10 million/£20 million) and eight years by the fraction contributed by eight-year bonds (0.5 = £10 million/£20 million). The present value duration is thus

$$0.5(6 \text{ years}) + 0.5(8 \text{ years}) = 7 \text{ years}$$

Knowing the cash flows in this example allows us to find the discount rate that makes the present value of the combined cash flows equal £20 million. This single internal rate of return is then used to discount the individual cash flows to obtain the weights on six and eight years for the MacAuley duration. By contrast, present value duration uses different discount rates to obtain the comparable weights on six years and eight years.

Example 23.18 also points out that the present value duration of a portfolio is the portfolio-weighted average of the durations of the individual bonds in the portfolio. MacAuley duration does not possess this property unless the term structure of interest rates is flat, in which case MacAuley duration and present value duration are the same.

Present Value Duration as a Derivative

If the term structure of interest rates is flat, then (as Section 23.3 noted) the negative of a bond's duration is the percentage change in a bond's price with respect to small changes in interest rates. Present value duration does not generally possess this derivative property. With present value duration, there is no single interest rate

[21] This method was developed by Frederick MacAuley (1938).

to take a derivative with respect to. Each cash flow has its own interest rate for discounting! However, it is possible to have a derivative interpretation for present value duration, too, if one makes a minor modification to the derivative; in this case, present value duration can be interpreted as the negative of the percentage change in the bond's value for a small parallel shift in the term structure of continuously compounded interest rates. That is, defining r_t as the appropriate continuously compounded rate for cash flows t years from now, and assuming that, for all ts, r_t shifts up by a constant δ, the derivative of the percentage change in the bond's price with respect to δ equals the negative of duration: that is,[22]

$$\text{(present value) DUR} = -\frac{1}{P}\frac{dP}{d\delta}$$

This derivative interpretation makes it possible to relate term structure PV01 to present value duration. Specifically, term structure PV01 can be written as a constant times a derivative:

$$\text{(term structure) PV01} = -0.0001\frac{dP}{d\delta}$$

Combining the last two equations implies

$$\text{(term structure) PV01} = \text{(present value) DUR} \times P \times 0.0001$$

23.7 Summary and Conclusions

This chapter described several tools that are important for bond portfolio management and corporate financial management of fixed-income securities and interest rate risk. Managers can use these tools to better understand the relation between yield and market price in order to manage interest rate risk. Among the tools discussed in the chapter were:

- the concept of PV01, in original and term structure variations, which is a measure of the slope of the price–yield curve
- the concept of duration, in MacAuley, modified and present value variations, which is a weighted average of the time at which a set of cash flows is received
- the link between duration and PV01 and the formulae needed to use either of them for hedging
- immunization and contingent immunization, using both duration and PV01, which are methods of converting the cash flows of a bond portfolio into the cash flows of a zero-coupon bond
- the link between immunization and hedging, and how to use this link for managing the asset base and capital structure of financial institutions, and for managing a bond portfolio
- the concept of convexity, which is similar to the slope of the price–yield curve, and how it can be properly used and misused.

The yield curve is not flat and does not shift in a parallel fashion, which complicates the use of these tools. Parallel shifts lead to arbitrage, thus making it incumbent upon those who desire a more rigorous analysis of interest rate hedging to develop a sophisticated model of the term structure of interest rates that precludes such arbitrage.

Final Remarks

Financial firms have developed some sophisticated models that are used to value complicated interest rate derivatives. The basic structure of these interest rate derivatives valuation models is similar to that of the binomial model in Chapter 7. However, here, the risk-neutral valuation accounts for interest rate factors that evolve along trees (or grids) with move sizes for these factors determined by the term structure of interest rates and volatility. The level of mathematical sophistication in these models is beyond the scope of any textbook geared towards those seeking a general understanding of corporate finance and financial markets. Indeed, the quantitative methods associated with these models has given the 'quants' – often

[22] Exercise 23.2 at the end of the chapter asks you to prove this. The adjustment for derivatives with respect to non-continuously compounded yields with present value duration is not as simple or straightforward. If each gross discount rate $1 + r_t$ for cash flows t years from now is multiplied by $1 + \delta$, then present value duration for a set of discount rates that reflect compounding m times a year is $-1/m$ times the derivative of the percentage change in the price of the bond (or portfolio) with respect to δ.

PhDs in financial mathematics, statistics, economics, physics and finance – an unprecedented degree of prestige, compensation and control over the management and valuation of interest rate derivatives.

The level of technical sophistication in corporate finance has also increased considerably over the last two decades. In some cases, non-financial corporations are hiring these same quants to oversee their hedging operations. However, this is still the exception. After 23 chapters, our message to you is that no matter how sophisticated either investment management or corporate management becomes, there are some fundamental principles in finance that will always be useful.

In short, one of the basic principles developed in this textbook – the formation of portfolios to track an investment with risks one is familiar with – can be used to understand the risk of a highly complex security. The lesson here is that one does not need advanced mathematics or sophisticated models to master finance. One must, however, go beyond a superficial understanding of finance and master its basic principles to succeed as a finance professional in the twenty-first century. We wrote this text in the hopes of contributing to such an understanding.

Key Concepts

Result 23.1: If the term structure of interest rates is flat, a bond portfolio with a PV01 of zero has no sensitivity to interest rate movements.

Result 23.2: Let r_n and r_m denote the annualized yield to maturity of the same bond computed with yields compounded n times a year and m times a year, respectively. The PV01 for a bond (or portfolio) using compounding of m times a year is $(1 + r_n/n)/(1 + r_m/m)$ times the PV01 of the bond using a compounding frequency of n times a year.

Result 23.3: Assuming that the term structure of interest rates is flat, the duration of a portfolio of bonds is the portfolio-weighted average of the durations of the respective bonds in the portfolio.

Result 23.4: Because PV01 can be translated into duration, and vice versa, PV01 and duration are equivalent as tools both for measuring interest rate risk and for hedging.

Result 23.5: If the term structure of interest rates is flat, immunization 'guarantees' a fixed value for an immunized portfolio at a horizon date. The value obtained is the same as the face value of a zero-coupon bond with (1) the same market value as the original portfolio and (2) a maturity date equal to the horizon date selected as the target date to which the duration of the immunized portfolio is fixed.

Key terms

Exercises

23.1 A three-year coupon bond has payments as follows:

Bond cash flow at year		
1	2	3
£8	£8	£108

This 8 per cent coupon bond is currently trading at par (£100).

a What is the annually compounded yield of the bond?

b Compute the MacAuley duration and ordinary PV01 (calculated with respect to the annually compounded bond yield).

c Using PV01, how much do you expect this bond's price to rise if the yield on the bond declines by 10 basis points compounded annually?

23.2 Prove that if the present value of a cash flow is represented by

$$\text{PV} = (\text{cash flow}) \times \exp(-r_t t)$$

and, for all *t*s, r_t shifts up by a constant δ, the derivative of the percentage change in the bond's price with respect to δ equals the negative of present value duration: that is,

$$(\text{present value}) \text{ DUR} = -\frac{1}{P}\frac{dP}{d\delta}$$

23.3 Bond A has a PV01 of €0.10 per €100 face value. Bond B has a PV01 of €0.05 per €100 face value.

a If Danny buys €1 million (face amount) of bond A, what should his position (face amount) in bond B be in order to hedge out all interest rate risk on the portfolio?

b If bond A and bond B are par bonds (that is, they have prices equal to their face values and have equal yields to maturity), what euro amount needs to be spent on bonds A and B to immunize the bond portfolio to a horizon of seven years if €1 million is spent on the portfolio? (Assume that the PV01s were calculated with respect to a one-basis-point decline in each bond's *continuously compounded* yield to maturity.)

23.4 The PV01 of a Treasury bond maturing on 15 November 2027, with an 8 per cent coupon (4 per cent paid semi-annually) and a €100 face value, is €0.10. The PV01 of a Treasury note maturing on 15 May 2018, with a 7 per cent coupon (3.5 per cent paid semi-annually) and a €100 face value, is €0.06.

a What is the accrued interest (per €100 face value) to be paid on both the bond and the note for a purchase with a settlement date of 11 June 2008, for each of these fixed-income securities? (*Hint:* see Chapter 2.)

b If you held a position of €1 million (face value) in the Treasury bond, what position should you hold in the Treasury note to eliminate all interest rate risk?

23.5 A two-year default-free straight-coupon bond has annual coupons of £8 per £100 of face value. Assume that a default-free zero-coupon bond with one year to maturity sells for £90 per £100 of face value, and that a default-free zero-coupon bond with two years to maturity sells for £80 per £100 of face value.

a What is the no-arbitrage price of the straight-coupon 8 per cent bond?

b What is the present value duration of the straight-coupon bond, given the market value of the bond computed in part *a?*

c Assume you hold £1 million face value of the straight-coupon bond. How much in market value of a three-year zero-coupon bond should you hold (in addition to the straight-coupon bond position) to have an overall position that is perfectly hedged against a parallel shift in the term structure?

23.6 Compute the duration, PV01 and convexity of a semi-annual straight-coupon bond with three years to maturity. The bond trades at par with a 6 per cent coupon. Assume the term structure of interest rates is flat.

23.7 Compute the duration, PV01 and convexity of a 6 per cent two-year par bond that pays semi-annual coupons. Assume the term structure of interest rates is flat.

23.8 Discuss how you might use the 6 per cent two-year bond in exercise 23.7 to hedge a position in the three-year bond from exercise 23.6.

23.9 How would your answer to exercise 23.8 change if the bond in exercise 23.7 were a 10 per cent two-year premium bond with a yield curve still at a flat 6 per cent?

23.10 Discuss qualitatively how your answer to exercise 23.8 would change if the bond in exercise 23.7 was a 10 per cent two-year par bond. (This means that the term structure of interest rates is not flat.)

References and Additional Reading

Fabozzi, F. (2010) *Bond Markets, Analysis, and Strategies,* 7th edn, Prentice-Hall, Englewood Cliffs, NJ.

Kopprasch, R. (1985) *Understanding Duration and Volatility,* Salomon Brothers, New York; reprinted in *The Handbook of Fixed-Income Securities,* Frank Fabozzi and Irving Pollack (eds), Irwin Professional Publishing, Burr Ridge, IL, 1996.

MacAuley, F. (1938) *Some Theoretical Problems Suggested by the Movement of Interest Rates, Bond Yields, and Stock Prices in the US since 1856,* National Bureau of Economic Research, New York.

Redington, F.M. (1952) Review of the principle of life-office valuations, *Journal of the Institute of Actuaries,* 78: 286–340.

Tuckman, B. (1995) *Fixed Income Securities: Tools for Today's Markets,* John Wiley, New York.

Practical Insights for Part 6

Allocating Capital for Real Investment

- Managers are likely to make better capital allocation decisions if they hedge their risks, because it forces them to use forward and futures prices in their calculations of NPV rather than potentially ad hoc estimates of expected value. (Section 21.2)
- Firms sometimes build plants in foreign countries in which they sell their products as a substitute for hedging when it is difficult to hedge real exchange rate risk effectively. (Section 21.8)

Financing the Firm

- The Modigliani–Miller Theorem is very general, and implies that, in the absence of market frictions, firms are indifferent about the currencies of their debt obligations and the maturity structure of their debt, as well as their debt–equity ratio. (Section 21.1)
- Firms that use derivatives to reduce their probability of financial distress can create value by increasing their debt ratio without increasing their probability of financial distress. (Section 21.2)
- Firms that have high leverage ratios, but also potentially have high financial distress costs, are more likely to use derivatives to hedge. (Section 21.2)
- In general, hedging will benefit debt holders at the expense of equity holders. (Section 21.6)
- Firms can sometimes reduce their funding costs by combining debt instruments with swaps and other derivatives. (Sections 21.7, 22.6)

Knowing Whether and How to Hedge Risk

- Firms can benefit from hedging even when shareholders are not averse to risk. (Section 21.2)
- Firms that are uncertain about whether or not they will have positive tax liabilities have an incentive to hedge. (Section 21.2)
- Firms benefit from hedging if it allows them to avoid the possibility of costly financial distress. (Section 21.2)
- Firms benefit from hedging when external sources of capital are more expensive than internal sources of capital. However, when investment opportunities are positively correlated with the hedgeable risk, firms should hedge only partially. Options may prove to be a particularly good hedging vehicle in this case. (Sections 21.2, 22.7)
- Management performance can be evaluated more accurately if managers are required to hedge extraneous risks. (Section 21.2)
- In most cases, firms benefit from hedging real rather than strictly nominal exchange rate changes. (Section 21.8)
- Factor models are perhaps the best way to think about a firm's risk exposure. (Sections 21.1, 22.1, 22.8)
- Regression slope coefficients give risk-minimizing hedge ratios. (Section 22.9)
- Even though futures and forward prices are often virtually identical, hedge ratios using futures can differ vastly from hedge ratios using forwards. In particular, hedges with futures need to be tailed, and thus are generally lower than hedge ratios involving forwards. (Section 22.3)
- The convenience yield of an asset or commodity affects the hedge ratio when hedging long-term commitments with short-term forwards or futures. The larger the convenience yield, the more correlated it is with the price of the commodity, and the more unpredictable it is, the lower is the risk-minimizing hedge ratio. (Sections 22.4, 22.5)

- Firms that set the ratio of the duration of assets and liabilities to the inverse of the ratios of their market values will have equity with a PV01 of 0, which means that their stock price is insensitive to interest rate risk. (Section 23.3)
- It is possible to lock in (that is, immunize) the future value of an interest-rate-sensitive liability or asset at a horizon date by managing the liability to have a duration that is matched to the horizon date. (Section 23.4)
- Even though PV01 and duration are relatively simple risk estimation and risk management tools in comparison with the techniques on Wall Street, they often provide good approximations to the interest rate risk of an asset or liability, and offer useful insights into risk and hedging. (Sections 23.1–23.3, 23.7)

Allocating Funds for Financial Investments

- Bond portfolios that are managed to have PV01s or durations of zero have no interest rate risk. (Section 23.3)

Index

Page numbers in italics are exhibits.